2 for 1

Terms: This voucher is valid at any venue specified as accepting vouchers within the AA 'The Days Out Guide 2003'. This voucher admits one adult or child free when presented at the time of purchase of one fully priced adult ticket. Valid until 31 Oct 2003. Subject to availability at the venue when presented. Photocopies will **not** be accepted.

2 for 1

when presented. Photocopies will **not** be accepted.

---

2 for 1

Terms: This voucher is valid at any venue specified as accepting vouchers within the AA 'The Days Out Guide 2003'. This voucher admits one adult or child free when presented at the time of purchase of one fully priced adult ticket. Valid until 31 Oct 2003. Subject to availability at the venue when presented. Photocopies will **not** be accepted.

2 for 1

Terms: This voucher is valid at any venue specified as accepting vouchers within the AA 'The Days Out Guide 2003'. This voucher admits one adult or child free when presented at the time of purchase of one fully priced adult ticket. Valid until 31 Oct 2003. Subject to availability at the venue when presented. Photocopies will **not** be accepted.

---

2 for 1

Terms: This voucher is valid at any venue specified as accepting vouchers within the AA 'The Days Out Guide 2003'. This voucher admits one adult or child free when presented at the time of purchase of one fully priced adult ticket. Valid until 31 Oct 2003. Subject to availability at the venue when presented. Photocopies will **not** be accepted.

2 for 1

Terms: This voucher is valid at any venue specified as accepting vouchers within the AA 'The Days Out Guide 2003'. This voucher admits one adult or child free when presented at the time of purchase of one fully priced adult ticket. Valid until 31 Oct 2003. Subject to availability at the venue when presented. Photocopies will **not** be accepted.

---

2 for 1

Terms: This voucher is valid at any venue specified as accepting vouchers within the AA 'The Days Out Guide 2003'. This voucher admits one adult or child free when presented at the time of purchase of one fully priced adult ticket. Valid until 31 Oct 2003. Subject to availability at the venue when presented. Photocopies will **not** be accepted.

2 for 1

Terms: This voucher is valid at any venue specified as accepting vouchers within the AA 'The Days Out Guide 2003'. This voucher admits one adult or child free when presented at the time of purchase of one fully priced adult ticket. Valid until 31 Oct 2003. Subject to availability at the venue when presented. Photocopies will **not** be accepted.

---

2 for 1

Terms: This voucher is valid at any venue specified as accepting vouchers within the AA 'The Days Out Guide 2003'. This voucher admits one adult or child free when presented at the time of purchase of one fully priced adult ticket. Valid until 31 Oct 2003. Subject to availability at the venue when presented. Photocopies will **not** be accepted.

2 for 1

Terms: This voucher is valid at any venue specified as accepting vouchers within the AA 'The Days Out Guide 2003'. This voucher admits one adult or child free when presented at the time of purchase of one fully priced adult ticket. Valid until 31 Oct 2003. Subject to availability at the venue when presented. Photocopies will **not** be accepted.

AA Lifestyle Guides

Conditions: Only one voucher per person or party accepted. No change given. This voucher is valid during the published opening times for the establishments concerned, and will not be valid after 31 Oct 2003. This voucher cannot be used in conjunction with any other discount voucher or special offer. Redeemable cash value .01p. No cash alternative available.

AA Lifestyle Guides

Conditions: Only one voucher per person or party accepted. No change given. This voucher is valid during the published opening times for the establishments concerned, and will not be valid after 31 Oct 2003. This voucher cannot be used in conjunction with any other discount voucher or special offer. Redeemable cash value .01p. No cash alternative available.

AA Lifestyle Guides

Conditions: Only one voucher per person or party accepted. No change given. This voucher is valid during the published opening times for the establishments concerned, and will not be valid after 31 Oct 2003. This voucher cannot be used in conjunction with any other discount voucher or special offer. Redeemable cash value .01p. No cash alternative available.

AA Lifestyle Guides

Conditions: Only one voucher per person or party accepted. No change given. This voucher is valid during the published opening times for the establishments concerned, and will not be valid after 31 Oct 2003. This voucher cannot be used in conjunction with any other discount voucher or special offer. Redeemable cash value .01p. No cash alternative available.

AA Lifestyle Guides

Conditions: Only one voucher per person or party accepted. No change given. This voucher is valid during the published opening times for the establishments concerned, and will not be valid after 31 Oct 2003. This voucher cannot be used in conjunction with any other discount voucher or special offer. Redeemable cash value .01p. No cash alternative available.

AA Lifestyle Guides

Conditions: Only one voucher per person or party accepted. No change given. This voucher is valid during the published opening times for the establishments concerned, and will not be valid after 31 Oct 2003. This voucher cannot be used in conjunction with any other discount voucher or special offer. Redeemable cash value .01p. No cash alternative available.

AA Lifestyle Guides

Conditions: Only one voucher per person or party accepted. No change given. This voucher is valid during the published opening times for the establishments concerned, and will not be valid after 31 Oct 2003. This voucher cannot be used in conjunction with any other discount voucher or special offer. Redeemable cash value .01p. No cash alternative available.

AA Lifestyle Guides

Conditions: Only one voucher per person or party accepted. No change given. This voucher is valid during the published opening times for the establishments concerned, and will not be valid after 31 Oct 2003. This voucher cannot be used in conjunction with any other discount voucher or special offer. Redeemable cash value .01p. No cash alternative available.

AA Lifestyle Guides

Conditions: Only one voucher per person or party accepted. No change given. This voucher is valid during the published opening times for the establishments concerned, and will not be valid after 31 Oct 2003. This voucher cannot be used in conjunction with any other discount voucher or special offer. Redeemable cash value .01p. No cash alternative available.

AA Lifestyle Guides

Conditions: Only one voucher per person or party accepted. No change given. This voucher is valid during the published opening times for the establishments concerned, and will not be valid after 31 Oct 2003. This voucher cannot be used in conjunction with any other discount voucher or special offer. Redeemable cash value .01p. No cash alternative available.

AA Lifestyle Guides

WIN one of **10 Family Breaks** with **AA Lifestyle Guides** in association with **Travel Inn**

See overleaf for terms & conditions

With our fantastic giveaway of 10 Family Breaks, there's no need to rush home after a great day out! Follow up your day's adventures with a good night's sleep at one of the conveniently located 280 Travel Inns throughout the country.

For more information on Travel Inn call 0870 242 8000 or visit www.travelinn.co.uk

---

HOW TO ENTER
Just complete (in capitals please) and send off this card or alternatively, send your name and address on a stamped postcard to the address overleaf (no purchase required). Entries are limited to one per household.
Closing date 28 November 2003.

MR/MRS/MISS/MS/OTHER, PLEASE STATE: _____
NAME: _____
ADDRESS: _____
_____
_____ POSTCODE: _____
TEL. NO: _____ E-MAIL: _____

Are you an AA Member?   Yes/No
Have you bought this or any other AA Lifestyle Guide before?   Yes/No
If yes, please indicate the year of the last edition you bought:

AA Hotel Guide	____	AA Caravan & Camping (Europe) ____
AA Bed and Breakfast Guide	____	AA Britain Guide ____
AA Restaurant Guide	____	AA Days Out Guide ____
AA Pub Guide	____	AA B&B France ____
AA Caravan & Camping (Britain & Ireland)	____	Other, please state _____

We may use information we hold about you to write, email or telephone you about other products and services offered by us and our carefully selected partners. Information may be disclosed to other companies in the Centrica group (including those using the British Gas, Scottish Gas, Goldfish, One-Tel and AA brands) but we can assure you that we will not disclose it to third parties. Please tick the box if you do not wish to receive details of other products and services from the AA ☐

DO03

Terms and Conditions

1. Two winners will be drawn from each of the five prize draws to take place on 03 March, 05 May, 01 September, 03 November and 01 December 2003.
2. Closing date for receipt of entries is midday on the relevant draw date. Final closing date for receipt of entries is **28 November 2003**.
3. Entries received after any draw date other than the final one will go forward into the next available draw. Each entry will only be entered in one draw. **Only one entry per household accepted.**
4. Winners will be notified by post within 14 days of the relevant draw date.
5. Prizes are not transferable and there is no cash alternative.
6. This prize cannot be used in conjunction with any other discount, promotion or special offer.
7. Each prize consists of 1 night's stay on a room only basis in a family room on any Friday, Saturday or Sunday night (for 2 adults and 2 children under 15). Any additional expenses will be charged as taken.
8. Travel Inn provides all hotel accommodation, services and facilities and AA Publishing is not party to your agreement with Travel Inn in this regard.
9. No purchase required.
10. The prize draw is open to UK residents over the age of 18, other than employees and agents of the Automobile Association or Travel Inn, members of their households or anyone else connected with the promotion.
11. For a list of winners, please send a stamped, self-addressed envelope to AA Lifestyle Guide Winners 2003, AA Publishing, Fanum House (14), Basingstoke, Hants, RG21 4EA.
12. This card must have an appropriate stamp.
13. Winners may be asked to participate in draw-related publicity.

Please Affix Stamp

AA Lifestyle Guide 2003 Prize Draw
AA PUBLISHING
FANUM HOUSE (14)
BASING VIEW
BASINGSTOKE
HANTS RG21 4EA

Fold along this line

Seal along this edge with sticky tape

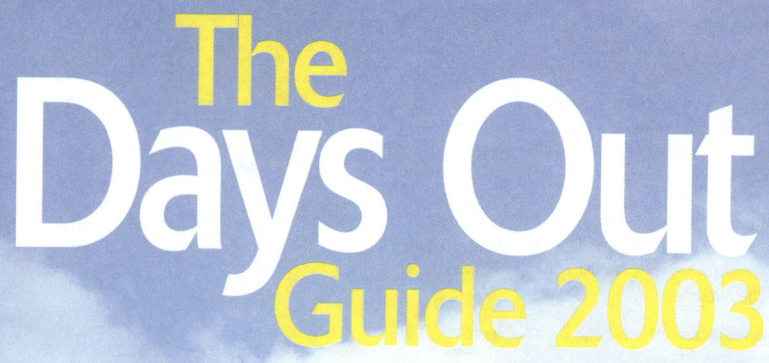

The Days Out Guide 2003

The AA Days Out Guide aims to provide useful information about a large number of museums, art galleries, theme parks, national parks, visitor centres and stately homes across Britain and Ireland. Entries include contact details for each attraction, along with a short description and details of opening times, prices and special facilities. Each county has an introductory page that gives a general overview of the area.

We hope that this guide will help you and your family get the most out of your time.

Happy Visiting!

Produced by AA Publishing

© Automobile Association Developments Limited 2002

All rights reserved. No part of this publication may be reproduced, stored in a retrieval system, or transmitted in any form or by any means – electronic, mechanical, photocopying, recording or otherwise – unless the written permission of the publisher has been given beforehand. This book may not be lent, resold, hired out or otherwise disposed of by way of trade in any form of binding or cover other than that in which it is published, without the prior consent of the publisher.

A CIP catalogue record for this book is available from the British Library

Directory generated by the AA Establishment Database, Information Research, AA Hotel Services

Design by Kingswood Graphics, Reading, Berkshire

Cover pictures: AA Picture Library

Advertisement Sales: advertisingsales@theAA.com

Lifestyle Guides: lifestyleguides@theAA.com

Typeset/Repro by Microset Graphics Ltd, Basingstoke, England

Printed in Italy by Graficas Estella, S.A., Navarra, Spain

The contents of this book are believed correct at the time of printing. Nevertheless, the Publisher cannot be held responsible for any errors or omissions or for changes in the details given in this guide or for the consequences of any reliance on the information provided in the same. This does not affect your statutory rights. We have tried to ensure accuracy in this guide but things do change and we would be grateful if readers would advise us of any inaccuracies they may encounter.

This product includes mapping data licensed from Ordnance Survey® with the permission of the Controller of Her Majesty's Stationery Office ©Crown copyright 2002. All rights reserved. Licence number 399221

Northern Ireland mapping reproduced by permission of the Director and Chief Executive, Ordnance Survey of Northern Ireland, acting on behalf of the Controller of Her Majesty's Stationery Office ©Crown copyright 2002. Permit No. 1674

Republic of Ireland mapping based on Ordnance Survey Ireland Permit No. MP004202 ©Ordnance Survey Ireland and Government of Ireland.

Maps prepared by the Cartographic Department of The Automobile Association Maps
© The Automobile Association 2002

Published by AA Publishing, which is a trading name of Automobile Association Developments Limited whose registered office is Millstream, Maidenhead Road, Windsor, Berkshire, SL4 5GD Registered number 1878835.

ISBN 0749535091

A1335

Contents

How to Use This Guide 4-5

Key to Symbols and Abbreviations 6

Animal Attractions 8-11

ENGLAND	.13
CHANNEL ISLANDS	.288
ISLE OF MAN	.293
SCOTLAND	.296
SCOTTISH ISLANDS	.343
WALES	.349
NORTHERN IRELAND	.372
REPUBLIC OF IRELAND	.383

County Maps 396

Atlas 398

Index 416

How to Use This Guide

THE DIRECTORY
The directory is arranged in countries, counties, then in alphabetical location order within each county. Each county has an introductory page that gives general information on the county as well as details of selected events and festivals. (These pages may mention places, landmarks or streets that do not have an entry in the directory.)

❶ MAP REFERENCES AND ATLAS
Map references for attractions are based on the National Grid, and can be used with the Atlas at the back of this book.

First comes the map page number, followed by the National Grid reference. To find the location, read the first figure horizontally and the second figure vertically within the lettered square.

❷ DIRECTIONS may be given after the address of each attraction and where shown have been provided by the places of interest themselves.

❸ TELEPHONE NUMBERS have the STD code shown before the telephone number. (If dialling Northern Ireland from England use the STD code, but for the Republic you need to prefix the number with 00353, and drop the first zero from the Irish area code).

❹ `2 for 1` **2-FOR-1 VOUCHER SCHEME**
This symbol indicates which attractions have chosen to participate in our new 2-for-1 voucher scheme. Visitors using one of the vouchers from the front of this guide will be able to buy 2 entries for the price of one, with certain restrictions that are detailed on the voucher itself.

❺ OPENING TIMES quoted in the guide are inclusive - for instance, where you see Apr-Oct, that place will be open from the beginning of April to the end of October.

❻ FEES quoted for the majority of entries are current. If no price is quoted, you should check with the attraction concerned before you visit. Places which are open 'at all reasonable times' are usually free, and many places which do not charge admission at all may ask for a voluntary donation. Remember that prices can go up, and those provided to us by the attractions are provisional.

❼ FACILITIES
This section includes parking, dogs allowed, refreshments etc. See page 6 for a key to Symbols and Abbreviations used in this guide.

(8) **VISITORS WITH MOBILITY DISABILITIES** should look for the wheelchair symbol showing where all or most of the establishment is accessible to the wheelchair-bound visitor. We strongly recommend that you telephone in advance of your visit to check the exact details, particularly regarding access to toilets and refreshment facilities. Assistance dogs are usually accepted where the attractions show the 'No Dogs' symbol 🐕 unless stated otherwise. For the hard of hearing induction loops are indicated by a symbol at the attraction itself.

(9) **CREDIT & CHARGE CARDS** are taken by a number of attractions for admission charges. To indicate which accept credit cards we have used this symbol at the end of the entry. 💳

PHOTOGRAPHY is restricted in some places and there are many where it is only allowed in specific areas. Visitors are advised to check with places of interest on the rules for taking photographs and the use of video cameras.

SPECIAL EVENTS are held at many of these attractions, and although we have listed a few of the more important ones on the county introduction pages, we cannot hope to give details of them all, so please ring the places of interest for details of exhibitions, themed days, talks, guided walks and more.

Sample Entry

🏛 **ANY TOWN**   Map 03 SP27 — (1)
ANY PLACE
ZE17 5ZE (off A14 at junc with B760 signed Old Weston) — (2)
(3) — ☎ 01002 293002   📠 01002 293007
e-mail: anyplace@demon.co.uk   **2 for 1** — (4)

A wildlife breeding centre, dedicated to the practical conservation of endangered species including gibbons, marmosets, lemurs, wildcats, meerkats, Britain's only group of breeding sloths and many more. There is also a large and varied bird collection, with several species unique to this location. Over 120 species in all. Other attractions include a children's play area, and undercover viewing of many mammals.

(5) — **Times:** open summer daily 10.30-6; winter daily 10.30-4. (Closed Xmas)
(6) — **Fees:** £3 (£1.50 children and OAP) **Facilities:** P 🍴 — (7)
(8) — ♿ toilets for disabled, shop 🐕 **Cards:** 💳 — (9)

ABBREVIATED ENTRIES Some attractions have abbreviated entries and the line 'Details not confirmed for 2003'. These are entries that were unable to provide the relevant information in time for publication.

...AND FINALLY Opening times and admission prices can be subject to change. Please check with the attraction before making your journey.

Public Holidays

New Year's Day	1 January	Battle of the Boyne (Orangemen's Day) (N.I. only)	14 July
Bank Holiday (Scotland only)	2 January		
St Patrick's Day (N.I. & R.O.I. only)	17 March	Summer Bank Holiday (Scotland & R.O.I. only)	4 August
Good Friday	18 April	Summer Bank Holiday (excluding R.O.I. - Scotland varies)	25 August
Easter Monday	21 April		
May Day Bank Holiday	5 May	Bank Holiday (R.O.I. only)	27 October
Spring Bank Holiday (excluding R.O.I.)	26 May	Christmas Day	25 December
June Bank Holiday (R.O.I. only)	2 June	Boxing Day (St Stephen's Day in R.O.I.)	26 December

Key to Symbols and Abbreviations

SYMBOLS
In order to give you as much information as possible in the space available, we have used the following symbols in the guide:

	ENGLISH	FRANÇAIS	DEUTSCH	ITALIANO	ESPAÑOL
☎	Telephone number	Numéro de téléphone	Telefonnummer	Numero telefonico	Número telefónico
📄	Fax number				
♿	Suitable for visitors in wheelchairs	Les invalidens fauteuils roulants pourrant y accéder	Für Rollstuhltahrer zugänglich	Accessibile agli handicappeti	Acondicionado para visitantes en silla de reudas
P	Parking at Establishment	Stationnement à l'établissement	Parken an Ort und Stelle	Parcheggio in loco	Aparcamiento en el establecimiento
P	Parking nearby	Stationnement tout près	Parken in der Nähe	Parcheggio nelle vicinanze	Aparcamiento cerca del
	Refreshments	Rafraîchissements	Erfrischungen	Snack-bar	Refrescos
✕	Restaurant	Restaurant	Restaurant	Ristorante	Restaurante
✈	No dogs	Chiens non permis	Hundeverbot	Cani non accettati	Se prohiben los perros
🚌	No coaches	Les groupes en cars pas admis	Keine Reisebusgesellschaften	Non si accettano comitive in pullman	Non se admiten los grupos de viajeros en autobús
*	Admission prices relate to 2002. It should be noted that in some entries the opening dates and times may also have been supplied as 2002. Please check with the establshment before making your journey.				
	Cadw (Welsh Historic Monuments)	Cadw Monument ancien (Pays de Galles)	Cadw Historiches Gebaude (Walisland)	Cadw Monumento storico (Galles)	Cadw Monumento histórico (Gales)
	English Heritage (opening times: see advert on opposite page)	English Heritage	English Heritage	English Heritage	English Heritage
	National Trust	National Trust	National Trust	National Trust	The National Trust
	National Trust for Scotland	National Trust en Ecosse	National Trust in Schottland	National Trust per la Scozia	The National Trust de Escocia
	Historic Scotland				

ABBREVIATIONS
In the same way, we have abbreviated certain pieces of information:

	ENGLISH	FRANÇAIS	DEUTSCH	ITALIAN	ESPAÑOL
BH	Bank Holidays	Jours fériés	Bankfeiertage	Festività nazionale	Días festivos (bancos y comercio)
PH	Public Holidays	Jours fériés	Feiertage	Festività nazionale	Días festivos
Etr	Easter	Pâques	Ostern	Pasqua	Semana Santa
ex	except	sauf	ausser	eccetto	excepto
Free	Admission free	Entrée gratuit	Freier eintritt	Ingresso gratuito	Entrada gratuita
£1	Admission £1	Entrée £1	Eintritt £1	Ingresso £1	Entrada £1
ch 50p	Children 50p	Enfants 50p	Kinder 50p	Bambini 50p	Niños 50p
ch 15 50p	Children under 15 50p	Enfants de moins de 15 ans 50p	Kinder unter 15 Jahren 50p	Bambini sotto i 15 anni 50p	Los niños de menores de 15 años 50p
Pen	Senior Citizens	Retraites	Rentner	Pensionati	Jubilados
Party	Special or reduced rates for parties booked in advance	Tarifs spéciaux ou réduits pour groupes réservés d'advance	Sondertarife oder Ermässigungen für im voraus bestellte Gesellschaften	Tariffe speciali o ridotte per comitive che prenotano in anticipo	Tarifas especiales o reducidas para los grupos de viajeros que reserven de anternano
Party 30+	Special or reduced rates for parties of 30 or more booked in advance	Tarifs spéciaux ou réduits pour groupes de 30 ou plus réservés d'advance	Sondertarife oder Ermässigungen für im voraus bestellte Gesellschaften von wenigstens 30 Personen	Tariffe speciali o ridotte per comitive di 30 o più persone che prenotano in anticipo	Tarifas especiales o reducidas para grupos de 30 viajeros, o más, que reserven de anternano

Animal Attractions

By Julia Hynard

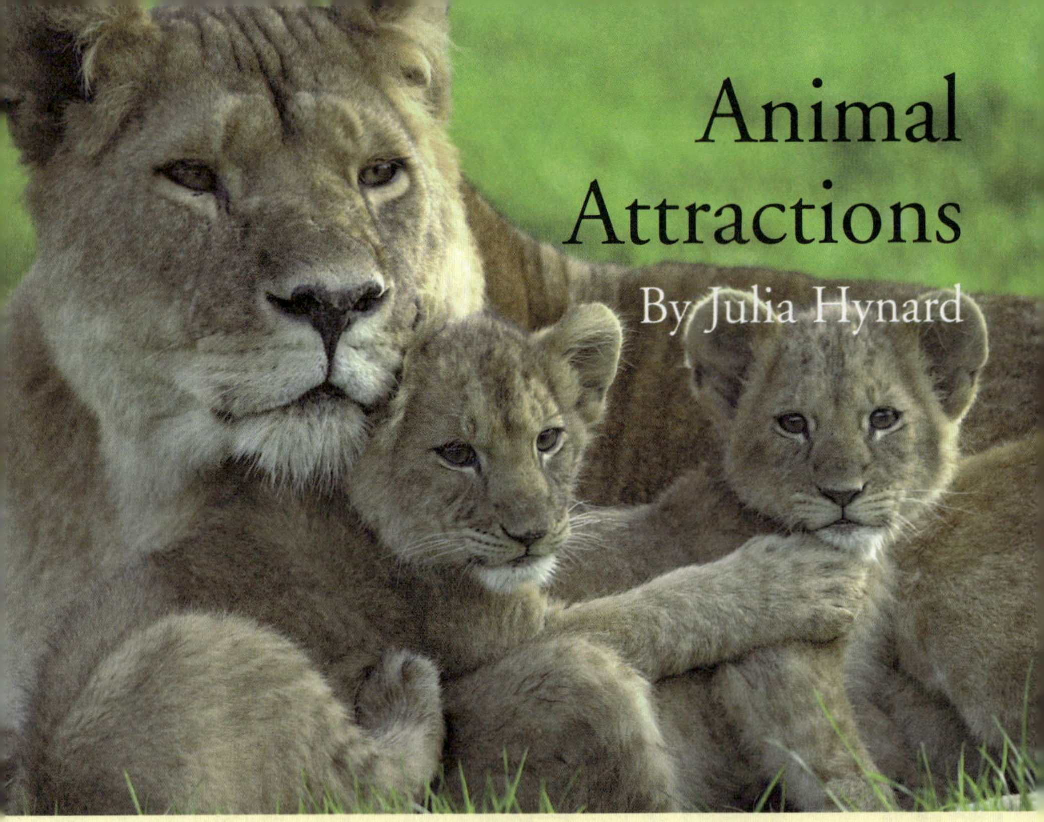

Given the nation's much vaunted susceptibility to our furry friends, it's no wonder that so many tourist attractions are trading on their animal magnetism. Options range from open farms where you can milk a cow, feed a goat or cuddle a bunny, to the drive-through safari park where you're more likely to encounter a hulking great white rhino.

Down on the Farm

Variations on a theme include **Finkley Down Farm Park** at Andover (page 97). Along with its countryside museum, Romany caravans exhibit, adventure playground and assortment of farm animals is the very popular pets' corner offering a memorable hands-on experience. Here, children (who are very quiet and good) may get to hold one of the captivating hand-reared animals. **White Post Modern Farm Centre** at Farnsfield (page 185) is actually a working farm where you see modern methods in practice as well as plenty of animals: llamas, deer, pigs, cows, snails and quails … plus mousetown and the reptile house.

One of Wales' leading tourist attractions, **Greenmeadow Community Farm** at Cwmbran (page 370), was built in the 1980s on land threatened by developers. Attractions include tractor and trailer rides, a dragon themed adventure playground, lambing and shearing, and special events at Halloween and Christmas.

If it's the horses you fancy, don't miss the **National Horseracing Museum** at Newmarket (page 217). The museum tells the story of horseracing and its heroes and runs two-hour minibus tours taking you behind the scenes at the stables and trainers' yards, giving you the chance to meet both horses and staff. You also get to see horses going through their paces on the gallops, and splashing in the horses' swimming pool.

On Safari

The first drive-through safari park outside Africa opened at **Longleat** (page 256) in 1966, allowing animals to roam freely across hundreds of acres on the estate of Longleat House – which in 1949 was the first English stately home to open its doors to the public. The park is divided into eight main sections: the East African Reserve, Elephant Country, Monkey Jungle, Big Game Park, Deer Park, Tiger Territory, Lion Country and Wolf Wood.

Also in the grounds of an impressive stately home is the safari park at **Woburn Abbey** (page 15), where in addition to the wide range of animals (antelopes, bears, bison, elephants, giraffes, lions, rhinos, tigers, wolves and zebra) attractions include the Elephant Encounter, a huge indoor adventure playground, treetop action trail, and a railway train running from Bison Halt to Elephant Junction.

Blair Drummond Safari and Adventure Park (page 340) features a sea lion show, pets' farm and chimpanzee island, and the four-mile drive-through safari at the **West Midland Safari Park** (page 261) in the heart of rural Worcestershire includes twice daily hippo feeding, live shows and plenty of animal encounter opportunities.

Going to the Zoo

Traditional zoos, like those in London, Edinburgh and Belfast, never lose their appeal. **London Zoo** (page 149), at Regents Park, first opened in 1828 for the purpose of scientific study and didn't actually admit the public until 1847, giving an expectant population their first glimpse of fantastic creatures beyond their wildest imaginings, long before the days of TV and accessible foreign travel. Today, 112 of the 650 species resident at London Zoo are listed as threatened with extinction, and conservation is the abiding theme, with the recent addition of the Web of Life exhibit combining a museum-style presentation with live animals.

Whipsnade in Bedfordshire (page 15), opening in 1931, was the first zoo park to recognise the need to keep large, exotic animals in more natural surroundings with plenty of space to wander at will. In the last 30 years eminent conservationists have taken up the theme, including John Knowles at **Marwell Zoological Park**, Hampshire (page 102), and the late John Aspinall at **Howletts** (page 117) and **Port Lympne Wild Animal Parks** (page 124) in Kent.

However worthy the objectives in terms of animal husbandry, academic study and conservation, and however didactic the message about bio-diversity and the threat to world habitats and species, there's no doubting that these zoos and wildlife parks offer a cracking day out, with an emphasis on fun – however much you learn on the way.

One of Britain's top tourist destinations, **Flamingo Land** at Kirby Misperton, North Yorkshire (page 271), combines the thrills of the UK's fourth most visited theme park with a fully-fledged zoo of over 1000 animals, all set in 375 acres of parkland. Many of the species represented are endangered and as such are included in the zoo's breeding programme. It also has a children's farm and the largest flock in the country of those flamboyantly pink eponymous birds.

Claiming Sanctuary

Concerned more with the conservation of individual creatures than of entire species are a growing breed of animal rescue centres, which have also been developed into engaging visitor attractions. Long established examples include **Monkey World** (page 76), set in 65 acres of woodland at Longthorns near Wareham in Dorset, which was started in 1987 by Jim and Alison Cronin to provide a sanctuary for Spanish beach monkeys. These poor creatures were taken as babies from Africa, dressed in human clothes and used as photographers' props. As they grew older and harder to control, many would be beaten into submission or drugged to keep them quiet.

Chimps have been rescued from many other countries, too, where they have been used and abused in circuses and private homes or in laboratories for experimental purposes. Chimps routinely arrive with drug addiction problems, physical injuries and malnutrition and need a long recovery period. The chimps are rehabilitated into large social groups, but are not permitted to breed, as there are always so many more who need rescuing.

Equally fascinating is the work of the **National Seal Santuary** at Gweek in Cornwall (page 39), which has been rescuing, rehabilitating and returning seals to the sea for 40 years, and the **Otter Trust** (page 215), the world's largest and longest established otter conservation organisation, which has its headquarters at Earsham in Suffolk. The Earsham sanctuary is located on the banks of the River Waveney, with resident birds on the marshes and an abundance of wild waterfowl. Facilities include a visitor centre and children's playground, and in the grounds you can also see wallabies, Muntjac and Fallow deer. The Trust has two other sanctuaries: at the North Pennines Reserve in County Durham, and Tamar in Cornwall, both with equally beautiful settings where you can enjoy your visit with the added satisfaction of helping to conserve these delightful creatures for posterity.

How can I get away without the hassle of finding a place to stay?

Booking a place to stay can be a time-consuming process. You choose a place you like, only to find it's fully booked. That means going back to the drawing board again. Why not ask us to find the place that best suits your needs? No fuss, no worries and no booking fee.

Whatever your preference, we have the place for you. From a rustic farm cottage to a smart city centre hotel - we have them all. Choose from around 8,000 quality rated hotels and B&Bs in Great Britain and Ireland.

Hotel Booking Service

0870 50 50 505

accommodation@aabookings.com

www.theAA.com

You may contact us using a Textphone on 0870 243 2456. Information is available in large print, audio and Braille on request. Please call for details.

Bedfordshire

One of England's smallest counties, Bedfordshire contains the picturesque villages of Woburn and Old Warden, and the large towns of Luton and Bedford. There's plenty of countryside to explore on foot or by bike, and plenty to see and do in Bedfordshire's towns and villages.

For many travellers, Luton is the gateway to London and Eastern England. London Luton Airport offers an increasing number of international flights, but that's not all there is to this bustling town. Once a centre for hat manufacture, Luton has a variety of attractions including gardens, museums, parks and a unique collection of horse-drawn carriages. Not far from the town there stands the magnificent Luton Hoo, a 19th-century house (now a hotel) with over 1,000 acres of `Capability' Brown garden and a collection of Fabergé eggs and art connected with the Russian royal family.

The county has some charming sights, set among its many small villages. Woburn is one of these, and is known not only for its Abbey and Safari Park, but also its fine Georgian houses and antique shops. At Shuttleworth, not far from Old Warden, the Swiss Garden is an ideal place to spend a quiet afternoon. In its ten-acre spread there are trees and shrubs from all over the world, as well as a tiny thatched Swiss cottage.

Dunstable boasts the Norman Church of St Peter, with medieval additions that include a 14th-century chancel screen. Ampthill, between Luton and Bedford, is full of fascinating architecture, including Avenue House and the 14th-century Church of St Andrew, which houses a cannon-ball monument to Richard Nicolls, a local man who named New York (after his patron the Duke of York) in 1664.

Top: Leighton Buzzard Narrow Gauge Railway

EVENTS & FESTIVALS

March
1st-8th Bedfordshire Festival of Music, Speech & Drama, various venues in Bedford

May
1st Ickwell May Festival, The Maypole, Ickwell Green
26th Luton Carnival, a multi-cultural showcase

July
4th-6th Popular Flying Association International Air Rally & Exhibition, Cranfield Airfield (provisional)

August
2nd Proms in the Park (10th anniversary), Bedford Park

September
13th-14th Bedfordshire Steam & Country Fayre, Old Warden Park, near Biggleswade

October
4th Bedford Beer Festival, Bedford Corn Exchange
12th National Apple Day at Bromham Mill: apples, cider, apple bobbing, farmers market & entertainment (provisional)

November
tbc Bedford Fireworks Display, Rugby Ground, Goldington Road, Bedford

December
tbc Bedford Victorian Fayre, Bedford town centre

14   Bedfordshire

AMPTHILL   Map 04 TL03
HOUGHTON HOUSE
(1m NE off A421)

Now a ruin, the mansion was built for Mary Countess of Pembroke, the sister of Sir Philip Sidney. Inigo Jones is thought to have been involved in work on the house, which may have been the original `House Beautiful' in Bunyan's 'Pilgrim's Progress'.
Times: Open all reasonable times. **Fee:** Free **Facilities:** P & ⚑

BEDFORD   Map 04 TL04
BEDFORD MUSEUM
Castle Ln MK40 3XD (close to town bridge and Embankment)
☎ 01234 353323   📠 01234 273401
e-mail: bmuseum@bedford.gov.uk

Embark on a fascinating journey through the human and natural history of north Bedfordshire, pausing briefly to glimpse at wonders from more distant lands. Go back in time and visit the delightful rural room sets and the Old School Museum, where Blackbeard's Sword, 'Old Billy' the record breaking longest-living horse and numerous other treasures and curiosities can be found. Housed in the former Higgins and Sons Brewery, Bedford Museum is situated within the gardens of what was once Bedford Castle, beside the Great Ouse embankment. The courtyard and galleries provide an excellent setting for the varied collections.
Times: Open all year, Tue-Sat 11-5, Sun 2-5. (Closed Mon ex BH Mon afternoon, Good Fri & Xmas). **Fee:** * £2.10 (ch, pen & con free). Fri free for everyone. Annual ticket £8.40. **Facilities:** P (50mtrs) 🍴 & (lift available on request, subject to staff availability) toilets for disabled shop ✖ (ex guide dogs)

CECIL HIGGINS ART GALLERY & MUSEUM
Castle Ln MK40 3RP (in the centre of the town, just off the Embankment)
☎ 01234 211222   📠 01234 327149
e-mail: chag@bedford.gov.uk

A recreated Victorian mansion, with the rooms arranged as though the house was still lived in. Includes a bedroom with furniture designed by Victorian architect William Burges, and the adjoining gallery has an outstanding collection of ceramics, glass and changing exhibition of prints, drawings and watercolours. Also includes the Thomas Lester lace collection.
Times: Open all year, Tue-Sat 11-5, Sun & BH Mon 2-5. (Closed Mon, Good Fri, 25-26 Dec & 1 Jan). **Fee:** * £2.10 (ch & concessions free) includes entry to Bedford Museum. Free to all visitors Fri **Facilities:** P (50yds) pay & display 🍴 & toilets for disabled shop ✖ (ex guide dogs)

ELSTOW   Map 04 TL04
MOOT HALL
MK42 9XT (signposted off Elstow Road)
☎ 01234 266889   📠 01234 228531

The restored medieval timber-framed market hall has a collection of 17th-century furniture and items relating to the life and times of John Bunyan, who was born nearby. These include a fine collection of his works, notably *Pilgrim's Progress*.
Times: Open 2 Apr-Sep, Tue-Thu, Sun & BH's 1-4 (Closed Sat & Mon ex BH's & Fri). Phone to confirm. **Fee:** * £1 (ch 5-16 & pen 50p). Disabled visitors free. **Facilities:** P & shop ✖

LEIGHTON BUZZARD   Map 04 SP92
LEIGHTON BUZZARD RAILWAY
Pages Park Station, Billington Rd LU7 4TN (0.75m SE on A4146 signposted in and around Leighton Buzzard. Nr rdbt junct with A505 Dunstable-Aylesbury)
☎ 01525 373888   📠 01525 377814   **2 for 1**
e-mail: info@buzzrail.co.uk

The Leighton Buzzard Railway offers a 65-minute journey into the vanished world of the English Light Railway, with its sharp curves, steep gradients, level crossings and unique roadside running. Built in 1919 to serve the local sand industry, the railway has carried a steam passenger service, operated by volunteers, since 1968.
Times: Open Mar-Oct, Sun & BH wknds; Jul, Wed; Aug, Tue-Thu, Sat & BH wknds. **Fee:** * Return ticket £5 (ch 2-15 £2, pen £4 & ch under 2 free). Party 10+. **Facilities:** P 🍴 & (platform & train access for wheelchairs) toilets for disabled shop 🛍

LUTON   Map 04 TL02
JOHN DONY FIELD CENTRE
Hancock Dr, Bushmead LU2 7SF (signposted from rdbt on A6, at Barnfield College on New Bedford Rd)
☎ 01582 486983   📠 01582 422805
e-mail: tweent@luton.gov.uk

This is a purpose built study centre for exploring the landscapes, plants and animals of the Luton area. Featuring permanent displays on local archaeology, natural history and the management of the local nature reserve, it explains how ancient grasslands and hedgerows are conserved and follows 4000 years of history from Bronze Age to modern times.
Times: Open all year, Mon-Fri 9.30-4.45, Sun 9.30-1. Closed BHs. **Fee:** Free. **Facilities:** P & toilets for disabled ✖ (ex guide/hearing dogs)

LUTON MUSEUM & GALLERY
Wardown Park, Old Bedford Rd LU2 7HA (Follow brown signs from the town centre & N of Luton)
☎ 01582 546722 & 546739   📠 01582 546763
e-mail: museum.gallery@luton.gov.uk

A Victorian mansion, with displays illustrating the natural and cultural history, archaeology and industries of the area, including the development of Luton's hat industry, and the Bedfordshire and Hertfordshire

continued

Bedfordshire

Regimental Collections. New 'Luton Life' displays are due to open in December 2002. Telephone for further details.
Times: Open all year, Tue-Sat 10-5, Sun 1-5 (Closed Xmas, 1 Jan & Mon ex open BH Mons). **Fee:** Free. **Facilities:** P ⬛ ♿ (parking adjacent to entrance, lift to 1st floor) toilets for disabled shop ✶ (ex guide dogs & hearing dogs)

STOCKWOOD CRAFT MUSEUM & GARDENS
Stockwood Country Park, Farley Hill LU1 4BH (signposted from M1 junct 10 and from Hitchin, Dunstable, Bedford and from Luton town centre)
☎ 01582 738714 & 546729   📄 01582 546763
e-mail: museum.gallery@luton.gov.uk

The Museum is set in period gardens which incorporate the Ian Hamilton Finlay Sculpture Gardens. The Mossman collection of horse-drawn vehicles traces the history of transport from Roman times to the 1940s. Craft demonstrations are held at weekends in the summer. Please telephone for details of special events.
Times: Open all year; Mar-Oct, Tue-Sat 10-5, Sun & BH Mons 10-6; Nov-Mar, wknds 10-4. (closed Xmas & 1 Jan) **Fee:** Free. **Facilities:** P ⬛ ♿ (stair lift, parking, induction loop, automatic door) toilets for disabled shop ✶ (ex guide & hearing dogs)

🏛 OLD WARDEN   Map 04 TL14
THE SHUTTLEWORTH COLLECTION
Old Warden Aerodrome SG18 9EA (2m W from rdbt on A1, Biggleswade by-pass)
☎ 01767 627288   📄 01767 626229
Times: Open Apr-Oct 10-5 (last admission 4), Nov-Mar 10-4 (last admission 3). Closed Xmas-New Year. **Facilities:** P ⬛ ✶ licensed ♿ toilets for disabled shop ✶ (ex guide dogs) *Details not confirmed for 2003* ✎

🏛 SANDY   Map 04 TL14
RSPB NATURE RESERVE
The Lodge SG19 2DL (1m E, on B1042 Potton Rd)
☎ 01767 680541   📄 01767 683508
e-mail: jo.davies@rspb.org.uk
Times: Open daily dawn-dusk. Visitor Centre 9-5.15. **Facilities:** P ♿ (partial access) toilets for disabled shop ✶ (ex guide dogs) *Details not confirmed for 2003* ✎

🏛 SILSOE   Map 04 TL03
WREST PARK HOUSE & GARDENS
MK45 4HS (0.75m E off A6)
☎ 01525 860152

The formal gardens designed over 150 years ago form a serene and beguiling setting for this elegant 19th-century mansion.
Times: Open 31 Mar-28 Oct, Sat, Sun & BH's only 10-5; Apr-Sep 10-6. Last admission one hour before closing time. **Fee:** * £3.80 (ch 5-15 £1.90, under 5's free, concessions £2.90). Personal stereo tour included in price. **Facilities:** P ⬛ ✶ (in certain areas) ♨

🏛 WHIPSNADE   Map 04 TL01
WHIPSNADE WILD ANIMAL PARK
LU6 2LF (signposted from M1 junct 9 & 12)
☎ 01582 872171   📄 01582 872649
Times: Open all year, daily. (Closed 25 Dec). Telephone 01582 872171 for opening times. **Facilities:** P (charged) ⬛ ♿ (free entry for disabled cars) toilets for disabled shop ✶ *Details not confirmed for 2003* ✎

🏛 WOBURN   Map 04 SP93
WOBURN ABBEY
MK17 9WA
☎ 01525 290666   📄 01525 290271
e-mail: enquiries@woburnabbey.co.uk

Standing in 3000 acres of parkland, this palatial 18th-century mansion was originally a Cistercian Abbey, and the Dukes of Bedford have lived here since 1547. The art collection includes works by Canaletto, Rembrandt, Van Dyck, and Gainsborough. 14 state apartments are on view, and the private apartments are shown when not in use. Special events are held during the year, including the De-Havilland Tiger Moth Fly-In and a garden show.
Times: Open Jan-23 Mar; Abbey Sat & Sun only 11-4, Deer park 10.30-3.45; 24 Mar-29 Sep; Abbey weekdays 11-4, Sun & BH 11-5; 5-27 Oct Sat & Sun only; Deer Park weekdays 10-4.30, Sun & BH 10-4.45. **Fee:** * Abbey & Deer Park £8 (ch over 12yrs £3.50, pen £7). Family ticket £20-£23. Deer Park only car & passengers £2. Motorcycles & passengers £2. **Facilities:** P (charged) ⬛ ✶ licensed ♿ (wheelchairs accommodated by prior arrangement) toilets for disabled shop ✶ ✎

WOBURN SAFARI PARK
Woburn Park MK17 9QN (Signposted from M1 junct 13)
☎ 01525 290407   📄 01525 290489
e-mail: info@woburnsafari.co.uk

Set in the 3000 acres of parkland belonging to Woburn Abbey, Woburn Safari Park has an extensive collection of many species. The safari road passes through an African plains area stocked with eland, zebra, hippo and rhino, then through well-kepeed tiger and lion enclosures and on past bears and monkeys. Animal encounters, sea lion and parrot shows, and elephant displays are all popular attractions. The large leisure complex also offers a boating lake, adventure playgrounds, railway train, walk-through aviary, squirrel monkey exhibit and `the Australian Walkabout', with friendly wallabies. A new attraction is underwater viewing at Sealion Cove.
Times: Open daily, 10 Mar-27 Oct, 10-5. **Fee:** * £12.50 (ch 3-17 £9, pen £9.50). Ch under 3 free. From 21 Jul-3 Sep prices increase by extra 50p during Bedfordshire School Holidays. **Facilities:** P ⬛ ✶ licensed ♿ toilets for disabled shop ✶ ✎

Berkshire

EVENTS & FESTIVALS

March
4th Shrove Tuesday Great Newbury Pancake Race

May
3rd-5th Crafty Craft Race, Kennet & Avon Canal
10th-24th Newbury International Spring Festival of music and the visual arts
14th-18th Royal Windsor Horse Show

June
28th-29th Newbury International Orchid Show
tbc Royal Ascot, Ascot Race Course

July
4th-6th Bracknell Festival
19th-20th Kennet Valley Kite Festival, Thatcham
tbc De Beers Diamond Day, Ascot Race Course
tbc Kennet & Avon Canal Trust Water Carnival
tbc WOMAD World Music & Arts Festival, Rivermead, Reading

August
tbc Carling Festival, Richfield Avenue, Reading
tbc Shergar Cup, Ascot Race Course

September
20th-21st Newbury & Royal County of Berkshire Show, Newbury Showground
tbc Ascot Festival of Racing
tbc Windsor Festival

October
tbc Michaelmas Fair, Northcroft, Newbury

Berkshire is a narrow county of wide variety, reaching from the edge of London on its eastern boundary to the relative isolation of the Lambourn Downs in the west, containing towns as diverse as Reading and Hungerford, Newbury and Windsor.

Waterways play an important part in Berkshire's character and history, not least the River Thames which forms the county's border with Oxfordshire. The Kennet, a tributary of the Thames that was partially converted into the Kennet and Avon Canal, had a major role in the growth and success of both Reading and Newbury, and flows the length of the county from Reading until it peters out somewhere in Wiltshire. Both of these rivers, as well as The Bourne and the River Pang, flow through some of England's prettiest countryside. The charm of these scenes has been preserved in one of Britain's best-loved children's books. Kenneth Graham used the river banks around Cookham as the setting for *The Wind in the Willows* in 1908. Cookham is also known as the birthplace of eccentric artist, Sir Stanley Spencer (1891-1959), whose work includes *Christ Carrying the Cross* and various religious murals. His birthplace and a gallery of his work are in the town.

Reading is the largest and liveliest town in Berkshire and has played an important role in the county's history. The town was founded by the Saxons and its 12th-century abbey was once a major pilgrimage site. Alfred defeated a Viking invasion nearby, and the town was also the home of the English Parliament for a while. During the Industrial era Reading was famous for Bacon, Biscuits and Beer – The Three B's, and the Huntley & Palmer biscuit factory can still be seen among the new office blocks and apartments near the centre of town.

Top: Bisham Church

Berkshire   **17**

🏛 BRACKNELL   Map 04 SU86
THE LOOK OUT DISCOVERY CENTRE
Nine Mile Ride RG12 7QW (3m S of town centre. From M3 junct 3, A322 to Bracknell from M4 junct 10, take A329M to Bracknell. Follow brown tourist signs)
☎ 01344 354400   📠 01344 354422
e-mail: thelookout@bracknell-forest.gov.uk

A hands-on, interactive science and nature exhibition where budding scientists can spend many hours exploring and discovering over 70 fun filled exhibits within five themed zones, the topics covered linked to the National Curriculum. There's the Sound and Music zone where visitors can see their own voice and make water dance. Other zones include Light and Colour, Forces and Movement and the Body and Perception. Enjoy a nature walk in the surrounding 2,600 acres.
Times: Open all year (Closed 25-26 Dec). **Fee:** * £4.50 (ch £3, concessions £2.70). Family (2 adults/2children or 1 adult/3children) £12. **Facilities:** 🅿 ☕ ♿ toilets for disabled shop ✈ (ex grounds)

🏛 ETON   Map 04 SU97
DORNEY COURT
Dorney SL4 6QP (signed from M4 junct 7, B3026)
☎ 01628 604638   📠 01628 665772   **2 for 1**
e-mail: palmer@dorneycourt.co.uk

An enchanting brick and timber manor house (c1440) in a tranquil setting. With tall Tudor chimneys and a splendid great hall, it has been the home of the present family since 1510.
Times: Open BH Sun & Mons in May; Sun 1.30-4.30. Aug every afternoon ex Sat 1.30-4.30. **Fee:** £5.50 (ch £3, under 10's free).
Facilities: 🅿 ☕ ♿ toilets for disabled garden centre ✈ (ex guide dogs)

🏛 LOWER BASILDON   Map 04 SU67
BASILDON PARK
RG8 9NR (7m NW of Reading on W side of A329)
☎ 0118 984 3040   📠 0118 984 1267   **2 for 1**
e-mail: tbdgen@smtp.ntrust.org.uk

This 18th-century house, built of Bath stone, fell into decay in the 20th Century, has been beautifully restored by Lord and Lady Iliffe. The classical front has a splendid central portico and pavilions, and inside there are delicate plasterwork decorations on the walls and ceilings. The Octagon drawing room has fine pictures and furniture. There is a small formal garden.
Times: House open Apr-end Oct, Wed-Sun & BH Mon 1-5.30. Park & garden Apr-end Oct, Wed-Sun & BH Mon 12-5.30. **Fee:** House & grounds £4.40, family ticket £11; Grounds only £2, family ticket £5.
Facilities: 🅿 ✖ licensed ♿ (driven buggy) toilets for disabled shop ✈ (ex on lead in grounds) 🐾

BEALE PARK
Lower Basildon RG8 9NH (M4 junct 12, follow brown tourist signs to Pangbourne, A329 towards Oxford)
☎ 0118 984 5172   📠 0118 984 5171
e-mail: bealepark@bun.com

Beale Park is home to an extraordinary bird collection and also offers a steam railway, rare breeds of farm animals, a pets' corner, meerkats, wallabies, a deer park, two splash pools, adventure playground, gardens and trails. Summer riverboat trips and excellent fishing.
Times: Open Mar-Dec. **Fee:** £4.80 (ch under 3 & disabled ch free, ch 3-16 £3.40, student, disabled adult & helper £2.40, pen £4). Family (2 adult & 2 ch) £14, (1 adult & 3 ch) £12. **Facilities:** 🅿 ☕ ♿ (parking, wheelchair available) toilets for disabled shop ✈ (ex guide dogs)

🏛 NEWBURY   Map 04 SU46
WEST BERKSHIRE MUSEUM
The Wharf RG14 5AS (M4 junct 13, then on A34 for 3m, follow signs for town centre)
☎ 01635 30511   📠 01635 38535
e-mail: heritage@westberks.gov.uk
Times: Open all year: Apr-Sep, Mon-Fri (Wed during school hols only) 10-5, Sat 10-4.30. Oct-Mar, Mon-Sat (Wed during school hols only) 10-4. (Closed Sun & BHs). **Facilities:** 🅿 (15yds) ♿ shop ✈ (ex guide dogs) Details not confirmed for 2003

🏛 READING   Map 04 SU77
MUSEUM OF ENGLISH RURAL LIFE
University of Reading, Whiteknights Park RG6 6AG (2m SE on A327)
☎ 0118 931 8660   📠 0118 975 1264
e-mail: info@rhc.ac.uk
Times: Open all year, Tue-Sat, 10-1 & 2-4.30. (Closed BH's & Xmas-New Year). **Facilities:** 🅿 ♿ shop ✈ Details not confirmed for 2003

🏛 RISELEY   Map 04 SU76
WELLINGTON COUNTRY PARK
RG7 1SP (signposted off A33)
☎ 0118 932 6444   📠 0118 932 6445

Times: Open all year Mar-Oct, daily 10-5.30, Nov-Feb wknds 10-4.30.
Facilities: 🅿 ☕ ♿ (fishing platform & nature trail for disabled) toilets for disabled shop Details not confirmed for 2003 🐾

18 Berkshire

WINDSOR   Map 04 SU97

Frogmore House
Home Park SL4 1NJ (entrance from B3021)
☎ 020 7321 2233 ≣ 020 7930 9365
e-mail: information@royalcollection.org.uk

The present building dates back to 1618, and residents have included Queen Charlotte, Queen Victoria and Queen Mary. An original mural, discovered only recently during redecoration, can be seen on the stairway.
Times: Open 21-23 May, 10-6 (last admission 5). 24-26 Aug, 10-5.30 (last admission 3.30). Prebooked guided tours 6 Aug-26 Sep. **Fee:** * Tours £7. **Facilities:** shop ✕

Household Cavalry Museum
Combermere Barracks, St Leonards Rd SL4 3DN (on St Leonards Rd opposite King Edward VII Hospital)
☎ 01753 755112 ≣ 01753 755161

One of the finest military museums in Britain, with comprehensive displays of the uniforms, weapons, horse furniture (tack, regalia, etc) and armour used by the Household Cavalry from 1600 to the present day.
Times: Open all year Mon-Fri (ex BH) 9-12.30 & 2-4.30. **Fee:** Free admission, however a donation is appreciated. **Facilities:** ♿ shop ✕

Legoland Windsor
Winkfield Rd SL4 4AY (on B3022 signed from M3 junct 3 & M4 junct 6)
☎ 08705 040404 ≣ 01753 626200
e-mail: sales@legoland.co.uk

With over 50 interactive rides, live shows, building workshops, driving schools and attractions. Set in 150 acres of beautiful parkland, LEGOLAND Windsor is a different sort of family theme park. An atmospheric and unique experience for the whole family, a visit here is more than a day out, it's a lifetime of memories.

Times: Open daily 10 Mar-3 Nov (Closed 10-11, 17-18 & 24-25 Sep; 1-2, 8-9, & 15-16 Oct). Xmas opening 21 Dec-5 Jan. (Closed 25 Dec).
Fee: * Adult £18.95-£22.95 (ch under 3 free, ch 3-15 £15.95-£19.95, pen £12.95-£16.95. Tickets can be booked in advance by telephoning 08705 040404. **Facilities:** 🅿 🍴 ✕ licensed ♿ (signing staff, wheelchair hire, parking) toilets for disabled shop ✕ (ex guide dogs)

St George's Chapel
SL4 1NJ (M4 junct 6 & M3 junct 3)
☎ 01753 865538 ≣ 01753 620165

Begun in 1475 by Edward IV, and completed in the reign of Henry VIII, the chapel is a fine example of Perpendicular architecture, with large windows adding to the effect of light and spaciousness. The fan vaulting on the ceiling is magnificent, as are the chantries and intricate carving on the choir stalls.
Times: Open Mon-Sat 10-4. (Closed 26 & 27 Apr, 16-19 Jun, 24-25 Dec & occasionally at short notice). Closed Sun, worshippers very welcome. **Fee:** Free entry to the Chapel is included in the price of entry to Windsor Castle. **Facilities:** ♿ shop ✕

Savill Garden (Windsor Great Park)
Wick Ln, Englefield Green TW20 0UU (Signposted off A30 between Egham & Virginia Water)   **2 for 1**
☎ 01753 847518 ≣ 01753 847536
e-mail: savillgarden@crownestate.org.uk

The magnificent 35-acre garden lies within Windsor Great Park. It has spectacular woodland displays in spring, sweeping herbaceous borders in summer, fiery autumn colours and misty winter vistas. The garden's temperate house is a year-round delight.
Times: Open all year, daily 10-6 (10-4 Nov -Feb). (Closed 25-26 Dec). **Fee:** * £5 (ch 6-16 £2, pen £4.50) Apr & May; £4 (ch 6-16 £1, pen £3.50) Jun-Oct; £3 (ch 6-16 £1, pen £2.50) Nov-Mar. Ch 1-5 free. Party 10+. **Facilities:** 🅿 🍴 ✕ licensed ♿ (wheelchairs available) toilets for disabled shop garden centre ✕ (ex guide dogs & on terrace)

Windsor Castle
SL4 1NJ (M4 junct 6 & M3 junct 3)
☎ 020 7321 2233 ≣ 020 7930 9365
e-mail: windsorcastle@royalcollection.org.uk

Covering 13 acres, this is the official residence of HM The Queen and the largest inhabited castle in the world. Begun as a wooden fort by William the Conqueror, it has been added to by almost every monarch since. The Upper Ward includes the State Apartments, magnificently restored following the fire of 1992, and the Lower Ward where St George's Chapel is situated. The Doll's House designed for Queen Mary in the 1920s by Lutyens, is also on display.
Times: Open all year, daily except Good Friday & 25-26 Dec. Nov-Feb, 9.45-4.15 (last admission 3), Mar-Oct 9.45-5.15 (last admission 4). As Windsor Castle is a royal residence the opening arrangements may be subject to change at short notice. **Fee:** * £11.50 (ch 5-17 £6, under 5's free, pen £9.50) Family ticket £29 (2 adults & 2 ch). **Facilities:** 🅿 (400yds) ♿ (ramps) toilets for disabled shop ✕ (ex guide dogs)

Bristol

Bristol was once one of the South of England's major ports but is now perhaps better known for its contributions to contemporary art and music. It is an ancient city with a modern outlook, and centuries of history are waiting, ready to be explored by the curious visitor.

For centuries ships sailed from Bristol to every part of the known world in search of new produce and markets, opening up international trade routes. In 1497 John Cabot (Giovanni Caboto), a Genoese pilot set sail from Bristol and within months had encountered North America. Four centuries later the Cabot Tower was built in commemoration. In 1843 Brunel launched his *SS Great Britain*, the largest iron ship then built. She now sits, rescued and restored, in the dock where she was constructed.

Clifton Suspension Bridge is 702ft (214m) long and spans the Avon gorge, which is over 200 ft (60m) deep. The Bridge was designed by Isombard Kingdom Brunel and took a while to build. Work started in 1836, but due to financial problems was not completed until 1864, five years after Brunel had died. The bridge remains a fitting monument to Victorian engineering.

The city's cathedral was founded as an Augustinian monastery and contains examples of Norman, early-English, Gothic and Victorian architecture. Other important church buildings include St Mary Redcliffe, which was built in the Middle Ages and carries a massive tower with a 285ft (87m) spire.

Post-war rebuilding of the blitz-damaged city centre has meant that Bristol's current identity is less defined by its history than by its recent contributions to popular culture and art. Redevelopment of the disused dockland has led to the creation of art spaces such as the Arnolfini and the Watershed, which are at the forefront of uncovering new talent.

Top: Clifton Suspension Bridge

EVENTS & FESTIVALS

February
tbc Bristol Beer Festival

May
5th North Somerset Show, Long Ashton

June
tbc Bristol Bike Fest
tbc UK Comics Festival

July
5th St Paul's Carnival, Bristol
19th-20th Bristol Community Festival, Long Ashton
26th-27th Bristol Harbour Regatta Festival
tbc Bristol Community Festival
tbc Bristol Motor & Classic Car Show, Long Ashton

August
7th-10th Bristol Balloon Fiesta, Long Ashton
27th-29th Bristol Flower Show, The Downs
tbc Bristol Children's Festival

September
6th-7th International Kite Festival, Long Ashton

September/October
tbc Bristol Half Marathon

October
2nd-11th Poetry Festival, various venues in Bristol

November
tbc Christmas lights switch on, Bristol city centre
tbc Firework Fiesta, Durdham Downs, Bristol

BRISTOL
Map 03 ST57

ARNOLFINI
16 Narrow Quay BS1 4QA
☎ 0117 929 9191 ≋ 0117 925 3872
e-mail: arnolfini@arnolfini.demon.co.uk
Times: Open Mon-Wed, Fri-Sat 10-7, Thu 10-9, Sun & BH's 12-7. (Closed Xmas). Closing for refurbishment summer 2003, phone for details **Facilities:** P 5mins walk 🍴 ✗ licensed & toilets for disabled shop ✈ (ex guide dogs) *Details not confirmed for 2003*

AT-BRISTOL
Anchor Rd, Harbourside BS1 5DB (from city centre, A4 to Anchor Rd. Located on left opposite Cathedral)
☎ 0845 345 1235 ≋ 0117 915 7200
e-mail: information@at-bristol.org.uk

For the interactive adventure of a lifetime head for At-Bristol's three attractions on the city's habourside. A clever fusion of sci-fi architecture and historic buildings are home to 'Wildwalk', a breathtaking journey through the plant and animal kingdoms; Explore, the UK's most exciting hands-on science centre; and the IMAX theatre, the largest cinema screen in the West of England.
Times: Open all year, daily 10-6. (Closed 25 Dec). **Fee:** Ticket for 3 attractions £16.50 (ch £11.45, concessions £13.45). Family ticket £52. **Facilities:** P (charged) 🍴 ✗ licensed & (induction loop) toilets for disabled shop ✈ (ex guide dogs)

BLAISE CASTLE HOUSE MUSEUM
Henbury Rd, Henbury BS10 7QS (4m NW of city, off B4057)
☎ 0117 950 6789 ≋ 0117 959 3475
e-mail: general_museum@bristol-city.gov.uk

Built in the 18th century for a Quaker banker, this mansion is now Bristol's Museum of Social History. Nearby Blaise Hamlet is a picturesque estate village, designed by John Nash.
Times: Open Apr-Oct, Sat-Wed, 10-5. **Fee:** Free. **Facilities:** P & shop ✈ (ex guide dogs)

BRISTOL CITY MUSEUM & ART GALLERY
Queen's Rd, Clifton BS8 1RL (follow signs to city centre, then follow tourist signs to City Museum & Art Gallery)
☎ 0117 922 3571 ≋ 0117 922 2047
e-mail: general_museum@bristol-city.gov.uk

Regional and international collections representing ancient history, natural sciences, and fine and applied arts. Displays include dinosaurs, Bristol ceramics, silver, Chinese and Japanese ceramics. A full programme of Special Exhibitions take place throughout the year. Ring for details.
Times: Open all year, daily 10-5. (Closed 25-26 Dec). **Fee:** Free. **Facilities:** P (NCP 400yds) 🍴 & (lift) toilets for disabled shop ✈ (ex guide dogs)

BRISTOL INDUSTRIAL MUSEUM
Prince's Wharf, Prince St, City Docks BS1 4RN
☎ 0117 925 1470 ≋ 0117 729 7318
e-mail: general_museum@bristol-city.gov.uk

The museum is housed in a converted dockside transit shed. Motor and horse-drawn vehicles from the Bristol area are shown, with locally built aircraft and aero-engines. Railway exhibits include the industrial locomotive 'Henbury'. At weekends from April to October there are trips around the harbour in either the tug 'John King' or the steam tug 'Mayflower' or the fire boat 'Pyronant; or trips around the dockside on the Bristol Harbour Railway. At certain weekends visitors can watch the steam crane and electric crane at work.
Times: Open Apr-Oct, Sat-Wed 10-5; Nov-Mar, Sat & Sun 10-5. **Fee:** Free. **Facilities:** P (charged) & toilets for disabled shop ✈ (ex guide dogs)

BRISTOL ZOO GARDENS
Clifton BS8 3HA (M5 junct 17, take A4018 then follow brown elephant signs. Also signed from city centre)
☎ 0117 973 8951 ≋ 0117 973 6814
e-mail: information@bristolzoo.org.uk

There is so much to experience at Bristol Zoo Gardens, with over 300 species of wildlife in beautiful gardens. Award-winning 'Seal and Penguin Coasts' with fantastic underwater viewing is exceptional, with landscaped beaches, cliffs and an amazing shipwreck. Other favourites include Bug World, Twilight World, the Monkey House, the Reptile House, and the children's play area. The new Brazilian exhibit boasts stunning birds, grazing tapirs, and the world's largest living rodent-the capybara. There is a 'hands-on' activity centre, special events and feeding-time talks.
Times: Open all year, daily (ex 25 Dec) from 9am. Closing times approx 5.30pm (summer) 4.30pm (winter). **Fee:** * £8.60 (ch 3-14 £5, pen £7.70). **Facilities:** P (charged) ✗ licensed & (wheelchairs for use in zoo grounds) toilets for disabled shop ✈

GEORGIAN HOUSE
7 Great George St, off Park St BS1 5RR (5 mins walk from Bristol City Centre)
☎ 0117 921 1362 ≋ 0117 922 2047
e-mail: general_museum@bristol-city.gov.uk

A carefully preserved example of a late 18th-century merchant's town house, with many original features and furnished to illustrate life both above and below stairs. A bedroom is now open, featuring a four-poster bed plus a small display recounting Bristol's involvement in the slave trade.
Times: Open Apr-Oct, Sat-Wed, 10-5. **Fee:** Free. **Facilities:** P (pay & display street parking) ✈ (ex guide dogs)

Bristol

Harveys Wine Museum
12 Denmark St BS1 5DQ (City Centre)
☎ 0117 927 5036   📠 0117 927 5001
e-mail: alun.cox@adsweu.com

Explore a world of wine in Harveys' 13th-century cellars, and discover the delights of tasting from a range of sherries, ports, wines and champagnes. The cellars depict Bristol's history as a trading port plus stunning silverware, glass and other items connected to the wine trade. Wine shop.
Times: Open all year (ex BH's). **Fee:** Open to pre-booked parties only. Prices depend on size of party and type of tasting. **Facilities:** P (5 mins walk) (parking meters) ✘ licensed shop ✈ 🎧

John Wesley's Chapel (The New Room)
36 The Horsefair, Broadmead BS1 3JE (M32 towards Broadmead)
☎ 0117 926 4740

The oldest Methodist chapel in the world, built in 1739 and extended in 1748. Above the chapel are the preacher's rooms where John Wesley, Charles Wesley and the early Methodist preachers stayed.
Times: Open all year, Mon-Sat 10-4. **Fee:** Free. **Facilities:** P (250yds) 💷 ♿ shop ✈ (ex guide dogs) 🎧

Maritime Heritage Centre
Gas Ferry Rd BS1 6UN (M5 junct 18, follow brown signs 'Anchor')
☎ 0117 926 0680
📠 0117 925 5788   **2 for 1**
e-mail: commerical@ss-great-britain.com

Exploring 200 years of Bristol shipbuilding, with special reference to Charles Hill & Son, and their predecessor, James Hillhouse. At the Great Western Dock the museum forms part of the *SS Great Britain* and John Cabot's *Matthew* experience.
Times: Open all year, daily 10-5.30, 4.30 in winter. (Closed 24 & 25 Dec). **Fee:** * Admission is for the museum, the SS Great Britain & the Matthew £6.25 (ch £3.75, pen £5.25). Family ticket (2 adults & 2 ch) £16.50. Party 20+. **Facilities:** P (charged) 💷 ♿ toilets for disabled shop ✈ (ex guide dogs) 🎧

Red Lodge
Park Row BS1 5LJ (5 mins walk from Bristol City Centre)
☎ 0117 921 1360   📠 0117 922 2047
e-mail: general_museum@bristol-city.gov.uk

The house was built in 1590 and then altered in 1730. It has fine oak panelling and carved stone chimney pieces and is furnished in the style of both periods. The garden has now been laid out in Elizabethan style.
Times: Open Apr-Oct, Sat-Wed 10-5. **Fee:** Free. **Facilities:** P (NCP, adjacent) ✈ (ex guide dogs) 🎧

SS Great Britain
Great Western Dock, Gas Ferry Rd BS1 6TY (off Cumberland Rd)
☎ 0117 926 0680   📠 0117 925 5788
Times: Open all year daily 10-5.30, 4.30 in winter. (Closed 24 & 25 Dec). **Facilities:** P (charged) 💷 ♿ shop ✈ *Details not confirmed for 2003* 🎧

Buckinghamshire

EVENTS & FESTIVALS

March
4th Shrove Tuesday Olney Pancake Day Race

April
tbc Stowe Kite Festival, Stowe Park, Buckingham

May
3rd-5th Milton Keynes Garden Show
5th Marlow Spring Regatta, Higginson Park, Marlow
24th-26th Wrest Park Garden Show

June
1st Coombe Hill Run, Wendover
6th-8th The Woburn Abbey Garden Show
15th Folk on the Green, Stony Stratford
26th-29th Milton Keynes International Festival
29th Milton Keynes Carnival

July
5th-12th Buckingham Festival
tbc North Bucks Show, Stowe Park, Buckingham

August
23rd-25th Wrest Park Crafts Festival

September
6th-7th Milton Keynes Garden Show
14th Thames Valley Grand Prix Raft Race, Marlow
20th Marlow Carnival, Marlow

November
tbc Milton Keynes Free Firework Display

December
6th Haddenham Festival

Visitors to Buckinghamshire cannot fail to be enchanted by the majestic sweep of the Chiltern Hills, and fascinated by the history and heritage of the county's many attractive towns and villages.

Richly wooded in the west but mainly windswept and bare near Ivinghoe in the east, the Chilterns extend in a line from Goring in the Thames Valley, across the breadth of Buckinghamshire, to a point near Hitchin in Hertfordshire. Its highest point is the 835ft Coombe Hill near Wendover, which is also the site of a Boer War memorial. Many of the chalk downs are crowned with ancient beech groves. Walkers can get to grips with the Chilterns by walking the North Bucks Way – 30 miles from Wolverton to Chequers near Great Missenden.

Chequers Court plays an important role as the official country residence of the British Prime Minister. It was given to the nation by Lord Lee of Fareham in 1921. The building was constructed in the 16th century, sits in 1,000 acres of farms and woodland, and ironically, contains some valuable Cromwellian relics.

Buckinghamshire is famous for its pretty villages and any one of them would make a visit here worthwhile. Not only are they pretty, but many have strong historical connections. Jordan is the site of the most famous of all Quaker Meeting Houses, which was built in 1688. British Prime Minister Benjamin Disraeli lived at Hughenden Manor in Hughenden; John Milton, author of *Paradise Lost*, lived in a cottage near Chalfont St Giles; Florence Nightingale lived at Claydon House near Buckingham; Roald Dahl lived at Great Missenden; and legendary jazz couple Johnny Dankworth and Cleo Laine live at Wavedon.

Top: Shell fountain at Cliveden, near Cookham.

Buckinghamshire 23

🏛 BEACONSFIELD   Map 04 SU99
BEKONSCOT MODEL VILLAGE
Warwick Rd HP9 2PL (2.7m M40 junct 2, 4m M25 junct 16)
☎ 01494 672919 📠 01494 675284   **2 for 1**
e-mail: bekonscot@dial.pipex.com

A miniature world, depicting rural England in the 1930s. A Gauge 1 model railway meanders through six little villages, each with their own tiny population. Rides on the sit-on miniature railway take place weekends and school holidays.
Times: Open 9 Feb-27 Oct, 10-5. **Fee:** £4.80 (ch £3, students £4). **Facilities:** 🅿 ⦿ ♿ (wheelchair loan) toilets for disabled shop ✈ (ex guide dogs) 🍴

🏛 CHALFONT ST GILES   Map 04 SU99
CHILTERN OPEN AIR MUSEUM
Newland Park, Gorelands Ln HP8 4AB (M25 junct 17, M40 junct 2. Follow brown signs)
☎ 01494 871117 & 875542 📠 01494 872774
Times: Open Apr-29 Oct, daily 10-5. **Facilities:** 🅿 ⦿ ♿ (Braille guide books & taped guides available, wheelchairs) toilets for disabled shop ✈ (ex on lead) *Details not confirmed for 2003* 🍴

MILTON'S COTTAGE
Dean Way HP8 4JH (0.5m W of A413. 3m N of M40 junct 2)
☎ 01494 872313
e-mail: pbirger@clara.net

A timber-framed, 16th-century cottage, with a charming garden, the only surviving home in which John Milton lived and worked. He completed *Paradise Lost* and started *Paradise Regained* here. First editions of these works are among the many rare books and artefacts on display.
Times: Open Mar-Oct, Tue-Sun 10-1 & 2-6. Also open Spring & Summer BH. **Fee:** * £2.50 (ch 15 £1). Party 20+ £2 each. **Facilities:** 🅿 ✈ licensed ♿ (special parking area closer to cottage) shop ✈ (ex guide dogs)

🏛 CLIVEDEN   Map 04 SU98
CLIVEDEN
SL6 0JA (2m N of Taplow, follow brown signs on A4)
☎ 01628 605069 📠 01628 669461   **2 for 1**
e-mail: cliveden@ntrust.org.uk

The 375 acres of garden and woodland overlook the River Thames, and include a magnificent parterre, topiary, lawns with box hedges, and water gardens. The palatial house, former home of the Astors, is now a hotel - The Great Hall and French Dining Room can be visited on certain afternoons.
Times: Open Grounds 12 Mar-Oct daily 11-6, Nov-Dec daily 11-4 (Woodlands open all year). House Apr-Oct, Thu & Sun 3-6 by timed ticket. (Last admission 5.30). **Fee:** Grounds: £6. House: £1 extra. Family ticket £15. **Facilities:** 🅿 ✈ licensed ♿ (powered vehicle & wheelchairs available, parking) toilets for disabled shop ✈ (ex in woodland) 🍴

🏛 HIGH WYCOMBE   Map 04 SU89
WYCOMBE LOCAL HISTORY & CHAIR MUSEUM
Castle Hill House, Priory Av HP13 6PX (follow brown tourist sign from A404 (Amersham Hill) N of High Wycombe town centre)
☎ 01494 421895 📠 01494 421897
e-mail: enquiries@wycombemuseum.demon.co.uk

Situated in an 18th-century house that is set in attractive grounds. The displays explore the history of the Wycombe area, focusing on the chair-making industry, with interactive displays, and changing exhibitions.
Times: Open all year, Mon-Sat 10-5, Sun 2-5. Closed on BHs except special events - ring for details. **Fee:** Free. **Facilities:** 🅿 ⦿ ♿ (large print guides, special parking/drop off point) toilets for disabled shop ✈ (ex guide dogs)

🏛 HUGHENDEN   Map 04 SU89
HUGHENDEN MANOR
HP14 4LA (1.5m N of High Wycombe, on W side of A4128)
☎ 01494 755573 📠 01494 474284

Benjamin Disraeli, later the Earl of Beaconsfield and twice Prime Minister, bought the house in 1847 and lived there until his death in 1881. It still has many of his books and other possessions. The gardens are a recreation of the colourful designs of Disraeli's wife, Mary-Anne.
Times: House open 1-30 Mar, Sat & Sun only. Apr-Oct, Wed-Sun & BH Mon 1-5. Last admission 4.30. Gardens same dates as house 12-5. Park open all year. **Fee:** * £4.40. Family ticket £11. Garden only £1.50 (ch 75p). Park free. **Facilities:** 🅿 ✈ licensed ♿ (braille leaflet, wheelchairs, ramp to house) toilets for disabled shop ✈ (ex in park & car park only) 🍴

Buckinghamshire

🏛 LONG CRENDON Map 04 SP60
COURTHOUSE
HP18 9AN (2m N of Thame, via B4011 when entering village turn right into the High St. Courthouse on left at end)
☎ 01494 528051   📠 01494 463310   `2 for 1`

Probably built as a wool store in the early 1400s, but also used as a manorial courthouse until the late 19th century, this timber-framed building stands out even in this picturesque village. Although the windows and doors have been altered and the chimney stack is Tudor, the magnificent timber roof is original. One of the finest examples of early timber framed building in the area.
Times: Open, Upper storey Apr-Sep, Wed 2-6, Sat, Sun & BH Mons 11-6. **Fee:** * £1 **Facilities:** P (street) (not suitable for large vehicles) 🐕 ♿

🏛 MIDDLE CLAYDON Map 04 SP72
CLAYDON HOUSE
MK18 2EY (Off A413 in Padbury, follow National Trust signs. Entrance by north drive only)
☎ 01296 730349   📠 01296 738511
e-mail: tcdgen@smtp.ntrust.org.uk   `2 for 1`

The rather sober exterior of this 18th-century house gives no clue to the extravagances that lie inside, in the form of fantastic rococo carvings. Ceilings, cornices, walls and overmantels are adorned with delicately carved fruits, birds, beasts and flowers by Luke Lightfoot. The Chinese room is particularly splendid.
Times: House open Sat-Wed 1-5 (Closed Thu & Good Fri). Grounds open 12-6. Last admission 4.30. **Fee:** £4.40 (ch £2.20). Family ticket £11. Grounds £1 (ch 50p) **Facilities:** P ♿ (Braille guide) toilets for disabled 🐕 (ex guide dogs or in park) ♿ 🍴

🏛 QUAINTON Map 04 SP72
BUCKINGHAMSHIRE RAILWAY CENTRE
Quainton Rd Station HP22 4BY (Off A41 Aylesbury to Bicester road. 7m NW of Aylesbury)
☎ 01296 655720 & 655450 (info)
📠 01296 655720
e-mail: bucksrailcentre@btopenworld.com

The Centre houses an interesting and varied collection of about 20 locomotives with 40 carriages and wagons from places as far afield as South Africa, Egypt and America. Items date from the 1800s up to the 1960s. Visitors can take a ride on full-size and miniature steam trains, and stroll around the 20-acre site to see locomotives and rolling stock. The Centre runs locomotive driving courses for visitors. Regular 'days out with Thomas' events take place throughout the year.
Times: Open with engines in steam Apr-Oct, Sun & BH Mon; Jun-Aug, Wed; 10.30-5.30. Dec Sat & Sun Santa's Magical Steamings-advanced booking recommended. Also open for static viewing Wed-Sun. **Fee:** * Steaming Days; £4.50 (ch & pen £3.50). Family ticket £14. BH wknds £6 (ch & pen £5). Family ticket £18. Static viewing £3 (ch & pen £2). **Facilities:** P 🍴 ♿ toilets for disabled shop 🛒

🏛 STOWE Map 04 SP63
STOWE HOUSE
MK18 5EH (From London M1 to Milton Keynes. 3m NW Buckingham)
☎ 01280 818282   📠 01280 818186
e-mail: sses@stowe.co.uk

Set in the National Trust's landscaped gardens, Stowe is a splendid 18th-century mansion. The leading designers of the day were called in to lay out the gardens, and leading architects - Vanbrugh, Gibbs, Kent and Leoni - commissioned to decorate them with garden temples. The house is now a major public school.
Times: Open 3 Jul-6 Sep, daily ex Mon & Tue (open BH Mon) 12-5. Last admission 4. 18-22 Dec daily ex Mon & Tue 11-3. Last admission 2. Please tel for further details on group bookings and other dates. House may close at times when being used for private functions, check before travelling. **Fee:** * £2 (ch £1). **Facilities:** P ♿ toilets for disabled 🐕 (ex guide dogs)

STOWE LANDSCAPE GARDENS
MK18 5EH (3m NW of Buckingham via Stoke Avenue, off A422 Buckingham-Banbury rd)
☎ 01280 822850   📠 01280 822437   `2 for 1`
e-mail: stowegarden@ntrust.org.uk

One of the finest Georgian landscape gardens, made up of valleys and vistas, narrow lakes and rivers with more than 30 temples and monuments designed by many of the leading architects of the 18th century. At the centre is Stowe House surrounded by the park. Many of the garden buildings have been conserved, and thousands of new trees and shrubs have been planted in recent years.
Times: Open 3 Mar-28 Oct (closed 26 May), Wed-Sun, 10-5.30, last admission 4; 1-23 Dec, Wed-Sun, last admission 3. Open all BH Mons. **Fee:** * £4.80 (ch £2.40). Family ticket £12. **Facilities:** P 🍴 licensed ♿ (manual wheelchairs unsuitable, powered batricars available) toilets for disabled shop 🛒

WADDESDON
Map 04 SP71
WADDESDON MANOR
HP18 0JH (gates off A41, 6m NW of Aylesbury)
☎ 01296 653211, 653226 & 653203
✉ 01296 653212
e-mail: twmsep@smtp.ntrust.org.uk

Waddesdon was built in the style of a French château of the 16th century and houses one of the finest collections of 18th-century French decorative arts in the world and includes French furniture, Savonnerie carpets and Sèvres porcelain. There is also a fine collection of important portraits by Gainsborough and Reynolds and works by Dutch and Flemish masters of the 17th century. The garden is renowned for its seasonal displays, colourful shrubs, mature trees and parterre. There is a rococo-style aviary housing many exotic birds, a rose and children's garden.
Times: Open, Grounds & Aviary only, 5 Mar-21 Dec, Wed-Sun & BH Mon 10-5. House 2 Apr-2 Nov, Wed-Sun & BH Mon 11-4. Entrance by timed ticket. **Fee:** Grounds & Aviary £4 (ch £2). House & grounds £11 (ch £8). Tickets bookable in advance at booking charge (tel 01296 653226). **Facilities:** ◨ ✕ licensed ♿ (wheelchairs, braille guide, parking, scented plants) toilets for disabled shop ✈ ❦ ⏾

WEST WYCOMBE
Map 04 SU89
WEST WYCOMBE CAVES
HP14 3AJ (on A40)
☎ 01494 524411 (office) & 533739 (caves)
✉ 01494 471617

The entrance to West Wycombe caves is halfway up the hill that dominates the village. On the summit stands the parish church and the mausoleum of the Dashwood family. The caves are not natural but were dug on the orders of Sir Francis Dashwood between 1748 and 1752. Sir Francis, the Chancellor of the Exchequer, was also the founder of the Hell Fire Club, whose members were reputed to have held outrageous and blasphemous parties in the caves, which extend approximately half a mile underground. The entrance, from a large forecourt, is a brick tunnel that leads into the caves, where tableaux and curiosities are exhibited.
Times: Open all year, Mar-Oct, daily 11-6; Nov-Feb, Sat & Sun 1-5.
Fee: * £3.75 (ch & pen £2.50, students £3). Party 20+. **Facilities:** ◨ ⌨ ♿ toilets for disabled shop ✈ (ex guide dogs)

Buckinghamshire 25

WEST WYCOMBE PARK
HP14 3AJ (S of A40)
☎ 01628 488675

Set in 300 acres of beautiful parkland, the house was rebuilt in the Palladian style, between 1745 and 1771, for Sir Francis Dashwood. Of particular note are the painted ceilings by Borgnis. The park was laid out in the 18th century and given an artificial lake and classical temples.
Times: Open, House & grounds Jun-Aug, Sun-Thu 2-6. Grounds only Apr-May, Sun-Thu 2-6 & Etr, May Day & Spring BH Sun & Mon 2-6. Last admission 5.15. Entry by timed tickets on wkdays. Parties must book in advance. **Fee:** * House & grounds £4.80. Grounds only £2.60. Family ticket £12. **Facilities:** ◨ ♿ (partial access to ground floor & gardens) ✈ (ex on lead in car park) ❦

WING
Map 04 SP82
ASCOTT
LU7 0PS (0.5m E of Wing, 3m SW of Leighton Buzzard on S side of A418)
☎ 01296 688242   ✉ 01296 681904
e-mail: info@ascottestate.co.uk

A National Trust property since 1946, Ascott holds an exceptional collection of paintings, Chinese porcelain and English and French furniture. The 30-acre garden is a fine example of Victorian gardening and the grounds are stunning at any time of year.
Times: House & Gardens: 2-30 Apr, 6 Aug-13 Sep daily 2-6 (ex Mon). Gardens: May-Jul every Wed & last Sun in month, 18 & 25 Sep, 2-6.
Fee: * House & Garden £5.60 (ch £2.80). Gardens only: £4 (ch £2). National Trust members free. **Facilities:** ◨ ♿ (wheelchairs available, all parts accessible with assistance) toilets for disabled ✈ ❦

Cambridgeshire

EVENTS & FESTIVALS

January
tbc Whittlesey Straw Bear Festival

March
15th-16th National Shire Horse Show, Alwalton

April
5th-6th Daffodil Weekend, Thriplow

May
5th Stilton Cheese Rolling
9th-11th East of England Garden Show, Alwalton
tbc Duxford Air Show
tbc St Neots Folk Festival

June
13th-16th East of England Show, Alwalton
28th-29th Hemingford Abbots Open Gardens
tbc Charles Wells Cambridge Folk Festival, Cambridge
tbc Children's Festival Family Day, Jesus Green, Cambridge
tbc Strawberry Fair, Cambridge

July
2nd-5th Wisbech Rose Fair
11th-13th Ely Folk Week, Ely
12th World Pea Shooting Championships, Witcham, Ely (provisional)
tbc Duxford Air Show

August
1st-24th Cambridge Shakespeare Festival
19th-24th Peterborough Beer Festival

September-October
tbc Duxford Air Show

October
12th The World Conker Championships, Ashton

The City of Cambridge is the place that most visitors will want to visit most, and who can blame them? Its ancient colleges, air of learning and rich history are guaranteed to be of interest to anyone looking for a special taste of England, yet there is so much more to the county.

Much of Cambridgeshire is unspoilt and ideal for exploration. Many of the peat-black Fens have been reclaimed over the centuries, and beautiful rivers such as the Ouse and the Nene, as well as miles of canal, are great for those looking for relaxation. Around 1000 acres of undrained fenland at Wicken Fen are run by the National Trust as a nature reserve.

Walkers are well catered for, with over 3,000 miles of public footpaths to explore. Routes include the Fen Rivers Way, the Nene Way, and the Hereward Way. This latter covers 43 miles of lowland, and is named after Hereward, who made a brave stand against Norman conquest in 1071.

But Cambridgeshire isn't all about walking and ancient goings-on. Peterborough has modern arcades as well as lots of old streets that have been pedestrianised. Huntingdon, Ely, Wisbech, St Neots and St Ives have all retained something of the atmosphere of the English market town, complete with family-run shops and busy market days.

The county also has connections with historical figures. Katherine of Aragon is buried in Peterborough cathedral, Wisbech is home to the Octavia Hill Birthplace Museum, commemorating the life and work of one of the founders of the National Trust, and Oliver Cromwell was born in Huntingdon.

A strange and forgotten chapter in the county's history concerns Coprolite-digging, "the extraction of phosphatised clay nodules for fertiliser" which caused a "coprolite rush" between 1850 and 1890.

Top: The Folly, Wimpole Park

Cambridgeshire

CAMBRIDGE   Map 05 TL45
CAMBRIDGE & COUNTY FOLK MUSEUM
2/3 Castle St CB3 0AQ (Turn off A14 onto A3019, museum NW of town)
☎ 01223 355159
e-mail: info@folkmuseum.org.uk

This timber-framed inn houses items covering the everyday life of the people of Cambridgeshire from the 17th century to the present day. Special exhibitions and children's activity days take place throughout the year. Please telephone for details.
Times: Open all year, Apr-Sep, Mon-Sat 10.30-5, Sun 2-5. Oct-Mar, Tue-Sat 10.30-5, Sun 2-5. (Last admissions 30 mins before closing). (Closed 1 Jan, Good Fri, 24-31 Dec). **Fee:** £2.50 (ch 5-12 75p, concessions £1.50) one free ch with every full paying adult. **Facilities:** P (300yds) (pay and display on street parking) & (braille touch tables, tape guides & large print guides) shop ✖ (ex guide dogs)

CAMBRIDGE UNIVERSITY BOTANIC GARDEN
Cory Lodge, Bateman St CB2 1JF (1m S of city centre)
☎ 01223 336265   01223 336278
e-mail: enquiries@botanic.cam.ac.uk

The Cambridge University Botanic Garden is a 40-acre oasis of beautifully landscaped gardens and glasshouses close to the heart of the city. Opened on its present site in 1846, the garden showcases a collection of some 8000 plant species. This Grade II heritage landscape features the Rock Garden, displaying alpine plants, the Winter and Autumn Gardens, tropical rainforest and seasonal displays in the Glasshouses, the historic Systematic Beds, the Scented Garden, Herbaceous Beds and the finest collection of trees in the east of England.
Times: Open all year daily 10-6 (summer), 10-5 (autumn & spring), (10-4) winter. Glasshouses 10-12.30 & 2-3.45. (Closed 25 Dec-1 Jan). Entry by Bateman St and Station Rd gates on weekdays & by Bateman St gate only at weekends & BH. **Fee:** £2.50 (ch & pen £2). **Facilities:** P (0.25m) (on street parking bays-pay & display) 🍴 & (scented garden for the visually impaired) toilets for disabled shop (open Mar-Oct) ✖ (ex guide dogs)

FITZWILLIAM MUSEUM
Trumpington St CB2 1RB (From M11 take either junct 11, 12 or 13. Museum near city centre)
☎ 01223 332900   01223 332923
e-mail: fitzwilliam-enquiries@lists.cam.ac.uk

The Fitzwilliam is the art museum of the University of Cambridge and one of the oldest public museums in Britain. Exhibits include ancient art and sculpture, furniture and rugs as well as masterpieces by painters including Picasso, Monet, Constable and Titian. Highlights of the paintings collection will be on display, and wheelchair access will be limited during the museums courtyard development 2002/2003; please telephone for details.
Times: Open all year Tue-Sat 10-5, Sun 2.15-5 plus Etr Mon & Summer BH. (Closed Good Fri, May Day & 23 Dec-1 Jan) **Fee:** Free. **Facilities:** P (400yds) (2hr max, metered) & (limited access 2002-2003, induction loop) toilets for disabled shop ✖ (ex guide dogs)

SCOTT POLAR RESEARCH INSTITUTE MUSEUM
Lensfield Rd CB2 1ER (1km S of City Centre)
☎ 01223 336540   01223 336549
e-mail: rkh10@cam.ac.uk

An international centre for polar studies, including a museum featuring displays of Arctic and Antarctic expeditions, with special emphasis on those of Captain Scott. Other exhibits include Eskimo work and other arts of the polar regions, as well as displays on current scientific exploration. Public lectures run from October to December and February to April.
Times: Open all year, Mon-Fri 2.30-4. Closed some public & university hols. Occasional Saturday opening. **Fee:** Free. **Facilities:** P (400mtrs) & shop ✖ (ex guide dogs)

UNIVERSITY MUSEUM OF ARCHAEOLOGY & ANTHROPOLOGY
Downing St CB2 3DZ (opposite Crowne Plaza Hotel)
☎ 01223 333516   01223 333517
e-mail: cumaa@hermes.cam.ac.uk

The museum is part of the Faculty of Archaeology and Anthropology of the University of Cambridge. It was established in 1884 and is still housed in its 1916 building on the Downing Site in the city centre. It has three floors displaying renowned archaeological and anthropological collections from around the world.
Times: Open all year Tue-Sat 2-4.30. (Closed 1wk Etr & 1wk Xmas). Telephone for extended summer hours. **Fee:** Free. **Facilities:** P (100yds) & (lift available) shop ✖ (ex guide dogs)

DUXFORD   Map 05 TL44
IMPERIAL WAR MUSEUM DUXFORD
CB2 4QR (off M11 junct 10, on A505)
☎ 01223 835000   01223 837267
e-mail: duxford@iwm.org.uk

This former Battle of Britain fighter station, with hangars dating from WW1, is home to most of the Imperial War Museum's collection of military aircraft, armoured fighting vehicles, midget submarines and other large exhibits. Also on display is the Duxford Aviation Society's collection of civil aircraft. Flying displays are held in summer.
Times: Open all year, mid Mar-mid Oct daily 10-6; mid Oct-mid Mar daily 10-4. (Closed 24-26 Dec) **Fee:** * £8 (pen £6 & concessions £4). Ch under 16yrs free. Different rates apply for air shows. **Facilities:** P 🍴 ✖ licensed & (wheelchair available-phone in advance) toilets for disabled shop ✖ (ex guide dogs) 🎧

28 Cambridgeshire

⌂ ELY Map 05 TL58
OLIVER CROMWELL'S HOUSE
29 Saint Mary's St CB7 4HF (adjacent to St Mary's church)
☎ 01353 662062 📠 01353 668518
e-mail: tic@eastcambs.gov.uk

Cromwell inherited the house and local estates from a maternal uncle and moved here in 1636, along with his mother, sisters, wife and eight children. There are displays and period rooms dealing with Cromwell's life, the Civil War and domestic life in the 17th century, as well as the history of The Fens and the house itself, from its medieval origins to its role as an inn in the 19th century.
Times: Open all year: Apr-Sep, daily 10-5.30; Oct-Mar, Mon-Sat 10-5. Winter, Sun, 11-3. **Fee:** £3.50 (concessions £3). Family ticket £8.50.
Facilities: P (100yds) ♿ shop ✖ (ex guide dogs) 🛍

ELY CATHEDRAL
CB7 4DL (A10 or A142, 15m from Cambridge)
☎ 01353 667735 📠 01353 665658

The Octagon Tower of Ely Cathedral can be seen for miles as it rises above the surrounding flat fenland. A monastery was founded on the site by St Etheldreda in 673, but the present cathedral church dates from 1083 and is a magnificent example of Romanesque architecture.
Times: Open daily, Summer 7-7, Winter 7.30-6 (5pm Sun). **Fee:** * £4 (concessions £3.50). Ch free in family group. **Facilities:** P (walking distance) 🍴 ✖ licensed ♿ (touch tour for blind/partially sighted) toilets for disabled shop ✖ (ex guide dogs)

THE STAINED GLASS MUSEUM
The Cathedral CB7 4DN (15m N of Cambridge via A10, situated inside Ely Cathedral)
☎ 01353 660347 📠 01223 327367
e-mail: stainedgm@lineone.net

2 for 1

Situated in the cathedral, this museum is the only one of its kind in the country. Case exhibits show how stained-glass windows are designed and made, and there is an exhibition of approximately 100 panels dating from the 13th century to the present day, displayed at eye level in back-lit cases. The museum is undergoing refurbishment and may be closed for one or two months. Please ring to avoid disappointment.
Times: Open Mon-Fri 10.30-4.30, Sat & BH 10.30-5 & Sun 12-6. **Fee:** * £3.50 (ch, students & pen £2.50). Party 10+ £2.50 (concessions £2). **Facilities:** P 400yds 🍴 (Inter-active video visit) shop ✖ (ex guide dogs) 🛍

⌂ HAMERTON Map 04 TL17
HAMERTON ZOO PARK
PE17 5RE (off A14 at junct with B660 signed Old Weston/Kimbolton)
☎ 01832 293362 📠 01832 293677
e-mail: office@hamertonzoopark.com
Times: Open Summer daily 10.30-6; winter daily 10.30-4. (Closed 25 Dec) **Facilities:** P 🍴 ♿ toilets for disabled shop ✖ Details not confirmed for 2003

⌂ LINTON Map 05 TL54
CHILFORD HALL VINEYARD
Chilford Hall, Balsham Rd CB1 6LE (signposted from A1307 and A11)
☎ 01223 892641 📠 01223 894056
e-mail: simonalper@chilfordhall.co.uk

Taste and buy award-winning wines from the largest vineyard in Cambridgeshire. See the grapes growing in the 18-acre vineyard and take a winery tour to learn how English wine is made and appreciate the subtle difference between each of the Chilford quality wines. Telephone for details of special events.
Times: Open Mar-23 Dec. **Fee:** * Guided tours £4.50 (ch free). Party 15+. Includes wine to taste, tour of the vineyards & a souvenir glass to take home. **Facilities:** P 🍴 ♿ toilets for disabled shop 🛍

LINTON ZOOLOGICAL GARDENS
Hadstock Rd CB1 6NT (exit M11 at junct 9/10, off A604/A1307 on B1052, signposted)
☎ 01223 891308 📠 01223 891308

Linton Zoo, as featured in Anglia Television's 'Wild At Heart' series, places emphasis on conservation and education where visitors can see a combination of beautiful gardens and a wealth of wildlife from all over the world. There are many rare and exotic creatures to see including tapirs, snow leopards, tigers, lions, Grevy's zebra, tamarin monkeys, owls, parrots, giant tortoises, snakes, tarantula spiders and many others. New arrivals include Parma wallabies and several species of rare lemur. The zoo is set in 16-acres of gardens with plenty of picnic areas, children's play area and bouncy castle.
Times: Open daily 10-6 or dusk if earlier (closed 25-26 Dec). Last admission 1 hour before closing. **Fee:** £6 (ch 2-13 £4.50, pen £5.50). **Facilities:** P 🍴 ♿ toilets for disabled shop ✖ 🛍

⌂ LODE Map 05 TL56
ANGLESEY ABBEY
CB5 9EJ (6m NE of Cambridge on B1102, signposted from A14)
☎ 01223 811200 📠 01223 811200
e-mail: angleseyabbey@ntrust.org.uk

A medieval undercroft has survived from the priory

continued

Cambridgeshire

founded here in 1135, but the house dates mainly from 1600. Thomas Hobson of 'Hobson's Choice' was one of the owners. A later owner was Lord Fairhaven, who amassed the huge collection of pictures, and laid out the beautiful gardens.
Times: Open House & Mill: 27 Mar-27 Oct, Wed-Sun & BH Mon's, 1-5. Gardens open Mar-Oct, daily, 10.30-5.30; 30 Oct-22 Dec & Jan-Mar, Wed-Sun, 10.30-4.30 or dusk if earlier. **Fee:** * £6.25. Garden & Mill only £3.85 (£3.25 in winter). Family & party discounts available.
Facilities: P ⬛ ✕ licensed ♿ (electric buggy, wheelchairs & braille guide) toilets for disabled shop garden centre 🐕 (ex guide dogs) ⚑

PETERBOROUGH
LONGTHORPE TOWER   Map 04 TL19
PE1 1EP
☎ 01733 268482

The main attraction of this medieval fortified house are the rare wall paintings of religious and educational subjects, the finest surviving in northern Europe.
Times: Open 29 Mar-Sep, daily 10-6; Oct, Sat-Sun & BH 12-5. **Fee:** * £1.70 (ch 5-15 90p, under 5's free, concessions £1.20). **Facilities:** 🐕 ⚑

PETERBOROUGH CATHEDRAL
PE1 1XS (access from A1 juncts with A605 or A47, follow signs)
☎ 01733 343342   📠 01733 552465

The cathedral has one of the most dramatic west fronts in the country, its three arches are an extraordinary creation of medieval architecture. The Romanesque interior is little altered since its completion 800 years ago, with a unique painted nave ceiling, the elaborate fan vaulting of the 'new' building, Saxon carvings from an earlier church and the burial place of two Queens. An exhibition in the north aisle tells the story of the cathedral. A range of tours can be booked in advance: please contact the Chapter office for details.
Times: Open all year, daily 8.30-5.15. **Fee:** Free - donations towards the cost of upkeep are requested & there is a charge for tours.
Facilities: P (300yds) (no parking within cathedral precincts) ⬛ ✕ ♿ (touch & hearing centre, braille guide, ramps) toilets for disabled shop 🐕 (ex guide dogs or in grounds)

RAMSEY
RAMSEY ABBEY GATEHOUSE   Map 04 TL28
Abbey School PE17 1DH (SE edge of Ramsey, where Chatteris Road joins B1096)
☎ 0870 609 5388   📠 01263 734924

The ruins of this 15th-century gatehouse, together with the 13th-century Lady Chapel, are all that remain of the abbey. Half of the gatehouse was taken away after the Dissolution. Built in ornate late-Gothic style, it has panelled buttresses and friezes.
Times: Open Apr-Oct, daily 10-5. **Fee:** Free. **Facilities:** 🐕 ⚑

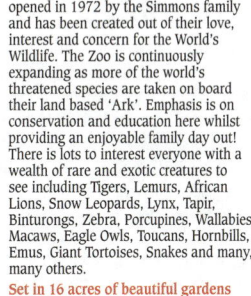

See the wonderful combination of Beautiful Gardens and Wildlife from all over the world at LINTON ZOO
"Cambridgeshire's Wildlife Breeding Centre"

This famous wildlife breeding centre was opened in 1972 by the Simmons family and has been created out of their love, interest and concern for the World's Wildlife. The Zoo is continuously expanding as more of the world's threatened species are taken on board their land based 'Ark'. Emphasis is on conservation and education here whilst providing an enjoyable family day out! There is lots to interest everyone with a wealth of rare and exotic creatures to see including Tigers, Lemurs, African Lions, Snow Leopards, Lynx, Tapir, Binturongs, Zebra, Porcupines, Wallabies, Macaws, Eagle Owls, Toucans, Hornbills, Emus, Giant Tortoises, Snakes and many, many others.

Set in 16 acres of beautiful gardens with pleasant country surroundings. Keeper talks and animal encounters usually during school holidays and at weekends. Please phone for details. Free car and coach park, cafeteria (busy season only). Plenty of picnic areas, exciting children's play area and all other usual facilities.

OPEN ALL YEAR, every day (Closed 25/26 December only) 10am to 6pm or dusk if earlier.
Admission 2003: Adults £6.00; OAPs £5.50; Children (2-13yrs) £4.50.
Tel. Cambridge 01223 891308 for further information, school information packs or party bookings.
www.lintonzoo.co.uk

Hadstock Road, Linton, Cambridgeshire. Situated along B1052 just off A1307, leave M11 at J9 from London

---

WANSFORD
NENE VALLEY RAILWAY   Map 04 TL09
Wansford Station, Stibbington PE8 6LR (A1 at Stibbington, W of Peterborough)
☎ 01780 784444 & 784404   📠 01780 784440
e-mail: nvrorg@aol.com

Visit Britain's International Steam Railway and see steam and diesel engines, carriages and wagons from Europe including the UK. All the sights and sounds of the golden age of steam come alive here. Travelling between Yarwell Junction, Wansford and Peterborough the 7.5 miles of track pass through the heart of the 500-acre Ferry Meadows Country Park. Neve Valley Railway is also the home of 'Thomas'- children's favourite engine.
Times: Train services operate on Sun from Jan; weekends from Apr-Oct; Wed from May, plus other mid-week services in summer.
Fee: * £10 (ch 3-15 £4, concessions £6). Family ticket £20. **Facilities:** P ⬛ ♿ (disabled access to trains) toilets for disabled shop ⚑

WIMPOLE
WIMPOLE HALL   Map 05 TL35
SG8 0BW (M11 junct 12, 8 m SW of Cambridge off A603)
☎ 01223 207257   📠 01223 207838
e-mail: aweusr@smtp.ntrust.org.uk

Wimpole Hall is one of the grandest mansions in East Anglia, and has 360 acres of parkland devised and planted by no less than four celebrated landscape

continued

30 Cambridgeshire

designers, Charles Bridgeman, `Capability' Brown, Sanderson Miller and Humphrey Repton. The house dates back to 1640, but was altered into a large 18th-century mansion with a Georgian façade. The chapel has a trompe l'oeil ceiling.
Times: Open 23 Mar-Jul & Sep-3 Nov, Tue-Thu & Sat-Sun, BH Mon's & Good Fri, 1-5; Aug Tue-Sun, BH Mon's 1-5; Nov, Sun only 1-5. Closes 4pm after 27 Oct. **Fee:** * £6.20 (ch under 13 free with one paying adult, ch 13-17 £2.80). Party. **Facilities:** P 🅿 ✗ licensed ♿ (braille guide, battery vehicle, stairlift, wheelchairs) toilets for disabled shop ✖ (ex park only) 🎒 🍽

WIMPOLE HOME FARM
SG8 0BW (M11 junct 12 8m SW of Cambridge off A603)
☎ 01223 208987   📠 01223 207838
e-mail: aweusr@smtp.ntrust.org.uk

When built in 1794, the Home Farm was one of the most advanced agricultural enterprises in the country. The Great Barn, now restored, holds a display of farm machinery and implements of the kind used at Wimpole over the past two centuries. On the farm there are rare breeds of domestic animals. Please ring for details of special events.
Times: Open 23 Mar-Jun & Sep-3 Nov, Tue-Thu & Sat-Sun, Good Fri & BH Mons 10.30-5; Jul & Aug, Tue-Sun 10.30-5; Nov-Mar, Sat & Sun 11-4. **Fee:** * £4.90 (ch £2.80). NT members £2.60 (ch £1.60).
Facilities: P 🅿 ✗ licensed ♿ (braille guide, wheelchairs, electric buggies) toilets for disabled shop ✖ (ex guide dogs) 🎒 🍽

🏛 WISBECH   Map 09 TF40

PECKOVER HOUSE & GARDEN
North Brink PE13 1JR (Leave A47 & take town centre signs, then follow brown signs)
☎ 01945 583463   📠 01945 583463
e-mail: info@peckoverhouse.co.uk

Dating from 1722, Peckover House is a beautiful Georgian brick townhouse with a two-acre walled town garden, one of the finest such gardens in Britain and home to over 70 types of rose. The Victorian glasshouses include a fern house, and an orangery with 300-year-old trees that still bear fruit.
Times: Open, House, Garden & Tearoom Apr-Oct, wknds, Wed & BH Mons 12.30-5 (house also open Thu May-Aug). Garden open Apr-Oct, Mon-Tue & Thu 12.30-5. **Fee:** * House & garden £4 (ch £1.50). Garden £2.50 on days when only garden is open. **Facilities:** P (400yds) 🅿 ✗ licensed ♿ (Batricar available on loan) toilets for disabled shop ✖ (ex guide dogs) 🎒

WISBECH & FENLAND MUSEUM
Museum Square PE13 1ES (on A47)
☎ 01945 583817   📠 01945 589050
Times: Open all year, Tue-Sat 10-5 (4pm Oct-Mar). Closed Xmas.
Facilities: P (100 yds) shop ✖ *Details not confirmed for 2003*

Cheshire

Bordered by Wales and the metropoli of Liverpool and Manchester, Cheshire has a rich history that can be seen in its wealth of Roman heritage, black and white buildings, and industrial waterways. The county also boasts some lovely countryside, a tradition of floral excellence, and some rather delicious cheese.

From the invasion of the Romans who made Chester one of their major garrisons, to skirmishes with Norsemen during the Dark Ages, Cheshire has been the scene of many conflicts. The area was also the base for Hugh the Wolf's violent reign in the 11th century, and the setting for the some of the fiercest battles of the Civil War, including the seige of Chester. Clearly, life is less stressful now, but the history of the county is far from forgotten.

Cheshire's canals, part of which form a ring of around 100 miles (151km) of waterways, are the ideal way to explore by foot or by boat. The county has over 200 miles (302 km) of man-made waterways – more than any other county in England – and is a centre for boating holidays. Ellesmere Port has a Boat Museum which has preserved many of the vessels used for both inland and sea travel, from a small weedcutter to a 300-ton coaster.

From a literary angle, Knutsford has a monument to Mrs Gaskell (1810-1865), a native of the town, whose novels dealt with subject matter surprisingly controversial for a female writer of her generation. Her novel, *Wives and Daughters*, was recently adapted by BBC TV.

Cheshire is full of gardens. From the acres of orangeries and Japanese gardens surrounding the stately homes, to the town parks of Crewe and Congleton, the county is a feast of flowers, lawns and landscaping. Even many private gardens are showpieces of gardening expertise.

EVENTS & FESTIVALS

May
3rd Knutsford Royal May Day
14th-17th Alderley Edge Music Festival
24th-27th Chester Folk Festival

June
17th-18th Cheshire County Show, The Showground, Tabley, nr Knutsford
tbc World Worm Charming Championship, Willaston Primary School, Willaston

July
5th Macclesfield Carnival
23rd-27th Royal Horticultural Society Flower Show, Tatton Park, Knutsford

August
17th Family Fun Day, West Park, Macclesfield
23rd Poynton Show

October
Macclesfield Festival for the Performing Arts, Ryles Park High School (2 wknds of autumn half term)
tbc Chrysanthemum Show, Wilmslow Royal British Legion

Top: Eastgate Clock, Chester

32 Cheshire

BEESTON
BEESTON CASTLE Map 07 SJ55
Tarporley CW6 9TX (on minor road off A49 or A41)
☎ 01829 260464

This ruined 13th-century stronghold was built by the Earl Ranuf of Chester on a steep and inaccessible hillside. The remains of the inner and outer wards can still be seen and there is an exhibition of the castle's history.
Times: Open all year, 29 Mar-Sep, daily 10-6 (Oct, daily 10-5); Nov-Mar, daily 10-4. (Closed 24-26 Dec & 1 Jan) **Fee:** * £3 (ch £1.50, under 5's free, concessions £2.30). **Facilities:** P shop ✈ (in certain areas) ♿

CAPESTHORNE
CAPESTHORNE HALL Map 07 SJ87
SK11 9JY (On A34 between Congleton and Wilmslow)
☎ 01625 861221 ▤ 01625 861619

Capesthorne has been the home of the Bromley-Davenport family and their ancestors since Domesday times. The present house dates from 1719 and was designed by the Smiths of Warwick. It was subsequently altered by Edward Blore in 1837 and after a disastrous fire in 1861 the whole of the centre portion was rebuilt by Anthony Salvin. Capesthorne contains a great variety of sculptures, paintings and other contents including a collection of American colonial furnishings.
Times: Open Apr-Oct, Wed-Sun & BH's (Closed Xmas & New Year). Park & Garden 12-5.30, Hall 1.30-3.30. **Fee:** * Park, Garden & Chapel £4 (ch £2). Park, Gardens, Chapel & Hall £6.50 (ch £3 & pen £5.50). Family ticket £12. Party 25+. Special deal on Wed's £5 per car (up to 4 persons) £25 per coach. **Facilities:** P ⏾ ✈ licensed ♿ (ramp access to ground floor of hall & gardens) toilets for disabled ✈ (ex guide dogs & in gardens)

CHESTER
CHESHIRE MILITARY MUSEUM Map 07 SJ46
The Castle CH1 2DN (follow signs to Military Museum from town centre)
☎ 01244 327617 ▤ 01244 401700 **2 for 1**

This military museum boasts exhibits from the history of the Cheshire Regiment, Cheshire Yeomanry, 5th Royal Inniskilling Dragoon Guards, and 3rd Carabiniers. Display of the work of George Jones, Victorian battle artist, and an exhibition of life in barracks in the 1950s. Research available by written appointment and donation. There are special events throughtout the year, please phone for details.
Times: Open all year, daily 10-5 (last entry 4.30pm). (Closed 22 Dec-2 Jan). **Fee:** * £2 (concessions £1). **Facilities:** P (400yds) ♿ shop ✈ (ex guide dogs)

CHESTER CATHEDRAL
Saint Werburgh St CH1 2HU (opposite the town hall)
☎ 01244 324756 ▤ 01244 341110
e-mail: office@chestercathedral.org.uk

Founded as a Benedictine monastery in 1092 on the sites of earlier churches, in 1541 it became the cathedral of the newly created Diocese of Chester and is a good example of a medieval monastic complex.

Restored in the 19th century, the building contains work by Gilbert Scott, Clayton, Pugin and Kempe. There are daily services and visitors are welcome to join in. A summer music festival is held in July.
Times: Open daily 8-6 (subject to alteration). **Fee:** * Donation of £3 per person requested. **Facilities:** P (200yds) (multi-storey) ⏾ ✈ licensed ♿ (induction loop, tactile model) toilets for disabled shop ✈ (ex guide dogs)

CHESTER VISITOR CENTRE
Vicars Ln CH1 1QX (opposite Roman Amphitheatre)
☎ 01244 402111 ▤ 01244 403188
e-mail: tis@chestercc.gov.uk

Among the attractions at this large visitor information centre are guided walks of Chester, brass rubbing, candle-making, World of Names which explores the history of family and first names, displays on the history of Chester, a café and a gift shop.
Times: Open all year Apr-Sep, Mon-Sat 9-5.30, Sun & BHs 10-4; Oct-Mar, Mon-Sat 10-5, Sun 10-4. **Fee:** Free. **Facilities:** P (200yds) (short stay visitor parking) ⏾ ♿ (ramped access from Vicars Lane) toilets for disabled shop ⌨

CHESTER ZOO
Upton-by-Chester CH2 1LH (2m N of city centre off A41 & M53 Junct 10 southbound, Junct 12 all other directions)
☎ 01244 380280 ▤ 01244 371273
e-mail: marketing@chesterzoo.co.uk

The largest zoological gardens in the UK, with 2000 plus animals in 500 plus species. There are large outdoor islands for chimps, orang-utans and monkeys, penguin pool, and birds of prey. The Bat Cave is the largest enclosure in the world for endangered bat species. New features include the 'Spirit of the Jaguar', Dragons in Danger, Marmot Mania, Tsavo Rhino experience & Red Panda's, a huge extension to the National Elephant Centre, and 'Noah's Ark' children's play area.
Times: Open all year, daily from 10. Last admission varies with season from 5.30pm high summer to 3.30pm winter. (Closed 25 Dec). **Fee:** £11 (ch 3-15 & pen £9). Family ticket (2 adult & 2 ch) £37.50.
Facilities: P ⏾ ✈ licensed ♿ (electric scooters, audio guide, induction loop, braille) toilets for disabled shop ✈ (ex guide & sensory dogs) ⌨

Cheshire

DEVA ROMAN EXPERIENCE
Pierpoint Ln, (off Bridge St) CH1 1NL (city centre)
☎ 01244 343407   📠 01244 347737

Stroll along reconstructed streets experiencing the sights, sounds and smells of Roman Chester. From the streets of Deva (the Roman name for Chester) you return to the present day on an extensive archeological 'dig', where you can discover the substantial Roman, Saxon and medieval remains beneath modern Chester.
Times: Open daily 9-5. (Closed 25-26 Dec). **Fee:** * £3.95 (ch £2.25, under 5's free, pen £3.50, student £3.50). Family ticket £11. Party. **Facilities:** P (200yds) ♿ shop ✕ (ex guide dogs)

🏛 CHOLMONDELEY   Map 07 SJ55
CHOLMONDELEY CASTLE GARDENS
SY14 8AH (off A49/A41)
☎ 01829 720383   📠 01829 720877

Dominated by a romantic Gothic Castle built in 1801 of local sandstone, the gardens are laid out with fine trees and water gardens, and have been replanted with rhododendrons, azaleas, cornus and acer. There is also a rose and lavender garden, lakeside and woodland walks, and rare breeds of farm animals.
Times: Open Apr-Sep, Wed-Thu, Sun & BH's 11.30-5. **Fee:** * £3 (ch £1.50). **Facilities:** P 🅿 ♿ (disabled car park near tearoom) toilets for disabled shop garden centre

🏛 DISLEY   Map 07 SJ98
LYME PARK
SK12 2NX (off A6, 6.5m SE of Stockport)
☎ 01663 762023   📠 01663 765035
e-mail: mlyrec@smtp.ntrust.org.uk

Home of the Legh family for 600 years and the largest house in Cheshire, Lyme Park featured as Pemberley in the BBC's production of *Pride and Prejudice*. It also featured in Granada's production of *The Forsyte Saga*. Parts of the original Elizabethan house remain, with 18th and 19th-century additions. Set in extensive historic gardens with a lake and also a 1,400-acre park, home to red and fallow deer.
Times: Open Park: Apr-Oct, daily 8-8.30; Nov-Mar, daily 8-6. Gardens: 29 Mar-Oct, Fri-Tue 11-5, Wed-Thu 1-5; Nov-18 Dec, wknds 12-3. House: 29 Mar-Oct, Fri-Tue 1-5 (last admission 4.30), BH Mon's 11-5. Cage: Apr-Oct, 2nd & 4th wknd of each month 12-4. Paddock Cottage Apr-Oct, 1st & 3rd wknd of each month, 12-4. **Fee:** * Park £3.50 per car (refundable on purchase of house & garden ticket). Garden £2.50 (ch £1.25), House only £4 (ch £2), House and Garden £5.50 (ch £2.75). Family ticket £12. NT members free, ch under 5 free.
Facilities: P (charged) 🅿 ✕ licensed ♿ (by arrangement) toilets for disabled shop ✕ (ex park on lead) 🚼 🍴

🏛 ELLESMERE PORT   Map 07 SJ47
BLUE PLANET AQUARIUM
Cheshire Oaks CH65 9LF (off M53 junct 10 at Cheshire Oaks. Follow signs for aquarium)
☎ 0151 357 8804   📠 0151 356 7288
e-mail: info@blueplanetaquarium.co.uk

A voyage of discovery on the longest moving walkway in the world. Beneath the waters of the Carribean Reef, see giant rays and menacing sharks pass inches from your face and stroke some favourite fish in the special rock pools or pay a visit to the incredible world of poisonous frogs. Divers hand feed the fish and sharks throughout the day and they can answer questions via state of the art communication systems.
Times: Open all year, daily; Apr-Oct 10-6, Nov-Mar 11-5 (wknds, BHs and school holidays 10-6). **Fee:** * £7.25 (ch £4.95, under 3's free, concessions £5.50). Family ticket £23-£25 (2 adults and up to 4 ch). Party. **Facilities:** P ✕ licensed ♿ toilets for disabled shop ✕ (ex guide dogs) 🍴

BOAT MUSEUM
South Pier Rd CH65 4FW (M53 junct 9)
☎ 0151 355 5017   📠 0151 355 4079   `2 for 1`
e-mail: bookings@boatmuseum.freeserve.co.uk

Occupying a historic dock complex at the junction of the Shropshire Union and Manchester Ship Canals, this museum has the world's largest collection of floating canal craft, from a small weedcutter to a 300-ton coaster. Boat trips are also available. There are indoor exhibitions on canal life and local history, together with period workers' cottages, a blacksmith's forge and working engines.
Times: Open Summer daily 10-5. Winter daily (ex Thu & Fri) 11-4. (Closed 25 & 26 Dec). **Fee:** * £5.50 (ch £3.70, pen & student £4.30). Family ticket £16.50, OAP family ticket £14.50. **Facilities:** P 🅿 ♿ (tactile Map for blind, wheelchair) toilets for disabled shop 🍴

🏛 GAWSWORTH   Map 07 SJ86
GAWSWORTH HALL
SK11 9RN (2.5m S of Macclesfield on A536)
☎ 01260 223456   📠 01260 223469
e-mail: gawsworth@lineone.net

This fine Tudor black-and-white manor house was the birthplace of Mary Fitton, thought by some to be the 'Dark Lady' of Shakespeare's sonnets. Pictures and

continued

Cheshire

armour can be seen in the house, which also has a tilting ground - now thought to be a rare example of an Elizabethan pleasure garden.
Times: Open daily, 28 Mar-6 Oct, closed certain days, phone for details. **Fee:** * £4.50 (ch £2.25). Party 20+ £3.50 each. **Facilities:** P 🍽 ✕ licensed ♿ (disabled parking in front of house) toilets for disabled shop 🐕 (guide dogs in garden only) 🍴

🏛 JODRELL BANK SCIENCE CENTRE & ARBORETUM   Map 07 SJ77
JODRELL BANK SCIENCE CENTRE, PLANETARIUM & ARBORETUM
SK11 9DL (M6 junct 18, A535 Holmes Chapel to Chelford Road)
☎ 01477 571339   📠 01477 571695
e-mail: visitorcentre@jb.man.ac.uk   `2 for 1`

Discover the Universe in the Science Centre beside one of the largest, fully steerable radio telescopes in the world, the Lovell Telescope. Explore exhibitions and hands-on exhibits on astronomy and space. View the mysteries of the night sky in the planetarium before walking in the tree-lined trails of the Arboretum. A 3D visual show is new for 2003.
Times: Open summer, 3rd wknd in Mar-last wknd in Oct, 10.30-5.30; winter, Nov-mid Mar, Tue-Sun 10.30-3.30. (ring for Xmas opening times). Closed Mon. **Fee:** £5 (ch £2.50, pen £3.50) extra charge for Planetarium and visual theatre show. Family ticket £15. Children under 4 not admitted to the visual shows. **Facilities:** P 🍽 ♿ (Audio loop, wheelchair loan, audio guide & tactile guide) toilets for disabled shop 🐕 (ex guide dogs)

🏛 KNUTSFORD   Map 07 SJ77
TABLEY HOUSE
WA16 0HB (leave M6 junct 19 onto A556 S towards Chester. Entrance for cars off A5033, 2m W of Knutsford)
☎ 01565 750151   📠 01565 653230
e-mail: enquiries@tableyhouse.co.uk

This finest Palladian House in the north west, holds the first great collection of English pictures, furniture by Chippendale, Gillow and Bullock, and fascinating Leicester family memorabilia. Friendly stewards are available to talk about the Leicester's 700 years at Tabley.
Times: Open Apr-end Oct, Thu-Sun & BHs, 2-5 (last entry 4.30). **Fee:** * £4 (ch & students £1.50) **Facilities:** P 🍽 ♿ (phone administrator in advance for help) toilets for disabled shop 🐕 (ex guide dogs)

TATTON PARK
WA16 6QN (5m from M6 junct 19, or M56 junct 7)
☎ 01625 534400   📠 01625 534403

Times: Open 29 Mar-28 Sep, daily except Mon; Oct Sat & Sun, opening times vary telephone to check. Gardens all year daily except Mon. Park Apr-Oct daily; 29 Sep-26 Mar 2004 daily except Mon. **Fee:** car entry charges £3.70, discovery saver tickets £4.60 (ch £2.60). **Facilities:** P (charged) 🍽 ♿ (Old Hall & areas of Farm not accessible) toilets for disabled shop garden centre 🐕 (ex in Park) 🍴

🏛 MACCLESFIELD   Map 07 SJ97
HARE HILL
SK10 4QB (4m N off B5087, follow brown signs to Hare Hill)
☎ 01625 584412

The beautiful parkland at Hare Hill also features a pretty walled garden and pergola. There are woodland paths and ponds, and in late spring, a brilliant display of rhododendrons and azaleas.
Times: Open Apr-Oct, Wed-Thu, Sat, Sun & BH Mons 10-5.30; 10-30 May daily 10-5.30; (Closed Nov-Mar). **Fee:** * £2.50 (ch £1.25). £1.50 per car (refundable on entry to garden). **Facilities:** P (charged) ♿ (wheelchair available, braille guides) 🐕 (ex guide dogs) 🍴

MACCLESFIELD SILK MUSEUM
Heritage Centre, Roe St SK11 6UT (Turn off A523 & follow brown signs. Museum in town centre)
☎ 01625 613210   📠 01625 617880
e-mail: postmaster@silk-macc.u-net.com

The story of silk in Macclesfield, told through a colourful audio-visual programme, exhibitions, textiles, garments, models and room settings. The Silk Museum is part of the Heritage Centre, a restored Georgian Sunday school, which runs a full programme of musical and artistic events throughout the year. The new

continued

Cheshire

museum opened in 2002 and has a changing temporary exhibition programme.
Times: Open all year, Mon-Sat 11-5, Sun & BH Mon 1-5. (Closed 24-26 Dec & 1 Jan) **Fee:** * £2.90 (concessions £2). Family ticket £7.75 Joint ticket with Paradise Mill £5.10 (concessions £2.90). Family ticket £11.15. **Facilities:** P (50mtrs) licensed (ramps, chairlift, audio guides) toilets for disabled shop (ex guide dogs)

PARADISE MILL
Park Ln SK11 6TJ (turn off A523 & follow brown signs)
☎ 01625 618228

A working silk mill until 1981, with restored jacquard hand looms in their original location. Knowledgeable guides, many of them former silk mill workers, illustrate the silk production process with the help of demonstrations from weavers. Exhibitions and room settings give an impression of working conditions at the mill during the 1930s.
Times: Open all year, BH Mon & Mon-Sat from 11am. (Closed 25-26 Dec & 1 Jan). **Fee:** Telephone for details. **Facilities:** P (100 yds) (care needed on uneven floors) toilets for disabled shop (ex guide dogs)

MOULDSWORTH   Map 07 SJ57
MOULDSWORTH MOTOR MUSEUM
Smithy Ln CH3 8AR (6m E of Chester, off B5393, close to Delamere Forest & Oulton Park Racing Circuit, signposted. Or M56 junct 12 into Frodsham then B5393 into Mouldsworth, follow brown signs in village)
☎ 01928 731781   **2 for 1**

Housed in an amazing 1937 large Art Deco building close to Delamere Forest, this is a superb collection of over 60 motor cars, motorcycles and bicycles. There is also a massive collection of automobilia - old signs, pumps, tools, mascots and badges, as well as old motoring toys, Dinky cars and pedal cars all complemented by a motoring art gallery, that has posters and advertising material. School parties are encouraged for a guided tour and structured talk. Motoring clubs visit on Sundays.
Times: Open Feb-Nov (Sun only), Etr wknd, early May BH Mon, Spring BH Sun-Mon & Aug BH wknd; Sun, Feb-Nov; also Wed, Jul-Aug, noon-5. **Fee:** £3 (ch £1.50, pen - reduction Wed only Jul-Aug £2.50) **Facilities:** P (hands on items) shop

NANTWICH   Map 07 SJ65
STAPELEY WATER GARDENS
London Rd, Stapeley CW5 7LH (off M6 junct 16, 1m S of Nantwich on A51)
☎ 01270 623868 & 628628 🖷 01270 624919
e-mail: stapeleywg@btinternet.com

Stapeley Water Gardens consists of three main areas. The Palms Tropical Oasis is a glass pavilion which is home to Koi carp, Giant Amazon water-lilies, sharks, piranhas, parrots and exotic flowers. The two-acre Water Garden Centre houses the National Collection of water-lilies.
Times: Open Summer: Mon-Sat 9-6, BHs 10-6, Sun 10-4, Wed 9-8; Winter: Mon-Sat 9-5, BHs 10-5, Sun 10-4, (Wed 10-7 Angling dept only). The Palms Tropical Oasis open from 10am. **Fee:** * The Palms Tropical Oasis £3.85 (ch £2.15, pen £3.40). **Facilities:** P licensed (free wheelchair loan service) toilets for disabled shop garden centre (ex guide dogs)

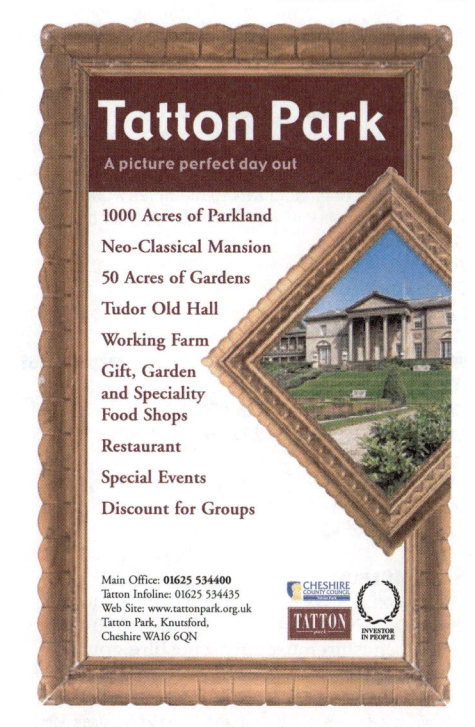

NESTON   Map 07 SJ27
LIVERPOOL UNIVERSITY BOTANIC GARDENS (NESS GARDENS)
Ness Gardens CH64 4AY (off A540 near Ness-on-Wirral, follow signs)
☎ 0151 353 0123 🖷 0151 353 1004
e-mail: ejs@liv.ac.uk

A long association with plant collectors ensures a wide range of plants, providing interest for academics, horticulturists and amateurs alike. There are tree and shrub collections, water and rock gardens, herbaceous borders and glasshouses. A regular programme of lectures, courses and special events take place throughout the year for which tickets must be obtained in advance.
Times: Open all year, Nov-Feb, daily 9.30-4; Mar-Oct, daily 9.30-5. (Closed 25 Dec). **Fee:** * £4.70 (ch free admission when accompanied with an adult, concessions £4.30) **Facilities:** P licensed (wheelchair route, induction loop in lecture theatre) toilets for disabled shop garden centre (ex guide dogs)

Tatton Park
A picture perfect day out

- 1000 Acres of Parkland
- Neo-Classical Mansion
- 50 Acres of Gardens
- Tudor Old Hall
- Working Farm
- Gift, Garden and Speciality Food Shops
- Restaurant
- Special Events
- Discount for Groups

Main Office: **01625 534400**
Tatton Infoline: 01625 534435
Web Site: www.tattonpark.org.uk
Tatton Park, Knutsford, Cheshire WA16 6QN

Cheshire

NETHER ALDERLEY
Map 07 SJ87
NETHER ALDERLEY MILL
Congleton Rd SK10 4TW (1.5m S of Alderley Edge)
☎ 01625 584412   📠 01625 584412

Built in the 15th century, this water-mill is much larger inside than it looks. Inside there are tandem overshot water-wheels, original Elizabethan timber work, and Victorian machinery which was restored after being derelict for 30 years.
Times: Open Apr-May & Oct, Wed, Sun & BH Mon 1-4.30; Jun-Sep, Tue-Sun & BH Mon 1-5. Parties by arrangement. **Fee:** * £2 (ch £1)
Facilities: 🅿 ✄ ♿

NORTHWICH
Map 07 SJ67
ARLEY HALL & GARDENS
Great Budworth CW9 6NA (N of Northwich on B5075.)
☎ 01565 777353 & 777284   📠 01565 777465
Times: Open Etr-end Sep, Tue-Sun & BH 11-5. Hall open Tue & Sun only. **Facilities:** 🅿 🍴 ✕ ♿ (ramps, parking by entrance) toilets for disabled shop garden centre ✈ (ex in gardens on lead) Details not confirmed for 2003 🎫

SALT MUSEUM
162 London Rd CW9 8AB (on A533 0.5m S of town)
☎ 01606 41331 & 40394   📠 01606 350420
e-mail: cheshiremuseums@cheshire.gov.uk
Times: Open Tue-Fri 10-5, wknds 2-5 (Sun 12-5 in Aug). Open BH & Mons in Aug 10-5. **Facilities:** 🅿 🍴 ♿ (inductory video with induction loop facilities) toilets for disabled shop ✈ (ex guide dogs) Details not confirmed for 2003

RUNCORN
Map 07 SJ58
NORTON PRIORY MUSEUM & GARDENS
Tudor Rd, Manor Park WA7 1SX (from M56 junct 11 in direction of Warrington, signposted)
☎ 01928 569895   📠 01928 589743   **2 for 1**
e-mail: info@nortonpriory.org

Thirty-eight acres of peaceful woodland gardens are the setting for the medieval priory remains, museum and Walled Garden. Displays tell the story of the transformation of the priory into a Tudor manor house and then into an elegant Georgian mansion. Please telephone for details of special events.

Times: Open all year, Apr-Oct, Mon-Fri 12-5; Sat, Sun & BHs 12-6; Nov-Mar daily 12-4. (Closed 24-26 Dec & 1 Jan). Walled Garden open Apr-Oct, daily 1.30-4.30) **Fee:** £3.95 (ch 5-16, students, UB40's & pen £2.75). Family ticket (2 adults & 3 ch) £10. **Facilities:** 🅿 🍴 ♿ (wheelchairs, large print & audio guides, induction loop) toilets for disabled shop garden centre (guide dogs only wall garden)

SCHOLAR GREEN
Map 07 SJ85
LITTLE MORETON HALL
Newcastle Rd CW12 4SD (4m SW of Congleton on A34)
☎ 01260 272018

One of the best examples of half-timbered architecture in England. By 1580 the house was much as it is today, and the long gallery, chapel and the great hall are very impressive. The garden has a knot garden, orchard and herbaceous borders. Ring for details of special events.
Times: Open all year mid Mar-early Nov, Wed-Sun 11.30-5 or dusk if earlier, BH Mon 11.30-5; early Nov-mid Dec, weekends 11.30-4. **Fee:** * £4.30. Joint ticket with Biddulph Grange Gardens £6.50. Dec free entry to ground floor and garden. Parking £2, refundable on entry to Hall. **Facilities:** 🅿 ✕ licensed ♿ (wheelchair, electric vehicle, Braille & large print guides) toilets for disabled shop ✈ (ex guide & hearing dogs) ♨ 🎫

STYAL
Map 07 SJ88
QUARRY BANK MILL & STYAL ESTATE
Quarry Bank Mill SK9 4LA (M56 junct 5, signposted)
☎ 01625 527468   📠 01625 539267
e-mail: quarrybankmill@ntrust.org.uk

Quarry Bank Mill is a working water and steam powered cotton mill. Spinning and weaving from the hand processes are demonstrated every day and items made from the cloth are sold in the shop. Lots of practical 'hands-on' activities plus a new children's playground and railway. The Apprentice House shows how life was for the mill apprentices.
Times: Mill open all year, Apr-Sep daily 10.30-5.30 (last admission 4); Oct-Mar, daily 10.30-5 (closed Mon in term time). Last admission 3.30. Apprentice House & Garden, Tue-Fri from 11 (2-4.30 term time), Sat-Sun & Aug from 11. Closed Mon (ex school hols). **Fee:** * Mill, Apprentice House & Gardens £6.50 (ch & concessions £3.70). Family ticket £16.50. Mill only £5 (ch & concessions £3.40). Family ticket £14.50. Estate fee £2.50 part refund on entry to Mill. **Facilities:** 🅿 (charged) 🍴 ✕ licensed ♿ (wheelchairs) toilets for disabled shop ✈ (ex in Park) ♨ 🎫

WIDNES
Map 07 SJ58
CATALYST SCIENCE DISCOVERY CENTRE
Mersey Rd WA8 0DF (signed from M62 junct 7 and M56 junct 12)
☎ 0151 420 1121   📠 0151 495 2030   **2 for 1**
e-mail: info@catalyst.org.uk

Discover a world where science and technology come alive, with over 100 interactive exhibits and hands-on displays. Take a trip in an all-glass lift to the Observatory, 100 feet above the River Mersey. Ring for details of special events.
Times: Open all year, BH Mon, Tue-Fri daily 10-5, wknds 11-5. (Closed Mon ex BH's, 24-26 Dec & 1 Jan). **Fee:** * £4.95 (ch £3.50, concessions £3.95). Family ticke t £14.95. **Facilities:** 🅿 🍴 ♿ toilets for disabled shop ✈ (ex guide dogs) 🎫

Cornwall & Isles of Scilly

Cornwall is a striking and majestic county, and also a land of contrasts. While small coastal towns like Mousehole, Mevagissey and Polperro remain largely untouched by time, the resort of Newquay is at the forefront of the European surfing scene.

Unsurprisingly, Cornwall's history is tied to the sea and seafaring, surrounded as it is by the Atlantic on three sides. For a long time the county was a centre for smuggling operations. The seclusion of its many coves and caves were ideal for the shady machinations of customs dodgers right up until the 20th century.

The isolation and ruggedness of the coastal landscape and its inhabitants has offered the perfect challenge for many religious groups and individuals. Some of Britain's earliest Christian churches and communities were started in Cornwall, including St Pirran's Church in Perranporth which was founded in the 6th century by the patron saint of tinners. Like many other missionaries of this time he came from Ireland and, local tales claim, was not the most sober of ministers. St Columba was another, perhaps more important influence on Christianity in England.

Legend has it that Cornwall was once the site of King Arthur's fabled Camelot. High on the cliffs near Tintagel is the ruined castle most strongly connected to the ancient hero, although its remains post-date Arthurian lore by some seven centuries. Some local legends state that nearby Camelford was once Camelot.

Top: Land's End

EVENTS & FESTIVALS

March
29th-30th Falmouth Spring Flower Show

April
13th-20th St Endellion Easter Festival of Music, St Endellion, Port Isaac
26th Trevithick Day, Camborne

May
1st Padstow 'Obby 'Oss celebrations
17th-18th Re-enactment of the Battle of Stamford Hill, Bude (provisional)
24th-30th Calstock Festival
tbc Daphne du Maurier Festival, Fowey
tbc Helston Flora

June
5th-7th Royal Cornwall Show
7th-8th Murdoch Weekend, Redruth (provisional)
20th-29th Golowan Festival incorporating Mazey Eve (27th), Mazey Day (28th) and Quay Fair Day (29th), Penzance

July
14th Stithians Show, Truro
27th-8th August St Endellion Summer Festival, St Endellion, Port Isaac
tbs RNAS Culdrose Air Day (provisional)

August
1st-3rd Re-enactment of Arthurian Battle of Camlann, Tintagel
8th-16th Falmouth Classics & Regatta
22nd-25th Cornwall Folk Festival
23rd-25th Morval Vintage Steam Rally
25th-30th Bude Jazz Festival
25th Newlyn Fish Festival

September
tbc Lanlivery Vintage Rally
tbc St Ives September Festival

October
9th-12th Falmouth Oyster Festival (provisional)
15th-19th Lowender Peran, Perranporth

November
17th-22nd Camborne Music Festival

December
23rd Tom Bawcock's Eve, Mousehole

BODMIN
Map 02 SX06
MILITARY MUSEUM
The Keep PL31 1EG (on B3268 beside steam railway station)
☎ 01208 72810   ≋ 01208 72810
e-mail: dclimus@talk21.com

The history of a famous County Regiment with fascinating displays of uniforms, weapons, medals, badges and much more.
Times: Open all year Mon-Fri, Sun during Jul & Aug 9-5. (Closed Etr & Xmas). **Fee:** * £2 (ch 50p). Parties 10+. **Facilities:** P shop

PENCARROW
Washaway PL30 3AG (4m NW of Bodmin, signposted off A389 & B3266)
☎ 01208 841369   ≋ 01208 841722
e-mail: pencarrow@aol.com

Still a family home, this Georgian house has a superb collection of pictures, furniture and porcelain. The 50 acres of formal and woodland gardens include a Victorian rockery, a lake, 700 different rhododendrons and an acclaimed conifer collection. There is also a craft centre and a children's play area.
Times: Open House: 30 Mar-30 Oct, Sun-Thu 11-5 (last house tour 4pm). Gardens open daily. **Fee:** House & Garden £6 (ch £3). Gardens only £3 (ch free). Party 20+ £5 each, Party 31+ £4.50 each. **Facilities:** P 🍴 ♿ (2 wheelchairs for use) toilets for disabled shop ✖ (ex in gardens)

CALSTOCK
Map 02 SX46
COTEHELE
St Dominick PL12 6TA (turn off A390 at St. Anne's Chapel, signposted 2.5m S of junct)
☎ 01579 351346 & 352739 (info)
≋ 01579 351222
e-mail: cotehele@ntrust.org.uk

A 15th-century house that contains tapestries, embroideries, furniture and armour; and outside, a beautiful garden on different levels, including a formal Italian-style garden, medieval stewpond, dovecote, and an 18th-century tower with lovely views. There is a restored water mill in the valley below, and at the Victorian riverside quay an outstation of the National Maritime Museum.
Times: Open 22 Mar-2 Nov daily ex Fri (open Good Fri), 11-5 (11-4.30 Oct & Nov). Garden open all year, daily 10.30-dusk. **Fee:** * House, Garden & Mill £6.20. Garden & Mill £3.60 (ch 1/2 price, under 5's & NT members free). Family ticket £16 for House, Garden and Mill, £9 for Garden and Mill only. Party £5.40 each. **Facilities:** P 🍴 ✖ licensed ♿ (garden limited access,braille guide,audio loop,wheelchairs) toilets for disabled shop garden centre 🐾 ⛔

CAMELFORD
Map 02 SX18
BRITISH CYCLING MUSEUM
The Old Station PL32 9TZ (1m N of Camelford on B3266 at junct with B3314)
☎ 01840 212811   ≋ 01840 212811

This is the nation's foremost museum of cycling history from 1818 to the present day, with over 400 cycles;

more than 1000 cycling medals, fobs and badges; an extensive library; displays of gas, candle, battery and oil lighting; and many ad posters and enamel signs.
Times: Open all year, Sun-Thu 10-5. **Fee:** £2.75 (ch 5-17 £1.50)
Facilities: P ♿ shop ✖ (ex guide dogs)

CHYSAUSTER ANCIENT VILLAGE
Map 02 SW43
CHYSAUSTER ANCIENT VILLAGE
TR20 8XA (2.5m NW of Gulval, off B3311)
☎ 07831 757934

This fascinating ancient Celtic village, 2000 years old, includes eight drystone houses ranged along the oldest known village street in England.
Times: Open all year, 24 Mar-Sep, daily 10-6 (Oct, daily 10-5); **Fee:** * £1.80 (concessions £1.40, ch 90p) **Facilities:** P ✖ ⛔

DOBWALLS
Map 02 SX26
DOBWALLS FAMILY ADVENTURE PARK
PL14 6HD (0.5 N of A38)
☎ 01579 320325 & 321129
e-mail: dobwallsadpk@aol.com
Times: Open 12 Apr-10 Sep, daily 10.30-5.30 (10am in high season); 11 Sep-29 Sep, Sat-Thu; 1-22 Oct, Sat-Wed; 23-29 Oct, daily.
Facilities: P 🍴 ♿ (motorised & manual wheelchairs available) toilets for disabled shop *Details not confirmed for 2003* ⛔

FALMOUTH
Map 02 SW83
NATIONAL MARITIME MUSEUM CORNWALL
Discovery Quay TR11 3QY (follow signs from A39, 300mtrs from Falmouth Station)
☎ 01326 313388   ≋ 01326 317878
e-mail: enquiries@nmmc.co.uk

After starting work in October 1999, this impressive tribute to the county's maritime history is scheduled to open in Autumn 2002, and seems likely to become one of Cornwall's major attractions. The waterfront museum includes more than 120 small craft from the National Maritime Museum in Greenwich, a massive maritime library, interactive displays on navigation and construction, and much more. Programme of temporary exhibitions, lectures, presentations and outside events through the year.
Times: Open daily 10-5 or 6. (Closed 25 Dec, 6-31 Jan). Telephone for further details. **Fee:** * £5.90 (concessions £3.90). Family ticket (up to 3 children) £15.50 **Facilities:** P (charged) 🍴 ✖ licensed ♿ toilets for disabled shop ✖ (ex guide dogs) ⛔

PENDENNIS CASTLE
TR11 4LP (1m SE)
☎ 01326 316594

The well preserved granite gun fort and outer ramparts testify to the strength of the coastal fortresses erected in the Tudor period by Henry VIII. It was eventually besieged and captured from the land during the Civil War in the 17th century.
Times: Open all year, 29 Mar-Sep, daily 10-6 (Oct, daily 10-5); Nov-Mar, daily 10-4. (Closed 24-26 Dec & 1 Jan). **Fee:** * £4 (ch £2, concessions £3). Family ticket £10 **Facilities:** P ♿ shop ✖ (in certain areas) ⛔

Cornwall & Isles of Scilly

🏛 FOWEY   Map 02 SX15
ST CATHERINE'S CASTLE
(0.75m along footpath off A3082)

The ruined stronghold (restored in 1855) was one of the many castles built by Henry VIII to defend the coast.
Times: Open all year, any reasonable time. **Fee:** *Free* **Facilities:** ♿

🏛 GODOLPHIN CROSS   Map 02 SW63
GODOLPHIN HOUSE
TR13 9RE (situated off A303 between Townshend and Godolphin)
☎ 01736 763194 📠 01736 763194
e-mail: godo@euphony.net

A romantic Tudor and Stuart mansion, begun in 1475 and considerably extended over the centuries. The Godolphin family's taste is evident throughout the mansion, and of particular note are examples of 16th and 17th-century English oak furniture and Wootton's 1731 painting, Godolphin Arabian, one of the three Arab stallion ancestors of all British bloodstock. The gardens are Tudor, with some areas even earlier. Major repair programme on the mansion funded by English Heritage.
Times: National Trust Estate open all year. House open Etr Mon-Sep.
Fee: Telephone for admission prices. **Facilities:** 🅿 ☕ ♿ (telephone prior to visit. Lift installed) toilets for disabled shop 🐕 (ex guide dogs)

🏛 GOONHAVERN   Map 02 SW75
WORLD IN MINIATURE
Bodmin Rd TR4 9QE (Turn off A30 at Boxheater junct onto B3285 to Perranporth)
☎ 01872 572828 📠 01872 572829
e-mail: info@worldinminiature.co.uk
Times: Open 24 Mar-26 Oct 10-4 (Jul/Aug 10-5) **Facilities:** 🅿 ☕ ♿ toilets for disabled shop garden centre *Details not confirmed for 2003* 🐕

🏛 GORRAN   Map 02 SW94
CAERHAYS CASTLE GARDENS
PL26 6LY (off A390 onto B3287)
☎ 01872 501144 📠 01872 501870
e-mail: estateoffice@caerhays.co.uk

For centuries this magnolia filled garden was a deer park, and it was not until the late 19th century that John Charles Williams ("JCW") inherited Caerhays and not until the early 20th that new and exotic plants were introduced here. Now the gardens are a blaze of plants from Chile, China, New Zealand, the Himalayas, and many other distant lands. Magnolias, Rhododendrons, Camellia, and japonicas can all be seen on marked walks, and the house can be visited in small groups during the spring.
Times: Open 10 Mar-May, daily 10-5.30 (last admission 4.30). House open mid Mar-Apr, telephone for details. **Fee:** * £4.50 (under 16's £1.50). **Facilities:** 🅿 440yds ☕ ♿ 🐕 (ex on leads)

🏛 GWEEK   Map 02 SW72
NATIONAL SEAL SANCTUARY
TR12 6UG (pass RNAS Culdrose & take A3293 & then B3291 to Gweek, the sanctuary is signposted from village)
☎ 01326 221361 & 221874
📠 01326 221210   **2 for 1**
e-mail: slcgweek@merlin-entertainments.com

Britain's largest seal rescue facility - offering a unique opportunity to learn more about these beautiful creatures. Every year it rescues, rehabilitates and releases around 30 sick or abandoned seal pups.
Times: Open all year, daily from 9am. (Closed 25 Dec). **Fee:** Please call for admission prices. **Facilities:** 🅿 ☕ ♿ toilets for disabled shop 🐕

🏛 HELSTON   Map 02 SW62
FLAMBARDS VILLAGE THEME PARK
Culdrose Manor TR13 0QA (0.5m SE of Helston on A3083, Lizard road)
☎ 01326 573404 📠 01326 573344
e-mail: info@flambards.co.uk

Three award-winning, all-weather attractions can be visited on one site here. Flambards Victorian Village is

continued

a recreation of streets, shops and houses from the turn of the century, including a chemist's shop. Britain in the Blitz is a life-size wartime street featuring shops, a pub and a living room with Morrison shelter; and Cornwall Aero Park covers the history of aviation. The Science Centre is a science playground for the whole family. There are many rides from the gentle to the daring, including the new Thunderbolt, Hornet Rollercoaster, Flambards Family Log Flume, Balloon Race and play areas for the very young. Award-winning gardens and live entertainment.
Times: Open Etr-Oct 10.30-5. End Jul-Aug 10-6. (Closed some Mon/Fri in low season) **Fee:** * £11.95 (ch 5-14 £8.95 pen £5.75) Family of 4 £38, family of 5 £44.50 family of 6 £49.95. **Facilities:** P ⌽ & (95% accessible, free loan of wheelchairs, route guides) toilets for disabled shop garden centre ✗ (ex guide dogs) ⚑

TREVARNO ESTATE GARDEN & MUSEUM OF GARDENING
Trevarno Manor, Crowntown TR13 8RU (signposted from B3302)
☎ 01326 574274 📠 01326 574282
e-mail: gardencoordinator@trevarnoestate.fsnet.co.uk

The Trevarno Estate got its name from Randolphus de Trevarno in 1246, and now more than 750 years later it is open to the public throughout the year. Visitors can walk through beautiful Victorian and Georgian gardens, look in on craft workshops, and learn more about the history of gardening in Britain. The National Museum of Gardening has a large collection of gardening antiques, ephemera, and models covering commercial and recreational gardening.
Times: Open daily 10.30-5 **Fee:** * £4.50 (ch 5-14 £1.50, pen £3.95, disabled 2.50). Group 12+ **Facilities:** P ⌽ & toilets for disabled shop ⚑

🏛 LANHYDROCK Map 02 SX06
LANHYDROCK
PL30 5AD (2.5m SE of Bodmin, signposted from A30, A38 & B3268)
☎ 01208 73320 📠 01208 74084
e-mail: clhan@smtp.ntrust.org.uk

Part-Tudor, part-Victorian building that gives a vivid picture of life in Victorian times. The 'below stairs' sections have a huge kitchen, larders, dairy, bakehouse, cellars, and servants' quarters. The long gallery has a moulded ceiling showing Old Testament scenes, and overlooks the formal gardens with their clipped yews and bronze urns. The higher garden, famed for its magnolias and rhododendrons, climbs the hillside behind the house.
Times: Open Apr-Oct: House daily (ex Mon), but open BH Mon 11-5.30 (11-5 in Oct). Gardens daily from mid Feb, last admission half hour before closing. Winter Gardens Nov-Feb during daylight hours. **Fee:** * House & Grounds £7 (ch £3.50). Grounds £3.80 (ch £1.90). Family ticket £17.50. Party £6. **Facilities:** P ⌽ ✗ licensed & (small lift, self drive buggy (pre-book) mannal wheelchairs) toilets for disabled shop garden centre ✗ (ex on lead in park) ⚐ ⚑

🏛 LANREATH Map 02 SX15
LANREATH FARM & FOLK MUSEUM
Churchtown PL13 2NX (A390 from Liskeard, then B3359 for Looe/Polperro, signposted)
☎ 01503 220321 **2 for 1**

A hands-on countryside museum reflecting bygone times in Cornwall. Implements and equipment from the farmhouse, dairy and farmyard are displayed, together with mill workings rescued from a derelict mill house. Demonstrations of local crafts are given on weekday afternoons from 2-4pm. Play phones, pets, and models to operate make it a fun place as well as educational.
Times: Open Etr-May & Oct, daily 11-5; Jun-Sep, daily 10-6. **Fee:** * £2.50 (ch £1.50, under 5 free). Party. **Facilities:** P & shop

🏛 LAUNCESTON Map 02 SX38
LAUNCESTON CASTLE
PL15 7DR
☎ 01566 772365

Dominating this old market town is the ruin of the 12th and 13th-century castle. Built in the early years of the Norman Conquest, it soon became a symbol of the authority of the Earls of Cornwall.
Times: Open all year, 29 Mar-Sep, daily 10-6 (Oct, daily 10-5); Nov-28 Mar, daily 10-4. (Closed 24-26 Dec & 1 Jan). **Fee:** * £2 (ch £1, concessions £1.50). **Facilities:** & (outer bailey only) ✗ ♿

LAUNCESTON STEAM RAILWAY
St Thomas Rd PL15 8DA (turn off A30, well signposted)
☎ 01566 775665 **2 for 1**

The Launceston Steam Railway links the historic town of Launceston with the hamlet of New Mills. Tickets are valid for unlimited travel on the day of issue and you can break your journey at various points along the track. Launceston Station houses railway workshops, a transport museum, gift and book shop.
Times: Open Good Fri: 8 days inclusive, Spring: BH Sun for 6 days, Jun: Sun-Wed inclusive, Jul-Sep: daily ex Sat, Oct: half-term week. **Fee:** * £5.50 (ch £3.80, pen £5). Family ticket £18. Dogs 50p. **Facilities:** P ⌽ & shop

🏛 LOOE Map 02 SX25
MONKEY SANCTUARY
St Martins PL13 1NZ (signposted on B3253 at No Man's Land between East Looe & Hessenford)
☎ 01503 262532 📠 01503 262532
e-mail: info@monkeysanctuary.org

Visitors can see a colony of Amazonian woolly monkeys in extensive indoor and outdoor territory. There are also conservation gardens, children's play area, activity room, and a display room. Vegetarian café.
Times: Open Sun-Thu 11-4.30 from the Sun before Etr-end Sep. **Fee:** £4 (under 5's free, ch £2 & concession £3). **Facilities:** P ⌽ & toilets for disabled shop ✗ ⚑

Cornwall & Isles of Scilly   **41**

⛪ MARAZION   Map 02 SW53
ST MICHAEL'S MOUNT
TR17 0HT (access is by causeway on foot at low tide. 0.5m S of A394 at Marazion)
☎ 01736 710507 & 710265   🖷 01736 711544
e-mail: godolphin@manor-office.co.uk

Reached on foot by causeway at low tide, or by ferry at high tide in the summer only, St Michael's Mount rises dramatically from the sea, a medieval castle to which a magnificent east wing was added in the 1870s. It is home to Lord St Leven, whose ancestor John St Aubyn acquired it in the 17th century.
Times: Open 31 Mar-Oct, Mon-Fri 10.30-5.30. Last admission 4.45; Nov-Mar, telephone for details. The Castle and grounds are open most weekends during the summer season. These are special charity open days and NT members are also asked to pay. Group bookings 01736 710507. **Fee:** * £4.60 (ch £2.30) Family ticket £13. Party 20+ £4.20 each. **Facilities:** P (on mainland) ⛔ ✘ licensed (braille guide) shop ✱ (ex guide dogs) 🛇 ▬

⛪ MAWNAN SMITH   Map 02 SW72
GLENDURGAN
TR11 5JZ (4m SW of Falmouth. 0.5m SW of Mawnan Smith on road to Helford Passage)
☎ 01872 862090   🖷 01872 865808
e-mail: ctlpmo@smtp.ntrust.org.uk
Times: Open 16 Feb-3 Nov, Tue-Sat & BH Mon (last admission 4.30). (Closed Good Fri). **Facilities:** P ⛔ ♿ (braille guide, limited access to gardens/ground floor) toilets for disabled shop garden centre ✱ (ex guide dogs) 🛇 *Details not confirmed for 2003* ▬

TREBAH GARDEN
TR11 5JZ (signposted at Treliever Cross rdbt at junct of A39/A394 & follow brown tourist signs)
☎ 01326 250448   🖷 01326 250781
e-mail: mail@trebah-garden.co.uk

A 25-acre wooded ravine garden, descending 200 feet from the 18th-century house down to a private cove on the Helford River. The cascading Water Garden has pools of giant koi and exotic water plants, winding through two acres of blue and white hydrangeas to the beach. There are glades of sub-tropical tree ferns and palms, as well as rhododendrons and many other trees and shrubs. The beach is open to visitors and there are children's trails and activities all year.
Times: Open daily 10.30-5 (last admission). **Fee:** * Mar-Oct £4.50 (ch & disabled £2.50, pen £4, ch under 5 free); Nov-Feb £2.25 (con £1.25). Party 12+ £4 each. **Facilities:** P ⛔ ✘ licensed ♿ (2 powered wheelchairs & 2 wheelchair routes) toilets for disabled shop garden centre (only on leads) ▬

⛪ NEWQUAY   Map 02 SW86
BLUE REEF AQUARIUM
Towan Promenade TR7 1DU (from A30 follow signs to Newquay, follow Blue Reef Aquarium signs to car park in town centre)
☎ 01637 878134   🖷 01637 872578
e-mail: info@bluereefaquarium.co.uk

The Blue Reef Aquarium, takes visitors from the dramatic Cornish coastline to the spectacular 'underwater gardens' of the Mediterranean and the dazzling beauty of a Caribbean coral reef. The centrepiece of the aquarium is a spectacular coral ocean display home to Black Tip sharks and stingrays as well as hundreds of brightly coloured fish. Visitors can enjoy the spectacle inside an underwater walk-through tunnel as well as from the surface, along a specially-constructed boardwalk. More than 30 living displays are home to everything from crabs and lobsters to seahorses and cuttlefish.
Times: Open all year, daily 10-5. (Closed 25 Dec). Open until 6 during summer holidays. **Fee:** * £4.95 (ch 3-16 £3.25, pen & student £4.25). Family ticket £14.95. **Facilities:** P 5mins walk ⛔ ♿ (lift) toilets for disabled shop ✱ (ex guide dogs) ▬

DAIRY LAND FARM WORLD
Summercourt TR8 5AA (Signposted from A30 at exit for Mitchell/Summercourt)
☎ 01872 510246   🖷 01872 510349
e-mail: farmworld@yahoo.com
Times: Open daily, late Mar-Oct 10.30-5. Xmas opening telephone for details. **Facilities:** P ⛔ ♿ (wheelchairs for loan; disabled viewing gallery - milking) toilets for disabled shop ✱ *Details not confirmed for 2003* ▬

NEWQUAY ZOO
Trenance Gardens TR7 2LZ (off A3075 and follow signs to Zoo)
☎ 01637 873342   🖷 01637 851318
e-mail: info@newquayzoo.co.uk

Education and conservation are the key issues at this exciting zoological centre. Apart from attractions such as the monkey enclosures, penguin pool, tropical house and lion house, the park also boasts a maze, an Oriental Garden, an activity Play Park, a Tarzan Trail assault course, wildlife hospital and a village farm.
Times: Open Apr-Oct, daily 9.30-6; Nov-Mar 10-5. (Closed 25 Dec) **Fee:** * £6.25 (ch 5-15 £3.95, ch 2-4 £1.50, pen £4.50). Family ticket £18.50. **Facilities:** P ⛔ ✘ ♿ (free wheelchairs, guided tours & sensory sculptures) toilets for disabled shop ✱ (ex guide dogs) ▬

Cornwall & Isles of Scilly

🏛 PADSTOW Map 02 SW97
PRIDEAUX PLACE
PL28 8RP (off B3276 Padstow to Newquay Rd. Follow brown heritage signs)
☎ 01841 532411
🖷 01841 532945
e-mail: office@prideauxplace.fsnet.co.uk

2 for 1

Built by Sir Nicholas Prideaux in 1592, this impressive country house has been inhabited by his family for fourteen generations, and is still in use by them today. Visitors can see relics of the English Civil War, including a pardon from Charles II and a double-sided brooch of Cromwell and the King, as well as fascinating rooms filled with antique furniture, paintings and a 16th-century ceiling depicting the biblical story of Susannah. The house was used as a location for Trevor Nunn's film version of *Twelfth Night*.
Times: Open Etr Sun-11 Apr & 12 May-3 Oct, Sun-Thu 1.30-4 (house tours). Grounds 12.30-5. Open all year to pre-booked groups (15+)
Fee: * House & grounds £6 (ch £2), Grounds only £2 (ch £1)
Facilities: 🅿 ⓟ ♿ shop ✖ (ex on leads in grounds)

🏛 PENTEWAN Map 02 SX04
THE LOST GARDENS OF HELIGAN
PL26 6EN (signposted from A390 & B3273)
☎ 01726 845100   🖷 01726 845101
e-mail: info@heligan.com

The largest garden reclamation project in Europe, covering 1000 acres. The gardens are being restored to their former glory including the re-planting of Victorian varieties of fruit and vegetables. Various events are held throughout the year including walks, horticultural events, theatrical events and educational courses.
Times: Open daily 10-6 (last admission 4.30pm): winter 10-dusk. Closed 24-25 Dec. **Fee:** * £6 (ch under 5 free, ch 5-15 £3, pen £5.50). Family £17. **Facilities:** 🅿 ⓟ ♿ (free loan of wheelchairs) toilets for disabled shop garden centre ⌘

🏛 PENZANCE Map 02 SW43
TRENGWAINTON GARDEN
TR20 8RZ (2m NW Penzance, 0.5m W of Heamoor off Penzance - Morvah rd (B3312), 0.5m off St Just rd (A3071))
☎ 01736 362297 & 01637 875404   🖷 01736 362297
e-mail: trengwainton@ntrust.org.uk

Rhododendrons and magnolias grow in profusion at Trengwainton, along with many plants that are difficult to grow in Britain. The mild climate means that seed collected on expeditions to the Far East and southern hemisphere have flourished to produce a magnificent display in this 20th-century garden.
Times: Open 16 Feb-2 Nov, daily 10-5.30 (closed Fri-Sat) but open Good Fri 10-5.30 (Feb, Mar & Oct 10-5). Last admission 30 mins before closing. **Fee:** * £3.90. Family ticket £9.75. Party £3.20 each.
Facilities: 🅿 ⓟ ♿ (braille guide, special route, 2 wheelchairs) toilets for disabled shop garden centre ⌘ ⓟ

🏛 POOL Map 02 SW64
CORNISH MINES & ENGINES
TR14 7AW (2m W of Redruth on A3047, signposted from A30, Pool exit)
☎ 01209 315027 & 210900   🖷 01209 315027
e-mail: info@trevithicktrust.com

Impressive relics of the tin mining industry, these great beam engines were used for pumping water from 2000ft down and for lifting men and ore from the workings below ground. The mine at East Pool has been converted into the Cornwall Industrial Heritage Centre which includes audio visual theatre giving background to all aspects of Cornwall's industrial heritage.
Times: Open 31 Mar-2 Nov, daily (ex Sat) 11-5; Aug open daily 11-5. Nov-Mar by arrangement. **Fee:** * £5 (concessions £4.60, students £3) Family ticket £13. Party. **Facilities:** 🅿 ♿ (lift to all levels, parking by arrangement, braille guide) toilets for disabled shop ✖ (ex guide dogs) ⌘ ⓟ

🏛 PROBUS Map 02 SW84
TREWITHEN GARDENS
Grampound Rd TR2 4DD (on A390 between Truro & St Austell)
☎ 01726 883647   🖷 01726 882301
e-mail: gardens@trewithen-estate.demon.co.uk

The Hawkins family has lived in this charming, intimate country house since it was built in 1720. The internationally renowned landscaped garden covers some 30 acres and grows camellias, magnolias and rhododendrons as well as many rare trees and shrubs seldom seen elsewhere. The nurseries are open all year.
Times: Open Mar-Sep Mon-Sat 10-4.30; Daily 10-4.30 Apr & May **Fee:** £4.25 (pen £4) group 20+ £4 **Facilities:** 🅿 ⓟ ♿ toilets for disabled garden centre ✖ (ex on lead) ⓟ

🏛 RESTORMEL Map 02 SX16
RESTORMEL CASTLE
PL22 OBD (1.5m N of Lostwithiel off A390)
☎ 01208 872687

On a high mound surrounded by a deep moat, the huge circular keep of this Norman castle is remarkably well preserved and commands the Fowey Valley.
Times: Open all year, 29 Mar-Sep, daily 10-6 (Oct, daily 10-5); **Fee:** * £1.90 (ch £1, concessions £1.40). **Facilities:** 🅿 ♿ ✖ ⌘

🏛 ST AUSTELL Map 02 SX05
CHARLESTOWN SHIPWRECK & HERITAGE CENTRE
Quay Rd, Charlestown PL25 3NJ (1.25m SE A3061)
☎ 01726 69897   🖷 01726 69897
e-mail: admin@shipwreckcharlestown.com

Charlestown is a small and unspoilt village with a unique sea-lock, china-clay port, purpose built in the 18th century. The Shipwreck and Heritage Centre houses the largest display of shipwreck artefacts in the

continued

Cornwall & Isles of Scilly

UK, along with local heritage and diving exhibits, and also a Titanic display.
Times: Open Mar-Oct, daily 10-5 (later in high season). Last admission 1 hour before closing. **Fee:** £4.95 (ch under 12 free if accompanied by paying adult, ch under 16 £1.95, concessions £3.45). **Facilities:** P (charged) 🍴 ✗ licensed ♿ (ramps) toilets for disabled shop 🐕

THE CHINA CLAY MUSEUM - WHEAL MARTYN
Carthew PL26 8XG (2m N on B3274)
☎ 01726 850362 📠 01726 850362
e-mail: info@wheal-martyn.com

This museum tells the story of Cornwall's most important present-day industry: china clay production. The open-air site includes a complete 19th-century clayworks, with huge granite-walled settling tanks, working water-wheels and a wooden slurry pump. There is a short audio-visual programme, nature trails and a children's adventure trail.
Times: Open Apr-Oct, 10-6 (last admission 5pm) phone for winter opening times. **Fee:** * £5 (ch & student £3, pen £4.60). **Facilities:** P 🍴 ♿ shop 🐕

EDEN PROJECT
Bodelva PL24 2SG (overlooking St Austell Bay signposted from A390/A30/A391)
☎ 01726 811911 📠 01726 811912
Times: Open daily Mar-Oct 10-6 (last admission 5pm), Nov-Feb 10-4.30 (last admission 3pm). Closed 24-25 Dec. **Facilities:** P 🍴 ✗ licensed ♿ (wheelchairs, car shuttle to visitor centre/biomes) toilets for disabled shop garden centre ✗ (ex guide dogs) *Details not confirmed for 2003* 🐕

🏛 ST IVES   Map 02 SW54

(Park your car at Lelant Station and take advantage of the park and ride service. The fee includes parking and journeys on the train between Lelant and St Ives during the day).

BARBARA HEPWORTH MUSEUM & SCULPTURE GARDEN
Barnoon Hill TR26 1AD (M5 to Exeter, A30 onto Penzance & St Ives, in town centre)
☎ 01736 796226 📠 01736 794480

Dame Barbara Hepworth lived here from 1949 until her death in 1975, and the house is now a museum displaying sculptures and drawings, photographs, documents and other memorabilia. Visitors can also visit her workshops, which house a selection of tools and some unfinished carvings. The garden contains a number of monumental sculptures, situated amongst semi-tropical plants.
Times: Open Mar-Oct, daily 10-5.30; Nov-Feb, Tue-Sun 10-4.30. **Fee:** * £3.75. (ch & pen free, concessions £2). **Facilities:** P (880 yds) ♿ (accessible with assistance) shop ✗ (ex guide dogs) 🐕

TATE ST IVES
Porthmeor Beach TR26 1TG (M5 to Exeter, then A30 onto Penzance & St Ives. Located on Porthmeor Beach)
☎ 01736 796226 📠 01736 794480

Tate St Ives offers a unique introduction to modern art, where many works can be seen in the surroundings and atmosphere, which inspired them. The gallery presents changing displays from the Tate Collection, focusing on the post-war modern movement St Ives is so famous for. Artists represented at the gallery include Alfred Wallis, Ben Nicholson, Barbara Hepworth, Naum Gabo, Peter Lanyon, Bryan Wynter, Roger Hilton, John Wells, Patrick Heron and Terry Frost. There is also a changing programme of temporary exhibitions by major contemporary artists.
Times: Open Mar-Oct, daily 10-5.30; Nov-Feb, Tue-Sun 10-4.30. **Fee:** * £4.25 (ch & pen free, concessions £2.50). **Facilities:** P (800yds) 🍴 ✗ licensed ♿ toilets for disabled shop ✗ (ex guide dogs) 🐕

🏛 ST MAWES   Map 02 SW83
ST MAWES CASTLE
TR2 3AA (on A3078)
☎ 01326 270526

Part of the coastal-defence system built in the reign of Henry VIII, the castle guarded the Fal estuary, together with Pendennis Castle (see Falmouth). A fine example of military architecture, it is of particular interest to military historians. Delightful gardens surround the castle.
Times: Open all year, 29 Mar-Sep, daily 10-6 (Oct, daily 10-5); Nov-Mar daily 10-1, 2-4 Wed-Sun. (Closed 24-26 Dec & 1 Jan). **Fee:** * £2.90 (ch £1.50, concessions £2.20) **Facilities:** P ♿ shop ✗ ♨

🏛 SANCREED   Map 02 SW42
CARN EUNY ANCIENT VILLAGE
(1.25m SW, off A30)

Four courtyard houses and several round houses dating from the 1st century BC can be seen at this site. There is also an impressive 'fogou', a subterranean passage leading to a circular chamber that may have served as a hiding place.
Times: Open any reasonable time. **Fee:** Free **Facilities:** P ♨

🏛 TINTAGEL   Map 02 SX08
TINTAGEL CASTLE
PL34 0HE (on Tintagel Head, 0.5m along uneven track from Tintagel, no vehicles)
☎ 01840 770328

These romantic ruins make a dramatic sight on the edge of the towering cliffs. Associated in popular legend with King Arthur and the magician, Merlin, theories as to its origins abound: a Celtic monastery, the stronghold of Cornish Kings of the Dark Ages, the Durocornovium of the Romans? Whatever the true

continued

Cornwall & Isles of Scilly

answer, it remains one of the most spectacular sites in Britain.
Times: Open 24 Mar-13 Jul, 10-6; 14 Jul-27 Aug 10-7 (later on Wed event evenings); 28 Aug-Sep, daily 10-6. 1-31 Oct daily 10-5. Nov-Mar, daily 10-4. (Closed 24-26 Dec & 1 Jan). **Fee:** * £3 (ch 5-15 £1.50, ch under 5 free, concessions £2.30). **Facilities:** P (in village) shop

TORPOINT   Map 02 SX45
ANTONY HOUSE
PL11 2QA (2m NW, off A374 from Trerulefoot rdbt, 2m from Torpoint Ferry)
☎ 01752 812191
e-mail: antony@ntrust.org.uk

A fine, largely unaltered mansion, built in brick and Pentewan stone for Sir William Carew between 1711 and 1721. The stable block and outhouses remain from an earlier 17th-century building. The house contains contemporary furniture and family portraits. The grounds include a dovecote and the Bath Pond House.
Times: Open 29 Mar-1 Nov, Tue-Thu & BH Mon 1.30-5.30 (last admission 4.45). Also open Sun in Jun-Aug. **Fee:** * House & Garden £4.80. Woodland garden £3. Combined Gardens only £3.70. Party rates available. **Facilities:** P (braille guide, recommended route in garden) toilets for disabled shop (ex guide dogs)

MOUNT EDGCUMBE HOUSE & COUNTRY PARK
Cremyll PL10 1HZ (from Plymouth via Cremyll Foot Ferry, Torpoint ferry or Saltash Bridge. Via Liskeard to A374, B3247 follow brown tourist signs)
☎ 01752 822236   01752 822199

Covering some 800 acres, the country park surrounding Mount Edgcumbe contains a deer park, an amphitheatre, formal gardens, sculpture, the 18th-century Earl's Garden, and woodlands containing California redwoods. The coastal footpath runs along the shores of the Park from Cremyll to Whitsand Bay. Sir Richard Edgcumbe of Cotehele built Mount Edgcumbe between 1547 and 1553. It survived a direct hit by bombs in 1941, and was restored in the 1950s. It now contains antique paintings and furniture, 16th-century tapestries, and 18th-century porcelain.
Times: Open - House & Earl's Garden Good Fri-29 Sep, Wed-Sun & BHs 11-4.30. Formal Gardens & Country Park open daily. Winter months wknds & wkdays depending on weather. Telephone for details. **Fee:** * House & Garden £4.50 (ch £2.25, concessions £3.50) Family ticket £10. Formal Gardens & Country Park, free. **Facilities:** P (charged) licensed toilets for disabled shop

TREDINNICK   Map 02 SW97
SHIRES FAMILY ADVENTURE PARK
Trelow Farm PL27 7RA (signposted off A39)
☎ 01841 540215

2 for 1

There's even more fun at this park this year with 'The Haunted Castle', full of demons, skeletons and ghosts. Enter the 'Dragon Kingdom', the Country's largest indoor adventure zone consisting of two floors of slides, climbs, ropes, balls and towers. Take a walk through the Enchanted Forest to Greengate Meadow and met fully animated moles, Mr Badger and their woodland friends. Acres of outdoor adventure play with the highest aerial bridges and the longest, steepest slides in Cornwall. Plus train rides around the lakes and the majestic shire horses including new born foals with farmyard friends.
Times: Open Good Fri-end Oct, daily 10-5. **Fee:** * £7 (ch 2-14 £6, pen £5) **Facilities:** P licensed (most areas are ramped) toilets for disabled shop

TRELISSICK GARDEN   Map 02 SW83
TRELISSICK GARDEN
TR3 6QL (4m S of Truro on both sides of B3289, King Harry Ferry Road)
☎ 01872 862090   01872 865808
e-mail: ctlpmo@smtp.ntrust.org.uk

Set amidst more than 500 acres of park and farmland, with panoramic views down the Carrick Roads to Falmouth and the sea. The garden is well known for its large collection of hydrangeas, camellias, rhododendrons and exotic and tender plants. The Cornish Apple Orchard contains the definitive collection of Cornish apple varieties and is particularly lovely in the spring.
Times: Open 15 Feb-2 Nov, Mon-Sat 10.30-5.30, Sun 12.30-5.30. Park & woodland walks open all year. **Fee:** * £4.50 (Family ticket £11.25). Party rate 15+ £3.70 each. Car park charge £1.60 (refundable on admission). **Facilities:** P (charged) licensed (audio guide, wheelchairs, batricar, induction loops) toilets for disabled shop garden centre

TRERICE   Map 02 SW85
TRERICE
TR8 4PG (3m SE of Newquay off A3058 at Kestle Mill)
☎ 01637 875404   01637 879300
e-mail: trerice@ntrust.org.uk

Built in 1571 for Sir John Arundell, this picturesque Elizabethan house has unusual curved and scrolled gables, which may have been influenced by Sir John's stay in the Netherlands. The hall has an imposing window with 576 panes. Throughout the house are plasterwork ceilings, fine furniture and a large clock collection. Ring for details of special events.
Times: Open 30 Mar-2 Nov, daily (ex Tue & Sat) 11-5.30 (11-5 Oct-Nov). Open daily from 16 Jul-10 Sep. **Fee:** * House: £4.40. Family ticket (2 adult & 3 ch) £11. Party £3.60 each. **Facilities:** P (braille/large print guide, tape tour, access leaflet) toilets for disabled shop (ex guide dogs)

TRURO   Map 02 SW84
ROYAL CORNWALL MUSEUM
River St TR1 2SJ (follow A390 towards town centre)
☎ 01872 272205   01872 240514
e-mail: enquiry@royal-cornwall-museum.freeserve.co.uk

Interesting displays on the history of the county, a world-famous collection of minerals, paintings and drawings, including a number of Old Masters. Other galleries house displays of archaeology, Cornish history,

continued

Cornwall & Isles of Scilly   **45**

and Egyptian artefacts. Also galleries of Cornish wildlife, fashion and textiles.
Times: Open all year, Mon-Sat 10-5. Library closes 1-2. (Closed BHs).
Fee: £3.95 (unaccompanied ch 50p, pen & students £2.50) **Facilities:** P (200 yds) (disabled parking on street) 💺 ✕ licensed ♿ (lift, ramps to main entrances) toilets for disabled shop 🐕 (ex guide dogs) ☕

WENDRON   Map 02 SW63
POLDARK MINE AND HERITAGE COMPLEX
TR13 0ER (3m from Helston on B3297 Redruth rd)
☎ 01326 573173 ✉ 01326 563166
e-mail: info@poldark-mine.com
Times: Open Oct-Apr, 10.30-4.30 (last tour 3pm). (Closed Fri ex 1/2 term week). Please check for winter opening times. **Facilities:** P 💺 ♿ (newly refurbished museum allowing disabled access) shop (ex grounds) *Details not confirmed for 2003* ☕

ZENNOR   Map 02 SW43
WAYSIDE FOLK MUSEUM
TR26 3DA (4m W of St Ives, on B3306)
☎ 01736 796945

Founded in 1937, this museum covers every aspect of life in Zennor and surrounding district from 3000BC to the 1930s. Over 5000 items are displayed in 14 workshops and rooms covering wheelwrights, blacksmiths, agriculture, fishing, wrecks, mining, domestic and archaeological artefacts. A photographic exhibition entitled 'People of the Past' tells the story of the village.
Times: Open Apr & Oct Sun-Fri 11-5, May-Sep Sun-Fri 10.30-5.30, also Sat during Summer school & BH's. **Fee:** * £2.50 (ch £1.50, over 60's £2.25). Party rates 10+. **Facilities:** P (50yds) 💺 ♿ (not suitable for wheelchair users) shop 🐕 (ex guide dogs) ☕

Cumbria

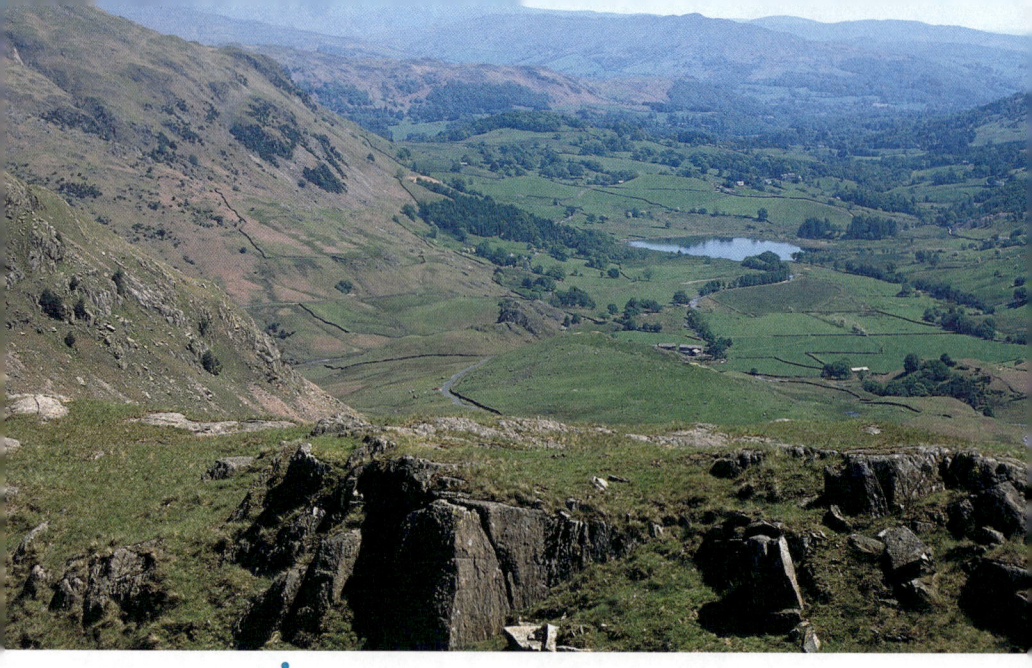

EVENTS & FESTIVALS

March
15th-22nd Mary Wakefield Westmorland Festival, Kendal

March/April
28th March-6th April Ulverston Walking Festival

May
4th-5th Carlisle & Borders Spring Flower Show, Carlisle
15th-18th Jennings Keswick Jazz Festival, Keswick
30th-1st June Great Garden & Countryside Festival, Cumbria
tbc Cumbria Brass Band Competition, Whitehaven

June
30th May-1st Great Garden & Countryside Festival
5th-11th Appleby Horse Fair, Appleby-in-Westmorland
9th-11th La'al Cumbrian Beer Festival, Wasdale Head, Seascale

July
19th Cumberland County Show
25th-27th Maryport Blues Festival
26th-27th The Cumbria Steam Gathering, Flookburgh

August
6th Cartmel Show, Cartmel
24th Grasmere Lakeland Sports & Show, Grasmere
tbc Yorkshire Dales & English Lakes Historic Vehicle Event

September
11th Westmorland County Show, Milnthorpe
20th Egremont Crab Fair & Sports (including gurning competition)
tbc Westmorland Beer Festival

November
8th-9th Kendal Mountain Film Festival, Highgate, Kendal

The heart of Cumbria is the massive and majestic Lake District National Park, approximately 1,200 square miles of woodland, hills, lakes, mountains, rivers, and small villages. This means that a visit to Cumbria is basically a visit to some of Britain's finest landscapes.

The highest of the Lake District's peaks is Scafell Pike, which at 3,210ft (978m) is also the highest point in England. Other notable peaks include Scafell itself, Helvellyn towering above Ullswater, Skiddaw looming in the north above Bassenthwaite Lake and the impressive Langdale Pikes towering above the fertile greenery of the Great Langdale valley. In all, there are more than 60 summits above 2,500ft (762m).

At the foot of the mountains are the lakes the district takes its name from. These were scooped out millions of years ago by Ice Age glaciers, and are mostly called 'mere' (Old English) or 'water'. Derwent Water is commonly regarded as the most beautiful of these, and is a haven for wildlife. Wast Water is much more sombre, hemmed in by grim mountains and scree slopes, while long and winding Ullswater is perhaps the most spectacular. Windermere is the busiest as well as the biggest at 10.5 miles (17km) long.

It wasn't until the 18th century that the Lake District began to be appreciated, and it wasn't until the 19th century that people came in large numbers to see it. Now, those wishing to visit may want to come in the spring or autumn, as the area can get crowded in summer. Fell-walking, rock climbing, pony trekking, and fishing are major Lake District activities.

The area has inspired writers as diverse as William Wordsworth, Beatrix Potter and Arthur Ransome, who set his novel *Swallows and Amazons* largely around Coniston Water.

Top: Little Langdale

Cumbria

ALSTON   Map 12 NY74
SOUTH TYNEDALE RAILWAY
The Railway Station, Hexham Rd CA9 3JB (0.25m N, on A686)
☎ 01434 381696

Running along the beautiful South Tyne valley, this narrow-gauge railway follows the route of the former Alston to Haltwhistle branch. At present the line runs between Alston and Kirkhaugh. **Times:** Open Apr-Oct & Dec, wknds and BH's; 20 Jul-Aug, daily. Also open some wknds in Dec. Please enquire for times of trains. **Fee:** * Return £4 (ch 3-15 £2). Single £2.50 (ch 3-15 £1.50). All day £10 (ch 3-15 £5). **Facilities:** P & (railway carriage for wheelchairs, pre-booking required) toilets for disabled shop

AMBLESIDE   Map 07 NY30
ARMITT MUSEUM
Rydal Rd LA22 9BL (beyond Bridge House opposite main car park)
☎ 015394 31212
📠 015394 31313   2 for 1
e-mail: mail@armitttrust.fsbusiness.co.uk

The story of Ambleside from Roman times to present day. Explore the area through the eyes of John Ruskin, Kurt Schwitters, photographer Herbert Bell and Beatrix Potter and admire a wonderful collection of local history material. Hands on activities for all the family. **Times:** Open all year, daily 10-5 (last entrance 4.30pm). Closed 25-26 Dec. **Fee:** * £2.50 (ch, students, pen £1.80) Family ticket £5.60. **Facilities:** P (50yds) & (chairlift to upstairs library, parking at establishment) toilets for disabled shop ✱ (ex guide dogs)

APPLEBY-IN-WESTMORLAND
                                                 Map 12 NY62
APPLEBY CASTLE
CA16 6XH (on A66, castle is top of the main street)
☎ 017683 51402   📠 017683 51082

Times: Open 4 Apr-Oct, daily 10-5 (last admission); Oct, daily 10-4. **Facilities:** P ✱ & (assistance available) toilets for disabled shop garden centre ✱ (ex on lead, guide dogs) *Details not confirmed for 2003*

BARROW-IN-FURNESS   Map 07 SD26
FURNESS ABBEY
LH13 0TJ (1.5m NE on unclass road)
☎ 01229 823420

Founded by the wealthy Cistercian Order in the 12th century, the red sandstone abbey is an impressive ruin. Its setting is the beautiful 'Glen of Deadly Nightshade' near Barrow. Fine stone carving is displayed in the site museum.
Times: Open all year, 29 Mar-Sep, daily 10-6 (Oct, daily 10-5); Nov-Mar, daily 10-4. (Closed 24-26 Dec & 1 Jan). **Fee:** * £2.80 (ch 5-15 £1.40, under 5's free, concessions £2.10). Personal stereo tour included in admission. **Facilities:** P & ✱ (in certain areas) ♿

BASSENTHWAITE   Map 11 NY23
TROTTERS WORLD OF ANIMALS
Coalbeck Farm CA12 4RD
☎ 017687 76239   2 for 1
📠 017687 76598
e-mail: info@trottersworld.com

Home to hundreds of friendly animals including lemurs, wallabies and other exotic animals along with reptiles and birds of prey and a family of gibbons which will keep families amused for hours. Informative, amusing demonstrations daily bring visitors closer to the animals. The new "Clown About" indoor play centre has soft play area and ballpools for toddlers upwards. **Times:** Open 9 Feb-3 Nov 10-5.30. Winter Sat-Sun & daily Xmas-New Year (ex 25 Dec & 1 Jan) **Fee:** * £4.25 (ch £3, under 3yrs free) **Facilities:** P 🍴 & toilets for disabled shop ✱ (ex guide dogs)

BIRDOSWALD   Map 12 NY66
BIRDOSWALD ROMAN FORT
CA8 7DD (signposted off A69 between Brampton & Hexham)
☎ 016977 47602   📠 016977 47605   2 for 1
e-mail: birdoswald@dial.pipex.com

A visitor centre introduces you to Hadrian's Wall and the Roman Fort. This unique section of Hadrian's Wall overlooks the Irthing Gorge, and is the only point along the Wall where all the components of the Roman frontier system can be found together. Birdoswald isn't just about the Romans, though, it's also about border raids in the Middle Ages, and recent archaeological discoveries.
Times: Open Mar-Oct 10-5.30. **Fee:** £3 (ch £1.75, concessions £2.50). Family ticket £7.75. English Heritage members half price. **Facilities:** P 🍴 & (ramp outside, disabled parking) toilets for disabled shop

BOWNESS-ON-WINDERMERE
                                                 Map 07 SD49
BLACKWELL THE ARTS & CRAFTS HOUSE
LA23 3JR (M6 junct 36. 1.5m S of Bowness on B5360, off A5074)
☎ 015394 46139   📠 015394 88486
e-mail: info@blackwell.org.uk

Blackwell was designed by architect M H Baillie Scott (1865-1945) and completed in 1900. Part of the late 19th-century Arts and Crafts Movement it houses changing exhibitions of high quality applied arts and crafts, as well as original design features including stained glass, stonework, carved oak panelling, and plasterwork.
Times: Open Apr-Oct daily 10-5; mid Feb-Mar & Nov-Xmas daily 10-4 **Fee:** * £4.50 (ch & students £2.50) Family ticket £12 **Facilities:** P 🍴 & toilets for disabled shop ✱ (ex guide dogs)

Cumbria

BRAMPTON
Map 12 NY56
LANERCOST PRIORY
CA8 2HQ (2.5m NE)
☎ 01697 73030

The Augustinian priory was founded around 1166. The nave of the church has survived and is now used as the local parish church, providing a striking contrast with the ruined chancel, transepts and priory buildings.
Times: Open all year, 29 Mar-Sep, daily 10-6 (Oct, daily 10-5); (parish church not managed by English Heritage) **Fee:** * £2.20 (ch 5-15 £1.10, under 5's free, concessions £1.70). **Facilities:** P & ✖ ♿

BROUGH
Map 12 NY71
BROUGH CASTLE
CA17 4EJ (S of A66)
☎ 0191 261 1585

Standing on the site of the Roman Verterae, the castle, of which the keep and curtain wall remain, was built in the 12th and 13th centuries to replace an earlier stronghold. The later castle also fell into ruin, but was restored in the 17th century.
Times: Open any reasonable time. **Fee:** Free. **Facilities:** P ✖ ♿

BROUGHAM
Map 12 NY52
BROUGHAM CASTLE
CA10 2AA (1.5m SE of Penrith on minor road off A66)
☎ 01768 62488

On the banks of the River Eamont lie the ruins of one of the strongest castles in the region, founded in the 13th century and restored in the 17th by the strong-minded Lady Anne Clifford.
Times: Open all year, 29 Mar-Sep, daily 10-6 (Oct, daily 10-5); **Fee:** * £2.20 (ch 5-15 £1.10, under 5's free, concessions £1.70) **Facilities:** P & (ex keep) ♿

CARLISLE
Map 11 NY35
CARLISLE CASTLE & BORDER REGIMENTS MUSEUM
CA3 8UR (north side of city centre, close to station)
☎ 01228 591992

This medieval castle has a long history of warfare. An exhibition marks the Jacobite Rising of 1745, when Bonnie Prince Charlie took the castle. It is also the home of the Museum of the King's Own Border Regiment.
Times: Open all year, 29 Mar-Sep, daily 10-6 (Oct, daily 10-5); Nov-Mar, daily 10-4. (Closed 24-26 Dec & 1 Jan). **Fee:** * £3.20 (ch 5-15 £1.60, under 5's free, concessions £2.40). **Facilities:** P (400 yds) & (parking for disabled at Castle) shop ✖ ♿

CARLISLE CATHEDRAL
Castle St CA3 8TZ (M6 junct 42,43 or 44)
☎ 01228 535169 & 548151 (office)
📠 01228 547049
e-mail: office@carlislecathedral.org.uk

Founded in 1122 as a Norman Priory for Augustinian canons. The chancel roof is magnificently decorated and the cathedral features an exquisite east window.
Times: Open daily throughout the year, Mon-Sat 7.30-6.15, Sun 7.30-5, summer BHs 9.45-6.15, winter BHs, Xmas & New Year 9.45-4.
Fee: Suggested donation of £2 per adult. **Facilities:** P (5 mins walk) (2xdisabled only at establishment) ✖ licensed & (parking, ramps, loop system, large print books, chairlifts) toilets for disabled shop ✖ (ex guide dogs)

GUILDHALL MUSEUM
Green Market CA3 8JE (town centre, opposite The Crown & Mitre Hotel)
☎ 01228 534781   📠 01228 810249
e-mail: barbaral@carlisle-city.gov.uk

One of Carlisle's oldest buildings, c.1405 and Grade I listed. The Guildhall was once the meeting place of Carlisle's eight trade guilds, few of which still meet today. Experience the cabin-like atmosphere of the shoemaker's room and the 'modernised' butcher's room with its Victorian features. There are amazing objects such as the medieval town chest, dating from around 1400, two small silver balls (one dated 1599)- reputed to be the earliest surviving horse racing prizes in the country.
Times: Open Apr-Oct, 12-4.30 **Fee:** Free. **Facilities:** P (500yds) (disc parking on street, 1 hr limit) ✖ (ex guide dogs)

TULLIE HOUSE MUSEUM & ART GALLERY
Castle St CA3 8TP (M6, junct 42, 43 or 44 follow signs to city centre. Car park located in Devonshire Walk)
☎ 01228 534781   📠 01228 810249
e-mail: barbaral@carlisle-city.gov.uk

Dramatic audio-visual displays, striking recreations of long vanished scenes and imaginative hands-on displays. There is something for everyone, no matter what age - the stunning new underground Millennium Gallery or Border River pathway linking to Carlisle Castle. This unique project combines the museum's own collections with the cutting edge of contemporary art. The new multi-media room features touch sensitive computer screens & a short film.
Times: Open: Nov-Mar, Mon-Sat 10-4, Sun 12-4; Apr-Jun & Sep-Oct, Mon-Sat 10-5, Sun 12-5. Jul-Aug, Mon-Sat 10-5, Sun 11-5. (Closed 25-26 Dec & 1 Jan). **Fee:** * Ground floor (including Art Gallery & Old Tullie House) - Free. Upper floors & New Millenium Gallery - £5 (concessions £3.50) Family ticket (2 adults 3 ch) £14. **Facilities:** P (5mins walk) (disabled parking on site by request) ✖ licensed & (chair lift) toilets for disabled shop ✖ (ex guide dogs) 🍽

COCKERMOUTH
Map 11 NY13
JENNINGS BREWERY TOUR
The Castle Brewery CA13 9NE
☎ 01900 821011   📠 01900 827462
e-mail: brewery@globalnet.co.uk
Times: Tours: 16-20 Feb & 23 Mar-30 Oct, Mon-Fri 11 & 2; 13 Jul-28 Aug, extra tour at 12.30; 4 Apr-19 Sep, Sats at 11; BHs 11 & 2. (Closed Sun). **Facilities:** P shop ✖ *Details not confirmed for 2003* 🍽

Cumbria

LAKELAND SHEEP & WOOL CENTRE
Egremont Rd CA13 0QX (M6 junct 40, W on A66 to rdbt at Cockermouth on A66/A586 junction)
☎ 01900 822673   ≣ 01900 822673
e-mail: reception@sheep-woolcentre.co.uk

Come face to face with 19 different breeds of live sheep. Stage show with 'One Man and his Dog' demonstration and our Jersey cow. Shows four times daily, March-end Oct. All indoors.
Times: Open all year, daily 9.30-5.30 (Closed 25 Dec & 4-17 Jan).
Fee: £4 (ch £3). **Facilities:** P ⦿ ✕ licensed ♿ (hearing loop system) toilets for disabled shop ✣ (ex guide/hearing dogs) ⚑

WORDSWORTH HOUSE
Main St CA13 9RX (W end of Main Street)
☎ 01900 824805   ≣ 01900 824805
e-mail: rworn@smtp.ntrust.org.uk
Times: Open 2 Apr-2 Nov Mon-Fri 10.30-4.30. Also Sats in Jun, Jul & Aug. **Facilities:** P ⦿ ♿ (braille guide) shop ✣ ⚘ Details not confirmed for 2003

🏛 CONISTON   Map 07 SD39
BRANTWOOD
LA21 8AD (2.5m SE off B5285, unclass road. Regular ferry services from Coniston Pier)
☎ 015394 41396   ≣ 015394 41263
e-mail: enquiries@brantwood.org.uk

Brantwood, home of John Ruskin, is a beautifully situated house with fine views across Coniston Water. Inside, there is a large collection of Ruskin paintings and memorabilia, and visitors can enjoy delightful nature walks through the Brantwood Estate.
Times: Open mid Mar-mid Nov, daily 11-5.30. Winter, Wed-Sun 11-4.30. (Closed 25-26 Dec). **Fee:** House & Estate £4.50 (ch £1, student £3). Family ticket £10. Estate only £2. **Facilities:** P ⦿ ✕ licensed ♿ (wheelchairs, photo albums of inaccessible areas) toilets for disabled shop ✣ (ex guide dogs & in grounds) ⚑

RUSKIN MUSEUM
The Institute, Yewdale Rd LA21 8DU (In village centre, accessed from A593, A595 & B5285)
☎ 015394 41164   ≣ 01539 441132   `2 for 1`
e-mail: rmj@ruskinmuseum.com

John Ruskin (1819-1900) was one of Britain's most versatile and important political thinkers and artists. The museum contains many of his watercolours, drawings, letters, sketchbooks and other relics. The geology, mines and quarries of the area, Arthur Ransome's *'Swallows and Amazons'* country, and Donald Campbell's *Bluebird* are also explored in the Museum.
Times: Open all year, mid Mar-mid Nov, daily 10-5.30; Winter opening, Wed-Sun 10.30-3.30. **Fee:** £3.50 (ch £1.75). Family ticket £9. Ruskin passport gives exclusive discount for cruise on S.Y. Gondola.
Facilities: P ♿ (audio guide, handling specimens) toilets for disabled shop ✣ (ex guide dogs) ⚑

STEAM YACHT GONDOLA
Pier Cottage LA21 8AJ
☎ 015394 63856   ≣ 015394 35353
e-mail: rcogon@smtp.ntrust.org.uk
Times: Open Apr-Oct to scheduled daily timetable. Trips commence 11 at Coniston Pier; 12 on Sat. Piers at Coniston, Park-a-Moor at SE end of lake & Brantwood. (Not NT). **Facilities:** P shop ✣ (ex guide dogs) ⚘ Details not confirmed for 2003

🏛 DALEMAIN   Map 12 NY42
DALEMAIN
CA11 0HB (between Penrith & Ullswater on A592)
☎ 017684 86450   ≣ 017684 86223   `2 for 1`
e-mail: admin@dalemain.com

Originally a medieval pele tower, Dalemain was added to in Tudor times, and the imposing Georgian façade was completed in 1745. It has oak panelling, Chinese wallpaper, Tudor plasterwork and fine period furniture. The tower contains the Westmorland and Cumberland Yeomanry Museum, and there is a countryside collection in the 16th-century Great Barn. The gardens include a collection of old fashioned roses, and in early summer a magnificent display of blue Himalayan poppies.
Times: Open Gardens, Mediaeval Hall and agricultural & countryside collections: 24 Mar-13 Oct , Sun-Thu 10.30-5. House open 11-4. **Fee:** * House £5.50 (ch £3.50) Family ticket £14.50. Gardens £3.50. (ch free when accompanied). Party. **Facilities:** P ⦿ ✕ licensed ♿ (ramp access at entrance, setting down & collection point) toilets for disabled shop garden centre ✣ (ex guide dogs) ⚑

🏛 DALTON-IN-FURNESS   Map 07 SD27
SOUTH LAKES WILD ANIMAL PARK
Crossgates LA15 8JR (M6 junct 36, A590 to Dalton-in-Furness, signed)
☎ 01229 466086   ≣ 01229 466086
e-mail: office@wildanimalpark.co.uk
Times: Open all year, daily 10-6, during Winter 10-dusk. (Closed 25 Dec) **Facilities:** P ⦿ ♿ (Sound system, wheelchair users may need help) toilets for disabled shop ✣ ⚘ Details not confirmed for 2003 ⚑

Cumbria

🏛 GRASMERE Map 11 NY30
DOVE COTTAGE & THE WORDSWORTH MUSEUM
LA22 9SH (S, off A591, immediately before Grasmere village)
☎ 015394 35544   📠 015394 35748
e-mail: enquiries@wordsworth.org.uk

Dove Cottage was the inspirational home of William Wordsworth for over eight years, and it was here that he wrote some of his best-known poetry. The cottage has been open to the public since 1891, and is kept in its original condition. The museum displays manuscripts, works of art and items that belonged to the poet.
Times: Open daily 9.30-5.30, last admission 5pm. (Closed mid Jan-mid Feb & 24-26 Dec). **Fee:** Admission charge, discount and concessions available. Reciprocal discount offer with Rydal Mount, Ambleside & Wordsworth House, Cockermouth. **Facilities:** 🅿 💺 ✕ licensed ♿ (ramps) toilets for disabled shop 🐕 (ex guide dogs) 🍴

🏛 GRETA BRIDGE Map 12 NZ01
CUMBERLAND PENCIL MUSEUM
Cumberland Pencil Museum, Southey Works CA12 5NG (M6 N onto A66 at Penrith. Left at 2nd Keswick exit, left at T-junct, left over Greta Bridge)
☎ 017687 73626   📠 017687 74679
e-mail: museum@acco-uk.co.uk

Investigating the history and technology of an object most of us take utterly for granted, this interesting museum includes a replica of the Borrowdale mine where graphite was first discovered, the world's largest pencil, and displays on brass-rubbing and various artistic techniques that use pencils.
Times: Open daily 9.30-4 (hours may be extended during peak season). (Closed 25-26 Dec & 1 Jan) **Fee:** * £2.50 (ch & pen £1.25, students £1.75). Family ticket (2 adults, 3 children) £6.25 **Facilities:** 🅿 ♿ toilets for disabled shop 🍴

🏛 HARDKNOTT CASTLE ROMAN FORT
Map 07 NY20
HARDKNOTT CASTLE ROMAN FORT
(at W end of Hardknott Pass)

Hair-raising hairpin bends on a steep hill are the feature for which Hardknott Pass is famous, and this astonishing Roman fort commands its western end, looking down over Eskdale.
Times: Open any reasonable time. Access may be hazardous in winter. **Fee:** Free **Facilities:** 🅿 ♿

🏛 HAWKSHEAD Map 07 SD39
BEATRIX POTTER GALLERY
Main St LA22 0NS
☎ 015394 36355   📠 015394 36118
e-mail: rhabpg@smtp.ntrust.org.uk
Times: Open Apr-1 Nov & Good Friday Sun-Thu 10.30-4.30 (last admission 4). Admission is by timed ticket including NT members.
Facilities: 🅿 (300metres) (braille guide) shop 🐕 ♿ 🦮 *Details not confirmed for 2003*

🏛 HOLKER Map 07 SD37
HOLKER HALL & GARDENS
Cark in Cartmel, Grange over Sands LA11 7PL (from M6 junct 36, on A590, signposted)
☎ 015395 58328   📠 015395 58378
e-mail: publicopening@holker.co.uk

Dating from the 16th century, the new wing of the Hall was rebuilt in 1871, after a fire. It has a notable woodcarving and many fine pieces of furniture which mix happily with family photographs from the present day. There are magnificent gardens, both formal and woodland and the Lakeland Motor Museum, exhibitions, deer park and adventure playground are further attractions.
Times: Open 20 Mar-3 Nov, Sun-Fri 10-6. Hall open 10.30-4.30. (Closed Sat). **Fee:** * Gardens & Grounds £3.95 (ch 6-15 £2.25) Family ticket £11.95. All 3 attractions £8.25 (ch £4.65) Family ticket £23.95.
Facilities: 🅿 💺 ✕ licensed ♿ (ramps, handrails, wheelchairs, scooters) toilets for disabled shop 🍴

🏛 KENDAL Map 07 SD59
ABBOT HALL ART GALLERY
LA9 5AL (M6 junct 36, follow signs to Kendal. Located at S end of town centre beside church)
☎ 01539 722464   📠 01539 722494
e-mail: info@abbothall.org.uk

The ground floor rooms of this splendid house have been restored to their former glory, with original carvings and fine panelling. The walls are hung with paintings by Romney, Gardner, Turner and Ruskin. The gallery has notable temporary exhibitions and a fine permanent collection of 18th and 19th-century watercolours of the Lake District, and 20th-century British art, including works by Hepworth, Frink, Nicholson, Sutherland, Riley and Freud.
Times: Open mid Feb-Xmas, Mon-Sat 10.30-5 (reduced hours in Feb, Mar, Nov & Dec) please telephone for details. **Fee:** £3.50 (ch & students £1.75). Family ticket £9. **Facilities:** 🅿 💺 ♿ (chair lifts in split level galleries, large print lables) toilets for disabled shop 🐕 (ex guide dogs) 🍴

KENDAL MUSEUM
Station Rd LA9 6BT (opposite railway station)
☎ 01539 721374   📠 01539 737976
e-mail: enquiries@kendalmuseum.org.uk

The archaeology and natural history of the Lakes is explored in this popular museum which also features a world wildlife exhibition and a display devoted to author Alfred Wainwright, who was honorary clerk to the museum.
Times: Open mid Feb-mid Dec, Mon-Sat 10.30-5. Reduced hours Feb-Mar; Nov & Dec, 10.30-4. Closed Sun. **Fee:** * £3.50 (ch, students £1.75). Family tickets £9. Groups 15+. Seasonal tickets available. Ticket provides reduced entry to Abbot Hall Art Gallery & Museum of Lakeland life & Industry. **Facilities:** 🅿 ♿ toilets for disabled shop 🐕 (ex guide dogs) 🍴

Cumbria   51

Museum of Lakeland Life
Abbot Hall LA9 5AL (M6 junct 36, follow signs to Kendal. Located at S end of Kendal beside Abbot Hall Art Gallery)
☎ 01539 722464   ◧ 01539 722494
e-mail: info@lakelandmuseum.org.uk

The life and history of the Lake District is captured by the displays in this museum, housed in Abbot Hall's stable block. The working and social life of the area are well illustrated by a variety of exhibits including period rooms, a Victorian Cumbrian street scene and a farming display. Two of the rooms are devoted to the memory of Arthur Ransome.
Times: Open mid Feb-Xmas, Mon-Sat 10.30-5. Reduced hours Feb, Mar, Nov & Dec, please telephone for details. Closed Sun **Fee:** £3.50 (ch & students £1.75). Family ticket £9. **Facilities:** P ⬛ ♿ (listening posts, large print lables) toilets for disabled shop ✖ (ex guide dogs) ⬛

KESWICK   Map 11 NY22
Keswick Museum & Gallery
Fitz Park, Station Rd CA12 4NF (M6 junct 40, A66 to Keswick, then follow tourist signs for Museum & Art Gallery)
☎ 017687 73263   ◧ 017687 80390
e-mail: keswick.museum@allerdale.gov.uk
Times: Open Good Friday-Oct, 10-4. **Facilities:** P (on road outside) (2 hour limit) ♿ (ramp at front entrance, with handrails) shop ✖ (ex guide & hearing dogs) Details not confirmed for 2003

Mirehouse
CA12 4QE (3m N of Keswick on A591)
☎ 017687 72287   ◧ 017687 72287
e-mail: info@mireho.freeserve.co.uk
Times: Open Apr-Oct. House: Wed, Sun, (also Fri in Aug) 2-last entry 4.30. Grounds: daily 10.30-5.30. Parties by arrangement. **Facilities:** P ⬛ ♿ (notes available listing facilities) toilets for disabled ✖ (ex guide dogs) Details not confirmed for 2003

LAKESIDE   Map 07 SD38
Aquarium of the Lakes
LA12 8AS (M6, junct 36, take A590 to Newby Bridge. Turn right over bridge, follow Hawkshead road to Lakeside. Well signposted)
☎ 015395 30153   ◧ 01539 530152
e-mail: aquariumofthelakes@reallive.co.uk

Discover the magic of the lakes at Britain's award winning freshwater aquarium. Over 30 displays, featuring the UK's largest collection of freshwater fish as well as mischievous otters and diving ducks. Walk on Windemere's re-created lakebed in the Lake District's only underwater tunnel, and come face to face with sharks and rays from around our coast in the fascinating Morecambe Bay displays.
Times: Open all year, daily from 9am. Closed 25 Dec. **Fee:** * £5.95 (ch £3.75, pen £4.75). Family ticket (2 adult & 2 ch £16.95, 2 adult & 3 ch £19.95, 2 adult & 4 ch £22.95). **Facilities:** P (charged) ⬛ ♿ (lift to first floor, wheelchairs, motorised scooters) toilets for disabled shop ✖ (ex guide dogs) ⬛

LEVENS   Map 07 SD48
Levens Hall
LA8 0PD (M6 junct 36. 5m S of Kendal, on A6)
☎ 015395 60321   ◧ 015395 60669
e-mail: email@levenshall.fsnet.co.uk

An Elizabethan mansion, built onto a 13th-century pele tower, with fine plasterwork and panelling. The topiary garden, laid out in 1694, has been little changed.
Times: Open: House & gardens Apr-late Oct, Sun-Thu. Gardens 10-5. House 12-5. Last admission 4.30. **Fee:** * House & garden £6.50 (ch £3.20), garden only £5 (ch 2.50). **Facilities:** P ⬛ ♿ (ramps within garden) toilets for disabled shop garden centre ✖ (ex guide dogs) ⬛

MUNCASTER   Map 06 SD19
Muncaster Castle, Gardens & Owl Centre
CA18 1RQ (1m S of Ravenglass on A595)
☎ 01229 717614 & 717393   **2 for 1**
(owl centre)   ◧ 01229 717010
e-mail: information@muncastercastle.co.uk

Muncaster Castle has been home to the Pennington family for 800 years. Treasures include a Gainsborough painted for a bet, John of Bologna's Alabaster Lady, and Henry VI's drinking bowl. The Castle stands in 77 acres of woodland and gardens, which also houses 50 species of owl in the World Owl Centre.
Times: Open Castle; late Mar-2 Nov, Sun-Fri 12-5. Garden & Owl Centre, all year, daily 10.30-6. Parties by arrangement. **Fee:** * Castle, Gardens & Owl Centre £7.50 (ch £5). Family ticket £20. Season & party tickets available. **Facilities:** P ⬛ ✖ licensed ♿ (wheelchair loan, induction loop, audio tour) toilets for disabled shop ✖ (ex on a lead in gardens) ⬛

NEAR SAWREY   Map 07 SD39
Hill Top
LA22 0LF (2m S of Hawkshead. Behind The Tower Bank Arms)
☎ 015394 36269   ◧ 015394 36118
e-mail: rpmhtop@smtp.ntrust.org.uk
Times: Open Mar-May & Sep-Oct 11-4.30, Jun-Aug 10.30-5.
Facilities: P (200 metres) (no parking for coaches) (braille guide, handling items, accessibility by arrangement) shop ✖ ⚤ Details not confirmed for 2003

PENRITH   Map 12 NY53
Wetheriggs Country Pottery
Clifton Dykes CA10 2DH (approx 2m off A6, S from Penrith, signposted)
☎ 01768 892733   ◧ 01768 892722
e-mail: info@wetheriggs-pottery.co.uk

Wetheriggs is the UK's only remaining steam-powered pottery. The Pots of Fun Studio is an interactive craft experience where you can throw a pot, paint a figurine, make candles or work with mosaics. There is also a newt pond and nature area.
Times: Contact establishment for details of opening times. **Fee:** Free.
Facilities: P ⬛ ♿ toilets for disabled shop ✖ (ex guide dogs & dogs on lead) ⬛

RAVENGLASS Map 06 SD09
Ravenglass & Eskdale Railway
CA18 1SW (close to A595)
☎ 01229 717171   01229 717011
e-mail: rer@netcomuk.co.uk

From the Lake District National Park's only coastal village of Ravenglass, small steam engines haul trains through 7 miles of outstanding, unspoilt beauty to the foot of England's highest mountains in Eskdale. Enjoy the freedom of open or cosy covered carriages. Children learn about steam with 'La'al Ratty', the water-vole stationmaster.
Times: Open: trains operate daily 29 Mar-Sun 2 Nov. Some winter wknds, plus daily in Feb Half term. **Fee:** * Return fare £7.40 (ch 5-15 £3.70). 1 adult half price with 2+ fare paying children. **Facilities:** P (charged) licensed (special coaches - prior notice advisable) toilets for disabled shop

RYDAL Map 11 NY30
Rydal Mount
LA22 9LU (1.5m from Ambleside on A591 to Grasmere)
☎ 015394 33002   015394 31738
e-mail: rydalmount@aol.com
Times: Open Mar-Oct daily 9.30-5; Nov-Feb daily (ex Tue) 10-4 (Closed 8 Jan-1 Feb). **Facilities:** P & shop (ex guide dogs & garden) *Details not confirmed for 2003*

SEDBERGH Map 07 SD69
National Park Centre
72 Main St LA10 5AS
☎ 015396 20125   015396 21732
Times: Open Apr-Oct, daily 10-5. Nov-Mar open 2 days a week.
Facilities: P (charged) & (accessible with help Radar key scheme) toilets for disabled shop *Details not confirmed for 2003*

SELLAFIELD Map 06 NY00
The Sellafield Visitors Centre
CA20 1PG (off A595, signposted)
☎ 019467 27027   019467 27021
Times: Open all year, Apr-Oct, 10-5; Nov-Mar daily 10-4. (Closed 25 Dec). **Facilities:** P & (induction loop) toilets for disabled shop (ex guide dogs) *Details not confirmed for 2003*

SHAP Map 12 NY51
Shap Abbey
CA10 3NB (1.5m W on bank of River Lowther)

Dedicated to St Mary Magdalene, the abbey was founded by the Premonstratensian order in 1199, but most of the ruins are of 13th-century date. The most impressive feature is the 16th-century west tower of the church.
Times: Open any reasonable time. **Fee:** Free **Facilities:** P &

SIZERGH Map 07 SD48
Sizergh Castle & Garden
LA8 8AE (3.5m S of Kendal)
☎ 015395 60070   015395 61621
e-mail: ntrust@sizerghcastle.fsnet.co.uk
Times: Open 28 May-Oct, Sun-Thu 1.30-5.30; Garden open 23 Apr-Oct, 12.30. Last admission 5pm. **Facilities:** P & (wheelchair and powered buggy for use, braille guide etc) toilets for disabled shop *Details not confirmed for 2003*

SKELTON Map 12 NY43
Hutton-in-the-Forest
CA11 9TH (6m NW of Penrith on B5305 to Wigton, 2.5m from M6 junct 41)
☎ 017684 84449   017684 84571
e-mail: hutton-in-the-forest@talk21.com

A beautiful house, set in woods which were once part of the medieval forest of Inglewood. The house consists of a 14th-century pele tower with later additions, and contains a fine collection of furniture, portraits, tapestries and china, a 17th-century gallery and cupid staircase. The walled garden has a large collection of herbaceous plants, and there are 19th-century topiary terraces, a 17th-century dovecote and a woodland walk with impressive specimen trees.
Times: Open, House; 18 Apr-28 Sep Thu, Fri, Sun & BH 12.30-4. Gardens Daily ex Sat 11-5 **Fee:** £4.50 (ch £2.50). Family ticket £12. Grounds £2.50 (ch free). **Facilities:** P & (electric wheelchair available) shop (ex in grounds on leads)

TEMPLE SOWERBY Map 12 NY62
Acorn Bank Garden
CA10 1SP (6m E of Penrith on A66)
☎ 017683 61893   017683 61467
e-mail: racon@smtp.ntrust.org.uk
Times: Open 31 Mar-4 Nov, daily 10-5 (last admission 5pm).
Facilities: P & (braille guide) toilets for disabled shop (ex on lead on woodland walk) *Details not confirmed for 2003*

Cumbria 53

🏛 TROUTBECK Map 07 NY40
TOWNEND
LA23 1LB (3m SE of Ambleside at S end of village)
☎ 015394 32628
e-mail: rtown@smtp.ntrust.org.uk
Times: Open 2 Apr-Oct, Tue-Fri, Sun & BH Mon 1-5 or dusk if earlier. Last admission 4.30pm. **Facilities:** 🅿 (braille guide) ✈ 🐾 *Details not confirmed for 2003*

🏛 WINDERMERE Map 07 SD49
LAKE DISTRICT VISITOR CENTRE AT BROCKHOLE
LA23 1LJ (on A591, between Windermere and Ambleside follow brown tourist signs)
☎ 015394 46601   📄 015394 45555
e-mail: infodesk@lake-district.gov.uk

Set in 32 acres of landscaped gardens and grounds, on the shore of Lake Windermere, this house became England's first National Park Visitor Centre in 1969. It offers exhibitions, audio-visual programmes, lake cruises, an adventure playground and an extensive events programme.

Lake District Visitor Centre at Brockhole

Times: Open Etr-Oct, 10-5 daily. Grounds & gardens open all year.
Fee: Free admission but parking charge £4 full day, £3 half day.
Facilities: 🅿 (charged) 💷 ✗ licensed ♿ (mannal & electric wheelchairs, lifts, induction loops) toilets for disabled shop 💳

WINDERMERE STEAMBOAT CENTRE
Rayrigg Rd LA23 1BN (0.5m N of Bowness-on-Windermere on A592)
☎ 015394 45565   📄 015394 48769
Times: Open 16 Mar-27 Oct daily, 10-5. Steamboat trips subject to availability & weather. **Facilities:** 🅿 💷 ♿ toilets for disabled shop 💳 *Details not confirmed for 2003*

Derbyshire

The natural features of this central English county range from the modest heights of the Peak District National Park, where Kinder Scout stands at 2,088 ft (636 m), to the depths of its remarkable underground caverns, floodlit to reveal exquisite Blue John stone.

These underground explorations may extend as far as a mile by boat at Speedwell Cavern, or half a mile by foot at Peak Cavern. Walkers and cyclists will enjoy the High Peak Trail which extends from the Derwent Valley to the limestone plateau near Buxton.

The county is well endowed with stately homes. Most notably Chatsworth, the home of the Duke and Duchess of Devonshire, with its outstanding collections of paintings, statuary and art. Other gems include Haddon Hall, a well preserved medieval house, the Elizabethan Hardwick Hall, and Kedleston Hall, created by the Scottish designer Robert Adam.

The spa town of Matlock is the county's administrative centre. Other major towns are Derby, home of Royal Crown Derby china, and the old coal mining town of Chesterfield, with its crooked spire. Bargain hunters will enjoy a browse around the huge open air market in Chesterfield on a Monday, Friday and Saturday, or the Flea Market on a Thursday.

Around the villages of Derbyshire, look out for the ancient tradition of well dressing, the decorating of springs and wells – the precious sources of life-sustaining water – with pictures formed from flowers.

The county also has links with angling. Izaak Walton, the 17th-century "Father of Angling" and his friend Charles Cotton together wrote *The Compleat Angler*, based on their fishing experiences in Derbyshire.

Top: Monsal Dale

EVENTS & FESTIVALS

March
4th Shrove Tuesday Pancake Races, Winster

April
22nd Flagg Races, Flagg Moor
tbc Steam Into Spring, Peak Rail, Rowsley South Station

May
2nd-3rd & 10th Buxton Music, Speech & Drama Festival
3rd-5th Derbyshire Steam Fair, Hartington Moor Showground
10th-11th Chatsworth Horse Trials
22nd Derbyshire County Show, Showground, Alvaston

June
tbc Derbyshire Summer Garden Festival, Bakewell

July
20th Ashbourne Highland Gathering
tbc Buxton Opera Festival
tbc Vintage Steam Weekend, Rowsley South Station

August
6th-7th Bakewell Show
30th Aug-25th Oct Matlock Bath Illuminations
25th Chesterfield Evening Fireworks
30th-31st Chatsworth Country Fair
tbc Ashbourne Show, Osmaston
tbc The Roaring Forties, Peak Rail, Rowsley South Station

September
13th-14th Buxton Country Music Festival, Pavilion Gardens, Buxton
13th-20th Chesterfield Well Dressings
19th-21st Derbyshire Autumn Gold Garden & Woodland Festival
tbc Wirksworth Festival

October
16th Ilkeston Charter Fair, (fun fair)

November
2nd Dovedale Dash, Thorpe

Derbyshire

BOLSOVER Map 08 SK47
BOLSOVER CASTLE
Castle St S44 6PR (on A632)
☎ 01246 822844

An enchanting and romantic spectacle, situated high on a wooded hilltop dominating the surrounding landscape, this 17th-century mansion was built on the site of a Norman castle. The keep displays elaborate fireplaces, panelling and wall paintings and there is also an impressive indoor Riding School, also of the 17th century.
Times: Open all year, 29 Mar-Sep, daily 10-6 (Oct daily 10-5); Nov-28 Mar, Wed-Sun 10-4. (Closed 24-26 Dec & 1 Jan). **Fee:** * £6 (ch 5-15 £3, under 5's free, concessions £4.50). Personal stereo tour included in admission. **Facilities:** P & (keep not accessible) shop ✕ ✿

BUXTON Map 07 SK07
POOLE'S CAVERN (BUXTON COUNTRY PARK)
Green Ln SK17 9DH (1m from Buxton town centre, off A6 and A515)
☎ 01298 26978 🖹 01298 73563
e-mail: info@poolescavern.co.uk **2 for 1**

Limestone rock, water and millions of years created this natural cavern containing thousands of crystal formations. A 45-minute guided tour leads the visitor through chambers used as a shelter by Bronze-Age cave dwellers, Roman metal workers and as a hideout by the infamous robber Poole. Attractions include the underground source of the River Wye, the 'Poached Egg Chamber', Mary, Queen of Scots' Pillar, the Grand Cascade and underground sculpture formations.
Times: Open Mar-Oct, daily 10-5. (Open in winter for groups only).
Fee: * £5.10 (ch £2.90, pen & students £4). Family ticket £14.50. Group rates available. **Facilities:** P & toilets for disabled shop ✕ (ex guide dogs or in park) 🍴

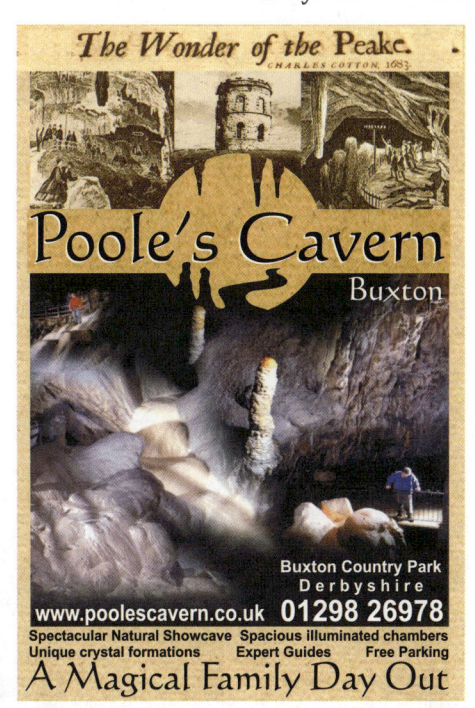

The Wonder of the Peake. CHARLES COTTON, 1683

Poole's Cavern
Buxton

www.poolescavern.co.uk **01298 26978**
Buxton Country Park
Derbyshire

Spectacular Natural Showcave Spacious illuminated chambers
Unique crystal formations Expert Guides Free Parking

A Magical Family Day Out

CALKE Map 08 SK32
CALKE ABBEY
DE73 1LE (9m S of Derby, on A514)
☎ 01332 863822 🖹 01332 865272
e-mail: eckxxx@smtp.ntrust.org.uk
Times: Open 23 Mar-3 Nov Sat-Wed & BH Mon; House & church 1-5.30 Gardens from 11am. Last admission 5pm. Park open all year until 9pm (dusk if earlier). House, church & garden closed Sat 17 Aug.
Facilities: P ✕ licensed & (braille guide, hearing system, buggy/wheelchair available) toilets for disabled shop ✕ (ex guide dogs) ⚹ *Details not confirmed for 2003*

CASTLETON Map 07 SK18
BLUE-JOHN CAVERN & MINE
Buxton Rd S33 8WP (follow brown "Blue-John Cavern" signs from Castleton)
☎ 01433 620638 & 620642 🖹 01433 621586
e-mail: lesley@bluejohn.gemsoft.co.uk

A remarkable example of a water-worn cave, over a third of a mile long, with chambers 200ft high. It contains 8 of the 14 veins of Blue John stone, and has been the major source of this unique form of fluorspar for nearly 300 years.
Times: Open all year daily 9.30-5 (or dusk). Guided tours of approx 1hr every 10 mins tour. **Fee:** * £6 (ch £3, pen & student £4.50) Family ticket £16. Party rates on request. **Facilities:** P 🍴 (not suitable for disabled visitors) shop 🍴

Derbyshire

PEAK CAVERN
S33 8WS (on A6187, in centre of Castleton)
☎ 01433 620285   📠 01433 623229
e-mail: info@peakcavern.co.uk   **2 for 1**

One of the most spectacular natural limestone caves in the Peak District, with an electrically-lit underground walk of about half a mile. Ropes have been made for over 500 years in the `Grand Entrance Hall', and traces of a row of cottages can be seen. Rope-making demonstrations are included on every tour.
Times: Open Etr-Oct, daily 10-5. Nov-Etr wknds only 10-5 **Fee:** * £5.25 (ch £3.25, other concessions £4.25). Family ticket £15.
Facilities: 🅿 (charged) shop

PEVERIL CASTLE
Market Place SW33 8WQ (on S side of Castleton)
☎ 01433 620613

William Peveril, one of William the Conqueror's trusted knights, guarded the King's manors in the Peak from this natural vantage point which commands spectacular views of the Hope Valley. The area is designated a Site of Special Scientific Interest.
Times: Open all year, 29 Mar-Sep, daily 10-6 (Oct daily 10-5); Nov-28 Mar, Wed-Sun 10-4. (Closed 24-26 Dec & 1 Jan). **Fee:** * £2.40 (ch 5-15 £1.20, under 5's free, concessions £1.80) **Facilities:** shop 🍴 ♿

SPEEDWELL CAVERN
Winnats Pass S33 8WA (off A625, (A625 becomes A6187 at Hathersage) 0.5m W of Castleton)
☎ 01433 620512   📠 01433 621888
e-mail: info@speedwellcavern.co.uk   **2 for 1**

Descend 105 steps to a boat that takes you on a one-mile underground exploration of the floodlit cavern.
Times: Open all year, Etr-Oct daily 9.30-5.30, Nov-Etr 10-5. (Closed 25 Dec). Phone to check Winter opening times due to weather. **Fee:** * £5.75 (ch £3.75). **Facilities:** 🅿 (charged) shop

TREAK CLIFF CAVERN
S33 8WP (0.75m W of Castleton on A6187)
☎ 01433 620571   📠 01433 620519
e-mail: treakcliff@bluejohnstone.com

An underground world of stalactites, stalagmites, flowstone, rock and cave formations, minerals and fossils. There are rich deposits of the rare and beautiful Blue John Stone, and the show caves include the Witch's Cave, Aladdin's Cave and Fairyland Grotto.

Times: Open all year, Mar-Oct, daily 10-last tour 4.20, Aug only, last tour 4.45; Nov-Feb daily 10-last tour at 3.20. Closed 24-26 & 31 Dec-1 Jan. All tours are guided & last about 40 mins. **Fee:** * Adults £5.50 (ch 5-15 £3). Family ticket (2 adult & 2 ch) £15. **Facilities:** 🅿 ♿ (establishment can only cater for walking disabled) shop

🏛 CHATSWORTH   Map 08 SK27
CHATSWORTH
DE45 1PP (8m N of Matlock on B6012)
☎ 01246 582204   📠 01246 583536
e-mail: visit@chatsworth-house.co.uk
Times: Open 15 Mar-29 Oct, House & garden 11-4.30, Farmyard 10.30-4.30 **Facilities:** 🅿 (charged) 🍴 ✕ licensed ♿ (3 electric wheelchairs available for garden) toilets for disabled shop garden centre 🐕 (ex park & gardens on lead) *Details not confirmed for 2003*

🏛 CRESWELL   Map 08 SK57
CRESWELL CRAGS VISITOR CENTRE
Crags Rd, Welbeck S80 3LH (1m E of Creswell village, off B6042)
☎ 01909 720378

This world famous archaeology site is a picturesque, limestone gorge with caves and a lake. Archaeological

continued

Derbyshire 57

finds from the caves include bones of mammoth and hyena as well as stone tools left by ice age hunters over 40,000 years ago. The museum offers displays, audio-visual, interactive computers and cave-site tours. (Booking is advised for tours).
Times: Open all year, Feb-Oct, daily, 10.30-4.30; Nov-Jan, Sun only 10.30-4.30. **Fee:** Free. Cave & site tour £2.75 (ch £2). £1 parking donation requested. **Facilities:** P & toilets for disabled shop

CRICH   Map 08 SK35
CRICH TRAMWAY VILLAGE
DE4 5DP (off B5034)
☎ 0870 758 7267 🖷 01773 852326
e-mail: info@tramway.co.uk   [2 for 1]

A mile-long scenic journey through a Period Street to open countryside with panoramic views. You can enjoy unlimited vintage tram rides, and the exhibition hall houses the largest collection of vintage electric trams in Britain. Ring for details of special events.
Times: Open Apr-Oct, daily 10-5.30 (6.30pm wknds Jun-Aug & BH wknds). Winter, open Sat-Sun & Mon, 10.30-4. **Fee:** * £7 (ch 3-15 £3.50, pen £6). Family ticket (2 adults & 3 ch) £19. **Facilities:** P 🍴 ✘ licensed & (Braille guidebooks, converted tram, talktype facilities) toilets for disabled shop 🐕

CROMFORD   Map 08 SK25
ARKWRIGHT'S CROMFORD MILL
Mill Ln DE4 3RQ (off A6, 3m S of Matlock)
☎ 01629 824297 🖷 01629 823356
e-mail: info@cromfordmill.co.uk

Sir Richard Arkwright established the world's first successful water-powered cotton spinning mill at Cromford in 1771. The Arkwright Society are involved in a major restoration to create a lasting monument to an extraordinary genius. Guided tours are available, and there is a programme of lectures and visits - ring for details. The Mill site is part of the Derwent Valley Mill World Heritage site.
Times: Open all year, daily 9-5 (Closed 25 Dec). **Fee:** Guided tour & exhibitions £2 (ch & pen £1.50). Mill site Free. **Facilities:** P ✘ & toilets for disabled shop 🐕

DENBY   Map 08 SK34
DENBY POTTERY VISITOR CENTRE
Derby Rd DE5 8NX (8m N of Derby off A38, on B6179, 2m S of Ripley)
☎ 01773 740799 🖷 01773 740749
e-mail: visitor.centre@denby.co.uk

Tours of the factory take place daily and include lots of hands-on activities including painting a plate and making a frog. Cookery demonstrations take place alongside the extensive Cookery Emporium, and a huge range of discounted seconds are available in the Denby Factory Shop.

Times: Open all year. Full factory tours, Mon-Thu 10.30 & 1. Craftroom tour only, daily 10-3.15. Visitor Centre Mon-Sat 9.30-5, Sun 10-5. Closed 25-26 Dec. **Fee:** Free. **Facilities:** P 🍴 ✘ licensed & (lift) toilets for disabled shop garden centre 🐕 (ex guide dogs) 🛍

DERBY   Map 08 SK33
DERBY MUSEUM & ART GALLERY
The Strand DE1 1BS (in city centre)
☎ 01332 716659 🖷 01332 716670
e-mail: david.fraser@derby.gov.uk

The museum has a wide range of displays, notably of Derby porcelain, and paintings by the local artist Joseph Wright (1734-97). Also antiquities, natural history and militaria, as well as many temporary exhibitions.
Times: Open all year, Mon 11-5, Tue-Sat 10-5, Sun & BHs 2-5. Closed Xmas & New Year, telephone for details. **Fee:** Free. **Facilities:** P (50yds) & (lift to all floors, portable mini-loop, large print labels) toilets for disabled shop 🐕 (ex guide dogs)

INDUSTRIAL MUSEUM
The Silk Mill, Silk Mill Ln, off Full St DE1 3AR (From Derby inner ring road, head for Cathedral & Assembly Rooms car park. Then 5 mins walk)
☎ 01332 255308 🖷 01332 716670
e-mail: david.fraser@derby.gov.uk

The museum is set in an early 18th-century silk mill and adjacent flour mill. Displays cover local mining, quarrying and industries, and include a major collection of Rolls Royce aero-engines from 1915 to the present. There is also a section covering the history of railway engineering in Derby.
Times: Open all year, Mon 11-5, Tue-Sat 10-5, Sun & BHs 2-5. (Closed Xmas & New Year, telephone for details). **Fee:** Free. **Facilities:** P & (lift to all floors) toilets for disabled shop 🐕 (ex guide dogs)

---

* An asterisk by an entry indicates that the prices shown are for 2002 only. Please contact the attraction for up-to-date price information.

Derbyshire

PICKFORD'S HOUSE MUSEUM OF GEORGIAN LIFE & COSTUME
41 Friar Gate DE1 1DA (from A38 into Derby, follow signs to city centre)
☎ 01332 255363   📄 01332 255527
e-mail: ellen.malin@derby.gov.uk

The house was built in 1770 by the architect Joseph Pickford as a combined workplace and family home. It now shows domestic life at different periods, with Georgian reception rooms and service areas and a 1930's bathroom. Other galleries are devoted to temporary exhibitions. There is also a display on the growth of Georgian Derby, and on Pickford's contribution to Midlands architecture.
Times: Open all year, Mon 11-5, Tue-Sat 10-5, Sun & BHs 2-5. (Closed Xmas & New Year, telephone for details). **Fee:** Free. **Facilities:** 🅿 ♿ (tape guides, video with sign language subtitles) shop 🐕 (ex guide dogs)

ROYAL CROWN DERBY VISITOR CENTRE
194 Osmaston Rd DE23 8JZ (10 mins walk from bus & rail stations & Derby city centre)
☎ 01332 712800 & 712841 (tours)
📄 01332 712863
e-mail: sjbirks@royal-doulton.com
Times: Open all year, daily. Factory tours twice daily, booking strongly advised. **Facilities:** 🅿 🍴 ✗ licensed ♿ (visitor entry accessible but not factory tour) toilets for disabled shop 🐕 (ex guide dogs) *Details not confirmed for 2003*

🏛 EYAM   Map 08 SK27
EYAM HALL
S32 5QW (in village centre)
☎ 01433 631976   📄 01433 631603   **2 for 1**
e-mail: nicwri@eyamhall.co.uk

An intimate 17th-century manor house in the heart of the famous "plague village". Home to the Wright family since 1671, the Hall offers a glimpse of domestic history through the eyes of one family, in portraits, furniture, tapestries, costumes and memorabilia. Converted farm buildings house the Eyam Hall Craft Centre. Please telephone for details of musical and theatrical events throughout the season.
Times: Open House: Jun-Aug. Garden: Wed-Thu, Sun & BH Mon 11-4. Craft Centre open all year Tue-Sun 11-5. **Fee:** House £4.50 (ch £3.50, pen £4). Family ticket £14.50. Garden £2 (ch £1). Family ticket £5. Craft centre free admission. **Facilities:** 🅿 ✗ licensed ♿ (disabled entrance via special gate, ramps) toilets for disabled shop 🐕 (ex guide & dogs in grounds)

🏛 HADDON HALL   Map 08 SK26
HADDON HALL
DE45 1LA (1.5m S of Bakewell off A6)
☎ 01629 812855   📄 01629 814379
e-mail: info@haddonhall.co.uk

Originally held by the illegitimate son of William the Conqueror, Haddon has been owned by the Manners family since the 16th century. Little has been added since the reign of Henry VIII, and, despite its time-worn steps, few medieval houses have so successfully withstood the ravages of time.

Times: Open Apr-Sep, daily 10.30-5; Oct, Thu-Sun 10.30-4.30. **Fee:** * £6.75 (ch £3.50 & pen £5.75). Family ticket £18. Party 15+. **Facilities:** 🅿 (charged) ✗ licensed ♿ (access is impossible for those in wheelchairs) toilets for disabled shop 🐕 (ex guide dogs)

🏛 HARDWICK HALL   Map 08 SK46
HARDWICK OLD HALL
Doe Lea S44 5QJ (2m S M1 junct 29)
☎ 01246 850431   📄 01246 854200
e-mail: ehwxxx@smtp.ntrust.org.uk
Times: Open 27 Mar-27 Oct, Wed- Thu, Sat-Sun, BH Mon & Good Fri, 12.30-5 (Oct 12.30-4). Last admission 30mins before closing. Garden open 27 Mar-27 Oct daily ex Tue, 11-5.30. **Facilities:** 🅿 ✗ licensed ♿ (hearing scheme, wheelchair if prebooked, braille guides) toilets for disabled shop 🐕 (ex in park on leads) 🐾 *Details not confirmed for 2003*

🏛 ILKESTON   Map 08 SK44
AMERICAN ADVENTURE THEME PARK
DE7 5SX (off M1 junct 26, signposted, take A610 to A608 then A6007)
☎ 0845 330 2929   **2 for 1**
📄 01773 716140
e-mail: sales@americanadventure.co.uk

This is one of Britain's few fully themed parks, based on the legend of a whole continent. The experiences here are widely varied, from the Missile Rollercoaster in Spaceport USA, to the wet and wild excitement of the Rocky Mountain Rapid's ride and the Nightmare Niagara log flume. Fort Adventure is an action packed challenge and the driving school is great for kids to find out if they've got what it takes to be an advanced driver. There's also a Mississippi paddle steamer, a horse-show in Silver City, glamorous Lazy Lil's Saloon Show Skycoaster, a 200ft free fall.
Times: Open 23 Mar-3 Nov, daily from 10. **Fee:** * £13.99 (ch under 1mtr free, otherwise 12yrs & under £10.99, pen £3.50). Family ticket (2 adult & 2 ch) £42.50, each additional person £10.99. **Facilities:** 🅿 🍴 ✗ licensed ♿ (free wheelchair hire, must pre book, call 0845 330 2929) toilets for disabled shop 🐕 (ex guide dogs)

Derbyshire

🏛 KEDLESTON HALL Map 08 SK34
KEDLESTON HALL
DE22 5JH (5m NW of Derby)
☎ 01332 842191 📠 01332 841972
e-mail: ekdxxx@smtp.ntrust.org.uk
Times: Open all year: House; 23 Mar-3 Nov, Sat-Wed 12-4.30. Last admission 5pm. (Closed Good Fri). Garden; same as house but open 10-6. Park open all year Mar-Nov daily ex Xmas & New Year, 10-6, Nov-Mar 10-4. **Facilities:** 🅿 ✖ licensed ♿ (braille guide, w/chair, self-drive vehicle) toilets for disabled shop 🐕 (ex in park, must be on leads) ♨ *Details not confirmed for 2003*

🏛 MATLOCK BATH Map 08 SK25
THE HEIGHTS OF ABRAHAM CABLE CARS, CAVERNS & HILLTOP PARK
DE4 3PD (on A6, signposted from M1 junct 28 & A6. Base station next to Matlock Bath railway station)
☎ 01629 582365 📠 01629 581128
e-mail: info@h-of-a.co.uk

The visit begins with a spectacular cable car journey across the Derwent Valley to the summit of the hill top country park. The most famous aspects of the Heights of Abraham are the two spectacular show caverns, which provide exciting tours to the underground world within the hillside. There's the 'miner's tale' in the Great Rutland Cavern-Nestus Mine and the 'story of the rock' at the Masson Cavern Pavilion. There is also an Explorer's Challenge, woodland walks and the Victoria Prospect Tower.
Times: Open daily Etr-Oct 10-5 (later in high season) for Autumn & Winter opening telephone for details. **Fee:** * £7.30 (ch £5, pen £6). Under 5's free - one per adult. **Facilities:** 🅿 (300mtrs) 💺 ✖ licensed ♿ (please ring for details) toilets for disabled shop 🐕 (ex in grounds & cable car) 🎁

PEAK DISTRICT MINING MUSEUM
The Pavilion DE4 3NR (On A6 alongside River Derwent)
☎ 01629 583834
e-mail: mail@peakmines.co.uk   `2 for 1`

A large display explains the history of the Derbyshire lead industry from Roman times to the present day. The geology of the area, mining and smelting processes, the quarrying and the people who worked in the industry,
are illustrated by a series of static and moving exhibits. The museum also features an early 19th-century water pressure pumping engine.
Times: Open all year, daily 11-4 (later in summer season). Closed 25 Dec. **Fee:** * Museum & Mine: £4 (ch, students, disabled & pen £2.50). Family £9. Museum only or mine only £2.50 (ch, students, disabled £1.50). Family £6. Party rates. **Facilities:** 🅿 (charged) 💺 ♿ (Chair lift to Mezanine) shop

TEMPLE MINE
Temple Rd DE4 3NR (off A6)
☎ 01629 583834   `2 for 1`

In the process of being restored to how it was in the 1920s and 1930s, this old lead and fluorspar workings makes interesting viewing. A self-guided tour illustrates the geology, mineralisation and mining techniques.
Times: Open all year, Summer 10-5, Winter timed visits during afternoon. **Fee:** * Museum & Mine: £4 (ch, pen, disabled £2.50). Family ticket £9. Museum only or mine only: £2.50 (ch, pen, disabled £1.50), Family £6. Party rates. **Facilities:** 🅿 (100mtrs) shop 🐕 (ex guide dogs)

🏛 MELBOURNE Map 08 SK32
MELBOURNE HALL & GARDENS
DE73 1EN (9m S of Derby on A514)
☎ 01332 862502 📠 01332 862263

Sir John Coke (Charles I's Secretary of State) bought the lease of Melbourne Hall in 1628 and the house has been home to two Prime Ministers: Lord Melbourne and Lord Palmerston. The glorious formal gardens are among the finest in Britain.
Times: Open, house daily throughout Aug only (ex first three Mons) 2-5 (last admission 4.15). Prebooked parties by appointment in Aug. Gardens Apr-Sep, Wed, Sat, Sun & BH Mon 1.30-5.30. **Fee:** House Tue-Sat (guided tour) £3 (ch £1.50, pen £2.50), Sun & BH Mon (no guided tour) £2.50 (ch £1, pen £2). House & Garden (Aug only) £5 (ch £3, pen £4). Garden only £3 (pen £2). Family £8. **Facilities:** 🅿 (200yds) 💺 ♿ (ramp at garden entrance) shop 🐕 (ex guide dogs)

🏛 MIDDLETON BY WIRKSWORTH Map 08 SK25
MIDDLETON TOP ENGINE HOUSE
Middleton Top Visitor Centre DE4 4LS (Signed off A6 in Cromford then, 0.5m S from B5036 Cromford/Wirksworth road)
☎ 01629 823204 📠 01629 825336
e-mail: middletontop@derbyshire.gov.uk

A beam engine built in 1829 for the Cromford and High Peak Railway, and its octagonal engine house. The engine's job was to haul wagons up the Middleton Incline, and its last trip was in 1963 after 134 years' work. The visitor centre tells the story of this historic railway.
Times: Open: Information Centre, daily, wknds only winter. Engine House Etr-Oct 1st wknd in month (engine in motion). **Fee:** * Static Engine 60p (ch 30p). Working Engine £1.20 (ch 60p). **Facilities:** 🅿 (charged) ♿ toilets for disabled shop 🎁

OLD WHITTINGTON
Map 08 SK37
REVOLUTION HOUSE
High St S41 9LA (3m N of Chesterfield town centre, on B6052 off A61, signposted)
☎ 01246 345727   🖹 01246 345720
e-mail: museum@chesterfieldbc.gov.uk

Originally the Cock and Pynot alehouse, this 17th-century cottage was the scene of a meeting between local noblemen to plan their part in the Revolution of 1688. The house is now furnished in 17th-century style. A video relates the story of the Revolution and there is a small exhibition room.
Times: Open Good Fri-29 Sep, daily 10-4. Xmas opening 14-24 Dec & 27 Dec-1 Jan, daily 10-4. **Fee:** Free. **Facilities:** P (100yds) & (signing available by prior arrangement) shop ✻ (ex guide dogs)

RIPLEY
Map 08 SK35
MIDLAND RAILWAY CENTRE
Butterley Station DE5 3QZ (1m N of Ripley on B6179, signposted from A38)
☎ 01773 747674 & 749788   2 for 1
🖹 01773 570721
e-mail: info@midlandrailwaycentre.co.uk

A regular steam-train passenger service runs here, to the centre where the aim is to depict every aspect of the golden days of the Midland Railway and its successors. Exhibits range from the steam locomotives of 1866 to an electric locomotive. There is also a large section of rolling stock spanning the last 100 years.
Times: Open all year, wknds. May-Oct also open Wed and most school hols. **Fee:** £7.95 (ch 5-16 £4, pen £6.50) children under 5 free. Party 15+. **Facilities:** P 🍴 & (special accommodation on trains) toilets for disabled shop 🍴

ROWSLEY
Map 08 SK26
THE WIND IN THE WILLOWS
Peak Village DE4 2NP (at junct of A6 & B6012)
☎ 01629 733433   🖹 01629 734850

Based on the charming book written by Kenneth Grahame and illustrated by E H Shepard, this attraction brings to life the characters Mole, Ratty, Toad and Badger in an indoor recreation of the English countryside.
Times: Open Apr-Sep, daily 10-5.30; Oct-Mar, daily 10-4.30. (Closed 25 Dec & 29-31 Jan). **Fee:** £3.75 (ch £2, under 4's free). **Facilities:** P 🍴 & toilets for disabled shop ✻ (ex guide dogs) 🍴

SUDBURY
Map 07 SK13
SUDBURY HALL
DE6 5HT (6m E of Uttoxeter)
☎ 01283 585305   🖹 01283 585139
e-mail: esuxxx@smtp.ntrust.org.uk
Times: Open 16 Mar-3 Nov, Wed-Sun, BH Mon & Good Fri 1-5 or sunset if earlier. Last admissions 30 mins before closing. Gardens open 10-5. **Facilities:** P 🍴 & (w/chair available, braille guide & hearing system) toilets for disabled shop ✻ (ex in grounds) 🦮 *Details not confirmed for 2003*

WIRKSWORTH
Map 08 SK25
WIRKSWORTH HERITAGE CENTRE
Crown Yard DE4 4ET (on B5023 off A6 in centre of Wirksworth)
☎ 01629 825225   2 for 1
e-mail: heritage@crownyard.fsnet.co.uk

The Centre has been created in an old silk and velvet mill. The three floors of the mill have interpretative displays of the town's past history as a prosperous lead-mining centre. Each floor offers many features of interest including a computer game called 'Rescue the injured lead-miner', a mock-up of a natural cavern, and a Quarryman's House. During the Spring Bank Holiday you can also see the famous Well Dressings.
Times: Open mid Feb-Etr & Nov, Wed-Sat, 11-4, Sun 1.30-4; Etr-Jun & Oct, Tue-Sat, 11-4, Sun 1.30-5; Jul-Sep, Tue-Sat 10-5. Also open BH Mon. Last admission 40 mins before closing. **Fee:** * £2 (ch & pen £1) Family (2 adults & 3 ch) £5. Party 20+. **Facilities:** P (80yds) (pay & display) 🍴 ✕ licensed shop ✻ (ex guide dogs)

Devon

A county of great contrasts, Devon encompasses wild moorland terrain and rolling farming country dotted with delightful villages. Exmoor extends to the spectacular northern coastline with England's highest cliffs, where there are excellent walks on the hills and coastal footpath.

In the south, stretching from Dartmoor to the seaside resort of Torbay, is the area alluringly dubbed the 'English Riviera'. Other major resorts are Torquay, Paignton and Teignmouth on the south coast, and Ilfracombe on the north. Perhaps more interesting to explore however, are the estuaries of Kingsbridge and Dartmouth, Sidmouth with its elegant seafront, and Salcombe with its flotilla of yachts.

Both Dartmoor and Exmoor have National Park status which preserves them from encroachment. Exmoor is home to the hardy little Exmoor pony and is the only remaining habitat in England for the native red deer. Dartmoor is the largest expanse of untamed country in Southern England, with Dartmoor Forest at its heart.

Devon's main cities are Exeter and Plymouth. The former was badly damaged in World War II, but the cathedral survives. Plymouth has been closely associated with naval history since Sir Francis Drake played his legendary game of bowls before facing the Spanish Armada, but as a centre for shipbuilding and a military base, it was also doomed to devastation by Luftwaffe bombing. The city is popular with Americans tracing their ancestors back to the launching of the Mayflower, which set sail from Plymouth docks in September 1620.

One of Devon's most famous natives is Agatha Christie (1890-1976). The queen of the mystery novel was born in Torquay and the town has a special walk and many plaques to commemorate the prolific novelist.

Top: Becky Falls, nr Bovey Tracey

EVENTS & FESTIVALS

February
17th-3rd March Animated Exeter (films, workshops, exhibitions, events)

May
15th-17th Devon County Show, Clyst St Mary
tbc Brixham Heritage Festival (music, dance, street theatre & fireworks)

July
4th-20th Exeter Festival of music, entertainment, jazz, comedy & dance
tbc Okehampton Arts Music Festival

August
1st-8th Sidmouth International Festival (folk music, dance & song)
2nd-3rd Exeter Living History Weekend (re-enactment groups, combat displays, tournament ring)
8th-10th Dartmoor Folk Festival
14th Okehampton Agricultural Show
21st Chagford Agricultural Show
22nd-24th West Country Balloon Fiesta, Tavistock College, Tavistock (provisional)

September
9th Widecombe Fair, Widecombe-in-the-Moor

November
tbc Plymouth American Thanksgiving Festival

APPLEDORE Map 02 SS43
NORTH DEVON MARITIME MUSEUM
Odun House, Odun Rd EX39 1PT
☎ 01237 422064
Times: Open Etr-Oct, daily 2-5; also May-Sep, Mon-Fri 11-1.
Facilities: P (opposite) & (hands-on items for visually impaired) toilets for disabled shop ✈ (ex guide dogs) *Details not confirmed for 2003*

ARLINGTON Map 02 SS64
ARLINGTON COURT
EX31 4LP (7m NE of Barnstaple, on A39)
☎ 01271 850296 ▪ 01271 850711
Times: Open 23 Mar-3 Nov, daily (ex Tue) 10.30-5.30. Last admission 4.30. Grounds open Nov-Mar during daylight hours. **Facilities:** P ● & (wh.chrs available, ramps at house, batricar, braille guide) toilets for disabled shop ✈ (ex in grounds on lead) ❀ *Details not confirmed for 2003*

BARNSTAPLE Map 02 SS53
MARWOOD HILL GARDENS
EX31 4EB (signposted off A361)
☎ 01271 342528
Times: Open daily, dawn to dusk. **Facilities:** P ● & garden centre *Details not confirmed for 2003*

BEER Map 03 SY28
PECORAMA PLEASURE GARDENS
Underleys EX12 3NA (from A3052 take B3174, Beer road, signed)
☎ 01297 21542 ▪ 01297 20229

The gardens are high on a hillside, overlooking Beer. A miniature steam and diesel passenger line offers visitors a stunning view of Lyme Bay as it runs through the Pleasure Gardens. Attractions include an aviary, crazy golf, children's activity area and the Peco Millennium Garden. The main building houses an exhibition of railway modelling in various small gauges. There are souvenir and railway model shops, plus full catering facilities.
Times: Open Etr-Sep (plus Autumn Half Term), Mon-Fri 10-5.30, Sat 10-1. Also Sun at Etr. **Fee:** * £2.75 (ch 4-14 £3.10, pen £4.25, over 80 & under 4 free) **Facilities:** P ● ✗ licensed & (access with helper, wheelchair. Garden steep in places) toilets for disabled shop ✈ (ex guide dogs)

BICKLEIGH Map 03 SS90
BICKLEIGH CASTLE
EX16 8RP (off A396 follow signs from Bickleigh Bridge)
☎ 01884 855363
Times: Open Etr wk (Sun-Fri), then Wed, Sun & BH to late May BH, then daily (ex Sat) to 1st Sun in Oct. **Facilities:** P ● & (specially arranged tours with experienced guide) shop garden centre ✈ (ex guide dogs) *Details not confirmed for 2003*

BICTON Map 03 SY08
BICTON PARK BOTANICAL GARDENS
East Budleigh EX9 7BJ (2m N of Budleigh Salterton on B3178, leave M5 at junct 30 & follow brown tourist signs)
☎ 01395 568465 ▪ 01395 568374
e-mail: info@bictongardens.co.uk

Times: Open Winter 10-5, Summer 10-6. (Closed 25 Dec) **Facilities:** P ● ✗ licensed & (adapted carriage on woodland railway, wheelchairs) toilets for disabled shop garden centre *Details not confirmed for 2003*

BLACKMOOR GATE Map 03 SS64
EXMOOR ZOOLOGICAL PARK
South Stowford, Bratton Fleming EX31 4SG (off A399. Follow brown tourist signs)
☎ 01598 763352 ▪ 01598 763352
e-mail: exmoorzoo@fsbdial.co.uk

Exmoor Zoo is both personal and friendly. Open since 1982 it is an ideal family venue, catering particularly for the younger generation. The zoo specialises in smaller animals, many endangered, such as the golden headed lion tamarins. Over 14 species of this type of primate are exhibited. Contact pens are provided throughout and children are encouraged to participate. Twice daily guided tours at feeding times along with handling sessions.
Times: Open daily, Apr-Oct 10-6; Nov-Mar 10-4. (Closed 21 Dec-1 Jan). **Fee:** * £5.25 (ch 3-16 £3.95, under 3 free, pen £4.75), Family £16. **Facilities:** P ● & toilets for disabled shop ✈ (ex guide dogs)

Devon 63

BUCKFASTLEIGH Map 03 SX76
BUCKFAST ABBEY
TQ11 0EE (off A38 on A384 Dartbridge turn off, follow tourist signs for 0.5m)
☎ 01364 645530 ▪ 01364 645533
Times: Open all year daily 5.30am-9.30pm. (visitor facilities 9-5 (summer) 10-4.30 (winter) **Facilities:** 🅿 🍴 ✗ licensed ♿ (level site, braille plan, wheelchair available) toilets for disabled shop ✱ (ex guide dogs) *Details not confirmed for 2003*

BUCKFAST BUTTERFLY FARM & DARTMOOR OTTER SANCTUARY
TQ11 0DZ (off A38, at Dart Bridge junct, follow tourist signs)
☎ 01364 642916 ▪ 01364 642916
e-mail: info@ottersandbutterflies.co.uk
Visitors can wander around a specially designed, undercover tropical garden, where free-flying butterflies and moths from around the world can be seen. The otter sanctuary has large enclosures with underwater viewing areas. Three types of otters can be seen including the native British otter along with Asian and North American otters.
Times: Open Good Fri-end Oct, daily 10-5.30 or dusk (if earlier). **Fee:** * £4.95 (ch £3.50, pen £4.50). Family ticket £15. **Facilities:** 🅿 🍴 ♿ (wheelchair ramps) shop ✱ (ex guide dogs) 🎫

BUCKLAND ABBEY Map 02 SX46
BUCKLAND ABBEY
PL20 6EY (off A386 0.25m S of Yelverton, signed)
☎ 01822 853607 ▪ 01822 855448
e-mail: dbamex@smtp.ntrust.org.uk
Times: Open Apr-Oct, daily (ex Thu) 10.30-5.30. Nov-end Mar, Sat & Sun 2-5. Closed Xmas to mid-Feb. Last admissions 45mins before closing. **Facilities:** 🅿 (charged) ✗ licensed ♿ (wheelchairs & motorised buggy available) toilets for disabled shop ✱ (ex guide dogs) 🎫 *Details not confirmed for 2003*

CHITTLEHAMPTON Map 03 SS62
COBBATON COMBAT COLLECTION
Cobbaton EX37 9RZ (signed from A361 & A377)
☎ 01769 540740 ▪ 01769 540141 **2 for 1**
e-mail: info@cobbatoncombat.co.uk
World War II British and Canadian military vehicles, war documents and military equipment can be seen in this private collection. There are over 50 vehicles including tanks, one a Gulf War Centurian, and a Warsaw Pact section. There is also a section on `Mum's War' and the home front.
Times: Open Apr-Oct, daily 10-5. Winter, most weekdays, phone for details. **Fee:** * £4.25 (ch £2.75, pen £3.75). **Facilities:** 🅿 🍴 ♿ (most areas accessible) toilets for disabled shop ✱ (ex guide dogs) 🎫

CHUDLEIGH Map 03 SX87
CANONTEIGN FALLS
EX6 7NT (off A38 at Chudleigh/Teign Valley juntion onto B3193 and follow tourist signs for 3m)
☎ 01647 252434 ▪ 01647 52617
e-mail: canonteignfalls@lineone.net
Times: Open all year, mid Mar-mid Nov, daily 10-5.30; Feb Half Term & Winter, Sun only 11-4. **Facilities:** 🅿 🍴 ✗ licensed (grounds partly accessible) shop *Details not confirmed for 2003* 🎫

CHURSTON FERRERS Map 03 SX95
GREENWAY GARDEN
TQ5 0ES (follow NT brown acorn signs)
☎ 01803 842382 ▪ 01803 661900
e-mail: dgwrtb@smtp.ntrust.org.uk
Times: Open Mar-Sep, Wed-Sat **Facilities:** 🅿 🍴 ♿ toilets for disabled shop ✱ (ex guide dogs & in Parkland) 🎫 *Details not confirmed for 2003*

CLOVELLY Map 02 SS32
THE MILKY WAY ADVENTURE PARK
EX39 5RY (on A39, 2m from Clovelly)
☎ 01237 431255 ▪ 01237 431735
e-mail: info@themilkyway.co.uk
One of the West Country's leading attractions for the biggest rides and the best shows. Attractions include Clone Zone - Europe's first interactive adventure ride featuring a suspended roller coaster; Time Warp indoor adventure play area; daily displays from the North Devon Bird of Prey Centre; archery centre; golf driving nets; railway; pets corner and more. The 'Droid Destroyers' attraction invites pilots to save the Earth from the Vega Asteroid.
Times: Open Etr-Oct, daily 10.30-6. Telephone for winter opening times. **Fee:** * £6.50 (ch £5.50). Family ticket £23 (2 adult & 2 ch) extra ch £4.50 each. **Facilities:** 🅿 🍴 ♿ (ramps) toilets for disabled shop ✱ (ex if dogs on leads) 🎫

CLYST ST MARY Map 03 SX99
CREALY ADVENTURE PARK
Sidmouth Rd EX5 1DR (leave M5 junct 30 onto A3052 Exeter to Sidmouth road)
☎ 01395 233200 ▪ 01395 233211
e-mail: fun@crealy.co.uk
Crealy Adventure Park offers indoor and outdoor adventures including the River Raiders' Challenge and the Children's Magical Kingdom. Go-karts, bumper boats and train rides, home of 'El Pastil Loco' and Sir Walter Raleigh's Swinging Queen Bess, plus lots of friendly animals.
Times: Open all year, Mar-Oct, daily 10-6; Nov-Mar 10-5. (Closed winter term time Mon-Tue, 24-26 Dec & 1 Jan). **Fee:** * £7.75 (ch £7.50, under 3 free, pen £4.89). Nov-Mar £4.50. Party 20+ £4.75. Annual ticket £27.50. **Facilities:** 🅿 🍴 ✗ licensed ♿ (Carers admitted free, restrictions on rollercoasters) toilets for disabled shop 🎫

---

2 for 1 This symbol indicates which attractions have chosen to participate in our new 2-for-1 voucher scheme.

COMBE MARTIN Map 02 SS54
Combe Martin Wildlife Park & Dinosaur Park
EX34 0NG (M5 junct 27 then A361 towards Barnstaple and turn right onto A399)
☎ 01271 882486   01271 883869
e-mail: combemartinpark@hotmail.com

The land that time forgot. A subtropical paradise with hundreds of birds and animals and animatronic dinosaurs, so real they're alive! Fantastic sealion shows, falconry displays & animal handling sessions. Snow leopards, meerkats, apes & monkeys and lots more.
Times: Open Etr-4 Nov, daily 10-4 (last admission). **Fee:** * £10 (ch 3-15 £6, ch under 3 free, pen £7). Family (2 adults & 2 ch) £29.
Facilities: P ⬤ shop ✖ (ex guide dogs)

COMPTON Map 03 SX86
Compton Castle
TQ3 1TA (off A381 Newton Abbot road. 4m W of Torquay)
☎ 01803 875740   01803 875740
e-mail: dpaset@smtp.ntrust.org.uk
Times: Open 2 Apr-Oct, Mon, Wed & Thu 10-12.15 & 2-5. **Facilities:** P ✖ (ex guide dogs) ❋ Details not confirmed for 2003

DARTMOUTH Map 03 SX85
Bayard's Cove Fort
TQ6 9AT (on riverfront)

Built by the townspeople to protect the harbour, the remains of the circular stronghold still stand at the southern end of the harbour.
Times: Open at all reasonable times. **Fee:** Free **Facilities:** P ✖ (in certain areas) ⛶

Dartmouth Castle
Castle Rd TQ6 0JN (1m SE off B3205, narrow approach road)
☎ 01803 833588

The castle dates from 1481 and was one of the first to be designed for artillery. It faces Kingswear Castle on the other side of the Dart estuary, and a chain could be drawn between the two in times of war.
Times: Open all year, 29 Mar-Sep, daily 10-6 (Oct, daily 10-5); Nov-Mar daily 10-1 & 2-4. (Closed 24-26 Dec & 1 Jan). **Fee:** * £3.20 (concessions £2.40, ch 5-15 £1.60, under 5's free). **Facilities:** P shop ✖ ⛶

Woodlands Leisure Park
Blackawton TQ9 7DQ (W, off A3122)
☎ 01803 712598   01803 712680
e-mail: fun@woodlandspark.com

All weather fun with an outstanding range of indoor and outdoor attractions. Experience the biggest indoor venture centre in the UK. Enjoy 60 acres of outdoor attractions for all the family including three watercoasters, a 500-metre toboggan run, Arctic Gliders, Mystic Maze and 15 massive play zones. There is an indoor falconry centre with flying displays, and a wide selection of animals and birds. The Master Blaster is the newest game for the whole family. Blast, propel & vortex thousands of balls around the alien planet.

Times: Open 26 Mar-5 Nov daily, also wknds & school holidays. **Fee:** * £6.75. Family ticket £24.95 (2 adult & 2 ch). **Facilities:** P ⬤ ♿ (ramps) toilets for disabled shop ✖ (ex guide dogs) ⛶

DREWSTEIGNTON Map 03 SX79
Castle Drogo
EX6 6PB (4m S of A30)
☎ 01647 433306   01647 433186
e-mail: dcdpjj@smtp.ntrust.org.uk
Times: Open Apr-Oct, daily (ex Fri but open Good Fri) 11-5.30. Garden open all year, daily 10.30-5.30 (or dusk if earlier). **Facilities:** P ⬤ ✖ licensed ♿ (wheelchairs available, lift to lower ground floor) toilets for disabled shop garden centre ✖ (ex guide/hearing dogs) ❋ Details not confirmed for 2003 ⛶

EXETER Map 03 SX99
Guildhall
High St EX4 3EB (city centre)
☎ 01392 665500
e-mail: guildhall@exeter.gov.uk
Times: Open when there are no mayoral functions. Times are posted outside weekly. Special opening by arrangement. **Facilities:** P (200yds) ♿ toilets for disabled ✖ (ex guide dogs) Details not confirmed for 2003

St Nicholas' Priory
Mint Ln, off Fore St EX4 3AT
☎ 01392 665858   01392 421252
e-mail: ramm-events@exeter.gov.uk
Times: Open Etr-Oct, Mon, Wed & Sat 3-4.30pm **Facilities:** P (200yds) shop ✖ (ex guide dogs) Details not confirmed for 2003

EXMOUTH Map 03 SY08
The World of Country Life
Sandy Bay EX8 5BU (M5 junct 30, take A376 to Exmouth. Follow signs to Sandy Bay)
☎ 01395 274533   01392 273457

All-weather family attraction including owl displays, and a safari train that rides through a 40-acre deer park. Kids will enjoy the friendly farm animals, pets' centre and animal nursery. There are also a Victorian

continued

Devon

street, working models and thousands of exhibits from a bygone age, including steam and vintage vehicles.
Times: Open Etr-Oct, daily 10-5. **Fee:** * £6 (ch 3-17 & pen £5). Family ticket (2 adult & 2 ch) £20, (2 adult & 3 ch) £23. Wheelchair user plus escort £5.50. **Facilities:** P ⬛ ✘ ♿ (all parts accessible ex 'safari train') toilets for disabled shop 🐕 (ex guide dogs) ⬛

🏛 GREAT TORRINGTON   Map 02 SS41
DARTINGTON CRYSTAL
EX38 7AN (Turn off A386 in centre of Great Torrington down School Lane (opposite church). Dartington Crystal is 200mtrs on left)
☎ 01805 626242 ✉ 01805 626363
e-mail: tours@dartington.co.uk   **2 for 1**

Dartington Crystal has won many international design awards in recognition of its excellence. The factory tour allows visitors to watch the glassware being crafted, from the safety of elevated viewing galleries. All age groups are encouraged to have fun in the glass activity area and to discover the fascinating story of glass and the history of Dartington in the Visitor Centre.
Times: Open all year. (Closed Xmas & Etr Sun). Visitor centre: Mon-Sat 9.30-4; Sun 10-4. Factory tour: Mon-Fri 9.30-3.15 (closed wknd & public holidays). Factory shops & restaurant: Mon-Sat 9.30-5; Sun 10.30-4.30. **Fee:** * £4 (ch 6-16 £2, pen £3). Family ticket £12. Party on application. **Facilities:** P ⬛ ✘ ♿ (special tours available, book in advance) toilets for disabled shop 🐕 (ex guide dogs) ⬛

RHS GARDEN ROSEMOOR
EX38 8PH (1m SE of town on A3124)
☎ 01805 624067 ✉ 01805 624717
e-mail: annet@rhs.org.uk
Times: Open: Gardens all year; Visitor Centre Apr-Sep 10-6, Oct-Mar 10-5. (Closed Xmas day) **Facilities:** P ⬛ ✘ licensed ♿ (Herb garden for disabled) toilets for disabled shop garden centre 🐕 (ex guide dogs) *Details not confirmed for 2003* ⬛

🏛 HONITON   Map 03 ST10
ALLHALLOWS MUSEUM
High St EX14 1PG (next to parish church of St Paul)
☎ 01404 44966 & 42996 ✉ 01404 46591
e-mail: dyateshoniton@msn.com

The museum, housed in a chapel dating back to around 1200, has a wonderful display of Honiton lace, and there are lace demonstrations from June to August. The town's history is also illustrated.
Times: Open Mon before Easter to end of Sep, Mon-Fri 10-5 & Sat 10-1.30. Oct, Mon-Fri 10-4, Sat 10-1.30. Winter opening by special arrangement. **Fee:** £2 (ch under 11 free, ch 50p, pen £1.50).
Facilities: P (400yds) ♿ (stair lift between floors) shop 🐕 (ex guide dogs)

🏛 ILFRACOMBE   Map 02 SS54
ILFRACOMBE MUSEUM
Runnymede Gardens, Wilder Rd EX34 8AF (next to the Landmark Theatre & TIC on seafront)
☎ 01271 863541
e-mail: ilfracombe@devonmuseums.net
Times: Open all year, Apr-Oct, daily 10-5; Nov-Mar Mon-Fri 10-12.30.
Facilities: P (10yds) ♿ (ramp to front door, wide aisles) shop 🐕 (ex guide dogs) *Details not confirmed for 2003*

WATERMOUTH CASTLE & FAMILY THEME PARK
EX34 9SL (3m NE off A399, midway between Ilfracombe & Combe Martin)
☎ 01271 863879 ✉ 01271 865864
e-mail: enquiries@watermouthcastle.com

Overlooking a beautiful bay, this 19th-century castle is one of North Devon's finest. It caters enthusiastically for the public, offering such unique experiences as a mechanical musical demonstration and the Watermouth Water Fountains. Other attractions include a tube slide, carousel and Gnomeland.
Times: Open Apr-Oct, closed Sat. (Also closed some Mon & Fri off season). Ring for further details. **Fee:** * £7 (ch 3-13 £6 & pen £5.50) **Facilities:** P ⬛ ♿ (special wheelchair route) toilets for disabled shop 🐕 (ex guide dogs) ⬛

🏛 KILLERTON HOUSE & GARDEN
                                Map 03 SS90
KILLERTON HOUSE & GARDEN
EX5 3LE (off B3181)
☎ 01392 881345
Times: Open: House, daily (ex Tue), Mar & Oct, Wed-Sun, Aug daily 11-5. Gardens open all year, daily from 10.30. House will close Sept 2002 until Etr 2003 for essential maintenance work. Gardens will remain open. **Facilities:** P ⬛ ✘ licensed ♿ (wheelchairs & motorised buggy available) toilets for disabled shop garden centre 🐕 (ex in park & guide dogs) ♿ *Details not confirmed for 2003*

🏛 KINGSBRIDGE   Map 03 SX74
COOKWORTHY MUSEUM OF RURAL LIFE
The Old Grammar School, 108 Fore St TQ7 1AW (A38 onto A384, then A381 to Kingsbridge, museum at the top of the town)
☎ 01548 853235
e-mail: wcookworthy@talk21.com
Times: Open all year, Apr-Sep Mon-Sat 10-5; Oct Mon-Fri 10-4. Nov-Mar groups by arrangement. Local history room Tue-Thu 10-12 & Wed also 2-4, other times by appointment. **Facilities:** P (100mtrs) ♿ (Braille labels on selected exhibits) toilets for disabled shop 🐕 (ex guide dogs) *Details not confirmed for 2003*

🏛 KINGSWEAR   Map 03 SX85
COLETON FISHACRE HOUSE & GARDEN
Brownstone Rd TQ6 0EQ (3m from Kingswear. Take Ferry Road and turn off at Toll House)
☎ 01803 752466 ✉ 01803 753017
e-mail: dcfdmx@smtp.ntrust.org.uk
Times: Garden open 3-17 Mar, Sat & Sun only 11-5; 23 Mar-3 Nov, Wed-Sun & BH Mon 10.30-5.30. House open 23 Mar-3 Nov, Wed-Sun & BH Mon 11-4.30. **Facilities:** P ⬛ ♿ (wheelchair available, braille guides) toilets for disabled shop garden centre 🐕 (ex guide dogs) ♿ *Details not confirmed for 2003* ⬛

Prices and opening times subject to change from March 2003. Please check with the property before visiting.

Devon

KNIGHTSHAYES COURT — Map 03 SS91
KNIGHTSHAYES COURT
EX16 7RQ (2m N of Tiverton off A396)
☎ 01884 254665 & 257381 📠 01884 243050
Times: House & garden open 23 Mar-Sep, daily ex Fri 11-5.30. Oct-early Nov, daily ex Thu & Fri. **Facilities:** 🅿 🍴 ✗ licensed ♿ (wheelchairs available, lift, braille & audio guide) toilets for disabled shop garden centre 🐕 (ex guide dogs & in park) 🎁 *Details not confirmed for 2003* 📖

LYDFORD — Map 02 SX58
LYDFORD CASTLE
EX20 4BH (off A386)

The great square stone keep dates from 1195. It is not built on a mound, as it seems to be, but had earth piled against the walls. The upper floor was a Stannary Court, which administered local tin mines, and the lower floor was used as a prison.
Times: Open all reasonable times. **Fee:** Free **Facilities:** 🅿 ♿

LYDFORD GORGE
EX20 4BH (off A386, between Okehampton & Tavistock)
☎ 01822 820320 & 820441 📠 01822 822000
e-mail: dlybhx@smpt.ntrust.org.uk
Times: Open Apr-Sep, daily 10-5.30; Oct, daily 10-4. (Nov-Mar, waterfall entrance only, daily 10.30-3). **Facilities:** 🅿 🍴 (easy access path above gorge, audio tapes) shop 🎁 *Details not confirmed for 2003*

MORWELLHAM — Map 02 SX47
MORWELLHAM QUAY
PL19 8JL (4m W of Tavistock, off A390. Midway between Gunnislake & Tavisock. Signposted)
☎ 01822 832766 & 833808 📠 01822 833808
Times: Open all year (ex Xmas wk) 10-5.30 (4.30 Nov-Etr). Last admission 3.30 (2.30 Nov-Etr). **Facilities:** 🅿 🍴 ✗ licensed ♿ (smooth paths, but difficult areas in Victorian village) toilets for disabled shop 🐕 (ex on lead) *Details not confirmed for 2003* 📖

NEWTON ABBOT — Map 03 SX87
BRADLEY MANOR
TQ12 6BN (SW of Newton Abbot on A381 Totnes rd. 1m from town centre)
☎ 01626 354513
Times: Open Apr-Sep, Wed & Thu, 2-5. **Facilities:** 🅿 🐕 ♿ 🎁 *Details not confirmed for 2003*

HEDGEHOG HOSPITAL AT PRICKLY BALL FARM
Denbury Rd, East Ogwell TQ12 6BZ (1.5m from Newton Abbot on A381 towards Totnes, follow brown tourist signs)
☎ 01626 362319 & 330685 📠 01626 330685
e-mail: hedgehog@hedgehog.org.uk

See, touch and learn about this wild animal. In mid-season see baby hogs bottle feeding. Find out how to encourage hedgehogs into your garden and how they are put back into the wild. Talks on hedgehogs throughout the day, short basic video information about hedgehogs available.
Times: Open Mar-Sep, 10.30-5. Last admission 1hr before closing. **Fee:** * £4.95 (ch 4-14 £3.95, pen £4.50, ch under 3 free). **Facilities:** 🅿 🍴 ♿ (large print menu, use of wheelchair, Braille menu) toilets for disabled shop garden centre 🐕 (ex guide dogs) 📖

TUCKERS MALTINGS
Teign Rd TQ12 4AA (follow brown tourist signs from Newton Abbot railway station)
☎ 01626 334734 📠 01626 330153
e-mail: info@tuckersmaltings.com

The only working malthouse in England open to the public, producing malt from barley for over 30 West Country breweries. Learn all about the process of malting - and taste the end product at the in-house brewery. Guided tours last an hour.
Times: Open Good Fri-end Oct, Mon-Sat (Closed Sun ex in Jul & Aug). Speciality bottled beer shop open throughout the year. **Fee:** * £4.95 (ch 5-15 £2.95, 16-17 £3.75, pen £4.45). Family ticket £13.85. **Facilities:** 🅿 ♿ toilets for disabled shop 📖

OKEHAMPTON — Map 02 SX59
MUSEUM OF DARTMOOR LIFE
3 West St EX20 1HQ (follow brown signs off all major roads into Okehampton. Museum on main road next to White Hart Hotel)
☎ 01837 52295   **2 for 1**
📠 01837 659330
e-mail: dartmoormuseum@eclipse.co.uk

Housed on three floors in an early 19th-century mill, the museum tells the story of how people have lived, worked and played on and around Dartmoor through the centuries. It shows how the moorland has shaped their lives just as their work has shaped the moorland. In the Cranmere Gallery, temporary exhibitions feature local history, art and crafts.
Times: Open Etr-Oct, Mon-Sat 10-5 (also Sun, Jun-Sep). Winter opening times, telephone for details. **Fee:** * £2 (ch 5-16 & students £1, pen £1.80). Family ticket £5.60. Party 10+. **Facilities:** 🅿 🍴 shop

OKEHAMPTON CASTLE
Castle Lodge EX20 1JB (1m SW of town centre)
☎ 01837 52844

The chapel, keep and hall date from the 11th to 14th centuries and stand on the northern fringe of Dartmoor National Park.
Times: Open all year, 29 Mar-Sep, daily 10-6 (9-6 in Jul & Aug) (Oct, daily 10-5); **Fee:** * £2.50 (ch 5-15 £1.30, ch under 5 free, concessions £1.90). **Facilities:** 🅿 ♿

OTTERTON — Map 03 SY08
OTTERTON MILL CENTRE
EX9 7HG (between North Poppleford & Budleigh Salterton on A3572)
☎ 01395 568521 📠 01395 568521
e-mail: ottertonmill@ukonline.co.uk
Times: Open all year, daily, summer 10.30-5.30; winter 11-4.
Facilities: 🅿 ✗ licensed ♿ (free entry to ground floor) shop garden centre *Details not confirmed for 2003* 📖

Devon 67

⚜ OTTERY ST MARY Map 03 SY19
CADHAY
EX11 1QT (1m NW of Ottery St Mary, near junct of A30 & B3167)
☎ 01404 812432 ▤ 01404 812432 **2 for 1**

A beautiful Tudor and Georgian house which stands around a courtyard and dates from 1550.
Times: Open Jul-Aug Tue, Wed & Thu. Also Sun & Mon of late spring & late summer BH's. 2-6 (last admission 5). **Fee:** * £4.50 (ch £2). Party 20+ by appointment. **Facilities:** 🅿 & ✈ (ex guide dogs)

⚜ PAIGNTON Map 03 SX86
PAIGNTON & DARTMOUTH STEAM RAILWAY
Queens Park Station, Torbay Rd TQ4 6AF (from Paignton follow brown tourist signs)
☎ 01803 555872 ▤ 01803 664313
e-mail: pdsr@talk21.com

Steam trains run for seven miles from Paignton to Kingswear on the former Great Western line, stopping at Goodrington Sands, Churston, and Kingswear, connecting with the ferry crossing to Dartmouth. Combined river excursions available. Ring for details of special events.
Times: Open Jun-Sep daily 9-5.30 & selected days Oct & Apr-May.
Fee: * Paignton to Kingswear £6.60 (ch £4.60, pen £6). Family £20. Paignton to Dartmouth (including ferry) £7.70 (ch £5.20, pen £7.10). Family £24. **Facilities:** 🅿 (5mins walk) 🍴 & (wheelchair ramp for boarding train) toilets for disabled shop 🐕

PAIGNTON ZOO ENVIRONMENTAL PARK
Totnes Rd TQ4 7EU (1m from Paignton town centre on A3022 Totnes road)
☎ 01803 697500 ▤ 01803 523457
e-mail: info@paigntonzoo.org.uk

Paignton is one of Britain's biggest zoos, set in a beautiful and secluded woodland valley, where new enclosures are spacious and naturalistic. A tour will take you through some of the world's threatened habitats - Forest, Savannah, Wetland and Desert, with hundreds of species, many of them endangered and part of conservation breeding programmes. There are regular keeper talks, a children's play area, and special events include an annual Easter Egg Safari.
Times: Open all year, daily 10-6 (5pm in winter). Last admission 5pm (4pm in winter). (Closed 25 Dec). **Fee:** * £8 (ch 3-15 £5.75, students & pen £6.50). Family ticket £24.70 (2 adult & 2 ch). Party 15+.
Facilities: 🅿 🍴 ✕ licensed & (some steep hills, wheelchair loan-booking essential) toilets for disabled shop 🐕 (ex guide dogs) 🎁

⚜ PLYMOUTH Map 02 SX45
CITY MUSEUM & ART GALLERY
Drake Circus PL4 8AJ (turn off A38 onto A374, follow signs to city centre, museum on NW of city centre, opposite university)
☎ 01752 304774 ▤ 01752 304775
e-mail: museum@plymouth.gov.uk
Times: Open all year, Tue-Fri 10-5.30, Sat 10-5, BH Mon 10-5. (Closed Good Fri & 25-26 Dec). **Facilities:** 🅿 200yds & (wheelchair available) toilets for disabled shop 🐕 ex guide dogs *Details not confirmed for 2003*

MERCHANT'S HOUSE MUSEUM
33 St Andrews St PL1 2AX (Turn off A38 onto A374, follow signs to city centre, house located behind St Andrew's Church)
☎ 01752 304774 ▤ 01752 304775
e-mail: museum@plymouth.gov.uk
Times: Open Apr-Sep, Tue-Fri 10-5.30, Sat 10-5, BH Mon 10-5 (summer), (closed 1-2) **Facilities:** 🅿 (400 yds) & shop 🐕 *Details not confirmed for 2003*

PLYMOUTH DOME
The Hoe PL1 2NZ
☎ 01752 603300 & 600608 (recorded message) ▤ 01752 256361

This high-tech visitor centre lets you explore the sounds and smells of an Elizabethan street, walk the gun-deck of a galleon, dodge the press gang, stroll with film stars on an ocean liner, and witness the devastation of the Blitz. Examine satellite weather pictures as they arrive from space, keep up to date with shipping movements and monitor the busy harbour on radar. An excellent introduction to Plymouth and a colourful interpretation of the past. Ring for details of special events.
Times: Open all year, daily, 10-5 **Fee:** * £4.50 (ch £3, ch under 5 free, pen & students £3.50). **Facilities:** 🅿 (200 yds) 🍴 & (audio descriptions, induction loop, wheelchairs available) toilets for disabled shop 🐕 ex guide dogs 🎁

ROYAL CITADEL
PL1 2PD (at the end of Plymouth Hoe)
☎ 01752 775841
Times: Open for guided tours only May-Sep, daily. For security reasons tours may be suspended at short notice. **Facilities:** 🐕 ♿
Details not confirmed for 2003

PLYMPTON Map 02 SX55
Saltram
PL7 1UH (2m W between A38 & A379)
☎ 01752 333500 & 01752 333503
🖷 01752 336474
Times: Open House: 24 Mar-3 Nov, Sat-Thu 12.30-4.30. Garden open all year, Mar-Nov 10.30-5.30, Nov-Feb 11-4. **Facilities:** P (charged) ⚫ ✕ licensed ♿ (wheelchairs available, lift, braille & audio guides) toilets for disabled shop 🐾 (ex in park on leads) 🌿 Details not confirmed for 2003

POWDERHAM Map 03 SX98
Powderham Castle
EX6 8JQ (signposted off A379 Exeter/Dawlish road)
☎ 01626 890243 🖷 01626 890729 **2 for 1**
e-mail: castle@powderham.co.uk

Built between 1390 and 1420, this ancestral home of the Earls of Devon was damaged in the Civil War. The house was restored and altered in later times and is set in beautiful rose gardens with views over the deer park to the Exe Estuary. Ring for details of special events.
Times: Open Etr-end Oct, 10-5.30 (last admission 5pm). Closed Sat.
Fee: * £6.45 (ch £2.95, pen £5.95). Family ticket £15.85. Party.
Facilities: P ⚫ ✕ licensed ♿ (ramps) toilets for disabled shop garden centre 🐾

SALCOMBE Map 03 SX73
Overbecks Museum & Garden
Sharpitor TQ8 8LW (2.5m SW of Salcombe)
☎ 01548 842893 🖷 01548 845020
e-mail: dovrcx@smtp.ntrust.org.uk
Times: Open Apr-Jul Sun-Fri 11-5.30; Aug daily 11-5.30; Sep Sun-Fri 11-5.30; Oct Sun-Thu 11-5. Gardens open all year, 10-8 (or sunset if earlier). **Facilities:** P (charged) ⚫ ♿ (ramp from garden, braille guide) shop 🐾 🚌 🌿 Details not confirmed for 2003

SOUTH MOLTON Map 03 SS72
Quince Honey Farm
EX36 3AZ (3.5m W of A361, on N edge of South Molton)
☎ 01769 572401 🖷 01769 574704
e-mail: info@quincehoney.co.uk

Follow the story of honey and beeswax from flower to table. The exhibition allows you to see the world of bees close up in complete safety; hives open at the press of a button revealing the honeybees' secret life. After viewing the bees at work, sample the fruits of their labour in the café or shop.
Times: Open daily, Apr-Sep 9-6; Oct 9-5; Shop only Nov-Etr 9-5. (Closed 25 Dec-4 Jan). **Fee:** * £3.20 (ch 5-16 £1.80, pen £2.60)
Facilities: P ⚫ ♿ toilets for disabled shop 🐾 (ex guide dogs) 🌿

STICKLEPATH Map 03 SX69
Finch Foundry
EX20 2NW (Turn off A30 at Okehampton junct, follow brown signs to Finch Foundry. Located in main street of village. Approx 7m from Okehampton)
☎ 01837 840046 🖷 01837 840046
Times: Open Apr-Nov, daily ex Tue, 11-5.30. **Facilities:** P ⚫ ♿ (access to shop/tea room, view main foundry via shop) shop Details not confirmed for 2003

TAVISTOCK
See Morwellham

TIVERTON Map 03 SS91
Tiverton Castle
EX16 6RP (M5 junct 27, then 7m on A361 towards Tiverton to rdbt where Castle is signposted)
☎ 01884 253200 & 255200 **2 for 1**
🖷 01884 254200
e-mail: tiverton.castle@ukf.net

The original castle, built in 1106 by order of Henry I, was rebuilt late 13th/early 14th centuries. It resisted General Fairfax during the Civil War but fell to him when a lucky shot hit the drawbridge chain. Now a private house, the gardens are lovely and there's a fine Civil War armoury.
Times: Open Etr-Jun & Sep, Sun,Thu & BH Mon's only 2.30-5.30; Jul & Aug, Sun-Thu 2.30-5.30. **Fee:** £4 (ch 7-16 £2, under 7 free). Disabled half price if accessing ground floor only. **Facilities:** P ♿ toilets for disabled shop 🐾 (ex guide dogs)

Tiverton Museum of Mid Devon Life
Beck's Square EX16 6PJ (in centre of town next to Beck's Square car park)
☎ 01884 256295 **2 for 1**
e-mail: su7711@eclipse.co.uk

This large and comprehensive museum now with 15 galleries, re-opened after extensive rebuilding and redisplayed throughout. It is housed in a 19th-century school and the exhibits include a Heathcote Lace Gallery featuring items from the local lace-making industry. There is also an agricultural section with a collection of farm wagons and implements. Other large exhibits include two waterwheels and a railway gauge.
Times: Open 3 Feb, Mon-Fri 10.30-4.30, Sat 10-1. **Fee:** * £3.50 (ch £1, pen £2.50) **Facilities:** P (100yds) ♿ (lift) toilets for disabled shop 🐾

TORQUAY Map 03 SX96
Babbacombe Model Village
Hampton Av, Babbacombe TQ1 3LA (follow brown tourist signs from outskirts of town)
☎ 01803 328669 & 315315 🖷 01803 315173
e-mail: ss@babbacombemodelvillage.co.uk

Set in four acres of beautifully maintained, miniature landscaped garden, the village contains over 400 models and 1200ft of model railway. City Lights, an evening illuminations feature, depicts Piccadilly Circus in miniature. Also a facility that offers breathtaking views over the model village. Open-top bus trips; computer presentation area; undercover display area; vintage model railway layout; and the new Aquaviva, an evening water, light and sound spectacular.
Times: Open all year, Good Fri-Jun, 9.30-10; Jul-Aug, 9-10; Sep, 9.30-10; Oct, 9.30-9; Nov-Good Fri, 10-dusk. Closed 25 Dec. **Fee:** * £5.80 (ch £3.80, pen £4.50). Family ticket £16.90. **Facilities:** P (charged) ⚫ ✕ ♿ (push button audio information) toilets for disabled shop garden centre 🐾

'BYGONES'
Fore St, St Marychurch TQ1 4PR (follow tourist signs into Torquay and St Marychurch)
☎ 01803 326108 📠 01803 326108   **2 for 1**

Step back in time in this life-size Victorian exhibition street of over 20 shops including a forge, pub and period display rooms, housed in a former cinema. Exhibits include a large model railway layout, illuminated fantasyland, railwayana and military exhibits including a walk-through World War I trench. At Christmas the street is turned into a winter wonderland.
Times: Open all year, Summer 10-10, (Fri-Sun 10-6); Spring & Autumn 10-6; Winter 10-4, wknds & school hols 10-5. Last entry 1hr before closing. **Fee:** * £4.20 (ch 4-14 £3, pen £3.95). Family ticket £13. Prices may change, contact in advance. **Facilities:** P (50yds) ☕ (ramp) shop ✻ (ex guide dogs)

KENTS CAVERN
Cavern House, 91 Ilsham Rd, Wellswood TQ1 2JF (1.25m NE off B3199, follow brown tourist signs. 1m from Torquay Harbour)
☎ 01803 215136 📠 01803 211034
e-mail: mail@kents-cavern.co.uk
Times: Open daily (ex 25 Dec). Oct-Mar 10-last tour 4pm; Apr-Jun & Sep 10-last tour 4.30pm; Jul-Aug 9.30-last tour 5pm. Evenings: Jul-Aug (Mon-Thu) 6-9.30. **Facilities:** P ☕ ♿ toilets for disabled shop ✻ (ex guide dogs) Details not confirmed for 2003 ⚑

TORRE ABBEY HISTORIC HOUSE & GALLERY
The Kings Dr TQ2 5JE (on seafront, next to Riviera Centre)
☎ 01803 293593 📠 01803 215948
e-mail: michael.rhodes@torbay.gov.uk
Times: Open daily Apr-1 Nov, 9.30-6. (Last admission 5pm).
Facilities: P (100 yds) ☕ ♿ shop ✻ (ex guide dogs) Details not confirmed for 2003

🏛 TOTNES   Map 03 SX86
BOWDEN HOUSE GHOSTLY TALES & THE BRITISH PHOTOGRAPHIC MUSEUM
TQ9 7PW (off A381 from Totnes)
☎ 01803 863664
Times: Open 27 May-27 Sep from noon. Bowden House & Museum Mon-Fri. **Facilities:** P ☕ ♿ (museum only suitable) toilets for disabled shop ✻ (ex guide/hearing dogs) Details not confirmed for 2003

GUILDHALL
Rampart Walk, off High St TQ9 5QH (behind St Mary's Church on the main street)
☎ 01803 862147 📠 01803 864275
e-mail: totnestowncouncil@btinternet.com

Originally the refectory, kitchens, brewery and bakery for the Benedictine Priory of Totnes (1088-1536), the building was established as the Guildhall in 1553 during the reign of Edward VI. A magistrates' court and a prison opened in 1624, and the council chamber is still used today.
Times: Open Apr-Oct, Mon-Fri 10.30-1 & 2-4; Other times by appointment. **Fee:** * £1 (ch 25p, concessions 50p). **Facilities:** P (50yds)

TOTNES CASTLE
TQ9 5NU (on hill overlooking town)
☎ 01803 864406

A classic example of the Norman motte-and-bailey castle, Totnes dates from the 11th, 13th and 14th centuries. The circular shell-keep, protected by a curtain wall, gives marvellous views.
Times: Open, 29 Mar-Sep, daily 10-6 (Oct, daily 10-5); **Fee:** * £1.80 (ch 5-15 90p, under 5 free, concessions £1.40) **Facilities:** P (70yds) ♿

TOTNES MUSEUM
70 Fore St TQ9 5RU (from bottom of Totnes, turn into Fore St by Royal Seven Stars Hotel. Museum on left of main street, just before East Gate Arch Clock Tower)
☎ 01803 863821 📠 01803 863821
e-mail: totnes.museum@virgin.net

An Elizabethan merchant's house, dating from 1575, said to have been built for Sir Walter Kelland, a wealthy merchant. The building houses archaeological and social history collection and room dedicated to Charles Babbage, inventor of the first computer. Study centre archives located at the rear of the museum.
Times: Open Etr-30 Oct, Mon-Fri & BHs 10.30-4.30, Sat group bookings only as arranged. **Fee:** * £1.50 (ch 5-16 25p, students & pen £1). **Facilities:** P (440yds) (restricted parking on main street) ♿ Personal guided tours available shop ✻ (ex small dogs & guide dogs)

🏛 UFFCULME   Map 03 ST01
COLDHARBOUR MILL WORKING WOOL MUSEUM
Coldharbour Mill EX15 3EE (2m from M5 junct 27, off B3181. Follow signs to Willand, then brown signs)
☎ 01884 840960 📠 01884 840858
e-mail: info@coldharbourmill.org.uk
Times: Open Apr-Oct, daily 10.30-5. Last tour 4pm. Nov-Mar, Mon-Fri (please telephone for times). **Facilities:** P ✻ licensed ♿ (helpful guides & lift) toilets for disabled shop ✻ (ex guide dogs) Details not confirmed for 2003 ⚑

🏛 YEALMPTON   Map 02 SX55
NATIONAL SHIRE HORSE CENTRE
PL8 2EL (On A379, Plymouth to Kingsbridge)
☎ 01752 880268 📠 01752 881014
Times: Open May-Sep. **Facilities:** P ☕ ✻ licensed ♿ toilets for disabled shop Details not confirmed for 2003 ⚑

🏛 YELVERTON   Map 02 SX56
YELVERTON PAPERWEIGHT CENTRE
4 Buckland Ter, Leg O'Mutton Corner PL20 6AD (at Yelverton off A386, Plymouth to Tavistock road)
☎ 01822 854250 📠 01822 854250
e-mail: paperweightcentre@btinternet.com

This unusual centre is the home of the Broughton Collection - a glittering permanent collection of glass paperweights of all sizes and designs. The centre also has an extensive range of modern glass paperweights for sale. Prices range from a few pounds to over £1000. Also oil and watercolour paintings by local artists.
Times: Open Apr-Oct, daily 10-5; 1-24 Dec, daily; Nov & Jan-Mar wknds only or by appointment. **Fee:** Free. **Facilities:** P (100yds) ♿ (ramp on request) shop ⚑

Dorset

One of England's most picturesque counties, Dorset has such a wealth of history, stunning scenery and coastal attractions on offer that one is spoilt for choice when writing about it, and it seems a shame that so many people simply drive through it on their way somewhere else.

Possibly the county's most famous landmark is the Cerne Abbas giant, a 180-foot high depiction of a naked man with a club, visible for miles around. However, those visiting this important remnant of Dorset's distant past shouldn't pass by Cerne Abbas itself, which contains a centuries-old church, and the remains of a 10th-century Abbey.

Rural Dorset has retained a great deal of the charm and tranquility of England before the Industrial Revolution. All of the market towns in this area (Gillingham, Blandford Forum, Stalbridge, Shaftesbury and Sturminster Newton) are well worth seeing. Shaftesbury is one of England's oldest towns and is the site of an abbey founded by Alfred The Great. The area around these towns, – known as 'Hardy Country', after Thomas Hardy, the 19th-century novelist, – has been designated an Area of Outstanding Natural Beauty, and includes Cranborne Chase, Blackmore Vale and the Dorset Downs.

The major coast resorts, – Weymouth, Poole and Bournemouth – offer a wide range of activities, combined with some beautiful scenery, and yet more of historic interest. The best example of the latter is probably Corfe Castle, which stands on the Isle of Purbeck. The keep was built by the Normans, and the whole thing was completed by 1300. Unfortunately for future generations, the castle was ruined during a Civil War siege. Local legend has it that a lone woman betrayed the castle to Cromwell, and that her headless ghost can be seen by the gate of the ruined structure.

Top: Corfe Castle

EVENTS & FESTIVALS

January
1st Annual Bath Race, Poole

May
tbc Trawler Race & Water Carnival, Weymouth
tbc Weymouth International Beach Kite Festival

June
13th-15th Wimborne Folk Festival
21st Dorchester Carnival (provisional)
tbc Annual Military & Veterans Festival, Weymouth Seafront
tbc Teddy Bears' Picnic, Borough Gardens, Dorchester (games, bouncy castle)

July
19th Tolpuddle Martyrs Memorial Rally & Festival
26th July-3rd Lyme Regis Lifeboat Week, The Cobb, Lyme Regis

August
26th July-3rd Lyme Regis Lifeboat Week, The Cobb, Lyme Regis
27th-31st Great Dorset Steam Fair, South Down Farm, Tarrant Hinton
tbc Weymouth Carnival, Weymouth Seafront

September
6th-7th Dorchester Show, Cokers Frome Showground

October
tbc Weymouth Beach Motocross Championship

November
tbc Weymouth Guy Fawkes, The Beach

ABBOTSBURY Map 03 SY58
ABBOTSBURY SWANNERY
New Barn Rd DT3 4JG (turn off A35 at Winterborne Steepleton near Dorchester. Abbotsbury on B3157 coastal road, between Weymouth and Bridport)
☎ 01305 871858   📠 01305 871092
e-mail: info@abbotsbury-tourism.co.uk

Abbotsbury is the breeding ground of the only managed colonial herd of mute swans. The swans can be seen safely at close quarters, and the site is also home or stopping point for many wild birds. The highlight of the year is the cygnet season, end of May to the end of June, when there may be over 100 nests on site. Visitors can often take pictures at close quarters of cygnets emerging from eggs. There is an audio-visual show, as well as mass feeding at noon & 4pm daily, and an ugly duckling trail.
Times: Open 24 Mar-2 Nov, daily 10-6, last admission 5. **Fee:** * £5.50 (ch £3.50 & pen £5.20). **Facilities:** 🅿 💷 ✗ licensed ♿ (free wheelchair loan, herb garden for blind) toilets for disabled shop 🐕

ATHELHAMPTON Map 03 SY79
ATHELHAMPTON HOUSE & GARDENS
DT2 7LG (off A35 Northbrook junct, follow brown tourist signs towards Puddletown, at traffic lights turn left, Athelhampton is approx 1m on left)
☎ 01305 848363   📠 01305 848135
e-mail: pcooke@athelhampton.co.uk

Athelhampton, one of the finest 15th-century houses in England, contains magnificently furnished rooms including The Great Hall of 1485 and the library. The glorious Grade I gardens contain the world-famous topiary pyramids, fountains, and collections of tulips, magnolias, roses, clematis and lilies in season.
Times: Open Mar-Nov, daily 10.30-5. Also Sun in winter (ex Xmas). (Closed Sat). **Fee:** * House & Garden £6.25 (ch free, pen £5.75, student & disabled £3.95). Garden only £4.50 (ch free). **Facilities:** 🅿 💷 ✗ licensed ♿ (motorised scooter for use in grounds) toilets for disabled shop 🐕 (ex assistance dogs)

BEAMINSTER Map 03 ST40
MAPPERTON
DT8 3NR (2m SE off A356 & B3163)
☎ 01308 862645   📠 01308 863348
e-mail: office@mapperton.com

Several acres of terraced valley gardens with specimen trees and shrubs, and formal borders surround a manor house that dates back to the 16th century. There are also fountains, grottoes, stone fishponds and an orangery, and the garden offers good views and walks. The Mapperton Courtyard Fair is held annually in August with craft demonstrations, stalls, house tours and local displays.
Times: Open Gardens: Mar-Oct, daily 2-6. House open weekday afternoons Jun-10 Jul, spring & summer BH's. **Fee:** Gardens £3.50 (ch 5-18 £1.50, under 5 free). **Facilities:** 🅿 💷 ♿ (ramp from parking area to garden) toilets for disabled shop 🐕 (ex guide dogs)

BLANDFORD FORUM Map 03 ST80
ROYAL SIGNALS MUSEUM
Blandford Camp DT11 8RH (signposted off B3082 Blandford/Wimborne road & A354 Salisbury road)
☎ 01258 482248   📠 01258 482084
e-mail: royalsignalsmuseum@army.mod.uk
Times: Open Mar-Oct, Mon-Fri 10-5, Sat-Sun 10-4. Closed 10 days over Xmas & New Year **Facilities:** 🅿 💷 ♿ (ramps & chair lift) toilets for disabled shop 🐕 (ex guide dogs) *Details not confirmed for 2003*

BOURNEMOUTH Map 04 SZ09
OCEANARIUM
Pier Approach BH2 5AA (from A338 Wessex Way, follow the Oceanarium tourist signs)
☎ 01202 311993   📠 01202 311990
e-mail: oceanarium@reallive.co.uk
Times: Open all year, daily from 10am. (Closed 25 Dec). **Facilities:** 🅿 (100mtrs) 💷 ♿ (wheelchair for hire) toilets for disabled shop 🐕 (ex guide dogs) *Details not confirmed for 2003*

BOVINGTON CAMP Map 03 SY88
CLOUDS HILL
BH20 7NQ (1m N of Bovington Camp)
☎ 01929 405616

T E Lawrence ('Lawrence of Arabia') bought this cottage in 1925 when he was a private in the Tank Corps at Bovington. He would escape here to play records and entertain friends to feasts of baked beans and China tea. The furniture and contents were Lawrence's own and a new display, opened in 2002, tells the story of his life.
Times: Open 2 Apr-Oct, Wed-Fri & Sun, also BH Mon, 12-5, or dusk if earlier. **Fee:** £2.90. **Facilities:** 🅿 (Braille guide) 🐕 🚲 ♿

THE TANK MUSEUM
BH20 6JG (off A352 or A35, follow brown tank signs from Bere Regis & Wool)
☎ 01929 405096   📠 01929 405360
e-mail: admin@tankmuseum.co.uk

The Tank Museum houses the world's finest international collection of Armoured Fighting Vehicles. Tanks in Action displays are held every Thursday at noon from July-September and every Tuesday from 23rd July to 29th August. Armoured vehicle rides are available throughout the summer, and various special events take place - please telephone for details.
Times: Open all year, daily 10-5 (Closed from 16-26 Dec). **Fee:** * £7.50 (ch £5, pen £6.50). Family saver £21 (2 adult & 2 ch); £17.50 (1 adult & 2 ch). Group rates available. **Facilities:** 🅿 💷 ✗ licensed ♿ (wheelchairs available, Braille & audio tours) toilets for disabled shop 🐕 (ex guide dogs)

BROWNSEA ISLAND Map 03 SZ08
BROWNSEA ISLAND
BH15 7EE (located in Poole Harbour)
☎ 01202 707744   📠 01202 701635
Times: Open Apr-1 Oct, daily 10-5 (10-6 Jul & Aug) **Facilities:** 💷 ✗ ♿ (Braille guide, 2 selfdrive vehicles- booking advisable) toilets for disabled shop 🐕 *Details not confirmed for 2003*

Dorset

🏛 CANFORD CLIFFS   Map 04 SZ08
Compton Acres Gardens
Canford Cliffs Rd BH13 7ES (on B3065, follow brown tourist signs)
☎ 01202 700778   📠 01202 707537
e-mail: sales@comptonacres.co.uk
Times: Open Apr-Dec 10-6 (last entry 5.15) **Facilities:** P 🍴 ✗ licensed ♿ (level paths and ramps into shops and cafe) toilets for disabled shop garden centre 🐕 (ex guide & hearing dogs) *Details not confirmed for 2003* 🎟

🏛 CHRISTCHURCH   Map 04 SZ19
Christchurch Castle & Norman House
(near Christchurch Priory)

All that remain of the castle buildings are a ruined keep and an interesting, well preserved Norman house, believed to have been the home of the castle's constable.
Times: Open any reasonable time. **Fee:** Free **Facilities:** ♿

Red House Museum & Gardens
Quay Rd BH23 1BU (follow brown tourist signs from Christchurch, Red House is on the corner of Quay Rd)
☎ 01202 482860   `2 for 1`
📠 01202 481924

A museum with plenty of variety, featuring local history, archaeology, and natural history, displayed in a beautiful Georgian house. There's an excellent costume collection, some Arthur Romney-Green furniture and gardens with a woodland walk and herb garden. Regularly changing temporary exhibitions include contemporary art.
Times: Open all year, Tue-Sat 10-5 Sun 2-5 (Closed Mon ex BH). Last admission 4.30pm. **Fee:** * £1.50 (concessions 80p). Family ticket £3.50. **Facilities:** P (200yds) 🍴 ♿ (hearing aid and loop in reception only) shop 🐕 (ex guide & hearing dogs)

🏛 CORFE CASTLE   Map 03 SY98
Corfe Castle
BH20 5EZ (follow A351 from Wareham to Swanage. Corfe Castle approx 5m along this road)
☎ 01929 481294   📠 01929 481294
e-mail: wcfgen@smpt.ntrust.org.uk

Built in Norman times, the castle was added to by King John. It was defended during the Civil War by Lady Bankes, who surrendered after a stout resistance. Parliament ordered the demolition of the castle, and today it is one of the most impressive ruins in England. Ring for details of special events.
Times: Open daily, Mar 10-5; Apr-end Oct 10-6; Nov-Feb 10-4. Last admission 30 mins before closing. (Closed 25-26 Dec). **Fee:** £4.30 (ch £2.15). Family ticket £10.80 (2 adults & 3 ch) or £6.50 (1 adult & 3 ch).
Facilities: P 🍴 ✗ licensed (Braille guide & menu) shop 🐾 🎟

Corfe Castle Museum
West St BH20 5HE (to side of church on West St)
☎ 01929 480974   📠 01929 480974
e-mail: kenwollaston@tesco.net

The tiny, rectangular building was partly rebuilt in brick after a fire in 1780, and is the smallest town hall building in England. It has old village relics, and dinosaur footprints, 130 million years old. A council chamber on the first floor is reached by a staircase at one end. The Ancient Order of Marblers meets here each Shrove Tuesday.
Times: Open all year, Apr-Oct, daily 9.30-6; Nov-Mar, wknds and Xmas holidays 10-5. **Fee:** Free. **Facilities:** P (200yds) ♿ 🐕

🏛 DORCHESTER   Map 03 SY69
Dinosaur Museum
Icen Way DT1 1EW (In town centre, just off High East Street)
☎ 01305 269880   📠 01305 268885
e-mail: info@dinosaur-museum.org.uk

This museum, devoted to dinosaurs, has an appealing mixture of fossils, skeletons, life-size reconstructions and interactive displays such as the 'feelies'. There are audio-visual presentations and computer displays providing an all-round family attraction with new displays each year.
Times: Open all year, daily 9.30-5.30 (10-4.30 Nov-Mar). (Closed 24-26 Dec). **Fee:** * £4.75 (ch £2.95, pen & student £3.75, under 4's free). Family ticket £13.75. **Facilities:** P (50yds) ♿ (Many low level displays) shop 🎟

Dorset County Museum
High West St DT1 1XA (turn off A354 signposted Dorchester, attraction on right half way up main street)
☎ 01305 262735   📠 01305 257180
e-mail: dorsetcountymuseum@dor-mus.demon.co.uk
Times: Open May-Oct, Mon-Sat, 10-5. Also open Sun during May-Oct. (Closed 25 Dec). **Facilities:** P (150 yds) ♿ (Free entry for disabled visitors) shop *Details not confirmed for 2003*

Dorset Teddy Bear Museum
Antelope Walk, Cornhill DT1 1BE (in town centre near Tourist Information Centre)
☎ 01305 263200   📠 01305 268885
e-mail: info@teddybearmuseum.co.uk

A visit to the museum begins with the home of Edward Bear and his extended family of human-sized teddy bears. Then, in a more traditional museum setting, view hundreds of teddy bears from throughout the last century in atmospheric and evocative displays.
Times: Open daily 9.30-5. (Closed 25-26 Dec) **Fee:** £2.95 (ch £1.50, under 4's free). Family £7.95. **Facilities:** P (500mtrs) shop 🐕 (ex guide dogs) 🎟

Dorset

Hardy's Cottage
Higher Bockhampton DT2 8QJ (3m NE of Dorchester, 0.5m S of A35. Turn off A35 at Kingston Maurward rdbt towards Stinsford and Bockhampton. Left onto Bockhampton Ln, signed to Hardy's Cottage)
☎ 01305 262366

The small cob and thatch cottage where novelist and poet Thomas Hardy was born in 1840 and from where he would walk 6 miles every day to school in Dorchester. It was built by his great-grandfather and is little altered since. The interior has been furnished by the trust.
Times: Open Apr-Oct, daily (ex Fri & Sat), 11-5 or dusk if earlier. Open Good Fri. **Fee:** £2.80. **Facilities:** P (10 min walk) (no coach parking) & (car parking by arrangement, large print guide) ✈ ♨

Maiden Castle
DT1 9PR (2m S, access off A354, N of bypass)

The Iron Age fort ranks among the finest in Britain. It covers 47 acres, and has daunting earthworks, with a complicated defensive system around the entrances. One of its main purposes may well have been to protect grain from marauding bands. The first single-rampart fort dates from around 700BC, and by 100BC the earthworks covered the whole plateau. It was finally overrun by Roman troops in AD43.
Times: Open any reasonable time. **Fee:** Free **Facilities:** P ♨

The Military Museum of Devon & Dorset
The Keep, Birdport DT1 1RN (near top of High West St, towards Bridport)
☎ 01305 264066   ≣ 01305 250373
e-mail: keep.museum@talk21.com

Three hundred years of military history, with displays on the Devon Regiment, Dorset Regiment, Dorset Militia and Volunteers, the Queen's Own Dorset Yeomanry, and Devonshire and Dorset Regiment (from 1958). The Museum uses modern technology and creative displays to tell the stories of the Infantry, Cavalry and Artillerymen.
Times: Open Apr-Sep, Mon-Sat 9-5; Oct-Mar, Tue-Sat 9-5; (also Jul & Aug, Sun 10-4). Closed Xmas & New Year. **Fee:** * £3 (ch, student & pen £2). Family ticket £9 **Facilities:** P ⛾ & (lift avalible to 3 floors) toilets for disabled shop ✈ (ex guide dogs)

Tutankhamun Exhibition
High West St DT1 1UW (In town centre)
☎ 01305 269571   ≣ 01305 268885
e-mail: info@tutankhamun-exhibition.co.uk

The exhibition recreates the excitement of one of the world's greatest discoveries of ancient treasure. A reconstruction of the tomb and recreations of its treasures are displayed. The superbly preserved mummified body of the boy king can be seen, wonderfully recreated in every detail. Facsimiles of some of the most famous treasures, including the golden funerary mask and the harpooner can be seen in the final gallery.
Times: Open all year, Apr-Oct, daily 9.30-5.30; Nov-Mar 9.30-5, wknds 10-4.30. (Closed 24-26 Dec). **Fee:** * £4.75 (ch £2.95, pen & student £3.75, under 5's free). Family ticket £13.75 **Facilities:** P (200yds) & shop ✈ (ex guide dogs) ♨

⛪ MINTERNE MAGNA   Map 03 ST60
Minterne Gardens
DT2 7AU (2m N of Cerne Abbas on A352 Dorchester-Sherborne road)
☎ 01300 341370   ≣ 01300 341747

Lakes, cascades, streams and many fine and rare trees will be found in these lovely landscaped gardens. The 18th-century design is a superb setting for the spring shows of rhododendrons, azaleas and spring bulbs, and the autumn colour.
Times: Open Mar-10 Nov, daily 10-7. **Fee:** * £3 (accompanied ch free). **Facilities:** P

⛪ POOLE   Map 03 SZ09
Waterfront Museum & Scaplen's Court
4 High St BH15 1BW (off Poole Quay)
☎ 01202 262600   ≣ 01202 262622
e-mail: museums@poole.gov.uk

The museum tells the story of Poole's seafaring past. Learn of the Roman occupation and see material raised from the Studland Bay wreck. Scaplen's Court, just a few yards from the museum, is a beautifully restored domestic building dating from the medieval period. There is a Victorian school room, a kitchen and scullery.
Times: Museum: open Apr-Oct, Mon-Sat 10-5, Sun noon-5; Nov-Mar, Mon-Sat 10-3, Sun noon-3. Scaplen's Court: Aug, Mon-Sat 10-5, Sun noon-5. **Fee:** Free. **Facilities:** P (250mtrs) & (Town Cellars & Scaplen's Court not accessible) toilets for disabled ✈ (ex guide dogs) ♨

⛪ PORTLAND   Map 03 SY67
Portland Castle
Castleton DT5 1AZ (overlooking Portland harbour)
☎ 01305 820539

One of the best preserved of Henry VIII's coastal forts, built of white Portland stone and originally intended to thwart attack by the Spanish and French. The castle was much fought over in the Civil War.
Times: Open all year, 29 Mar-Sep, daily 10-6 (Oct, daily 10-5); Nov-Mar, daily 10-4. (Closed 24-26 Dec & 1 Jan). **Fee:** * £3.50 (ch 5-15 £1.80, under 5 free, concessions £2.60). **Facilities:** P & shop ✈ ♨

Portland Museum
217 Wakeham DT5 1HS (A354, through Fortuneswell to Portland Heights Hotel, then English Heritage signs)
☎ 01305 821804   ≣ 01305 761654
e-mail: tourism@weymouth.gov.uk
Times: Open Etr-Oct, Fri-Tue (ex school holidays open daily), 10.30-5 (Closed 1-1.30 daily). **Facilities:** P 50yds (coach parking on roadside) & shop *Details not confirmed for 2003*

SHAFTESBURY Map 03 ST82
SHAFTESBURY ABBEY MUSEUM & GARDEN
Park Walk SP7 8JR (follow signs to Shaftesbury town centre. Shaftesbury Abbey is signed outside King Alfred's Restaurant)
☎ 01747 852910 ▤ 01747 852910
e-mail: user@shaftesburyabbey.fsnet.co.uk

The Abbey at Shaftesbury was part of a nunnery founded by King Alfred in 888. It became one of the wealthiest in the country but was destroyed during the Dissolution in 1539. The excavated ruins show the foundations of the abbey church. The story is told through the use of carved stone and medieval floor tiles and illustrations from ancient manuscripts.
Times: Open Apr-Oct, daily, 10-5. **Fee:** * £1.50 (ch 60p, pen & concessions £1). **Facilities:** P (250yds) ♿ (large print guides, audio tour) toilets for disabled shop

SHERBORNE Map 03 ST61
SHERBORNE CASTLE
New Rd DT9 5NR (off A30, 0.5m E of Sherborne)
☎ 01935 813182 ▤ 01935 816727
e-mail: enquiries@sherbornecastle.com

Built by Sir Walter Raleigh in 1594, Sherborne Castle has been the home of the Digby family since 1617. Prince William of Orange was entertained here in 1688, and George III visited in 1789. Splendid collections of art, furniture and porcelain are on show in the Castle. Lancelot 'Capability' Brown created the lake in 1753.
Times: Open Apr-Oct, Tue-Thu, Sun & BH Mon 11-4.30. Castle opens from 2.30 on Sat. Last admission 4.30. **Fee:** £6 (pen £5.75). Gardens only £3.20. Ch under 15 free (max 4 ch per adult). Party 15+
Facilities: P 🍴 ♿ (braille guide book) toilets for disabled shop garden centre ✖ (ex guide dogs & in garden) 🚭

SHERBORNE MUSEUM
Abbey Gate House, Church Ln DT9 3BP (Turn off A303 to B3145 to Sherborne)
☎ 01935 812252
e-mail: admin@shermus.fsnet.co.uk

The museum features a model of Sherborne's original Norman castle, as well as a fine Victorian doll's house and other domestic and agricultural bygones. There are also items of local geological, natural history and archaeological interest, including Roman material.
Times: Open Apr-Oct, Tue-Sat 10.30-4.30, Sun 2.30-4.30; BH Mon 2.30-4.30 **Fee:** * £1 (ch & students free) **Facilities:** P (200yds) ♿ toilets for disabled shop ✖ (ex guide dogs)

SHERBORNE OLD CASTLE
Castleton D19 3SA (0.5m E off B3145)
☎ 01935 812730

The 12th-century castle was built by Roger, Bishop of Salisbury. In Elizabethan times it belonged to Sir Walter Raleigh, but was largely destroyed by Cromwell in the Civil War. The ruined Norman buildings remain.
Times: Open 29 Mar-Sep, daily 10-6 (Oct, 10-1 & 2-5); Nov-Mar, Wed-Sun 10-1 & 2-4. (Closed 24-26 Dec & 1 Jan). **Fee:** * £1.80 (ch 90p, concessions £1.40). **Facilities:** P ♿ ✖ ♿

SWANAGE Map 03 SZ07
SWANAGE RAILWAY
Station House BH19 1HB (signed from A351)
☎ 01929 425800 ▤ 01929 426680

Times: Open every weekend throughout the year, daily Apr-Oct.
Facilities: P 🍴 ✖ licensed ♿ (special disabled persons coach) toilets for disabled shop (shop at Swanage Station) *Details not confirmed for 2003*

TOLPUDDLE Map 03 SY79
TOLPUDDLE MARTYRS MUSEUM
DT2 7EH (off A35 from Dorchester, Tolpuddle is signposted at Troytown turn off. Continue on A35, Museum has brown heritage signpost giving clear directions)
☎ 01305 848237 ▤ 01305 848237
e-mail: jpickering@tuc.org.uk

One dawn, in the bitter February of 1834, six Tolpuddle farm labourers were arrested after forming a trade union. A frightened squire's trumped up charge triggered one of the most celebrated stories in the history of human rights. That dawn arrest created the Tolpuddle Martyrs, who were punished with transportation as convicts to Australia. Packed with illustrative displays, this new state-of-the-art, interactive exhibition tells the Tolpuddle Martyrs story. Every summer in July, the museum holds the Tolpuddle Martyrs Festival. The weekend combines celebration with tradition offering traditional and contemporary music as well as many other attractions.
Times: Open all year, Apr-Oct, Tue-Sat 10-5.30, Sun 11-5.30; Nov-Mar, Tue-Sat 10-4, Sun 11-4. Open BH Mon. (Closed 20 Dec-2 Jan). **Fee:** Free. **Facilities:** P (outside museum) ♿ (interactive computers at wheelchair height & parking) toilets for disabled shop ✖ (ex guide dogs)

WAREHAM
See WOOL for gazetteer entry

Dorset   75

WEST LULWORTH   Map 03 SY88
LULWORTH CASTLE
BH20 5QS (from Wareham, W on A352 for 1m, left onto B3070 to E Lulworth, follow tourist signs)
☎ 01929 400352   01929 400352   **2 for 1**
e-mail: estate.office@lulworth.com

Glimpse life below stairs in the restored kitchen, and enjoy beautiful views from the top of the tower of this historic castle set in beautiful parkland. The 18th-century chapel is reputed to be the first Catholic chapel built in England after the Reformation. Children will enjoy the animal farm, play area, indoor activity room and pitch and putt.
Times: Open Castle: 31 Mar-27 Oct, 10.30-6; 28 Oct-23 Dec 10.30-4. Lulworth Castle House open 12 Jun-25 Sep 2-5. **Fee:** * £5.50 (ch 5-16 £3.50, concessions £5). Family £15. English Heritage Members half price. Lulworth Castle House £4 (ch £1.50, concessions £3.50). Family £10. **Facilities:** P ⌘ & (limited in castle due to grade one listing) toilets for disabled shop

WEYMOUTH   Map 03 SY67
DEEP SEA ADVENTURE & SHARKY'S PLAY ZONE
9 Custom House Quay, Old Harbour DT4 8BG (follow signs on A35 from Weymouth. Located on the Old Harbour between pavilion and town bridge)
☎ 01305 760690   01305 760690
e-mail: deepsea_adventure.co.uk

A fascinating attraction telling the story of underwater exploration and marine exploits. Discover the history of Weymouth's Old Harbour, compelling tales of shipwreck survival, explore the Black Hole and search for Ollie the Oyster. Also a unique display telling the gripping tale of the *Titanic* disaster. Sharky's Play Area is four floors of fun-packed adventure. Separate toddler area for the under fives.
Times: Open all year, daily 9.30-7 (high season 9.30-8). (Closed 25 & 26 Dec & 1 Jan). **Fee:** * Sharky's Play Area: Adults free (ch £3). Deep Sea Adventure: £3.75 (ch 5-15 £2.75, pen & student £3.25). Family ticket £11.95. Combined ticket for both attractions, ch £4.75. **Facilities:** P (100yds) ✘ licensed & (lift & sign language for deaf) toilets for disabled shop ✘ (ex guide dogs)

RSPB NATURE RESERVE RADIPOLE LAKE
The Swannery Car Park DT4 7TZ (within the town, close to seafront & railway station)
☎ 01305 778313   01305 778313
Times: Open daily 9-5 **Facilities:** P (concessions for members from centre) & shop *Details not confirmed for 2003*

SEA LIFE PARK
Lodmoor Country Park DT4 7SX (on A353)
☎ 01305 788255   01305 760165
Times: Open all year, daily from 10am. (Closed 25 Dec). **Facilities:** P (charged) ⌘ & toilets for disabled shop ✘ *Details not confirmed for 2003*

WIMBORNE   Map 03 SZ09
KINGSTON LACY HOUSE, GARDEN & PARK
BH21 4EA (1.5m W of Wimborne, B3082)
☎ 01202 883402 (Mon-Fri) & 842913 (wknds)
 01202 882402

This house was the home of the Bankes family for over 300 years. The original house is 17th century, but in the 1830s it was given a stone façade. The Italian marble staircase, Venetian ceiling, treasures from Spain and an Egyptian oberlisk were also added. There are outstanding pictures by Titian, Rubens, Velásquez, Reynolds and Van Dyck. No photography is allowed in the house.
Times: House: 22 Mar-2 Nov, Wed-Sun 11-5 (last admission 4). Garden & Park: 22 Mar-2 Nov, daily 10.30-6; Feb - 21 Mar, Sat & Sun 10.30-4; 7 Nov-21 Dec, Fri-Sun 10.30-4.
Fee: £6 (ch £3.40). Park & Gardens only - £3.50 (ch £1.75).
Facilities: P ✘ licensed & (parking by arrangement) toilets for disabled shop ✘ (ex on leads in park & wood) *Details not confirmed for 2003*

NOW OPEN PHASE 1 OF THE LARGEST CHILDREN'S PLAY AREA IN SOUTHERN ENGLAND

FoLLOw that MoNKeY
MONKEY WORLD
APE RESCUE CENTRE • 0800 456 600
www.monkeyworld.org
Longthorns • Wareham • Dorset
(one mile from Wool on the Bere Regis Road)
COME SEE THE STARS OF MONKEY BUSINESS
VOTED DORSET'S BEST DAY OUT

Dorset

Knoll Gardens & Nursery
Stapehill Rd, Hampreston BH21 7ND (3m E between Wimborne and Ferndown off A31, at Canford Bottom rdbt, into B3073 signed Ham Lane)
☎ 01202 873931   📠 01202 870842   **2 for 1**
e-mail: enquiries@knollgardens.co.uk

Over 6000 plant species from all over the world thrive here, within a six-acre site. There are water gardens with waterfalls, pools and a stream, herbaceous borders, and many other features. There is also a 'Dragon' formal garden and a Mediterranean-style gravel garden. The nursery offers a wide range of plants; best known for its range of Ornamental Grasses and 'plants for the modern lifestyle'.
Times: Open all year, Oct-Mar Sun-Thu, 10-4 (or dusk if earlier); Apr-Sep, daily 10-5. Closed Xmas & New Year hols. **Fee:** * £3.50 (ch 5-15 £2, student & pen £3). Party 15+. **Facilities:** P ☕ ♿ (wheelchairs available) toilets for disabled garden centre ✈ (ex guide dogs) 🐕

Priest's House Museum and Garden
23-27 High St BH21 1HR
☎ 01202 882533   📠 01202 882533

An award-winning local history museum, set in an historic house with a Victorian kitchen where regular cooking demonstrations are held (4th Saturday in the month, 2-5pm). There are nine other rooms to see, along with regular special exhibitions, and a beautiful 300ft-long walled garden.
Times: Open Apr-Oct, Mon-Sat, 10-4.30. Also every Sun Jul-Aug & BH wknds 2-5. **Fee:** £2.50 (ch £1.90, pen & students £1.90). Family ticket £6.50. Season ticket £6.50. **Facilities:** P (200 yds) ☕ ♿ (hands on archaeology gallery, audio tapes) shop ✈ (ex guide dogs)

Stapehill Abbey
Wimborne Rd West BH21 2EB (2.5m E, off A31)
☎ 01202 861686   📠 01202 894589   **2 for 1**

This early 19th-century abbey, home for nearly 200 years to Cistercian nuns, is now a busy working crafts centre with many attractions under cover. There are award-winning landscaped gardens, parkland and picnic spots, and the Power to the Land exhibition. Telephone for details of special events.
Times: Open Etr-Sep, daily 10-5; Oct-Etr Wed-Sun 10-4. (Closed 22 Dec-2 Feb). **Fee:** * £7 (ch 4-16 £4.50, students & pen £6.50). Family ticket (2 adults & 2 ch) £19.50. **Facilities:** P ☕ ♿ toilets for disabled shop garden centre ✈ (ex guide dogs) 🐕

🏛 WOOL   Map 03 SY88
Monkey World
Longthorns BH20 6HH (1m N of Wool on Bere Regis road)
☎ 01929 462537 & 0800 456600
📠 01929 405414
e-mail: apes@monkeyworld.org

Set up in order to rescue monkeys and apes from abuse and illegal smuggling, Monkey World houses over 100 primates in 60 acres of woodland. There are 45 chimps, the largest grouping outside Africa, as well as orang-utans, gibbons, woolly monkeys, lemurs, macaques and marmosets. Those wishing to help the centre continue in its quest to rescue primates from lives of misery may like to take part in the adoption scheme which includes free admission to the park for one year.
Times: Open daily 10-5 (Jul-Aug 10-6). Last admission 1 hour before closing **Fee:** * £6 (ch & concessions £5). Family ticket (1 adult, 2 children) £14, (2 adults, 2 children) £19. Group15+ **Facilities:** P ☕ ✖ ♿ toilets for disabled shop ✈ (ex guide dogs) 🐕

See advert on page 75

County Durham

The Durham Dales lie between the Northumberland National Park and the Yorkshire Dales, and form around a third of the county's area. This huge expanse of waterfalls, meadows, heath and river valleys contains some beautiful scenery.

There are two record-holding geographic features in the area. The road from Killhope to Nenthead in Cumbria rises to over 2,000 feet, and is the highest classified road in England. The waterfall at High Force, where the River Tees falls 70 feet, is the highest waterfall in England.

The history of the area is as rich as the scenery. In the middle ages the Prince Bishops ruled the County Palatine with a blend of political and ecclesiastic power. This power extended into Northumberland and Yorkshire, and was the first line of defence against the marauding Scots. These unusual figures maintained their own armies, had their own courts and nobility, and minted their own coins. Essentially they were the rulers of virtually independent states. The best expression of this dual worldly and heavenly power is Durham's cathedral, once described as "Half Church of God, half Castle 'gainst the Scot."

In the 19th century the area around Weardale was the centre of the lead-mining industry. The industry has long since disappeared, and the 34-foot waterwheel and mine at the Killhope Lead Mining Centre are among the few reminders that this work ever took place.

Co. Durham was the birthplace of pop singer and organist, Alan Price. Born in Fatfield he was a member of 60s band The Animals, and then a solo artist whose down-to-earth music encapsulated many of the area's political and social concerns. Other famous Durhamites include Roxy Music singer Bryan Ferry, author and vet James Herriot, and football manager Bobby Robson.

EVENTS & FESTIVALS

May
3rd-5th Teesdale Thrash - concerts, ceilidhs, music sessions and morris dancing in Barnard Castle
tbc Morgan Car Meet, Beamish, North of England Open Air Museum

June
7th-8th Durham Regatta (provisional)

July
5th-6th Summer Festival, Durham city centre
12th Durham Miners Gala - colourful miners' banners paraded through the city of Durham (provisional)
tbc Chester-le-Street Traction Engine Rally
tbc Durham County Show, nr Chester-le-Street

August
24th-25th Durham Light Infantry Vehicle Rally, DLI Museum & Durham Art Gallery (provisional)
30th-31st Weardale Agricultural Show, Showfield, St John's Chapel (provisional)
tbc Billingham International Folklore Festival
tbc Ploughing Match, Beamish

September
6th-7th Wolsingham & Wear Valley Agricultural Show, Wolsingham (provisional)
13th-14th Stanhope Agricultural Show & Country Fair, Stanhope (provisional)
tbc Classic Car Day, Beamish

Top: Durham Cathedral

County Durham

BARNARD CASTLE   Map 12 NZ01
BARNARD CASTLE
DL12 8NP
☎ 01833 638212

The town's name comes from Bernard Baliol, who built the castle in 1125. The impressive ruins cling to the steep banks of the River Tees.
Times: Open all year, 29 Mar-Sep, daily 10-6 (Oct, daily 10-5); Nov-Mar, Wed-Sun 10-4. (Closed 1-2pm all year & 24-26 Dec & 1 Jan)
Fee: * £2.50 (ch £1.30, under 5's free, concessions £1.90)
Facilities: P & shop ✱

THE BOWES MUSEUM
DL12 8NP (on outskirts of town)
☎ 01833 690606   01833 637163

This splendid château-style mansion was built in 1869 by John Bowes, who made his fortune in Durham coal and married a French actress. They amassed an outstanding collection of works of art, and built the flamboyant château to house them. The museum contains paintings by El Greco, Goya and Canaletto among others; porcelain and silver, furniture, ceramics and textiles.
Times: Open daily 11-5. **Fee:** * £4 (concessions £3.90). Family ticket £12. **Facilities:** P ⌘ & (lift, ramped entrance, reserved parking) toilets for disabled shop (grounds only) ⟲

EGGLESTONE ABBEY
DL12 8QN (1m S on minor road off B6277)

The remains of this Premonstratensian abbey make a picturesque sight on the bank of the River Tees. A large part of the church can be seen, as can remnants of monastic buildings.
Times: Open any reasonable time. **Fee:** Free **Facilities:** P & ✱

Are there any great Days Out that we've missed? Use the Readers' Report form at the back of the book to tell us about them

---

BEAMISH   Map 12 NZ25
BEAMISH, THE NORTH OF ENGLAND OPEN-AIR MUSEUM
DH9 0RG (off A693 & A6076 signposted off A1(M) junct 63. Midway between Durham and Newcastle-upon-Tyne)
☎ 0191 370 4000   0191 370 4001
e-mail: museum@beamish.org.uk

Set in 200 acres of countryside, award-winning Beamish recreates life in the early 1800s and 1900s. Costumed staff welcome visitors to a 1913 town street, colliery village, farm and railway station; a display of how people lived and worked. Ride on early electric tramcars, take a ride on a replica of an 1825 steam railway and visit Pockerley Manor where a yeoman farmer and his family would have lived.
Times: Open 23 Mar-27 Oct, daily 10-5; 28 Oct-4 Apr daily (ex Mon & Fri) 10-4. Closed 16 Dec-1 Jan. **Fee:** * Summer £12 (ch £6, over 60's £9). Winter £4 (ch £4, over 60's £4). NB a winter visit is centered on the town and tramway only, other areas are closed. **Facilities:** P ⌘ & (not ideal for wheelchairs, free entry for essential helpers) toilets for disabled shop ⟲

BISHOP AUCKLAND   Map 08 NZ22
AUCKLAND CASTLE
DL14 7NR (from A1(M), exit at junct 61 and join A688 signposted to Bishop Auckland, follow signs to Bishop Auckland Market Place and then brown tourist sign for Auckland Castle)
☎ 01388 601627   01388 609323
e-mail: auckland.castle@zetnet.co.uk

Serving as the principal county residence of the Prince Bishops since the 12th century, Auckland Castle is the home of the Bishop of Durham. Built on a promontory overlooking the River Wear and the Roman Fort of Binchester, the Castle has been added to and adapted over the centuries. St Peter's Chapel houses many of the treasures of past Bishops.
Times: Open Apr-Sep, Mon & Thu 12.30-5 & Sun 2-5. (Closed 13 Jun, 1 & 26 Sep). **Fee:** * £3.50 (ch under 8 free, ch 9-16 & concessions £2.50). **Facilities:** P ⌘ & (chair walker available by prior arrangement) toilets for disabled shop ✈ (ex guide dogs)

County Durham 79

BOWES
BOWES CASTLE Map 12 NY91
DL12 9LD (on A66)

Built inside the earthworks of the Roman fort of 'Lavatrae', the castle dates from the 12th century and its great ruined Norman keep still stands to a height of three storeys.
Times: Open any reasonable time. **Fee:** Free. **Facilities:**

COWSHILL
KILLHOPE LEAD MINING MUSEUM Map 12 NY84
DL13 1AR (beside A689 midway between Stanhope & Alston)
☎ 01388 537505   01388 537617
e-mail: killhope@durham.gov.uk   **2 for 1**

Equipped with hard hats and lamps, you can descend into the depths of the earth and explore the working conditions of lead miners. The mine and 19th-century crushing mill have been restored to look as they would have done in the 1870s, and the 34ft water wheel has been restored to working order. There is also a visitor centre and mineral exhibition, based on the life of miners and their families, a woodland walk, children's play area and a red squirrel and bird hide.
Times: Open Apr-Sep, Oct wknds & Oct half term, daily 10.30-5 (BHs & summer school hols open till 5.30); Dec open for santa wknds. Telephone for details. **Fee:** £3.40 (ch, disabled, & UB40 £1.70). Additional charge for mine visit £1.60 (ch, disabled, UB40 80p)
Facilities: (electric scooter) toilets for disabled shop

DARLINGTON
DARLINGTON RAILWAY CENTRE & MUSEUM Map 08 NZ21
North Rd Station DL3 6ST (0.75m N, off A167)
☎ 01325 460532   01325 287746   **2 for 1**

Housed in the carefully restored North Road Station, this museum's prize exhibit is 'Locomotion', which pulled the first passenger train on the Stockton to Darlington railway and was built by Robert Stephenson & Co in 1825. Several other steam locomotives are also shown, together with models and other exhibits relating to the Stockton and Darlington and the North Eastern Railway companies.
Times: Open daily 10-5. May be subject to amendment. **Fee:** * £2.10 (ch £1.05, pen £1.50). **Facilities:** toilets for disabled shop (ex guide dogs)

DURHAM
DURHAM CATHEDRAL Map 12 NZ24
DH1 3EH (A1(M) to Durham, turn off at A690 into city take turn into Market Place & follow signs)
☎ 0191 386 4266   0191 386 4267
e-mail: enquiries@durhamcathedral.co.uk
Times: Open daily, 9.30-6.15, 21 Jun-8 Sep 9.30-8. (Sun 12.30-5). Cathedral is closed to visitors during evening recitals & concerts.
Facilities: (in city centre) (very poor parking) licensed & (braille guide touch/hearing centre, stairclimber) toilets for disabled shop (ex guide dogs) Details not confirmed for 2003

DURHAM LIGHT INFANTRY MUSEUM & DURHAM ART GALLERY
Aykley Heads DH1 5TU (0.5m NW, turn right off A691)
☎ 0191 384 2214   0191 386 1770
e-mail: dli@durham.gov.uk

The history of the Regiment is told in displays of artefacts, medals, uniforms and vehicles. The Art Gallery has a continuous programme of temporary exhibitions, and holds regular lectures and concerts.
Times: Open all year, Apr-Oct, daily 10-5; Nov-Mar, daily 10-4 (closed 25 Dec). **Fee:** £2.50 (£1.25 concessions). family ticket £6.25
Facilities: (wheelchair available, lift, ramps) toilets for disabled shop (ex guide dogs)

FINCHALE PRIORY
Brasside, Newton Hall DH1 5SH (3m NE)
☎ 0191 386 3828

This lovely setting was the refuge chosen by St Godric in 1110 for his years of solitary meditation, and the priory, used by monks from Durham Cathedral, was founded in 1180. Remains of the 13th-century church can be seen.
Times: Open 29 Mar-Sep, daily 10-6 (Oct 10-5). **Fee:** * £1.40 (ch 5-15 70p, under 5's free, concessions £1.10) **Facilities:** (charged) &

ORIENTAL MUSEUM
University of Durham, Elvet Hill DH1 3TH (signposted from A167 & A177)
☎ 0191 374 7911
 0191 374 7911   **2 for 1**
e-mail: oriental.museum@durham.ac.uk

The Marvels of China gallery introduces the visitor to contemporary China, its history and decorative arts. Other displays cover the Islamic World, Buddhism, Chinese archaeology, the story of writing, and there is a Javanese Gamelan Orchestra.
Times: Open Mon-Fri 10-5, wknds 12-5. (Closed Xmas-New Year). **Fee:** * £1.50 (ch, pen & students 75p) **Facilities:** (lifts to all floors) toilets for disabled shop

HARTLEPOOL
HARTLEPOOL HISTORIC QUAY Map 08 NZ53
Maritime Av TS24 0XZ (from A19 take A179 and follow signs for Marina then Historic Quay)
☎ 01429 860077   01429 867332
Times: Open daily 10-5 (10-7 in summer). Closed 25 Dec & 1 Jan.
Facilities: licensed & (all areas ramped or lift access) toilets for disabled shop Details not confirmed for 2003

HMS TRINCOMALEE
Jackson Dock TS24 0SQ (From A19 take A689 or A179, follow signs for Hartlepool Historic Quay)
☎ 01429 223193   01429 864385
e-mail: office@hms-trincomalee.co.uk

HMS 'Trincomalee', is the oldest ship afloat in the UK and the last of Nelson's frigates. Now fully restored in

continued

an award-winning project. Come aboard for a unique experience of navy life two centuries ago.
Times: Open all year, Summer: 10-5, Winter: 10.30-4. Closed Xmas & New Year. **Fee:** * £3.70 (ch, students & disabled £2.70, pen & unemployed £2.70. Family ticket (2 adults & 3 ch) £10. Group tickets available. **Facilities:** P & (3 out of the 4 decks are accessible by lift) shop ✖ (ex guide dogs)

MUSEUM OF HARTLEPOOL
Jackson Dock, Maritime Av TS24 0XZ (Historic Quay & Museum towards the Marina)
☎ 01429 860077   ▯ 01429 523477
Times: Open all year, daily (closed 25-26 Dec & 1 Jan). **Facilities:** P & toilets for disabled shop ✖ (ex guide dogs) Details not confirmed for 2003

⛁ SHILDON   Map 08 NZ22
TIMOTHY HACKWORTH VICTORIAN & RAILWAY MUSEUM
Soho Cottages, Hackworth Close DL4 1PQ (SE of town centre. Signed from A6072 & B6282)
☎ 01388 777999   ▯ 01388 777999

Timothy Hackwood (1786-1850) was an important figure in the development of steam travel. He constructed "Puffing Billy" for William Hedley, ran Stephenson's Newcastle Works, and also became the first superintendent of the Stockton & Darlington Railway. The museum and house detail Hackwood's life and the steam transport revolution, as well as displaying working models and locomotives from various periods. Steam train rides are available throughout the year.
Times: Open Good Fri-end Oct, Wed-Sun & BH's 10-5 **Fee:** * £2 (ch & pen £1). Family ticket £5 **Facilities:** P & toilets for disabled shop ✖ (ex guide dogs)

⛁ STAINDROP   Map 12 NZ12
RABY CASTLE
DL2 3AH (on A688, Barnard Castle to Bishop Auckland road, 1m N of Staindrop. Travelling S, leave A1(M) junct 58 on A68, turning left onto A688 towards Barnard Castle, Castle on right)
☎ 01833 660202   ▯ 01833 660169
e-mail: admin@rabycastle.com

The castle was built during Saxon times but is predominantly 14th century, with many later additions.

It has an impressive gateway; nine towers; a vast medieval hall; and a splendid restored Victorian octagonal drawing room which has re-emerged as one of the most striking interiors from the 19th century. The castle contains fine pictures, interesting furniture and ceramics, and a carriage collection.
Times: Open May & Sep, Wed & Sun only. Jun-Aug, Sun-Fri. Castle open 1-5. Park & gardens 11-5.30, (last admission 4.30pm). Open BH wknds Sat-Wed. **Fee:** * Castle, Park & Gardens £5 (ch £2 & pen £4). Family ticket £12 (2 adults & 3 ch). Park & Gardens £3 (ch & pen £2). Party 20+. **Facilities:** P & (most of ground floor accessible) toilets for disabled shop ✖ (ex guide dogs & on lead)

⛁ TANFIELD   Map 12 NZ15
TANFIELD RAILWAY
Old Marley Hill NE16 5ET (on A6076 1m S of Sunniside)
☎ 0191 388 7545   ▯ 0191 387 4784 |2 for 1|
e-mail: tanfield@ingsoc.demon.co.uk

A 3-mile working steam railway and the oldest existing railway in the world. The Causey Arch, the first large railway bridge of its era, is the centrepiece of a deep wooded valley, with picturesque walks. You can ride in carriages that were first used in Victorian times, and visit Marley Hill shed, the home of 35 engines; inside is the stationary steam engine at work driving some of the vintage machine tools. The blacksmith is also often at work forging new parts for the restoration work. Special events are held throughout the year, please telephone for details.
Times: Open all year, summer daily 10-5; winter daily 10-4. Trains: Sun & Summer BH's wknds; also Thu & Sat mid Jul-Aug. Santa's Specials Sat & Sun in Dec (booking essential). Mince pie specials Boxing Day. **Fee:** * Admission free. Train travel £4 (under 5 free, ch & pen £2). Family discount tickets avalible £10. **Facilities:** P & (all trains carry ramps for wheelchair access) toilets for disabled shop

Essex

Essex and its inhabitants have for some time been the butt of jokes that imply financial acuity but a lack of taste, discernment and sophistication. This might be due to the county's proximity to London, which has led to the development of commuter towns and changed the nature of a once rural area.

However, moving northeast into East Anglia there are some fine country towns and villages, and, approaching the Suffolk border, all the scenic delights of Constable country around the Stour Valley.

The big resorts of Southend and Clacton are the best known on the Essex coast, but by contrast there are pretty places on the Tendring Peninsula, the sailing centres of Burnham-on-Crouch and Maldon, the marshy headland of the Naze, and the birdlife of Maplin Sands.

From medieval times to the 18th century, Saffron Walden was the centre of the saffron crocus industry. It was saffron wealth that bought the town the largest parish church in Essex, and the streets around the church reflect this historic prosperity.

Colchester lays claim to being England's oldest town, and is a fascinating place to visit. There is evidence of a settlement from the fifth century BC, and the town was King Cymbeline's capital in the first century AD. The Romans also made it their capital in 43 AD and the town prospered despite being burned by Boudicca/Boadicea in 60 AD. The Roman walls are largely intact, and the remains of the Norman castle are there to be seen.

Famous natives of Essex include Noel Edmonds, Lee Evans, Helen Mirren, two members of The Prodigy, Samuel Pepys, Dick Turpin and Matthew Hopkins - Witchfynder General.

Top: Beach Huts, Walton-on-the-Naze

EVENTS & FESTIVALS

May
18th Essex Young Farmers Show, Great Leighs
tbc Southend Air Show (Europe's largest free show)
tbc Tour de Tendring Cycle Ride, Tendring area

June
26th-27th Thaxted Morris Ring Meet (various venues), annual meeting of morris men
tbc Concert in the Park, Southend
tbc Essex County Show, Great Leighs

July
12th Tendring Hundred Show, Lawford House Park, Manningtree - agricultural show
tbc Classic Car rally London-Southend
tbc Cressing Temple Festival - jazz, classical music, drama

August
21st-25th Clacton Jazz Festival (provisional)
tbc Clacton Air Show, Clacton Seafront
tbc Clacton Carnival
tbc Southend Carnival, Chalkwell Park
tbc Southend Jazz Festival (various venues)

September
tbc Colchester Festival - street and arts festival
tbc Maldon Town Regatta
tbc Old Leigh Regatta

Essex

AUDLEY END
Map 05 TL53
AUDLEY END HOUSE & GARDENS
CB11 4JF (1m W of Saffron Walden on B1383)
☎ 01799 522399

Built on a grandiose scale by Thomas Howard, Earl of Suffolk, to entertain King James I, Audley End House was gradually reduced in size over the next century, but what we see today is still impressive in scale and the 30 rooms open to the public display a stunning collection of art, as well as period furnishings. Gardens and a landscaped park surround the mansion.
Times: Open 29 Mar-Sep; Wed-Sun & BH; Grounds 11-6 (last entry 5pm); House, 12-5 (last entry 4pm). 2-31 Oct: Grounds 11-4 Wed-Fri (last entry 3pm), 11-5 Sat-Sun (last entry 4pm); House 11-3 Wed-Sun (Site closes at 4pm) Guided tours by arrangement. Times may vary during music on a Summer's eve Concerts. Phone for details **Fee:** House & grounds: £6.95 (ch 5-15 £3.50, concessions £5.20). Family ticket (2 adults & 3 ch) £17.40. Grounds only: £4 (ch £2, concessions £3) Family ticket £10. **Facilities:** ℗ (charged) 🍽 ♿ shop ✗ ♿

BRAINTREE
Map 05 TL72
THE WORKING SILK MILL
New Mills, South St CM7 3GB (follow brown tourist signs)
☎ 01376 553393 📠 01376 330642
Times: Open Mon-Fri, 10-12.30 & 1.30-5. Last admission to mill 12 noon and 4pm. **Facilities:** ℗ ♿ (ramps) toilets for disabled shop ✗ (ex guide dogs) *Details not confirmed for 2003*

CASTLE HEDINGHAM
Map 05 TL73
COLNE VALLEY RAILWAY & MUSEUM
Castle Hedingham Station CO9 3DZ (4m NW of Halstead on A1017)
☎ 01787 461174

The old Colne Valley and Halstead railway buildings have been rebuilt here. Stock includes seven steam locomotives plus 70 other engines, carriages and wagons, in steam from Easter to December. Visitors can dine in style in restored Pullman carriages while travelling along the line. Please telephone for a free timetable and details of the many special events.
Times: Open all year, daily 10-dusk. Steam days, rides from 12-4. (Closed 23 Dec-1 Feb). Steam days every Sun and BH from Mothering Sunday to end Oct, Wed of school summer holidays & special events. Railway Farm Park open May-Sep. Phone 01787 461174 for timetable information. **Fee:** Steam days £6 (ch £3 pen £5); Family ticket £17. Non-steam days (to view static exhibits only) £3 (ch £1.50); Family ticket £7.50. **Facilities:** ℗ 🍽 ✗ licensed ♿ (ramps for wheelchairs to get onto carriages) shop ✗ (ex guide dogs)

HEDINGHAM CASTLE
CO9 3DJ (on B1058, 1m off A1017)
Colchester/Cambridge. Follow brown tourist signs to Hedingham Castle)
☎ 01787 460261 📠 01787 461373
e-mail: hedinghamcastle@aspects.net   **2 for 1**

This impressive Norman castle was built in 1140. It was besieged by King John, and visited by Henry VII, Henry VIII and Elizabeth I, and was home to the de Veres,
Earls of Oxford, for over 500 years. During the summer months Hedinghams colourful heritage comes to life with a full programme of special events. There are medieval jousts and sieges with authentic living history displays and encampments. Please telephone for details civil ceremony weddings and corporate hire.

Times: Open wk before Etr-end Oct, daily 10-5. **Fee:** * £4 (ch £3, concessions £3.50). Family ticket £14. **Facilities:** ℗ 🍽 shop ✗ (ex in grounds)

CHELMSFORD
Map 05 TL20
RHS GARDEN HYDE HALL
Rettendon CM3 8ET (on A130 follow signs from Rettendon village)
☎ 01245 400256 📠 01245 402100
e-mail: hydehall@rhs.org.uk

Calling itself "A garden of beauty and surprises", RHS Garden Hyde Hall is a great day out for flower-lovers, and includes highlights such as the Dry Garden, a modern rose garden designed by Robin Williams, a colour themed herbaceous border, a farmhouse garden, and the NCCPG National Collection™ of Viburnum.
Times: Open 18 Mar-10 Nov daily 10-6, (10-5 Sep-Nov) **Fee:** * £4 (ch 6-16 £1, ch under 6 free, disabled carer/companion free. Groups 10+) **Facilities:** ℗ ✗ licensed ♿ toilets for disabled shop garden centre ✗ (ex assistance dogs)

COGGESHALL
Map 05 TL82
PAYCOCKE'S
West St CO6 1NS (Signposted from A120, on S side of West Street)
☎ 01376 561305

This timber-framed house is a fine example of a medieval merchant's home. It was completed in about 1505 and has interesting carvings on the outside timbers, including the Paycocke trade sign. Inside there are further elaborate carvings and linenfold panelling. Behind the house is a pretty garden.
Times: Open 31 Mar-13 Oct Tue, Thu, Sun & BH Mon 2-5.30. **Fee:** * £2.30, joint ticket with Coggeshall Grange Barn £3.40. **Facilities:** ℗ (400yds) ♿ ✗ (ex guide dogs) 🐕

Essex 83

COLCHESTER Map 05 TL92
BETH CHATTO GARDENS
Elmstead Market CO7 7DB (5m E of Colchester on A133)
☎ 01206 822007   📠 01206 825933
e-mail: info@bethchatto.fsnet.co.uk

Begun almost 40 years ago, when Beth Chatto and her late husband began working on acres of wasteland. Today the wasteland has become a garden of three distinctive areas. The south-west facing dry garden is on gravel, and has plants such as yucca and pineapple broom. It faces a group of oaks which shade the second area, with woodland and other shade-loving plants. Lastly, there is the wetland garden, with five large pools filled with fish and surrounded by swathes of bog plants.
Times: Open all year, Mar-Oct, Mon-Sat 9-5; Nov-Feb, Mon-Fri 9-4. (Closed Sun). **Fee:** £3.50 (accompanied ch under 14 free) **Facilities:** P 🍴 ♿ (access to parts of garden may be difficult) toilets for disabled garden centre 🐕 (ex guide dogs)

COLCHESTER CASTLE MUSEUM
Castle Park, High St CO1 1TJ (at E end of High St)
☎ 01206 282931   📠 01206 282925
Times: Open all year, Mon-Sat 10-5, Sun 11-5. **Facilities:** P (town centre) ♿ (ramps to all areas & lift) toilets for disabled shop 🐕 Details not confirmed for 2003

COLCHESTER ZOO
Stanway, Maldon Rd CO3 0SL (turn off A12 onto A1124 and follow elephant signs)
☎ 01206 331292   📠 01206 331392
e-mail: enquiries@colchester-zoo.co.uk

One of England's finest zoos, Colchester Zoo has over 200 types of animals. Visitors can meet the elephants, handle a snake, and see parrots, seals, penguins and birds of prey all appearing in informative daily displays. New enclosures include Spirit of Africa, Elephant Kingdom, Penguin Shores, the Wilds of Asia for orang-utans, and Chimp World. There is also an undercover soft play complex, road train, four adventure play areas, eating places and gift shops, all set in 40 acres of gardens.
Times: Open all year, daily from 9.30. Last admission 5.30 (1hr before dusk out of season). Closed 25 Dec. **Fee:** * £9 (ch 3-14 & pen £5.75, disabled £4). **Facilities:** P 🍴 ✕ licensed ♿ (easy route developed) toilets for disabled shop garden centre 🐕

HADLEIGH Map 05 TQ88
HADLEIGH CASTLE
(0.75m S of A13)
☎ 01536 402840

The subject of several of Constable's paintings, the castle has fine views of the Thames estuary. It is defended by ditches on three sides, and the north-east and south-east towers are still impressive.
Times: Open any reasonable time. **Fee:** Free. **Facilities:** ♿

HARLOW Map 05 TL41
HARLOW MUSEUM
Passmores House, Third Av CM18 6YL
☎ 01279 454959   📠 01279 626094
Times: Open all year, Tue-Fri 9.30-4.30 & Sat 10-12.30 & 1.30-4.30. Last admission 4.15pm. **Facilities:** P ♿ shop 🐕 Details not confirmed for 2003

HARWICH Map 05 TM23
HARWICH REDOUBT FORT
CO12 3TE (behind 29 Main Rd)
☎ 01255 503429   📠 01255 503429   `2 for 1`
e-mail: theharwichsociety@quista.net

The 180ft-diameter circular fort was built in 1808 in case of invasion by Napoleon. It has a dry moat and 8ft-thick walls, with 18 rooms for stores, ammunition and quarters for 300 men. The Redoubt is being restored by the Harwich Society, and contains three small museums. Ten guns can be seen on the battlements.
Times: Open May-Aug, daily 10-5; Sep-Apr, Sun only 10-4. **Fee:** £1 (accompanied ch free). **Facilities:** P (200yds) shop

HEDINGHAM
See Castle Hedingham

LAYER MARNEY Map 05 TL91
LAYER MARNEY TOWER
CO5 9US (off B1022 Colchester to Maldon road, signposted)
☎ 01206 330784   📠 01206 330884   `2 for 1`
e-mail: info@layermarneytower.co.uk

The tallest Tudor gatehouse in the country, intended to be the entrance to a courtyard which would have rivalled Hampton Court Palace. The death of Henry, the 1st Lord Marney, in 1523, and of his son in 1525, meant that the building work ceased before completion. The beautiful parish church lies within the grounds and a wildlife walk offers the chance to see a range of livestock.
Times: Open Apr-Sep, Mon-Fri 12-5, Sun 12-5 & BHs 11-5. **Fee:** * £3.50 (ch £2). Family ticket £10. Guided tour £4.75. Party 20+.
Facilities: P 🍴 ✕ licensed ♿ (ramps in garden and farm) toilets for disabled shop 🐕 (ex guide dogs & dogs on lead)

MISTLEY Map 05 TM13
MISTLEY TOWERS
CO11 1NJ (on B1352, 1.5m E of A137 at Lawford)

All that remains of the grand hall and church, designed by Robert Adam, are the lodges built in 1782 for the hall, and two square towers, topped with drums and domes which came from an earlier church.
Times: Open all reasonable times. Key available from Mistley Quay Workshops & Teashop. **Fee:** Free. **Facilities:** ♿ (exterior only) 🐕 (in certain areas)

NEWPORT Map 05 TL53
MOLE HALL WILDLIFE PARK
Widdington CB11 3SS (between Stansted & Saffron Walden, off B1383)
☎ 01799 540400   ≣ 01799 540400
e-mail: enquiries@molehall.co.uk
Times: Open all year, daily 10.30-6 (or dusk). (Closed 25 Dec). Butterfly House open mid Mar-Oct. **Facilities:** P ⏣ ♿ (Difficult in wet weather for wheelchairs) toilets for disabled shop garden centre ✱ (ex guide dogs) *Details not confirmed for 2003*

SAFFRON WALDEN Map 05 TL53
SAFFRON WALDEN MUSEUM
Museum St CB10 1JL (take B184 & follow signs to Saffron Walden)
☎ 01799 510333   ≣ 01799 510334
e-mail: museum@uttesford.gov.uk
Times: Open all year, Mar-Oct, Mon-Sat 10-5, Sun & BHs 2-5; Nov-Feb, Mon-Sat, 10-4.30, Sun & BHs 2-4.30. (Closed 24 & 25 Dec).
Facilities: P ♿ (ramped entrance,spare wheelchairs,stairlift to upper floor) toilets for disabled shop ✱ (ex guide dogs) *Details not confirmed for 2003*

SOUTHEND-ON-SEA Map 05 TQ88
SOUTHEND MUSEUM, PLANETARIUM & DISCOVERY CENTRE
Victoria Av SS2 6EW (take A127 or A13 towards town centre. Museum is adjacent to Southend Victoria Railway Station)
☎ 01702 434449   ≣ 01702 349806
e-mail: southendmuseum@hotmail.com

A fine Edwardian building housing displays of archaeology, natural history and local history, telling the story of man in the south-east Essex area. Also the only planetarium in the south east outside London. Ring for details of special events.
Times: Open Central Museum: Tue-Sat 10-5 (Closed Sun-Mon & BH); Planetarium: Wed-Sat, shows at 11, 2 & 4. **Fee:** * Central Museum free. Planetarium £2.25 (ch & pen £1.60). Family tickets £7. Party rates on request. **Facilities:** P (50mtrs) (disabled only behind museum) ♿ (planetarium not accessible, disabled access to centre) shop ✱ (ex guide dogs)

STANSTED Map 05 TL52
HOUSE ON THE HILL MUSEUM ADVENTURE
CM24 8SP (off B1383, in the centre of Stansted Mountfitchet)
☎ 01279 813567   ≣ 01279 816391
e-mail: gold@enta.net

A large, privately-owned toy museum, housed on two floors covering 7,000 sq. ft. A huge variety of toys, books and games from the late Victorian period up to the 1970s. There is a space display, Teddy Bears' picnic, Action Men, Sindy, Barbie, military displays and much more. Additional displays of film, theatre and television memorabilia are on show, plus end-of-the-pier slot machines.
Times: Open daily, 10-5; (closed for a few days over the Xmas period) **Fee:** £3.80 (ch under 14's £3, pen £3.50). Party 15+.
Facilities: P (charged) shop ✱ (ex guide dogs)

MOUNTFITCHET CASTLE & NORMAN VILLAGE
CM24 8SP (off B1383, in centre of village. 5 min from M11 junct 8)
☎ 01279 813237   ≣ 01279 816391
e-mail: gold@enta.net

Norman motte and bailey castle and village reconstructed as it was in Norman England of 1066, on its original historic site. A vivid illustration of village life in Domesday England, complete with houses, church, seige tower, seige weapons, and many types of animals roaming freely. Animated wax figures in all the buildings give historical information to visitors.
Times: Open daily, 16 Mar-16 Nov, 10-5. **Fee:** £5 (ch under 14's £4, pen £4). Party 15+.£4.50 (ch £3.50). **Facilities:** P (charged) ⏣ ♿ (laser commentaries) toilets for disabled shop ✱ (ex guide dogs)

TILBURY Map 05 TQ67
TILBURY FORT
No 2 Office Block, The Fort RM18 7NR (0.5 mile E off A126)
☎ 01375 858489

The largest English example of 17th-century military engineering, the fort originally dates from the earlier Tudor period, and is most famous for Queen Elizabeth I's review of her troops before the defeat of the Spanish Armada. It defended the country again in the 17th century against the Dutch and the French.
Times: Open all year, 29 Mar-Sep, daily 10-6 (Oct, daily 10-5); Nov-28 Mar, Wed-Sun 10-1, 2-4. (Closed 24-26 Dec & 1 Jan). **Fee:** * £2.90 (ch 5-15 £1.50, under 5's free, concessions £2.20). £1.30 to fire AA gun.
Facilities: ♿ shop ✱ (in certain areas)

WALTHAM ABBEY Map 05 TL30
LEE VALLEY PARK FARMS
Stubbings Hall Ln, Crooked Mile EN9 2EG (off B194)
☎ 01992 892781 & 892291
≣ 01992 892291   **2 for 1**

Two different views of farming methods. Hayes Hill Farm has a traditional-style farmyard and you can also look round Holyfield Hall Farm, a working commercial dairy and arable farm of some 700 acres. There are 140 Friesian cows, and milking takes place at 2.45pm every day. Booked guided tours are available.
Times: Open all year, Mon-Fri 10-4.30, wknds & BH 10-5.30. **Fee:** * £3.15 (concessions £2.10). **Facilities:** P ⏣ ♿ (graded concrete paths, signed routes) toilets for disabled shop

WALTHAM ABBEY GATEHOUSE, BRIDGE & ENTRANCE TO CLOISTERS

Beside the great Norman church at Waltham are the slight remains of the abbey buildings - bridge, gatehouse and part of the north cloister. The bridge is named after King Harold, founder of the abbey.
Times: Open any reasonable time. **Fee:** Free. **Facilities:**

Gloucestershire

Most of the Cotswolds lie in the county of Gloucestershire; limestone hills dotted with picturesque villages built from local stone, varying in hue from honey gold to silver grey. The large churches and substantial manor houses are a legacy of the medieval wool trade.

The bits of Gloucestershire outside the Cotswolds include the county town of Gloucester, the Regency spa town of Cheltenham and the countryside around the Severn estuary, the site of the Slimbridge wildfowl reserve. The county's other major natural feature is the Forest of Dean, a mining area exploited from Roman times until the 20th century.

Gloucester has plenty to see and do. The Victorian docks now house offices, shops, and cafés, while the canal is busy with pleasure craft.

Nearby Cheltenham is more upmarket, with Regency architecture and exclusive boutiques. The mineral spring was discovered in 1715 through the observation of pigeons coming and going. Pigeons are incorporated into the town's crest to this day, though Cheltenham is probably better known for horse-racing.

South of Cheltenham is the charming and rather less self-conscious Cirencester, the 'capital of the Cotswolds'. It was once an immensely powerful town known as Corinium by the Romans, and in those days was second only to Londinium. Little of its Roman heritage remains, although some replicas of ancient mosaics have been made.

Laurie Lee (1914-1997), a native of Slad near Stroud, wrote the classic novel *Cider With Rosie*, which explored his childhood in the 1920s among the rolling Cotswold hills. His carefree writing captures the spirit of the area.

Top: Owlpen Manor

EVENTS & FESTIVALS

February
7th-9th Cheltenham Folk Festival

March
11th-13th National Hunt Festival (Gold Cup Week), Cheltenham

April
4th-6th Cheltenham Festival of Literature Spring Weekend
26th-5th May Nailsworth Festival
tbc Wotton Arts Festival

May
1st-5th Cheltenham International Jazz Festival
2nd-5th Badminton Horse Trials
5th Cheese Roll, A46 nr Brockworth
7th-18th Cheltenham Competitive Festival, (provisional)
tbc Coleford Music & Arts Festival
tbc Robert Dover's Cotswold Olimpick Games, Dover's Hill, Chipping Coopers Hill

June
4th-8th Cheltenham Science Festival
13th-15th Three Counties Show, Malvern

July
4th-20th Cheltenham Fringe and Music Festivals
12th-13th Tewkesbury Medieval Festival
18th-20th Tewkesbury Water Festival
19th-20th Royal International Air Tattoo, RAF Fairford
26th-27th International Kite Festival
tbc Cotswold Show & Country Fair
tbc Gloucester Festival

August
1st-10th Gloucester Blues Festival
tbc Twyning to Tewkesbury Raft Race

September
6th Moreton Show
27th-28th The Malvern Autumn Show, Malvern

Gloucestershire

BERKELEY Map 03 ST69
BERKELEY CASTLE
GL13 9BQ (just off A38 midway between Bristol & Gloucester. From M5 take junct 14 or 15)
☎ 01453 810332
e-mail: berkeley.castle@ukf.net

Home of the Berkeleys for almost 850 years, the castle is a rambling and romantic fortress surrounded by 14ft thick walls, with a Norman keep, a great hall, medieval kitchens, and the dungeon where Edward II was murdered. Outside there are Elizabethan terraced gardens overlooking rolling countryside towards the River Severn. See also the beautiful butterfly house; an enclosed, tranquil glasshouse garden with hundreds of exotic butterflies in free flight among unusual plants and flowers.
Times: Open Apr-May, Tue-Sun 2-5; Jun, Tue-Sat 11-5, Sun 2-5; Jul-Aug, Mon-Sat 11-5, Sun 2-5; Sep, Tue-Sat 11-5, Sun 2-5. Oct, Sun only 2-5. Also open BH Mon 11-5. Last admission 30mins before closing. **Fee:** * Castle & Gardens: £5.70 (ch £3.10, pen £4.70). Family ticket (2 adult & 2 ch) £15.50. Gardens only £2 (ch £1). Party 25+. Butterfly farm £2 (ch & pen £1). School groups 80p each. Family ticket (2 adult & 2 ch) £5. **Facilities:** P shop (ex guide dogs)

JENNER MUSEUM
Church Ln, High St GL13 9BH (follow tourist signs from A38 to town centre, left into High St & left again)
☎ 01453 810631   01453 811690
e-mail: manager@jennermuseum.com
2 for 1

This beautiful Georgian house was the home of Edward Jenner, the discoverer of vaccination against smallpox. The house and the garden, with its Temple of Vaccinia, are much as they were in Jenner's day. The displays record Jenner's life as an 18th-century country doctor, his work and his interest in natural history.
Times: Open Apr-Sep, Tue-Sat 12.30-5.30, Sun 1-5.30. Oct, Sun 1-5.30. (Closed Mon, ex BH Mon 12.30-5.30). **Fee:** * £3 (ch £1.50, students & pen £2.30). Family ticket £7.50. Party 20+. **Facilities:** P toilets for disabled shop (ex guide dogs)

BOURTON-ON-THE-WATER Map 04 SP12
BIRDLAND PARK & GARDENS
Risssington Rd GL54 2BN (on A429)
☎ 01451 820480   01451 822398
e-mail: sb.birdland@virgin.net
Times: Open all year, Apr-Oct, daily 10-6; Nov-Mar, daily 10-4. Last admission 1hr before closing. (Closed 25 Dec). **Facilities:** P (adjacent) & toilets for disabled shop *Details not confirmed for 2003*

MODEL VILLAGE
Old New Inn GL54 2AF
☎ 01451 820467   01451 810236
e-mail: old_new_inn@compuserve.com
Times: Open all year 9-5.45 (summer), 10-dusk (winter). (Closed 25 Dec). **Facilities:** P licensed shop *Details not confirmed for 2003*

CHEDWORTH Map 04 SP01
CHEDWORTH ROMAN VILLA
Yanworth GL54 3LJ (3m NW of Fossebridge on A429)
☎ 01242 890256   01242 890544
e-mail: chedworth@smtp.ntrust.org.uk

The remains of a Romano-British villa, excavated 1864-66. Set in a beautiful wooded combe, there are fine 4th-century mosaics, two bath houses, and a temple with spring. The museum houses the smaller finds. Telephone for details of special events.
Times: Open 26 Feb-22 Mar, daily (ex Mon) 11-4; 23 Mar-20 Oct, daily (ex Mon) 10-5; 22 Oct-17 Nov, daily (ex Mon) 11-4. Closed Mon (ex BH Mon's). **Fee:** * £3.80 (ch £1.90). Family ticket £9.50. **Facilities:** P & (audio tour) toilets for disabled shop

CHELTENHAM Map 03 SO92
CHELTENHAM ART GALLERY & MUSEUM
Clarence St GL50 3JT (close to town centre)
☎ 01242 237431   01242 262334
e-mail: artgallery@cheltenham.gov.uk

The museum has an outstanding collection relating to the Arts and Crafts Movement, including fine furniture and exquisite metalwork. The Art Gallery contains Dutch and British paintings from the 17th century to the present day. The Oriental Gallery features pottery, costumes and treasures from the Ming Dynasty to the reign of the last Chinese Emperor. There is also a display about Edward Wilson who journeyed with Captain Scott in 1911-12, together with the history of Britain's most complete Regency town and archaeological treasures from the neighbouring Cotswolds. Special exhibitions are held throughout the year.
Times: Open all year, Mon-Sat 10-5.20, Sun 2-4.20. (Closed BHs & Etr Sun). **Fee:** Free. **Facilities:** P (500 metres) disabled parking on site & (handling tables; speech reinforcement system) toilets for disabled shop (ex guide dogs)

Details subject to change from March 2003. Please check before visiting.

Gloucestershire

HOLST BIRTHPLACE MUSEUM
4 Clarence Rd GL52 2AY (opposite gateway of Pittville Park. 10 min walk from town centre)
☎ 01242 524846 📠 01242 580182 **2 for 1**
e-mail: holstmuseum@btconnect.com

Gustav Holst, composer of *The Planets* was born at this Regency house in 1874. The museum contains unique displays on Holst's life, including his original piano. The rooms of the house have been carefully restored, each area evoking a different period in the history of the house from Regency to Edwardian times.
Times: Open Tue-Sat 10-4 (Closed Mon & Dec-Jan, ex pre-booked groups) **Fee:** * £2.50 (concessions £2). Family ticket (2 adults & 3 ch) £7 **Facilities:** P (250yds) (large print & braille guide, special hands-on tours) shop ✕ (ex guide dogs)

🏛 CIRENCESTER   Map 04 SP00
CORINIUM MUSEUM
Park St GL7 2BX (in town centre)
☎ 01285 655611 📠 01285 643286
e-mail: simone.clark@cotswold.gov.uk

Cirencester was the second largest town in Roman Britain and the Corinium Museum brings the period to life with full-scale reconstructions. Due to re-open in October 2003, the museum will boast a new Anglo-Saxon gallery, a new ground floor life-long learning centre, new displays on the Roman history and archaeology of Cirencester and the Cotswolds and new 18th and 19th century displays.
Times: Closed for refurbishment from Sep 2002 to Oct 2003. **Fee:** * £2.50 (ch £1, students £1, pen £2). Family ticket £5. Party. Fri after 3.30pm free admission. **Facilities:** P (440yds town centre) 🍴 ✕ licensed ♿ (large print & braille guide for exhibits) toilets for disabled shop 🛍

🏛 CLEARWELL   Map 03 SO50
CLEARWELL CAVES ANCIENT IRON MINES
GL16 8JR (1.5m S of Coleford town centre, off B4228 follow brown tourism signs)
☎ 01594 832535 📠 01594 833362 **2 for 1**
e-mail: jw@clearwellcaves.com

These impressive natural caves have also been mined since the earliest times for paint pigment and iron ore. Today visitors explore nine large caverns with displays of local mining and geology. Colour room where ochre pigments are still produced and blacksmith shop.
Times: Open Mar-Oct daily 10-5. Jan-Feb Sat-Sun 10-5. Christmas Fantasy 1-24 Dec, daily 10-5. **Fee:** * £3.80 (ch £2.40, concessions £3.20) Family ticket £11. **Facilities:** P 🍴 ♿ (hands-on exhibits, contact in advance) toilets for disabled shop ✕ (ex guide & hearing dogs) 🛍

🏛 CRANHAM   Map 03 SO81
PRINKNASH ABBEY AND POTTERY
GL4 8EX (on A46 between Cheltenham & Stroud)
☎ 01452 812066 📠 01452 812529
e-mail: bjnicholls@prinknash.fsnet.co.uk

Set in a large park, the old priory building is a 12th to 16th-century house, used by Benedictine monks and guests of Gloucester Abbey until 1539. It became an abbey for Benedictine monks from Caldey in 1928. Rich beds of clay were discovered when foundations were being dug for the new abbey building, and so the pottery was established, employing local craftspeople.
Times: Open all year. Abbey Church: daily 5am-8pm. Pottery: Mon-Sat 11-4.30 (Sun pm). Pottery shop & tearoom 9-5.30. (Closed Good Fri, 25 & 26 Dec). **Fee:** * Guided tour fee £2 (ch £1) Family ticket £5. **Facilities:** P 🍴 ♿ toilets for disabled shop

PRINKNASH BIRD & DEER PARK
GL4 8EX (M5 junct 11a, A417 Cirencester. Take 1st exit signposted A46 Stroud. Follow brown tourist signs)
☎ 01452 812727

Nine acres of parkland and lakes make a beautiful home for black swans, geese and other water birds. There are also exotic birds such as white and Indian blue peacocks and crown cranes, as well as tame fallow deer and pygmy goats. The Golden Wood is stocked with ornamental pheasants, and leads to the reputedly haunted monks' fishpond, which contains trout. Also an 80-year old, free-standing, 16ft-tall wendy house in the style of a Tudor house.
Times: Open all year, daily 10-5 (4pm in winter). Park closes at 6pm (5pm in winter). (Closed 25-26 Dec, 1 Jan & Good Fri). **Fee:** * £3.70 (ch £1.90, pen £2.90). Party 10+ £2.90 (ch £1.70, pen £1.90). Prices under review. **Facilities:** P 🍴 shop ✕

🏛 DEERHURST   Map 03 SO82
ODDA'S CHAPEL
(off B4213 near River Severn at Abbots Court SW of parish church)

This rare Saxon chapel was built by Earl Odda and dedicated in 1056. When it was discovered, it had been incorporated into a farmhouse. It has now been carefully restored.
Times: Open any reasonable time. **Fee:** *Free*. **Facilities:** ♿

🏛 DYRHAM   Map 03 ST77
DYRHAM PARK
SN14 8ER (8m N of Bath, 2m from M4 junct 18)
☎ 0117 937 2501
e-mail: wfijew@smtp.ntrust.org.uk

Dyrham Park is a splendid William and Mary house, with interiors which have hardly altered since the late 17th century. It has contemporary Dutch-style furnishings, Dutch pictures and blue-and-white Delft ware. Around the house is an ancient park with fallow deer.
Times: Open 28 Mar-2 Nov. Contact for details. **Fee:** £7.90 (ch £3.90). Family £19.50. Grounds only £3 (ch £2). Family £7. Park only ticket on days when house & gardens closed: £2 (ch £1). Winter: park & domestic rooms £4 (ch £2). Party. **Facilities:** P 🍴 ✕ licensed ♿ (Braille & audio guides, stairclimber, free bus from carpark toilets for disabled shop ✕ (ex in dog walk area). 🛍

GLOUCESTER
Map 03 SO81

CITY MUSEUM & ART GALLERY
Brunswick Rd GL1 1HP
☎ 01452 396131 01452 410898
e-mail: city.museum@gloucester.gov.uk
Times: Open all year, Mon-Sat 10-5. (Also Jul-Sep, Sun 10-4).
Facilities: P (adjacent) & (lift suitable only for manual wheelchairs) toilets for disabled shop ✈ *Details not confirmed for 2003*

FOLK MUSEUM
99-103 Westgate St GL1 2PG
☎ 01452 526467 01452 330495
e-mail: irenez@gloscity.gov.uk
Times: Open all year, Mon-Sat 10-5. (Also Jul-Sep, Sun 10-4). Open BH Mon. **Facilities:** P (200yds) & (parking on request, ramps) shop ✈ (ex guide dogs) *Details not confirmed for 2003*

NATIONAL WATERWAYS MUSEUM
Llanthony Warehouse, The Docks GL1 2EH (follow signs for historic docks off M5 and also within the city, situated to the south of the city)
☎ 01452 318054 01452 318066
e-mail: info@nwm.demon.co.uk
Times: Open all year, daily 10-5 (Closed 25 Dec). **Facilities:** P (charged) & (wheelchair, lifts, limited access to floating exhibits) toilets for disabled shop ✈ (ex guide dogs) *Details not confirmed for 2003*

NATURE IN ART
Wallsworth Hall, Tewkesbury Rd, Twigworth GL2 9PA (2m N of Gloucester on A38, from village follow tourist signs)
☎ 01452 731422 01452 730937
e-mail: ninart@globalnet.co.uk

2 for 1

Nature is the theme at this gallery, and there are many outstanding exhibits including sculpture, tapestries and ceramics. There is a comprehensive 'artist in residence' programme for ten months of the year, and events include regular monthly talks, film showings and a full programme of temporary exhibitions and art courses. Work from over 60 countries spanning 1,500 years is included in the collection which has been specially commended twice in the National Heritage Museum of the Year Awards.
Times: Open all year, Tue-Sun & BH's 10-5. Mon by arrangement. (Closed 24-26 Dec). **Fee:** * £3.35 (ch, pen & students £2.75, ch under 8 free). Family ticket £10. Party 15+. **Facilities:** P ⌑ & (lift & ramps at entrance) toilets for disabled shop ✈ (ex guide dogs)

ROBERT OPIE COLLECTION-MUSEUM OF ADVERTISING & PACKAGING
Albert Warehouse, Gloucester Docks GL1 2EH (follow signs for Gloucester 'Historic Docks')
☎ 01452 302309 01452 308507
e-mail: sales@robertopie.telme.com
Times: Open all year, daily, 10-6; winter Tue-Fri 10-5, Sat & Sun 10-6. (Closed 25-26 Dec). **Facilities:** P (charged) ⌑ & shop ✈ (ex guide dogs) *Details not confirmed for 2003*

GREAT WITCOMBE
Map 03 SO91

WITCOMBE ROMAN VILLA
(off A417, 0.5m S of reservoir in Witcombe Park)

Several mosaic pavements and evidence of a hypocaust have been preserved in the remains of this large Roman villa.
Times: Open any reasonable time. Guided tours may be available contact 01451 862000. **Fee:** *Free.* **Facilities:** P ⌑

GUITING POWER
Map 04 SP02

COTSWOLD FARM PARK
GL54 5UG (signposted off B4077 from M5 Junct 9)
☎ 01451 850307 01451 850423
e-mail: info@cotswoldfarmpark.co.uk

At the Cotswold Farm Park there are nearly 50 breeding herds and flocks of the rarest British breeds of sheep, cattle, pigs, goats, horses, poultry and waterfowl. Set on the very top of the Cotswold Hills, this is the perfect opportunity to get to know a Bagot goat, cuddle a Cotswold lamb, stroke a mighty Longhorn ox, and admire generations of our living agricultural heritage. New born lambs and goat kids can be seen from April to May, spring calves in May, foals and sheep shearing in June and piglets throughout the year. Lambing takes

continued

Gloucestershire

place in front of visitors from mid March to the end of April and milking during July, August and September. **Times:** Open 23 Mar-15 Sep, daily 10.30-5 (also open wknds only untill end Oct 10.30-4). **Fee:** * £4.75 (ch £3, pen £4.25). Family ticket £14.50. **Facilities:** 🅿 ☕ ♿ (ramps, wheelchair to let) toilets for disabled shop 🐕 (ex guide dogs) 🎟

🏛 HAILES   Map 04 SP02
HAILES ABBEY
GL54 5PB (2m NE of Winchcombe off B4632)
☎ 01242 602398

This Cistercian abbey was, in the Middle Ages, one of the main centres of pilgrimage in England because it possessed a phial reputed to contain some of Christ's blood. Good medieval sculpture and floor tiles are displayed in the museum.
Times: Open all year, 29 Mar-Sep, daily 10-6 (Oct, daily 10-5); **Fee:** * £2.80 (ch under 5 free, ch £1.40 & concessions £2.10). **Facilities:** 🅿 ♿ shop 🐕 ♿ ♻

🏛 LITTLEDEAN   Map 03 SO61
LITTLEDEAN HALL
GL14 3NR
☎ 01594 824213   📠 01594 824213
e-mail: sheila@lttledean.com
Times: Open - House, Grounds & Archaeological site, Apr-Oct, daily 11-5. **Facilities:** 🅿 🐕 (ex in grounds) *Details not confirmed for 2003*

🏛 LYDNEY   Map 03 SO60
DEAN FOREST RAILWAY
Norchard Railway Centre, New Mills, Forest Rd GL15 4ET (At Lydney, turn off the Gloucester to Chepstow (A48) road and follow brown tourist signs to Norchard Railway Centre, on B4234 Lydney-Parkend road)
☎ 01594 843123 (info) & 845340   📠 01594 845840

Just north of Lydney lies the headquarters of the Dean Forest Railway where a number of steam locomotives, plus lots of coaches, wagons and railway equipment are on show and guided tours are available by prior arrangement. Standard gauge passenger service on steam haulage runs from Norchard to Lydney Junction and back to Norchard, the diesel train runs from Lydney Junction to Tufts and back to Lydney Junction.
Times: Open all year, daily for static displays. Steam days: Oct, Sun only; Jun-Sep, Wed & Sun; Aug, Thu & Sat. Diesel only days: Jun-Jul, Sat only. (Additional days & school holidays telephone 01594 843420 for details). **Fee:** No entry fee on non passenger opening days. Fares on standard Steam days £5.50 (ch 5-16 £3.50 & pen £4.50, under 5's free on standard days only). Various fares during Special events.
Facilities: 🅿 ☕ ♿ (specially adapted coach for wheelchairs, phone for details) toilets for disabled shop

---

| 2 for 1 | This symbol indicates which attractions have chosen to participate in our new 2-for-1 voucher scheme. |

🏛 MICKLETON   Map 04 SP14
HIDCOTE MANOR GARDEN
Chipping Campden GL55 6LR (1m E of B4632)
☎ 01386 438333   📠 01386 438817
Times: Open 23 Mar-end May, Aug to 3 Nov daily (ex Thu/Fri) but open Good Fri. Jun/Jul daily ex Fri. Mar-end Sep 10.30-6.30, Oct 10.30-5.30. Last admission 1hr before closing. **Facilities:** 🅿 ☕ ✖ licensed ♿ (limited due to stone paths) toilets for disabled shop garden centre 🐕 ♻ *Details not confirmed for 2003*

KIFTSGATE COURT GARDEN
Mickleton GL55 6LN (0.5m S off A46, adjacent Hidcote NT garden)
☎ 01386 438777   📠 01386 438777
e-mail: kiftsgte@aol.com

Kiftsgate Garden is spectacularly set on the edge of the Cotswold Escarpment, with views over the Vale of Evesham. It contains many rare plants collected by three generations of women gardeners, including the largest rose in England, the R. Filipes Kiftsgate.
Times: Open Apr-May & Aug-Sep; Wed, Thu, Sun & BH Mon 2-6. Jun-Jul Wed, Thu, Sat & Sun 12-6. **Fee:** * £4.30 (ch £1). **Facilities:** 🅿 ☕ garden centre 🐕 (ex guide dogs)

🏛 MORETON-IN-MARSH   Map 04 SP23
BATSFORD ARBORETUM
Admissions Centre, Batsford Park GL56 9QB (1.5m NW, off A44 from Moreton-in-Marsh)
☎ 01386 701441
📠 01386 701829
e-mail: batsarb@batsfound.freeserve.co.uk   **2 for 1**

Batsford Arboretum has one of the largest private collections of trees in Great Britain and wonderful views across the Vale of Evenlode. Visitors can stroll amongst the spring flowers that cascade down the hillside, and see many rare and unusual trees. There is an impressive display of colour during autumn, and peace and tranquillity are ever present. View the Buddha and cave, and try and negotiate the waterfall without getting too wet.
Times: Open Feb-mid Nov, daily 10-5; mid Nov-Jan, wknds only 10-4. **Fee:** £4 (ch under 4-15 (inc) £1, con £3). Party 12+. **Facilities:** 🅿 ☕ ♿ (some steep & slippery paths not suited to wheelchairs) toilets for disabled shop garden centre 🎟

COTSWOLD FALCONRY CENTRE
Batsford Park GL56 9QB (1m W of Moreton-in-Marsh on A44)
☎ 01386 701043
e-mail: geoffdalton@yahoo.co.uk   **2 for 1**

Conveniently located by the Batsford Park Arboretum, the Cotswold Falconry gives daily demonstrations in the art of falconry. The emphasis here is on breeding and conservation, and eagles, hawks, owls and falcons can be seen.
Times: Open mid Feb-mid Nov, 10.30-5.30. (Last admission 5pm). **Fee:** £4 (ch 4-15 £2.50, concession £3.50). Joint ticket with Batsford Arboretum £6.50 (ch 4-15 £3, concession £6). **Facilities:** 🅿 ♿ (no steps, wide doorways) toilets for disabled shop garden centre 🐕 (ex on leads in car park) 🎟

Gloucestershire

SEZINCOTE
GL56 9AW (1.5m out of Moreton-in-Marsh on A44, Evesham road)

The Indian-style house at Sezincote was the inspiration for Brighton Pavilion; its charming water garden adds to its exotic aura and features trees of unusual size.
Times: Open: House, May-Jul & Sep, Thu & Fri 2.30-6. Garden only, all year (ex Dec) Thu, Fri & BH Mon 2-6 or dusk if earlier. **Fee:** * House & garden £5. Garden only £3.50 (ch £1 under 5 free). Children not allowed in the House. Groups by appointment only. **Facilities:** P ✱ (ex guide dogs)

NEWENT   Map 03 SO72
THE NATIONAL BIRDS OF PREY CENTRE
GL18 1JJ (follow A40, right onto B4219 towards Newent. Then follow brown tourist signs)
☎ 0870 9901992   📠 01531 821389
e-mail: jpj@nbpc.demon.co.uk

Trained birds can be seen at close quarters in the Hawk Walk and the Owl Courtyard and there are also breeding aviaries, a gift shop, bookshop, picnic areas, coffee shop and children's play area. Birds are flown three times daily in summer and winter, giving an exciting and educational display. There are over 110 aviaries on view with 85 species. The centre leads the world in the field of captive breeding.
Times: Open Feb-Oct, daily 10.30-5.30 or dusk if earlier. Also open in Nov-Dec for evening events. **Fee:** £5.95 (ch £3.65, pen £4.95). Family ticket £17. Party 12+. **Facilities:** P 🍴 ♿ (special tours available, pre-booking required) toilets for disabled shop ✱ 🛒

THE SHAMBLES
Church St GL18 1PP (close to town centre near church)
☎ 01531 822144   📠 01531 821120

Cobbled streets, alleyways, cottages and houses set in over an acre with display shops and trades, even a tin chapel and cottage garden all helping to recreate the feel and atmosphere of a small Victorian town.
Times: Open 15 Mar-end Oct, Tue-Sun & BH's 10-5 (or dusk); Nov-Dec wknds only. **Fee:** * £3.60 (ch £1.95, pen £2.95). **Facilities:** P (100yds) 🍴 ♿ toilets for disabled shop 🛒

NORTHLEACH   Map 04 SP11
COTSWOLD HERITAGE CENTRE
Fosseway GL54 3JH (12m E of Cheltenham on A429 at Northleach crossroads)
☎ 01451 860715   📠 01451 860091   **2 for 1**
e-mail: simone.clark@cotswold.gov.uk

The story of everyday rural life in the Cotswolds is told here, in the remaining buildings of the Northleach House of Correction. There's a unique collection of Gloucestershire harvest-wagons; a 'below stairs' gallery showing a dairy, kitchen and laundry; and the work of local craftsmen and artists is promoted through exhibitions, workshops and demonstrations.
Times: Open 23 Mar-3 Nov, Mon-Sat 10.30-5; Sun 12-5. Open at other times by arrangement only. **Fee:** £2.50 (ch & student £1 & pen £2). Family ticket £5. Party. **Facilities:** P 🍴 ♿ (wheelchair, special parking, photos of unaccessable areas) toilets for disabled shop 🛒

KEITH HARDING'S WORLD OF MECHANICAL MUSIC
Oak House, High St GL54 3ET (at crossroads of A40 & A429)
☎ 01451 860181   📠 01451 861333
e-mail: keith@mechanicalmusic.co.uk
Times: Open all year, daily 10-6. Closed 25-26 Dec. **Facilities:** P ♿ toilets for disabled shop ✱ (ex guide dogs) Details not confirmed for 2003 🛒

OWLPEN   Map 03 ST79
OWLPEN MANOR
GL11 5BZ (3m E of Dursley off B4066, follow brown tourist signs)
☎ 01453 860261   📠 01453 860819
e-mail: sales@owlpen.com
Times: Open Apr-15 Oct, Tue-Sun & BH Mon, 2-5. **Facilities:** P 🍴 ✘ licensed ✱ Details not confirmed for 2003 🛒

PAINSWICK   Map 03 SO80
PAINSWICK ROCOCO GARDEN
GL6 6TH (on B4073 0.5m NW of Painswick)
☎ 01452 813204   📠 01452 814888
e-mail: info@rococogarden.co.uk

This beautiful Rococo garden (a compromise between formality and informality) is the only one of its period to survive complete. There are ponds, woodland walks, a maze, kitchen garden and herbacious borders, all set in a Cotswold valley famous for snowdrops in the early spring. Ring for details of special events.
Times: Open 10 Jan-Oct, daily 11-5. **Fee:** £3.60 (ch £1.80, pen £3.30). **Facilities:** P 🍴 ✘ licensed shop garden centre 🛒

SLIMBRIDGE   Map 03 SO70
WWT SLIMBRIDGE
GL2 7BT (off A38, signed from M5 junct 13 & 14)
☎ 01453 890333   📠 01453 890827   **2 for 1**
e-mail: slimbridge@wwt.org.uk

Slimbridge is home to the world's largest collection of exotic wildfowl - and the only place in Europe where all six types of flamingo can be seen. Up to 8,000 wild

continued

Gloucestershire

birds winter on the 800-acre reserve of flat fields, marsh and mudflats on the River Severn.
Times: Open all year, daily from 9.30-5 (winter 4pm). (Closed 25 Dec). **Fee:** * £6.30 (ch £3.80, pen £5). Family ticket £16.40. Party 10+.
Facilities: 🅿 💺 ✖ licensed ♿ (wheelchair loan, tapes for blind, hearing pads & loops) toilets for disabled shop 🐕 (ex guide/hearing dogs) ☕

🏛 SNOWSHILL   Map 04 SP03
SNOWSHILL MANOR
WR12 7JU (3m SW of Broadway, off A44)
☎ 01386 852410 📠 01386 852410   `2 for 1`
e-mail: snowshill@nationaltrust.org.uk

A traditional Cotswold manor house, best known for Charles Paget Wade's collections of craftmanship and design, including musical instruments, clocks, toys, bicycles, weavers' and spinners' tools, and Japanese armour.
Times: Open 29 Mar-3 Nov daily (ex Mon/Tue) 12-5. (Open BH Mon & Mon in July & Aug). 4 Sep-3 Nov Garden, Shop & Restaurant open Wed-Sun 11-5. **Fee:** £6 (ch £3). Family ticket £15. Grounds only £3.50 (ch £1.50). **Facilities:** 🅿 ✖ licensed ♿ (Braille guides, audio tapes) toilets for disabled shop 🐕 (ex guide dogs) 🌿 ☕

🏛 SOUDLEY   Map 03 SO61
DEAN HERITAGE CENTRE
Camp Mill GL14 2UB (on B4287, in Forest of Dean)
☎ 01594 822170 📠 01594 823711
e-mail: deanmuse@btinternet.com
Times: Open all year, daily, Apr-Sep 10-6, last admission 5.30, Oct-Mar 10-4. (Closed 24-26 Dec). **Facilities:** 🅿 💺 ♿ (help from establishment staff) toilets for disabled shop 🐕 (ex guide dogs) *Details not confirmed for 2003* ☕

🏛 TETBURY   Map 03 ST89
CHAVENAGE HOUSE
GL8 8XP (2m NW of Tetbury signposted off B4014. 1m SE of Stroud off A46)
☎ 01666 502329 & 01453 832700   `2 for 1`
📠 01453 836778
e-mail: info@chavenage.com

Built in 1576, this unspoilt Elizabethan house contains stained glass from the 16th century and earlier with some good furniture and tapestries. The owner during the Civil War was a Parliamentarian, and the house contains Cromwellian relics. In more recent years, the house has been the location for *Grace and Favour, Poirot, The House of Elliot, Berkeley Square, Casualty* and *Cider with Rosie*. Tours of the house are enlivened by ghost stories.
Times: Open May-Sep, Thu, Sun & BHs 2-5. Also Etr Sun & Mon. Other days by appointment only. **Fee:** £5 (ch £2.50). **Facilities:** 🅿 ♿ 🐕 (ex guide dogs)

🏛 ULEY   Map 03 ST79
ULEY TUMULUS
(3.5m NE of Dursley on B4066)

This 180ft Neolithic long barrow is popularly known as Hetty Pegler's Tump. The mound, surrounded by a wall,

is about 85ft wide. It contains a stone central passage, and three burial chambers.
Times: Open any reasonable time. **Fee:** *Free.* **Facilities:** ♿

🏛 WESTBURY ON SEVERN   Map 03 SO71
WESTBURY COURT GARDEN
GL14 1PD (9m SW of Gloucester on A48)
☎ 01452 760461
e-mail: westbury@smtp.ntrust.org.uk
Times: Open Mar-Jun daily (ex Mon/Tue) but open BH Mon's. Jul-Aug, daily 10-6. Sep-27Oct, Wed-Sun, 10-6. Other months by appointment. **Facilities:** 🅿 ♿ (braille guide, w/chair available) toilets for disabled shop 🐕 (ex guide dogs) 🌿 *Details not confirmed for 2003*

🏛 WESTONBIRT   Map 03 ST88
WESTONBIRT ARBORETUM
GL8 8QS (3m S Tetbury on A433)
☎ 01666 880220 📠 01666 880559

Begun in 1829, this arboretum contains one of the finest and most important collections of trees and shrubs in the world. There are 18,000 specimens, planted from 1829 to the present day, covering 600 acres of landscaped Cotswold countryside. Magnificent displays of rhododendrons, azaleas, magnolias and wild flowers, and ablaze with colour in the autumn from the national collection of Japanese maples.
Times: Open all year, daily 10-8 or sunset. Visitor centre & shop all year. (Closed Xmas & New Year) **Fee:** * £5 (ch £1, pen £4).
Facilities: 🅿 💺 ✖ ♿ (electric & manual wheelchair for loan, telephone to book) toilets for disabled shop garden centre ☕

🏛 WINCHCOMBE   Map 04 SP02
SUDELEY CASTLE & GARDENS
GL54 5JD (B4632 to Winchcombe, Castle is signposted from town)
☎ 01242 602308 📠 01242 602959
e-mail: marketing@sudeley.org.uk

Times: Open daily 3 Mar-28 Oct, Grounds, Gardens, exhibition, shop & plant centre 10.30-5.30. Apr-28 Oct, Castle apartments & Church & restaurant 11-5. **Facilities:** 🅿 ✖ licensed ♿ (partial access to disabled) toilets for disabled shop garden centre 🐕 (by request on arrival) *Details not confirmed for 2003* ☕

Greater Manchester

A conurbation in the northwest of England, Greater Manchester incorporates the towns of Bolton, Oldham, Rochdale, Salford, Stockport and Wigan, with the vibrant city of Manchester as its administrative headquarters.

Manchester was founded in Roman times, and developed during the 17th century as a textile town, becoming the centre of the English cotton industry. Magnificent Victorian Gothic public buildings are reminders of Manchester's prosperous heyday. These include the town hall designed by Alfred Waterhouse which takes up one side of Albert Square. Also look out for the recently restored Royal Exchange, – severely damaged in a IRA bombing of 1996, which left some 75,000 sq ft of buildings to be reconstructed – the Athenaeum, The Theatre Royal, and the Free Trade Hall. The Castlefield area, 15 minutes' walk southwest of the town hall, has been redeveloped in recent times to include a reconstruction of the Roman fort that once stood on the site. This area is also home to the world's longest-running soap opera – *Coronation Street*.

Another feature is the Manchester Ship Canal, completed in 1894, linking the Mersey with the sea and bringing ocean-going vessels into Manchester and enabling the city to compete with its rival, Liverpool.

The city of Manchester is alive with a vibrant youth culture (it has England's largest student population), a flourishing club scene, and a whole range of multi-cultural festivals and events. Musical groups from Manchester include Magazine, Oasis, New Order and James. To take in the atmosphere, take a stroll around Britain's biggest Chinatown (between Charlotte Street and Princess Street), or wander down to Rusholme to take in the tempting aromas of curry houses and browse among the sari shops, Asian grocers, and Indian sweet shops.

Top: Albert Square

EVENTS & FESTIVALS

January
26th Rochdale District Annual Brass Band Contest
tbc Chinese New Year Celebrations
tbc Winter Ales Festival

February
7th-9th Manchester Championship Dog Show, G-Mex Centre

May
2nd-5th X.TRAX on the Streets

June
14th-15th Greater Manchester Youth Games, Wigan
15th-29th Manchester Jazz Festival, (provisional)

July
5th Unity Festival, Chorlton Park
7th Italian Procession, through city centre to St John's Cathedral, Salford
19th-20th North Manchester Mela, Heaton Park
26th-28th Chadkirk Festival, Stockport
tbc Manchester Show
tbc National Children's Art Day, Manchester Museum

August
1st-3rd Catalan Fever, Manchester city centre
9th Bramhall Horticultural Show

October
18th-26th International Short Film Festival, various venues
tbc Manchester Food & Drink Festival, city-wide

November
23rd Manchester District Annual Brass Band Contest

Greater Manchester   93

ALTRINCHAM   Map 07 SJ78
DUNHAM MASSEY
WA14 4SJ (3m SW of Altrincham (off A56), off M6 junct 19 or off M56 junct 7, then follow brown signs)
☎ 0161 941 1025   ▤ 0161 929 7508
e-mail: mdmjxf@smtp.ntrust.org.uk

A fine 18th-century house, garden and park, home of the Earls of Stamford until 1976. The house contains fine furniture and silverware, and some thirty rooms, including the library, billiard room, fully-equipped kitchen, butler's pantry and laundry. The garden is on an ancient site with waterside plantings, mixed borders and fine lawns. There is also a 300-acre deer park. Telephone for details of special events.
Times: Open: Park open all year. House open Apr-Oct, 12-5 (11 Sun & BH Mon, closes at 4 during Oct). Garden Apr-Oct, 11-5.30 (closes 4.30 in Oct). Last entry to house & Gardens 30mins before closing time. **Fee:** * House & Garden £5.50 (ch £2.75). House only £3.50 (ch £1.75). Garden only £3.50 (ch £1.75). Family ticket £13.75. Park only, £3 per car. **Facilities:** ▣ (charged) ✘ licensed ♿ (loan of batricar/wheelchairs, lift, braille guide, parking) toilets for disabled shop ✖ (ex on lead in Park) ♨ ☕

ASHTON-UNDER-LYNE   Map 07 SJ99
CENTRAL ART GALLERY
Central Library Building, Old St OL6 7SG
☎ 0161 342 2650
e-mail: portland.basin@mail.gov.uk

Set in a fine Victorian Gothic building, the Central Art Gallery has three areas, each of which offers a varied programme of temporary exhibitions. The range covers painting, sculpture and textiles.
Times: Open all year, Tue, Wed & Fri 10-5; Thu 1-7.30 & Sat 9-4. **Fee:** Free. **Facilities:** ▣ ♿ toilets for disabled shop ✖ (ex guide dogs)

MUSEUM OF THE MANCHESTER REGIMENT
The Town Hall, Market Place OL6 6DL (in town centre, follow signs for museum)
☎ 0161 342 3078 & 0161 342 3710
▤ 0161 343 2869
e-mail: portland.basin@mail.tameside.gov.uk

The social and regimental history of the Manchesters is explored at this museum, tracing the story back to its origins in the 18th century. The Manchesters fought in both World Wars, the Boer War, and the Crimea.
Times: Open all year, Mon-Sat, 10-4. (Closed Sun). **Fee:** Free. **Facilities:** ▣ (50yds) (pay & display) ♿ toilets for disabled shop ✖ (ex guide dogs)

PORTLAND BASIN MUSEUM
Portland Place OL7 0QA (off A635)
☎ 0161 343 2878   ▤ 0161 343 2869
e-mail: portland.basin@mail.gov.uk

Exploring the social and industrial history of Tameside, this museum is part of the rebuilt Ashton Canal Warehouse, originally dating from 1834. Visitors can walk around a 1920s street, dress up in old hats and gloves, steer a virtual canal boat, and see the original canal powered waterwheel that once drove the warehouse machinery.
Times: Open all year, Tue-Sun 10-5. (Closed Mon, ex BH's) **Fee:** Free. **Facilities:** ▣ ♿ (Wheelchair, lift, loop system) toilets for disabled shop ✖ (ex guide dogs)

BRAMHALL   Map 07 SJ88
BRAMALL HALL & PARK
SK7 3NX (from A6 turn right at Blossoms public house through Davenport village then turn right - signposted)
☎ 0161 485 3708   ▤ 0161 486 6959
Times: Open all year, Good Fri-Sep Mon-Sat 1-5, Sun 11-5; Oct-New Year's Day Tue-Sat 1-4, Sun 11-4; 2 Jan-Good Fri Sat & Sun 12-4. Closed 25-26 Dec. **Facilities:** ▣ (charged) ☕ ♿ (access for wheelchair users) toilets for disabled shop ✖ (ex guide dogs) Details not confirmed for 2003 ☜

MANCHESTER   Map 07 SJ89
CITY ART GALLERY
Mosley St/Princess St M2 3JL
☎ 0161 234 1456   ▤ 0161 236 7369
e-mail: cityart@mcrl.poptel.org.uk
Times: Gallery now reopened after expansion scheme. Unfortunately at the time of going to print we have not received confirmation of new details. **Facilities:** Details not confirmed for 2003

GALLERY OF COSTUME
Platt Hall, Rusholme M14 5LL (situated in Platt Fields Park, access from Wilmslow Rd. 2m S of city centre)
☎ 0161 224 5217   ▤ 0161 256 3278

With one of the most comprehensive costume collections in Great Britain, this gallery makes captivating viewing. Housed in a fine Georgian mansion, the displays focus on the changing styles of everyday fashion and accessories over the last 400 years. Contemporary fashion is also illustrated. Because of the vast amount of material in the collection, no one period is permanently illustrated.
Times: Open Tue-Sun 10-4 (5pm during summer). Also open BH Mon's. **Fee:** Free. **Facilities:** ▣ ♿ shop ✖ (ex guide dogs)

JOHN RYLANDS LIBRARY
150 Deansgate M3 3EH (in city centre, A56. Next to Manchester Evening News building)
☎ 0161 834 5343   ▤ 0161 834 5574
e-mail: spcoll72@fs1.li.man.ac.uk

Founded as a memorial to Manchester cotton-magnate and millionaire John Rylands, this is a public library, and also the Special Collections Division of the John Rylands University Library of Manchester. Internationally renowned, it extends to two million books, manuscripts and archival items representing some 50 cultures and ranging in date from the third millennium BC to the present day.
Times: Open all year, Mon-Fri 10-5.30, Sat 10-1. (Closed Sun, BH & Xmas-New Year). **Fee:** Free. **Facilities:** ▣ (400yds) (pay and display) shop ✖ (ex guide dogs by arrangement)

Greater Manchester

MANCHESTER MUSEUM
The University, Oxford Rd M13 9PL (S of city centre on B5117)
☎ 0161 275 2634   📠 0161 275 2676
e-mail: dot.fenton@man.ac.uk/museum
Times: Open all year, Mon-Sat 10-5, Sun & BHs 11-4. Phase 2 of a major refurbishment is due to be completed by Jun 2002. **Facilities:** 🅿 (350mtrs) ♿ (Provision for disabled telephone in advance) shop ✈ (ex guide dogs) *Details not confirmed for 2003*

MANCHESTER UNITED MUSEUM & TOUR CENTRE
Sir Matt Busby Way, Old Trafford M16 0RA (2m from city centre, off A56)
☎ 0161 868 8631   📠 0161 868 8861   **2 for 1**
e-mail: tours@manutd.co.uk

This museum was opened in 1986 and is the first purpose-built British football museum. It covers the history of Manchester United in words, pictures, sound and vision, from its inception in 1878 to the present day.
Times: Open daily 9.30-5 (open until 1/2hr before kick off on Match Days). (Closed some days over Xmas & New Year) **Fee:** * Stadium tour & Museum: £8.50 (ch & pen £5.75) Family ticket £23.50. Museum only: £5.50 (ch & pen £3.75) Family ticket £15.50. **Facilities:** 🅿 🍴 ✕ licensed ♿ (wheelchair, audio visual scrips, part of tour not accessible) toilets for disabled shop ✈ (ex dogs only) 🛍

THE MUSEUM OF SCIENCE AND INDUSTRY IN MANCHESTER
Liverpool Rd, Castlefield M3 4FP (follow brown tourist signs from city centre)
☎ 0161 832 2244 & 0161 832 1830
📠 0161 833 1471
e-mail: marketing@msim.org.uk

This museum is housed in the buildings of the world's oldest passenger railway station. Colourful galleries packed full of fascinating facts and amazing artefacts bring the past to life. Walk away from your own shadow in Xperiment! The mind bending science centre, see wheels of industry turning in the Power Hall, and the planes that made flying history in the Air and Space Hall. A programme of changing exhibitions.
Times: Open all year, daily 10-5. Last admission 4.30. (Closed 24-26 Dec). **Fee:** Free. **Facilities:** 🅿 (charged) ✕ licensed ♿ (lifts, wheelchair loan service) toilets for disabled shop ✈ (ex guide dogs) 🛍

MUSEUM OF TRANSPORT
Boyle St, Cheetham M8 8UW (museum adjacent to Queens Rd bus depot. 1.25m N of city centre)
☎ 0161 205 2122   📠 0161 205 2122   **2 for 1**
e-mail: Gmts.enquire@btinternet.com

This museum is a must-see for fans of public transport! Among the many interesting exhibits are more than 80 beautifully restored buses and coaches from the region - the biggest collection in the UK. Displays of old photographs, tickets and other memorabilia complement the vehicles, some of which date back to 1890. Please telephone for details of special events.

Times: Open all year, Wed, Sat, Sun & BH 10-5 ex Xmas. **Fee:** * £3 (ch u5 free, ch 5-15 & pen £1.75, registered disabled, UB40 free). Family ticket £9 (2ad+3ch). Adult season ticket (unlimited visits for 6 months) £8, ch & pen season ticket £6, family season ticket £20.
Facilities: 🅿 🍴 ♿ toilets for disabled shop 🛍

THE WHITWORTH ART GALLERY
The University of Manchester, Oxford Rd M15 6ER (follow brown tourist signs, on Oxford road on B5117)
☎ 0161 275 7450   📠 0161 275 7451
e-mail: whitworth@man.ac.uk

The gallery houses an impressive range of modern and historic drawings, prints, paintings and sculpture, as well as the largest collection of textiles and wallpapers outside London and an internationally famous collection of British watercolours. An innovative programme of touring exhibitions and tour lectures, workshops and concerts.
Times: Open Mon-Sat 10-5, Sun 2-5. (Closed Good Fri & Xmas-New Year). **Fee:** Free. **Facilities:** 🅿 🍴 ✕ licensed ♿ (wheelchair available, induction loop, Braille lift buttons) toilets for disabled shop ✈ (ex guide dogs)

🏛 PRESTWICH   Map 07 SD80
HEATON HALL
Heaton Park M25 2SW
☎ 0161 773 1231 or 0161 234 1456
📠 0161 236 2880
Times: Open Etr-end Oct, but phone for time details on 0161-234 1456. **Facilities:** 🅿 (charged) ♿ (occasional 'touch tours'. Phone for details) toilets for disabled shop ✈ (ex guide dogs) *Details not confirmed for 2003*

🏛 SALFORD   Map 07 SJ89
THE LOWRY
Pier Eight, Salford Quays M50 3AZ (from M60 junct 12 for M602. Salford Quays 0.25m from M602 junct 3, follow Lowry signs)
☎ 0161 876 2000   📠 0161 876 2001   **2 for 1**
e-mail: info@thelowry.com

The Lowry proves to be a lot more than just an art gallery – everything from West End plays to live bands, famous comedians to ballet. And with a restaurant, stylish

continued

Greater Manchester 95

waterside café-bars and gift shops it gives you the opportunity to make a day of your visit.

Times: Open daily from 10am. (Closed 25 Dec). **Fee:** Free. **Facilities:** P (charged) ☕ ✗ licensed ♿ toilets for disabled shop 🐕 (ex guide dogs) 🎥

SALFORD MUSEUM & ART GALLERY
Peel Park, Crescent M5 4WU (from N leave M60 junct 13, A666. From S follow signs from end of M602. Museum on A6)
☎ 0161 736 2649   ▤ 0161 745 9390
e-mail: salford.museum@salford.gov.uk

The museum features a reconstruction of a 19th-20th century northern street with original shop fronts. There are temporary exhibitions and the lifetimes gallery, featuring audio, IT zones, a spectacular Pickington's display and lots of hands-on activities.
Times: Open all year, Mon-Fri 10-4.45, Sat & Sun 1-5. (Closed Good Fri, Etr Sat, 25 & 26 Dec, 1 Jan). **Fee:** Free. **Facilities:** P ☕ ♿ (Braille & large print labels & visitor packs, hearing loop) toilets for disabled shop 🐕 (guide dogs) 🎥

🏛 STALYBRIDGE   Map 07 SJ99
ASTLEY CHEETHAM ART GALLERY
Trinity St
☎ 0161 338 2708
e-mail: portland.basin@mail.tameside.uk

Built as a gift to the town in 1901 by mill owner John Frederick Cheetham, this one-time lecture hall has been an art gallery since 1932 when Cheetham left his collection to the town. Among the works are Italian paintings from the Renaissance, British masters such as Cox and Burne-Jones, and more recent gifts such as works by Turner and local artist Harry Rutherford.
Times: Open all year, Mon-Tue, Wed & Fri 1-7.30; Sat 9-4. **Fee:** Free.
Facilities: P shop 🐕 (ex guide dogs)

🏛 UPPERMILL   Map 07 SD90
SADDLEWORTH MUSEUM & ART GALLERY
High St OL3 6HS (From M62 E exit at junct 22 or from M62 W exit at junct 21. On A670)
☎ 01457 874093   ▤ 01457 870336

Based in an old mill building next to the Huddersfield

MUSEUM of TRANSPORT
Boyle Street, Cheetham, Manchester M8 8UW
Tel/Fax: 0161 205 2122

A trip down memory lane

Over 80 buses, coaches and trams representing over a century of road public transport in Greater Manchester.

Special events including a Vintage vehicle rally, themed displays, a weekend for people with disabilities and participation in the National Heritage Weekend.

The Museum has tearooms, shop, facilities for the disabled. A small exhibits area and archive and research facilities.

canal, the museum explores the history of the Saddleworth area. Wool weaving is displayed in the 18th-century Weaver's Cottage and the Victoria Mill Gallery. The textile machinery is run regularly by arrangement.
Times: Open all year, Nov-late Mar, daily 1-4; late Mar-Oct, Mon-Sat 10-5, Sun 12-5. **Fee:** * £2 (concessions £1) Family ticket £4. **Facilities:** P ♿ (stairlift, ramps, braille & large print guides, wheelchair) toilets for disabled shop 🐕 (ex guide dogs) 🎥

🏛 WIGAN   Map 07 SD50
WIGAN PIER
Trencherfield Mill WN3 4EF (follow brown tourist signs from motorway)
☎ 01942 323666   ▤ 01942 701927   **2 for 1**
e-mail: wigan.pier@wiganmbc.gov.uk

Wigan Pier is a journey never to be forgotten. Part museum, part theatre, it is a mixture of entertainment and education. Step back in time at 'The Way We Were' heritage centre, visit Trencherfield Mill and The Machinery Hall, and then the newest attraction the Museum of Memories. Other on-site attractions include walks, talks and boat trips.
Times: Open all year, Mon-Thu 10-5; Sat & Sun 11-5. Also open Good Fri. (Closed 25-26 Dec, 1 Jan & Fri). **Fee:** * £7.50 (concessions £5.95). Family ticket £21.95 (2 adult & 2 concessions). **Facilities:** P ☕ ✗ licensed ♿ toilets for disabled shop 🐕 (ex guide dogs) 🎥

Hampshire

EVENTS & FESTIVALS

February
24th-28th Children's Festival (theatre, arts, workshops) Winchester

June
tbc Butser Festival of Flight, Portsmouth
tbc Kite Festival, Southampton
tbc Power in the Park, pop concert, Southampton
tbc Southsea Spectacular, Southsea Common

July
4th-6th Hat Fair (oldest street fair in England), Winchester
4th-6th Southampton Balloon & Flower Festival, The Common, Southampton
4th-13th Winchester Festival (multi-arts festival)
25th-27th Netley Marsh Steam Engine Rally, Southampton
25th-10th August Basingstoke Festival
tbc Gay Pride Festival, Mayflower Park, Southampton
tbc New Forest Show
tbc Southampton Carnival, Mayflower Park/City Centre

August
tbc Kite Festival, Southsea
tbc Portsmouth & Southsea Show, Southsea Common

September
13th Romsey Show, Broadlands Park, Romsey
tbc Southampton International Boat Show, Southampton

November
tbc Bonfire Night Firework Spectacular, Cosham
tbc Winchester Grand Firework Display

Hampshire is mainly rural with a gentle landscape and coastal cities – Portsmouth and Southampton – that enjoy a proud maritime history.

Portsmouth has been an important naval base since the 12th century, and Southampton has long been associated with the romance of the ocean liner. Both cities were badly bombed in World War II. These days they are both ideal for shopping, nights out and fans of maritime history. Portsmouth has the 16th-century Mary Rose, while Southampton was the port of departure for the ill-fated Titanic in 1912.

A more attractive destination is the charming town of Lyndhurst at the heart of the glorious New Forest. Recently celebrating its 900th anniversary, the Forest is a huge expanse of woodland, heath and hills set aside as a royal hunting ground by William the Conqueror in 1079, and covers some 93,000 acres. Now millions visit every year. 'Forest' can seem a bit of a misnomer as large areas are quite open and covered only by heather and gorse. Wildlife flourishes, and walkers can see red, fallow, roe and muntjac deer, as well as badgers, adders, and the famous ponies. Lyndhurst was home to Alice Hargreaves, (née Liddell) the inspiration for Alice in Lewis Carroll's world-famous books. Her grave is behind St Michael and All Angels Church.

Winchester is a town with a historic atmosphere and a vibrant present. The cathedral dominates the town once used as Alfred the Great's capital. William the Conqueror claimed his crown here, and Jane Austen is buried in the nave. The town is well known for street entertainment.

Hampshire has many picturesque villages. Alresford has the Watercress Line, Silchester has nearby Roman remains including an amphitheatre, and Old Basing has the delightful River Loddon and the remains of Basing House, once the largest private house in England.

Top: Deer in the New Forest

Hampshire

ALDERSHOT
Map 04 SU85

AIRBORNE FORCES MUSEUM
Browning Barracks, Queens Av GU11 2BU (from motorway take A325 to Aldershot then take next left)
☎ 01252 349619   📠 01252 349203
e-mail: airborneforcesmuseum@army.mod.uk.net
Times: Open all year, Mon-Fri 10-4.30 (last admission 3.45), Sat-Sun & BH 10-4. (Closed Xmas). **Facilities:** P & (wheelchair ramps) shop ✗ (ex guide dogs) *Details not confirmed for 2003*

ALDERSHOT MILITARY MUSEUM
Evelyn Woods Rd, Queens Av GU11 2LG (A331 exit for 'Aldershot Military Town (North)', attraction near North Camp)
☎ 01252 314598   📠 01252 342942   **2 for 1**
e-mail: musmim@hants.gov.uk
Follow the development of the 'Home of the British army' and the 'Birthplace of British aviation' through brand new displays. Also discover the fascinating local history of Aldershot and Farnborough including first British powered flight.
Times: Open Mar-Oct, daily 10-5; Nov-Feb, daily 10-5. **Fee:** * £2 (ch & unemployed £1, pen £1.50) **Facilities:** P & shop ✗ (ex guide dogs)

ALRESFORD
Map 04 SU53

WATERCRESS LINE
The Railway Station SO24 9JG (stations at Alton & Alresford signposted off A31)
☎ 01962 733810   📠 01962 735448   **2 for 1**
e-mail: info@watercressline.co.uk

The Watercress Line runs through ten miles of rolling scenic countryside between Alton and Alresford. All four stations are 'dressed' in period style, and there's a locomotive yard and picnic area at Ropley.
Times: * Open May-Sep Tue-Thu & wknds; Jan-Apr & Oct wknds only.
Fee: Unlimited travel for the day, £9 (ch £2, pen £8). Family ticket £20. **Facilities:** P (charged) 🍴 ✗ licensed & (ramp access to trains) shop (at Alresford, Alton & Ropley stations)

COME AND FIRE UP YOUR IMAGINATION!

Regular steam services run from Alresford or Alton every weekend from March to October, or weekdays during May to September. Call us for details on any of our services on 01962 733810.

Fancy learning to drive a steam engine? For an unforgettable present, contact us for a gift voucher, or to arrange a date!

Privately hire your own train, make your venue a talking point! Why not try our Real Ale trains for a pub crawl with a difference, or treat yourself to dinner on one of our evening dining trains.

Mid-hants WATERCRESS LINE
HAMPSHIRE'S HERITAGE RAILWAY

The Railway Station, Alresford,
Hampshire SO24 9JG
Tel: 01962 733 810
Fax: 01962 735 448

Talking Timetable
01962 734 866

AMPFIELD
Map 04 SU42

THE SIR HAROLD HILLIER GARDENS & ARBORETUM
Jermyns Ln SO51 OQA (3m NE of Romsey, signposted off A3090 & B3057)
☎ 01794 368787   📠 01794 368027
Times: Open all year, Apr-Oct wkdays 10.30-6, wknds & BHs 9.30-6. Nov-Mar daily 10.30-5 or dusk if earlier (closed Xmas). **Facilities:** P ✗ licensed & (all ability path) toilets for disabled garden centre ✗ (ex guide dogs) *Details not confirmed for 2003*

ANDOVER
Map 04 SU34

FINKLEY DOWN FARM PARK
SP11 6NF (signposted from A303 & A343, 1.5m N of A303 and 2m E of Andover)
☎ 01264 352195   📠 01264 363172
e-mail: a1finkley@aol.com

A wide range of farm animals and poultry can be seen here, including some rare breeds. The pets corner has tame, hand-reared animals that can be stroked and petted. There are also a Countryside Museum, housed in a barn, Romany caravans and rural bygones to see, an adventure playground and a large picnic area.
Times: Open 17 Mar-3 Nov, daily 10-6. Last admission 5pm. **Fee:** * £4.50 (ch £3.50, pen £4). Family ticket £15. **Facilities:** P 🍴 & toilets for disabled shop ✗ (ex guide dogs)

Hampshire

ASHURST
Map 04 SU31
LONGDOWN DAIRY FARM
Longdown SO40 4UH (off A35 between Lyndhurst & Southampton)
☎ 023 8029 3326   📠 023 8029 3376
e-mail: annette@longdown.uk.com
Times: Open Etr-Oct, daily. **Facilities:** 🅿 ♿ toilets for disabled shop 🐕 (kennels provided) *Details not confirmed for 2003*

BASINGSTOKE
Map 04 SU65
MILESTONES - HAMPSHIRE'S LIVING HISTORY MUSEUM
Basingstoke Leisure Park, Churchill Way West RG21 6YR (M3 junct 6, clockwise around ringroad to Town Centre West rdbt, follow Leisure Park signs)
☎ 01256 477766   📠 01256 477784
e-mail: jacqui.hendy@hants.gov.uk

Milestones brings Hampshire's recent past to life through stunning period street scenes and exciting interactive areas, all under one roof. Nationally important collections of transport, technology and everyday life are presented in an entertaining way. Staff in period costumes, mannequins and sounds will bring the streets to life.
Times: Open Tue-Fri & BH's 10-5, Sat-Sun 11-5 (Closed 24-26 Dec & 1 Jan). Prices may increase, please telephone for details. **Fee:** * £6.60 (ch £3.50, concessions £5.25). Family ticket (2 adults & 2 ch) £16. Group discounts 17+. **Facilities:** 🅿 🍴 ♿ (induction loops & audio trails) toilets for disabled shop 🐕 (ex guide dogs)

BEAULIEU
Map 04 SU30
BEAULIEU : NATIONAL MOTOR MUSEUM
SO42 7ZN (M27 junct 2, A326, B3054, then follow tourist signs)
☎ 01590 612345   📠 01590 612624
e-mail: info@beaulieu.co.uk

Set in the heart of William the Conqueror's New Forest, on the banks of the Beaulieu River, stands this 16th-century house. It has become most famous as the home of the National Motor Museum. The site also contains the picturesque abbey building ruins, which have an exhibition on life in the middle ages, and various family treasures and memorabilia. In 2002-2003 a display of 'James Bond' boats is also on view.

Times: Open all year - Palace House & Gardens, National Motor Museum, Beaulieu Abbey & Exhibition of Monastic Life, May-Sep 10-6; Oct-Apr 10-5. (Closed 25 Dec). **Fee:** * £11.95 (ch £6.95, pen £9.95). Family ticket £33.95. **Facilities:** 🅿 🍴 ♿ (ramp access to most areas, lift to upper level) toilets for disabled shop

BISHOP'S WALTHAM
Map 04 SU51
BISHOP'S WALTHAM PALACE
SO32 1DH (on A333)
☎ 01489 892460

Bishop's Waltham Palace was once among the greatest stately homes of the medieval period. Although mostly destroyed in the Civil War, remains are still impressive.
Times: Open all year, 29 Mar-Sep, daily 10-6 (Oct, daily 10-5) **Fee:** * £2.50 (ch 5-15 £1.20, under 5's free, concessions £1.70). **Facilities:** 🅿 ♿ 🐕 (in certain areas)

BOLDRE
Map 04 SZ39
SPINNERS
School Ln SO41 5QE (off A337, between Brockenhurst & Lymington)
☎ 01590 673347   **2 for 1**

The garden has been entirely created by the owners since 1960. It has azaleas, rhododendrons, camellias and magnolias, interspersed with primulas, blue poppies and other woodland and ground-cover plants. The nursery is famed for its rare trees, shrubs and plants.
Times: Open 14 Apr-14 Sep, daily 10-5. Other times on application. 14 Sep-14 Apr Nursery and part of garden open, free entry. **Fee:** £2 **Facilities:** 🅿 garden centre 🐕 (ex guide dogs)

BREAMORE
Map 04 SU11
BREAMORE HOUSE & COUNTRYSIDE
SP6 2DF (turn off A338, between Salisbury & Fordingbridge and follow signs for 1m)
☎ 01725 512468   📠 01725 512858   **2 for 1**
e-mail: breamore@ukonline.co.uk

The handsome manor house was completed in around 1583 and has a fine collection of paintings, china and tapestries. The museum has good examples of steam

continued

Hampshire 99

engines, and uses reconstructed workshops and other displays to show how people lived and worked a century or so ago. There is also a children's playground.
Times: Open Apr, Tue, Wed, Sun & Etr, May-Jul & Sep, Tue-Thu & Sat, Sun & all BH, Aug, daily 2-5.30 (Countryside Museum 1pm). **Fee:** * Combined tickets £5 (ch £3.50). Party £4.50 each. **Facilities:** 🅿 💷 ♿ (ramps, parking by house) toilets for disabled shop ✂ (ex guide dogs)

🏛 BUCKLER'S HARD   Map 04 SU40
BUCKLER'S HARD VILLAGE & MARITIME MUSEUM
SO42 7XB (M27 junct 2, A326, B3054 then follow tourist signs to Beaulieu & Buckler's Hard)
☎ 01590 616203   📠 01590 612624
e-mail: info@bucklershard.co.uk

An interesting port of call, the historic and picturesque shipbuilding village of Buckler's Hard is where ships from Nelson's fleet were built. After visiting the Buckler's Hard Story and authentically reconstructed 18th-century Historic Cottages savour the sight and sounds of the countryside on a ramble along the Riverside Walk or enjoy a cruise on the Beaulieu River on *'Swiftsure'* during the summer months.
Times: Open all year, Etr-Sep 10.30-5, winter 11-4. (Closed 25 Dec).
Fee: * £4 (ch & pen £3). **Facilities:** 🅿 💷 ✗ licensed ♿ shop 🛍

🏛 BURGHCLERE   Map 04 SU46
SANDHAM MEMORIAL CHAPEL
RG20 9JT (4m S Newbury off A34)
☎ 01635 278394   📠 01635 278394
e-mail: sandham@ntrust.org.uk

This red brick chapel was built in the 1920s for the artist Stanley Spencer to fill with murals inspired by his experiences in WWI. Influenced by Giotto's Avena Chapel in Padua, Spencer took five years to complete what is arguably his finest achievement. The chapel is set amongst lawns and orchards with views over Watership Down.
Times: Open Apr-Oct, Wed-Sun, 11.30-5 & BH Mon. Nov & Mar, Sat & Sun 11.30-4. Dec-Feb by appointment only. **Fee:** * £2.80 (ch £1.40).
Facilities: 🅿 ♿ (Braille guide, large print guide, ramps) ✂ (ex on leads in garden) 🐕 🛍

🏛 CHAWTON   Map 04 SU73
JANE AUSTEN'S HOUSE
GU34 1SD (1m SW of Alton, in centre of village)
☎ 01420 83262   📠 01420 83262
e-mail: museum@janeausten.demon.co.uk

Jane Austen lived and wrote here from 1809 to 1817. Restored to look as it would have done in the early

---

JANE AUSTEN'S HOUSE
CHAWTON, ALTON, HANTS
Telephone: 01420 83262

17th-century house where Jane Austen lived from 1809 to 1817

OPEN 11 – 4.00pm
1st Mar–30 Nov: daily
Dec, Jan and Feb: Sats and Suns only, and 27 Dec– 2 Jan
(Closed Christmas Day and Boxing Day)
Adult £4, Child 50p
Groups and Concessions £3.00
Refreshments available in village   Bookshop

1800s, with items such as the author's donkey cart and writing table to be seen.

Jane Austen's House

Times: Open daily Mar-Nov; Dec-Feb wknds only. Also open 27 Dec-1 Jan & Feb half term. **Fee:** £4 (ch 8-18 50p, pen & students £3). Party £3 each. **Facilities:** 🅿 (300yds) ♿ (wheelchair ramp) toilets for disabled shop ✂ (ex guide dogs & service dogs) 🛍

🏛 EXBURY   Map 04 SU40
EXBURY GARDENS & RAILWAY
Exbury Estate Office SO45 1AZ (from M27 junct 2, 3m from Beaulieu, off B3054)
☎ 023 8089 1203   📠 023 8089 9940

A 200-acre landscaped woodland garden on the east

continued

bank of the Beaulieu River, with one of the finest collections of rhododendrons, azaleas, camellias and magnolias in the world - as well as many rare and beautiful shrubs and trees. A labyrinth of tracks and paths enable you to explore, as well as the popular steam railway that winds its way through the gardens.
Times: Open 2 Mar-3 Nov, daily 10-5.30; 9 Nov-8 Dec, wknds only 10-4. **Fee:** * £3.50-£5 (ch under 10 free, ch 10-15 £2.50-£3, pen £3-£4.50). Train £2-£2.50. **Facilities:** P X licensed & (free wheelchair loans & access maps, buggy tours £3) toilets for disabled shop garden centre

FAREHAM   Map 04 SU50
ROYAL ARMOURIES FORT NELSON
Downend Rd PO17 6AN (from M27 junct 11, follow brown tourist signs for Royal Armouries)
☎ 01329 233734   ▪ 01329 822092
e-mail: fnenquiries@armouries.org.uk

Wonderfully restored 19-acre Victorian fort overlooking Portsmouth Harbour that commands spectacular views. Built in the 1860s to deter a threatened French invasion there are secret tunnels, underground chambers and grass ramparts to explore. Home to the Royal Armouries' collection of artillery, part of the National Museum of Arms and Armour, with over 350 pieces from the Romans to the infamous Iraqi supergun.
Times: Open all year, daily. Closed Xmas & Boxing Day. **Fee:** Free. **Facilities:** P ▪ & (access guide, ramps, audio guide, induction loop) toilets for disabled shop X (ex guide & hearing dogs)

GOSPORT   Map 04 SZ69
EXPLOSION! MUSUEM OF NAVAL FIREPOWER
Priddy's Hard PO12 4LE (A32 and follow signs)
☎ 023 9250 5600   ▪ 023 9250 5605   `2 for 1`
e-mail: info@explosion.org.uk

This museum is set in the heritage area of Priddy's Hard in Gosport on the shores of Portsmouth Harbour, and tells the story of naval firepower from the days of gunpowder to modern missiles. Come face to face with the atom bomb, the Exocet missile and the Gatling Gun and follow the fascinating story of the men and woman of the Royal Navy. Walk round the buildings that were a state secret for 200 years and discover the Grand Magazine, an amazing vault once packed full of gunpowder – now a stunning multimedia film show.
Times: Open all year, Apr-Oct, daily 10-5.30; Nov-Mar, daily 10-4.30. (Closed 25-26 Dec & 1 Jan) **Fee:** * £5 (ch £3, pen £4). Family ticket £13 **Facilities:** P ▪ & toilets for disabled shop X (ex guide dogs)

ROYAL NAVY SUBMARINE MUSEUM & HMS ALLIANCE
Haslar Jetty Rd PO12 2AS (M27 junct 11, follow signs for Submarine Museum)
☎ 023 9252 9217 & 9251 0354   `2 for 1`
▪ 023 9251 1209
e-mail: rnsubs@rnsubmus.co.uk

The great attraction of this museum is the chance to see inside a submarine, and there are guided tours of HMS Alliance, as well as displays exploring the development of submarines. Two periscopes from HMS Conqueror can be seen in the reconstruction of a nuclear submarine control room, giving panoramic views of Portsmouth Harbour. A gallery shows the development of submarine weapons from the tiny torpedo to the huge polaris nuclear missile and the Navy's first submarine is back on display.
Times: Open all year, Apr-Oct 10-5.30; Nov-Mar 10-4.30. (Closed 24 Dec-1 Jan). Allow 3 hrs for visit. Last tour 1 hour before closing. **Fee:** * £4 (ch & pen £2.75). Family ticket £11 (2 adults & 4 ch). Party 12+. Discounted entry scheme "Defence of the Realm", in association with Southern Military Museums. **Facilities:** P ▪ & (information in Braille, lift to upper gallery) toilets for disabled shop X (ex guide dogs)

HARTLEY WINTNEY   Map 04 SU75
WEST GREEN HOUSE GARDENS
West Green RG27 8JB (off A30, at Phoenix Green take sign to West Green, along Thackhams Lane. House last left)
☎ 01252 844611   ▪ 01252 844611

The gardens surrounding this Queen Anne house date back 300 years. Restoration work is ongoing and there will be ten acres of garden and pleasure grounds - four walled gardens, a lake, follies, green theatre, nymphaeum, mixed border and potager.
Times: Open May-Aug, Wed-Sun 11-4. **Fee:** £4.50 (ch under 7 free). **Facilities:** P ▪ & (most areas accessible) toilets for disabled shop X (ex guide dogs)

HAVANT   Map 04 SU70
STAUNTON COUNTRY PARK
Middle Park Way PO9 5HB (off B2149, between Havant & Horndean)
☎ 023 9245 3405   `2 for 1`
▪ 023 9249 8156
e-mail: amanda.fallbrown@hants.gov.uk

This colourful Victorian park offers a wonderful range of attractions for all ages. Meet and feed the friendly animals at the Ornamental Farm where you'll find a broad range of animals from llama and shirehorses to pigs and pigmy goats. Explore the Victorian tropical

continued

Hampshire

glasshouses with exotic flowers from around the world, including the giant Amazonian waterlily (summer months only). 1000 acres of parkland and lakes to explore.
Times: Open 10-5 (4pm winter). **Fee:** * £4.10 (ch £3.10, pen £3.70). Family ticket (2 adults & 2 ch) £13.40. **Facilities:** P ⬛ & (wheelchair for visitors, most areas accessible) toilets for disabled shop ✘ (dogs in parkland only) 🗨

🏛 HIGHCLERE Map 04 SU45
Highclere Castle & Gardens
RG20 9RN (4.5m S of Newbury, off A34)
☎ 01635 253210   📠 01635 255315
e-mail: theoffice@highclerecastle.co.uk
Times: Open Jul-Aug (may occasionally be subject to closure during this period), Mon-Fri & Sun 11-5 (last admission 4pm); Sat 11-3.30 (last admission 2.30pm) **Facilities:** P ⬛ ✘ licensed & (wheelchair available) toilets for disabled shop ✘ (ex guide dogs) *Details not confirmed for 2003* 🗨

🏛 HINTON AMPNER Map 04 SU62
Hinton Ampner Garden
SO24 0LA (off A272, 1m W of Bramdean)
☎ 01962 771305   📠 01962 793101
e-mail: shigen@smtp.ntrust.org.uk

Set in superb Hampshire countryside, this delightful garden combines formality of design with informality of planting. Full of scent and colour, the walks open up into unexpected vistas. The house, restored after a fire in 1960, displays a fine collection of Regency furniture and Italian paintings.
Times: Open Garden: Apr-Sep, Sat-Wed 11-5. House: Apr-Sep, Tue & Wed 1.30-5 (also Aug, Sat & Sun 1.30-5). **Fee:** * House and Garden £5, garden only £4. **Facilities:** P ⬛ & (Braille guides, special parking, Map for wheelchair users) toilets for disabled ✘ ♿

🏛 HURST CASTLE Map 04 SZ38
Hurst Castle
SO4 0FF (on Pebble Spit S of Keyhaven)
☎ 01590 642344
Times: Open Apr-Oct, daily 10-5 or dawn till dusk **Facilities:** ⬛ ✘ (in certain areas) ‡ *Details not confirmed for 2003*

🏛 LIPHOOK Map 04 SU83
Bohunt Manor
GU30 7DL (on old A3)
☎ 01428 727936   📠 01428 727936
e-mail: eddie@bohuntmanor.freeserve.co.uk

Bohunt includes woodland gardens with a lakeside walk, a water garden, roses, tulips and herbaceous borders, and a collection of ornamental ducks, white swans, and geese. Several unusual trees and shrubs include a handkerchief tree and a Judas tree. The property has been given to the Worldwide Fund for Nature.
Times: Open all year, daily 10-5. **Fee:** * £1.50 (ch free, pen £1). **Facilities:** P ✘

Hollycombe Steam Collection
Iron Hill, Midhurst Rd GU30 7LP (1.5m SE Liphook on Midhurst road, follow brown tourist signs)
☎ 01428 724900   📠 01428 723682
e-mail: hollycombe@talk21.com

2 for 1

A comprehensive collection of working steam power, including a large Edwardian fairground, three railways, including one with spectacular views of the South Downs, traction engine hauled rides, steam agricultural machinery, sawmill, pets corner and even a paddle steamer engine.
Times: Open Apr-13 Oct, Sun & BH's; 21 Jul-26 Aug, daily 12-5. Rides open from 1. **Fee:** * £7.50 (ch & pen £6). Saver ticket (2 ad & 2ch) £24. Party 15+. **Facilities:** P ⬛ & shop ✘ (guide dogs on request) 🗨

🏛 LYMINGTON Map 04 SZ39
Braxton Gardens
Braxton Courtyard, Lymore Ln SO41 0TX (leave A337 at Everton onto B3058 then turn left into Lymore Ln, Braxton Courtyard on left)
☎ 01590 642008
Times: Open daily 10-5. Shorter opening hours in winter, please telephone for details. **Facilities:** P ⬛ & shop garden centre ✘ (ex guide dogs) *Details not confirmed for 2003* 🗨

🏛 LYNDHURST Map 04 SU30
New Forest Museum & Visitor Centre
Main Car Park, High St SO43 7NY (leave M27 at Cadnam & follow A337 to Lyndhurst. Museum signposted)
☎ 023 8028 3914   📠 023 8028 4236
e-mail: nfmuseum@lineone.net

The story of the New Forest - history, traditions, character and wildlife, told through an audio-visual show and exhibition displays. With life-size models of Forest characters, and the famous New Forest embroidery.
Times: Closed for redevelopment Sep 2002-Jun 2003. Museum expected to re-open Jun-Jul 2003. **Fee:** *Prices not confirmed for 2003.* **Facilities:** P & toilets for disabled shop 🗨

MARWELL
Map 04 SU52
MARWELL ZOOLOGICAL PARK
Colden Common SO21 1JH (M3 junct 11 or M27 junct 5. Zoo on B2177)
☎ 01962 777407   📠 01962 777511
e-mail: marwell@marwell.org.uk

Devoted to the conservation and breeding of rare wild animals, Marwell has a worldwide reputation. There is an encounter village where animals can be approached and stroked by children. Covering 100 acres of parkland, the collection includes over 1000 animals, and some of the species here no longer exist in the wild. There is also a gift shop and many attractions for younger children, including a children's farmyard, Tropical World, Penguin World and road trains.
Times: Open all year, daily (ex 25 Dec), 10-6 (in summer), 10-4 (in winter). Last admission 90 min before closing. **Fee:** £9.50-£10 (ch 3-14 £7, pen £8.50). Family ticket (2 adults and 2 ch) £31.50-£32.50. **Facilities:** 🅿 💷 ✕ licensed ♿ (tours for visually impaired, disabled groups by arrangement) toilets for disabled shop 🐕 🍴

MIDDLE WALLOP
Map 04 SU23
MUSEUM OF ARMY FLYING
SO20 8DY (on A343, between Andover & Salisbury)
☎ 01980 674421   📠 01264 781694
e-mail: et@flyingmuseum.org.uk
Times: Open all year, daily 10-4.30. Closed week prior to Xmas. Evening visits by special arrangement. **Facilities:** 🅿 💷 ✕ licensed ♿ (lifts to upper levels) toilets for disabled shop 🐕 (ex guide dogs or in grounds) *Details not confirmed for 2003* 🍴

MINSTEAD
Map 04 SU21
FURZEY GARDENS
SO43 7GL (1m S of junct A31/M3 Cadnam off A31 or A337 near Lyndhurst)
☎ 023 8081 2464 & 023 8081 2297   📠 023 8081 2297   `2 for 1`
e-mail: mtp@milestonenet.co.uk

A large thatched gallery is the venue for refreshments and displays of local arts and crafts, and the eight acres of peaceful glades which surround it include winter and summer heathers, rare flowering trees and shrubs and a mass of spring bulbs. There is a 16th-century cottage, lake, and the nursery, run by the Minstead Training Project for Young People with Learning Disabilities, sells a wide range of produce.
Times: Gardens open daily 10-5 (or dusk if earlier). (Closed Xmas). Gallery Open: Mar-Oct, 10-5. **Fee:** * Mar-Oct: £3.50 (ch £1.50, pen £2.80) Family £9. Nov-Feb: £1.50 (ch 50p, pen £1) Family £3. Party 10+. **Facilities:** 🅿 💷 ♿ (garden access for wheelchair visitors with assistance) toilets for disabled shop garden centre 🐕 (guide dogs)

MOTTISFONT
Map 04 SU32
MOTTISFONT ABBEY GARDEN
SO51 0LP (4.5m NW Romsey, 1m W of A3057)
☎ 01794 340757   📠 01794 341492
e-mail: smogen@smtp.ntrust.org.uk
Times: Open Garden & Grounds: 17 Mar-4 Nov, Sat-Wed 11-6 (or dusk if earlier). 9-24 June special opening daily from 11-8.30. Last admission to grounds 1hr before closing. House: 1-5. Derek Hill Picture Collection: Sun-Tue 1-5. **Facilities:** 🅿 💷 ✕ licensed ♿ (Braille guide, wheelchair available, volunteer driven buggy) toilets for disabled shop garden centre 🐕 🍴 *Details not confirmed for 2003* 🍴

NETLEY
Map 04 SU40
NETLEY ABBEY
SO31 5FB (4m SE of Southampton, facing Southampton Water)
☎ 023 80453076

A romantic ruin, set among green lawns and trees, this 13th-century Cistercian abbey was founded by Peter des Roches, tutor to Henry III. Nearby is the 19th-century, Gothic Netley Castle.
Times: Open any reasonable time. **Fee:** Free. **Facilities:** 🅿 ♿ 🐕 ♯

NEW MILTON
Map 04 SZ29
SAMMY MILLER MOTORCYCLE MUSEUM
Bashley Cross Rd BH25 5SZ (signposted off A35)
☎ 01425 620777   📠 01425 619896   `2 for 1`
e-mail: info@sammymiller.co.uk

With machines dating back to 1900, some are the only surviving examples of their type. The Racing Collection features World Record breaking bikes and their history, including the first bike to lap a Grand Prix Course at over 100 miles per hour. Special events include marquee days.
Times: Open all year, daily 10-4.30. **Fee:** * £3.50 (ch £1.50). **Facilities:** 🅿 💷 ♿ toilets for disabled shop 🐕 🍴

OLD BASING
Map 04 SU65
BASING HOUSE
Redbridge Ln RG24 7HB (signed from Basingstoke ring road)
☎ 01256 467294   📠 01256 326283   `2 for 1`

The largest house of Tudor England, almost entirely destroyed by Parliament during a two-year siege ending in 1645. Built on the site of a Norman castle in 1530, the ruins include a 300ft-long tunnel. There is a re-creation of a garden of 1600 and exhibitions

continued

Hampshire

showing the history of the house. A fine 16th-century barn stands nearby.

Times: Open Apr-Sep, Wed-Sun & BH 2-6. **Fee:** * £1.50 (ch & pen 70p). Registered disabled free. **Facilities:** P & (disabled parking by prior arangement) toilets for disabled shop

OWER   Map 04 SU31
PAULTONS PARK
SO51 6AL (exit M27 junct 2, near junct A31 & A36)
☎ 023 8081 4442   📠 023 8081 3025
e-mail: info@paultons.co.uk

Paultons Park offers a great day out for all the family with over 40 different attractions. Many fun activities include Stinger Roller coaster, bumper boats, 6-lane astroglide, teacup ride, raging river ride log flume, Pirate Ship Swingboat, Dragon Ride Roundabout and Viking Boats Water Ride. Attractions for younger children include Kid's Kingdom, Tiny Tots Town, Rabbit Ride, the Magic Forest where nursery rhymes come to life, Wonderful World of Wind in the Willows and the Ladybird ride. In beautiful parkland setting with extensive 'Capability' Brown gardens landscaped with ponds and aviaries for exotic birds; lake and hedge maze.
Times: Open mid Mar-end Oct, daily 10-6, earlier closing at certain times of the year - daily info on hotline. Nov & Dec, wknds only until Xmas. **Fee:** * £11 (ch under 14 & pen £10). Children under 1m tall enter for free. Range of Family Supersavers. **Facilities:** P 🍴 ✕ & (Pre-booked wheelchair hire, some rides unsuitable) toilets for disabled shop ✕ (ex guide dogs) 🛍

PETERSFIELD   Map 04 SU72
BEAR MUSEUM & STEIFF CLUB STORE
38 Dragon St GU31 4JJ (100yds from bottom of the High Street, turn right and museum signed)
☎ 01730 265108

This was the world's first Teddy Bear Museum, and children are allowed to cuddle and play with some of the exhibits. The exhibition houses one of the best labelled collections and people are on hand to help identify visitors old teddy bears if needed. The Teddy Bear Museum also restores old bears and downstairs in the museum you will find the 'Teddy Bear's Picnic'.
Times: Open Tue-Sat 10-4.30. **Fee:** Free entry. Contributions welcomed. **Facilities:** P (200yds) shop ✕ (ex guide dogs) 🚗 🛍

PORTCHESTER   Map 04 SU60
PORTCHESTER CASTLE
Castel St PO16 9QW (off A27)
☎ 01705 378291

Built on the site of a Roman fort, the castle has witnessed many famous events of English history. From here Henry V embarked for France and the Battle of Agincourt; here Henry VIII courted Anne Boleyn, and later still the castle was 'home' to prisoners during the Napoleonic wars. The castle has the most complete Roman walls in Europe; remains of the church and other medieval buildings can also be seen.
Times: Open all year, 29 Mar-Sep, daily 10-6 (Oct, daily 10-5); Nov-Mar, daily 10-4. (Closed 24-26 Dec & 1 Jan). **Fee:** * £3.20 (ch 5-15 £1.60, under 5's free, concessions £2.40). **Facilities:** P & shop ✕ (in certain areas) ♿

PORTSMOUTH   Map 04 SU60
CHARLES DICKENS' BIRTHPLACE MUSEUM
393 Old Commercial Rd PO1 4QL (accessible from M27, 1st left at 1st rdbt)
☎ 023 9282 7261   📠 023 9287 5276
e-mail: cspendlove@portsmouthcc.gov.uk

A small terraced house built in 1805 which became the birthplace and early home of the famous novelist, born in 1812. On display are items pertaining to Dickens' work, portraits of the Dickens' family, and the couch on which he died. Dickens readings are given in the exhibition room on the first Sunday of each month.
Times: Open Apr-Sep, daily 10-5.30; Oct, daily 10-5. (Last admission 5pm). **Fee:** * £2.50 (ch & student £1.50, accompanied ch 13 free, pen £1.80). Family ticket £6.50. **Facilities:** P (150mtrs) shop ✕ (ex guide & helper dogs) 🛍

CITY MUSEUM & RECORDS OFFICE
Museum Rd PO1 2LJ (M27/M275 into Portsmouth, follow museum symbol signs)
☎ 023 9282 7261   📠 023 9287 5276
e-mail: cspendlove@portsmouthcc.gov.uk

Dedicated to local history, fine and decorative art, 'The Story of Portsmouth' displays room settings showing life here from the 17th century to the 1950s. The 'Portsmouth at Play' exhibition features leisure pursuits from the Victorian period to the 1970s. Temporary exhibitions are also held.
Times: Open all year, Apr-Oct daily 10-5.30; Nov-Mar daily 10-5. Closed 24-26 Dec and Record Office closed on public holidays. **Fee:** Free. **Facilities:** P 🍴 & (induction loops, lift & wheelchairs available, parking) toilets for disabled shop ✕ (ex guide & helper dogs)

Are there any great Days Out that we've missed?
Use the Readers' Report form at the back of the book to tell us about them

104　Hampshire

D-Day Museum & Overlord Embroidery
Clarence Esplanade PO5 3NT (M27/M275 into Portsmouth, follow D-Day Museum & seafront signs)
☎ 023 9282 7261　✉ 023 9287 5276
e-mail: cspendlove@portsmouthcc.gov.uk

Portsmouth's D-Day Museum tells the dramatic story of the Allied landings in Normandy in 1944. Centrepiece is the magnificent 'Overlord Embroidery', 34 individual panels and 83 metres in length. Experience the world's largest ever seaborne invasion, and step back in time to scenes of wartime Britain. Also military equipment, vehicles, landing craft and personal memories.
Times: Open all year, Apr-Oct daily 10-5.30. Nov-Mar, 10-5. **Fee:** * £5 (ch £3, pen £3.75). Family ticket £13. **Facilities:** P (charged) 🅿 ♿ (induction loops, sound aids for blind, wheelchairs available) toilets for disabled shop ✱ (ex guide & helper dogs)

Eastney Beam Engine House
Henderson Rd, Eastney PO4 9JF (from A3(M), A27 & A2030, turn left at Bransbury Park lights)
☎ 023 9282 7261　✉ 023 9287 5276
e-mail: cspendlove@portsmouthcc.gov.uk

The main attraction here is a magnificent pair of James Watt Beam Engines still housed in their original High-Victorian engine house opened in 1887. One of these engines is in steam when the museum is open. A variety of other pumping engines, many in running order are also on display.
Times: Open all year, last (whole) weekend of every month, 1-5 (last admission 30 minutes before closing). **Fee:** * £2.50 (ch & student £1.50, accompanied ch under 13 free & pen £1.80). Family ticket £6.50. **Facilities:** P (300mtrs) ✱ (ex guide & helper dogs)

Natural History Museum & Butterfly House
Cumberland House, Eastern Pde PO4 9RF (From A3(M), A27 or A2030, follow seafront signs)
☎ 023 9282 7261　✉ 023 9282 5276
e-mail: cspendlove@portsmouthcc.gov.uk

Focusing on the natural history and geology of the area, with wildlife dioramas including a riverbank scene with fresh water aquarium. During the summer British and European butterflies fly free in the Butterfly House.
Times: Open all year daily, Apr-Oct 10-5.30; Nov-Mar 10-5. **Fee:** * £2.50 (ch £1.50, accompanied ch under 13 free & pen £1.80). Family ticket £6.50. **Facilities:** P (200mtrs) shop ✱ (ex guide & helper dogs)

Portsmouth Historic Dockyard
HM Naval Base PO1 3LJ (follow brown historic ships sign from M27/M275)
☎ 023 9287 0999　✉ 023 9229 5252　**2 for 1**
e-mail: mail@historicdockyard.co.uk

Portsmouth Historic Dockyard is home to the world's greatest historic ships: *Mary Rose*, *HMS Victory*, *HMS Warrior* and the Royal Naval Museum. The Action Stations attraction demonstrates life aboard a modern naval frigate. Many special events held throughout the year. Telephone for details.
Times: Open all year, Apr-Oct, daily 10-5.30; Nov-Mar, daily 10-5. (Closed 25 Dec). **Fee:** * Passport ticket: £18 (ch & pen £14.50); HMS Victory: £7 (ch & pen £6); Mary Rose or HMS Warrior: £6.75 (ch & pen £5.75). **Facilities:** P (charged) 🅿 ✕ ♿ toilets for disabled shop

The Royal Marines Museum
Southsea PO4 9PX (signposted from seafront)
☎ 023 9281 9385　　　　　　　　　　**2 for 1**
✉ 023 9283 8420
e-mail: info@royalmarinesmuseum.co.uk

Telling the story of the 330-year history of the Marines through dramatic displays, exciting films and videos, state of the art interactives and there's even a live snake and scorpion! Also a world famous medal collection, portraits and silverware.
Times: Open all year, Jun-Aug, daily 10-5; Sep-May, daily 10-4.30. (Closed 3 days Xmas). **Fee:** * £4 (ch £2.25, pen £3). Family ticket £12.
Facilities: P 🅿 ♿ (wheelchairs, hearing loops, special tours-prior notice) toilets for disabled shop ✱ (ex guide dogs or in grounds)

Southsea Castle
Clarence Esplanade PO5 3PA (accessible from M27, A27, A3M, A2030, follow castle signs)
☎ 023 9282 7261　✉ 023 9287 5276
e-mail: cspendlove@portsmouthcc.gov.uk

Part of Henry VIII's national coastal defences, this fort was built in 1544. In the 'Time Tunnel' experience, the ghost of the castle's first master gunner guides you through the dramatic scenes from the castle's eventful history. Audio-visual presentation, underground passages, Tudor military history displays, artillery, and panoramic views of the Solent and Isle of Wight.
Times: Open all year, Apr-Sep, daily 10-5.30; Oct-Mar, daily 10-5. **Fee:** * £2.50 (ch & students £1.50, ch accompanied under 13 free, pen £1.80). Family ticket £6.50. **Facilities:** P (charged) ♿ (wheelchair available) shop ✱ (ex guide & helper dogs)

Hampshire

SPITBANK FORT
(ferries depart from HM Naval Base Portsmouth, Portsmouth Hard & Gosport ferry pontoon)
☎ 01329 664286 & 07977 066560
Times: Open May-Sep, Tue-Sun. (Weather permitting). **Facilities:** P
Details not confirmed for 2003

RINGWOOD   Map 04 SU10
MOORS VALLEY COUNTRY PARK
Horton Rd, Ashley Heath BH24 2ET (1.5m from Ashley Heath rdbt on A31 near Three Legged Cross)
☎ 01425 470721   01425 471656
e-mail: mvalley@eastdorsetdc.gov.uk
Times: Open all year (ex 25 Dec), 8-dusk. Visitor centre open 9.30-4.30 (later in summer). **Facilities:** P (charged) (visitor centre & park mostly accessible, wheelchairs) toilets for disabled shop (ex in park on lead) *Details not confirmed for 2003*

ROCKBOURNE   Map 04 SU11
ROCKBOURNE ROMAN VILLA
SP6 3PG (from Salisbury exit A338 at Fordingbridge, take B3078 through Sandleheath & follow signs. Or turn off A354 Salisbury to Blandford road, W of Coombe Bissett)
☎ 01725 518541
2 for 1

Discovered in 1942, the site features the remains of a 40-room Roman villa and is the largest in the area. Displays include mosaics and a very rare hypocaust system. The museum displays the many artefacts found on the site during excavations. Roman re-enactments are performed - please ring for details.
Times: Open Apr-Sep, daily 10.30-6. Last admission 5.30pm. **Fee:** * £1.75 (concessions 95p). **Facilities:** P (ramps in & out of museum) toilets for disabled shop (ex guide/hearing dogs)

ROMSEY   Map 04 SU32
BROADLANDS
SO51 9ZD (main entrance on A3090 Romsey by-pass)
☎ 01794 505010   01794 505040
e-mail: admin@broadlands.net

Famous as the home of the late Lord Mountbatten, Broadlands is now home to his grandson Lord Romsey. An elegant Palladian mansion in a beautiful landscaped setting on the banks of the River Test, Broadlands was also the country residence of Lord Palmerston, the great Victorian statesman.
Times: Open daily, 10 Jun-1 Sep, 12-5.30. Last admission 4pm. **Fee:** * £5.95 (ch 12-16 £3.95, pen, students & disabled £4.95). Party 15+.
Facilities: P toilets for disabled shop (ex guide dogs)

SELBORNE   Map 04 SU73
GILBERT WHITE'S HOUSE & THE OATES MUSEUM
The Wakes, High St GU34 3JH (on village High St)
☎ 01420 511275   01420 511040

Charming 18th-century house, home of famous naturalist, the Rev. Gilbert White, author of *The Natural History and Antiquities of Selborne*. There are also exhibitions on two famous members of the Oates family - Captain Oates who accompanied Scott to the South Pole, and Frank Oates, a Victorian explorer. Special events include an Unusual Plants Fair in June.
Times: Open daily Jan-24 Dec, 11-5. **Fee:** £4.50 (ch £1, pen £4).
Facilities: P (200yds) shop (ex guide dogs)

SHERBORNE ST JOHN   Map 04 SU65
THE VYNE
RG24 9HL (4m N of Basingstoke, off A340, signposted)
☎ 01256 881337   01256 881720
Times: Open House Apr-29 Oct daily ex Mon & Fri 1-5. Grounds open wknds in Feb & Mar, 11-4; Apr-29 Oct daily ex Mon & Fri, 11-6. Open Good Fri & BH Mons. **Facilities:** P licensed (Braille guide) shop (ex guide & hearing dogs) *Details not confirmed for 2003*

SILCHESTER   Map 04 SU66
CALLEVA MUSEUM
Bramley Rd RG7 2LU (between Basingstoke & Reading. Reached from A340, follow brown tourist signs)

Little remains of the Roman town of Calleva Atrebatum except the 1.5 miles of city wall, still an impressive sight, and the ampitheatre. This small museum shows what life may have been like in a Roman town, while the main artefacts from the site can be seen in the Silchester Gallery at Reading Museum.
Times: Open daily 9am-sunset. Closed 25 Dec. **Fee:** Free. **Facilities:** P

Hampshire

SOUTHAMPTON — Map 04 SU41
MUSEUM OF ARCHAEOLOGY
God's House Tower, Winkle St SO14 2NY (near the waterfront close to Queen's Park and the Town Quay)
☎ 023 8063 5904 & 8083 2768
📠 023 8033 9601
e-mail: historic.sites@southampton.gov.uk
Times: Open Tue-Fri 10-12 & 1-5; Sat 10-12 & 1-4; Sun 2-5. Also open BH Mon. **Facilities:** P (400 yds) (designated areas only, parking charges) shop ✕ (ex guide dogs) *Details not confirmed for 2003*

SOUTHAMPTON CITY ART GALLERY
Civic Centre, Commercial Rd SO14 7LP (on Watts Park side of Civic Centre, a short walk from the station)
☎ 023 8063 2601 📠 023 8083 2153
e-mail: artgallery@southampton.gov.uk
Times: Open all year, Tue, Wed & Fri 10-5, Thu 10-5, Sat 10-5, Sun 1-4. (Closed 25-27 & 31 Dec). **Facilities:** P (250yds) 🍽 & toilets for disabled shop ✕ *Details not confirmed for 2003*

SOUTHAMPTON MARITIME MUSEUM
The Wool House, Town Quay SO14 2AR (on the waterfront, near to the Town Quay)
☎ 023 8022 3941 & 8063 5904
📠 023 8033 9601
e-mail: historic.sites@southampton.gov.uk
Times: Open all year, Tue-Fri 10-12 & 1-5, Sat 10-12 & 1-4, Sun 2-5. Also open BH Mon. **Facilities:** P (400 yds) (metered parking adjacent) & shop ✕ (ex guide dogs) *Details not confirmed for 2003*

TUDOR HOUSE MUSEUM
St Michael's Square, Bugle St SO14 2AD (follow signs for Old Town & Waterfront. 500 yards from the Wool House)
☎ 023 8033 2513 & 8063 5904
📠 023 8033 9601
e-mail: historic.sites@southampton.gov.uk
Times: Open Tue-Fri 10-5 (closed between 12-1), Sat 10-4 (closed between 12-1), Sun 2-5. Open BH Mon. **Facilities:** P (20yds) (metered & disabled parking opposite) & toilets for disabled shop ✕ (ex guide dogs) *Details not confirmed for 2003*

STRATFIELD SAYE — Map 04 SU66
STRATFIELD SAYE HOUSE
RG7 2BZ (off A33 between Reading & Basingstoke)
☎ 01256 882882 📠 01256 882882

Given by the nation to the first Duke of Wellington in 1817, after his victory over Napoleon at the Battle of Waterloo. Stratfield Saye remains the home of the Duke of Wellington and contains many mementoes of the 1st Duke, including his magnificent funeral carriage. Please telephone for details of special events.
Times: At the time of going to print Stratfield Saye House is closed for restoration, but will open during 2003. Please telephone for details.
Fee: Please telephone for details **Facilities:** P ✕ licensed & toilets for disabled shop ✕ (ex in grounds)

TITCHFIELD — Map 04 SU50
TITCHFIELD ABBEY
PO15 5RA (0.5m N off A27)
☎ 023 9252 7667

Also known as `Palace House', in Tudor times this was the seat of the Earl of Southampton, built on the site of the abbey founded in 1232. He incorporated the gatehouse and the nave of the church into his house.
Times: Open Apr-Sep, daily 10-6; Oct, daily 10-5; Nov-Mar, daily 10-4.
Fee: *Free.* **Facilities:** P & ✕ ♿

WEYHILL — Map 04 SU34
THE HAWK CONSERVANCY AND COUNTRY PARK
SP11 8DY (3m W of Andover, signposted from A303)
☎ 01264 772252 📠 01264 773772
e-mail: info@hawk-conservancy.org

This is the largest centre in the South for birds of prey from all over the world including eagles, hawks, falcons, owls, vultures and kites. Exciting birds of prey demonstrations are held daily at noon, 2pm, and 3.30pm, including the 'Valley of the Eagles' at 2pm. Different birds are flown at these times and visitors may have the opportunity to hold a bird.
Times: Open mid Feb-last Sun in Oct, daily from 10.30 (last admission 4pm). **Fee:** * £6.25 (ch £3.60, pen £5.70). Family ticket £18.50. **Facilities:** P 🍽 & (wheelchair area in flying grounds) toilets for disabled shop ✕ 🍴

WHITCHURCH — Map 04 SU44
WHITCHURCH SILK MILL
28 Winchester St RG28 7AL (halfway between Winchester & Newbury signposted clearly on A34. In village centre)
☎ 01256 892065 📠 01256 893882   **2 for 1**
e-mail: silkmill@btinternet.com

The mill is idyllically located on the River Test. Whitchurch Silk Mill is the oldest surviving textile mill in southern England. Fine silks and ribbons are still woven. See the 19th-century waterwheel working and learn about winding, warping and weaving. There is a programme of exhibitions, workshops and children's activities.
Times: Open Tue-Sun & BH Mon 10.30-5 (last admission 4.15). Closed 24 Dec-1 Jan. **Fee:** * £3.50 (ch £1.75, pen & students £3). Family ticket (2 adults & 3 ch) £8.75. **Facilities:** P 🍽 & (disabled parking adjacent site) toilets for disabled shop ✕ (ex guide dogs) 🍴

WINCHESTER — Map 04 SU42
GURKHA MUSEUM
Peninsula Barracks, Romsey Rd SO23 8TS (Exit M3 junct 9 to Winchester, follow traffic circuit into High St, 1st left after Westgate)
☎ 01962 842832 📠 01962 877597   **2 for 1**
e-mail: curator@thegurkhamuseum.co.uk

This museum tells the fascinating story of the Gurkha's involvement with the British Army. Travel from Nepal to

continued

Hampshire

the North-West Frontier and beyond, with the help of life-sized dioramas and interactive exhibits.
Times: Open all year, BH Mon, Tue-Sat 10-5, Sun 12-4. Telephone for Xmas opening times. (Closed 25-26 Dec, 1 Jan and Tue following BH Mon) **Fee:** £1.50 (pen 75p). Party 15+ 75p each. **Facilities:** P & (lift & chair lift) toilets for disabled shop ✱ (ex guide dogs)

HOSPITAL OF ST CROSS
St Cross SO23 9SD (1.5m S of city, on A3335)
☎ 01962 851375 ≣ 01962 878221 **2 for 1**
e-mail: visitors@stcrosshospital.co.uk

Founded in 1132 for the benefit of 13 poor men, and still functioning as an almshouse. Throughout the Middle Ages the Hospital handed out the Dole - bread and beer - to travellers, and this is still done. The Church of St Cross, Brethrens Hall and the walled Master's Garden are all worthy of note.
Times: Open all year, Apr-Oct, Mon-Sat 9.30-5; Nov-Mar 10.30-3.30. (Closed Sun, Good Fri & 25 Dec). **Fee:** * £2 (ch 50p, students & pen £1.25). **Facilities:** P (200yds) (2 hrs) ☕ & (A resident Brother can act as guide and assistant) toilets for disabled shop ✱ (ex guide dogs) 🛈

THE KING'S ROYAL HUSSARS REGIMENTAL MUSEUM
Peninsula Barracks, Romsey Rd SO23 8TS (exit M3 junct 9/10 follow signs for city centre, then hospital A&E red signs to Romsey road. Vehicle access is from Romsey road)
☎ 01962 828539 & 828541 ≣ 01962 828538
e-mail: beresford@krhmuseum.freeserve.co.uk

The Royal Hussars were formed by the amalgamation of two regiments raised at the time of the Jacobite Rebellion in 1715. The museum was formed by the amalgamation in 1992 of the Royal Hussars and the 14th/20th King's Hussars. This museum tells their story.
Times: Open 5 Jan-18 Dec, Tue-Fri 10-4, wknds, BH's & 1/2 term Mon, 12-4. Closed daily between 12.45-1.15. **Fee:** Free. **Facilities:** P & (lift to first floor) toilets for disabled shop ✱ (ex guide dogs)

ROYAL HAMPSHIRE REGIMENT MUSEUM & MEMORIAL GARDEN
Serle's House, Southgate St SO23 9EG (Near city centre, 150mtrs from traffic lights in High St)
☎ 01962 863658 ≣ 01962 888302

The Regimental Museum of the Royal Hampshire Regiment 1702-1992 is set in an 18th-century house by the regiment's Memorial Garden, and tells the complete history of the regiment.
Times: Open all year (ex 2 wks Xmas & New Year), Mon-Fri 11-3.30; Apr-Oct wknds & BH 12-4. **Fee:** Free. **Facilities:** P (800mtrs) & shop ✱ (ex guide dogs)

THE GREAT HALL
Castle Av SO23 8PJ (At top of High St. Pedestrians only - turn left into Castle Ave nearest public car park is Tower St. Park & Ride recommended)
☎ 01962 846176 ≣ 01962 841326

The only surviving part of Winchester Castle, once home to the Domesday Book, this 13th-century hall was the centre of court and government life. The round table, closely associated with the legendary King Arthur, has hung here for over 600 years. A visitor centre and the Winch Castle exhibition.
Times: Open all year, Mar-Oct daily 10-5; Nov-Feb, daily 10-5, wknds 10-4. (Closed 25-26 Dec). **Fee:** Free. **Facilities:** P (200yds) & toilets for disabled shop ✱ (ex guide/hearing dogs) 🛈

WINCHESTER CATHEDRAL
SO23 9LS (in city centre - follow city heritage signs)
☎ 01962 857200 & 866854 ≣ 01962 857201
e-mail: cathedral.office@winchester-cathedral.org.uk
Times: Open all year, daily 8.30-6.30. Subject to services and special events. **Facilities:** P 500mtrs ☕ ✕ licensed & (chair lift to east end of Cathedral, touch & hearing model) toilets for disabled shop ✱ (ex guide dogs) *Details not confirmed for 2003*

WINCHESTER CITY MILL
Bridge St SO23 8EJ (by the city bridge between King Alfred's statue & Chesil St)
☎ 01962 870057 ≣ 01962 870057
e-mail: swigen@smtp.ntrust.org.uk
Times: Open Apr-Oct, Wed-Sun & BH Mons 11-4.45; Mar wknds only. Last admission 15 mins before closing. **Facilities:** P (200 yds) shop ✱ *Details not confirmed for 2003* 🛈

WINCHESTER CITY MUSEUM
The Square SO23 9ES
☎ 01962 848269 ≣ 01962 848299
Times: Open all year, Mon-Sat 10-5, Sun 2-5 (Closed Mon Oct-Mar, Good Fri, Xmas & 1 Jan). **Facilities:** & shop ✱ *Details not confirmed for 2003*

WINCHESTER COLLEGE
College St SO23 9NA (In city centre, S of Cathedral Close, beyond Kingsgate arch)
☎ 01962 621209 ≣ 01962 621166
e-mail: enterprises@wincoll.ac.uk

Founded in 1382, Winchester College is believed to be the oldest continuously running school in England. The college has greatly expanded over the years but the original buildings remain intact. See the college's many historic buildings, including a schoolhouse thought to have been designed by Christopher Wren. The 14th-century chapel with one of the earliest examples of a Jan vaulted roof, the original scholars' dining room and the cloister containing memorials including one to Mallory, the mountaineer.
Times: Open all year (ex Xmas & New Year). Guided tours available Mon, Wed, Fri & Sat; 10.45, 12, 2.15 & 3.30. Tue & Thu 10.45 & 12. Sun 2.15 & 3.15. Groups of 10+ by arrangement only. **Fee:** * Booked tours £3 (pen & students 18 £2.50), unbooked tours £2.50 (pen & students £2). **Facilities:** P (250yds) (Street parking 1hr) & (access ramps) toilets for disabled shop ✱ (ex guide dogs)

Herefordshire

EVENTS & FESTIVALS

May
4th-5th Blossom Time Weekend, Putley, nr Ledbury
6th-8th Hereford May Fair
30th-8th June Leominster Festival (mixed arts, various venues)
tbc Bromyard Spring Festival

June
30th May-8th Leominster Festival (mixed arts, various venues)
27th-28th Music Festival, Dore Abbey, Abbeydore

July
4th-13th Ledbury Poetry Festival
tbc Madley Festival

August
17th-22nd Three Choirs Festival, Hereford Cathedral
17th-22nd Three Choirs Fringe Festival, Hereford
tbc Eardisland Annual Duck Races
tbc Ross-on-Wye International Festival

September
12th-14th Bromyard Folk Festival

October
11th-12th Big Apple Weekend, Much Marcle, nr Ledbury

October/November
tbc Herefordshire Photography Festival

Herefordshire is split in two by the River Wye which meanders through the county on its way to the Severn and the sea. The entire county is largely rural, with Hereford, Leominster and Ross-on-Wye the only towns or cities of any size.

The countryside and ancient villages of Herefordshire are probably the county's major asset, and visitors can take advantage of a number of trails which will guide them through much of interest. These are set out on leaflets available from Tourist Information Centres. Those especially interested in villages should try the Black and White Village Trail, which takes the motorist on a 35 - mile drive around timber-framed villages in the northwest of the county from Leominster to Weobley, (established in the 7th century and known as a centre of witchcraft in the 18th), Kinnersley Castle, Eardisley (where the Church of St Mary Magdalene boasts a early 12th-century carved font), Great Oak, Kington (one of the five market towns of Herefordshire), Pembridge, and others.

Other trails include the Mortimer Trail; – a 30 - mile walk through unspoilt countryside between Ludlow and Kington – the Hop Trail; – which goes from Bromyard to Ledbury through fields which display the varying stages of hop growing – and the Hidden Highway, which begins at Ross-on-Wye and ends in Chester, taking in much of the area's dramatic countryside and many secret places on the way.

Hereford has a glorious 11th-century cathedral situated on the River Wye. It contains a 13th-century Mappa Mundi, and the world's largest chained library that dates from the 8th century.

Top: Goodrich Castle

Herefordshire

ASHTON Map 03 SO56
BERRINGTON HALL
Berrington HR6 0DW (3m N of Leominster, on A49)
☎ 01568 615721 ⌨ 01568 613363
e-mail: berrington@smtp.ntrust.org.uk **2 for 1**

An elegant neo-classical house of the late 18th century, designed by Henry Holland and set in a park landscape by `Capability' Brown. There is a restored bedroom suite, a nursery, a Victorian laundry and a tiled Georgian dairy.
Times: Open 23 Mar-3 Nov, Sat-Wed & Good Fri 1-5 (4.30pm in Oct/Nov). Last admission 30min before closing. Garden open 12-4 (4.30pm in Oct). Park walk open Jul-3 Nov, same times as house.
Fee: * £4.40 (ch £2.20) Family ticket £11. Garden only £3. **Facilities:** 🅿 ✕ licensed ♿ (by arrangement, Braille guide, 2 wheelchairs, audio guides) toilets for disabled shop ✱ (ex guide dogs) 🎗 🔔

BROCKHAMPTON Map 03 SO65
LOWER BROCKHAMPTON
WR6 5TB (2m E of Bromyard on A44)
☎ 01885 482077 & 488099 ⌨ 01885 482151

A late 14th-century moated manor house, with an attractive half-timbered 15th-century gatehouse, a rare example of this type of structure, and the ruins of a 12th-century chapel. It is part of a larger National Trust property covering over 1,700 acres of Herefordshire countryside with various walks including a Sculpture Trail.
Times: Open Apr-3 Nov daily (ex Mon/Tue) but open BH Mon's Apr-Nov 12-5 (12-4 in Oct/Nov). **Fee:** * £3 (ch £1.25) Family £7.50
Facilities: 🅿 🍴 ♿ (special parking for disabled) toilets for disabled shop ✱ (ex in woodland area) 🎗

CROFT Map 03 SO46
CROFT CASTLE
HR6 9PW (off B4362)
☎ 01568 780246 ⌨ 01568 780462
e-mail: croft@smtp.ntrust.org.uk
Times: This property will be under going major structural works during 2002. **Facilities:** 🅿 (charged) 🍴 ♿ (parking available, braille guide) ✱ (ex in parkland) 🎗 *Details not confirmed for 2003*

GOODRICH Map 03 SO51
GOODRICH CASTLE
HR9 6HY (5m S of Ross-on-Wye, off A40)
☎ 01600 890538

Goodrich Castle dominates an ancient crossing of the River Wye. Its huge towers, graceful arches and chapel are well worth the visit, and there is a maze of rooms, passages and a gloomy dungeon to be explored. It was besieged in the Civil War, and the locally made canon used to bombard it, and nicknamed 'Roaring Meg', is on display in Hereford Cathedral.
Times: Open all year, 29 Mar-Sep, daily 10-6 (Oct, daily 10-5); Nov-Mar, daily 10-1 & 2-4 Wed-Sun. (Closed 24-26 Dec & 1 Jan). **Fee:** £3.60 (ch 5-15 £1.80, under 5's free, concessions £2.70). Family £9
Facilities: 🅿 ✱ ♿

HEREFORD Map 03 SO53
CIDER MUSEUM & KING OFFA DISTILLERY
21 Ryelands St HR4 0LW (off A438 Hereford to Brecon road)
☎ 01432 354207 ⌨ 01432 371641 **2 for 1**
e-mail: info@cidermuseum.co.uk

Explore the fascinating history of cider making - old cider-making equipment, the cooper's workshop and Vat House with hydraulic presses and bottling machinery. An annual international cider competition is held and cider-making festival weekends take place.
Times: Open all year, Apr-Oct, daily 10-5.30; Nov-Dec, daily 11-3. Jan-Mar, Tue-Sun 11-3. Pre-booked groups at anytime. **Fee:** £2.70 (concessions £2.20). Party 15+. **Facilities:** 🅿 🍴 ♿ (audiotapes, large print guide sheets) shop ✱ (ex guide dogs)

HEREFORD CATHEDRAL
HR1 2NG (A49 to Hereford, signed from city inner ring roads)
☎ 01432 374200 ⌨ 01432 374220
e-mail: office@herefordcathedral.co.uk
Times: Cathedral open daily for visitors 9.30-5; Mappa Mundi & Chained Library Exhibition Summer: Mon-Sat 10-4.15, Sun 11-3.15. Winter: Mon-Sat 11-3.15 (closed Sun). **Facilities:** 🅿 (0.25m) 🍴 ♿ (touch facility for blind, braille & large print info) toilets for disabled shop ✱ (ex guide dogs) *Details not confirmed for 2003*

OLD HOUSE
High Town HR1 2AA (in the centre of High Town)
☎ 01432 260694

The Old House is a fine Jacobean building dating from around 1621, and was once in a row of similar houses. Its rooms are furnished in 17th-century style and give visitors the chance to learn what life was like in Cromwell's time.
Times: Open all year, 10-5. Apr-Sep, Tue-Sat 10-5, Sun & BH Mon 10-4. **Fee:** Free. **Facilities:** 🅿 ♿ shop (very small) ✱ (ex guide dogs)

KINGTON Map 03 SO25
HERGEST CROFT GARDENS
HR5 3EG (turn off A44 W of Kington and follow signs)
☎ 01544 230160 ⌨ 01544 232031
e-mail: gardens@hergest.kc3.co.uk

From spring bulbs to autumn colour, this is a garden for all seasons. A fine collection of trees and shrubs surrounds the Edwardian house. There's an old fashioned kitchen garden with spring and summer borders, and Park Wood, a hidden valley with splendid rhododendrons.
Times: Open 30 Mar-Oct, 1.30-6. (May & Jun noon-6). **Fee:** * £4 (ch under 16 free). Party 20+ £3.50 **Facilities:** 🅿 🍴 ♿ (portable ramp & wheelchair available) toilets for disabled shop garden centre ✱ (ex on lead) 🔔

Herefordshire

🏛 LEDBURY   Map 03 SO73
EASTNOR CASTLE
Eastnor HR8 1RL (2.5m E of Ledbury on A438, Tewkesbury road)
☎ 01531 633160 📠 01531 631776
e-mail: eastnorcastle@eastnorcastle.com

Times: Open Etr-7 Oct, Sun & BH Mon; Jul & Aug, Sun-Fri 11-5. Last admission 4.30pm. **Facilities:** 🅿 💷 ✕ ♿ shop garden centre *Details not confirmed for 2003* 🏷

🏛 SWAINSHILL   Map 03 SO44
THE WEIR GARDENS
HR4 8BS (5m W of Hereford, on A438)
☎ 01684 855372
e-mail: sevinfo@smtp.ntrust.org.uk
Times: Open 19 Jan-10 Feb, Sat & Sun 11-4; 13 Feb-3 Nov, Wed-Sun 11-6, BH Mon's 11-6. **Facilities:** 🅿 ✕ 🚐 ♿ *Details not confirmed for 2003*

Hertfordshire

This southeastern county of England is close to London, making its county town of Hertford and the towns of Hemel Hempstead, Watford and Harpenden a haven for commuters to the capital.

St Albans, less than 19 miles (30km) from London, has retained its distinctive character, along with many historic remains. The Roman city of Verulamiun is situated in a nearby park, and excavations have revealed an amphitheatre, a temple, parts of the city walls and the foundations of houses. Some spectacular mosaic pavements are displayed in the Verulamium Museum.

The abbey church at St Albans is built on the site where St Alban, the first British Christian martyr, was executed in the 3rd century. The abbey was founded in 793 by King Offa of Mercia, and contains his shrine, made of Purbeck marble. Lost for years, it was discovered in the 19th century, in pieces, and restored by Sir Giles Gilbert Scott. Rebuilt by the Normans, the abbey contains some wonderful medieval wall paintings.

Nicholas Breakspear was born in St Albans, the son of an abbey tenant. In 1154 he took the name Adrian IV, and became the first, and so far only, English pope. His Papal Bull of 1155 empowered Henry II to conquer Ireland.

Another famous historic son of Hertfordshire was Sir Francis Bacon, Elizabethan scholar and Lord High Chancellor, who some believe was the real author of Shakespeare's plays. He was born at Gorhambury House near Hemel Hempstead in 1561.

The county has also produced some famous daughters, namely two of the world famous Spice Girls, now both well-known in their own right: Geri Halliwell, and Victoria Beckham, whose perhaps even more famous husband, David, plays for Manchester United and England.

EVENTS & FESTIVALS

May
24th-25th Herts County Show, Herts County Showground, Redbourn
tbc Herts Garden Show, Knebworth House

June
7th-8th Festival of Gardening, Hatfield House
tbc Hertford Carnival

July
12th-20th St Albans Organ Festival, cathedral and various venues
tbc Families' Day Out in Meadow Park, Borehamwood
tbc Fireworks & Laser Concert, Knebworth House

August
25th St Albans Carnival

September
5th-7th Homes, Gardens & Flower Show, Hatfield House
13th Hoddeson Carnival
tbc Discover St Albans Festival

October
tbc Apple Day Fair & Market, city center, St Albans

November
tbc Firework display, Verulamium Park, St Albans

Top: Rose, Chiswellgreen

Hertfordshire

AYOT ST LAWRENCE Map 04 TL11
SHAW'S CORNER
AL6 9BX (A1(M) junct 4 or M1 junct 10. Follow B653 signed Wheathampstead & follow signs to Luton and The Ayots. Turn right, and establishment is signed)
☎ 01438 820307   🖹 01438 820307
e-mail: tscgen@smtp.ntrust.org.uk
Times: Open Apr-4 Nov **Facilities:** P ♿ (braille guide to house, scented plants, items to touch) ✖ (ex on lead in car park) ♻ *Details not confirmed for 2003*

BERKHAMSTED Map 04 SP90
BERKHAMSTED CASTLE
HP4 1HF
☎ 01536 402840

Roads and a railway have cut into the castle site, but its huge banks and ditches remain impressive. The original motte-and-bailey was built after the Norman Conquest, and there is a later stone keep, owned by the Black Prince, eldest son of King Edward III, where King John of France was imprisoned.
Times: Open all year, daily 10-4. Keykeeper. **Fee:** *Free.* **Facilities:** P ♿ ⚏

HATFIELD Map 04 TL20
HATFIELD HOUSE, PARK AND GARDENS
AL9 5NQ (2m from junct 4 A1(M) on A1000, 7m from M25 junct 23. House is opposite Hatfield railway station)
☎ 01707 287010   🖹 01707 287033   **2 for 1**
e-mail: curator@hatfield-house.co.uk

Home of the Cecil family for 400 years, this celebrated Jacobean house is steeped in Elizabethan and Victorian political history and is famous for its exquisite furniture, tapestries and paintings. The extensive formal gardens reflect their historic origins, were designed and developed by Lady Salisbury and are managed entirely organically. A children's play area and nature trails are also open to the public.
Times: Open Etr Sat-Sep. House: daily 12-4, guided tours only on weekdays. Park & gardens: daily 11-5.30. **Fee:** House Park & Gardens: £7.50 (ch £4). Park only £2 (ch £1). Park & gardens: £4.50 (ch 3.50). Park only £2 (ch £1). Fri (Connoisseurs' Day), £10.50 (no concessions). **Facilities:** P ✖ licensed ♿ (lift) toilets for disabled shop garden centre (not in garden) ♻

KNEBWORTH Map 04 TL22
KNEBWORTH HOUSE, GARDENS & COUNTRY PARK
SG3 6PY (direct access from A1(M) junct 7 Stevenage South)
☎ 01438 812661   🖹 01438 811908
e-mail: info@knebworthhouse.com

Home of the Lytton family since 1490, the original Tudor manor was transformed in 1843 by the spectacular high Gothic decoration of Victorian novelist Sir Edward Bulwer Lytton. The formal gardens, laid out by Edwin Lutyens in 1908, include a Gertrude Jekyll herb garden, a maze, a restored walled garden and wilderness walks. The 250-acre park includes a miniature railway, an adventure playground and a deer park.
Times: Please contact for 2003 details **Fee:** Please contact for 2003 details **Facilities:** P 🍴 ♿ (with prior notice visitors can be driven to front door) toilets for disabled shop (2 shops) garden centre ✖ (ex guide dogs & in park) ♻

LETCHWORTH Map 04 TL23
MUSEUM & ART GALLERY
Broadway SG6 3PF (next door to the Public Library, near the Broadway Cinema)
☎ 01462 685647   🖹 01462 481879
e-mail: letchworth.museum@north-herts.gov.uk

Opened in 1914 to house the collections of the Letchworth Naturalists' Society, this local museum has exhibits on local wildlife, geology, arts and crafts, and archaeology. There is also a museum shop and a regular programme of workshops. 2003 is Letchworth Garden City's Centenary year and a number of Centenary exhibitions will take place, including one on the work of artist William Ratcliff (1878-1955) as well as small exhibitions displaying the work of the original Garden City architects.
Times: Open Mon-Tue, Thu-Sat (Closed BHs). **Fee:** *Free.* **Facilities:** P (100 yds) ♿ (special provisions on request) shop ✖ (ex guide dogs)

Hertfordshire **113**

LONDON COLNEY Map 04 TL10
DE HAVILLAND AIRCRAFT HERITAGE CENTRE
Salisbury Hall AL2 1EX (signposted from M25 junct. Follow signs for 'Mosquito Aircraft Museum' onto B556)
☎ 01727 822051 & 826400
📠 01727 826400

2 for 1

The oldest aircraft museum in Britain, opened in 1959 to preserve and display the de Havilland Mosquito prototype on the site of its conception. A working museum with displays of 20 de Havilland aircraft and sections together with a comprehensive collection of de Havilland engines and memorabilia. Selective cockpits are open for visitors to enter.
Times: Open first Sun Mar-last Sun Oct, Sun & BH Mons 10.30-5.30, Tue, Thu & Sat 2-5.30. **Fee:** * £5 (ch under 5 free, ch & pen £3) Family ticket £13 (2 adults & 2 ch) **Facilities:** 🅿 🍴 ♿ (wheelchairs available) toilets for disabled shop (not accessible for wheelchairs) ✈ (ex on lead & under control) 🛍

ST ALBANS Map 04 TL10
CLOCK TOWER
Market Place AL3 3DR (City centre, junct of High St (A1081) & Market Place)
☎ 01727 855843

This early 15th-century curfew tower, which faces the High Street, provides fine views over the city (especially of the abbey) and the surrounding countryside. This is one of the only two medieval curfew towers in the country. It has a bell, older than the tower itself, which strikes on the hour.
Times: Open Good Fri-mid Sep, Sat, Sun & BH 10.30-5. **Facilities:** 🅿 (400yds) shop ✈ *Details not confirmed for 2003*

Knebworth
HOUSE, GARDENS & PARK

Home of the Lytton family for over 500 years, where Elizabeth I visited, Charles Dickens acted and Winston Churchill painted. Extensive Gardens, Maze, Indian Raj Display, Adventure Playground, Miniature Railway, Gift Shops and Tea Room.

FULL PROGRAMME OF EXCITING EVENTS IN THE PARK, FROM EASTER TO SEPTEMBER - PLEASE TELEPHONE FOR DETAILS.

So much to see – So much to do!

For further information, please contact:
The Estate Office, Knebworth Park, Near Stevenage, Herts SG3 6PY
Tel: 01438 812661
www.knebworthhouse.com

Direct access at Junction 7 - A1(M), 15 miles from M25 (J23). Ample free parking.

Hertfordshire

GARDENS OF THE ROSE (ROYAL NATIONAL ROSE SOCIETY)
Chiswell Green Ln AL2 3NR (2m S off B4630 Watford Rd in Chiswell Green Ln)
☎ 01727 850461 📧 01727 850360
e-mail: mail@rnrs.org.uk

Times: Open 2 Jun-Sep, Mon-Sat 9-5 (Sun & BH Mon 10-6).
Facilities: 🅿 🍴 ♿ (ramps where necessary) toilets for disabled shop *Details not confirmed for 2003*

GORHAMBURY
AL3 6AH (entry via lodge gates on A414)
☎ 01727 855000 📧 01727 843675

This house was built by Sir Robert Taylor between 1774 and 1784 to house an extensive picture collection of 17th-century portraits of the Grimston and Bacon families and their contemporaries. Also of note is the 16th-century enamelled glass collection and an early English pile carpet.
Times: Open May-Sep, Thu 2-5. **Fee:** * £6 (ch £3, pen £4). Party.
Facilities: 🅿 shop 🐕

MUSEUM OF ST ALBANS
Hatfield Rd AL1 3RR (city centre on A1057 Hatfield road)
☎ 01727 819340 📧 01727 837472
e-mail: a.wheeler@stalbans.gov.uk

Exhibits include the Salaman collection of craft tools, and reconstructed workshops. The history of St Albans is traced from the departure of the Romans up to the present day. There is a special exhibition gallery with a surprising variety of exhibitions and a wildlife garden with picnic area.
Times: Open all year, daily 10-5, Sun 2-5. (Closed 25 & 26 Dec). **Fee:** Free. **Facilities:** 🅿 ♿ toilets for disabled shop 🐕 (ex guide dogs)

ROMAN THEATRE OF VERULAMIUM
St Michaels AL3 6AH (Off of A4147)
☎ 01727 835035 📧 01727 843675

The theatre was discovered in 1847 and excavated in 1935. It is unique in England. First constructed around AD160, it is semicircular in shape, 180ft across and could hold over 2000 spectators.
Times: Open all year, daily 10-5 (4 in winter). Closed 25-26 Dec. 1 Jan by appointment only. **Fee:** * £1.50 (ch 50p, students & pen £1). Ch under 5yrs & disabled free. **Facilities:** 🅿 ♿ (limited access to viewing path) shop (on leads only)

ST ALBANS CATHEDRAL
Sumpter Yard AL1 1BY (exit M25 junct 22a, in the town centre)
☎ 01727 860780 📧 01727 850944
e-mail: admin@stalbanscathedal.org.uk

An imposing Norman abbey church built on the site of the execution of St Alban, Britain's first martyr (c250AD). The cathedral is constructed from recycled Roman brick taken from nearby Verulamium.
Times: Open daily, 9-5.45 **Fee:** Free. **Facilities:** 🅿 (200mtrs) ✕ licensed ♿ (touch & hearing centre, braille guides) toilets for disabled shop 🐕 (ex guide dogs)

VERULAMIUM MUSEUM
St Michaels AL3 4SW (follow signs for St Albans, museum signposted)
☎ 01727 751810 📧 01727 859919
e-mail: a.coles@stalbans.gov.uk **2 for 1**

Verulamium was one of the largest and most important Roman towns in Britain - by the lst century AD it was declared a `municipium', giving its inhabitants the rights of Roman citizenship, the only British city granted this honour. A mosaic and underfloor heating system can be seen, and the museum has wall paintings, jewellery, pottery and other domestic items. On the second weekend of every month legionaries occupy the galleries and describe the tactics and equipment of the Roman Imperial Army and the life of a legionary.
Times: Open all year wkdys 10-5.30, Sun 2-5.30. (Closed 25-26 Dec). **Fee:** £3.30 (ch, pen & students £2). Family ticket £8. Subject to change. **Facilities:** 🅿 (charged) ♿ (ramp access to main entrance) toilets for disabled shop 🐕 (ex guide dogs)

> * An asterisk by an entry indicates that the prices shown are for 2002 only. Please contact the attraction for up-to-date price information.

Hertfordshire

🏛 TRING   Map 04 SP91
THE WALTER ROTHSCHILD ZOOLOGICAL MUSEUM
Akeman St HP23 6AP (signposted from A41)
☎ 020 7942 6171   📠 020 7942 6150
e-mail: tring-enquiries@nhm.ac.uk

An unusual museum, founded in the 1890s by Lionel Walter, 2nd Baron Rothschild, scientist, eccentric and natural history enthusiast. Now part of the Natural History Museum, it houses more than 4000 specimens from whales to fleas, and humming birds to tigers.
Times: Open all year, Mon-Sat 10-5, Sun 2-5. (Closed 24-26 Dec).
Fee: Free. **Facilities:** 🅿 ☕ ♿ (ramps to shop & cafe, disabled parking space) toilets for disabled shop ✈ (ex guide dogs)

🏛 WARE   Map 05 TL31
SCOTT'S GROTTO
Scott's Rd SG12 9JQ (off A119)
☎ 01920 464131

Scott's Grotto, built in the 1760s by the Quaker poet John Scott, has been described by English Heritage as 'one of the finest in England'. Restored by the Ware Society, it consists of underground passages and chambers decorated with flints, shells, minerals and stones, and extends 67ft into the side of the hill. Please wear flat shoes and bring a torch.
Times: Open Apr-end Sep, Sat & BH Mon 2-4.30. Other times by appointment only. **Fee:** Free. **Facilities:** 🅿 (on street)

Kent

Often called the 'garden of England', Kent is renowned for its fruit in the agricultural area of the Weald, and its hop growing for the brewing industry. Historically, hops were picked by itinerant workers, many from London, who moved in for the season.

For many years, Londoners have flocked to the seaside resorts of the Isle of Thanet, Margate, Broadstairs and Ramsgate. Of these, Broadstairs retains a quiet charm, and is probably best known as Charles Dickens' resort of choice, where he lived overlooking the bay in a rather forbidding residence since known as Bleak House. More popular yet with visitors from all over the world is the ancient city of Canterbury, the metropolis of the Anglican church since Augustine's mission to England in 597, and site of a magnificent cathedral.

The Channel Tunnel and the Channel ports of Dover, Folkestone and Ramsgate ensure good transport links into the county. The administrative centre is Maidstone, and other main towns are: Chatham, home of the historic Royal Naval Dockyard, part of which has become a film set used in films such as *The Mummy* and *Tomorrow Never Dies*; Rochester with its lovely cathedral; and the elegant spa town of Royal Tunbridge Wells.

Kent is blessed with some fine castles, houses and gardens. Chief among these are Leeds Castle, east of Maidstone; Hever Castle, birthplace of Anne Boleyn; Knole, England's largest house with 365 rooms; Churchill's house, Chartwell, near Westerham; Penshurst Place, a 14th-century house with a splendid hall and long gallery; and the inspirational Sissinghurst Garden created by Vita Sackville-West.

EVENTS & FESTIVALS

May
3rd-4th Kent Garden Show, Kent & County Showground (provisional)
tbc Art & Soul Festival and open studios, in Dover, Deal and Sandwich
tbc Sellindge Steam Festival, Ashford
tbc Tonbridge Carnival

June
14th-22nd Broadstairs Dickens Festival
22nd Witstable Umbrella Fun Day
tbc Canterbury Carnival
tbc Ramsgate Spring Festival
tbc Stour Music Festival, Canterbury

July
19th grassrootz music festival, Tunbridge Wells
tbc Deal Summer Music Festival
tbc Dover Carnival
tbc Kent County Show, Maidstone
tbc Whitstable Oyster Festival
tbc Whitstable Regatta, Whitstable

August
8th-15th Broadstairs Folk Week
9th Herne Bay Carnival, Herne Bay
10th Broadstairs & St Peters Carnival
16th-17th Autorama vintage/classic car show, Tunbridge Wells
23rd Swale Barge & Smack Race
25th Sedan Chair Race, Tunbridge Wells
tbc Broadstairs Water Gala
tbc Dover Regatta
tbc Margate Summer Carnival
tbc Sandwich Festival
tbc Whitstable Barge Race

September
tbc Battle of Britain Day, Herne Bay
tbc Deal Maritime Folk Festival
tbc Sandwich Carnival

October
11th-25th Canterbury Festival

December
6th Tankerton Christmas Street Market

Top: Lullingstone viaduct

Kent

AYLESFORD
Map 05 TQ75
AYLESFORD PRIORY
The Friars ME20 7BX (M20 junct 6, M2 junct 3, signposted)
☎ 01622 717272 01622 715575
e-mail: friarsevents@hotmail.com

Built in the 13th and 14th centuries, the Priory has been restored and is now a house of prayer, guest house, conference centre and a place of pilgrimage and retreat. It has fine cloisters, and displays sculpture and ceramics by modern artists.
Times: Open all year, daily 9-dusk. Gift & book shop May-Sep, 10-5; Oct-Apr, 10-4 (Sun 11am). Guided tours of the priory by arrangement.
Fee: Donations. £2 for annual fund-raising day. **Facilities:** P ⌑ & (wheelchairs available, ramps) toilets for disabled shop ✖ (ex guide & hearing dogs) ⌕

BEKESBOURNE
Map 05 TR15
HOWLETTS WILD ANIMAL PARK
CT4 5EL (off A2, 3m S of Canterbury, follow brown tourist signs)
☎ 01227 721286 01227 721853
e-mail: karenw@howletts.net
Times: Open all year, daily 10-5, (3.30pm in winter). Closed 25 Dec.
Facilities: P ⌑ ✖ licensed & toilets for disabled shop ✖ Details not confirmed for 2003 ⌕

BELTRING
Map 05 TQ64
HOP FARM & COUNTRY PARK
TN12 6PY (on A228 at Paddock Wood)
☎ 01622 872068 01622 872630
e-mail: enquiry@thehopfarm.co.uk

The largest group of Victorian oast houses and galleried barns in the country, with features including the Hop Story Exhibition, Shire Horse Centre and pottery workshop.
Times: Open all year from 10am (Closed 24-26 Dec) **Fee:** * £6.50 (ch 4-15 & pen £4.50). Family ticket £18 (2 adults & 2 children) under 4's free. **Facilities:** P ⌑ ✖ licensed & toilets for disabled shop ⌕

BIDDENDEN
Map 05 TQ83
BIDDENDEN VINEYARDS & CIDER WORKS
Little Whatmans, Gribble Bridge Ln TN27 8DH (0.5m S off A262, between Biddenden & Tenterden)
☎ 01580 291726 01580 291933
e-mail: info@biddendenvineyards.co.uk

The present vineyard was established in 1969 and now covers 22 acres. Visitors are welcome to stroll around the vineyard and to taste wines, ciders and apple juice available at the shop.
Times: Open all year, Shop: Mon-Fri 10-5, Sat 10-5, Sun & BH 11-5. Closed noon 24 Dec-2 Jan & Sun in Jan & Feb. **Fee:** * Non-guided groups and individuals free. Pre-booked guided tours (minimum 15 adults) £3.20 (ch 10-18 £1, ch under 10 free). **Facilities:** P ⌑ & shop ⌕

BIRCHINGTON
Map 05 TR36
POWELL-COTTON MUSEUM, QUEX HOUSE & GARDENS
Quex Park CT7 0BH (W of Margate on A28)
☎ 01843 842168 01843 846661
e-mail: powell-cotton.museum@virgin.net

Major Powell-Cotton spent much of his life on the study of African animals and many different cultures. This museum, founded in 1895, is his legacy, consisting of animal dioramas, photographs, extensive notes, and artefacts from around the world. Also on display in Quex House, the family home, are collections of Eastern and Asian furniture, Kashmir walnut wall carvings, Chinese silk embroidery, and English period furniture.
Times: Open Apr-Oct Tue-Thu, Sun & BH 11-5, Quex House 2-4.30. Nov & Mar Sun 11-4, Quex House closed. (Closed Dec-Feb) **Fee:** * Summer £4 (ch & pen £3, under 5's free), Family ticket (2 adults & 3 children) £12. Winter £3 (ch & pen £2.50), Family ticket (2 adults & 3 children) £8. Garden only £1 (ch & pen 50p) **Facilities:** P ⌑ ✖ licensed & toilets for disabled shop ✖ (ex assistance dogs)

BOROUGH GREEN
Map 05 TQ65
GREAT COMP GARDEN
TN15 8QS (2m E off B2016)
☎ 01732 882669 & 886154
Times: Open Apr-Oct, daily 11-6. **Facilities:** P ⌑ ✖ & (wheelchair for hire) toilets for disabled garden centre ✖ (ex guide dogs) Details not confirmed for 2003

BRASTED
Map 05 TQ45
EMMETTS GARDEN
Ide Hill TN14 6AY (1m S of A25, Sundridge-Ide Hill road)
☎ 01732 868381 & 866368 01732 868193
e-mail: kchxxx@smtp.ntrust.org.uk

Emmetts is a charming hillside shrub garden, with bluebells, azaleas and rhododendrons in spring and fine autumn colours. It has magnificent views over Bough Beech Reservoir and the Weald. Emmetts Blues Concert in July.
Times: Open 22 Mar-29 Jun, Wed-Sun & BH 11-5 (last admission 4.15); 2 Jul-2 Nov Wed, Sat & Sun **Fee:** £3.60 (ch £1.80). Family ticket £9. **Facilities:** P ⌑ & (wheelchairs & buggy service from car park to garden) toilets for disabled shop ⌕

BROADSTAIRS
Map 05 TR36
BLEAK HOUSE DICKENS MARITIME & SMUGGLING
Fort Rd CT10 1EY (off Eastern Esplanade, near Viking Bay)
☎ 01843 862224

The house was a favourite seaside residence of Charles Dickens, and he wrote all of *'David Copperfield'* and other works here, and drafted the idea for Bleak House. There are also exhibitions of relics salvaged from the Goodwin Sands and Kents' only smuggling museum.
Times: Open mid Feb-mid Dec, daily; Jan-mid Feb wknds only.10-6
Fee: * £3 (ch under 12 £2.20, pen £2.80, students £2.50).
Facilities: P (100 yds) & (provisions made for blind) shop

Kent

Dickens House Museum
Victoria Pde CT10 1QS (on the seafront)
☎ 01843 863453 📠 01843 863453
e-mail: aleeault@aol.com
Times: Open Apr-mid Oct, daily 2-5, also Sat-Sun during summer 10.30-5. **Facilities:** P (400yds) (play & display) shop ✈ (ex guide dogs) Details not confirmed for 2003

CANTERBURY Map 05 TR15

Canterbury Roman Museum
Butchery Ln, Longmarket CT1 2RA (in town centre close to cathedral and car parks)
☎ 01227 785575 📠 01227 455047
e-mail: museums@canterbury.gov.uk

Step below today's Canterbury to discover an exciting part of the Roman town including the real remains of a house with fine mosaics. Experience everyday life in the reconstructed market place and see exquisite silver and glass. Try your skills on the touch screen computer, and in the hands-on area with actual finds. Use the computer animation of Roman Canterbury to join the search for the lost temple.
Times: Open all year, Mon-Sat 10-5 & Sun (Jun-Oct) 1.30-5. Last admission 4pm. (Closed Good Fri & Xmas period). **Fee:** £2.60 (ch 5-18, disabled, pen and students £1.65). Family ticket £6.80. **Facilities:** P (500mtrs) ♿ (lift) toilets for disabled shop ✈

The Canterbury Tales
Saint Margaret's St CT1 2TG (In heart of city centre, follow finger sign-posting)
☎ 01227 479227 📠 01227 765584 **2 for 1**
e-mail: info@canterburytales.org.uk

Step back in time to experience the sights sounds and smells of the Middle Ages in this reconstruction of 14th century England. Travel from the Tabard Inn, in London, to St. Thomas Becket's Shrine in Canterbury with Chaucer's colourful pilgrims. Their tales of chivalry, romance and intrigue are vividly brought to life along your journey.
Times: Open all year. Jan-mid Feb, 10-4.30; mid Feb-end Jun, 10-5; Jul-early Sep, 9.30-5; early Sep-end Oct, 10-5; end Oct-end Dec, 10-4.30. (Closed 25 Dec). **Fee:** * £6.50 (ch 5-16 £5, pen & student £5.50) Family ticket (2 adults & 2 ch) £20. **Facilities:** P (200mtrs) ☕ ♿ (notice required for wheelchairs) toilets for disabled shop ✈ (except guide dogs) 🎧

Canterbury West Gate Museum
Saint Peter's St CT1 2RA (at end of main street beside the river. Entrance under main arch)
☎ 01227 452747 📠 01227 455047
e-mail: museums@canterbury.gov.uk

The last of the city's fortified gatehouses sits astride the London road with the river as a moat. Rebuilt in around 1380 by Archbishop Sudbury, it was used as a prison for many years. The battlements give a splendid panoramic view of the city and make a good vantage point for photographs. Arms and armour can be seen in the guardroom, and there are cells in the towers. Brass rubbings can be taken and children can try on replica armour.
Times: Open all year (ex Good Fri & Xmas period), Mon-Sat; 11-12.30 & 1.30-3.30. Last admission 15 mins before closure **Fee:** * £1 (ch, disabled, pen, students & UB40 65p). Family ticket £2.50. Party 10+.
Facilities: P (100 yds) shop ✈

Druidstone Park & Art Park
Honey Hill, Blean CT2 9JR (3m NW on A290 from Canterbury)
☎ 01227 765168 📠 01227 768860 **2 for 1**

Idyllic garden setting for a range of sculptures. Enchanted woodland walks where the sleeping dragon dwells. See the mystical Oak Circle with the old man of the oaks. Children's farmyard, play areas and gift shop.
Times: Open Etr-Nov, daily, 10-5.30. **Fee:** * £3.90 (ch £2.60 & concessions £3.50). Family ticket £11. **Facilities:** P ☕ ♿ toilets for disabled shop ✈ (ex guide dogs)

Museum of Canterbury
Stour St CT1 2RA (in the Medieval Poor Priests' Hospital, just off St Margaret's St & High St)
☎ 01227 452747 📠 01227 455047
e-mail: museums@canterbury.gov.uk

The museum is housed in the beautiful medieval Poor Priests' Hospital built in 1973. One of the most striking features is the magnificent oak roof of the Great Hall. Many of the city's treasures are on display including the Anglo Saxon Canterbury Cross, medieval pilgrim badges and Stephenson's very first passenger steam locomotive, the *'Invicta'*. There is a medieval discovery

continued

gallery, interactive displays of archaeology, and Rupert Bear Museum.
Times: Open all year, Mon-Sat 10.30-5 & Sun (Jun-Sep) 1.30-5 (last admission 4pm). (Closed Good Fri & Xmas period). **Fee:** £2.60 (ch 5-18, disabled & pen & students £1.65). Family ticket £6.80. **Facilities:** P & shop ✱

ROYAL MUSEUM & ART GALLERY WITH BUFFS MUSEUM
High St CT1 2RA (in the Beaney Institute in the High St)
☎ 01227 452747   ≣ 01227 455047
e-mail: museums@canterbury.gov.uk

A splendid Victorian building, houses decorative arts and the city's picture collections, including a gallery for T.S. Cooper, England's finest cattle painter. The art gallery is the arena for the visual arts with a varied exhibition programme. Here too is the Buffs Museum, which tells the story of one of England's oldest infantry regiments.
Times: Open all year, Mon-Sat 10-5. (Closed Good Fri and Xmas period). **Fee:** Free. **Facilities:** P 500 mtrs shop ✱

ST AUGUSTINE'S ABBEY
Longport CT1 1TF (off A28) ☎ 01227 767345

The abbey, founded by St Augustine in 598, when he brought Christianity from Rome to England, is one of the oldest monastic sites in the country. Its long and fascinating history can be traced in the ruins.
Times: Open all year, 29 Mar-Sep, daily 10-6 (Oct, daily 10-5); Nov-Mar, daily 10-4. (Closed 24-26 Dec & 1 Jan). **Fee:** * £3 (ch 5-15 £1.50, under 5's free, concessions £2.30). Prices and opening times subject to change from Mar 2003, please check. **Facilities:** P & shop ♿

⛫ CHARTWELL   Map 05 TQ45
CHARTWELL
TN16 1PS (2m S of Westerham, off B2026)
☎ 01732 866368 (info line) & 868381
≣ 01732 868193
e-mail: kchxxx@smpt.ntrust.org.uk

The former home of Sir Winston Churchill is filled with reminders of the great statesman, from his hats and uniforms to gifts presented by Stalin, Roosevelt & de Gaulle. There are paintings of Churchill and other works by notable artists, and also many paintings by Churchill himself.
Times: Open 22 Mar-9 Nov, house, garden & studio, Wed-Sun 11-5. Tue Jul/Aug Open BH Mon's & Tue in Jul/Aug. Last admission 4.15pm (5.30pm BH) **Fee:** House, Garden & studio £6.50 (ch £3.25). Gardens and studio only £3.25 (ch £1.65). Family ticket £16.25. **Facilities:** P ✱ licensed & (2 steps to lift, grounds partially accessible, parking) toilets for disabled shop ✱ (ex guide dogs or in garden) 🌿 ♿

⛫ CHATHAM   Map 05 TQ76
FORT AMHERST
Dock Rd ME4 4UB (adjacent to A231 dock road, 0.5m from Chatham Dockyard)
☎ 01634 847747   ≣ 01634 830612   **2 for 1**
e-mail: amherstman2@hotmail.com

A fine Georgian fortress set in over 15 acres of attractive parkland. A fascinating collection of caves, tunnels, gun-batteries and barracks gives visitors an insight into the life of the Napoleonic soldier. Please telephone for details of special events, including historic re-enactments.
Times: Open daily Nov-Mar Sat/Sun 10-3.30. Apr-Oct daily 10-4 **Fee:** * £4.50 (ch, pen & students £2.50) Family tickets £11.50. **Facilities:** P ♿ & (wheelchair provided, road access up to fort) toilets for disabled shop ✱ (ex guide dogs) ⚑

THE HISTORIC DOCKYARD
ME4 4TZ (short distance from M25. Signposted as 'Historic Dockyard' from junct 1, 3 & 4 of M2)
☎ 01634 823800   ≣ 01634 823801
e-mail: info@chdt.org.uk
Times: Open Apr-Oct, daily 10-5; Feb, Mar & Nov, Wed, Sat & Sun 10-4. **Facilities:** P ♿ ✱ licensed & (wheelchair available, Braille guides) toilets for disabled shop Details not confirmed for 2003 ⚑

⛫ CHIDDINGSTONE   Map 05 TQ54
CHIDDINGSTONE CASTLE
TN8 7AD (off B2027, at Bough Beech)
☎ 01892 870347
Times: Open Apr-May, Oct, Easter & Public Holidays, Jun-Sep, Wed-Fri & Sun. Weekdays 2-5.30; Sun & BH 11.30-5.30. **Facilities:** P ♿ & shop ✱ (ex guide dogs on lead) Details not confirmed for 2003 ⚑

⛫ DEAL   Map 05 TR35
DEAL CASTLE
Victoria Rd CT14 7BA (SW of Deal town centre)
☎ 01304 372762

This huge, austere structure, shaped like a Tudor rose, was an important part of the coastal defences built by Henry VIII. Its unrelenting walls are rounded to deflect cannon shot and inside, the dark passages tell the reality of garrison life.
Times: Open all year, 29 Mar- Sep, daily 10-6 (Oct, daily 10-5); Nov-Mar, daily 10-4. (Closed 24-26 Dec & 1 Jan). **Fee:** * £3.20 (ch £1.60, concessions £2.40). **Facilities:** & shop ♿

WALMER CASTLE
Walmer, Kingsdown Rd CT14 7LJ (1m S on coast, off A258)
☎ 01304 364288

Of similar design to Deal Castle, Walmer was also part of the defences of Tudor England. It is the official residence of the Lord Warden of the Cinque Ports (Dover, Sandwich, Hythe, Romney and Hastings were the original five) an honorary post mostly recently held by Queen Elizabeth, the Queen Mother.
Times: Open all year, 29 Mar-Sep, daily 10-6 (Oct, daily 10-5); Nov-Dec & Mar, Wed-Sun 10-4; Jan-Feb 2003 10-4 Sat & Sun only. (Closed 24-26 Dec, 1 Jan & when Lord Warden is in Residence). **Fee:** * £5 (ch £2.50, under 5's free, concessions £3.80). Family ticket £12.50. **Facilities:** P & shop ✱ (in certain areas) ♿

Kent

DOVER Map 05 TR34
CRABBLE CORN MILL
Lower Rd CT17 0UY (Exit M20 onto A20 into Dover. Follow brown tourist signs)
☎ 01304 823292
e-mail: mill@ccmt.freeserve.co.uk
Times: Open all year, Etr-Jun & Sep, Sat & Sun 11-5; Jul-Aug, Wed-Sun 11-5; Winter Sun 11-5. **Facilities:** P 🍽 shop ✖ (ex guide/hearing dogs) *Details not confirmed for 2003*

DOVER CASTLE & SECRET WARTIME TUNNELS
CT16 1HU
☎ 01304 201628

A giant among England's castles, set high on the famous white cliffs, Dover Castle traces its history back to the Iron Age, and many relics of its different periods remain. The underground tunnel system, nicknamed Hellfire Corner, was originally built in medieval times.
Times: Open all year, 29 Mar-Sep, daily 10-6 (Oct, daily 10-5); Nov-Mar, daily 10-4. (Closed 24-26 Dec & 1 Jan). **Fee:** * £7.50 (ch 5-15 £3.80, under 5's free, concessions £5.60). Family ticket (2 adults & 3ch includes admission to tours of the Secret Wartime tunnels) £18.80 **Facilities:** P ✖ ♿ shop ✖ (in certain areas) ✡

ROMAN PAINTED HOUSE
New St CT17 9AJ (follow A20 to York St bypass, located in town centre)
☎ 01304 203279

Visit five rooms of a Roman hotel built 1800 years ago, famous for its unique, well-preserved Bacchic frescos. The Roman underfloor heating system and part of a late-Roman defensive wall are also on view. There are extensive displays on Roman Dover, and special events are held throughout the year.
Times: Open Apr-Sep, Tue-Sun 10-5, also BH Mon & Mon Jul & Aug.
Fee: £2 (ch & pen 80p) **Facilities:** P ♿ (touch table, glass panels on gallery for wheelchairs) shop ✖

DUNGENESS Map 05 TR01
DUNGENESS POWER STATIONS' VISITOR CENTRE
TN29 9PP (follow A259 to New Romney, right turn signposted B2075 to Lydd, power station signposted)
☎ 01797 321815 📠 01797 321844

The 'A' and 'B' power stations at Dungeness make an extraordinary sight in a landscape of shingle, fishing boats and houses. There is a high-tech information centre, with 'hands-on' interactive videos and many other displays and models including an environmental exhibition which depicts Dungeness from the Ice Age to the present day.
Times: Open Mar-Oct, Mon-Fri, 10-4. Nov-Feb by appointment only.
Fee: Free. **Facilities:** P ♿ (information centre only/shortened tour by appointment) toilets for disabled shop ✖ (ex guide dogs)

DYMCHURCH Map 05 TR12
MARTELLO TOWER
TN29 0NU (access from High St not seafront)
Times: Telephone 01304 211267 for opening details. **Facilities:** ✖ ✡
Details not confirmed for 2003

EDENBRIDGE
See Hever

EYNSFORD Map 05 TQ56
EYNSFORD CASTLE
(off A225)

The walls of this Norman castle, still 30ft high, come as a surprise in the pretty little village. Its founder, William de Eynsford, ended his days as a monk.
Times: Open all year, Mar-Sep, daily 10-6; Oct-Feb, daily 10-4. **Fee:** Free. **Facilities:** P ♿ ✡

LULLINGSTONE CASTLE
DA4 0JA (1m SW of Eynsford via A225 & Lullingstone Roman villa)
☎ 01322 862114 📠 01322 862115

The house was altered extensively in Queen Anne's time, and has fine state rooms and beautiful grounds. The 15th-century gate tower was one of the first gatehouses in England to be made entirely of bricks, and there is a church with family monuments. Please telephone for details of special events.
Times: Open, House May-Aug, Sat, Sun & BH 2-6. Parties by arrangement. **Fee:** * House & Gardens £5 (ch £2 & pen £4) family £10. **Facilities:** P ♿ shop ✖

LULLINGSTONE ROMAN VILLA
DA4 0JA (0.5m SW off A225)
☎ 01322 863467

The excavation of this Roman villa in 1939 uncovered one of the most exciting archaeological finds of the 20th century. These remarkable villa remains include wonderful mosaic floors, wall paintings and one of the earliest Christian chapels.
Times: Open all year, 29 Mar-Sep, daily 10-6 (Oct, daily 10-5); Nov-Mar, daily 10-4. (Closed 24-26 Dec & 1 Jan). 3pm during Jun & Jul due to Opera evenings **Fee:** * £2.80 (ch 5-15 £1.40, ch under 5 free, concessions £2.10). Personal stereo tour included in admission price. **Facilities:** P ✖ ✡

FAVERSHAM Map 05 TR06
FLEUR DE LIS HERITAGE CENTRE
10-13 Preston St ME13 8NS (3 minutes' drive from M2 junct 6)
☎ 01795 534542
e-mail: faversham@btinternet.com   **2 for 1**

Housed in 16th-century premises, the Centre features colourful displays and room settings that vividly evoke the 2000 years history in Faversham. Special features include the 'Gunpowder Experience' and a working old-style village telephone exchange, one of only two remaining in Britain. In July, during the Faversham Open House Scheme, over 20 historic properties in the town are opened to the public.
Times: Open all year, Mon-Sat, 10-4; Sun 10-1. **Fee:** £2 (ch & pen £1)
Facilities: P (200 yds) ♿ toilets for disabled shop 🛍

Kent **121**

🏛 FOLKESTONE   Map 05 TR23
RUSSIAN SUBMARINE
South Quay, Folkestone Harbour CT20 1QH (adjacent to Hoverspeed Seacat Terminal)
☎ 01303 240400
e-mail: info@sovietsub.co.uk

2 for 1

The fascinating history of U475 (known as The Black Widow) is shrouded in secrecy. Only the select few, the Chiefs of Staff of the former Soviet Navy, know the full history. Was it part of their plan for the U475 to patrol the waters off Cuba after the successful deployment of missiles on the island in 1963? A mysterious and sometimes chilling day out.
Times: Open all year, Mon-Fri 10-dusk, wknds 10-6. (Closed 25 Dec).
Fee: * £3.95 (ch £2.50 con £3.50). Family ticket £10. Party. **Facilities:** P (20mtrs) shop ✈ 🍴

🏛 FORDWICH   Map 05 TR15
TOWN HALL
The Square CT2 0DW (off A28)
☎ 01227 710756   📠 01227 713773
Times: Open Etr, Jun-Sep, Sun 2-4 & Wed in Aug 2-4. **Facilities:** P
Details not confirmed for 2003

🏛 GILLINGHAM   Map 05 TQ76
ROYAL ENGINEERS MUSEUM
Prince Arthur Rd ME4 4UG (follow brown signs from Gillingham & Chatham town centres)
☎ 01634 406397   📠 01634 822371
e-mail: remuseum.rhqre@gtnet.gov.uk
Times: Open all year, Mon-Thu 10-5, Sat-Sun & BH Mon 11.30-5. (Closed Good Fri, 25-26 Dec & 1 Jan). Friday by appointment only.
Facilities: P ♿ (help available if required, chair lift to upper level) toilets for disabled shop ✈ (ex guide dogs) *Details not confirmed for 2003* 🍴

🏛 GOUDHURST   Map 05 TQ73
FINCHCOCKS
TN17 1HH (off A262)
☎ 01580 211702   📠 01580 211007
e-mail: katrina@finchcocks.co.uk

This fine early Georgian house stands in a spacious park with a beautiful garden, and contains an outstanding collection of keyboard instruments from the 17th century onwards. They have been restored to playing condition, and there are musical tours on all open days and private visits. Visually handicapped visitors may touch the instruments as well as hear them.
Times: Open Etr-Sep, Sun & BH Mon 2-6; Aug, Wed, Thu & Sun only 2-6. Private groups on other days by appointment Apr-Oct. **Fee:** * £7.
Facilities: P 🍽 ✕ licensed ♿ (wheelchair available) toilets for disabled shop garden centre ✈ (ex guide dogs)

GROOMBRIDGE PLACE GARDENS
& ENCHANTED FOREST

These award winning gardens, set in 200 acres of wooded parkland, feature a series of magnificent walled gardens set against the romantic backdrop of a 17th century moated manor house, including -

- Secret Garden
- Paradise Walk
- Knot Garden
- Herbaceous borders
- White Rose Garden

In complete contrast, in the ancient woodland of the 'Enchanted Forest' there's mystery, magic and excitement to challenge the imagination of young and old alike. Children love the -

- Giant Swings Walk
- Tree Fern Valley
- Village of the Groms
- Mystic Pool
- Canal Boat Rides
- Birds of Prey Flying Displays

RESTAURANT, PICNIC AREA AND GIFT SHOP. SPECIAL EVENTS PROGRAMME
Open daily: 9.00am - 6.00 pm 5th April to 1st November, 2003.
Groombridge Place, Groombridge, Nr. Tunbridge Wells, Kent TN3 9QG. Only 25 minutes south of the M25 Junction 5.
Info Hotline 01892 863999 or visit the website www.groombridge.co.uk

GROOMBRIDGE PLACE　　Map 05 TQ53
GROOMBRIDGE PLACE GARDENS & ENCHANTED FOREST
TN3 9QG (turn off A264 onto B2110, 0.5m from Langton Green. Follow signs to Groombridge. Entrance at bottom of Groombridge Hill in Groombridge village)
☎ 01892 861444 (office) & 863999 (info line)
📠 01892 863996
e-mail: office@groombridge.co.uk

These award-winning gardens, set in 200 acres, feature magnificent walled gardens and herbaceous borders, rose gardens, secret gardens, drunken topiary and much more, against the romantic backdrop of a 17th-century moated manor. In the ancient woodland of the 'Enchanted Forest' there's mystery, innovation and excitement for all ages.
Times: Open 29 Mar-2 Nov, daily 9-6. **Fee:** * £8 (ch 3-12 & pen £6.50) Family ticket (2 adults & 2 ch 3-12) £26. Groups 20+. Prices subject to change on event days. **Facilities:** 🅿 🍴 ♿ (ramps, canal boat) toilets for disabled shop ✶ (ex guide/hearing dogs) 🍽
See advert on page 121

HAWKINGE　　Map 05 TR23
KENT BATTLE OF BRITAIN MUSEUM
Aerodrome Rd CT18 7AG (off A260, 1m along Aerodrome road)
☎ 01303 893140
e-mail: kentbattleofbritainmuseum@btinternet.com

Once a Battle of Britain Station, today it houses the largest collection of relics and related memorabilia of British and German aircraft involved in the fighting. Also shown full-size replicas of the Hurricane, Spitfire and Me109 used in Battle of Britain films. The year 2000 was the 60th anniversary of the Battle of Britain and a memorial has been dedicated. Artefacts on show, recovered from over 600 battle of Britain aircraft all forming a lasting memorial to all those involved in the conflict.
Times: Open Etr-Sep, daily 10-5; Oct, daily 11-4. Closed Oct-Etr. Last admission 1 hour before closing. **Fee:** * £3.50 (ch £2, pen £3). Group 20+. **Facilities:** 🅿 🍴 ♿ shop ✶ (ex guide dogs)

HEVER　　Map 05 TQ44
HEVER CASTLE & GARDENS
TN8 7NG (M25 junct 5 or 6, 3m SE of Edenbridge, off B2026)
☎ 01732 865224　📠 01732 866796
e-mail: mail@hevercastle.co.uk

This enchanting, double-moated, 13th-century castle was the childhood home of Anne Boleyn. Restored by the American millionaire William Waldorf Astor at the beginning of the 20th century, it shows superb Edwardian craftsmanship. Astor also transformed the grounds, creating a lake, a spectacular Italian garden filled with antique sculptures; and a maze. Additions to the gardens include a 110-metre herbaceous border and a 'splashing' water maze on the Sixteen Acre Island.
Times: Open Mar-Nov, daily. Castle 12-6, Gardens 11-6. Last admission 5pm. (Closes 4pm Mar & Nov). **Fee:** * Castle & Gardens £8.20 (ch 5-14 £4.50, pen £7). Family ticket £20.80. Gardens only £6.50 (ch 5-14 £4.30, pen £5.60). Family ticket £17.30. Party 15+.
Facilities: 🅿 🍴 ✶ licensed ♿ (wheelchairs available, book in advance) toilets for disabled shop garden centre ✶ (ex on leads in grounds) 🍽

HYTHE　　Map 05 TR13
ROMNEY, HYTHE & DYMCHURCH RAILWAY
TN28 8PL (off M20 junct 11, off A259 signed New Romney)
☎ 01797 362353 & 363256　　**2 for 1**
📠 01797 363591
e-mail: rhdr@dels.demon.co.uk

The world's smallest public railway has its headquarters here. The concept of two enthusiasts coincided with Southern Railway's plans for expansion, and so the 13.5 mile stretch of 15-inch gauge railway came into being,
continued

Kent **123**

running from Hythe through New Romney and Dymchurch to Dungeness Lighthouse.

Times: Open daily Etr-Sep, also wknds in Mar & Oct. For times apply to: The Manager, RH & DR, New Romney, Kent. **Fee:** Charged according to journey. **Facilities:** 🅿 (charged) 🍴 ♿ (stairlift to Toy & Model Museum) toilets for disabled shop (Dymchurch & Dungeness high season only) 🏷

🏛 IGHTHAM   Map 05 TQ55
IGHTHAM MOTE
TN15 0NT (2.5m S off A227, 6m E of Sevenoaks)
☎ 01732 810378 & 811145 (info line)
📠 01732 811029
e-mail: igthammote@nationaltrust.org.uk

This moated manor house, nestling in a sunken valley, dates from 1330. The main features of the house span many centuries and include the Great Hall, old chapel and crypt, Tudor chapel with painted ceiling, drawing room with Jacobean fireplace, frieze and 18th-century handpainted Chinese wallpaper and the billiards room. There is an extensive garden and interesting walks in the surrounding woodland.
Times: Open Apr-Nov, daily ex Tue & Sat, 10-5.30. Open Good Fri. Last admission 5pm. **Fee:** * £5.40 (ch £2.70). Family ticket £13.50.
Facilities: 🅿 🍴 ✖ licensed ♿ (wheelchairs available,special parking ask at ticket office) toilets for disabled shop 🐾 🎒

🏛 LAMBERHURST   Map 05 TQ63
BAYHAM ABBEY
TN3 8DE (off B2169, 2m W in East Sussex)
☎ 01892 890381
Times: Open Apr-Sep, daily 10-6 (Oct 10-5). Nov-28 Mar, wknds 10-4. Closed 24-26 Dec & 1 Jan **Facilities:** 🅿 ♿ ♿ Details not confirmed for 2003

SCOTNEY CASTLE GARDEN
TN3 8JN (1m S, of Lamberhurst on A21)
☎ 01892 891081 📠 01892 890110
e-mail: kscxxx@smtp.ntrust.org.uk

The beautiful gardens at Scotney were planned in the 19th century around the remains of the old, moated Scotney Castle. There is something to see at every time of year, with spring flowers followed by rhododendrons, azaleas and a mass of roses, and then superb autumn

colours. Estate walks all year through 770 acres of woodlands and meadows; walker's guide available.
Times: Open Garden: Apr-end Oct. Old Castle open May-mid Sep, Wed-Sun, 11-6 or sunset if earlier. BH Mon 11-6. (Closed Good Fri). Last admission 1hr before closing. **Fee:** Telephone for details.
Facilities: 🅿 ♿ (wheelchair hire,braille & large print guidebook, audio tape) toilets for disabled shop 🐾 (ex guide & hearing dogs) 🎒

🏛 LEEDS
For Leeds Castle see Maidstone

🏛 LYDD   Map 05 TR02
RSPB NATURE RESERVE
Boulderwall Farm, Dungeness Rd TN29 9PN (off Lydd to Dungeness road, 1m SE of Lydd)
☎ 01797 320588 📠 01797 321962
e-mail: dungeness@rspb.org.uk

This coastal reserve comprises 2,106 acres of shingle beach and flooded pits. An excellent place to watch breeding terns, gulls and other water birds. Wheatears, great crested and little grebes also nest here, and outside the breeding season there are large flocks of teals, shovelers, and goldeneyes, goosanders, smews and both Slavonian and red-necked grebes.
Times: Open daily 9am-9pm (or sunset if earlier). Visitor Centre daily 10-5 Mar-Oct, 10-4 Nov-Feb. (Closed 25 & 26 Dec). **Fee:** * £3 (ch £1, concessions £2). Family ticket £6. **Facilities:** 🅿 ♿ (access by car to some hides) toilets for disabled shop 🐾 (ex guide dogs) 🏷

"Two of the best wild animal parks in the world" BBC TV

TWO WILD ANIMAL PARKS TWO GREAT DAYS OUT!
THE JOHN ASPINALL WILD ANIMAL PARKS AND GARDENS

Port Lympne Nr Hythe. Set in 400 acres over looking the English Channel, home to the largest gorillarium in the world "The Palace of the Apes", safari trailer rides, historic Port Lympne Mansion & Gardens, restaurant and gift shops. Barbary lions, tigers, Asian elephants, hunting dogs, snow leopards, red pandas and many more rare & endangered animals.

Howletts Nr Canterbury. Set in 90 acres, contains the worlds largest group of captive-bred Lowland gorillas, England's largest herd of African elephants, tigers, buffalo, wolves, tapirs and many rare monkeys and small cats. Cave of Gems, gift shops and restaurant.

HOWLETTS & PORT LYMPNE
WILD · ANIMAL · PARKS
www.howletts.net

09068 800605
Calls cost 60p per min at all times.
Prices correct at time of going to print.

GETTING THERE AND OPENING TIMES. Port Lympne nr Hythe is off the M20 junction 11. Howletts is at Bekesbourne just south of Canterbury off the A2. Parks are open everyday from 10am, last admission 4pm. (Last admission winter 3pm) Parks close at 6pm.

Kent

LYMPNE
Map 05 TR13
PORT LYMPNE WILD ANIMAL PARK, MANSION & GARDEN
CT21 4PD (off M20 junct 11, follow brown tourist signs. Also follow brown tourist signs from A20 between Ashford and Folkestone)
☎ 01303 264647   📠 01303 264944
e-mail: karenw@howletts.net

A 300-acre wild animal park that houses hundreds of rare animals: Indian elephants, rhinos, wolves, bison, snow leopards, Siberian and Indian tigers, gorillas and monkeys. The mansion designed by Sir Herbert Baker is surrounded by 15 acres of spectacular gardens. Inside, the most notable features include the restored Rex Whistler Tent Room, Moroccan Patio and hexagonal library where the Treaty of Paris was signed after World War I. New additions to the mansion are the Spencer Roberts Mural room and the Martin Jordan animal mural room.
Times: Open all year, daily 10am-4.30pm, last admission 5pm summer, 3.30pm winter. (Closed 25 Dec). **Fee:** £11.95 (ch 4-14 & pen £8.95). Family ticket £34 (2 adults & 2 ch) £39 (2 adults & 3 ch).
Facilities: 🅿 🍴 ✕ licensed ♿ (very limited access for disabled) toilets for disabled shop garden centre (in season) 🐕 🚭

See advert on page 123

MAIDSTONE
Map 05 TQ75
LEEDS CASTLE
ME17 1PL (7m E of Maidstone at junct 8 of M20/A20, clearly signposted)
☎ 01622 765400   📠 01622 735616
e-mail: enquiries@leeds-castle.co.uk

Set on two islands in the centre of a lake, Leeds Castle has been called the 'loveliest castle in the world', and was home to six medieval Queens of England, as well as being Henry VIII's Royal Palace. Among the treasures inside are many paintings, tapestries and furnishings. Attractions in the grounds include formal gardens, two mazes, exotic bird aviary, dog collar museum, vineyard, woodland walks and show greenhouses.

Times: Open all year daily, Mar-Oct 10-5 (Castle 11-5.30). Nov-Feb 10-3 (Castle 10.15-3.30). Closed 28 Jun; 5 Jul; 8 Nov; 25 Dec **Fee:** * Mar-Oct, Castle, Park & Gardens, £11 (ch 4-15 £7.50, students & pen £9.50); Family ticket £32. Party 15+. Nov-Feb, Castle Park & gardens £9.50 (ch £6, students & pen £8). Family ticket £27 **Facilities:** 🅿 🍴 ✕ licensed ♿ (Braille information, induction loops & wheelchair, lift) toilets for disabled shop garden centre 🐕 (ex guide dogs) 🚭

MAIDSTONE MUSEUM & BENTLIF ART GALLERY
Saint Faith's St ME14 1LH (close to County Hall & Maidstone E train station)
☎ 01622 754497   📠 01622 685022

Set in an Elizabethan manor house which has been much extended over the years, this museum houses an outstanding collection of fine and applied arts, including watercolours, furniture, ceramics, and a collection of Japanese art and artefacts. The museum of the Queen's Own Royal West Kent Regiment is also housed here. Please apply for details of temporary exhibitions, workshops etc.
Times: Open all year, Mon-Sat 10-5.15, Sun & BH Mon 11-4. (Closed 25-26 Dec). **Fee:** Free. **Facilities:** 🅿 (50 yds) 🍴 ♿ shop 🐕 (ex guide dogs)

MUSEUM OF KENT LIFE
Lock Ln, Sandling ME14 3AU (from A229, follow signs for Aylesford. From M20 junct 6 onto A229 Maidstone road)
☎ 01622 763936
📠 01622 662024   **2 for 1**
e-mail: enquiries@museum-kentlife.co.uk

Kent's award-winning open air museum is home to an outstanding collection of historic buildings which house exhibitions on life in Kent over the last 100 years. An early 20th-century village hall and reconstruction of
continued

---

2 for 1 — This symbol indicates which attractions have chosen to participate in our new 2-for-1 voucher scheme.

cottages from the 17th & 20th centuries are more recent buildings to be viewed.

venture playground, woodland trail and 10 acres of walled formal gardens.

Times: Open Mar-end Oct, daily 10-5.30. **Fee:** * £4.90 (concessions £3.50). Family ticket £15. **Facilities:** 🅿 🍴 ✕ licensed ♿ (wheelchairs available, ramps) toilets for disabled shop 🐕

TYRWHITT DRAKE MUSEUM OF CARRIAGES
The Archbishop's Stables, Mill St ME15 6YE (close to River Medway & Archbishops Palace, just off A229 in town centre)
☎ 01622 754497 ✉ 01622 682451

A wide array of horse-drawn carriages and vehicles is displayed in these late-medieval stables, which are interesting in themselves. The exhibits include state, official and private carriages, and some are on loan from royal collections.
Times: Open all year, Apr-Oct daily 10.30-4.30. Last admission 3.45. **Fee:** * £1.60 (ch & pen £1.05). **Facilities:** 🅿 (50 yds) ♿ shop 🐕 (ex guide dogs)

🏛 MINSTER-IN-THANET   Map 05 TR36
MINSTER ABBEY
CT12 4HF (turn off A253 at Minster rdbt. Down the hill through the village. Turn left at St. Mary's Church).
☎ 01843 821254
Times: Open all year, May-Sep, Mon-Fri 11-12 & 2.30-4, Sat 11-12; Oct-Apr, Mon-Sat 11-12. **Facilities:** 🅿 ♿ toilets for disabled shop (ex guide dogs) *Details not confirmed for 2003*

🏛 PENSHURST   Map 05 TQ54
PENSHURST PLACE & GARDENS
TN11 8DG (from M25 junct 5 take A21 Hastings road then exit at Hildenborough, then follow signs)
☎ 01892 870307 ✉ 01892 870866
e-mail: enquiries@penshurstplace.com

Built between 1340 and 1345, the original house is perfectly preserved. Enlarged by successive owners during the 15th, 16th and 17th centuries, the great variety of architectural styles creates a dramatic backdrop for the extensive collections of English, French and Italian furniture, tapestries and paintings. The chestnut-beamed Baron's Hall is the oldest and finest in the country, and the house is set in magnificent formal gardens. There is a toy museum,

Times: Open: House Apr-Oct daily. Gardens, Grounds & venture playground open 10.30-6 and also wknds from 4 Mar. **Fee:** House & Grounds £6.50 (ch 5-16 £4.50, pen & students £6). Family (2ad & 2 ch) £18. Grounds only £5 (ch 5-16 £4, pen & students £4.50) Family (2ad & 2ch) £15. Party 20+. Garden season ticket £30. **Facilities:** 🅿 ✕ licensed ♿ (ramp into Barons Hall, Braille room guides) toilets for disabled shop garden centre 🐕 (ex guide dogs) 🐕

🏛 RAMSGATE   Map 05 TR36
MARITIME MUSEUM
Clock House, Pier Yard, Royal Harbour CT11 8LS (follow Harbour signs)
☎ 01843 587765 & 570622 ✉ 01843 582359
e-mail: museum@ekmt.fsnet.co.uk

This museum is housed in the early 19th-century Clock House, and contains four galleries depicting various aspects of the maritime heritage of the East Kent area. The adjacent restored dry dock and floating exhibits from the museum's historic ship collection include the steam tug *Cervia* and the Dunkirk little ship motor yacht *Sundowner*.
Times: Open Mar-Sep 10am-5pm. Oct-Mar 4 days a week 10am-4.30pm. (Closed Mon). **Fee:** * Combined ticket for museum & steam tug £1.50. (ch & pen 75p). Family £4. **Facilities:** 🅿 (charged) ♿ (restricted) shop 🐕

🏛 RECULVER   Map 05 TR26
RECULVER TOWERS & ROMAN FORT
CT6 6SU (3m E of Herne Bay)
☎ 01227 740676

Regulbium was one of the forts built during the 3rd century AD by the Romans to defend the Saxon Shore. It suffered some damage in the 18th century when erosion of the cliff on which it stands caused part of its walls to collapse. The towers are the remains of a Norman church, built on the site of a 7th-century Anglo-Saxon church.
Times: Open any reasonable time. **Fee:** *Free.* **Facilities:** 🅿 ♿ 🐕 ♿

Kent

🏛 RICHBOROUGH Map 05 TR36
RICHBOROUGH CASTLE
CT13 9JW (1.5m N of Sandwich off A257)
☎ 01304 612013
Times: Open Apr-Oct, daily 10-6 (Oct 10-5); Nov-Mar, 10-4 Wed-Sun (wknds only Dec-Feb). **Facilities:** P & ✗ (in certain areas) ⚌
Details not confirmed for 2003

🏛 ROCHESTER Map 05 TQ76
CHARLES DICKENS CENTRE
Eastgate House, High St ME1 1EW
☎ 01634 844176 📧 01634 827980
Times: Open all year, daily 10-5.30. (Closed Xmas). Last admission 4.45pm. **Facilities:** P (250 yds) shop ✗ *Details not confirmed for 2003* 🍴

GUILDHALL MUSEUM
High St ME1 1PY (follow signs from A2 to Rochester city centre, museum is at N end of High St)
☎ 01634 848717 📧 01634 832919
e-mail: guildhall.museum@medway.gov.uk

Housed in two adjacent buildings, one dating from 1687 and the other from 1909. The collections are arranged chronologically from Pre-history to the Victorian and Edwardian periods. They cover local history and archaeology, fine and decorative art. There is a gallery devoted to the prison hulks of the River Medway. There's a regular programme of temporary exhibitions.
Times: Open all year, daily 10-4.30. Last admissions 4 (Closed Xmas & New Year). **Fee:** Free. **Facilities:** P (250 yds) & shop ✗ (ex guide & hearing dogs)

ROCHESTER CASTLE
ME1 1SX (by Rochester Bridge, A2, M2 junct 1, M25 junct 2)
☎ 01634 402276
Times: Open all year, Apr-Sep, daily 10-6; Oct, daily 10-5; Nov-Mar, daily 10-4. (Closed 24-26 Dec & 1 Jan). **Facilities:** shop ⚌ *Details not confirmed for 2003*

🏛 ROLVENDEN Map 05 TQ83
C M BOOTH COLLECTION OF HISTORIC VEHICLES
Falstaff Antiques, 63 High St TN17 4LP (on A28)
☎ 01580 241234
Times: Open all year, Mon-Sat 10-6. (Closed 25-26 Dec). **Facilities:** P (roadside) shop *Details not confirmed for 2003* 🍴

🏛 SEVENOAKS Map 05 TQ55
KNOLE
TN15 0RP (S end of Sevenoaks, E of A225)
☎ 01732 462100 & 450608 (info line)
📧 01732 465528
e-mail: kknxxx@smtp.ntrust.org.uk
Times: Open Apr-Oct, telephone for details. **Facilities:** P (charged) 🍴 & toilets for disabled shop ✗ (ex in park on lead) 🍴 *Details not confirmed for 2003* 🍴

🏛 SISSINGHURST Map 05 TQ73
SISSINGHURST CASTLE GARDEN
TN17 2AB (1m E of Sissinghurst village on A262)
☎ 01580 710700 📧 01580 710702
e-mail: ksixxx@smtp.ntrust.org.uk
Times: Open: Gardens 23 Mar-3 Nov, Mon, Tue & Fri 11-6.30 (last admission 5.30), Sat, Sun & BHs 10-6.30 (last admission 5.30). Limited capacity timed tickets in operation so visitors may have to wait for admission, garden may be closed when its capacity has been reached. Garden is least crowded in Apr, Sep & Oct. **Fee:** Admission charged (telephone for details). **Facilities:** P ✗ licensed & (Admission restricted to 2 wheelchairs at any one time) toilets for disabled shop ✗ (ex guide dogs) 🍴 🍴

🏛 SITTINGBOURNE Map 05 TQ96
DOLPHIN SAILING BARGE MUSEUM
Crown Quay Ln ME10 3SN (N on A2, signed)
☎ 01795 423215 & 421549

The museum presents the history of the Thames spritsail sailing barge, many of which were built along the banks of Milton Creek. Tools of the trade, photographs and associated artefacts can be seen at the barge yard along with the sailing barge *Cambria*. Privately owned barges are repaired - there's a forge, shipwright's shop and sail loft.
Times: Open Etr-Oct, Sun & BHs 11-5. Other times by arrangement. **Fee:** * £1.50 (concession £1). **Facilities:** P & toilets for disabled shop

🏛 SMALLHYTHE Map 05 TQ83
SMALLHYTHE PLACE
TN30 7NG (2m S of Tenterden, on E side of the Rye road on B2082)
☎ 01580 762334 📧 01580 762334
e-mail: smallhytheplace.ntrust.org.uk

Once a Tudor harbour master's house, this half-timbered, 16th-century building was Dame Ellen Terry's last home, and is now a museum of Ellen Terry memorabilia. The barn is situated in the grounds and is a theatre that is open most days courtesy of the Barn Theatre Society.
Times: Open Apr-Oct, Sat-Wed 11-5, also Good Fri. Last admission 30 mins before closing. **Fee:** £3.40 (ch £1.70). Family ticket £8.50.
Facilities: P & (album of descriptions & photos of upstairs, braille guide) ✗ (ex guide dogs) 🍴

🏛 SWINGFIELD MINNIS Map 05 TR24
THE BUTTERFLY CENTRE
McFarlanes Garden Centre CT15 7HX (on A260 by junction with Elham-Lydden road)
☎ 01303 844244
Times: Open Apr-1 Oct, daily 10-5. Closed Easter Sunday. **Facilities:** P 🍴 & shop garden centre ✗ (ex guide dogs) *Details not confirmed for 2003* 🍴

Kent

TUNBRIDGE WELLS Map 05 TQ53
A Day at the Wells
The Corn Exchange, The Pantiles TN2 5QJ (Accessible via A26/A21/A267)
☎ 01892 546545 📄 01892 513857 **2 for 1**

Take a journey through Georgian England. Experience the sights, sounds and smells of a summer's day in 1740's Tunbridge Wells. Meet the 18th-century socialites of this popular spa town and watch as they take the spring waters, parade and waltz around the ballrooms.
Times: Open daily, Apr-Oct 10-5, Nov-Mar 10-4. (Closed 25 Dec). **Fee:** * £5.10 (ch & pen/student £4.50). Family (2 adults & 2 ch £17.50) (2 adults & 1 ch £13) **Facilities:** P (charged) ♿ (specially designed flat route) shop ✘ (ex guide dogs) 🍴

Tunbridge Wells Museum and Art Gallery
Civic Centre, Mount Pleasant TN1 1JN (adjacent to Town Hall, off A264)
☎ 01892 554171 & 526121 📄 01892 534227

The museum displays local history, along with Tunbridge ware, archaeology, toys and dolls, and domestic and agricultural bygones. The art gallery has regularly changing art and craft exhibitions and touring displays from British and European museums.
Times: Open all year, daily 9.30-5. (Closed Sun, BH's & Etr Sat). **Fee:** Free. **Facilities:** P (200 yds) ♿ parking adjacent to building shop ✘ (ex guide dogs)

UPNOR Map 05 TQ77
Upnor Castle
ME2 4XG (on unclass road off A228)
☎ 01634 718742
Times: Open Apr-Sep, daily 10-6. **Facilities:** P ♿ ✘ (in certain areas) ♻ Details not confirmed for 2003

WESTERHAM Map 05 TQ45
Quebec House
TN16 1TD (at E end of village on N side of A25 facing junct with B2026 Edenbridge road)
☎ 01892 890651 📄 01892 890110

Westerham was the birthplace of General Wolfe, who spent his childhood in this multi-gabled, square brick house, now renamed Quebec House. The house probably dates from the 16th century and was extended and altered in the 17th century. It contains a Wolfe museum and an exhibition on Wolfe and the Quebec campaign.
Times: Open Apr-Oct, Tue & Sun only 2-6 (last admission 5.30pm). Parties by written arrangement. **Fee:** * Telephone 0870 458 4000 for prices. £2.60 (ch £1.30). Family ticket £6.50 booked groups £2.20 **Facilities:** P (150m) ♿ (tactile items) toilets for disabled ✘ (ex guide dogs) 🍴

Squerryes Court Manor House & Gardens
TN16 1SJ (0.5m W of town centre, signposted off A25)
☎ 01959 562345 & 563118 **2 for 1**
📄 01959 565949
e-mail: squerryes.court@squerryes.co.uk

This beautiful manor house, built in 1681, has been the home of the Wardes since 1731. It contains a fine collection of pictures, furniture, porcelain and tapestries. The garden was landscaped in the 18th century and has a lake, restored formal garden, and woodland walks.
Times: Open Apr-Sep (Days not yet known) **Fee:** * House & grounds £4.60 (ch £2.50 & pen £4.10) family ticket £12. Grounds £3 (ch £1.50 & pen £2.50) **Facilities:** P 🍴 ♿ (telephone in advance, part of grounds accessible) toilets for disabled shop ✘ (ex on leads in grounds)

WEST MALLING Map 05 TQ65
St Leonard's Tower
ME19 6PE (on unclass road W of A228)

The fine early Norman tower, dating from the 11th century, is all that remains of a castle or fortified manor house built by Gundulf, Bishop of Rochester.
Times: Open any reasonable time for exterior viewing. Contact West Malling Parish Council for interior viewing - 01732 870872. **Fee:** Free. **Facilities:** ♿ ♻

Lancashire

Lancashire was at the centre of the British cotton industry in the 19th century, which lead to the urbanisation of great tracts of the area. The cotton boom came and went, but the industrial profile remains.

These days Preston is the county's administrative headquarters, and is part of the Central Lancashire New Town, along with Fulwood, Bamber Bridge, Leyland and Chorley. Preston is also the birthplace of Oscar-winning animator Nick Park, creator of Wallace and Gromit.

The former county town, Lancaster, boasts one of the younger English universities, dating from 1964. Other towns, built up to accommodate the mill-workers with back-to-back terraced houses, are Burnley, Blackburn, Rochdale and Accrington. The last of these is home to Accrington Stanley FC one of the original members of the Football League.

Lancashire's resorts, Blackpool, Southport and Morecambe Bay, were developed to meet the leisure needs of the cotton mill town workers. Blackpool is the biggest and brashest, celebrated for its tower, miles of promenade, and the coloured light 'illuminations'. Amusements are taken very seriously here, day and night, and visitors can be entertained in a thousand different ways.

Famous names from Lancashire include actor David Thewlis, comic genius Eric Morecambe (born in Morecambe naturally), and ukelele-playing film star of the 30s and 40s, George Formby.

To get out of town, you can head for the Pennines, the 'backbone of England', a series of hills stretching from the Peak District National Park to the Scottish borders. To the north of the county is the Forest of Bowland, which despite its name is fairly open country, high up, with great views.

Top: Forest of Bowland

EVENTS & FESTIVALS

January
18th-19th Pigeon Racing: British Homing World Show of the Year, Blackpool

February
9th Youth Brass Band Entertainment, Blackpool

March
9th Brass Band Championships, Blackpool

April
18th-21st Easter Maritime Festival, Lancaster
21st-26th Blackpool Junior Dance Festival

May
3rd-18th Blackpool Festival of Puppetry (provisional)
23rd-30th British Open Dance Festival, Blackpool
tbc Lancashire Clog-Dancing Festival, Accrington

June
6th-8th Clitheroe Great Days
22nd Blackpool Marathon

July
tbc Streetbands Festival, Morecambe (provisional)

August
25th National Sedan Chair Carrying Championships
29th-2nd Nov Blackpool Illuminations

September
tbc Heritage Gala, Morecambe
tbc Lancaster Jazz Festival

October
tbc Lancaster Litfest
tbc Morecambe Festival of Comedy

November
20th-22nd British National Dance Championships, Blackpool

Lancashire 129

🏛 BLACKPOOL Map 07 SD33
BLACKPOOL ZOO PARK
East Park Dr FY3 8PP (M55 junct 4, follow brown tourist signs)
☎ 01253 830830   📠 01253 830800   **2 for 1**
e-mail: zookeeper@blackpool-zoo.freeserve.co.uk

This modern zoo, built in 1972, houses over 400 animals within its 32 acres of landscaped gardens. There is a miniature railway, the chance to ride with dolphins in the 'Swimulator', a children's play area, animal feeding times and keeper talks throughout the day.
Times: Open all year daily, summer 10-6; winter 10-5 or dusk. (Closed 25 Dec). **Fee:** * £6.75 (concessions £5.25 ch £4.75). Family (2 adults & 3 ch) £23. **Facilities:** P 💺 ✕ licensed ♿ (wheelchair loan, braille factsheets, sensory experiences) toilets for disabled shop 🐕

🏛 CHARNOCK RICHARD Map 07 SD51
CAMELOT THEME PARK
PR7 5LP (from M6 junct 27/28, or M61 junct 8 follow brown tourism signs)
☎ 01257 453044   📠 01257 452320
e-mail: kingarthur@camelotthemepark.co.uk

Times: Open Apr-Oct. Telephone for further details. **Facilities:** P 💺 ♿ (disabled car parking) toilets for disabled shop 🐕 (ex guide dogs) Details not confirmed for 2003

🏛 CHORLEY Map 07 SD51
ASTLEY HALL MUSEUM & ART GALLERY
Astley Park PR7 1NP (2m W of Chorley off A581 Southport road)
☎ 01257 515555   📠 01257 515556   **2 for 1**
e-mail: astleyhall@lineone.net

A charming Tudor/Stuart building set in beautiful parkland, this lovely Hall retains a comfortable 'lived-in' atmosphere. There are pictures and pottery to see, as well as fine furniture and rare plasterwork ceilings.
Times: Open Apr-Oct, Tue-Sun 12-5; Nov-Mar Sat-Sun 12-4. **Fee:** * £2.95 (concessions £1.95). Family ticket £7.50. Party 10+. **Facilities:** P ♿ (video of upper floors, print/braille guide, CD audio guide) shop 🐕 (ex guide dogs)

🏛 CLITHEROE Map 07 SD74
CLITHEROE CASTLE MUSEUM
Castle Gate, Castle St BB7 1BA (follow Clitheroe signs from A59 by-pass. Museum located in castle grounds near town centre)
☎ 01200 424635   **2 for 1**
e-mail: museum@ribblevalley.gov.uk

The museum has a good collection of carboniferous fossils, and items of local interest. Displays include local history and the industrial archaeology of the Ribble Valley, while special features include the restored Hacking ferry boat believed to be the inspiration for "Buckleberry Ferry" featured in JRR Tolkien's *Fellowship of the Ring*, printer's and clogger's shops and Edwardian kitchen. The area is renowned for its early 17th-century witches, and the museum has a small display on witchcraft.
Times: Open 11-4.30; Mar-Etr, Sat-Wed; Etr-Oct, daily inc BH; Nov, Dec & Feb, wknds & school half terms. (Closed Jan) **Fee:** £1.65 (ch 25p, pen 80p). Family ticket £3.50 **Facilities:** P (500yds) (disabled only parking at establishment) ♿ shop 🐕 (ex guide dogs)

🏛 LANCASTER Map 07 SD46
CITY MUSEUM (ALSO 15 CASTLE HILL)
Market Sq LA1 1HT (In city centre just off A6)
☎ 01524 64637   📠 01524 841692   **2 for 1**
e-mail: awhite@lancaster.gov.uk

The fine Georgian town hall is the setting for the museum, which explores the history and archaeology of the city from prehistoric and Roman times onwards. Also housed here is the museum of the King's Own Royal Lancaster Regiment. The Cottage Museum, furnished in the style of an artisan's house of around 1820, faces Lancaster Castle.
Times: Open all year, Mon-Sat 10-5, (Closed 25 Dec-1 Jan). 15 Castle Hill, Etr-Sep, daily 2-5. **Fee:** City Museum free. 15 Castle Hill £1 (concessions 25p). **Facilities:** P (5 mins walk) ♿ (ramp to entrance/ground floor, 2 stairlifts) shop 🐕 (ex guide dogs)

Lancashire

LANCASTER MARITIME MUSEUM
St George's Quay LA1 1RB (close to M6, junct 33 & 34. From A6 follow signs to Lancaster town centre)
☎ 01524 64637   🖷 01524 841692   2 for 1
e-mail: awhite@lancaster.gov.uk

Graceful Ionic columns adorn the front of the Custom House, built in 1764. Inside, the histories of the 18th-century transatlantic maritime trade of Lancaster, the Lancaster Canal and the fishing industry of Morecambe Bay are well illustrated.
Times: Open all year, daily, Etr-Oct 11am-5pm; Nov-Etr 12.30-4pm.
Fee: £3 (concessions £1). **Facilities:** P ⌴ ♿ (ramped access, lift to all floors, ground floor entry) toilets for disabled shop ✖ (ex guide dogs)

SHIRE HALL
Lancaster Castle, Castle Pde LA1 1YJ (follow brown tourist signs from M6 junct 33/34)
☎ 01524 64998   🖷 01524 847914
e-mail: christine.goodier@property.lancscc.gov.uk

Founded on the site of three Roman forts, Lancaster Castle dominates Castle Hill, above the River Lune. The Norman keep was built in about 1170 and King John added a curtain wall and Hadrian's Tower. The Shire Hall, noted for its Gothic revival design, contains a splendid display of heraldry. The Crown Court was notorious as having handed out the greatest number of death sentences of any court in the land.
Times: Open daily ex Xmas/New Year 10.30 (1st tour)-4 (last tour). Court sittings permitting -it is advisable to telephone before visiting except in August or at weekends. **Fee:** * £4 (ch, pen & students £2.50). **Facilities:** P (100mtrs) (voucher system) ♿ shop ✖ (ex guide dogs) 🍴

🏛 LEIGHTON HALL   Map 07 SD47
LEIGHTON HALL
LA5 9ST (off M6 at junct 35 onto A6 & follow signs)
☎ 01524 734474   🖷 01524 720357   2 for 1
e-mail: leightonhall@yahoo.co.uk

Early Gillow furniture is displayed among other treasures in the fine interior of this neo-Gothic mansion. Outside a large collection of birds of prey can be seen,

and flying displays are given each afternoon. There are also fine gardens, a maze and a woodland walk.
Times: Open May-Sep, Sun, Tue-Fri & BH Mon from 2pm. For Aug only open from 12.30. (Last admission 4.30pm). **Fee:** * £4.50 (ch 5-16 £3, pen £4). Family ticket £13.75 **Facilities:** P ⌴ ♿ shop garden centre ✖ (ex guide dogs & in park)

🏛 LEYLAND   Map 07 SD52
BRITISH COMMERCIAL VEHICLE MUSEUM
King St PR5 1LE (0.75m from M6 junct 28)
☎ 01772 451011   🖷 01772 623404
Times: Open 2 Apr-Sep, Sun, Tue & BH (Oct Sun only). **Facilities:** P ⌴ ♿ (ramps to decked viewing area) toilets for disabled shop ✖ (ex guide dogs) *Details not confirmed for 2003*

🏛 LYTHAM ST ANNES   Map 07 SD32
TOY & TEDDY BEAR MUSEUM
373 Clifton Dr North FY8 2PA (350yds from town centre, on A584 towards Blackpool)
☎ 01253 713705   2 for 1

This museum has a collection of old toys arranged in five large rooms and the Toytown Arcade. Charming displays include: Teddy Bears' Picnic and Bears at the Seaside. Other attractions include a Mini Motor Museum, a collection of more than 200 dolls, 35 dolls' houses, toy trains, working layouts, Dinky cars, aeroplanes, meccano, books and games.
Times: Open all BHs & school holidays, daily 1-5 ex Xmas; Jul-Aug, daily Wed, Thur,Sat,Sun 11-5. Winter open for groups & schools daily by appointment. **Fee:** * £2.95 (ch & pen £2.50) **Facilities:** P ♿ shop

🏛 MARTIN MERE   Map 07 SD41
WWT MARTIN MERE
L40 0TA (signposted from M61, M58 &M6, 6m from Ormskirk, off A59)
☎ 01704 895181   🖷 01704 892343   2 for 1
e-mail: info@martinmere.co.uk

One of Britain's most important wetland sites, where you can get really close to a variety of ducks, geese and swans from all over the world as well as two flocks of flamingos. Thousands of wildfowl, including Pink-Footed geese, Bewick's and Whooper swans, winter here. Other features include a children's adventure playground, exhibition gallery, craft area and an educational centre. The Annual North West Bird Fair takes place on 15th & 16th of November and wild swans by floodlight from 1st November to 31st January.
Times: Open all year, daily 9.30-5.30 (5 in winter). (Closed 25 Dec).
Fee: * £5.50 (ch £3.30, pen £4.40). Family ticket £14.30. **Facilities:** P ⌴ ♿ (wheelchair loan, Braille trail, heated hide, audio tours) toilets for disabled shop ✖ (ex guide dogs) 🍴

🏛 MORECAMBE   Map 07 SD46
FRONTIERLAND - FAMILY PARK
The Promenade LA4 4DG (from M6 take junct 34 northbound and junct 35 southbound)
☎ 01524 410024   🖷 01524 831399
Times: Open 8 Apr-3 Sep, days & times vary, telephone for details.
Facilities: P (charged) ⌴ ♿ toilets for disabled shop ✖ *Details not confirmed for 2003* 🍴

Lancashire

PADIHAM
Map 07 SD73
GAWTHORPE HALL
BB12 8UA (off A671)
☎ 01282 771004 📠 01282 770178
e-mail: rpmgaw@smtp.ntrust.org.uk
Times: Open 31 Mar-Oct, Garden: daily 10-6. Hall: Tue-Thu, Sat & Sun 1-5. Also open BH Mon & Good Fri. (Last admission 4.30). **Facilities:** P ⌁ ♿ toilets for disabled shop ✖ (ex in grounds) 🐕 Details not confirmed for 2003

PRESTON
Map 07 SD52
HARRIS MUSEUM & ART GALLERY
Market Square PR1 2PP (exit M6 at junct 31, follow signs for Preston town centre)
☎ 01772 258248 📠 01772 886764
e-mail: harris.museum@preston.gov.uk

An impressive Grade I listed Greek Revival building containing extensive collections of fine and decorative art including a gallery of Clothes and Fashion. The Story of Preston covers the town's history and the lively exhibition programmes of contemporary art and social history are accompanied by events and activities throughout the year. The National Art Collections Fund Centenary Exhibition takes place between March and April 2003, and will consist of the best fine and decorative art acquired by museums and galleries in the North over the last 100 years.
Times: Open all year, Mon-Sat 10-5. (Closed Sun & BHs). **Fee:** Free. **Facilities:** P (5 mins walk) (blue badge disabled parking only) ⌁ ♿ (Wheelchair available. Chair lift to mezzanine galleries) toilets for disabled shop ✖ (ex guide/assistance dogs)

THE NATIONAL FOOTBALL MUSEUM
Sir Tom Finney Way, Deepdale PR1 6RY (2m from M6 juncts 31, 31A or 32. Follow brown tourist signs in Preston)
☎ 01772 908442 📠 01772 908433
e-mail: enquiries@nationalfootballmuseum.com

2 for 1

What location could be more fitting for a National Football Museum than Deepdale Stadium, the home of Preston North End, first winners of the professional football league in 1888-9? This fascinating trip through football past and present includes the FIFA Museum Collection, a fine display of memorabilia and artefacts; interactive displays that allow visitors to commentate on matches, and take virtual trips to every League ground in the country; and an art gallery dedicated to the Beautiful Game.
Times: Open Tue-Sat 10-5, Sun 11-5. (Closed Mon ex BH's). Contact for opening times on match days. **Fee:** * £6.95 (ch 5-15 & concessions £4.95). Under 5's free **Facilities:** P ⌁ ♿ (Lifts, multi-sensory exhibitions) toilets for disabled shop ✖ (ex guide dogs) 🎁

ROSSENDALE
Map 07 SD72
WHITAKER PARK & ROSSENDALE MUSEUM
Whitaker Park, Haslingden Rd, Rawtenstall BB4 6RE (off A681, 0.25m W of Rawtenstall centre)
☎ 01706 244682 📠 01706 250037

Former mill owner's house, built in 1840 and set in the delightful Whitaker Park. Displays include fine and decorative arts, a Victorian drawing room, natural history, costume, local and social history.
Times: Open Mon-Fri, 1-5; Sat 10-5 (Apr-Oct), 10-4 (Nov-Mar); Sun noon-5 (Apr-Oct), noon-4 (Nov-Mar). BH's 1-5. (Closed 24-26 Dec & 1 Jan). **Fee:** Free. **Facilities:** P ♿ (large print, audio guides, induction loop) toilets for disabled shop ✖ (ex guide dogs)

RUFFORD
Map 07 SD41
RUFFORD OLD HALL
L40 1SG (off A59, 7m North of Ormskirk)
☎ 01704 821254 📠 01704 821254
Times: Open 31 Mar-4 Nov, Sat-Wed, (but open 31 May, 2, 9, 16, 23 Aug). Hall 1-5 (Last admission 4.30pm); Garden & shop 12-5.30.
Facilities: P ✖ ♿ (braille guide, wheelchairs, adapted cutlery etc) shop ✖ (ex in grounds) 🐕 Details not confirmed for 2003

SAMLESBURY
Map 07 SD53
SAMLESBURY HALL
Preston New Rd PR5 OUP (M6 junct 31/A677 for 3m)
☎ 01254 812010 & 812229
📠 01254 812174
e-mail: dhornby@btinternet.com

2 for 1

A well restored half-timbered manor house, built during the 14th and 15th centuries, and set in 5 acres of beautiful grounds. Sales of antiques and collector's items, craft shows and temporary exhibitions are held all year round.
Times: Open all year ex last wk Dec & 1st 2 wks Jan, Tue-Sun 11-4.30. Closed Sat for weddings, newer part of hall open Sat for antiques sales. **Fee:** * £2.50 (ch 4-16 £1). **Facilities:** P ✖ licensed ♿ toilets for disabled ✖ (ex guide dogs)

---

†Lancaster Castle†
Owned by HM The Queen in right of her Duchy of Lancaster

Used as a Court and a Prison – *see*
- where the Lancashire Witches were tried, convicted and condemned to die
- the Shire Hall, with its display of heraldic shields
- the dungeons, 'Drop Room' and 'Hanging Corner'
- the court from which convicts were transported to Australia
- the Grand Jury Room where Queen Victoria dined

Open daily except Christmas/New Year
Tours every half-hour from 10.30am-4pm
(Court sittings permitting)

Check by telephoning (01524) 64998
http://www.lancastercastle.com

🏛 SILVERDALE   Map 07 SD47
RSPB NATURE RESERVE
Myers Farm LA5 0SW (M6 junct 35, then N along A6 for several miles, follow brown tourist signs to reserve)
☎ 01524 701601   📠 01524 701601   **2 for 1**

A large reed swamp with meres with willow and alder scrub in a valley with woodland on its limestone slopes. The reserve covers 321 acres, and is home to the North West's largest concentration of bitterns, together with bearded tits, reed, sedge and grasshopper warblers, shovelers, pochards, tufted ducks and marsh harriers. Black terns and ospreys regularly pass through in spring, and greenshanks and various sandpipers in the autumn. Wintering wildfowl include large flocks of mallards, teals, wigeons, and shovelers.
Times: Open daily 9am-9pm (or sunset if earlier). Visitor Centre daily 9.30-5. Feb-Oct 9.30-4.30 Nov-Jan (closed Xmas Day). **Fee:** £4.50 (ch £1, concessions £3) Family £9. **Facilities:** 🅿 ☕ ♿ (chair lift to 1st floor, ramp access to 4 hides) toilets for disabled shop ✖ (ex guide dogs) 🚭

🏛 TURTON BOTTOMS   Map 07 SD71
TURTON TOWER
BL7 0HG (on B6391, off A666 or A676)
☎ 01204 852203   **2 for 1**
📠 01204 853759
e-mail: turtontower.lcc@btinternet.com

A historic house incorporating a 15th-century tower house and Elizabethan half-timbered buildings, and displaying a major collection of carved wood furniture. During the 19th century, the house became associated with the Gothic revival and later typified the idealism of the Arts and Crafts movement. The gardens are being restored in late-Victorian style. The exhibition gallery houses three exhibitions per season, usually consisting of one high profile, one by regional artists and finally a touring show from elsewhere in the country.
Times: Open May-Sep, Mon-Thu 11-5, wknds 1-5; Mar-Oct, Mon-Wed 1-5, wknds 1-4; Apr Sat-Wed 1-5; Nov & Feb, Sun 1-4. Other times by prior arrangement. **Fee:** £3 (concessions £1.50). Guided tour with supper/lunch, prices vary. **Facilities:** 🅿 ☕ ♿ toilets for disabled shop ✖ (ex in grounds) 🚭

🏛 WHALLEY   Map 07 SD73
WHALLEY ABBEY
BB7 9SS (Just off A59 4m S of Clitheroe)
☎ 01254 828400   📠 01254 828401

The ruins of a 14th-century Cistercian abbey, set in the delightful gardens of the Blackburn Diocesan Retreat and Conference House, a 17th-century manor house with gardens reaching down to the River Calder. The remains include two gateways, a chapter house and the abbot's lodgings and kitchen.
Times: Grounds open all year; coffee shop, shop & exhibition area, Jan-Dec daily 11-5. (Closed 24 & 25 Dec 2002 & 6-9 Jan 2003). **Fee:** * £2 (ch 50p, pen £1.25). **Facilities:** 🅿 ☕ ✖ licensed ♿ (chair lifts, ramps) toilets for disabled shop ✖ (ex guide dogs)

Leicestershire

Leicestershire is divided between the large country estates of its eastern side and the industrial towns of the East Midlands to its west.

Coal mining was an important part of the county's industrial development in the 19th and early 20th centuries, and this is reflected in its heritage, including a reclaimed mine near Coalville, now divided between a nature reserve and Snibston Discovery Park, where children can find out about the mining industry.

Agricultural areas are concentrated around the pleasant market towns of Market Harborough and Market Bosworth. The latter was the site of the Battle of Bosworth Field, the final engagement of the War of the Roses in 1485, where Richard III, the Yorkist king was defeated and killed by Henry of Richmond, who was then crowned Henry VII, the first of the Tudors.

The administrative centre is the city of Leicester, and other major towns are Loughborough, which includes bell-founding among its many industries, and Melton Mowbray, home of Stilton cheese and a particularly English item, the pork pie. One shop in Leicester has been specialising in this meaty delicacy since 1851. Northeast of Melton Mowbray is the lovely Vale of Belvoir, beneath which are large deposits of coal.

Charnwood Forest, with fewer trees than one would expect, provides a wild and rugged landscape conveniently situated for escape from the city. It lies to the northwest of Leicester extending to Loughborough and Coalville, with some interruptions.

Famous locals include footballer and broadcaster Gary Lineker, the "Elephant Man" John Merrick, singer Englebert Humperdinck, and Thomas Cook, 19th-century travel agent, who opened his first shop in Leicester.

EVENTS & FESTIVALS

February
7th-16th Comedy Festival, Leicester

March
tbc Leicester Jazz Festival

May
4th-5th Leicestershire County Show, Loughborough
tbc Heart Link Street Organ Festival, Leicester
tbc Leicester Early Music Festival

June
tbc Everybody's Reading, celebration of reading & writing
tbc International Music Festival, Leicester
tbc Melton Show, Melton Mowbray

July
20th Riverside Festival, Leicester (provisional)
20th-27th Spokesfest
tbc Belgrave Mela, Leicester

August
1st-3rd Leicestershire Country Music Festival
2nd Caribbean Carnival, Victoria Park, Leicester
tbc Castle Park Festival, Leicester
tbc Leicester Horticultural Show

October
tbc Dashera, Hindu festival
tbc Navrati, Asian religious festival

October/November
tbc Diwali Celebrations

November
tbc Abbey Park Bonfire & Fireworks Display

Top: Bede House, Lyddington

Leicestershire

ASHBY-DE-LA-ZOUCH Map 08 SK31
ASHBY-DE-LA-ZOUCH CASTLE
LE65 1BR
☎ 01530 413343
Times: Open Apr-Sep, daily 10-6; Oct, daily 10-5; Nov-Mar, daily 10-4. (Closed 24-26 Dec & 1 Jan). **Facilities:** P & ✗ # *Details not confirmed for 2003*

BELVOIR Map 08 SK83
BELVOIR CASTLE
NG32 1PD (between A52 & A607, follow the brown heritage signs from A1, A52, A607 & A46)
☎ 01476 870262   📠 01476 870443
e-mail: info@belvoircastle.com
Times: Open Etr wknd-Sep daily 11-5 & Sun in Oct **Facilities:** P ⬛ ✗ licensed & (permitted to be driven/drive right up to castle entrance) toilets for disabled shop ✗ (ex guide dogs) *Details not confirmed for 2003*

CASTLE DONINGTON Map 08 SK42
DONINGTON GRAND PRIX COLLECTION
Donington Park DE74 2RP (2m from M1 junct 23a/24 and M42/A42)
☎ 01332 811027   **2 for 1**
📠 01332 812829
e-mail: enquiries@doningtoncollection.co.uk

From the turn of the 20th century to the new millennium, it's all here – the largest collection of Mclaren racing cars on public display, the world's only complete collection of Racing Green Vanwalls, every Williams F1 car from 1983 to 1999, a superb BRM display and Ferraris driven by Asvar. Ickx, Senna's winning Mclaren from the 1993 European Grand Prix at Donington, Stirling Moss's Lotus which defeated the works Ferraris at Monaco and Jim Clark's beautiful Lotus 25 . . . they're all here, and many, many more.
Times: Open daily 10-5 (last admission 4pm). Open later on race days. (Closed over Xmas period - telephone to confirm opening times over this period). **Fee:** £7 (ch 6-16 £2.50 pen & students £5). Family ticket (2 adults & up to 3 ch) £14. Party. **Facilities:** P ⬛ ✗ licensed & shop ✗ (ex guide dogs) ⚑

COALVILLE Map 08 SK41
SNIBSTON DISCOVERY PARK
County Hall LE3 8TB (4.5m from M1 junct 22/2m or from A42/M42 junct 13 on A511 on the west side of Coalville)
☎ 01530 278444   📠 01530 813301
e-mail: snibston@leics.gov.uk
Times: Open all year, 10-5 (Closed 25-26 Dec). **Facilities:** P ⬛ & (Braille labels, touch tables, parking available) toilets for disabled shop ✗ (ex guide dogs) *Details not confirmed for 2003* ⚑

DONINGTON-LE-HEATH Map 05 SK41
DONINGTON-LE-HEATH MANOR HOUSE
Manor Rd LE67 2FW (S of Coalville)
☎ 01530 831259   📠 01530 831259
e-mail: museum@leics.gov.uk
Times: Open all year: Apr-Sep, 11-5; Oct-Mar, 11-3. **Facilities:** P ⬛ ✗ & shop ✗ (ex guide dogs) *Details not confirmed for 2003*

KIRBY MUXLOE Map 04 SK50
KIRBY MUXLOE CASTLE
Oakcroft St LE9 9MD (off B5380)
☎ 0116 238 6886

When Lord Hastings drew up designs for his castle in the late 15th century, he first had to obtain 'licence to crenellate', but his moated, fortified manor was never completed as he was executed only a few years after the work was begun. It stands as a ruin in his memory.
Times: Open 29 Mar-Oct, wknds & BH's 12-5. **Fee:** * £2.10 (ch 5-15 £1.10, under 5's free, con £1.60) **Facilities:** P & #

LEICESTER Map 04 SK50
ABBEY PUMPING STATION
Corporation Rd, Abbey Ln LE4 5PX (off A6, 1m N from city centre)
☎ 0116 299 5111   📠 0116 299 5125
Times: Open Apr-Oct, Mon-Sat 10-5, Sun 2-5; Nov-Mar, Mon-Sat 10-4.30, Sun 2-4.30 (Closed 24-26 & 31 Dec & 1 Jan). Subject to change. **Facilities:** P & (loan of wheelchairs) toilets for disabled shop ✗ (ex guide dogs) *Details not confirmed for 2003*

BELGRAVE HALL & GARDENS
Church Rd, off Thurcaston Rd, Belgrave LE4 5PE (off Belgrave/Loughborough road, 1m from city centre)
☎ 0116 266 6590   📠 0116 261 3063
e-mail: marteool@leicester.gov.uk

A delightful three-storey Queen Anne house dating from 1709 with beautiful period and botanic gardens. Authentic room settings contrast Georgian elegance with Victorian cosiness and include the kitchen, drawing room, music room and nursery. The home of the celebrated Arts and Crafts collection owned by Leicester City Museums.
Times: Open all year, Apr-Oct, Mon-Sat 10-5, Sun 2-5; Nov-Mar, Mon-Sat 10-4.30, Sun 2-4.30. Closed 24-26 Dec/New Year. Opening times subject to change, ring Hall for details. **Fee:** Free. **Facilities:** P & (loan of wheelchair) toilets for disabled shop ✗

JEWRY WALL MUSEUM & SITE
St Nicholas Circle LE1 4LB (opposite The Holiday Inn)
☎ 0116 225 4971   📠 0116 225 4966

Behind the massive fragment of the Roman Jewry wall and a Roman Baths site of the 2nd century AD is the Museum of Leicestershire Archaeology, which covers finds from the earliest times to the Middle Ages.
Times: Open Apr-Oct, Mon-Sat 10-5, Sun 2-5; Nov-Mar, Mon-Sat 10-4, Sun 2-4 (Closed 31 Dec & 1 Jan). Subject to change. **Fee:** Admission free, however a charge is made for some events. Donations welcome. **Facilities:** P (300yds) (limited on-street parking) & toilets for disabled shop ✗ (ex guide dogs)

Leicestershire

LEICESTERSHIRE MUSEUM & ART GALLERY
53 New Walk LE1 7EA (From A6 onto Waterloo Way at Railway Stn. Right into Regent Rd, right onto West St, right onto Princess Rd which leads to car park)
☎ 0116 255 4100   ▤ 0116 247 3005

This major regional venue houses local and national collections. There's an internationally famous collection of German Expressionism and other displays include the Rutland Dinosaur and thousands of butterflies. An extensive Natural History collection augmented by art from the renaissance to contemporary.
Times: Open all year, Apr-Oct, Mon-Sat 10-5, Sun 2-5. Nov-Mar, Mon-Sat 10-4.30, Sun 2-4.30. (Closed 24-26 Dec/New Year). **Fee:** Free. **Facilities:** P ☕ ♿ (wheelchairs for loan, minicom, induction loop) toilets for disabled shop ✖ (ex guide dogs) 🍴

NATIONAL SPACE CENTRE
Exploration Dr LE4 5NS (off A6, 2m N of city centre)
☎ 0116 261 0261   ▤ 0116 258 2100
e-mail: info@spacecentre.co.uk

Offering five themed galleries, cutting-edge audio-visual technology and glimpses into genuine space research, the National Space Centre is a unique experience. Learn about the planets, astronaut life, weather forecasting, space-stations and satellites. Visit the Space Theatre and the Newsdesk, and take a look at the scientists and astronomers doing genuine research in the Space Science Research Unit.
Times: Open all year, Tue-Fri 9.30-last entry 4pm, Sat-Sun 9.30-4.30. School holidays, Mon 12-4.30 & Tue-Sun 9.30-4.30. **Fee:** * £7.95 (ch 5-14 & concessions £5.95). Family ticket £24-£29 **Facilities:** P ☕ ✖ licensed ♿ toilets for disabled shop ✖ (ex guide dogs) 🍴

NEWARKE HOUSES
The Newarke LE2 7BY
☎ 0116 247 3222   ▤ 0116 247 0403

This museum follows Leicestershire's social history from the 15th century to the present, showing everyday life and social change throughout the county. Clocks, toys, domestic life objects, greetings cards and Asian arts are among the many collections. A reconstructed street scene gives a glimpse of Victorian life and the fascinating story of Daniel Lambert, the famous 52-stone gaoler of the 18th century, is also told.
Times: Telephone Newarke Houses Museum on 0116 247 3222 for details of opening hours. **Fee:** Free. **Facilities:** P (200 yds) shop ✖ (ex guide dogs) 🍴

THE RECORD OFFICE FOR LEICESTERSHIRE, ER & RUTLAND
Long St, Wigston Magna LE18 2AH (Old A50, S of Leicester City)
☎ 0116 257 1080   ▤ 0116 257 1120
e-mail: museums@leics.gov.uk
Times: Open all year, Mon, Tue & Thu 9.15-5, Wed 9.15-7.30, Fri 9.15-4.45, Sat 9.15-12.15. (Closed Sun & BH wknds Sat-Tue). **Facilities:** P ♿ toilets for disabled ✖ 🚻 Details not confirmed for 2003

UNIVERSITY OF LEICESTER HAROLD MARTIN BOTANIC GARDEN
Beaumont Hall, Stoughton Dr South, Oadby LE2 2NA (3m SE A6, entrance at 'The Knoll', Glebe Rd)
☎ 0116 271 7725

The grounds of four houses, now used as student residences and not open to the public, make up this 16-acre garden. A great variety of plants in different settings provide a delightful place to walk, including rock, water and sunken gardens, trees, borders, heathers and glasshouses.
Times: Open Mon-Fri 10-4 (ex 25-26 Dec & 1 Jan), Sat & Sun 10-4 (from 3rd weekend in Mar to 2nd weekend in Nov inclusive). **Fee:** Free. **Facilities:** P (adjacent) ♿ toilets for disabled ✖ (ex guide dogs)

WYGSTON'S HOUSE MUSEUM OF COSTUME
12 Applegate, St Nicholas Circle LE1 5LD
☎ 0116 247 3056   ▤ 0116 262 0964
Times: Open Apr-Oct, Mon-Sat 10-5, Sun 2-5; Nov-Mar, Mon-Sat, 10-4.30, Sun 2-4.30 (Closed Good Fri & 25-26 & 31 Dec & 1 Jan).
Facilities: P (150 yds) ♿ shop ✖ Details not confirmed for 2003

🚂 LOUGHBOROUGH   Map 08 SK51
GREAT CENTRAL RAILWAY
Great Central Rd LE11 1RW (signposted from A6)
☎ 01509 230726   ▤ 01509 239791
e-mail: booking_office@gcrailway.co.uk
Times: Open Sat, Sun & BH Mon & midweek Jun-Sep. **Facilities:** P ☕ ✖ licensed ♿ (Disabled coach available on most trains, check beforehand) toilets for disabled shop Details not confirmed for 2003 🍴

🚂 MARKET BOSWORTH   Map 04 SK40
THE BATTLEFIELD LINE
Shackerstone Station, Shackerstone, Nuneaton CV13 6NW (from A444/A447 take B585 to Market Bosworth and follow signs for Congerstone/Shackerstone. Follow brown tourist signs from M42 junct 11)
☎ 01827 880754   ▤ 01827 881050   `2 for 1`
e-mail: robertlep@aol.com

Together with a regular railway service (mainly steam) from Shackerstone to Shenton, there is an extensive railway museum featuring a collection of rolling stock and many other relics from the age of steam.
Times: Open all year, Passenger steam train service operates Apr-Oct, Sat, Sun & BH Mon. Heritage Railcar Wed Jul-Aug **Fee:** Return train fare £6 (ch £3, Sen £4). Family ticket £16. **Facilities:** P ☕ ✖ ♿ toilets for disabled shop 🍴

BOSWORTH BATTLEFIELD VISITOR CENTRE & COUNTRY PARK
Ambion Hill, Sutton Cheney CV13 0AD (follow brown tourist signs from A447, A444 & A5)
☎ 01455 290429   ▤ 01455 292841   `2 for 1`
e-mail: bosworth@leics.gov.uk

The Battle of Bosworth Field was fought in 1485 between the armies of Richard III and the future Henry VII. The visitor centre offers a comprehensive

continued

136 Leicestershire

interpretation of the battle, with exhibitions, models and a film theatre. Special medieval attractions are held in the summer months.

Bosworth Battlefield Visitor Centre & Country Park

Times: Open all year, Country Park and Battle Trails daily 11-5. Nov & Dec Sun 11-dusk; Mar wknds 11-5. Visitor Centre open Apr-Oct. Parties all year by arrangement. **Fee:** * Visitor Centre £3 (concessions £2). Family ticket £8.50. Special charges apply on event days. Subject to review. **Facilities:** P (charged) (wheelchair & electric scooter hire, tactile exhibits) toilets for disabled shop.

MOIRA   Map 08 SK31
Conkers
Millennium Av, Rawdon Rd DE12 6GA (on B5003 in Moira, signposted from A444 and A42)
☎ 01283 216633   01283 210321
e-mail: info@visitconkers.com

Conkers the 120-acre attraction in the Heart of the National Forest, two award-winning buildings linked by a train! Relax and enjoy amazing indoor exhibits and outdoor experiences. Feel a leaf breath, touch a toad...tackle the assault course or rise to the challenge of Billy Bonkers playpark. Enjoy the Artscape sculpture trail, water play area and Forest Garden. Discover wildlife through the woodland and wetland walks; tree canopy walk way and bird hide. Relax in one of two lakeside restaurants. Enjoy events all year round, explore our innovative education program and browse in the shops.
Times: Open daily, summer 10-6, winter 10-5. (Closed 25 Dec). **Fee:** * £5.25 (ch £3.25, pen & concessions £4.25). Family ticket (2 adults & 2 ch) £14.95. **Facilities:** P X licensed (multi access walks & trails accessible to wheelchairs) toilets for disabled shop garden centre (ex guide dogs).

SWINFORD   Map 04 SP57
Stanford Hall
LE17 6DH (7.5m NE of Rugby, 1.5m from Swinford. 2m from the M1, M6, A14 junct)
☎ 01788 860250   01788 860870
e-mail: enquiries@stanfordhall.co.uk

A beautiful William and Mary house, built in 1697 by Sir Roger Cave, ancestor of the present owner. The house contains antique furniture, paintings (including the Stuart Collection) and family costumes. Special events include car and motorcycle owners' club rallies.
Times: Open Etr Sat-end Sep, Sat, Sun, BH Mon & Tue following 1.30-5.30; noon on BH & Event Days (House 1.30). Last admission 5pm. Motorcycle Museum: Sun & BH Mons only, 1.30-5. **Fee:** * House & Grounds £4.50 (ch £2); Grounds only £2.50 (ch £1); Motorcycle Museum £1 (ch 35p). Party 20+. **Facilities:** P (museum also accessible) toilets for disabled shop (ex guide dogs & in park).

TWYCROSS   Map 04 SK30
Twycross Zoo Park
CV9 3PX (On A444 Burton to Nuneaton road, directly off M42 junct 11)
☎ 01827 880250   01827 880700

Set in 50 acres of parkland, the zoo is home to around 1000 animals, most of which are from endangered species. Twycross is the only zoo in Britain to house Bonobos - humans' 'closest living relative'. There are also various other animals such as lions, tigers, elephants and giraffes, and a pets' corner for younger children. Other attractions include a Penguin Pool with underwater viewing and a Children's Adventure Playground.
Times: Open all year, daily 10-6 (4pm in winter). (Closed 25 Dec). **Fee:** Please telephone for prices. **Facilities:** P (charged) toilets for disabled shop (ex guide dogs).

Lincolnshire

Lincolnshire is an east coast county with an agricultural economy, attractive seaside resorts, some lovely countryside, and quintessentially English market towns.

Much of the fenland around the Wash has been drained of its marshes and reclaimed as highly productive farmland. Further north, the coastline, with its sandy beaches, has been developed to accommodate the holiday industry, with caravans, campsites and the usual seaside paraphernalia. The main resorts are Skegness, Mablethorpe, Cleethorpes and Ingoldmells. Inland, the chalky margin of the Lincolnshire Wolds offers an undulating landscape of hills and valleys, designated as an Area of Outstanding Natural Beauty.

Lincoln, the county town, is dominated by its magnificent cathedral. Most of interest in the city is in the uphill area, Steep Hill, ascending from the River Witham; the Bailgate spanned by the Newport Arch, and the Minster Yard with its medieval and Georgian architecture. During World War II the county was the base for Bomber Command, and it was from Scampton that the famous Dambuster mission of May 1943 took off.

Boston, on the banks of the Witham, was England's second biggest seaport in the 13th and 14th centuries, when the wool trade was at its height. The town is distinguished by the Boston Stump, the 272-ft (83m) tower on the church of St Boltoph, which can be seen for miles around.

There are market towns all over the county still holding weekly markets, including Barton-upon-Humber, Boston, Bourne, Brigg, Crowland, Gainsborough, Grantham, Great Grimsby, Holbeach, Horncastle, Long Sutton, Louth, Market Rasen, Scunthorpe, Sleaford, Spalding (the centre of the flower industry), and the elegant Edwardian spa resort of Woodhall Spa.

Top: Flower Festival at Spalding

EVENTS & FESTIVALS

January
26th The Great Australian Breakfast, University of Lincoln

April
6th Lincoln 10km Run

May
3rd-5th Spalding Flower Parade & Country Fair
tbc Beer Festival, Cleethorpes
tbc Folk Festival, Cleethorpes
tbc Lincoln Grand Prix Cycle Race
tbc Tallington Beer Festival (real ale & live music)

June
18th-19th Lincolnshire Show, Lincolnshire Showground
28th-29th RAF Waddington International Air Show

July
26th-27th Heckington Show, Estate Showground, Heckington
tbc Lincoln Water Carnival, Brayford Pool
tbc Scarecrow Weekend & Flower Festival, Tetney

July/August
tbc Cleethorpes Carnival Parade

August
23rd-24th Lincolnshire Steam & Vintage Rally, Lincoln

November
tbc Bonfire night celebrations, Cleethorpes

December
tbc Lincoln Christmas Market

Lincolnshire

ALFORD
Map 09 TF47
Manor House Museum
West St LN13 9DJ (on the A1104, in centre of town)
☎ 01507 463073

Alford Manor House dates back to around c1540. It has been extended, altered and adopted over the centuries, and is probably the largest thatched building of its kind in the country. New for 2003 is a display detailing the history of the Manor House. Plus, a photographic record of Alford in years gone by, links with America and (Tuesdays only) farm machinery in the Hackett Barn. **Times:** Open Etr-Sep daily, Mon-Sat 10.30-4.30, Sun 12-4. **Fee:** * £1.50 (accompanied ch 50p). **Facilities:** P ⌘ (photographs of inaccessible areas) shop ✸ (ex guide dogs)

BELTON
Map 08 SK93
Belton House Park & Gardens
NG32 2LS (3m NE Grantham on A607)
☎ 01476 566116   📠 01476 579371
e-mail: ebahah@smtp.ntrust.org.uk
Times: Open 23 Mar-3 Nov, Wed-Sun & BH Mon. Closed Good Fri. House open 12.30-5 (last admission 4.30). Grounds open 11-5.30, 10.30-5.30 in Aug. Garden open 9 Nov-22 Dec, Sat & Sun 12-4. **Facilities:** P ✸ licensed ♿ (braille guide, hearing scheme) toilets for disabled shop ✸ (ex in grounds) ♨ *Details not confirmed for 2003*

CLEETHORPES
Map 08 TA30
Pleasure Island Theme Park
Kings Rd DN35 0PL (From A46, follow signs to Cleethorpes, then brown tourist signs)
☎ 01472 211511   📠 01472 211087
e-mail: pleasureisland@btinternet.com
Times: Open from Apr-Oct, daily. **Facilities:** P ⌘ ✕ ✸ ♿ toilets for disabled shop *Details not confirmed for 2003*

CONINGSBY
Map 08 TF25
Battle of Britain Memorial Flight Visitor Centre
LN4 4SY (on A153)
☎ 01526 344041   📠 01526 342330
e-mail: bbmf@lincolnshire.gov.uk

View the aircraft of the Battle of Britain Memorial Flight, comprising the only flying Lancaster in Europe, five Spitfires, two Hurricanes, a Dakota and two Chipmunks. Because of operational commitments, specific aircraft may not be available. Ring for information before planning a visit.
Times: Open all year, Mon-Fri, conducted tours 10-3.30. (Closed 2 wks Xmas). (Phone prior to visiting to check security situation) **Fee:** £3.50 (ch £1.50, pen £2, u5's free). **Facilities:** P ⌘ ♿ (electric wheelchairs not allowed in hangers) toilets for disabled shop (ex guide dogs)

EPWORTH
Map 08 SE70
Old Rectory
1 Rectory St DN9 1HX (on A161, 3m S of M180 junct 2)
☎ 01427 872268
e-mail: curator@epwortholdrectory.org.uk

John and Charles Wesley were brought up in this handsome rectory, built in 1709. Maintained by the World Methodist Council as 'The Home of the Wesleys', the house displays items which belonged to John and Charles Wesley and their parents Samuel and Susanna. The house is a registered museum.
Times: Open daily Mar-Oct, Mon-Sat 10-12 & 2-4, Sun 2-4 (only in Mar, Apr & Oct) May-Sep Mon-Sat 10-4.30. Sun 2-4.30. Other times by prior arrangement. **Fee:** * £3 (ch £1, OAP £2.50) Family £7. **Facilities:** P ⌘ ✕ ♿ shop ✸ (ex guide dogs)

GAINSBOROUGH
Map 08 SK88
Old Hall
Parnell St DN21 2NB (turn off A1 onto A57 to Gainsborough. Follow brown heritage signs in city centre. Old Hall is adjacent to town centre.)
☎ 01427 612669   📠 01427 612779   **2 for 1**
e-mail: crawleyg@lincolnshire.gov.uk

A complete medieval manor house dating back to 1460-80 and containing a remarkable Great Hall and original kitchen with a variety of room settings. Richard III, Henry VIII, the Mayflower Pilgrims and John Wesley all visited the Old Hall.
Times: Open all year, Mon-Sat 10-5; Etr-Oct, Sun 2-5.30. (Closed 25-26 Dec, 1 Jan). **Fee:** * £2.50 (ch £1, pen £1.50). **Facilities:** P (100 yds) (unrestricted parking 100yds from Hall) ⌘ ♿ (audio tour, induction loop, wheelchair for visitors use) shop ✸ (ex guide dogs)

GRANTHAM
See Belvoir, Leicestershire

GRIMSBY
Map 08 TA20
National Fishing Heritage Centre
Alexandra Dock DN31 1UZ (follow signs off M180)
☎ 01472 323345   📠 01472 323555
Times: Open Apr-Sep, Mon-Thu 10-4, Sat-Sun 11-5 (10.30-5.30 Jul-Sep). **Facilities:** P ⌘ ♿ (easy access route) toilets for disabled shop ✸ (ex guide dogs) *Details not confirmed for 2003*

GRIMSTHORPE
Map 08 TF02
Grimsthorpe Castle
PE10 0NB (on A151, 8m E of Colsterworth rbt on A1)
☎ 01778 591205   📠 01778 591259
e-mail: ray@grimsthorpe.co.uk
Times: Open 22 Apr-Sep, Sun, Thu & BH's. Daily in Aug ex Fri & Sat. Park & Gardens 11-6, Castle 1-6 (last admission 4.30). **Facilities:** P ⌘ ✕ licensed ♿ toilets for disabled shop *Details not confirmed for 2003*

HECKINGTON
Map 08 TF14
The Pearoom
Station Yard NG34 9JJ (4m E of Sleaford, off A17)
☎ 01529 460765   📠 01529 460948
Times: Open all year, Mon-Sat & BHs 10-5, Sun 12-5. **Facilities:** P ⌘ ♿ toilets for disabled shop ✸ (ex guide dogs) *Details not confirmed for 2003*

LINCOLN

LINCOLN CASTLE
Map 08 SK97

Castle Hill LN1 3AA
☎ 01522 511068   📠 01522 512150

Situated in the centre of Lincoln, the Castle, built in 1068 by William the Conqueror, dominates the Bailgate area alongside the great Cathedral. In addition to its many medieval features, Lincoln Castle has strong 19th-century connections and the unique Victorian prison chapel is perhaps the most awe-inspiring. The beautiful surroundings are ideal for historical adventures, picnics and special events that include jousting, Roman re-enactments, and Vintage vehicle rallies. The Castle is the home of the Magna Carta and there is an exhibition interpreting and displaying this important document.
Times: Open - Summer: Mon-Sat 9.30-5.30, Sun 11-5.30. Winter: Mon-Sat 9.30-4.30, Sun 11-4.30. (Closed 24-8 & 31 Dec & 1 Jan).
Fee: * £2.50 (ch £1) Family ticket (2 adults & 3 children) £6.50
Facilities: P (100yds) 🍴 & (hearing loop) toilets for disabled shop ✘ (ex guide dogs) ⚑

MUSEUM OF LINCOLNSHIRE LIFE
Burton Rd LN1 3LY (100mtr, walk from Lincoln Castle)
☎ 01522 528448   📠 01522 521264
e-mail: finchj@lincolnshire.gov.uk
Times: Open all year, May-Sep, daily 10-5.30; Oct-Apr, Mon-Sat 10-5.30, Sun 2-5.30. **Facilities:** P 🍴 & (wheelchair available, parking space) toilets for disabled shop ✘ Details not confirmed for 2003

USHER GALLERY
Lindum Rd LN2 1NN (in city centre, signed)
☎ 01522 527980   📠 01522 560165
e-mail: usher.gallery@lincolnshire.gov.uk
Times: Open all year, Tue-Sat 10-5.30 (last entry 4.30pm), Sun 2.30-5. (Closed 25/26 Dec & 1 Jan). Open BHs. **Facilities:** P (150yds) 🍴 & (large print exhibition guides) toilets for disabled shop ✘ (ex guide dogs) Details not confirmed for 2003 ⚑

LONG SUTTON
See Spalding

SCUNTHORPE
Map 08 SE81

NORMANBY HALL COUNTRY PARK
Normanby DN15 9HU (4m N of Scunthorpe off B1430)
☎ 01724 720588   **2 for 1**
📠 01724 721248
e-mail: normanbyhall@northlincs.gov.uk

A whole host of activities and attractions are offered in the 300 acres of grounds that surround Normanby Hall, including riding, nature trails and a farming museum. Inside the Regency mansion the fine rooms are decorated and furnished in period style. Fully restored and working Victorian kitchen garden. There is also a

Lincolnshire **139**

Victorian walled garden with a new nursery selling a wide range of Victorian and other unusual plants.
Times: Open, Park all year, daily 9am-dusk. Walled garden: daily 10.30-5 (4pm winter). Hall & Farming Museum: Apr-Sep daily 1-5.
Fee: Mar-1 Oct £3.50 (concessions £2.50). Family ticket £9.50. Season ticket (resident) £7 (non resident) £14 2 Oct-26 Mar £2.20 per car.
Facilities: P (charged) 🍴 ✘ licensed & (audio tour & sensory bed in walled garden) toilets for disabled shop garden centre ✘ (ex guide dogs & park on lead) ⚑

SKEGNESS
Map 09 TF56

CHURCH FARM MUSEUM
Church Rd South PE25 2HF (on entering Skegness follow brown Museum signs)
☎ 01754 766658   📠 01754 898243   **2 for 1**
e-mail: walkerr@lincolnshire.gov.uk

A farmhouse and outbuildings, restored to show the way of life on a Lincolnshire farm at the end of the 19th century, with farm implements and machinery plus household equipment on display. Temporary exhibitions are held in the barn with special events throughout the season. A timber framed mud & stud cottage is restored on site.
Times: Open Apr-Oct, daily 10.30-5.30 **Fee:** * £1 (ch 50p). **Facilities:** P 🍴 & (wheelchair available, grounds accessible with care) toilets for disabled shop ✘ (ex guide dogs) ⚑

SKEGNESS NATURELAND SEAL SANCTUARY
North Pde PE25 1DB (north end of seafront)
☎ 01754 764345   📠 01754 764345
e-mail: natureland@fsbdial.co.uk

Natureland houses seals, penguins, tropical birds, reptiles, aquarium, pets' corner. Also free-flight tropical butterflies (May-Oct). Natureland is well known for its rescue of abandoned seal pups, and has successfully reared and returned to the wild a large number of them. The hospital unit incorporates a public viewing area, and a large seascape seal pool (with underwater viewing).
Times: Open all year, daily at 10am. Closing times vary according to season. (Closed 25-26 Dec & 1 Jan). **Fee:** * £4.50 (ch u3 free, ch £2.95, pen £3.45). Family ticket £13.40. **Facilities:** P (100 yds) 🍴 & toilets for disabled shop ⚑

SPALDING
Map 08 TF22

BUTTERFLY & WILDLIFE PARK
Long Sutton PE12 9LE (off A17 at Long Sutton)
☎ 01406 363833 & 363209   **2 for 1**
📠 01406 363182
e-mail: butterflypark@hotmail.com

The Park contains one of Britain's largest walk-through tropical houses, in which hundreds of butterflies and birds from all over the world fly freely. Outside are 15 acres of butterfly and bee gardens, wildflower meadows, nature trail, farm animals, a pets' corner and a large adventure playground. At The Lincolnshire Birds of Prey Centre there are daily birds of prey displays. See an ant room where visitors can observe leaf-cutting

continued

140   Lincolnshire

ants in their natural habitat, plus Reptile Land, home to crocodiles and snakes.
Times: Open end Mar-end Oct, daily 10-5. (Sep & Oct 10-4). **Fee:** £5 (ch 3-16 £3.60, pen £4.60). Family ticket £16-£18. Party rates on application. **Facilities:** P ✕ licensed ♿ (wheelchairs available) toilets for disabled shop ✱ (ex guide dogs) ⚑

Spalding Tropical Forest
Glenside North, Pinchbeck PE11 3SD (signposted when approaching Pinchbeck)
☎ 01775 710822   🖷 01775 710882
e-mail: mike@rosecottagewgc.co.uk
Times: Open daily summer 10-5.30, winter 10-4. Closed 25 Dec-2 Jan.
Facilities: P ♿ (disabled parking close to establishment) toilets for disabled shop garden centre ✱ *Details not confirmed for 2003* ⚑

Springfields Gardens
Camelgate PE12 6ET (1m E on A151, signposted from the Spalding by-pass)
☎ 01775 724843 & 713295
🖷 01755 711209
e-mail: brianwillonghby@springfields.net

2 for 1

The 25-acre gardens provide an amazing spectacle in the spring when thousands of bulbs are blooming among the lawns and lakes. Special events for 2003: Flower Festival and Parade 3-5 May 2003.
Times: Open 10 Mar-12 May, daily 10-6 (last admission 5pm) **Fee:** * £3.50 (accompanied ch free, pen £3). Prices vary for special events.
Facilities: P ♿ ✕ licensed ♿ (free wheelchair hire) toilets for disabled shop garden centre ✱ (guide dogs) ⚑

⛪ STAMFORD   Map 04 TF00
Burghley House
PE9 3JY (1.5m off A1 at Stamford)
☎ 01780 752451   🖷 01780 480125
e-mail: burghley@burghley.co.uk

This great Elizabethan palace, built by William Cecil, has all the hallmarks of that ostentatious period. The vast house is three storeys high and the roof is a riot of pinnacles, cupolas and paired chimneys in classic Tudor style. However, the interior was restyled in the 17th century, and the state rooms are now Baroque, with silver fireplaces, elaborate plasterwork and painted ceilings. These were painted by Antonio Verrio, whose Heaven Room is quite awe-inspiring.
Times: Open 29 Mar-27 Oct, daily, 11-4.30. (Closed 1 Sep). **Fee:** £7.10 (ch 5-12 £3.50 or free with every paying adult, pen £6.50)
Facilities: P ♿ ✕ licensed ♿ (chairlift access to restaurant and staterooms) toilets for disabled shop ✱ (guide dogs) ⚑

Stamford Museum
Broad St PE9 1PJ (from A1 follow town centre signs from any Stamford exit)
☎ 01780 766317   🖷 01780 480363
e-mail: stamford_museum@lincolnshire.gov.uk

Displays illustrate the history of this fine stone town and include Stamford Ware pottery, the visit of Daniel Lambert and the town's more recent industrial past. The new Stamford Tapestry depicts the history of the town in wool.
Times: Open all year, Apr-Sep, Mon-Sat 10-5, Sun 2-5; Oct-Mar Mon-Sat 10-5. (Closed 24-26 & 31 Dec & 1 Jan). **Fee:** Free. **Facilities:** P (200 yds) (on street parking is limited waiting) ♿ (info on 1st floor gallery available) shop ✱ (ex guide dogs) ⚑

Stamford Shakespeare Company
Rutland Open Air Theatre, Tolethorpe Hall, Little Casterton PE9 4BH (off A6121, follow heritage signs to Tolethorpe Hall)
☎ 01780 54381   🖷 01780 481954
Times: Open daily 10-4, May-Sep. Rutland Open Air Theatre performances Jun-29 Aug. **Facilities:** P ♿ ♿ toilets for disabled shop ✱ *Details not confirmed for 2003*

⛪ TATTERSHALL   Map 08 TF25
Tattershall Castle
LN4 4LR (S of A153)
☎ 01526 342543   🖷 01526 342543
e-mail: etcxxx@smtp.ntrust.org.uk
Times: Open 23 Mar-3 Nov, Sat-Wed, 11-5.30 (11-4 Oct); also open Thu in Aug. 9 Nov-15 Dec, Sat & Sun 12-4. **Facilities:** P ♿ toilets for disabled shop ✱ (ex guide dogs) ♥ *Details not confirmed for 2003*

⛪ THORNTON   Map 08 TA11
Thornton Abbey
DN39 6TU
☎ 01469 40357

A magnificent 14th-century gatehouse and the ruins of the church and other buildings survive from the 12th-century Augustinian abbey. The approach is across a long bridge, spanning a dry moat.
Times: Open Apr-Sep, 1st & 3rd Sun of month 12-6; Oct-Mar, 3rd Sun of month 12-4. Grounds open any reasonable time. **Fee:** Free.
Facilities: P ♿ ✱ (in certain areas) ✡

⛪ WOOLSTHORPE   Map 08 SK92
Woolsthorpe Manor
23 Newton Way NG33 5NR (7m S of Grantham, 1m W of A1)
☎ 01476 860338   🖷 01746 860338
e-mail: ewmxxx@smtp.ntrust.org.uk
Times: Open 23 Mar-29 Sep, Wed-Sun, BH Mon & Good Fri 1-5, Jun-Aug 1-6; 5 Oct-3 Nov Sat & Sun 1-5 but Wed-Sun 1-5 during half term. **Facilities:** P ✱ (ex guide dogs) ♥ *Details not confirmed for 2003*

London

The capital of England and the United Kingdom, London is the largest city in Europe with a population of nearly seven million people.

Londinium was established in 43 AD, at the lowest crossing point of the River Thames. In the second century the city walls were built, but London soon grew beyond them to merge with Westminster and, by the 11th century, was the main city in England and the home of William the Conqueror.

London continued to flourish until the plague of 1665 and the Great Fire of London in 1666. Much of the city was rebuilt at this time under the direction of Sir Christopher Wren. During WWII the Blitz did immense damage to the city, razing whole streets and destroying domestic and public buildings alike. Post-war architecture introduced modern structures of concrete and glass. Ancient sights include the Tower of London, built by William the Conqueror on a Roman site; the 15th-century Guildhall; and the Monument, designed by Wren to commemorate the Great Fire. Most of the public buildings are 18th-century or Victorian.

London's role as a port has declined, with most activity now outside the metropolitan area. The East End docks have been redeveloped to provide housing, offices, factories and the Docklands Light Railway. London is a major financial centre, and the focus of the national media, including film and publishing.

London has been a cosmopolitan centre for centuries, and much of the excitement of the city is derived from its cultural diversity. The foods, dress, languages, art and music of every continent can be experienced on its streets. As Dr Samuel Johnson put it, "When a man is tired of London, he is tired of life, for there is in London all that life can afford."

Top: London Eye

EVENTS & FESTIVALS

January
1st New Year's Day Parade
2nd-12th Boat Show, Earls Court

March
29th Head of the River Race, Mortlake to Putney
Oxford & Cambridge Boat Race

April
13th London Marathon

May
20th-23rd Chelsea Flower Show
Hampstead & Highgate Festival

June
7th-8th Biggin Hill International Air Fair, Biggin Hill
8th London to Brighton Classic Car Run
9th-27th Spitalfields Festival, Christ Church, Commercial Street E1
14th Trooping the Colour, Horse Guards Parade SW1
tbc Beating the Retreat by the Household Division Massed Bands Chelsea Festival
Covent Garden Flower Festival

June/July
tbc City of London Festival

July
tbc Greenwich & Docklands International Festival

August
24th-25th Notting Hill Carnival

September
1st-2nd City of London Flower Show, Gresham Street EC2

October
19th Trafalgar Day Parade, Trafalgar Square (provisional)

November
2nd London to Brighton Veteran Car Run, Hyde Park W2
8th Lord Mayor's Show
9th Remembrance Day Service

London

W1
APSLEY HOUSE, THE WELLINGTON MUSEUM
Hyde Park Corner W1J 7NT (Underground - Hyde Park Corner, exit 1 overlooking rdbt)
☎ 020 7499 5676   ▤ 020 7493 6576

Number One, London, is the popular name for one of the Capital's finest private residences, 19th-century home of the first Duke of Wellington. Built in the 1770s, its rich interiors have been returned to their former glory, and house the Duke's magnificent collection of paintings, silver, porcelain, sculpture and furniture. **Times:** Open Tue-Sun 11-5. (Closed Mon ex BH Mon, Good Fri, May Day BH, 24-26 Dec & 1 Jan). Last admission 4.30pm. **Fee:** * £4.50 (ch under 18 & pen free, disabled & UB40 £3). Includes the use of a soundguide. **Facilities:** P (NCP 10mins walk) & lift, learning disabilities shop ✈ (ex guide dogs) ⬤

EC2
BANK OF ENGLAND MUSEUM
Threadneedle St EC2R 8AH (museum housed in Bank of London, entrance in Bartholomew Lane)
☎ 020 7601 5545
▤ 020 7601 5808   **2 for 1**
e-mail: museum@bankofengland.co.uk

Located in the heart of The City, this museum traces the history of the Bank from its foundation in 1694, and includes a collection of gold bars, old and new. New interactive programme.
Times: Open all year, Mon-Fri 10-5. (Closed wknds & BH's). Open on the day of the Lord Major's Show and Open House Weekend. **Fee:** Free. P (10 mins walk) & (special need presentation, advance notice helpful) toilets for disabled shop

SE1
BANKSIDE GALLERY
48 Hopton St SE1 9JH (E of Blackfriars Bridge, South Bank of the Thames, adjacent to Tate Modern and the Millennium Bridge)
☎ 020 7928 7521   ▤ 020 7928 2820
e-mail: info@banksidegallery.com

Bankside Gallery is the home of the Royal Watercolour Society (RWS) and the Royal Society of Painter-Printmakers (RE). A series of regularly changing exhibitions throughout the year displays the work of both societies.
Times: Opening dates vary according to exhibitions programme - Tue 10-8, Wed-Fri 10-5, Sat & Sun 11-5. (Closed Mon) **Fee:** * £3.50 (concessions £2). Some exhibitions are free. P & shop ✈ ⬤

SW1
BANQUETING HOUSE AT WHITEHALL PALACE
Whitehall SW1A 2ER (Underground - Westminster, Charing Cross or Embankment)
☎ 020 7930 4179   ▤ 020 7930 8268
e-mail: valerie.jarvis@hrp.org.uk

Designed by Inigo Jones, this is the only surviving building of the vast Whitehall Palace, destroyed by fire 300 years ago. The Palace has seen many significant royal events, including the execution of Charles I in 1649. The Banqueting House's ceiling paintings by Rubens are stunning examples of the larger works of the Flemish Master and its classical Palladian style set the fashion for much of London's later architecture.

Times: Open all year, Mon-Sat 10-5. (Closed Good Fri, 24 Dec-1 Jan & BH's). Liable to close at short notice for Government functions. **Fee:** * £4 (ch 16 £2.60 (under 5 free) students & pen £3). P 5 minutes (no parking in Whitehall) & toilets for disabled shop ✈ (ex guide/hearing dogs) ⬤

SE1
BRITISH AIRWAYS LONDON EYE
Riverside Building, County Hall, Westminster Bridge Rd SE1 7PB (Underground - Waterloo/Westminster)
☎ 0870 500 0600   ▤ 0870 990 8884

The skyline of central London drastically changed in the year 2000, with the opening of this amazing sightseeing wheel. The London Eye is 135 metres in diameter and weighs 1,900 tonnes. It takes 30 minutes to revolve once and allows passengers, who travel in one of the 32 capsules, to see for about 25 miles (40km). As the Eye is operated by British Airways, in-flight meals are offered for those who hire a private capsule for a romantic interlude or a meeting.
Times: Open - Summer: May-Sep daily 9.30am-10pm. Winter: 2 Feb-Apr & Oct-Dec daily 9.30am-8pm. (Closed 25 Dec & Jan-1 Feb) **Fee:** * Summer £10.50 (ch £5, pen & disabled £8.50); Winter £9.50 (ch £5, pen & disabled £7.50). Group rates available. **Facilities:** P ⌑ & toilets for disabled shop ✈ (ex guide dogs) ⬤

W12
BBC TELEVISION CENTRE TOURS
BBC Television Centre, Wood Ln W12 7RJ (Underground - Central Line/ White City)
☎ 0870 6030304

Take a look behind the scenes at the world's most famous TV centre. As the BBC TV Centre is a working building, no guarantees can be made as to what visitors will see, although dressing rooms, the News Centre, the Weather Centre, and various studios are all possible. The uncertain nature of the visit means that no two are

continued

the same, and that only pre-booked guided tours are available.
Times: Open Mon-Sat. Tours at 10.20, 10.40, 1, 1.20, 2.40 & 3. (Closed 24 Dec-2 Jan). All tours must be pre-booked. **Fee:** * £7.95 (concessions £6.95, student £5.95). Family ticket £21.95 **Facilities:** P (5min walk) no parking on road outside & (wheelchair available) toilets for disabled shop ✈ (ex guide/hearing dogs) ⚑

WC1
BRITISH MUSEUM
Great Russell St WC1B 3DG (Underground - Russell Sq, Tottenham Court Rd, Holborn)
☎ 020 7323 8000 📠 020 7323 8616
e-mail: information@thebritishmuseum.ac.uk
Times: Open all year, Gallery: Mon-Sat 10-5.30 & Thu-Fri 10-8.30. Great Court: Mon 9-6, Tue-Wed & Sun 9-9, Thu-Sat 9am-11pm. (Closed Good Fri, 24-26 Dec & 1 Jan). **Facilities:** P (5 mins walk) 🍽 ✕ licensed & (parking by arrangement) toilets for disabled shop ✈ (ex guide/companion dogs) *Details not confirmed for 2003*

SW1
BUCKINGHAM PALACE
Buckingham Palace Rd SW1 1AA (Underground - Victoria, Green Park)
☎ 020 7321 2233 📠 020 7930 9625
e-mail: buckinghampalace@royalcollection.org.uk

The official London residence of Her Majesty The Queen, whose personal standard flies when Her Majesty is in residence. Each August and September the State Rooms are open to visitors. These principle rooms now include the Ballroom, the largest room in the Palace. The rooms occupy the main west front overlooking the garden and are all opulently decorated with the finest pictures and works of art from the Royal Collection.
Times: Open 5 Aug-29 Sep 9.30-4.30 last admission 4.15 **Fee:** * £11.50 (ch under 17 £6, pen £9.50) Family ticket (2 adults & 2 ch) £29. Tickets bought in advance £1 booking fee P (200yds) (very limited, driving not recommended) & (ex gardens, pre-booking essential) toilets for disabled shop ✈ (ex guide dogs) ⚑

SW1
CABINET WAR ROOMS
Clive Steps, King Charles St SW1A 2AQ (Underground - Westminster or St James Park)
☎ 020 7930 6961 📠 020 7839 5897
e-mail: cwr@iwm.org.uk

The underground emergency accommodation used to protect the Prime Minister, Winston Churchill, his War Cabinet and the Chiefs of Staff during WWII provides a fascinating insight into those tense days and nights. Among the 21 rooms are the Cabinet Room, the Map Room (where information about operations on all fronts was collected) and the Prime Minister's room, all carefully preserved since the end of the war. There is a changing exhibition of war documents.
Times: Open all year, daily 9.30-6. (10-6 Oct-Mar) last admission 5.15 (Closed 24-26 Dec). **Fee:** * £5.80 (ch under 16 free, students & pen £4.20). Party 10+. P (10 mins walk) & (education service, object handling session) toilets for disabled shop ✈ ⚑

SW3
CARLYLE'S HOUSE
24 Cheyne Row SW3 5HL (Underground - Sloane Square. Off Cheyne Walk between Battersea & Albert Bridges)
☎ 020 7352 7087 📠 020 7352 5108
Times: Open Apr-Oct, Wed-Sun & BH Mons 11-5. Last admission 4.30. (Closed Good Fri). **Facilities:** P (street metered) ✈ 🚲 🛒
Details not confirmed for 2003

WC1
THE CHARLES DICKENS MUSEUM
48 Doughty St WC1N 2LX (Underground - Russell Square or Chancery Lane)
☎ 020 7405 2127
📠 020 7831 5175
e-mail: dhmuseum@rmplc.co.uk

2 for 1

Charles Dickens lived in Doughty Street in his twenties and it was here he worked on his first full-length novel, *The Pickwick Papers*, and later *Oliver Twist* and *Nicholas Nickelby*. Pages of the original manuscripts are on display, together with valuable first editions, his marriage licence and many other personal mementoes.
Times: Open all year, Mon-Sat 10-5. Sun 11-5 **Fee:** * £4 (ch under 16 £2, concession £3). Family ticket £9. P (in street) (metered, 2 hrs max) & shop ✈ ⚑

SW3
CHELSEA PHYSIC GARDEN
66 Royal Hospital Rd, SW3 4HS (Underground - Sloane Square, entrance in Swan Walk)
☎ 020 7352 5646 📠 020 7376 3910

Begun in 1673 for the study of plants used by the Society of Apothecaries. This garden is one of Europe's oldest botanic gardens and is the only one to retain the title 'Physic' after the old name for the healing arts. The garden is still used for botanical and medicinal research, and offers displays of many fascinating plants in lovely surroundings.
Times: Open Apr-Oct, Wed 12-5, Sun 2-6. Additional opening during Chelsea Flower Show week, late May & Chelsea Festival week late Jun. Groups at other times by appointment. **Fee:** * £4 (ch 5-15, students & UB40 £2). **Facilities:** P (0.5m) (west end of Battersea Park) 🍽 & (disabled parking) toilets for disabled shop garden centre ✈ (ex guide dogs)

W4
CHISWICK HOUSE
Burlington Ln, Chiswick W4 2RD (Underground - Gunnersbury)
☎ 020 8995 0508

Built by Lord Burlington in the 1720s, Chiswick House is inspired by the architecture of ancient Rome. The interior has a fine collection of art and the Italianate gardens delight visitors with their statues, temples, urns and obelisks.
Times: Open all year, 29 Mar-Sep, daily 10-6 (Oct daily 10-5). **Fee:** * £3.30 (ch 5-15 £1.70, under 5's free, concessions £2.50). Personal stereo tour included in admission, also available for the partially sighted, those with learning difficulties, and in French & German)
Facilities: P & shop ✱ (in certain areas) ✿

W8
COMMONWEALTH INSTITUTE
Kensington High St W8 6NQ (Underground - High Street Kensington)
☎ 020 7603 4535   ≣ 020 7602 7374
e-mail: info@commonwealth.org.uk
Times: Commonwealth Institute is being redeveloped please ring 020 7603 4535 for details. **Facilities:** P (500yds) 🍴 & (lift from car park, intercom at Holland Park gate) toilets for disabled shop ✱
Details not confirmed for 2003

WC2
COURTAULD GALLERY
Somerset House, Strand WC2R 0RN (Underground - Temple, Embankment)
☎ 020 7848 2526   ≣ 020 7848 2589   **2 for 1**
e-mail: galleryinfo@courtauld.ac.uk

The Galleries contain the superb collection of paintings begun by Samuel Courtauld in the 1920s and 1930s and presented to the University of London in memory of his wife. This is the most important collection of Impressionist and post-Impressionist works in Britain and includes paintings by Monet, Renoir, Degas, Cézanne, Van Gogh and Gauguin. There are also works by Michelangelo, Rubens, Goya, and other notable Masters, as well as early Italian paintings.
Times: Open daily 10-6. Last admission 5.15 **Fee:** * £5 (concessions £4). P (NCP Drury Lane) 🍴 & (parking by arrangement only, call 020 7836 8686, lift) toilets for disabled shop ✱ (ex guide dogs)

SE17
CUMING MUSEUM
155-157 Walworth Rd SE17 1RS (Underground - Elephant & Castle, North line exit follow signs for the shopping centre)
☎ 020 7701 1342   ≣ 020 7703 7415
Times: Open all year, Tue-Sat 10-5. (Closed BH's & Sat of BH wknd).
Facilities: P (20 yds) (on street pay & display meters) shop ✱ (ex guide dogs) *Details not confirmed for 2003*

SE10
CUTTY SARK CLIPPER SHIP
King William Walk, Greenwich SE10 9HT (situated in dry dock beside Greenwich Pier)
☎ 020 8858 3445 & 020 8858 2698   ≣ 020 8853 3589
e-mail: info@cuttysark.org.uk

The fastest tea clipper ever, built in 1869, she once sailed 363 miles in a single day. Preserved in dry dock since 1957, her graceful lines dominate the riverside at Greenwich. Exhibitions and a video presentation the story of the ship, and restoration work can be seen.
Times: Open all year, daily 10-5 (Closed 24-26 Dec). Last ticket 30 mins before closing. **Fee:** £3.90(concessions £2.90). Family ticket £9.70. Party 10+ 20% reduction. P (500mtrs) & shop ✱ (ex guide dogs)

SE1
DALI UNIVERSE
County Hall, Riverside Building SE1 7PB (Adjacent to the London Eye and opposite Big Ben)
☎ 020 7620 2720   ≣ 020 7620 3120   **2 for 1**
e-mail: info@daliuniverse.com

The Dali Universe is a conceptual exhibition dedicated to one of the 20th century's most important artistic forces, Salvador Dali (1904-1989). Arranged thematically to cover the major influences in his life and work, The Dali Universe boasts over 500 works of art, from sculpture to rare etchings, from furniture to gold jewellery. Highlights include the Lobster Telephone and the Mae West Lips sofa.
Times: Open daily 10-5.30 (ex 25 Dec) **Fee:** * £8.50 (children under 5 free, ch 10-16 £4.95, concessions £7.50)under 10's free P & shop ✱

SE1
DESIGN MUSEUM
Shad Thames SE1 2YD (Turn off Tooley St onto Shad Thames. Underground - London Bridge & Tower Hill)
☎ 020 7403 6933   ≣ 020 7378 6540

The Design Museum is the first museum in the world to be dedicated to 20th and 21st century design. Since opening in 1989, it has become one of London's most

continued

inspiring attractions and has won international acclaims for its ground-breaking exhibition and education programmes. The museum aims to excite everyone about design by stimulating the public interest in design, fashion, creative technology and architecture. Permanent collections of design classics and temporary exhibitions ranging from retrospectives on the work of great designers to thematic shows on Bauhaus Dessau and Erotic design. As well as exploring the history of modern design, the Design Museum showcases the best of contemporary designs and technologies, which will shape our future.
Times: Open all year, daily 10-5.45 (last entry 5.15). Closed 25-26 Dec only. **Fee:** * £6 (concessions £4) Family ticket £16. **Facilities:** P (3 mins walk) (Gainsford St car park is chargeable) ♿ ✗ licensed ♿ (ramped entrance, wheelchair & lift) toilets for disabled shop ✗ (ex guide dogs)

EC4
Dr Johnson's House
17 Gough Square EC4A 3DE (Underground - Temple, Blackfriars, Chancery Lane)
☎ 020 7353 3745   📠 020 7353 3745
e-mail: curator@drjh.dircon.co.uk

The celebrated literary figure, Dr Samuel Johnson, lived here between 1748 and 1759. He wrote his English Dictionary here, and a facsimile third edition is on display at the house. The dictionary took nine and a half years to complete and contained 40,000 words. Johnson then undertook the formidable task of editing the complete works of Shakespeare. The house is a handsome example of early 18th-century architecture, and includes a collection of prints, letters and other Johnson memorabilia.
Times: Open all year, May-Sep, daily 11-5.30; Oct-Apr 11-5. (Closed Sun, BH's, Good Fri & 24 Dec). **Fee:** * £4 (ch £1, under 10 free, students & pen £3). Family £9. P (500 yards) (limited meters) (Large print info sheets, handrails, seating) shop ✗

SE21
Dulwich Picture Gallery
Gallery Rd, Dulwich SE21 7AD (off South Circular A205 follow signs to Dulwich village)
☎ 020 8693 5254   **2 for 1**
📠 020 8299 8700
e-mail: info@dulwichpicturegallery.org.uk

This is the oldest public picture gallery in England, housing a magnificent collection of Old Masters, including works by Poussin, Claude, Rubens, Murillo, Van Dyck, Rembrandt, Watteau and Gainsborough. The gallery was designed by Sir John Soane in 1811. The collection, the building and the critically acclaimed loan exhibitions make the gallery a must see for art lovers.
Times: Open all year, Tue-Fri 10-5, wknds & BH Mon 11-5. (Closed Mon). **Fee:** * £4 (pen £3, students, UB40, disabled & ch free). P ✗ licensed ♿ (wheelchairs available, hearing loop) toilets for disabled shop ✗ (ex guide dogs)

SE9
Eltham Palace House & Gardens
Court Yard SE9 5QE
☎ 020 8294 2548

Stephen and Virginia Courtauld's stunning country house in 1930s art-deco style, incorporating a medieval Great Hall. One of its most charming features is the old bridge, spanning the moat.
Times: Open all year, 29 Mar-Sep, Wed-Fri & Sun 10-6 (Oct, Wed-Fri & Sun10-5); Nov-Mar, Wed-Fri & Sun 10-4. Also open BH's. Palace and grounds closed 23 Dec-1 Feb. Pre-book tours 2 weeks in advance **Fee:** * House & Gardens: £6.20 (ch 5-15 £3.10, ch under 5 free, concessions £4.70). Family ticket £15.50. Gardens only: £3.60 (ch 5-15 £1.80, under 5's free, con cessions £2.70) **Facilities:** ✗ ⚔ ♿

NW3
Fenton House
Windmill Hill NW3 6RT (Underground - Hampstead, right out of station. Cross Heath St, up Holly Hill. Take right fork at top of hill into Hampstead Grove. Entrance on left of Hampstead Grove)
☎ 020 7435 3471   **2 for 1**
📠 020 7435 3471
e-mail: fentonhouse@smtp.ntrust.org.uk

A William and Mary mansion built about 1693 and set in a walled garden, Fenton House is now owned by the National Trust. It contains a display of furniture and some notable pieces of Oriental and European porcelain as well as the Benton Fletcher collection of early keyboard instruments.
Times: Open Mar, Sat & Sun 2-5; Apr-Oct, Sat-Sun & BH Mon 11-5pm, Wed-Fri 2-5pm. Last admission 30mins before closing. (Closed Good Fri). **Fee:** £4.40 (ch £2.20). Family ticket £11. Group 15+ £3.70 ♿ (photographs of upper floors which are not accessible) ✗

SE18
Firepower
Royal Arsenal, Woolwich SE18 6ST (A205, right at Woolwich ferry onto A206, Firepower is signposted from there)
☎ 020 8855 7755   📠 020 8855 7100
e-mail: info@firepower.org.uk

Firepower is the Royal Artillery Museum in the historic Royal Arsenal spans 2000 years of artillery and shows how it developed from Roman catapult to guided missile to self-propelled gun. The dramatic and moving field of fire tells the stories of the men and woman in the 20th century, and visitors can put science into action with touchscreen displays and be awed by the big guns.
Times: Open from Apr 2003 Wed-Sun & BH's 11-5.30. Phone for winter opening times or check website. **Fee:** * £6.50 (ch 4.50, concessions £5.50) Family tickets & group discounts (10+) available. P (charged) ♿ (wheelchairs available) toilets for disabled shop ✗ (ex guide dogs)

SE1
FLORENCE NIGHTINGALE MUSEUM
Gassiot House, 2 Lambeth Palace Rd SE1 7EW (Underground - Westminster, Waterloo. On the site of St Thomas' Hospital)
☎ 020 7620 0374
🖷 020 7928 1760
e-mail: curator@florence-nightingale.co.uk

2 for 1

Florence Nightingale needs no introduction, but this museum shows clearly that she was more than 'The Lady with the Lamp'. Beautifully designed, the museum creates a personal setting in which are displayed some of Florence's possessions, a lamp from the Crimean War, and nursing artefacts. There are audio and visual displays and a life-size reconstruction of a Crimean ward scene.
Times: Open all year, Mon-Fri 10-5; wknds & BH's 11.30-4.30. Last admission 1hr before closing. (Closed 24 Dec-2 Jan, Good Fri & Etr Sun). **Fee:** £4.80 (concessions £3.80) Family ticket (2 adults & 2 ch) £12. P (20mtrs) hospital parking limited and charged ♿ toilets for disabled shop ✕ (ex guide dogs) 🍴

NW3
FREUD MUSEUM
20 Maresfield Gardens, Hampstead NW3 5SX (Underground - Finchley Road)
☎ 020 7435 2002 & 7435 5167
🖷 020 7431 5452
e-mail: freud@gn.apc.org

In 1938, Sigmund Freud left Vienna as a refugee from the Nazi occupation and chose exile in England, transferring his entire domestic and working environment to this house. He worked here until his death a year later. His extraordinary collection of Egyptian, Greek, Roman and Oriental antiquities, his working library and papers, and his fine furniture including the famous desk and couch are all here.
Times: Open all year, Wed-Sun 12-5 (Closed BH's, telephone for Xmas Holiday times). **Fee:** £5 (ch 12-18, students, UB40 & pen £2, ch under 12 free). P ♿ (personal tours can be arranged if booked in advance) shop ✕ (ex guide dogs) 🍴

E2
GEFFRYE MUSEUM
Kingsland Rd E2 8EA (at southern end of Kingsland Rd, A10 in Shoreditch)
☎ 020 7739 9893 🖷 020 7729 5647
e-mail: info@geffrye-museum.org.uk

The only museum in the UK to specialise in the domestic interiors and furniture of the urban middle classes. Displays span the 400 years from 1600 to the present day, forming a sequence of period rooms which capture the nature of English interior style. The museum is set in elegant, 18th-century buildings, surrounded by delightful gardens including an award-winning walled herb garden and a series of historical gardens which highlight changes in urban middle-class gardens from the 17th to 20th centuries. One of the museum's historic almshouses will shortly be restored, furnished and opened to the public.
Times: Open all year, Tue-Sat 10-5, Sun & BH Mons 12-5 (Closed Mon, Good Fri, 24/25 Dec & New Year). **Fee:** Free. Prices for special lectures on request. P (150yds) (meter parking) ✕ licensed ♿ (wheelchair available) toilets for disabled shop ✕ (ex guide dogs)

WC2
GILBERT COLLECTION
Somerset House, Strand WC2R 1LN (Underground - Temple, Covent Garden)
☎ 020 7420 9400 🖷 020 7420 9440
e-mail: info@gilbert-collection.org.uk

2 for 1

An oustanding collection of decorative arts and an important bequest to the nation. The Gilbert Collection is the gift of Sir Arthur Gilbert and is on permanent display at Somerset House. This new museum includes European silver, gold snuff boxes and Italian mosaics, the displays will also include furniture, clocks and potrait miniatures.
Times: Open daily 10-6, last admission 5.15. **Fee:** * £5 (concessions £4, under 18, uk students, unemployed & admission after 4.30 free). Combined ticket with Courtauld & Hermitage Gallery. P (400mtrs) 💷 ✕ licensed ♿ (lifts, hearing loop, wheelchair hire, disabled parking) toilets for disabled shop ✕ (ex guide dogs) 🍴

SE1
GOLDEN HINDE EDUCATIONAL MUSEUM
St Mary Overie Dock, Cathedral St SE1 9DE (On the Thames path between Southwark Cathedral and Globe Theatre)
☎ 020 7403 0123 🖷 020 7407 5908
e-mail: info@goldenhinde.co.uk

2 for 1

A full size replica of Sir Francis Drake's famous 16th-century galleon. Just like the original, this *Golden Hinde* has circumnavigated the globe. You can explore the five decks, and costumed crew add to the atmosphere. Special events include Living History re-enactments. There are holiday workshops for children and the ship is also available for private hire.
Times: Open all year, 9.30-5.30. Visitors are advised to check opening times as they may vary due to closures for functions. **Fee:** * £2.50 (ch 4-13 £1.75, under 4's free, concessions £2.10) P (on street parking) 💷 shop (ex guide dogs) 🍴

EC2
THE GUILDHALL
Gresham St EC2V 5AE (Underground - Bank, St Paul's)
☎ 020 7606 3030 🖷 020 7260 1119
Times: Open all year, May-Sep, daily 10-5; Oct-Apr, Mon-Sat 10-5. (Closed Xmas, New Year, Good Fri, Etr Mon & infrequently for Civic occasions). **Facilities:** ♿ shop ✕ *Details not confirmed for 2003*

London   147

W1
HANDEL HOUSE MUSEUM
25 Brook St W1K 4HB (off Park Lane into Brook Gate, then Upper Brook Street. Pass Claridge's Hotel on right. The entrance is Lancashire Court)
☎ 020 7495 1685   📠 020 7495 1759   **2 for 1**
e-mail: mail@handelhouse.org

The composer of Messiah, Music for the Royal Fireworks and numerous other works, lived here from 1723 until his death in 1759. As well as living there, the house was used by Handel for rehearsals, and as a kind of ticket office and shop where he sold copies of scores. The refurbished interior includes furniture based on the inventory taken after the composer's death, as well as fine art. The house next door contains an exhibition on the restoration of Handel's house.
Times: Open Tue, Wed & Sat 10-6, Thu 10-8, Sun & BH Mon 12-6. (Closed 25-26 Dec & 1 Jan) **Fee:** * £4.50 (ch £2, concessions £3.50) P & toilets for disabled shop ✖ (ex guide dogs) 🍴

N6
HIGHGATE CEMETERY
Swains Ln N6 6PJ (Underground - Archway, see directions posted at exit)
☎ 020 8340 1834
Times: Open all year. Eastern Cemetery: daily 10 (11 wknds)-5 (4 in winter). Western Cemetery by guided tour only: Sat & Sun 11-4 (3 in winter); midweek tours 12, 2 & 4 (12, 2 & 3 in winter). No weekday tours in Dec, Jan & Feb. Special tours by arrangement. (Closed 25-26 Dec & during funerals). **Facilities:** P shop ✖ Details not confirmed for 2003

SE1
HMS BELFAST
Morgans Ln, Tooley St SE1 2JH (Underground - London Bridge/Tower Hill/Monument. Rail: London Bridge)
☎ 020 7940 6300   📠 020 7403 0719
e-mail: hmsbelfast@iwm.org.uk

Europe's last surviving big gun armoured warship from WWII, HMS Belfast was launched in 1938 and served in the North Atlantic and Arctic with the Home Fleet. She led the Allied naval bombardment of German positions on D-Day, and was saved for the nation in 1971. A tour of the ship will take you from the Captain's Bridge through nine decks to the massive Boiler and Engine Rooms. You can visit the cramped Messdecks, Officers' Cabins, Galley, Sick Bay, Dentist and Laundry.
Times: Open all year, daily. Mar-Oct 10-6, last admission 5.15; Nov-28 Feb 10-5, last admission 4.15. (Closed 24-26 Dec). **Fee:** * £5.80 (ch under 16 free, concessions £3.80). Party £4.60 p.p. P (150yds) 🍴 & (wheelchair lift for access on board) toilets for disabled shop ✖ (ex guide dogs) 🍴

W4
HOGARTH HOUSE
Hogarth Ln, Great West Rd W4 2QN (50yds W of Hogarth rdbt on Great West Road A4).
☎ 020 8994 6757   📠 0845 456 2880

This 18th-century house was the country home of artist William Hogarth (1697-1764) during the last 15 years of his life. The house contains displays on the artist's life, and many of his satirical engravings.
Times: Open Apr-Oct, Tue-Fri 1-5, Sat-Sun 1-6; Nov-Mar, Tue-Fri 1-4, Sat-Sun 1-5. (Closed Mon (ex BH's), Jan, 25-26 Dec, Good Fri). **Fee:** Free. **Facilities:** P (25 & 50yds) (spaces marked in Axis Centre car park) & toilets for disabled shop ✖ (ex guide dogs)

SE23
THE HORNIMAN MUSEUM & GARDENS
London Rd, Forest Hill SE23 3PQ (situated on A205)
☎ 020 8699 2339 (rec info) 020 8699 1872
📠 020 8291 5506
e-mail: marketing@horniman.ac.uko.uk
Times: Open all year, Mon-Sat 10.30-5.30, Sun 2-5.30 (Closed 24-26 Dec). Gardens close at sunset. **Facilities:** P (opposite museum) 🍴 & (chair lift to parts of upper floor) toilets for disabled shop (closed until 2001) ✖ (ex guide dogs or in gardens) Details not confirmed for 2003

SW1
HOUSES OF PARLIAMENT
Westminster SW1A 0AA (Underground - Westminster)
☎ 020 7219 4272   📠 020 7219 5839
e-mail: poi@parliament.uk
Times: Telephone well in advance for information on how to go about arranging permits for a tour of the building, or to listen to debates from the Strangers Gallery. Tours must be arranged through a Member of Parliament. **Facilities:** P (250yds) & (by arrangement) toilets for disabled shop ✖ 🍴 Details not confirmed for 2003

SE1
IMPERIAL WAR MUSEUM
Lambeth Rd SE1 6HZ (Underground - Lambeth North, Elephant & Castle or Waterloo)
☎ 020 7416 5000   📠 020 7416 5374
e-mail: mail@iwm.org.uk
Times: Open all year, daily 10-6. (Closed 24-26 Dec). **Facilities:** P (on street 100mtrs) (metered Mon-Fri) 🍴 & (disabled parking, wheelchair hire & access, study room) toilets for disabled shop ✖ (ex guide dogs) Details not confirmed for 2003 🍴

N3
THE JEWISH MUSEUM
The Sternberg Centre, 80 East End Rd, Finchley N3 2SY (Underground - Finchley Central, 10 mins walk via Station Rd & Manor View)
☎ 020 8349 1143   📠 020 8343 2162
e-mail: enquiries@jewishmuseum.org.uk

The Jewish Museum traces the story of Jewish immigration and settlement in London, including a reconstruction of an East End tailoring workshop. It also has a Holocaust Education Gallery with an exhibition on Leon Greenman - British Citizen and Auschwitz survivor. There is a regular programme of changing exhibitions and events.
Times: Open all year, Sun 10.30-4.30, Mon-Thu 10.30-5. Closed Jewish festivals, public holidays & 24 Dec-4 Jan. Also closed Sun in Aug & BH wknds. **Fee:** £2 (concessions £1, ch free) P (50m) (on street parking) 🍴 & toilets for disabled shop ✖

NW1
The Jewish Museum
Raymond Burton House, 129-131 Albert St, Camden Town NW1 7NB (Underground - Camden Town, 3 mins walk from station)
☎ 020 7284 1997   020 7267 9008
e-mail: admin@jmus.org.uk

Times: Open Mon-Thu, 10-4, Sun 10-5. Closed Jewish Festivals & public holidays. **Facilities:** P (outside museum) (pay & display parking) & (induction loop in lecture room linked to audio-visual unit) toilets for disabled shop ✕ (ex guide dogs) *Details not confirmed for 2003*

NW3
Keats House
Keats Grove, Hampstead NW3 2RR (Underground - Hampstead, about 15mins walk from station)
☎ 020 7435 2062   020 7431 9293
e-mail: keatshouse@corpoflondon.gov.uk

Times: Open 23 Apr-10 Dec, Tue-Sat 12-5. Tue-Sat between 10-12 guided tours, schools & visits by appointment take place. Wed between 5-8 a programme of tours & lectures are available. Sun & BH'S 12-5. **Facilities:** P (500yds) (residents parking in operation) & shop ✕ (ex guide dogs) *Details not confirmed for 2003*

W8
Kensington Palace State Apartments & Royal Ceremonial Dress Collection
Kensington Gardens W8 4PX (Underground - High Street Kensington or Notting Hill Gate)
☎ 0870 751 5170   020 7376 0198

Highlights of a visit to Kensington include the restored Kings Apartments with a fine collection of Old Masters; Tintoretto and Van Dyke amongst them. The Royal Ceremonial Dress Collection includes a selection of HM The Queen's dresses, representations of tailor's and dressmaker's workshops, and a display of dresses that belonged to Diana, Princess of Wales.

Times: Open Mar-Oct 10-6, last admission 5; Nov-end Feb 10-5, last admission 4. (Closed 24-26 Dec). **Fee:** * £10 (ch £6.50, concessions £7.50) **Facilities:** P (500yds) ✕ & (cafeteria has wheelchair access ramp) toilets for disabled shop ✕ (ex guide dogs)

NW3
Kenwood
Hampstead Ln NW3 7JR (Underground - Hampstead)
☎ 020 8348 1286   020 8348 7325

Times: Open all year, Apr-Oct, daily 10-6 (Sun 10-8 in Aug); Oct, daily 10-5; Nov-Mar, daily 10-4. (Closed 24-25 Dec & 1 Jan). **Facilities:** P ✕ licensed & toilets for disabled shop ✕ (ex grounds) *Details not confirmed for 2003*

W14
Leighton House Museum & Art Gallery
12 Holland Park Rd W14 8LZ (Underground - High Street Kensington. Museum is N of Kensington High Street, off Melbury rd)
☎ 020 7602 3316   020 7371 2467
e-mail: leightonhousemuseum@rbkc.gov.uk

Times: Open all year, daily 11-5.30. Garden open Apr-Sep 11-5. (Closed Tue). Open Spring & Summer BH's. **Facilities:** shop ✕ *Details not confirmed for 2003*

W8
Linley Sambourne House
18 Stafford Ter W8 7BH (Underground - High Street Kensington)
☎ 020 7602 3316   020 7602 3316

Times: Due to reopen January 2003, telephone for details. **Facilities:** P (metered parking) shop ✕ *Details not confirmed for 2003*

SE1
London Aquarium
County Hall, Riverside Building, Westminster Bridge Rd SE1 7PB (Underground-Waterloo & Westminster. On south bank next to Westminster Bridge, near Big Ben & London Eye)
☎ 020 7967 8000   020 7967 8029
e-mail: info@londonaquarium.co.uk

One of Europe's largest displays of global aquatic life.

continued

London 149

Explore the waters of the world and witness breathtakingly beautiful and dramatic underwater scenes, featuring thousands of living specimens from rivers, oceans and seas across our planet.
Times: Open all year, daily 10-6. Last admission 1hr before closing. Closed 25 Dec. late opening over summer months see website for details **Fee:** * £8.75 (ch 3-14 £5.25, concessions £6.50, ch under 3yrs free, registered disabled £3.50). Family ticket (2 adults, 2 children) £25. P (1km) 💶 ♿ (wheelchairs available) toilets for disabled shop 🗙 (ex guide & hearing dogs) 💬

N1
THE LONDON CANAL MUSEUM
12/13 New Wharf Rd N1 9RT (Underground - Kings Cross. Follow York Way along East side of King's Cross Stn, turn right at Wharfedale Rd, then left into New Wharf Rd.
☎ 020 7713 0836 & 📠 020 7689 6679
e-mail: info@canalmuseum.org.uk

The museum covers the development of London's canals (particularly Regent's Canal), canal vessels and trade, and the way of life of the canal people. Housed in a former ice warehouse and stables, it also illustrates horse transport and the unusual trade of importing ice from Norway; there are two large ice wells under the floor. Facilities include temporary moorings, so you can arrive by boat if you want. There are regular special exhibitions.
Times: Open all year, Tue-Sun & BH Mon 10-4.30 (last admission 3.45). Closed 24-26 & 31 Dec. **Fee:** £2.50 (ch, students, pen & UB40s £1.25, under 8's free). Groups 10+ P (metered parking Mon-Fri before 6.30pm) ♿ (Large print guides) toilets for disabled shop 🗙 (ex guide dogs) 💬

SE1
LONDON DUNGEON
28-34 Tooley St SE1 2SZ (Next to London Bridge Stn)
☎ 0870 8460666 📠 020 7378 1529
e-mail: londondungeon@merlin-entertainments.com
Times: Open all year, daily, Apr-Sep 10-5.30; Oct-Mar 10.30-5. Late night opening in the Summer. Telephone for exact times. **Facilities:** P (NCP 200yds) 💶 ♿ toilets for disabled shop 🗙 (ex guide dogs) Details not confirmed for 2003 💬

NW1
LONDON PLANETARIUM
Marylebone Rd NW1 5LR (Underground - Baker Street)
☎ 020 7935 6861 📠 020 7465 0862
e-mail: firstname.lastname@madame-tussauds.com
Times: Open daily (ex 25 Dec), star shows from 12.20, every 40 mins (10.20am wknds & holidays). **Facilities:** P (200 mtrs) ♿ (induction loop) toilets for disabled shop 🗙 (ex guide dogs) Details not confirmed for 2003 💬

WC2
LONDON'S TRANSPORT MUSEUM
The Piazza, Covent Garden WC2E 7BB (Underground - Covent Garden, Leicester Sq or Holburn)
☎ 020 7379 6344 & 020 7565 7299
📠 020 7565 7250
e-mail: resourced@ltmuseum.co.uk

Covent Garden's original Victorian flower market is home to this excellent museum which explores the colourful story of London and its famous transport system from 1800 to the present day. There are buses, trams, tube trains, and posters, as well as touch-screen displays, videos, working models and tube simulators to bring the story to life.
Times: Open all year, daily 10-6, Fri 11-6. Last admission 5.15pm. (Closed 24-26 Dec). **Fee:** * £5.95 (concessions £4.50, under 16 free). P (5 mins walk) (parking meters) 💶 ♿ (lift & ramps, touch & sign tours) toilets for disabled shop 🗙 (ex guide dogs) 💬

SW13
LONDON WETLAND CENTRE
Queen Elizabeth Walk SW13 9WT (Underground - Hammersmith)
☎ 020 8409 4400 📠 020 8409 4401 `2 for 1`
e-mail: info@wetlandcentre.org.uk

An inspiring wetland landscape that stretches over 105 acres, almost in the heart of London, in Barnes. 30 wild wetland habitats have been created from reservoir lagoon to ponds, lakes and reedbeds and all are home to a wealth of wildlife.
Times: Winter 9.30-4, Summer 9.30-5 **Fee:** * £6.75 (ch £4 & pen £5.50). Family ticket £17.50. Groups 10+ P (charged) 💶 🗙 licensed ♿ (99% accessible, ramps, lifts) toilets for disabled shop 🗙 (ex guide dogs) 💬

NW1
LONDON ZOO
Regents Park NW1 4RY (Underground - Camden Town or Regents Park)
☎ 020 7722 3333 📠 020 7586 5743
e-mail: marketing@zsl.org
Times: Open all year, daily from 10am. (Closed 25 Dec). **Facilities:** P (charged) 💶 🗙 licensed ♿ (wheelchairs & booster scooter available) toilets for disabled shop 🗙 Details not confirmed for 2003 💬

NW8
LORD'S TOUR & M.C.C. MUSEUM
Lord's Ground NW8 8QN (Underground - St John's Wood)
☎ 020 7432 1033 📠 020 7266 3825 `2 for 1`
e-mail: tours@mcc.org.uk

Established in 1787, Lord's is the home of the MCC and cricket. Guided tours take you behind the scenes, and highlights include the Long Room and the MCC Museum, where the Ashes and a large collection of

continued

London

paintings and memorabilia are displayed. The Museum is open on match days for spectators.
Times: Open all year, Oct-Mar tours at 12 & 2pm. Apr-Sep 10am, 12 & 2pm (restrictions on some match days). Telephone for details & bookings. **Fee:** * Guided tour £6.50 (ch £4.50, students & pen £5). Family ticket (2 adults & 2 ch) £19. Party 25+. Museum only £2.50 (concessions £1) plus ground admission (match days only). 🅿 ✘ licensed ♿ (by arrangement) toilets for disabled shop ✘ (ex guide dogs) 📞

NW1
MADAME TUSSAUD'S
Marylebone Rd NW1 5LR (Underground - Baker Street)
☎ 020 7935 6861   📠 020 7465 0862
e-mail: firstname.lastname@madame-tussauds.com
Times: Open all year 10-5.30 (9.30am wknds, 9am summer). (Closed 25 Dec). **Facilities:** 🅿 (200 mtrs) 🚻 ♿ (All parts accessible except Spirit of London ride) toilets for disabled shop ✘ (ex guide dogs) *Details not confirmed for 2003* 📞

SW1
MALL GALLERIES
The Mall SW1Y 5BD (Underground - Charing Cross)
☎ 020 7930 6844   📠 020 7839 7830
e-mail: jdestonmallgalleries@dial.pipex.com

The venue for the annual open exhibitions of eight national art societies. There is also a wide range of individual and group shows.
Times: Open all year, daily 10-5. Closed between exhibitions please phone for details **Fee:** £2.50 Depending on exhibition (ch & pen £1). groups 10+ £1 p.p 🅿 (50 yds) (no parking at the Mall) ♿ (chairlift to galleries) toilets for disabled ✘ 📞

EC4
MIDDLE TEMPLE HALL
The Temple EC4Y 9AT (Underground - Temple, Blackfriars. Turn left at the embankment & left into Middle Temple Lane. Hall half way up on left)
☎ 020 7427 4800   📠 020 7427 4801
e-mail: library@middletemple.org.uk
Times: Open all year, Mon-Fri 10-12 & 3-4 (Closed BH & legal vacations). **Facilities:** ♿ ✘ 🍴 *Details not confirmed for 2003*

EC3
THE MONUMENT
Monument St EC3R 8AH (Underground - Monument)
☎ 020 7626 2717   📠 020 7403 4477
Times: Open Mon-Sun, 10-6. Last admission 5.40pm. **Facilities:** ✘ *Details not confirmed for 2003*

E2
MUSEUM OF CHILDHOOD AT BETHNAL GREEN
Cambridge Heath Rd E2 9PA (Underground - Bethnal Green)
☎ 020 8980 2415   📠 020 8983 5225
e-mail: bgmc@vam.ac.uk

The Museum of Childhood houses a multitude of childhood delights. Toys, dolls and dolls' houses, model soldiers, puppets, games, model theatres, children's costume and nursery antiques are all included in its well planned displays. Art cart and soft play every weekend throughout the school holidays. Permanent under 5's play area and games zone with board games and giant snakes & ladders.
Times: Open all year, Mon-Thu & Sat-Sun 10-5.50 (Closed Fri, 24-26 Dec & 1 Jan). **Fee:** Free. 🅿 (Metered parking) 🚻 ♿ (disabled parking by arrangement) toilets for disabled shop ✘

SE1
MUSEUM OF GARDEN HISTORY
Lambeth Palace Rd SE1 7LB (Underground - Waterloo/Lambeth North, next to Lambeth Palace opposite Houses of Parliament)
☎ 020 7401 8865   📠 020 7401 8869
e-mail: info@museumgardenhistory.org

Adjacent to the south gateway of Lambeth Palace is the former church of St Mary-at-Lambeth, now the Museum of Garden History. There is a permanent exhibition on the history of gardens and a collection of ancient tools. The shop sells souvenirs, books, gifts and seeds from the plant collection. Admiral Bligh of the *Bounty* is buried in the garden.
Times: Open 2 Feb-mid Dec, daily, 10.30-5. **Fee:** Free. 🅿 (100yds) (metered) 🚻 ♿ shop ✘ (ex guide dogs) 📞

EC2
MUSEUM OF LONDON
150 London Wall EC2Y 5HN (Underground - St Paul's, Barbican)
☎ 020 7600 3699   📠 020 7600 1058
e-mail: info@museumoflondon.org.uk
Times: Open all year, Mon-Sat 10-5.50, Sun 12-5.50 (closed 24-26 Dec & 1 Jan). **Facilities:** 🅿 🚻 ♿ (wheelchairs available, lifts & induction loops, parking) toilets for disabled shop ✘ (ex guide dogs) *Details not confirmed for 2003* 📞

EC1
MUSEUM OF THE ORDER OF ST JOHN
St John's Gate, St John's Ln EC1M 4DA (Underground - Farringdon, Barbican)
☎ 020 7253 6644   📠 020 7336 0587
Times: Open all year, Mon-Sat 10-5, Sat 10-4 (Closed Etr, Xmas wk & BH wknds). Guided tours 11 & 2.30 Tue, Fri & Sat. **Facilities:** 🅿 (meters/ NCP 300yds) ♿ toilets for disabled shop ✘ (ex guide dogs) *Details not confirmed for 2003*

WC2
MUSEUMS OF THE ROYAL COLLEGE OF SURGEONS
35-43 Lincoln's Inn Fields WC2A 3PN (Underground - Holborn)
☎ 020 7869 6560   📠 020 7869 6564
e-mail: museums@rcseng.ac.uk

Two museums are housed here - the Hunterian Museum contains the anatomical and pathological specimens collected by John Hunter FRS (1728-1793), a renowned surgeon and teacher of anatomy, and displays relating to the work of Sir Joseph Lister, pioneer of antiseptic surgery. The Odontological

continued

Museum contains an extensive collection of human and animal skulls and teeth as well as dental instruments.
Times: Closed for refurbishment 2003, please telephone for details
Fee: Free. P (25 metres) (pay & display 8-6pm) & (prior notice required) shop ✘ (ex guide dogs)

SW3
NATIONAL ARMY MUSEUM
Royal Hospital Rd, Chelsea SW3 4HT (Underground - Sloane Square)
☎ 020 7730 0717   📠 020 7823 6573
e-mail: info@national-army-museum.ac.uk
Times: Open all year, daily 10-5.30. (Closed Good Fri, May Day, 24-26 Dec & 1 Jan). **Facilities:** P 🍴 & (wheelchair lift to access lower ground floor) toilets for disabled shop ✘ (ex guide dogs)
Details not confirmed for 2003

WC2
NATIONAL GALLERY
Trafalgar Square WC2N 5DN (Underground - Charing Cross, Leicester Square, Embankment & Piccadilly Circus. Rail: Charing Cross. Located on N side of Trafalgar Sq)
☎ 020 7747 2885   📠 020 7747 2423
e-mail: information@ng-london.org.uk

All the great periods of Western European painting from 1260-1900 are represented here, although most of the national collection of British works is housed at the Tate. The Gallery's particular treasures include Velázquez's *Toilet of Venus*, Leonardo da Vinci's Cartoon (The *Virgin and Child with Saints Anne and John the Baptist*), Rembrandt's *Belshazzar's Feast*, Van Gogh's *Sunflowers*, and Titian's *Bacchus and Ariadne*. The British paintings include Gainsborough's *Mr and Mrs Andrews* and Constable's *Haywain*.
Times: Open all year, daily 10-6, (Wed until 9pm). Special major charging exhibitions open normal gallery times. Closed Good Fri, 24-26 Dec & 1 Jan. **Fee:** Free. P (100yds) 🍴 ✘ licensed & (wheelchair,induction loop,lift,deaf/blind visitor tours) toilets for disabled shop ✘ (ex guide & hearing dogs) 📖

SE10
NATIONAL MARITIME MUSEUM
Romney Rd SE10 9NF (central Greenwich)
☎ 020 8858 4422 & 8312 6565 info line
📠 020 8312 6632
Times: Open all year, daily 10-5. (Closed 24-26 Dec & 1 Jan)
Facilities: P (50 yds) (parking in Greenwich limited) ✘ licensed & (wheelchairs, advisory service for hearing/sight impaired) toilets for disabled shop ✘ *Details not confirmed for 2003* 📖

WC2
NATIONAL PORTRAIT GALLERY
St Martin's Place WC2H 0HE (Underground - Charing Cross, Leicester Square)
☎ 020 7306 0055   📠 020 7306 0056

The National Portrait Gallery is home to the largest collection of portraiture in the world featuring famous British men and woman who have created history from the Middle Ages until the present day. Over 1000 portraits are on display across three floors form Henry VIII and Florence Nightingale to The Beatles and The Queen. And, if you want to rest those weary feet, visit the fabulous Portrait Restaurant on the top floor with roof-top views across London.
Times: Open all year, Mon-Wed & Sat-Sun 10-6, Thu-Fri 10-9. (Closed Good Fri, 24-26 Dec & 1 Jan). Gallery closure commences 10mins prior to stated time. **Fee:** Free. **Facilities:** P (200yds) 🍴 ✘ licensed & (stair climber,touch tours,audio guide,large print captions) toilets for disabled shop ✘ (ex guide dogs) 📖

SW7
THE NATURAL HISTORY MUSEUM
Cromwell Rd SW7 5BD (Underground - South Kensington)
☎ 020 7942 5000   📠 020 7942 5536
e-mail: marketing@nhm.ac.uk

This vast and elaborate Romanesque-style building, with its terracotta facing showing relief mouldings of animals, birds and fishes, covers an area of four acres. A multitude of fascinating galleries cover every aspect of natural history. A major permanent exhibition on dinosaurs includes new skeletons, recreated robotic models, and displays on how dinosaurs lived, why they became extinct, and how they were dug up and studied by scientists.
Times: Mon-Sat 10-5.50, Sun 11-5.50 (last admission 5.30) Closed 24-26 Dec **Fee:** Free. P (metered 180yds) limited parking,public transport advised 🍴 ✘ licensed & (ex top floor & one gallery, wheelchairs available) toilets for disabled shop (4 giftshops) ✘ (ex guide dogs) 📖

SE10
OLD ROYAL OBSERVATORY
Greenwich Park, Greenwich SE10 9NF (off A2)
☎ 020 8858 4422 & 8312 6565 recording
📠 020 8312 6632
Times: Open all year, daily 10-5 (Closed 24-26 Dec & 1 Jan)
Facilities: P & toilets for disabled shop ✘ *Details not confirmed for 2003* 📖

WC1
PETRIE MUSEUM OF EGYPTIAN ARCHAEOLOGY
Malet Place, Univerity College London WC1E 6BT (on 1st floor of the D M S Watson building, in Malet Place, off Torrington Place)
☎ 020 76792884   📠 020 7679 2886
e-mail: petrie.museum@ucl.ac.uk

One of the largest and most inspiring collections of Egyptian archaeology anywhere in the world. The displays illustrate life in the Nile Valley from prehistory, through the era of the Pharoahs to Roman and Islamic timsa. Especially noted for its collection of the personal items that illustrate life and death in Ancient Egypt, including the world's earliest surviving dress (c 2800BC).
Times: Open all year, Tue-Fri 1-5, Sat 10-1. Closed for 1 wk at Xmas/Etr. **Fee:** Free. 🍴 ✘ & shop ✘ (ex guide dogs)

W1
Pollock's Toy Museum
1 Scala St W1T 2HL (Underground - Goodge Street)
☎ 020 7636 3452   **2 for 1**
e-mail: toymuseum@hotmail.com

Teddy bears, wax and china dolls, dolls' houses, board games, toy theatres, tin toys, mechanical and optical toys, folk toys and nursery furniture, are among the attractions to be seen in this appealing museum. Items from all over the world and from all periods are displayed in two small, interconnecting houses with winding staircases and charming little rooms. Toy theatre performances available for groups.
Times: Open all year, Mon-Sat 10-5. (Closed BH's, Sun & Xmas). **Fee:** £3 (ch 3-18 £1.50). P (100 yds) (Central London restrictions) & shop ⌦

SW1
The Queen's Gallery
Buckingham Palace, Buckingham Palace Rd SW1A 1AA (Underground - Victoria/Green Park/St. James' Park)
☎ 020 7321 2233   🕮 020 7930 9625
e-mail: buckinghampalace@royalcollection.org.uk

The Queen's Gallery at Buckingham Palace was first opened to the public in 1962 to display paintings, drawings, furniture and other works of art in the Royal Collection.
Times: Open all year, daily, 10-5.30. Last admission 4.30. Closed 25&26 Dec **Fee:** * £6.50 (pen £5, under 17's £3), family (2ad+2ch) £16, under 5's free P (200yds) & shop ✖ (ex guide dogs)

SE10
The Queens House
Romney Rd SE10 9NF (central Greenwich)
☎ 020 8858 4422 & 8312 6565 info line
🕮 020 8312 6632
Times: Open from Dec-24 Sep. **Facilities:** P (50 yds) ✖ licensed & (Blind kit/stairclimber/wheelchairs) toilets for disabled shop ✖ Details not confirmed for 2003 ⌦

SE3
Rangers House (The Wernher Collection)
Chesterfield Walk SE10 8QY
☎ 020 8853 0035

This beautiful villa, built around 1700 on the edge of Greenwich Park, houses two important collections: one of Jacobean and Stuart portraits, the second of musical instruments. The house is the new home of the Wernher Collection - a magnificent collection of international importance.
Times: Open Oct, Wed-Sun, 10-5; Nov & Dec, Wed-Sun 10-4. (Closed 24-4 Mar 2003). Times subject to change 1 Apr 2003, please telephone for further details. **Fee:** * £4.50 (ch 5-15 £2.30, under 5's free, concessions £3.40). Prices subject to change from 1 April 2003, please telephone for further details. **Facilities:** P & toilets for disabled ✖ (in certain areas) ⌗

W1
Royal Academy Of Arts
Burlington House, Piccadilly W1V 0DS (Underground - Piccadilly Circus)
☎ 020 7300 8000   🕮 020 7300 8001

Known principally for its exhibitions, the Royal Academy of Arts was founded in 1768 and is Britain's oldest Fine Arts institution. Two of its founding principles were to provide a free school and to mount 'an annual exhibition open to all artists of distinguished merit', now known as the Summer Exhibition. Both continue today. The Royal Academy's most prized possession, Michelangelo's Tondo, "The Virgin and Child with the Infant St John", one of only four marble sculptures by the artist outside Italy, is on permanent display in the Sackler Wing. Visit our website www.royalacademy.org.uk for details of current and forthcoming exhibitions
Times: Open daily 10-6. (Closed 25 Dec & Good Fri) late night opening Fridays 10am-10pm. **Fee:** £6-£8 (ch, students, pen & group visitors reduced price). Prices vary for each exhibition **Facilities:** 🍴 ✖ licensed & toilets for disabled shop ✖ ex guide dogs ⌦

NW9
Royal Air Force Museum
Grahame Park Way, Hendon NW9 5LL (Underground - Colindale)
☎ 020 8205 2266   🕮 020 8358 4981
e-mail: groupbusiness@rafmuseum.com

This museum now offers free admission, and visitors can see the world-class collection of over 70 aircraft, artefacts and memorabilia celebrating over 100 years of aviation development. The fun 'n' flight gallery offers interactive entertainment for all ages including sitting in an aircraft cockpit.
Times: Open daily 10-6. (Closed 24-26 Dec & 1 Jan). **Fee:** Free. P 🍴 ✖ licensed & (lifts, ramps & wheelchairs available) toilets for disabled shop ✖ (ex guide dogs) ⌦

SW1
The Royal Mews
Buckingham Palace, Buckingham Palace Rd SW1W 0QH (Underground - Green Park/St. James' Park)
☎ 020 7321 2233 (info line)   🕮 020 7930 9625
e-mail: buckinghampalace@royalcollection.org.uk

Designed by John Nash and completed in 1825, the Royal Mews houses the State Coaches, horse drawn carriages and motor cars used for coronations, state visits, royal weddings and the State Opening of Parliament. These include the Gold State Coach, made in 1762, with panels painted by the Florentine artist Cipriani. As one of the finest working stables in existence, the Royal Mews provides a unique opportunity for you to see a working department of the Royal Household.
Times: Open 30 Mar-Oct 11-4 last admission 3.15 **Fee:** * £5 (ch 5-17 £2.50, under 5's free, pen £4) Family ticket (2 adults & 2 ch) £12.50. P (200yds) & toilets for disabled shop ✖ (ex guide dogs) ⌦

London 153

Let us on your imaginary forces work

Shakespeare's Globe
Bankside ~ London
Theatre Tour and Exhibition
Tel: 020 7902 1500 Fax: 020 7902 1515

www.shakespeares-globe.org   Bankside Marketing Group

SE10
ROYAL NAVAL COLLEGE
Greenwich SE10 9NN (In centre of Greenwich, off the one way system, college approach, located on the Thames next to the Cutty Sark)
☎ 020 8269 4791   📠 020 8269 4786
e-mail: info@greenwichfoundation.org.uk
Times: Open all year (Painted Hall and Chapel only), daily 10-5 (last admission 4.15). **Facilities:** 🅿 (200m) (all local streets: yellow line roads) ☕ ✕ licensed (can be given access if prior notice given) shop 🐕 (ex guide dogs) *Details not confirmed for 2003* 🔔

EC4
ST PAUL'S CATHEDRAL
St Pauls Courtyard EC4M 8AD
☎ 020 7246 8348   📠 020 7248 3104
e-mail: chapterhouse@stpaulscathedral.org.uk

Completed in 1710, Sir Christopher Wren's architectural masterpiece is the cathedral church of the Bishop of London, and arose, like so much of this area of London, from the ashes of the Great Fire of London in 1666. Among the worthies buried here are Nelson and the Duke of Wellington, while Holman Hunt's masterpiece, *Light of the World* hangs in the nave. Impressive views of London can be seen from the Golden Gallery.
Times: Open Mon-Sat 8.30-4.15pm. Cathedral may close for special services. **Fee:** * £6 (ch £3, concessions £5) 🅿 ☕ ✕ licensed ♿ toilets for disabled shop 🐕 (ex guide dogs) 🔔

SW7
SCIENCE MUSEUM
Exhibition Rd, South Kensington SW7 2DD (Underground - South Kensington. Signposted from tube station)
☎ 020 7942 4000   📠 020 7942 4421
e-mail: sciencemuseum@nmsi.ac.uk
Times: Open all year, daily 10-6. (Closed 24-26 Dec). **Facilities:** ☕ ✕ licensed ♿ (personal 2hr tour of museum) toilets for disabled shop 🐕 (ex guide dogs) *Details not confirmed for 2003* 🔔

SE1
SHAKESPEARE'S GLOBE EXHIBITION AND THEATRE TOUR
21 New Globe Walk, Bankside SE1 9DT (Underground - London Bridge, walk along Bankside. Mansion House, walk across Southwark Bridge)
☎ 020 7902 1500   📠 020 7902 1515
e-mail: info@shakespearesglobe.com

Guides help to bring England's theatrical heritage to life at the 'unparalleled and astonishing' recreation of this famous theatre. Discover what an Elizabethan audience would have been like, find out about the rivalry between the bankside theatres, the bear baiting and the stews, hear about the penny stinkards and find out what a bodger is.

Times: Open all year, May-Sep, daily 9-12 (12-5 virtual theatre tour); Oct-Apr 10-6. **Fee:** £8 (ch £5.50, pen & students £6.50). Group rates available. 🅿 (0.5m) (on-street parking forbidden) ☕ ✕ licensed ♿ toilets for disabled shop 🐕 (ex guide & hearing dogs) 🔔
See advert on page 153

WC2
SIR JOHN SOANE'S MUSEUM
13 Lincoln's Inn Fields WC2A 3BP (Underground - Holborn)
☎ 020 7405 2107   📠 020 7831 3957

Sir John Soane was responsible for some of the most splendid architecture in London, and his house, built in 1812, contains his collections of antiquities, sculpture, paintings, drawings and books. Included are the *Rake's Progess* and *Election* series of paintings by Hogarth.
Times: Open all year, Tue-Sat 10-5. Also first Tue of month 6-9pm. (Closed BH). Lecture tour Sat 2.30 (limited no of tickets sold from 2pm) **Fee:** Free. **Facilities:** 🅿 (200yds) (metered parking) ♿ (w/chair available, phone for details of accessibility) shop 🐕 (ex guide dogs) 🔔

SE5
SOUTH LONDON GALLERY
65 Peckham Rd SE5 8UH (from Vauxhall take A202 to Camberwell Green. SLG is halfway between Camberwell Green and Peckham)
☎ 020 7703 6120 7703 9799-taped info
📠 020 7252 4730
e-mail: mail@southlondongallery.org

The gallery presents a programme of up to eight exhibitions a year of cutting-edge contemporary art, and has established itself as South East London's premier venue for contemporary visual arts. The Gallery also aims to bring contemporary art of the highest standards to audiences in South London and to assist in the regeneration of the area by attracting audiences from across Britain and abroad.
Times: Open only when exhibitions are in progress, Tue-Fri 11-6, Thu 11-7, wknds 2-6 (Closed Mon). **Fee:** Free. 🅿 (50yds) 🐕 (ex guide dogs)

SE1
SOUTHWARK CATHEDRAL
Montague Close SE1 9DA (Adjacent to London Bridge (Rd & Station), off Borough High Street)
☎ 020 7367 6700 📄 020 7367 6730
e-mail: cathedral@dswark.org.uk

Originally an Augustinian priory, this is London's oldest gothic church building, and has been a place of worship for more than 1,000 years. It became a cathedral for the Diocese of Southwark in 1905, and has links with Chaucer, Dickens and Shakespeare. John Gower, John Harvard and Shakespeare's brother Edmund are all buried here, and visitors can also view part of a Roman road, 14th-century cloister work, and kilns used for Southwark delftware in the 17th & 18th centuries.
Times: Open daily: Cathedral 9-6, Cathedral exhibition 10-6. (No tourism permitted on Good Fri & 25 Dec) **Fee:** Free, suggested donation £2.50. Exhibition £3 (concessions £2.50) P ✗ licensed ♿ toilets for disabled shop 🐕 (ex service dogs) 🍽

E9
SUTTON HOUSE
2 & 4 Homerton High St E9 6JQ (Hackney Central train station)
☎ 020 8986 2264
e-mail: suttonhouse@ntrust.org.uk

In London's East End, the building is a rare example of a Tudor red-brick house. Built in 1535 by Sir Rufe Sadleir, Principal Secretary of State for Henry VIII, the house has 18th-century alterations and later additions.
Times: Open 7 Feb-Nov, Fri & Sat 1-5.30; Sun &BH Mon 11.30-5.30.
Fee: £2.10. Family ticket £4.80. P (on street parking) (meters) 💷 ♿ (induction loop braille guide) toilets for disabled shop (ex guide dogs) 🎵

SW1
TATE BRITAIN
Millbank SW1P 4RG (Underground - Pimlico)
☎ 020 7887 8000 & rec info 020 7887 8008
e-mail: information@tate.org.uk

Tate Britain is the national gallery of British art from 1500 to the present day, from Tudors to the Turner Prize. Tate holds the greatest collection of British art in the world, including works by Blake, Constable, Epstein, Gainsborough, Gilbert and George, Hatoum, Hirst, Hockney, Hodgkin, Hogarth, Moore, Rossetti, Sickert, Spencer, Stubbs and Turner. The gallery is the world centre for the understanding and enjoyment of British art. The opening of the Tate Centenary provides Tate Britain with ten new and five refurbished galleries used for special exhibitions and the permanent collection.
Times: Open daily 10-5.50. (Closed 24-26 Dec). **Fee:** Free. Donations welcomed. Prices vary for special exhibitions. P (100mtrs) (1hr stay) 💷 ✗ licensed ♿ (wheelchairs on request, parking by prior arrangement) toilets for disabled shop 🐕 (ex guide & hearing dogs) 🍽

London   **155**

SE1
TATE MODERN
Bankside SE1 9TG
☎ 020 7887 8008 (info) & 020 7887 8888
📄 020 7401 5052
e-mail: information@tate.org.uk
Times: Open all year, Sun-Thu 10-6, Fri & Sat 10am-10pm. (Closed 24-26 Dec). **Facilities:** P (limited) 💷 ✗ licensed ♿ (parking available) toilets for disabled shop 🐕 (ex guide dogs) *Details not confirmed for 2003* 🍽

SE18
THAMES BARRIER VISITORS CENTRE
Unity Way SE18 5NJ
☎ 020 8305 4188 📄 020 8855 2146
e-mail: jane.finch@environment-agency.gov.uk
Times: Open all year, telephone for opening times. (Closed Xmas - telephone for details). **Facilities:** P (charged) 💷 ♿ (lift from river pier approach) toilets for disabled shop 🐕 *Details not confirmed for 2003* 🍽

WC2
THEATRE MUSEUM
Russell St, Covent Garden WC2E 7PR (Underground - Covent Garden, Leicester Sq)
☎ 020 7943 4700 📄 020 7943 4777
e-mail: tmeducation@vam.ac.uk

Major developments, events and personalities from the performing arts, including stage models, costumes, prints, drawings, posters, puppets, props and a variety of other theatre memorabilia. There are guided tours, demonstrations on the art of stage make-up, and you can dress up in costumes from National Theatre companies. Groups are advised to book in advance.
Times: Open all year, Tue-Sun 10-6. (closed 25 Dec & other public hols) **Fee:** Free. P (meters, NCP 250yds) ♿ toilets for disabled shop 🐕 (ex guide dogs) 🍽

SE1
THE TOWER BRIDGE EXPERIENCE
SE1 2UP (Underground - Tower Hill or London Bridge)
☎ 020 7940 3985 📄 020 7357 7935
e-mail: towerbridge@corpoflondon.gov.uk

One of the capital's most famous landmarks, its glass-covered walkways stand 142ft above the Thames, affording panoramic views of the river. Much of the original machinery for working the bridge can be seen in the engine rooms. The exhibition, The Tower Bridge Experience, uses state-of-the-art effects to present the story of the bridge in a dramatic and exciting fashion.
Times: Open all year, 9.30-6 (last ticket sold 5pm). (Closed 24-25 Dec). **Fee:** * £4.50 (ch 5+, Pen, Student £3) Family ticket £14. Party 10+. P (100yds) ♿ toilets for disabled shop 🐕 🍽

156 London

EC3
TOWER OF LONDON
Tower Hill EC3N 4AB (Underground - Tower Hill)
☎ 0870 756 6060

Perhaps the most famous castle in the world, the Tower of London has played a central part in British history. The White Tower, built by William the Conqueror as a show of strength to the people of London, remains one of the most outstanding examples of Norman military architecture in Europe. For hundreds of years the Tower was used, among other things, as the State Prison. It was here that Henry VIII had two of his wives executed, here that Lady Jane Grey died and here that Sir Walter Raleigh was imprisoned. The Yeoman Warders, or 'Beefeaters' play an important role in the protection of the Tower - home of the Crown Jewels - and are informative and entertaining. Look out for the ravens, whose continued residence is said to ensure that the Kingdom does not fall. The Crowns and Diamonds exhibition features a number of crowns never displayed to the public before and more than 12,000 rough and polished diamonds. Also open to the public are the Royal Armouries, which received their first recorded visitor as long ago as 1489. The displays include an extensive range of arms and armour dating from the Norman ages, a collection of Spanish arms and the Line of Kings.
Times: Open all year, Mar-Oct, Mon-Sat 9-6, Sun 10-6 (last admission 5pm); Nov-Feb, Tue-Sun 9-5, Sun 10-5 (last admission 4pm). (Closed 24-26 Dec & 1 Jan). **Fee:** * £11.50 (ch £7.50, concessions £8.75). Family ticket £34. **Facilities:** P (100yds) (NCP Lower Thames St) 💺 ✘ licensed ♿ (access guide can be obtained in advance call 020 7488 5694) toilets for disabled shop 🐕 (ex guide dogs) 🅢

SW7
VICTORIA AND ALBERT MUSEUM
Cromwell Rd, South Kensington SW7 2RL
(Underground - South Kensington)
☎ 020 7942 2000 📠 020 7942 2266
e-mail: infodome@vam.ac.uk
Times: Open all year, Mon-Sun 10-5.45. (Closed 24-26 Dec). Wed & last Fri of month open late, 10-10. **Facilities:** P (500yds) 💺 ✘ licensed ♿ (braille guide, tour tape. for further info, please phone) toilets for disabled shop 🐕 (ex guide dogs) Details not confirmed for 2003 🅢

SE1
VINOPOLIS, CITY OF WINE
1 Bank End SE1 9BU (Underground-London Bridge. Borough High Street West exit, right into Stoney St, then left into Park St)
☎ 0870 241 4040 📠 020 7403 7093
e-mail: sales@vinopolis.co.uk
Times: Open all year, Tue-Fri 10-5.30 (last admission 3.30pm); Sat-Mon from 10 (last admisssion 6pm). Closed 25 Dec & 1 Jan. **Facilities:** P (5-10 min walk) (NCP parking) 💺 ✘ licensed ♿ (lifts & ramps) toilets for disabled shop 🐕 (ex guide dogs) Details not confirmed for 2003 🅢

W1
WALLACE COLLECTION
Hertford House, Manchester Square W1U 3BN (Underground - Bond Street, Baker Street)
☎ 020 7935 0687 📠 020 7224 2155
e-mail: admin@wallcoll.demon.co.uk
Times: Open all year, Mon-Sat 10-5, Sun 2-5. Apr-Sep, Sun 11-5 (Closed Good Fri, May Day, 24-26 Dec & 1 Jan). **Facilities:** P (NCP & meters) ♿ (ramp wheelchair available upon request) shop 🐕 Details not confirmed for 2003 🅢

EC1
WESLEY'S CHAPEL, HOUSE & MUSEUM OF METHODISM
49 City Rd EC1Y 1AU (Underground - Old Street- exit number 4)
☎ 020 7253 2262 📠 020 7608 3825
Times: Open all year, Mon-Sat & BH 10-4 (Closed BH's, 25 & 26 Dec). Main service 11am Sun followed by an opportunity to tour the museum and house. **Facilities:** P (NCP at Finsbury Square) ♿ (lift to the crypt of the chapel) toilets for disabled shop 🐕 (ex guide dogs) Details not confirmed for 2003

SW1
WESTMINSTER ABBEY
Broad Sanctuary SW1P 3PA (Underground - Westminster, St James's Park. Next to Parliament Square and opposite the Houses of Parliament)
☎ 020 7222 5152 7654 4900 📠 020 7233 2072
e-mail: info@westminster-abbey.org

Westminster Abbey was originally a Benedictine monastery. In the 11th century, it was re-founded by

continued

St. Edward the Confessor. The great Romanesque abbey Edward built next to his royal palace became his burial place shortly after it was completed. Over the centuries that followed, many more kings and queens have been buried, and many great figures commemorated, in the abbey. The abbey has been the setting for nearly every coronation since that of William the Conqueror in 1066, and for numerous other royal occasions. The present building, begun by Henry III in 1245, is one of the most visited churches in the world.
Times: Abbey: Mon-Fri 9.30-3.45, Sat 9-1.45. Wed late night opening 6-7pm. Last admission 60 mins before closing. Cloister: daily 8-6. No tourist visiting on Sundays, however visitors are welcome at services. The Abbey may at short notice be closed for special services & other events. **Fee:** * £6 (ch 11-15 £3, under 11's free, pen & students £3). Family ticket (2 adults & 2 ch) £12. 🍴 ♿ (areas accessible induction loop) shop ✈ (ex guide dogs) 🔊

SW1
WESTMINSTER CATHEDRAL
Victoria St SW1P 1QW (300yds from Victoria Station)
☎ 020 7798 9055 📠 020 7798 9090
e-mail: bpalmer@westminstercathedral.org.uk

Westminster Cathedral is a fascinating example of Victorian architecture. Designed in the early Christian Byzantine style by John Francis Bentley, its strongly oriental appearance makes it very distinctive. The foundation stone was laid in 1895 but the interior decorations are not fully completed. The Campanile Bell Tower is 273ft high and has a four-sided viewing gallery with magnificent views over London. The lift is open daily 9am-5pm Mar-Nov but shut Mon-Wed from Dec-Feb.
Times: Open all year, daily 7-7. **Fee:** Free. 🅿 (0.25m) (2hr metered parking) 🍴 ♿ (all parts accessible except side chapels) shop ✈ (ex guide dogs)

SW1
WESTMINSTER HALL
Westminster SW1A 0AA (Underground - Westminster Hall)
☎ 020 7219 4272
Times: Westminster Hall can only be viewed by those on a tour of the Houses of Parliament, which must be arranged by an MP or Peer.
Facilities: ♿ toilets for disabled shop ✈ *Details not confirmed for 2003*

Prices and opening times subject to change from March 2003. Please check with the property before visiting.

E17
WILLIAM MORRIS GALLERY
Lloyd Park, Forest Rd E17 4PP (Underground -Blackhorse Rd)
☎ 020 8527 3782 📠 020 8527 7070

Victorian artist, craftsman, poet and free thinker William Morris lived here from 1848 to 1856, and the house has been devoted to his life and work. Displays include fabrics, stained glass, wallpaper and furniture, as well as Pre-Raphaelite paintings, sculpture by Rodin, ceramics and a collection of pictures by Frank Brangwyn, who worked briefly for Morris.
Times: Open all year, Tue-Sat and 1st Sun in each month 10-1 & 2-5. (Closed Mon & BH's). Telephone for Xmas/New Year opening times.
Fee: Free. **Facilities:** 🅿 ♿ shop ✈ 🔊

SW19
WIMBLEDON LAWN TENNIS MUSEUM
Centre Court, Church Rd SW19 5AE (Underground - Southfields, 15mins walk)
☎ 020 8946 6131 📠 020 8944 6497
e-mail: museum@aeltc.com

Pictures, displays and memorabilia trace the development of the game over the last century. See the world famous Championship's trophies, as well as film and video footage of great players in action from the 1920s to the present day. There is also the chance to go for a behind-the-scenes guided tour of Centre Court, No. 1 Court, and the press interview room.
Times: Open daily all year, 10.30-5. (Closed middle Sun of Championships, Mon immediately following the Championships, 24-26 Dec & 1 Jan). **Fee:** £5.50 (ch under 5 free, ch £3.50, con £4.50). Party 15+. 🅿 🍴 ✖ licensed ♿ (lift, stairlift to cafe) toilets for disabled shop ✈ (ex guide dogs) 🔊

SE1
WINSTON CHURCHILL'S BRITAIN AT WAR EXPERIENCE
64/66 Tooley St SE1 2TF (Midway down Tooley St, between London Bridge & Tower Bridge. 2min walk from London Bridge Stn)
☎ 020 7403 3171 📠 020 7403 5104 **2 for 1**
e-mail: britainatwar@dial.pipex.com

The Britain at War Experience pays tribute to the ordinary people who lived through the Second World War. Huddle in the Anderson shelter, share the excitement and anxiety of the evacuees as they wait to be transported to new homes and experience the fury of the London Blitz. An exciting adventure for all ages.
Times: Open all year, Apr-Sep 10-5.30pm; Oct-Mar 10-4.30. (Closed 24-26 Dec) **Fee:** £6.50 (ch 16 £3.50, student, pen & UB40 £4.50). Family ticket £15. 🅿 (100mtrs) ♿ (wheelchair for loan) shop (small) ✈ (ex guide dogs) 🔊

London Outer

BARNET   Map 04 TQ29
MUSEUM OF DOMESTIC DESIGN & ARCHITECTURE
Middlesex University, Cat Hill EN4 8HT (from M25, junct 24, signposted A111 Cockfosters to Cat Hill)
☎ 020 8411 5244   📧 020 8411 6639   **2 for 1**
e-mail: moda@mdx.ac.uk

Located on Middlesex University's Cat Hill campus, the MoDA houses one of the most comprehensive collections of late 19th and 20th century decorative design for the home. A wide ranging exhibition programme is offered throughout the year, alongside the permanent exhibit, Exploring Interiors: Decoration of the Home 1900-1960.
Times: Open Tue-Sat 10-5, Sun 2-5. (Closed Mon, Etr, Xmas & New Year). **Fee:** Free. **Facilities:** P & toilets for disabled shop ✶ (ex guide dogs)

BEXLEY   Map 05 TQ47
HALL PLACE
Bourne Rd DA5 1PQ (near junction of A2 & A233)
☎ 01322 526574   📧 01322 522921
Times: Open all year, House: Mon-Sat 10-5, Sun & BHs 11-5 (summer); Tue-Sat 10-4.15 (winter). Gardens: Mon-Fri 7.30-dusk, Sat & Sun 9-dusk. **Facilities:** P 🍴 ✶ licensed & toilets for disabled shop garden centre ✶ (ex guide/hearing dogs) *Details not confirmed for 2003*

BRENTFORD   Map 04 TQ17
KEW BRIDGE STEAM MUSEUM
Green Dragon Ln TW8 0EN (Underground - Kew Gardens, district line then 391 bus. Museum 100yds from N side of Kew Bridge. From M4 junct 2 follow A4 to Chiswick rdbt, take A315 to Kew Bridge, Green Dragon Ln 1st right after lights)
☎ 020 8568 4757   📧 020 8569 9978
e-mail: info@kbsm.org

This Victorian pumping station has steam engines and six beam engines, of which five are working and one is the largest in the world. A forge, diesel house, waterwheel and old workshops can also be seen along with London's only steam narrow-gauge railway which operates on the second and last weekend of each month (Mar-Nov). The Water for Life Gallery tells the story of London's water supply from pre-Roman times.
Times: Open all year, daily 11-5. In steam wknds & BHs. (Closed Good Fri & Xmas wk). **Fee:** * Weekdays: £3.50 (ch 5-15 £1, pen & students £2.50) Family ticket £8. Weekends: £4.50 (ch £2, pen & students £3.50) Family ticket £11.50. **Facilities:** P 🍴 & (tours for partially sighted, wheelchairs,large print guide) toilets for disabled shop 🛍

MUSICAL MUSEUM
368 High St TW8 0BD (Underground - Gunnersbury, nr Kew Bridge)
☎ 020 8560 8108
Times: Open Apr-Oct, Sat & Sun 2-5. Also Jul-Aug, Wed 2-4.
Facilities: P (200 yds) & shop ✶ (guide dogs) *Details not confirmed for 2003*

CHESSINGTON   Map 04 TQ16
CHESSINGTON WORLD OF ADVENTURES
Leatherhead Rd KT9 2NE (M25 junct 9/10, on A243)
☎ 0870 444 7777   📧 01372 725050

Fasten your seat belts for a fang-tastic family flight that everyone will be batty about as Vampire strikes back. Take on the quick fire challenge of Tomb Blaster in an action packed interactive adventure ride. Plus, a no-go zone for all softies, Dennis's Madhouse is the latest addition to the mischief making mayhem in Beanoland. Explore the Trail of the Kings jungle themed experience and enjoy plenty of fun in Toytown where there's Toadie's Crazy Cars, cheeky Berry Bouncers and Tiny Truckers. With plenty firm favourites there's more to explore then ever before!
Times: Open end Mar-beginning Nov (excluding some off peak days) either 10-5, 10-6 or 10-7 (telephone for details). Open until 7.30 during Halloween week. **Fee:** * £17-£21 (ch under 4 free, ch 4-11 £14.50-£17). Family ticket (2 adults & 2ch) from £52. Advance booking saves money and allows fast track entry. **Facilities:** P 🍴 ✶ licensed & (some rides not accessible, disabled guide available) toilets for disabled shop ✶ (ex guide dogs & hearing dogs) 🛍

CHISLEHURST   Map 05 TQ47
CHISLEHURST CAVES
Old Hill BR7 5NB (off A222 near Chislehurst railway stn. Turn into station road, then right & right again into Caveside Close)
☎ 020 8467 3264
📧 020 8295 0407   **2 for 1**
e-mail: enquiries@chislehurstcaves.co.uk

Take a 45-minute guided tour through the darkness of these unique manmade caves. You will hear of the Druids, Romans and Saxons, see the tunnels made famous as a shelter during WW2, visit the haunted pool and more.
Times: Open all year, daily during school hols (incl half terms). All other times Wed-Sun, 10-4. Closed Xmas. **Fee:** £4 (ch & pen £2).
Facilities: P 🍴 ✶ licensed (ramps) shop ✶ (ex guide dogs) 🛍

London Outer 159

🏛 DOWNE Map 05 TQ46
DOWN HOUSE - HOME OF CHARLES DARWIN
Luxted Rd BR6 7JT (Off A233, signposted)
☎ 01689 859119

The home of Charles Darwin for forty years. The drawing room and Old Study are furnished as they were when he was working on his famous book *On the Origin of Species by means of Natural Selection*. The Museum includes memorabilia from his voyage on HMS *Beagle*. The garden is also maintained, including the famous Sand Walk or thinking path, along which he took his daily walk.
Times: Open all year, 29 Mar-Sep, Wed-Sun 10-6 (last admission 5.30) (Oct 10-5); Nov- Mar, Wed-Sun 10-4. Also BH Mon. (Closed 23 Dec-4 Feb). **Fee:** * £6 (ch 5-15 £3, under 5's free, con £4.50). Family ticket £15. Group visits 11+ must be booked in advance. **Facilities:** P ♿ shop ✈

🏛 ENFIELD Map 04 TQ39
FORTY HALL MUSEUM
Forty Hill EN2 9HA (M25 junct 25 onto A10, turn right into Bullsmoor Lane)
☎ 020 8363 8196 & 020 8363 4046
📠 020 8367 9098
Times: Open all year, Thu-Sun 11-5 & BH's. **Facilities:** P 🍴 ♿ (Disabled parking in main carpark & 3 near house) toilets for disabled shop ✈ (ex guide dogs) *Details not confirmed for 2003*

🏛 ESHER Map 04 TQ16
CLAREMONT LANDSCAPE GARDEN
Portsmouth Rd KT10 9JG (E of A307)
☎ 01372 467806 📠 01372 464394
e-mail: claremont@ntrust.org.uk
Times: Open all year Apr-end of Oct daily, Nov-end Dec & Jan-end Mar daily (ex Mon). Apr-Oct Mon-Fri 10-6, Sat-Sun & BH Mon 10-7 (closed all day 10 & 11 Jul closes 2pm 12-15 Jul); Nov-Mar 10-5 or sunset if earlier. Closed 25 Dec & 1 Jan. House open Feb-Nov, 1st wknd of month 2-3 (ex 1st Sat in Jul). House not National Trust.
Facilities: P 🍴 ♿ (wheelchairs available, Braille guide) toilets for disabled shop ✈ (ex on leads, Nov-Mar only) 🐕 *Details not confirmed for 2003*

🏛 HAM Map 04 TQ17
HAM HOUSE
TW10 7RS (W of A307, between Kingston & Richmond)
☎ 020 8940 1950 📠 020 8332 6903
e-mail: hamhouse@ntrust.org.uk

Built in 1610 and extended in the 1670s, Ham House is one of the most outstanding Stuart houses from that period. It was home to the Duchess of Lauderdale, who was renowned as a political schemer and during the 17th century the house was at the heart of Civil War politics and Restoration court intrigues. The beautiful gardens include the Cherry Garden featuring lavender parterres flanked by two Berceaux of pleached Hornbeam and a statue of Bacchus at its centre. There are also eight grass plats, including, a 17th-century

---

Take a lamplit guided tour lasting approximately 45 minutes through the miles of darkness beneath Chislehurst. See the caves, church and hospital from World War II. The Druid Altar and much more!.

CHISLEHURST CAVES

Telephone (020) 8467 3264 for further details
OLD HILL · CHISLEHURST
KENT BR7 5NB (off the A222)

• Open – Wednesday-Sunday. Daily during School Holidays
• Guided tours hourly from 10am-4pm
• All children must be accompanied by an adult • Reduced rates for school or group bookings •

GIFT SHOP – CAFE
FREE CAR PARK
OPEN ALL YEAR

Orangery; a tea terrace; an outer courtyard with Walnut and Chestnut trees that act as a roost and nesting site for a large flock of green parakeets; and formal listed avenues of over 250 trees.
Times: Open Gardens: all year, Sat-Wed 11-6 or dusk if earlier. (Closed 25-26 Dec & 1 Jan). House: Apr-Oct, Sat-Wed 1-5. Last admission 4.30. **Fee:** * House £6 (ch £3). Family ticket £15. Garden only £2 (ch £1). Family £5. Discount for groups 15+. **Facilities:** P (500 yds) 🍴 ♿ (Braille guide, wheelchairs & stairclimber, lift access) toilets for disabled shop ✈ (ex guide/hearing dogs) 🐕 🛍

🏛 HAMPTON COURT Map 04 TQ16
HAMPTON COURT PALACE
KT8 9AU (on A308, close to A3, M3 & M25 exits. Train from Waterloo - Hampton Court, 2mins walk from station)
☎ 0870 752 7777 & 8781 9501
📠 020 8781 9669

With over 500 years of royal history Hampton Court Palace has something to offer everyone, from the magnificent State Apartments to the domestic reality of the Tudor Kitchens. Costumed guides and audio tours bring the palace to life and provide an insight into how

continued

life in the palace would have been in the time of Henry VIII and William III.

Hampton Court Palace

Times: Open 31 Mar-26 Oct Mon 10.15-6; Tue-Sun 9.30-6. 27 Oct-30 Mar Mon 10.15-4 Tue-Sun 9.30-4. Closed 24-26 Dec **Fee:** * £11 (ch 5-16 £7.25, pen, students £8.25). Family £33. **Facilities:** P (charged) ☕ ✕ licensed ♿ (lifts, buggies for gardens, wheelchairs, wardens to assist) toilets for disabled shop (4 shops on site) ✕ (ex guide/hearing dogs) 🎩

ISLEWORTH Map 04 TQ17
SYON HOUSE
TW8 8JF (Approach via A310 Twickenham road into Park Rd)
☎ 020 8560 0882/3 📠 020 8568 0936 **2 for 1**
e-mail: info@syonpark.co.uk

Set in 200 acres of parkland, Syon House is the London home of the Duke of Northumberland, whose family have lived here since the late 16th century. During the second half of the 18th century the first Duke of Northumberland engaged Robert Adam to remodel the interior and `Capability' Brown to landscape the grounds. Adam was also responsible for the furniture and decorations, and the result is particularly spectacular in the superbly coloured Ante-Room and Long Gallery.
Times: Open 27 Mar-3 Nov, Wed-Thu, Sun & BH 11-5 (last ticket 4.15pm). **Fee:** * Combined ticket for house and gardens £6.95 (ch £5.95 concessions £6.20). Family ticket £15. **Facilities:** P ☕ ♿ (only accessible if visitor can walk 9 stairs to entrance) toilets for disabled shop garden centre ✕ 🎩

SYON PARK
TW8 8JF (A310 Twickenham Road into Park Rd)
☎ 020 8560 0882 📠 020 8568 0936
e-mail: info@syonpark.co.uk

Contained within the 40 acres that make up Syon Park Gardens is one of the inspirations for the Crystal Palace at the Great Exhibition of 1851: a vast crescent of metal and glass, the first construction of its kind in the world and known as the Great Conservatory. Although the horticultural reputation of Syon Park goes back to the 16th century, its beauty today is thanks to the master of landscape design, `Capability' Brown.
Times: Open all year, daily 10-5.30 or dusk if earlier. (Closed 25 & 26 Dec). **Fee:** * £3.50 (concessions £2.50). Combined ticket for house & gardens £6.95 (ch £5.95 concessions £6.50). Family ticket £15.
Facilities: P ☕ ♿ toilets for disabled shop garden centre ✕ (ex guide dogs) 🎩

KEW Map 04 TQ17
KEW GARDENS (ROYAL BOTANIC GARDENS)
TW9 3AB (Underground - Kew Gdns)
☎ 020 8940 1171 📠 020 8332 5197
e-mail: info@kew.org
Times: Open all year, Gardens daily 9.30-between 4 & 6.30pm on weekdays, between 4-7.30pm Suns & BH's, depending on the time of sunset.(Closed 25 Dec & 1 Jan) **Facilities:** P (charged) ☕ ✕ licensed ♿ (16 seat bus tour: enquiries ring 020 8332 5623) toilets for disabled shop ✕ (ex guide dogs) *Details not confirmed for 2003* 🎩

KEW PALACE
Royal Botanic Gardens TW9 3AB (Underground - Kew Bridge)
☎ 020 8781 9540
Times: Please telephone for details 020 8332 5655 **Facilities:** *Details not confirmed for 2003*

PUBLIC RECORD OFFICE MUSEUM
Ruskin Av TW9 4DU (Underground - Kew Gardens)
☎ 020 8392 5202 020 8392 5323
📠 020 8392 5345
e-mail: events@pro.gov.uk
Times: Open Mon, Wed & Fri, 9-5; Tue, 10-7; Thu, 9-7 (closed 1st wk in Dec, Sun & public holiday wkends). **Facilities:** P ☕ ♿ (hearing loops & large print text in museum) toilets for disabled shop ✕ *Details not confirmed for 2003*

QUEEN CHARLOTTE'S COTTAGE
Royal Botanic Gardens TW9 3AB (Underground - Kew Bridge)
☎ 020 8332 5189
Times: Open weekends only between May & Sep. **Facilities:** shop ✕ *Details not confirmed for 2003*

OSTERLEY Map 04 TQ17
OSTERLEY PARK HOUSE
TW7 4RB (Underground - Osterley)
☎ 020 8560 7714 📠 020 8568 7714
e-mail: tsogen@smtp.ntrust.org.uk
Times: Open all year: Park & pleasure grounds, daily 9-7.30 or sunset if earlier. House: Apr-1 Nov, Wed-Sun 2-5, BH Sun & Mon 1-5. Last admission 4.30. (Closed Good Fri & 25-26 Dec). **Facilities:** P (charged) ☕ ♿ toilets for disabled shop ✕ (ex on lead in park) 🎒 *Details not confirmed for 2003*

TWICKENHAM Map 04 TQ17
MARBLE HILL HOUSE
Richmond Rd TW1 1NL
☎ 020 8892 5115

An example of the English Palladian school of architecture, Marble Hill House was built in the 18th century for a mistress of George II. The perfectly

continued

proportioned Thames-side villa, contains a notable collection of paintings and furniture, as well as the Lazenby Chinoiserie Bequest.
Times: Open daily, 29 Mar-Sep 10-6 (Oct, daily 10-5); **Fee:** * £3.30 (ch 5-15 £1.70, under 5's free, concessions £2.50) **Facilities:** P ⬛ ✗ licensed ♿ toilets for disabled shop ✈ (ex in grounds) ♯

MUSEUM OF RUGBY & TWICKENHAM STADIUM TOURS
Rugby Football Union, Rugby Rd TW1 1DZ (M3 into London, A316 follow signs to museum)
☎ 020 8892 8877 ✉ 020 8892 2817
e-mail: museum@rfu.com

Times: Museum: open Tue-Sat 10-5, Sun 2-5. Last admission 4.30pm. Tours: 10.30am, noon, 1.30pm, & 3pm; Sun 3pm. No tours on match days. Museum open on match days for ticket holders only. Ground closed Mon (ex BH), 24-26 Dec, Good Fri & the Sunday after a match. **Facilities:** P ⬛ ✗ licensed ♿ (special tours and lifts to all floors) toilets for disabled shop ✈ (ex guide dogs) *Details not confirmed for 2003*

ORLEANS HOUSE GALLERY
Riverside TW1 3DJ (From Twickenham along Richmond road (A305), Orleans Rd on right just past Orleans Park School)
☎ 020 8892 0221 ✉ 020 8744 0501
e-mail: m.denovellis@richmond.gov.uk
Times: Open Oct-Mar, Tue-Sat 1-4.30, Sun & BH 2-4.30; Apr-Sep Tue-Sat 1-5.30, Sun & BH 2-5.30. **Facilities:** P ♿ (handling objects & large print labels for some exhibitions) toilets for disabled shop ✈ (ex guide dogs) *Details not confirmed for 2003*

Prepare to be inspired – Spend a day in the life of rugby

MUSEUM OF RUGBY
TWICKENHAM

From the moment you pass through the authentic Twickenham turnstile at the Museum of Rugby, you'll be immersed in a world of Rugby Union history. Enjoy the finest and most extensive collection of rugby memorabilia in the world. Let interactive touch-screen computers, video footage and period set pieces take you on a journey through the history of the game. Also operating from the Museum are tours of the Stadium. Expert Tour Guides will take you on an awe-inspiring journey through the home of England rugby. Walk alongside the hallowed turf, visit England's dressing room and experience the excitement of match day as you enter the stadium through the players' tunnel.

Open daily: Tuesdays to Saturdays and Bank Holidays 10am to 5pm, Sundays 11am to 5pm.
Match days: Museum only open to match ticket holders only.
Closed: Post Twickenham match day Sundays. Also closed Mondays, Easter Sunday, Xmas Eve, Xmas Day, Boxing Day, New Year's Day. *For more information:* telephone 020 8892 8877

Merseyside

A Northwestern metropolitan county on the River Mersey, with Liverpool as its administrative centre, Merseyside incorporates the towns of Bootle, Birkenhead, St Helens, Wallasey, and Southport.

The fortunes of the city have declined since the 19th century when Liverpool was England's second greatest port, and the area has been dogged by urban deprivation and unemployment. However, Merseyside is on the upturn, due in part to that indomitable Scouse spirit.

When the port of Chester silted up in medieval times, Liverpool took up the slack. The first dock was built in 1715 and the port came to prominence with the slave trade. Following abolition, the port grew to a seven-mile stretch of docks, busy with cargoes of cotton, tobacco and sugar and the huge wave of emigration from Europe to the New World in the 19th and early 20th centuries. In its turn, immigration brought an influx of people to Merseyside to join its expanding population, including many from Ireland fleeing the potato famines of the mid-19th century.

In the second half of the 20th century, accessible air travel brought to an end the era of the ocean-going liners. At the same time, trade with Europe was picked up by the southeastern ports. Merseyside waned and its population dwindled, although it remains one of Britain's most vibrant and interesting areas.

Liverpool's shipping heritage is part of its attraction today, in the museums and galleries of the redeveloped Albert Dock, and in the impressive architecture reflecting the city's civic pride. Look out for the Royal Liver Building and the Cunard Building on the waterfront, and the architecture around St George's Hall, Dale Street, Water Street and William Brown Street.

Top: The Liver Building overlooking the Mersey

EVENTS & FESTIVALS

February
tbc Chinese New Year, Liverpool

April
3rd-5th Grand National, Aintree

May
18th Liverpool Princes Women's 10k Run, Liverpool
tbc Liverpool Show, Wavertree Playground

June
13th-16th The Mersey River Festival, Liverpool
tbc Hope Street Festival, Liverpool

July
25th-27th St Helens Show, Sherdley Park, St Helens
tbc Middlesbrough Mela, Albert Park, Middlesbrough

August
23rd-25th International Beatles Week & Convention, Liverpool
29th-31st Ness Botanic Gardens Garden Festival, Wirral
tbc Southport Flower Show, Victoria Park, Southport

August/September
tbc British Musical Firework Championships, Southport

September
14th Liverpool Corporate Cup Run, 5km course in city centre
tbc The Southport Airshow

November
22nd-23rd British Ministrada Festival of Gymnastics & Dance
tbc City of Liverpool Fireworks Display, various venues

Merseyside **163**

BIRKENHEAD Map 07 SJ38
BIRKENHEAD PRIORY
Priory St CH41 5JH
☎ 0151 666 1249
Times: Open all year, Sat & Sun 1-5 (in summer), 12-4 (in winter) & Tue-Sun 1-5 (school holidays), 12-4 (Oct & Feb half term). Telephone to confirm. **Facilities:** P & toilets for disabled shop ✱ (ex guide dogs) *Details not confirmed for 2003*

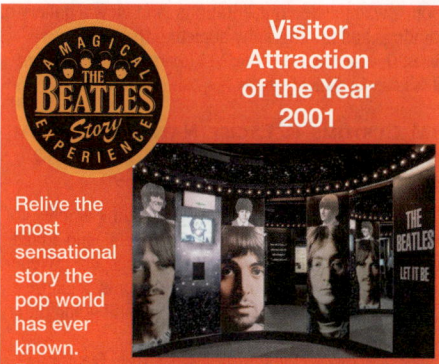

HISTORIC WARSHIPS
East Float, Dock Rd CH41 1DJ (end of M53 all docks turn off follow tourist signs, from Liverpool Wallasey tunnel 1st exit after toll & follow brown heritage signs)
☎ 0151 650 1573
📠 0151 650 1473   **2 for 1**
e-mail: manager@warships.freeserve.co.uk

HMS Onyx served in the Falklands and is the only submarine afloat in the UK that visitors can explore; *HMS Plymouth*, an anti-submarine frigate also served in the Falklands. The U534 is the only WWII German U-Boat to be raised from the sea bed. Pre-booking is required, adults only admitted to U-Boat.
Times: Open all year, Sep-Mar daily 10-4, Apr-Aug daily 10-5. (Closed 24-26 Dec). **Fee:** £5.50 (ch £3.50, pen £4.50). Family ticket £15. Combined ships & U-Boat £13.50 (adults only). U-Boat £8. **Facilities:** P 🍽 & museum only, access to HMS Plymouth, multimedia tour of U534 shop ✱ (ex guide dogs) 🍽

WILLIAMSON ART GALLERY & MUSEUM
Slatey Rd CH43 4UE
☎ 0151 652 4177   📠 0151 670 0253
e-mail: wag@museum-service.freeserve.co.uk
Times: Open all year, Tue-Sun & BHs 1-5, (Closed Xmas & Good Fri).
Facilities: P & toilets for disabled shop ✱ *Details not confirmed for 2003*

LIVERPOOL Map 07 SJ39
THE BEATLES STORY
Britannia Pavilion, Albert Dock L3 4AA
☎ 0151 709 1963   📠 0151 708 0039

Visitor Attraction of the Year 2001

A MAGICAL BEATLES Story EXPERIENCE

Relive the most sensational story the pop world has ever known.

Four lads from Liverpool took the world by storm and changed the face of music for generations to come. Live and breathe the whole 60s experience and see how it all happened. This spectacular walk through experience is situated in the basement vaults of the Britannia Pavilion in the award winning Albert Dock. New: "Through the lenses of Lennon".

The Beatles Story
Britannia Pavilion · Albert Dock
Liverpool · L3 4AA Tel: 0151-709 1963
www.beatlesstory.com

CENTRAL LIBRARY
William Brown St L3 8EW (Adjacent to St. George's Hall, which is opposite Lime St. Station. Central Library is between the museum and the art gallery)
☎ 0151 233 5858   📠 0151 233 5824
e-mail: refham.central.library@liverpool.gov.uk
Times: Open all year, Mon-Thu 9-7.30, Fri 9-5, Sat 10-4 & Sun 12-4 Closed BHs. **Facilities:** P (50 yds) (pay & display parking only) & (lift, text magnification, reading machine) toilets for disabled ✱ (ex guide dogs) *Details not confirmed for 2003*

CONSERVATION CENTRE
White Chapel L1 6HZ
☎ 0151 478 4999   📠 0151 478 4990

Award-winning centre, the only one of its kind, gives the public an insight into the world of museum and gallery conservation.
Times: Mon-Sat 10-5, Sun 12-5, Closed 23-26 Dec & 1 Jan **Fee:** Free.
Facilities: P (charged) 🍽 & toilets for disabled shop ✱ ex guide dogs 🍽

THE GRAND NATIONAL EXPERIENCE
Aintree Racecourse, Ormskirk Rd L9 5AS
☎ 0151 522 2921   📠 0151 522 2920
e-mail: aintree@rht.net

A fascinating look at Britain's most famous horserace, the Martell Grand National. Visitors can sit in the jockey's weighing-in chair, walk around the dressing

continued

rooms, watch video presentations, and view a gallery of paintings and photography depicting the race.
Times: Open 26 May-17 Oct **Fee:** * £7 (concessions £4) **Facilities:** P & toilets for disabled shop ✖ (ex guide dogs)

HM Customs & Excise National Museum
Merseyside Maritime Museum, Albert Dock L3 4AQ
☎ 0151 478 4499   📠 0151 478 4590

Enter the exciting world of smuggle busting where everyday items reveal their hidden secrets. Find a fake, rummage for hidden goods and spot a suspect traveller. Look into illustrious history of HM Customs & Excise – it's the longest battle in history and it's still going on today!
Times: Open daily 10-5. (Closed 23-26 Dec & 1 Jan) **Fee:** Free.
Facilities: P 🍽 ✖ licensed & (restricted wheelchair access, no access to basement) toilets for disabled shop ✖ (ex guide dogs)

Liverpool Football Club Visitors Centre Tour
Anfield Rd L4 0TH
☎ 0151 260 6677   📠 0151 264 0149
e-mail: stephen.done@liverpoolfc.tv

See all the first team kit set out for a match day, listen to a recorded 'team talk' from Gerard Houllier, and then touch the famous 'This is Anfield' sign to the sound of 45,000 cheering fans - a marvellous experience for any Liverpool fan!
Times: Open all year: Museum daily 10-5 last admission 4pm. (Closed 25-26 Dec). Match days 9am until last admission 1hr before kick off. Museum & Tour - tours are run subject to daily demand. Advance booking is essential to avoid disappointment. **Fee:** * Museum only, £5 (ch under 6 & pen £3) Family £13. Museum & Tour £8.50 (ch under 16 & pen £5.50) Family £23. **Facilities:** P 🍽 ✖ licensed & (lifts to all areas for wheelchairs) toilets for disabled shop ✖ (ex guide dogs)

Merseyside Maritime Museum
Albert Dock L3 4AQ (Albert Dock is near Liverpool's historic waterfront. Entry into the dock is from the Strand)
☎ 0151 478 4499   📠 0151 478 4590

Set in the heart of Liverpool's magnificent waterfront, the Merseyside Maritime Museum offers a unique insight into the history of the great port of Liverpool, its ships and its people.
Times: Open daily 10-5 (Closed 23-26 Dec & 1 Jan). **Fee:** Free.
Facilities: P ✖ licensed & (lifts, wheelchairs, ramps, ex pilot boat & basement) toilets for disabled shop ✖ (ex guide dogs)

Metropolitan Cathedral of Christ the King
Mount Pleasant L3 5TQ (5 mins walk from either Liverpool Lime Street or Liverpool Central Railway Station. 'Smart' buses stop outside)
☎ 0151 709 9222   📠 0151 708 7274
e-mail: met.cathedral@cwcom.net

A modern Roman Catholic cathedral which provides a focal point on the Liverpool skyline. The imposing structure of curving concrete ribs and stained glass was designed by Sir Frederick Gibberd and consecrated in 1967.
Times: Open daily 8-6 (Sun 5pm in winter). **Fee:** Free. **Facilities:** P & (lift, loop system, no access to Crypt) toilets for disabled shop ✖ (ex guide dogs)

Museum of Liverpool Life
Pier Head L3 4AA (follow signs for Albert Dock, museum is on Pier Head side)
☎ 0151 478 4080   📠 0151 478 4090
e-mail: liverpoollife@nmgm.org

The Museum of Liverpool Life celebrates the contribution of the people of Liverpool to national life. Recently expanded to include three new galleries, City Lives exploring the richness of Liverpool's cultural diversity, The River Room featuring life around the river Mersey and City Soldiers about the King's Regiment. Other galleries include Mersey Culture from Brookside to the Grand National, Making a Living and Demanding a Voice.
Times: Open daily 10-5. (Closed 23-26 Dec & 1 Jan). **Fee:** Free.
Facilities: P (charged) & (wheelchairs, audio handsets, subtitles on video terminals) toilets for disabled shop ✖ (ex guide/hearing dogs)

---

* An asterisk by an entry indicates that the prices shown are for 2002 only. Please contact the attraction for up-to-date price information.

Merseyside 165

National Museums & Galleries on Merseyside

Merseyside Maritime Museum   the Walker

Museum of Liverpool Life

Conservation Centre

Sudley House

HM Customs & Excise National Museum

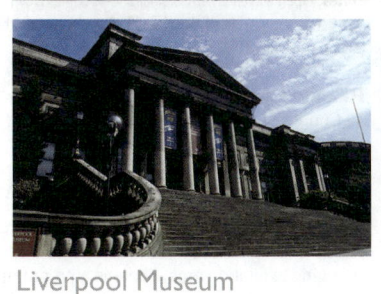

Liverpool Museum   Lady Lever Art Gallery

Liverpool's Cultural Heart

Telephone 0151 207 0001

LIVERPOOL 2008 EUROPEAN CAPITAL OF CULTURE

FREE for ALL

NMGM
NATIONAL MUSEUMS & GALLERIES ON MERSEYSIDE

www.nmgm.org.uk

Merseyside

NATIONAL WILDFLOWER CENTRE
Court Hey Park L16 3NA (M62 junct 5, take A5080 to rdbt. Exit into Roby Rd, entrance 0.5m on left)
☎ 0151 737 1819 0151 737 1820   2 for 1
e-mail: info@nwc.org.uk

Set in a public park on the outskirts of Liverpool, the National Wildflower Centre promotes the creation of wildflower habitats around the country and provides educational materials, wildflower seeds and interactive facilities. The Centre has demonstration areas, children's activities, a working nursery, compost display and rooftop walk. The centre has a comprehensive programme of events through the summer.
Times: Open Apr-Sep, daily 10-5. **Fee:** £3 (ch 5-16, pen, students & unemployed £1.50). Family ticket (2 adults & 2 ch) £7.50. Season tickets & group discount tickets available. **Facilities:** P ⌑ & Electric buggy & wheelchair available for use. toilets for disabled shop garden centre ✈ (ex guide dogs & in park) ⌑

TATE LIVERPOOL
Albert Dock L3 4BB (within walking distance of Liverpool Lime Street train station)
☎ 0151 702 7400 & 0151 702 7402
 0151 702 7401
e-mail: liverpoolinfo@tate.org.uk

A converted Victorian warehouse with stunning views across the River Mersey, Tate Liverpool displays the best of the National Collection of 20th-century Art. A changing programme of exhibitions draws on works from public and private collections across the world.
Times: Open Tue-Sun, 10-5.30. (Closed Mon ex BH Mon, 25-26 Dec, 1 Jan & Good Fri). **Fee:** Free. **Facilities:** P ⌑ & (wheelchairs available, leaflets in braille, hearing loop) toilets for disabled shop ✈ ⌑

WALKER ART GALLERY
William Brown St L3 8EL (follow brown tourist signs)
☎ 0151 478 4199   0151 478 4390

For over 120 years, visitors have been surprised, charmed & moved by The Walker's world-famous collection including masterpieces by Rembrandt, Poussin, Rubens & Murillo. Newly refurbished galleries will display and exciting and varied programme of must see exhibitions.
Times: Open Mon-Sat 10-5, Sun 12-5 (Closed 23-26 & 1 Jan) **Fee:** Free. **Facilities:** P (charged) ⌑ ✕ & (prior notice appreciated, wheelchair on request) toilets for disabled shop ✈ (ex guide dogs)
See advert on page 165

⌑ PORT SUNLIGHT   Map 07 SJ38
LADY LEVER ART GALLERY
CH62 5EQ (Follow brown heritage signs)
☎ 0151 478 4136   0151 478 4140
e-mail: ladyleverartgallery@nmgm.org

The Lady Lever Art Gallery houses many world famous works of art, including Pre-Raphaelite masterpieces by Millais, Burnejoues and Rossetti. Dramatic landscapes by the great British painters, Turner & Constable are also displayed alongside portraits by Gainsborough, Romney & Reynolds.
Times: Open all year, Mon-Sat 10-5, Sun 12-5. (Closed 23-26 Dec & 1 Jan) **Fee:** Free. **Facilities:** P (charged) ⌑ & (prior notice appreciated, wheelchair no request) toilets for disabled ✈ (ex guide dogs).
See advert on page 165

⌑ PRESCOT   Map 07 SJ49
KNOWSLEY SAFARI PARK
L34 4AN (M62 junct 6 onto M57 junct 2. Follow 'safari park' signs)
☎ 0151 430 9009   0151 426 3677
e-mail: safari.park@knowsley.com

A five-mile drive through the reserves enables visitors to see lions, tigers, elephants, rhinos, monkeys and many other animals in spacious, natural surroundings. Also a children's amusement park, reptile house, pets' corner plus sealion shows. Other attractions include an amusement park and a miniature railway.
Times: Open all year, Mar-Oct., daily 10-4. Winter Nov-Feb 11-3. **Fee:** * £8 (ch & pen £5). **Facilities:** P ⌑ & toilets for disabled shop ✈ (kennels provided) ⌑

PRESCOT MUSEUM
34 Church St L34 3LA (on corner of High St (A57) & Church St. Follow the brown tourist signs)
☎ 0151 430 7787   0151 430 7219
e-mail: prescot.museum.dlcs@knowsley.gov.uk

Permanent exhibitions reflecting the clock and watch-making industry of the area; with a special changing exhibition area. There is a programme of events and holiday activities, telephone for details.
Times: Open all year, Tue-Sat 10-5 (closed between 1-2), Sun 2-5 (also BH Mon 10-1 & 2-5). (Closed 24-26 Dec, 1 Jan & Good Fri). **Fee:** Free. **Facilities:** P (100 yds) & (ramp to ground floor) shop ✈ (ex guide dogs).

🏛 SOUTHPORT Map 07 SD31
ATKINSON ART GALLERY
Lord St PR8 1DH (located in centre of Lord Street, next to the Town Hall)
☎ 01704 533133 ext 2110   📠 0151 934 2110

The gallery specialises in 19th and 20th-century oil paintings, watercolours, drawings and prints, as well as 20th-century sculpture. Temporary exhibitions are shown regularly at the art gallery.
Times: Open all year, Mon-Wed & Fri 10-5, Thu & Sat 10-1. (Closed 25-26 Dec & 1 Jan). **Fee:** Free. **Facilities:** P (next street) (pay & display) ✗ licensed ♿ shop ✱ (ex guide dogs)

THE BRITISH LAWNMOWER MUSEUM
106-114 Shakespeare St PR8 5AJ (From M6, M58 or M57 follow signs towards town centre, then brown heritage signs to museum)
☎ 01704 501336   📠 01704 500564
e-mail: info@lawnmowerworld.co.uk

The award-winning museum houses a private collection of over 200 rare exhibits of garden machinery of special interest. In addition to grass cutting and garden machinery dating from 1799, there is also the largest collection of vintage toy lawnmowers and games in the world. See the lawnmowers of the rich and famous. A tribute to the garden machine industry over the last 200 years.
Times: Open daily, 9-5.30, ex Sun & BH Mon. **Fee:** £1 (ch 50p). Guided tour £4. **Facilities:** P shop ✱ 🍴

PLEASURELAND
Marine Dr PR18 1RX
☎ 0870 220 0204   📠 01704 537936
e-mail: mail@pleasurelandltd.freeserve.co.uk

Home to five rollercoasters, including TRAUMAtizer, the UK's tallest, fastest suspended coaster. Lucozade Space Shot at 125ft is a vertical reality thrill ride. There is something for all the family at Pleasureland, including more leisurely family entertainment.
Times: Open Mar-Nov opening times vary please call for information. **Fee:** * £15 all day (juniors £10) **Facilities:** P (charged) 🍽 ✗ licensed ♿ toilets for disabled shop ✱ (ex guide dogs) 🍴

SOUTHPORT ZOO & CONSERVATION TRUST
Princes Park PR8 1RX (from outskirts of Southport follow brown heritage signs, situated next to Pleasureland)
☎ 01704 538102 & 548894   📠 01704 538102
e-mail: info@southportzoo.com

Among the animals here are lions, snow leopards, lynx, chimpanzees, parrots, otters and llamas. An extension houses a pets' corner barn, a giant tortoise house, primate house and porcupines. There is also a reptile house with an aquarium. During the summer there are snake handling sessions with talks. There is an education centre for schools who have booked in advance. There is also new primate house and a new otter pool.
Times: Summer: 10-6, Winter: 10-4. Closed 25 Dec. **Fee:** £4 (ch 2-13 £3, pen £3.50) Party 20+ **Facilities:** P (100 yds) (metered) 🍽 ♿ (wide pathways, wide doorways) toilets for disabled shop

🏛 SPEKE Map 07 SJ48
SPEKE HALL
The Walk L24 1XD (follow signs for Liverpool Airport and brown heritage signs marked 'Speke hall')
☎ 0151 427 7231   📠 0151 427 9860   `2 for 1`

A remarkable timber-framed manor house set in tranquil gardens and grounds. The house has a Tudor Great Hall, Stuart plasterwork, and William Morris' wallpapers. Outside are varied grounds, including a rose garden, bluebell woods and woodland walks. Special events include Open Air Shakespeare, hands-on family activities, guided walks and tours.
Times: House open: Apr-Oct, daily (ex Mon but open BH Mon) 1-5.30; Nov-mid Dec, Sat & Sun 1-4.30. Garden open daily (ex Mon & closed 24-26 Dec, 31 Dec, 1 Jan & Good Fri). **Fee:** * Hall & Gardens: £5 (ch £2.50). Gardens only: £2.50 (ch 1.50p). Family ticket £14.
Facilities: P (charged) 🍽 ✗ ♿ (Wheelchairs & Electric car) toilets for disabled shop ✱ (on estate only) 🐾 🍴

Norfolk

A fertile agricultural county in the east of the country, sparsely populated, with plenty of fresh air and wide open spaces.

Norfolk is the northern bit of East Anglia, en route to nowhere, and too far from London to be colonised. Its coastline encompasses fenland round the Wash, the wonderfully unspoilt seaside towns of the north coast, and two of the country's most important nature reserves at Blakeney Point and the Cley marshes. Common features of the countryside are windmills, and attractive houses built of Norfolk flint with Dutch gables, a relic of the area's historical trade links with the Low Countries.

The Norfolk Broads are the county's main tourist attraction. The 'broads' are waterways set in marshy fenland, which came about from extensive peat cutting and subsequent flooding in the 13th and 14th centuries. Reed cutting for local thatching helped to keep the waterways clear. The Broads now has National Park status, to help protect the important wetland site from the demands of tourism and agriculture. The best way to see the Broads is to hire a boat, and there is plenty of opportunity for this at boatyards in Wroxham and Hoveton.

The county town is the city of Norwich, the largest in East Anglia, with a fine cathedral, a Norman keep, a huge market place and a medieval centre. Norwich came to prominence in the 17th century as a centre for the textile industry. Today it is most famously associated with Coleman's, the mustard company. The city also has a beautiful art nouveau shopping precinct.

Famous Norfolk natives include Horatio Nelson, Edith Cavell, Anna Sewell (author of *Black Beauty*), and Delia Smith, the TV celebrity cook who is also a director on the board of Norwich City Football Club.

EVENTS & FESTIVALS

May
1st King's Lynn May Garland Procession
31st Norwich Bike Ride
tbc Norfolk & Norwich Festival
tbc Norfolk Open Studios

June
25th-26th Royal Norfolk Show

July
4th-5th Morris & Folk Festival, Sheringham
18th-20th Weeting Steam Rally, Weeting
25th-27th Worstead Village Festival
31st Sandringham Flower Show (provisional)
tbc Lord Mayor's Celebrations, Norwich
tbc Norwich Music Festival
tbc Theatre in the Park, Norwich

August
3rd-9th Mundesley Festival
14th-17th West Norfolk CAMRA Rhythm & Booze Festival
20th Cromer Carnival
24th-25th Deepdale Jazz Festival, Burnham Deepdale
24th-25th Village at War re-enactment, Gressenhall

September
tbc Great Yarmouth Carnival
tbc Great Yarmouth Maritime Festival

November
tbc Sparks in the Park, Earlham Park, Norwich

December
tbc Norwegian Christmas Fayre, Great Yarmouth

Top: Hickling Broad in the Norfolk Broads

Norfolk

BACONSTHORPE   Map 09 TG13
BACONSTHORPE CASTLE
NR25 6LN (0.75m N off unclass road)

The 'castle' was really a moated and semi-fortified house, built by the Heydon family in the 15th century. Gatehouses, curtain walls and towers still remain.
Times: Open all year, daily 10-4. **Fee:** Free. **Facilities:** P ♿

BANHAM   Map 05 TM08
BANHAM ZOO
The Grove NR16 2HE (on B1113, signed off A11 and A140. Follow brown tourist signs)
☎ 01953 887771 & 887793   ≣ 01953 887445

Set in 35 acres of magnificent parkland, see hundreds of animals ranging from big cats to birds of prey and siamangs to shire horses. Tiger Territory is a purpose-built enclosure for Siberian tigers, including a rock pool and woodland setting. See also Lemur Island and Tamarin and Marmoset Islands. The Heritage Farm Stables & Falconry displays Norfolk's rural heritage with majestic shire horses and birds of prey. Other attractions include Children's Farmyard Barn and an adventure play area.
Times: Open all year, daily from 10-5 (10-4.30 Jan-mid Mar & Nov-Dec, 10-5.30 Jul-Sep). (Closed 25-26 Dec). Last admission 1 hour before closing. **Fee:** * £6.95-£8.95 (ch under 3 free, ch 3-14 £4.95-£6.50). Special rates for concessions. Party. **Facilities:** P 🍴 ✗ licensed ♿ (3 wheelchairs for hire, special parking) toilets for disabled shop ✗ 🐕

BLICKLING   Map 09 TG12
BLICKLING HALL
NR11 6NF (on B1354, 1.5m NW of Aylsham, signposted off A140 Norwich to Cromer road)
☎ 01263 738030   ≣ 01263 731689
e-mail: abgusr@smtp.ntrust.org.uk
Times: Hall open 31 Mar-28 Oct, Wed-Sun & BH, 1-4.30 (1-3.30 Oct). Also open Tue in Aug. Garden, shop & restaurant same days as hall 10.15-5.15. **Facilities:** P 🍴 ✗ licensed ♿ (wheelchairs & batricars, Braille guide, lift, parking) toilets for disabled shop garden centre ✗ (ex guide dogs) 🐾 *Details not confirmed for 2003* 🐕

BRESSINGHAM   Map 05 TM08
BRESSINGHAM STEAM MUSEUM & GARDENS
IP22 2AB (on A1066 2.5m W of Diss. Between Thetford & Diss)
☎ 01379 686900 & 687386   ≣ 01379 688085
e-mail: info@bressingham.co.uk

Alan Bloom is an internationally recognised nurseryman and a steam enthusiast, and has combined his interests to great effect at Bressingham. There are three miniature steam-hauled trains, including a 15in gauge running through two and a half miles of the wooded Waveney Valley. The Dell Garden has 5,000 species of perennials and alpines; Foggy Bottom has wide vistas, pathways, trees, shrubs, conifers and winter colour (restricted opening). A steam roundabout is another attraction, and the Norfolk fire museum is housed here. Various events are held, including Friends of Thomas the Tank Engine, please telephone for details.
Times: Open: Steam Museum, Dad's Army collection, Foggy Bottom & Dell Garden Apr-Sep, daily 10.30-5.30 (10.30-4.30 Mar & Oct). Museum & collections open all year (ex 24 Dec-8 Jan). Last admission 1 hour before closing time. **Fee:** * £7-£10 (ch 3-16 £5-£8, pen £6-£8). Family £21-£30. Season tickets available. **Facilities:** P 🍴 ✗ licensed ♿ (wheelchairs can be taken onto Nursery & Waveney lines) toilets for disabled shop garden centre ✗ (ex guide dogs) 🐕

BURGH CASTLE   Map 05 TG40
BERNEY ARMS WINDMILL
NR30 1SB
☎ 01493 700605

Access is by boat from Great Yarmouth or by rail to Berney Arms station: the road is unsuitable for cars. The seven-storey landmark was built in the 19th century to grind clinker for cement and then to help drain the marshes.
Times: Open 29 Mar-Oct, daily 9-1 & 2-5. **Fee:** * £1.60 (ch 80p, concessions £1.20). Phone 01493 700605 for opening details.
Facilities: ✗ 🐕

THE CASTLE
NR31 9PZ (off A143)

Burgh Castle was built in the third century AD by the Romans, as one of a chain of forts along the Saxon Shore - the coast where Saxon invaders landed. Sections of the massive walls still stand.
Times: Open any reasonable time. **Fee:** Free. **Facilities:** 🐕

CAISTER-ON-SEA   Map 09 TG51
ROMAN TOWN

The name Caister has Roman origins, and this was in fact a Roman naval base. The remains include the south gateway, a town wall built of flint with brick courses and part of what may have been a seamen's hostel.
Times: Open any reasonable time. **Fee:** Free. **Facilities:** 🐕

CASTLE ACRE   Map 09 TF81
CASTLE ACRE PRIORY & CASTLE
Stocks Green PE32 2XD
☎ 01760 755394

The priory was built for the Cluniac order in the Norman period. After the Dissolution under Henry VIII, the priory fell into ruin, but its extensive remains are dominated by the glorious, arcaded west front of the priory church, a reminder of past splendour. The chapel and 15th-century gatehouse also remain, and there are impressive ruins of a great castle which also stood nearby.
Times: Open all year 29 Mar-Sep, daily 10-6 (Oct daily 10-5); Nov-28 Mar, Wed-Sun 10-4. Closed 24-26 Dec & 1 Jan. **Fee:** * £3.70 (ch 5-15 £1.90, under 5's free, concessions £2.80). Family ticket £9.30
Facilities: P ♿ shop ✗ (in certain areas) 🐕

CASTLE RISING   Map 09 TF62
CASTLE RISING CASTLE
PE31 6AH (off A149)
☎ 01553 631330
Times: Open all year, Apr-Sep, daily 10-6; Oct, daily 10-5; Nov-Mar, Wed-Sun 10-4. (Closed 24-26 Dec & 1 Jan). **Facilities:** P & (exterior only) toilets for disabled shop ✈ ♿ *Details not confirmed for 2003*

CROMER   Map 09 TG24
HENRY BLOGG MUSEUM
No 2 Boathouse, The Promenade NR27 9HE (located at the bottom of East Gangway)
☎ 01263 511294   ▤ 01263 513018
e-mail: rfmuirhead@csma-netlink.co.uk

A lifeboat has been stationed at the Cromer since 1804, and the museum in No 2 boat house at the bottom of The Gangway covers local lifeboat history and the RNLI in general. The main exhibit is the WWII Watson Class lifeboat "H F Bailey", the boat Henry Blogg coxed. In ten years he helped to save over 500 lives.
Times: Open Etr-Oct, daily 10-4. Or by appointment with the Curator.
Fee: Donations welcome. **Facilities:** P (pay & display in town) & shop

ERPINGHAM   Map 09 TG13
WOLTERTON PARK
NR11 7LY (signposted from A140 Norwich to Cromer)
☎ 01263 584175   ▤ 01263 761214

Covering some 800 hectares this estate contains managed conservation areas, 18th-century landscaped gardens, a Heritage rose garden, lakes, a scented garden, a ruined church, horses graves, and Wolterton Hall, built in the 1720s. Special events include gardening demonstrations, concerts, craft fairs, guided walks and history lectures.
Times: Open: Park & walled garden daily; Hall, late Apr-Oct, Fri 2-5 (last entry 4). **Fee:** Free. **Facilities:** P (charged) & toilets for disabled shop ✈ (ex on lead & guide dogs)

FAKENHAM   Map 09 TF93
See also **Thursford Green**

PENSTHORPE WATERFOWL PARK & NATURE RESERVE
Pensthorpe NR21 0LN (signed off A1067 Norwich to Fakenham road)
☎ 01328 851465   ▤ 01328 855905
Times: Open all year, daily 10-5 mid Mar-end of year. **Facilities:** P ⊕ ✗ licensed & (network of hard surfaced pathways ensures access to shore) toilets for disabled shop ✈ (ex guide dogs) *Details not confirmed for 2003*

FELBRIGG   Map 09 TG23
FELBRIGG HALL
NR11 8PR (off B1436 betweeen A148 Cromer to Kings Lynn & A140 Cromer to Norwich)
☎ 01263 837444   ▤ 01263 837032   [2 for 1]
e-mail: afgusr@smtp.ntrust.org.uk

Felbrigg is a 17th-century house built on the site of an existing medieval hall. It contains a superb collection of 18th-century furniture and pictures and an outstanding library. A 550-acre wood shelters the house from the North Sea and contains waymarked walks and a working dovecot.
Times: Open house and garden: late Mar-early Nov, Sat-Wed, house 1-5, garden 11-5.30. BH Sun & BH Mon 11-5. Park walks available daily dawn-dusk. **Fee:** * House & garden £5.80 (ch £2.90). Family ticket £14.20. Garden only £2.20. Party. **Facilities:** P (charged) ⊕ ✗ licensed & (battery operated wheelchair for garden, braille guide) toilets for disabled shop ✈ (ex guide or on lead in park) ♿ ⚑

FILBY   Map 09 TG41
THRIGBY HALL WILDLIFE GARDENS
NR29 3DR (on unclass road off A1064, between Acle & Caister on Sea)
☎ 01493 369477   ▤ 01493 368256
e-mail: mail@thrigbyhall.co.uk

The 250-year-old park of Thrigby Hall is now the home of animals and birds from Asia, and the lake has ornamental wildfowl. There are tropical bird houses, a unique blue willow pattern garden and tree walk and a summer house as old as the park. The enormous jungle swamp hall has special features such as underwater viewing of large crocodiles.
Times: Open all year, daily from 10. **Fee:** * £5.90 (ch 4-14 £3.90, pen £4.90). **Facilities:** P ⊕ & (wheelchairs available) toilets for disabled shop ✈ (ex guide dogs) ⚑

FLEGGBURGH   Map 09 TG41
THE VILLAGE
Burgh St. Margaret NR29 3AF (7m from Great Yarmouth, on A1064 between Acle and Caister-on-Sea)
☎ 01493 369770   ▤ 01493 369318
Times: Open 24 Mar-end Oct, daily 10-5. Other times not confirmed. Saturday is grounds only day (admission reduced accordingly)
Facilities: P ⊕ ✗ licensed & toilets for disabled shop ✈ (ex guide dogs) *Details not confirmed for 2003* ⚑

GREAT BIRCHAM   Map 09 TF73
BIRCHAM WINDMILL
PE31 6SJ (0.5m W off unclassified Snettisham road)
☎ 01485 578393
e-mail: birchamwindmill@btinternet.com

This windmill is one of the last remaining in Norfolk. Sails turn on windy days, and the adjacent tea room serves home-made cakes, light lunches and cream teas. There is also a bakery shop and cycle hire.
Times: Open Etr-Sep, 10-5. **Fee:** * £2.75 (ch £1.50, pen £2.50)
Facilities: P ⊕ & toilets for disabled shop

GREAT YARMOUTH   Map 05 TG50
ELIZABETHAN HOUSE MUSEUM
4 South Quay NR30 2QH
☎ 01493 855746

A wealthy merchant built this house in 1596. It has been completely re-displayed to show a wealthy household through time from the 16th to 19th centuries. Visitors can see a Victorian kitchen, scullery

continued

Norfolk   **171**

and parlour, a Tudor bedroom and dining room, a Stuart (Civil War) 'conspiracy' room and a children's toy room.
Times: Open 25 Mar-Oct, Mon-Fri 10-5; Sat & Sun 1.15-5. **Fee:** * £2 (ch £1, concessions £1.50). Family ticket £4.70. **Facilities:** P (100yds) & shop ✖

MARITIME MUSEUM
Marine Pde NR30 2EN
☎ 01493 842267

The sea and the fishing industry have played an enormous part in East Anglia's history and this museum has exhibits on the herring fishery, the wherry, life-saving and the most recent industry - oil and gas in the North Sea.
Times: Open 25 Mar-7 Apr & 26 May-27 Sep, Mon-Fri 10-5; Sat & Sun 1.15-5. **Fee:** * £1.10 (ch 70p, concessions 90p). **Facilities:** P shop ✖

MERRIVALE MODEL VILLAGE
Wellington Pier Gardens, Marine Pde NR30 3JG (Marine parade seafront. Next to Wellington Pier)
☎ 01493 842097

Set in attractive landscaped gardens, this comprehensive miniature village is built on a scale of 1:12. The layout includes a two and a half inch gauge model railway, radio-controlled boats, and over 200 models set in an acre of landscaped gardens. There are additional amusements and remote-controlled cars and boats.
Times: Open Etr 9.30-6, Jun-Oct 9.30-10. **Fee:** * £3 (ch 3-14 £1.50, pen £2.50). **Facilities:** P (opposite) ⬛ & shop ✖ (ex on leads)

OLD MERCHANT'S HOUSE
Row 111, Greyfriar's Cloister NR30 2RQ (follow signs to dock and south quay)
☎ 01493 857900
Times: Open Apr-Sep 10-6. Oct 10-5 (closed 1-2). **Facilities:** ✖ ♿
Details not confirmed for 2003

TOLHOUSE MUSEUM
Tolhouse St NR30 2SH
☎ 01493 858900   📠 01493 745459

This late 13th-century building was once the town's court house and gaol and has dungeons which can be visited. The rooms above contain exhibits on local history. The museum has become a brass rubbing centre and has a wide range of replica brasses from which rubbings can be made. Prices start at 50p and include materials and instructions.
Times: Open 28 May-28 Sep, Mon-Fri 10-5; Sat & Sun 1.15-5. **Fee:** £2 (ch £1, concessions £1.50). Family ticket £4.70. **Facilities:** P (100yds) (lift to ground & 2nd floor) shop ✖

🏛 GRESSENHALL   Map 09 TF91
NORFOLK RURAL LIFE MUSEUM & UNION FARM
Beech House NR20 4DR (A47, B1110 through East Dereham towards Holt, onto B1146 to Fakenham, museum is 1.5m on right)
☎ 01362 860563   📠 01362 860385
e-mail: gressenhall.museum@norfolk.gov.uk

Housed in a former workhouse, the museum reflects the rural history of the county over the past 200 years. Displays include Cherry Tree Cottage and garden, a typical farm labourer's home of the early 20th century, as well as reconstructed craftsmen's workshops. Union Farm is a working farm, which is worked with heavy horses and stocked with rare breeds of sheep, cattle, pigs and poultry. Farm trail, woodland and riverside walk, osier beds. Special events and demonstrations throughout the season.
Times: Open Mar-Oct, Tue-Sun, also BH & School Hol Mon, 10.30-5.30; Nov & Dec Sun only 11-4. **Fee:** * £4.70 (ch £3.30, concessions £4). Family ticket £13. **Facilities:** P ⬛ & (sound guide & wheelchair loan) toilets for disabled shop ✖ 🍴

🏛 GRIMES GRAVES   Map 05 TL88
GRIMES GRAVES
Lynford IP26 5DE (7m NW of Thetford off A134)
☎ 01842 810656

Grimes Graves is the largest known group of Neolithic flint mines in Britain. It consists of a network of hundreds of pits, the oldest dating from about 3000BC. Vertical shafts lead through the flint seams to galleries. Visitors can descend 10 metres (30 feet) into an excavated shaft and there are regular demonstrations of the craft of flint-knapping.
Times: Open all year, 29 Mar-Sep, daily 10-6 (Oct 10-5); Nov-28 Mar, Wed-Sun 10-4. Last visit to pit 30 minutes before closing). **Fee:** * £2.30 (ch 5-15 £1.20 under 5's free, concessions £1.70). A torch is useful. **Facilities:** P & (exhibition area, grounds only; access track rough) shop ✖ (in certain areas) ♿

🏛 HEACHAM   Map 09 TF63
NORFOLK LAVENDER
Caley Mill PE31 7JE (on A149 at junct with B1454)
☎ 01485 570384   📠 01485 571176
e-mail: admin@norfolk-lavender.co.uk
Times: Open all year, daily 10-5. (Closed 25-26 Dec & 1 Jan).
Facilities: P ⬛ ✖ licensed & (wheelchairs for loan) toilets for disabled shop garden centre *Details not confirmed for 2003*

🏛 HOLKHAM   Map 09 TF84
HOLKHAM HALL & BYGONES MUSEUM
NR23 1AB (off A149, 2m W of Wells-next-the-Sea)
☎ 01328 710227   📠 01328 711707

This classic Palladian mansion was built between 1734 and 1764 by Thomas Coke, 1st Earl of Leicester, and is home to his descendants. It has a magnificent alabaster entrance hall and the sumptuous state rooms house Greek and Roman statues, fine furniture and paintings by Rubens, Van Dyck, Gainsborough and others. The

continued

Norfolk

Bygones Museum, housed in the stable block, has over 5,000 items of domestic and agricultural display - from gramophones to fire engines.
Times: Open 26 May-Sep, Sun-Thu 1-5; Etr, May & Summer BHs, Sun & Mon 11.30-5. **Fee:** * Hall £5 (ch £2.50). Bygones £5 (ch £2.50). Combined ticket Hall & Bygones: £8 (ch £4). **Facilities:** P X licensed & (wheelchair ramps at all entrances) toilets for disabled shop garden centre X (ex guide & on lead in park)

HORSEY   Map 09 TG42
Horsey Windpump
NR29 4EF (2.5m NE of Potter Heigham. On B1159 N of Martham)
☎ 01493 393904

The windpump mill was built 200 years ago to drain the area, and then rebuilt in 1912 by Dan England, a noted Norfolk millwright. It has been restored since being struck by lightning in 1943, and overlooks Horsey Mere and marshes, noted for their wild birds and insects.
Times: Open Apr-Oct, daily 11-5. (Closed Good Fri). **Fee:** * £1.50 (ch 80p). National Trust members free entry & parking. Mooring fees payable to the Horsey Estate (inc NT members). **Facilities:** P (charged) & toilets for disabled shop X (ex guide dogs)

HORSHAM ST FAITH   Map 09 TG21
City of Norwich Aviation Museum
Old Norwich Rd NR10 3JF (follow brown tourist signs from A140 Norwich to Cromer Road)
☎ 01603 893080
e-mail: derek.waters@virgin.net
Times: Open all year, Apr-Oct Tue-Sat, 10-5. Sun 12-5. Nov-Mar, Wed & Sat 10-4. Sun 12-4. **Facilities:** P & (assistance available) shop X (ex guide dogs) *Details not confirmed for 2003*

HOUGHTON   Map 09 TF72
Houghton Hall
PE31 6UE (1.25m off A148)
☎ 01485 528569   01485 528167
e-mail: administrator@houghtonhall.com
Times: Open Etr Sun-last Sun Sep, Thu, Sun & BH's.House open 2-5.30, grounds 1-5.30. **Facilities:** P & toilets for disabled shop X *Details not confirmed for 2003*

HUNSTANTON   Map 09 TF64
Sea Life Aquarium & Marine Sanctuary
Southern Promenade PE36 5BH
☎ 01485 533576   01485 533531
Times: Open all year, daily from 10. (Closed 25 Dec) **Facilities:** P (charged) X & toilets for disabled shop X (ex guide dogs)
Details not confirmed for 2003

KING'S LYNN   Map 09 TF62
African Violet Centre
Terrington St Clement PE34 4PL (4m W of Kings Lynn, on A17)
☎ 01553 828374   01553 828376
Times: Open daily Mon-Sat 9-5, Sun 10-5. (Closed Xmas & New Year). **Facilities:** P & (ramps to reach tea room & outside sales areas) toilets for disabled shop garden centre X (ex guide dogs) *Details not confirmed for 2003*

King's Lynn Arts Centre
27-29 King St PE30 1HA (just off Tuesday Market Place in King Street, next to Globe Hotel)
☎ 01553 765565 & 01553 764864
 01553 762141

Although it has been used for many purposes, the theatrical associations of this 15th-century Guildhall are strongest: Shakespeare himself is said to have performed here. The annual King's Lynn Festival takes place towards the end of July.
Times: Open Mon-Fri, 10-2. Closed show days, Sun, BHs, Good Fri & 24 Dec-1st Mon in Jan. **Fee:** Free. **Facilities:** P P X & (hearing loop, ramp) toilets for disabled X

Lynn Museum
Market St PE30 1NL (Town centre)
☎ 01553 775001   01553 775001
e-mail: lynn.museum@norfolk.gov.uk

Once it was a walled city of considerable importance; its two great churches, two marketplaces and two Guildhalls testify to its size. King's Lynn was also a noted port and a stop on the Pilgrim's Way to Walsingham. The geology, archaeology and natural history of the area are the main collections in the local museum. Objects in the archaeology gallery include Bronze Age weapons and the skeleton of a Saxon warrior. Relics from the medieval town of Lynn include an important collection of pilgrim badges. Also see the Snarling Tiger, the Medieval Stonemason, the Victorian Ironmonger's Shop and the beautiful 19th-century fairground roundabout horses of Frederick Savage.
Times: Open all year, Tue-Sat, 10-5. **Fee:** * £1 (ch 60p, concessions 80p). **Facilities:** P (500yds) & shop X

LENWADE   Map 09 TG01
Dinosaur Adventure Park
Weston Park NR9 5JW (9m from Norwich. Follow signs from A47 or A1067)
☎ 01603 870245 & 01603 876312
 01603 876315
e-mail: info@dinosaurpark.co.uk

Children will have great fun coming face to face with lots of friendly farm animals (real), and giant dinosaurs (thankfully not real). Alongside the animals there are adventure play areas, a fossil workshop, raptor racers, Jurassic putt, a Victorian walled garden, and the Neanderthal walk.
Times: Open Etr-8 Sep & Oct half term, daily; 9 Sep-20 Oct, Fri, Sat & Sun. **Fee:** * £6.50 (ch & pen £5.50). Please telephone for 2003 prices.
Facilities: P P & toilets for disabled shop X (ex guide dogs)

LITTLE WALSINGHAM   Map 09 TF93
Walsingham Abbey Grounds & Shirehall Museum
NR22 6BP (Follow B1105 from Fakenham. Entrance to museum through tourist info centre in village)
☎ 01328 820510 & 820259   01328 820098
e-mail: walsingham.museum@farmline.com

In the grounds of the Abbey are the ruins of the original

continued

Norfolk   173

Augustinian priory built in the 1100s. The priory was built over the shrine of Our Lady of Walsingham which had been established in 1061. Shirehall Museum consists of an original Georgian Courthouse, displays on the history of Walsingham and local artefacts. The museum is situated in 20 acres of tranquil and picturesque gardens with access to woodland and river walks across the historic parkland.
Times: Open Apr-late Oct, daily 10-4.30; Oct-Dec, wknds only 10-4; late Jan-late Feb, daily 10-4. Other times through Estate office Mon-Fri, 10-4. Closed between 1-2. **Fee:** * £3 (concessions £1.50) **Facilities:** P (100yds) & toilets for disabled shop garden centre (ex on leads)

🏛 NORTH CREAKE   Map 09 TF83
CREAKE ABBEY
NR21 9LF (1m N off B1355)

Church ruin with crossing and eastern arm belonging to a house of Augustinian canons founded in 1206.
Times: Open any reasonable time. **Fee:** Free. **Facilities:** ‡

🏛 NORWICH   Map 05 TG20
BRIDEWELL MUSEUM
Bridewell Alley NR2 1AQ (in town centre)
☎ 01603 667228   📠 01603 765651
e-mail: museums@norfolk.gov.uk

Built in the late 14th century, this flint-faced merchant's house was used as a prison from 1583 to 1828. It now houses displays illustrating the trades and industries of Norwich during the past 200 years, including a large collection of locally made boots and shoes. There is also a reconstructed 1920s pharmacy, a 1930s pawnbrokers shop and a blacksmith's smithy. Special for children: Hunt the Animals quiz trail.
Times: Open Feb-Oct. **Fee:** £2 (ch £1, concessions £1.50) Family ticket £5. **Facilities:** P 5min walk shop 🐕 (ex guide dogs)

NORWICH CASTLE MUSEUM
Castle Meadow NR1 3JU (city centre)
☎ 01603 493625   📠 01603 493323
e-mail: museums@norfolk.gov.uk

The Castle keep was built in the 12th century, and the museum houses displays of art, archaeology, natural history, Lowestoft porcelain, Norwich silver, a large collection of paintings (with special emphasis on the Norwich School of Painters) and British ceramic teapots. There are also guided tours of the dungeons and battlements. A programme of exhibitions, children's events, gallery and evening talks takes place throughout the year. Please ring for details.
Times: Open all year, Mon-Sat 10.30-5, Sun 2-5; School holidays: Etr & half terms Mon-Sat 10.30-6, Sun 12-5; Summer Mon-Sat 10-7, Sun 12-5. (Closed Good Fri & 25-26 Dec). **Fee:** * Castle Keep & Archaeology or Exhibitions & Art Galleries: £2.90 (ch £2.25, concessions £2.55) Whole museum: £4.70 (ch £3.50, concessions £4.10). **Facilities:** P (200yds) 🍴 & (lift to first floor, special parking by prior arrangement) toilets for disabled shop 🐕

NORWICH CATHEDRAL
The Close NR1 4DH (A47, A11 to city centre, inner ring road to Barrack St rdbt, take road towards city centre to Tombland)
☎ 01603 218321   📠 01603 766032
e-mail: vis-profficer@cathedral.org.uk

For more than 900 years the splendour and tranquillity of Norwich Cathedral has attracted pilgrims and visitors. Founded in 1096 as part of a Benedictine priory, the cathedral boasts several superlatives. It stands as one of the finest complete Romanesque buildings in Europe, with the second tallest spire and largest monastic cloisters in England. There is a collection of over 1,000 beautifully carved roof bosses, which is one of the great treasures of medieval art.
Times: Open daily, 7.30-7 (6pm mid Sep-mid May). **Fee:** Free. **Facilities:** P (440yds) 🍴 licensed & (lift, touch & hearing centre, audio-induction loop) toilets for disabled shop 🐕 (ex guide dogs)

ROYAL NORFOLK REGIMENTAL MUSEUM
Shirehall, Market Av NR1 3JQ (adjacent to Norwich Castle Museum)
☎ 01603 493623   📠 01603 493623

Museum displays deal with the social as well as military history of the county regiment from 1685, including the daily life of a soldier. Audio-visual displays and graphics complement the collection and there's a programme of temporary exhibitions.
Times: Open all year, Mon-Sat 10-5, Sun 2-5. (Closed Xmas period & 1 Jan). **Fee:** * £1.80 (ch 90p, concessions £1.40). Joint ticket with Castle Museum available if visiting Castle first. **Facilities:** P (400yds) & (stair lift available, ring for details) shop 🐕 (ex guide dogs)

SAINSBURY CENTRE FOR VISUAL ARTS
University of East Anglia NR4 7TJ
☎ 01603 456060 & 593199   📠 01603 259401
e-mail: scva@uea.ac.uk
Times: Open Tue-Sun 11-5. (Closed Mon & University closure at Xmas). **Facilities:** P 🍴 licensed & (parking at main entrance, wheelchair available on loan) toilets for disabled shop 🐕 (guide dogs by arrangement) *Details not confirmed for 2003*

🏛 OXBOROUGH   Map 05 TF70
OXBURGH HALL
PE33 9PS (7m SW of Swaffham. Signposted from A134 at Stoke ferry & Swaffham)
☎ 01366 328258   📠 01366 328066   **2 for 1**
e-mail: aohusr@smtp.ntrust.org.uk

The outstanding feature of this 15th-century moated building is the 80ft high Tudor gatehouse which has remained unaltered throughout the centuries. Henry VII lodged in the King's Room in 1487. A parterre garden of French design stands outside the moat, and rare needlework by Mary, Queen of Scots and Bess of Hardwick is on display. A particular attraction is a

continued

genuine 17th-century priests' hole, which is accessible to members of the public.
Times: Open House: 22 Mar-2 Nov, daily (ex Thu & Fri) 1-5, BH Mon 11-5, last admission 4.30. Garden: 1-16 Mar, wknds, 11-4; 23 Mar-3 Nov daily (ex Thu & Fri) 11-5.30; Aug daily 11-5.30. **Fee:** Please telephone for details. **Facilities:** P X licensed & (braille guide, wheelchairs available) toilets for disabled shop X (ex guide dogs)

REEDHAM   Map 05 TG40
PETTITTS ANIMAL ADVENTURE PARK
NR13 3UA (off A47 at Acle)
☎ 01493 700094 & 701403   📠 01493 700933
Times: Open Etr Sun-Oct, daily 10-5.30. (Closed Sat). **Facilities:** P ⬛ X & (ramps to all areas) toilets for disabled shop *Details not confirmed for 2003*

ST OLAVES   Map 05 TM49
ST OLAVES PRIORY
(5.5m SW of Great Yarmouth on A143)

The fine brick undercroft in the cloister is one of the most notable features of the ruin of this small 13th-century Augustinian priory.
Times: Open any reasonable time. **Fee:** Free. **Facilities:** ♿

SANDRINGHAM   Map 09 TF62
SANDRINGHAM HOUSE, GROUNDS, MUSEUM & COUNTRY PARK
PE35 6EN (off A148)
☎ 01553 772675   📠 01485 541571
e-mail: enquiries@sandringhamestate.co.uk

The private country retreat of Her Majesty The Queen, this neo-Jacobean house was built in 1870 for King Edward VII. The main rooms used by the Royal Family when in residence are all open to the public. Sixty acres of glorious grounds surround the House and offer beauty and colour throughout the season. Sandringham Museum contains fascinating displays of royal memorabilia.
Times: Open Etr Sat-mid Jul & early Aug-Oct. House open 11-4.45, Museum 11-5 & Grounds 10.30-5. **Fee:** House, Museum & Grounds: £6.50 (ch £4, pen £5). Family ticket £17. **Facilities:** P ⬛ X licensed & (wheelchair loan, free transport in grounds, braille guide) toilets for disabled shop garden centre X (ex guide dogs)

SAXTHORPE   Map 09 TG13
MANNINGTON GARDENS & COUNTRYSIDE
Mannington Hall NR11 7BB (signposted from Corpusty/Saxthorpe on B1149 Norwich-Holt road. Follow brown tourist signs)
☎ 01263 584175   📠 01263 761214

The moated manor house, built in 1460 and still a family home, forms a centrepiece for the pretty gardens which surround it. Enjoy the roses, the chief feature of the gardens, and lovely countryside walks.
Times: Open: Gardens Jun-Aug, Wed-Fri 11-5; also Sun noon-5; 30 Apr-1 Oct. Walks open every day from 9am. Hall open by prior appointment only. **Fee:** * Garden £3 (accompanied ch 16 free, students & pen £2.50). Walks free (car park for walkers £1). **Facilities:** P ⬛ & (boardwalk across meadow, wheelchair ramps) toilets for disabled shop X (ex guide dogs)

SHERINGHAM   Map 09 TG14
NORTH NORFOLK RAILWAY
Sheringham Station, Station Approach NR26 8RA (from A148 take A1082. Next to large car park by rdbt in town centre)
☎ 01263 820800   📠 01263 820801   **2 for 1**

A steam railway with trains operating on most days (Apr-Sep), with extra days as the season progresses and a daily service in the summer. At Weybourne Station there is a collection of steam locomotives and rolling stock, some of which are undergoing or awaiting restoration. There is also a museum of railway memorabilia.
Times: Open Apr-Sep; daily during summer season; Dec (Santa specials). Telephone for details of other running days. **Fee:** Return £7.50 (ch £4, pen £6.50). Family ticket £21. **Facilities:** P ⬛ & (ramps to trains, carriage converted for wheelchair access) toilets for disabled shop

SNETTISHAM   Map 09 TF63
PARK FARM
PE31 7NQ (signposted on A149, Park Farm is close to the church)
☎ 01485 542425   📠 01485 543503
e-mail: parkfarm@supanet.com

You can see farming in action here with lambing in the spring, sheep shearing in May and deer calving in June and July. Sheep, goats, lambs, rabbits, turkeys, ducks, chickens, ponies, piglets etc can be seen in the paddocks, and the sheep centre has over 40 different breeds. Other attractions include a large adventure playground, horse and pony rides, 2.5 miles of farm trails, visitor centre and craft workshops, including pottery studio and leather worker.
Times: Open Mar-Oct, daily 10-5; Nov-Feb (ring for details). Closed 25 Dec & 1st Jan. **Fee:** * £4.50 (ch £3.50, pen £3.75). Family ticket £15. **Facilities:** P ⬛ & (gravel paths, ramps where needed) toilets for disabled shop X (ex on farm trails)

SOUTH WALSHAM   Map 09 TG31
FAIRHAVEN WOODLAND & WATER GARDEN
School Rd NR13 6EA (follow brown heritage signs from A47 onto B1140 to South Walsham through village towards Gt Yarmouth. Turn left into School Road, 100yds past South Walsham Hall)
☎ 01603 270449   **2 for 1**
📠 01603 270449
e-mail: fairhavengardens@norfolkbroads.com

These delightful woodland and water gardens offer a combination of cultivated and wild flowers. In spring there are masses of primroses and bluebells, with azaleas and rhododendrons in several areas. Candelabra primulas and some unusual plants grow

continued

near the waterways, and in summer the wild flowers provide a habitat for butterflies, bees and dragonflies.

Times: Open daily 10-5, extended opening until 9pm Wed & Thu, May-Aug. (Closed 25 Dec). **Fee:** £3.50 (ch £1.25, under 5 free, pen & concessions £3). Single membership tickets £12.50. Family membership ticket £30. **Facilities:** P 🍴 ✕ ♿ (ramp, grab rail) toilets for disabled shop garden centre 🐕 (ex on lead) 🎟

🏛 THETFORD Map 05 TL88
ANCIENT HOUSE MUSEUM
White Hart St IP24 1AA (in town centre)
☎ 01842 752599
e-mail: ancient.house.museum@norfolk.gov.uk

An early Tudor timber-framed house with beautifully carved beamed ceilings, it now houses an exhibition on Thetford and Breckland life. This has been traced back to very early times, and there are examples from local Neolithic settlements. Brass rubbing facilities are available and there is a small period garden recreated in the rear courtyard.
Times: Open all year, Mon-Sat, 10-5 (Closed Mon 12.30-1); Jun-Aug also Sun 2-5. (Closed Good Fri, Xmas period & New Year's Day). **Fee:** Free (ex Jul & Aug £1, ch 60p, concessions 80p). **Facilities:** P (20yds) shop garden centre 🐕

THETFORD PRIORY
(on W side of Thetford near station)

Extensive remains of the Cluniac monastery founded in 1103 include the 14th-century gatehouse and complete ground plan of the cloisters.
Times: Open any reasonable time. **Fee:** Free. **Facilities:** 🐕 ♿

WARREN LODGE
(2m NW, on B1107)

The remains of a two-storey hunting lodge, built in 15th-century of flint with stone dressings.
Times: Open any reasonable time. **Fee:** Free. **Facilities:** ♿

🏛 THURSFORD GREEN Map 09 TF93
THURSFORD COLLECTION
NR21 0AS (1m off A148. Halfway between Fakenham and Holt)
☎ 01328 878477
🖷 01328 878415
e-mail: admin@thursfordcollection.co.uk

2 for 1

This exciting collection specialises in organs, with a Wurlitzer cinema organ, fairground organs, barrel organs and street organs among its treasures. There are live musical shows every day. The collection also includes showmen's engines, ploughing engines and farm machinery. There is a children's play area and a breathtaking `Venetian gondola' switchback ride.
Times: Open Good Fri-mid Oct, daily, 12-5. Closed Sat. **Fee:** £5 (ch under 4 free, ch 4-14 £2.50, pen £4.70). Party 15+ £4.25 each.
Facilities: P 🍴 ✕ ♿ toilets for disabled shop 🐕 (ex guide dogs) 🎟

🏛 TITCHWELL Map 09 TF74
RSPB NATURE RESERVE
PE31 8BB (6m E of Hunstanton on A149, signposted entrance)
☎ 01485 210779 🖷 01485 210779
e-mail: titchwell@rspb.org.uk
Times: Open at all times. Visitor Centre daily 10-5 (4pm Nov-Mar).
Facilities: P (charged) 🍴 ♿ (ramps to hides, wheelchair bays in hides) toilets for disabled shop Details not confirmed for 2003 🎟

🏛 WEETING Map 05 TL78
WEETING CASTLE
IP27 0RQ (2m N of Brandon off B1106)

This ruined 11th-century fortified manor house stands in a moated enclosure. There are interesting but slight remains of a three-storey cross-wing.
Times: Open any reasonable time. **Fee:** Free. **Facilities:** ♿

🏛 WELLS-NEXT-THE-SEA Map 09 TF94
WELLS & WALSINGHAM LIGHT RAILWAY
NR23 1QB (A149 Cromer road)
☎ 01328 710631 & 711630

The railway covers the four miles between Wells and Walsingham, and is the longest ten and a quarter inch gauge track in the world. The line passes through some very attractive countryside, particularly noted for its wild flowers and butterflies. This is the home of the unique Garratt Steam Locomotive specially built for this line.
Times: Open daily Good Fri-Oct. **Fee:** * £6 return (ch £4 return).
Facilities: P 🍴 ♿ shop

🏛 WELNEY Map 05 TL59
WWT WELNEY
Hundred Foot Bank PE14 9TN (off A1101, N of Ely)
☎ 01353 860711   📠 01353 860711
e-mail: welney@wwt.org.uk

2 for 1

This important wetland site on the beautiful Ouse Washes is famed for the breathtaking spectacle of wild ducks, geese and swans which spend the winter here. Impressive observation facilities, including hides, towers and an observatory, offer outstanding views of the huge numbers of wildfowl which include Bewick's and whooper swans, wigeon, teal and shoveler. Floodlit evening swan feeds take place between November and February. There are two hides for wheelchair users. **Times:** Open all year, daily 10-5. (Closed 25 Dec). **Fee:** * £3.65 (ch £2, pen £2.90). Family ticket £9.25. **Facilities:** 🅿 🍴 ♿ toilets for disabled shop ✖ (ex guide/hearing dogs) 🍴

🏛 WEST RUNTON Map 09 TG14
NORFOLK SHIRE HORSE CENTRE
West Runton Stables NR27 9QH (off A149)
☎ 01263 837339   📠 01263 837132
e-mail: bakewell@norfolkshirehorse.fsnet.co.uk
Times: Open 9 Apr-Oct, Sun-Fri; also Sats Jul-Aug & BHs. **Facilities:** 🅿 🍴 ✖ licensed ♿ toilets for disabled shop ✖ (ex on lead) *Details not confirmed for 2003* 🍴

🏛 WEYBOURNE Map 09 TG14
THE MUCKLEBURGH COLLECTION
Weybourne Military Camp NR25 7EG (on A149, coast road, 3m W of Sheringham)
☎ 01263 588210 & 588608
📠 01263 588425
e-mail: info@muckleburgh.co.uk

2 for 1

The largest privately-owned military collection of its kind in the country, which incorporates the Museum of the Suffolk and Norfolk Yeomanry. Exhibits include restored and working tanks, armoured cars, trucks and artillery of WWII, and equipment and weapons from the Falklands and the Gulf War. Live tank demonstrations are run daily (except Saturdays) during school holidays. **Times:** Open 10 Feb-27 Oct, daily 10-5. **Fee:** * £4.95 (ch £2.50 & pen £4). Family ticket £12.60. **Facilities:** 🅿 🍴 ✖ ♿ (ramped access, wheelchairs available) toilets for disabled shop ✖ (ex guide, kennels provided) 🍴

Northamptonshire

Northamptonshire is a mainly rural county of gentle beauty, with farmland, forest and great country estates. Rivers, canals and watermeadows are all part of the tranquil scene, providing a haven for wildlife.

Northamptonshire is ideal country for touring, walking and exploring lovely villages of stone and thatch, and visiting some particularly impressive churches. Among the most interesting of these are the Saxon churches at Brixworth and Earls Barton.

In the main square of the pretty village of Geddington stands one of the three surviving Eleanor Crosses. Edward I (King of England 1272-1307), grief-stricken at the death of his queen, erected a series of these crosses to mark the resting place of her body, each night, on its journey south from Leicestershire to London. Another such cross can be seen on the southern outskirts of Northampton at Hardingstone. In recent times, Althorp, home of the Spencer family and last resting place of Diana Princess of Wales, has put the county firmly on the tourist map, in quite a similar way.

Northampton is the county town, and along with Kettering, has long been associated with the production of footwear. Kettering was the second largest town until it was overtaken by the rapid development of Corby as a major centre of the steel industry. With the decline of the steel industry, Corby, has fought back as an enterprise zone to provide a home for modern industries.

Jane Austen's novel *Mansfield Park* is set in Northamptonshire, although it seems that Austen never actually visited the county. Other famous connections include the poet John Dryden; King Richard III; and George Washington, whose family came from Sulgrave Manor.

EVENTS & FESTIVALS

May
24th-26th British Waterways Annual Boat Show, Crick
11th-18th Moulton Village Festival

June
1st-30th Northampton Music & Arts Festival
21st Proms in the Park (music, laser & firework spectacular), Delapre Park, Northampton

July
5th-6th Hollowell Steam & Heavy Horse Show, Hollowell nr Northampton
tbc Northampton Town Show, Abington Park, Northampton

August
15th-17th Northampton Hot Air Balloon Festival, Northampton Racecourse, Northampton

Top: Stoke Park, Stoke Bruerne

Northamptonshire

ALTHORP
Map 04 SP66
ALTHORP
NN7 4HQ (M1 junct 16 and follow signs to Althorp)
☎ 01604 770107 0870 167 9000 📠 01604 770042
e-mail: mail@althorp.com

Althorp House has been the home of the Spencer family since 1508. The House was built in the 16th century, but has been changed since, most notably by Henry Holland in the 18th century. Restored by the present Earl, the House is carefully maintained and in immaculate condition. The award-winning exhibition 'Diana, A Celebration' is located in six rooms and depicts the life and work of Diana, Princess of Wales. There is in addition, a room which depicts the work of the Diana, Princess of Wales Memorial Fund.
Times: Open Jul-30 Sep, daily 10-5. Closed 31 Aug. **Fee:** * £11.50 (ch £5.50 & pen £9.50). Family ticket £28.50. Tickets discounted if pre-booked. **Facilities:** 🅿 🍽 ♿ disabled parking, wheelchairs, audio tour, shuttle toilets for disabled shop ✈ (ex guide dogs) 🚭

CANONS ASHBY
Map 04 SP55
CANONS ASHBY HOUSE
NN11 3SD (easy access from either M40, junct 11 or M1, junct 16)
☎ 01327 860044 📠 01327 860168
e-mail: ecaxxx@smtp.ntrust.org.uk
Times: Open 23 Mar-3 Nov, Sat-Wed & BH Mon 1-5.30 (12-4.30 Oct-Nov) or dusk if earlier. Closed Good Fri. **Facilities:** 🅿 🍽 ♿ (hearing scheme, taped guide, w/lchair available) toilets for disabled shop ✈ (ex on lead in home paddock) 🐕 *Details not confirmed for 2003*

DEENE
Map 04 SP99
DEENE PARK
NN17 3EW (0.5m off A43, between Kettering & Stamford)
☎ 01780 450278 450223 📠 01780 450282
e-mail: admin@deenepark.com

A mainly 16th-century house of great architectural importance, and home of the Brudenell family since 1514 (including the 7th Earl of Cardigan who led the Charge of the Light Brigade). There's a large lake and park, and extensive gardens with old-fashioned roses, rare trees and shrubs. Phone for details of garden openings and any other special events.
Times: Open 2-5 BH's (Sun & Mon) Etr, May, Spring & Aug; Jun-Aug, Sun. Party 20+ by prior arrangement with House Keeper. **Fee:** * House & Gardens: £5.50 (ch 10-14 £2.50, concessions £5). Gardens only: £3 (ch £1.50). Children under 10 free admission with accompanying adult. **Facilities:** 🅿 🍽 ♿ (ramps to cafeteria and gardens) toilets for disabled shop ✈ (ex guide dogs in garden only)

KIRBY HALL
NN17 5EN (on unclass road off A43, 4m NE of Corby)
☎ 01536 203230

A beautiful Elizabethan manor house boasting an unusual richness and variety of architectural detail in the Renaissance style. The extensive gardens were among the finest in England at their peak during the 17th century.
Times: Open all year, 29 Mar-Sep, daily 10-6 (Oct daily 10-5); Nov-28 Mar, Sat-Sun 10-4. Closed 24-26 Dec & 1 Jan & 7, 8, 9, 12, 13 &14 Aug.
Fee: * £3.30 (ch 5-15 £1.70, under 5's free, concessions £2.50). Family ticket £8.30 **Facilities:** 🅿 ♿ shop ✈ (in certain areas) 🚭

HOLDENBY
Map 04 SP66
HOLDENBY HOUSE, GARDENS & FALCONRY CENTRE
NN6 8DJ (7m NW of Northampton, off A5199 or A428)
☎ 01604 770074 📠 01604 770962
e-mail: sarah@holdenby.com

Just across the fields from Althorp, this former palace and prison of Charles I provides a stately backdrop to a beautiful garden and host of attractions. Falconry, 17th-century farmstead, children's amusements, shop and tearoom.
Times: Open; Gardens & Falconry Centre Apr-end Sep, Sun 1-5. 14 Jul to end Aug open daily 1-5 (ex Sat). House open Etr, Whitsun & Aug BH. Contact for details of additional Falconry Centre opening days. **Fee:** * Gardens & Falconry Centre £3 (ch £1.75, pen £2.50). House, Gardens & Falconry Centre £5 (ch £3, pen £4.50). **Facilities:** 🅿 🍽 ♿ (gravel paths with ramps) toilets for disabled shop (on leads)

KETTERING
Map 04 SP87
ALFRED EAST GALLERY
Sheep St NN16 0AN (A43/A6, located in town centre)
☎ 01536 534274 📠 01536 534370

The Gallery has a permanent exhibition space showing work by Sir Alfred East, Thomas Cooper Gotch and other local artists, as well as selections from the Gallery's contemporary collection, including Sir Howard Hodgkin and John Bevan. Two further display spaces are dedicated to monthly changing sales exhibitions of art, craft and photography.
Times: Open all year, Mon-Sat 9.30-5 (ex Wed closed until 10am & closed BHs). **Fee:** Free. **Facilities:** 🅿 (300yds) ♿ shop ✈ (ex guide dogs)

LYVEDEN NEW BIELD
Map 04 SP98
LYVEDEN NEW BIELD
PE8 5AT (4m SW Oundle via A427)
☎ 01832 205358
e-mail: elnbxx@smtp.ntrust.org.uk
Times: House, Elizabethan Water Garden & Visitor Information Room open 23 Mar-3 Nov Wed-Sun 10.30-5, 4 Nov-Mar Sat & Sun 10.30-4.
Facilities: 🅿 (0.5 m along track) ✈ (ex on leads) 🐕 *Details not confirmed for 2003*

NASSINGTON
Map 04 TL09
PREBENDAL MANOR HOUSE
PE8 6QG
☎ 01780 782575
e-mail: info@prebendal-manor.demon.co.uk
Times: Open Etr Mon- end Sep Wed-Sun 1-5.30; open BH Mon (Closed Xmas) **Fee:** * House & garden £4.50 (ch £1.50) Party 20+; Garden only £3.80. **Facilities:** 🅿 🍽 ♿ (ramps) shop ✈ (guide dogs)

Northamptonshire

🏛 NORTHAMPTON Map 04 SP76
NORTHAMPTON MUSEUM & ART GALLERY
Guildhall Rd NN1 1DP (town centre)
☎ 01604 238548 📠 01604 238720
e-mail: museums@northhampton.gov.uk

Reflecting Northampton's proud standing as Britain's boot and shoe capital, the museum houses a collection of boots and shoes which is considered one of the finest in the world. Other displays include the History of Northampton, Decorative Arts, the Art Gallery, and special temporary exhibitions.
Times: Open all year, Mon-Sat 10-5, Sun 2-5. **Fee:** Free. **Facilities:** P (200 yds) ♿ (wheelchairs available, large print catalogues) toilets for disabled shop 🐾 (ex guide/assistance dogs) 🏷

🏛 ROCKINGHAM Map 04 SP89
ROCKINGHAM CASTLE
LE16 8TH (2m N of Corby, off A6003)
☎ 01536 770240 📠 01536 771692 **2 for 1**
e-mail: gilesarnold@lineone.net

Set on a hill overlooking five counties, the castle was built by William the Conqueror. The site of the original keep is now a rose garden, but the outline of the curtain wall remains, as do the foundations of the Norman hall, and the twin towers of the gatehouse. A royal residence for 450 years, the castle was granted to Edward Watson in the 16th century, and the Watson family have lived there ever since.
Times: Open Jul-Aug, Tue & Thu, BH Mon 1-5. Grounds open at 11.30 am on Sun & BH Mon. **Fee:** * £5.50 (ch £3.50 & pen £5). Family ticket £15. Party. Grounds only £3.50. **Facilities:** P 🍴 ♿ (may alight at entrance, ramped) shop 🐾 (ex in grounds) 🏷

🏛 RUSHTON Map 04 SP88
TRIANGULAR LODGE
NN14 1RP
☎ 01536 710761
Times: Open Apr-Sep, daily 10-6; Oct, daily 10-5. **Facilities:** ♿ 🐾 ⛲
Details not confirmed for 2003

🏛 STOKE BRUERNE Map 04 SP74
CANAL MUSEUM
NN12 7SE (A508, 4m S of M1 junct 15)
☎ 01604 862229 📠 01604 864199
e-mail: britishwaterways@sosb.globalnet.co.uk
Times: Open Etr-Oct daily, 10-5; Nov-Etr Tue-Sun, 10-4. Closed 25-26 Dec. Last admission 30 mins before closing time. **Facilities:** P (charged) ♿ toilets for disabled shop 🐾 (ex guide dogs) Details not confirmed for 2003 🏷

🏛 SULGRAVE Map 04 SP54
SULGRAVE MANOR
Manor Rd OX17 2SD (off B4525 Banbury to Northampton road. 6m from M40 junct 11, 15m From M1 junct 15a)
☎ 01295 760205 📠 01295 768056 **2 for 1**
e-mail: sulgrave-manor@talk21.com

Home to George Washington's ancestors until 1656 when his great grandfather, John, emigrated to Virginia. Inside the house there are many relics of George Washington. Though much of the house is a 20th-century restoration, original parts include the porch (with a carving of the original American flag), a screens passage, the great hall and the great Chamber.
Times: Open 29 Mar-Oct 2-5.30 Closed Mon & Fri ex BH's and special event days. Other times by appointment (closed 25-26 Dec & Jan) **Fee:** * £5 (ch £2.50). Party 15+. £4.50 (ch £2.25) Special event days £6.50 (ch £3.25). Family ticket £17.50. **Facilities:** P 🍴 ✕ licensed ♿ (induction loop available in shop or ticket office) toilets for disabled shop garden centre 🐾 (ex guide & outside on leads) 🏷

---

2 for 1
This symbol indicates which attractions have chosen to participate in our new 2-for-1 voucher scheme.

The AA Hotel Guide 2003
Britain's best-selling hotel guide for all your business and leisure needs.
AA Lifestyle Guides www.theAA.com

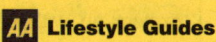

Northumberland

EVENTS & FESTIVALS

April
tbc Morpeth Northumbrian Gathering

May
1st Riding the Bounds, Berwick-upon-Tweed (traditional horseback ride)
tbc Border Marches, Berwick-upon-Tweed
tbc Northumberland County Show, Corbridge

June
21st Ovingham Goose Fair, Goose Fair Cross, Ovingham
29th-6th July Alnwick Fair
tbc Allendale Fair, Market Square, Northumberland

July
29th June-6th Alnwick Fair
5th-6th Amble Sea Fair
11-13th Rothbury Traditional Music Festival, Rothbury
27th Alnwick Castle Tournament, Alnwick

August
2nd Powburn Show & Sheepdog Trials
2nd-8th Alnwick International Music Festival (provisional)
9th Slaley Show, Townhead Field, Slaley
30th-31st Military Tattoo, Barracks, Berwick-upon-Tweed

September
6th Alnwick District Horticultural Show

November
1st Northumbrian Gathering

Northumberland is a county of wide open spaces taking in the Northumberland National Park to the northwest, with miles of moorland around Hadrian's Wall rising to the Cheviot Hills on the Scottish border, and incorporating great swathes of Forestry Commission planted conifers.

The Pennine Way walking trail runs through the park from Hadrian's Wall to The Cheviot, the National Park's highest peak at 2,674 feet (815 metres), and crosses the border into Scotland. Towards the east, the park changes character in the gentle valleys of the rivers Coquet, Redesdale and North Tyne.

Hadrian's Wall, an astonishing feat of engineering built by the Romans to mark the limit of the empire in the 2nd century AD, runs for 73 miles across northern England, and there are several well preserved forts, including Housestead's, one of the most popular sites on the wall.

The long, low lying coastline of Northumberland, designated an Area of Outstanding Natural Beauty, is dotted with a series of magnificent castles, Warworth, Alnick, Bamburgh, plus the remains of the 12th-century castle at Berwick-upon-Tweed and the impressive Elizabethan ramparts. Berwick is England's northernmost town, held alternately by the Scottish and English over centuries of bitter struggle.

The county town is Morpeth, which is the administrative centre, though this is disputed to some extent by Alnwick, the seat of the Duke of Northumberland. The attractive market town of Hexham warrants some exploration, with its Abbey, Moot Hall and other medieval remains, and also makes a good base for visiting Hadrian's Wall.

Top: Lindisfarne Castle, Holy Island

Northumberland   181

ALNWICK   Map 12 NU11
ALNWICK CASTLE
NE66 1NQ (off A1 on outskirts of town, follow signs for The Alnwick Garden & Castle)
☎ 01665 510777   ▤ 01665 510876
e-mail: enquiries@alnwickcastle.com

Alnwick Castle is the main seat of the Duke of Northumberland whose family have lived here since 1309. The stern, medieval exterior belies the treasure house within, furnished in Renaissance style, with paintings by Titian, Van Dyck and Canaletto, and an exquisite collection of Meissen china. The Regiment Museum of Royal Northumberland Fusiliers is housed in the Abbot's Tower of the Castle. Refurbished towers include museums of local archaeology and the Percy Tenantry volunteers.
Times: Open 28 Mar-25 Oct, daily 11-5 (last admission 4.15). **Fee:** * £6.95 (child 16 & under free if accompanied by adult, concessions £5.95). Family ticket £15.50. Party 14+. **Facilities:** P ⬛ & (Castle lift for those able to walk a little) toilets for disabled shop ✖ (ex guide dogs) ⚑

BAMBURGH   Map 12 NU13
BAMBURGH CASTLE
NE69 7DF (A1 Belford by-pass, E on B1342 to Bamburgh)
☎ 01668 214515 & 214208   ▤ 01668 214060
e-mail: bamburghcastle@aol.com

Rising dramatically from a rocky outcrop, Bamburgh Castle is a huge, square Norman castle. Last restored in the 19th century, it has an impressive hall and an armoury with a large collection of armour from the Tower of London. Guide services are available.
Times: Open 15 Mar-Oct, daily 11-5 (last admission 4.30pm). Other times by prior arrangement. **Fee:** £5 (ch £2 & pen £4). Party 15+ £3.50 (ch £1.50 & pen £2.50) **Facilities:** P (charged) ⬛ & shop ✖ (ex guide dogs)

GRACE DARLING MUSEUM
Radcliffe Rd NE69 7AE (follow A1, turn off at Bamburgh & follow signposts to Northumbria Coastal route, museum on right)
☎ 01668 214465   ▤ 01668 214365
Times: Open Etr-Oct, daily 10-5 (Sun 12-5). **Facilities:** P (400yds) & (ramps) shop ✖ (ex guide dogs) *Details not confirmed for 2003*

BARDON MILL   Map 12 NY76
VINDOLANDA (CHESTERHOLM)
Vindolanda Trust NE47 7JN (signposted from A69 or B6318)
☎ 01434 344217   ▤ 01434 344060
e-mail: info@vindolanda.com

Vindolanda was a Roman fort and frontier town. It was started well before Hadrian's Wall, and became a base for 500 soldiers. The civilian settlement lay just west of the fort and has been excavated. The excellent museum in the country house of Chesterholm nearby, has displays and reconstructions. There are also formal gardens and an open-air museum with Roman Temple, shop, house and Northumbrian croft.
Times: Open daily from 10am, all facilities mid Feb-mid Nov. **Fee:** * £3.90 (ch £2.80, student & pen £3.30, free admission for disabled). Saver ticket for joint admission to sister site - The Roman Army Museum £5.60 (ch £4.10, pen £4.80) Party. **Facilities:** P ⬛ & toilets for disabled shop ✖ (ex guide dogs) ⚑

BELSAY   Map 12 NZ07
BELSAY HALL, CASTLE AND GARDENS
NE20 0DX (on A696)
☎ 01661 881636

Belsay Castle, with its splendid turrets and battlements, dates from 1370 and was the home of the Middleton family, until they built the Jacobean manor house beside it, and then the magnificent Grecian-style Hall. There are also wonderful gardens.
Times: Open all year, daily 29 Mar-Sep 10-6 (Oct 10-5); Nov-Mar, daily 10-4. Closed 24-26 Dec & 1 Jan. **Fee:** * £4 (ch 5-15 £2, under 5's free, concessions £3). **Facilities:** P ✖ & toilets for disabled shop ✖ (in certain areas) ⚏

BERWICK-UPON-TWEED   Map 12 NT95
BERWICK BARRACKS, MUSEUM & ART GALLERY
TD15 1DF (on the Parade, off Church St, in town centre)
☎ 01289 304493

Enclosed by its Elizabethan ramparts, Berwick is an outstanding example of a fortified town, and the barracks have changed little since 1721. The museum covers 200 years of military and regimental history, and the Art Gallery houses the important Burrell collection.
Times: Open all year, 29 Mar-Sep, daily 10-6 (Oct daily 10-5); Nov-Mar, Wed-Sun 10-4. Closed 24-26 Dec & 1 Jan, during tattoo event and 1-2pm in winter **Fee:** * £2.80 (ch 5-15 £1.40, under 5's free, concessions £2.10). **Facilities:** P & shop ✖ ⚏

PAXTON HOUSE
TD15 1SZ (3m from A1 Berwick-upon-Tweed bypass on B6461 Kelso road)
☎ 01289 386291   ▤ 01289 386660
e-mail: info@paxtonhouse.com
Times: Open daily from Apr-Oct, House & gallery 11-5 (last tour of house 4.15pm). Grounds 10-sunset. **Facilities:** P ⬛ ✖ licensed & (lifts to main areas of house, parking close to reception) toilets for disabled shop ✖ (ex guide/on lead in grounds) *Details not confirmed for 2003* ⚑

CAMBO   Map 12 NZ08
WALLINGTON HOUSE WALLED GARDEN & GROUNDS
NE61 4AR (6m NW of Belsay)
☎ 01670 773600   ▤ 01670 774420
e-mail: nwaplr@smtp.ntrust.org.uk

The house is set in a great moorland estate of over 12,000 acres. It features delicate plasterwork, 'Capability' Brown gardens and William Bell Scott murals. In the 19th century Ruskin and other writers

continued

Northumberland

and artists came here as guests. Special events include open air concerts and theatre productions.
Times: Open: House Apr-Sep, daily (ex Tue) 1-5.30, Oct daily (ex Tue) 1-4.30. Last admission half hour before closing. Walled garden Apr-Oct, daily 10-7 or dusk; Nov-Mar, 10-4 or dusk if earlier. Grounds open all year. House will be closed 2003 due to restorations **Fee:** * House, walled garden & grounds: £5.70, family ticket £14.25. Walled gardens & grounds only: £4.10. Party £5.20 each. **Facilities:** P ⬛ ✗ ♿ (Vessa Ventura scooter, braille guide) toilets for disabled shop garden centre 🍴 ☕

CARRAWBROUGH   Map 12 NY87
ROMAN WALL (MITHRAIC TEMPLE)
(on B6318)

This fascinating Mithraic temple was uncovered by a farmer in 1949. Its three altars to the war god, Mithras date from the third century AD, and are now in the Museum of Antiquities in Newcastle, but there are copies on site.
Times: Open any reasonable time. **Fee:** Free. **Facilities:** P ♿

CHILLINGHAM   Map 12 NU02
CHILLINGHAM CASTLE
NE66 5NJ (signposted from A1 & A697)
☎ 01668 215359   📠 01668 215463
e-mail: enquiries@chillingham.castle.com
Times: Open Etr wknd & May-Sep, daily (ex closed Tue in May, Jun & Sep) 12-5 (Last admission 4.30pm). Other times by prior arrangement.
Facilities: P ⬛ ✗ licensed ♿ shop ✈ *Details not confirmed for 2003*

CHILLINGHAM WILD CATTLE PARK
NE66 5NP (off B6348, follow brown tourist signs off A1 and A697)
☎ 01668 215250   📠 01668 215250

The park at Chillingham, a registered charity, boasts an extraordinary survival: a herd of wild white cattle descended from animals trapped in the park when the wall was built in the 13th century; they are the sole surviving pure-bred examples of their breed in the world. Binoculars are recommended for a close view. Visitors are accompanied into the park by the Warden.
Times: Open Apr-Oct, daily 10-12 & 2-5, Sun 2-5. (Closed Tue). **Fee:** * £3 (ch £1 & pen £2.50). **Facilities:** P shop ✈

CORBRIDGE   Map 12 NY96
CORBRIDGE ROMAN STATION
NE45 5NT (0.5m NW on minor road - signposted)
☎ 01434 632349

The remains of Roman 'Corstopitum', built around AD210, include granaries, portico columns and the probable site of legionary headquarters.
Times: Open all year, Apr-Sep, daily 10-6 (Oct daily 10-5); Nov-28 Mar, Wed-Sun 10-1 & 2-4. Closed 24-26 Dec & 1 Jan. **Fee:** * £2.70 (ch 5-15 £1.40, under 5's free, concessions £2). **Facilities:** P ♿ ✈ (in certain areas) ☕

EMBLETON   Map 12 NU22
DUNSTANBURGH CASTLE
Craster NE66 2RD (1.5m E on footpaths from Craster or Embleton)
☎ 01665 576231

The skeletal ruins of the huge castle, partly built by John of Gaunt, stand on cliffs 100ft above the North Sea. Already a ruin by Tudor times, its setting has inspired many paintings, including three by Turner.
Times: Open all year, 29 Mar-Sep, daily 10-6 (Oct daily 10-5) 10-4; Nov-Mar, Wed-Sun 10-4. Last admission 30 min before closing. Closed 24-26 Dec & 1 Jan. **Fee:** * £2 Ch 5-15 £1, under 5's free, concessions £1.50) **Facilities:** P (charged) ☕

HOLY ISLAND (LINDISFARNE)
                                   Map 12 NU14
LINDISFARNE CASTLE
TD15 2SH (8m S Berwick from A1 on Holy Island)
☎ 01289 389244   📠 01289 389349

The 16th-century castle was restored by Sir Edwin Lutyens in 1903 for the owner of *Country Life* magazine. The austere outside walls belie the Edwardian comfort within, and there is a little garden designed by Gertrude Jekyll.
Times: Open Apr-Oct, daily (closed Fri ex Good Fri) as Lindisfarne is a tidal island, the Castle will open 4.5 hrs which will always include 12-3 and then either earlier opening or later closing as the tide allows.
Fee: * £4.20 (ch £2.10) Family ticket £10.50. **Facilities:** P (1m in village) ✈ 🍴

LINDISFARNE PRIORY
TD15 2RX (Can only be reached at low tide across a causeway. Tide tables posted at each end of the causeway)
☎ 01289 389200

St Aidan and monks from Iona founded the first monastery on the island in the 7th century, and from here preached the gospel to much of Northern England, also producing the illuminated Lindisfarne Gospels, now in the British Library. The priory ruins date from the 11th century and the island can be reached by a causeway at low tide (tide tables are displayed), or phone the custodian for details.
Times: Open all year, 29 Mar-Sep, daily 10-6 (Oct daily 10-5); Nov-Mar, daily 10-4. Subject to tides. Closed 24-26 Dec & 1 Jan. **Fee:** * £3 (ch 5-15 £1.50, under 5's free, concessions £2.30) **Facilities:** shop ✈ (in certain areas) ☕

HOUSESTEADS   Map 12 NY76
HOUSESTEADS ROMAN FORT
Bardon Mills NE47 6NN (2.5m NE of Bardon Mill on B6318)
☎ 01434 344363

Housesteads was the Roman fort of *Vercovicium*. It has a spectacular site on Hadrian's Wall, and is also one of the best preserved Roman forts. It covers five acres,

continued

Northumberland 183

including the only known Roman hospital in Britain, and a 24-seater latrine with a flushing tank.
Times: Open all year, 29 Mar-Sep, daily 10-6 (Oct daily 10-5); Nov-Mar, daily 10-4. Closed 24-26 Dec & 1 Jan. **Fee:** * £3 (ch £1.50, pen £2.30). **Facilities:** P (0.25m from fort) shop ✕ ♿ ♨

LONGFRAMLINGTON   Map 12 NU10
BRINKBURN PRIORY
NE65 8AR (off B6344)
☎ 01665 570628

The priory was founded in 1135 for Augustinian canons, and stands on a bend of the River Coquet. After the Dissolution of the Monasteries it fell into disrepair, but was restored in 1858.
Times: Open 29 Mar-Sep, daily 10-6, (Oct, daily 10-5). **Fee:** * £1.70 (ch 5-15 90p, under 5's free, concessions £1.30). **Facilities:** P ✕ (in certain areas) ♿

MORPETH   Map 12 NZ28
MORPETH CHANTRY BAGPIPE MUSEUM
Bridge St NE61 1PJ (off A1)
☎ 01670 519466   📠 01670 511326

This unusual museum specialises in the history and development of Northumbrian small pipes and their music. They are set in the context of bagpipes from around the world, from India to Inverness.
Times: Open all year, Mon-Sat 10-5. (Closed 25-26 Dec, 1 Jan & Etr Mon). **Fee:** * £1.50 (concessions 80p). Family ticket £3.50. **Facilities:** P (100 metres) ♿ (induction loop, not suitable for wheelchairs) shop ♨

NORHAM   Map 12 NT94
CASTLE
TD15 2JY
☎ 01289 382329
Times: Open Apr-Oct, 10-6 (Oct 10-5). **Facilities:** P ♿ ✕ ♨ Details not confirmed for 2003

PRUDHOE   Map 12 NZ06
PRUDHOE CASTLE
NE42 6NA (on minor road off A695)
☎ 01661 833459

Standing on the River Tyne, this medieval castle was the stronghold of the d'Umfravelles and Percys. The keep stands in the inner bailey and a notable gatehouse guards the outer bailey. Access is to the Pele Yard only.
Times: Open 29 Mar-Sep, daily 10-6 (Oct daily 10-5). **Fee:** * £1.90 (ch 5-15 £1, under 5's free, concessions £1.40). **Facilities:** P shop ✕ (in certain areas) ♨

ROTHBURY   Map 12 NU00
CRAGSIDE
NE65 7PX (1m NW of Morpeth on A697, turn L onto B6341, entrance 1m N of Rothbury)
☎ 01669 620333 & 620150   📠 01669 620066
e-mail: ncrvmx@smtp.ntrust.org.uk

This Victorian mansion was the first building in the world to be lit by hydro-electricity. In the 1880s the house had hot and cold running water, central heating, telephones and a passenger lift. There is a vast forest garden to explore containing one of Europe's largest rock gardens, formal gardens, lakes and an adventure play area.
Times: Open, Estate & Gardens: 23 Mar-4 Nov, Tue-Sun & BH Mons 10.30-7 last admission 5;. House: 23 Mar-Sep 1-5.30. Oct-3 Nov 1-4. Last admission 1hr before closing. **Fee:** * House, Estate & Gardens £6.90 (ch £3.50) Family £17.30 (2ad+3ch). Estate & Gardens £4.40 (ch 2.20) Family £11 (2ad+3ch). **Facilities:** P ✕ licensed ♿ (ltd access, braille guide, wheelchair path, lift) toilets for disabled shop ✕ (ex in grounds on lead) ♨

WALWICK   Map 12 NY97
CHESTERS ROMAN FORT & MUSEUM
Chollerford NE46 4EP (0.5m W of Chollerford on B6318)
☎ 01434 681379

One of the Roman forts on Hadrian's Wall is now in the park of Chesters, an 18th-century mansion. The fort named *Cilurnum* housed 500 soldiers and covered nearly 6 acres. Excavations have shown that it was destroyed and rebuilt three times. Evidence of an aqueduct and substantial remains of a bath house show that the standard of living was high.
Times: Open all year, 29 Mar-Sep, daily 9.30-6; Oct, daily 10-5; Nov-Mar, daily 10-4. Closed 24-26 Dec & 1Jan. **Fee:** * £3 (ch 5-15 £1.50, under 5's free, concessions £2.30) **Facilities:** P 🍴 ♿ shop ✕ (in certain areas) ♨

WARKWORTH   Map 12 NU20
WARKWORTH CASTLE
NE66 0UJ
☎ 01665 711423
Times: Open all year, Apr-Oct, daily 10-6 (Oct 10-5); Nov-Mar, daily 10-4 (or dusk if earlier, closed 1-2pm). Closed 24-26 Dec & 1 Jan. **Facilities:** P ♿ ✕ (in certain areas) ♨ Details not confirmed for 2003

WARKWORTH HERMITAGE
NE65 0UJ
☎ 01665 711423

Upstream from Warkworth Castle is the Hermitage, a refuge dug into the rockface by a 14th-century hermit. It consists of a chapel and two living chambers. Nearby is Coquet Island, which was also the home of hermit monks.
Times: Open 29 Mar-Sep, daily 10-6, (Oct, daily 10-5); Nov-Mar, daily 10-1 & 2-4.. Closed 24-26 Dec & 1 Jan. Hermitage 29 Mar-Sep 11-5 Wed, Sun & BH wknds. Closed 24-26 Dec & 1 Jan **Fee:** * Castle £2.60 (ch 5-15 £1.30, under 5's free, concessions £2) Hermitage £1.70 (ch 90p concessions £1.30) **Facilities:** P ♿ ✕ ♨

Nottinghamshire

EVENTS & FESTIVALS

February
8th-22nd Art Sparks youth arts festival, Nottingham
tbc Eid Mela, Nottingham (Muslim festival)

May
10th-11th Nottingham County Show, Winthorpe, Newark

June
tbc Motor Show, Nottingham

July
6th Mansfield Fun Run
10th-13th Americana International Festival, Winthorpe, Newark
28th-3rd August Annual Robin Hood Festival, Edwinstowe
tbc Newark Festival
tbc Transport Festival, Winthorpe, Newark

August
28th July-3rd Annual Robin Hood Festival, Edwinstowe
tbc Caribbean Carnival, Nottingham
tbc Riverside Festival, Nottingham

September
28th Robin Hood Marathon, Nottingham
tbc Rushcliffe Festival

October
1st-4th Goose Fair, Nottingham
tbc Dusshera Mela, Nottingham (Hindu festival)

October/November
tbc Now Festival, Nottingham (contemporary arts festival)

November
tbc Robin Hood Pageant, Nottingham Castle

The inland county of Nottinghamshire in eastern England is strongly associated with the legend of Robin Hood, though Robin's territory, the former royal hunting ground of Sherwood Forest, has been somewhat tamed since his outlaw days.

The county is divided between the old coalfields north of the city of Nottingham, the commuter belt of the Wolds to the south, and the area of most interest, that of Sherwood Forest and the great country estates known as the 'Dukeries'. One of these, Clumber Park, was formerly home to the Dukes of Newcastle, and is now owned by the National Trust.

The traditional industry of Nottinghamshire, alongside agriculture, was coal mining, though this has declined in recent years. It is also an oil producing area, and during World War II produced the only oil out of reach of the German U-Boats.

D H Lawrence was a Nottinghamshire man, born in Eastwood, the son of a miner and former schoolteacher. He grew up in poverty, and his book *Sons and Lovers* reflects the experiences of his early years. There is a D H Lawrence commemorative walk from his home at Eastwood to Old Brinsley Colliery.

Other Nottinghamshire notables include Thomas Cranmer, the first Protestant Archbishop; Jesse Boot, founder of the Boots pharmaceutical company; Henry Ireton, the man who signed Charles I's death warrant; Torvill & Dean, Olympic skaters; Brian Clough, Yorkshire-born outspoken manager of Nottingham Forest Football Club; and Paul Smith, fashion designer.

Other towns of note are the river port and market town of Newark, which hosts a major antiques fair six times a year, and Southwell, known for the medieval minster with exquisite carvings of Sherwood Forest.

Top: Nottingham Council House

Nottinghamshire

🏛 EASTWOOD Map 08 SK44
DURBAN HOUSE HERITAGE CENTRE
Mansfield Rd NG16 3DZ (signed on A610)
☎ 01773 717353   📠 01773 713509
Times: Open all year, Apr-Oct, daily 10-5; Nov-Mar, daily 10-4. Closed 24 Dec-1 Jan. **Facilities:** 🅿 ⬛ ✗ ♿ (lift to exhibition) toilets for disabled shop 🐕 (ex guide dogs) *Details not confirmed for 2003*

🏛 EDWINSTOWE Map 08 SK66
SHERWOOD FOREST COUNTRY PARK & VISITOR CENTRE
NG21 9HN (on B6034 N of village between A6075 and A616)
☎ 01623 823202 & 824490   📠 01623 823202
e-mail: sherwood.forest@nottscc.gov.uk

At the heart of the Robin Hood legend is Sherwood Forest. Today it is a country park and visitor centre with 450 acres of ancient oaks and shimmering silver birches. Waymarked pathways guide you through the forest. A year round programme of events includes the spectacular Robin Hood Festival.
Times: Country Park: open daily dawn to dusk. Visitor Centre: open daily 10.30-5 (4.30pm Nov-Mar) **Fee:** Free. **Facilities:** 🅿 (charged) ✗ ♿ toilets for disabled shop (ex guide dogs)

See advert on page 187

🏛 FARNSFIELD Map 08 SK65
WHITE POST MODERN FARM CENTRE
NG22 8HL (12m N of Nottingham on A614)
☎ 01623 882977 & 882026   📠 01623 883499
e-mail: tim@whitepostfarmcentre.co.uk

This award-winning working farm gives an introduction to a variety of modern farming methods. It explains how farms work, with exhibits such as llamas, deer, pigs, cows, snails, quails, snakes and fish. There's a lot to see indoors, including the incubator room, mousetown and a reptile house. There is also a large indoor play area including a sledge run, trampoline and a large bouncy slide.

Times: Open daily 10-5 **Fee:** * £5.50 (ch 3-16 £4.50) **Facilities:** 🅿 ⬛ ♿ (sign language, free hire wheelchairs, book if more than 6) toilets for disabled shop 🐕 (ex guide dogs)

🏛 HAUGHTON Map 08 SK67
WORLD OF ROBIN HOOD
Haughton Farm DN22 8DZ (on B6387 just outside Walesby, signposted off A1)
☎ 01623 860210   📠 01623 836003
e-mail: worldofrobinhood@talk21.com
Times: Open 10.30-4. Telephone for winter opening times. **Facilities:** 🅿 ⬛ ✗ licensed ♿ toilets for disabled shop 🐕 (outside areas only) *Details not confirmed for 2003*

🏛 NEWARK-ON-TRENT Map 08 SK75
MILLGATE MUSEUM
48 Millgate NG24 4TS (easy access from A1 & A46)
☎ 01636 655730   📠 01636 655735
e-mail: museums@newark-sherwooddc.gov.uk
Times: Open all year, Mon-Fri 10-5, Sat & Sun & BH 1-5. Last admission 4.30. **Facilities:** 🅿 (250yds) ⬛ ♿ toilets for disabled shop 🐕 (ex aid dogs) *Details not confirmed for 2003*

NEWARK AIR MUSEUM
The Airfield, Winthorpe NG24 2NY (easy access from A1, A46, A17 & Newark relief road, follow tourist signs)
☎ 01636 707170   📠 01636 707170   **2 for 1**
e-mail: newarkair@lineone.net

A diverse collection of transport, training and reconnaisance aircraft, jet fighters, bombers and helicopters, now numbering more than fifty. An Undercover Aircraft Display Hall and an Engine Hall make the museum an all-weather attraction. Everything is displayed around a WWII airfield.
Times: Open all year, Mar-Sep daily 10-5; Oct-Feb, daily 10-4. (Closed 24-26 Dec). Other times by appointment. **Fee:** * £4.25 (ch £2.50, pen £3.50). Family ticket £11.50. Party 10+. **Facilities:** 🅿 ⬛ ♿ toilets for disabled shop

Nottinghamshire

VINA COOKE MUSEUM OF DOLLS & BYGONE CHILDHOOD
The Old Rectory, Cromwell NG23 6JE (5m N of Newark off A1)
☎ 01636 821364

All kinds of childhood memorabilia are displayed in this 17th-century house: prams, toys, dolls' houses, costumes and a large collection of Victorian and Edwardian dolls including Vina Cooke hand-made character dolls.
Times: Open Mar-Oct Tue-Thu 10.30-12 & 2-5. Sat, Sun & BH Mon 10.30-5. Mon, Fri & other times by appointment. **Fee:** * £2.50 (ch £1.50, pen £2). **Facilities:** P & shop

NEWSTEAD   Map 09 SK55
NEWSTEAD ABBEY
Newstead Abbey Park NG15 8NA (off A60, between Nottingham & Mansfield)
☎ 01623 455900 🖷 01623 455904

This beautiful house is best known as the home of poet Lord Byron. Visitors can see Byron's own rooms, mementoes and other splendidly decorated rooms. The grounds of over 300 acres include waterfalls, ponds, water gardens and Japanese gardens. Special events include outdoor theatre and opera, Christmas events and Ghost Tours.
Times: Open: Grounds all year, daily 9-dusk (ex last Fri in Nov); House Apr-Sep, daily 12-5. Last admission 4pm **Fee:** * House & Grounds £4 (ch £1.50, concessions £2) Family ticket (2 adults & 3 ch) £10. Grounds only £2 (ch & concessions £1.50) Family ticket £6. Subject to change. **Facilities:** P 🍴 ✗ licensed & (audio tour, mobility car & wheelchair for loan Apr-Sep) toilets for disabled shop (open Apr-Sep) ✗ (ex guide or garden on lead) 🍴

NOTTINGHAM   Map 08 SK53
BREWHOUSE YARD MUSEUM
Castle Boulevard NG7 1FB
☎ 0115 915 3600 & 0115 915 3640
🖷 0115 915 3601
Times: Open all year 10-4.30. (Closed Fri Nov-Mar & 25-26 Dec).
Facilities: P (100yds) & toilets for disabled shop ✗ (ex guide dogs)
Details not confirmed for 2003

CASTLE MUSEUM
NG1 6EL
☎ 0115 915 3700 🖷 0115 915 3653
Times: Open all year, daily 10-5. (ex Fri Nov-Feb) Grounds 8-dusk. (Closed 25 & 26 Dec). **Facilities:** P (400yds) 🍴 & (chair lift, mobility car available) toilets for disabled shop ✗ (ex guide dogs)
Details not confirmed for 2003

THE CAVES OF NOTTINGHAM
Upper Level, Broadmarsh Shopping Centre NG1 7LS (within Broadmarsh Shopping Centre, on the first floor)
☎ 0115 924 1424 🖷 0115 924 1430
e-mail: info@cavesofnottingham.co.uk

A unique 750-year-old cave system situated beneath a modern day shopping centre. A digital audio tour guides you through the only remaining underground medieval tannery in England, beer cellars, an air raid shelter and the remains of Drury Hill, one of the oldest streets in Nottingham.
Times: Open daily 10-5, Sun 11-5 (last admission 4.15pm, Sun 4pm). (Closed 24-26 Dec, 1 Jan & Etr Sun). **Fee:** * £3.75 (concessions £2.75). Family ticket £11.50. **Facilities:** P (charged) & (non-accessible to wheelchairs, induction loop, textual guide) shop ✗ (ex guide dogs) 🍴

GALLERIES OF JUSTICE
The Shire Hall, High Pavement, Lace Market NG1 1HN (follow signs to City Centre, brown tourist signs to Lace Market & Galleries of Justice)
☎ 0115 952 0555 🖷 0115 993 9828   **2 for 1**
e-mail: info@galleriesofjustice.org.uk

The Galleries of Justice are located on the site of an original Court and County Gaol. Visitors can take an authentic tour through three centuries of Crime and Punishment and witness a trial re-created in the authentic Victorian courtroom before being 'sent down' to the original cells and medieval caves. In the genuine Edwardian police station, an interactive forensic science display allows visitors to 'crack the case'. A series of innovative and stimulating temporary exhibitions run throughout the year. Special activities for all the family run in school holidays. Voted visitor attraction and family attraction of the year.
Times: Open all year, Tue-Sun & BH Mon's 10-5 (also open Mon in school hols). Last admission one hour before closing. Contact for Xmas opening times. **Fee:** * £6.95 (ch £5.25, concessions £5.95). Family ticket £19.95 (2 adult & 2 ch). Ticket vaild for one visit to all exhibitions for 12 months from date of purchase. **Facilities:** P (5 mins walk) 🍴 & (braille control lifts, induction loop, large print lables) toilets for disabled shop ✗ (ex guide dogs) 🍴

THE LACE CENTRE
Severns Building, Castle Rd NG1 6AA (follow signs for the Castle, situated opposite the Robin Hood statue)
☎ 0115 941 3539 🖷 0115 941 3539

Exquisite Nottingham lace fills this small building, with panels also hanging from the beamed ceiling. There are weekly demonstrations of lace-making on Thursday afternoons from Easter to October. Telephone for details.
Times: Open Jan-Mar, daily 10-4; Apr-Nov, 10-5. Every Sun 11am-4pm. (Closed Xmas & New Year) **Fee:** Free. **Facilities:** P (100yds) (metered street parking) & shop 🍴

MUSEUM OF COSTUME & TEXTILES
43-51 Castle Gate NG1 6AF (Close to city centre, near the Robin Hood statue & Nottingham Castle Museum & Art Gallery)
☎ 0115 915 3500 🖷 0115 915 3653
Times: Open all year, Wed-Sun & BHs 10-4. **Facilities:** P (200yds) & shop ✗ (ex guide dogs) *Details not confirmed for 2003*

Museum of Nottingham Lace
3-5 High Pavement, The Lace Market NG1 1HF (Follow signs for Lace Market Parking in the city centre)
☎ 0115 988 1849   📠 0115 950 5166
e-mail: info@nottinghamlace.org

'Nottingham Lace and its People' is a free exhibition that includes a photographic story, hand-lace and machine-lace demonstrations. The Lace Market Trail, which takes about an hour, guides you to all the points of interest around this historical part of the city.
Times: Open Mon-Sat, 10-5: Sun 10.30-4 (Closed Xmas). **Fee:** Free.
Facilities: P (100yds) ♿ (counters at lower level, lift, audio & written tour) shop ✈ (ex guide dogs) 💳

Natural History Museum
Wollaton Hall, Wollaton NG8 2AE (3m W, off A52 & A6514)
☎ 0115 915 3911   📠 0115 915 3932
Times: Open all year, daily 11-5 (Closed Fri Nov-Mar & 25-26 Dec).
Facilities: P (charged) ♿ toilets for disabled shop ✈ Details not confirmed for 2003

Nottingham Industrial Museum
Courtyard Buildings, Wollaton Park NG8 2AE (4m from city centre off A6514)
☎ 0115 915 3910   📠 0115 915 3941
Times: Open Apr-Sep, daily 11-5; Oct-Mar only open on steaming days, contact for details. **Facilities:** P (charged) ♿ (hand & powered wheelchairs available) toilets for disabled shop ✈ (ex guide dogs)
Details not confirmed for 2003

Tales of Robin Hood
30-38 Maid Marian Way NG1 6GF (in city centre, follow brown tourist signs. Situated minutes from Nottingham Castle)
☎ 0115 948 3284   📠 0115 950 1536   **2 for 1**
e-mail: robinhoodcentre@mail.com

Special effects and adventure cars transport the visitor back to medieval Nottingham and Sherwood Forest, legendary home of Robin Hood. There is commentary in seven languages via portable CD players. Medieval banquets and other events take place throughout the year.
Times: Open all year, daily 10-6 Spring/Summer. 10-5.30 Autumn/Winter (Closed 25-26 Dec). **Fee:** * £6.50 (ch £4.50, pen & students £5.25) Family ticket £19.95 (2ad+2ch), £23 (2ad+3ch). Party.
Facilities: P (NCP 200 yds) 🍴 ♿ (specially adapted 'car') toilets for disabled shop ✈ (ex guide dogs) 💳

Wollaton Hall & Park
Wollaton NG8 2AE (M1 junct 25 signed from A52, A609, A6154, A60 and city centre)
☎ 0115 915 3900   📠 0115 915 3932
e-mail: carolb@notmusbhy.demon.co.uk

Built in the late 16th century, and extended in the 19th, Wollaton Hall and Park holds Nottingham's Natural History Museum, Nottingham's Industrial Museum, the Wollaton Park Visitor Centre, and the Yard Gallery,

continued

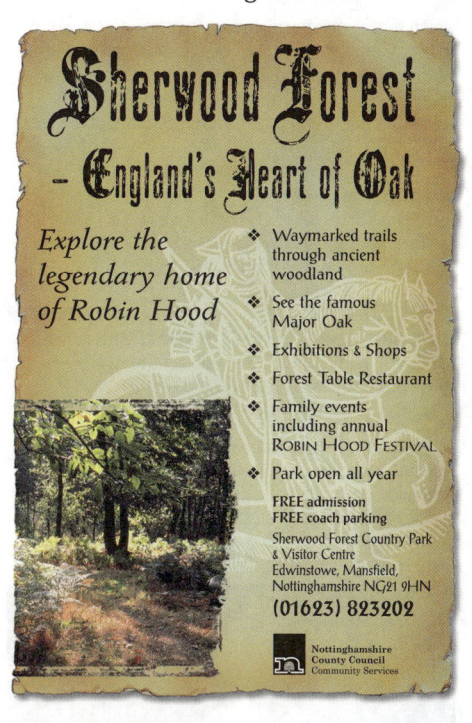

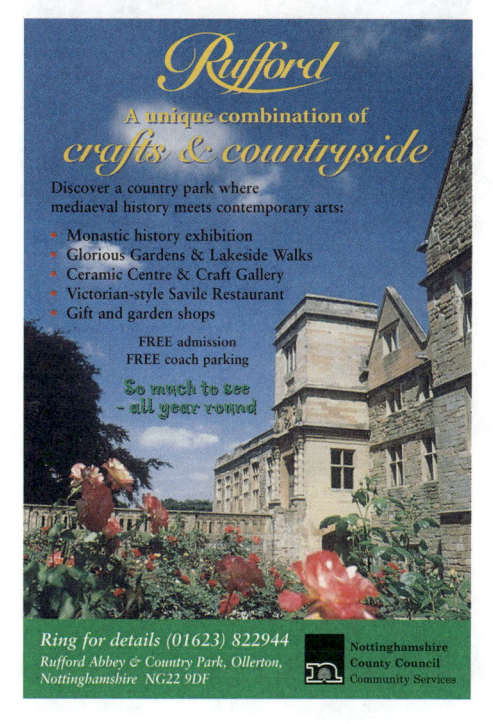

Sherwood Forest
– England's Heart of Oak

Explore the legendary home of Robin Hood

❖ Waymarked trails through ancient woodland
❖ See the famous Major Oak
❖ Exhibitions & Shops
❖ Forest Table Restaurant
❖ Family events including annual Robin Hood Festival
❖ Park open all year

FREE admission
FREE coach parking

Sherwood Forest Country Park & Visitor Centre
Edwinstowe, Mansfield,
Nottinghamshire NG21 9HN

(01623) 823202

Nottinghamshire County Council Community Services

Rufford
A unique combination of
crafts & countryside

Discover a country park where mediaeval history meets contemporary arts:

* Monastic history exhibition
* Glorious Gardens & Lakeside Walks
* Ceramic Centre & Craft Gallery
* Victorian-style Savile Restaurant
* Gift and garden shops

FREE admission
FREE coach parking

So much to see – all year round

Ring for details (01623) 822944
Rufford Abbey & Country Park, Ollerton,
Nottinghamshire NG22 9DF

Nottinghamshire County Council Community Services

188 Nottinghamshire

which has changing exhibitions exploring art and the environment. The Hall itself is set in 500 acres of deer park, with herds of red and fallow deer roaming wild. There are also formal gardens, a lake, nature trails, adventure playgrounds, a sensory garden and a water garden. The many events throughout the year include pop concerts, opera, and twilight bat walks.
Times: Open daily 11-5 (Nov-Mar 11-4). (Closed 24-26 Dec & 1 Jan)
Fee: * £2 (ch & concessions £1). Charge made at wknds & BH's only
Facilities: P (charged) ⬛ ♿ sensory garden toilets for disabled shop ✘ (ex guide dogs/leads in park) ♨

OLLERTON   Map 08 SK66
RUFFORD ABBEY AND COUNTRY PARK
NG22 9DF (2m S of Ollerton, adjacent to A614)
☎ 01623 822944   🖷 01623 824840
e-mail: marilyn.louden@nottscc.org.uk

At the heart of the wooded country park stand the remains of a 12th-century Cistercian Abbey, housing an exhibition on the life of a monk at Rufford. Many species of wildlife can be seen on the lake, and there are lovely formal gardens, with sculptures and Britain's first centre for studio ceramics.

Times: Open all year 10.30-5.30 (closes 4pm Jan & Feb). For further details of opening times telephone establishment. **Fee:** Free.
Facilities: P (charged) ⬛ ✘ licensed ♿ (lift to craft centre gallery, free parking,wheelchair loan) toilets for disabled shop garden centre ✘ (ex guide dogs or in park)

See advert on page 187

SUTTON-CUM-LOUND   Map 08 SK68
WETLANDS WATERFOWL RESERVE & EXOTIC BIRD PARK
Off Loundlow Rd DN22 8SB (Signposted on A638)
☎ 01777 818099   **2 for 1**

The Reserve is a 32-acre site for both wild and exotic waterfowl. Visitors can see a collection of birds of prey, parrots, geese, ducks, and wigeon among others. There are also many small mammals and farm and wild animals, including llamas, wallabies, emus, monkeys, red squirrels, deer and goats.
Times: Open all year, daily 10-5.30 (or dusk - whichever is earlier). (Closed 25 Dec). **Fee:** * £2.50 (ch & pen £2). **Facilities:** P ⬛ ♿ (wheelchair available) shop ✘ (ex guide dogs)

WORKSOP   Map 08 SK57
CLUMBER PARK
The Estate Office, Clumber Park S80 3AZ (4.5m SE of Worksop, signposted from A1)
☎ 01909 476592   🖷 01909 500721
Times: Open: Walled Garden, Victorian Apiary, Fig House, Vineries & Garden Tools exhibition Apr-Sep Wed & Thu 10.30-5.30, Sat, Sun & BH Mon 10.30-6. Chapel: Apr-Sep, daily 10.30-5.30 (until 6 Sat & Sun); Oct-Jan daily 10.30-4. Contact warden for conservation centre opening times. **Facilities:** P (charged) ⬛ ✘ licensed ♿ (powered self-drive vehicle available if booked) toilets for disabled shop garden centre 🌿
Details not confirmed for 2003

Oxfordshire

The city of Oxford, situated on the River Thames (known locally as the Isis), is renowned for its ancient buildings and 'dreaming spires'. It is home to Britain's oldest university, established during the 12th century, with a collegiate system dating from the 13th.

Other well-known towns include Banbury, though the Banbury Cross of nursery rhyme fame was destroyed in the 1600s by the Puritans. The current cross was built to commemorate one of Queen Victoria's daughters in 1859. Henley-on-Thames is home to the Royal Regatta, an amateur rowing competition of world renown and a highlight of the social calendar. Witney is a blanket-making town, using two important local resources, wool, and power from the River Windrush.

The Cotswold Hills extend over the border from Gloucestershire into the east of Oxfordshire, dotted with pretty towns and villages built of mellow Cotswold stone hewn from the hillsides. These settlements prospered from the sheep who grazed the hills, producing wool for the flourishing medieval wool trade. Great churches are a feature of the area, an enduring symbol of medieval wool wealth.

To the southeast of the county are the Chiltern Hills, chalk downlands excellent for walking. The Chilterns range from the Berkshire Downs to the East Anglian Ridge, passing through Oxfordshire and reaching their highest point at Coombe Hill, near Wendover in Buckinghamshire, at 852 ft (260m).

Southwest of Oxford is the Vale of the White Horse, a prehistoric figure, 374 ft (114m) long, carved into the chalk, some 18 miles (29km) from the city. Theories on its meaning differ, some claim it is an image of the Celtic horse goddess, Epona, while others think it is the dragon slain by St George.

EVENTS & FESTIVALS

March
16th Poohsticks World Championships, Little Wittenham

May
1st May 6am Morning Choir, singing from Magdalen Tower, Magdalen College, Oxford
26th Lord Mayor's Parade

June
25th Encaenia (Oxford University graduation event with gowned procession through the city)

July
2nd-6th Henley Royal Regatta, Henley-on-Thames
9th-13th Henley Festival (various venues)
14th-18th Swan Upping, River Thames, Sunbury-Abingdon

September
1st-2nd St Giles Fair, Oxford
13th Banbury Street Organ Festival
14th Henley Show
19th Thame & Oxfordshire County Agricultural Show
tbc Charlbury Street Fair, Charlbury

October
5th Ploughing Match, Bishopsland Farm, Dunsden, nr Reading
tbc Banbury Folk & Good Music Day
tbc Abingdon Fair

Top: Thame

Oxfordshire

BANBURY
Map 04 SP44
BANBURY MUSEUM
Spiceball Park Rd OX16 2PQ (M40 Junct 11 straight across at first rdbt into Hennef Way, left at next rdbt into Concord Avenue, right at next rdbt & left at next rdbt, Castle Quay Shopping Centre & Museum on right)
☎ 01295 259855   ▤ 01295 270556
e-mail: banburymuseum@cherwell-dc.gov.uk

A stunning new museum situated in an attractive canal-side location in the centre of Banbury. Exciting modern displays tell of Banbury's origins and historic past. The Civil War, the plush manufacturing industry, the Victorian market town, costume from the 17th century to the present day, Tooley's Boatyard and the Oxford Canal, are just some of the subjects illustrated.
Times: Open all year, Mon-Sat, 10-5, (tel. for Sun details). **Fee:** Free.
Facilities: ℗ (500yds) ✗ ⚹ toilets for disabled shop ✈ (ex guide dogs)

BROUGHTON
Map 04 SP43
BROUGHTON CASTLE
OX15 5EB (2m W of Banbury Cross on B4035)
☎ 01295 276070
▤ 01869 337126 & 01295 276070   **2 for 1**
e-mail: info@broughtoncastle.demon.co.uk

Built by Sir John de Broughton then, owned by William of Wykeham, and later by the first Lord Saye and Sele, the castle is an early 14th and mid 16th-century house with a moat and gatehouse. Period furniture, paintings and Civil War relics are displayed. There are fine borders in the knot garden.
Times: Open Etr & 19 May-12 Sep, Wed Sun (also Thu in Jul & Aug) & all BHs, Sun & Mon's 2-5. **Fee:** * £5 (ch 5-15 £2, pen & students £4). **Facilities:** ℗ ▤ ⚹ toilets for disabled shop ✈ (ex in grounds on leads)

BURFORD
Map 04 SP21
COTSWOLD WILDLIFE PARK
OX18 4JW (2m S of Burford on the A361)
☎ 01993 823006   ▤ 01993 823807

This 160-acre landscaped zoological park, surrounds a listed Gothic-style manor house. There is a varied collection of animals from all over the world, many of which are endangered species such as Asiatic Lions Leopards, White Rhinos and Red Pandas. There's an adventure playground, a children's farmyard, and train rides during the summer. The park has also become one of the Cotswold's leading attractions for garden enthusiasts, with its exotic summer displays and varied plantings offering interest all year.
Times: Open all year, daily (ex 25 Dec) from 10am, last admission 4.30pm Mar-Sep, 4pm Oct, 3.30pm Nov-Feb. **Fee:** * £7 (ch 3-16 & pen £4.50). Party: £6 (ch £3.50 pen £4) **Facilities:** ℗ ▤ ✗ licensed ⚹ (parking, free hire of wheelchairs) toilets for disabled shop ✈

BUSCOT
Map 04 SU29
BUSCOT PARK
SN7 8BU (on A417 between Faringdon & Lechdale)
☎ 01367 240786 & 0845 345 3387   **2 for 1**
▤ 01367 241794
e-mail: estbuscot@aol.com

A highlight of this 18th-century house is the Faringdon Collection which includes work by Reynolds, Gainsborough, Rembrandt, Murillo, several of the Pre-Raphaelites, and some 20th-century artists. The charming formal water gardens were laid out by Harold Peto in the early 20th century. There is also an attractively planted kitchen garden, with unusual concentric walls.
Times: House & grounds Apr-Sep Wed-Fri 2-6. Grounds only Mon-Fri 2-6. Also most wknds & BH's, Mid Apr-Sep 2-6. **Fee:** * House & Gardens £5 Grounds only £4. **Facilities:** ℗ ▤ ⚹ ✈ ✿

DEDDINGTON
Map 04 SP43
DEDDINGTON CASTLE
OX5 4TE (S of B4031 on E side of Deddington)

The large earthworks of the outer and inner baileys can be seen; the remains of 12th-century castle buildings have been excavated, but they are not now visible.
Times: Open any reasonable time. **Fee:** Free. **Facilities:** ✿

DIDCOT
Map 04 SU58
DIDCOT RAILWAY CENTRE
OX11 7NJ (on A4130 at Didcot Parkway Station)
☎ 01235 817200   ▤ 01235 510621   **2 for 1**
e-mail: didrlyc@globalnet.co.uk

Based around the original GWR engine shed, the Centre is home to the biggest collection anywhere of Great Western Railway steam locomotives, carriages and wagons. A typical GWR station has been re-created and a section of Brunel's original broad gauge track relaid.
Times: Open all year, Sat & Sun. Daily 12-27 Apr, 24 May-Aug 10-5. (closes 4 Nov-Feb). Steamdays first and last Sun from Mar, BHs, all Suns Jul-Aug. Wed 16 Jul -26 Aug & Sat in Aug. **Fee:** * £4-£8 depending on event (ch £3-£7.50, over 60's £3.50-£6.50).
Facilities: ℗ (100yds) ▤ ⚹ (advance notice recommended, some awkward steps) toilets for disabled shop ✈

Oxfordshire   **191**

🏛 GREAT COXWELL   Map 04 SU29
GREAT COXWELL BARN
(2m SW of Faringdon between A420 & B4019)
☎ 01793 762209
e-mail: tbcjaw@smtp.ntrust.org.uk
Times: Open all reasonable times. For details please contact Estate Office. **Facilities:** 🅿 ✖ (ex on leads) 🐕 *Details not confirmed for 2003*

🏛 HENLEY-ON-THAMES   Map 04 SU78
GREYS COURT
Rotherfield Greys RG9 4PG (M4 junct 8 or 9, take A404 (M) to Henley-on-Thames. From Nettlebed mini rdbt on A4130 take B481. Property is signposted 3m on left)
☎ 01491 628529
e-mail: tgrgen@smtp.ntrust.org.uk
Times: Open: House: part of ground floor only, 4 Apr-Sep Wed-Fri & BH Mons (closed Good Fri). Garden 3 Apr-Sep daily ex Sun & Mon (closed Good Fri, open BH Mon. **Facilities:** 🅿 ♿ shop (bookshop) ✖ (ex on lead in car park) 🐕 *Details not confirmed for 2003*

RIVER & ROWING MUSEUM
Mill Meadows RG9 1BF (off A4130, signposted to Mill Meadows)
☎ 01491 415600   📠 01491 415601
e-mail: museum@rrm.co.uk
Times: Open Summer: May-Aug 10-5.30. Winter: Sep-Apr 10-5. (museum closed 24-25 & 31 Dec & 1 Jan). **Facilities:** 🅿 🍽 ✖ licensed ♿ toilets for disabled shop ✖ (ex guide dogs) *Details not confirmed for 2003* 🐕

🏛 LONG WITTENHAM   Map 04 SU59
PENDON MUSEUM
OX14 4QD (follow brown signs from A4130 Didcot-Wallingford or A415 Abingdon-Wallingford road)
☎ 01865 407365
Times: Open Sat & Sun 2-5, BH wknds 11-5 also Wed in Jul & Aug 2-5. (Closed Dec). **Facilities:** 🅿 🍽 ♿ (phone in advance, special seating with handrails) toilets for disabled shop ✖ (ex guide dogs) *Details not confirmed for 2003* 🐕

🏛 MAPLEDURHAM   Map 04 SU67
MAPLEDURHAM HOUSE
RG4 7TR (off A4074, follow brown heritage signs from Reading)
☎ 0118 972 3350   📠 0118 972 4016
e-mail: mtrust1997@aol.com

The small community at Mapledurham includes the house, a watermill and a church. The fine Elizabethan mansion, surrounded by quiet parkland that runs down to the River Thames, was built by the Blount family in the 16th century. The estate has literary connections with the poet Alexander Pope, with Galsworthy's *Forsyte Saga* and Kenneth Graham's *Wind in the Willows*, and was a location for the film *The Eagle has Landed*.
Times: Open Etr-Sep, Sat, Sun & BH's 2-5.30. Picnic area 2-5.30. Last admission 5pm. Group visits midweek by arrangement. **Fee:** * Combined house, watermill & grounds £6 (ch £3). House & grounds £4 (ch £2). Watermill & grounds £3 (ch £1.50). **Facilities:** 🅿 🍽 ♿ shop ✖ (ex park area) 🐕

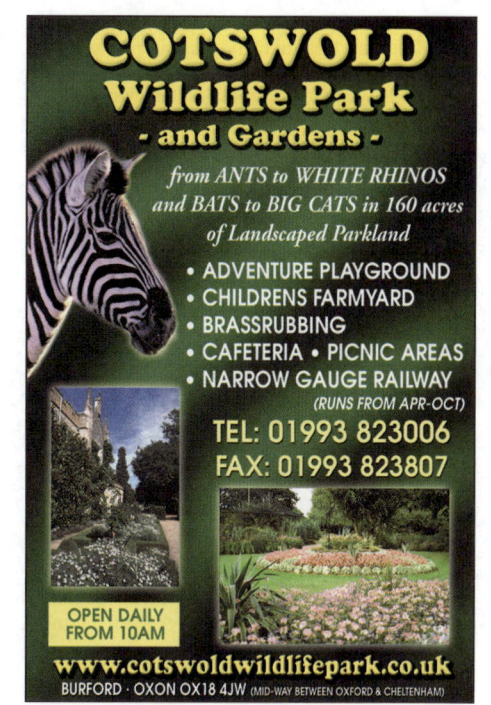

MAPLEDURHAM WATERMILL
RG4 7TR (off A4074, follow brown heritage signs from Reading)
☎ 0118 972 3350   📠 0118 972 4016
e-mail: mtrust1997@aol.com

Close to Mapledurham House stands the last working corn and grist mill on the Thames, still using traditional wooden machinery and producing flour for local bakers and shops. The watermill's products can be purchased in the shop. When Mapledurham House is open the mill can be reached by river launch.
Times: Open Etr-Sep, Sat, Sun & BHs 2-5.30. Picnic area 2-5.30. Last admission 5. Groups midweek by arrangement. **Fee:** * Watermill & grounds £3 (ch £1.50) **Facilities:** 🅿 🍽 ♿ shop ✖ (ex in country park) 🐕

🏛 MINSTER LOVELL   Map 04 SP31
MINSTER LOVELL HALL & DOVECOT
OX8 5RN (adjacent to Minster Lovell church, 3m W of Witney off A40)
☎ 01993 775315

Home of the ill-fated Lovell family, the ruins of the

continued

COTSWOLD Wildlife Park - and Gardens -

from ANTS to WHITE RHINOS and BATS to BIG CATS in 160 acres of Landscaped Parkland

- ADVENTURE PLAYGROUND
- CHILDRENS FARMYARD
- BRASSRUBBING
- CAFETERIA • PICNIC AREAS
- NARROW GAUGE RAILWAY
  (RUNS FROM APR-OCT)

TEL: 01993 823006
FAX: 01993 823807

OPEN DAILY FROM 10AM

www.cotswoldwildlifepark.co.uk
BURFORD • OXON OX18 4JW (MID-WAY BETWEEN OXFORD & CHELTENHAM)

15th-century house are steeped in history and legend. One of the main features of the estate is the medieval dovecote.
Times: Open any reasonable time. **Fee:** Free. **Facilities:** P (ex Dovecot)

NORTH LEIGH   Map 04 SP31
NORTH LEIGH ROMAN VILLA
OX8 6QB (2m N)

Excavations show that the villa was occupied from the second to fourth centuries AD. A tessellated pavement and a 2-3ft high wall span are on show.
Times: Open, grounds all year. No access to mosaic. Pedestrian access only from the main road - 600 yds. **Fee:** Free. **Facilities:**

OXFORD   Map 04 SP50
ASHMOLEAN MUSEUM OF ART & ARCHAEOLOGY
Beaumont St OX1 2PH (city centre, opposite The Randolph Hotel)
☎ 01865 278000   ▤ 01865 278018

The oldest museum in the country, opened in 1683, the Ashmolean contains Oxford University's priceless collections. Many important historical art pieces and artefacts are on display, including work from Ancient Greece through to the 20th century.
Times: Open all year, Tue-Sat 10-5, Sun & BH Mons 2-5. (Closed Etr & during St.Giles Fair in early Sep, Xmas & 1 Jan). **Fee:** Free. Guided tours by arrangement. **Facilities:** P (100-200metres) (pay & display) ▇✕ licensed ♿ (entry ramp from Beaumont St. Tel. before visit) toilets for disabled shop

HARCOURT ARBORETUM
Nuneham Courtenay OX44 9PX (400 yds S of Nuneham Courtenay on A4074)
☎ 01865 343501   ▤ 01865 341828
e-mail: piers.newth@botanic-garden.ox.ac.uk

The gardens consist of 75 acres of mixed woodland, meadow, pond, rhododendron walks and fine specimen trees.
Times: Open May-Oct, daily 10-5; Nov-Apr, Mon-Fri 10-4.30. Closed 22 Dec-4 Jan & Good Fri-Etr Mon. **Fee:** £2 pay & display for car park or £5 for 1yr season ticket. **Facilities:** P (charged) ♿ (ex guide dogs)

MUSEUM OF OXFORD
St Aldate's OX1 1DZ
☎ 01865 252761   ▤ 01865 252254
e-mail: museum@oxford.gov.uk

Permanent displays depict the archaeology and history of the city through the ages. There are temporary exhibitions, facilities for school parties and groups, and an audio tour.
Times: Open all year, Tue-Fri 10-4, Sat 10-5 & Sun 12-4. (Closed 25-26 Dec, Good Fri & Etr Sun). **Fee:** * £2 (ch 5-17 & concessions £1.50). Family ticket £5 **Facilities:** shop (ex guide dogs)

MUSEUM OF THE HISTORY OF SCIENCE
Old Ashmolean Building, Broad St OX1 3AZ (Next to Sheldonian Theatre in city centre)
☎ 01865 277280   ▤ 01865 277288
e-mail: museum@mhs.ox.ac.uk

The first purpose built museum in Britain, containing the world's finest collection of early scientific instruments used in astronomy, navigation, surveying, physics and chemistry.
Times: Open Tue-Sat 12-4 (closed Xmas wk) **Fee:** Free. **Facilities:** P (300 metres) (limited street parking, meters) ♿ (lift) toilets for disabled shop (ex guide dogs)

THE OXFORD STORY
6 Broad St OX1 3AJ (Follow signs)
☎ 01865 728822   ▤ 01865 791716   **2 for 1**
e-mail: info@oxfordstory.co.uk

The Oxford Story offers the very best introduction to the city's world famous University. Climb aboard our indoor 'dark' ride to travel through the university's 900 years of history. In our interactive exhibition, 'Innovate' you can quiz experts from Oxford University on modern day issues, from heart disease to climate change.
Times: Open: Jan-Jun & Sep-Dec, Mon-Sat 10-4.30 & Sun 11-4.30. Jul & Aug daily 9.30-5. Closed 25 Dec. **Fee:** * £6.50 (ch £5, pen & students £5.50), Family ticket £20 (2ad+2ch) **Facilities:** P (300 metres) (Park & Ride all round city) ♿ (advisable to phone in advance) toilets for disabled shop (ex guide dogs)

OXFORD UNIVERSITY MUSEUM OF NATURAL HISTORY
Parks Rd OX1 3PW (opposite Keble College)
☎ 01865 272950   ▤ 01865 272970
e-mail: info@oum.ox.ac.uk

Built between 1855 and 1860, this museum of "the natural sciences" was intended to satisfy a growing interest in biology, botany, archaeology, zoology, entomology and so on. The museum reflects Oxford University's position as a 19th-century centre of learning, with displays of early dinosaur discoveries, Darwinian evolution and Elias Ashmole's collection of

continued

preserved animals. Although visitors to the Pitt-Rivers Museum must pass through the University Museum, the two should not be confused.
Times: Open daily 12-5. Times vary at Xmas & Etr. **Fee:** Free.
Facilities: P (meter parking at 100yds) & toilets for disabled shop ✈

PITT RIVERS MUSEUM
South Parks Rd OX1 3PP (10 min walk from Oxford city centre)
☎ 01865 270927 ✉ 01865 270943
e-mail: prm@prm.ox.ac.uk

The museum, one of the city's most popular attractions, is part of the University of Oxford and was founded in 1884. The collections held at the museum are internationally acclaimed, and contain many objects from different cultures of the world and from various periods, all grouped by type, or purpose. Special exhibitions during 2002 & 2003. 5th Oct 2002-17 Aug 2003: 'Visions of Lost Lhasa' the Tibetan capital explored through imagery from the 1930s. 6 Sep 2003 onwards 'Objects talk' a range of personal responses to the collections.
Times: Open Mon-Sat 12-4.30 & Sun 2-4.30. (Closed Xmas & Etr, open BH's) **Fee:** Free. **Facilities:** & (audio guide, wheelchair trail, Map to ground floor) toilets for disabled shop ✈ (ex guide dogs)

ST EDMUND HALL
College of Oxford University OX1 4AR (Queen's Lane Oxford nr the High St)
☎ 01865 279000 ✉ 01865 279090
Times: Open all year. (Closed 23 Dec-3 Jan, 9-17 Apr & 28-31 Aug).
Facilities: 🅿 & toilets for disabled shop ✈ *Details not confirmed for 2003*

UNIVERSITY OF OXFORD BOTANIC GARDEN
High St OX1 4AZ (E end of High St on banks of river Cherwell)
☎ 01865 286690 ✉ 01865 286693
e-mail: postmaster@botanic-garden.ox.ac.uk
Times: Open all year, daily 9-4.45 (9-4.30 Oct-Mar), Greenhouses, daily 10-4.30. Last admission 4.15. (Closed Good Fri & 25 Dec).
Facilities: P (0.5 mile) & toilets for disabled ✈ (ex guide dogs)
Details not confirmed for 2003

🏛 ROUSHAM   Map 04 SP42
ROUSHAM HOUSE
OX25 4QX (1m E of A4260. 0.5m S of B4030)
☎ 01869 347110 ✉ 01869 347110

This attractive mansion was built by Sir Robert Dormer in 1635. During the Civil War it was a Royalist garrison. The house contains over 150 portraits and other pictures, and also much fine contemporary furniture. The gardens are a masterpiece by William Kent, and are his only work to survive unspoiled.
Times: Open all year, garden only, daily 10-4.30. House, Apr-Sep, Wed, Sun & BH Mon 2-4.30 (last entry). **Fee:** * House £3, Garden £3. Groups by arrangement. No children under 15. **Facilities:** P & ✈ (ex guide dogs)

Oxfordshire   *193*

🏛 RYCOTE   Map 04 SP60
RYCOTE CHAPEL
OX9 2PE (off B4013)

This small private chapel was founded in 1449 by Richard Quatremayne. It has its original font, and a particularly fine 17th-century interior. The chapel was visited by both Elizabeth I and Charles I.
Times: Open 29 Mar-Sep Fri-Sun & BH 2-6 **Fee:** * £2 (ch £1, concessions £1.50) **Facilities:** P & (if assisted) ✈ ♿

🏛 STONOR   Map 04 SU78
STONOR HOUSE & PARK
RG9 6HF (M40 junct 6, through Wattington, towards Nettlebed. At top of hill, left along B480 towards Henley. Stonor approx 3m further on left just before Stonor village)
☎ 01491 638587 ✉ 01491 639348
e-mail: jweaver@stonor.com

The house dates back to 1190 but features a Tudor façade. It has a medieval Catholic chapel which is still in use today, and shows some of the earliest domestic architecture in Oxfordshire. Its treasures include rare furniture, paintings, sculptures and tapestries from Britain, Europe and America. The house is set in beautiful gardens commanding views of the surrounding deer park.
Times: Open Apr-Sep, Sun 2-5.30; Jul & Aug, also Wed 2-5.30; BH Mons. Parties by appointment Tue-Thu, Apr-Sep. **Fee:** * £5.50 (ch 14 accompanied free). Gardens only £3.50. Party 12+ £5. Private guided tours £6 each. **Facilities:** P 🍽 & shop ✈ (ex in grounds on lead)

🏛 UFFINGTON   Map 04 SU38
CASTLE, WHITE HORSE & DRAGON HILL
(S of B4507)

The 'castle' is an Iron Age fort on the ancient Ridgeway Path. It covers about eight acres and has only one gateway. On the hill below the fort is the White Horse, a 375ft prehistoric figure carved in the chalky hillside and thought to be about 2000 years old.
Times: Open - accessible any reasonable time. **Fee:** Free.
Facilities: P ♿

🏛 WATERPERRY   Map 04 SP60
WATERPERRY GARDENS
OX33 1JZ (2.5m from A40, turn off at Wheatley)
☎ 01844 339226 & 339254   **2 for 1**
✉ 01844 339883

The manor of Waterperry is mentioned in the Domesday Book. The present house (not open) was rebuilt by Sir John Curson in 1713. The peaceful gardens and nurseries which surround the house were the home of a celebrated horticultural school between 1932 and 1971, and have fine herbaceous borders, a rock garden, riverside walk, shrub borders, lawns and trees. Please phone for details of special events.
Times: Open all year, Gardens (ex Xmas & New Year & during "Art in Action" 15-18 Jul). Apr-Oct 9-5.30, Nov-Mar 9-5 daily. **Fee:** Apr-Oct, £3.25 (ch 10-16 £1.75, ch under 10 free, pen £2.75). Nov-Mar £1.50 Party 20+. **Facilities:** P 🍽 ✗ licensed & (grounds mostly accessible) shop garden centre ✈ (ex on leads) 🚌

WITNEY Map 04 SP31
COGGES MANOR FARM MUSEUM
Church Ln, Cogges OX28 3LA (0.5m SE off A4022)
☎ 01993 772602 📄 01993 703056 `2 for 1`

The museum includes the Manor, dairy and walled garden, and has breeds of animals typical of the Victorian period. The first floor of the manor contains period rooms. Special events take place through the season.
Times: Open Apr-Nov, Tue-Fri & BH Mon 10.30-5.30, Sat & Sun 12-5.30. Early closing Oct. (Closed Good Fri). **Fee:** * £4.20 (ch £2.10, pen, students & UB40 £2.65). Family ticket £11.55 (2ad+2ch)
Facilities: 🅿 🍴 ♿ (wheelchair available, commentary/history file for 1st floor) toilets for disabled shop 🛍

WOODSTOCK Map 04 SP41
BLENHEIM PALACE
OX20 1PX (M40 junct 9, follow signs to Blenheim, on A44 8m N of Oxford)
☎ 01993 811091 & 811325 (information line)
📄 01993 813527
e-mail: admin@blenheimpalace.com

Home of the 11th Duke of Marlborough and birthplace of Sir Winston Churchill, Blenheim Palace is an English Baroque masterpiece. Fine furniture, sculpture, paintings and tapestries are set in magnificent gilded staterooms that overlook sweeping lawns and formal gardens. 'Capability' Brown landscaped the 2,100-acre grounds, which are open to visitors for pleasant walks and beautiful views.
Times: Palace & Gardens mid Mar-Oct, daily 10.30-5.30 (last admission 4.45pm). Park daily all year. **Fee:** * £10 (ch £5, pen & students £7.50). Family ticket £26. Group rates for coach parties.
Facilities: 🅿 🍴 ✗ licensed ♿ (ramps to front door, disabled parking) toilets for disabled shop ✗ (ex in park on leads) 🛍

OXFORDSHIRE MUSEUM
Fletcher's House OX20 1SN (A44 Stratford-upon-Avon road from Oxford, opposite church)
☎ 01993 811456 `2 for 1`
📄 01993 813239
e-mail: oxon.museum@oxfordshire.go.uk

Situated in the heart of the historic town, Fletcher's House has undergone an award-winning redevelopment. The museum presents Oxfordshire's heritage, environmental diversity and contemporary innovation. A number of exhibitions take place throughout the year, including 'Hand to Eye': an insight into the processes a selection of craft makers use to produce their work. 'A Century of Comfort': quilts from Oxford County, Ontario, Canada 1900-2000. 'Food for Thought': a look at the amazing range of food consumed throughout the ages, its origins, cultural traditions, and the ways we prepare and serve it.
Times: Open all year, Tue-Sat 10-5. Last admission 4.30. (Closed Good Fri, 25-26 Dec & 1 Jan). Galleries are closed on Mon. **Fee:** £2.50 (ch 50p, concessions £1) Family ticket £4.50. Free admission to some temporary exhibitions. **Facilities:** 🅿 (outside entrance) (3hr free, no return within 1hr) 🍴 ♿ (chair lifts to all galleries) toilets for disabled ✗ (ex guide dogs)

Rutland

A mere twenty miles across, the county of Rutland was reinstated in 1997 due to public demand from Rutlanders who had fiercely maintained their identity through twenty years as part of Leicestershire. The county motto is "Multum in Parvo", which is Latin for 'much in little'.

Oakham is the only town of any size in the county, and as Rutland only has a population of around 35,000 it's not hard to imagine what kind of size that is! Those who don't live there inhabit one of the fifty or so villages, or the other two towns, Uppingham and Stamford.

Many of these villages have their own little oddities which are so tantalising to students of eccentric England. For example, Wing has a strange ancient turf maze, the story of the fools who tried to fence a cuckoo in, and the Wise Woman of Wing.

Some famous connections with Rutland are John Clare, the 18th-century pastoral poet; the Gunpowder Plotters (who are said to have met at Stoke Dry); Thomas Barker, a pioneer of modern weather forecasting, and more recently the TV production of George Eliot's *Middlemarch*, which was filmed at Stamford.

Apart from its small attractions, Rutland also has a large one. Rutland Water is, at 5,000 acres, the largest man-made reservoir in Europe. As well as a mass of wildlife and water pursuits such as windsurfing and sailing, Rutland Water has its own church, Normanton Church, which sits on an outcrop that juts out onto the Water itself.

Top: The village of Ketton

EVENTS & FESTIVALS

August
22nd-24th British Birdwatching Fair, Egleton
tbc Models & Miniatures, Stapleford Steam Railway, nr Melton Mowbray

Rutland

LYDDINGTON
BEDE HOUSE   Map 04 SP89
Blue Coat Ln LE15 9LZ
☎ 01572 822438
Times: Open Apr-Sep, daily 10-6 (Oct 10-5). **Facilities:** ♿ ✈ ♯
Details not confirmed for 2003

OAKHAM
OAKHAM CASTLE   Map 04 SK80
off Market Place LE15 6HW (off Market place)
☎ 01572 758440   01572 758445
e-mail: museum@rutland.gov.uk

An exceptionally fine Norman Great Hall of a 12th-century fortified manor house. Earthworks, walls and remains of an earlier motte can be seen along with medieval sculptures and unique presentation horseshoes forfeited by peers of the realm and royalty to the Lord of the Manor. Licensed for civil marriages. Please enquire for details of the Oakham Festival.
Times: Open all year, late Mar-late Oct, Mon-Sat, 10-1 & 1.30-5, & Sun 1-5; late Oct-late Mar Castle closes at 4. Closed Good Fri & Xmas. **Fee:** Free. **Facilities:** P (400 yds) (disabled parking only by notification) ♿ shop ✈ (ex guide dogs)

RUTLAND COUNTY MUSEUM
Catmos St LE15 6HW (on A6003, S of town centre)
☎ 01572 758440   01572 758445
e-mail: museum@rutland.gov.uk

The Museum of Rutland Life has displays of farming equipment, machinery and wagons, rural tradesmen's tools, domestic collections and local archaeology, all housed in a splendid late 18th-century cavalry riding school. There is a special gallery on the Volunteer Soldier in Leicestershire and Rutland.
Times: Open all year, Mon-Sat 10-5. (Also open Sun 2-5 Apr-Oct & 2-4 Nov-Mar). Closed Good Fri & Xmas. **Fee:** Free. **Facilities:** P (adjacent) (pay & display. free on Sun) ♿ (induction loop in meeting room) toilets for disabled shop ✈ (ex guide dogs)

Shropshire

Shropshire is a mainly agricultural county in the west of England, on the Welsh border. Home to beautiful rivers and lakes, as well as spectacular walking opportunities, the county is sparsely populated and has some fine market towns.

Britain's longest river, the Severn, flows from northwest to southeast. Other natural features are the 'Shropshire Lakes' at Ellesmere in the northwest, and the Clee Hills in the south, between Ludlow and Kidderminster, rising to 1,800 ft (610m). The two ridges, Wenlock Edge and the Long Mynd, running either side of Church Stretton, are much favoured by walkers. This part of the country was immortalised in A E Houseman's poem, *A Shropshire Lad*, published in 1896.

The two largest centres of population in a sparsely populated county are Shrewsbury, the county town, situated on a hilly site in a loop of the River Severn, and Telford New Town, named after the engineer, Thomas Telford. In the 5th century, Shrewsbury was the capital of the kingdom of Powys, with the name Pengwern (later part of Mercia). A rich legacy of half-timbered Tudor buildings and red brick Georgian buildings remains, along with the castle, which has Norman origins.

Telford was created about 30 years ago, and is now home to some of the Far East's most successful electronics firms, as well as monuments to British engineering of the 19th century, such as Abraham Darby's Ironbridge.

There are some fine market towns, well worth a visit. Chief among these are Ludlow, capital of the Marches, and widely held to be one of the most beautiful of British towns, with its intricately decorated black and white buildings; Bishop's Castle, retaining much of its medieval character, and the dramatically located hilltop town of Bridgnorth.

Top: Ludlow Castle

EVENTS & FESTIVALS

June
14th Shrewsbury Carnival & Show, Quarry Park
20th-21st Shropshire & West Midlands Show, Showground, Berwick Road, Shrewsbury
21st-6th July Ludlow Festival
tbc International Kite & Boomerang Festival, Shrewsbury
tbc Royal Air Force Show

July
21st June-6th Ludlow Festival in the ruins of Ludlow Castle
18th-20th Festival at the Edge (storytelling), Stokes Barn, Much Wenlock
19th-20th Wem Sweet Pea Festival, Wem

August
2nd Oswestry Show
15th-16th Shrewsbury Flower Festival
22nd-24th Bridgnorth Folk Festival
24th-25th County of Salop Steam Rally
25th-26th Shropshire Game Fair, Chetwynd Park, Telford

September
5th-6th Shrewsbury Real Ale Festival
13th-14th The Midland Game & Country Fair, Weston-under-Lizard, Nr Shifnel
tbc Ludlow & the Marches Food Festival, Ludlow

December
tbc Music Hall Pantomime, Shrewsbury

Shropshire

ACTON BURNELL　　　　Map 07 SJ50
ACTON BURNELL CASTLE
SY5 7PE (on unclass road 8m S of Shrewsbury)

Now ruined, this fortified manor house was built in the late 13th century by Robert Burnell, the Chancellor of the time.
Times: Open at all reasonable times. **Fee:** Free. **Facilities:** & #

ATCHAM　　　　Map 07 SJ50
ATTINGHAM PARK
SY4 4TP (4m SE of Shrewsbury on B4380)
☎ 01743 708123　📠 01743 708175
e-mail: matsec@smtp.ntrust.org.uk
Times: House open mid Mar-Oct, Fri-Tue 1.30-5, BH Mon 11-5. Deer park & grounds daily Mar-Oct 9am-8pm, Nov-Feb 9am-5pm.
Facilities: P ⬛ & (2 electric self drive buggies) toilets for disabled shop ✖ (ex guide & hearing dogs) ✿ *Details not confirmed for 2003*

BENTHALL　　　　Map 07 SJ60
BENTHALL HALL
TF12 5RX (on B4375)
☎ 01952 882159
e-mail: benthall@ntrust.org.uk　　**2 for 1**

The exact date of the house is not known, but it seems to have been started in the 1530s and then altered in the 1580s. It is an attractive sandstone building with mullioned windows, fine oak panelling and a splendid carved staircase.
Times: Open Apr-Sep, Wed, Sun & BH Mon 1.30-5.30. Last admission 5pm. Other days by appointment only. **Fee:** *Prices not confirmed for 2003.* **Facilities:** P & ✖ ✿ 🍴

BOSCOBEL　　　　Map 07 SJ80
BOSCOBEL HOUSE AND THE ROYAL OAK
Brewood ST19 9AR (on unclass road between A41 and A5)
☎ 01902 850244

The house was built around 1600 by John Giffard, a Roman Catholic, and includes a number of secret hiding places. One of them was used by King Charles II after his defeat at the Battle of Worcester in 1651.
Times: Open, Mar-Sep, daily 10-6 (Oct, daily 10-5); Nov 10-4 Wed-Sun (Closed Dec-Feb). **Fee:** * £4.40 (ch 5-15 £2.20, under 5's free, concessions £3.30). Family ticket £11 **Facilities:** P ⬛ & shop ✖ #

WHITELADIES PRIORY (ST LEONARDS PRIORY)

Only the ruins are left of this Augustinian nunnery, which dates from 1158 and was destroyed in the Civil War. After the Battle of Worcester Charles II hid here and in the nearby woods before going on to Boscobel House.
Times: Open any reasonable time. **Fee:** Free. **Facilities:** #

BUILDWAS　　　　Map 07 SJ60
BUILDWAS ABBEY
TF8 7BW (on S bank of River Severn on B4378)
☎ 01952 433274

The beautiful, ruined, Cistercian abbey was founded in 1135, and stands in a picturesque setting. The church with its stout round pillars is roofless but otherwise almost complete.
Times: Open all year, 29 Mar-Sep, daily 10-5 **Fee:** * £2.10 (ch £1.10, ch u5 free, concessions £1.60) **Facilities:** & #

BURFORD　　　　Map 03 SO56
BURFORD HOUSE GARDENS
WR15 8HQ (off A456, 1m W of Tenbury Wells, 8m from Ludlow)
☎ 01584 810777　📠 01584 810673　**2 for 1**
e-mail: treasures@burford.co.uk

The beauty of Burford House Gardens is a tribute to the late John Treasure who, since the early 1950s, transformed the setting of this early Georgian house into a garden of quiet serenity and fascination. Harmonising combinations of colour have been achieved, and special use has been made of clematis - the garden, now boasting over 150 varieties is home to the National Collection. The garden is famous for its range of unusual plants, many of which are sold in Treasures Plant Centre adjacent, who specialise in clematis, herbaceous, shrubs, trees and climbers. Also on site are the Burford House Gallery, Burford Buttery, Craft Shop and Craft Workshops. Special events this year: 4th Annual Botanical Exhibition and two contemporary art shows (April-October), Christmas Fair (early Nov-24 Dec). Ring for further details.
Times: Open all year 10-5 or dusk if earlier. **Fee:** * £3.50 (ch £1). Party 10+ £3. **Facilities:** P ⬛ ✖ licensed & (ramp into gardens, sloping paths) toilets for disabled shop garden centre ✖ (ex in Plant Centre) 🍴

COSFORD　　　　Map 07 SJ70
ROYAL AIR FORCE MUSEUM
TF11 8UP (on A41, 1m S of M54 junct 3. From S M6 junct 10a, from N M6 junct 12 then follow A5 W)
☎ 01902 376200　📠 01902 376211
e-mail: cosford@rafmuseum.com
Times: Open all year daily, 10-6 (last admission 4). Closed 24-26 Dec & 1 Jan. **Facilities:** P ✖ licensed & (limited amount of wheelchairs on request) toilets for disabled shop ✖ (ex guide dogs) *Details not confirmed for 2003* 🍴

CRAVEN ARMS　　　　Map 07 SO48
SHROPSHIRE HILLS DISCOVERY CENTRE
School Rd SY7 9RS (on A49, on southern edge of Craven Arms)
☎ 01588 676000　📠 01588 676030
e-mail: hope.alderson@shropshire-cc.gov.uk
Times: Open all year, daily from 10am. **Facilities:** P ⬛ ✖ licensed & (Wheelchair available) toilets for disabled shop ✖ (ex assistance dogs) *Details not confirmed for 2003* 🍴

Shropshire

🏛 HAUGHMOND ABBEY   Map 07 SJ51
HAUGHMOND ABBEY
Upton Magna SY4 4RW (off B5062)
☎ 01743 709661

The ruined abbey was founded for Augustinian canons around 1135, and partly converted into a house during the Dissolution. The chapter house has a fine Norman doorway, and the abbot's lodging and the kitchens are well preserved.
Times: Open all year, 29 Mar-Sep, daily 11-5 **Fee:** * £2.10 (ch £1.10, concessions £1.60). **Facilities:** 🅿 ♿ ✖ ♿

🏛 HODNET   Map 07 SJ62
HODNET HALL GARDENS
TF9 3NN (M6 junct 12/15 or M54 junct 3. Hodnet is on A442, Telford-Whitchurch road and A53 Shrewsbury-Market Drayton road)
☎ 01630 685202   📠 01630 685853

Sixty acres of landscaped gardens offer tranquillity among pools, lush plants and trees. Big game trophies adorn the 17th-century tearooms, and plants are usually for sale in the kitchen gardens. The house, rebuilt in Victorian-Elizabethan style, is not open.
Times: Open Apr-Sep, Tue-Sun & BH Mon 12-5. **Fee:** £3.50 (ch £1.50, pen £3). Party £3. **Facilities:** 🅿 🍴 ♿ (2 wheelchairs available) toilets for disabled shop garden centre

🏛 IRONBRIDGE   Map 07 SJ60
IRONBRIDGE GORGE MUSEUMS
TF8 7AW (M54 junct 4, signposted)
☎ 01952 433522 & 0800 590258
📠 01952 432204
e-mail: info@ironbridge.org.uk
Times: Open all year, 10-5. Some small sites closed Nov-Mar. Telephone or write for exact winter details. **Facilities:** 🅿 🍴 ✖ licensed ♿ (wheelchairs,potters wheel,braille guide,lifts,hearing loop) toilets for disabled shop ✖ (ex Blists Hill & guide dogs) *Details not confirmed for 2003* 🏷

🏛 LILLESHALL   Map 07 SJ71
LILLESHALL ABBEY
TF10 9HW (1.5m SW off A518 on unclass road)

In the beautiful grounds of Lilleshall Hall, ruined Lilleshall Abbey was founded shortly before the middle of the 12th century and from the high west front visitors can look down the entire 228ft length of the abbey church.
Times: Open Apr-Oct, any reasonable time. (Closed Nov-Mar). **Fee:** Free. **Facilities:** 🅿 ✖ ♿

🏛 LUDLOW   Map 07 SO57
LUDLOW CASTLE
Castle Square SY8 1AY (A49, turn off into town centre)
☎ 01584 873355

Ludlow Castle dates from about 1086. In 1473, Edward IV sent the Prince of Wales and his brother - later to become the Princes in the Tower - to live here and Ludlow Castle became a seat of government. John Milton's *Comus* was first performed at Ludlow Castle in 1634; now contemporary performances of Shakespeare's plays, together with concerts, are put on in the castle grounds during the Ludlow Festival (2 weeks, end June-early July).
Times: Open all year, Jan Sat-Sun 10-4; Feb-Mar daily 10-4; Apr-Jul daily 10-5; Aug daily 10-7; Sep daily 10-5; Oct-Dec daily 10-4 (last admission 30 minutes before closing). **Fee:** £3.50 (ch under 6 free, ch £1.50, pen £3). Family ticket £9.50. **Facilities:** 🅿 (100 yds) ♿ toilets for disabled shop 🏷

🏛 LYDBURY NORTH   Map 07 SO38
WALCOT HALL
SY7 8AZ (3m E of Bishops Castle, on B4385, beside the Powis Arms)
☎ 01568 610693   📠 01568 610693
e-mail: lesley@walcothall.com

Re-designed by Sir William Chambers for Lord Clive of India in 1763. The Georgian House possesses a free-standing and restored Ballroom, stableyard with matching clock towers and extensive walled garden. There is an Arboretum, noted for its rhododendrons and azaleas, specimen trees, pools and a lake. The Ballroom is available for hire and the Hall holds a licence for civil weddings.
Times: Open 25 & 26 May. Arboretum & gardens open Apr-Oct. **Fee:** £3 (ch under 15 free) **Facilities:** 🅿 ♿ (lift to 1st floor)

🏛 MORETON CORBET   Map 07 SJ52
CASTLE

A small 13th-century keep and the ruins of an impressive Elizabethan house are all that remain: the house was destroyed in the Civil War.
Times: Open all reasonable times. **Fee:** Free. **Facilities:** 🅿 ♿ ♿

🏛 MUCH WENLOCK   Map 07 SO69
MUCH WENLOCK PRIORY
TA3 6HS
☎ 01952 727466
Times: Open all year, Apr-Oct, daily 10-6 (Oct 10-5); Nov-Mar, Wed-Sun 10-4. Closed 24-26 Dec & 1 Jan. **Facilities:** 🅿 ♿ *Details not confirmed for 2003*

🏛 OSWESTRY   Map 07 SJ22
OLD OSWESTRY HILL FORT
(1m N, accessible from unclass road off A483)

This Iron Age hill-fort covers 68 acres, has five ramparts and an elaborate western portal. Part of the prehistoric Wat's Dyke abuts the site.
Times: Open any reasonable time. **Fee:** Free. **Facilities:** ♿

🏛 QUATT   Map 07 SO78
DUDMASTON
WV15 6QN (4m SE of Bridgnorth on A442)
☎ 01746 780866   📠 01746 780744
e-mail: mouefe@smtp.ntrust.org.uk
Times: Open Apr-Sep, Tue, Wed & Sun & BH Mons, 2-5.30. Garden noon-6. Closed Good Fri. **Facilities:** 🅿 🍴 ♿ (Braille guides, taped tours) toilets for disabled shop ✖ (ex in grounds) ♿ *Details not confirmed for 2003* 🏷

SHREWSBURY   Map 07 SJ41
SHREWSBURY CASTLE AND SHROPSHIRE REGIMENTAL MUSEUM
The Castle, Castle St SY1 2AT (in town centre, adjacent to railway station)
☎ 01743 358516   📠 01743 354811
e-mail: shropsrm@zoom.co.uk
Times: Open Tue-Sat 10-4.30, also Sun from Etr-1 Oct & BH Mon. Closed Dec & Jan. Telephone for winter opening times. Castle grounds open Mon-Sat & Sun as above, 9-5 **Facilities:** P (3 mins NCP) (on street parking by voucher only) ♿ (please ask staff for assistance) toilets for disabled shop 🐕 (ex guide dogs) *Details not confirmed for 2003*

SHREWSBURY QUEST
193 Abbey Foregate SY2 6AH (opposite Shrewsbury Abbey)
☎ 01743 243324   📠 01743 244342
Times: Open Apr-Oct 10-5 (last admission); Nov-Mar 10-4 (last admission). Closed 25-26 Dec & 1 Jan. **Facilities:** P (charged) ✗ licensed ♿ (Braille maps, lift) toilets for disabled shop 🐕 (ex assistance dogs) *Details not confirmed for 2003*

STOKESAY   Map 07 SO48
STOKESAY CASTLE
SY7 9AH (1m S of Craven Arms off A49)
☎ 01588 672544

Well-preserved and little altered, this 13th-century manor house has a romantic setting. It has a fine timber-framed Jacobean gatehouse, a great hall and a solar with 17th-century panelling.
Times: Open all year, 29 Mar-Sep, daily 10-6 (Oct, daily 10-5); Nov-Mar Wed-Sun 10-1 & 2-4 (Closed 24-26 Dec & 1 Jan). **Fee:** * £4.40 (ch 2.20, pen £3.30) family ticket £11 **Facilities:** P ♿ (tape tour for visually handicapped, ramp for wheelchairs) toilets for disabled 🐕

TELFORD   Map 07 SU60
HOO FARM ANIMAL KINGDOM
Preston-on-the-Weald Moors TF6 6DJ (M54 junct 6, follow brown tourist signs)
☎ 01952 677917   📠 01952 677944
e-mail: info@hoofarm.com

Along with the pig and baby lamb feeding, egg collecting, craft demonstrations, junior quad bikes, candle dipping, the rifle range, a petting zoo, and large play areas, Hoo Farm Animal Kingdom is host to the wonderful Sheep Steeplechase, held everyday between Easter Monday and September. A great day out for kids and adults alike.
Times: Open 23 Mar-8 Sep, daily 10-6 (last admission 5). 10 Sep-22 Nov, Tue-Sun 10-5 (last admission 4. Closed Mon ex Halloween). 23 Nov-24 Dec daily 10-5 (closes at 1pm 24 Dec). (Closed 25 Dec-mid Mar). **Fee:** * £3.95 (ch £3.25 & pen £3.50). Family ticket (2 adults & 3 children) £15 **Facilities:** P 🍴 ♿ toilets for disabled shop 🐕 (ex guide dogs)

WESTON-UNDER-REDCASTLE   Map 07 SJ52
HAWKSTONE HISTORIC PARK & FOLLIES
SY4 5UY (3m from Hodnet off A53, follow the brown heritage signs)
☎ 01939 200611   📠 01939 200311   [2 for 1]
e-mail: info@hawkstone.co.uk

Created in the 18th century by the Hill family, Hawkstone was once one of the greatest historic parklands in history. After almost one hundred years of neglect it has now been restored and designated a Grade I historic park. Visitors can once again experience the magical world of intricate pathways, arches and bridges, towering cliffs and follies, and an awesome grotto. The Grand Valley and woodlands have centuries-old oaks, wild rhododendrons and lofty monkey puzzle trees. The park covers nearly 100 acres of hilly terrian and vistors are advised to wear sensible shoes and clothing and to bring a torch. Allow 3-4 hours for the tour, which is well signposted and a map is provided. Attractions include 'Hear King Arthur' and meeting the Duke of Wellington in the White Tower to discuss the Battle of Waterloo.
Times: Open Sat & Sun Jan-Mar; Wed-Sun, Apr-May & Sep-Oct, Jun-Aug, daily. Closed Nov & Dec. Open from 10am **Fee:** Weekdays £5.50 (ch £3.50 pen/students £4.50). Family ticket £15. **Facilities:** P 🍴 ✗ licensed ♿ (no access to follies due to terrain access Valley only) toilets for disabled shop 🐕 (ex on lead)

WROXETER   Map 07 SJ50
ROMAN TOWN
SY5 6PH (5m E of Shrewsbury, 1m S of A5)
☎ 01743 761330
Times: Open all year, Apr-Oct, daily 10-6 (Oct 10-5); Nov-Mar, Wed-Sun 10-4 (closed 1-2pm). Closed 24-26 Dec & 1 Jan. **Facilities:** P ♿ shop 🐕 ⚿ *Details not confirmed for 2003*

Somerset

Somerset is rich with history and legend, as well as having some beautiful coastline and countryside. The name of the county comes from the Saxon, and literally translated means 'Land of the Summer People.'

One of the county's most famous landmarks is Glastonbury Tor, a hill that once gave refuge to the ancient Britons. One legend has it that Joseph of Arimathea came to Glastonbury in a bid to convert the English. It is also the place where King Arthur and Gwynevere are said to be buried. (Those interested in Arthurian legend should also visit South Cadbury, an Iron Age hill fort reputed to be the site of Camelot.) The tor is connected to many more legends, but in more recent years, the area has been host to a more concrete, if no less fabulous event, Glastonbury Festival.

At the other end of the county lies the timeless, rugged beauty of Exmoor, most of which is now a National Park. R. D. Blackmore's novel of 1869, *Lorna Doone: A Romance of Exmoor* is set here.

Bath is the biggest town in Somerset, and is ideal for shopping, spa relaxation and architecture buffs. Jane Austen lived here, and set two of her novels in the town.

The seaside resorts of Minehead, Burnham-on-Sea and Weston-super-Mare are great places to enjoy a family holiday. Dunster is further inland and walking through it is a little like taking a time machine through 900 years of history. The town is overshadowed by the Norman splendour of Dunster Castle, owned by the National Trust.

In the heart of Somerset lies Wells, the smallest city in England, with only 10,000 inhabitants. The cathedral was begun in the late 12th century, and completed in the mid-13th. It is well known for its stone figures, and its 600-year old clock.

Top: Hadspen Garden

EVENTS & FESTIVALS

March
tbc Bath Literature Festival
tbc Bath Shakespeare Festival

May
3rd-4th Bath Annual Spring Flower Show
16th-1st June Bath International Music Festival
16th-1st June Bath Fringe Festival (various venues)
28th-31st The Royal Bath & West Show, Royal Bath & West Showground, Shepton Mallet

June
16th May-1st Bath International Music Festival (various venues)
16th May-1st Bath Fringe Festival (various venues)
tbc Glastonbury Festival, Worthy Farm, Pilton, Glastonbury

July
12th Glastonbury Pilgrimage, Glastonbury Abbey
tbc Glastonbury International Dance Festival

August
6th-7th Flower Show, Taunton

September
27th Wellington Carnival

October
18th Taunton Carnival

November
tbc Bridgwater Guy Fawkes Carnival, Bridgwater
tbc Glastonbury Chilkwell Guy Fawkes Carnival

Somerset

🏛 AXBRIDGE
Map 03 ST45
KING JOHN'S HUNTING LODGE
The Square BS26 2AP
☎ 01934 732012
Times: Open 29 Mar-Sep, daily 1-4. **Facilities:** ♿ shop ✖ ⚭ *Details not confirmed for 2003*

🏛 BARRINGTON
Map 03 ST31
BARRINGTON COURT GARDEN
TA19 0NQ (5m NE of Ilminster on B3168)
☎ 01460 241938 📄 01460 241938
e-mail: barringtoncourt@ntrust.org.uk

The house dates from the 17th century, but the gardens were created in the 1920s, with the help (through the post) of Gertrude Jekyll. They are laid out in 'rooms' and there is a large walled kitchen garden supplying fresh fruit and vegetables to the restaurant.
Times: Open Mar & Oct: Thu, Fri, Sat & Sun 11-4.30: Apr-Sep: daily (ex Wed) 11-5.30; Oct Tue, Fri, Sat & Sun 11-4.30. **Fee:** £5.20 (ch £2.50). Family £13. **Facilities:** P 🍴 ✖ licensed ♿ (batricars available, braille guides, wheelchairs) toilets for disabled shop garden centre ✖ ⚭

🏛 BATH
Map 03 ST76
AMERICAN MUSEUM
Claverton Manor BA2 7BD (2.5m SE)
☎ 01225 460503 📄 01225 480726
e-mail: amibbath@aol.com

Claverton Manor is just south east of Bath, in a beautiful setting above the River Avon. The house was built in 1820 by Sir Jeffrey Wyatville, and is now a museum of American decorative arts. The gardens are well worth seeing, and include an American arboretum and a replica of George Washington's garden at Mount Vernon. The Folk Art Gallery and the New Gallery are among the many exhibits in the grounds along with seasonal exhibitions.
Times: Open 24 Mar-4 Nov, Tue-Sun 2-5. Gardens 1-6. BH Sun & Mon 11-5. **Fee:** £6 (ch £3.50, pen £5.50). **Facilities:** P 🍴 ♿ toilets for disabled shop ⚭

BATH ABBEY
BA1 1LY (centre of Bath, next to Pump Rooms)
☎ 01225 422462 & 446300 📄 01225 429990
e-mail: office@bathabbey.org

The 15th-century abbey church was built on the site of the Saxon abbey where King Edgar was crowned in 973. The church is Perpendicular style with Norman arches and superb fan-vaulting. The famous West Front carvings represent the founder-bishop's dream of angels ascending and descending from heaven.
Times: Open all year, Apr-Oct, Mon-Sat 9-6; Nov-Mar 9-4.30. Sun all year 1-2.30 & 4.30-5.30. **Fee:** Free. **Facilities:** ♿ 📄 (5 mins) (limited street parking) ♿ toilets for disabled shop ✖ (ex guide dogs)

BATH POSTAL MUSEUM
8 Broad St BA1 5LJ
☎ 01225 460333 📄 01225 460333 **2 for 1**
e-mail: info@bathpostalmuseum.org

Discover how 18th-century Bath influenced and developed the Postal System, including the story of the Penny Post. The first letter sent with a stamp was sent from this very building. Visitors can explore the history of written communication from Egyptian clay tablets, thousands of years ago, to the first Airmail flight from Bath to London in 1912. See the Victorian Post Office and then visit the tearoom and shop. You can even discover how the Romans communicated across their Empire.
Times: Open all year, Mon-Sat 11-5. Parties by appointment. (Closed Sun, 25-26 Dec & 1 Jan). **Fee:** * £2.90 (ch £1.50 & students, ch up to 6 yrs free, pen, £2.40). Party 10+. **Facilities:** P (200yds) 🍴 ♿ toilets for disabled shop ✖ 🍴

THE BUILDING OF BATH MUSEUM
Countess of Huntingdons Chapel, The Vineyards, The Paragon BA1 5NA (M4 junct 18 down A46 towards Bath city centre. Take A4, 2nd exit at mini rdbt. Along road on right)
☎ 01225 333895 📄 01225 445473
e-mail: cathryn@bathmuseum.co.uk

This new museum relates the fascinating story of how Georgian Bath was created. 17th-century Bath was a medieval market town but in the space of 100 years it was transformed into one of the most beautiful and glamorous cities in Europe. The exhibition depicts elegant society life in 'Beau' Nash's spa resort and explains how the houses were constructed. After a visit, the street scene outside seems like an extension of the exhibition. Ring for details of special events such as concerts and lectures.
Times: Open 15 Feb-1 Dec, Tue-Sun & BH's 10.30-5. **Fee:** * £4 (ch £1.50, concessions £3). Family ticket £10. Party 10+ **Facilities:** P (500yds) ♿ shop ✖ (ex guide dogs) 🍴

HOLBURNE MUSEUM OF ART
Great Pulteney St BA2 4DB (M4 junct 18, follow brown tourist signs from Bristol via A4 or A431)
☎ 01225 466669 📄 01225 333121 **2 for 1**
e-mail: holburne@bath.ac.uk

This elegant building shows 17th and 18th-century collections of fine and decorative art, notably silver, porcelain, glass, furniture and Old Master paintings. There is an annual programme of events and lively lectures. The biggest Gainsborough painting in Britain, of The Byam Family, previously unseen by the general public is on loan to the museum for three years.
Times: Open mid Feb-mid Dec, Mon-Sat & BHs 10-5, Sun 2.30-5.30 (Closed Mon ex group bookings). **Fee:** * £3.50 (ch £1.50, unemployed & student £2, other concessions £3). Family ticket £7.
Facilities: P 🍴 ♿ (lift to all floors) toilets for disabled shop ✖ (ex guide dogs)

MUSEUM OF BATH AT WORK
Julian Rd BA1 2RH (from city centre, off Lansdown Rd into Julian Rd. Museum is next to church on right)
☎ 01225 318348 📄 01225 318348
e-mail: mobaw@hotmail.com

The centre houses the Bowler collection, and the entire stock-in-trade of various Victorian craftsmen. Also here

continued

Somerset

is 'The Story of Bath Stone', with a replica of a mine face before mechanisation, and a Bath cabinet-maker's workshop. Also Horstmann Car Gallery plus a computerised information point of Bath's heritage at work.
Times: Open all year, Etr-1 Nov, daily 10-5; Nov-Etr, wknds 10-5. (Closed 25-26 Dec). **Fee:** * £3.50 (ch, pen & students £2.50). Family ticket £10. **Facilities:** P (0.25m) 💷 shop ✘ (ex guide dogs)

Museum of Costume
Bennett St BA1 2QH (M4 junct 18, follow A46 into Bath. Museum near city centre)
☎ 01225 477785   01225 477743
e-mail: costume_bookings@bathnes.gov.uk

The Museum of Costume is one of the finest collections of fashionable dress in the world, covering the period from the late 16th-century to the present day. It is housed in Bath's famous 18th-century Assembly Rooms designed by John Wood the Younger in 1771. Entrance to the Assembly Rooms is free.
Times: Open all year, daily 10-4.30 (Closed 25 & 26 Dec). **Fee:** * £5 (ch £3.50). Family ticket £14. Combined ticket with Roman Baths, £10.50 (ch £5.90) **Facilities:** P (5 mins walk) (park & ride recommended) ♿ (audio guides available) toilets for disabled shop ✘ (ex guide dogs) 🍴

No 1 Royal Crescent
BA1 2LR
☎ 01225 428126   01225 481850
e-mail: no1@bptrust.demon.co.uk

Bath is very much a Georgian city, but most of its houses have naturally altered over the years to suit changing tastes and lifestyles. Built in 1768 by John Wood the Elder, No 1 Royal Crescent has been restored to look as it would have done some 200 years ago.
Times: Open 15 Feb-29 Oct, Tue-Sun 10.30-5; 31 Oct-26 Nov, Tue-Sun 10.30-4. Open BH Mon & Bath Festival Mon 22 May. (Closed Good Fri). Last admission 30 mins before closing. **Fee:** * £4 (concessions £3.50). Family ticket £10. Party 10+. **Facilities:** P (5 mins walk) (street parking with card £1 per hour) shop ✘ (ex guide dogs)

Roman Baths & Pump Room
Abbey Church Yard BA1 1LZ (M4 junct 18, A46 into city centre)
☎ 01225 477785   01225 477743
e-mail: romanbaths_bookings@bathnes.gov.uk

The remains of the Roman baths and temple give a vivid impression of life nearly 2000 years ago. Built next to Britain's only hot spring, the baths served the sick, and the pilgrims visiting the adjacent Temple of Sulis Minerva. Above the Temple Courtyard, the Pump Room became a popular meeting place in the 18th century. The site still flows with natural hot water and no visit is complete without a taste of the famous hot spa water.
Times: Open all year, Mar-Jun & Sep-Oct, daily 9-5; Jul & Aug daily 9am-9pm; Jan-Feb & Nov-Dec, daily 9.30-4-30. (Closed 25 & 26 Dec). Last exit 1hr before closing. **Fee:** * £8 (ch £4.60). Family ticket £20.50. Combined ticket with Museum of Costume £10.50 (ch £5.90). Disabled visitors free admission to ground floor areas. **Facilities:** P (5 mins walk) (park & ride recommended) ✘ licensed ♿ (sign language & audio tours) toilets for disabled shop ✘ (ex guide dogs) 🍴

Sally Lunn's Refreshment House & Museum
4 North Pde Passage BA1 1NX (city centre, follow signs, next to Bath Abbey)
☎ 01225 461634   01225 447090
e-mail: info@sallylunns.co.uk

This Tudor building is Bath's oldest house and was a popular 17th-century meeting place. The traditional 'Sally Lunn' is similar to a brioche, and it is popularly believed to carry the name of its first maker who came to Bath in 1680. The bun is still served in the restaurant, and the original oven, Georgian cooking range and a collection of baking utensils are displayed in the museum.
Times: Open all year, Museum - Mon-Fri 10-6, Sat 10-5, Sun 11-5. (Closed 25-26 Dec & 1 Jan). **Fee:** 30p (concessions free) **Facilities:** P 2-3 min walk (cards required for street parking) 💷 ✘ licensed ♿ (braille menu for the blind) shop ✘ (ex guide dogs) 🍴

Somerset

CASTLE CARY — Map 03 ST63
HADSPEN GARDEN & NURSERY
Hadspen House BA7 7NG (2m SE off A371)
☎ 01749 813707 📠 01749 813707

Situated within a 17th-century curved wall, this five acre garden has borders planted with roses and herbaceous plants, many of which have been developed here. Plants grown in the garden are available in the adjoining nursery.
Times: Open 6 Mar-28 Sep, Thu-Sun & BHs 10-5. **Fee:** * £3 (ch 50p). Free admission for wheelchair users. **Facilities:** 🅿 ✗ ♿ toilets for disabled garden centre 🍴 (ex guide dogs)

CHARD — Map 03 ST30
FORDE ABBEY
TA20 4LU (4m S of Chard, follow brown tourist signs)
☎ 01460 221290 📠 01460 220296   2 for 1
e-mail: forde.abbey@virgin.net

This 12th-century Cistercian monastery was converted into a private dwelling in the mid-17th century by Cromwell's attorney general. In the house there are good pictures and furniture and an outstanding set of Mortlake tapestries. The large gardens are some of the finest in the area and include a kitchen garden, rock garden and bog garden as well as herbaceous borders and many outstanding trees.
Times: Gardens, open all year, daily 10-4.30. Abbey & gardens Apr-Oct, Tue-Fri, Sun & BH 1-4.30. **Fee:** * Gardens £4.75 (ch free, pen £4.40). House & Gardens £6.50 (ch free, pen £5.95). **Facilities:** 🅿 ☕ ♿ (wheelchair can be borrowed) toilets for disabled shop garden centre 🍴 (ex in the garden)

CLEVEDON — Map 03 ST47
CLEVEDON COURT
Tickenham Rd BS21 6QU (off B3130 1.5m E of Clevedon)
☎ 01275 872257
Times: Open 31 Mar-29 Sep, Wed-Thu, Sun & BH Mon 2-5.
Facilities: 🅿 ♿ (ground floor accessible via 4 steps) 🍴 🐕 Details not confirmed for 2003

CRANMORE — Map 03 ST64
EAST SOMERSET RAILWAY
Cranmore Railway Station BA4 4QP (on A361 between Frome & Shepton Mallet)
☎ 01749 880417 📠 01749 880764
Times: Open daily Mar-24 Dec from 10am. For days when steam trains are operating phone 01749 880417. **Facilities:** 🅿 ☕ ✗ licensed ♿ (ramp from road to platform) toilets for disabled shop Details not confirmed for 2003

CRICKET ST THOMAS — Map 03 ST30
THE WILDLIFE PARK AT CRICKET ST THOMAS
TA20 4DB (3m E of Chard on A30, follow brown tourist signs. Clearly signposted from M5 junct 25)
☎ 01460 30111   2 for 1
📠 01460 30817
e-mail: teresa.white2@bourne-leisure.co.uk

The Wildlife Park offers you the chance to see more than 60 species of animals at close quarters. Visitors can learn about what is being done to save endangered species, take a walk through the Lemur Wood, ride on the Safari Train or visit the Children's Farm. During peak season, park mascot Larry the Lemur stars in his own show.
Times: Open all year, daily 10-dusk, last admission 4pm in summer. (Closed 25 Dec). **Fee:** * £6.50 (ch 3-14 £4.95 & pen £5.50, under 3's free). Family ticket £20. **Facilities:** 🅿 ☕ ✗ licensed ♿ (some steep slopes) toilets for disabled shop 🍴 (ex guide dogs) 🐕

DUNSTER — Map 03 SS94
DUNSTER CASTLE
TA24 6SL (3m SE of Minehead, approach from A39. Approx 2m from Dunster Stn)
☎ 01643 821314 📠 01643 823000
e-mail: wdugen@smtp.ntrust.org.uk

The castle's picturesque appearance is largely due to 19th-century work, but older features can also be seen, the superb 17th-century oak staircase for example. Sub-tropical plants flourish in the 28-acre park and the terraced gardens are noted for exotica such as a giant lemon tree, yuccas, mimosa and palms.
Times: Open: Castle: 31 Mar-Sep, Sat-Wed 11-5; Oct-4 Nov, Sat-Wed 11-4. Garden & Park: Apr-29 Sep daily 10-5; Oct-Mar 11-4. **Fee:** * Castle, Garden & Park £6.20 (ch under 16 £3.10). Family ticket £15.50. Garden & park only £3 (ch under 16 £1.50). Family ticket £7.50.
Facilities: 🅿 ♿ (Braille & audio guides, large print guides & Batricar) toilets for disabled shop 🍴 (in park only) 🐕

EAST HUNTSPILL — Map 03 ST34
SECRET WORLD-BADGER & WILDLIFE RESERVE CENTRE
New Rd TA9 3PZ (Signposted from A38, 1m S of Highbridge)
☎ 01278 783250 📠 01278 793109
Times: Open Mar-Nov, daily 10-6. Nov-Dec, daily 10-5. Feb- Mar, daily 10-5. **Facilities:** 🅿 ☕ ✗ ♿ toilets for disabled shop garden centre Details not confirmed for 2003

EAST LAMBROOK — Map 03 ST41
EAST LAMBROOK MANOR GARDEN
TA13 5HH (signed off A303, at South Petherton roundabout)
☎ 01460 240328 📠 01460 242344
e-mail: enquiries@eastlambrook.com

It was the late Margery Fish who created the concept of 'cottage gardening' in the 1930s. Her wonderful Grade I listed gardens are known to garden lovers throughout the world. The gardens now house the National Collection of Geraniums, a specialist plant nursery, a tea shop and art gallery.
Times: Open Feb-Oct, daily 10-5. **Fee:** * £3.50 (ch £1 & pen £3.25). Party £3.25 each. **Facilities:** 🅿 ☕ ♿ (Gardens partly accessible) shop garden centre 🍴 (ex guide dogs) 🐕

FARLEIGH HUNGERFORD   Map 03 ST85
Farleigh Hungerford Castle
BA3 6RS (3.5m W of Trowbridge on A366)
☎ 01225 754026

The ruined 14th-century castle has a chapel containing wall paintings, stained glass and the fine tomb of Sir Thomas Hungerford who built the castle. His powerful family and the castle are linked with various grim tales.
Times: Open all year, 29 Mar-Sep, daily 10-6 (Oct, daily 10-5); Nov-Mar, daily 10-1 & 2-4. (Closed 24-26 Dec & 1 Jan). **Fee:** * £2.50 (concessions £1.70, ch 5-15 £1.20, under 5's free). **Facilities:** 🅿 ♿ ✖ 🚻

GLASTONBURY   Map 03 ST43
Glastonbury Abbey
Abbey Gatehouse, Magdalene St BA6 9EL (on A361 between Frome & Taunton. M5 junct 23 then take A39 to Glastonbury)
☎ 01458 832267
🖷 01458 832267   **2 for 1**
e-mail: glastonbury.abbey@dial.pipex.com

Few places in Britain are as rich in myth and legend as Glastonbury. Tradition maintains that the impressive ruins mark the birth place of Christianity in Britain. Joseph of Arimathea is said to have founded a chapel here in AD61, planting his staff in the ground where it flowered both at Christmas and Easter. Later, it is said, King Arthur and Guinevere were buried here, and the abbey has been a place of pilgrimage since the Middle Ages. The present abbey ruins date mostly from the 12th and 13th centuries, fell into decay after the Dissolution. The display area contains artefacts and a model of the Abbey as it might have been in 1539. During the summer months meet brother Thomas, who will tell you how the monks used to live.
Times: Open all year, daily, Jun-Aug 9-6; Sep-May 9.30-6 or dusk, whichever is the earliest. Dec-Feb open at 10am. (Closed 25 Dec).
Fee: £3.50 (ch 5-15 £1.50, pen & students £3). Family ticket £8 (2ad+2ch) **Facilities:** 🅿 (charged) 🍴 ♿ (no access in Lady Chapel,audio tape,deaf loop,wheelchairs) toilets for disabled shop ✖ (on leads only)

KINGSDON   Map 03 ST52
Lytes Cary Manor
TA11 7HU (off A303)
☎ 01458 224471   🖷 01458 224471
e-mail: lytescarymanor@ntrust.org.uk

Much of the present house was built in the 16th century although the oldest part, the chapel, dates from 1343. The Great Hall was a 15th-century addition. Unfortunately the gardens did not survive, but the present formal gardens are being restocked with plants that were commonly grown at the time of building.
Times: Open Apr-Oct, Mon, Wed & Fri 11-5 **Fee:** * £4.60 (ch £2)
Facilities: 🅿 ♿ (braille guide, scented plants) toilets for disabled ✖ (ex guide dogs) 🚻

MONTACUTE   Map 03 ST41
Montacute House
TA15 6XP (off A3088)
☎ 01935 823289   🖷 01935 826921   **2 for 1**
e-mail: wmogen@smtp.ntrust.org.uk

Set amidst formal gardens, Montacute House was built by Sir Edward Phelips. He was a successful lawyer, and became Speaker of the House of Commons in 1604. Inside there are decorated ceilings, ornate fireplaces, heraldic glass and fine wood panelling. The Long Gallery displays a permanent collection of Tudor and Jacobean portraits from the National Portrait Gallery in London.
Times: Open, Garden & Park: Apr-30 Oct daily (ex Tue) 11-5.30. Nov-Mar Wed-Sun 11-5. House: Apr-30 Oct, daily (ex Tue) 11-5 **Fee:** House, Garden & Park £6.50 (ch £3). Garden & Park only £3.50 (ch £1.50). **Facilities:** 🅿 🍴 ✖ licensed ♿ (Braille guide) toilets for disabled shop garden centre ✖ (ex in park) 🚻

MUCHELNEY   Map 03 ST42
Muchelney Abbey
TA10 0DQ
☎ 01458 250664

Encircled by marshes, Muchelney seemed a suitably remote spot in the 8th century for a Benedictine Abbey. The ruins that remain date from the 15th and 16th centuries, however, and there is also a 14th-century priest's house nearby. Exhibitions include Stuart furnishings and examples of the work of modern potter, John Leach.
Times: Open all year, 29 Mar-Sep, daily 10-6 (Oct, daily 10-5); **Fee:** * £2 (ch 5-15 £1, under 5's free, concessions £1.50) **Facilities:** 🅿 ♿ ✖ 🚻

NETHER STOWEY   Map 03 ST13
Coleridge Cottage
35 Lime St TA5 1NQ (At W end of Nether Stowey, on S Side of A39, 8m W of Bridgwater)
☎ 01278 732662

It was in this small cottage that Coleridge was most inspired as a poet and here that he wrote *The Rime of the Ancient Mariner*, part of *Christabel* and *Frost at Midnight*. The Coleridge family moved to Nether Stowey in 1797 and became friendly with the Wordsworths who lived nearby.
Times: Open Apr-Sep, Tue-Thu & Sun 2-5. **Fee:** * £3. (ch £1.50).
Facilities: 🅿 ✖ 🚻

NUNNEY   Map 03 ST74
Nunney Castle
(3.5m SW of Frome, off A361)

Built in 1373, and supposedly modelled on France's Bastille, this crenellated manor house has one of the deepest moats in England. It was ruined by Parliamentarian forces in the Civil War.
Times: Open any reasonable time. **Fee:** Free. **Facilities:** ♿ 🚻

SPARKFORD
Haynes Motor Museum
BA22 7LH (from A303 follow A359 road towards Castle Cary, the museum is clearly signposted)
☎ 01963 440804
📠 01963 441004
e-mail: info@haynesmotormuseum.co.uk

2 for 1

Spectacular collection of historic cars, motorcycles and motoring memorabilia. Vehicles range from a 1903 Oldsmobile to sports cars of the 50s and 60s and modern day classics. Also at the Museum is a video cinema, the Hall of Motorsports, a millennium hall, picnic area and children's adventure playground.
Times: Open all year, Mar-Oct , daily 9.30-5.30; Nov-Feb, 10-4.30. Etr-summer hols open to 6.30pm. (Closed 25 & 26 Dec & 1 Jan). **Fee:** * Adult £6 (ch £3.50, concessions £5) family £7.50 (1ad+ 1ch) £17 (2ad+3ch) **Facilities:** 🅿 ⊇ ♿ (ramps & loan wheelchairs available) toilets for disabled shop ✈ (ex guide dogs & in grounds) 🍴

STOKE ST GREGORY
Willow & Wetlands Visitor Centre
Meare Green Court TA3 6HY (between North Curry & Stoke St Gregory, signed from A361 & A378)
☎ 01823 490249   📠 01823 490814
e-mail: phcoate@globalnet.co.uk

2 for 1

The centre is owned and run by Somerset Basketmakers and willow growers P H Coate & Son. The environmental exhibition gives a fascinating insight into the Somerset Levels and Moors. Guided tours.
Times: Open all year, Mon-Fri 9-5 (guided tours 10-4), Sat (no tours) 9-5. Closed Sun. **Fee:** Free. **Facilities:** 🅿 ⊇ ♿ toilets for disabled shop 🍴

STOKE-SUB-HAMDON
Stoke-Sub-Hamdon Priory
North St TA4 6QP (between A303 & A3088)
☎ 01985 843600

A complex of buildings, begun in the 14th century for the priests of the Chantry Chapel of St Nicholas (now destroyed).
Times: Open 29 Mar-2 Nov, daily 10-6 or dusk if earlier. **Fee:** Free. **Facilities:** 🅿 (5mtrs) 🚗 (on road parking only) 🐕

STREET
The Shoe Museum
C & J Clark Ltd, High St BA16 0YA (M5 Junct 23, take A39 to Street, follow signs for Clarks Village)
☎ 01458 842169   📠 01458 443196

The museum is in the oldest part of the shoe factory set up by Cyrus and James Clark in 1825. It contains shoes from Roman times to the present, buckles, engravings,

fashion plates, machinery, hand tools and advertising material.

Times: Open all year. (ex 10 days over xmas) **Fee:** Free. **Facilities:** 🅿 ⊇ ✕ ♿ toilets for disabled shop 🍴

TAUNTON
Hestercombe Gardens
Cheddon Fitzpaine TA2 8LG (3m N, off A361)
☎ 01823 413747   📠 01823 413747
e-mail: info@hestercombegardens.com

There are three period gardens to enjoy at Hestercombe: the 40-acre Georgian pleasure grounds with woodland walks, temples, Witch House and Great Cascade; the Victorian terrace and the Edwardian gardens, showing the work of Gertrude Jekyll and architect Edwin Lutyens.
Times: Open every day, 10-6 (last admission 5). **Fee:** * £4.50 (ch 5-15 £1, pen £4.20). Family ticket £10 **Facilities:** 🅿 ⊇ ♿ (gardens partially accessible) toilets for disabled shop garden centre (Apr-Oct) 🍴 (ex on lead) 🍴

TINTINHULL
Tintinhull House Garden
BA22 9PZ (0.5m S off A303. Follow signs to Tintinhull village, garden is well signposted from village)
☎ 01935 822545   📠 01935 826357
e-mail: wtifxs@smtp.ntrust.org.uk

An attractive, mainly 17th-century farmhouse with a Queen Anne façade, it stands in beautiful formal gardens. The gardens were largely created by Mrs Reiss, who gave the property to the National Trust.
Times: Open Apr-Sep, Wed-Sun & BH Mons 12-6. **Fee:** * £3.80 (ch £1.80). **Facilities:** 🅿 ⊇ 🍴 (ex guide dogs) 🐕

WASHFORD
Cleeve Abbey
TA23 0PS (0.25m S of A39)
☎ 01984 640377

The now ruined Cistercian abbey was founded at the end of the 12th century. Little remains of the church,

continued

but the gatehouse, dormitory and refectory are in good condition, with traceried windows, a fine timbered roof and wall paintings to be seen.
Times: Open all year, 29 Mar-Sep, daily 10-6 (Oct, daily 10-5); Nov-Mar daily 10-1.2-4 **Fee:** * £2.80 (concessions £2.10, ch 5-15 £1.40, under 5's free). **Facilities:** P & shop ✗ (in certain areas) ♿

TROPIQUARIA ANIMAL AND ADVENTURE PARK
TA23 0QB (on A39, between Williton and Minehead)
☎ 01984 640688   📠 01984 641105
e-mail: office@tropiquaria.co.uk

Housed in a 1930s BBC transmitting station, the main hall has been converted into an indoor jungle with a 15-foot waterfall, tropical plants and free-flying birds. Downstairs is the submarine crypt with local and tropical marine life. Other features include landscaped gardens, and the Shadowstring Puppet Theatre. Also two pirate adventure ships are moored on the front lawn.
Times: Open Apr-Sep, daily 10-5; Oct daily 11-5, Nov -Mar wknds 11-4. **Fee:** * £5.50 (ch & pen £4.50). **Facilities:** P 🍴 & ramp to pirate galleon+indoor castle toilets for disabled shop ✗ (ex guide dogs) 🛍

🏛 WELLS   Map 03 ST54
THE BISHOP'S PALACE
Henderson Rooms BA5 2PD (next to cathedral)
☎ 01749 678691   📠 01749 678691

Close to the cathedral is the moated bishop's palace. The early part of the palace, the bishop's chapel and the ruins of the banqueting hall date from the 13th century. There are several state rooms and a long gallery which houses portraits of former Bishops. Events include a Living History re-enactment.
Times: Open Apr-Oct, Tue-Fri & BH's; daily in Aug 10.30-5 Sun 1-5. Gates close at exactly 6pm. **Fee:** * £3.50 (ch 12 accompanied free, pen £2.50 & UB40's, disabled £1.50). Party 10+ £2.50 each. **Facilities:** P (100yds) 🍴 ✗ licensed & (free use of electric wheelchair) shop

🏛 WESTON-SUPER-MARE   Map 03 ST36
THE HELICOPTER MUSEUM
The Heliport, Locking Moor Rd BS24 8PP (outskirts of town on A371, nr M5 Junct 21)
☎ 01934 635227   📠 01934 645230
e-mail: office@helimuseum.fsnet.co.uk
Times: Open all year, Nov-Mar Wed-Sun 10-4. Apr-Oct 10-6. (closed 24-26 Dec & 1 Jan) Open daily during Etr & Summer school hols. **Facilities:** P 🍴 & toilets for disabled shop Details not confirmed for 2003 🛍

NORTH SOMERSET MUSEUM
Burlington St BS23 1PR
☎ 01934 621028   📠 01934 612526   **2 for 1**
e-mail: nickgoff@n-somerset.org.uk

This museum, housed in the former workshops of the Edwardian Gaslight Company, has displays on the seaside holiday, an old chemist's shop, a dairy and Victorian pavement mosaics. Adjoining the museum is

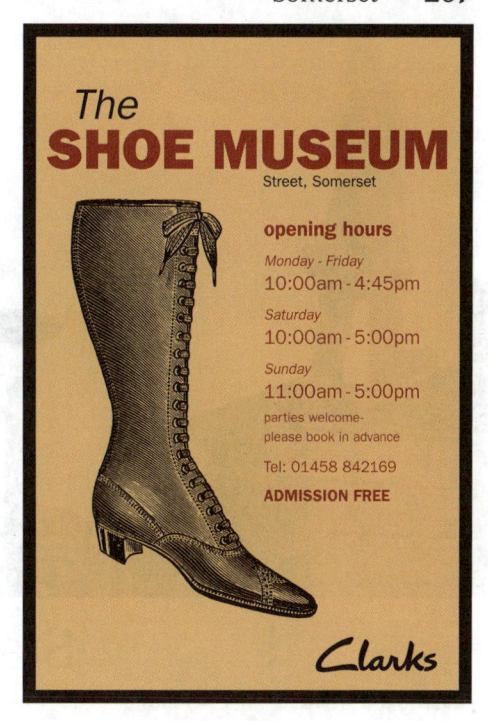

The SHOE MUSEUM
Street, Somerset

opening hours

Monday - Friday
10:00am - 4:45pm

Saturday
10:00am - 5:00pm

Sunday
11:00am - 5:00pm

parties welcome-
please book in advance

Tel: 01458 842169

ADMISSION FREE

Clarks

Clara's Cottage, a Westonian home of the 1900s with period kitchen, parlour, bedroom and back yard.
Times: Open all year: Mon-Sat 10-4.30, (Closed 25-26 Dec & 1 Jan). **Fee:** £3.50 (ch £1.50, pen £2.50). Family ticket (2 adults & 3 ch or 1 adult & 4 ch) £8. **Facilities:** P (800 yds) (some disabled parking outside museum) 🍴 & toilets for disabled shop garden centre ✗ (ex guide dogs) 🛍

🏛 WOOKEY HOLE   Map 03 ST54
WOOKEY HOLE CAVES & PAPERMILL
BA5 1BB (M5 junct 22 follow signs via A38 & A371, A39 to Wells then 2m to Wookey Hole)
☎ 01749 672243   📠 01749 677749
e-mail: witch@wookey.co.uk

A 40-minute guided tour leads visitors through this amazing complex of caves, with stalagmites, stalactites and other interesting geological features. There is also a Victorian papermill, with handmade papermaking and an old penny pier with mirror maze and penny arcade.
Times: Open all year, Mar-Oct 10-5; Nov-Feb 10.30-4.30. (Closed 16-28 Dec). **Fee:** * £8 (ch £5) **Facilities:** P ✗ licensed & (Papermill only) toilets for disabled shop ✗ (ex guide dogs) 🛍

🏛 YEOVILTON   Map 03 ST52
FLEET AIR ARM MUSEUM
Royal Naval Air Station BA22 8HT (on B3151)
☎ 01935 840565   📠 01935 842630
e-mail: info@fleetairarm.com
Times: Open all year, daily (ex 24-26 Dec) 10-5.30 (4.30 Nov-Mar). **Facilities:** P 🍴 ✗ licensed & (wheelchairs available) toilets for disabled shop ✗ (ex guide dogs) Details not confirmed for 2003 🛍

Staffordshire

For many, the main attractions of Staffordshire are the rollercoaster entertainment of Alton Towers or the precision craftsmanship of the world-famous potteries of Stoke-on-Trent. Yet the county also has some beautiful countryside and historic sites.

Part of the Peak District National Park – the first in Britain – forms the top right-hand corner of the county, and contains landscape ideal for hiking or pony trekking, as well as more adventurous pastimes such as rock climbing, hang-gliding, potholing, mountain biking, windsurfing, kayaking, abseiling and orienteering.

Toward the south lies Cannock Chase, 30,000 acres of forest and heathland that was once a royal hunting preserve, and where a large herd of fallow deer still run free. The Chase is also home to cemeteries of fallen servicemen, including all the German servicemen (nearly 5,000) Germans who died in Britain during two World Wars.

The Vale of Trent is known for its gentle beauty, and provides a welcome contrast to the craggy splendour of the moorland. Miles of rural canals (more than in any other county) are also a welcoming sight, now very popular with holidaymakers hiring boats.

Staffordshire has many historic attractions, including Lichfield's three-spired cathedral which contains the 8th-century Gospels of St Chad. The town was also the birthplace of Dr Samuel Johnson, who was born in a bookshop, and each year there are celebrations to commemorate the man who gave us the first Dictionary of the English Language.

Burton-upon-Trent is the 'Brewing Capital of England', and the Bass Museum Visitors' Centre will surely provide a certain something to banish the thirst.

EVENTS & FESTIVALS

June
1st Midland Counties Show, Uttoxeter Racecourse, Wood Lane, Uttoxeter (provisional)
20th-22nd Lichfield Folk Festival (various venues)
tbc Staffordshire County Show, County Showground
tbc World Toe Wrestling Championships, Ye Olde Royal Oak, Wetton

July
3rd-13th Lichfield International Arts Festival (various venues)
10th-13th Lichfield Free Festival in the Park
26th-29th Lichfield Real Ale, Jazz & Blues Festival
tbc Back to the Roots Folk & Blues Festival, Stafford Castle, Newport Road, Stafford
tbc Staffordshire Bull Terrier Show, Staffordshire County Showground
tbc Stafford Festival, Stafford

August
tbc Victorian Street Market & Circus, Shugborough Estate

September
8th Abbots Bromley Horn Dance (throughout village)
tbc National Chrysanthemum Show, Staffordshire County Showground

Top: Sir Henry Doulton, Burslem

Staffordshire

ALTON
ALTON TOWERS Map 07 SK04
ST10 4DB (signposted from M1 junct 23A, M6 junct 15, M1 junct 28 or M6 junct 16)
☎ 08705 204060   📠 01538 704097
e-mail: info@alton-towers.com

Alton Towers offers rides, shows and attractions to suit every member of the family. There are enchanting children's areas and the theme park has more thrill rides than any other in Europe. The Alton Towers Hotel displays a wonderful array of artefacts and memorabilia from a bygone age. On top of all this, there are 200 acres of landscaped gardens and the majestic ruins of the Towers themselves.
Times: Open 16 Mar-3 Nov, daily 9.30-5/7 depending on season.
Fee: * £18.50 (ch £15.50, under 4's free); Please telephone for price confirmation **Facilities:** 🅿 (charged) 🍴 ✕ licensed ♿ (disabled guest guide books) toilets for disabled shop ✕ (ex guide dogs) 🎁

BIDDULPH
BIDDULPH GRANGE GARDEN Map 07 SJ85
Grange Rd ST8 7SD (off A527, 0.5m N of Biddulph)
☎ 01782 517999   📠 01782 510624
e-mail: mbgwxm@smtp.ntrust.org.uk

This exciting and rare survival of a high Victorian garden has undergone extensive restoration. Conceived by James Bateman, the 15 acres are divided into a number of smaller gardens which were designed to house specimens from his extensive plant collection.
Times: Open mid Mar-Oct, Wed-Fri 12-5.30. Sat-Sun & BH Mon 11-5.30 (last admission 5.30 or dusk if earlier); early Nov-mid Dec, Sat-Sun 12-4 or dusk. **Fee:** * Mar-Oct; £4.50 (ch £2.40). Family ticket £11.50. Nov-Dec free **Facilities:** 🅿 🍴 (not suitable for people with mobility problems) shop ✕ (ex guide dogs) 🎁

BURTON-UPON-TRENT Map 08 SK22
THE BASS MUSEUM
PO Box 220, Horninglow St DE14 1YQ (from N junct 28 M1, A38, A511; from S junct 24 A564, A38)
☎ 01283 511000   📠 01283 513613   **2 for 1**
e-mail: enquiries@bass-museum.com

This museum is housed in the original Engineers Dept and Joiners shop, and was opened in 1977, the bi-centenary of the founding of the Bass brewery. Visitors can explore the history of brewing through a wide range of visual and interactive displays, including a state of the art virtual reality model allowing visitors to ask questions to historical figures from Burton, and take a trip around town. Visit the famous Bass Shire horse team.
Times: Open all year, Mon-Fri 10-5, Sat & Sun 11-5. Last admission 4pm. (Closed 25-26 Dec & 1 Jan). **Fee:** £5.50 (ch £3, pen £4). Family ticket £15. Brewery tours by arrangement only, at extra charge (inc free glass of beer/lager/soft drink) **Facilities:** 🅿 ✕ licensed ♿ (lift to all floors) toilets for disabled shop ✕ (ex guide dogs) 🎁

CHEDDLETON
CHEDDLETON FLINT MILL Map 07 SJ95
Beside Caldon Canal, Leek Rd ST13 7HL (3m S of Leek on A520)
☎ 01782 502907

Two water mills complete with wheels are preserved here, and both are in running order. The 17th-century south mill was used to grind corn, while the north mill was built to grind flint for the pottery industry. The restored buildings have displays on aspects of the pottery industry. Exhibits include examples of motive power, such as a Robey steam engine, and of transport, such as the restored 70ft horse-drawn narrow boat 'Vienna'. There is a learning room suitable for school and adult parties.
Times: Open all year, Sat & Sun 2-5, Mon-Fri 10-5 (on most days).
Fee: Free. **Facilities:** 🅿 ♿

CHURNET VALLEY RAILWAY
The Station
☎ 01538 360522   📠 01538 361848
e-mail: mgt@cheddcur.freeserve.co.uk

The Churnet Valley Railway goes through some lovely countryside, from Leekbrook Junction to Froghall passing through Cheddleton, with its Victorian station and historic flint mill, and Consall, with its nature reserve. Special events throughout the year include a day out with Thomas the Tank, the Ghost Train, steam and canal trips, and the Wizard's Express.
Times: Open every Sun Etr-end Sep, Sat Jul-Aug and Wed in Aug
Fee: * Return ticket £7 (ch £4, pen £6) **Facilities:** 🅿 🍴 ♿ ramps shop 🎁

HALFPENNY GREEN Map 07 SO89
HALFPENNY GREEN VINEYARDS
DY7 5EP (0.5m off B4176 Dudley to Telford road)
☎ 01384 221122   📠 01384 221101
e-mail: enquiries@halfpenny-green-vineyards.co.uk

Using German, French and hybrid varieties that can prosper even in the poorest British summer, this vineyard offers 'The complete English wine experience.' This includes a self-guided vineyard trail as well as

continued

guided tours, wine-tasting, a craft centre and a visitor centre. Visitors can purchase wines with personalised labels for special occasions. Coarse fishing is also available.
Times: Open all year, daily 10.30-5. **Fee:** Free. **Facilities:** P 🍽 ♿ toilets for disabled shop ✕ (ex guide dogs) 🏴

🏛 HIMLEY   Map 07 SO89
HIMLEY HALL & PARK
DY3 4DF (off A449, on B4176)
☎ 01902 324093 & 326665 📠 01902 894163
e-mail: himley.pls@mbc.dudley.gov.uk

The extensive parkland offers a range of attractions, including a 9-hole golf course and coarse fishing. The hall is open to the public when exhibitions are taking place. Permanent orienteering course (a charge is made for the maps). Guided tours at the hall available by prior arrangement. The Hall is available for private hire. There are also a large variety of outdoor events and concerts.
Times: Open Hall: Apr-mid Sep, 2-5. Closed Mon ex BH. Park open all year. **Fee:** Free. **Facilities:** P (charged) 🍽 ♿ toilets for disabled ✕ (ex guide dogs & in park)

🏛 LICHFIELD   Map 07 SK10
ERASMUS DARWIN CENTRE
Beacon St WS13 7AD (signposted to Lichfield Cathedral. Access by foot through the cathedral close)
☎ 01543 306260 📠 01543 306261
e-mail: erasmus.d@virgin.net

The Centre is dedicated to Erasmus Darwin, Charles Darwin's grandfather, a talented doctor, inventor, philosopher and poet, who resided in Lichfield for more than 20 years. It is contained in a beautiful 18th-century house complete with a delightful period garden. Period rooms, audio-visual and interactive displays re-create the story of Erasmus' life, ideas and inventions.
Times: Open Thu-Sat 10-4.30, Sun & BH Mon noon-4.30. Last admission 3.45. (Closed Good Fri, Xmas & New Year) **Fee:** * £2.50 (concessions £2). Family ticket (2 adults & 2 children) £6. **Facilities:** P (200mtrs) ♿ toilets for disabled shop ✕ (ex guide dogs)

LICHFIELD CATHEDRAL
WS13 7LD (signposted from all major roads and within city)
☎ 01543 306240 & 306100 📠 01543 306109
e-mail: enquiries@lichfield-cathedral.org

The Cathedral's three spires, known as the Ladies of the Vale, dominate the landscape. The first cathedral here was founded in 700AD to house the shrine of St Chad. The present building, with its elaborate carvings, has been much restored since it was attacked during the Civil War. Among its treasures is an 8th-century illuminated manuscript, the Lichfield Gospels. Many musical events take place here.
Times: Open daily 7.45-6.30. **Fee:** Suggested donation of £3 for each adult visitor. **Facilities:** P (200mtrs) (no parking ex disabled in close) 🍽 ✕ licensed ♿ (Touch & hearing centre for blind) toilets for disabled shop ✕ (ex guide/hearing dogs)

LICHFIELD HERITAGE CENTRE
Market Square WS13 6LG
☎ 01543 256611 📠 01543 414749
Times: Open all year, daily 10-5. Last admission 4.14pm. (Closed Xmas & New Year) **Facilities:** P (200yds) 🍽 ♿ (lift) toilets for disabled shop ✕ (ex guide dogs) *Details not confirmed for 2003* 🏴

SAMUEL JOHNSON BIRTHPLACE MUSEUM
Breadmarket St WS13 6LG (in city centre market place)
☎ 01543 264972 📠 01543 414779
e-mail: sjmuseum@lichfield.gov.uk

Dr Samuel Johnson, author of the famous English dictionary 1755 lexicographer, poet, critic, biographer & personality. One of England's greatest writers, Dr Johnson was born in this house in 1709. The birthplace now houses a museum dedicated to his extraordinary life, work and personality. Five floors of exhibits featuring period room settings, introductory video and personal items owned by Johnson, his family and his famous friends.
Times: Open daily Apr-Sep 10.30-4.30; Oct-Mar 12-4.30; last admission 4pm **Fee:** £2.20 (ch & pen £1.30). Joint ticket with Lichfield Heritage Centre £4 (ch & pen £3). Family ticket £5.80. **Facilities:** P (500yds) (large print text literature) shop ✕ (ex guide dogs/in shop)

🏛 MOSELEY   Map 07 SJ90
MOSELEY OLD HALL
V10 7HY (4m N of Wolverhampton, off A460)
☎ 01902 782808 📠 01902 782808   **2 for 1**
e-mail: mmodxl@smtp.ntrust.org.uk

Charles II sheltered in Moseley Old Hall after the Battle of Worcester in 1651. There are numerous pictures and other reminders of the king. The house itself is an Elizabethan timber-framed building which was encased in brick in the 19th century. The small garden has a nut walk, period herbs and plants, and a formal knot

continued

garden. For details of special events please send a 9" x 4" envelope.
Times: Open 23 Mar-15 Dec; Mar-Nov Wed, Sat-Sun, BH Mon and Tue 1-5 (BH 11-5). Nov & Dec: Sun 1-4 **Fee:** £4.30 (ch £2.15). Family ticket £10.75. Party 15+ £3.65. **Facilities:** P ⬛ ✕ ♿ (braille & large print, 1 wheelchair, thick handled cutlery) toilets for disabled shop 🐕 (ex guide dogs) 🍴 ☕

SHUGBOROUGH   Map 07 SJ92
SHUGBOROUGH ESTATE
ST17 OXB (6m E of Stafford off A513, signposted from M6 junct 13)
☎ 01889 881388 ✉ 01889 881323
e-mail: promotions@staffordshire.gov.uk
Times: Open 25 Mar-1 Oct, daily (ex Mon, but open BH Mon) 11-5. Sun only during Oct. Site open all year to pre-booked parties.
Facilities: P (charged) ⬛ ✕ licensed ♿ (step climber for wheelchairs, 2 Batricars) toilets for disabled shop 🐕 (ex guide dogs & in parkland) 🍴 *Details not confirmed for 2003* ☕

STAFFORD   Map 07 SJ92
SHIRE HALL GALLERY
Market Square ST16 2LD (M6 junct 13 or 14, follow signs to town centre & Gallery is signed from there)
☎ 01785 278345 ✉ 01785 278327
e-mail: shirehallgallery@staffordshire.gov.uk
Times: Open all year, Mon & Fri 9.30-6, Tue-Thu 9.30-5, Sat 10-5. Closed BH. **Facilities:** P (200yds) ⬛ ♿ (minicom telephone & hearing loop) toilets for disabled shop 🐕 (ex guide dogs) *Details not confirmed for 2003* ☕

STOKE-ON-TRENT   Map 07 SJ84
CERAMICA
Wedgewood Place, Burslem ST6 3DS (M6 junct 15/16 take A500 leave at B5051 Burslem. Ceramica in centre of Burslem)
☎ 01782 832001 ✉ 01782 823300
Times: Please contact for dates & times. **Facilities:** P (charged) ♿ toilets for disabled shop 🐕 (ex guide dogs) *Details not confirmed for 2003* ☕

ETRURIA INDUSTRIAL MUSEUM
Lower Bedford St, Etruria ST4 7AF (M6 junct 16, A500 onto Stoke Rd (A5006))
☎ 01782 233144 ✉ 01782 233145
Times: Open all year, Wed-Sun 10-4. (Closed Xmas & New Year).
Facilities: P ⬛ ♿ toilets for disabled shop 🐕 (ex guide dogs) *Details not confirmed for 2003*

GLADSTONE WORKING POTTERY MUSEUM
Uttoxeter Rd, Longton ST3 1PQ (M6 junct 15, follow A500 to A50 then follow brown heritage signs)
☎ 01782 319232 ✉ 01782 598640
e-mail: gladstone@stoke.gov.uk

Located at the heart of the Potteries, Gladstone Pottery Museum is the last remaining Victorian Pottery industry. Whilst touring the original factory building discover what it was like for the men, woman and children to live and work during the era of the coal firing bottle ovens. In original workshops working potters can be found demonstrating traditional pottery

Staffordshire   *211*

skills. There are also lots of opportunities for you to have a go at pottery making, throw your own pot on the potters wheel, make china flowers and decorate pottery items to take home. Also explore 'Flushed with Pride' and The Tile Gallery
Times: Open all year, daily 10-5 (last admission 4pm). Limited opening Xmas & New Year. **Fee:** * £4.95 (ch £3.50, students & pen £3.95). Family ticket £14 (2ad+2ch 4-16yrs) **Facilities:** P ⬛ ✕ licensed ♿ special potters wheel for wheelchair users to experiment on toilets for disabled shop 🐕 (ex guide dogs) ☕

ROYAL DOULTON VISITOR CENTRE
Nile St, Burslem ST6 2AJ (M6 junct 15 from S or 16 from N. Join A500 leaving at exit for Tunstall A527, follow tourist signs)
☎ 01782 292434 ✉ 01782 292324   **2 for 1**
e-mail: visitor@royal-doulton.com

The centre has extensive displays of both current products and out of production pieces together with ranges from our museum tracing the history of Royal Doulton. Live demonstrations showing the skill and craftsmanship in the creation and hand painting of figurines. Behind the scenes look on the working factory weekdays only, prior booking advised)
Times: Open all year, Mon-Sat 9.30-5, Sun 10.30-4.30. Factory tours by advance booking Mon-Fri 10.30-2 (1.30 Fri). (Closed Xmas week). No tours during factory holidays. **Fee:** * Visitor Centre only £3 (concessions £2.25); Factory Tour & Visitor Centre £6.50 (concessions £5). Parties 12+. Visitor centre £2. Factory tour and visitor centre £4.50. **Facilities:** P ⬛ ✕ licensed ♿ (only Visitor Centre accessible) toilets for disabled shop 🐕 (ex guide dogs) ☕

SPODE
Church St ST4 1BX (M6 junct 15, then A500 to Stoke. Ignore city centre signs. Turn left at Stoke roundabout, follow brown tourist signs)
☎ 01782 744011 ✉ 01782 744012
e-mail: visitorcentre@spode.co.uk
Times: Visitor Centre, Museum, Factory Shops, concessions & licensed restaurant. Mon-Sat 9-5, Sun 10-4. Factory Tours by prior appointment weekdays only, not available during factory closures-please ring for details. **Facilities:** P (charged) ✕ licensed ♿ (ramps) toilets for disabled shop 🐕 (ex guide dogs) *Details not confirmed for 2003* ☕

THE POTTERIES MUSEUM & ART GALLERY
Bethesda St, Hanley ST1 3DW (M6 junct 15/16 take A500 to Stoke-on-Trent. Follow signs for city centre (Hanley), cultural quarters & the Potteries museum)
☎ 01782 232323 ✉ 01782 232500
e-mail: museums@stoke.gov.uk

The history of the Potteries under one roof, including a dazzling display of the world's finest collection of Staffordshire ceramics. Other displays introduce natural, local and archaeological history from in and around The Potteries, and a Mark 16 Spitfire

continued

Staffordshire

commemorating its locally born designer - Reginald Mitchell.

The Potteries Museum & Art Gallery

Times: Open Mar-Oct Mon-Sat 10-5 Sun 2-5; Nov-Feb Mon-Sat 10-4 Sun 1-4; closed 25 Dec-1Jan **Fee:** Free. **Facilities:** P (500mtrs) ⬛ & (lift, induction loop, 2 wheelchairs available) toilets for disabled shop ✈ (ex guide/helping dogs) ⬛

Wedgwood Visitor Centre
Barlaston ST12 9ES (5m S)
☎ 01782 204141 & 204218   📠 01782 204402
Times: Open all year, Mon-Fri 9-5, Sat & Sun 10-5; (Closed Xmas & 1 Jan). **Facilities:** P ✖ licensed & toilets for disabled shop ✈ *Details not confirmed for 2003*

🏛 TAMWORTH   Map 07 SK20
Drayton Manor Theme Park & Zoo
B78 3TW (M42, junct 9, follow brown tourist board signs on A4091)
☎ 01827 287979   📠 01827 288916
e-mail: info@draytonmanor.co.uk

A popular family theme park with over 100 rides set in 250 acres of parkland and lakes. There are world-class rides like 'Maelstrom', 'Apocalypse' - the world's first stand-up tower drop, 'Shockwave' - Europe's only stand-up rollercoaster and 'Stormforce 10' (bring your waterproofs!). There are also many children's rides, plus a zoo and exotic creature reserve and 'Dinosaurland'.
Times: Park open end Mar-end Oct, 9-6 daily, Zoo open 10-5, 6 or 7, Rides open 10.30-5, 6, & 7 (depending on season). **Fee:** Please telephone for admission prices. **Facilities:** P ⬛ ✖ licensed (ramps or lifts to most rides, some rides limited access) shop garden centre ✈ (ex in park) ⬛

Tamworth Castle
The Holloway, Ladybank B79 7NA (from M42 junct 10 & M6 junct 12, access via A5)
☎ 01827 709629 & 709626   📠 01827 709630
e-mail: heritage@tamworth.gov.uk

The dramatic Norman motte and bailey castle was once the home of England's Royal Champions and today is (reputedly) haunted by two lady ghosts. Quizzes, dressing-up and brass-rubbing make it a great family destination.
Times: Open Tue-Sun 12-5.15. Last admission 4.30. Telephone to confirm opening times before visiting. **Fee:** * £4.30 (ch £2.20). Family £11.90. Prices subject to change. **Facilities:** P (100yds & 400yds) & (one wheelchair for use inside the castle) shop ✈ (ex guide dogs & hearing dogs)

🏛 WALL   Map 07 SK10
Wall Roman Site
Watling St WS15 0AW (off A5)
☎ 01543 480768

Wall was originally the Roman fort of Letocetum, standing at the crossroads of Watling Street and Rykneild Street. It was an important military base from about AD50. Excavations have revealed the most complete bath house ever found in Britain.
Times: Open all year, 29 Mar-Sep, daily 10-6 **Fee:** * £2.50 (ch 5-15 £1.30, under 5's free, concessions £1.90). **Facilities:** ✈ ♿ ⬛

🏛 WESTON PARK   Map 07 SJ81
Weston Park
TF11 8LE (on A5 at Weston-under-Lizard, 3m off M54 junct 3 and 8m off M6 junct 12)
☎ 01952 852100   📠 01952 850430
e-mail: enquiries@weston-park.com

Built in 1671, this fine mansion stands in elegant gardens and a vast park designed by 'Capability' Brown. Three lakes, a miniature railway, and a woodland adventure playground are to be found in the grounds, and in the house itself there is a magnificent collection of pictures, furniture and tapestries. There is also a miniature railway, animal centre and deer park.
Times: Open wknds until Jul then daily until 8 Sep **Fee:** Park & Gardens £2.50 (ch £1.50, pen £2). House, £2 (ch £1, pen £1.50). Family ticket (inc house) £7.50 (up to 2ad+3ch). **Facilities:** P ⬛ ✖ licensed & (disabled route, access to restaurant & shop) toilets for disabled shop ⬛

Staffordshire   *213*

WHITTINGTON   Map 07 SK10
STAFFORDSHIRE REGIMENT MUSEUM, WHITTINGTON BARRACKS
WS14 9PY (on A51 between Lichfield/Tamworth)
☎ 0121 311 3240/3229   0121 311 3205
Times: Open all year, Tue-Fri 10-4.30 (last admission 4); also Apr-Oct wknds and BH 1-4.30. (Closed Xmas-New Year). Parties at other times by arrangement. **Facilities:** P & (ramps) toilets for disabled shop ✈ (outside only ex guide dogs) *Details not confirmed for 2003*

WILLOUGHBRIDGE   Map 07 SJ74
THE DOROTHY CLIVE GARDEN
TF9 4EU (on A51 between Nantwich & Stone)
☎ 01630 647237   01630 647902
Times: Open Apr-Oct, daily 10-5.30. **Facilities:** P ⌧ & (wheelchairs for use, special route) toilets for disabled *Details not confirmed for 2003*

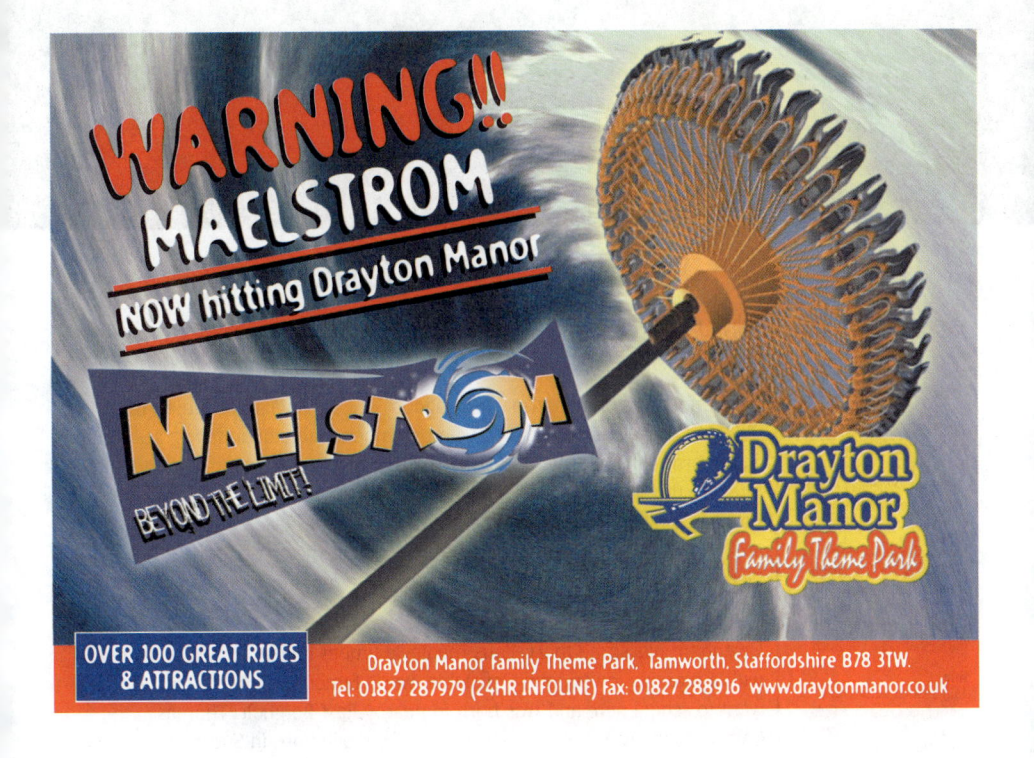

Suffolk

Britain's most easterly county has plenty to offer to visitors, aside from the enviable fact that it has the driest regional climate in England.

EVENTS & FESTIVALS

May
9th-25th Bury St Edmunds Festival, arts festival (various venues)
11th South Suffolk Show, Point-to-Point Course, Ampton Park, Ingham
24th-25th Mildenhall Air Fete, US Airforce, Mildenhall

June
6th-22nd Aldeburgh Festival of Music & the Arts, Snape Maltings Concert Hall, Snape
28th-29th Suffolk Show, Suffolk Showground, Bucklesham Road, Ipswich

July
13th Ipswich Music Day
tbc Suffolk Coast Bike Ride (in aid of Anthony Nolan Bone Marrow Trust)

August
24th-25th Eye Show, Eye Show Ground, Eye

November
tbc November Big Night Out, fireworks, bonfire & fair, Melford Hall Park, Long Melford

Suffolk was once part of the kingdom of East Anglia. Back then the kingdom was protected by almost impenetrable boundaries; sea to the north and east, the undrained Fens to the west, and a barrier of oak forest to the south. However, these natural defences didn't stop invasion from Romans, Angles, Vikings, and Saxons, all of whom have left their mark on the area. In later years Icelandic fisherfolk settled in the coastal towns, and Flemish weavers helped the wool towns boom and also took part in the brewing industry.

Lavenham has some marvellous medieval timber houses as well as a church with a massive tower. John Constable, world-famous painter of *The Haywain*, went to school here and was born in nearby East Bergholt. Thomas Gainsborough was another artistic son of Suffolk, born in Sudbury, where a statue of him stands in the village square. Sudbury also features as 'Eatanswill' in Dickens' *The Pickwick Papers*.

Ipswich is said to be the oldest continuously-inhabited Anglo-Saxon town in England, and has some very attractive municipal parks. The dock area has been massively redeveloped after the decline of the town as a major port.

Known as the Sunrise Coast, the resorts of Lowestoft, Kessingland and Southwold have won awards for the cleanliness and safety of their beaches. Lowestoft is Britain's most easterly town and sits between sandy beaches on one side and beautiful broadland on the other. Sparrow's Nest Park is located just below the lighthouse and the town also features a maritime museum, a War Memorial Museum, which contains displays on the WWII bombing of the town, and the Royal Naval Patrol Museum.

Top: Framlingham Castle

Suffolk   **215**

🏛 BUNGAY   Map 05 TM38
OTTER TRUST
Earsham NR35 2AF (off A143, 1m W of Bungay)
☎ 01986 893470   📠 01986 892461
Times: Open Apr (or Good Fri if earlier)-Oct, daily 10.30-6. **Facilities:**
🅿 ♿ ♿ toilets for disabled shop ✖ (ex guide dogs) *Details not confirmed for 2003*

🏛 BURY ST EDMUNDS   Map 05 TL86
MANOR HOUSE MUSEUM
Honey Hill IP33 1HF (Edge of town centre, follow signs to Police Station, opposite is museum car park)
☎ 01284 757072   `2 for 1`
📠 01284 747231
e-mail: stedmundsbury@burybo.stedbc.gov.uk

The Georgian mansion specialises in costumes, textiles, horology and fine and decorative art from the 17th to the 20th centuries. There is a temporary exhibition gallery as well as workshops in textiles and horology. Interactive horological room and feely pictures and boxes.
Times: Open all year Wed-Sun, 11-4. Other times by arrangement.
Fee: £2.50 (ch & concessions £2). **Facilities:** 🅿 (charged) 🍴 ✖ licensed ♿ (Special tours can be arranged for disabled groups) toilets for disabled shop ✖ (ex guide dogs) 🎒 🛒

MOYSE'S HALL MUSEUM
Cornhill IP33 1DX (Take Bury central exit from A14, follow signs for town centre, museum in town centre)
☎ 01284 757488   `2 for 1`
📠 01284 757079
e-mail: maggie.goodger@stedsbc/gov.uk

Moyse's Hall is a 12th-century Norman house built of flint and stone which now serves as a local history museum, and among the fascinating exhibits are memorabilia of the notorious William Corder "Murder in the Red Barn".
Times: Open all year, Mon-Fri 10.30-4.30, Sat & Sun 11-4. (Closed 25-26 Dec & Good Fri) **Fee:** * £2.50 (ch & concessions £1.80). Guided tour £1; free for residents of St Edmondsbury **Facilities:** 🅿 (200yds) ♿ stairlift, lift, hearing loop, braille pictures shop ✖ (ex guide dogs) 🛒

🏛 CAVENDISH   Map 05 TL84
THE SUE RYDER FOUNDATION MUSEUM
PO Box 5736 CO10 8RN (on A1092 Long Melford to Clare road)
☎ 01787 282591   📠 01787 280548
Times: Open all year, daily 10-5.30. (Closed 25 Dec). **Facilities:** 🅿 ✖ ♿ toilets for disabled shop ✖ *Details not confirmed for 2003*

🏛 EASTON   Map 05 TM25
EASTON FARM PARK
IP13 0EQ (signed from A12 at Wickam Market, and from A1120)
☎ 01728 746475   📠 01728 747861   `2 for 1`
e-mail: easton@eastonfarmpark.co.uk

Award-winning Farm Park on the banks of the River Deben. There are lots of breeds of farm animals, including Suffolk Punch horses, ponies, pigs, lambs, calves, goats, rabbits, guinea pigs & poultry. Chicks hatching and egg collecting daily. Free pat-a-pet & pony rides every day.
Times: Open Mar-end Sep, daily 10.30-6. Also open Feb & Oct half term hols. **Fee:** * £5 (ch under 3 free, ch 3-16 £3.50 pen £4.25). Party 20+ **Facilities:** 🅿 🍴 ♿ (special parking) toilets for disabled shop 🛒

🏛 EUSTON   Map 05 TL87
EUSTON HALL
IP24 2QP (on A1088, 3m S of Thetford)
☎ 01842 766366   📠 01842 766764
e-mail: lcampbell@euston-estate.co.uk

Home of the Duke and Duchess of Grafton, this 18th-century house is notable for its fine collection of pictures, by Stubbs, Lely, Van Dyck and other Masters. The grounds were laid out by John Evelyn, William Kent and 'Capability' Brown, and include a 17th-century church in the style of Wren and a river walk to the newly restored watermill.
Times: Open 6 Jun-26 Sep, Thu only. 30 Jun-1 Sep, Thu & Sun 2.30-5. **Fee:** * £4 (ch £2, pen £3). **Facilities:** 🅿 🍴 ♿ shop ✖ (guide dogs by permission)

🏛 FLIXTON   Map 05 TM38
NORFOLK & SUFFOLK AVIATION MUSEUM
Buckeroo Way, The Street NR35 1NZ (off A143, take B1062, 2m W of Bungay)
☎ 01986 896644
e-mail: nsam.flixton@virgin.net

Situated in the Waveney Valley, the museum has over 30 historic aircraft. There is also a Bloodhound surface-to-air missile, the 446th Bomb Group Museum, RAF Bomber Command Museum, the Royal Observer Corps Museum, RAF Air-Sea Rescue and Coastal Command and a souvenir shop. Among the displays are Decoy Sites and Wartime Deception, and Fallen Eagles - Wartime Luftwaffe Crashes.
Times: Open Apr-Oct, Sun-Thu 10-5 (last admission 4); Nov-Mar 10-4 (last admission 3) Tue, Wed, Sun. New Year closed 2 weeks either side. **Fee:** Free. **Facilities:** 🅿 🍴 ♿ (helper advised. ramps to all buildings) toilets for disabled shop ✖ (ex guide dogs)

🏛 FRAMLINGHAM   Map 05 TM26
FRAMLINGHAM CASTLE
IP13 9BP (on B1116)
☎ 01728 724189

Built by Hugh Bigod between 1177 and 1215, the castle has fine curtain walls, 13 towers and an array of Tudor chimneys. In the 17th century the castle was bequeathed to Pembroke College, Cambridge, which built almshouses inside the walls.
Times: Open all year, 29 Mar-Sep, daily 10-6 (5pm in Oct); Nov-28 Mar, daily 10-4. Closed 24-26 Dec & 1 Jan. **Fee:** * £3.90 (ch 5-15 £2, under 5's free, concessions £2.90). **Facilities:** 🅿 ♿ shop ✖ 🚻

Suffolk

🏛 HORRINGER   Map 05 TL86
ICKWORTH HOUSE, PARK & GARDENS
The Rotunda IP29 5QE (2.5m S of Bury St Edmunds, on A143)
☎ 01284 735270   📠 01284 735175
e-mail: ickworth@ntrust.org.uk

The eccentric Earl of Bristol created this equally eccentric house, begun in 1795, to display his collection of European art. The Georgian Silver Collection is considered the finest in private hands. 'Capability' Brown designed the parkland, and also featured are a deer enclosure, waymarked walks and an adventure playground.
Times: Open: House 24 Mar-28 Oct, Tue, Wed, Fri, wknds & BH Mons 1-5 (4.30 in Oct) last admission 4.30; Garden open daily 24 Mar-28 Oct 10-5. 29 Oct-Mar 10-4 wkdays; Park daily 7am-7pm. **Fee:** * House, Garden & Park £5.70 (National Trust members & ch under 5 free, ch £2.50) Garden & park £2.50 (ch 80p). Discount for pre-booked parties. **Facilities:** 🅿 ✘ licensed ♿ (braille guide batricars stairlift to shop & restaurant) toilets for disabled shop garden centre ✘ (ex guide dogs & in park) 🐕

🏛 IPSWICH   Map 05 TM14
CHRISTCHURCH MANSION
Soane St IP4 2BE (South side of Christchurch Park)
☎ 01473 253246 & 213761   📠 01473 210328
e-mail: mansion@ipswich.gov.uk

The house was built in 1548 on the site of an Augustinian priory. Set in a beautiful park, it displays period rooms and an art gallery which has changing exhibitions. The Suffolk Artists' Gallery has a collection of Constables and Gainsboroughs.
Times: Open all year, Tue-Sat 10-5 (dusk in winter), Sun 2.30-4.30 (dusk in winter). (Closed Good Fri & 24-26 Dec & 1-2 Jan). Open BH Mon. **Fee:** Free. **Facilities:** 🅿 ♿ (tape guide for partially sighted) shop ✘

IPSWICH MUSEUM
High St IP1 3QH (Follow tourist signs to Crown St car park. Museum 3 mins walk from here)
☎ 01473 433550   📠 01473 433558
e-mail: museum.service@ipswich.gov.uk

The Museum has sections on Victorian Natural History, Suffolk wildlife, Suffolk geology, Roman Suffolk, Anglo-Saxon Ipswich and Peoples of the World. There is also one of the best bird collections in the country.
Times: Open all year, Tue-Sat 10-5. (Closed Sun, BH's, 24-26 Dec & 1 Jan). **Fee:** Free. **Facilities:** 🅿 (3 min walk) ♿ (lift) toilets for disabled shop ✘ (ex guide dogs)

🏛 LAVENHAM   Map 05 TL94
LAVENHAM GUILDHALL
Market Place CO10 9QZ (Lavenham Market Place. A1141 & B1071)
☎ 01787 247646
e-mail: almjtg@smtp.ntrust.org.uk

The Guildhall of Corpus Christi is one of the finest timber framed buildings in Britain. It was built around 1530 by the prosperous Corpus Christi Guild, for religious rather than commercial reasons. The hall now houses a local history museum telling the story of Lavenham's 15th and 16th-century cloth-trade riches. Visitors can also see the walled garden with its 19th-century lock-up and mortuary.
Times: Open Mar & Nov, Sat/Sun 11-4; Apr, Wed-Sun 11-5; May-Oct daily 11-5. (Closed Good Fri but open BH Mon) **Fee:** £3 (accompanied ch free). Parties £2.50 each. School parties by arrangement 60p per ch. **Facilities:** 🅿 (adjacent) ☕ (shop & tea room accessible) shop ✘ (ex guide dogs) 🐕

🏛 LEISTON   Map 05 TM46
LEISTON ABBEY
(1m N off B1069)

For hundreds of years this 14th-century abbey was used as a farm and its church became a barn. A Georgian house, now used as a retreat house, was built into its fabric and remains of the choir, the church transepts and parts of the cloisters still stand.
Times: Open any reasonable time. **Fee:** Free. **Facilities:** 🅿 ♿ 🚻

LONG SHOP MUSEUM
Main St IP16 4ES (Turn off A12, follow B1119 from Saxmundham to Leiston. Museum is in the middle of town)
☎ 01728 832189   📠 01728 832189   `2 for 1`
e-mail: longshop@care4free.net

Discover the Magic of Steam through a visit to the world famous traction engine manufacturers. Trace the history of the factory and Richard Garrett engineering. See the traction engines and road rollers in the very place that they were built. Soak up the atmosphere of the Long Shop, built in 1852 as one of the first production line engineering halls in the world. An award-winning museum with three exhibition halls full of items from the glorious age of steam and covering 200 years of local, social and industrial history.
Times: Open Apr-Oct, Mon-Sat 10-5, Sun 11-5. **Fee:** * £3 (ch 75p, under 5's free, concessions £2.50) **Facilities:** 🅿 ♿ toilets for disabled shop ✘ (ex guide dogs)

🏛 LINDSEY   Map 05 TL94
ST JAMES'S CHAPEL
Rose Green

Built mainly in the 13th century, this small thatched, flint-and-stone chapel incorporates some earlier work.
Times: Open all year. **Fee:** Free. **Facilities:** ♿ 🚻

🏛 LONG MELFORD   Map 05 TL84
KENTWELL HALL
CO10 9BA (signposted off A134)
☎ 01787 310207   📠 01787 379318   `2 for 1`
e-mail: info@kentwell.co.uk

Kentwell Hall is a moated red brick Tudor manor with gardens, woodland walks and a rare breeds farm. The house and grounds are open to the public at certain

continued

Suffolk *217*

times of the year, and recreations of Tudor and 1940s life take place at weekends. Ring for details.
Times: Open: Gardens & Farm, Sun during Mar. House, Gardens & Farm: Apr-11 Jun, Sun only; Also 16-28 Apr, 30 May-2 Jun & 12 Jul-24 Sep daily. 27 Sep-29 Oct, Sun only. open 23-27 Oct daily. Historical re-creations on selected wknds & BH through the year. **Fee:** * Inclusive ticket £6.50 (ch £4.50, pen £5.50). Garden & Farm only £4.50 (ch £2.30, pen £3.20). Special prices apply for Re-Creations. **Facilities:** P 🍽 ♿ (wheelchair ramp & 2 wheelchairs for loan) toilets for disabled shop ✕ (ex guide dogs) 🚭

MELFORD HALL
CO10 9AA (off A134, 3m N of Sudbury, next to village green)
☎ 01787 880286
e-mail: amdklx@smtp.ntrust.org.uk

Queen Elizabeth I was a guest at this turreted, brick-built Tudor house in 1578. It features an 18th-century drawing room, a Regency library and a Victorian bedroom. There is also a large collection of Chinese porcelain, and a display on Beatrix Potter, who was related to the owners and often stayed here. The garden has a Tudor pavilion, which may have been built as a banqueting house.
Times: Open Etr wknd & Etr Mon; Apr & Oct wknds only; May-Sep, daily Wed-Sun (open BH Mon) 2-5.30. **Fee:** * £4.50 National Trust Members free **Facilities:** P ♿ (stairlift, braille/large print guides, ramps) toilets for disabled ✕ (ex guide dogs & dogs in park) 🐕

🏛 LOWESTOFT   Map 05 TM59
EAST ANGLIA TRANSPORT MUSEUM
Chapel Rd, Carlton Colville NR33 8BL (3m SW of Lowestoft, on B1384. Follow brown signs from A12 & A146))
☎ 01502 518459 📠 01502 584658
e-mail: enquiries@eatm.org.uk

A particular attraction of this museum is the reconstructed 1930's street scene which is used as a setting for working vehicles: visitors can ride by tram, trolley bus and narrow gauge railway. Other motor, steam and electrical vehicles are exhibited. There is also a woodland picnic area served by trams.
Times: Open Good Fri & Etr Sat 2-4, Etr Sun-Etr Mon 11-5. May-Sep, Sun & BH's 11-5; Wed & Sat 2-5 (last entry 1 hour before closing). **Fee:** £4.50 (ch 5-15 & pen £3). Price includes rides. Party. **Facilities:** P 🍽 ♿ toilets for disabled shop 🚭

MARITIME MUSEUM
Sparrow Nest Gardens, Whapload Rd NR32 1XG (on A12, 100mtrs N of Lowestoft Lighthouse, turn right down Ravine)
☎ 01502 561963 & 511260   **2 for 1**

Models of ancient and modern fishing and commercial boats, fishing gear and shipwrights' tools are among the exhibits. Exhibition of the evolution of lifeboats, a replica of the aft cabin of a steam drifter. There is also an art gallery.
Times: Open 18 Apr-5 Oct, daily, 10-5. **Fee:** 75p (ch, students 25p, pen 50p) **Facilities:** P ♿ shop ✕ (ex guide & small dogs)

NEW PLEASUREWOOD HILLS
Leisure Way, Corton NR32 5DZ (off A12 at Lowestoft)
☎ 01502 586000 (Admin) & 508200 (info)
📠 01502 567393
e-mail: info@pleasurewoodhills.co.uk

There are over 40 rides, shows and attractions at New Pleasurewood Hills, set in 50 acres of beautiful parkland. Old favourites such as the Tidal Wave Watercoaster and the Fairytale Fantasy Ride combine with more recent attractions such as Formula K Raceway Go-Karts, the new 100ft Drop Tower, the Crazy Coaster and the Double Decker Carousel.
Times: Open Apr-Oct & Xmas. Phone 01502 586000 for details. **Fee:** £13.50 over 1.25mtr, £11.50 under 1.25mtr, under 1mtr free, family (2ad+2ch) £48. Telephone 01502 586000 for admission prices. **Facilities:** P 🍽 ✕ licensed ♿ all shows accessible. Most ride operators are able to assist toilets for disabled shop ✕ (ex guide dogs) 🚭

🏛 NEWMARKET   Map 05 TL66
NATIONAL HORSERACING MUSEUM AND TOURS
99 High St CB8 8JL (In centre of Newmarket High St)
☎ 01638 667333 📠 01638 665600   **2 for 1**

A chance to meet the horses and stable staff at close quarters, watch the horses on the historic gallops and see them in the equine swimming pool. Retired jockeys will answer questions and let you ride the horse

continued

218 Suffolk

simulator at up to 40mph. Ring for details of special tours.

National Horseracing Museum & Tours

Times: Open 15 Apr-3 Nov, Tue-Sun (also BH Mons & Mon in Jul & Aug) 11-5. (10 on race days). **Fee:** £4.50 (ch £1.50, concessions £3.50). Family tickets (2 adults & 2 ch) £10. **Facilities:** P (300yds) (coach drop off in front of museum) 🍴 ✗ licensed ♿ (ramps) toilets for disabled shop ✗ (ex guide dogs) 🛍

ORFORD
Map 05 TM45
ORFORD CASTLE
IP12 2ND (on B1084)
☎ 01394 450472

Built by Henry II circa 1165, the castle's magnificent keep survives almost intact with three immense towers reaching to 90 feet. Inside there are many rooms to explore.
Times: Open all year, Apr-Sep, daily 10-6; (Oct 10-5); Nov-28 Mar, Wed-Sun, 10-1 & 2-4. Closed 24-26 Dec & 1 Jan. **Fee:** * £3.42 (ch 5-15 £1.60, under 5's free, concessions £2.40). **Facilities:** P ✗ ♿

SAXMUNDHAM
Map 05 TM36
BRUISYARD WINES & HERBS
Church Rd, Bruisyard IP17 2EF (4m W of Saxmundham bypass (A12))
☎ 01728 638281
📠 0870 136 3708
e-mail: ian@bruisyardwines.fsnet.co.uk

2 for 1

Well established vineyard with winery in traditional Suffolk farm buildings in the beautiful Alde Valley. Bruisyard Wines is the first producer of quality wine in East Anglia. Tranquil water and herb gardens, with peaceful wooded picnic area and children's play area. Sony Walkman tours and tastings. The Country Shop sells a range of international award-winning wines, and choice things to eat and drink. Large variety of interesting and unusual potted herbs and seeds for sale.
Times: Open 16 Jan-23 Dec, Tue-Sun & BHs. Summer 10.30-5, Winter 11-4. **Fee:** Free. **Facilities:** P 🍴 ♿ shop garden centre ✗ (ex in vineyard & guide dogs) 🚌 🛍

SAXTEAD GREEN
Map 05 TM26
SAXTEAD GREEN POST MILL
The Mill House IP13 9QQ (2.5m NW of Framlingham on A1120)
☎ 01728 685789

Dating from 1854, this is one of the finest examples of a traditional Suffolk post-mill. Machinery and millstones are in perfect order.
Times: Open 29 Mar-Sep daily 10-6 (Oct 10-5). Closed 1-2pm; Nov-28 Mar 10-1 & 2-4 Wed-Sun. **Fee:** * £2.30 (ch £1.20 pen £1.60). **Facilities:** (exterior only) ✗ ♿

STOWMARKET
Map 05 TM05
MUSEUM OF EAST ANGLIAN LIFE
IP14 1DL (in centre of Stowmarket opposite ASDA Supermarket & is signposted from A14 & B1115)
☎ 01449 612229   📠 01449 672307
e-mail: meal@meal.fsnet.co.uk

This 70-acre, all-weather museum is set in an attractive valley site. There are reconstructed buildings, including a water mill, a smithy and also a wind pump, and the Boby Building houses craft workshops. There are displays on Victorian domestic life, gypsies, farming and industry. These include working steam traction engines, the only surviving pair of Burrell ploughing engines of 1879, and a working Suffolk Punch horse. New: William Bone Building illustrating history of ransomes of Ipswich.
Times: Open Apr-Oct. **Fee:** * £5 (ch 4-16 £3.25, concessions £4.25). Family ticket £15. Party 10+. **Facilities:** P (adjacent) 🍴 ♿ (wheelchairs available, special vehicle facilities) toilets for disabled shop 🛍

SUDBURY
Map 05 TL84
GAINSBOROUGH'S HOUSE
46 Gainsborough St CO10 2EU (in the centre of Sudbury. Follow pedestrian signs from town centre car parks or from train stn)
☎ 01787 372958   📠 01787 376991
e-mail: mail@gainsborough.org

2 for 1

The birthplace of Thomas Gainsborough RA (1727-88). The Georgian-fronted town house, with an attractive walled garden, displays more of the artist's work than any other gallery, together with 18th-century furniture and memorabilia. There's a varied programme of exhibitions throughout the year including fine art, craft, photography, printmaking and sculpture.
Times: Open all year - House Tue-Sat 10-5, Sun & BH Mons 2-5; (4pm Nov-Mar). (Closed Good Fri & Xmas-New Year). **Fee:** £3 (ch, students & disabled £1.50, pen £2.50). Party rates available. **Facilities:** P (300 yds) (no parking in Gainsborough Street) ♿ toilets for disabled shop ✗ (ex guide dogs) 🛍

SUFFOLK WILDLIFE PARK Map 05 TM58
Suffolk Wildlife Park
Kessingland NR33 7TF (Just S of Lowestoft off A12)
☎ 01502 740291   📠 01502 741104

Enjoy the atmosphere and excitement of your very own African Adventure at Suffolk Wildlife Park. Spend the whole day exploring 100 acres of dramatic coastal parkland, filled with animals from the African continent and around the world. Guide your expedition to giraffe, lion, buffalo, hyena and many more exciting animals. Capture the true splendour and atmosphere of the park by going walkabout amongst the large open paddocks or join the children's favourite - the Safari Roadtrain with its live commentary of fascinating animal facts.
Times: Open all year, daily from 10am. (Closed 25-26 Dec). Closes at 4pm Jan-15 Mar & Nov-Dec; 5pm 16 Mar-Jun & Oct; 5.30pm Jul-Sep.
Fee: * £5.95-£7.95 (ch 3-14 £4.50-£5.95). **Facilities:** 🅿 🍴 ✕ ♿ (wheelchairs available for hire) toilets for disabled shop 🐕 🍴

WESTLETON Map 05 TM46
RSPB Nature Reserve Minsmere
IP17 3BY (signposted from A12 & Westleton)
☎ 01728 648281   📠 01728 648770
e-mail: minsmere@rspb.org.uk

One of the RSPB's most popular sites. It is famous for its nesting avocets, marsh harriers and bitterns. Ideal for families and birdwatchers alike, there are countryside walks of varying lengths and eight hides. The Visitor Centre provides information about the reserve, as well as a shop and tearoom. Education programmes for school groups are also available.
Times: Open Wed-Mon 9am-9pm (or sunset if earlier). Visitor centre & shop Feb-Oct 9-5, Nov-Jan 9-4. Closed Xmas & Boxing day. **Fee:** * £5 (ch £1.50, concessions £3). Family ticket £10. RSPB members free.
Facilities: 🅿 🍴 ♿ (ramps, viewing areas, wheelchair) toilets for disabled shop 🐕 (ex guide dogs) 🍴

WEST STOW Map 05 TL87
West Stow Anglo Saxon Village
West Stow Country Park, Icklingham Rd IP28 6HG (off A1101, follow brown heritage signs. 6m NW of Bury St Edmunds)
☎ 01284 728718   📠 01284 728277   `2 for 1`
e-mail: weststow@stedsbc.gov.uk

The village is a reconstruction of a pagan Anglo-Saxon settlement dated 420-650 AD. Seven buildings have been reconstructed on the site of the excavated settlement. There is a visitors' centre and a children's play area. A new Anglo-Saxon centre houses the original objects found on the site. The village is located in the West Stow Country Park. The park is 125 acres with river, lake, woodland and heath and has many trails and paths.
Times: Open all year, daily 10-5. Last entry 4pm (3.30 in Winter) **Fee:** £5 (ch £4). Family ticket £15. (prices subject to changes for special events) **Facilities:** 🅿 🍴 ♿ (ramps) toilets for disabled shop 🐕 (ex guide dogs) 🍴

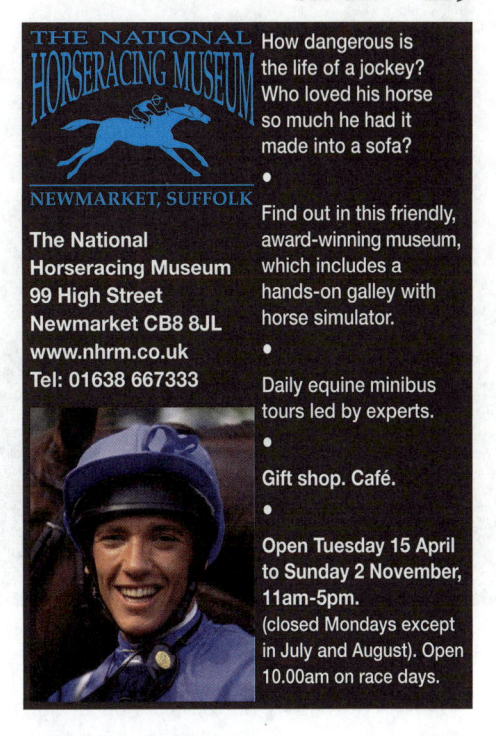

THE NATIONAL HORSERACING MUSEUM
NEWMARKET, SUFFOLK

The National Horseracing Museum
99 High Street
Newmarket CB8 8JL
www.nhrm.co.uk
Tel: 01638 667333

How dangerous is the life of a jockey? Who loved his horse so much he had it made into a sofa?

• Find out in this friendly, award-winning museum, which includes a hands-on galley with horse simulator.

• Daily equine minibus tours led by experts.

• Gift shop. Café.

Open Tuesday 15 April to Sunday 2 November, 11am-5pm.
(closed Mondays except in July and August). Open 10.00am on race days.

WOODBRIDGE Map 05 TM24
Woodbridge Tide Mill
Tide Mill Way IP12 4SR (follow signs for Woodbridge off A12, 7m E of Ipswich - Tide Mill is on riverside)
☎ 01473 626618
e-mail: geoffgostling@aol.com

The machinery of this 18th-century mill has been completely restored. There are photographs and working models on display. Situated on a busy quayside, the unique building looks over towards the historic site of the Sutton Hoo Ship Burial. Every effort is made to run the machinery for a while whenever the mill is open and the tides are favourable.
Times: Open Etr, then daily May-Sep. Apr, Oct wknds only. 11-5 **Fee:** £1.50 (concessions £1, accompanied ch free). **Facilities:** 🅿 (400 yds) (no parking or turning in Tide Mill Way) ♿ shop 🐕 (ex guide dogs)

Surrey

EVENTS & FESTIVALS

March
tbc Guildford International Music Festival

June
24th-26th Wisley Flower Show
tbc Surrey County Show, Stoke Park, Guildford

July
26th Classic Car & Country Fair, Queen Elizabeth's Foundation, Woodlands Road, Leatherhead (provisional)
tbc Guildford Live Music Festival
tbc Guildford Summer Spectacular (various events throughout the month)

August
3rd Cranleigh Show, Showground, Cranleigh
19th-21st Wisley Flower Show

October
20th-3rd Nov Guildford Book Festival

November
20th Oct-3rd Guildford Book Festival

Top: View from Box Hill, early morning.

Surrey is profoundly affected by its proximity to London, and much of the county has been developed to accommodate affluent commuters to the capital. Despite this, it has the reputation of being Britain's most wooded county, and it has some lovely countryside.

Particularly attractive are the areas around Haslemere and Shere. High points are the North Downs west of Guildford rising to a peak at Box Hill near Dorking, and Leith Hill which is 970 ft (294m) tall, making it the highest point in the southeast of England.

There are a number of attractions located within the area bounded by the M25 motorway. These include Sandown Park and Epsom racecourses, and the south's two huge theme parks, Thorpe Park and Chessington World of Adventures, where you can enjoy all the thrills and spills of white knuckle rides and a variety of themed areas.

Kingston-upon-Thames is the county's administrative headquarters. Other main towns are Woking, Farnham, Dorking and Guildford. The latter has a modern cathedral, consecrated in 1961, and the Keep of the Norman Castle still survives. The castle was frequented by King John, who signed the Magna Carta at Runnymede, a meadow on the south bank of the Thames, in 1215. The castle at Farnham is still in one piece, it dates from 1160 and was occupied until 1927. Farnham is a pleasant town with some graceful Georgian buildings, particularly in Castle Street.

Woking has a peculiar claim to fame. It was here, in 1898, that Martians landed on Horsell Common. The invasion was part of H.G.Wells' classic sci-fi novel *The War of the Worlds*. Wells lived in Woking, and Horsell Common is 750 acres of open space that are home to deer, bees and the spider-hunting wasp! The town was also the birthplace of singer/songwriter Paul Weller.

Surrey **221**

ASH VALE Map 04 SU85
ARMY MEDICAL SERVICES MUSEUM
Keogh Barracks GU12 5RQ (M3 junct 4 on A331 to Mytchett then follow tourist signs)
☎ 01252 868612 01252 868832
e-mail: museum@keogh72.freeserve.co.uk

The museum traces the history of Army medicine, nursing and dentistry and veterinary science from 1660 until the present day. Medical equipment and ambulances complement displays including uniforms and medals. **Times:** Open all year, Mon-Fri 10-3.30. (Closed Xmas, New Year & BH). Wknds & BH by appointment only. **Fee:** Free. **Facilities:** P & hand rails, wide doors toilets for disabled shop (large shop selling souvenirs) ✈ (ex guide dogs)

CHERTSEY Map 04 TQ06
THORPE PARK
Staines Rd KT16 8PN (M25 junct 11 or 13 and follow signs via A320 to Thorpe Park)
☎ 0870 444 4466 01932 566367

Prepare for total thrill immersion at the UK's fastest changing theme park in 2002 as the world's first ten-looping coaster, Colossus, joins and unbeatable line of thrilling experiences at Thorpe Park. Back for the second sense-ational season and now firmly on the thrill seekers 'must ride' list are the terrifying trio-Detonator, Vortex and Zodiac. Plus Ribena Rumba Rapids is a white water thrill-fest that twists and turns, tosses and twirls riders through an adrenaline charged river ride. And the thrills don't stop there with Tidal Wave, Pirates-4D, Loggers Leap, Neptune's Beach and Thorpe Farm. **Times:** Open from 22 Mar-3 Nov (ex some off-peak days) 9/10-5/6 (times vary) 7.30pm from 27 Jul-1 Sep and on fireworks night. **Fee:** * £17-£23 (ch under 4 free, ch 4-11 £14-£18). Family £52-£65 (2ad+2ch under 13). **Facilities:** P ✕ licensed & (some rides not accessible, free w.chr loan) toilets for disabled shop ✈ (ex guide dogs)

EAST CLANDON Map 04 TQ05
HATCHLANDS PARK
GU4 7RT (E off Guildford, off A246)
☎ 01483 222482 01483 223176
e-mail: hatchlands@ntrust.org.uk

Built in the 1750s for Admiral Boscawen, hero of the Battle of Louisburg and set in a beautiful 430-acre Repton Park offering a variety of park and woodlands walks, Hatchlands boasts the earliest known decorative works by Robert Adam. Hatchlands is home to the Cobbe collection, the world's largest group of keyboard instrument associated with famous composers. There is also a small garden by Gertrude Jekyll, flowering from late May to early July and a beautiful bluebell wood in May. **Times:** House & Gardens: Apr-Oct, Tue-Thu & Sun, 2-5.30 (also open BH & Fri in Aug). Park Walks open Apr-Oct, daily, 11-6. **Fee:** £6. Grounds and Park walks £2.50. Family ticket £15. combined ticket with Clandon Park £9 **Facilities:** P ✕ licensed & (wheelchair available & special parking) toilets for disabled shop ✈ (ex guide dogs)

FARNHAM Map 04 SU84
BIRDWORLD & UNDERWATERWORLD
Holt Pound GU10 4LD (3m S of Farnham on A325)
☎ 01420 22140 01420 23715
e-mail: bookings@birdworld.co.uk

Birdworld is the largest bird collection in the country and includes toucans, pelicans, flamingoes, ostriches and many others. Underwaterworld is a tropical aquarium with brilliant lighting that shows off collections of marine and freshwater fish, as well as the swampy depths of the alligator exhibit. Visitors can also visit some beautiful gardens, the Jenny Wren farm and the Heron Theatre. **Times:** Open 5 Jan-Feb weekends only, daily mid Feb-End Oct, Wknds only Nov-Dec, Dec-early Jan daily. **Fee:** * £9.25 (ch 3-14 £6.25, pen £6.95) Family ticket £27.95 (2 adults & 2 ch) **Facilities:** P & (wheelchairs available) toilets for disabled shop ✈ (ex guide dogs)

FARNHAM CASTLE KEEP
Castle Hill GU6 0AG (0.5m N on A287)
☎ 01252 713393

Built by an 11th-century bishop of Winchester, the castle made a convenient resting place on the journey to London. His tower, standing on a mound, was later encircled by high walls. **Times:** Open all year, 29 Mar-Sep, daily 10-6 (Oct, daily 10-5). **Fee:** * £2.30 (ch 5-15 £1.20, under 5's free, concessions £1.70). **Facilities:** P ✈ ⌬

GODSTONE Map 05 TQ35
GODSTONE FARM
RH9 8LX (M26 junct 6, south of village, signposted)
☎ 01883 742546 01883 740380
e-mail: havefun@godstonefarm.co.uk

An ideal day out for children, Godstone Farm has lots of friendly animals, big sand pits and play areas. The Indoor Play Barn costs 80p extra on rainy days. **Times:** Open Mar-Oct, 10-6 (last admission 5); Nov-Feb 10-5 (last admission 4). **Fee:** Admission charged **Facilities:** P & toilets for disabled shop ✈

GREAT BOOKHAM   Map 04 TQ15
POLESDEN LACEY
RH5 6BD (2m S off A246 from village of Bookham)
☎ 01372 452048   📠 01372 452023
e-mail: spljxd@smtp.n.trust.org.uk

King George VI and Queen Elizabeth (the Queen Mother) spent part of their honeymoon here, and photographs of other notable guests can be seen. The house is handsomely furnished and full of charm, and it is set in spacious grounds. There is also a summer festival, where concerts and plays are performed. Please phone for details of special events.
Times: Open all year. Grounds, Garden & Landscape walks: daily 11-6. House: 23 Mar-3 Nov, Wed-Sun 11-5. Also BH Mon 11-5 (last admission 30mins before closing) **Fee:** * Ground, Garden & Landscape walks: £4 (Family ticket £10); House: £3 extra (Family £7.50 extra). Ch under 17 half price, ch under 5's free. Party 15+ **Facilities:** 🅿 ☕ ✖ licensed ♿ (braille guide & disabled parking by arrangement) toilets for disabled shop garden centre ✖ (ex guide dogs or in grounds) 🐕

GUILDFORD   Map 04 SU94
DAPDUNE WHARF
Wharf Rd GU1 4RR (off Woodbridge Road to rear of Surrey County Cricket Ground)
☎ 01483 561389   📠 01483 531667
e-mail: riverwey@ntrust.org.uk

The visitor centre at Dapdune Wharf is the centrepiece of one of the National Trust's most unusual properties, the River Way Navigations. A series of interactive exhibits and displays allow you to discover the fascinating story of Surrey's secret waterway, one of the first British rivers to be made navigable. See where huge Wey barges were built and climb aboard *Reliance*, one of the last surviving barges. Children's trails and special events run throughout the season.
Times: Open Apr-Oct, Thu-Mon 11-5. River trips Thu-Mon 11-5 (conditions permitting) **Fee:** * £2.50 (ch £1.50). Family ticket £6.50. National Trust Members Free **Facilities:** 🅿 ☕ ♿ (braille guide) toilets for disabled shop ✖ (ex on lead) 🐕

GUILDFORD CASTLE
GU1 3TU
☎ 01483 444718   📠 01483 444444
e-mail: dandol@guildford.gov.uk
Times: Open: Grounds daily 8-dusk (Closed 25 Dec); Keep Apr-Sep 10.30-6. **Facilities:** 🅿 (50yds) ♿ *Details not confirmed for 2003*

GUILDFORD HOUSE GALLERY
155 High St GU1 3AJ (N side of High St, opposite Sainsbury's)
☎ 01483 444740   📠 01483 444742
e-mail: guildfordhouse@remote.guildford.gov.uk

An impressive building in its own right, Guildford House dates from 1660 and has been Guildford's art gallery since 1959. A changing selection from the Borough's Art Collection is on display, including pastel portraits by John Russell, topographical paintings and contemporary craftwork, as well as temporary exhibitions.
Times: Open Tue-Sat 10-4.45. **Fee:** Free. **Facilities:** 🅿 (100yds) ☕ ♿ shop ✖

LOSELEY PARK
GU3 1HS (2m SW of Guildford, off A3 onto B3000)
☎ 01483 304440 & 505501   📠 01483 302036
e-mail: enquiries@loseley-park.com

Magnificent Elizabethan mansion, home of the More-Molyneux family for over 450 years. Set in magnificent parkland scenery. Based on a Gertude Jekyll design. The walled garden contains five gardens each with its own theme and character. These include the award-winning Rose Garden, Vine Walk, Fruit, Flower Garden & the Serene White Fountain Garden.
Times: Walled Garden open 5 May-Sep, Wed-Sun & BH 11-5. House open 26 May-25 Aug, Wed-Sun & BH Mon 1-5 (last tour 4pm). **Fee:** * House & Gardens £6 (ch £3, ch under 5 free, concessions £5). Gardens only £3 (ch £1.50, concessions £2.50). Party. Garden summer ticket £15, admits ticket holder & guest from May-Sep. **Facilities:** 🅿 ☕ ✖ licensed ♿ (wheelchair available, parking outside house) toilets for disabled shop garden centre ✖ (ex guide dogs)

HASCOMBE   Map 04 SU94
WINKWORTH ARBORETUM
Hascombe Rd GU8 4AD (2m NW on B2130, follow brown tourist signs from Godalming)
☎ 01483 208477   📠 01483 208252
e-mail: swagen@smtp.ntrust.org.uk   **2 for 1**

This lovely woodland covers a hillside of nearly 100 acres, with fine views over the North Downs. The best times to visit are April and May, for the azaleas, bluebells and other flowers, and October for the autumn colours. A delightful Victorian boathouse is open Apr-Oct with fine views over Rowes Flashe Lake. With many rare trees and shrubs in group plantings for spring and autumn colour effect.
Times: Open all year, daily during daylight hours. (Could close when weather is bad) **Fee:** * £3.50 (ch £1.75). Family ticket £8.75, additional family member £1.50. **Facilities:** 🅿 ☕ ♿ (suggested route, free entry for helpers) toilets for disabled shop ✖ (ex on leads) 🐕 🍴

OUTWOOD   Map 04 TQ34
OUTWOOD WINDMILL
Outwood Common RH1 5PW (M25 junct 6, take A25 through Godstone towards Redhill, after 1m turn S off A25 at Bletchingly, between The Prince Albert & the White Hart Mill is 3m on left)
☎ 01342 843458 & 843644   📠 01342 843458
e-mail: sheila@outwoodwindmill.co.uk

This award-winning example of a post-mill dates from 1665 and is the oldest working windmill in England and one of the best preserved in existence. Standing 400ft above sea level, it is surrounded by common land and

continued

National Trust property. Ducks and geese wander freely in the grounds.
Times: Open Etr Sun-last Sun in Oct, Sun & BH Mons only 2-6. Other days & evening tours by arrangement. **Fee:** * £2 (ch £1). **Facilities:** P (10yds) & toilets for disabled shop ✈ (on leads only)

PAINSHILL PARK   Map 04 TQ06
PAINSHILL LANDSCAPE GARDEN
KT11 1JE (W of Cobham, on A245, in between streets)
☎ 01932 868113   📠 01932 868001
e-mail: info@painshill.co.uk

Painshill, created by the Hon. Charles Hamilton between 1738 and 1773, it was a pleasure ground for fashionable society. The garden has been described as landscape theatre in which the spectator moves from scene to scene. Staged around a huge serpentine lake, surprises come at every turn – a Gothic Temple, Chinese Bridge, Ruined Abbey, Grotto, Turkish Tent, Gothic Tower, spectacular waterwheel, 18th-century planting and a working vineyard.
Times: Open Apr-Oct, Tue-Sun & BH, 10.30-6. (gates close 4.30pm). Nov-Mar, Tue-Thu, wknds & BH 11-3 (gates close 4pm). Closed 25-26 Dec. **Fee:** * £4.50 (ch 5-16 £2, concessions £4). Pre-booked adult groups 10+ £3.60. Please telephone 01932 864674 for 2003 prices
Facilities: P 🍴 ✗ & (wheelchairs & buggies available - pre-booked) toilets for disabled shop ✈ (ex guide dogs) 🛍

REIGATE   Map 04 TQ24
REIGATE PRIORY MUSEUM
Bell St RH2 7RL (off A217)
☎ 01737 222550

The Priory Museum is housed in Reigate Priory which was originally founded before 1200, this Grade I listed building was converted to a mansion in Tudor times. Notable features include the magnificent Holbein fireplace, 17th-century oak staircase and murals. The small museum has changing exhibitions on a wide range of subjects, designed to appeal to both adults and children. The collection includes domestic bygones, local history and costume.
Times: Open Etr-early Dec Wed & Sat 2-4.30 in term time. **Fee:** Free.
Facilities: P (50yds) & ("Hands On" facilities) shop ✈

TILFORD   Map 04 SU48
RURAL LIFE CENTRE
Reeds Rd GU10 2DL (off A287, 3m S of Farnham, signposted)
☎ 01252 795571   📠 01252 795571   **2 for 1**
e-mail: rural.life@lineone.net

The museum covers village life from 1750 to 1960. It is set in over ten acres of garden and woodland and incorporates purpose-built and reconstructed buildings, including a chapel. Displays show village crafts and trades, such as wheelwrighting, thatching, ploughing and gardening. The historic village playground provides entertainment for children and there is an arboretum featuring over 100 trees from around the world.
Times: Open Apr-Sep, Wed-Sun & BH 11-6. Winter Wed only 11-4
Fee: £5 (ch £3 & pen £4). Family ticket £12 (2 adults & 2 ch)
Facilities: P 🍴 & (3 wheelchairs for use) toilets for disabled shop

Surrey   223

RHS Garden Wisley
A spectacular garden to visit throughout the year.
RHS Plant Centre and Shop, Café & Restaurant.

RHS Garden Wisley
Woking, Surrey, GU23 6QB   Tel: 01483 224234
On the A3, J10 of the M25 in Surrey

www.rhs.org.uk

WEST CLANDON   Map 04 TQ05
CLANDON PARK
GU4 7RQ (E of Guildford on A247)
☎ 01483 222482   📠 01483 223479
e-mail: clandonpark@ntrust.org.uk

A grand Palladian mansion built c.1730 by the Venetian architect Giacomo Leoni, and notable for its magnificent marble hall. The house is filled with the superb Gubbay collection of 18th-century furniture, porcelain, textiles and carpets. The attractive gardens contain a parterre, grotto, sunken Dutch garden and a Maori meeting house.
Times: House and garden open Apr-Oct, Tue-Thu & Sun 11-5 (also BH's) **Fee:** House & Garden £6 (ch £2.20). Family ticket £15. Combined ticket with Hatchlands Park £9. **Facilities:** P ✗ licensed & (wheelchairs, braille guide & disabled parking) toilets for disabled shop ✈ (ex guide dogs) 🌿 🛍

AA Bed & Breakfast Guide 2003
Britain's best-selling B&B guide featuring over 3500 great places to stay.

AA Lifestyle Guides   www.theAA.com

🏛 WEYBRIDGE　　　　　　　　　Map 04 TQ06
Brooklands Museum
Brooklands Rd KT13 0QN (M25 junct 10/11, museum off B374)
☎ 01932 857381　📠 01932 855465
e-mail: info@brooklandsmuseum.com

Brooklands racing circuit was the birthplace of British motorsport and aviation. From 1907 to 1987 it was a world-renowned centre of engineering excellence. The Museum features old banked track and the 1-in-4 Test Hill. Many of the original buildings have been restored including the Clubhouse, the Shell and BP Petrol Pagodas, and the Malcolm Campbell Sheds in the Motoring Village. Many motorcycles, cars and aircraft are on display. Ring for details of special events.
Times: Open Tue-Sun & BHs 10-5 (4pm in winter). **Fee:** * £7 (ch u5 free, ch 6-16 £5, pen & students £6). Family ticket (2ad+3ch) £18.
Facilities: 🅿 ☕ ♿ toilets for disabled shop ✖ (ex guide dogs) 🎁

🏛 WISLEY　　　　　　　　　　Map 04 TQ05
RHS Garden Wisley
GU23 6QB (on A3, close to M25 junct 10)
☎ 01483 224234　📠 01483 211750

Covering over 240 acres, Wisley is the flagship of the Royal Horticultural Society demonstrating the very best in gardening practices. The gardens have a wide variety of trees, shrubs and plants, many of which are unusual in Britain. Whatever the season the garden serves as a working encyclopedia for gardeners of all levels.
Times: Open all year, Mon-Fri 10-6 (4.30pm Nov-Feb), opens 9am Sat. (Closed 25 Dec). Glasshouses close at 4.15 or sunset Mon-Sun & Jun. **Fee:** * £6 (ch 6-16 £2). Party 10+ £5 each ch £1.60. **Facilities:** 🅿 ☕ ✖ licensed ♿ (free wheelchairs) toilets for disabled shop garden centre ✖ (ex guide dogs) 🎁

See advert on page 223

East Sussex

Natural features of East Sussex include Beachy Head, the highest headland on the South Coast at 590 feet (180m), and the South Downs, the great chalky ridge that once connected England and the Continent, which stretches from Beachy Head into Hampshire.

The heathlands of Ashdown Forest are Winnie the Pooh country, including the bridge where Poohsticks was first played and a monument to A A Milne on Gill's Lap, the Enchanted Place of the much loved Pooh Bear stories.

The coastline is almost entirely built up, and major resorts are Brighton, Hastings and Eastbourne, with Newhaven as the cross channel port. Eastbourne enjoys the reputation of being one of Britain's sunniest seaside destinations, consistently at the top of the sunshine league tables. It is the most respectable of 19th-century resorts with a shingle beach and a fine Victorian pier. Hastings has a fading grandeur, but the Old Town is the most interesting quarter, which can be reached by the West Hill Cliff funicular railway. Brighton is one of Britain's most vibrant cities, with an impressive seafront, lots of artistic activity and entertainment, and plenty of nightlife. Watch out for the occasional wild party on the beach, hosted by Brighton's resident DJ, Norman Cook (aka Fatboy Slim).

Lewes, the county town, is set either side of the River Ouse, where it cuts through the South Downs and provides some dramatic vistas. Attractive streets and lanes known as 'twittens' are overlooked by the Norman castle.

There are castles in abundance in East Sussex: Hastings, Herstmonceux, Pevensey and Bodiam. The town of Battle, six miles (10km) from Hastings, is the site of the famous Battle of Hastings, where the Normans led by William I, defeated Wessex led by Harold II, on 14 October 1066.

Top: Seven Sisters

EVENTS & FESTIVALS

January
25th-26th Rye Festival (literary)

February
1st-2nd Rye Festival (literary)

May
3rd-5th Hastings Traditional Morris Dance Festival
3rd-25th Brighton International Festival, (England's largest arts festival)
11th East Sussex Young Farmers Country Fayre, Laughton
11th MG Regency Run, London to Brighton run for MG cars
tbc Glyndebourne Festival Opera, Glyndebourne

June
8th London to Brighton Classic Car Run
25th-26th Battle Medieval Fair
29th Party in the Park, Brighton
tbc London to Brighton Bike Race

July
3rd Battle Abbey Classic Car Show & Country Fayre, Battle
tbc Hastings Beer & Music Festival, Hastings

August
tbc Pride in Brighton & Hove, gay pride parade
tbc Rye Medieval Festival

September
6th-21st Rye Festival

October
11th-19th Hastings Week

November
2nd London to Brighton Veteran Car Run

December
tbc Burning of the Clocks Parade with lanterns and fireworks

Sussex, East

⛪ ALFRISTON Map 05 TQ50
Alfriston Clergy House
The Tye BN26 5TL (4m NE of Seaford, E of B2108, next to church)
☎ 01323 870001   📠 01323 871318
e-mail: ksdxxx@smtp.ntrust.org.uk
Times: Open Apr-Oct Sat-Mon, daily (ex Tue & Fri), 10-5. **Facilities:** P (0.25 mile) (braille guide) shop ✖ (ex guide dogs) 🌿 *Details not confirmed for 2003*

Drusillas Park
BN26 5QS (off A27 near Alfriston between Lewes & Eastbourne)
☎ 01323 874100   📠 01323 874101
e-mail: drusilla@drusilla.demon.co.uk

An award-winning small zoo in a stunning valley setting. Animals kept here include meerkats, bats, penguins, monkeys, reptiles and creepy-crawlies. Children are well catered for with keeper talks, animal encounters, extensive play areas and activities such as panning for gold and the Zoolympics trail.
Times: Open all year, daily 10-5 (winter 10-4). (Closed 24-26 Dec).
Fee: * £8.99 (ch under 2 free, ch under 12 & pen £7.99, disabled & carers £6.99). Family of 3 £23.95, family of 4 £31.95 & family of 5 £38.95. Party 15+. **Facilities:** P 🍴 ✖ licensed ♿ (rear train carriage & sensory trails) toilets for disabled shop ✖ (ex guide dogs) 🌿

⛪ BATTLE Map 05 TQ71
Battle Museum of Local History
The Almonry, High St TN33 0EA (A21 towards Hastings. Turn right onto A2001 on entering Battle at rdbt, cross & park on Market Sq. Museum on High Street adjacent to Market Square, N end of town)
☎ 01424 772827   📠 01424 772827   **2 for 1**
e-mail: ann@battlehill.freeserve.co.uk

The focal point of this museum is a diorama of the Battle of Hastings and a reproduction of the Bayeux Tapestry. There are also local history exhibits. The museum re-opens in April 2003 after moving to new premises. The opening special exhibition will be "Romans in Sussex" displaying the wealth of finds at the Beauport Park Roman Bath House excavated just outside Battle.
Times: Open Apr-Oct, daily 10.30-4.30 (Sun 2-5). Museum moving from Memorial Hall to The Almonry and due to open April 2003. **Fee:** £1 (ch 20p, ch accompanied free). **Facilities:** P (20yds) ♿ (stair lift & toilet due to be installed) toilets for disabled shop ✖ (ex guide dogs)

Buckleys Yesterday's World
89-90 High St TN33 0AQ (A21 onto A2100 towards Battle, opposite Battle Abbey)
☎ 01424 775378   📠 01424 775174   **2 for 1**
e-mail: info@yesterdaysworld.co.uk

A fun day out for all the family, as the past is brought to life. Walk down the cobbled streets of yesteryear and meet the colourful characters in over 30 shop and room settings including a 1930's grocer's and a Victorian kitchen. The exhibition contains many rarities from the 1850s onwards, including some of Queen Victoria's personal effects and letters written by the present queen. The museum is housed in beautiful gardens with children's play village, miniature golf and summer tea rooms.
Times: Open all year, daily 10-6 (last admission 5pm). Oct to Mar closing times subject to minor change. Closed 25-26 Dec & 1 Jan.
Fee: * £4.75 (ch 4-15 £3.25, pen £4.25). Family ticket £14.75. Discount for special needs & parties of 15+. **Facilities:** P (100yds) (50p per day) 🍴 ♿ (limited access for wheelchairs) toilets for disabled shop 🌿

1066 Battle of Hastings Abbey & Battlefield
High St TN33 0AD (A21 onto A2100)
☎ 01424 773792
Times: Open all year, Apr-Sep, daily 10-6 (Oct 10-5); Nov-28 Mar, daily 10-4. Closed 24-26 Dec & 1 Jan. **Facilities:** P (charged) ♿ shop ✖ (allowed in certain areas) ⚑ *Details not confirmed for 2003*

⛪ BODIAM Map 05 TQ72
Bodiam Castle
TN32 5UA (2m E of A21 Hurst Green)
☎ 01580 830436   📠 01580 830398
e-mail: kboxxx@smtp.ntrust.org.uk
Times: Open 16 Feb-Oct, daily 10-6 or dusk if earlier; Nov-15 Feb, Sat & Sun 10-4 or dusk. Last admission 1 hour before closing. **Facilities:** P (charged) 🍴 ♿ (Braille/large print guides, special parking on request) toilets for disabled shop ✖ (ex in grounds on a lead) 🌿 *Details not confirmed for 2003*

⛪ BRIGHTON Map 04 TQ30
Booth Museum of Natural History
194 Dyke Rd BN1 5AA (from A27 Brighton by pass, 1.5m NW of town centre, opposite Dyke Rd Park)
☎ 01273 292777   📠 01273 292778
e-mail: boothmus@pavilion.co.uk
Times: Open all year, Mon-Sat (ex Thu) 10-5, Sun 2-5. (Closed Good Fri, Xmas & 1 Jan). **Facilities:** P (road opposite) (two hour limit) ♿ shop ✖ (ex guide dogs) *Details not confirmed for 2003*

Museum & Art Gallery
Church St BN1 1UE (A23/M23 from London, in city centre near seafront. New entrance in the Royal Pavilion Gardens)
☎ 01273 290900   📧 01273 292841

A £10 million redevelopment has transformed Brighton Museum into a state-of-the-art visitor attraction. Dynamic and innovative new galleries, including fashion, 20th-century design and world art, featuring exciting interactive displays appealing to all ages. The museum also benefits from a spacious new entrance located in the Royal Pavilion gardens and full disabled access.
Times: Open all year, Tue 10-7, Wed-Sat 10-5 & Sun 2-5. (closed Mon ex BHs). **Fee:** Free. **Facilities:** P (5 mins walk) (Church St NCP & on Street) 🅿 ♿ (lift,tactile exhibits,induction loops,ramps,automatic door) toilets for disabled shop ✘ (ex guide dogs)

Preston Manor
Preston Drove BN1 6SD (off A23, 2m N of Brighton)
☎ 01273 292770   📧 01273 292771
e-mail: visitor.services@brighton-hove.gov.uk

This charming Edwardian manor house is beautifully furnished with notable collections of silver, furniture and paintings and presents a unique opportunity to see an Edwardian home both `upstairs' and `downstairs'. The servants' quarters can also be seen, featuring kitchen, butler's pantry and boot hall. The house is set in beautiful gardens, which include a pet cemetery and the 13th-century parish church of St Peter. The restored walled garden now enables disabled people to explore the garden.
Times: Open all year, Tue-Sat 10-5, Sun 2-5, Mon 1-5 (BH Mons 10-5). (Closed Good Fri & 25-26 Dec). **Fee:** * £3.40 (ch 5-15 £2.10, pen, students & UB40 £2.90). Family ticket £5.50-£8.90. Party 20+ £2.90 each. Joint ticket with Royal Pavilion £7.60. **Facilities:** P ♿ (access to ground floor with prior notice) shop ✘ (ex guide dogs)

Royal Pavilion
BN1 1EE (M23/A23 from London, situated in city centre near seafront. 15 min walk from Brighton train station)
☎ 01273 290900   📧 01273 292871
e-mail: visitor.services@brighton-hove.gov.uk

Acclaimed as one of the most exotically beautiful buildings in the British Isles, the Royal Pavilion was the magnificent seaside residence of George IV. The breathtaking Regency palace is decorated in Chinese style, with a romanticised Indian exterior, and surrounded by restored Regency gardens.
Times: Open all year, Apr-Sep, daily 9.30-5.45 (last admission 5); Oct-May, daily 10-5.15 (last admission 4.30). **Fee:** * £5.35 (ch £3.30, concessions £3.85) Family ticket £8.65-£14. Joint ticket with Preston Manor £7.60 Groups 20+.£4.55 each. **Facilities:** P (5 mins walk) (NCP & on street) 🅿 ♿ (tours for the blind by arrangement, wheelchairs) toilets for disabled shop ✘ (ex guide dogs) 🍴

Sea Life Centre
Marine Pde BN2 1TB
☎ 01273 604234 & 604233 (rec info)
📧 01273 681840
Times: Open all year, daily (ex 25 Dec), 10-5. Last admission 4. (Open later on wknds in summer & school holidays) **Facilities:** P (200 yds) 🅿 ♿ toilets for disabled shop ✘ (ex guide dogs) *Details not confirmed for 2003*

🏛 BURWASH   Map 05 TQ62
Bateman's
TN19 7DS (0.5m SW off A265)
☎ 01435 882302   📧 01435 882811
e-mail: kbaxxx@smtp.ntrust.org.uk

Rudyard Kipling lived for over 34 years in this 17th-century manor house and it remains much the same as it was during his lifetime. His 1928 Rolls Royce Phantom is on display, and the watermill at the bottom of the garden grinds wheat into flour on Saturday afternoons.
Times: Open Apr-1 Nov, Sat-Wed 11-5.30, also open Good Fri, (last admission 4.30pm). House closes at 5pm. **Fee:** * £5.20 (ch £2.60). Family ticket £13. Party 15+. **Facilities:** P 🅿 ✘ licensed ♿ (braille guide,touch test,computerised tour of upper floors) toilets for disabled shop ✘ (ex guide/hearing dogs) 🐕 🍴

🏛 EASTBOURNE   Map 05 TV69
"How We Lived Then" Museum of Shops & Social History
20 Cornfield Ter BN21 4NS (just off seafront, between town centre & theatres)
☎ 01323 737143

Over the last 40 years, Jan and Graham Upton have collected over 100,000 items which are now displayed on four floors of authentic old shops and room-settings, transporting visitors back to their grandparents' era. Other displays, such as seaside souvenirs, wartime rationing and Royal mementoes, help to capture 100 years of social history.
Times: Open daily all year, 10-5.30 (last entry 5pm). Winter times subject to change, telephone establishment. **Fee:** £3.50 (ch 5-15 £2.50, under 5's free, pen £3). Party 10+. **Facilities:** P (outside) ♿ (no charge for disabled) shop

Sussex, East

Redoubt Fortress and Museum
Royal Pde BN22 7AQ
☎ 01323 410300   ▤ 01323 732240
Times: Open Etr-5 Nov, 9.30-5.30. **Facilities:** P (200yds) shop
Details not confirmed for 2003

Wish Tower Puppet Museum
Martello Tower No 73, King Edward Pde BN21 4BU
(on seafront, W of pier)
☎ 01323 417776   ▤ 01323 644440 or 728319
e-mail: puppet.workshop@virgin.net
Times: Open May-mid Jul & Sep, wknds 11-5; mid Jul-Aug, daily 11-5.
Facilities: P (100mtrs) shop ✻ *Details not confirmed for 2003*

⛪ FIRLE   Map 05 TQ40
Firle Place
BN8 6LP (off A27, Eastbourne to Brighton road)
☎ 01273 858307   ▤ 01273 858188
e-mail: firleestate@aol.com

Home of the Gage family for over 500 years, the house has a Tudor core but was remodelled in the 18th century. Its treasures include important European and English Old Master paintings, fine English and French furniture, and porcelain, including notable examples from Sèvres and English factories. There are family monuments and brasses in the church at West Firle.
Times: Open 12 May-Sep, Sun, Wed, Thu & BHs 1.45-4.15. **Fee:** £5 (ch £2.50, concessions £4.50). Groups 25+. Connoisseurs Day £6 each. Private viewing 25+ by appointment only. **Facilities:** P ✗ licensed ♿ toilets for disabled shop ✻ (ex in garden)

⛪ GLYNDE   Map 05 TQ40
Glynde Place
Lewes BN8 6SX (off A27 between Lewes & Eastbourne)
☎ 01273 858224   ▤ 01273 858224
Times: Open Jun & Sep, Wed & Sun 2-5, Jul & Aug Wed, Thu & Sun.
Facilities: P shop ✻ *Details not confirmed for 2003*

⛪ HAILSHAM   Map 05 TQ50
Michelham Priory
Upper Dicker BN27 3QS (off A22 & A27, 2m W of Hailsham, 8m NW of Eastbourne, signposted from A27 & A22).
☎ 01323 844224   ▤ 01323 844030
e-mail: adminmich@sussexpast.co.uk

Set on a moated island surrounded by gardens, Michelham Priory is one of the most beautiful historic houses in Sussex. Founded in 1229 for Augustinian canons, the Priory is approached through a 14th-century gatehouse spanning the longest medieval moat in the country. Most of the original priory was demolished during the Dissolution, but the remains were incorporated into a Tudor farm that became a country house. Outside, the gardens are enhanced by a

working watermill, physic garden, smithy, rope museum and the dramatic Elizabethan Great Barn.
Times: Open Mar-Oct, Wed-Sun (daily in Aug & BH Mons). Mar & Oct 10.30-4, Apr-Jul & Sep 10.30-5, Aug 10.30-5.30. **Fee:** * £4.80 (ch 5-15 £2.50, pen & student £4.20). Family ticket (2 adult & 2 ch) £12.50. **Facilities:** P ✗ licensed ♿ (wheelchairs & braille guide available) ✻

⛪ HALLAND   Map 05 TQ51
Bentley Wildfowl & Motor Museum
BN8 5AF (7m NE of Lewes, signposted off A22, A26 & B2192)
☎ 01825 840573
▤ 01825 841322   **2 for 1**
e-mail: barrysutherland@pavilion.co.uk

Hundreds of swans, geese and ducks from all over the world can be seen on lakes and ponds along with flamingos and peacocks. There is a fine array of Veteran, Edwardian and Vintage vehicles, and the house has splendid antiques and wildfowl paintings. The gardens specialise in old fashioned roses. Other attractions include woodland walks, a nature trail, Education Centre, adventure playground and a miniature train.
Times: Open 20 Mar-Oct, daily 10.30-4.30. House open from noon, Apr-Nov, Feb & part of Mar, wknds only. Estate closed Dec & Jan. House closed all winter. **Fee:** * Summer £5.20 (ch 4-15 £3.50, pen & students £4.20). Family ticket (2 adults & 4 ch) £16. Winter £4.20. Special rates for disabled. **Facilities:** P ♿ (wheelchairs available) toilets for disabled shop ✻ (ex guide dogs)

⛪ HASTINGS   Map 05 TQ80
Old Town Hall Museum of Local History
Old Town Hall, High St TN34 3EW (off A529 coast road into High St in Hastings old town. Signposted)
☎ 01424 781166   ▤ 01424 781165
e-mail: oldtownmuseum@hastings.gov.uk

Situated in the heart of Hastings Old Town, the museum was originally a Georgian Town Hall built in 1823. Refurbished displays tell the story of Hastings Old Town as a walk back in time, with features including a Cinque Ports ship, and interactive displays.
Times: Open Apr-Sep, daily 10-5; Oct-Mar, daily 11-4. **Fee:** Free.
Facilities: P (150yds) (parking metres in operation) ♿ (lift, evac chair, low-level displays, audio tour) toilets for disabled shop ✻ (ex guide dogs)

Smugglers Adventure
St Clements Caves, West Hill TN34 3HY (follow brown signs along A259 coast road through Hastings. Use seafront carpark and then take West Cliff railway or follow signed footpath)
☎ 01424 422964
▤ 01424 721483   **2 for 1**
e-mail: bookings@discoverhastings.co.uk

A Smuggler's Adventure is a themed experience housed in a labyrinth of caverns and passages deep below the West Hill. Visitors first tour a comprehensive exhibition and museum, followed by a video theatre, before embarking on the Adventure Walk - a trip through

continued

several acres of caves with life-size tableaux, push-button automated models and dramatic scenic effects depicting life in the days of 18th-century smuggling.
Times: Open all year daily, Etr-Sep 10-5.30; Oct-Etr 11-4.30. (Closed 24-26 Dec). **Fee:** * £5.50 (ch £3.50, concessions £4.50). Family ticket £15.75. **Facilities:** P (500yds) (parking meters) shop ✻ (ex guide dogs)

1066 STORY IN HASTINGS CASTLE
Castle Hill Rd, West Hill TN34 3RG (close to A259 seafront, 2m from B2093)
☎ 01424 781111 & 781112 (info line) 2 for 1
📠 01424 781186

The ruins of the Norman castle stand on the cliffs, close to the site of William the Conqueror's first motte-and-bailey castle in England. It was excavated in 1825 and 1968, and old dungeons were discovered in 1894. An unusual approach to the castle can be made via the West Hill Cliff Railway.
Times: Open Mar-Sep 10-5 (5.30 summer school hols); Oct-Feb 11-3.30 (Closed 24-26 Dec). **Fee:** £3.20 (ch £2.10, pen & students £2.60, disabled free). Family ticket £9.50, extra ch 75p each. **Facilities:** P (seafront) (time restrictions, pay & display) & (ramps) shop ✻ (ex guide dogs)

⛪ HERSTMONCEUX   Map 05 TQ61
THE OBSERVATORY SCIENCE CENTRE
BN27 1RG (2m E of village on Boreham Street to Pevensey Road)
☎ 01323 832731 📠 01323 832741
e-mail: info@the-observatory.org

From the 1950s to the 1980s this was part of the Royal Greenwich Observatory, and was used by astronomers to observe and chart movements in the night sky. Visitors can learn about not only astronomy, but also other areas of science in a series of interactive and engaging displays. There are also exhibitions, a discovery park, and a collection of unusual giant exhibits.
Times: Open 9-17 Feb & 23 Mar-3 Nov, 10-6 (last admission 5 in Feb, Oct & Nov) **Fee:** * £4.95 (ch 4-15 £3.65). Family ticket (2 ad & 2 ch or 1 ad & 3 ch) £14.50 **Facilities:** P 💺 & ramps+ disabled entrance toilets for disabled shop ✻ (ex guide dogs)

THE TRUGGERY
Coopers Croft BN27 1QL (from A22 at Hailsham, Boship rdbt, take A271 towards Bexhill for 4m)
☎ 01323 832314 📠 01323 832314
e-mail: sarah@truggery.fsnet.co.uk

The art of Sussex trug making can be seen through all the work processes including preparing timber, use of the draw knife and assembly of trug.
Times: Open Tue-Fri 10-5, Sat 10-1. Closed Sun & Mon. Oct-Apr opening times may vary. **Fee:** Free. **Facilities:** P & shop ⚒

Sussex, East   229

⛪ HOVE   Map 04 TQ20
BRITISH ENGINEERIUM-MUSEUM OF STEAM & MECHANICAL ANTIQUITIES
off Nevill Rd BN3 7QA (signposted off A27 from Worthing & Eastbourne)
☎ 01273 559583 📠 01273 566403
e-mail: info@britishengineerium.com   2 for 1

This restored Victorian water pumping station has an original working beam engine of 1876, and a French Corliss horizontal engine which won first prize at the Paris International Exhibition of 1889. There are also traction engines, fire engines, and many other full-size and model engines. Also an exhibition of craftsmen's tools and domestic appliances. Boilers are fired up and in steam on special days.
Times: Open all year, daily 10-4. In steam first Sun in month & Sun & Mon of BH's. Telephone for details of days closed prior to Xmas. **Fee:** £4 (ch, students & pen £3, ch under 5 free). Family ticket £12. **Facilities:** P & shop ✻ (ex guide dogs)

⛪ LEWES   Map 05 TQ41
ANNE OF CLEVES HOUSE
52 Southover High St BN7 1JA (S of town centre off A27/A26/A275)
☎ 01273 474610 📠 01273 486990
e-mail: anne@sussexpast.co.uk

Henry VIII gave this beautiful timber-framed house to Anne of Cleves, his fourth wife, as part of her divorce settlement. Today there are collections of early English furniture, Sussex pottery and stone from Lewes Priory, plus a local social history exhibition. The Wealden Iron Gallery tells the story of the industrial past of Sussex and contains a large collection of iron artefacts.
Times: Open Jan-Feb & Nov-Dec, Tue-Sat 10-5; Mar-Oct, Mon-Sat 10-5 Sun 12-5. Closed 24-26 Dec. **Fee:** * £2.80 (ch 5-15 £1.40, pen & student £2.50). Family ticket £7 (2 adult & 2 ch), £5.50 (1 adult & 4 ch). **Facilities:** P (25yds) (on street-2hr restriction) & shop ✻ (ex guide dogs)

LEWES CASTLE & BARBICAN HOUSE MUSEUM
169 High St BN7 1YE (N of High St off A27/A26/A275)
☎ 01273 486290 📠 01273 486990
e-mail: castle@sussexpast.co.uk

High above the medieval streets stands Lewes Castle, begun soon after the Norman Conquest by William de Warenne as his stronghold in Sussex and added to over the next 300 years, culminating in the magnificent Barbican. Thomas Read Kemp and his family owned and updated the ruins during Georgian times. Barbican House is next to the castle, and now houses a museum covering the area from pre-history to the late medieval period. Visitors can climb to the top of the castle, from where they are rewarded by stunning views. A 'sound and light' show in the museum below tells the story of the town of Lewes through the ages.
Times: Open daily, Tue-Sat 10-5.30, Sun & Mon 11-5.30. Last admission 30 mins before closing. Closed Mon's in Jan & Xmas. **Fee:** * £4.20 (ch £2.10, pen & student £3.70). Family ticket (2 adults & 2 ch) £11.40, (1 adult & 4 ch) £8.40. **Facilities:** P (on street parking) (touch screen) shop ✻ (ex castle & guide dogs)

Sussex, East

NEWHAVEN Map 05 TQ40
Paradise Park & Gardens
Avis Rd BN9 0DH (signposted off A26 & A259)
☎ 01273 512123 ▤ 01273 616005
e-mail: enquiries@paradisepark.co.uk **2 for 1**

A perfect day out for plant lovers whatever the season. Discover the unusual garden designs with waterfalls, fountains and lakes, including the Caribbean garden and the tranquil Oriental garden. The Conservatory Gardens complex contains a large variety of the world's flora divided into several zones. There's also a Sussex history trail and Planet Earth with moving dinosaurs and interactive displays, plus rides and amusements for children.
Times: Open all year, daily 9-6 (Closed 25-26 Dec) **Fee:** * £4.99 (ch £3.99). Family ticket £16.99 (2ad+2ch) **Facilities:** P ▤ ✗ licensed ♿ (all areas level or ramped) toilets for disabled shop garden centre ✗ (ex guide dogs) ▤

NORTHIAM Map 05 TQ82
Great Dixter
TN31 6PH (off A28, signposted)
☎ 01797 252878 ▤ 01797 252879
e-mail: office@greatdixter.co.uk

Birthplace and home of Christopher Lloyd, gardening writer, Great Dixter was built in 1460 and boasts one of the largest timber-framed buildings in the country. Lutyens was employed to restore both the house and gardens in 1910. The gardens are now a combination of meadows, ponds, topiary and notably the Long Border and Exotic Garden.
Times: Open 29 Mar-26 Oct, Tue-Sun & BH Mon, 2-5.30 (last admission 5); Gardens only open from 11am on Sun & Mon BH wknds only. **Fee:** * House & Gardens £6 (ch £1.50). Gardens only £4.50 (ch £1). Party 25+. **Facilities:** P ♿ (one wheelchair available free of charge) toilets for disabled shop garden centre ✗ (ex guide dogs) ▤

PEVENSEY Map 05 TQ60
Pevensey Castle
BN24 5LE (off A259)
☎ 01323 762604

Witness to 17 centuries of conflict, from its origins as a Roman fortress to its use as a coastal base during the Second World War, this powerful castle has never been taken by force.
Times: Open all year, 29 Mar-Sep, daily 10-6 (Oct, daily 10-5); Nov-Mar daily 10-4. (Closed 24-26 Dec & 1 Jan). **Fee:** * £2.80 (ch 5-15 £1.40, ch under 5 free, concessions £2.10). **Facilities:** P (charged) ▤ ♿ ✗ (in certain areas) ⛉

RYE Map 05 TQ92
Lamb House
West St TN31 7ES (facing W end of Church)
☎ 01892 890651 ▤ 01892 890110

This 18th-century house was the home of novelist Henry James from 1898 until his death in 1916, and was later occupied by the writer, E F Benson. Some of James' personal posessions can be seen. There is also a charming walled garden.
Times: Open Apr-2 Nov; Wed & Sat 2-6, (last admission 5.30). **Fee:** * £2.60 (ch £1.30). Family ticket £6.50. Groups by arrangement. **Facilities:** P (200mtrs) (scented plants & herbs) ✗ (ex guide dogs) ▤

Rye Castle Museum
3 East St TN31 7JY (In town centre, on A259)
☎ 01797 226728

Part of the museum is housed in a stone tower built as a fortification in 1249. The museum's collection of ironwork, medieval pots and smuggling items are on display here, while the East Street site contains the rest of the collection, including pottery made in Rye, fashions, an 18th-century fire engine, toys, cinque port regalia and a special exhibition on Rye in WWII. The museum tells the story of Rye's long and illustrious history.
Times: Open all year Nov-Mar wknds only 10.30-3; Apr-Oct Thu-Mon 10.30-5. (last entry 4.30). Closed between 1-2pm. **Fee:** * Entrance to both sites: £2.90 (ch 7-16 £1.50, concessions £2). Family ticket £5.90. Single entry only: £1.90 (ch 7-16) £1, concessions £1.50). Family ticket £4.50. Party 8+. **Facilities:** P (30yds) (street limited to 1hr) ♿ (only East Street accessible) toilets for disabled shop ✗ (ex guide dogs) ▤

SHEFFIELD PARK Map 05 TQ42
Sheffield Park Garden
TN22 3QX (5m E of Haywards Heath off A275)
☎ 01825 790231 ▤ 01825 791264
e-mail: kshxxx@smtp.ntrust.org.uk
Times: Open Jan-Feb Sat-Sun 10.30-4; Mar-Oct Tue-Sun (open BH Mons) 10.30-6; Nov-Dec Tue-Sun 10.30-4 (Last admission 1 hour before closing). **Facilities:** P ▤ ♿ (powered self drive cars & wheelchairs available) toilets for disabled shop ✗ (ex guide/hearing dogs) ▤ Details not confirmed for 2003 ▤

SHEFFIELD PARK STATION Map 05 TQ42
Bluebell Railway
Sheffield Park Station TN22 3QL (4.5m E of Haywards Heath, off A275)
☎ 01825 723777, 722370 & 722008
▤ 01825 724084

A volunteer-run heritage steam railway with nine miles of track running through pretty Sussex countryside. Please note that there is no parking at Kingscote Station. If you wish to board the train here, catch the bus (service 473) which connects Kingscote and East Grinstead.
Times: Open all year, Sat & Sun, daily May-Sep & during school holidays. Santa Specials run Dec. For timetable and information regarding trains contact above. **Fee:** * 3rd class return fare £8 (ch £4). Family ticket £21.50. Admission to Sheffield Park Station only £1.60 (ch 80p). Other tickets available on request. **Facilities:** P ▤ ✗ licensed ♿ (special carriage for wheelchairs & carers) toilets for disabled shop ▤

West Sussex

West Sussex is a county of weald and downland, once dominated by the forest that stretched through The Weald from Kent into Hampshire. The oaks of the forest were used to smelt the local iron ore, and though the forest is now somewhat diminished, the country remains green and lush.

The county town of Chichester, the only city in Sussex, is a gem in its own right. Building on the cathedral began in 1076, and has been added to since then. St Richard was Bishop here in the 13th century, and his shrine was an important pilgrimage centre until its destruction by Henry VIII. South of the city is the headland of Selsey. Selsey was originally an island and is still almost encircled by water, it offers a number of different beaches, including the Witterings and Pagham Harbour which is notable for its birdlife. Pre-Norman Selsey was lost to the sea long ago.

Further east, the county's main seaside resorts are Bognor Regis, Littlehampton and Worthing. Bognor Regis was one of the first bathing resorts in the late 18th century, and Queen Victoria was particularly fond of the place. Bognor gained the addition 'Regis' after George V convalesced there in 1929.

Outside Worthing, at Highdown Hill, there is a Bronze Age settlement beneath an Iron Age hill fort, where the Saxons later buried their dead. These may include Aella, thought to have died in battle against King Arthur in 516AD.

The main towns are Horsham, Haywards Heath, and Crawley. The third of these is the only new town south of London, and is close to Gatwick Airport. Despite its new town status it has several buildings dating back to the 15th century. Arundel is a particularly handsome town, at a crossing point on the River Arun, dominated by the sprawling, much restored castle and the Roman Catholic Cathedral.

Top: Mysterious yew trees in Kingsley Vale

EVENTS & FESTIVALS

April
18th British & World Marbles Championships, Crawley

June
2nd Spring Carnival, Crawley
6th-8th South of England Agricultural Show, Haywards Heath
14th-15th Parham Steam Rally, Pulborough
18th-19th Corpus Christi Carpet of Flowers & Floral Festival, Cathedral of Our Lady & St Philip Howard, Arundel
27th-29th Crawley Folk Festival, Crawley

July
11th-27th Petworth Festival (various Venues)
tbc Bognor Birdman, Bognor Regis (provisional)
tbc Chichester Festivities

August
2nd-3rd Littlehampton Regatta, River Arun, Littlehampton
tbc Arundel Festival
tbc Crawley International Mela, The Hawth, Crawley
tbc Juggling Festival, The Hawth, Crawley

September
13th Findon Great Sheep Fair, Nepcote Green, Findon (provisional)

October
tbc South of England Autumn Show, Haywards Heath

AMBERLEY
Map 04 TQ01

AMBERLEY WORKING MUSEUM
BN18 9LT (on B2139, between Arundel and Storrington, adjacent to Amberley railway station)
☎ 01798 831370 01798 831831
e-mail: office@amberleymuseum.co.uk

This exciting working museum reflects the industrial history of the south east of England. Here you can visit the craftsmen - the blacksmith, potter, printer or boat-builder, and experience the sights, sounds and smells of their workshops. Take a ride on the workmen's train or on the narrow gauge railway, or enjoy the delights of the vintage motor buses. There are many other exhibits and displays to capture your interest and imagination within the magnificent 36-acre site including the Rural Telephone Exchange, Wheelwright's Shop, the Seeboard Electricity Hall, and Paviors' Museum of Roads and Roadmaking. Allow at least three hours for a visit.
Times: Open 20 Mar-3 Nov, Wed-Sun & BH Mon 10-5. Also open daily during school holidays. **Fee:** * £6.75 (ch 5-16 £3.75, pen & students £6). Family ticket (2 adults & 3 children) £19 **Facilities:** 🅿 🍴 ♿ toilets for disabled shop 🚫

ARDINGLY
Map 05 TQ32

WAKEHURST PLACE & MILLENNIUM SEED BANK
RH17 6TN (1.5m NW of Ardingley, on B2028)
☎ 01444 894066 01444 894069
e-mail: wakehurst@kew.org

Woodland and lakes linked by a pretty watercourse make this large garden a beautiful place to walk, and it also has an amazing variety of interesting trees and shrubs, a winter garden, and a rock walk. It is administered and maintained by the Royal Botanic Gardens at Kew.
Times: Open all year, Nov-Jan 10-4; Feb & Oct 10-5; Mar 10-6; Apr-Sep 10-7. (Closed 25 Dec & 1 Jan). Last admission 30 mins before closing. Mansion Restaurant, shop & exhibition closes one hour before garden & car park. **Fee:** * £6.50 (ch under 16, free) **Facilities:** 🅿 🍴 🚫 licensed ♿ (wheelchair available) toilets for disabled shop garden centre 🚫 (ex guide dogs)

ARUNDEL
Map 04 TQ00

ARUNDEL CASTLE
BN18 9AB (on A27 between Chichester & Worthing)
☎ 01903 882173 01903 884581
e-mail: info@arundelcastle.org

Set high on a hill in West Sussex, this magnificent castle and stately home, seat of the Dukes of Norfolk for nearly 1000 years, commands stunning views across the River Arun and out to sea. Climb to the keep and battlements; marvel at a fine collection of 16th-century furniture; portraits by Van Dyke, Gainsborough, Canaletto and others; tapestries and the personal possessions of Mary, Queen of Scots; wander in the grounds and renovated Victorian flower and vegetable gardens.

Times: Open 31 Mar-Oct, Sun-Fri 12-5. Last admission 4pm (Closed Sat & Good Fri). **Fee:** * £8.50 (ch 5-16 £5.50, pen £6). Family ticket £24.50. Party 20+ **Facilities:** 🅿 🍴 ♿ toilets for disabled shop 🚫 (ex guide dogs)

WWT ARUNDEL
Mill Rd BN18 9PB (signposted from A27 & A29)
☎ 01903 883355 01903 884834   **2 for 1**
e-mail: arundel@wwt.org.uk

More than a thousand ducks, geese and swans from all over the world can be found here; many are so friendly that they will eat from your hand. The wild reserve attracts a variety of birds and includes a reedbed habitat considered so vital to the wetland wildlife it shelters that it has been designated a Site of Special Scientific Interest. Visitors can walk right through this reedbed on a specially designed boardwalk. There is a packed programme of events and activities throughout the year.
Times: Open all year, daily. Summer 9.30-5; Winter 9.30-4.30. Last admission Summer 5pm; Winter 4pm. (Closed 25 Dec). **Fee:** * £5.50 (ch £3.30, pen £4.40). Family ticket £14.30 **Facilities:** 🅿 🍴 🚫 licensed ♿ (level paths, free wheelchair loan) toilets for disabled shop 🚫 (ex guide/hearing dogs)

ASHINGTON
Map 04 TQ11

HOLLY GATE CACTUS GARDEN
Billingshurst Rd RH20 3BB (off A24, towards Ashington then B2133 towards Billingshurst for 0.5m)
☎ 01903 892930
e-mail: hollygate@tmh.globalnet.co.uk   **2 for 1**

A mecca for the cactus enthusiast, with more than 30,000 succulent and cactus plants, including many rare types. They come from both arid and tropical parts of the world, and are housed in over 10,000 sq ft of greenhouses.
Times: Open all year, daily 9-5. (Closed 25-26 Dec). **Fee:** £2 (ch & pen £1.50). Family ticket £6. Party 20+ 25p deduction. **Facilities:** 🅿 ♿ shop garden centre 🚫 (ex guide dogs)

Sussex, West

BIGNOR Map 04 SU91
BIGNOR ROMAN VILLA & MUSEUM
RH20 1PH (between A29 & A285)
☎ 01798 869259 ▤ 01798 869259
e-mail: bignorromanvilla@care4free.net

Rediscovered in 1811, this Roman house was built on a grand scale. It is one of the largest known, and has spectacular mosaics. The heating system can also be seen, and various finds from excavations are on show. The longest mosaic in Britain (82ft) is on display here in its original position.
Times: Open Mar-Apr Tue-Sun & BH 10-5, May 10-5 daily, Jun-Sep 10-6 daily, Oct 10-5 daily **Fee:** * £3.65 (ch 5-15 £1.55, pen £2.60). Party 10+. Guided tours by arrangement. **Facilities:** P ▤ & Most areas accessible shop ✕ (ex guide dogs) ❦

BRAMBER Map 04 TQ11
BRAMBER CASTLE
BN4 3FB (on W side of village off A283)

A former home of the Dukes of Norfolk, this ruined Norman stronghold lies on a ridge of the South Downs and gives wonderful views.
Times: Open any reasonable time. **Fee:** Free. **Facilities:** P ❦

CHICHESTER Map 04 SU80
CHICHESTER CATHEDRAL
West St PO19 1PX (in city centre)
☎ 01243 782595 ▤ 01243 536190
e-mail: vo@chicath.freeserve.co.uk

The beauty of the 900-year-old cathedral, site of the shrine of St Richard, is enhanced by many art treasures, ancient and modern.
Times: Open daily end Mar-end Sep 7.15am-7pm; end Sep-end Mar 7.15am-6pm **Fee:** Free. **Facilities:** P (within city walls) ▤ ✕ & (touch & hearing centre, loop system) toilets for disabled shop ✕ (ex guide dogs)

MECHANICAL MUSIC & DOLL COLLECTION
Church Rd, Portfield PO19 4HN (1m E of Chichester, signposted off A27)
☎ 01243 372646 ▤ 01243 370299

A unique opportunity to see and hear barrel organs, polyphons, musical boxes, fair organs etc - all fully restored and playing. A magical musical tour to fascinate and entertain all ages. The doll collection contains fine examples of Victorian china and wax dolls, and felt and velvet dolls of the 1920s.
Times: Open Jun-Sep, Wed 1-4; Group bookings anytime in the year by prior arrangement. **Fee:** £2.50 (ch £1.25). **Facilities:** P & shop ✕ (ex guide dogs)

PALLANT HOUSE GALLERY
9 North Pallant PO19 1TJ (in city centre off East Street)
☎ 01243 774557 ▤ 01243 536038
e-mail: pallant@pallant.co.uk
Times: Open all year, Tue-Sat 10-5, Sun & BHs 12.30-5. **Facilities:** P (100 yds) ▤ & shop ✕ (ex guide dogs) *Details not confirmed for 2003* ❦

EAST GRINSTEAD Map 05 TQ33
STANDEN
RH19 4NE (2m S of East Grinstead, signposted from B2110)
☎ 01342 323029 ▤ 01342 316424
e-mail: standen@ntrust.org.uk

Standen is a showpiece of the 19th-century Arts and Crafts movement. It was designed by Philip Webb for the Beale family, and was intended for decoration with William Morris wallpapers and fabrics. The interior has been carefully preserved. Webb also designed some of the furniture and details. There is a beautiful hillside garden. Telephone for details of special events.
Times: House open Apr-Nov, Wed-Sun & BH 11-5. Garden open same dates as house 11-6 & Nov-mid Dec, Fri-Sun 11-3. Last entry to house 4.30 **Fee:** * House & garden £5.50. Garden only £3. Children half price. Family ticket £13.75. Joint ticket which includes same day entry to Nymans garden £9, available Wed-Fri. **Facilities:** P ✕ licensed & (braille guide & touch list) shop ✕ (ex guide dogs & on wood walk) ▤ ❦

FISHBOURNE Map 04 SU80
FISHBOURNE ROMAN PALACE
Salthill Rd PO19 3QR (off A27 onto A259 into Fishbourne. Turn right into Salthill Rd & right into Roman Way)
☎ 01243 785859 ▤ 01243 539266
e-mail: adminfish@sussexpast.co.uk

This is the largest known Roman residence in Britain. It was occupied from the 1st to the 3rd centuries AD, and has mosaic floors and painted walls. 25 of these mosaic floors can still be seen in varying states of completeness, including others rescued from elsewhere in the area. Outside, part of the garden has been replanted to its original 1st-century plan. The museum displays a collection of finds from the excavations and tells the story of the site's discovery. An audio-visual presentation helps bring the site back to life, as it would have been many centuries ago.
Times: Open all year, daily Feb-15 Dec. Feb, Nov-Dec 10-4; Mar-Jul & Sep-Oct 10-5; Aug 10-6. Winter wknds 10-4. **Fee:** * £4.70 (ch £2.50, pen & students £4, registered disabled £3.80). Family ticket £12.20 (2ad+2ch). Group rates available. **Facilities:** P ▤ & (self guiding tapes & tactile objects for the blind) toilets for disabled shop garden centre ✕ (ex guide dogs) ❦

FONTWELL Map 04 SU90
DENMANS GARDEN
Denmans Ln BN18 0SU (5m E of Chichester off A27 W between Chichester and Arundel, adjacent to Fontwell racecourse)
☎ 01243 542808 ▤ 01243 544064
Times: Open Mar-Oct daily 9-5. **Facilities:** P & shop garden centre ✕ (ex guide dogs) *Details not confirmed for 2003* ❦

Sussex, West

GOODWOOD
Map 04 SU81
GOODWOOD HOUSE
PO18 0PX (3m NE of Chichester)
☎ 01243 755000 📠 01243 755005
e-mail: curator@goodwood.co.uk

Ancestral home of the Dukes of Richmond for 300 years. Following refurbishment the State Apartments have taken on new life, including the restored tapestry drawing room. Goodwood was the country home of the scandalous and glamorous Lennox sisters, immortalised in the BBC TV production of *Aristocrats*. Unrivalled as an English ancestral collection, the paintings include works by Van Dyck, Reynolds, Stubbs and Canaletto.
Times: Open 31 Mar-Sep, Sun & Mon; 4-29 Aug, Sun-Thu 1-5. (Closed 21 Apr, 23 & 24 Jun 8, 14 & 15 Jul, 8 Sep). **Fee:** £6.50 (ch, disabled & student £3, pen £6). Groups 20+ £5.50 each. **Facilities:** 🅿 ☕ ♿ (ramp at front of house, disabled parking area) toilets for disabled shop ✈ 🛍

HANDCROSS
Map 04 TQ22
NYMANS GARDEN
RH17 6EB (on B2114)
☎ 01444 400321 & 400777 📠 01444 400253
Times: Open Garden: Mar-29 Oct, daily Wed, Thu & wknds, (also open BH Mon) 11-6 or sunset if earlier. Nov-Mar, wknds, 11-4, restricted according to ground conditions. Closed 25-26 & 30-31 Dec. Phone for more information. House open 29 Mar-29 Oct 12-4.
Facilities: 🅿 ☕ ♿ (wheelchair route, wheelchair available, braille guide) toilets for disabled shop ✈ (ex guide dogs & hearing dogs) 🛍
Details not confirmed for 2003

HAYWARDS HEATH
Map 05 TQ32
BORDE HILL GARDEN
Balcombe Rd RH16 1XP (0.5m N of Haywards Heath on Balcombe Road, 3m from A23)
☎ 01444 450326 📠 01444 440427
e-mail: info@bordehill.co.uk

Beauty for all seasons with formal 'garden rooms' such as the Rose and Italian Garden, combine with informal areas like the Azalea Ring, the Garden of Allah and the Round Dell. A plantsman's paradise, with rare trees and shrubs introduced in the early 1900s by the Great Plant Collectors from all corners of the world. Spring is heralded early by a magnificent collection of magnolias, rhododendron and azaleas, blending into summer with fragrant roses and herbaceous plants, developing into rich autumn borders before winter's architectural splendour. Magical woodland and parkland walks with outstanding views across the impressive Victorian viaduct.
Times: Open all year, 10-6 or dusk if earlier. **Fee:** * £5.50 (ch £3.50). Family ticket £17. Party 20+ £5 (ch £2.50) each. **Facilities:** 🅿 ☕ ✖ licensed ♿ (wheelchairs available, audio/braille guides) toilets for disabled shop garden centre (must be on lead) 🛍

LOWER BEEDING
Map 04 TQ22
LEONARDSLEE GARDENS
RH13 6PP (4m SW from Handcross, at junct of B2110 & A281)
☎ 01403 891212 📠 01403 891305
e-mail: gardens@leonardslee.com

This Grade I listed garden is set in a peaceful valley with walks around seven beautiful lakes. It is a paradise in spring, with banks of rhododendrons and azaleas along paths lined with bluebells. Wallabies live in parts of the valley, deer in the parks and wildfowl on the lakes. Enjoy the Rock Garden, the fascinating Bonsai, the new 'Behind the Doll's House' exhibition and the collection of Victorian Motorcars (1889-1900).
Times: Open Apr-Oct, daily 9.30-6 **Fee:** Apr & Jun-Oct £6, May (Mon-Fri) £7, (wknds & BH) £8 (ch £4 anytime). **Facilities:** 🅿 ☕ ✖ licensed (No wheelchair access) shop garden centre ✈

PETWORTH
Map 04 SU92
PETWORTH HOUSE & PARK
GU28 0AE (in town centre, A272/283)
☎ 01798 342207 & 343929 📠 01798 342963
e-mail: petworth@ntrust.org.uk

Petworth house is an impressive 17th-century mansion set in a 700 acre Deer Park, landscaped by 'Capability' Brown, and immortalised in Turner's paintings. At Petworth you will find the National Trust's finest art collection including work by Van Dyck, Titian, and Turner as well as sculpture ceramics and fine furniture. Fascinating servants' quarters show the domestic side of life of this great estate.
Times: Open 23 Mar-3 Nov (closed Thu & Fri) 11-5.30 last entry 5
Fee: £7 (ch £4). Family ticket £18. Party 15+ £6.50 p.p. NT members free Pleasure Ground £1.50 (ch free). **Facilities:** 🅿 ☕ ✖ licensed ♿ (wheelchairs available, braille guide) toilets for disabled shop ✈ (ex guide/hearing dogs) 🛍

PULBOROUGH
Map 04 TQ01
PARHAM HOUSE & GARDENS
Parham Park RH20 4HS (3m SE off A283, between Pulborough & Storrington)
☎ 01903 744888 (info line) & 742021
📠 01903 746557
e-mail: parham@dial.pipex.com
Times: Open 4 Apr-Oct, Wed, Thu, Sun & BH. Gardens 12-6; House 2-6 (last entry 5). Guided tours on Wed & Thu mornings and Tue & Fri afternoons by special arrangement. **Facilities:** 🅿 ☕ ♿ (wheelchairs available by arrangement/tape tour) shop garden centre (ex guide dogs & in grounds) *Details not confirmed for 2003* 🛍

Sussex, West 235

RSPB Pulborough Brooks Nature Reserve
Uppertons Barn Visitor Centre, Wiggonholt RH20 2EL (signposted on A283, 2m SE of Pulborough & 2m NW of Storrington)
☎ 01798 875851 ▪ 01798 873816
e-mail: pulborough.brooks@rspb.org.uk

Set in the scenic Arun Valley and easily reached via the visitor centre at Wiggonholt, this is an excellent reserve for year-round family visits. A nature trail winds through hedgerow-lined lanes to viewing hides overlooking water-meadows. Breeding summer birds include nightingales and warblers, ducks and wading birds, and nightjars and hobbies on nearby heathland. Unusual wading birds and hedgerow birds regularly pass through on spring and autumn migration.
Times: Open daily, Reserve: 9-9, (or sunset if earlier). Visitor centre: 10-5. Reserve closed 25 Dec, Visitor Centre closed 25-26 Dec. **Fee:** * £3.50 (ch 5-16 £1, concessions £2.50) Family £7 (2ad+4ch) **Facilities:** P ● & (ramps at some hides/batricar bookable/easy gradient trail) toilets for disabled shop ✕ (ex guide dogs)

SINGLETON   Map 04 SU81
Weald & Downland Open Air Museum
PO18 0EU (6m N of Chichester on A286)
☎ 01243 811348 ▪ 01243 811475
e-mail: office@wealddown.co.uk

A showcase of English architectural heritage, where historic buildings have been rescued from destruction and rebuilt in a parkland setting. Vividly demonstrating the evolution of building techniques and use of local materials, these fascinating buildings bring to life the homes, farms and rural industries of the past 500 years.
Times: Open all year, Mar-Oct, daily 10.30-6 (last admission 5); Nov-Feb, Sat & Sun 10.30-4, also 26 Dec-1 Jan daily & Feb half term, 10.30-4. **Fee:** * £7 (ch & students £4, pen £6.50). Family ticket (2 adults & 3 ch) £19. Party. **Facilities:** P ● & toilets for disabled shop (ex on leads)

SOUTH HARTING   Map 04 SU71
Uppark
GU31 5QR (A3 take A272, B2146 to South Harting, follow signs to Uppark.)
☎ 01730 825415 825857 ▪ 01730 825873
e-mail: uppark@ntrust.org.uk

Times: Open 24 Mar-Oct, Sun-Thu. House 1-5. Car park, woodland walk, garden & Exhibition 11-5. Last admission to house 4pm. Timed tickets will be in operation on BH Sun & Mon & Sun in Aug. House open 12-5 on Sun in Aug. **Facilities:** P ● ✕ licensed & (ramps, lift to basement,chair lift in exhibition) toilets for disabled shop ✕ (ex woodland walk & car park) 🌿 *Details not confirmed for 2003*

TANGMERE   Map 04 SU90
Tangmere Military Aviation Museum Trust
PO20 2ES (off A27, 3m E of Chichester on the Arundel side)
☎ 01243 775223 ▪ 01243 789490
e-mail: admin@tangmere-museum.org.uk

Based at an airfield that played an important role during the World Wars, this museum spans 80 years of military aviation. There are photographs, documents, aircraft and aircraft parts on display along with a Hurricane replica, Spitfire replica and cockpit simulator. A hangar houses a Supermarine Swift and the record-breaking aircraft Meteor and Hunter.
Times: Open Mar-Oct, daily 10-5.30; Feb & Nov, daily 10-4.30. **Fee:** £4 (ch £1.50 & pen £3) Family £9.50 (2ad+2ch) **Facilities:** P ● & (wheelchairs available) toilets for disabled shop ✕ (ex guide dogs)

WEST DEAN   Map 04 SU81
West Dean Gardens
Estate Office PO18 0QZ (on A286, 6m N of Chichester)
☎ 01243 818210 & 811301 ▪ 01243 811342
e-mail: gardens@westdean.org.uk

Award-winning historic garden of 35 acres in a tranquil downland setting. Noted for its 300ft-long Harold Peto pergola, mixed and herbaceous borders, rustic summerhouses and specimen trees. Walled kitchen garden with magnificent collection of 16 Victorian glasshouses and frames. The visitors' centre provides a high level of facilities with a beautiful prospect of the River Lavant and West Dean Park.
Times: Open Mar, Apr & Oct, daily 11-5; May-Sep 10.30-5. Last ticket 4.30pm. **Fee:** £5 (ch £2, pen £4.50). Party+ £4.50. **Facilities:** P ✕ licensed & (reserved parking, 2 wheelchairs available) toilets for disabled shop ✕ (ex guide dogs)

Tyne & Wear

EVENTS & FESTIVALS

April
12th-13th Gateshead Spring Flower Show, Gateshead Central Nursery

July
5th All Ireland Pipe Band Championships, Newcastle
11th-13th Whitby Bay International Jazz Festival
25th-27th Gateshead Summer Flower Show, Gateshead Central Nursery
26th-27th Sunderland International Air Show, Promenade, Seaburn, Sunderland (provisional)

August
24th-25th Newcastle Mela (free Asian festival), Exhibition Park, Newcastle-upon-Tyne
tbc North of England Motorshow, Newcastle Racecourse

September/October
tbc Junior Great North Run, Gateshead International Stadium, Gateshead
tbc Great North Run (Newcastle-upon-Tyne to South Shields)

November
tbc Newcastle Comedy Festival (various venues), Newcastle-upon-Tyne

Top: Marsden Rock

Tyne & Wear is a metropolitan county, created by local government reorganisation in 1974. It includes the towns of Newcastle-upon-Tyne, Gateshead, South Shields and Sunderland. It is cut through by the two rivers the Tyne and the Wear, and includes a section of Hadrian's Wall.

The area grew prosperous on coal and shipbuilding, and buildings of Victorian grandeur reflect its heyday. George Stephenson established an ironworks here in 1826, and the first engine on the Stockton and Darlington railway was made in Newcastle. Industrial decline has hit hard, but the Geordie spirit survives and brings immense vitality to the place.

Newcastle's 'new castle' is believed to date from the 11th century, though the present keep dates from the 12th. Other ancient buildings include the 14th-century cathedral, and the 17th-century Guildhall. Contemporary constructions include the Metro, which links Newcastle to Gateshead (along with several bridges), and the Metro Centre in Gateshead, Europe's largest indoor shopping and leisure complex. The most famous of the bridges are High Level Bridge, a road and rail bridge, built by Robert Stephenson in 1849, and the Tyne Bridge dating from 1929.

Jarrow, five miles east of Newcastle, is remembered for the Jarrow Crusade of 1936, when 200 men marched to London to bring attention to the plight of unemployed shipbuilders. The town was also the home of monk-scholar, the Venerable Bede, whose 8th-century work, *Historia Ecclesiastica Gentis Anglorum*, was the first important history written about the English. He was buried at Jarrow, and his bones remained there until the 11th century when they were moved to Durham. Other notable citizens include footballer Paul "Gazza" Gascoine, singer/songwriters Sting and Jimmy Nail, actor James Bolam, footballing brothers Jackie and Bobby Charlton, and writers Vera Brittan and Catherine Cookson.

Tyne & Wear

🏛 JARROW Map 12 NZ36
BEDES WORLD & ST PAUL'S CHURCH
Church Bank NE32 3DY (off A185 near south end of Tyne tunnel)
☎ 0191 489 2106 📠 0191 428 2361
e-mail: visitor.info@bedesworld.co.uk

The Venerable Bede lived over 1,300 years ago and was one of early Britain's greatest scholars, author of the *Historia Ecclesiastica Gentis Anglorum* - the definitive history of the early medieval period. As well as exhibits detailing Bede's monastic life and work, the museum re-creates an Anglo-Saxon farm and incorporates the ruins of the medieval monastery.
Times: Open all year, Apr-Oct, Mon-Sat 10-5.30, Sun noon-5.30; Nov-Mar, Mon-Sat 10.4.30 & Sun 12-4.30; Xmas-New Year opening times vary. Church open Mon-Sat 10-4 & Sun 2.30-4, unless service being held. **Fee:** * £4.50 (ch & concessions £2.50). Family ticket £9. UB40 family ticket £6. Party rates 15+. **Facilities:** 🅿 ☕ ♿ (electric wheelchair on request) toilets for disabled shop 🎁 (ex guide dogs) 📷

🏛 NEWCASTLE UPON TYNE Map 12 NZ26
CENTRE FOR LIFE
Times Square NE1 4EP (next to Newcastle Central station)
☎ 0191 243 8223 & 0191 243 8210 **2 for 1**
e-mail: bookings@centre-for-life.co.uk

This colourful attraction has chosen one of the biggest subjects possible for its theme: Life itself. With three spectacular shows that explore the Secret of Life, the workings of the brain, and how your body reacts to motion, along with exhibits dealing with cells, the senses, pregnancy, emotion and the beginnings of life, this is an educational as well as entertaining day out.
Times: Open daily Mon-Sat 10-6, Sun 11-6. Last entry 4.30pm. Closed 25 Dec & 1 Jan. **Fee:** £6.95 (ch £4.50, concessions £5.50). Family ticket £19.95. **Facilities:** 🅿 (charged) ☕ ✖ licensed ♿ (ramps, wheelchairs, induction loops) toilets for disabled shop 🎁 (ex guide dogs) 📷

HANCOCK MUSEUM
Barras Bridge NE2 4PT (Follow exit signs for city centre A167 off the A1(M))
☎ 0191 222 7418 📠 0191 222 6753
e-mail: hancock.museum@ncl.ac.uk

Newcastle's premier natural history museum unravels the natural world, through sensational galleries and close encounters with resident reptiles and insects. For more than 100 years the Hancock Museum has provided visitors with a glimpse of the animal kingdom and the powerful and often destructive forces of nature. The Hancock is home to creatures past and present and the odd Egyptian mummy or two.
Times: Open all year, Mon-Sat, 10-5, Sun 2-5. Closed 25 & 26 Dec & 1 Jan. **Fee:** £2.50 (ch & concessions £1.75). Family ticket (2 adults & 2 ch) £7.25. Prices vary with special exhibitions, call 0191 222 7418 for details. **Facilities:** 🅿 ☕ ♿ (stair lift, audio/braille guide, sign language) toilets for disabled shop 🎁 (ex guide dogs) 📷

MUSEUM OF ANTIQUITIES
The University NE1 7RU (on campus of Newcastle University)
☎ 0191 222 7849 📠 0191 222 8561
e-mail: m.o.antiquities@ncl.ac.uk

Artefacts from north-east England from prehistoric times to AD 1600 are on display here. The principal museum for Hadrian's Wall, this collection includes models of the wall, life-size Roman soldiers and a reconstruction of the Temple of Mithras.
Times: Open all year, daily (ex Sun), 10-5 (Closed Good Fri, 24-26 Dec & 1 Jan). **Fee:** Free. **Facilities:** 🅿 (400yds) ♿ (Large print guide) shop 🎁 (ex guide dogs) 📷

🏛 ROWLANDS GILL Map 12 NZ15
GIBSIDE
NE16 6BG (turn off A1 western Bypass following brown tourist signs from Gibside & Gibside Chapel, 3m W of Metro Centre & 6m SW of Gateshead, on B6314)
☎ 01207 542255
e-mail: tony.walton@ntrust.org.uk

The important early 18th-century landscaped park contains a chapel - an outstanding example of Palladian architecture, built to a design by James Paine as the mausoleum for members of the Bowes family. It stands at one end of the Great Walk of Turkey oaks, looking towards the column of British Liberty.
Times: Open: Grounds all year (ex Mon), 10-4.30. Open BH Mon (Mar-Oct 10-5, Nov-Feb 10-3.30). Chapel: Apr-Oct as grounds 11-5, otherwise by prior arrangment. **Fee:** £3.50 (ch £1.75). Family ticket £9 (single parent with family £7). **Facilities:** 🅿 ☕ ♿ (braille guide, wheelchairs & wheelchair carrier) toilets for disabled shop 🎁 📷

🏛 SOUTH SHIELDS Map 12 NZ36
ARBEIA ROMAN FORT & MUSEUM
Baring St NE33 2BB (5 mins walk from South Shields town centre)
☎ 0191 456 1369 & 454 4093
📠 0191 427 6862

In the town are the extensive remains of Arbeia, a Roman fort in use from the 2nd to 4th century. It was the supply base for the Roman army's campaign against Scotland. On site there are full size reconstructions of a fort gateway, a barrack block and part of the commanding officer's house. Archaeological evacuations are in progress throughout the summer.
Times: Open all year, Etr-Sep, Mon-Sat 10.30-5.30, Sun 1-5; Oct-Etr, Mon-Sat 10-4. Closed 25-26 Dec, 1 Jan & Good Fri. **Fee:** * Fort & Museum free of charge ex for 'Timequest' Archaeological Interpretation Gallery £1.50 (ch & concessions 80p). **Facilities:** 🅿 ♿ (Minicom system) toilets for disabled shop 📷

🏛 SUNDERLAND Map 12 NZ35
MUSEUM & WINTER GARDENS
Burdon Rd SR1 1PP (situated in Sunderland City Centre)
☎ 0191 553 2323 📠 0191 553 7828
e-mail: sunderland.museum@tyne-wear-museums.org.uk

This award-winning attraction re-opened in 2001. The

continued

Tyne & Wear

wide-ranging displays, with many hands-on exhibits, cover the archaeology and geology of Sunderland, the coal mines and shipyards of the area and the spectacular glass and pottery made on Wearside. Other galleries show the changes in the lifestyles of Sunderland women over the past century, works by LS Lowry and wildlife from all corners of the globe. Exotic plants from around the world can be seen in The Winter Gardens, growing to their full natural height in a spectacular glass and steel rotunda.
Times: Open all year, Mon 10-4, Tue-Sat 10-5, Sun 2-5. **Fee:** Free. **Facilities:** P (150 yds) ✖ licensed ♿ (lifts to all floors, induction loops) toilets for disabled shop 🍴 (ex guide dogs) 🛍

NATIONAL GLASS CENTRE
Liberty Way SR6 0GL
☎ 0191 515 5555 📠 0191 515 5556   **2 for 1**
e-mail: info@nationalglasscentre.com

Housed in a striking modern building, the National Glass Centre celebrates this unique material and explains its history. Visitors can see the changing exhibitions of glass art, featuring pieces by leading artists. There is also the opportunity to witness the glass-making process, to learn more about glass and how it impacts on our lives. The brave can even walk on the glass roof 30 feet above the riverside.
Times: Open daily 10-5 (last admission to glass tour 4pm). Closed 25 Dec & 1 Jan. **Fee:** * £5 (concessions £3). Family ticket £12. **Facilities:** P ✖ licensed ♿ (lifts, ramps, parking facilites) toilets for disabled shop 🍴 (ex guide dogs) 🛍

TYNEMOUTH   Map 12 NZ36
TYNEMOUTH CASTLE & PRIORY
NE30 4BZ (near North Pier)
☎ 0191 257 1090

The castle and priory are a testament to the strategic importance of the site and its great religious significance. The soaring arches of the presbytery are an eloquent reminder of the priory's former wealth, and the Percy Chantry is still almost complete.
Times: Open all year, 29 Mar-Sep, daily 10-6 (Oct, daily 10-5); Nov-Mar, Wed-Sun 10-1 & 10-4. Closed 24-26 Dec & 1 Jan. Gun battery Apr-Sep: Sat-Sun & BH 10-6 **Fee:** * £2.20 (ch 5-15 £1.10, under 5's free, concessions £1.70). Family ticket £5.50 **Facilities:** ♿ shop 🍴 ❈

WALLSEND   Map 12 NZ26
SEGEDUNUM ROMAN FORT, BATHS & MUSEUM
Buddle St NE28 6HR (A187 from Tyne Tunnel, signposted)
☎ 0191 236 9347 📠 0191 295 5858   **2 for 1**
e-mail: segedunum@tyne-wear-museums.org.uk

Hadrian's Wall was built by the Roman Emperor, Hadrian in 122AD, Segedunum was built as part of the Wall, serving as a garrison for 600 soldiers until the collapse of Roman rule around 410AD. This major historical venture shows what life would have been like then, using artefacts, audio-visuals, reconstructed buildings and a 34mtr-high viewing tower.
Times: Open all year, Apr-Oct, daily 10-5; Nov-Mar, daily 10-3.30. (Closed 25-26 Dec & 1 Jan) **Fee:** * £3.50 (ch, pen & concessions £1.95). Family ticket £9. **Facilities:** P 🍽 ♿ (lifts) toilets for disabled shop 🍴 (ex guide dogs) 🛍

WASHINGTON   Map 12 NZ35
WASHINGTON OLD HALL
The Avenue, Washington Village NE38 7LE (from A1 and A19 follow signs to Washington, District 4 on The Avenue, next to Holy Trinity Church)
☎ 0191 416 6879 📠 0191 4192065
e-mail: nwohal@smtp.ntrust.org.uk

The home of George Washington's ancestors from 1183 to 1613, the Old Hall was originally an early medieval manor, but was rebuilt in the 17th century. The house has been restored and filled with period furniture. Exhibitions include stepping back in time and enjoying the peace and quite in the beautifully-planted Knot Parterre gardens, The Jacobean Great Hall, Kitchen, Panelled room and the Liberty Room celebrating American Independence and the life of George Washington.
Times: Open Apr-Oct, Sun-Wed & Good Fri 11-5. Last admission 4.30. **Fee:** £3 (ch £1.50). Family ticket £7.50. Group £2.50 each. **Facilities:** P 🍽 ♿ (braille guide, sensory scented gardens, handrails, ramps) toilets for disabled shop 🍴 (ex guide dogs) 🛍

WWT WASHINGTON
District 15 NE38 8LE (signposted off A195, A1231 & A182)
☎ 0191 416 5454 📠 0191 416 5801   **2 for 1**
e-mail: washington@wwt.org.uk

In a parkland setting, on the north bank of the River Wear, WWT Washington is the home of a wonderful collection of exotic wildfowl from all over the world. There is also a heronry where visitors can watch a colony of wild Grey Herons on CCTV. The 100-acre site includes an area for wintering wildfowl which can be observed from hides, and a flock of Chilean Flamingos. Other features include a discovery centre, waterfowl nursery, picture windows and a viewing gallery from which to observe the birds.
Times: Open all year, daily 9.30-5 (summer) or 9.30-4 (winter). Closed 25 Dec. **Fee:** * £5.20 (ch £3.20, pen £4.20). Family £13.50. **Facilities:** P 🍽 ✖ licensed ♿ (lowered windows in certain hides, wheelchairs to hire free) toilets for disabled shop 🍴 (ex guide/hearing dogs) 🛍

WHITBURN   Map 12 NZ46
SOUTER LIGHTHOUSE
Coast Rd SR6 7NH (On A183 coast road, 2m S of South Shields, 3m N of Sunderland)
☎ 0191 529 3161 & 01670 773966
📠 0191 529 0902
e-mail: nslhse@smtp.ntrust.org.uk
Times: Open Apr-Oct daily ex Fri, (open Good Fri), 11-5. Last admission 4.30. Please contact for opening at other times. **Facilities:** P ✖ ♿ braille guide, induction loops, tactile exhibits toilets for disabled shop 🍴 (ex guide dogs) 🛍 *Details not confirmed for 2003* 🛍

Warwickshire

The countryside of south Warwickshire, located in the Heart of England, was beloved of William Shakespeare. The bard is forever associated with the town of Stratford-upon-Avon, the place of his birth and death, which now has two theatres built in his honour.

These days, the small market town he knew as home is packed with tourists – it is the most visited British tourist destination outside London. North of the county, around Coventry, which is itself officially part of the West Midlands, the scene is much more industrial/urban and seems a world away from this mainly rural area.

Warwickshire has some fine towns, including Warwick itself, the county town, which boasts one of the greatest English castles. The castle is medieval, though it was comprehensively restored in the 19th century, and its enormous bulk dominates the town. The centre of Warwick is mainly Georgian, built following a fire in 1694 that destroyed the earlier medieval buildings, though some do remain on the periphery. The county's other great castle is Kenilworth, a Norman fortress built of sandstone standing to the west of Kenilworth town.

Leamington Spa came to prominence when the fashion for 'taking the waters' was at its height in the late 18th and early 19th centuries. Rugby, however, is best known as the home of one of England's most elevated public schools, immortalised in Thomas Hughes' *Tom Brown's Schooldays*. The school was also the birthplace of the sport that bears its name.

Residents of the county have included singer-songwriter Nick Drake; author George Eliot; and Sir Francis Galton, anthropologist and cousin of Charles Darwin, who established that everybody's fingerprints are unique.

Top: Warwick Castle

EVENTS & FESTIVALS

February
tbc February Frolics (during lambing), Hatton Country World, February half-term

March
22nd-23rd Spring Craft Fair, Ragley Hall, Alcester

April
12th-13th Gardeners Weekend, Alcester

May
31st-1st June Transport Show, Alcester (provisional)

June
31st May-1st Transport Show, Alcester (provisional)
30th-3rd July The Royal Show, Stoneleigh

July
13th Caspian Horses Show, Alcester (provisional)
30th June-3rd The Royal Show, Stoneleigh
3rd-14th Warwick & Leamington Festival
25th-27th Warwickshire Folk Festival (various venues)

August
2nd Fireworks & Laser Show, Alcester (provisional)
6th-7th Gardeners Weekend, Alcester (provisional)
16th-17th Warwickshire & West Midlands Game Fair, Alcester (provisional)
23rd-25th Town & Country Festival, Stoneleigh

October
18th-19th Autumn Craft Fair, Alcester (provisional)

November
29th-30th Yuletide Craft Fair, Alcester (provisional)

ALCESTER
Map 04 SP05
RAGLEY HALL
B49 5NJ (8m of Stratford upon Avon, off A46/A435)
☎ 01789 762090   ▤ 01789 764791
e-mail: info@ragleyhall.com

Built in 1680, Ragley is the family home of the Marquess and Marchioness of Hertford and houses a superb collection of 18th-century paintings, porcelain and furniture. Set in 27 acres of gardens and 400 acres of parkland, the house contains a stunning mural by Graham Rust *The Temptation* and England's finest Baroque plasterwork dated 1750. Ticket includes the House, Terrace Tea Rooms overlooking the Rose Garden, gift shop, adventure playground, unique 3D maze, lakeside picnic area, woodland walk and stables containing equestrian memorabilia. Location for BBC production of *Scarlet Pimpernel*.
Times: Open mid Apr-early Oct, Thu-Sun & BH Mon. Park & Garden open daily, late Jul-early Sep. **Fee:** * House (including garden & park) £6 (ch £4.50, pen £5). **Facilities:** ▯ ◳ ♿ (lift to first floor) toilets for disabled shop (on leads in park only)

BADDESLEY CLINTON
Map 04 SP27
BADDESLEY CLINTON HALL
B93 0DQ (0.75m W off A4141, 7.5m NW of Warwick)
☎ 01564 783294
▤ 01564 782706   **2 for 1**
e-mail: baddesleyclinton@ntrust.org.uk

A romantically-sited medieval moated house, dating from the 14th century, that has changed very little since 1634. With family portraits, priest holes, chapel, garden, ponds, nature trail and lake walk. An autumn lecture programme is planned.
Times: House open 6 Mar-3 Nov, Wed-Sun & BH Mon. Mar-Apr & Oct-Nov 1.30-5; May-Sep 1.30-5.30. (Last admissions 30 mins before closing). Grounds open Good Fri-3 Nov 12-5; May-Sep 12-5.30; 6 Nov-15 Dec. **Fee:** * £5.80. Family ticket £14.50. Grounds, restaurant & shop only £2.90. **Facilities:** ▯ ✕ licensed ♿ (w/chairs avail, braille guides, tactile route) toilets for disabled shop ✈ (ex guide dogs) ⚘

CHARLECOTE
Map 04 SP25
CHARLECOTE PARK
CV35 9ER (5m E of Stratford, 1m W of Wellesbourne on B4086)
☎ 01789 470277   ▤ 01789 470544   **2 for 1**
e-mail: charlecote@smtp.ntrust.org.uk

Built in the 1550s and later visited by Queen Elizabeth I, Charlecote Park was landscaped by 'Capability' Brown. Fallow deer, reputedly poached by Shakespeare, and a flock of Jacob sheep first introduced in 1756. The principal rooms are decorated in Elizabethan Revival style.

Times: Open 6 Mar-2 Nov; 12-5. Fri-Tue 12-5. Gardens 11-6 **Fee:** * £5.80 (ch £2.90). Family ticket £14.50 Grounds £3. **Facilities:** ▯ ◳ ✕ licensed ♿ (Braille guides & hearing scheme available) toilets for disabled shop ✈ ⚘ ▱

COUGHTON
Map 04 SP06
COUGHTON COURT
B49 5JA (2m N of Alcester on E side of A435)
☎ 01789 762435   ▤ 01789 765544
Times: Open 23 Mar-Jul & Sep daily (ex Mon/Tue) but open BH Mon/Tue. (Closed Good Fri & 23 Jun). Aug daily ex Mon (open BH Mon). 5-26 Oct Sat/Sun. **Facilities:** ▯ ✕ licensed ♿ (braille guide, wheelchair available) toilets for disabled shop ✈ ⚘ *Details not confirmed for 2003* ▱

FARNBOROUGH
Map 04 SP44
FARNBOROUGH HALL
OX17 1DU (6m N of Banbury, 0.5m W of A423)
☎ 01295 690002
e-mail: upton@smtp.ntrust.org.uk
Times: House, grounds & terrace walk open Apr-Sep, Wed & Sat, 5 & 6 May 2-6. Terrace walk Thu & Fri only, 2-6. Last admission 5.30pm. (Closed Good Friday). **Facilities:** ▯ ♿ ✈ (ex guide dogs) ⚘ *Details not confirmed for 2003*

GAYDON
Map 04 SP35
HERITAGE MOTOR CENTRE
Banbury Rd CV35 0BJ (M40 Junct 12 and take B4100. Motor centre is signposted from this junct)
☎ 01926 641188   ▤ 01926 641555
e-mail: enquiries@heritagemotorcentre.org.uk

Home to the largest collection of historic British cars anywhere in the world. Set in 63 acres of grounds, the centre boasts a Land Rover demonstration course and

continued

Warwickshire 241

has children's quad bikes and electric cars on offer at weekends and during school holidays.

Times: Open daily 10-5. (Closed 24-26 Dec). **Fee:** * £8 (ch 5-16 £6, under 5 free, & pen £7). Family ticket £25. subject to changes for 2003 **Facilities:** 🅿 🍴 ♿ (lifts, wide doors, graded ramps & pathways, wheelchairs) toilets for disabled shop 🐕 (ex guide/hearing dogs) 🍼

🏛 KENILWORTH   Map 04 SP27
KENILWORTH CASTLE
CV8 1NE
☎ 01926 852078

Kenilworth is the largest castle ruin in England, its massive walls towering over the countryside. Originally founded in the 11th century, it was already ancient when Queen Elizabeth I visited her favourite, Robert Dudley, Earl of Leicester, here in 1575; he built a new wing for her use.
Times: Open all year, 29 Mar-Sep, daily 10-6 (Oct, daily 10-5); Nov-Mar daily 10-4. (Closed 24-26 Dec & 1 Jan). **Fee:** * £4.40 (ch 5-15 £2.20, under 5's free, concessions £3.30). Family ticket £11 **Facilities:** 🅿 ♿ shop 🐕 ♿

STONELEIGH ABBEY
CV8 2LF (Entrance to the abbey is off the B4115 close to junction of A46 and A452)
☎ 01926 858535 & 858585   📠 01926 850724
e-mail: enquire@stoneleigh.org

Stoneleigh Abbey is one of the finest country house estates in the Midlands and has seen the subject of considerable restoration work. Set in 690 acres of parkland, the abbey, founded in the reign of Henry II, is now managed by a charitable trust. Visitors will experience a wealth of architectural styles spanning more than 800 years. The magnificent state rooms and chapel, the medieval Gatehouse and the Regency stables are some of the major areas to be admired.
Times: Open Apr-Oct, Tue-Thu, Sun & BHs for guided tours at 11, 1 & 3pm **Fee:** * £5 (one child free with every paying adult, additional ch £2.50, pen £3.50) Party rates available. **Facilities:** 🅿 🍴 ♿ (West Wing, Ground Level and grounds) toilets for disabled shop

🏛 MIDDLETON   Map 07 SP19
ASH END HOUSE CHILDRENS FARM
Middleton Ln, Middleton B78 2BL (signposted from A4091)
☎ 0121 329 3240   📠 0121 329 3240
e-mail: childrensfarm@ashendhouse.fsnet.co.uk
Times: Open daily 10-5 or dusk in winter. (Closed 25-28 Dec & 1 Jan). **Facilities:** 🅿 🍴 ♿ toilets for disabled shop 🐕 (ex guide dogs) *Details not confirmed for 2003* 🍼

MIDDLETON HALL
B78 2AE (M42 junct 9, on A4091 midway between Belfry & Drayton Manor, follow brown heritage signs)
☎ 01827 283095   📠 01827 285717
e-mail: middletonhall@btconnect.com

Once the home of two great 17th-century naturalists, Francis Willughby and John Ray, the Hall shows several architectural styles, from c1300 to a Georgian west wing. The grounds include a nature reserve, lake, meadow, orchard and woodland, all Sites of Special Scientific Interest.
Times: Open Apr-13 Oct, Sun 2-5, BH 11-5. **Fee:** * £2.50 (ch free, pen £1.50). BH & some Sun £4 (ch 50p, pen £3) **Facilities:** 🅿 🍴 ♿ (wheelchair available) toilets for disabled shop

🏛 NUNEATON   Map 04 SP39
ARBURY HALL
CV10 7PT (2m SW of Nuneaton, off B4102 Meriden road)
☎ 024 7638 2804   📠 024 7664 1147
e-mail: brenda.newell@arburyhall.net

The 16th-century Elizabethan house, Gothicised in the 18th century, has been the home of the Newdegate family for over 450 years. It is the finest complete example of Gothic revival architecture in existence, and contains pictures, furniture, and beautiful plasterwork ceilings. The 17th-century stable block, with a central doorway by Wren, houses the tearooms and lovely gardens with lakes and wooded walks.
Times: Open Etr-Sep 2-5.30 (last admission 5pm). Hall & gardens: Sun & Mon of BH weekends only. For other opening days & times, contact the Administrator. **Fee:** * £6 (ch £3.50) gardens only £4. (ch £2.50) **Facilities:** 🅿 🍴 ♿ shop 🐕 (ex guide dogs & in grounds)

🏛 PACKWOOD HOUSE   Map 07 SP17
PACKWOOD HOUSE
B94 6AT (on unclass road off A34)
☎ 01564 782024   📠 01564 782912
e-mail: baddesley@smtp.ntrust.org.uk

Dating from the 16th century, Packwood House has been extended and much changed over the years. An important collection of tapestries and textiles is displayed. Equally important are the stunning gardens with renowned herbaceous borders, attracting many visitors, and the almost surreal topiary garden based on the Sermon on the Mount.
Times: Open 6 Mar-3 Nov Wed-Sun, BH Mon & Good Fri. Mar/Oct/Nov 11-4.30. May-Sep 11-5.30. **Fee:** * £5.20 (ch £2.60). Family ticket £13. Garden only £2.60 (ch £1.30). **Facilities:** 🅿 ♿ (w/chairs available, tactile tour, braille guide) toilets for disabled shop 🐕 (ex guide dogs) 🍴 🍼

Warwickshire

🏛 RUGBY　　　　　　　　　Map 04 SP57
THE JAMES GILBERT RUGBY FOOTBALL MUSEUM
5 Saint Matthew's St CV21 3BY (On A428 opposite Rugby school)
☎ 01788 333889　📠 01788 540795
e-mail: museum@james-gilbert.com
Times: Open all year, Mon-Sat 9-5. Phone for holiday opening times.
Facilities: P (500 yds) & shop ✱ (ex guide dogs) *Details not confirmed for 2003*

🏛 RYTON-ON-DUNSMORE　　Map 04 SP37
RYTON ORGANIC GARDENS
CV8 3LG (5m SE of Coventry signposted off A45, on road to village of Wolston)
☎ 024 7630 3517　📠 024 7663 9229　**2 for 1**
e-mail: enquiry@hdra.org.uk

Eight acres of glorious gardens show how you can grow flowers, fruit and vegetables nature's way without added chemicals. More than thirty individual gardens to look at and enjoy. New in 2003 'The Vegetable Kingdom' - learn all about vegetables, their history, varieties, and how they help to keep us healthy, in a fully interactive visitor centre. Special events, tours and a restaurant.
Times: Daily 10-5. (Closed Xmas). **Fee:** * £3.95 (child £1.50).
Facilities: P ✱ licensed & (wheelchairs available) toilets for disabled shop garden centre ✱ (ex guide dogs)

🏛 SHOTTERY　　　　　　　Map 04 SP15
ANNE HATHAWAY'S COTTAGE
CV37 9HH (House in Shottery Village, N of town)
☎ 01789 292100
e-mail: info@shakespeare.org.uk　**2 for 1**

Before her marriage to William Shakespeare, Anne Hathaway lived in this substantial 12-roomed thatched Tudor farmhouse with her prosperous yeoman family. The house now shows many aspects of domestic life in 16th-century England, and has a lovely traditional cottage garden and Shakespeare tree garden.
Times: Open Nov-Mar, Mon-Sat; 10-4. Sun 10.30-4. Apr-May & Sep-Oct, Mon-Sat; 10-5. Sun 10.30-5. Jun-Aug, Mon-Sat; 9-5. Sun 9.30-5. **Fee:** * £5 (ch £2, concessions £4). Family ticket £11. Inclusive ticket to 3 Shakespearian properties £8.50 (ch £4.20, concessions £7.50). Family £20. Ticket to 5 houses £12 (ch £6, concessions £11) Family £29. Party **Facilities:** P (charged) ✱ & toilets for disabled shop garden centre ✱ (ex guide dogs)

🏛 STRATFORD-UPON-AVON　Map 04 SP25
BUTTERFLY FARM
Tramway Walk, Swan's Nest Ln CV37 7LS (south bank of River Avon opposite RSC)
☎ 01789 299288　📠 01789 415878
e-mail: sales@butterflyfarm.co.uk

Europe's largest live butterfly and insect exhibit. Hundreds of the world's most spectacular and colourful butterflies, in the unique setting of a lush tropical landscape, with splashing waterfalls and fish-filled pools. See also the strange and fascinating Insect City, a bustling metropolis of ants, bees, stick insects, beetles and other remarkable insects. See the dangerous and deadly in Arachnoland!
Times: Open daily 10-6 (winter 10-dusk). Closed 25 Dec. **Fee:** * £4.25 (ch £3.25, pen & students £3.75). Family £12.50 **Facilities:** P (opposite entrance) (site parking orange badge holders only) & toilets for disabled shop ✱

HALL'S CROFT
Old Town CV37 6EP (In town centre)
☎ 01789 292107　📠 01789 296083　**2 for 1**
e-mail: info@shakespeare.org.uk

A Tudor house with outstanding furniture and paintings where Shakespeare's daughter Susanna, and her husband, Dr John Hall, lived before moving to New Place on the dramatist's death. There is an exhibition on Tudor medicine, and fine walled gardens can also be seen.
Times: Open Nov-Mar, Mon-Sat; 11-4, Sun, 12-4. Apr-May & Sep-Oct daily; 11-5. Jun-Aug Mon-Sat; 9.30-5. Sun 10-5. **Fee:** * £3.50 (ch £1.70 concessions £3) Family ticket £8.50. Five House Properties ticket: £12 (ch £6, concessions £11) Family ticket £29. Multiple House ticket: £8.50 (ch £4.20, concessions £7.50) Family £20. Party **Facilities:** P (100mtrs) (2hr limit on-street parking) ✱ licensed & (ramp access for garden & lawns) toilets for disabled shop ✱ (ex guide dogs)

NEW PLACE / NASH'S HOUSE
Chapel St CV37 6EP (In town centre)
☎ 01789 292325　📠 01789 263138　**2 for 1**
e-mail: info@shakespeare.org.uk

Only the foundations remain of the house where Shakespeare spent the last five years of his life and died in 1616. The house was destroyed in 1759, but the picturesque garden has been planted as an Elizabethan

continued

knot garden. There is a small museum of furniture and local history in the adjacent Nash's House.
Times: Open Nov-Mar, Mon-Sat 11-4, Sun 12-4. Apr-May & Sep-Oct, daily 11-5. Jun-Aug Mon-Sat; 9.30-5, Sun 10-5. **Fee:** * £3.50 (ch £1.70, concessions £3.70) Family ticket £8.50. 3 properties £8.50 (ch £4.20, concessions £7.50) Family £20. 5 Properties Ticket £12 (ch £6, concessions £11) Family £29 **Facilities:** P (250yds) & toilets for disabled shop ✖ (ex guide dogs)

ROYAL SHAKESPEARE COMPANY COLLECTION
Royal Shakespeare Theatre, Waterside CV37 6BB (M40 Junct 14 take A46 S. At 1st rdbt take 1st exit (A439). Parking in town centre, follow RSC signposted)
☎ 01789 262870 01789 262870
e-mail: info@rsc.org.uk

The RSC gallery opened in 1881, and was first part of the first Shakespeare Memorial Theatre. In 1926 fire destroyed the theatre leaving only a semi circular wall around the gallery. The exhibition space now displays costumes from past RSC productions, paintings and other Theatre Memorabilia.

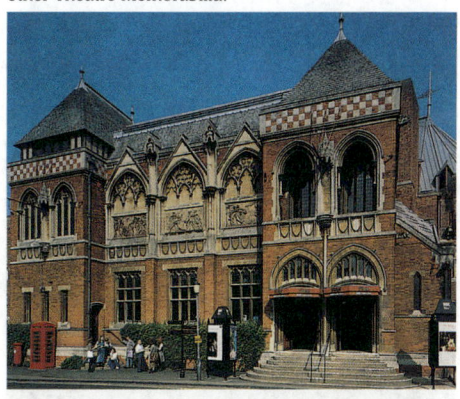

Times: Open all year, Mon-Fri 1.30-6.30, Sat 10.30-6.30 & Sun 11.30-6.30. (Closed 24 & 25 Dec).Theatre tours usually Mon-Fri (ex matinee days), 1.30 & 5.30, Sun 12, 1, 2 & 3. **Fee:** * Exhibition £1.50 (ch, pen & students £1). Family ticket £4. Theatre Tours £4 (ch, pen & students £3) - advisable to book in advance. **Facilities:** P (200yds) (street parking restricted to 2hrs) 🍽 ✖ & services for hearing impaired, braille books/reading rooms toilets for disabled shop ✖ (ex guide dogs)

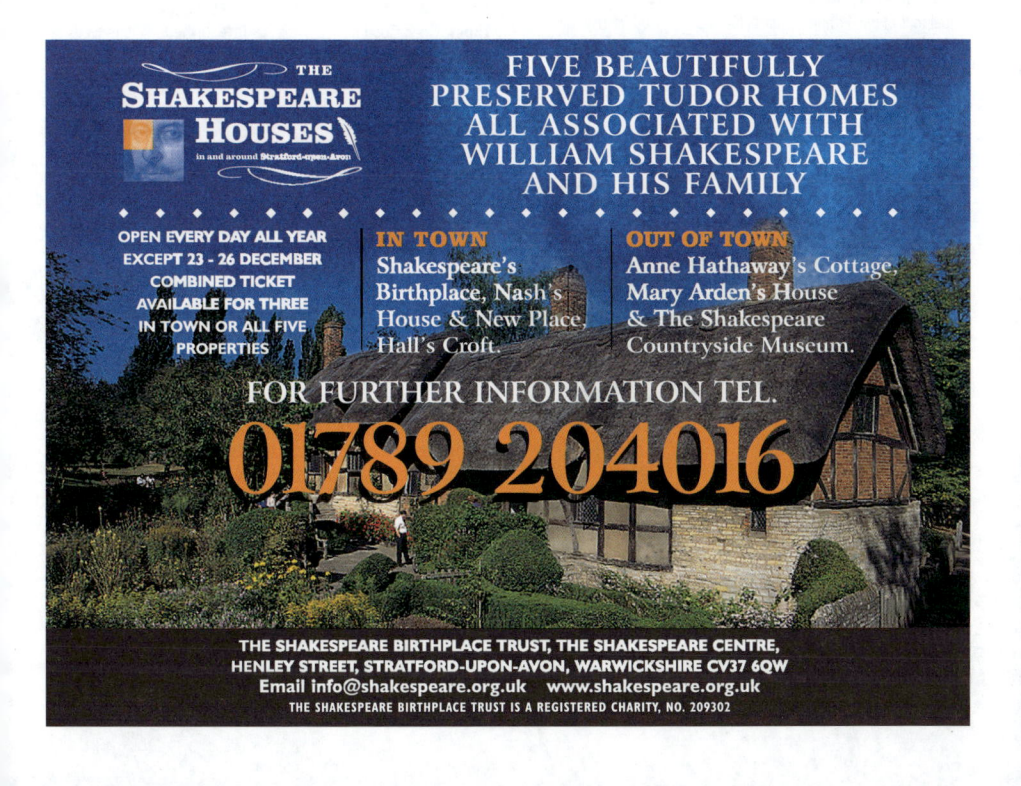

THE SHAKESPEARE HOUSES
in and around Stratford-upon-Avon

FIVE BEAUTIFULLY PRESERVED TUDOR HOMES ALL ASSOCIATED WITH WILLIAM SHAKESPEARE AND HIS FAMILY

OPEN EVERY DAY ALL YEAR
EXCEPT 23 - 26 DECEMBER
COMBINED TICKET
AVAILABLE FOR THREE
IN TOWN OR ALL FIVE
PROPERTIES

IN TOWN
Shakespeare's Birthplace, Nash's House & New Place, Hall's Croft.

OUT OF TOWN
Anne Hathaway's Cottage, Mary Arden's House & The Shakespeare Countryside Museum.

FOR FURTHER INFORMATION TEL.
01789 204016

THE SHAKESPEARE BIRTHPLACE TRUST, THE SHAKESPEARE CENTRE,
HENLEY STREET, STRATFORD-UPON-AVON, WARWICKSHIRE CV37 6QW
Email info@shakespeare.org.uk   www.shakespeare.org.uk
THE SHAKESPEARE BIRTHPLACE TRUST IS A REGISTERED CHARITY, NO. 209302

Warwickshire

Shakespeare's Birthplace
Henley St CV37 6QW (in town centre)
☎ 01789 204016   ▤ 01789 296343
e-mail: info@shakespeare.org.uk

2 for 1

Shakespeare was born in the timber-framed house in 1564. It contains numerous exhibits of the Elizabethan period and Shakespeare memorabilia, and the acclaimed exhibition, Shakespeare; His Life and Background.
Times: Open all year, Nov-Mar, Mon-Sat, 10-4, Sun 10.30-4; Apr-May & Sep-Oct, Mon-Sat, 10-5, Sun 10.30-5; Jun-Aug, Mon-Sat, 9-5, Sun 9.30-5. **Fee:** £6.50 (ch £2.50, concessions £5.50). Family ticket £15. 3 properties ticket £8.50 (ch £4.20, concessions £7.50). Family ticket £20. 5 properties ticket £12 (ch £6, concessions £11). Family ticket £29. **Facilities:** P (100 yds) (no vehicle access to Henley Street) & virtual tour of the birthplace. toilets for disabled shop ✘ (ex guide dogs)

See advert on page 243

The Teddy Bear Museum
19 Greenhill St CV37 6LF (M40 junct 15, follow signs to Stratford Town Centre)
☎ 01789 293160
e-mail: info@theteddybearmuseum.com

2 for 1

Collection of some of the oldest and rarest teddy bears in the world, housed in a small house once owned by Henry VIII. Lots of modern teddy bear stars too,
including the original Fozzie Bear, Paddington Bear, Mr. Bean's bear and many more.
Times: Open all year, daily 9.30-5.30. Closed 25-26 Dec. **Fee:** £2.50 (ch £1.50, concessions £1.95). Family ticket £7.50. Party 20+.
Facilities: P (30yds & 200yds) (access to ground floor shop only) shop ✘ (ex guide dogs)

🏛 UPTON HOUSE   Map 04 SP34
Upton House
OX15 6HT (on A422, 7m NW of Banbury)
☎ 01295 670266   ▤ 01295 670266
e-mail: upton@smtp.ntrust.org.uk
Times: Open 23 Mar-3 Nov daily (ex Thu/Fri) 1-5, last admission 4.30. **Facilities:** P 🍴 & (Braille guide, parking nr house, buggy for lower garden) toilets for disabled shop ✘ (ex guide dogs) ✿ *Details not confirmed for 2003*

🏛 WARWICK   Map 04 SP26
Warwick Castle
CV34 4QU (2m from M40 exit 15)
☎ 0870 442 2000   ▤ 01926 401692
e-mail: customer.information@warwick-castle.com
Times: Open daily 10-6 (5pm Nov-Mar). Closed 25 Dec. **Facilities:** P (charged) 🍴 ✘ licensed & (Free admission to wheelchair bound visitors) toilets for disabled shop ✘ (ex assistance dogs) *Details not confirmed for 2003*

Warwickshire Yeomanry Museum
The Court House Vaults, Jury St CV34 4EW (corner of Jury St & Castle Street)
☎ 01926 492212   ▤ 01926 494837
Times: Open Good Fri-Sep, Fri-Sun & BHs 10-1 & 2-4. Other times by prior arrangement. **Facilities:** P (300yds) (2hr max in nearby streets) shop ✘ *Details not confirmed for 2003*

🏛 WILMCOTE   Map 04 SP15
Mary Arden's House and the Shakespeare Countryside Museum
CV37 6BG (3m NW off A34)
☎ 01789 293455   ▤ 01789 296083
e-mail: info@shakespeare.org.uk

2 for 1

Mary Arden was William Shakespeare's mother, and this picturesque, half-timbered Tudor house was her childhood home. The house is the main historic feature of an extensive complex of farm buildings which house displays of farming and country life, including a remarkable dovecote, kitchen circa 1900, a smithy and cooper's workshop. Daily demonstrations by The Heart of England Falconry. Rare breeds and field walk.
Times: Open all year, Nov-Mar, 10-4; Sun, 10.30-4; Apr-May & Sep-Oct, Mon-Sat 10-5; Sun 10.30-5; Jun-Aug, Mon-Sat 9.30-5, Sun 10-5. **Fee:** * £5.50 (ch £2.50, concessions £5) Family ticket £13.50. Three Properties Ticket £8.50 (ch £4.20, concessions £7.50) Family £20. Five Properties Ticket £12 (ch £6, concessions £11) Family ticket £29. **Facilities:** P 🍴 & toilets for disabled shop ✘ (ex guide dogs)

West Midlands

At the centre of England, the West Midlands is a metropolitan county with a mainly industrial base. Birmingham is the administrative centre and the other main towns are Coventry, Dudley, Smethick, Walsall, West Bromwich and Wolverhampton.

The area was badly affected by the decline in British manufacturing, but has fought back by diversification into the service sector; impressive conference and exhibition facilities are offered in Birmingham, in the form of the International Convention Centre and National Exhibition Centre, home to many of the country's biggest trade fairs. Industrial heritage museums have blossomed, including the Black Country Museum at Dudley, and Cadbury World, which tells the story of chocolate and the chocolate factory established at Bournville by the renowned Quaker family.

Birmingham, AKA 'Brum', is Britain's second largest city, its position at the hub of things emphasised by the miles of canals criss-crossing the city and its amazing tangle of flyovers. There are some splendid public buildings, notably the Town Hall and the City Museum and Art Gallery. Modern developments include an ongoing rejuvenation of the infamous 60s-designed Bull Ring shopping centre. Birmingham's urban sprawl produced bands like Electric Light Orchestra, Led Zeppelin and Black Sabbath in the 60s and 70s. Ozzy Osbourne of Black Sabbath has recently become an unlikely TV star.

The West Midland's multi-racial population gives a buzz to its cultural life, which offers a feast of arts, products, foods and festivals from around the world. In the late 1970s, Coventry was the home of the Two-Tone record label, and band The Specials, mixing punk and ska and gaining plenty of chart success.

Fans of *The Lord of the Rings* trilogy may be interested to learn that JRR Tolkien, although actually born in South Africa, was the child of Brummie parents, and grew up in the city.

EVENTS & FESTIVALS

March
6th-9th Crufts Dog Show, National Exhibition Centre, Birmingham
17th St Patrick's Day Pageant, Coventry

June
11th-15th BBC Gardeners' World Live, National Exhibition Centre, Birmingham
tbc Coventry Classic Car Run, War Memorial Park, Coventry
tbc Godiva Festival, War Memorial Park, Coventry

July
4th-13th Birmingham International Jazz Festival
5th-6th City of Wolverhampton Show (provisional)
26th-27th Wolvestock Music Festival, Hickman Park, Bilston (provisional)

August
tbc Coventry Jazz Festival
tbc Italian Festival, School Street, Wolverhampton
tbc Steam & Vintage Rally, West Park, Wolverhampton

September
tbc Birmingham Arts Festival
tbc Dudley Glass Festival

November
tbc Coombe Fireworks, Coventry
tbc Firework Display, West Park, Wolverhampton

Top: Aston Hall, Birmingham

BIRMINGHAM Map 07 SP08
Aston Hall
Trinity Rd, Aston B6 6JD (M6 junct 6 follow A38(M) Aston Expressway towards city centre. Leave at Aston Waterlinks and follow brown signs to Aston Hall)
☎ 0121 327 0062   📠 0121 327 7162
e-mail: bmag-enquiries@birmingham.gov.uk

Built by Sir Thomas Holte, Aston Hall is a fine Jacobean mansion complete with a panelled Long Gallery, balustraded staircase and magnificent plaster friezes and ceilings. King Charles I spent a night here during the Civil War and the house was damaged by Parliamentary troops. It was also leased to James Watt Junior, the son of the great industrial pioneer.
Times: Open Etr-Oct, Tue-Fri 1-4; Sat & Sun 12-4. Closed Mon ex BH's. **Fee:** Free. **Facilities:** P 🍴 ♿ (ground floor only partially accessible) shop ✘ (ex guide dogs)

Birmingham Botanical Gardens & Glasshouses
Westbourne Rd, Edgbaston B15 3TR (2m W of city centre, follow signs for Edgbaston, then brown heritage signs)
☎ 0121 454 1860   📠 0121 454 7835
e-mail: admin@birminghambotanicalgardens.org.uk

Originally opened in 1832, the gardens include the Tropical House, which has 24ft-wide lily pool and lush vegetation. The Mediterranean house features a wide variety of citrus fruits and the Arid House has a desert scene with its giant agaves and opuntias. Outside, a tour of the gardens includes rhododendrons and azalea borders and a collection of over 200 trees. Young children's discovery garden & a sculpture trail.
Times: Open daily all year, wkdays 9-7 or dusk, Sun 10-7 or dusk whichever is earlier. (Closed 25 Dec). **Fee:** £5.50 (concessions £3); £5 summer Sun & BH's. Family £15 (£16 summer & BH's) Groups 10+ £4.50 (concessions £2.70). **Facilities:** P 🍴 ✘ licensed ♿ (3 wheelchairs, 2 electric scooters & braille guides) toilets for disabled shop garden centre ✘ (ex guide dogs) 🍴

Birmingham Museum & Art Gallery
Chamberlain Sq B3 3DH
☎ 0121 303 2834   📠 0121 303 1394
Times: Open all year Mon-Thu & Sat 10-5, Fri 10.30-5 and Sun 12.30-5. **Facilities:** P 🍴 ✘ licensed ♿ (lift) toilets for disabled shop ✘ *Details not confirmed for 2003* 🍴

The Jewellery Quarter Discovery Centre
75-79 Vyse St, Hockley B18 6HA (turn off A41 into Vyse St, museum on left after 1st side street)
☎ 0121 554 3598   **2 for 1**
📠 0121 554 9700
e-mail: louise_evans@birmingham.gov.uk

The Museum tells the story of jewellery making in Birmingham from its origins in the Middle Ages right through to the present day. Discover the skill of the jeweller's craft and enjoy a unique tour of an original jewellery factory frozen in time. For over 80 years the family firm of Smith and Pepper produced jewellery from the factory. This perfectly preserved 'time capsule' workshop has changed little since the beginning of the century. The Jewellery Quarter is still very much at the forefront of jewellery manufacture in Britain and the Museum showcases the work of the city's most exciting new designers.
Times: Open all year, Mon-Fri 10-4, Sat 11-5. (Closed Sun). Open BHs but closed Xmas/New Year **Fee:** * £3 (concessions £2.50). Family ticket £8. Party 10+ booked in advance. **Facilities:** P (limited 2hr stay/pay & display) 🍴 ♿ (tours for hearing/visually impaired booked in advance) toilets for disabled shop ✘ (ex guide dogs) 🍴

Sarehole Mill
Cole Bank Rd, Hall Green B13 0BD (M42 Junct 4. Take A34 towards Birmingham. After 5m turn left on B4146 Sarehole mill on left)
☎ 0121 777 6712   📠 0121 303 2891

Home to Birmingham's only working watermill; Sarehole Mill was built in the 1760s. Used for both flour production and metal rolling up to the last century, the Mill can still be seen in action during the summer months. Restored with financial backing from JRR Tolkien, who grew up in the area and cites Sarehole as an influence for writing *The Hobbit* and *Lord of the Rings*.
Times: Open Apr-Oct, Tue-Fri 1-4, Sat-Sun & BH 12-4, (Closed Mon) **Fee:** Free. **Facilities:** P ✘ (ex guide dogs)

Selly Manor Museum
Maple Rd, Bournville B30 2AE (off A38)
☎ 0121 472 0199   📠 0121 471 4101
e-mail: gillianellis@bvt.org.uk
Times: Open mid Jan-mid Dec, Tue-Fri & BH 10-5 (Apr-Sep, Sat-Sun 2-5), phone for details. **Facilities:** P ♿ toilets for disabled shop *Details not confirmed for 2003*

Soho House

Soho Av, Handsworth B18 5LB (from city centre follow A41 to Soho Rd, follow brown heritage signs to Soho Ave)
☎ 0121 554 9122 🖷 0121 554 5329 **2 for 1**
e-mail: soho.house.bmag@dnet.co.uk

Soho House was the elegant home of industrial pioneer Matthew Boulton between 1766 and 1809. Here, he met with some of the most important thinkers and scientists of his day. The house has been carefully restored and contains many of Boulton's possessions including furniture, clocks, silverware and the original dining table where the Lunar Society met.
Times: Open all year, Tue-Sat 10-5 & Sun 12-5; also BH Mon. **Fee:** * £3 (concessions £2.50). Family ticket (2 adults & 3 ch) £8. Party 10+
Facilities: P 🍴 & (induction loop) toilets for disabled shop ✖ (ex guide dogs) 🍵

BOURNVILLE Map 07 SP08
Cadbury World

Linden Rd B30 2LD (1m S of A38 Bristol Rd, on A4040 Ring Rd)
☎ 0121 451 4159 🖷 0121 451 1366
e-mail: cadbury.world@csplc.com
Times: Contact information line 0121 451 4180 for opening times.
Facilities: P 🍴 ✖ & (adapted ride & lift to 2nd floor) toilets for disabled shop ✖ (ex guide dogs) *Details not confirmed for 2003* 🍵

COVENTRY Map 04 SP37
Coventry Cathedral & Visitor Centre

7 Priory Row CV1 5ES (signposted on all approaches to the city)
☎ 024 7622 7597 🖷 024 7663 1448
e-mail: information@coventrycathedral.org

Coventry's old cathedral was bombed during an air raid of November 1940 which devastated the city. The remains have been carefully preserved. The new cathedral was designed by Sir Basil Spence and consecrated in May 1962. It contains outstanding modern works of art, including a huge tapestry designed by Graham Sutherland, the west screen (a wall of glass engraved by John Hutton with saints and angels), bronzes by Epstein, and the great baptistry window by John Piper.
Times: Open all year, daily 8.30-6. **Fee:** * Cathedral £3 donation. Camera charge £1. Video charge £2. **Facilities:** P (250yds) 🍴 & (lift, touch and hearing centre, paved wheelchair access) toilets for disabled shop ✖ (ex guide dogs)

Herbert Art Gallery & Museum

Jordan Well CV1 5QP (in city centre near Cathedral)
☎ 024 7683 2381 & 7683 2565
🖷 024 7683 2410
e-mail: artsandheritage@coventry.gov.uk

'Godiva City', tells Coventry's story over 1,000 years, through interactive exhibits, objects, pictures and words. Changing displays of art, craft, social and

THE BIRMINGHAM BOTANICAL GARDENS & GLASSHOUSES
Garden of the World

Open in 1832, the Gardens are a 15 acre "Oasis of Delight" with over 200 trees and the finest collection of plants in the Midlands. Tropical, Mediterranean and Arid glasshouses. National Bonsai Collection. Children's Playground, Children's Discovery Garden, exotic birds, art gallery and Sculpture Trail. Gift shop. Plant sales. Restaurant. Bands play summer Sunday afternoons and Bank Holidays. Open Daily.

Westbourne Road, Edgbaston, Birmingham
West Midlands B15 3TR
Tel: 0121 454 1860 Fax: 0121 454 7835
Email: admin@birminghambotanicalgardens.org.uk
Internet: www.birminghambotanicalgardens.org.uk

industrial history. It is Coventry's premier museum hosting a range of exhibitions and events.
Times: Open all year, Mon-Sat 10-5.30, Sun 12-5. (Closed 25-27 Dec & 1-2 Jan) **Fee:** Free. **Facilities:** P (500yds) 🍴 & (disabled parking, automatic doors, tactile/audio displays) toilets for disabled shop ✖ (ex guide/assistance dogs)

Jaguar Daimler Heritage Centre

Browns Ln, Allesley CV5 9DR (on A45, follow signs for Browns Lane Plant)
☎ 024 7640 2121 🖷 024 7620 2777
e-mail: tokeeffe@jaguar.com
Times: Open Mon-Fri 9.30-4.30 & last Sun of month 10-4. **Facilities:** P & toilets for disabled shop ✖ (ex guide dogs) *Details not confirmed for 2003*

Lunt Roman Fort

Coventry Rd, Baginton CV8 3AJ (S side of city, off Stonebridge highway, A45)
☎ 024 7683 2381 & 7683 2565
🖷 024 7683 2410
e-mail: artsandheritage@coventry.co.uk

The turf and timber Roman fort from around the end of the 1st century has been faithfully reconstructed. An Interpretation Centre is housed in the granary.
Times: Open 15 Jul-3 Sep, Thu-Tue 10-5; Spring BH wk daily 10-5; Apr-29 Oct wknds & BH Mons 10-5. **Fee:** * £2 (concessions £1). Audio tour 80p. **Facilities:** P & (ramp to Granary Interpretation Centre) toilets for disabled shop ✖ (ex guide/assistance dogs)

West Midlands

Museum of British Road Transport
St Agnes Ln, Hales St CV1 1PN (just off junct 1 Coventry ring road, Tower Street in city centre)
☎ 024 7683 2425 ▪ 024 7683 2465
e-mail: museum@mbrt.co.uk

Coventry is the traditional home of the motor industry. The Museum of British Road Transport displays the largest collection of British cars, buses, cycles and motorcycles in the world. Visitors can learn about motoring's early days in 'landmarques', how Royalty travelled, and see Thrust 2 and Thrust SSC, the world land speed record cars.
Times: Open all year, daily 10-5. (Closed 24-26 Dec). **Fee:** Free.
Facilities: P (adjacent) (pay & display) 🍴 ♿ (audio tour, tactile floor & models, wheelchairs for hire) toilets for disabled shop 🐕 (ex guide dogs) 🎧

DUDLEY Map 07 SO99
Black Country Living Museum
Tipton Rd DY1 4SQ (on A4037, nr Showcase cinema)
☎ 0121 557 9643 & 0121 520 8054
▪ 0121 557 4242
e-mail: info@bclm.co.uk

On the 26-acre site is a recreated canal-side village, with shops, houses and workplaces. Meet the costumed guides and find out what life was like around 1900. Ride on a tramcar, take a trip down the underground mine, venture into the limestone caverns or visit the olde tyme fairground (additional charge). There are also demonstrations of chainmaking, glass engraving and sweet-making. Watch a silent movie in the Limelight cinema, taste fish and chips cooked on a 1930's range, and finish your visit with a glass of real ale in the Bottle and Glass Inn.
Times: Open all year, Mar-Oct daily 10-5; Nov-Feb, Wed-Sun 10-4. (Telephone for Christmas closing) **Fee:** * £8.25 (ch 5-17 £4.75, pen £7.25). Family ticket (2ad+2ch) £22.50. Party 10+ (rates available on application). Prices subject to change. **Facilities:** P (charged) 🍴 ✕ licensed ♿ (ramps available) toilets for disabled shop 🐕 (ex guide dogs) 🎧

Dudley Zoo & Castle
2 The Broadway DY1 4QB (M5 junct 2 towards Wolverhampton/Dudley. Signposted)
☎ 01384 215313 ▪ 01384 456048 **2 for 1**
e-mail: marketing@dudleyzoo.org.uk

Set in 40 acres, the castle ruins are an impressive example of feudal splendour, whilst the zoo houses one of the most diverse collections of animals in the country. Home to many endangered species, there is the opportunity to see and learn about animals from every continent.
Times: Open all year, Etr-mid Sep, daily 10-4; mid Sep-Etr, daily 10-3. (Closed 25 Dec). **Fee:** * £7.50 (ch 4-15 £5, concessions £5.25). Family ticket £26 (2ad+3ch) **Facilities:** P (charged) 🍴 ✕ licensed ♿ (land train from gates-castle, wheelchair hire) toilets for disabled shop 🐕 🎧

Museum & Art Gallery
St James's Rd DY1 1HU (M5 northbound, exit at junct 2. Take A4123 signposted to Dudley)
☎ 01384 815575 ▪ 01384 815576
e-mail: museum.pls@mbc.dudley.gov.uk
Times: Open all year, Mon-Sat 10-4. (Closed BHs). **Facilities:** P (25mtrs) ♿ (Braille & large print text. Tactile objects) shop 🐕 (ex guide dogs) *Details not confirmed for 2003*

SOLIHULL Map 07 SP17
National Motorcycle Museum
Coventry Rd, Bickenhill B92 0EJ (near junct 6, of M42, off A45 near NEC)
☎ 01675 443311 ▪ 0121 711 3153

Five exhibition halls showing British motorcycles built during the Golden Age of motorcycling. Spanning 90 years, the immaculately restored machines are the products of around 150 different factories. Over 700 machines are on show, most are owned by the museum, others are from collections or private owners. Restoration work is carried out by enthusiasts, and new motorcycles are acquired from all over the world.
Times: Open all year, daily 10-6. (Closed 24-26 Dec). **Fee:** * £4.50 (ch 12 & pen £3.25). Party 20+. **Facilities:** P ✕ licensed ♿ toilets for disabled shop 🐕 (ex guide dogs) 🎧

STOURBRIDGE Map 07 SO88
The Falconry Centre
Hurrans Garden Centre, Kidderminster Rd South, Hagley DY9 0JB (off A456)
☎ 01562 700014 ▪ 01562 700014 **2 for 1**

The centre houses some 80 birds of prey including owls, hawks and falcons and is also a rehabilitation centre for sick and injured birds of prey. Spectacular flying displays are put on daily from midday. There are picnic areas.
Times: Open all year, daily 10-5 & Sun 11-5. (Closed 25 & 26 Dec). Sun 11-5 **Fee:** * £2.50 (ch, pen & disabled £1.50). Party 25+.
Facilities: P 🍴 ♿ toilets for disabled shop garden centre 🐕 (ex guide dogs) 🎧

WALSALL   Map 07 SP09
NEW ART GALLERY WALSALL
Gallery Square WS2 8LG
☎ 01922 654200 ▤ 01922 654401
e-mail: info@artatwalsall.org.uk
Times: Open all year Tue-Sat 10-5, Sun noon-5. Closed Mon ex BH Mons. **Facilities:** P 🅿 ✗ ♿ (lift access to facilties) toilets for disabled shop ✗ (ex guide dogs) *Details not confirmed for 2003*

WALSALL LEATHER MUSEUM
Littleton St West WS2 8EQ (On Walsall ring road on north side of town)
☎ 01922 721153 ▤ 01922 725827
e-mail: leathermuseum@walsall.gov.uk

Award-winning working museum in the saddlery and leathergoods 'capital' of Britain. Watch skilled craftsmen and women at work in this restored Victorian leather factory. Displays tell the story of Walsall's leatherworkers past and present. Large shop stocks range of Walsall made leathergoods, many at bargain prices. Saddle Room Café serves delicious home-cooked cakes and light lunches. Groups very welcome, guided tours available.
Times: Open all year, Tue-Sat 10-5 (Nov-Mar 4pm), Sun noon-5 (Nov-Mar 4pm). Open BH Mon. (Closed 24-26 Dec, 1 Jan, Good Fri, Etr Sun & May Day). **Fee:** Free. **Facilities:** P (10metres) 🅿 ♿ (staff with sign language skills,tactile activities,parking) toilets for disabled shop ✗ (ex guide dogs) 🍴

WOLVERHAMPTON   Map 07 SO99
WIGHTWICK MANOR
WV6 8EE (3m W, beside Mermaid Inn off A454 Bridgenorth)
☎ 01902 761400 ▤ 01902 764663
e-mail: mwtman@smtp.ntrust.org.uk   **2 for 1**

This house was begun in 1887 and is one of the finest examples of 19th-century decorative style. All aspects of William Morris's talents are shown in the house - wallpapers, textiles, carpets, tiles, embroidery and even books. The garden reflects late Victorian and Edwardian design.
Times: Open Mar-Dec, Thu, Sat & BH Sun & Mon 1.30-5. Last admission 4.30 **Fee:** * £5.00 (accompanied ch & students £2.80). Gardens only £2.50 ch free in garden **Facilities:** P 🅿 ♿ (car parking call 01902 761400 for details) shop ✗ (ex on leads) 🍴

Isle of Wight

Despite being less than 23 miles (39km) across at its widest point – the Isle of Wight offers plenty of variety, and is popular with holidaymakers for its lovely countryside, pleasant resorts and mild climate.

There's lots to see and do, with an abundance of museums, children's activity parks, and leisure facilities including watersports, riding, cycling, paragliding, golf, and sea and freshwater fishing. Local specialities are freshly caught crab and lobster, which can be enjoyed with a glass of wine from one of the island's five vineyards.

A chalk ridge runs east to west of the island, popular with walkers for the fine views afforded from its vantage points. The interesting coastline takes in the chalky pinnacles of The Needles, some splendid cliffs, and the curious multi-coloured sand at Alum Bay, which can be bought bottled in colourful layers from local souvenir shops. Coastal paths follow the shoreline from Totland to St Lawrence on the south coast, and Yarmouth to Cowes on the north coast.

The east coast has the most developed seaside resorts, with Ryde, Sandown, Shanklin and Ventnor, and their sandy beaches. Newport, the island's capital, is the only inland town and is a good shopping centre.

In addition to its natural features, the island has some fine castles and historic houses. Chief among these are medieval Carisbrooke Castle outside Newport, Osborne House at East Cowes, Brading Roman Villa, and lovely manor houses at Arreton, Barton, Haseley, Nunwell, Appuldurcombe and Morton.

Among its illustrious residents past and present the Isle can claim author J B Priestly; Sir Christopher Cockerell, inventor of the Hovercraft; Barnes Wallace, inventor of the Bouncing Bomb; actors Sheila Hancock and Jeremy Irons; and conspiracy theorist extraordinaire, David Icke.

EVENTS & FESTIVALS

May
tbc Isle of Wight Walking Festival

June
tbc Isle of Wight Festival

July
19th-20th Isle of Wight County Show

August
2nd-9th Cowes Week, sailing event
22nd-25th The Island Steam Show, Havenstreet
tbc Isle of Wight Garlic Festival, Newchurch

September
tbc Isle of Wight Cycling Festival

Top: Alum Bay

Wight, Isle of

ALUM BAY
Map 04 SZ38
The Needles Old Battery
West High Down PO39 0JH (0.75m SW)
☎ 01983 754772
Times: Open 26 Mar-29 Jun Sun-Thu & Jul-Aug daily 10.30-5. Property closes in bad weather. **Facilities:** P (0.75m) 🍴 shop ✱
Details not confirmed for 2003

The Needles Park
PO39 0JD (signposted, on B3322)
☎ 0870 458 0022 ▪ 01983 755260
e-mail: info@theneedles.co.uk

Overlooking the Needles on the western edge of the Island, the park has attractions for all the family: included in the wide range facilities is the spectacular chair lift to the beach to view the famous coloured sandcliffs, Needles Rocks and lighthouse. Other popular attractions include Alum Bay Glass and the Isle of Wight Sweet Manufactory.
Times: Open 5 Apr-early Nov, daily 10-5. Hours extended in high season. **Fee:** * No admission charged for entrance to Park. Supersaver Attraction Discount ticket £7 (ch £5), or chargeable attractions individually priced. **Facilities:** P (charged) 🍴 ✗ licensed ♿ toilets for disabled shop ✱

ARRETON
Map 04 SZ58
Haseley Manor
PO30 3AN (on Sandown to Newport road)
☎ 01983 865420 ▪ 01983 867547
Times: Open Etr-Sep, Mon-Fri 10-5.30. (Closed Sat & Sun). **Facilities:** P 🍴 ✗ licensed ♿ (wheelchair ramps) toilets for disabled shop
Details not confirmed for 2003 ✱

Robin Hill Country Park
Downend PO30 2NU (0.5m from Allerton village next door to the Hare and Hounds pub)
☎ 01983 527352 ▪ 01983 527347

Set in 88 acres of downland and woods, Robin Hill offers a Tree Top Trail, Mazes, Snake Slides, Troll Island, Toboggan Run Ride, Squirrel Tower, Forest Sculptures and a Countryside Centre and the 3 largest rides on the island - the Hoom Toboggan Rub, Motion Platform Cinema.
Times: Open 25 Mar-3 Nov, daily 10-5 (last admission 4). **Fee:** * Over 1.1m £5.50 (under 1.1m £4, pen £5, disabled £3) **Facilities:** P 🍴 ✗ ♿ (most areas are accessible. ramps access) toilets for disabled shop ✈ (ex on leads) ✱

BEMBRIDGE
Map 04 SZ68
Bembridge Windmill
PO30 4EB (0.5m S of Bembridge on B3395)
☎ 01983 873945
Times: Open 27 Mar-Jun & Sep-27 Oct, Sun-Fri (Closed Sat ex Etr Sat) & Jul-Aug, daily 10-5. Last admission 4.45. **Facilities:** P shop ✈
✱ Details not confirmed for 2003

BLACKGANG
Map 04 SZ47
Blackgang Chine Fantasy Park
PO38 2HN (follow signs from Ventnor for Whitnell & Niton. From Niton follow signs for Blackgang).
☎ 01983 730330 ▪ 01983 731267
e-mail: vectisventureltd@btinternet.com

Opened as scenic gardens in 1843 c overing some 40 acres, the park has imaginative play areas, water gardens, maze and coastal gardens. Set on the steep wooded slopes of the chine are the themed areas Smugglerland, Nurseryland, Dinosaurland, Fantasyland and Frontierland. St Catherine's Quay has a maritime exhibition showing the history of local and maritime affairs.
Times: Open 25 Mar-3 Nov daily, 10-5.30. Whitsun & high season floodlit every evening (phone for details). **Fee:** * Combined ticket to chine, sawmill & quay £6.50 (ch 3-13 & pen £5.50, disabled £3.50). Family £21.50. Return within 4 days - £1 each. **Facilities:** P (charged) 🍴 ✗ ♿ (some paths steep) toilets for disabled shop ✱

BRADING
Map 04 SZ68
Isle of Wight Wax Works
46 High St PO36 0DQ (on A3055, in Brading High St)
☎ 01983 407286 ▪ 01983 402112
e-mail: waxworks@bradingisleofwight.fsnet.co.uk

Set in 3/4 acre in the historic 'Kynge's Towne' of Brading, this attraction comprises the Rectory mansion filled with famous and infamous characters from the past, the chamber of horrors, world of nature, Professor Copperthwaithe's extraordinary collection of oddities and the art of candle carving.
Times: Open all year, Summer 10-5, extended in high season. Telephone for Dec & Jan opening times. **Fee:** * £5.25 (ch £3.50, under 5 free, pen £4). Family £16 (2ad+2ch), Family £19 (2ad+3ch). Party 20+. Includes free entry into "Chamber of Horrors" & Animal World of Natural History. **Facilities:** P ♿ (Disabled route planner) shop ✱

Lilliput Antique Doll & Toy Museum
High St PO36 0DJ (A3055 Ryde/Sandown road, in Brading High Street)
☎ 01983 407231
e-mail: lilliput.museum@btconnect.com

This private museum contains one of the finest collections of antique dolls and toys in Britain. There are over 2000 exhibits, ranging in age from 2000BC to 1945 with examples of almost every seriously collectable doll, many with royal connections. Also dolls' houses, teddy bears and rare and unusual toys.
Times: Open all year, daily, 10-5. **Fee:** * £1.95 (ch & pen £1, ch under 5 free). Party. **Facilities:** P (200 yds) ♿ (ramps provided on request) shop ✱

Morton Manor
PO36 0EP (off A3055 in Brading, well signposted)
☎ 01983 406168   `2 for 1`

The manor dates back to 1249, but was rebuilt in 1680 with further changes during the Georgian period. The
continued

house contains furniture of both the 18th and 19th centuries, but its main attraction lies in the gardens and vineyard. The garden is landscaped into terraces, with ornamental ponds, a sunken garden and a traditional Elizabethan turf maze. In recent years Morton Manor has become one of the places to have an established vineyard and winery.
Times: Open Apr-Oct, daily 10-5.30 (Closed Sat) Last admissions 4.30. **Fee:** * £4.50 (ch £2, pen £4). Party 15+ £3.50each. **Facilities:** P ⏣ ✕ licensed ♿ shop garden centre ✱ (ex in garden on lead)

Nunwell House & Gardens
Coach Ln PO36 0JQ (Off Ryde-Sandown Rd, A3055)
☎ 01983 407240   **2 for 1**

Set in beautiful gardens, Nunwell is an impressive, lived-in and much loved house where King Charles I spent his last night of freedom. It has fine furniture and interesting collections of family militaria. In summer, concerts are occasionally held in the music room.
Times: Open House & Gardens: 25-26 May then 1 Jul-3 Sep, Mon-Wed 1-5. Groups welcome when house open & at other times by appointment. **Fee:** * £4 inc guide book. **Facilities:** P shop ✱ (ex guide dogs)

🏛 CARISBROOKE   Map 04 SZ48
Carisbrooke Castle
PO30 1XY (1.25m SW of Newport, off B3401)
☎ 01983 522107

This is the only medieval castle on the island and its most famous resident was King Charles I who was imprisoned here. There are two medieval wells: the one in the keep can be reached by climbing down 71 steps; the one in the courtyard had winding gear traditionally driven by a donkey, and displays of it working are still given.
Times: Open all year, 29 Mar-Sep, daily 10-6 (Oct, daily 10-5); Nov-Mar daily 10-4. (Closed 24-26 Dec & 1 Jan). **Fee:** * £4.60 (ch under 5 free, ch £2.30 & con £3.50). Family ticket (2 adults & 3 ch) £11.50. **Facilities:** P ⏣ ♿ shop ♯

🏛 FRESHWATER   Map 04 SZ38
Dimbola Lodge
Terrace Ln, Freshwater Bay PO40 9QE (off A3054)
☎ 01983 756814   🖬 01983 755578
e-mail: administrator@dimbola.co.uk

Home of Julia Margaret Cameron, the pioneer Victorian portrait photographer. The house has the largest permanent collection of Cameron prints on display in the UK, as well as galleries exhibiting work by young,

up and coming, and acclaimed modern photographers; and a large display of cameras and accessories.

Times: Open all year 10-5 (Closed 5 days at Xmas). **Fee:** £3.50 (ch 16 free) **Facilities:** P ✕ ♿ chairlifts toilets for disabled shop ✱ (ex guide dogs) ⎘

🏛 HAVENSTREET   Map 04 SZ58
Isle of Wight Steam Railway
The Railway Station PO33 4DS (Situated between Ryde & Newport. Railway well signposted)
☎ 01983 882204   🖬 01983 884515
e-mail: havenstreet@iwsteamrailway.co.uk

When the Newport to Ryde railway was closed, Haven Street Station was taken over by a private company, the Isle of Wight Steam Railway. A number of volunteers restored the station, locomotives and rolling stock, and steam trains now run the five miles from Wootton, via Haven Street to Smallbrook Junction where there is a direct interchange with the Ryde-Shanklin electric trains.
Times: Open selected days Mar-Oct (Jun-Sep daily) **Fee:** * Return Fares £7.50 (ch 5-15 £4). Family ticket £19. **Facilities:** P ⏣ ♿ (with assistance) toilets for disabled shop ⎘

🏛 NEWPORT   Map 04 SZ48
Roman Villa
Cypress Rd PO30 1EX (S of Newport, signposted 'Roman Villa')
☎ 01983 529720   🖬 01983 823841
Times: Open Etr-Oct, daily 10-4.30. Other times by appointment.
Facilities: P (100 yds) ♿ shop ✱ *Details not confirmed for 2003*

🏛 NEWTOWN   Map 04 SZ49
Old Town Hall
Town Ln PO30 4PA (1m N of A3054 between Yarmouth & Newport)
☎ 01983 531785
Times: Open 27 Mar-end Jun, Sep-25 Oct, Mon Wed & Sun (also open Good Fri & Etr Sat); Jul & Aug Sun-Thu, 2-5. Last admission 4.45pm. **Facilities:** P (Braille guide books available) ✱ ⚘ *Details not confirmed for 2003*

Wight, Isle of   **253**

OSBORNE HOUSE   Map 04 SZ59
OSBORNE HOUSE
PO32 6JY (1m SE of East Cowes)
☎ 01983 200022

Designed by Prince Albert and Thomas Cubitt in the mid 19th century, Osborne was Queen Victoria's favourite home, especially after the death of Prince Albert. She died here in 1901. The interior of the house is largely unchanged since Victorain times, and is a fascinating insight into the private life of the Royal family of that day.
Times: Open House & Gardens, 29 Mar-Sep, daily 10-6 last admission 4pm (Oct, daily 10-5); house and gardens closes 4pm on 20 Jul phone for events, Spring and winter opning times. **Fee:** * House & Grounds: £7.50 (ch £3.80 con £5.20). Family ticket 2ad+3ch)£18.80. Grounds: £4 (ch £2, ch u5 free, con £3) Family ticket £10 **Facilities:** P 🍽 ♿ shop ✈ ♿

SHANKLIN   Map 04 SZ58
SHANKLIN CHINE
12 Pomona Rd PO37 6PF (turn off A3055 into Chine Hollow, Shanklin Old Village (between Crab Inn & Pencil Cottage) to Upper entrance or turn off A3055 at lights, left into Hope Rd & continue onto Esplanade. Lower entrance Western end)
☎ 01983 866432   📠 01983 874215   **2 for 1**
e-mail: jill@shanklinchine.co.uk

This historic gorge at Shanklin, is a magical world of unique beauty and a rich haven of rare plants, woodland and wildlife, including red squirrels and enchanting waterfalls. A path winds down through the ravine with overhanging trees, ferns and other flora covering steep sides. New for 2003 , the Exhibition "The Island - Then and Now", is in the Heritage Centre, together with PLUTO (Pipe Line Under The Ocean) which carried petrol to the Allied troops in Normandy, and the 40 Royal Marines Commando display, commemorating their link with the Chine - they trained here during the war in preparation for the Dieppe Raid of 1942. After dusk, during the summer months, subtle illuminations create a different world.
Times: Open 31 Mar-22 May 10-5; 23 May-28 Sep, 10-10 (illuminated at night); 29 Sep-2 Nov 10-5. (Opening period may be extended depending on weather conditions). **Fee:** £3.50 (ch under 16 £2, pen & students £2.50). Family ticket £9 (2 adult & 2 ch), £11 (2 adult & 3 ch). Group rates available. **Facilities:** P (450yds) 🍽 (very restricted access) shop (on lead)

SHORWELL   Map 04 SZ48
YAFFORD WATER MILL FARM PARK
PO30 3LH (on B3399, Shorwell to Brightstone Road)
☎ 01983 740610 & 741725   📠 01983 740610
Times: Open all year, daily 10-6 or dusk in winter. (Last admission 5pm). **Facilities:** P 🍽 ♿ toilets for disabled shop ✈ (ex guide dogs) Details not confirmed for 2003

VENTNOR   Map 04 SZ57
MUSEUM OF THE HISTORY OF SMUGGLING
Botanic Gardens PO38 1UL (on A3055, 1m W of Ventnor)
☎ 01983 853677

Situated underground in extensive vaults, this unique museum shows methods of smuggling used over a 700-year period right up to the present day. There is an adventure playground in the Botanic Gardens.
Times: Open Apr-Sep, daily 10-5. **Fee:** * £2.80 (ch & pen £1.40). Parties by arrangement. school parties £1.80 **Facilities:** P (charged) 🍽 ✈ licensed shop garden centre

WROXALL   Map 04 SZ57
APPULDURCOMBE HOUSE
PO38 3EW (off B3327, 0.5 miles W)
☎ 01983 852484
Times: Open 2 Jan-Apr 10-4, May-Sep, daily 10-5. **Facilities:** P ♿ ♿ Details not confirmed for 2003

YARMOUTH   Map 04 SZ38
YARMOUTH CASTLE
Quay St PO41 0PB (adjacent to car ferry terminal)
☎ 01983 760678

Modern buildings surround this well preserved castle, the last addition to Henry VIII's coastal defences completed in 1547. Fine views of the harbour can be obtained from the gun platform.
Times: Open all year, 29 Mar-Sep, daily 10-6 (Oct, daily 10-5). **Fee:** * £2.30 (ch 5-15 £1.20, ch under 5 free, con £1.70) **Facilities:** P (200yds) ♿ ✈ ♿

Wiltshire

EVENTS & FESTIVALS

May
1st-17th Swindon Festival of Literature
3rd Downton Cuckoo Fair, medieval fair in village centre
tbc Chippenham Folk Festival
tbc Salisbury Festival (various venues)
tbc Swindon Kite Festival

June
21st-28th Corsham Festival

July
4th-6th Calne Country Music Festival
11th-13th Marlborough International Jazz Festival
17th-19th Southern Cathedrals Festival, Salisbury Cathedral
17th-20th Larmer Tree Festival, Larmer Tree Victorian Pleasure Gardens, Cranbourne Chase (festival of world music)
tbc Marlborough Festival Open Studios, artists' studios within 8 mile radius

August
tbc Wiltshire Festival (music), Lydiard Park, Lydiard Tregoze, West Swindon

October
3rd-5th Calne Music & Arts Festival
10th-12th North Wilts Classic Car Tour
tbc Cricklade Festival

To many visiting the county, Wiltshire has three attractions: Salisbury, Stonehenge and Longleat. While these are all worthwhile, (indeed Stonehenge could be rightly called one of the wonders of the world) there is still plenty more to be discovered in the county.

After seeing Stonehenge, those interested in prehistoric sites should visit Avebury, where the stones are more approachable. Even though there is a lot of tourist activity in the village, the area remains relatively untouched, mostly given over to farmland and moor. This is also a good area for encountering crop circles.

Stonehenge and the Avebury circles seem to be part of a larger complex which still baffles investigators, and includes nearby features such as Windmill Hill with the remains of an earthwork camp some 5,500 years old; Silbury Hill, a man-made mound of earth which covers 5.5 acres; West Kennet Long Barrow, a burial mound; and possibly the chalk-carved White Horses on surrounding hillsides.

Miss Matilda Talbot left the village of Lacock to the National Trust in the 1940s. Another Talbot, William Henry Fox, produced the first ever photographic negative here in 1831. The village was also used for the recent BBC production of Jane Austen's *Pride & Prejudice*.

Malmesbury in Northern Wiltshire is the oldest borough in England and is home to a partially ruined 12th-century abbey, notable for a very impressive porch carving of the Apostles.

Well-known personalities from the county include model and TV presenter Melinda Messenger; pop singer Billie Piper; and actors Joseph Fiennes and Michael Crawford.

Top: Stonehenge

Wiltshire

🏛 AVEBURY   Map 04 SU06
ALEXANDER KEILLER MUSEUM
High St SN8 1RF (Turn off A4 onto A4361/B4003)
☎ 01672 539250   📠 01672 539388
e-mail: wavgen@smtp.ntrust.org.uk

This is one of the most important prehistoric sites in Europe, and was built before Stonehenge. An avenue of great stones leads to the site, which may have been a place of great religious significance. The museum now has the addition of the barn gallery. This interactive museum uses the latest interpretative techniques to explain the history of the Avebury landscape.
Times: Open Apr-Oct, daily 10-6 or dusk if earlier; Nov-Mar, 10-4. (Closed 24-26 Dec & 1 Jan). **Fee:** * £3.50 (ch £1.50). **Facilities:** 🅿 🍴 ✕ licensed ♿ toilets for disabled shop 🐕 (ex guide dogs) 🚻 ♨ 🛍

AVEBURY MANOR
SN8 1RF (from A4 take A4361/B4003)
☎ 01672 539250   📠 01672 539388
e-mail: wavgen@smtp.ntrust.org.uk

Avebury Manor has a monastic origin, and has been much altered since then. The present buildings date from the early 16th century, with notable Queen Anne alterations and Edwardian renovation. The flower gardens contain medieval walls, and there are examples of topiary.
Times: Open: House 2 Apr-Oct, Tue-Wed, Sun & BH Mon 2-5.30 (last admission 5pm or dusk if earlier). Garden 2 Apr-Oct daily ex Mon & Thu (open BH Mon). **Fee:** * Manor & garden £3.60 (ch £1.80). Garden £2.60 (ch £1.30). **Facilities:** 🅿 (charged) ♿ shop 🐕 ♨ 🛍

🏛 BRADFORD-ON-AVON   Map 03 ST86
GREAT CHALFIELD MANOR
SN12 8NJ (3m SW of Melksham)
☎ 01225 782239

`2 for 1`

Built during the Wars of the Roses, the manor is a beautiful, mellow, moated house which still has its great hall. It was restored in the 1920s. There is a small 13th-century church next to the house.
Times: Open Apr-Oct, Tue-Thu, guided tours only at 12.15, 2.15, 3, 3.45, 4.30. **Fee:** £4.20. **Facilities:** 🅿 🐕 ♨

TITHE BARN

This impressive tithe barn, over 160ft long by 30ft wide, once belonged to Shaftesbury Abbey. The roof is of stone slates, supported outside by buttresses and inside by massive beams and a network of rafters.
Times: Open all year, daily 10.30-4. (Closed 25 Dec). Keykeeper. **Fee:** Free. **Facilities:** 🅿 ♿ 🐕 🚻

🏛 CALNE   Map 03 ST97
BOWOOD HOUSE & GARDENS
SN11 0LZ (off A4 Chippenham to Calne rd, in Derry Hill village)
☎ 01249 812102
📠 01249 821757
e-mail: houseandgardens@bowood.org

`2 for 1`

Built in 1624, the house was finished by the first Earl of

CORSHAM COURT
HOME OF THE METHUEN FAMILY

Corsham Court is one of England's finest Stately Homes. It was a Royal Manor in the days of the Saxon Kings, and the present building is based upon an Elizabethan Manor dating from 1582. Magnificent Georgian State Rooms were added in 1760. It houses one of the oldest and most distinguished collections of Old Masters and Furniture in the country, and with its 'Capability' Brown gardens and arboretum, and architecture by John Nash and Thomas Bellamy, Corsham Court provides the visitor with a wonderful opportunity to enjoy the many delights of the historic and beautiful Stately Home.

Tel/Fax: 01249 701610
For opening times see gazetteer entry

Shelburne, who employed celebrated architects, notably Robert Adam, to complete the work. Adam's library is particularly admired, and also in the house is the laboratory where Dr Joseph Priestley discovered the existence of oxygen in 1774. The chief glory of Bowood, however, is its 2000-acre expanse, 100 acres of which are pleasure gardens. They were laid out by 'Capability' Brown in the 1760s, and are carpeted with daffodils, narcissi and bluebells in spring. There are also an adventure playground and new soft play area.
Times: Open Apr-Oct, daily 11-6, including BH. Rhododendron Gardens (separate entrance off A342) open 6 weeks during mid Apr-early Jun, 11-6. **Fee:** * House & Gardens £6.05 (ch 2-4 £3; 5-15 £3.85; pen £5). Rhododendrons only £3.30 **Facilities:** 🅿 🍴 ✕ licensed ♿ (parking by arrangement) toilets for disabled shop 🐕 (ex guide & hearing dogs) 🛍

🏛 CORSHAM   Map 03 ST87
CORSHAM COURT
SN13 0BZ (4m W of Chippenham off A4)
☎ 01249 701610   📠 01249 701610

The Elizabethan manor was built in 1582, and then bought by the Methuen family in the 18th century to house their collections of paintings and statues. 'Capability' Brown made additions to the house and laid out the park, and later John Nash made further changes. There is furniture by Chippendale, Adam, Cobb and Johnson inside, as well as the Methuen

continued

Wiltshire

collection of Old Master paintings. The garden has flowering shrubs, herbaceous borders, a Georgian bath house and peacocks.

Corsham Court

Times: Open Summer: 20 Mar-Sep daily ex Mon but incl BH's 2-5.30. Winter: Oct-19 Mar open wknds only 2-4.30pm. Last admission 30 minutes before closing. (Closed Dec). Open throughout year by appointment for groups 15+. **Fee:** * House & Gardens: £5 (ch £2.50, pen £4.50). Gardens only £2 (ch £1 & pen £1.50). Party 15+ **Facilities:** P 🍴 & shop 🐕 (on leads only)

See advert on page 255

HOLT   Map 03 ST86
THE COURTS
BA14 6RR (3m N of Trowbridge, on B3107)
☎ 01225 782340   📠 01225 782340   **2 for 1**

Weavers came to The Courts to have their disputes settled until the end of the 18th century. The house is not open, but it makes an attractive backdrop to the gardens - a network of stone paths, yew hedges, pools and borders with a strange, almost magical atmosphere.
Times: Open 30 Mar-12 Oct daily (ex Wed) 11-5 out of season by appointment only **Fee:** £4.20 (ch £2.10). Parties by arrangement.
Facilities: P 🍴 & 🐕 (ex guide dogs) 🦽

LACOCK   Map 03 ST96
LACKHAM COUNTRYSIDE CENTRE
SN15 2NY (3m S of Chippenham, on A350)
☎ 01249 466800   📠 01249 466818
e-mail: adavies@lackcoll.ac.uk
Times: Open Etr-Aug, Sun & BH Mon 10-5. Last admission 4pm.
Facilities: P 🍴 ✗ & (wheelchair available) toilets for disabled shop *Details not confirmed for 2003*

LACOCK ABBEY
SN15 2LG (3m S of Chippenham, E of A350)   **2 for 1**
☎ 01249 730227 (abbey)

Lacock Abbey was the venue for a series of innovative photographic experiments by William Henry Fox Talbot. The abbey was founded in the 13th century. At the Dissolution it was sold to William Sharington, who destroyed the chuch and turned the quarters into a grand home.
Times: Museum, Cloisters & Grounds, Mar-2 Nov, daily 11-5.30. Closed Good Fri. Abbey, 29 Mar-2 Nov daily, ex Tue, 1-5.30. Closed Good Fri. Museum open winter wknds, but closed 20-28 Dec. **Fee:** Museum, Abbey, Grounds & Cloisters £6.50 (ch £3.60), family ticket £17.60. Grounds, Cloisters & Museum only £4.20 (ch £2.50), family ticket £11.80. Abbey & garden only £5.30 (ch £3), family ticket £13.30.
Facilities: P & (taped guides) toilets for disabled shop 🐕 🦽

LONGLEAT   Map 03 ST84
LONGLEAT
The Estate Office BA12 7NW (Turn off A36 Bath-Salisbury onto A362 Warminster-Frome)
☎ 01985 844400   📠 01985 844885
e-mail: enquiries@longleat.co.uk

Times: Open Attractions: 5 Apr-2 Nov daily. House: 5 Apr-Dec (ex Xmas Day) daily. Ring to confirm opening arrangements out of season. **Fee:** Passport ticket £15 (ch & pen £12). Prices under review.
Facilities: P 🍴 ✗ licensed & (Informative leaflet available or see website) toilets for disabled shop (free kennels for Safari park) 🦽

LUDGERSHALL   Map 04 SU25
LUDGERSHALL CASTLE
SP11 9QR (7m NW of Andover on A342)

Although a ruin since the 16th century, this was once a royal castle and hunting palace. The visitor can see large earthworks of the Norman motte-and-bailey castle and the flint walls of the later hunting palace. The stump of a medieval cross stands in the village street.
Times: Open all reasonable times. **Fee:** Free. **Facilities:** P & ♿

LYDIARD PARK   Map 04 SU18
LYDIARD PARK
Lydiard Tregoze SN5 9PA (from M4 junct 16. Follow brown Tourist Information signs)
☎ 01793 770401   📠 01793 877909
Times: Open all year, House: Mon-Fri 10-1 & 2-5, Sat 10-5, Sun 2-5 (last Sun in every month, 11-5). Winter closing 4pm (Nov-Feb). Park: all year, daily closing at dusk each day. **Facilities:** P 🍴 & (telephone 01793 770401 for access information sheet) toilets for disabled shop 🐕 (ex guide dogs in house) *Details not confirmed for 2003*

MARLBOROUGH Map 04 SU16
CROFTON BEAM ENGINES
Crofton Pumping Station, Crofton SN8 3DW (signposted from A338/A346/B3087 at Burbage and from A4 at Froxfield)
☎ 01672 870300
e-mail: administration@katrust.org

2 for 1

The oldest working beam engine in the world still in its original building and still doing its original job. The Boulton and Watt 1812, can be found in this rural spot. Its companion is a Harvey's of Hayle of 1845. Both are steam driven, from a hand-stoked, coal-fired boiler, and pump water into the summit level of the Kennet and Avon Canal with a lift of 40ft.
Times: Open daily from Etr-late Sep, 10.30-5 (last entry 4.30). Steaming on Bank Holiday weekends and last wknd of Jun, Jul & Sep **Fee:** * Steaming weekend: £4 (ch £1, under 5 free & pen £3). Family ticket £9. Non-steaming days £2.50 (ch £1, pen £2). **Facilities:** P ⌒ ⌂ (phone warden in advance, sighted guides provided) shop ✗

MIDDLE WOODFORD Map 04 SU13
HEALE GARDENS, PLANT CENTRE & SHOP
SP4 6NT (4m N of Salisbury, between A360 & A345)
☎ 01722 782504

Heale House and its eight acres of beautiful garden lie beside the River Avon at Middle Woodford. Much of the house is unchanged since King Charles II sheltered here after the Battle of Worcester in 1651. The garden provides a wonderfully varied collection of plants, shrubs, and musk and other roses, growing in the formal setting of clipped hedges and mellow stonework.
Times: Gardens & Plant cafe open all year, daily 10-5. Closed Mon. Open BH Mons. **Fee:** £3.75 (ch 5-15 £1.50 under 5's free). **Facilities:** P ⌒ ⌂ shop garden centre ✗ (ex guide dogs) ⌒

SALISBURY Map 04 SU12
THE MEDIEVAL HALL (SECRETS OF SALISBURY)
Cathedral Close SP1 2EY (follow signs within Salisbury Cathedral Close)
☎ 01722 412472 & 324731 ▤ 01722 339983
e-mail: medihall@aol.com
Times: Open Apr-Sep, from 11-5. Also open throughout year for pre-booked groups. **Facilities:** P (charged) ⌂ Details not confirmed for 2003

MOMPESSON HOUSE
Chorister's Green, Cathedral Close SP1 2EL
☎ 01722 335659 ▤ 01722 335659
e-mail: wmpkxr@smtp.ntrust.org.uk
Times: Open Apr-Oct, daily (ex Thu & Fri) 12-5.30. **Facilities:** P ⌒ ⌂ shop ✗ ⌂ Details not confirmed for 2003

OLD SARUM
Castle Rd SP1 3SD (2m N on A345)
☎ 01722 335398

Impressive remains of an Iron-Age camp surround what was the original site of Salisbury cathedral and its thriving community. It was abandoned in medieval times, and the bishop and his flock moved to found a new cathedral where the present city stands. However, for many hundreds of years after its desertion, until the Reform Bill of 1832, ten voters continued to return two MPs to parliament at Westminster.
Times: Open all year,29 Mar-Sep, daily 10-6 (9-6 Jul-Aug) (Oct daily 10-5); Nov-Mar daily 10-4. **Fee:** * £2 (ch 5-15 £1, under 5's free, con £1.50). **Facilities:** P ⌒ ⌂

SALISBURY CATHEDRAL
33 The Close SP1 2EJ (South of the city centre & market Sq)
☎ 01722 555120 ▤ 01722 555116
e-mail: visitors@salcath.co.uk

Built in one phase between 1220 and 1258, the cathedral is probably Britain's finest piece of medieval architecture. The spire is 123 metres tall, making it the tallest in England. The chapter house displays a frieze depicting scenes from Genesis and Exodus, also the finest surviving Magna Carta. The choir continue a tradition that began around 750 years ago, with performances at daily services. They are accompanied by Europe's finest romantic church organ. The surrounding cathedral close contains two museums, two small stately homes and acres of lawn.
Times: Open all year, Jan-May, Sep-Dec, daily 7.15-6.15; Jun-Aug, Mon-Sat 7.15-8.15. **Fee:** Voluntary donation. **Facilities:** P (100yds) (limited spaces) ⌒ ✗ licensed ⌂ (loop system, interpretative model for blind, wheelchairs) toilets for disabled shop ⌒

SALISBURY & SOUTH WILTSHIRE MUSEUM
The King's House, 65 The Close SP1 2EN (in Cathedral Close)
☎ 01722 332151 ▤ 01722 325611
e-mail: museum@salisburymuseum.freeserve.co.uk
Times: Open all year Mon-Sat 10-5; also Suns Jul & Aug, 2-5. (Closed Xmas). **Facilities:** P (100 metres) (nearby parking charge) ✗ ⌂ parking by prior arrangement,induction loop in lecture hall toilets for disabled shop ✗ (ex guide dogs) Details not confirmed for 2003 ⌒

Wiltshire

STONEHENGE   Map 04 SU14
STONEHENGE
SP4 7DE (2m W of Amesbury on junct A303 and A344/A360)
☎ 01980 624715

One of the most famous prehistoric monuments in Europe, the henge was started about 5,000 years ago, but redesigned several times during the following 1,500 years. Enormous sarsens, each weighing more than 50 tons, were dragged from the Marlborough Downs, and were then worked into the design we see today - an outer ring of upright stones with lintels, and an inner horseshoe of five pairs of uprights, also with lintels. The axis of the horseshoe points towards the midsummer sunrise.
Times: Open all year, daily, 16 Mar-May, daily 9.30-6. Jun-Aug, 9-7; Sep-15 Oct, daily 9.30-6. 16-23 Oct, 9.30-5; 24 Oct-15 Mar 9.30-4. Closed 24-26 Dec. Last admission no later than 30 mins before the advertised closing time. Stonehenge will close promptly 20 mins after the advertised closing time. **Fee:** * £4.40 (ch £2.20, concessions £3.30). Family ticket (2ad+3ch)£11 **Facilities:** P ⌑ & shop ✗ ♿

STOURHEAD   Map 03 ST73
STOURHEAD HOUSE & GARDEN
Estate Office BA12 6QD (At Stourton off B3092, 3m NW Mere, follow brown tourist signs)
☎ 01747 841152 ▤ 01747 842005   2 for 1
e-mail: wstest@smtp.ntrust.org.uk
Times: garden open all year 9-7 (or dusk if earlier). house open 28 Mar-31 Oct 11-5 (closed on Wed & Thu); King Alfred tower open daily 28 Mar-31 Oct 12-5 **Fee:** Garden & House £8.90, Garden or House £5.10; Garden only (1 Nov- end Feb) £3.95; King Alfred Tower £1.85
Facilities: P ⌑ ✗ licensed & (wheelchairs, electric buggy, telephone in advance) toilets for disabled shop garden centre ✗ (ex in gardens Nov-Feb only) ♿ ⌑

STOURTON   Map 03 ST73
STOURTON HOUSE FLOWER GARDEN
Stourton House BA12 6QF (3m NW of Mere, on A303)
☎ 01747 840417

Set in the attractive village of Stourton, the house has more than four acres of beautifully maintained flower gardens. Many grass paths lead through varied and colourful shrubs and trees. Stourton House also specialises in unusual plants and dried flowers, many of which are for sale. It also has collections of daffodils, delphiniums and hydrangeas.
Times: Open Apr-end Nov, Wed, Thu, Sun & BH Mon 11-6 (or dusk if earlier). Also open Dec-Mar, wkdays for plant/dried flower sales. **Fee:** * £3 (ch 50p). **Facilities:** P ⌑ & (wheelchairs available) toilets for disabled shop (plants for sale) garden centre ✗ (ex by arrangement)

SWINDON   Map 04 SU18
STEAM - MUSEUM OF THE GREAT WESTERN RAILWAY
Kemble Dr SN2 2TA (from junct 16 of M4 & A420 follow brown signs to 'Outlet Centre')
☎ 01793 466646   2 for 1
▤ 01793 466615
e-mail: steampostbox@swindon.gov.uk

Nominated for European Museum of the Year, this fascinating day out tells the story of the men and women who built, operated and travelled on the Great Western Railway. Hands on displays, world-famous locomotives, archive film footage and the testimonies of ex-railway workers bring the story to life. A reconstructed station platform, posters and holiday memorabilia recreate the glamour and excitement of the golden age of steam. Located next door to the McArthurGlen Designer Outlet Great Western, Steam offers a great day out for all. Good value group packages, special events and exhibitions, shop and café.
Times: Open Nov-Mar, Mon-Sat 10-5, Sun 11-5. Apr-Oct, Mon-Sat 10-5.30, Sun 11-5.30. **Fee:** * £5.95 (ch £3.80, pen £3.90) Family ticket £14.70 (2ad+2ch) **Facilities:** P (100 yds) (disabled parking only at establisment) ⌑ & audio guide, wheelchair or scooter can be pre-booked toilets for disabled shop ✗ (ex guide dogs) ⌑

TEFFONT MAGNA   Map 03 ST93
FARMER GILES FARMSTEAD
SP3 5QY (11m W of Salisbury, off A303 at Teffont)
☎ 01722 716338 ▤ 01722 716993
e-mail: tdeane6995@aol.com

Set in 175 acres of Wiltshire downland, this is a real working dairy farm. You can watch the cows being milked, bottle feed lambs and get to know a host of other animals and pets. There is an adventure

continued

Wiltshire 259

playground with tractors and a relaxing walk along the picturesque Beech belt, meeting Highland cattle and Shire horses along the way. There are also exhibition areas and a restaurant.
Times: Open 18 Mar-5 Nov, daily 10-6, wknds in winters, 10-dusk. Party bookings all year. **Fee:** * £3.95 (ch £2.85, under 2's free & pen £3.50) Family ticket £13. **Facilities:** P ✕ licensed ♿ (complete access for disabled/wheelchairs available for use) toilets for disabled shop 🛒

TISBURY   Map 03 ST92
OLD WARDOUR CASTLE
SP3 6RR (2m SW)
☎ 01747 870487

Substantial remains of this hexagonal 14th-century castle are still standing, with walls 60ft high. It was twice besieged, and finally ruined during the Civil War. These ruins are considered among the most attractive in England.
Times: Open all year, 29 Mar-Sep, daily 10-6 (Oct, daily 10-5); Nov-Mar 10-1, 2-4 Wed-Sun closed 24-26 Dec & 1 Jan. **Fee:** * £2.50 (ch 5-15 £1.30, ch under 5 free, concessions £1.90) **Facilities:** P ♿ ♿

WESTBURY   Map 03 ST85
BROKERSWOOD COUNTRY PARK
Brokerswood BA13 4EH (turn off A36 at Bell Inn, Standerwick. Follow brown heritage signs)
☎ 01373 822238 & 823890   📠 01373 858474
e-mail: woodland.park@virgin.net

Brokerswood Country Park's nature walk leads through 80 acres of woodlands, with a lake and wildfowl. Facilities include a woodland visitor centre (covering wildlife and forestry), two children's adventure playgrounds, indoor soft play area, guided walks and the woodland railway, over a third of a mile long.
Times: Open all year; Park open daily 10-5. Closed Christmas Day, Boxing Day & New Years Day. Ring for museum opening hours. **Fee:** £3 (ch 6-16yrs £1.25, pen £2.25) **Facilities:** P 🍽 ♿ shop 🛒

WESTWOOD   Map 03 ST85
WESTWOOD MANOR
BA15 2AF (1.5m SW of Bradford on Avon, off B3109)
☎ 01225 863374

[2 for 1]

This late 15th-century stone manor house has some particularly fine Jacobean plasterwork. The house, which is situated by the parish church, was altered in 1610, but still retains its late Gothic and Jacobean windows.
Times: Open Apr-Sep, Sun, Tue & Wed 2-5. **Fee:** £4.20. **Facilities:** P ✕ ♿ *Details not confirmed for 2003*

WILTON (near Salisbury)   Map 02 SU03
WILTON HOUSE
SP2 0BJ (3m W of Salisbury, on the A30, 10m from Stonehenge & A303)
☎ 01722 746720 & 746729(24 hr line)
📠 01722 744447
e-mail: tourism@wiltonhouse.com

[2 for 1]

Beauty, pleasure, fascination - a visitor's experience of Wilton House. This fabulous Palladian mansion amazes visitors with its treasures, including magnificent art, fine furniture and interiors by Indigo Jones. The traditional and modern gardens, some designed by Lord Pembroke himself, are fabulous throughout the season and continue to delight visitors, whilst the adventure playground is a firm favourite with children.
Times: Open 11 Apr-26 Oct daily 10.30-5.30. Last admission 4.30. **Fee:** £9.25 (ch 5-15 £4.50, under 5 £1, students & pen £7.50). Family ticket £22. **Facilities:** P ✕ licensed ♿ (induction loop) toilets for disabled shop garden centre ✕ (ex guide dogs) 🛒

WOODHENGE   Map 04 SU14
WOODHENGE
(1.5m N of Amesbury, off A345 just S of Durrington)

A Neolithic ceremonial monument dating from about 2300 BC, consisting of six concentric rings of timber posts, now marked by concrete piles. The long axis of the rings, which are oval, points to the rising sun on Midsummer Day.
Times: Open all reasonable times. **Fee:** Free. **Facilities:** P ♿ ♿

Worcestershire

In Worcestershire, the fertile plains of the Vale of Evesham and the Severn Valley climb to the Malvern Hills in the west, and the Cotswolds in the south. To the north of the county lies the industrialised area of the Black Country, in sharp contrast to the south's rural idyll.

Worcester is the county town, and home to the Worcestershire County Cricket Club, which has what some regard as the most attractive grounds in the country, in a delightful setting with views of Worcester Cathedral. Worcester Racecourse is one of the oldest in the country, in Pitchcroft Park, close to the city, beside the River Severn. During the Civil War, Worcester was the first city to declare for the King, and the last to surrender to Cromwell.

Sir Edward Elgar was a Worcester man, and his statue stands in the High Street of the city, facing the cathedral. The cottage where he was born, in Lower Broadheath just west of Worcester, is now open as a museum. He is also commemorated on the £20 note.

Southeast of Worcester is the Vale of Evesham, the main fruit-growing area of the country, dotted with orchards and market gardens – a picture in the spring with the blossom in the trees. The main town in this area is Evesham, set in a loop of the River Avon.

The Malverns, Great and Little, set on the slopes of the Malvern Hills, are renowned for their refinement. Great Malvern, terraced on its hillside site, came to prominence as a genteel spa for well-to-do Victorians, rivalling the likes of Bath, Buxton and Cheltenham with its glorious surroundings.

Imortant figures in the county include poet A E Housman; chocolate magnate George Cadbury; and Lea and Perrins, who invented Worcestershire sauce.

EVENTS & FESTIVALS

May
tbc Upton Folk Festival (various venues), Upton-upon-Severn

June
9th-11th Spring Garden Show, Three Counties Showground, Malvern
13th-15th Three Counties Show, Three Counties Showground, Malvern
tbc Upton Jazz Festival (various venues), Upton-upon-Severn

July
tbc Worcester Carnival

September
27th-28th The Malvern Autumn Show, Three Counties Showground, Malvern

Top: Malvern Hills

Worcestershire

BEWDLEY Map 07 SO77
SEVERN VALLEY RAILWAY
Comberton Hill DY10 1QN
☎ 01299 403816   ▤ 01299 400839
(For full entry see Kidderminster)

WEST MIDLAND SAFARI & LEISURE PARK
Spring Grove DY12 1LF (on A456 between Kidderminster & Bewdley)
☎ 01299 402114   ▤ 01299 404519
e-mail: info@wmsp.co.uk

Located in the heart of rural Worcestershire, this 200-acre site is the home to a drive-through safari and Tiger World. There are a variety of rides, amusements and live shows suitable for all members of the family. Other features include Pets Corner, Hippo Lakes, Goat Walk, Seal Aquarium, Creepy Crawlies exhibit, animal and reptile encounters and Sealion Theatre.
Times: Open Apr-Oct, daily from 10am including BH's. **Fee:** * £6.25 (ch 4 free). Multi ride wristband £7.50. Junior restricted £6 (restricted rides only). Ride tickets £1 each from machines (various no of tickets per ride). **Facilities:** 🅿 🍴 ✕ licensed ♿ (most area accessible slopes/tarmac paths) shop 🐾 (ex guide dogs) ☕

BROADWAY Map 04 SP03
BROADWAY TOWER & ANIMAL PARK
WR12 7LB (off A44, 1m SE of village)
☎ 01386 852390   ▤ 01386 858038
e-mail: broadway-cotswold.co.uk/tower.html

The 65ft tower was designed by James Wyatt for the 6th Earl of Coventry, and built in 1799. The unique building now houses exhibitions depicting its colourful past and various uses such as holiday retreat to artist and designer William Morris. The viewing platform is equipped with a telescope, giving wonderful views over 13 counties. Around the Tower is a park with adventure playground, children's farm, BBQs, giant chess and draughts, and animal enclosures.
Times: Open Apr-Oct, daily 10.30-5. Nov-Mar (tower only) wknds weather permitting 11-3 or by prior booking. **Fee:** * Tower; £4 (£1.50, concessions £2.50). Animal Park; £3 (ch £2, concessions £2.50).
Facilities: 🅿 🍴 ✕ licensed ♿ toilets for disabled shop ☕

BROMSGROVE Map 07 SO97
AVONCROFT MUSEUM OF HISTORIC BUILDINGS
Stoke Heath B60 4JR (2m S, off A38)
☎ 01527 831886   ▤ 01527 876934   2 for 1
e-mail: avoncroft1@compuserve.com

A visit to Avoncroft takes you through nearly 700 years of history. Here you can see 25 buildings rescued from destruction and authentically restored on a 15-acre rural site. There are 15th and 16th-century timber framed buildings, 18th-century agricultural buildings and a cockpit. There are industrial buildings and a working windmill from the 19th century, and from the 20th a fully furnished pre-fab.
Times: Open Jul-Aug daily 10.30-5; Apr-Jun & Sep-Oct 10.30-4.30 (wknds 5.30), (Closed Mon); Mar & Nov 10.30-4, (Closed Mon & Fri). Open BHs. **Fee:** £5.20 (ch £2.60, pen £4.20). Family ticket £14.
Facilities: 🅿 🍴 ♿ (ramps, wheelchair available) toilets for disabled shop ☕

EVESHAM Map 04 SP04
THE ALMONRY HERITAGE CENTRE
Abbey Gate WR11 4EJ (on A4184, opposite Merstow Green, main North/South route through Evesham)
☎ 01386 446944   ▤ 01386 442348
e-mail: almonry@eveshamtc.ndirect.co.uk

The 14th-century stone and timber building was the home of the Almoner of the Benedictine Abbey in Evesham. It now houses exhibitions relating to the history of Evesham Abbey, the Battle of Evesham, and the culture and trade of Evesham. Evesham Tourist Information Centre is also located here.
Times: Open all year, Mon-Sat & BHs (ex Xmas & Sun in Nov, Dec & Jan) 10-5, Sun 2-5. **Fee:** * £2 (ch 16 free, pen & students £1).
Facilities: 🅿 (110yds) shop 🐾

GREAT WITLEY Map 03 SO76
WITLEY COURT
WR6 6JT (on A433)
☎ 01299 896636

Spectacular ruins of a once great house. An earlier Jacobean manor house was converted in the 19th-century into a vast Italianate mansion with porticoes by John Nash. The adjoining church by James Gibbs, has a remarkable 18th-century baroque interior. The gardens were equally elaborate and contained immense stone fountains which still survive today, the largest is the Poseidon Fountain
Times: Open all year, 29 Mar-Sep, daily 10-6 (Oct, daily 10-5); Nov-Mar 10-1, 2-4. Wed-Sun. (Closed 24-26 Dec & 1 Jan). **Fee:** * £4 (ch 5-15 £2, under 5's free, concessions £3) **Facilities:** 🅿 🍴 ♿ 🚻

HANBURY Map 03 SO96
HANBURY HALL
School Rd WR9 7EA (4.5m E of Droitwich, 1m N of B4090 and 1.5m W of B4091)
☎ 01527 821214   ▤ 01527 821251   2 for 1
e-mail: hanbury@smtp.ntrust.org.uk

This William and Mary style red-brick house, completed in 1701, was built by a prosperous local family. The house contains outstanding painted ceilings and staircase by Thornhill, and the Watney collection of porcelain. The 18th-century garden has recently been

continued

restored with many features including parterre, bowling green and working orangery.

Hanbury Hall

Times: Open 30 Mar-29 Oct Sun-Wed 1.30-5.30 (open Good Friday). Last admission 5 or dusk if earlier. Garden & tearoom opens 12 noon. **Fee:** * House & Garden £4.60 (ch £2.30). Family ticket £11.50. Garden only £2.90 (ch £1.45). **Facilities:** P ⏸ & (Braille guide) toilets for disabled shop ✈ (ex in park) ♨ 🛒

KIDDERMINSTER   Map 07 SO87
SEVERN VALLEY RAILWAY
Comberton Hill DY10 1QN (on A448, clearly signposted)
☎ 01299 403816   📠 01299 400839

The leading standard gauge steam railway, with one of the largest collections of locomotives and rolling stock in the country. Services operate from Kidderminster and Bewdley to Bridgnorth through 16 miles of picturesque scenery along the River Severn. Special steam galas and "Day out with Thomas" weekends take place during the year along with Santa Specials.
Times: Trains operate wknds throughout year, daily early May to end Sep, plus school holidays & half terms, Santa Specials, phone for details. **Fee:** * Subject to Review. (Train fares vary according to journey. Main through ticket £10 return, Family ticket £27) **Facilities:** P ⏸ & (some specially adapted trains, call for details) toilets for disabled shop (at Kidderminster/Bridgnorth) 🛒

WORCESTERSHIRE COUNTY MUSEUM
Hartlebury Castle, Hartlebury DY11 7XZ (4m S of Kidderminster clearly signed from A449)
☎ **01299 250416**
📠 **01299 251890**   **2 for 1**
e-mail: museum@worcestershire.gov.uk

Housed in the north wing of Hartlebury Castle, the County Museum contains a delightful display of crafts and industries. There are unique collections of toys, costume, domestic life, room settings and horse-drawn vehicles as well as a reconstructed forge, schoolroom, wheelwright's and tailor's shop.
Times: Open Feb-Nov, Mon-Thu 10-5, BH's 11-5, Fri & Sun 2-5. (Closed Sat & Good Fri). **Fee:** * £2.50 (ch & pen £1.20). Family ticket £6.50. **Facilities:** P ⏸ & (car parking spaces, close to main building) toilets for disabled shop ✈ (ex guide dogs & in grounds) 🛒

REDDITCH   Map 03 SP06
FORGE MILL NEEDLE MUSEUM & BORDESLEY ABBEY VISITOR CENTRE
Forge Mill, Needle Mill Ln, Riverside B98 8HY (N side of Redditch, off A441. M42 junct 2)
☎ 01527 62509
e-mail: museum@redditchbc.gov.uk   **2 for 1**

The Needle Museum tells the fascinating and sometimes gruesome story of how needles are made. Working, water-powered machinery can be seen in an original needle-scouring mill. The Visitor Centre is an archaeological museum showing finds from excavations at the nearby Bordesley Abbey.
Times: Open Etr-Sep, Mon-Fri 11-4.30, Sat-Sun 2-5; Feb-Etr & Oct-Nov, Mon-Thu 11-4 & Sun 2-5. Parties by arrangement. **Fee:** * £3.50 (ch 50p, pen £2.50). Family ticket £7.50. Reduced admission charge for holders of a Reddicard. **Facilities:** P ⏸ & (wheelchair available) toilets for disabled shop ✈ (ex guide dogs) 🛒

SPETCHLEY   Map 03 SO85
SPETCHLEY PARK GARDENS
Spetchley Park WR5 1RS (3m E of Worcester, off A422)
☎ 01905 345213 or 345224   📠 01453 511915
e-mail: hb@spetchleygardens.co.uk

The 110-acre deer park and the 30-acre gardens

continued

surround an early 19th-century mansion (not open), with sweeping lawns and herbaceous borders, a rose lawn and enclosed gardens with low box and yew hedges. There is a large collection of trees (including 17th-century Cedars of Lebanon), shrubs and plants, many of which are rare or unusual.
Times: Open Apr-Sep, Tue-Fri 11-5, Sun 2-5; BH Mons 11-5. Other days by appointment. **Fee:** * £3.50 (ch £1.70). Party 25+ £3.30.
Facilities: P ⬛ & (most of garden accessible) ✗ (ex guide dogs)

STONE
Map 07 SO87
STONE HOUSE COTTAGE GARDENS
DY10 4BG (2m SE of Kidderminster, on A448)
☎ 01562 69902   ▤ 01562 69960
e-mail: louisa@shcn.co.uk   **2 for 1**

A beautiful walled garden with towers provides a sheltered area of about one acre for rare shrubs, climbers and interesting herbaceous plants. Adjacent to the garden is a nursery with a large selection of unusual plants.
Times: Open Gardens & nursery Mar-end Sep, Wed-Sat 10-5.30. **Fee:** £2.50 (ch free). **Facilities:** P & garden centre ✗

WORCESTER
Map 03 SO85
CITY MUSEUM & ART GALLERY
Foregate St WR1 1DT (In city centre, 150mtrs from Foregate St train station)
☎ 01905 25371   ▤ 01905 616979
e-mail: artgalleryandmuseum@cityofworcester.gov.uk

The gallery has temporary art exhibitions from both local and national sources. Museum exhibits cover geology, local and natural history. Of particular interest is a complete 19th-century chemist's shop. There are collections relating to the Worcestershire Regiment and the Worcestershire Yeomanry Cavalry.
Times: Open all year, Mon, Tue-Fri 9.30-5.30, Sat 9.30-5.(Closed 25-26 Dec & 1 Jan also Good Fri) **Fee:** Free. **Facilities:** P (city centre) ⬛ & (lift, induction loop) toilets for disabled shop ✗ 🗨

THE COMMANDERY
Sidbury WR1 2HU (M5 junct 7, A44, signposted)
☎ 01905 361821   ▤ 01905 361822
e-mail: thecommandery@cityof
worcester.gov.uk
Times: Open all year, Mon-Sat 10-5, Sun 1.30-5. (Closed 25-26 Dec & 1 Jan) **Facilities:** P (100yds) shop ✗ (ex guide dogs) *Details not confirmed for 2003* 🗨

ELGAR'S BIRTHPLACE MUSEUM
Crown East Ln, Lower Broadheath WR2 6RH (3m W, signposted off A44 to Leominster)
☎ 01905 333224   ▤ 01905 333426   **2 for 1**
e-mail: birthplace@elgar.org

In 2000, the Elgar Centre was opened, to compliment the historic Birthplace Cottage and to provide additional exhibition space for more treasures from this unique collection, telling the story of Elgar's musical

Worcestershire 263

SEVERN VALLEY RAILWAY
the line for all seasons

T The SVR is a steam railway running the 16-miles between Bridgnorth and Kidderminster. Your journey provides excellent views of the River Severn and offers many opportunities for walking and visiting other attractions.

Kidderminster-Bewdley-Bridgnorth

Refreshments are available at stations and on most trains, and Luncheon is served most Sundays on our restaurant car train. There are special events throughout the year with visits by 'Thomas the Tank Engine' in May and September and Santa in December being popular with children. Older visitors will enjoy Heavy Horse Power Weekend in June, 1940's Weekends in late June and early July, and Classic Car and Bike Day in October.

THE RAILWAY STATION, BEWDLEY, WORCESTERSHIRE, DY12 1BG
Tel: 01299 403816
www.svr.co.uk

development and inspirations. Listen to his music as the audio tour guides you round the easily accessible displays.
Times: Open daily 11-5, Feb-Xmas. Last admission 4.15. (Closed 23 Dec-end Jan). **Fee:** * £3.50 (ch £1.75 & pen £3). Family ticket £8.75. Party rates available. **Facilities:** P & (large print guides, audio facilities, wheelchair access) toilets for disabled shop ✗ (ex guide dogs) 🗨

HAWFORD DOVECOTE
(3m N on A449)
☎ 01684 855300
Times: Open Apr-Oct, daily 9-6 or sunset. (Closed Good Fri). Other times by prior appointment only. **Facilities:** P (on street parking) ✗ ❧ *Details not confirmed for 2003*

MUSEUM OF LOCAL LIFE
Friar St WR1 2NA (City centre, 5min walk from Cathedral)
☎ 01905 722349

This interesting 500-year-old timber-framed house has a squint and an ornate plaster ceiling. It is now a museum of local life and displays show life here over the last 200 years.
Times: Open all year, Mon-Wed & Fri-Sat 10.30-5. Also BH's. (Closed 25-26 Dec & 1 Jan). **Fee:** Free. **Facilities:** P (200yds) & toilets for disabled shop ✗ (ex guide dogs) 🗨

Worcestershire

Museum of Worcester Porcelain
Severn St WR1 2NE (M5 Junct 7, follow signs to city centre, at 5th set of lights take 1st left into Edger Street & bear left into Severn St. At T-junct bear right & after 100yds take 1st left. Museum on left)
☎ 01905 23221 📠 01905 617807
e-mail: museum@royal-worcester.co.uk
Times: Open all year, Mon-Sat 9-5.30, Sun 11-5. **Facilities:** P (charged) ✗ licensed & (ex factory) toilets for disabled shop ✗
Details not confirmed for 2003

Worcester Cathedral
WR1 2LH (Worcester city centre, signed from M5 junct 7)
☎ 01905 28854 & 21004 📠 01905 611139
e-mail: info@worcestercathedral.org.uk

Worcester Cathedral is England's loveliest cathedral, with Royal Tombs, medieval cloisters, an ancient crypt and Chapter House and magnificent Victorian stained glass. The tower is open in the summer. There is nearby parking, bus and train stations.
Times: Open all year, daily 7.30-6. **Fee:** Donations. (Suggested £3 per adult.) **Facilities:** P (500yds) 🍽 & (Access from College Green) toilets for disabled shop ✗ (ex guide dogs)

East Riding of Yorkshire

From the imposing chalk cliffs at Flamborough, to the rolling green pastures of the Yorkshire Wolds, and the flourishing port of Hull, the East Riding of Yorkshire boasts some of the finest unspoilt countryside in England, and some wonderful places to visit.

Beverley Minster is big enough to be a cathedral. Among its treasures are a 1000-year old sanctuary chair and some wonderfully intricate wooden carvings. The magnificent Percy Tomb is a fine example of 14th-century stonemasonry. Beverley is also home to the Museum of Army Transport.

Driffield is known as the 'Capital of the Wolds', and is home to an annual agricultural show that attracts visitors from all around. Close by is Sledmere House, an impressive manor house set among parkland designed by `Capability' Brown.

Coastal areas of the East Riding can be a little daunting. Flamborough Head is a plateau of rolling turf 150ft high, surrounded on three sides by the sea. The Heritage Coast Project puts on a wide range of events which includes lectures, guided walks and nature expeditions. The lighthouse has defied the elements since 1806.

Hull has been one of the North of England's most vital ports since it was founded in the 12th century, and now has a justified reputation as an important cultural centre, in spite of attempts to label it as "Dull Hull". Famous folk from the city include thoughtful pop band The Housemartins, which fragmented into The Beautiful South and Fat Boy Slim; actor Tom Courtenay; comedienne Maureen Lipman; and the innovative Hull Truck Theatre Company.

Top: Hull's Maritime Museum

EVENTS & FESTIVALS

April
26th-5th May Bridlington Arts Festival (various venues)

May
26th April-5th Bridlington Arts Festival (various venues)
4th-5th East Riding Garden & Kite Festival, Beverley Racecourse
22nd-26th Beverley & East Riding Early Music Festival

June
20th-22nd Beverley & East Riding Folk Festival, various venues in Beverley

July
16th Driffield Agricultural Show, Driffield Showground
tbc Hornsea Music Festival, various venues

August
30th-31st International Sea Shanty Festival, Hull

September
tbc Beverley & East Riding Chamber Music Festival
tbc Hull Show, East Park, Hull
tbc International Sequence Dance Festival, Royal Hall Ballroom, Bridlington

October
25th-26th Beverley Christmas Fayre, Beverley Racecourse
tbc Hull Fair, Walton Street Fairground, Hull

November
tbc Hull Literature Festival (various venues)

Yorkshire, East Riding of

BEMPTON
Map 08 TA17
RSPB Nature Reserve
YO15 1JD (take cliff road from B1229, Bempton Village and follow brown tourist signs)
☎ 01262 851179 📠 01262 851533

Part of the spectacular chalk cliffs that stretch from Flamborough Head to Speeton. This is one of the sites in England to see thousands of nesting seabirds including gannets and puffins at close quarters. Viewpoints overlook the cliffs, which are best visited from April to July. Over two miles of chalk cliffs rising to 400ft with numerus cracks and ledges. Enormous numbers of seabirds nest on these cliffs including guilleots, razorbills, kittiwakes, fulmars, herring gulls and several pairs of shag. This is the only gannetry in England and is growing annually. Many migrants pass off-shore including terns, skuas and shearwaters. Wheatears, ring ouzels and merlins frequent the clifftop on migration. Grey seal and porpoise are sometimes seen offshore.
Times: Open for visitor centre daily, Mar-Nov 10-5. Winter wknds only 9.30-4. Closed Jan. **Fee:** £3 per car, £5 per minibus, £8 per coach.
Facilities: 🅿 (charged) 🍴 & toilets for disabled shop (must be on lead) 🐕

BEVERLEY
Map 08 TA03
Museum of Army Transport
Flemingate HU17 0NG (follow brown tourist signs once in Beverley. 5 mins walk from Minster)
☎ 01482 860445 📠 01482 872767

The museum tells the story of army transport from horse drawn waggons to the Gulf conflict: everything from prototype vehicles to Montgomery's Rolls Royce and the last Blackburn Beverley aircraft. There are also other exhibits to be explored including 'Monty's Men and D-Day Dodgers".
Times: Open all year, daily 10-5. (Closed 24 Dec-2 Jan). **Fee:** * £4.50 (ch 5-15, pen & student £3). Family ticket £12 (2 adults & 2 ch). Under 5's free. **Facilities:** 🅿 (charged) 🍴 & (parking next to entrance) toilets for disabled shop ✖

BURTON AGNES
Map 08 TA16
Burton Agnes Hall
Estate Office YO25 0ND (on A614)
☎ 01262 490324 📠 01262 490513
e-mail: burton.agnes@farmline.com

Built in 1598, this is a magnificent Elizabethan house, with furniture, pictures and china amassed by the family owners over four centuries. There is a walled garden with maze, potager, herbaceous borders, clematis, campanula and geranium collections, and jungle garden, as well as woodland walks.

Times: Open Apr-Oct, daily 11-5. **Fee:** * Hall & grounds £5.20 (ch £2.60, pen £4.70). Grounds only £2.60 (ch £1.15, pen £2.35). Party 30+. **Facilities:** 🅿 🍴 & (scented garden for the blind) toilets for disabled shop garden centre 🐕

Norman Manor House

This rare survivor from Norman times was replaced by Burton Agnes Hall. Some interesting Norman architectural features can still be seen, but the building was encased in brick at a later period.
Times: Open all year. **Fee:** Free. **Facilities:** ♿

HORNSEA
Map 08 TA14
Hornsea Museum
11 Newbegin HU18 1AB (turn off A165 onto B1244)
☎ 01964 533443

A former farmhouse whose outbuildings now illustrate local life and history. There are 19th-century period rooms and a dairy, plus craft tools and farming implements. Photographs, local personalities and industries are also featured.
Times: Open Etr-mid Oct, Tue-Sat 11-5, Sun 2-5 (last admission 4). **Fee:** £2 (concessions £1.50). Family ticket £6 **Facilities:** 🅿 (50yds) & toilets for disabled shop ✖

HULL
Map 08 TA02
Maister House
160 High St HU1 1NL (city centre)
☎ 01482 324114 📠 01482 227003
Times: Open all year, Mon-Fri 10-4 (Closed BH). **Facilities:** 🅿 ✖
♿ ✖ *Details not confirmed for 2003*

Maritime Museum
Queen Victoria Square HU1 3DX (from M62 follow A63 to town centre, museum is within pedestrian area of town centre)
☎ 01482 613902 📠 01482 613710
e-mail: museums@hullcc.gov.uk

Hull's maritime history is illustrated here, with displays on whales and whaling, ships and shipping, and other

continued

aspects of this Humber port. There is also a Victorian court room which is used for temporary exhibitions. The restored dock area, with its fine Victorian and Georgian buildings, is well worth exploring too.
Times: Open all year, Mon-Sat 10-5 & Sun 1.30-4.30. (Closed 25-2 Jan & Good Fri). **Fee:** Free. **Facilities:** P (100yds) & shop ✱ (ex guide dogs)

'STREETLIFE' - HULL MUSEUM OF TRANSPORT
High St HU1 1PS (A63 from M62, follow signs for Old Town)
☎ 01482 613902   📠 01482 613710
e-mail: museums@hullcc.gov.uk

This purpose built museum uses a 'hands-on' approach to trace 200 years of transport history. With a vehicle collection of national importance, state of the art animatronic displays and authentic scenarios, you can see Hull's Old Town brought vividly to life. The mail coach ride uses the very latest in computer technology to recreate a Victorian journey by four-in-hand.
Times: Open all year, Mon-Sat 10-5, Sun 1.30-4.30. (Closed 24-25 Dec & Good Fri). **Fee:** Free. **Facilities:** P (500mtrs) & toilets for disabled shop ✱ (ex guide dogs)

THE DEEP
HU1 4DP (follow signs from Hull City Centre)
☎ 01482 381000   📠 01482 381010
e-mail: info@thedeep.co.uk

Billing itself as "The World's Only Submarium", this fascinating aquarium centre is Europe's deepest, containing 2.5 million litres of water and 87 tonnes of salt. Dynamic displays recreate the birth of the universe, allow visitors to pilot a submarine and walk the ocean floor, and ride in the world's only underwater glass lift surrounded by sharks, eels, Napoleon Wrasse, and hundreds of other creatures.
Times: Open daily 10-7. (Closed 24-25 Dec) **Fee:** * £6 (ch under 16 £4). Family ticket (2 adults & 3 ch) £18 **Facilities:** P (charged) 🍴 & toilets for disabled shop ✱ (ex guide dogs)

WILBERFORCE HOUSE
23-25 High St HU1 1NE (A63 from M62 or A1079 from York, follow signs for Old Town)
☎ 01482 613902   📠 01482 613710
e-mail: museums@hullcc.gov.uk

The early 17th-century Merchant's house was the birthplace of William Wilberforce, who became a leading campaigner against slavery. There are Jacobean and Georgian rooms and displays on Wilberforce, the anti-slavery campaign. The house also has secluded gardens. There are special exhibitions throughout the year.
Times: Open all year, Mon-Sat 10-5 & Sun 1.30-4.30. (Closed 25-26 Dec, 1 Jan & Good Fri). **Fee:** Free. **Facilities:** P (500mtrs) (meters on street) & (large print, video area & audio guides) shop ✱ (ex guide dogs)

Yorkshire, East Riding of 267

🏛 POCKLINGTON   Map 08 SE84
BURNBY HALL GARDEN & STEWART COLLECTION
The Balk YO42 2QF (off A1079 at turning for Pocklington off B1247)
☎ 01759 302068
e-mail: burnbyhallgardens@hotmail.com

The two lakes in this garden have an outstanding collection of 80 varieties of hardy water lilies, designated a National Collection. The lakes stand within nine acres of beautiful gardens including heather beds, a rock garden, a spring and summer bedding area, woodland walk and Victorian garden. The museum contains sporting trophies and ethnic material gathered on world-wide travels.
Times: Open 29 Mar-Sep, daily 10-1 & 2-6. Oct, daily 10-1, 2-5 (last admission 5pm). **Fee:** * £1.70 (ch 5-15 90p, pen £1.70). Party 20+ £1.50 each. RHS members free. **Facilities:** P 🍴 & (free wheelchair hire, viewing platform for wheelchairs) toilets for disabled shop ✱ (ex guide dogs)

🏛 SEWERBY   Map 08 TA16
SEWERBY HALL & GARDENS
YO15 1EA (1m NE of Bridlington on B1255 towards Flamborough)
☎ 01262 673769   📠 01262 673090
e-mail: sewerby.hall@eastring.gov.uk

Sewerby Hall and Gardens, set in 50 acres of parkland overlooking Bridlington Bay, dates back to 1715. The Georgian House, with its 19th-century Orangery, contains art galleries, archaeological displays and an Amy Johnson Room with a collection of her trophies and mementoes. The grounds include magnificent walled Old English and Rose gardens and host many events throughout the year. Activities for all the family include a children's zoo and play areas, golf, putting, bowls, plus woodland and clifftop walks. Phone for details of special events.
Times: Estate open all year, dawn-dusk. Hall - contact office for further details **Fee:** * £3.10 (ch 5-15 £1.20, pen £2.30). Family ticket £7.50. Group 10+ **Facilities:** P 🍴 & toilets for disabled shop ✱

🏛 SPROATLEY   Map 08 TA13
BURTON CONSTABLE HALL
HU11 4LN (1.5m N of Sproatley. 14m from Beverley, follow A165 Bridlington road)
☎ 01964 562400   📠 01964 563229
e-mail: enquiries@burtonconstable.com

This superb Elizabethan house was built in 1570, but much of the interior was remodelled in the 18th century. There are magnificent reception rooms and a Tudor long gallery with a pendant roof: the contents range from pictures and furniture to a unique collection of 18th-century scientific instruments. Outside are 200 acres of parkland landscaped by `Capability' Brown, with oaks and chestnuts, and a lake with an island.
Times: Open, Hall & grounds Etr Sun-end Oct. Grounds 12.30-5, Hall 1-5. Last admission 4pm. **Fee:** House £5 (ch £2, pen £4.50). Family ticket £11. **Facilities:** P 🍴 & (stair lift to first foor, wheelchairs) toilets for disabled shop

EVENTS & FESTIVALS

January
30th-2nd Feb Harrogate Winter Antiques Fair

February
16th Kall Kwick National Rally, Pickering (motorsport event)

March
10th-15th Eskdale Festival of the Arts
tbc Selby Game Fair, Goole

April
10th-13th Harrogate Spring Antiques & Fine Art Fair
12th-13th Yorkshire Beautiful Homes & Gardens Show
18th-24th Harrogate International Youth Music Festival
tbc Knaresborough Spring Fayre

May
3rd-4th Busking Festival, York
3rd-5th Ripon Spring Festival
25th-26th Teeside Garden Festival & Woodland Festival

June
13th-28th Grassington Festival
tbc Nidderdale Festival
tbc North Yorkshire County Show
tbc Whitby Festival

July
4th-13th York Early Music Festival
8th-10th Great Yorkshire Show
17th-2nd August Harrogate International Festival
tbc Northern Aldeborough Festival

August
9th Ripley Show, Ripley
tbc Yorkshire Air Show, York

September
6th-7th Teeside Autumn Gold Garden Festival & Woodland Festival, Yarm
6th-20th Ripon International Festival
tbc Harrogate Autumn Show

October
18th-19th York Christmas Fayre
tbc Captain Cook Festival, Whitby

North Yorkshire

England's largest county has a stunning landscape, covering part of the Pennines, the rolling farmlands of the Vale of York, the Cleveland Hills and the North York Moors, plus the Yorkshire Dales National Park, which includes Swaledale and Wensleydale.

The coastline offers its own treasures, from the fishing villages of Staithes and Robin Hood Bay to Scarborough, one time Regency spa and Victorian bathing resort. In the 1890s, the quaint but bustling town of Whitby provided inspiration for Bram Stoker, who set much of his novel, *Dracula*, in the town.

York, traditionally the capital of the North of England, was second only to London prior to the Industrial Revolution. It is a city of immense historical significance: capital of the British province under the Romans in AD 71 and a Viking settlement in the 10th century. In the Middle Ages its prosperity depended on the wool trade. The city's earliest surviving building is the Roman Multangular Tower, and the city walls, dating from the 14th century, are among the finest in Europe, including four gates or 'bars'. However, the gothic Minster is York's crowning glory, built between 1220 and 1470.

These days it is Northallerton, that is the administrative centre of the county. Harrogate is a traditional spa resort renowned for its gentility and tea rooms. To the south of the town, an area of some 200 acres of common land known as The Stray is popular for walking and picnicking.

TV and movie fans may like to visit Goathland, which features in the chart-topping *Harry Potter* movies and also the TV series *Heartbeat*, Castle Howard which served as the location of *Brideshead Revisited*, or Scarborough, which was the set for *Little Voice* in 1998. *Top: Barns and drystone wall in Wharfedale*

Yorkshire, North

ALDBOROUGH Map 08 SE46
ROMAN TOWN
YO51 9ES (0.75m SE of Boroughbridge, on minor road off B6265 within 1m of junction of A1 & A6055)
☎ 01423 322768
Times: Open Apr-Sep, daily 10-1 & 2-6 (Oct 10-1 & 2-5). (Closed Nov-28 Mar) **Facilities:** ✗ ‡ *Details not confirmed for 2003*

AYSGARTH Map 07 SE08
NATIONAL PARK CENTRE
DL8 3TH (off A684, at Falls junct then down hill over river, centre 500yds on left)
☎ 01969 663424   📠 01969 663105
e-mail: aysgarth@ytbtic.co.uk
Times: Open Apr-Oct, daily 10-5; Winter, wknds only. **Facilities:** P (charged) 🍴 ✗ & toilets for disabled shop ✗ (ex guide dogs) 🚲
Details not confirmed for 2003

YORKSHIRE CARRIAGE MUSEUM
Yore Mill DL8 3SR (1.75m E on unclass rd N of A684. Turn right at Palmer Flatt Hotel, museum 300yds)
☎ 01969 663399
Times: Open Apr-Oct, daily 9.30-7.30, other times 9.30-dusk. Closed 24 Dec-12 Jan. **Facilities:** P (150 yds) 🍴 shop *Details not confirmed for 2003*

BEDALE Map 08 SE28
BEDALE MUSEUM
DL8 1AA (on A684, 1.5m W of A1 at Leeming Bar)
☎ 01677 423797   📠 01677 425393

Situated in a building dating back to the 17th-century, the Bedale is a fascinating museum. The central attraction is the Bedale fire engine, which dates back to 1742. Other artefacts include documents, toys, craft tools and household utensils, which all help to give an absorbing picture of the lifestyle of the times.
Times: Open Tue & Fri 10-12.30 & 2-4, Wed 2-4, Thu-Sat 10-12 **Fee:** Free. **Facilities:** P & ✗ (ex guide dogs)

BENINGBROUGH Map 08 SE55
BENINGBROUGH HALL
YO6 1DD (off A19, 8m NW of York. Entrance at Newton Lodge)
☎ 01904 470666   📠 01904 470002
e-mail: ybbrgb@smtp.ntrust.org.uk
Times: Open 23 Mar-3 Nov daily (ex Thu/Fri) open Good Friday, Jul/Aug daily ex Thu 12-5. Grounds 11-5.30. **Facilities:** P ✗ licensed & (access to Victorian laundry, shop & restaurant) toilets for disabled shop ✗ ⚐ *Details not confirmed for 2003*

BRIMHAM Map 08 SE26
BRIMHAM ROCKS
Summerbridge HG3 4DW (off B6265)
☎ 01423 780688   📠 01423 781020
e-mail: yorkbm@smtp.ntrust.org.uk
Times: Open 8-dusk, (may close in bad weather): shop with exhibition room, 16Mar/Apr/May/Oct, Sat/Sun, B Hols and local school hols 11-5. 25May/Jun-Sep, daily 11-5, Nov/Dec Suns 26 Dec & 1 Jan
Facilities: P 🍴 & (specially adapted path, braille guide) toilets for disabled shop ⚐ *Details not confirmed for 2003*

CASTLE BOLTON Map 07 SE09
BOLTON CASTLE
DL8 4ET (off A684, 6m W of Leyburn)
☎ 01969 623981   📠 01969 623332
e-mail: harry@boltoncastle.co.uk

A medieval castle completed in 1399, overlooking Wensleydale that was the stronghold of the Scrope family. Mary, Queen of Scots was imprisoned here for 6 months. The Castle was besieged and taken by Parliamentary forces in 1645. Tapestries, tableaux, arms and armour can be seen and medieval gardens have been developed.
Times: Open Apr-Oct 10-5, Nov-Mar 10-4. **Fee:** * £4 (ch & pen £3). Family ticket £10. **Facilities:** P 🍴 shop ✗ ⚐

CASTLE HOWARD
See Malton

CLAPHAM Map 07 SD76
CLAPHAM NATIONAL PARK CENTRE
LA2 8ED (signposted off A65 at Clapham)
☎ 015242 51419
Times: Open Apr-Oct, daily 10-5.Limited opening Nov-Mar. **Facilities:** P (charged) (Radar key scheme) shop *Details not confirmed for 2003* ⚐

COXWOLD Map 08 SE57
BYLAND ABBEY
YO6 4BD (2m S of A170 between Thirsk & Helmsley, near Coxwold village)
☎ 01347 868614

The abbey was built for the Cistercians in the 12th and 13th centuries and enough remains of the buildings to show how beautiful it most have been. There are well preserved floor tiles, carved stones and other finds.
Times: Open Apr-Sep, daily 10-6 (Oct 10-5). Closed 1-2pm. **Fee:** £1.70 (ch 90p, concessions £1.30). **Facilities:** P & garden/grounds partly accessible toilets for disabled ‡ ⚐

DANBY Map 08 NZ70
MOORS CENTRE
Lodge Ln YO21 2NB (turn S off A171 signed "Moors Centre Danby". Turn left at cross roads in Danby follow road for 2m, Moors Centre on right)
☎ 01287 660654   📠 01287 660308
e-mail: moorscentre@ytbtic.co.uk

The ideal place to start exploring the North York Moors National Park. There is an exhibition about the area as well as events, video, a shop and local walks. The Moors bus service also operates from this site - phone for details.
Times: Open all year, Apr-Oct, daily 10-5. Nov, Dec & Mar daily 11-4. Jan & Feb wknds only 11-4. **Fee:** Free. **Facilities:** P (charged) 🍴 & (woodland & garden trails, motorised & manual wheelchairs) toilets for disabled shop ✗ (ex guide dogs & in grounds)

EASBY
Map 08 NZ10
EASBY ABBEY
(1m SE of Richmond off B6271)

Set beside the River Swale, the Premonstratensian Abbey was founded in 1155 and dedicated to St Agatha. Extensive remains of the monks' domestic buildings can be seen.
Times: Open any reasonable time. **Fee:** Free. **Facilities:** P ♿

ELVINGTON
Map 08 SE74
YORKSHIRE AIR MUSEUM & ALLIED AIR FORCES MEMORIAL
Halifax Way YO41 4AU (from York take A1079 then immediate right onto B1228, museum is signposted on right)
☎ 01904 608595 📠 01904 608246

Unique WW2 bomber command station. Fascinating exhibitions, 43 aircraft, including the Halifax Bomber, covering aviation to modern jets like the Harrier GR3.
Times: Open all year, Mon-Fri 10-4, Sat & Sun 10-5, BH's 10.30-5. In winter times vary, telephone establishment. **Fee:** * £4 (ch & pen £3).
Facilities: P 🍽 ✖ licensed ♿ toilets for disabled shop 🐕

FAIRBURN
Map 08 SE42
RSPB NATURE RESERVE
Fairburn Ings, The Visitor Centre, Newton Ln WF10 2BH (W of A1, N of Ferrybridge. Signed from Allerton Bywater off A656. Signed Fairburn off A1)
☎ 01977 603796
e-mail: chris.drake@rspb.org.uk
Times: Access to the reserve via car park, open 9-dusk. Centre open 10-5 weekends and 11-4 weekdays (closed 25-26 Dec). **Facilities:** P ♿ (raised boardwalk for wheelchair) toilets for disabled shop (ex guide dogs) *Details not confirmed for 2003*

GRASSINGTON
Map 07 SE06
NATIONAL PARK CENTRE
Colvend, Hebden Rd BD23 5LB (follow B6265 to Grassington, located in car park on B6265 (Hebden Rd), heading to Pateley Bridge)
☎ 01756 752774 📠 01756 753358
e-mail: grassington@ytbtic.co.uk
Times: Open Apr-Oct daily, 9.30-5. Also limited wknds Nov-Mar.
Facilities: P (charged) ♿ (Radar key scheme) toilets for disabled shop *Details not confirmed for 2003* 🐕

GUISBOROUGH
Map 08 NZ61
GISBOROUGH PRIORY
TS14 6HG (next to parish church)
☎ 01287 633801
Times: Open all year Apr-Sep, Tue-Sun 9-5; Oct-Mar, Wed-Sun 9-5. (Closed 24 Dec & 1 Jan). **Facilities:** ♿ 🐕 ♿ *Details not confirmed for 2003*

HARROGATE
Map 08 SE35
RHS GARDEN, HARLOW CARR
Crag Ln, Otley Rd HG3 1QB (off B6162,1.5 miles from Harrogate centre)
☎ 01423 565418 📠 01423 530663
e-mail: admin@harlowcarr.fsnet.co.uk
Times: Open all year, daily 9.30 until dusk. **Facilities:** P 🍽 ✖ licensed ♿ (electric wheelchairs available) toilets for disabled shop garden centre 🐕 (ex guide dogs) *Details not confirmed for 2003*

THE ROYAL PUMP ROOM MUSEUM
Crown Place HG1 2RY (Take A61 into Harrogate town centre and follow brown heritage signs to museum)
☎ 01423 556188 📠 01423 556130
e-mail: lg23@harrogate.gov.uk

Housed in delightful early Victorian pump room. Over the town's sulphur wells, the museum tells the story of Harrogate's heyday as England's European spa. Visitors discover some of the amazing spa treatments; taste the sulphur water; and explore stories of Russian royalty, communal yo-roasts and early bicycles, among many others. Changing exhibitions complement permanent displays. Explore "The Land of The Pharaohs" in 2002, and "The New Elizabethans, a festival of the 50s" in 2003.
Times: Open all year, Apr-Oct, Mon-Sat 10-5, Sun 2-5, (Nov-Mar close at 4pm). (Closed 24-26 Dec & 1 Jan). **Fee:** * £2 (ch £1.25, concession £1.50). Family rate £5.50 (2 adults & 2 ch). Party. Combined seasonal tickets available for The Royal Pump Room Museum & Knaresborough Castle & Museum. **Facilities:** P (100yds) (restricted to 3hrs, need parking disc) ♿ toilets for disabled shop 🐕 (guide dogs only) 🐕

HAWES
Map 07 SD88
DALES COUNTRYSIDE MUSEUM CENTRE
Station Yard DL8 3NT (Off A684 in the Old Station Yard)
☎ 01969 667450 & 667494 📠 01969 667165
e-mail: hawes@ytbtic.co.uk
Times: Open all year 10-5. **Facilities:** P (charged) ♿ toilets for disabled shop 🐕 (ex guide dogs) *Details not confirmed for 2003* 🐕

HELMSLEY
Map 08 SE68
DUNCOMBE PARK
YO62 5EB (Within the North York Moors National Park, off A170 Thirsk-Scarborough road)
☎ 01439 770213 📠 01439 771114
e-mail: sally@duncombepark.com

Duncombe Park stands at the heart of a spectacular 30-acre early 18th-century landscape garden which is set in 300 acres of dramatic parkland around the River Rye. The house, originally built in 1713, was gutted by fire in 1879 and rebuilt in 1895. Its principal rooms are a fine example of the type of grand interior popular at the turn of the century. Home of the Duncombes for 300 years, for much of this century the house was a girls' school. In 1985 the present Lord and Lady Feversham decided to make it a family home again and after major restoration, the house opened to the public. Part of the garden and parkland were designated a 250-acre National Nature Reserve. Special events include a

continued

Country Fair (May), an Antiques Fair (June), Steam Fair (July), Antiques Fair (November). Please telephone for details.
Times: Open: 28 Apr-27 Oct Sun-Thu; Gardens, Parkland Centre tea room & shop & Parkland walks 11-5.30. House by guided tour only every 30 mins from 12.30 - 3.30 **Fee:** * House & Gardens £6 (ch 10-16, £3, concessions £5) Gardens & Parkland £3 (ch £1.50, concessions £2) Parkland only £2 (ch £1). **Facilities:** P ✗ licensed & portable ramp, lift toilets for disabled shop ✱ (ex park)

HELMSLEY CASTLE
YO5 5AB
☎ 01439 770442

The ruined castle dates from the 12th century and later, and stands within enormous earthworks. It was besieged in the Civil War, and destroyed in 1644.
Times: Open all year, 29 Mar-Sep, daily 10-6 (Oct, daily 10-5); Nov-Mar, daily 10-4. Closed 1pm-2pm throughout the year (ex 29 Mar-Sep) (Closed 24-26 Dec & 1 Jan). **Fee:** * £2.50 (ch £1.30, under 5's free, con £1.90). Family ticket £6.30 **Facilities:** P (charged) ✱ (in certain areas)

KIRBY MISPERTON   Map 08 SE77
FLAMINGO LAND THEME PARK & ZOO
The Rectory YO17 6UX (off A169 & A64)
☎ 01653 668287   ■ 01653 668280
Times: Open 28 Mar-26 Sep, as well as weekends and full half term week in Oct. **Facilities:** P ■ ✗ & (parking) toilets for disabled shop *Details not confirmed for 2003*

KIRKHAM   Map 08 SE76
KIRKHAM PRIORY
Whitwell-on-the-Hill YO6 7JS (5m SW of Malton on minor road off A64)
☎ 01653 618768

The ruins of this former house of Augustinian canons stand on an entrancing site on the banks of the River Derwent. The remains of the finely sculpted 13th-century gatehouse and lavatorium, where the monks washed in leaded troughs, are memorable.
Times: Open all year, 29 Mar-Sep, daily 10-6 (Oct , daily 10-5); closed between 1&2pm **Fee:** * £1.70 (ch 5-15 90p, under 5's free, con £1.30) **Facilities:** P & ✱

KNARESBOROUGH   Map 08 SE35
KNARESBOROUGH CASTLE & MUSEUM
Castleyard HG5 8AS (turn off the High St, continue past Market Square, turn right at police station into the Castleyard)
☎ 01423 556188   ■ 01423 556130
e-mail: lg23@harrogate.gov.uk

High above the town of Knaresborough, the ruins of this 14th-century castle look down over the gorge of the River Nidd. This imposing fortress was once the hiding place of Thomas Becket's murderers and served as a prison for Richard II. Remains include the keep, the sally-port, parts of the curtain wall and the Old Court of

Yorkshire, North   **271**

Knaresborough. It now houses a local museum, and entrance is part of the combined ticket price.
Times: Open Good Fri-end Sep, daily 10.30-5. Guided tours regulary available. **Fee:** * £2 (ch £1.25, concessions £1.50). Family ticket (2 adults & 2 ch) £5.50. Party 10+. Joint & season tickets available for Knaresborough Castle & Museum & The Royal Pump Room Museum.
Facilities: P (charged) & toilets for disabled shop ✱ (ex guide dogs)

MALHAM   Map 07 SD96
MALHAM NATIONAL PARK CENTRE
BD23 4DA (Turn off A65 at Gargrave opposite petrol station. Malham 7m)
☎ 01729 830053
e-mail: malham@ytbtic.org
Times: Open Apr-Oct, daily 10-5. Limited winter opening. **Facilities:** P (charged) & (Radar key scheme for toilet) toilets for disabled shop *Details not confirmed for 2003*

MALTON   Map 08 SE77
CASTLE HOWARD
YO60 7DA (15m NE of York, off A64, follow the brown heritage signs to Castle Howard)
☎ 01653 648333 648444   ■ 01653 648501
e-mail: house@castlehoward.co.uk

In its dramatic setting of lakes, fountains and extensive gardens, this 18th-century palace was designed by Sir John Vanbrugh. Castle Howard was begun in 1699 for the 3rd Earl of Carlisle, Charles Howard. The interior has a 192ft Long Gallery, as well as a Chapel with magnificent stained glass windows by the 19th-century artist, Edward Burne-Jones. The Castle contains a portrait of Henry VIII by Holbein and works by Rubens, Reynolds and Gainsborough. The grounds include the domed Temple of the Four Winds by Vanbrugh, and the family mausoleum.
Times: Open Mar-2 Nov, grounds, exhibition wing, plant centre & stable court yard, daily from 10. House 11. Last admissions 4.30. Grounds close 6.30. **Fee:** £8.50 (ch £5.50, pen £7.50). Grounds only £5.50(ch £3.50). **Facilities:** P ■ ✗ licensed & (wheelchair lift, free adapted transport to house) toilets for dis*abled shop garden centre (ex guide dogs)

Eden Camp Modern History Theme Museum
Eden Camp YO17 6RT (junct of A64 & A169, between York & Scarborough)
☎ 01653 697777   ✉ 01653 698243
e-mail: admin@edencamp.co.uk   **2 for 1**

The story of the peoples' war unfolds in this museum devoted to civilian life in World War II. The displays, covering the blackout, rationing, the Blitz, the Homeguard and others, are housed in a former prisoner-of-war camp built in 1942 for German and Italian soldiers. Hut 13, part of a millennium project, covers the conflicts that Britain has been involved with from 1945 to present day.
Times: Open 2nd Mon in Jan-23 Dec, daily 10-5. Last admission 4pm. Allow at least 3-4hrs for a visit. **Fee:** * £4 (ch & pen £3) Party 10+.
Facilities: P ⬤ ♿ (taped tours, Braille guides) toilets for disabled shop

Malton Museum
Old Town Hall, Market Place YO17 7LP (leave A64, follow signs for Malton town centre)
☎ 01653 695136

The extensive Roman settlements in the area are represented and illustrated in this museum, including collections from the Roman fort of Derventio. There are also displays of local prehistoric and medieval finds plus changing exhibitions of local interest.
Times: Open Etr Sat-Oct, Mon-Sat 10-4. **Fee:** * £1.50 (ch, pen & students £1) Family ticket £4 (2 adults & 2 ch) **Facilities:** P (adjacent) (pay & display-2hrs) ♿ shop ✈ (ex guide dogs)

MASHAM   Map 08 SE28
Theakston Brewery & Visitor Centre
The Brewery HG4 4YD (on A6108)
☎ 01765 684333   ✉ 01765 684383
e-mail: bookings@theakstons.co.uk   **2 for 1**

Visit the Theakston Brewery in Masham, home of the legendary 'Old Peculier' and witness the creation of real taste first-hand. Discover how traditional brewing techniques are still being applied to create today's award-winning pint. As these tours are thirsty work, you'll be invited, to round off your visit in the bar with a glass of real British beer at its best.
Times: Open 21 Jul-1 Sep, 19 Oct-27 Oct, 15 Feb-23 Feb, 12 Apr-5 May 10.30-4.30. All other times Fri-Mon 10.30-4.30. Closed 27 Oct-15 Feb **Fee:** * £4.50 (ch 10-17yrs £2, pen £3.50) **Facilities:** P (400yds) ♿ (ex brewery tours) toilets for disabled shop ✈

MIDDLEHAM   Map 07 SE18
Middleham Castle
DL8 4RJ (2m S of Leyburn on A6108)
☎ 01969 623899

The historic town of Middleham is dominated by the 12th-century keep which saw its great days during the Wars of the Roses. The seat of the Neville family, Earls of Warwick, it was the home for a time of the young King Richard III, then Duke of Gloucester.
Times: Open all year, 29 Mar-Sep, daily 10-6 (Oct, daily 10-5); Nov-Dec, daily, 10-1 & 2-4. Jan-Mar 10-1& 2-4 (Closed 24-26 Dec & 1 Jan). **Fee:** * £2.60 (ch 5-15 £1.30, under 5's free, con £2). **Facilities:** P ♿ (ex tower) shop

MIDDLESBROUGH   Map 08 NZ42
Captain Cook Birthplace Museum
Stewart Park, Marton TS7 6AS (3m S on A172)
☎ 01642 311211   ✉ 01642 317419
e-mail: jeanette_grainger@middlesbrough.gov.uk
Times: Open all year: Tue-Sun, Summer hrs 10am-5.30pm. Winter hrs 9am-4pm. Last entry 45 mins before closure. (Closed Mon except BH, 25-26 Dec & 1 Jan). **Facilities:** P ⬤ ♿ (lift to all floors, car parking) toilets for disabled shop ✈ (ex guide dogs) *Details not confirmed for 2003*

NEWBY HALL & GARDENS   Map 08 SE36
Newby Hall & Gardens
HG4 5AE (4m SE of Ripon & 2m W of A1M, off B6265, between Boroughbridge and Ripon)
☎ 01423 322583   ✉ 01423 324452
e-mail: info@newbyhall.com

A late 17th-century house with beautifully restored Robert Adam interiors containing an important collection of classical sculpture and Gobelin tapestries. 25 acres of award-winning gardens include a miniature

continued

railway, an adventure garden for children and a woodland discovery walk.
Times: Open Apr-Sep, Tue-Sun & BH's; Gardens 11-5.30; House 12-5. Last admission 5pm (gardens), 4.30pm (house), **Fee:** * House & Garden £7, (ch & disabled £4.50, pen £6). Gardens only £5.50 (ch & disabled £4, pen £4.50). Party rates and family tickets on application. Under 4's go free. **Facilities:** P ☕ ✕ licensed ♿ (wheelchairs available, maps of wheelchair routes) toilets for disabled shop garden centre ✕ (ex guide dogs) 🦮

NORTH STAINLEY Map 08 SE27
LIGHTWATER VALLEY THEME PARK
HG4 3HT (3m N of Ripon on the A6108)
☎ 0870 458 0060 & 458 0040
📠 01765 635359
e-mail: leisure@lightwatervalley.co.uk

The family sized theme park with thrills of all sizes, from Europe's longest rollercoaster; 'The Ultimate' and 'Beaver rapids' log flume to family favourite such as the 'ladybird' rollercoaster and Grand Prix go carting along with spinning teacups, vintage cars and much more for younger children. You just pay once and enjoy the fun all day long!
Times: Open 23 Mar-7 Apr, weekends only; 13 Apr-26 May inc BH Mon; daily from Jun-2 Sep, weekends only 7 Sep-13 Oct. daily 19 Oct-27 Oct. **Fee:** * £13.50 over 1.1 metres, £12 under 1.1 metres, free under 0.9m; senior citizens £5.95. Family ticket £48 (2ad + 2ch) or (1ad + 3ch u16), **Facilities:** P ☕ ✕ licensed ♿ (even pathways) toilets for disabled shop ✕ (ex guide dogs) 🦮

NUNNINGTON Map 08 SE67
NUNNINGTON HALL
YO6 5UY (4.5m SE of Helmsley)
☎ 01439 748283   📠 01439 748284
e-mail: yorknu@smtp.ntrust.org.uk
Times: Open 23 Mar-3 Nov, Mar-May & Sep-Nov, daily (ex Mon/Tue) open BH Mons 1.30-4.30 (last admission 5pm May & Sep); Jun-Aug; daily ex Mon (open BH Mon) 1.30-5. **Facilities:** P ☕ ♿ (w/chairs, braille guide, scented garden) toilets for disabled shop 🦮 *Details not confirmed for 2003*

ORMESBY Map 08 NZ51
ORMESBY HALL
TS7 9AS (3m SE of Middlesborough, W of A19 take the A174 to the A172. Follow signs for Ormesby Hall. Car entrance on Ladgate Lane)
☎ 01642 324188   📠 01642 300937
e-mail: yorkor@smtp.ntrust.org.uk
Times: Open 24 Mar-3 Nov: daily ex Mon, Fri & Sat (open Good Fri & BH Mons) 2-5. **Facilities:** P ☕ ♿ (parking, braille guide, special tours) toilets for disabled shop ✕ 🦮 *Details not confirmed for 2003*

OSMOTHERLEY Map 08 SE49
MOUNT GRACE PRIORY
DL6 3JG (1m NW)
☎ 01609 883494

A ruined 14th-century Carthusian priory, next to a 17th-century house. One of the monks cells has been fully restored to show how what monastic life was like

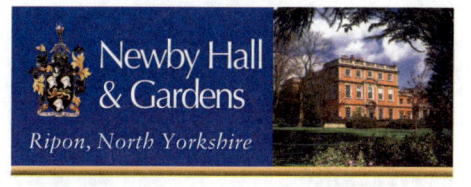

Yorkshire, North 273

Newby Hall & Gardens
Ripon, North Yorkshire

This graceful country house presents Robert Adam at his very best and the spectacular gardens are a must.

Come and Enjoy
- The famous Adam house
- 25 acres of award-winning gardens
- National Collection of CORNUS (dogwoods)
- Exciting Children's Adventure Garden
- Miniature Railway (10 1/4" gauge)
- Quality licensed Garden Restaurant
- Irresistible Shop and Plant Centre
- Enchanting Woodland Discovery Walk

Full visitor information
Tel: 01423 322583
Fax: 01423 324452
Email: info@newbyhall.com
Web site: www.newbyhall.com

Open daily except Mondays (but including Bank Holidays)
1st April – end September from 11am.

Simply a great day out!

---

here, and there are also interesting remains of the cloister, church and outer court.
Times: Open 19 Mar-Sep, daily 10-6 ; Nov-Mar 10-1, 2-4. Wed-Sun Last admission 30 minutes before closing time (Closed 24-26 Dec & 1 Jan). **Fee:** * £3 (ch £1.50, concessions £2.30). **Facilities:** P ♿ shop ✕ ♿ 🦮

PARCEVALL HALL GARDENS Map 07 SE06
PARCEVALL HALL GARDENS
BD23 6DE (Off B6265 between Grassington and Pateley Bridge)
☎ 01756 720311   📠 01756 720311
e-mail: info@parcevallhallgardens.co.uk

Enjoying a hillside setting east of the main Wharfedale Valley, these beautiful gardens surround a Grade II listed house which is used as the Bradford Diocesan Retreat House (not open to the public).
Times: Open Apr-Oct, daily 10-6. Winter visitors by appointment. **Fee:** * £3 (ch up to 16 50p). **Facilities:** P ☕ shop

PATELEY BRIDGE Map 07 SE16
STUMP CROSS CAVERNS
Greenhow HG3 5JL (situated on the B6265 between Pateley Bridge and Grassington)
☎ 01756 752780   📠 01756 752780

Discovered by the brothers Mark and William Newbould in 1860, Stump Cross Caverns have been an attraction for visitors since 1863 when one shilling was charged for entrance. Among the few limestone show caves in Britain, these require no special clothing, experience or

continued

equipment, as walkways are level and floodlighting is provided. Stalagmites, stalagtites and calcite precipitation make this an eerie day out.
Times: Open daily, mid Mar-9 Nov, then wknds 10-4 until mid Mar **Fee:** * £4.60 (ch £2.40 ch under 4 free) **Facilities:** P 🍴 shop ✗ (ex guide dogs) 🦮

🏛 PICKERING   Map 08 SE78
NORTH YORKSHIRE MOORS RAILWAY
Pickering Station YO18 7AJ (from A169 take the road towards Kirkbymoorside at traffic lights turn R. Station 400yds on L)
☎ 01751 472508   📠 01751 476970
e-mail: admin@nymr.pickering.fsnet.co.uk

Operating through the heart of the North York Moors National Park between Pickering and Grosmont, steam trains cover a distance of 18 miles. The locomotive sheds at Grosmont are open to the public. Events throughout the year include 'Day Out with Thomas' events, Steam Gala and Santa Specials.
Times: Open 23 Mar-3 Nov, daily; Dec, Santa specials and Christmas to New Year running. Further information available from Pickering Station. **Fee:** * Return: £10 (ch £5, pen £8.50). Family ticket £27 (2ad+3ch), others on request). All-line ticket £10 (ch £8, pen £8.50). Party 20+. **Facilities:** P (charged) 🍴 ✗ licensed ♿ (ramp for trains) toilets for disabled shop (at Pickering, Goathland & Grosmont) 🦮

PICKERING CASTLE
YO6 5AB
☎ 01751 474989

Standing upon its mound high above the town, the 12th-century keep and baileys are among the interesting remains of what was once a favourite royal hunting lodge. An exhibition tells the castle's history.
Times: Open, 29 Mar-Sep, daily 10-6 (Oct, daily 10-1 2-5); Nov-Mar Wed-Sun 10-1 & 2-4. (Closed 24-26 Dec & 1 Jan). **Fee:** * £2.50 (ch 5-15 £1.30 under 5's free, concessions £1.90). **Facilities:** P ♿ (ex motte) shop ✗ ♿

🏛 REDCAR   Map 08 NZ62
RNLI ZETLAND MUSEUM
5 King St TS10 3AH (on corner of King St and The Promenade)
☎ 01642 485370 & 471813
Times: Open May-Sep, Mon-Fri 1-4, Sat & Sun 12-4. Also Etr. Other times by appointment. **Facilities:** P (20m) (50p per hour) ♿ (ground floor accessible only) shop *Details not confirmed for 2003*

🏛 RICHMOND   Map 07 NZ10
GREEN HOWARDS MUSEUM
Trinity Church Square, Market Place DL10 4QN (Take any turning off A1, between Catterick & South Corner, signposted to Richmond. Located in centre market square, in Old Trinity Church).
☎ 01748 822133   📠 01748 826561
Times: Open Feb, Mon-Fri 10-4.30; Mar, Mon-Fri 10-4.30; mid Apr-Oct, Mon-Sat 9.30-4.30 & Sun 2-4.30; Nov, Mon-Sat 10-4.30. **Facilities:** P (in market place) (disk parking, 2hr max) ♿ (stairlift for access to all floors) shop ✗ *Details not confirmed for 2003*

RICHMOND CASTLE
DL10 4QW
☎ 01748 822493

Built high upon sheer rocks overlooking the River Swale, the castle dates from 1071. Its splendid keep and curtain walls, with two massive towers, are among the impressive remains. Scollard's Hall, built in 1080, may well be the oldest domestic building surviving in Britain.
Times: Open all year, 29 Mar-Sep, daily 10-6 (17 Jul-Aug, daily, 9.30-7); Oct, daily, 10-5; Nov-28 Mar, daily 10-4. (15-23 Feb, daily, 10-5) (Closed 24-26 Dec & 1 Jan). **Fee:** * £2.90 (ch 5-15 £1.50, under 5's free, concessions £2.20). **Facilities:** P (800 yds) ♿ shop ✗ ♿

🏛 RIEVAULX   Map 08 SE58
RIEVAULX ABBEY
YO6 5LB (2.25m W of Helmsley on minor road off B1257)
☎ 01439 798228

The site for this magnificent abbey was given to a small group of Cistercian monks in 1131; building was completed by the end of the century. In its heyday, this was a prosperous foundation, but its fortunes later declined. Surrounded by wooded hills, the site is beautiful, and the remains impressive. From Rievaulx Terrace, at the top of the hill, there is an excellent bird's eye view of the abbey ruins.
Times: Open 29 Mar-Sep, daily 10-6 (17 Jul-13 Aug, 9.30-6); Oct, daily, 10-5; Nov-Mar 10-4 daily (15-23 Feb 2003, 10-5 daily). Closed 24-26 Dec & 1 Jan **Fee:** * £3.60 (ch 5-15 £1.80, under 5's free, concessions £2.70). **Facilities:** P ♿ shop 🅿️ ♿

RIEVAULX TERRACE & TEMPLES
YO62 5LJ (2m NW of Helmsley on B1257)
☎ 01439 798340   📠 01439 748284
Times: Open 23 Mar-3 Nov: daily 10.30-6 (5pm Oct & Nov). Last admission 1hr before closing. **Facilities:** P ♿ (w/chair/runaround vehicle/braille guide/ramp) shop 🦮 *Details not confirmed for 2003*

🏛 RIPLEY   Map 08 SE26
RIPLEY CASTLE
HG3 3AY (off A61, Harrogate to Ripon road)
☎ 01423 770152   📠 01423 771745
e-mail: enquiries@ripleycastle.co.uk

Ripley Castle has been home to the Ingilby family since
continued

Yorkshire, North

1320, and stands at the heart of an estate with deer park, lake and Victorian walled gardens. The Castle has a rich history and a fine collection of Royalist armour housed in the 1555 tower. There are also walled gardens, tropical hot houses, woodland walks, pleasure grounds and the National Hyacinth collection in spring. **Times:** Open Sep-May, Tue, Thu, Sat & Sun 10.30-3; Jun-Aug daily 10.30-3, also BH and school holidays. Groups by prior arrangement. **Fee:** Castle & Gardens £5.50 (ch £3, pen £4.50). Gardens only £3 (ch £1.50, pen £2.50). Party **Facilities:** P ⬛ ✗ licensed & toilets for disabled shop garden centre ✈ (ex guide dogs) 🔔

RIPON   Map 08 SE37
FOUNTAINS ABBEY & STUDLEY ROYAL
HG4 3DY (4m W of Ripon off B6265)
☎ 01765 608888 ≡ 01765 608889
Times: Open all year, daily (except Fri in Nov, Dec & Jan); Apr-Sep, 10-6 (closes at 4pm 12/13Jul & one day in Aug); Oct-Mar 10-4 or dusk if earlier. Last admission one hour before closing. **Facilities:** P ⬛ ✗ licensed & (W/chairs, braille/large print guides) toilets for disabled shop ✄ *Details not confirmed for 2003*

NORTON CONYERS HALL
HG4 5EQ (from Ripon take A61 to Thirsk. At top of hill just outside Ripon, turn sharp left onto Wath Road)
☎ 01765 640337 ≡ 01765 692772

This late medieval house with Stuart and Georgian additions has belonged to the Grahams since 1624. It was visited by Charles I and James II. Another visitor was Charlotte Brontë: a family legend of a mad woman confined in the attics is said to have given her the idea for the mad Mrs Rochester in *Jane Eyre*. Family costumes are on display. (Please note that ladies are requested not to wear stiletto-heeled shoes).
Times: Open - House & garden Etr Sun & Mon; BH Sun & Mon;Sun between 11 May-7 Sep. Open daily 7-12 Jul. House open 2-5, garden open 12-5. Telephone for further details. **Fee:** £4 (ch 10-16, pen, concessions £3). Garden entry is free, with donations welcome, although a charge is made at garden charity openings. Parties by arrangement **Facilities:** P & (ramp at entrance) toilets for disabled shop ✄ (ex guide dogs or lead)

SALTBURN-BY-THE-SEA   Map 08 NZ62
SALTBURN SMUGGLERS HERITAGE CENTRE
Old Saltburn TS12 1HF (adjoining Ship Inn, on A174)
☎ 01287 625252 ≡ 01287 625252   **2 for 1**

Set in old fisherman's cottages, this centre skilfully blends costumed characters with authentic sounds and smells. Follow the story of John Andrew "King of Smugglers", who was at the heart of illicit local trade 200 years ago.
Times: Open Apr-Sep, daily 10-6: Winter open by arrangement only telephone 01642 444318. **Fee:** * £1.90 (ch £1.40). Family ticket £5.50. Party. **Facilities:** P (200 mtrs) (charged) shop ✄

SCARBOROUGH   Map 08 TA08
SCARBOROUGH CASTLE
Castle Rd YO1 1HY (E of town centre)
☎ 01723 372451

The ruins of Scarborough Castle stand on a narrow headland which was once the site of British and Roman encampments. The curtain wall is thought to have pre-dated the keep, the shell of which, with the later barbican and remains of medieval buildings, are all that remain.
Times: Open all year, 29 Mar-Sep, daily 10-6; Oct, daily 10-5; Nov-Mar, daily 10-4. (15-23 Feb, daily, 10-5) (Closed 24-26 Dec & 1 Jan). **Fee:** * £2.80 (ch 5-15 £1.40, under 5's free, £2.10). Family ticket £7 **Facilities:** P (100 yds) & (ex in keep) ✱

SEA LIFE & MARINE SANCTUARY
Scalby Mills Rd, North Bay YO12 6RP (follow brown signs after entering Scarborough. Centre is in 'North Bay Leisure Parks' area of town)
☎ 01723 376125 ≡ 01723 376285
Times: Open daily ex 25 Dec. **Facilities:** P (charged) ⬛ & (lift to cafe) toilets for disabled shop ✄ *Details not confirmed for 2003* 🔔

SKINNINGROVE   Map 08 NZ71
TOM LEONARD MINING MUSEUM
Deepdale TS13 4AP (Located in Skinningrove Valley, just off A174 between Middlesbrough and Whitby)
☎ 01287 642877 ≡ 01287 642970
e-mail: visits@ironstonemuseum.co.uk
Times: Open Apr-Oct, daily from 1 (last admission 3.45pm). Nov-Mar, schools & parties only. Parties by arrangement. **Facilities:** P (telephone for details) shop ✄ (ex guide dogs) *Details not confirmed for 2003*

SKIPTON   Map 07 SD95
SKIPTON CASTLE
BD23 1AQ (Centre of Skipton, at top of high street)
☎ 01756 792442 ≡ 01756 796100
e-mail: info@skiptoncastle.co.uk

Skipton is one of the most complete and well-preserved medieval castles in England. Some of the castle dates from the 1650s when it was rebuilt after being partially damaged following the Civil War. However, the original

continued

castle was erected in Norman times and became the home of the Clifford family in 1310 and remained so until 1676. Illustrated tour sheets are available in a number of languages.
Times: Open daily from 10am (Sun noon). Last admission 6pm (4pm Oct-Feb). (Closed 25 Dec). **Fee:** * £4.60 (inc illustrated tour sheet) (ch under 18 £2.30, under 5 free, concessions £4). Family ticket £12.50. Party 15+. **Facilities:** P (200m) 🍴 shop 🎁

SUTTON-ON-THE-FOREST   Map 08 SE56
SUTTON PARK
YO61 1DP (off A1237onto B1363 York to Helmsley road. 8m north of York)
☎ 01347 810249 & 811239   📠 01347 811251
e-mail: suttonpark@fsbdial.co.uk

The early Georgian house contains fine furniture, paintings and porcelain. The grounds have superb, award-winning terraced gardens, a lily pond and a Georgian ice house. There are also delightful woodland walks as well as spaces for caravans.
Times: Gardens 2 Apr-end Sept, daily 11am-5pm. House open 2 Apr-27 Sep, Wed & Sun, also Good Fri, Etr Mon and all BH Mons. **Fee:** * Gardens only £2.50 (ch 50p, pen £1.50). House & Gardens £5 (ch £2.50, pen £4) **Facilities:** P 🍴 ♿ 🐕 (ex guide dogs in garden)

WHITBY   Map 08 NZ81
WHITBY ABBEY
YO22 4JT (on clifftop E of Whitby town centre)
☎ 01947 603568

Dominating the skyline above the fishing port of Whitby the haunting ruins of the 13th-century Benedictine abbey are an impressive site. St Hilda built the first abbey on the site in 657.
Times: Open all year, 29 Mar-Sep, daily, 10-6; Oct, daily 10-5); Nov-Mar, daily 10-4. (15-23 Feb, daily, 10-5) (Closed 24-26 Dec & 1 Jan). **Fee:** * £3.60 (ch 5-15 £1.80, under 5's free, concessions £2.70). Family ticket £9 **Facilities:** P (charged) shop ♿

YORK   Map 08 SE65
THE ARC
St Saviourgate YO1 8NN (City centre, follow pedestrian signs for Archaeological Resource Centre)
☎ 01904 643211   📠 01904 627097   **2 for 1**
e-mail: enquiries@vikingjorvik.com

The ARC is a 'hands-on' experience of archaeology, housed in the beautifully restored medieval church of St Saviour. Be an archaeologist yourself - sift through the remains of centuries - bones, shell, pottery and much more.
Times: Open: School holidays Mon-Sat 11-3.30. Closed mid Dec-early Jan. Open for schools & groups all year Mon-Fri 10-3.30. **Fee:** * £4.50. (ch, stu & pen £4) Family £15. Group rates available on request.
Facilities: P (50yds) ♿ (induction loop, sensory garden, hands on) toilets for disabled shop 🐕 (ex guide dogs) 🎁

BORTHWICK INSTITUTE OF HISTORICAL RESEARCH
St Anthony's Hall, Peasholme Green YO1 7PW
☎ 01904 642315
Times: Open all year, Mon-Fri 9.30-12.50 & 2-4.50. Closed Etr & Xmas. **Facilities:** P (max 5mins walk) (public car park) 🐕 ♿
Details not confirmed for 2003

CLIFFORD'S TOWER
Tower St YO1 1SA
☎ 01904 646940

Named for the unfortunate Roger de Clifford, who was hung in chains from the castle, the tower was unused for centuries, as the first castle burned down and its replacement cracked from top to bottom as a result of subsidence. The walk around the old city walls offers the best way of seeing the ancient city.
Times: Open 29 Mar-Sep; daily, 10-6. (17 Jul-Aug, 9.30-7); Oct, daily, 10-5. Nov-Mar, daily, 10-4. (15-23 Feb, daily, 10-5). Closed 24-26 Dec & 1 Jan. **Fee:** * £2.10 (ch 5-15 £1.10, under 5's free, con £1.60). Family ticket £5.30 **Facilities:** P 🐕 ♿ 🎁

FAIRFAX HOUSE
Castlegate YO1 9RN (city centre, close to Jorvik Centre and Cliffords Tower)
☎ 01904 655543   **2 for 1**
📠 01904 652262
e-mail: peterbrown@fairfaxhouse.co.uk

An outstanding mid 18th-century house with a richly decorated interior, Fairfax House was acquired by the York Civic Trust in 1983 and restored. The house contains fine examples of Georgian furniture, porcelain, paintings and clocks which were donated by Mr Noel Terry, the great grandson of the founder of the York-based confectionery business. There is a special display of a recreated meal dating from 1763 in the dining room and kitchen.
Times: Open 20 Feb-5 Jan, Mon-Sun 11-5, (Fri guided tours only at 11am & 2pm). Sun 1.30-5. Last admission 4.30pm. **Fee:** £4.50 (ch £1.50, pen & student £3.75) **Facilities:** P (50yds) (3hr short stay) ♿ (with assistance, phone before visit) shop 🐕 🎁

GUILDHALL
Off Coney St YO1 9QN (5mins walk from the rail station)
☎ 01904 613161   📠 01904 552015
Times: Open all year, May-Oct, Mon-Fri 9-5, Sat 10-5, Sun 2-5; Nov-Apr, Mon-Fri 9-5.(Closed Good Fri, Spring BH, 25-26 Dec & 1 Jan). **Facilities:** P (15-20 mins walk) ♿ (electric chair lift/ramps) toilets for disabled 🐕 (ex guide dogs) ♿ *Details not confirmed for 2003*

JORVIK VIKING CENTRE
Coppergate YO1 9WT (Situated in the Coppergate shopping area follow the signs to Jorvik Viking centre)
☎ 01904 643211   📠 01904 627097
e-mail: enquiries@vikingjorvik.com

Travel back through time and discover what life really was like in Viking Age York in a life-size reconstruction of the street of Coppergate exactly as it would have

continued

been in AD 975. With the aid of 21st-century technology, you will travel through 1000 years of history, witnessing much change along the way. On reaching the 10th century, step aboard your time capsule and journey through the backyards and houses leading to the bustling street of Coppergate. Everything, down to the finest detail, has been thoroughly researched and is based on archaeological evidence unearthed on the very site.
Times: Open all year, Apr-Oct daily 9-5.30; and Viking festival Nov-Mar daily 10-4.30 (Closed 25 Dec). Opening times subject to change, please telephone for up to date details. **Fee:** * £6.95 (ch 5-15 £5.10, under 5 free, student & pen £6.10) Family £21.95. Telephone bookings on 01904 543403 (£1 booking fee per person). **Facilities:** P (400 yds) (limited to 3 hours) 🍴 & (lift & time car designed to take wheelchair, hearing loop) toilets for disabled shop ✖ (ex guide dogs) 🎟

MERCHANT ADVENTURERS' HALL
Fossgate YO1 9XD (located in town centre)
☎ 01904 654818   📠 01904 654818
e-mail: the.clerk@mahall-york.demon.co.uk

The medieval guild hall of the powerful Merchant Adventurers' Company was built 1357/1361 and is one of the finest in Europe. The Hall contains early furniture, one piece dating from the 13th century, paintings, silver, and weights and measures.
Times: Open, end Mar-early Nov, daily 9-5 (ex Sun 12-4). Closed Sun, 10 days at Xmas & 1 Jan-24 Mar. **Fee:** * £2 (ch under 7 free, ch 70p, pen & students £1.70). **Facilities:** P (500yds) & toilets for disabled ✖

NATIONAL RAILWAY MUSEUM
Leeman Rd YO26 4XJ (NRM is situated behind the railway station. Signposted from all major approach roads)
☎ 01904 621261   📠 01904 611112
e-mail: nrm@nmsi.ac.uk

Among the impressive exhibits are a reconstruction of Stephenson's Rocket; the record-breaking Mallard; a life-size section of the Channel Tunnel; a Japanese bullet train and Royal Palaces on Wheels. A wing features the Workshop, the Warehouse, and the Working Railway Gallery.
Times: Open all year, Mon-Sun 10-6. (Closed 24-26 Dec). **Fee:** Free.
Facilities: P (charged) 🍴 ✖ licensed & ("Please Touch" evenings) toilets for disabled shop ✖ (ex guide/hearing dogs) 🎟

ST WILLIAMS COLLEGE
5 College St YO1 7JF (adjacent to York Minster at east end)
☎ 01904 557233   📠 01904 557234
e-mail: info@yorkminster.org

St Williams College, a 15th-century timber-framed building, housed chantry priests until 1549. It now contains York Minster's Conference & Banquet Centre, shop, restaurant and the medieval rooms are open to view when not being used for functions an ideal venue for wedding receptions and medieval banquets. Craft Fairs most weekends.
Times: Open all year 10-5 for viewing of medieval rooms subject to private bookings - phone for details. Closed 24-26 Dec & Good Fri.
Fee: Medieval Rooms £1 (ch 50p) subject to functions. **Facilities:** P 🍴 ✖ licensed shop ✖

TREASURER'S HOUSE
Chapter House St YO1 7JL (in Minster Yard, on N side of Minster)
☎ 01904 624247   📠 01904 647372
e-mail: yorkth@smtp.ntrust.org.uk
Times: Open 23 Mar-3 Nov, daily except Fri, 11-5. **Facilities:** P (400 yds) ✖ licensed & (braille guide/tactile pictures/induction loop/scented path) ✖ 🎟 Details not confirmed for 2003

YORK CASTLE MUSEUM
The Eye of York YO1 1RY (city centre, next to Clifford's Tower)
☎ 01904 653611   📠 01904 671078
Times: Open all year, Apr-Oct Mon-Sat 9.30-5.30, Sun 10-5.30; Nov-Mar, Mon-Sat 9.30-4, Sun 10-4. (Closed 25-26 Dec & 1 Jan).
Facilities: 🍴 & toilets for disabled shop ✖ Details not confirmed for 2003 🎟

YORK CITY ART GALLERY
Exhibition Square YO1 7EW (3min walk from the minster in the centre of York)
☎ 01904 551861   📠 01904 551866
e-mail: art.gallery@york.gov.uk
Times: Open all year, daily 10-5. (Closed 25 & 26 Dec & 1 Jan).
Facilities: P (500mtrs) & (chair lift) toilets for disabled shop ✖ (ex guide dogs) Details not confirmed for 2003 🎟

THE YORK DUNGEON
12 Clifford St YO1 9RD (A64/A19/A59 - towards city centre)
☎ 01904 632599   📠 01904 612602   **2 for 1**
e-mail: yorkdungeons@merlin-entertainments.com

Deep in the heart of historic York, buried beneath its paving stones, lies the North's most chillingly famous museum of horror. The York Dungeon brings more than 2,000 years of gruesomely authentic history vividly back to life...and death. As you delve into the darkest chapters of our grim and bloody past, recreated in all its detail remember - everything you experience really happened. The 'exhibits' have an unnerving habit of coming back to life. The journey includes features of

continued

Dick Turpin, Guy Fawkes, Witch Trails, Clifford's Tower, Pit of Despair and Gorvik - the real viking experience.
Times: Open all year, daily 10.30-5 (closes 4.30 Oct-Mar). Closed 25 Dec. **Fee:** * £7.50 (ch & pen £5.50, students £6.50). Family ticket (2 adult & 2 ch) £22. **Facilities:** P (500yds) & (wheelchair ramps, stairlifts, award winning access) toilets for disabled shop

York Minster
Deangate YO1 7HH (Easy access via A19, A1 or A64)
☎ 01904 557216 01904 557218
e-mail: visitors@yorkminster.org
Times: Open daily, Mon-Sat 7-6 (later in summer), Sun after 1pm.
Facilities: P (440yds) & (loop system, tactile model, braille guide) toilets for disabled shop (ex guide dogs) *Details not confirmed for 2003*

York Model Railway
Tearoom Square, York Station YO2 2AB (next to York Station)
☎ 01904 630169
Times: Open daily, Mar-Oct 9.30-6, Nov-Feb 10.30-5 (Closed 25-26 Dec). **Facilities:** P (100 yds) & shop *Details not confirmed for 2003*

Yorkshire Museum
Museum Gardens YO1 7FR (park & ride service from 4 sites near A64/A19/A1079 & A166, also 3 car parks within short walk)
☎ 01904 551800 01904 551802
e-mail: yorkshire.museum@york.gov.uk

Yorkshire Museum is set in 10 acres of botanical gardens in the heart of the historic City of York, and displays some of the finest Roman, Anglo-Saxon, Viking and Medieval treasures ever discovered in Britain. The Middleham jewel, a fine example of English Gothic jewellery, is on display, and in the Roman Gallery, visitors can see a marble head of Constantine the Great. The Anglo-Saxon Gallery houses the delicate silver-gilt Ormside bowl and the Gilling sword.
Times: Open all year, daily 10-5. **Fee:** * £3.95 (concessions £2.50) Family ticket £11.50. **Facilities:** P (5 mins walk) & (ramps & lift) toilets for disabled shop

South Yorkshire

South Yorkshire is an industrial area and all of its main towns are traditionally steel and coal producing centres. Both of these industries have declined in recent years and have been replaced to some extent by other forms of manufacturing, as well as tourism based around the area's beautiful Pennine countryside

Barnsley is the county's administrative centre, located on of one Britain's richest coalfields. The town has an entry in the Domesday Book, and was built on land belonging to the priories of Pontefract and Monk Bretton.

Doncaster, originally a Roman station, is set on the River Don. It is known particularly for its racecourse. The best known race on its calendar is the celebrated St Leger, which is held in September. In 1875, Charles Dickens watched it from the 18th-century Italianate grandstand at the Town Moor racecourse. The Lincolnshire Handicap is held in March. The town also possesses some fine Georgian architecture, particularly James Paine's house which was built in 1748.

Rotheram, on the outskirts of Sheffield, has a fine 15th-century church, and a bridge with an old chapel over the Don river.

South Yorkshire claims part of the Peak District National park, whose hills and dales provide relief to the millions of city dwellers within its vicinity. The county has produced such luminaries as William Hague, Conservative Party leader in the 90s; Arthur Scargill, leader of the National Union of Miners; England goalkeeper David Seaman; and Michael Palin of Monty Python fame. A strong musical tradition has produced Joe Cocker, Def Leppard, Moloko, ABC, The Human League, Pulp, and Saxon.

EVENTS & FESTIVALS

January
6th The Ancient Haxey Hood Game, Doncaster

May
tbc Sheffield Mayfest, Hillsborough Park (provisional)

June/July
tbc Sheffield Childrenís Festival

July
6th Abbey Field Park Multicultural Festival
tbc City Centre Carnival, Sheffield
tbc Dore Gala, Sheffield
tbc South Yorkshire Festival, Wortley Hall, Sheffield
tbc Stannington Carnival, Sheffield

August
tbc The Sheffield Show, Graves Park, Sheffield

October
tbc Off the Shelf Literature Festival, Sheffield
tbc Sheffield International Documentary Festival

Top: Watermill in Worsbrough Country Park

Yorkshire, South

BARNSLEY Map 08 SE30
MONK BRETTON PRIORY
S71 5QD (1m E of Barnsley town centre, off A633)
☎ 01226 204089

The priory was an important Cluniac house, founded in 1135. The considerable remains of the gatehouse, church and other buildings can be seen.
Times: Open all year, Apr-Sep, daily 10-6; Oct, daily 10-5; Nov-Mar, daily 10-4. Keykeeper. **Fee:** *Prices not confirmed for 2003.* **Facilities:** 🅿 ♿ ✡

CONISBROUGH Map 08 SK59
CONISBROUGH CASTLE
DN12 3HH (NE of town centre off A630)
☎ 01709 863329

Times: Open all year, Apr-Sep, Mon-Sat 10-5, Sun 10-6; Oct-Mar, daily 10-4. Last admission 40mins before closing. (Closed 24-26 Dec & 1 Jan). **Facilities:** 🅿 ♿ ✖ ✡ *Details not confirmed for 2003*

CUSWORTH Map 08 SE50
THE MUSEUM OF SOUTH YORKSHIRE LIFE CUSWORTH H HALL
Cusworth Ln DN5 7TU (3m NW of Doncaster)
☎ 01302 782342 📠 01302 782342
e-mail: museum@doncaster.gov.uk

This museum is located in Cusworth Hall, an 18th-century country house set in a landscaped park. It has displays which illustrate the way local people here lived, worked and entertained themselves over the last 200 years.
Times: Open Mon-Fri 10-5, Sat 11-5 & Sun 1-5. (4pm Dec & Jan). Closed Good Fri, Xmas & 1 Jan. **Fee:** Free. **Facilities:** 🅿 🍽 ♿ (wheelchair available) toilets for disabled shop ✖ (ex guide dogs)

DONCASTER Map 08 SE50
BRODSWORTH HALL & GARDENS
Brodsworth DN5 7XJ (between A635 & A638)
☎ 01302 722598 📠 01302 337165

Brodsworth Hall is a Victorian country house which has survived largely intact. The faded grandeur of the family rooms contrasts with the functional austerity of the servant's wing. There are fine gardens.
Times: Open House: 29 Mar-27 Oct, 1-6 Tue-Sun & BH (last admission 5pm). Gardens, 29 Mar-27 Oct, noon-6 daily. gardens open winter weekends 11-4. Pre-booked guided tours for house in mornings Apr-Oct. **Fee:** * £5.50 (ch £2.80, concessions £4.10), Gardens £3.50 (ch £1.80, concessions £2.60) winter £2(ch £1, concessions £1.50) **Facilities:** 🅿 🍽 ♿ toilets for disabled shop (12-6) ✖ ✡ 🎟

DONCASTER MUSEUM & ART GALLERY
Chequer Rd DN1 2AE (off inner ring road)
☎ 01302 734293 📠 01302 735409
e-mail: museum@doncaster.gov.uk

The wide-ranging collections include fine and decorative art and sculpture. Also ceramics, glass, silver, and displays on history, archaeology and natural history. The historical collection of the Kings Own Yorkshire Light Infantry is housed here. Temporary exhibitions are held.
Times: Open all year, Mon-Sat 10-5, Sun 2-5. (Closed Good Fri, 25-26 Dec & 1 Jan). **Fee:** Free. **Facilities:** 🅿 ♿ (lift, hearing loop in lecture room) toilets for disabled shop ✖ (ex guide dogs)

EARTH CENTRE
Denaby Main DN12 4EA (follow brown signs from A1(M). From junct 36 follow brown Earth Centre signs along A630, then A6023 towards Mexborough. Centre next right after Coniston Train Stn)
☎ 01709 513933 📠 01709 512010 **2 for 1**
e-mail: info@earthcentre.org.uk

Earth Centre is an amazing adventure with lots to do in one day. Whether you want to fly down the zip wire, climb the tower, ride the Water Simulator, be amazed at the galleries, go pond dipping, or just stroll through the unusual gardens there is something for all ages and interests. Special events throughout the year, telephone for details.
Times: Open all year, daily (ex Xmas day) 10-5 (peak), 10-4 (off peak). **Fee:** * £4.50 (ch & concessions £3.50, ch under 5 & essential carers free). **Facilities:** 🅿 🍽 ✖ licensed ♿ (wheelchairs & electric vehicles for hire) toilets for disabled shop ✖ (ex guide dogs) 🎟

MALTBY Map 08 SK59
ROCHE ABBEY
S66 8NW (1.5m S off A634)
☎ 01709 812739

The walls of the south and north transepts of this 12th-century Cistercian abbey still stand to their full height, providing a dramatic sight for the visitor. There is also a fine gatehouse.
Times: Open all year, 29 Mar-Sep, daily 10-6; Oct, daily 10-5. **Fee:** * £1.70 (ch 5-15 90p, under 5's free, concessions £1.30) **Facilities:** 🅿 ♿ ✡

Brodsworth Hall is a Victorian country house which has survived largely intact. The faded grandeur of the family

Yorkshire, South **281**

ROTHERHAM Map 08 SK49
CLIFTON PARK MUSEUM
Clifton Park, Clifton Ln S65 2AA (Follow directions from inner ring road)
☎ 01709 823635   📠 01709 823631
e-mail: steve.blackbourn@rotherham.gov.uk

Housed in a mansion designed by John Carr, the museum is noted for its collection of Rockingham china. Other attractions include the 18th-century rooms, family portraits, the period kitchen, and Victoriana. Regular programme of temporary exhibitions.
Times: Closed for refurbishments during 2003, please phone for details. **Fee:** Free. **Facilities:** P & toilets for disabled shop ✈ (ex guide dogs)

MAGNA SCIENCE ADVENTURE CENTRE
Sheffield Rd, Templeborough S60 1DX (M1 junct 34, follow Templeborough sign off rdbt, then follow brown heritage signs)
☎ 01709 720002   📠 01709 820092
e-mail: jeyre@magnatrust.co.uk

Magna is the UK's first Science Adventure Centre, an exciting exploration of Earth, Air, Fire and Water; a chance for visitors to create their own adventure through hands-on interactive challenges. Visit the four Adventure Pavilions, two shows and the outdoor adventure park and have fun unearthing the mysteries of our world.
Times: Please phone for 2003 details **Fee:** * £7 (ch & concessions £5.99). Family (2ad+2ch) ticket £23.99, (2ad+3ch) £25.99 Party.
Facilities: P 🍴 ✕ licensed & (lifts, big melt scripts, portable seating, whchair hire) toilets for disabled shop ✈ (ex guide dogs) 🎁

SHEFFIELD Map 08 SK38
BISHOPS HOUSE
Meersbrook Park, Norton Lees Ln S8 9BE (2m S of Sheffield, on A61 Chesterfield road)
☎ 0114 278 2600
e-mail: info@sheffieldgalleries.org.uk

This 15th and 16th-century yeoman's house has been restored and opened as a museum of local and social history. Several rooms have been furnished and there are displays of life in Tudor and Stuart times. Special educational facilities can be arranged for schools and colleges. Please ring for details.
Times: Open Sat 10-4.30. Sun 11-4.30 **Fee:** Free. **Facilities:** P (roadside parking on nearby streets) & shop ✈ (ex guide dogs)

KELHAM ISLAND MUSEUM
Alma St S3 8RY (0.5m NW of city centre, take A61 N to West Bar, follow signs)
☎ 0114 272 2106   📠 0114 275 7847
e-mail: postmaster@simt.co.uk
Times: Open Mon-Thu 10-4, Sun 11-4.45. Closed Fri and Sat. Check opening days/times at Christmas & New Year before travelling.
Facilities: P 🍴 & (wheelchair on request) toilets for disabled shop ✈ Details not confirmed for 2003

MILLENNIUM GALLERIES
Arundel Gate S1 2PP
☎ 0114 278 2600   📠 0114 278 2604
e-mail: info@sheffieldgalleries.org.uk

With four different galleries under one roof the Millennium Galleries has something for everyone. Enjoy new blockbuster exhibitions drawn from the collections of Britain's national galleries and museums, including the Victoria & Albert Museum and Tate. See the best of contemporary craft and design in a range of exhibitions by established and up-and-coming makers. Be dazzled by Sheffield's magnificent and internationally important collection of decorative and domestic metalwork and silverware. Discover the Ruskin Gallery with its wonderful array of treasures by Victorian artist and writer John Ruskin.
Times: Open daily Mon-Sat 10-5, Sun 11-5. **Fee:** Free. Special Exhibitions: £4 (ch 5-16 £2, concessions £3) family ticket £9.
Facilities: P 🍴 ✕ licensed & (hearing loop) toilets for disabled shop ✈ (ex guide dogs) 🎁

West Yorkshire

EVENTS & FESTIVALS

March
14th-29th Bradford Film Festival
26th-27th Complementary Medicine Festival, Ilkley
tbc Daffodil Week, Haworth

April
21st World Coal Carrying Championship, Ossett

May
10th-17th Wharfedale Music Festival, various venues in Ilkley (competitive performing arts festival)
tbc Forties Weekend, Haworth
tbc Todmorden Gang Show

June
tbc Celtic Weekend, Howarth
tbc Todmorden Agricultural Show, Todmorden
tbc Wetherby Agricultural Show, Wetherby

July
4th-6th Cleckheaton Folk Festival (various venues)
20th Arthington Show, Bramhope
tbc Bradford Festival & Mela

October
2nd-12th Leeds International Film Festival, (provisional)
tbc Complementary Medicine Festival, Ilkley

November
19th-30th Huddersfield Contemporary Music Festival
tbc Scroggling the Holly,

December
tbc Torchlight Weekend
tbc Wassail Wednesday
tbc Christmas Cracker

The West Riding has long been industrialised, and not only produced coal but was also home to the wool industry. The tall mill chimneys, set against the Pennine Hills, are characteristic of its industrial heritage.

The county includes the towns of Wakefield, Halifax, Huddersfield and Bradford, centres of the wool industry from the 13th century. Huddersfield is known particularly for its fine wool worsted. Well-known personalities from the county include Thomas Chippendale, 18th-century cabinet maker and designer; Harold Wilson, British Prime Minister of the 60s and 70s; Spice Girl Mel B; and Pop Idol Gareth Gates.

Leeds sprawls over its hilly site and includes a great variety of manufacturing and other industries, notably clothing. These days it has a vibrant club scene, and is also home to the celebrated Yorkshire County Cricket Club at Headingley, and Premiership football side, Leeds United. ITV's popular soap, *Emmerdale*, is filmed around Leeds, in places such as Otley and Esholt.

Many visitors to the region come in the wake of the extraordinary Brontë family. A motherless family with the curate of Haworth, Patrick Brontë, at its head. The children, Charlotte, Branwell (Patrick), Emily and Anne created a rich fantasy world, feeding their literary imaginations. Their poems and novels evoked the nature of their moorland home, particularly Emily's *Wuthering Heights*, published in December 1847, a year before her death from consumption at the age of 30. The Brontë Society was founded in 1893. In 1926 the American publisher Henry Houston Bonnell bequeathed his collection to the society, who bought the parsonage, the Brontë's former home to accommodate it.

Natural features of the county encompass Ilkley Moor, Haworth Moor, and parts of the Peak District National Park.

Top: Roman Road at Blackstone Edge

Yorkshire, West

🏛 BRADFORD   Map 07 SE13

BOLLING HALL
Bowling Hall Rd BD4 7LP (off A650)
☎ 01274 723057   🖷 01274 726220
e-mail: abickley@legend.co.uk
Times: Open all year, Wed-Fri 11-4, Sat 10-5, Sun 12-5. (Closed Mon ex BH, Good Fri, 25 & 26 Dec). **Facilities:** P & shop ✘ Details not confirmed for 2003

BRADFORD INDUSTRIAL MUSEUM AND HORSES AT WORK
Moorside Rd, Ecclesdhill BD2 3HP (off A658)
☎ 01274 631756   🖷 01274 636362
Times: Open all year, Tue-Sat 10-5, Sun 12-5. (Closed Mon ex BH) **Facilities:** P 💻 & (induction loop in lecture theatre) toilets for disabled shop ✘ Details not confirmed for 2003

CARTWRIGHT HALL ART GALLERY
Lister Park BD9 4NS (1m from city centre on A650)
☎ 01274 751212   🖷 01274 481045
Times: Open all year Apr-Sep, Tue-Sat 10-5, Sun 1-5. (Closed Mon ex BH, Good Fri, 25 & 26 Dec). **Facilities:** 💻 & (wheelchair available) toilets for disabled shop ✘ Details not confirmed for 2003

COLOUR MUSEUM
Perkin House, 1 Providence St BD1 2PW (from city centre follow sign B6144, then follow brown heritage signs)
☎ 01274 390955   🖷 01274 392888   **2 for 1**
e-mail: museum@sdc.org.uk

Europe's only Museum of Colour comprises two galleries packed with visitor-operated exhibits demonstrating the effects of light and colour, including optical illusions, and the story of dyeing and textile printing. There is a programme of special exhibitions and events. Please telephone for details.
Times: Open 2 Jan-20 Dec, Tue-Sat, 10-4. **Fee:** £2 (concessions £1.50). Family ticket £4 **Facilities:** P (300 yds) & (lift from street level) toilets for disabled shop ✘ (ex guide dogs) 🚩

NATIONAL MUSEUM OF PHOTOGRAPHY, FILM & TELEVISION
BD1 1NQ (2m from M606, follow city centre signs)
☎ 01274 202030   🖷 01274 394540
e-mail: talk.nmpft@nmsi.ac.uk

Experience the past, present and future of photography, film and television with amazing interactive displays and spectacular 3D IMAX cinema.
Times: Open all year, Tue-Sun, BH's & main school hols 10-6. (Closed Mon). **Fee:** * Admission to permanent galleries free, IMAX Cinema £5.80 (concessions £4). Groups 20% discount. **Facilities:** P (adjacent) 💻 ✘ licensed & (tailored tours,braille signs,induction loop,cinema seating) toilets for disabled shop ✘ (ex guide dogs) 🚩

🏛 BRAMHAM   Map 08 SE44

BRAMHAM PARK
LS23 6ND (on A1 take Bramham slip road, follow signs)
☎ 01937 846000   **2 for 1**
🖷 01937 846007
e-mail: lucy.finucane@bramhampark.co.uk

This fine Queen Anne house was built by Robert Benson and is the home of his descendants. The garden has ornamental ponds, cascades, temples and avenues.
Times: Open Apr-Sep, daily 10.30-5.30. **Fee:** * Gardens only £4 (ch under 16 & pen £2, under 5's free). House open by appointment only. **Facilities:** P & toilets for disabled woodlands only

🏛 GOMERSAL   Map 08 SE22

RED HOUSE
Oxford Rd BD19 4JP (M62 junct 26, take A58 towards Leeds then right onto A651 towards Gomersal. Red House on right)
☎ 01274 335100   🖷 01274 335105

Displayed as 1830s home of a Yorkshire wool clothier and merchant. The house was visited by Charlotte Brontë and featured in her novel *Shirley*. Exhibitions on the Brontë connection. Gardens have been reconstructed in period style.
Times: Open all year, Mon-Fri 11-5, Sat-Sun 12-5. Telephone for Xmas opening. (Closed Good Fri & 1 Jan). **Fee:** Free. **Facilities:** P & (Braille & T-setting hearing aid available) toilets for disabled shop ✘ (ex guide dogs) 🚩

🏛 HALIFAX   Map 07 SE02

BANKFIELD MUSEUM
Boothtown Rd, Akroyd Park HX3 6HG (On A647, 0.5m from Halifax town centre)
☎ 01422 354823 & 352734   🖷 01422 349020
e-mail: bankfield-museum@calderdale.gov.uk
Times: Open all year, Tue-Sat 10-5, Sun 2-5, BH Mon 10-5.(extended closing times at Xmas and New Year, phone for details) **Facilities:** P & audio guide & tactile objects toilets for disabled shop ✘ (ex guide dogs) *Details not confirmed for 2003* 🚩

EUREKA! THE MUSEUM FOR CHILDREN
Discovery Rd HX1 2NE (M62 junct 24 follow brown heritage signs to Halifax centre (A629))
☎ 01422 330069 & 01426 983191
🖷 01422 330275
e-mail: info@eureka.org.uk

A 'hands on' museum designed especially for children aged 12 and under. Four main exhibition areas - Me and My Body, Living and Working Together, Invent, Create, Communicate and Things - find out how the body and senses work, investigate everyday objects, role-play in town square buildings and explore the world of communications.
Times: Open all year, daily 10-5 (except 24-26 Dec) **Fee:** £5.50. Family Saver ticket £25. **Facilities:** P (charged) 💻 & (lift,staff trained in sign language,audio guide,workshop) toilets for disabled shop ✘ (ex guide dogs) 🚩

Yorkshire, West

PIECE HALL
HX1 1RE (follow brown tourist signs)
☎ 01422 358087   📠 01422 349310
e-mail: karen.belshaw@calderdale.gov.uk
Times: Open all year daily (Closed 25-26 Dec). Art Gallery; Tue-Sun & BH Mons 10-5. **Facilities:** P (50 yds) 🅿 & (lifts, shopmobility on site & audio guide available) toilets for disabled shop *Details not confirmed for 2003*

SHIBDEN HALL
Lister's Rd HX3 6XG (2km E of Halifax on A58)
☎ 01422 352246 & 321455   📠 01422 348440
e-mail: shibden.hall@calderdale.gov
Times: Open Mar-Nov, Mon-Sat 10-5, Sun 12-5. Dec-Feb, Mon-Sat 10-4, Sun 12-4 **Facilities:** P 🅿 & (garden only partially accesible) toilets for disabled shop ✱ *Details not confirmed for 2003*

🏛 HAREWOOD   Map 08 SE34
HAREWOOD HOUSE & BIRD GARDEN
LS17 9LQ (junc A61/A659 Leeds/Harrogate Rd)
☎ 0113 218 1010   📠 0113 218 1002
e-mail: business@harewood.org

Designed in 1759 by John Carr, Harewood House is the home of the Queen's cousin, the Earl of Harewood. His mother, HRH Princess Mary, Princess Royal lived at Harewood for 35 years and much of her memorabilia is still displayed. The House, renowned for its stunning architecture and exquisite Adam interiors, contains a rich collection of Chippendale furniture, fine porcelain and outstanding art collections from Italian Renaissance masterpieces and Turner watercolours to contemporary works. The Victorian kitchen, contains the best collection of noble household copperware in the country. The grounds include a restored parterre terrace, oriental rock garden, walled garden, lakeside and woodland walks, a bird garden and for youngsters, and an adventure playground.
Times: Open 7 Mar-3 Nov, daily Bird Garden from 10am, House from 11am. Grounds & Bird Garden open wknds 9/10 - 14/15 Nov-Dec. Closed 11 Jul. **Fee:** * 'Freedom ticket' (house, grounds, bird garden, terrace gallery) Mon-Sat £9 (ch £5, pen £7.50) Family £30. Sun & BH £10 (ch £5.50, pen £6.50) Family £22. 'Grounds ticket' (garden, grounds, terrace gallery £6.50 (ch £4 pen £5.50) Family £20. Sun & BH £7.50 (ch £4.50, pen £6.50) Family £22. **Facilities:** P 🅿 ✗ licensed & (electric ramp, lift, free audio tour) toilets for disabled shop garden centre ✱ (ex guide dogs or in gardens)

🏛 HAWORTH   Map 07 SE03
BRONTË PARSONAGE MUSEUM
BD22 8DR (A629 & A6033 follow signs for Haworth, take Rawdon Rd, pass 2 car parks, next left, then right)
☎ 01535 642323   📠 01535 647131   **2 for 1**
e-mail: bronte@bronte.prestel.org.uk

Haworth Parsonage was the lifelong family home of the Brontës. An intensely close-knit family, the Brontës saw the parsonage as the heart of their world and the moorland setting provided them with inspiration for their writing. The house contains much personal memorabilia, including the furniture Charlotte bought with the proceeds of her literary success, Branwell's portraits of local worthies, Emily's writing desk and Anne's books and drawings.
Times: Open Apr-Sep, daily 10-5.30; Oct-Mar daily 11-5 (final admission 30 min before closing). Closed 24-27 Dec & 2-31 Jan. **Fee:** * £4.80 (ch 5-16 £1.50, concessions £3.50). Family ticket £10.50. **Facilities:** P (charged) & (Information in large type & braille) shop ✱ (ex guide dogs)

KEIGHLEY & WORTH VALLEY RAILWAY & MUSEUM
Keighley BD22 8NJ (1m from Keighley on A629 Halifax rd, follow the brown sign)
☎ 01535 645214 & 677777   📠 01535 647317

The line was built mainly to serve the valley's mills, and goes through the heart of Brontë country. Beginning at Keighley (shared with Railtrack), it climbs up to Haworth, and terminates at Oxenhope, which has a storage and restoration building. At Haworth there are locomotive workshops and at Ingrow West, an award-winning museum.
Times: All year weekend service, but daily all BH wks & 19 Jun-1 Sep.
Fee: * Full line return ticket £6 reduced fares for ch & pen. Family return ticket £16. Day rover (unlimited travel) £8, Family day rover £20. Under 5's free. Party rates. **Facilities:** P (charged) 🅿 & (wheelchairs can be accommodated in brake car). toilets for disabled shop

🏛 HUDDERSFIELD   Map 07 SE11
TOLSON MEMORIAL MUSEUM
Ravensknowle Park, Wakefield Rd HD5 8DJ (on A629)
☎ 01484 223830   📠 01484 223843
Times: Open all year. Mon-Fri 11-5, Sat & Sun noon-5. (Closed Xmas).
Facilities: P & toilets for disabled shop ✱ *Details not confirmed for 2003*

🏛 ILKLEY   Map 07 SE14
MANOR HOUSE GALLERY & MUSEUM
Castle Yard, Church St LS29 9DT (behind Ilkley Parish Church, on A65)
☎ 01943 600066   📠 01943 817079
Times: Open all year, Wed-Sat 11-5, Sun 1-4. (Closed Good Fri, 25-28 Dec). **Facilities:** & shop ✱ *Details not confirmed for 2003*

🏛 KEIGHLEY   Map 07 SE04
CLIFFE CASTLE MUSEUM & GALLERY
Spring Gardens Ln BD20 6LH (NW of town off A629)
☎ 01535 618230   📠 01535 610536
Times: Open all year, Tue-Sat 10-5, Sun 12-5. Also open BH Mon. (Closed Good Fri & 25-28 Dec). **Facilities:** P 🅿 & toilets for disabled shop ✱ *Details not confirmed for 2003*

EAST RIDDLESDEN HALL
Bradford Rd BD20 4EA (1m NE of Keighley on south side of Bradford Rd)
☎ 01535 607075   📠 01535 691462
e-mail: yorker@smtp.ntrust.org.uk
Times: Open 23Mar-3Nov daily (ex Mon/thu/Fri) open Good Fri, BH Mons and Mons in Jul/Aug 12-5 (Sat 1-5) **Facilities:** P 🅿 & shop ✱ 🐾 *Details not confirmed for 2003*

Yorkshire, West

LEEDS   Map 08 SE33

ABBEY HOUSE MUSEUM
Abbey Walk, Abbey Rd, Kirkstall LS5 3EH (3m W of Leeds city centre on A65)
☎ 0113 230 5492   ▤ 0113 230 5499

Displays at this museum include an interactive childhood gallery, a look at Kirkstall Abbey, and an exploration of life in Victorian Leeds. Three reconstructed streets allow the visitor to immerse themselves in the sights and sounds of the late 19th century, from the glamorous art furnisher's shops to the impoverished widow washerwoman.
Times: Open all year Tue-Fri 10-5, Sat noon-5, Sun 10-5. Closed Mon **Fee:** * £3 (ch £1 accompanied by an adult, concessions £2). Family ticket £5 **Facilities:** ▣ 🅿 ✕ licensed ♿ (braille plaques on wall) toilets for disabled shop 🐕 (ex guide dogs) 📧

CITY ART GALLERY
The Headrow LS1 3AA (city centre, next to town hall and library)
☎ 0113 247 8248   ▤ 0113 244 9689
Times: Open all year, Mon-Sat 10-5, Wed until 8, Sun 1-5.Closed BHs.
Facilities: ▣ 🅿 ✕ licensed ♿ (restricted access to upper floor) toilets for disabled shop 🐕 (ex guide dogs) *Details not confirmed for 2003*

KIRKSTALL ABBEY
Abbey Rd, Kirkstall LS5 3EH (off A65, W of city centre)
☎ 0113 275 5821
Times: Open all year. Abbey site open dawn-dusk. **Facilities:** ▣ ♿ toilets for disabled shop 🐕 *Details not confirmed for 2003*

LEEDS INDUSTRIAL MUSEUM AT ARMLEY MILLS
Canal Rd, Armley LS12 2QF (2m W of city centre, off A65)
☎ 0113 263 7861
Times: Open all year, Tue-Sat 10-5, Sun 1-5. Last entry 1 hr before closing. (Closed Mon ex BHs). **Facilities:** ▣ ♿ (chair-lifts between floors) toilets for disabled shop 🐕 *Details not confirmed for 2003* 📧

MIDDLETON RAILWAY
Moor Rd, Hunslet LS10 2JQ (M621 junct 5 or follow signs from A61)
☎ 0113 271 0320 (ansaphone)
▤ 01977 620585   **2 for 1**
e-mail: info@middletonrailway.org.uk

This was the first railway authorised by an Act of Parliament (in 1758) and the first to succeed with steam locomotives (in 1812). Steam trains run each weekend in season from Tunstall Road roundabout to Middleton Park. There is a programme of special events.
Times: Moor Road Station open for viewing every wknd. Trains run Sat, Sun & BH, Apr-July. **Fee:** * Entry to station free. £2.50 (ch £1.50) Return train fare. Family ticket £7. **Facilities:** ▣ 🅿 ♿ (ramped access to all areas) toilets for disabled shop 📧

ROYAL ARMOURIES MUSEUM
Armouries Dr LS10 1LT (off A61 close to Leeds centre, follow brown heritage signs)
☎ 0113 220 1999 & 0990 106 666   ▤ 0113 220 1934
e-mail: enquiries@armouries.org.uk

The museum is an impressive contemporary home for the renowned national collection of arms and armour. The collection is divided between five galleries: War, Tournament, Self-Defence, Hunting and Oriental. The Hall of Steel features a 100ft-high mass of 3,000 pieces of arms and armour. Extensive interactive displays, dramatisations of jousting tournaments and the chance to see leather workers and armourers at work.
Times: Open daily, from 10-5. (Closed Xmas eve & day) **Fee:** Free. **Facilities:** ▣ (charged) 🅿 ✕ licensed ♿ (induction loops, wheelchairs, signers) toilets for disabled shop 🐕 (ex guide/hearing dogs) 📧

TEMPLE NEWSAM HOUSE & PARK
LS15 0AE (off A63)
☎ 0113 264 7321 (House) & 264 5535 (Park)
▤ 0113 260 2285
Times: Open all year. House: Tue-Sat 10-5, Sun 1-5; Nov-28 Dec & Mar, Tue-Sat 10-4, Sun 12-5. Open Bank Hols. Home Farm: 10-4 (3 in winter) ; Gardens: 10-dusk. Estate: daily, dawn-dusk. Closed Jan-Feb re-opens 28 Feb. **Facilities:** ▣ (charged) 🅿 ♿ (ramps giving full accesss to parkland,wheelchairs for hire) toilets for disabled shop 🐕 *Details not confirmed for 2003* 📧

THACKRAY MUSEUM
Beckett St LS9 7LN (From M1 South. Leave M1 Junction 43, Take M621 to junction 4. Follow signs for Harrogate and St James's Hospital)
☎ 0113 244 4343   ▤ 0113 247 0219   **2 for 1**
e-mail: info@thackraymuseum.org

Housed in a large Victorian building, next to the famous St James's Hospital, the Thackray Museum offers a unique hands-on experience. A cow from Gloucester, green mould and smelly toilets - all these things have helped transform our lives. Find out how by walking

continued

Yorkshire, West

back in time and exploring the sights, sounds and smells of Victorian slum life.
Times: Open all year, Tue-Sun & (Mon School Holidays) 10-5. Closed 24-26 & 31 Dec & 1 Jan **Fee:** * £4.40 (ch 4-16 £3.30, pen, students & unemployed £3.60). Family ticket £14. Party 12+ group rates available.
Facilities: P (charged) 🅿 ♿ (wheelchairs, induction loop) toilets for disabled shop 🍴 (ex guide dogs) 📞

THWAITE MILLS WATERMILL
Thwaite Ln, Stourton LS10 1RP (2m S of city centre, off A61)
☎ 0113 249 6453 📠 0113 246 5561
Times: Open Tues-Sat 10am-5pm & Sun 1-5pm. Nov-Dec & March Tues-Sat 10am-4pm, Sun 12-4pm. Open BH Mon. Closed Jan & Feb.
Facilities: P ♿ (wheelchair lifts) toilets for disabled shop 🍴 Details not confirmed for 2003 📞

TROPICAL WORLD
Canal Gardens, Roundhay Park LS8 2ER (3m N of city centre off A58 at Oakwood)
☎ 0113 266 1850 📠 0113 237 0077
Times: Open daily, 10-early evening (dusk in winter), special times at Christmas. Closed 25 Dec **Facilities:** P 🅿 ♿ toilets for disabled shop 🍴 (ex guide dogs) Details not confirmed for 2003 📞

🏛 LOTHERTON HALL   Map 08 SE43
LOTHERTON HALL
Aberford LS25 3EB (off the A1, 0.75m E of junct with B1217)
☎ 0113 281 3259
Times: Open Tue-Sat 10-5. Sun 1-5. Bank Hols. Nov-Dec & Mar Tue-Sat 10-4, Sun 12-4. **Facilities:** P (charged) 🅿 ✕ licensed ♿ shop 🍴 (ex in park) Details not confirmed for 2003 📞

🏛 MIDDLESTOWN   Map 08 SE21
NATIONAL COAL MINING MUSEUM FOR ENGLAND
Caphouse Colliery, New Rd WF4 4RH (on A642 between Wakefield & Huddersfield)
☎ 01924 848806 📠 01924 840694
e-mail: info@ncm.org.uk

Times: Open all year, daily 10-5. (Closed 24-26 Dec & 1 Jan).
Facilities: P 🅿 ✕ licensed ♿ (nature trail not accessible) toilets for disabled shop Details not confirmed for 2003 📞

🏛 NOSTELL PRIORY   Map 08 SE41
NOSTELL PRIORY
Doncaster Rd WF4 1QE (5m SE of Wakefield towards Doncaster, on A638)
☎ 01924 863892 📠 01924 865282
e-mail: yorknp@smtp.ntrust.org.uk
Times: Open 2-17 Mar, Sat & Sun only, grounds, shop & tearoom 11-4. House closed 23 Mar-3 Nov, daily ex Mon/Tue (open Good Fri & BH Mon) 1-5.30. grounds open 11-6, shop & tearoom 11.30-5.30. 9 Nov-15 Dec: Sat/Suns only 12-4. Grounds, shop & tea room 11-4.30
Facilities: P 🅿 ♿ (lift, braille guide/tactile books, w/hchair) toilets for disabled shop (ex around vista) ♨ Details not confirmed for 2003

🏛 OAKWELL HALL   Map 08 SE22
OAKWELL HALL
Nutter Ln, Birstall WF17 9LG (6m SE of Bradford, off M62 junct 26/27, follow brown heritage signs, turn off A652 onto Nutter Lane)
☎ 01924 326240 📠 01924 326249
e-mail: oakwell.hall@kirkleesmc.gov.uk

A moated Elizabethan manor house, furnished as it might have looked in the 1690s. Extensive 110-acre country park with visitor information centre, period gardens, nature trails, arboretum and children's adventure playground.
Times: Open all year, daily Mon-Fri 11-5; Sat & Sun 12-5. (ex Good Fri, 24 Dec-1 Jan). **Fee:** * Hall £1.40 (ch & wheelchair users 50p). Family ticket £3. Charges Mar -Oct. Free admission Nov-Feb. Vistor centre and park free all year. **Facilities:** P 🅿 ♿ (herb garden for the blind, large print & braille guide) toilets for disabled shop 🍴 (park only ex guide dogs) 📞

🏛 WAKEFIELD   Map 08 SE21
WAKEFIELD ART GALLERY
Wentworth Ter WF1 3QW (N of city centre by Wakefield College and Clayton Hospital)
☎ 01924 305796 📠 01924 305770

Wakefield was home to two of Britain's greatest modern sculptors - Barbara Hepworth and Henry Moore. The art gallery, which has an important collection of 20th-century paintings and sculptures, has a special room devoted to these two local artists. There are frequent temporary exhibitions of both modern and earlier works.
Times: Open all year, Tue-Sat 10.30-4.30, Sun 2-4.30. **Fee:** Free.
Facilities: P (on street) (on street parking restricted to 2hrs) shop 🍴 (ex guide dogs)

Are there any great Days Out that we've missed? Use the Readers' Report form at the back of the book to tell us about them

Yorkshire, West   *287*

🏛 WEST BRETTON   Map 08 SE21
YORKSHIRE SCULPTURE PARK
WF4 4LG (Follow brown heritage signs to A637. Turn left at the rdbt signed to Yorkshire Sculpture park)
☎ 01924 830302 📠 01924 830044
e-mail: office@ysp.co.uk

Set in the beautiful grounds and gardens of a 500-acre, 18th-century country estate, Yorkshire Sculpture Park is one of the world's leading open-air galleries and presents a changing programme of international sculpture exhibitions. The landscape provides a variety of magnificent scenic vistas of the valley, lakes and 18th century estate buildings and bridges. By organising a number of temporary exhibitions each year, the park ensures that there is always something new to see. A Visitor's Centre, opened in 2002 provides all-weather facilities including a large restaurant, shop, coffee bar, audio-visual auditorium and meeting rooms.

Times: Open all year 10-6 (summer) 10-4 (winter). (Closed 24 & 25 Dec) **Fee:** Free. **Facilities:** 🅿 (charged) 🍴 ♿ (free scooters, parking, trail accessible for wheelchairs) toilets for disabled shop

Guernsey

If it's sunshine, shopping and sea you're interested in, then the island of Guernsey is the ideal location for a break that combines the feeling of being abroad with the familiarity of the English language and the British ways of life.

When William conquered England, he didn't need to conquer Guernsey. It was already part of the Duchy of Normandy. The strategic importance of the island has been recognised through the centuries, from the 13th-century Castle Cornet to the fortifications of the German occupying forces during WWII. There are also many ancient structures, some of which are believed to be among the oldest in Europe.

Guernsey enjoys some 2,000 hours of sunshine a year. This makes its 27 beaches great places to spend time. No matter which way the wind is blowing, you'll be sure to find one that's sheltered.

The island is also known for its conservation. Both the National Trust and the home-grown La Société Guernesiaise maintain beautiful areas, including a wooded valley and a number of fields.

Shopping is a major attraction on Guernsey, not necessarily for what's on sale, although the shops cover a wide variety and there are some local specialities including Guernsey sweaters and flowers. The real attraction is the low local taxation and lack of VAT, which makes the island a bargain hunter's paradise.

Close to Guernsey are three smaller islands well worth visiting. Sark, Alderney and Aurigny. Sark was the setting for Mervyn Peake's novel, *Mr Pye*. It was also the location for the 1985 TV version starring Derek Jacobi. During the 1850s Victor Hugo was exiled in Guernsey, and wrote *Les Miserables* there.

Top: Haublet Bay

EVENTS & FESTIVALS

February
28th-8th March Guernsey Eisteddfod Festival

May
9th Liberation Day Celebrations, St Peter Port

June
1st-9th Floral Guernsey Festival Week
8th Guernsey Classic Vehicle Show & Mini Owners Club Show, St Saumarez Park
22nd-28th Guernsey Square Dance Festival, Beu Sejour
28th-29th Little Russell Regatta
28th-4th July Guernsey Natwest Island Games

July
7th Le Viaer Marchi (the Old Market), traditional arts, crafts, dance and music
12th-13th North Regatta
25th Harbour Carnival
26th-2nd Aug St Peter Port Town Carnival

August
6th-7th South Show
13th-14th West Show
20th-21st North Show, inc Battle of Flowers
27th-31st Horse of the Year Show

September
13th-15th Guernsey International Air Rally

October
3rd-5th Guernsey Jazz Festival
3rd-5th Guernsey Lily International Amateur Film Festival & Video Festival

🏛 FOREST
Map 16
GERMAN OCCUPATION MUSEUM
GY8 0BG (Behind Forest Church near the airport)
☎ 01481 238205
Times: Open Apr-Oct 10-5, Nov-Mar 10-1 (Closed Jan). **Facilities:** P 🍴 ♿ (ramps & handrails) *Details not confirmed for 2003*

🏛 ROCQUAINE BAY
Map 16
FORT GREY AND SHIPWRECK MUSEUM
GY7 9BY (on coast road at Rocquaine Bay)
☎ 01481 265036 ▪ 01481 263279
e-mail: education@museum.guernsey.net
Times: Open Apr-Oct, 10-5. **Facilities:** P (opposite fort) shop 🐕 *Details not confirmed for 2003*

🏛 ST ANDREW
Map 16
GERMAN MILITARY UNDERGROUND HOSPITAL & AMMUNITION STORE
La Vassalerie GY6 8XR
☎ 01481 239100

The largest structure created during the German Occupation of the Channel Islands, a concrete maze of about 75,000 sq. ft, which took slave workers three-and-a-half years to complete, at the cost of many lives. Most of the equipment has been removed, but the central heating plant, hospital beds and cooking facilities can still be seen.
Times: Open Jul-Aug, daily 10-noon & 2-4.30; May-Jun & Sep, daily 10-noon & 2-4; Apr & Oct, daily 2-4; Mar & Nov, Sun & Thu 2-3. **Fee:** * £2.60 (ch 60p). **Facilities:** P ♿ shop

🏛 ST MARTIN
Map 16
SAUSMAREZ MANOR
Sausmarez Rd GY4 6SG (Halfway between airport & St. Peter Port)
☎ 01481 235571 ▪ 01481 235572
e-mail: peter@lesausmarez.fsnet.co.uk

The Manor has been owned and lived in by the same family for centuries. The style of each room is different, with collections of Oriental, French and English furniture and paintings. Outside the Formal Garden has herbaceous borders, and the Woodland Garden, set around two small lakes and a stream, is planted with colourful shrubs, bulbs and wild flowers from the subtropics. Also on view, a comprehensive sculpture park.
Times: Open Etr-Oct 10.30 & 11.30, Mon-Thu; Jun-Aug 10.30, 11.30 & 2 Mon-Thu; or by appointment. **Fee:** * House £4.90 (ch £2, pen £4.50). Woodland Garden £2.50 (accompanied ch £1, pen £2, disabled free). Dolls House Collection £2.50 (ch £1, stu & pen £1.50). Family ticket £5. Sculpture Park £2.50 (accompanied ch £1, pen £2, disabled free). **Facilities:** P 🍴 ♿ (free admission, partial access to garden, wheelchair loan) shop (Specialises in dolls houses etc) 🐕 (ex dogs for blind and deaf)

🏛 ST PETER PORT
Map 16
CASTLE CORNET
GY1 UG (0.5m from town centre)
☎ 01481 721657 ▪ 01481 715177
e-mail: education@museum.guernsey.net
Times: Open Apr-Oct, daily 10-5. **Facilities:** P (100 yds) (2 hr time zone, 10hr within 200 yards) 🍴 shop 🐕 (ex guide dogs) *Details not confirmed for 2003*

GUERNSEY MUSEUM & ART GALLERY
Candie Gardens GY1 1UG (On the outskirts of St. Peter Port)
☎ 01481 726518 ▪ 01481 715177
e-mail: education@museum.guernsey.net
Times: Open all year, daily 10-5 (summer), 10-4 (winter). **Facilities:** P (outside museum) (2hr & 5hr) 🍴 ♿ toilets for disabled shop 🐕 (ex guide dogs) *Details not confirmed for 2003*

🏛 VALE
Map 16
ROUSSE TOWER
Rousse Tower Headland (on W coast, signposted)
☎ 01481 726518 726965 ▪ 01481 715177
e-mail: peter@museum.guernsey.net

One of the original fifteen towers built in 1778-9 in prime defensive positions around the coast of Guernsey. They were designed primarily to prevent the landing of troops on nearby beaches. Musket fire could be directed on invading forces through the loopholes. An interpretation centre displays replica guns.
Times: Open Apr-Oct 9-dusk, Nov-Mar Wed, Sat & Sun 9-4. **Fee:** Free. **Facilities:** P 🐕 (ex guide dogs)

Jersey

EVENTS & FESTIVALS

February
9th-16th Jersey Comedy Festival (various venues around the island)

March
21st-24th Spring Garden Festival 'Daffodils & Dunes'

April
13th-20th Spring Walking Week

May
3rd-10th International Arts Festival (various events around the island)
10th-18th Jersey International Food Festival (various events around the island)
24th-26th Country Fayre - traditional country fayre
tbc Jersey International Air Rally

June
6th-8th Jersey Festival of Motoring
tbc Early Summer Flower Show
tbc Maritime Festival

July
5th-11th Jersey Garden Festival - open gardens, guided walks & demonstrations

August
14th-15th Jersey Battle of Flowers - spectacular carnival
20th-21st Summer Flower Show, Howard Davis Park

September
tbc International Air Display
19th-21st Clipper Sailing Race, Jersey stopover
21st-28th Autumn Walking Week

October
tbc Artisans Showcase

November/December
tbc Fête de Noué (Christmas festival)

The Channel Islands are renowned for their hospitality, prosperity and beauty, with their fine cliffs, sandy beaches, splendid harbours and impressive marinas.

The mild climate is ideal for an enjoyable holiday, and ensures an abundance of flowers, fruit and vegetables. Notably the Channel Island tomato and the deliciously earthy early Jersey Royal potato, a delicacy in its own right with a knob of Jersey butter.

Like Guernsey, Jersey has its own breed of cow, and its own sweater, the jersey, incorporating an anchor into its design under the neckline at the front. Agriculture and fishing are traditional industries. The conger eel is particularly associated with the island, and conger eel soup is a popular local dish.

Jersey is the largest of the Channel Islands, and the most southerly, just 30 miles (48km) from St Malo. The unique combination of the French and British ways of life contributes much to the island's undoubtable charm. The island is infused with Gallic culture, as you can see by the names of the streets and the baguettes in the bakers'. The local language is traditionally a Norman-French Patois, though this is in decline and English is generally spoken. The islands also have their own banknotes, though the currency is sterling.

The financial industry has transformed the lives of islanders, bringing great prosperity to its economy. Banks of all nationalities are in residence on the island, taking advantage of its low-tax base and proximity to the City of London. Checking out the multi-million pound properties of the rich and famous tax exiles is part of the sightseeing itinerary.

Top: Rock formation on Green Island

Jersey

GOREY Map 16
Mont Orgueil Castle
JE3 6ET (A3 or coast road to Gorey)
☎ 01534 853292 ▤ 01534 854303
e-mail: marketing@jerseyheritagetrust.org
Times: Open daily throughout the year 9.30-6; Last admission 5pm. Times in winter change (Fri-Mon 10-dusk) **Facilities:** P (200 yds) (discs required at harbour) shop ✱ (ex guide dogs) *Details not confirmed for 2003*

GREVE DE LECQ BAY Map 16
Greve de Lecq Barracks

☎ 01534 483193 482238
e-mail: nationaltrust@jerseymail.co.uk

Originally serving as an outpost of the British Empire, these barracks, built in 1810, were used for civilian housing from the end of WWI to 1972, when they were bought by the National Trust and made into a museum that depicts the life of soldiers who were stationed here in the 19th century. Also includes a collection of old horse-drawn carriages.
Times: Open Etr wknd & 2 May-15 Sep, Tue-Sat 11-5 & Sun 2-5. (Closed Mon). **Fee:** Free. **Facilities:** P ⚐ shop ✱ (ex guide dogs)

GROUVILLE Map 16
La Hougue Bie
JE2 7UA (A6 or A7 to Five Oaks then Prines Tower Rd)
☎ 01534 853823 ▤ 01534 856472
e-mail: marketing@jerseyheritagetrust.org
Times: Open 29 Mar-Oct, daily 10-5. **Facilities:** P ⚐ shop ✱ (ex guide dogs) *Details not confirmed for 2003*

ST BRELADE Map 16
Jersey Lavender Farm
Rue du Pont Marquet JE3 8DS (on B25 from St.Aubin's Bay to Redhouses)
☎ 01534 742933 ▤ 01534 745613
e-mail: admin@jerseylavender.co.uk

At Jersey Lavender we grow seven acres of lavender, distil out the essential oil and create a range of fine toiletry products. Visitors are able to see the whole process from cultivating, through to harvesting, distillation and the production of the final product. There is a national collection of lavenders. Extensive gardens, herb beds and walks among the lavender fields.
Times: Open 20 May-21 Sep, Mon-Sat 10-5. **Fee:** * £2.90 (ch under 14 free) **Facilities:** P ⚐ (wheelchair loan, wide doors, grab rails etc) toilets for disabled shop garden centre ✱

ST CLEMENT Map 16
Samarès Manor
JE2 6QW (2m E of St Helier on St Clements inner road)
☎ 01534 870551 ▤ 01534 768349

The manor stands in 14 acres of beautiful gardens. The Japanese Garden occupies an artificial hill, and has a series of waterfalls cascading over Cumberland limestone. There's a craft centre, farm animals and a children's play area. Falconry displays mornings and afternoons except Sundays.
Times: Open 31 Mar-12 Oct. **Fee:** * £4.60 (ch under 16 £1.95, pen £3.90). Sat prices: £3.50 (ch under 16 £1.50, pen £3) **Facilities:** P ⚐ ✗ licensed ⚐ toilets for disabled shop garden centre ✱ (ex guide dogs)

ST HELIER Map 16
Elizabeth Castle
JE2 3WU (access by causeway or amphibious vehicle)
☎ 01534 723971 ▤ 01534 610338
e-mail: marketing@jerseyheritagetrust.org
Times: Open 29 Mar-Oct, daily 9.30-6. Last admission 5. **Facilities:** P ⚐ shop ✱ (ex guide dogs) *Details not confirmed for 2003*

Jersey Museum
The Weighbridge JE2 3NF (near bus station on weighbridge)
☎ 01534 633300 ▤ 01534 633301
e-mail: marketing@jerseyheritagetrust.org
Times: Open all year, daily 10-5. Winter daily 10-4. (Closed 24-26 Dec & 1 Jan). **Facilities:** P (100yds) (paycard at most public parking) ✗ licensed ⚐ (audio loop, audio guide for partially sighted, car park) toilets for disabled shop ✱ (ex guide dogs) *Details not confirmed for 2003*

Maritime Museum & Occupation Tapestry Gallery
New North Quay JE2 3ND (alongside Marina, opposite Liberation Square)
☎ 01534 811022 ▤ 01534 874099
e-mail: marketing@jerseyheritagetrust
Times: Open all year, daily 10-5 (winter closing at 4pm). **Facilities:** P (paycards in public car parks) ⚐ (braille books, audio guide etc) toilets for disabled shop ✱ (ex guide dogs) *Details not confirmed for 2003*

ST LAWRENCE Map 16
Flying Flowers
Jersey Flower Centre JE3 1GX
☎ 01534 865553 ▤ 01534 866000
Times: Open Apr-Oct, daily 10-5. **Facilities:** P ⚐ ✗ ⚐ (Wheelchairs available) toilets for disabled shop ✱ (ex guide dogs) *Details not confirmed for 2003*

German Underground Hospital
Les Charrieres Maloney JE3 1FU (bus route 8A from St Helier)
☎ 01534 863442 ▤ 01534 865970
e-mail: info@germanundergroundhospital.co.uk

On 1 July 1940 the Channel Islands were occupied by German forces, and this vast complex dug deep into a hillside is the most evocative reminder of that Occupation. A video presentation, along with a large collection of memorabilia, illustrates the lives of the

continued

Jersey

islanders at war and a further exhibition records their impressions during 1945, the year of liberation.
Times: Open 10 Feb-11 Nov, daily 9.30-5.30 Last admission 4.15. 16 Nov-8 Dec 9.30-1.30 last admission 12 **Fee:** * £6.50 (ch under 15 £3.00, ch under 6 free) **Facilities:** 🅿 🚌 ✕ licensed ♿ (ramp to restaurant & lift in Visitor Centre to restaurant) toilets for disabled shop 🐕 (ex guide dogs) 📧

HAMPTONNE COUNTRY LIFE MUSEUM
La Rue de la Patente JE3 1HS (5m from St Helier on A1, A10 & follow signs)
☎ 01534 863955 📠 01534 863935
e-mail: marketing@jerseyheritagetrust.org
Times: Open 29 Mar-Oct, daily 10-4. **Facilities:** 🅿 🚌 ♿ toilets for disabled shop 🐕 (ex guide dogs) *Details not confirmed for 2003* 📧

ST OUEN Map 16
THE CHANNEL ISLANDS MILITARY MUSEUM
Smile Rd (Northern end of Five Mile Rd, at the rear of the Jersey Woollen Mill & across the road from Jersey Pearl)
☎ 01534 723136 📠 01534 485647
e-mail: damienhorn@jerseymail.co.uk

German uniforms, motorcycles, weapons, documents, photographs and other items from the 1940-45 occupation are displayed in a wartime bunker that was part of the Nazis' Atlantic defences. Many of the items on display are not to be found anywhere else on the islands.
Times: Open week before Etr-Oct **Fee:** * £3 (ch £1). **Facilities:** 🅿 🚌 ♿ (All parts accessible ex 1 small room) toilets for disabled shop 🐕 (ex guide dogs)

KEMPT TOWER VISITOR CENTRE
Five Mile Rd
☎ 01534 483651 & 483140 📠 01534 485289
Times: Open BH's & Apr & Oct, Thu & Sun only 2-5; May-Sep, daily (ex Mon) 2-5. **Facilities:** 🅿 shop 🐕 *Details not confirmed for 2003*

ST PETER Map 16
THE LIVING LEGEND
Rue de Petit Aleval JE3 7ET (From main town of St Helier. Along main esplanade-turn right to Bel Royal. Turn left and follow road to The Living Legend (signposted from the German underground Hospital))
☎ 01534 485496 📠 01534 485855
e-mail: info@jerseylivinglegend.co.je

Pass through the granite archways into the landscaped gardens and the world of the Jersey Experience where Jersey's exciting past is recreated in a three dimensional spectacle. Learn of the heroes and villains, the folklore and the story of the island's links with the UK and her struggles with Europe. Other attractions include an adventure playground, street entertainment, the Jersey Craft and Shopping Village, a range of shops and the Jersey Kitchen Restaurant.
Times: Open Apr-Oct, daily 9.30-5; Mar & Nov, Mon-Wed & Sat-Sun 10-5. **Fee:** * £6.50 (ch £4.35, pen £6.20, student £5, disabled £5.10).
Facilities: 🅿 ✕ licensed ♿ (wheelchair available) toilets for disabled shop 🐕 (ex guide dogs) 📧

LE MOULIN DE QUETIVEL
St Peters Valley, Le Mont Fallu JE3 3EN (from St Helier via first tower (A1) heading W. Take A11 through St Peter's Valley. The mill located on left, with junct of Le Mont Fallu (B58))
☎ 01534 483193 01534 745408

There has been a water mill on this site since 1309. The present granite-built mill was worked until the end of the 19th century, when it fell into disrepair; during the German Occupation it was reactivated for grinding locally grown corn, but after 1945 a fire destroyed the remaining machinery, roof and internal woodwork. In 1971 the National Trust for Jersey began restoration, and the mill is now producing stoneground flour again.
Times: Open 14 May-3 Oct, Tue-Thu 10-4. **Fee:** * £2 (ch £1, pen & student £1.50). Trust Members free. **Facilities:** 🅿 ♿ shop 🐕 (ex guide dogs) 🚌 🐎

TRINITY Map 16
DURRELL WILDLIFE CONSERVATION TRUST
Les Augres Manor JE3 5BP
☎ 01534 860000 📠 01534 860001
Times: Open all year, daily 9.30-6 (dusk in winter). (Closed 25 Dec).
Facilities: 🅿 ✕ licensed ♿ (trail for the blind, auditory loop in pavilion) toilets for disabled shop 🐕 *Details not confirmed for 2003* 📧

Isle of Man

Going to the Isle of Man is, in many ways, like visiting a foreign country. The island is not ruled by the British monarch, and has its own parliament (the Tynwald) which makes laws that apply only to the island.

The Isle of Man is only 33 miles by 13, yet packs in so much. Celtic crosses, ancient Viking burial grounds and medieval castles are all around, and the history of the island is well chronicled by the award-winning Manx Museum. Inside, visitors can explore the National Art Gallery, the Map Gallery with its large-scale relief map of the island, and see a specially-produced film, 'Story of Mann'.

One of the island's main attractions is its railway network, which began over a century ago and still runs a regular service. 19th-century electric and mountain railways are also still in operation. The Snaefell Mountain Railway is the only electric mountain railway in Britain, and starts its journey from Laxey, home of the world's largest working waterwheel. Douglas also has horse trams, which have been in continuous operation since 1876, except for wartime breaks.

The island is probably best known for its TT (Tourist Trophy) racing, which is staged in May-June each year. The race, originally for cars only, has been run since 1907, and with motorbikes only since 1911. Other races include the Ramsey Sprint, the Manx Grand Prix, the Manx International Car Rally, and the Kart Racing Grand Prix.

The Isle of Man also serves as something of a celebrity retirement colony, currently being the home of British comic actor Norman Wisdom, and keyboard wizard Rick Wakeman.

EVENTS & FESTIVALS

May
24th-6th June Isle of Man TT Motorcycle Festival (various venues)

June
24th May -6th Isle of Man TT Motorcycle Festival (various venues)
tbc Mananan International Festival of Music (various venues)

July
19th-25th Yn Chruinnaght Inter-Celtic Festival (various venues)
31st-2nd Aug Manx International Car Rally (various venues)
31st-2rd Aug Conister Trust Historic Car Rally (various venues)
tbc Manx Heritage Flower Show (various venues)

August
31st July-2nd Manx International Car Rally (various venues)
31st July-2rd Conister Trust Historic Car Rally (various venues)
16th-19th Manx Grand Prix Motorcycle Fortnight (various venues)

September
tbc Mananan Opera Festival, Erin Arts Centre, Port Erin

Top: Cathedral of St German, Peel

BALLASALLA
Map 06 SC27
Rushen Abbey
IM9 3DB (signed from Ballasalla)
☎ 01624 648000 📧 01624 648001
e-mail: enquiries@mnh.gov.im

This important medieval religious site is the remains of an old abbey, and contains interpretative displays and changing archaeological investigations.
Times: Open Etr-3 Oct, daily 10-5 **Fee:** * £3 (ch £1.50) family ticket £7.50 **Facilities:** P & toilets for disabled shop ✖ (ex guide dogs)

BALLAUGH
Map 06 SC39
Curraghs Wild Life Park
IM7 5EA (on main road halfway between Kirk Michael & Ramsey)
☎ 01624 897323 📧 01624 897327
e-mail: curraghswlp@gov.im
Times: Open all year Etr-Oct, daily 10-6. Last admission 5.15pm. Oct-Etr, Sat & Sun 10-4. **Facilities:** P ⛽ & (loan of wheelchair & electric wheelchair) toilets for disabled shop ✖ (ex guide dogs by arrangement) *Details not confirmed for 2003*

CASTLETOWN
Map 06 SC26
Castle Rushen
(centre of Castletown)
☎ 01624 648000 📧 01624 648001
e-mail: enquiries@mnh.gov.im

One of Britain's most complete medieval castles, Castle Rushen is a limestone fortress rising out of the heart of the old Capital of the island, Castletown. Once the fortress of the Kings and Lords of Mann, Rushen is brought alive with rich decorations, and the sounds and smells of a bygone era. In summer battles are re-enacted and the lifestyle of the period re-created by enthusiasts.
Times: Open daily 10-5 Etr-end Oct **Fee:** * £4.25 (ch £2.25) Family £10.75. Group bookings available from £3.40. **Facilities:** P (100 yds) Disc Zone Parking & shop ✖ (ex guide dogs)

Nautical Museum
(From Castletown centre, cross footbridge over harbour. Museum on right)
☎ 01624 648000 📧 01624 648001
e-mail: enquiries@mnh.gov.im

Set at the mouth of Castletown harbour this museum is home to an 18th-century armed yacht, The Peggy, built by a Manxman in 1971. A replica sailmaker's loft, ship model and photographs bring alive Manx Maritime life and trade in the days of sail.
Times: Open daily 10-5, Etr-Oct. **Fee:** * £3 (ch £1.50). Family £7.50. Group bookings available from £2.40 pp **Facilities:** P (50 yds) & shop ✖ (ex guide dogs)

Old Grammar School
(centre of Castletown just off the square)
☎ 01624 648000 📧 01624 648001
e-mail: enquiries@mnh.gov.im

Built in the 12th century, the Island's first church, St Mary's, has had a significant role in Manx education. The school dates back to 1570 and evokes memories of Victorian school life.
Times: Open daily 10-5 Easter-end Oct. **Fee:** Fee. **Facilities:** P shop ✖ (ex guide dogs)

The Old House of Keys
(opposite Castletown Castle)
☎ 01624 648000 📧 01624 648001
e-mail: enquiries@mnh.gov.im

This reconstruction of the mid 19th-century House of Keys, the Manx Parliamentary Chamber, has interactive audio-visual presentations on key Manx Constitutional issues.
Times: Open Etr-Oct, daily 10-5 **Fee:** * £3 (ch £1.50) Family ticket £7.50 **Facilities:** P 30yds disk zone parking &

CREGNEISH
Map 06 SC16
Cregneash Village Folk Museum
(2m from Port Erin/Port St Mary, signposted)
☎ 01624 648000 📧 01624 648001
e-mail: enquiries@mnh.gov.im

The Cregneash story begins in Cummal Beg - the village information centre where you can experience what life was really like in a Manx crofting village during the early 19th century. As you stroll around this attractive village, set in beautiful countryside, call into Harry Kelly's cottage, a Turner's shed, a Weaver's house, and the Blacksmith's smithy. The Manx four-horned Loghtan Sheep can be seen grazing along with other animals from the village farm.
Times: Open Etr-end Oct, daily 10-5. **Fee:** * £3 (ch £1.50) Family £7.50. Group rates from £2.40 **Facilities:** P ⛽ shop ✖ (ex guide dogs)

DOUGLAS
Map 06 SC37
Manx Museum
IM1 3LY
☎ 01624 648000 📧 01624 648001
e-mail: enquiries@mnh.gov.im

The 'Story of Mann' begins at Manx Museum, where a specially produced film portrayal of Manx history complements the award-winning gallery displays of Manx archaeology, history, folk life and natural sciences. Also houses the National Art Gallery, the island's national archive and reference library.
Times: Open daily all year, Mon-Sat 10-5. (Closed 25/26 Dec, 1 Jan & am 5 Jul). **Fee:** Free. **Facilities:** P ✖ licensed & (Lift) toilets for disabled shop ✖ (ex guide dogs)

Isle of Man

SNAEFELL MOUNTAIN RAILWAY
Banks Circus IM1 5PT (change from Manx Electric Railway from Douglas at Laxey)
☎ 01624 663366 📠 01624 663637

Snaefell is the Isle of Man's highest mountain. Running up it is Britain's oldest working mountain railway, which was laid in 1895. From the top of Snaefell, on a clear day, England, Ireland, Scotland and Wales are all visible. It is only accessible by railway.
Times: Open 29 Apr-29 Sep **Fee:** Various fares charged. **Facilities:** 🅿 💺 shop 🍴

🏛 LAXEY   Map 06 SC48
GREAT LAXEY WHEEL & MINES TRAIL
(signposted in Laxey village)
☎ 01624 648000 📠 01624 648001
e-mail: enquiries@mnh.gov.im

Built in 1854, the Great Laxey Wheel, 22 metres in diameter, is the largest working water wheel in the world. It was designed to pump water from the lead and zinc mines and is an acknowledged masterpiece of Victorian engineering. The wheel was christened by Lady Isabella, the wife of the Lieutenant Governor of the Isle of Man.
Times: Open Etr-end Oct, daily 10-5. **Fee:** * £3 (ch £1.50) Family £7.50. Group rates from £2.40. **Facilities:** 🅿 ♿ shop 🐕 (ex guide dogs)

🏛 PEEL   Map 06 SC28
HOUSE OF MANANNAN
Mill Rd IM5 1TA (on quayside)
☎ 01624 648000 📠 01624 648001
e-mail: enquiries@mnh.gov.im

Interpretation of the Celtic, Viking and maritime traditions of the Isle of Man through reconstructions, interactive displays, audio-visual presentations and original material.
Times: Open daily. (Closed 25-26 Dec & 1 Jan). **Fee:** * £5 (ch £2.50) family (2ad & 2ch) £12.50. Group rates from £4 per person **Facilities:** 🅿 ♿ toilets for disabled shop 🐕 (ex guide dogs) 💳

PEEL CASTLE
(on Patricks Isle, facing Peel Bay, signposted in Peel)
☎ 01624 648000 📠 01624 648001
e-mail: enquiries@mnh.gov.im

History, mystery and suspense is all around as you discover the secrets of Peel Castle, one of the island's principal historic centres. This great natural fortress, with its imposing curtain wall, and set majestically at the mouth of Peel harbour is steeped in Viking heritage. In the 11th century the castle was the ruling seat of the Norse Kingdom of Mann and the isles. Today you can stroll through the remains of the Round Tower, 13th-century cathedral and site of the 90ft-long giant's grave. There are fantastic views of the town of Peel and the coast.
Times: Open Etr-end Oct, daily 10-5. **Fee:** £3. (ch £1.50). Family £7.50. Group rates from £2.40 per person **Facilities:** 🅿 shop 🐕 (ex guide dogs)

🏛 RAMSEY   Map 06 SC49
'THE GROVE' RURAL LIFE MUSEUM
(on W side of Andreas Road. Signposted)
☎ 01624 648000 📠 01624 648001
e-mail: enquiries@mnh.gov.im

The story of traditional farming is revealed by this Victorian time capsule, a country house built as a summer retreat for a Liverpool shipping merchant. Rooms are filled with period, and in some cases original furnishings, and the outbuildings house 19th-century vehicles and farming tools.
Times: Open Etr-end Oct, daily 10-5. **Fee:** £3 (ch £1.50). Family £7.50, group rates from £2.40 **Facilities:** 🅿 💺 ♿ shop 🐕 (ex guide dogs) 💳

Bla Bheinn, Cullin Hills, Isle of Skye

Scotland
EVENTS & FESTIVALS

January
31st Dec 02-1st Stonehaven Fireballing Festival, Stonehaven, Aberdeenshire
1st Men's & Boy's 'Ba', mass football game, Kirkwall, Orkney Isles
15th-2nd Feb Celtic Connections Festival (International Celtic music festival), Glasgow Royal Concert Hall
25th Burns Night (celebrations throughout Scotland)
25th-26th Royal Canin Sled Dog Rally at Glen Forest Park, Aviemore
28th Up Helly Aa, Lerwick, Shetland Islands

February
15th Jan-2nd Celtic Connections Festival (International Celtic music festival), Glasgow Royal Concert Hall
11th-16th Scottish Curling Championships, Dewar's Centre, Ice Rink, Perth

April
5th-6th City of Dundee Spring Flower Show
11th-22nd Edinburgh International Science Festival (various venues), Edinburgh
12th Scottish Grand National, Ayr Racecourse

May
1st-4th Shetland Folk Festival, Lerwick
23rd-26th International Festival of the Sea, Edinburgh
24th-25th Atholl Gathering & Highland Games, Perth & Kinross
26th-4th June Scottish International Children's Festival, Edinburgh
28th-29th Angus Show, Haughmuir by Brechin, Angus
tbc Dundee Jazz Festival, Dundee Rep Theatre, Tay Square, Dundee

June
26th May-4th Scottish International Children's Festival, Edinburgh
1st Borders Historic Motoring Extravaganza, Borders
8th Forfar Highland Games, Forfar, Angus
8th Kildrummy Castle Rally, veteran and vintage classic cars, Kildrummy nr Alford
12th Lanimer Day, Lanark, South Lanarkshire
19th-22nd Royal Highland Show, Edinburgh (provisional)

20th-25th St Magnus Festival, Orkney, annual festival of music, drama, dance and visual art
27th-6th July Glasgow International Jazz Festival (provisional)

July
27th June-6th Glasgow International Jazz Festival (provisional)
13th Stirling Highland Games, Stirlingshire (provisional)
25th Langholm Common Riding, Dumfries & Galloway
30th Stranraer Show, Dumfries & Galloway
30th-9th Aug Aberdeen International Youth Festival (various venues)
tbc Dundee Blues Bonanza, various venues in Dundee

August
30th July-9th Aberdeen International Youth Festival (various venues throughout the NE)
1st-23rd Edinburgh Military Tattoo
2nd Aboyne Highland Games, Aboyne, Aberdeenshire
7th-10th Border Gathering, Dumfries & Galloway College
10th-30th Edinburgh International Festival
14th Highland Games, Monaltrie Park, Ballater, Aberdeenshire
17th Crieff Highland Games, Perth & Kinross
tbc Arbroath Seafest, various venues in Arbroath, Angus
tbc Edinburgh International Film Festival (provisional)

September
5th-7th City of Dundee Summer Flower Show
5th-7th Kirriemuir Festival of Traditional Music & Song, Angus
6th Braemar Gathering, Princess Royal & Duke of Fife Memorial Park, Braemar, Aberdeenshire
7th-14th Techfest, Aberdeen, various venues
8th Blairgowrie Highland Games, Perth & Kinross

October
tbc Scottish International Storytelling Festival, Edinburgh

November
28th-30th Dundee Mountain Film Festival, Bonar Hall, Dundee

Above: Robert the Bruce

ABERDEEN CITY

🏛 ABERDEEN   Map 15 NJ90
ABERDEEN ART GALLERY
Schoolhill AB10 1FQ (located in city centre)
☎ 01224 523700   📠 01224 632133
e-mail: info@aagm.co.uk
Times: Open all year ex Xmas/New Year. Mon-Sat 10-5, Sun 2-5.
Facilities: P (500yds) 🍴 & toilets for disabled shop 🐕 (ex guide dogs) *Details not confirmed for 2003*

ABERDEEN MARITIME MUSEUM
Shiprow AB11 5BY (located in city centre)
☎ 01224 337700
e-mail: info@aagm.co.uk
Times: Open all year (ex Xmas & New Year). Mon-Sat 10-5, Sun 12-3. Telephone for details. **Facilities:** P (250yds) 🍴 ✕ licensed & toilets for disabled shop 🐕 *Details not confirmed for 2003*

CRUICKSHANK BOTANIC GARDEN
University of Aberdeen, St Machar Dr AB24 3UU (enter by gate in Chanonry, in Old Aberdeen)
☎ 01224 272704   📠 01224 272703
e-mail: pss@abdn.ac.uk

Developed at the end of the 19th century, the 11 acres include rock and water gardens, a rose garden, a fine herbaceous border, an arboretum and a patio garden. There are collections of spring bulbs, gentians and alpine plants, and a fine array of trees and shrubs.
Times: Open all year, Mon-Fri 9-4.30; also Sat & Sun, May-Sep 2-5.
Fee: Free. **Facilities:** P (200metres) & 🐕

THE GORDON HIGHLANDERS MUSEUM
St Lukes, Viewfield Rd AB15 7XH
☎ 01224 311200   📠 01224 319323
e-mail: museum@gordonhighlanders.com

Presenting a large collection of artefacts, interactive displays, audio-visual theatre, and reconstructions, the Gordon Highlanders Museum is the perfect day out for anyone interested in British military history. Also a tea room, the paintings of Scottish artist, Sir George Reid, and gardens.
Times: Open Apr-Oct Tue-Sat 10.30-4.30, Sun 1.30-4.30. (Closed Mon). Open by appointment only at other times. **Fee:** * £2.50 (ch £1, con £1.50) **Facilities:** P 🍴 & low level cases, hearing loop toilets for disabled shop 🐕 (ex guide dogs) 🍴

PROVOST SKENE'S HOUSE
Guestrow, (off Broad St) AB10 1AS
☎ 01224 641086
e-mail: info@aagm.co.uk
Times: Open all year Mon-Sat 10-5, Sun 1-4. closed Xmas & New Year). Telephone for details. **Facilities:** P (200yds) 🍴 & 🐕 (ex guide dogs) *Details not confirmed for 2003*

Aberdeen City - Aberdeenshire   297

SATROSPHERE ("HANDS-ON" SCIENCE & TECHNOLOGY CENTRE)
179 Constitution St AB24 5TU (5min from town centre, and very close to Aberdeen Beach Esplanade)
☎ 01224 640340   📠 01224 622211   **2 for 1**
e-mail: info@satrosphere.net

Satrosphere, the Discovery Place, is different from many museums or exhibition centres. It is an Interactive Centre where everything is 'hands-on'. Displays aren't locked in glass cases and there are certainly no "Do Not Touch" signs. The emphasis is on doing and finding out, not just looking and standing back. Over 100 hands-on exhibits, interactive shows, workshops and special weekend events.
Times: Open all year, Mon-Sat 10-5, Sun 11.30-5. (Closed 25-26 Dec & 1-2 Jan). **Fee:** * £5 (ch under 3 free, pen £3). **Facilities:** P 🍴 & toilets for disabled shop 🐕 (ex guide dogs) 🍴

🏛 PETERCULTER   Map 15 NJ80
DRUM CASTLE
AB31 5EY (3m W, off A93)
☎ 01330 811204   📠 01330 811962
e-mail: drum@nts.org.uk

The great 13th-century Square Tower is one of the three oldest tower houses in Scotland and has associations with Robert the Bruce. The handsome mansion, added in 1619, houses a collection of family memorabilia. The grounds contain the 100-acre Old Wood of Drum, a natural oak wood and an old rose garden.
Times: Open 25 Mar-28 Jun & 2 Sep-27 Oct, daily 12-5, 29 Jun-1 Sep, daily 10-6. **Fee:** Admission free to NTS members. For other details please phone (0131) 243 9387 or check website. **Facilities:** P 🍴 & (wheelchair available) shop 🐕 (ex guide dogs) 🍴

ABERDEENSHIRE

🏛 ALFORD   Map 15 NJ51
ALFORD VALLEY RAILWAY
AB33 8AD (A944 Alford Village)
☎ 019755 62326 & 62811   📠 019755 63182

Narrow-gauge passenger railway in two sections: Alford-Haughton Park and Haughton Park-Murray Park approx one mile each. Steam on peak weekends. Diesel traction. Exhibitions.
Times: Open Apr, May & Sep wknds 1-5, Jun-Aug daily from 1pm (30 min service). Party bookings also available at other times. **Fee:** * £2 (ch £1) return fare. **Facilities:** P & (ramps at station platforms) toilets for disabled shop

🏛 BALMORAL   Map 15 NO29
BALMORAL CASTLE GROUNDS & EXHIBITION
AB35 5TB (on A93 between Ballater & Braemar)
☎ 013397 42334 & 42335   📠 013397 42271
e-mail: info@balmoral-castle.co.uk
Times: Open 12 Apr-Jul, daily 10-5. **Facilities:** P (150yds) 🍴 & (wheelchairs available & free parking enquire at main gate) toilets for disabled shop 🐕 (ex guide dogs/in grounds) *Details not confirmed for 2003* 🍴

Aberdeenshire

🏛 BANCHORY
Map 15 NO69
BANCHORY MUSEUM
Bridge St AB31 5SX (beside tourist information centre, 100yds from main car park and 25yds from High St through Scott Skinner Square)
☎ 01771 622906 📠 01771 622884
e-mail: heritage@aberdeenshire.gov.uk

The museum has displays on Scott Skinner (The 'Strathspey King'), natural history, royal commemorative china, local silver artefacts and a variety of local history displays.
Times: Open May, Jun & Sep, Mon-Sat 11-1 & 2-4.30; Jul-Aug, Mon-Sat 11-1, 2-4.30 & Sun 2-4.30. Tel. for Apr & Oct opening times.
Fee: Free. **Facilities:** P (100yds) (limited) ♿ (toilet in staff area, ask museum asst) toilets for disabled shop ✱ (ex guide dogs)

🏛 BANFF
Map 15 NJ66
BANFF MUSEUM
High St AB45 1AE
☎ 01771 622906 📠 01771 622884
e-mail: heritage@aberdeenshire.gov.uk

Displays of geology, natural history, local history, Banff silver, arms and armour, and displays relating to James Ferguson (18th-century astronomer) and Thomas Edward (19th-century Banff naturalist).
Times: Open Jun-Sep, Mon-Sat 2-4.30. **Fee:** Free. **Facilities:** P (200yds) ♿ shop ✱ (ex guide dogs)

DUFF HOUSE
AB45 3SX (0.5m S, access south of town)
☎ 01261 818181

The house was designed by William Adam for William Duff, later Earl of Fife. The main block was roofed in 1739, but the planned wings were never built. Although it is incomplete, the house is still considered one of Britain's finest Georgian baroque buildings. Duff House is a Country House Gallery of the National Galleries of Scotland.
Times: Telephone for details of opening dates and times. **Fee:** Telephone for details of admission charges. **Facilities:** P ✱ ♿ toilets for disabled shop ✱ ■

🏛 CORGARFF
Map 15 NJ20
CORGARFF CASTLE
AB36 8YL (8m W of Strathdon village)
☎ 01975 651460

The 16th-century tower was besieged in 1571 and is associated with the Jacobite risings of 1715 and 1745. It later became a military barracks. Its last military use was to control the smuggling of whisky between 1827 and 1831.
Times: Open all year, Apr-Sep, daily 9.30-6.30; Oct-Mar, wknds only. (Closed 25-26 Dec). Telephone for 2003 details **Fee:** * £2.80 (ch £1, concessions £2). **Facilities:** P shop ■

🏛 CRATHES
Map 15 NO79
CRATHES CASTLE & GARDENS
AB31 3QJ (On A93, 3m E of Banchory)
☎ 01330 844525 📠 01330 844797
e-mail: crathes@nts.org.uk

This impressive 16th-century castle with magnificent interiors has royal associations dating from 1323. There is a large walled garden and a notable collection of unusual plants, including yew hedges dating from 1702. The grounds contain six nature trails, one suitable for disabled visitors, and an adventure playground.
Times: Open: Castle & Visitor Centre: 25 Mar-Sep, daily 10-5.30, Oct daily 10-4.30. **Fee:** Admission free to NTS members. For other details please phone (0131) 243 9387 or check website. **Facilities:** P ✱ licensed ♿ (tape for visually impaired) toilets for disabled shop ✱ (ex guide dogs) ♘

🏛 FETTERCAIRN
Map 15 NO67
FASQUE
AB30 1DN (0.5m N on B974)
☎ 01561 340569 & 340202 📠 01561 340325 & 340569
Times: Open Jul-Aug, daily 11-5. (Closed 5.30). Groups at all other times by arrangement at any other time all year round. **Facilities:** P 🍴 ♿ (wheelchairs available) shop ✱ *Details not confirmed for 2003*

🏛 HUNTLY
Map 15 NJ53
BRANDER MUSEUM
The Square AB54 8AE (In centre of Huntly, sharing building with library, museum on ground floor)
☎ 01771 622906 📠 01771 622884
e-mail: heritage@aberdeenshire.gov.uk

The museum has displays of local and church history, plus the 19th-century Anderson Bey and the Sudanese campaigns. Exhibits connected with George MacDonald, author and playwright can also be seen.
Times: Open all year, Tue-Sat 2-4.30. **Fee:** Free. **Facilities:** P (25yds) ♿ (access difficult due to 3 large steps at entrance) shop ✱ (ex guide dogs)

HUNTLY CASTLE
AB54 4SH
☎ 01466 793191

The original medieval castle was rebuilt a number of times and destroyed, once by Mary, Queen of Scots. It was rebuilt for the last time in 1602, in palatial style, and is now an impressive ruin, noted for its ornate heraldic decorations. It stands in wooded parkland.
Times: Open all year, Apr-Sep, daily 9.30-6.30; Oct-Mar, Mon-Sat 9.30-4.30, Sun 2-4.30. (Closed Thu pm, Fri & Sun in winter & 25-26 Dec). **Fee:** * £3 (ch £1, concessions £2). **Facilities:** P shop ■

Aberdeenshire **299**

⌂ INVERURIE   Map 15 NJ72
Carnegie Museum
Town House, The Square AB51 3SN (In town centre, on left of townhouse building, above library)
☎ 01771 622906   ▤ 01771 622884
e-mail: heritage@aberdeenshire.gov.uk

This fine museum contains displays on local history and archaeology, including Pictish stones, Bronze Age material and the Great North of Scotland Railway.
Times: Open all year, Mon & Wed-Fri 2-4.30, Sat 10-1 & 2-4. (Closed Tue & public holidays) **Fee:** Free. **Facilities:** P (50yds) shop ✖ (ex guide dogs)

⌂ KEMNAY   Map 15 NJ71
Castle Fraser
AB51 7LD (off A944, 4m N of Dunecht)
☎ 01330 833463
e-mail: castlefraser@nts.org.uk

The massive Z-plan castle was built between 1575 and 1636 and is one of the grandest of the Castles of Mar. The interior was remodelled in 1838 and decoration and furnishings of that period survive in some of the rooms. A formal garden inside the old walled garden, estate trails, a children's play area and a programme of concerts are among the attractions.
Times: 25 Mar-28 Jun & 2 Sep-27 Oct, Fri-Tue 12-5, 29 Jun-1 Sep, daily 10-5 **Fee:** Admission free to NTS members. For other details please phone (0131) 243 9387 or check website. **Facilities:** P ■ & shop garden centre ✖ (ex guide dogs, certain areas) ⚑

⌂ KILDRUMMY   Map 15 NJ41
Kildrummy Castle
AB54 7XT (10m SW of Alford)
☎ 01975 571331

An important part of Scottish history, at least until it was dismantled in 1717, this fortress was the seat of the Earls of Mar. Now it is a ruined, but splendid, example of a 13th-century castle, with four round towers, hall and chapel all discernible. Some parts of the building, including the Great Gatehouse, are from the 15th and 16th centuries.
Times: Open Apr-Sep, daily 9.30-6.30. **Fee:** * £2 (ch 75p, concessions £1.50). **Facilities:** P & toilets for disabled shop ▮

Kildrummy Castle Gardens
AB33 8RA (on A97 off A944. 10m west of Alford)
☎ 019755 71277 & 71203   ▤ 019755 71277
e-mail: information@kildrummy-castle-gardens.co.uk

With the picturesque ruin as a backdrop, these beautiful gardens include an alpine garden in an ancient quarry and a water garden. There's a small museum and a children's play area.
Times: Open Apr-Oct, daily 10-5. **Fee:** £2.50 (ch free) **Facilities:** P ■ & toilets for disabled shop garden centre

⌂ MACDUFF   Map 15 NJ76
Macduff Marine Aquarium
11 High Shore AB44 1SL (off A947 to Macduff, museum signposted)
☎ 01261 833369   ▤ 01261 831052
e-mail: macduffaquarium.ed@aberdeenshire.gov.uk

This aquarium has an unusual circular design that encloses a central tank open to the air. Visitors can see into this tank, containing 400,000 litres of seawater, from several angles, and observe many unusual undersea creatures. There are regular opportunities to see divers in the tank, undertaking maintenance and feeding the inhabitants. Lots of educational programmes for schools.
Times: Open 10-5 daily (last admission 4.15). (Closed 25-26 Dec & 1-2 Jan) **Fee:** £4 (ch £1.70, concessions £2.20). Family ticket (2 adults & 2 ch) £10.50. Groups 10+ **Facilities:** P & audio tour for visually impaired toilets for disabled shop ✖ (ex guide dogs) ⚑

⌂ MARYCULTER   Map 15 NO89
Storybook Glen   **2 for 1**
AB12 5FT (5m W of Aberdeen on B9077)
☎ 01224 732941   ▤ 01224 732941

This is a child's fantasy land, where favourite nursery rhyme and fairytale characters are brought to life. Grown-ups can enjoy the nostalgia and also the 20 acres of Deeside country, full of flowers, plants, trees and waterfalls.
Times: Open Mar-Oct, daily 10-6; Nov-Feb, daily 10-4. **Fee:** * £3.90 (ch £1.95, pen £3). **Facilities:** P ■ ✖ licensed & toilets for disabled shop garden centre ✖ (ex guide dogs) ⚑

⌂ METHLICK   Map 15 NJ83
Haddo House
AB41 7EQ (off B999, 4m N of Pitmedden)
☎ 01651 851440   ▤ 01651 851888
e-mail: haddo@nts.org.uk

Haddo House is renowned for its association with the Haddo Choral Society and is the venue for international concerts. It is a splendid Palladian-style mansion built in the 1730s to designs by William Adam. Home to the Earls of Aberdeen, the house was refurbished in the 1880s in the 'Adam Revival' style. The adjoining country park offers beautiful woodland walks.
Times: Open, House: 29 Jun-1 Sep, daily, 10-5. Park: all year, daily, 9.30-sunset. **Fee:** Admission free to NTS members. For other details please phone (0131) 243 9387 or check website. **Facilities:** P ✖ & (lift to first floor of house & wheelchair) toilets for disabled shop ✖ (ex in grounds & guide dogs) ⚑

⌂ MINTLAW   Map 15 NJ94
Aberdeenshire Farming Museum
Aden Country Park AB42 5FQ (1m W of Mintlaw on A950)
☎ 01771 622906   ▤ 01771 622884
e-mail: heritage@aberdeenshire.gov.uk

Housed in 19th-century farm buildings, once part of the estate which now makes up the Aden Country Park.

continued

Aberdeenshire

Two centuries of farming history and innovation are illustrated, and the story of the estate is also told. The reconstructed farm of Hareshowe shows how a family in the north-east farmed during the 1950s - access by guided tour only.
Times: Open May-Sep, daily 11-4.30; Apr & Oct, wknds only noon-4.30. Last admission 30 mins before closing. Park open all year, Apr-Sep 7-10, winter 7-7. To be confirmed. **Fee:** Free. **Facilities:** P (charged) 🍽 ♿ (sensory garden) toilets for disabled shop 🐕 (ex guide dogs)

🏛 OLD DEER   Map 15 NJ94
Deer Abbey
(10m W of Peterhead)
☎ 0131 668 8800

The remains of the Cistercian Abbey, founded in 1218, include the infirmary, Abbot's House and the southern claustral range. The University Library at Cambridge now houses the famous Book of Deer.
Times: Open at all reasonable times. **Fee:** Free. **Facilities:** P 🐕 🚻

🏛 OYNE   Map 15 NJ62
Archaeolink
Berryhill AB52 6QP (1m off A96 on B9002)
☎ 01464 851500   📠 01464 851544   **2 for 1**
e-mail: info@archaeolink.co.uk

A stunning audio-visual show, a Myths and Legends Gallery and a whole range of interpretation techniques help visitors to explore what it was like to live 6,000 years ago. In addition there are landscaped walkways, and outdoor activity areas including an Iron Age farm, Roman marching camp and Stone Age settlement in the 40-acre park.
Times: Open Apr-Oct, daily 11-5. **Fee:** * £4.25 (ch 3-6 £2.50, 7-16 £3, concessions £3.50) Family £13-£19. **Facilities:** P 🍽 ✕ licensed ♿ toilets for disabled shop 🐕 (ex guide dogs) ☕

🏛 PETERHEAD   Map 15 NK14
Arbuthnot Museum & Art Gallery
St Peter St AB42 1QD (in town centre, at St. Peter Street & Queen Street x-roads, above library)
☎ 01771 622906   📠 01771 622884
e-mail: heritage@aberdeenshire.gov.uk

Specialising in local exhibits, particularly those relating to the fishing industry, this museum also displays Arctic and whaling specimens and a British coin collection. The regular programme of exhibitions changes approximately every six weeks.
Times: Open all year, Mon, Tue & Thu-Sat 11-1 & 2-4.30, Wed 11-1. (Closed Sun and BHs). **Fee:** Free. **Facilities:** P (150 yds) shop 🐕 (ex guide dogs)

🏛 PITMEDDEN   Map 15 NJ82
Pitmedden Garden
AB41 7PA (1m W of Pitmedden on A920)
☎ 01651 842352   📠 01651 843188
e-mail: aclipson@nts.scot.demon.co.uk

The fine 17th-century walled garden, with sundials, pavilions and fountains dotted among the parterres, has been authentically restored, and there is a Museum of Farming Life and a woodland walk.
Times: Open - May-1 Sep, daily 10-5. Grounds: all year, daily. **Fee:** Admission free to NTS members. For other details please phone (0131) 243 9387 or check website. **Facilities:** P 🍽 ♿ (2 wheelchairs available) toilets for disabled shop ☕

Tolquhon Castle
AB41 7LP (2m NE off B999)
☎ 01651 851286

Now roofless, this late 16th-century quadrangular mansion encloses an early 15th-century tower. There is a fine gatehouse and a splendid courtyard.
Times: Open all year, Apr-Sep, daily 9.30-6.30; Oct-Mar, wknds only. (Closed 25-26 Dec). Telephone for 2003 details **Fee:** * £2 (ch 75p, concessions £1.50). Telephone for 2003 details **Facilities:** P ♿ toilets for disabled shop 🐕 🚻

🏛 RHYNIE   Map 15 NJ42
Leith Hall & Garden
Kennethmont AB54 4NQ (on B9002, 1m W of Kennethmont)
☎ 01464 831216   📠 01464 831594
e-mail: leithhall@nts.org.uk

Home of the Leith family for over 300 years, the house dates back to 1650, and has a number of Jacobite relics and fine examples of needlework. It is surrounded by charming gardens and extensive grounds.
Times: Open - House: 25 Mar-27 Oct, Wed-Sun 12-5. Garden: All year, daily 9.30-sunset. **Fee:** Admission free to NTS members. For other details please phone (0131) 243 9387 or check website.
Facilities: P 🍽 ♿ (parking next to hall, scented garden for the blind) toilets for disabled 🐕 (ex guide dogs) ☕

🏛 STONEHAVEN   Map 15 NO88
Dunnottar Castle
AB39 2TL (2m S of Stonehaven on A92)
☎ 01569 762173

This once-impregnable fortress, now a spectacular ruin, was the site of the successful protection of the Scottish Crown Jewels from the might of Cromwell. A must for anyone who takes Scottish history seriously.
Times: Open all year, summer Mon-Sat 9-6, Sun 2-5; winter open Fri-Mon only. Last entry 30mins before closing. (Closed 25-26 Dec & New Year). **Fee:** * £3.50 (ch 5-15 £1) **Facilities:** P 🐕 (ex on lead)

Tolbooth Museum
Old Pier AB39 2JU (On harbour front)
☎ 01771 622906   📠 01771 622884
e-mail: heritage@aberdeenshire.gov.uk

Built in the late 16th century as a storehouse for the Earls Marischal at Dunnottar Castle, the building was the Kincardineshire County Tollbooth from 1600-1767. Displays feature local history and fishing.
Times: Open May-Oct, Wed-Mon, 1.30-4.30. (Closed Tue). **Fee:** Free. **Facilities:** P (20yds) ♿ shop 🐕 (ex guide dogs)

Aberdeenshire - Angus

🏛 TURRIFF
Map 15 NJ75
FYVIE CASTLE
Fyvie AB53 8JS (8m SE of Turriff on A947)
☎ 01651 891266 📠 01651 891107
e-mail: aclipson@nts.scot.demon.co.uk

This superb castle, founded in the 13th century, has five towers, each built in a different century, and is one of the grandest examples of Scottish Baronial. It contains the finest wheel stair in Scotland, and a 17th-century morning room, lavishly furnished in Edwarian style. The collection of portraits is exceptional, and there are also displays of arms and armour and tapestries.
Times: Open 25 Mar-28 Jun & 2 Sep-27 Oct, Sat-Wed 12-5, 29 Jun-1 Sep, daily 10-5. **Fee:** Admission free to NTS members. For other details please phone (0131) 243 9387 or check website. **Facilities:** P 🍴 & (small lift, braille sheets) toilets for disabled shop ✂ (ex guide dogs) ⚘

ANGUS

🏛 ARBROATH
Map 12 NO64
ARBROATH ABBEY
DD11 1EG
☎ 01241 878756

The 'Declaration of Arbroath' - declaring Robert the Bruce as king - was signed at the 12th-century abbey on 6 April 1320. The abbot's house is well preserved, and the church remains are also interesting.
Times: Open all year, Apr-Sep, daily 9.30-6.30; Oct-Mar, Mon-Sat 9.30-4.30, Sun 2-4.30. (Closed Thu pm, Fri & Sun am in winter). please phone for 2003 details **Fee:** * £2.50 (ch 75p, concessions £1.90). **Facilities:** P & ✂ ¶

ARBROATH MUSEUM
Signal Tower, Ladyloan DD11 1PU (on A92 adjacent to harbour. 16m NE of Dundee)
☎ 01241 875598 📠 01241 439363
e-mail: signal.tower@angus.gov.uk

Fish and Arbroath Smokies, textiles and engineering feature at this local history museum housed in the 1813 shore station of Stevenson's Bell Rock lighthouse.
Times: Open all year, Mon-Sat 10-5; Jul-Aug, Sun 2-5. (Closed 25-26 Dec & 1-2 Jan). **Fee:** Free. **Facilities:** P & (induction loop) shop ✂ (ex guide dogs)

🏛 BARRY
Map 12 NO53
BARRY WATER MILL
DD7 7RJ (2m W of Carnoustie)
☎ 01241 856761

This restored 18th-century mill works on a demonstration basis. Records show that the site has been used for milling since the 16th century. Displays highlight the important place the mill held in the community. There is a waymarked walk and picnic area.
Times: Open 25 Mar-27 Oct, Thu-Mon 12-5 **Fee:** Admission free to NTS members. For other details please phone (0131) 243 9387 or check website. **Facilities:** P & ramp from car park to mill toilets for disabled (grounds only) ⚘

🏛 BRECHIN
Map 15 NO66
PICTAVIA VISITOR CENTRE
DD9 6RL (off A90)
☎ 01356 626813 📠 01356 626814
e-mail: laffertyc@angus.gov.uk

Find about more about the ancient pagan nation of the Picts, who lived in Scotland nearly 2000 years ago. Visitors can learn about Pictish culture, art and religion through film, interactive displays and music. There are also nature and farm trails, a pets' corner, and an adventure playground.
Times: Open daily; Summer Mon-Sat 9-6, Sun 10-5; Winter Mon-Sat 9-5, Sun 10-5. (Closed 25-26 Dec & 1 Jan) **Fee:** * £3.25 (ch & concessions £2.25) **Facilities:** P 🍴 ✕ licensed & toilets for disabled shop garden centre

🏛 EDZELL
Map 15 NO56
EDZELL CASTLE
DD9 7UE (on B966)
☎ 01356 648631

The 16th-century castle has a remarkable walled garden built in 1604 by Sir David Lindsay. Flower-filled recesses in the walls are alternated with heraldic and symbolic sculptures of a sort not seen elsewhere in Scotland. There are ornamental and border gardens and a garden house.
Times: Open all year, Apr-Sep, daily 9.30-6.30; Oct-Mar, Mon-Sat 9.30-4.30, Sun 2-4.30. (Closed Thu pm, Fri in winter & 25-26 Dec). Telephone for 2003 details **Fee:** * £2.80 (ch £1, concessions £2). **Facilities:** P & shop ¶

🏛 FORFAR
Map 15 NO45
THE MEFFAN ART GALLERY & MUSEUM
20 West High St DD8 1BB (13m N of Dundee, turn off A90, into Forfar town centre. Museum in town centre)
☎ 01307 464123 467017 📠 01307 468451
e-mail: the.meffan@angus.gov.uk

This lively, ever-changing contemporary art gallery and museum are full of surprises. Walk down a cobbled street full of shops, ending up at a witch-burning scene! Carved Pictish stones and a diorama of an archaeological dig complete the vibrant displays.
Times: Open all year. (Closed 25-26 Dec & 1-2 Jan). **Fee:** Free. **Facilities:** P (150yds) 30 mins limit on street & handrails and wide door toilets for disabled shop ✂ (ex guide dogs) 🍴

🏛 GLAMIS
Map 15 NO34
ANGUS FOLK MUSEUM
Kirkwynd Cottages DD8 1RT (off A94, in Glamis)
☎ 01307 840288 📠 01307 840233

A row of stone-roofed, late 18th-century cottages now houses the splendid Angus Folk Collection of domestic equipment and cottage furniture. Across the wynd, an Angus stone steading houses 'The Life on the Land' exhibition.
Times: Open 25 Mar-27 Oct, Sat-Wed 12-5. **Fee:** Admission free to NTS members. For other details please phone (0131) 243 9387 or check website. **Facilities:** P & toilets for disabled ✂ (ex guide dogs) ⚘

Angus - Argyll & Bute

GLAMIS CASTLE
DD8 1RJ (5m W of Forfar on A94)
☎ 01307 840393 📠 01307 840733
e-mail: admin@glamis-castle.co.uk

Glamis Castle is the family home of the Earls of Strathmore and Kinghorne and has been a royal residence since 1372. It was the childhood home of Queen Elizabeth, The Queen Mother, the birthplace of Princess Margaret and the setting for Shakespeare's play 'Macbeth'. Though the Castle is open to visitors it remains the home of the Strathmore family.
Times: Open 29 Mar-27 Oct, 10.30-5.30. Last admission 4.45pm. **Fee:** * Castle & grounds £6.50 (ch £3.20, pen & students £4.80). Family ticket £18. Grounds only £3.20 (ch, pen & students £2). Group 20+ £5.50 (ch £3, stu £4.30 & pen £2.20) **Facilities:** P ✗ licensed ♿ toilets for disabled shop ✱ (ex in grounds) 🐕

🏛 KIRRIEMUIR   Map 15 NO35
J M BARRIE'S BIRTHPLACE
9 Brechin Rd DD8 4BX (on A90/A926 6m NW of Forfar)
☎ 01575 572646
e-mail: aclipson@nts.scot.demon.co.uk

The creator of Peter Pan, Sir James Barrie, was born in Kirriemuir in 1860. The upper floors of No 9 Brechin Road are furnished as they may have been when Barrie lived there, and the adjacent house, No 11, houses an exhibition about him. The wash-house outside was his first 'theatre' and gave him the idea for Wendy's house in 'Peter Pan'.
Times: Open 25 Mar-27 Oct, Sat-Wed, 12-5 **Fee:** Admission free to NTS members. For other details please phone (0131) 243 9387 or check website. **Facilities:** P (100yds) 🍴 ♿ (stairlift, audio programmes) shop ✱ (ex guide dogs) 🐕

🏛 MONTROSE   Map 15 NO75
HOUSE OF DUN
DD10 9LQ (on A935, 3m W of Montrose)
☎ 01674 810264 📠 01674 810722
e-mail: houseofdun@nts.org.uk

This Georgian house, overlooking the Montrose Basin, was built for Lord Dun in 1730 and is noted for the exuberant plasterwork of the interior. Family portraits, fine furniture and porcelain are on display, and royal mementos connected with a daughter of King William IV and the actress Mrs Jordan, who lived here in the 19th century. There is a walled garden and woodland walks.
Times: House: 25 Mar-27 Oct, Fri-Tue 12-5, 29 Jun-1 Sep, Fri-Tue guided tours only. Garden: all year daily 9.30-sunset. **Fee:** Admission free to NTS members. For other details please phone (0131) 243 9387 or check website. **Facilities:** P ✗ ♿ (braille sheets, house wheelchair & stair lift) toilets for disabled shop ✱ (ex guide dogs) 🐕

MONTROSE MUSEUM & ART GALLERY
Panmure Place DD10 8HE (opposite Montrose Academy in town centre, approach via A92 from Aberdeen or Dundee)
☎ 01674 673232
e-mail: montrose.museum@angus.gov.uk

Extensive local collections cover the history of Montrose from prehistoric times, the maritime history of the port, the natural history of Angus, and local art.
Times: Open all year, Mon-Sat 10-5. (Closed 25-26 Dec & 1-2 Jan). **Fee:** Free. **Facilities:** P ♿ shop ✱ (ex guide dogs)

ARGYLL & BUTE

🏛 ARDUAINE   Map 10 NM71
ARDUAINE GARDEN
PA34 4XQ (20m S of Oban, on A816)
☎ 01852 200233 📠 01852 200233

An outstanding 18-acre garden on a promontory bounded by Loch Melfort and the Sound of Jura, climatically favoured by the North Atlantic Drift. It is famous for its rhododendrons and azalea species and other rare trees and shrubs.
Times: Open all year, daily 9.30-sunset. **Fee:** Admission free to NTS members. For other details please phone (0131) 243 9387 or check website. **Facilities:** P ♿ toilets for disabled ✱ (ex guide dogs) 🐕

🏛 ARROCHAR   Map 10 NN20
ARGYLL FOREST PARK
Forest Enterprise, Ardgartan Visitor Centre G83 7AR (on A83 at the foot of "The Rest and Be Thankful")
☎ 01301 702597 📠 01301 702597
e-mail: fekilmun@forestry.gov.uk
Times: Open all year. **Facilities:** P shop *Details not confirmed for 2003* 🐕

🏛 AUCHINDRAIN   Map 10 NN00
AUCHINDRAIN TOWNSHIP-OPEN AIR MUSEUM
PA32 8XN (5.5m SW of Inverarary on A83)
☎ 01499 500235

Auchindrain is an original West Highland township of great antiquity, and the only communal tenancy township to have survived on its centuries-old site. The buildings are furnished and equipped to present a fascinating glimpse of Highland life in the last century.
Times: Open Apr-Sep, daily 10-5. **Fee:** £3.80 (ch £1.80, pen £3). Family ticket £9.50. **Facilities:** P shop

🏛 BARCALDINE   Map 10 NM94
BARCALDINE CASTLE
Benderloch PA37 1SA (9m N of Oban on A828 Oban/Fort William road. Take left turn to Tralee in Benderloch)
☎ 01631 720598 📠 01631 720598
e-mail: barcaldine.castle@tesco.net

The 16th-century home of the Campbells of Barcaldine. The last of the seven castles built by Black Duncan to be held in Campbell hands, and associated with the Appin Murder and Glencoe Massacre. Said to be

continued

Argyll & Bute   303

haunted by the Blue Lady, the castle has secret passages and bottle dungeon; there is also a family quiz trail. 2002 Regional Winners of the National family and parenting institutes 'family friendly award'.
Times: Open Jul-Aug afternoons. **Fee:** * £3.50 (ch £1.75, concessions £2.95) **Facilities:** P ⌘ shop ✖ ⚐ ⚑

SCOTTISH SEALIFE & MARINE SANCTUARY
PA37 1SE (10m N of Oban on A828, Oban to Fort William rd)
☎ 01631 720386 ▤ 01631 720529
e-mail: oban@sealife.fsbusiness.co.uk
Times: Open all year, Feb-Nov, daily 9.30-5. Dec & Jan, Sat, Sun & school holidays only. **Facilities:** P ✖ licensed ♿ (assistance available for wheelchairs) toilets for disabled shop ✖ (ex guide dogs) *Details not confirmed for 2003* ⚑

🏛 BENMORE   Map 10 NS18
BENMORE BOTANIC GARDEN
PA23 8QU (7m N of Dunoon on A815)
☎ 01369 706261 ▤ 01369 706369
e-mail: info@rbge.org.uk

From the formal gardens, through the hillside woodlands, follow the paths to a stunning viewpoint with a spectacular outlook across the garden and the Holy Loch to the Firth of Clyde and beyond. Amongst many highlights are the stately conifers, the magnificent avenue of Giant Redwoods, and an extensive magnolia collection.
Times: Open Mar-Oct, daily, 10; Mar & Oct, close 5, Apr -Sep, close 6. **Fee:** £3 (ch £1, concessions £2.50). Family £7. Season ticket and group rates available. **Facilities:** P ⌘ ✖ licensed ♿ toilets for disabled shop garden centre ⚑

🏛 CARNASSARIE CASTLE   Map 10 NM80
CARNASSARIE CASTLE
PA31 8RQ (2m N of Kilmartin off A816)
☎ 0131 668 8800

Built in the 16th century by John Carswell, first Protestant Bishop of the Isles, the castle was taken and partly destroyed in Argyll's rebellion of 1685. It consists of a tower house with a courtyard built around.
Times: Open at all reasonable times. **Fee:** Free. **Facilities:** P ✖ ⚐

🏛 GIGHA ISLAND   Map 10 NR64
ACHAMORE GARDENS
PA41 7AD
☎ 01583 505267 & 505254 ▤ 01583 505244
e-mail: william@isle-of-gigha.co.uk
Times: Open all year, daily. **Facilities:** P ♿ *Details not confirmed for 2003*

🏛 INVERARAY   Map 10 NN00
BELL TOWER OF ALL SAINTS' CHURCH
The Avenue PA32 8YX
☎ 01499 302259
Times: Open mid May-Sep, daily 10-1 & 2-5. **Facilities:** P (adjacent to tower) ♿ shop ✖ (ex guide dogs) *Details not confirmed for 2003* ⚑

INVERARAY CASTLE
PA32 8XE (on A83 Glasgow to Campbeltown road)
☎ 01499 302203 ▤ 01499 302421
e-mail: enquiries@inveraray-castle.com

The third Duke of Argyll engaged Roger Morris to build the present castle in 1743; in the process the old Burgh of Inveraray was demolished and a new town built nearby. The 5th Duke commissioned the beautiful interior decoration. The great armoury hall and staterooms are of particular note.
Times: Open 5 Apr -26 Oct. Apr-Jun, Sep & Oct, Mon-Thu & Sat 10-1 & 2-5.45. Sun 1-5.45; Jul & Aug, Mon-Sat 10-5.45, Sun 1-5.45. Last admission 12.30 & 5. **Fee:** * £5.50 (ch under 16 £3.50, concessions £4.50) Family ticket £14. School parties. Groups 20+. **Facilities:** P ⌘ ♿ shop ✖ (ex guide dogs) ⚑

INVERARAY JAIL
Church Sq PA32 8TX (on main Campbeltown road, A82/A83)
☎ 01499 302381 ▤ 01499 302195
e-mail: inverarayjail@btclick.com

Enter Inveraray Jail and step back in time. See furnished cells and experience prison sounds and smells. Ask the `prisoner' how to pick oakum. Turn the heavy handle of an original crank machine, take 40 winks in a hammock or listen to Matron's tales of day-to-day prison life. Visit the magnificent 1820 courtroom and hear trials in progress. Imaginative exhibitions including `Torture, Death and Damnation' and `In Prison Today'.
Times: Open all year, Nov-Mar, daily 10-5 (last admisssion 4); Apr-Oct, daily 9.30-6 (last admission 5). (Closed 25 Dec & 1 Jan). **Fee:** £5.10 (ch £2.60, pen £3.30). Family ticket £14.10. **Facilities:** P (100 yds) ♿ (wheelchair ramp at rear, induction loop in courtroom) toilets for disabled shop ⚑

🏛 KILMARTIN   Map 10 NR89
DUNADD FORT
(1m W of Kilmichael Glassary)
☎ 0131 668 8800

Dunadd was one of the ancient capitals of Dalriada from which the Celtic kingdom of Scotland was formed. Near to this prehistoric hill fort (now little more than an isolated hillock) are carvings of a boar and a footprint; these probably marked the spot where early kings were invested with their royal power.
Times: Open & accessible at all reasonable times. **Fee:** Free. **Facilities:** ✖ ⚐

🏛 LOCHAWE   Map 10 NN12
CRUACHAN POWER STATION
Dalmally PA33 1AN (A85 18m E of Oban)
☎ 01866 822618 ▤ 01866 822509

A vast cavern hidden 1km inside Ben Cruachan, which contains a 400,000-kilowatt hydro-electric power station, driven by water drawn from a high-level reservoir up the mountain. A guided tour takes you

continued

304 Argyll & Bute - City of Edinburgh

inside the mountain and reveals the generators in their underground cavern.
Times: Open Etr-Nov, daily 9.30-5 (last tour 4.15). Aug 9.30-6 (last tour 5.15) **Fee:** * £3 (ch 6-16 £1.50, concessions £2.75) **Facilities:** P ⚌ & toilets for disabled shop ✖ (ex guide dogs) 🍴

⛪ OBAN   Map 10 NM83
CAITHNESS GLASS VISITOR CENTRE
The Waterfront, Railway Pier PA34 4LW (centre of Oban on the pier beside the train station)
☎ 01631 566523   ✉ 01631 566523

Factory shop selling a wide range of perfect and slightly imperfect paperweights and glassware, as well as ceramics, crystal and jewellery.
Times: Open all year, Mon-Sat 9-5 (open late Jun-Sep). Etr-Oct Sun 10-4; **Fee:** Free. **Facilities:** P (100yds) & shop ✖ (ex guide dogs)

DUNSTAFFNAGE CASTLE
PA37 1PZ (3m N on peninsula)
☎ 01631 562465

Now ruined, this four-sided stronghold has a gatehouse, two round towers and walls 10ft thick. It was once the prison of Flora MacDonald.
Times: Open all year, Apr-Sep, daily 9.30-6.30; Oct-Mar, Sat-Wed Sun 9.30-4.30. (Closed 25-26 Dec). **Fee:** * £2.20 (ch 75p, concessions £1.60). **Facilities:** P shop 🍴

⛪ TAYNUILT   Map 10 NN03
BONAWE IRON FURNACE
PA35 1JQ (0.75m NE off B845)
☎ 01866 822432

The furnace is a restored charcoal blast-furnace for iron-smelting and making cast-iron. It was established in 1753 and worked until 1876. The works exploited the Forest of Lorne to provide charcoal for fuel.
Times: Open Apr-Sep, daily 9.30-6.30. Telephone for 2003 details **Fee:** * £2.80 (ch £1, concessions £2). **Facilities:** P & toilets for disabled shop 🍴

CITY OF EDINBURGH

⛪ BALERNO   Map 11 NT16
MALLENY GARDEN
EH14 7AF (off Lanark Rd A70)
☎ 0131 449 2283

The delightful gardens are set round a 17th-century house (not open to the public). Shrub roses, a woodland garden, and a group of four clipped yews, survivors of a group planted in 1603, are among its notable features. The National Bonsai Collection for Scotland is also at Malleny.
Times: Garden: daily 10-6 or dusk if earlier. House closed. **Fee:** Admission free to NTS Members. For other details please phone (0131) 243 9387 or check website. **Facilities:** P & ✖ (ex guide dogs) 🌿

⛪ EDINBURGH   Map 11 NT27
BRASS RUBBING CENTRE
Trinity Apse, Chalmers Close, High St EH1 1SS (on the Royal Mile)
☎ 0131 556 4364   ✉ 0131 557 3364

Housed in the 15th-century remnant of Trinity Apse, the Centre offers the chance to make your own rubbing from a wide range of replica monumental brasses and Pictish stones. Tuition is available.
Times: Open Apr-Sep, Mon-Sat 10-5 (during Edinburgh Festival Sun 12-5). **Fee:** Free. Charge for brass rubbing. **Facilities:** P (250mtrs) shop ✖ (ex guide dogs)

CAMERA OBSCURA
Castlehill, Royal Mile EH1 2LZ (next to Edinburgh Castle)
☎ 0131 226 3709   ✉ 0131 225 4239
e-mail: info@camera-obscura.co.uk
Times: Open all year, daily, Apr-Oct 9.30-6; Nov-Mar 10-5. (Closed 25 Dec). Open later Jul-Aug, phone for details. **Facilities:** P (300mtrs) shop ✖ (ex guide dogs) *Details not confirmed for 2003* 🍴

CITY ART CENTRE
2 Market St EH1 1DE (opposite rear of Waverley Stn)
☎ 0131 529 3993   ✉ 0131 529 3986
e-mail: enquiries@city-art-centre.demon.uk

The City Art Centre houses the city's permanent fine art collection and stages a constantly changing programme of temporary exhibitions from all parts of the world. It has six floors of display galleries (linked by an escalator).
Times: Open Mon-Sat 10-5 (& Sun 12-5 Jul-Aug). **Fee:** Free. Admission charged for some exhibitions. **Facilities:** P (500yds) ⚌ & (induction loop, lifts, braille signage, escalator) toilets for disabled shop ✖ (ex guide dogs) 🍴

CRAIGMILLAR CASTLE
EH16 4SY (2.5m SE, off A68)
☎ 0131 661 4445

Mary, Queen of Scots retreated to this 14th-century stronghold after the murder of Rizzio. The plot to murder Darnley, her second husband, was also hatched here. There are 16th and 17th century apartments.
Times: Open all year, Apr-Sep, daily 9.30-6.30; Oct-Mar, Mon-Sat 9.30-4.30. Sun 2-4.30. (Closed Thu pm & Fri in winter & 25-26 Dec). **Fee:** * £2.20 (ch 75p, concessions £1.60). **Facilities:** P & toilets for disabled shop 🍴

DEAN GALLERY
73 Belford Rd EH4 3DS (20 min walk from Edinburgh Haymarket stn & Princes St)
☎ 0131 624 6200   ✉ 0131 343 3250
e-mail: enquiries@natgalscot.ac.uk
Times: Open all year, Mon-Sat 10-5, Sun 12-5. Extended opening during Edinburgh Festival. (Closed 25-26 Dec). **Facilities:** P ⚌ & (ramps & lift) toilets for disabled shop ✖ (ex guide dogs) *Details not confirmed for 2003* 🍴

City of Edinburgh

Dynamic Earth
Holyrood Rd EH8 8AS (on the edge of Holyrood Park, opposite the Palace of Holyroodhouse)
☎ 0131 550 7800   ▤ 0131 550 7801
e-mail: enquiries@dynamicearth.co.uk

Dynamic Earth takes you on a fantastic journey of discovery back through time to learn why the Earth has changed. Amazing interactive displays let you see, hear, smell and feel the planet as it was in the past, as it is today and how it will be in the future.
Times: Open Apr-Oct, daily 10-6; Nov-Mar, Wed-Sat 10-5. (Closed 24-26 Dec). **Fee:** * £7.95 (ch £4.50). Family ticket (2ad & 2ch) £21.
Facilities: ℗ (charged) ⬛ ✖ licensed ♿ (audio guides, large print gallery guides) toilets for disabled shop ✖ (ex guide dogs) ⛄

Edinburgh Castle
EH1 2NG
☎ 0131 225 9846

This historic stronghold stands on the precipitous crag of Castle Rock. One of the oldest parts is the 11th-century chapel of the saintly Queen Margaret, but most of the present castle evolved later, during its stormy history of sieges and wars, and was altered again in Victorian times. The Scottish crown and other royal regalia are displayed in the Crown Room. Also notable is the Scottish National War Memorial.
Times: Open Apr-Sep, daily 9.30-6; Oct-Mar, daily 9.30-5. Last ticket sold 45 mins before closing time. (Closed 25-26 Dec). **Fee:** * £8 (ch £2, concessions £6). **Facilities:** ℗ (charged) ⬛ ✖ licensed ♿ (free transport to top of Castle Hill site) toilets for disabled shop ✖ ▮

Edinburgh Zoo
Murrayfield EH12 6TS (3m W of Edinburgh city centre on A8 towards Glasgow)
☎ 0131 334 9171   ▤ 0131 316 4050
e-mail: marketing@rzss.org.uk
Times: Open all year, Apr-Sep, daily 9-6. (Closes 4.30pm Oct-Mar).
Facilities: ℗ (charged) ⬛ ✖ licensed ♿ (wheelchair loan free, 1 helper free - phone in advance) toilets for disabled shop ✖ (ex guide dogs) *Details not confirmed for 2003* ⛄

General Register House
(East end of Princes St) EH1 3YY
☎ 0131 535 1314   ▤ 0131 535 1360
e-mail: enquiries@nas.gov.uk
Times: Open Mon-Fri 9-4.45. Exhibitions 10-4. (Closed certain BHs & part of Nov). **Facilities:** ♿ toilets for disabled shop ✖ (ex guide dogs) ⛄ *Details not confirmed for 2003* ⛄

Georgian House
7 Charlotte Square EH2 4DR (2 mins walk W end of Princes Street)
☎ 0131 226 3318   ▤ 0131 226 3318
e-mail: thegeorgianhouse@nts.org.uk

The house is part of Robert Adam's splendid north side of Charlotte Square, the epitome of Edinburgh New Town architecture. The lower floors of No 7 have been restored in the style of the early 1800s, when the house was new. There also videos of life in the New Town, and this house in particular.
Times: Open Apr-Oct, Mon-Sat 10-5, Sun 2-5. Last admission 4.30pm. **Fee:** Admission free for NTS members. For other details please phone (0131) 243 9387 or check website. **Facilities:** ℗ (100 yds) (meters, disabled directly outside) ♿ (induction loop, braille guide) shop ✖ (ex guide dogs) ⛄

Gladstone's Land
477b Lawnmarket EH1 2NT (5 mins walk from Princes Street via Mound)
☎ 0131 226 5856   ▤ 0131 226 4851

Built in 1620, this six-storey tenement, once a merchant's house, still has its arcaded front - a rare feature now. Visitors can also see unusual tempera paintings on the walls and ceilings. It is furnished as a typical 17th-century merchant's home, complete with ground-floor shop front and goods of the period.
Times: 25 Mar-27 Oct, Mon-Sat, 10-5, Sun 1-5 **Fee:** Admission free to NTS members. For other details please phone 0131 243 9387 or check website. **Facilities:** ℗ (440yds) (outside for disabled) ♿ (tours for the blind can be arranged) shop ✖ (ex guide dogs) ⛄

John Knox House
The Netherbow, 43-45 High St EH1 1SR (between The Castle and Holyrood House)
☎ 0131 556 9579   ▤ 0131 557 5224

John Knox, the Reformer is said to have died in the house, which was built by the goldsmith to Mary, Queen of Scots. Renovation work has revealed the original floor in the Oak Room, and a magnificent painted ceiling.
Times: Open all year, Mon-Sat 10-5 & Sun in Jul-Aug 12-4. (Closed Xmas). Closed for part of 2003 for refurbishment. Phone for details. **Fee:** £2.25 (ch 75p, under 7's free, concessions £1.75). **Facilities:** ℗ (paying car park) ⬛ ♿ (House on 3 levels) toilets for disabled shop ✖ (ex guide dogs) ⛄

Lauriston Castle
Cramond Rd South, Davidson's Mains EH4 6AG (NW outskirts of Edinburgh, 1m E of Cramond)
☎ 0131 336 2060   ▤ 0131 557 3346

The castle is a late 16th-century tower house with 19th-century additions but is most notable as a classic example of the Edwardian age. It has a beautifully preserved Edwardian interior and the feel of a country house, and the spacious grounds are very pleasant.
Times: Open all year by guided tour only; Apr-Oct, 11-1 & 2-5; Nov-Mar, wknds 2-4. (Closed Fri). **Fee:** * £4 (ch £3). **Facilities:** ℗ ♿ toilets for disabled shop ✖ (ex guide dogs)

Museum of Childhood
42 High St Royal Mile EH1 1TG (on the Royal Mile)
☎ 0131 529 4142   ▤ 0131 558 3103

One of the first museums of its kind, it was reopened after major expansion. It has a wonderful collection of toys, games and other belongings of children through

continued

City of Edinburgh

the ages, to delight visitors both old and young. Ring for details of special events.
Times: Open all year, Mon-Sat, Jun-Sep 10-6; Oct-May 10-5; (also Sun 12-5 in Jul-Aug). **Fee:** Free. **Facilities:** P & (3 floors only) toilets for disabled shop ✱ (ex guide dogs)

MUSEUM OF EDINBURGH
142 Canongate, Royal Mile EH8 8DD (on the Royal Mile)
☎ 0131 529 4143 ▤ 0131 557 3346

Housed in one of the best-preserved 16th-century buildings in the Old Town. It was built in 1570 and later became the headquarters of the Incorporation of Hammermen. Now a museum of local history, it has collections of silver, glassware, pottery, and street signs.
Times: Open all year, Mon-Sat 10-5. (During Festival period only, Sun 2-5). **Fee:** Free. **Facilities:** P (200yds) & shop ✱ (ex guide dogs)

MUSEUM OF SCOTLAND
Chambers St EH1 1JF
☎ 0131 247 4422 ▤ 0131 220 4819
e-mail: info@nms.ac.uk

The museum is a striking landmark in Edinburgh's historic Old Town. It houses more than 10,000 of the nation's most precious artefacts, as well as everyday objects which throw light on life in Scotland through the ages. Admission to the Royal Museum which is adjacent to the Museum of Scotland, is also free.
Times: Open all year - Mon, Wed-Sat 10-5, Tue 10-8 & Sun 12-5. **Fee:** Free. **Facilities:** P ⌘ ✗ licensed & toilets for disabled shop ✱ (ex guide dogs) ⊜

NATIONAL GALLERY OF SCOTLAND
The Mound EH2 2EL (off Princes Street)
☎ 0131 624 6200 ▤ 0131 343 3250
e-mail: enquiries@natgalscot.ac.uk
Times: Open all year, Mon-Sat 10-5, Sun 12-5. Extended opening hours during the Edinburgh Festival period. (Closed 25-26 Dec).
Facilities: P (150yds) & (ramps & lift, room A1 not accessible) toilets for disabled shop ✱ (ex guide dogs) *Details not confirmed for 2003* ⊜

NATIONAL WAR MUSEUM OF SCOTLAND
Edinburgh Castle EH1 2NG
☎ 0131 225 7534 ▤ 0131 225 3848
e-mail: info@nms.ac.uk

Explore the Scottish experience of war and military service over the last 400 years.
Times: Open all year, Apr-Oct, Mon-Sat 9.30-6, Sun 11-6; Nov-Mar, Mon-Sat 9.30-5, Sun 12.30-5 **Fee:** Free admission after paying entrance fee to Castle. **Facilities:** P & toilets for disabled shop ✱

NELSON MONUMENT
Calton Hill (Overlooking East end of city)
☎ 0131 556 2716 ▤ 0131 557 3346

Designed in 1807 the monument dominates the east end of Princes Street. The views are superb, and every day except Sunday the time ball drops at 1pm as the gun at the castle goes off.
Times: Open all year, Apr-Sep, Mon 1-6 & Tue-Sat 10-6; Oct-Mar Mon-Sat 10-3. **Fee:** * £2 **Facilities:** ▣ shop ✱ (ex guide dogs)

PALACE OF HOLYROODHOUSE
EH8 8DX (at east end of Royal Mile)
☎ 020 7321 2233 ▤ 020 7930 9625
e-mail: information@royalcollection.org.uk

The Palace grew from the guest house of the Abbey of the Holyrood, said to have been founded by David I after a miraculous apparition. Mary, Queen of Scots had her court here from 1561 to 1567, and 'Bonnie' Prince Charlie held levees at the Palace during his occupation of Edinburgh. The Palace is still used by the Royal Family, but can be visited when they are not in residence. The picture gallery is notable for its series of Scottish monarchs.
Times: Open daily, Apr-Oct 9.30-6 (last admission 5.15); Nov-Mar 9.30-4.30 (last admission 3.45). Closed 25-26 Dec and when Queen in residence. **Fee:** * £6.50 (ch under 17 £3.30, pen £5). Family ticket (2ad+2ch) £16.30. Under 5 free **Facilities:** ▣ (charged) & (first floor by lift, wheelchair available) toilets for disabled shop ✱ (ex guide dogs) ⊜

PARLIAMENT HOUSE
Supreme Courts, 2-11 Parliament Square EH1 1RQ (behind St Giles Cathedral)
☎ 0131 225 2595 ▤ 0131 240 6755

Scotland's independent parliament last sat in 1707, in this 17th-century building hidden behind an 1829 façade, now the seat of the Supreme Law Courts of Scotland. A large stained glass window depicts the inauguration of the Court of Session in 1540.
Times: Open all year, Mon-Fri 10-4. **Fee:** Free. **Facilities:** P (400 mtrs) metered parking in high street ⌘ ✗ & toilets for disabled ✱ (ex guide dogs)

THE PEOPLE'S STORY
Canongate Tolbooth, 163 Canongate EH8 8BN (on the Royal Mile)
☎ 0131 529 4057 ▤ 0131 557 3439

The museum, housed in the 16th-century tolbooth, tells the story of the ordinary people of Edinburgh from the late 18th century to the present day. Reconstructions include a prison cell, 1930's pub and 1940's kitchen supported by photographs, displays, sounds and smells.
Times: Open, Mon-Sat 10-5. Also, open Sun during Edinburgh Festival 2-5. **Fee:** Free. **Facilities:** P (100yds) meters & (first floor accessible by lift) toilets for disabled shop ✱ (ex guide dogs)

ROYAL BOTANIC GARDEN EDINBURGH
20A Inverleith Row EH3 5LR (1m N of city centre)
☎ 0131 552 7171 ▤ 0131 248 2901
e-mail: info@rbge.org.uk

Established in 1670, on an area the size of a tennis court, the Garden is now over 70 acres of beautifully landscaped grounds. Spectacular features include the

continued

City of Edinburgh

Rock Garden, the Pringle Chinese Collection. The amazing glasshouse experience features Britain's tallest palm house and the magnificent woodland gardens and arboretum.
Times: Open all year, daily; Apr-Aug & Sep, 10-7; Mar & Oct, 10-6; Nov-Feb, 10-4. (Closed 25 Dec & 1 Jan). Facilities close 30 mins before the Garden. **Fee:** Free. Donations welcome. **Facilities:** P (restricted at certain times) 🍴 ✗ licensed ♿ (wheelchairs available at east/west gates) toilets for disabled shop garden centre 🐕 (ex guide dogs) 📢

ROYAL MUSEUM
Chambers St EH1 1JF (5min from Edinburgh Castle and the Royal Mile)
☎ 0131 247 4219 (info)   📠 0131 220 4819
e-mail: info@nms.ac.uk

This magnificent museum houses extensive international collections covering the Decorative Arts, Natural History, Science, Technology and Working Life, and Geology. Temporary exhibitions, films, lectures and concerts take place throughout the year.
Times: Open all year, Mon-Sat 10-5, Sun 12-5 (Tue late opening till 8). (Closed 25 Dec. Phone for times on 26 Dec/1 Jan). **Fee:** Free.
Facilities: P 🍴 ✗ licensed ♿ (induction loops) toilets for disabled shop 🐕 (ex guide dogs) 📢

ROYAL OBSERVATORY VISITOR CENTRE
Blackford Hill EH9 3HJ
☎ 0131 668 8405   📠 0131 668 8429
e-mail: vis@roe.ac.uk
Times: Open all year, Mon-Sat 10-5, Sun noon-5. (Closed 22 Dec-2 Jan). **Facilities:** P 🍴 ✗ ♿ (lift, no access to history zone & dome telescopes) toilets for disabled shop 🐕 (ex guide dogs) *Details not confirmed for 2003* 📢

THE ROYAL YACHT BRITANNIA
Ocean Dr, Leith EH6 6JJ (Situated within Ocean Terminal)
☎ 0131 555 5566   📠 0131 555 8835
e-mail: enquiries@tryb.co.uk

Visit the Royal Yacht Britannia, now in Edinburgh's historic port of Leith. The experience starts in the Visitor Centre where you can discover Britannia's fascinating story. Then step aboard for a self-led audio tour which takes you around five decks giving you a unique insight into what life was like for the Royal Family, Officers and Yachtsmen. Highlights include the State Apartments, Admirals Cabin, Engine Room, Laundry, Sick Bay and Royal Marine Barracks.
Times: Open Jan-Mar & Oct-Dec: 10-3.30 (close 5). Apr-Sep 9.30-4.30 (close 6) **Fee:** * £7.75 (ch under 5 free, 5-17 £3.75, pen £5.95). Family ticket (2adults & 3 ch) £20. **Facilities:** P ♿ (lift to ship, all areas ramped) toilets for disabled shop 🐕 (ex guide dogs) 📢

SCOTCH WHISKY HERITAGE CENTRE
354 Castlehill, The Royal Mile EH1 2NE
☎ 0131 220 0441   📠 0131 220 6288
e-mail: enquiry@whisky-heritage.co.uk

This fascinating heritage centre reveals the history of the Scottish Whisky industry. The tour has four main areas: The Making of Scotch Whisky, The Distillery, The Blender's Ghost, and Whisky Barrel Ride. The Whisky Bond Bar has over 270 different whiskies available.
Times: Open daily, 10-5.30 (extended in summer). (Closed 25 Dec).
Fee: £6.95 (ch 5-17 £3.40, concessions £4.75). Family ticket £15
Facilities: P (0.25m) 🍴 ♿ (braille script) toilets for disabled shop 🐕 (ex guide dogs) 📢

SCOTTISH NATIONAL GALLERY OF MODERN ART
Belford Rd EH4 3DR (in the West End, 20min walk from Haymarket station)
☎ 0131 624 6200   📠 0131 343 3250
e-mail: enquiries@natgalscot.ac.uk
Times: Open all year, Mon-Sat 10-5 & Sun 12-5. Extended opening hours during the Edinburgh Festival. (Closed 25-26 Dec). **Facilities:** P 🍴 ♿ (ramps & lift) toilets for disabled shop 🐕 (ex guide dogs) *Details not confirmed for 2003* 📢

SCOTTISH NATIONAL PORTRAIT GALLERY
1 Queen St EH2 1JD (parallel to Princes Street, just behind St Andrew Square)
☎ 0131 624 6200   📠 0131 558 3691
e-mail: enquiries@natgalscot.ac.uk
Times: Open all year, daily, Mon-Sat 10-5, Sun 12-5. Extended opening hours during the Edinburgh Festival. (Closed 25-26 Dec).
Facilities: P (200yds) 🍴 ♿ (ramps & lift) toilets for disabled shop 🐕 (ex guide dogs) *Details not confirmed for 2003* 📢

WEST REGISTER HOUSE
Charlotte Square EH1 3YY
☎ 0131 535 1314   📠 0131 535 1360
e-mail: enquiries@nas.gov.uk
Times: Open Mon-Fri 9-4.45. Exhibitions 10-4. (Closed certain PHs & part of Nov). **Facilities:** ♿ toilets for disabled shop 🐕 (ex guide dogs) 🚍 *Details not confirmed for 2003* 📢

THE WRITERS' MUSEUM
Lady Stair's House, Lady Stair's Close, Lawnmarket EH1 2PA (off the Royal Mile)
☎ 0131 529 4901   📠 0131 557 3346
e-mail: enquiries@writersmuseum.demon.co.uk

Situated in the historic Lady Stair's House which dates

continued

from 1622, the museum houses various objects associated with Robert Burns, Sir Walter Scott and Robert Louis Stevenson. Temporary exhibitions are planned throughout the year.
Times: Open all year, Mon-Sat 10-5. (During Festival period only, Sun 2-5). **Fee:** Free. **Facilities:** P (500mtrs) shop ✖ (ex guide dogs)

🏛 GOGAR Map 11 NT17
SUNTRAP GARDEN
43 Gogarbank EH12 9BY (between A8 & A71 W of city bypass)
☎ 0131 339 7283 📠 0131 339 2891
e-mail: suntrap@btopenworld.com

The three-acre garden comprises of many gardens within a single garden, including Italian, Rock, Peat and Woodland. Please refer to the Garden Guide under section headed Garden.
Times: Open all year, Oct-Apr, 10-4; May-Sep, 10-6 **Fee:** £1 (accompanied ch and NT members free). **Facilities:** P & toilets for disabled garden centre ✖ (ex on lead)

🏛 SOUTH QUEENSFERRY Map 11 NT17
DALMENY HOUSE
EH30 9TQ
☎ 0131 331 1888 📠 0131 331 1788
e-mail: events@dalmeny.co.uk
Times: Open Jul-Aug, Sun, Mon & Tue 2-5.30. Last admission 4.45. Open other times by arrangement for groups. **Facilities:** P 🍴 & toilets for disabled ✖ (ex guide dogs or in grounds) *Details not confirmed for 2003*

HOPETOUN HOUSE
EH30 9SL (2m W of Forth Road Bridge, off A904)
☎ 0131 331 2451 📠 0131 319 1885
e-mail: marketing@hopetounhouse.com

Hopetoun House at South Queensferry is just a short drive from Edinburgh and has all the ingredients for a great family day out. Built some 300 years ago, it is a delight to wander the corridors and historical rooms of one of the most splendid examples of the work of Scottish architects Sir William Bruce and William Adam. It shows some of the finest examples in Scotland of carving, wainscoting and ceiling painting. With 100 acres of parkland including a deep park, the gardens are a colourful carpet of seasonal flowers.
Times: Open daily Apr-Sep **Fee:** * £5.30 (ch £2.70). Grounds £2.90 (ch £1.70). **Facilities:** P 🍴 ✖ licensed & (ramps) toilets for disabled ✖ (ex on leads) 🍽

INCHCOLM ABBEY
Inchcolm Island (1.5m S of Aberdour Access by ferry Apr-Sep)
☎ 01383 823332

Situated on a green island on the Firth of Forth, the Augustinian abbey was founded in about 1192 by Alexander I. The well-preserved remains include a fine 13th-century octagonal chapter house and a 13th-century wall painting.
Times: Open Apr-Sep, daily 9.30-6.30. **Fee:** * £2.80 (ch £1, concessions £2). Additional charge for ferry trip. **Facilities:** & toilets for disabled shop ✖ 🍽

QUEENSFERRY MUSEUM
53 High St EH30 9HP
☎ 0131 331 5545 📠 0131 557 3346

The museum commands magnificent views of the two great bridges spanning the Forth and traces the history of the people of Queensferry and Dalmeny, the historic passage to Fife, the construction of the rail and road bridges, and the wildlife of the Forth estuary. An ancient annual custom, in August, is Burry Man, who is clad from head to toe in burrs, and parades through the town.
Times: Open all year, Mon & Thu-Sat 10-1, 2.15-5 (Sun noon-5) **Fee:** Free. **Facilities:** P (0.25m) shop ✖ (ex guide dogs)

CITY OF GLASGOW

🏛 GLASGOW Map 11 NS56
BURRELL COLLECTION
Pollok Country Park G43 1AT (2m S of city centre)
☎ 0141 649 7151 📠 0141 636 0086
Times: Open all year, Mon-Sat 10-5, Sun 11-5. **Facilities:** P (charged) ✖ licensed & (wheelchairs available, tape guides for blind) toilets for disabled shop ✖ *Details not confirmed for 2003*

CATHEDRAL
Castle St G4 0QZ
☎ 0141 552 6891

The most complete medieval cathedral surviving on the Scottish mainland, founded in the 6th century by St Kentigern, better known as Mungo ('dear one'), Glasgow's patron saint, and dates from the 13th and 14th centuries. The Cathedral was threatened at the time of the Reformation, but the city's trade guilds formed an armed guard to ensure that no damage was done.
Times: Open all year, Apr-Sep, Mon-Sat 9.30-6, Sun 2-5; Oct-Mar, Mon-Sat 9.30-4, Sun 2-4. (Closed 25-26 Dec). **Fee:** Free. **Facilities:** & shop ✖ 🍽

CLYDEBUILT
Braehead Shopping Centre, King Inch Rd G51 4BN (M8 junct 25A, 26, follow signs for Braehead Shopping Centre)
☎ 0141 886 1013 📠 0141 886 1015
e-mail: clydebuilt@tinyworld.co.uk

On the banks of the River Clyde, home of the Scottish shipbuilding industry, visitors can discover how Glasgow's famous ships were built, from the design stages through to the launch. There are also displays on the textile and cotton industries, iron and steel, and tobacco. Hands-on activities allow you to operate a real

continued

City of Glasgow

ship's engine, become a ship's riveter, and steer a virtual ship up the Clyde.
Times: Open Mon-Thu & Sat 10-6; Sun 11-5. (Closed Fri) **Fee:** * £3.50 (ch & concessions £1.75). Family ticket £8 **Facilities:** P & lift toilets for disabled shop ✈ (ex guide dogs)

GALLERY OF MODERN ART
Queen St G1 3AZ
☎ 0141 229 1996 📧 0141 204 5316
Times: Open all year, Mon-Thu & Sat 10-5, Fri & Sun 11-5. **Facilities:** P (200yds) ✗ licensed & toilets for disabled shop ✈ *Details not confirmed for 2003*

GLASGOW ART GALLERY & MUSEUM
Kelvingrove G3 8AG (1m W of city centre)
☎ 0141 287 2699 📧 0141 287 2690
Times: Open all year, Mon-Thu & Sat 10-5; Fri & Sun 11-5. **Facilities:** P 🍽 ✗ licensed & toilets for disabled shop ✈ *Details not confirmed for 2003*

GLASGOW BOTANIC GARDENS
730 Great Western Rd G12 0UE (From M8 junct 17 onto A82)
☎ 0141 334 2422 📧 0141 339 6964
Home of the national collections of Dendrobium Orchids, Begonias and tree ferns. The Victorian Kibble Palace has marble statuary secreted among the plant collections. The Gardens consist of an arboretum, herbaceous borders, an herb garden and unusual vegetables.
Times: Open all year. Gardens open daily 7am-dusk, Glasshouses 10-4.45 (4.15 in winter). **Fee:** Free. **Facilities:** P street parking 🍽 & toilets for disabled (ex in grounds)

GLASGOW SCIENCE CENTRE
50 Pacific Quay G51 1EA
☎ 0141 420 5000 📧 0141 420 5001
e-mail: admin@gsc.org.uk
Times: Open daily, all year. **Facilities:** P 🍽 & toilets for disabled shop *Details not confirmed for 2003*

GREENBANK GARDEN
Flenders Rd, Clarkston G76 8RB (off A726 on southern outskirts of the city)
☎ 0141 639 3281
The spacious, walled woodland gardens are attractively laid out in the grounds of an elegant Georgian house, and best seen between April and October. A wide range of flowers and shrubs are grown, with the idea of helping private gardeners to look at possibilities for their own gardens. A greenhouse and garden designed for the disabled gardener also displays specialised tools.
Times: Open daily 10-sunset **Fee:** Admission free to NTS members. For other details please phone (0131) 243 9387 or check website **Facilities:** P 🍽 & (wheelchairs available) toilets for disabled shop (& plant sales) ✈ (ex guide dogs) 🌱

HOUSE FOR AN ART LOVER
10 Dumbreck Rd, Bellahouston Park G41 5BW (Exit M8 W junct 23 marked B768, left at top of slip road onto Dumbreck Road. Bellahouston Park on right)
☎ 0141 353 4770 📧 0141 353 4771
e-mail: info@houseforanartlover.co.uk
Originally designed by Glasgow's most celebrated architect, Charles Rennie Mackintosh, in 1901, this unusual cultural, corporate and academic resource began construction in 1989 and was completed in 1996. Contains art galleries and rooms that can be hired for conferences and events.
Times: Open Apr-Sep, Sun-Thu 10-4 & Sat 10-3; Oct-Mar, Sat-Sun 10-4, telephone for wkday opening details. **Fee:** * £3.50 (ch under 10 free, concessions £2.50). **Facilities:** P 🍽 ✗ licensed & (lift to 2nd floor) toilets for disabled shop ✈ (ex guide dogs) 🌱

HUNTERIAN ART GALLERY
The University of Glasgow G12 8QQ
☎ 0141 330 5431 📧 0141 330 3618
e-mail: hunter@museum.gla.ac.uk
Times: Open all year. Main gallery Mon-Sat 9.30-5. Mackintosh House Mon-Sat 9.30-12.30 & 1.30-5. Telephone for BH closures. **Facilities:** P (500 yds) (pay & display) & (lift, wheelchair available) toilets for disabled shop ✈ (ex guide dogs) *Details not confirmed for 2003* 🌱

HUNTERIAN MUSEUM
The University of Glasgow G12 8QQ (2m W of city centre)
☎ 0141 330 4221 📧 0141 330 3617
e-mail: rpurss@museum.gla.ac.uk
Times: Open all year, Mon-Sat 9.30-5. (Closed certain BH's phone for details). **Facilities:** P (100yds) & (access by lift by prior arrangement) toilets for disabled shop ✈ (ex guide dogs) *Details not confirmed for 2003* 🌱

HUTCHESONS' HALL
158 Ingram St G1 1EJ (near SE corner of George Square)
☎ 0141 552 8391 📧 0141 552 7031
e-mail: hutchesonshall@nts.org.uk
This handsome early 19th-century building was designed by David Hamilton and houses a visitor centre and shop. There is a video about Glasgow's merchant city, and the Hall can be booked for functions. Telephone for details of concerts, recitals, etc.
Times: Gallery: open Mon-Sat, 10-5. Closed 24 Dec-21 Jan. Hall: open subject to functions. **Fee:** Free. **Facilities:** P (on street) (meters)(outside for disabled) & toilets for disabled shop ✈ 🌱

McLELLAN GALLERIES
270 Sauchiehall St G2 3EH
☎ 0141 331 1854 📧 0141 332 9957
Times: Open Mon-Thu & Sat 10-5, Fri & Sun 11-5. Closed 25-26 Dec & 1-2 Jan. **Facilities:** P (500mtrs) & (assistance available) toilets for disabled shop ✈ *Details not confirmed for 2003* 🌱

City of Glasgow - Clackmannanshire

Museum of Transport
Kelvin Hall, 1 Bunhouse Rd G3 8DP (1.5m W of city centre)
☎ 0141 287 2000 ▤ 0141 287 2692
Times: Open all year, Mon-Sat 10-5, Sun 11-5. **Facilities:** P (charged) ✗ licensed ♿ (assistance available) toilets for disabled shop ✱ Details not confirmed for 2003

People's Palace
Glasgow Green G40 1AT (1m SE of city centre)
☎ 0141 554 0223 ▤ 0141 550 0892
Times: Phone for details of opening times. **Facilities:** P ⏸ ♿ toilets for disabled shop garden centre ✱ Details not confirmed for 2003

Pollok House
Pollok Country Park G43 1AT (2m S of city centre)
☎ 0141 616 6410 ▤ 0141 649 0823
e-mail: pollokhouse@nts.org.uk

Given to the city at the same time as the land for Pollok Country Park, the house contains the remarkable Stirling Maxwell collection of Spanish paintings, including works by El Greco, Murillo and Goya. Silver, ceramics and furniture collected by the family over the generations are also on display.
Times: House: open daily 10-5, closed 25/26 Dec & 1/2 Jan. Gardens open all year daily. **Fee:** Admission free to NTS members. For other details please phone (0131) 243 9387 or check website. **Facilities:** P ⏸ ♿ shop ✱

Provand's Lordship
3 Castle St G4 0RB (1m E of city centre)
☎ 0141 552 8819 ▤ 0141 552 4744
Times: Open all year, Mon-Sat 10-5, Sun 11-5. **Facilities:** P shop ✱ Details not confirmed for 2003

St Mungo Religious Life & Art Museum
2 Castle St G4 0RH (1m NE of city centre)
☎ 0141 553 2557 ▤ 0141 552 4744
Times: Open all year, Mon-Sat 10-5; Sun 11-5. **Facilities:** P (charged) ⏸ ♿ (taped information & lift) toilets for disabled shop ✱ Details not confirmed for 2003

The Tall Ship at Glasgow Harbour
100 Stobcross Rd G3 8QQ (from M8 junct 19 onto A814 follow signs for 'the tall ship')
☎ 0141 222 2513 ▤ 0141 222 2536 **2 for 1**
e-mail: info@thetallship.com

Visit The Tall Ship at Glasgow Harbour and step back in time to the days of sail. Experience Glasgow's maritime history at first hand and explore the UK's only remaining Clyde-built sailing ship, the Glenlee. Exhibitions on board and in our visitor centre on the quayside tell the story of the ship and the Glasgow harbour area. If you have ever wondered what it would have been like to be a sailor on a tall ship, this is your chance to find out! Children can have fun by joining in the hunt for Jock, the ship's cat. An unmissable experience, The Tall Ship offers guided tours, changing exhibitions, children's activities, a nautical gift shop and pier 17 restaurant.
Times: Open daily Mar-Oct 10-5, Nov-Feb 11-4. **Fee:** * £4.50 (concessions £3.25, 1 ch free with paying adult/concession, additional ch £2.50). **Facilities:** P ⏸ ✗ licensed ♿ toilets for disabled shop 🍴

Tenement House
145 Buccleuch St, Garnethill G3 6QN (N of Charing Cross)
☎ 0141 333 0183
e-mail: tenementhouse@nts.org.uk

This shows an unsung but once-typical side of Glasgow life: it is a first-floor flat, built in 1892, with a parlour, bedroom, kitchen and bathroom, furnished with the original recess beds, kitchen range, sink, and coal bunker, among other articles. The home of Agnes Toward from 1911 to 1965, the flat was bought by an actress who preserved it as a `time capsule'. The contents vividly portray the life of one section of Glasgow society.
Times: Open Mar-27 Oct, daily 2-5. **Fee:** Admission free to NTS members. For other details please phone (0131) 243 9387 or check website. **Facilities:** P (100yds) (restricted, recommend parking in town) (braille guide) ✱ (ex guide dogs) ☕

University of Glasgow Visitor Centre
University Av G12 8QQ (M8 junct 19 (E) or junct 18(W))
☎ 0141 330 5511 ▤ 0141 330 5225
e-mail: visitorcentre@gla.ac.uk

The Visitor Centre is spacious and pleasant, with leaflets, publications and video displays explaining how the university works and its history, plus what courses are available and which university events are open to the public. It forms the starting point for guided tours of the university's historic attractions, including the Hunterian Museum, Memorial Chapel, Bute and Randolph Halls, Professors' Square and Lion and Unicorn Staircase.
Times: Open all year, Mon-Sat 9.30-5. Also May-Sep, Sun 2-5. In summer guided tours of the university start from the Visitor Centre at 2pm on Mon- Sat, telephone 0141 330 5511. **Fee:** Free. Charge made for tour. **Facilities:** P (880yds) ⏸ ♿ toilets for disabled shop ✱ 🍴

CLACKMANNANSHIRE

ALLOA   Map 11 NS89
Alloa Tower
Alloa Park FK10 1PP (on A907)
☎ 01259 211701 ▤ 01259 218744

Beautifully restored, the tower, completed in 1467, is the only remaining part of the ancestral home of the Earls of Mar. The structure retains rare medieval features, notably the complete timber roof structure and groin vaulting. A superb loan collection of portraits and chattels of the Erskine family includes paintings by Raeburn.
Times: Open 25 Mar-27 Oct, daily 1-5. **Fee:** Admission free to NTS members. For other details please phone (0131) 243 9387 or check website. **Facilities:** P ♿ toilets for disabled ✱ ☕

ALVA
Map 11 NS89
MILL TRAIL VISITOR CENTRE
Glentana Mill, West Stirling St FK12 5EN (on A91 approx 8m E of Stirling)
☎ 01259 769696 📠 01259 763100

In the heart of Scotland's woollen mill country, the Centre recounts the history of Scotland's woollen and tweed traditions, and features machines from spinning wheels to large motorised looms of the type in use today. Hear 12 year old Mary describe her working day as a mill girl 150 years ago, and then contrast her story with our modern working woollen mill. Factory bargains and local crafts. Tourist information centre, café.
Times: Open all year, Jan-Jun 10-5; Jul-Aug 9-5; Sep-Dec 10-5. **Fee:** Free. **Facilities:** 📒 🍴 ♿ toilets for disabled shop 🐕 (ex guide dogs) 🎧

DOLLAR
Map 11 NS99
CASTLE CAMPBELL
FK14 7PP (10m E of Stirling on A91)
☎ 01259 742408

Traditionally known as the 'Castle of Gloom', the 15th to 17th-century tower stands in the picturesque Ochil Hills, gives wonderful views, and can be reached by a walk through the magnificent Dollar Glen. Care must be taken in or after rain when the path may be dangerous.
Times: Open all year, Apr-Sep, daily 9.30-6.30; Oct-Mar, Mon-Sat 9.30-4.30, Sun 2-4.30. (Closed Thu & Fri in winter & 25-26 Dec). **Fee:** * £2.80 (ch £1, concessions £2). **Facilities:** 📒 🍴 shop 🎧 🐾

DUMFRIES & GALLOWAY

ARDWELL
Map 10 NX14
ARDWELL HOUSE GARDENS
DG9 9LY (10m S of Stranraer, on A716)
☎ 01776 860227 📠 01776 860288

Country house gardens and grounds with flowering shrubs and woodland walks. Plants for sale. House not open to the public.
Times: Open Mar-Oct, 10-5. Walled garden & greenhouses close at 5pm. **Fee:** * £2 (ch & pen £1). **Facilities:** 📒 garden centre

CAERLAVEROCK
Map 11 NY06
CAERLAVEROCK CASTLE
Glencaple DG1 4RU (8m SE of Dumfries, on B725)
☎ 01387 770244

This ancient seat of the Maxwell family is a splendid medieval stronghold dating back to the 13th century. It has high walls and round towers, with machicolations added in the 15th century.
Times: Open all year, Apr-Sep, daily 9.30-6.30; Oct-Mar, Mon-Sat 9.30-4.30, Sun 2-4.30. (Closed Thu pm, Fri & Sun am in winter). Please telephone for 2003 details. **Fee:** * £2.80 (ch £1, concessions £2) **Facilities:** 📒 🍴 ♿ toilets for disabled shop 🐾

WWT CAERLAVEROCK
Eastpark Farm DG1 4RS (9m SE of Dumfries, signposted from A75)
☎ 01387 770200 📠 01387 770539
e-mail: caerlaverock@wwt.org.uk

2 for 1

This internationally important wetland is the winter habitat of the entire Svalbard population of Barnacle Geese which spends the winter on the Solway Firth. Observation facilities include twenty hides, three towers and a heated observatory. A wide variety of other wildlife can be seen, notably the rare Natterjack Toad and a family of Barn Owls which can be observed via CCTV.
Times: Open daily 10-5. (Closed 25 Dec). **Fee:** * £4 (ch £2.50 & concessions £3.25). Family ticket £10.50 **Facilities:** 📒 🍴 ♿ toilets for disabled shop 🐕 (ex guide dogs)

CARDONESS CASTLE
Map 11 NX55
CARDONESS CASTLE
DG7 2EH (1m SW of Gatehouse of Fleet off A75)
☎ 01557 814427

A 15th-century stronghold overlooking the Water of Fleet. It was once the home of the McCullochs of Galloway. The architectural details inside the tower are of very high quality.
Times: Open all year, Apr-Sep, daily 9.30-6.30; Oct-Mar, wknds only. (Closed 25-26 Dec). **Fee:** * £2.20 (ch 75p, concessions £1.60). phone for 2003 details **Facilities:** 📒 shop 🐾

CASTLE DOUGLAS
Map 11 NX76
THREAVE CASTLE
DG7 1RX (3m W on A75)
☎ 0411 223101

Archibald the Grim built this lonely castle in the late 14th century. It stands on an islet in the River Dee, and is four storeys high with round towers guarding the outer wall. The island is reached by boat.
Times: Open Apr-Sep, daily 9.30-6.30. Telephone for 2003 details **Fee:** * £2.20 (ch 75p, concessions £1.60). Charge includes ferry trip.phone for 2003 details **Facilities:** 📒 🐕 🐾

THREAVE GARDEN & ESTATE
DG7 1RX (1m W of Castle Douglas off A75)
☎ 01556 502575 📠 01556 502683
e-mail: threave@nts.org.uk

The best time to visit is in spring when there is a dazzling display of daffodils. The garden is a delight in all seasons, however, and is home to the National Trust for Scotland's School of Practical Gardening.
Times: Estate & Garden: daily 9.30-sunset. Walled Garden & Glasshouse daily 9.30-5 **Fee:** Free entry for National Trust for Scotland members. For other admission details please phone (0131) 243 9387 or check website. **Facilities:** 📒 🍴 licensed ♿ (wheelchairs available incl. electric wheelchair) toilets for disabled shop garden centre 🐕 (ex guide dogs) 🎧

CREETOWN
CREETOWN GEM ROCK MUSEUM
Chain Rd DG8 7HJ (follow signs from A75 at Creetown bypass)
☎ 01671 820357 & 820554
📠 01671 820554
e-mail: gem.rock@btinternet.com

`2 for 1`

A spectacular collection of gems, crystals, minerals and fossils. Interactive computer displays provide an opportunity to learn more, and audiovisual displays explain how minerals are formed. World-class British specimens e.g. flounte, calcite and hemalite.
Times: Open Etr-Sep, daily 9.30-5.30; Oct-Nov & Mar-Etr, daily 10-4; Dec-Feb, wknds 10-4 or by appointment wkdays. (Closed 23 Dec-Jan).
Fee: * £2.90 (ch £1.75, concessions £2.40). Family ticket £7.55 (2ad+3ch). Party. **Facilities:** P 🍴 ♿ toilets for disabled shop ✈ (ex guide dogs) 🐕

DRUMCOLTRAN TOWER Map 11 NX86
DRUMCOLTRAN TOWER
(7m NE of Dalbeattie)
☎ 0131 668 8800

This 16th-century tower house stands three storeys high and has a simple, functional design.
Times: Open at any reasonable time. **Fee:** Free. **Facilities:** ✈ 🐕

DUMFRIES Map 11 NX97
BURNS HOUSE
Burns St DG1 2PS
☎ 01387 255297   📠 01387 265081
e-mail: info@dumfriesmuseum.demon.co.uk

It was here that Robert Burns spent the last three years of his short life; he died here in 1796. The house retains much of its 18th-century character and contains many fascinating items connected with the poet. There is the chair in which he wrote his last poems, many original letters and manuscripts, and the famous Kilmarnock and Edinburgh editions of his work.
Times: Open all year, Apr-Sep, Mon-Sat 10-5, Sun 2-5; Oct-Mar Tue-Sat 10-1 & 2-5. **Fee:** Free. **Facilities:** P (100yds) shop

BURNS MAUSOLEUM
St Michael's Churchyard
☎ 01387 255297   📠 01387 265081
e-mail: info@dumfriesmuseum.demon.co.uk

The mausoleum is in the form of a Greek temple, and contains the tombs of Robert Burns, his wife Jean Armour, and their five sons. A sculptured group shows the Muse of Poetry flinging her cloak over Burns at the plough.
Times: Unrestricted access. **Fee:** Free. **Facilities:** P (100yds) ♿ (visitors with mobility difficulties tel 01387 255297)

DUMFRIES MUSEUM & CAMERA OBSCURA
The Observatory DG2 7SW (Take A75 from S Carlisle or SW from Castle Douglas, museum situated in Maxwellton area)
☎ 01387 253374
📠 01387 265081
e-mail: dumfriesmuseum@dumgal.gov.uk

`2 for 1`

Situated in and around the 18th-century windmill tower, the museum's collections were started over 150 years ago and exhibitions trace the history of the people and landscape of Dumfries and Galloway. The Camera Obscura is to be found on the top floor of the windmill tower.
Times: Open all year, Apr-Sep Mon-Sat 10-5, Sun, 2-5; Oct-Mar, Tue-Sat 10-1 & 2-5. **Fee:** * Free except Camera Obscura £1.50 (concessions 75p) **Facilities:** P ♿ (camera obscura not accessible, parking available) toilets for disabled shop

OLD BRIDGE HOUSE MUSEUM
Mill Rd DG2 7BE
☎ 01387 256904   📠 01387 265081
e-mail: info@dumfriesmuseum.demon.co.uk

The Old Bridge House was built in 1660, and is the oldest house in Dumfries. A museum of everyday life in the town, it has an early 20th-century dentist's surgery, a Victorian nursery and kitchens of the 1850s and 1900s.
Times: Open Apr-Sep, Mon-Sat 10-5 & Sun 2-5. **Fee:** Free. **Facilities:** P ♿ shop

ROBERT BURNS CENTRE
Mill Rd DG2 7BE
☎ 01387 264808   📠 01387 265081
e-mail: postmaster@dumfriesmuseum.demon.co.uk

This award-winning centre explores the connections between Robert Burns and the town of Dumfries. Situated in the town's 18th-century watermill, the centre tells the story of Burns' last years spent in the busy streets and lively atmosphere of Dumfries in the 1790s. In the evening the centre shows feature films in the Film Theatre.
Times: Open all year, Apr-Sep, daily 10-8 (Sun 2-5); Oct-Mar, Tue-Sat 10-1 & 2-5. **Fee:** * Free ex audio-visual theatre £1.50 (concessions 75p). **Facilities:** P 🍴 ✗ licensed ♿ (induction loop hearing system in auditorium) toilets for disabled shop 🐕

DUNDRENNAN Map 11 NX74
DUNDRENNAN ABBEY
DG6 4QH (6.5m SE of Kirkcudbright, on A711)
☎ 01557 500262

The now ruined abbey was founded for the Cistercians. The east end of the church and the chapter house are of exceptional architectural quality. Mary, Queen of Scots is thought to have spent her last night in Scotland here on 15 May 1568, before seeking shelter in England, where she was imprisoned and eventually executed.
Times: Open, Apr-Sep, daily 9.30-6.30; Oct-Mar weekends 9.30-4.30, closed Thu pm & Fri. (Closed 25-26 Dec). **Fee:** * £1.80 (ch 75p, concessions £1.30). Telephone for 2003 details **Facilities:** P ♿ ✈ 🐕

GLENLUCE Map 10 NX15
GLENLUCE ABBEY
DG8 0AF (2m NW, off A75)
☎ 01581 300541

The abbey was founded for the Cistercians in 1192 by

continued

Roland, Earl of Galloway. The ruins include a vaulted chapter house, and stand in a beautiful setting.
Times: Open all year, Apr-Sep, daily 9.30-6.30; Oct-Mar, wknds only. (Closed 25-26 Dec). Telephone for 2003 details **Fee:** * £1.80 (ch 75p, concessions £1.30). **Facilities:** P ⬛ ♿ ✱ ♫

🏛 KIRKCUDBRIGHT   Map 11 NX65
BROUGHTON HOUSE & GARDEN
12 High St DG6 4JX (off A711/A755)
☎ 08457 090510
e-mail: aclipson@nts.scot.demon.co.uk

An 18th-century house where Edward A Hornel, one of the 'Glasgow Boys' group of artists, lived and worked from 1901-1933. It features a collection of his work, an extensive library of local history, including rare editions of Burns' works, and a Japanese-style garden that he created.
Times: 25 Mar-28 Jun & 2 Sep-27 Oct, Mon-Sat 12-5 Sun 1-5, 29 Jun-1 Sep Mon-Sat 10-6 Sun 1-5 **Fee:** Admission free for NTS members. For other price details please phone (0131) 243 9387 or check website. **Facilities:** P (on street) (limited space) ✱ (ex guide dogs) ❦

MACLELLAN'S CASTLE
(in Kirkcudbright on A711)
☎ 01557 331856

This handsome structure has been a ruin since the mid 18th-century. It was once an imposing castellated mansion, elaborately planned with fine architectural detail. Something of its 16th-century grandeur still remains.
Times: Open Apr-Sep, daily 9.30-6.30. Telephone for 2003 details. **Fee:** * £2 (ch 75p, concessions £1.50). Telephone for 2003 details **Facilities:** P shop ✱ 🚻 ♫

STEWARTRY MUSEUM
Saint Mary St DG6 4AQ (from A711 through town, pass the parish church, museum approx 200 mtrs on right)
☎ 01557 331643   📧 01557 330005
e-mail: davidd@dumgal.gov.uk

A large and varied collection of archaeological, social history and natural history exhibits relating to the Stewartry district.
Times: Open Mar-Oct, Mon-Sat 11-4 (5pm in May, Jun & Sep; 6pm in Jul & Aug also Sun 2-5); Nov-Feb, Mon-Sat 11-4. **Fee:** Free. **Facilities:** P (outside) ♿ shop ✱ (ex guide dogs)

TOLBOOTH ART CENTRE
High St DG6 4JL (From A711, through town pass parish church & Stewartry Museum, take 1st right into High St)
☎ 01557 331556   📧 01557 331643
e-mail: DavidD@dumgal.gov.uk

Dating from 1629, the Tolbooth was converted into an art centre and provides an interpretive introduction to the Kirkcudbright artists's colony, which flourished in the town from the 1880s. It also provides studio and exhibition space for contemporary local and visiting artists. A programe of exhibitions from March to October.
Times: Open Mar & Oct, Mon-Sat 11-4; May-Jun & Sep, Mon-Sat 10-6; Nov-Feb, Mon-Sat 11-4. Open Sun Jun-Sep 2-5. **Fee:** * £1.50 (ch free, concessions £1) **Facilities:** P (on street parking) ⬛ ♿ (lift) toilets for disabled shop ✱ (ex guide dogs)

Dumfries & Galloway   313

🏛 MONIAIVE   Map 11 NX79
MAXWELTON HOUSE TRUST
DG3 4DX (A76 from Dumfries to Thornhill, after 2m take B729 to Monavie, then 11m to Maxwelton House)
☎ 01848 200385
Times: Open last Sun in May-Sep, Sun-Fri 11-5. Etr-May by booking only. **Facilities:** P shop *Details not confirmed for 2003*

🏛 NEW ABBEY   Map 11 NX96
NEW ABBEY CORN MILL
DG2 8BX (7m S of Dumfries on A710)
☎ 01387 850260

Built in the late 18th century, this water-driven corn mill is still in working order. Regular demonstrations.
Times: Open all year, Apr-Sep, daily 9.30-6.30; Oct-Mar, Mon-Sat 9.30-4.30, Sun 2-4.30. (Closed Thu pm & Fri in winter & 25-26 Dec). Telephone for 2003 details **Fee:** £2.80 (ch £1, concessions £2). Telephone for 2003 details **Facilities:** P (100yds) shop ✱ ♫

SHAMBELLIE HOUSE MUSEUM OF COSTUME
DG2 8HQ (7m S of Dumfries, on A710)
☎ 01387 850375   📧 01387 850461
e-mail: info@nms.ac.uk

A beautiful Victorian country house set in wooded grounds. Step back in time and experience Victorian and Edwardian grace and refinement. Period costumes from 1850s to 1950s.
Times: Open Apr (or Good Fri if earlier)-Oct, 11-5. **Fee:** Free. **Facilities:** P ⬛ ♿ (house inaccessible for wheelchair users) shop ✱ (ex guide/hearing dogs)

SWEETHEART ABBEY
DG2 8BU (on A710)
☎ 01387 850397

Lady Devorgilla of Galloway founded Balliol College, Oxford in memory of her husband John Balliol; she also founded this abbey in his memory in 1273. When she died in 1289 she was buried in front of the high altar with the heart of her husband resting on her bosom; hence the name 'Sweetheart Abbey'. An unusual precinct wall of enormous boulders.
Times: Open all year, Apr-Sep, daily 9.30-6.30; Oct-Mar, Mon-Sat 9.30-4.30, Sun 2-4.30. (Closed Thu pm & Fri & Sun am in winter & 25-26 Dec). Telephone for 2003 details **Fee:** * £1.80 (ch 75p, concessions £1.30). Telephone for 2003 details **Facilities:** P ♿ (with assistance) ✱ ♫

🏛 PALNACKIE   Map 11 NX85
ORCHARDTON TOWER
(6m SE of Castle Douglas)
☎ 0131 668 8800

John Cairns built this rare example of a circular tower in the late 15th century.
Times: Open all reasonable times, on application to key keeper. (Closed 25-26 Dec). **Fee:** Free. **Facilities:** P ✱ ♫

Dumfries & Galloway

PORT LOGAN
Map 10 NX04
LOGAN BOTANIC GARDEN
DG9 9ND (on B7065, 14m S of Stranraer)
☎ 01776 860231 📠 01776 860333
e-mail: info@rbge.org.uk

Logan's exceptionally mild climate allows a colourful array of tender plants to thrive out-of-doors. Amongst the many highlights are tree ferns, cabbage palms, unusual shrubs, climbers and tender perennials found within the setting of the walled, water, terrace and woodland gardens.
Times: Open Mar-Oct, Mar & Oct daily 10-5. Apr-Sep 10-6 **Fee:** £3 (ch £1, concessions £2.50). Family ticket £7. **Facilities:** 🅿 ✕ licensed ♿ (access limited, wheelchairs available for loan) toilets for disabled shop garden centre 🐕 (ex guide dogs)

RUTHWELL
Map 11 NY16
RUTHWELL CROSS
(off B724)
☎ 0131 668 8800

Now in a specially built apse in the parish church, the carved cross dates from the 7th or 8th centuries. Two faces show scenes from the Life of Christ; the others show scroll work, and parts of an ancient poem in Runic characters. It was broken up in the 18th century, but pieced together by a 19th-century minister.
Times: Open all reasonable times. Key from Key Keeper, Kirkyett Cottage, Ruthwell. **Fee:** Free. **Facilities:** 🅿 🐕 ♿

SAVINGS BANKS MUSEUM
DG1 4NN (off B724, 10m E of Dumfries & 6m W of Annan)
☎ 01387 870640
e-mail: tsbmuseum@btinternet.com

Housed in the building where Savings Banks first began, the museum traces their growth and development from 1810 up to the present day. The museum also traces the life of Dr Henry Duncan, father of savings banks, and restorer of the Ruthwell Cross. Multi-lingual leaflets available.
Times: Open all year, daily (ex Sun & Mon Oct-Etr), 10-1 & 2-5. **Fee:** Free. **Facilities:** 🅿 ♿ (touch facilities for blind, guide available) 🐕 (ex guide dogs)

SANQUHAR
Map 11 NS70
SANQUHAR TOLBOOTH MUSEUM
High St DG4 6BN (on A76 Dumfries-Kilmarnock rd)
☎ 01659 250186 📠 01387 265081
e-mail: info@dumfriesmuseum.demon.co.uk

Housed in the town's fine 18th-century tolbooth, the museum tells the story of the mines and miners of the area, its earliest inhabitants, native and Roman, the history and customs of the Royal Burgh of Sanquhar and local traditions.
Times: Open Apr-Sep, Tue-Sat 10-1 & 2-5, Sun 2-5. **Fee:** Free. **Facilities:** 🅿 shop

STRANRAER
Map 10 NX06
CASTLE KENNEDY GARDENS
Stair Estates DG9 8BX (5m E on A75)
☎ 01776 702024 📠 01776 706248
Times: Open Apr-Sep, daily 10-5. **Facilities:** 🅿 🍴 ♿ toilets for disabled shop garden centre *Details not confirmed for 2003*

GLENWHAN GARDENS
Dunragit DG9 8PH (7m E of Stranraer)
☎ 01581 400222 📠 01581 400222
e-mail: tess@glenwhan.freeserve.co.uk

Enjoying spectacular views over the Mull of Galloway and Luce Bay, Glenwhan is a beautiful 12-acre garden set on a hillside. There are two lakes filled with rare species, alpines, scree plants, heathers, conifers, roses, woodland walks and fascinating garden sculpture.
Times: Open Apr-Sep 10-5 **Fee:** * £3 (ch £1.50, concessions £2.50). **Facilities:** 🅿 🍴 ✕ licensed ♿ (wheelchairs provided) toilets for disabled shop garden centre 🐕 (ex on lead)

THORNHILL
Map 11 NX89
DRUMLANRIG CASTLE
DG3 4AQ (4m N of Thornhill off A76)
☎ 01848 330248 📠 01848 331682
e-mail: bre@drumlanrigcastle.org.uk

This unusual pink sandstone castle was built in the late 17th century in Renaissance style. It contains a collection of paintings by Rembrandt, Da Vinci, Holbein, and many others. There is also French furniture, as well as silver and relics of Bonnie Prince Charlie. The old stable block has a craft centre with resident craft workers, and the grounds offer extensive gardens, working forge and woodland walks. For details of special events phone 01848 331555.
Times: Open early May-late Aug, Castle open seven days a week. Guided tours and restricted route may operate at various times, please verify before visiting. **Fee:** * £6 (ch £2 & pen £4. Grounds only £3. Party 20+ £4 each. **Facilities:** 🅿 ✕ licensed ♿ (lift for wheelchair users) toilets for disabled shop 🐕 (ex in park on lead)

🏛 WANLOCKHEAD Map 11 NS81
MUSEUM OF LEAD MINING
ML12 6UT (Signposted from M74 and A76)
☎ 01659 74387 📠 01659 74481
e-mail: ggodfrey@goldpan.co.uk

2 for 1

Wanlockhead is Scotland's highest village, set in the beautiful Lowther Hills. Visitors can see miners' cottages, the miners' library as well as the 18th-century lead mine, and there is a Gold Panning Centre.
Times: Open Apr-2 Nov, daily 10.30-4.30, Jul & Aug 10-5. **Fee:** * £4.95 (ch £3.25, concessions £3.25). Family ticket £12. **Facilities:** 🅿 🍴 licensed ♿ toilets for disabled shop 🐕 (ex guide dogs) 🍃

🏛 WHITHORN Map 15 NX44
WHITHORN-CRADLE OF CHRISTIANITY
45-47 George St DG8 8NS (Follow directions S from junct at Newton Stewart & Glenluce A75. Centre is on main street in centre of Whithorn)
☎ 01988 500508
e-mail: enquiries@whithorn.com
Times: Open daily, Apr-Oct 10.30-5. **Facilities:** 🅿 🍴 ♿ (one short staircase with 'stairmatic') toilets for disabled shop *Details not confirmed for 2003* 🍃

WHITHORN PRIORY
DG8 8PY (on A746)
☎ 01988 500508

The first Christian church in Scotland was founded here by St Ninian in 397AD, but the present ruins date from the 12th century. The ruins are sparse but there is a notable Norman door, the Latinus stone of the 5th century and other early Christian monuments.
Times: Open Apr-Sep daily 10-5 **Fee:** * £2.70 (ch & concessions £1.50) Family ticket £7.50. **Facilities:** 🅿 ♿ 🐕 🍃

DRUMLANRIG CASTLE

Dumfriesshire home of the
Duke of Buccleuch and Queensberry KT.
17th century house, with extensive gardens and Country Park. Renowned art collection, including works by Leonardo, Holbein and Rembrandt. French furniture.
Bonnie Prince Charlie relics.

Castle shop with quality goods – Tearoom
Working Forge – Craft Workshops
Adventure Playground – Visitor Centre

18 miles north of Dumfries on A76
16 miles from Elvanfoot off M74

Tel: 01848-330248

DUNDEE CITY

🏛 DUNDEE Map 11 NO43
BROUGHTY CASTLE MUSEUM
Broughty Ferry DD5 2TF (Turn S off A930 at traffic lights by Eastern Primary School in Broughty Ferry)
☎ 01382 436916 📠 01382 436950
e-mail: broughty@dundeecity.gov.uk

The 15th-century castle was rebuilt to defend the estuary in the 19th century. It now houses displays on Dundee's whaling history, arms and armour, local history and seashore life. There are superb views across the Tay estuary from the observation room.
Times: Open all year Apr-Sep, Mon-Sat 10-4, Sun 12.30-4; Oct-Mar, Tue-Sat 10-4, Sun 12.30-4. (Closed Mons, 25-26 Dec & 1-3 Jan). **Fee:** Free. **Facilities:** 🅿 🍴 (unsuitable for wheelchairs) shop 🐕 (ex guide dogs)

CAMPERDOWN COUNTRY PARK
DD2 4TF (A90 to Dundee and turn onto A923 Coupar Angus rd, turn left at 1st rdbt to Camperdown Country Park)
☎ 01382 432659 📠 01382 433211
Times: Open all year - park. Wildlife Centre - daily, Apr-Sep 10-3.45, Oct-Mar 10-2.45. **Facilities:** 🅿 ♿ (ramps) toilets for disabled shop 🐕 (ex guide dogs) *Details not confirmed for 2003*

Dundee City - East Ayrshire

Discovery Point & RRS Discovery
Discovery Quay DD1 4XA (in Dundee follow the brown heritage signs for Historic Ships)
☎ 01382 201245   ≣ 01382 225891
e-mail: info@dundeeheritage.sol.co.uk

Discovery Point is the home of RRS Discovery, Captain Scott's famous Antarctic ship. Spectacular lighting, graphics and special effects re-create key moments in the Discovery story. The restored bridge gives a captain's view over the ship and the River Tay. Learn what happened to the ship after the expedition, during the First World War and the Russian Revolution, and find out about her involvement in the first survey of whales' migratory patterns.
Times: Open all year, Mon-Sat 10-6. Sun 11-6 **Fee:** £6.25 (ch £3.85, pen & concessions £4.80). Group £5.15 (ch £3.50, pen & concessions £4) **Facilities:** ℗ (charged) 🍴 ♿ (in-house wheelchairs & lifts, parking, ramps onto ship) toilets for disabled shop 🐕 (ex guide & hearing dogs) 🎧

HM Frigate Unicorn
Victory Dock DD1 3JA (From W follow A85 from A90 at Invergowrie. From E follow A92. Located near N end of Tay Road Bridge)
☎ 01382 200900 & 200893   `2 for 1`
≣ 01382 200923
e-mail: frigateunicorn@hotmail.com

The *Unicorn* is the oldest British-built warship afloat, and Scotland's only example of a wooden warship. Today she houses a museum of life in the Royal Navy during the days of sail, with guns, models and displays.
Times: Open all year Apr-Oct daily 10-5. Nov-Mar daily 10-5 (closed Mon/Tue & 2 weeks at Xmas & New Year). **Fee:** * £3.50 (concessions £2.50). Family ticket £7.50-£9.50. Groups 10+ £2 each. **Facilities:** ℗ 🍴 ♿ (audio visual presentations) shop 🐕

McManus Galleries
Albert Square DD1 1DA (Turn off A90 & follow signs for Dundee city centre, located in city centre)
☎ 01382 432084   ≣ 01382 432052
e-mail: mcmanus.galleries@dundeecity.gov.uk

A remarkable Gothic building housing one of Scotland's most impressive collections of fine and decorative art. There are also displays on local archaeology, civic and social history, trades and industries and wildlife and the environment. Touring exhibitions are a regular feature.
Times: Open all year. Mon-Sat 10.30-5, Thu 10.30-7, Sun 12.30-4. (closed 25-26 Dec & 1-3 Jan) **Fee:** Free. **Facilities:** ℗ (100 yds) 🍴 ♿ (wheelchair available, lift, high arm chairs & audio loop) toilets for disabled shop 🐕 (ex guide dogs) 🎧

Mills Observatory
Balgay Park, Glamis Rd DD2 2UB (1m W of Dundee city centre, in Balgay Park)
☎ 01382 435846   ≣ 01382 435962
e-mail: mills.observatory@dundeecity.gov.uk

The observatory was built in 1935, and has a Victorian 10in Cooke refracting telescope among its instruments. The gallery has displays on astronomy and space exploration; visitors can view a safe projection of the sun on bright days. There is a small planetarium for booked groups only. Open nights during the winter months, children's activities during the summer holidays.
Times: Open all year, Apr-Sep, Tue-Fri 11-5, Sat & Sun 12.30-4; Oct-Mar, Mon-Fri 4-10, Sat & Sun 12.30-4. (Closed 25-26 Dec & 1-3 Jan). **Fee:** Free except for planetarium shows extra, £1 (ch 50p) Groups £10. **Facilities:** ℗ 🍴 shop 🐕 (ex guide dogs)

Verdant Works
West Henderson's Wynd DD2 5BT (follow brown tourist signs in Dundee)
☎ 01382 225282   ≣ 01382 221612
e-mail: info@dundeeheritage.sol.co.uk
Times: Open Apr-Oct, Mon-Sat 10-5, Sun 11-5. Nov-Mar, Mon-Sat 10-4, Sun 11-4. Venue closes 1hr after last entry. Please check for winter opening times. (Closed 25 Dec & 1-2 Jan). **Facilities:** ℗ (charged) ♿ (wheelchairs, induction loops) toilets for disabled shop 🐕 (ex guide & hearing dogs) *Details not confirmed for 2003* 🎧

EAST AYRSHIRE

🏛 GALSTON   Map 11 NS53
Loudoun Castle Theme Park
KA4 8PE (signposted from A74(M), from A77 and from A71)
☎ 01563 822296   ≣ 01563 822408
e-mail: loudouncastle@btinternet.com
Times: Open Apr-Aug & following days in Sep 3, 9-10, 16-17, 22-25, 29-30. Also 1-2, 7-8, 14-22 Oct. **Facilities:** ℗ 🍴 ✗ licensed ♿ toilets for disabled shop 🐕 (ex guide dogs) *Details not confirmed for 2003* 🎧

🏛 KILMARNOCK   Map 10 NS43
Dick Institute Museum & Art Galleries
Elmbank Ave KA1 3BU (Follow brown tourist signs from A77 S of Glasgow, into Kilmarnock town centre. Parking at front of building)
☎ 01563 554343   ≣ 01563 554344

Temporary and permanent exhibitions spread over two floors of this grand Victorian building. Fine art, social and natural history feature upstairs, whilst the

continued

downstairs galleries house temporary exhibitions of art and craft.
Times: Open all year, Gallery & Museum: Mon-Tue, Thu-Fri 10-8, Wed & Sat 10-5. (Closed Sun & BH's). **Fee:** Free except for special exhibitions when a charge may be made. **Facilities:** P & (wheelchair available) toilets for disabled shop ✈ (ex guide dogs)

EAST DUNBARTONSHIRE

BEARSDEN   Map 11 NS57
ROMAN BATH-HOUSE
Roman Rd G61 2SG
☎ 0131 668 8800

Considered to be the best surviving visible Roman building in Scotland, the bath-house was discovered in 1973 during excavations for a construction site. It was originally built for use by the Roman garrison at Bearsden Fort, which is part of the Antonine Wall defences.
Times: Open all reasonable times. **Fee:** Free. **Facilities:** & ✈ ¶

MILNGAVIE   Map 11 NS57
MUGDOCK COUNTRY PARK
Craigallian Rd G62 8EL (N of Glasgow on A81, signed)
☎ 0141 956 6100   🖃 0141 956 5624
e-mail: lain@mcp.ndo.co.uk

This country park incorporates the remains of Mugdock and Craigend castles, set in beautiful landscapes as well as an exhibition centre, craft shops, orienteering course and many walks.
Times: Open all year, daily. **Fee:** Free. **Facilities:** P 🍴 & shop garden centre

EAST LOTHIAN

ABERLADY   Map 12 NT47
MYRETON MOTOR MUSEUM
EH32 0PZ (1.5m from A198, 2m from A1)
☎ 01875 870288 & 07957 066666   **2 for 1**

The museum has on show a large collection, from 1899, of cars, bicycles, motor cycles and commercials. There is also a large collection of period advertising, posters and enamel signs etc.
Times: Open, Apr-Sep daily 11-4, Oct-Mar Sun only 1-3 **Fee:** £5 (ch 16 £2). **Facilities:** P 🍴 & shop ✈ (ex guide dogs)

DIRLETON   Map 12 NT58
DIRLETON CASTLE
EH39 5ER (on A198)
☎ 01620 850330

The oldest part of this romantic castle dates from the 13th century. It was besieged by Edward I in 1298, rebuilt and expanded, and then destroyed in 1650. Now the sandstone ruins have a beautiful mellow quality. Within the castle grounds is a garden established in the 16th century, with ancient yews and hedges around a bowling green.
Times: Open all year, Apr-Sep, daily 9.30-6.30; Oct-Mar, Mon-Sat 9.30-4.30, Sun 2-4.30. (Closed 25-26 Dec). Telephone for 2003 details **Fee:** * £2.80 (ch £1, concessions £2). Telephone for 2003 details **Facilities:** P shop ¶

DISCOVERY POINT
DUNDEE
STEP ABOARD ROYAL RESEARCH SHIP DISCOVERY

Take your own voyage of Discovery and see how Captain Scott and his men survived two winters trapped in the ice of the Antarctic. A great fun day out for all the family.
Café • Gift Shop • Parking • Access for all
Open all year: April-Oct 10am-5pm, Nov-March 10am-4pm. (Closed 1 hour after last entry. Sun open from 11am)
Discovery Point, Discovery Quay, Dundee DD1 4XA
Telephone: 01382 201245
Web: www.rrsdiscovery.com

EAST FORTUNE   Map 12 NT57
MUSEUM OF FLIGHT
East Fortune Airfield EH39 5LF (Signposted from A1 near Haddington. Turn onto B1347, past Athelstaneford)
☎ 01620 880308   🖃 01620 880355   **2 for 1**
e-mail: info@nms.ac.uk

Situated on 63 acres of one of Britain's best preserved wartime airfields, the museum has three hangars, with more than 50 aeroplanes, plus engines, rockets and memorabilia. Items on display include two Spitfires, a Vulcan bomber and Britain's oldest surviving aeroplane,

continued

East Lothian - Falkirk

built in 1896; exhibits include a phantom jet fighter and harrier jump-jet.
Times: Open daily, 10.30-5, Jun & Jul open until 6. (Closed 25 & 31 Dec, 1 Jan). **Fee:** * £3 (ch free, concessions £1.50). Season ticket available. **Facilities:** P ☕ ♿ toilets for disabled shop ✕ (ex guide dogs) 🐕

🏛 EAST LINTON   Map 12 NT57
HAILES CASTLE
(1m SW on unclass rd)
☎ 0131 668 8800

The castle was a fortified manor house of the Gourlays and Hepburns. Bothwell brought Mary, Queen of Scots here when they were fleeing from Borthwick Castle. The substantial ruins include a 16th-century chapel.
Times: Open at all reasonable times. **Fee:** Free. **Facilities:** ✕ 🐕

PRESTON MILL & PHANTASSIE DOOCOT
EH40 3DS (signposted from A1)
☎ 01620 860426

This attractive mill, with conical, pantiled roof, is the oldest working water-driven meal mill to survive in Scotland, and was last used commercially in 1957. Nearby is the charming Phantassie Doocot (dovecote), built for 500 birds.
Times: Open 25 Mar-27 Oct, Thu-Mon 12-5, Sun 1-5 **Fee:** Admission free to NTS members. For other deails please phone (0131) 243 9387 or check website **Facilities:** P ♿ toilets for disabled shop ✕ (ex guide dogs) 🐕

🏛 INVERESK   Map 11 NT37
INVERESK LODGE GARDEN
EH21 7TE (A6124 S of Musselburgh)
☎ 01721 722502

This charming terraced garden, set in the historic village of Inveresk, specialises in plants, shrubs and roses suitable for growing on small plots. The 17th-century house makes an elegant backdrop.
Times: Open Nov-Mar daily 10-4.30 or dusk if earlier. 25 Mar-Oct, daily 10-6. **Fee:** Admission free to NTS members. For other details please phone (0131) 243 9387 or check website. **Facilities:** P ♿ ✕ (ex guide dogs) 🐕

🏛 NORTH BERWICK   Map 12 NT58
SCOTTISH SEABIRD CENTRE
The Harbour EH39 4SS
☎ 01620 890202 📠 01620 890222
e-mail: info@seabird.org

2 for 1

Get close to nature with a visit to this award-winning centre. With panoramic views across the islands of the Firth of Forth and sand fringed bays of North Berwick, the area is a haven for wildlife. Use state-of-the-art cameras to see wide variety of wildlife action live - including gannet colony, hundreds of puffins, seals and sometimes bottlenose dolphins close to shore.
Times: Open - Summer, daily 10-6; Winter, daily 10-4. **Fee:** * £4.95 (concessions £3.50). Family ticket (4 persons) £13.50. **Facilities:** P ☕ ✕ licensed ♿ 1 w/chair, parking on site, walking frame available toilets for disabled shop ✕ (ex guide dogs)

TANTALLON CASTLE
EH39 5PN (3m E, off A198)
☎ 01620 892727

A famous 14th-century stronghold of the Douglases facing towards the lonely Bass Rock from the rocky Firth of Forth shore. Nearby 16th and 17th-century earthworks.
Times: Open all year, Apr-Sep, daily 9.30-6.30; Oct-Mar, Mon-Sat 9.30-4.30, Sun 2-4.30. (Closed Thu pm, Fri & Sun am in winter & 25-26 Dec). Telephone for 2003 details **Fee:** * £2.80 (ch £1, concessions £2).Telephone for 2003 details **Facilities:** P shop ✕ 🐕

🏛 PRESTONPANS   Map 11 NT37
PRESTONGRANGE MUSEUM
Prestongrange (on B1348)
☎ 0131 653 2904 📠 01620 828201
e-mail: elms@eastlothian.gov.uk

The oldest documented coal mining site in Britain, with 800 years of history, this museum shows a Cornish Beam Engine and on-site evidence of associated industries such as brickmaking and pottery. It is located next to a 16th-century customs port. Special weekend events for families and children in July and August.
Times: Open end Mar-mid Oct, daily 11-4. Last tour 3pm. **Fee:** Free. **Facilities:** P ☕ ♿ toilets for disabled shop ✕ (ex guide dogs or outside)

FALKIRK

🏛 BIRKHILL   Map 11 NS97
THE BIRKHILL FIRECLAY MINE
(via A706 from Linlithgow, A904 from Grangemouth)
☎ 01506 825855 📠 01506 828766
e-mail: mine@srps.org.uk
Times: Open Apr-22 Oct wknds only; Jul-27 Aug Tue-Sun. BH Mon's, 1 & 29 May. **Facilities:** P Details not confirmed for 2003 🐕

🏛 BO'NESS   Map 11 NT08
BO'NESS & KINNEIL RAILWAY
Bo'ness Station, Union St EH51 9AQ (A904 from all directions, signposted)
☎ 01506 822298 📠 01506 828233
e-mail: railway@srps.org.uk

Historic railway buildings, including the station and train shed, have been relocated from sites all over Scotland. The Scottish Railway Exhibition tells the story of the development of railways and their impact on the people of Scotland. Take a seven mile return trip by steam train to the tranquil country station at Birkhill. Special events take place throughout the year.
Times: Open Apr-Jun & Sep-Oct, Sat-Sun; Steam trains depart 11 (ex Apr), 12.15, 1.45, 3 & diesel at 4.15. Jul-Aug, Tue-Sun; 23 May-27 Jun, special timetable, ring for details. **Fee:** * Return fare £4.50 (ch 5-15 £2, concessions £3.50). Family ticket £11. Ticket for return train fare and tour of Birkhill Fireclay Mine £7.50 (ch £3.50, concessions £5.30), Family ticket £17.50. **Facilities:** P ☕ ✕ ♿ (ramps to station & adapted carriage) toilets for disabled shop (ex in cafe) 🐕

Falkirk - Fife 319

KINNEIL MUSEUM & ROMAN FORTLET
Duchess Anne Cottages, Kinniel Estate EH51 0PR
(Follow tourist signs from Heritage Railway, off M9.
Establishment is at the E end of town accessed via
Dean Rd)
☎ 01506 778530
Times: Open all year, Mon-Sat 12.30-4. **Facilities:** 🅿 & shop ✈ (ex
guide dogs) *Details not confirmed for 2003*

🏛 FALKIRK Map 11 NS88
CALLENDAR HOUSE
Callendar Park FK1 1YR (from W M80 junct 4; from E
M9 junct 4/5; A803 to Falkirk, follow signs into
Callendar Park)
☎ 01324 503770 📠 01324 503771

Mary, Queen of Scots, Oliver Cromwell, Bonnie Prince
Charlie, noble earls and wealthy merchants all feature
in the history of Callendar House. Costumed
interpreters describe early 19th-century life in the
kitchens and the 900-year history of the house is
illustrated in the 'Story of Callendar House' exhibition.
The house is set in parkland, offering boating and
woodland walks. Christmas at Callendar House will
include spitroasting goose in the kitchen, traditional
tree and carols in the main hall.
Times: Open all year, Mon-Sat 10-5. Apr-Sep Sun 2-5. **Fee:** £3 (ch £1
pen £1.50). Family ticket £7. **Facilities:** 🅿 🍴 ✈ & (ramps & lift)
toilets for disabled shop ✈ (ex guide dogs) 🎁

ROUGH CASTLE
(1m E of Bonnybridge)
☎ 0131 668 8800

The impressive earthworks of a large Roman fort on the
Antonine Wall can be seen here. The buildings have
disappeared, but the mounds and terraces are the sites
of barracks, and granary and bath buildings. Running
between them is the military road, which once linked
all the forts on the wall and is still well defined.
Times: Open any reasonable time. **Fee:** Free. **Facilities:** 🅿 ✈ 🎁

FIFE

🏛 ABERDOUR Map 11 NT18
ABERDOUR CASTLE
KY3 0SL (In Aberdour, 5m E of Forth Bridges on A921)
☎ 01383 860519

The earliest surviving part of the castle is the
14th-century keep. There are also later buildings, and
the remains of a terraced garden, a bowling green and
a fine 16th-century doocot (dovecote).
Times: Open all year, Apr-Sep, daily 9.30-6.30; Oct-Mar, Mon-Sat
9.30-4.30, Sun 2-4.30. (Closed Thu pm, Fri & Sun am in winter).
Telephone for 2003 details. **Fee:** * £2.20 (ch 75p, concessions £1.60).
Please telephone for further details **Facilities:** 🅿 ✕ & (wheelchairs)
toilets for disabled shop 🎁

🏛 ANSTRUTHER Map 12 NO50
SCOTTISH FISHERIES MUSEUM
St Ayles, Harbour Head KY10 3AB (from Edinburgh A90
take A92 to Kirkcaldy & then A915 to Upper Largo,
A917 then B942 through Colinsburgh to Pittenweem,
then A917 to Anstruther)
☎ 01333 310628 📠 01333 310628
e-mail: andrew@scottish-fisheries-museum.org

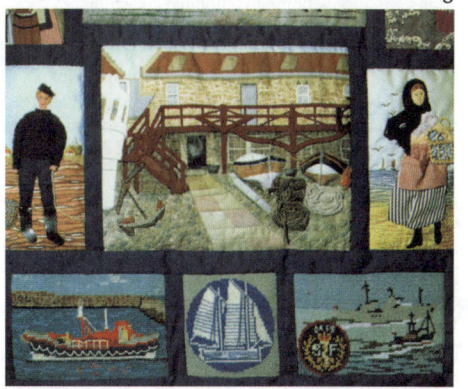

This award-winning national museum tells the story of
Scottish fishing and its people from the earliest times to
the present. With 10 galleries, 2 large boatyards, and a
restored fisherman's cottage to see, many fine paintings
and photographs, boat models and actual boats,
clothing and items of daily life, a visit to the museum
makes for an exceptional day out.
Times: Open all year, Apr-Sep, Mon-Sat 10-5.30, Sun 11-5; Oct-Mar,
Mon-Sat 10-4.30, Sun 12-4.30. (Closed 25-26 Dec & 1-2 Jan). Last
admission 45 mins before closing. **Fee:** * £3.50 (concessions £2.50).
Party 12+ £3 (con £2, primary ch £1) Accompanied ch free. **Facilities:**
🅿 (20yds) (charge in summer) 🍴 & (ramps) toilets for disabled
shop ✈ (ex guide dogs)

🏛 BURNTISLAND Map 11 NT28
BURNTISLAND EDWARDIAN FAIR MUSEUM
102 High St KY3 9AS (in the centre of Burntisland)
☎ 01592 412860 📠 01592 412870

Burntisland Museum has recreated a walk through the
continued

320 Fife

sights and sounds of the town's fair in 1910, based on a painting of the scene by local artist Andrew Young. See reconstructed rides, stalls and side shows of the time.
Times: Open all year, Mon, Wed, Fri & Sat 10-1 & 2-5; Tue & Thu 10-1 & 2-7pm. Closed public holidays. **Fee:** Free. **Facilities:** P (on street parking) ✈

CULROSS   Map 11 NS98
CULROSS PALACE, TOWN HOUSE & THE STUDY
West Green House KY12 8JH (off A985, 3m E of Kincardine Bridge)
☎ 01383 880359   ▤ 01383 882675
Times: Open - Palace & Town House: Apr-May & Sep, daily 1-5; Jun-Aug, daily 10-5; Oct, wknds 1-5 (last admission to Palace 4pm, Town House 4.30pm). Study: same dates, 1-5. Groups at other times by appointment. **Facilities:** P ▣ ♿ toilets for disabled shop ✈ (ex guide dogs) ☕ *Details not confirmed for 2003*

CUPAR   Map 11 NO31
HILL OF TARVIT MANSIONHOUSE & GARDEN
KY15 5PB (2.5m S of Cupar, off A916)
☎ 01334 653127   ▤ 01334 653127

Built in the first decade of the 20th century, the Mansionhouse is home to a notable collection of paintings, tapestries, furniture and Chinese porcelain. The grounds include formal gardens, and there is a regular programme of concerts and art exhibitions.
Times: 25 Mar-27 Oct, daily 12-5. Garden: all year, daily 9.30-sunset.
Fee: Admission free to NTS members. For other details please phone (0131) 243 9387 or check website. **Facilities:** P ▣ ♿ toilets for disabled shop ✈ (ex guide dogs) ☕

THE SCOTTISH DEER CENTRE
Bow-of-Fife KY15 4NQ (3m W of Cupar on A91)
☎ 01337 810391   ▤ 01337 810477   **2 for 1**

Guided tours take about 30 minutes and allow you to meet and stroke deer. There are indoor and outdoor adventure play areas. Other features include regular falconry displays, viewing platform and a tree top walkway. 'Wolf Wood' opened in 2002 – where visitors can meet at first hand these magnificent hunters.
Times: Open daily, Etr-Oct 10-6, Nov-Etr 10-5. **Fee:** * £4.50 (ch 3-15 £3, concessions £3.50) **Facilities:** P ▣ ♿ (special parking bay, loan of wheelchairs) toilets for disabled shop ✈ (ex guide dogs) ☕

DUNFERMLINE   Map 11 NT08
ABBOT HOUSE HERITAGE CENTRE
Abbot House, Maygate KY12 7NE (City Centre)
☎ 01383 733266   ▤ 01383 624908
e-mail: dht@abbothouse.fsnet.co.uk

For the better part of a millennium, pilgrims have beaten a path to Dumfermline's door. Today visitors can still share the rich royal heritage of the capital of Fife's magic Kingdom. The volunteer-run Abbot House Heritage Centre - dubbed 'The People's Tardis' - propels the traveller through time from the days of the Picts. Scotland's royal saint, *Braveheart's* Wallace and Bruce, Scotland's Chaucer, steel magnate Andrew Carnegie

and a whole panoply of kings, ending with the birth of ill-starred Charles I.
Times: Open daily 10-5. Last entry to upper exhibitions 4.15pm. (Closed 25 Dec & 1 Jan). **Fee:** * £3 (accompanied ch under 16 free, ch 5-16 £1.25 & concessions £2). Party 20+ **Facilities:** P (150yds) (disabled parking at establishment) ▣ ♿ (parking on site, videos of inaccesible areas) toilets for disabled shop ✈ (ex guide dogs) ☕

ANDREW CARNEGIE BIRTHPLACE MUSEUM
Moodie St KY12 7PL (400yds S from Dunfermline Abbey)
☎ 01383 724302   ▤ 01383 721862
e-mail: carnegiebirthplace@hotmail.com

The museum tells the story of the handloom weaver's son, born here in 1835, who created the biggest steel works in the USA and then became a philanthropist on a huge scale. The present-day work of the philanthropic Carnegie Trust is also explained.
Times: Open Apr-Oct, Mon-Sat 11-5, Sun 2-5. **Fee:** £2 (ch under 16 free, concessions £1). **Facilities:** P ♿ toilets for disabled shop ✈ (ex guide dogs)

DUNFERMLINE ABBEY
Pittencrieff Park
☎ 01383 739026

The monastery was a powerful Benedictine house, founded by Queen Margaret in the 11th century. A modern brass in the choir marks the grave of King Robert the Bruce. The monastery guest house became a royal palace, and was the birthplace of Charles I.
Times: Open all year, Apr-Sep, daily 9.30-6.30: Oct-Mar, Mon-Sat 9.30-4.30, Sun 2-4.30. (Closed Thu pm, Fri in winter & 25-26 Dec). Telephone for 2003 details **Fee:** * £2.20 (ch 75p, concessions £1.60). Telephone for 2003 details **Facilities:** P shop ✈ ♫

PITTENCRIEFF HOUSE MUSEUM
Pittencrieff Park KY12 8QH
☎ 01383 722935 & 313838   ▤ 01383 313837
Times: Open daily Apr-Sep 11-5, Oct-Mar 11-4. **Facilities:** P ♿ (ramp) toilets for disabled shop ✈ (ex guide dogs) *Details not confirmed for 2003*

FALKLAND   Map 11 NO20
FALKLAND PALACE & GARDEN
KY15 7BU (off A912, 11m N of Kirkaldy)
☎ 01337 857397   ▤ 01337 857980

The hunting palace of the Stuart monarchs, this fine building, with a French-Renaissance style south wing, stands in the shelter of the Lomond Hills. The beautiful Chapel Royal and King's Bedchamber are its most notable features, and it is also home to the oldest royal tennis court in Britain (1539). The garden has a spectacular delphinium border. Recorded sacred music is played hourly in the Chapel. Please telephone for details of concerts, recitals etc.
Times: Open Mar-27 Oct, Mon-Sat 10-6, Sun 1-5 **Fee:** Admission free to NTS members. For other details please phone (0131) 243 9387 or check website. **Facilities:** P ♿ shop ✈ (ex guide dogs) ☕

KELLIE CASTLE & GARDENS Map 12 NO50
KELLIE CASTLE & GARDENS
KY10 2RF (3m NW of Pittenweem on B9171)
☎ 01333 720271 ◈ 01333 720326
e-mail: aclipson@nts-scot.demon.co.uk

The oldest part dates from about 1360, but it is for its 16th and 17th-century domestic architecture that Kellie is renowned. It has notable plasterwork and painted panelling, and there are also interesting Victorian gardens.
Times: Open, Castle: 25 Mar-29 Sep, Thu-Mon 12-5. Garden: all year, daily 9.30-sunset. **Fee:** Admission free to NTS members. For other details please phone (0131) 243 9387 or check website. **Facilities:** P ♨ & (Induction loop for the hard of hearing) shop ✻ (ex guide dogs) ♀

KIRKCALDY Map 11 NT29
KIRKCALDY MUSEUM & ART GALLERY
War Memorial Gardens KY1 1YG (next to Kirkcaldy train station)
☎ 01592 412860 ◈ 01592 412870

Set in the town's lovely memorial gardens, the museum houses a collection of fine and decorative art, including 18th to 21st-century Scottish paintings among them the works of William McTaggart and S J Peploe. An award-winning display 'Changing Places' tells the story of the social, industrial and natural heritage of the area.
Times: Open all year, Mon-Sat 10.30-5, Sun 2-5. (Closed local hols).
Fee: Free. **Facilities:** P ♨ & (ramp to main entrance & lift to 1st floor galleries) toilets for disabled shop ✻ (ex guide dogs)

NORTH QUEENSFERRY Map 11 NT17
DEEP SEA WORLD
KY11 1JR (from N, M90 take exit for Inverkeithing. From S follow signs to Forth Road bridge, first exit left)
☎ 01383 411880 ◈ 01383 410514
e-mail: info@deepseaworld.com

The world's longest underwater tunnel gives you a diver's eye view of an underwater world. Come face to face with Sand Tiger sharks, and watch divers hand feed a wide array of sea life. Visit the Amazon experience with ferocious piranhas and electric eels and the amazing amphibian display featuring the world's most poisonous frog. The really brave will enjoy the dangerous animals tank.
Times: Open all year, daily, 27 Mar-Jun Mon-Fri 10-6; Jul-Aug, Mon-Fri 10-6.30; Sep-1 Nov, Mon-Fri 10-6; 2 Nov-26 Mar, Mon-Fri 11-5. Wknds, BH & school holidays 10-6. **Fee:** * £6.95 (ch 3-5 £4.95, concessions £5.50). Family ticket & group discounts available.
Facilities: P ♨ & (ramps & disabled parking) toilets for disabled shop ✻ (ex guide dogs) ⚓

ST ANDREWS Map 12 NO51
BRITISH GOLF MUSEUM
Bruce Embankment KY16 9AB (opposite Royal & Ancient Golf Club)
☎ 01334 460046 ◈ 01334 460064
e-mail: hilarywebster@randagc.org

2 for 1

A visit to the museum will transport you down a pathway of surprising facts and striking feats from 500 years of golf history. Using diverse displays and exciting exhibits, the museum traces the history of the game, both in Britain and abroad from the middle ages to the present day. There are also displays exploring St Andrews' golfing heritage. Find out more about the growth of the St Andrews clubmakers as well as the impact these businesses made upon the town.
Times: Open all year, Etr-mid Oct daily 9.30-5.30; mid Oct-Etr Thu-Mon 11-3. (closed Tue & Wed). **Fee:** * £4 (ch 15 £2, pen & students £3). Family ticket £9.50. Group 10+ **Facilities:** P (charged) & toilets for disabled shop ✻ (ex guide dogs)

CASTLE & VISITOR CENTRE
KY16 9AR
☎ 01334 477196

This 13th-century stronghold castle was the scene of the murder of Cardinal Beaton in 1546. The new visitor centre incorporates an exciting multi-media exhibition describing the history of the castle and nearby cathedral.
Times: Open all year, Apr-Sep, daily 9.30-6.30; Oct-Mar, Mon-Sat 9.30-4.30, Sun 2-4.30 (winter open 9.30am on Sun). (Closed 25-26 Dec). **Fee:** * £2.80 (ch £1, concessions £2). Joint ticket with St Andrews Cathedral available. **Facilities:** P & toilets for disabled shop ✻ ⚓

CATHEDRAL (& MUSEUM)
KY16 9QU
☎ 01334 472563

The cathedral was the largest in Scotland, and is now an extensive ruin. The remains date mainly from the 12th and 13th centuries, and large parts of the precinct walls have survived intact. Close by is St Rule's church, which the cathedral was built to replace. St Rule's probably dates from before the Norman Conquest, and is considered the most interesting Romanesque church in Scotland.
Times: Open all year, Apr-Sep, daily 9.30-6.30; Oct-Mar, Mon-Sat 9.30-4.30, Sun 2-4.30 (winter open 9.30am Sun). (Closed 25-26 Dec).
Fee: * £2.20 (ch 75p, concessions £1.60). Joint ticket for St Andrews Castle available. **Facilities:** P shop ✻ ⚓

ST ANDREWS AQUARIUM
The Scores KY16 9AS (Signposted in town centre)
☎ 01334 474786 ◈ 01334 475985

This continually expanding aquarium is home to shrimps, sharks, eels, octopi, seals and much much more. Special features include the Seahorse Parade, and the Sea Mammal Research Unit, which is committed to the care of sea mammals and their environment.
Times: Open daily from 10. Please phone for winter opening **Fee:** * £4.85 (ch & student £3.75, pen £4). Family ticket (2 adults & 2 ch) £14
Facilities: P (charged) ♨ ✕ licensed & toilets for disabled shop ⚓

Highland

HIGHLAND

AVIEMORE Map 14 NH81
STRATHSPEY STEAM RAILWAY
Aviemore Station, Dalfaber Rd PH22 1PY (off B970)
☎ 01479 810725
e-mail: information@strathspey-railway.co.uk

This steam railway covers the ten miles from Aviemore via Boat of Garten to Broomhill. The journey takes about 40 minutes, but allow around two hours for the round trip. Shorter trips are possible and timetables are available from the station and the tourist information centre. Special events include Thomas the Tank Engine, telephone for details of dates.
Times: Open late Mar-Oct, Wed-Thu, Sat-Sun; May-Sep, daily. Closed Sat in Apr (ex Etr). **Fee:** £8.20 basic roundtrip; £21 Family roundtrip.
Facilities: 🅿 ▣ & (ramps) toilets for disabled shop 🍴

BALMACARA Map 14 NG82
BALMACARA ESTATE & LOCHALSH WOODLAND GARDEN
IV40 8DN (3m E of Kyle of Lochalsh, off A87)
☎ 01599 566325 📠 01599 566359
e-mail: balmacara@nts.org.uk

The Balmacara estate comprises some 5,600 acres and seven crofting villages, including Plockton, a conservation area. There are excellent views of Skye, Kintail and Applecross. The main attraction is the Lochalsh Woodland Garden, but the whole area is excellent for walking.
Times: Open - Estate: all year. Woodland garden & Balmacara Square, daily, 10-6. **Fee:** Admission free to NTS members. For other details please phone (0131) 243 9387 or check website. **Facilities:** 🅿 ♿

BETTYHILL Map 14 NC76
STRATHNAVER MUSEUM
KW14 7SS
☎ 01641 521418
e-mail: strathnavermus@ukonline.co.uk

The museum has displays on the Clearances, with a fine collection of Strathnaver Clearances furnishings, domestic and farm implements, and local books. There is also a Clan Mackay room. The museum's setting is a former church, a handsome stone building with a magnificent canopied pulpit dated 1774. The churchyard contains a carved stone known as the Farr Stone, which dates back to the 9th-century and is a fine example of Pictish art.
Times: Open Apr-Oct, Mon-Sat 10-1 & 2-5; Nov-Mar restricted opening. **Fee:** * £1.90 (pen £1.20 ch 50p). **Facilities:** 🅿 & shop 🐕 (ex guide dogs)

BOAT OF GARTEN Map 14 NH91
RSPB NATURE RESERVE ABERNETHY FOREST
Forest Lodge, Nethybridge PH25 3EF (Signposted from B970 & A9 at Aviemore, follow 'RSPB Ospreys' signs)
☎ 01479 831694 📠 01479 821069
Times: Reserve open at all times. Osprey Centre daily, Apr-Aug 10-5.
Facilities: 🅿 & toilets for disabled shop 🐕 (ex guide dogs in centre)
Details not confirmed for 2003

CARRBRIDGE Map 14 NH92
LANDMARK HIGHLAND HERITAGE & ADVENTURE PARK
PH23 3AJ (off A9 between Aviemore & Inverness)
☎ 01479 841613 & 0800 731 3446 📠 01479 841384
e-mail: landmark@compuserve.com

This innovative centre is designed to provide a fun and educational visit for all ages. Microworld takes a close look at the incredible microscopic world around us. There is a 65ft forest viewing tower and a treetop trail. There are demonstrations of timber sawing, on a steam-powered sawmill and log hauling by a Clydesdale horse throughout the day. Attractions include a 3-track Watercoaster, a maze and a large covered adventure play area.
Times: Open all year, daily, Apr-mid Jul 10-6; mid Jul-mid Aug 10-7; Sep-Oct 10-5.30; Nov-Mar 10-5. **Fee:** Apr -Oct: £7.25 (ch £5.30); Nov-Mar £2.75 (ch £2.25). Family tickets available. **Facilities:** 🅿 ▣ ✗ licensed & toilets for disabled shop 🍴

CAWDOR Map 14 NH85
CAWDOR CASTLE
IV12 5RD (on B9090 off A96)
☎ 01667 404615 📠 01667 404674
e-mail: info@cawdorcastle.com

Home of the Thanes of Cawdor since the 14th century, this lovely castle has a drawbridge, an ancient tower built round a tree, and a freshwater well inside the house. Gardens Weekend takes place in June - guided tours of gardens and Bluebell Walk in Cawdor Big Wood.
Times: Open May-12 Oct, daily 10-5.30. (Last admission 5pm). **Fee:** £6.30 (ch 5-15 £3.50, pen £5.30). Family ticket £18.60. Party 20+ £5.50 each. Gardens, grounds & nature trails only £3.50. **Facilities:** 🅿 ▣ ✗ licensed & (ramps) toilets for disabled shop 🐕 (ex guide dogs)

CLAVA CAIRNS Map 14 NH74
CLAVA CAIRNS
(6m E of Inverness)
☎ 0131 668 8800

On the south bank of the River Nairn, this group of circular burial cairns is surrounded by three concentric rings of great stones. It dates from around 1600BC, and ranks among Scotland's finest prehistoric monuments.
Times: Open at all reasonable times. **Fee:** Free. **Facilities:** 🅿 🐕 ♿

CROMARTY Map 14 NH76
HUGH MILLER'S COTTAGE
Church St IV11 8XA
☎ 01381 600245

The cottage houses an exhibition on the life and work of Hugh Miller, a stonemason born here in 1802 who became an eminent geologist and writer. It was built by his great-grandfather around 1698, and now has a charming cottage garden.
Times: Open May-29 Sep, daily 12-5. **Fee:** Admission free to NTS members. For other details please phone (0131) 243 9387 or check website. **Facilities:** 🅿 (5mins) (disabled is directly outside) & 🐕 (ex guide dogs) ♿

Highland 323

🏛 CULLODEN MOOR Map 14 NH74
CULLODEN BATTLEFIELD
IV2 5ED (5m E of Inverness)
☎ 01463 790607 📠 01463 794294
e-mail: culloden@nts.org.uk

A cairn recalls this last battle fought on mainland Britain, on 16 April 1746, when the Duke of Cumberland's forces routed 'Bonnie' Prince Charles Edward Stuart's army. The battlefield has been restored to its state on the day of the battle, and in summer there are 'living history' enactments. This is a most atmospheric evocation of tragic events. Telephone for details of guided tours.
Times: Open - site always. Visitor Centre: 20 Jan-24 Mar & 28 Oct- 24 Dec, daily 10-4, 25 Mar-27 Oct, daily 9-6 **Fee:** Admission free to NTS members. For other details please phone (0131) 243 9387 or check website. **Facilities:** 🅿 ✕ ♿ (wheelchair, induction loop, raised map) toilets for disabled shop 🍴 (ex guide dogs) 🚻

🏛 DRUMNADROCHIT Map 14 NH52
OFFICIAL LOCH NESS MONSTER EXHIBITION CENTRE
IV3 6TU (on A82, 12m S Inverness)
☎ 01456 450573 & 450218
📠 01456 450770
e-mail: brem@loch-ness-scotland.com

`2 for 1`

A fascinating and popular multi-media presentation lasting 30 minutes. Seven themed areas cover the story from the pre-history of Scotland, through the cultural roots of the legend in Highland folklore, and into the 50-year controversy which surrounds it. Using latest technology in computer animation, lasers and multi-media projection systems.
Times: Open all year; Etr-May 9.30-5.30; Jun-Sep 9.30-6 (9-8.30 Jul & Aug); Winter 10-4. Last admission 30mins before closing. **Fee:** * £5.95 (ch £3.50, pen & students £4.50, ch under 7 & disabled free). Family ticket £14.95. Group. **Facilities:** 🅿 🍽 ✕ licensed ♿ (parking) toilets for disabled shop 🍴 (ex in grounds outside) 🎁

URQUHART CASTLE
IV63 6XJ (on A82)
☎ 01456 450551

The castle was once Scotland's biggest and overlooks Loch Ness. It dates mainly from the 14th century, when it was built on the site of an earlier fort, and was destroyed before the 1715 Jacobite rebellion.
Times: Open all year, Apr-Sep, daily 9.30-6.30; Oct-Mar, daily 9.30-4.30. Last admission 45mins before closing. (Closed 25-26 Dec).
Fee: * £5 (ch £1.20, concessions £3.75). **Facilities:** 🅿 shop 🍴🍽

🏛 DUNBEATH Map 15 ND12
LAIDHAY CROFT MUSEUM
KW6 6EH (1m N on A9 off Dunbeath)
☎ 01593 731244

The museum gives visitors a glimpse of a long-vanished way of life. The main building is a thatched Caithness longhouse, with the dwelling quarters, byre and stable all under one roof. It dates back some 200 years, and is furnished as it might have been 100 years ago. A collection of early farm tools and machinery is also shown. Near the house is a thatched winnowing barn with its roof supported on three 'Highland couples', or crucks.
Times: Open Etr-Oct, daily 10-6. **Fee:** £2 (ch 50p) **Facilities:** 🅿 🍽 ♿ toilets for disabled

🏛 ELPHIN Map 14 NC21
HIGHLAND & RARE BREEDS FARM
IV27 4HH (on A835 in Elphin)
☎ 01854 666204 📠 01854 666204

`2 for 1`

There are highland cattle, traditional 4-horned sheep with coloured fleeces, traditional Scottish ewes and lambs, rare breeds of pigs and goats. Many types of poultry, duck ponds, and a farm walk among the animals. Also on display are farm tools, crofting history, wool crafts and hand-spinning.
Times: Open Jul & Aug only **Fee:** * £3.50 (ch £2.50, students & pen £3) **Facilities:** 🅿 ♿ (assistance available) toilets for disabled shop 🍴 🎁

🏛 FORT GEORGE Map 14 NH75
FORT GEORGE
IV1 2TD (11m NE of Inverness)
☎ 01667 462777

Built following the Battle of Culloden as a Highland fortress for the army of George II, this is one of the outstanding artillery fortifications in Europe and still an active army barracks.
Times: Open all year, Apr-Sep, daily 9.30-6.30; Oct-Mar, Mon-Sat 9.30-4.30, Sun 2-4.30. Last admission 45mins before closing. (Closed 25-26 Dec). Telephone for 2003 details. **Fee:** * Summer: £5 (ch £1.50, concessions £3.50); Telephone for 2003 details **Facilities:** 🅿 ✕ ♿ toilets for disabled shop 🍴🍽

QUEEN'S OWN HIGHLANDERS REGIMENTAL MUSEUM COLLECTION
IV2 7TD (turn off A96 5 miles from Inverness)
☎ 01463 224380 📠 01463 224380

Fort George has been a military barracks since it was built in 1748-69, and was the Depot of the Seaforth Highlanders until 1961. The museum of the Queen's Own Highlanders (Seaforth and Camerons) is sited in

continued

the former Lieutenant Governor's house, where uniforms, medals and pictures are displayed.
Times: Open Apr-Sep, daily 10-6; Oct-Mar, Mon-Fri 10-4. (Closed Good Fri-Etr Mon, Xmas, New Year & CB). **Fee:** Free. (Admission charged by Historic Scotland for entry to Fort George). **Facilities:** P & (stair lift to 1st floor, wheelchair on 1st floor) toilets for disabled shop ✈ (ex guide dogs)

FORT WILLIAM   Map 14 NN17
INVERLOCHY CASTLE
PH33 6SN (2m NE)
☎ 0131 668 8800

The castle was begun in the 13th century and added to later. It is noted in Scottish history for the battle fought nearby in 1645, when Montrose defeated the Campbells.
Times: Open Apr-Sep. Key available from keykeeper. **Fee:** Free.
Facilities: ✈ ♫

WEST HIGHLAND MUSEUM
Cameron Square PH33 6AJ (follow signs to tourist office, museum is next door)
☎ 01397 702169   🖷 01397 701927

The displays illustrate traditional Highland life and history, with numerous Jacobite relics. One of them is the 'secret portrait' of 'Bonnie' Prince Charlie, which looks like meaningless daubs of paint but reveals a portrait when reflected in a metal cylinder.
Times: Open all year Jun-Sep, Mon-Sat 10-5 (also Sun 2-5 Jul-Aug); Oct-May, Mon-Sat 10-4. **Fee:** £2 (ch 50p, concessions £1.50)
Facilities: P (100yds) (charge May-Oct, max. 2hrs stay) & toilets for disabled shop ✈ (ex guide dogs)

GAIRLOCH   Map 14 NG87
GAIRLOCH HERITAGE MUSEUM
Auchtercairn IV21 2BP (At junct of A382 & B8021, near Police station & public car park)
☎ 01445 712287
e-mail: info@gairlochheritagemuseum.org.uk

A converted farmstead now houses the award-winning museum, which shows the way of life in this typical West Highland parish from early times to the 20th century. There are hands-on activities for children and reconstructions of a croft house room, a school room, a shop, and a smugglers' cave. You can also view Gairloch through one of the largest lenses assembled by the Northern Lighthouse Board.
Times: Open Apr-Sep, Mon-Sat 10-5; Oct, Mon-Fri 10-1.30 last admission 4.30. Winter months by arrangement. **Fee:** * £2.50 (ch 50p & pen £2). Group 10+ £1.50 each. **Facilities:** P ♨ ✗ licensed & shop ✈ (ex guide dogs)

GLENCOE   Map 14 NN15
GLENCOE & NORTH LORN FOLK MUSEUM
PH49 4HS (Turn off A82 at Glencoe crossroads then immediately right again into Glencoe village)
☎ 01855 811664

Two heather-thatched cottages in the main street of Glencoe now house items connected with the Macdonalds and the Jacobite risings. A variety of local domestic and farming exhibits, dairying and slate-working equipment, costumes and embroidery are also shown.
Times: Open mid May-Sep, Mon-Sat 10-5.30. **Fee:** * £2 (ch free, concessions £1.50). **Facilities:** P & shop

GLENCOE VISITOR CENTRE
PA39 4HX (on A82, 17m S of Fort William)
☎ 01855 811307 & 811729   🖷 01855 811772
Times: Open - Site all year, daily. Visitor Centre May-Aug, daily 9.30-5.30; Mar-Apr & Sep-Oct, daily 10-5; (last admission 30 mins before closing). **Facilities:** P ♨ & (induction loop in video programme room) toilets for disabled shop ✈ (ex guide dogs) ♨
Details not confirmed for 2003

HIGHLAND MYSTERYWORLD
PA39 4HL (on A82, 10m S of Fort William)
☎ 01855 811660   🖷 01855 821463
e-mail: monster@mysteryworld.co.uk
Times: Open Etr-Oct, daily, 10-5 (last entry 4.30). **Facilities:** P ♨ ✗ licensed & toilets for disabled shop (ex guide dogs) *Details not confirmed for 2003*

GLENFINNAN   Map 14 NM98
GLENFINNAN MONUMENT
PH37 4LT (on A830, 18.5m W of Fort William)
☎ 01397 722250
e-mail: glenfinnan@nts.org.uk

The monument commemorates Highlanders who fought for 'Bonnie' Prince Charlie in 1745. It stands in an awe-inspiring setting at the head of Loch Shiel. There is a visitor centre with information (commentary in four languages) on the Prince's campaign.
Times: Site open all year, daily. Visitor centre: 25 Mar-18 May & 2 Sep-27 Oct, daily 10-5, 19 May-1 Sep, daily 9.30-6. **Fee:** Admission free to NTS members. For other details please phone (0131) 243 9387 or check website. **Facilities:** P ♨ & (information centre only) shop ♨

GOLSPIE   Map 14 NH89
DUNROBIN CASTLE
KW10 6SF (1m NE on A9, from Golspie)
☎ 01408 633177 & 633268   🖷 01408 634081
e-mail: info@dunrobincastle.net

The ancient seat of the Earls and Dukes of Sutherland is a splendid, gleaming, turreted structure, thanks largely to 19th-century rebuilding, and has a beautiful setting overlooking the sea. Paintings, furniture and family heirlooms are on display, and the gardens are on a grand scale to match the house. There are also falconry displays in the gardens.
Times: Open Apr-15 Oct, Mon-Sat 10.30-5.30, Sun 12-5.30. Closes 1 hr earlier Apr, May & Oct. Last admission half hour before closing.
Fee: * £6.25 (ch & pen £5.70). Family ticket £17. Party. **Facilities:** P ♨ (access by arrangement only) shop ✈ ♨

Highland

HELMSDALE Map 14 ND01
TIMESPAN
Dunrobin St KW8 6JX (off A9 in centre of village, by Telford Bridge)
☎ 01431 821327 📠 01431 821058
e-mail: admin@timespan.org.uk
Times: Open Apr-Oct, Mon-Sat 9.30-5, Sun 2-5. Last admission to museum 4pm. **Facilities:** 🅿 💷 ♿ (lifts) toilets for disabled shop garden centre 🐶 (ex guide dogs) *Details not confirmed for 2003* ☕

KINCRAIG Map 14 NH80
HIGHLAND WILDLIFE PARK
PH21 1NL (on B9152, 7m S of Aviemore)
☎ 01540 651270 📠 01540 651236
e-mail: wildlife@rzss.org.uk
Times: Open throughout the year, weather permitting. Apr-Oct, 10-6; Jun-Aug 10-7; Nov-Mar 10-4. last entry 2 hours before closing.
Facilities: 🅿 💷 ♿ toilets for disabled shop 🐶 *Details not confirmed for 2003* ☕

KINGUSSIE Map 14 NH70
HIGHLAND FOLK MUSEUM
Duke St PH21 1JG (12m SW of Aviemore off A9 at Kingussie)
☎ 01540 661307 📠 01540 661631
e-mail: highland.folk@highland.gov.uk

First established on Iona in 1935 this was Britain's first open air museum. It has an extensive collection of everyday domestic objects together with major exhibits providing an insight into the social history of the Highland people. Visitors will see domestic and agricultural items and trade and craft tools.
Times: Open Apr-Sep, Mon-Sat 9.30-5.30; Oct Mon-Fri 9.30-4.30; Nov-Mar guided tours Mon-Fri, check for details. **Fee:** * £1 (ch & pen 50p). **Facilities:** 🅿 ♿ (ramp) toilets for disabled shop 🐶 (ex guide dogs) ☕

RUTHVEN BARRACKS
(0.5m SE of Kingussie)
☎ 0131 668 8800

Despite being blown up by 'Bonnie' Prince Charlie's Highlanders, these infantry barracks are still the best preserved of the four that were built after the Jacobite uprising. The considerable ruins are the remains of a building completed in 1716 on the site of a fortress of the 'Wolf of Badenoch'.
Times: Open at any reasonable time. **Fee:** Free. **Facilities:** 🅿 🐶 🍴

KIRKHILL Map 14 NH54
MONIACK CASTLE (HIGHLAND WINERY)
IV5 7PQ (7m from Inverness on A862, near village of Beauly, on S side of Beauly Firth)
☎ 01463 831283 📠 01463 831419

Commercial wine-making is not a typically Scottish industry, but nevertheless a wide range of 'country'-style wines is produced, including elderflower and silver birch; mead and sloe gin, are also made here. A selection of related products and tours of the production area are available at this unique attraction, situated in a 16th-century castle.
Times: Open all year, Mon-Sat 10-5. (11-4 in winter). **Fee:** £2.
Facilities: 🅿 shop 🐶 ☕

NEWTONMORE Map 14 NN79
CLAN MACPHERSON HOUSE & MUSEUM
Main St PH20 1DE (off A9 at junct of Newtonmore and Kingussie, museum on left after entering village)
☎ 01540 673332

Containing relics and memorials of the clan chiefs and other Macpherson families as well as those of Prince Edward Stuart, this museum also displays the Prince's letters to the Clan Chief of 1745 and one to the Prince from his father the Old Pretender, along with royal warrants and the green banner of the clan. Other interesting historic exhibits include James Macpherson's fiddle, swords, pictures, decorations and medals.
Times: Open Apr-Oct, Mon-Sat 10-5, Sun 2-5. Other times by appointment. **Fee:** Free. Donations welcome. **Facilities:** 🅿 ♿ toilets for disabled shop 🐶 (ex guide dogs)

HIGHLAND FOLK MUSEUM
Aultlarie Croft PH20 1AY (on A86, follow signs off A9)
☎ 01540 661307 📠 01540 661631
e-mail: highland.folk@highland.gov.uk

An early 18th-century farming township with turf houses has been reconstructed at this award-winning museum. A 1930's school houses old world maps, little wooden desks and a Coates library. Other attractions include a working croft with rare breed animals and tailor's workshop. Vintage buses run throughout the site.
Times: Open Apr-Aug, Mon-Sun 10.30-5.30; Sep-Oct, Mon-Fri 11-4.30.
Fee: * £5 (ch & pen £3) **Facilities:** 🅿 💷 ♿ (vintage bus with full disabled access) toilets for disabled shop 🐶 (ex guide dogs) ☕

POOLEWE Map 14 NG88
INVEREWE GARDEN
IV22 2LG (6m NE of Gairloch, on A832)
☎ 01445 781200 📠 01445 781497
e-mail: inverewe@nts.org.uk

The influence of the North Atlantic Drift enables this remarkable garden to grow rare and sub-tropical plants. At its best in early June, but full of beauty from March to October, Inverewe has a backdrop of magnificent mountains and stands to the north of Loch Maree.
Times: Open - Garden all year, 25 Mar-Oct, daily 9.30-9. Nov-24 Mar, 9.30-5. Visitor Centre 25 Mar-Oct, daily 10-5. **Fee:** Admission free to NTS members. For other details please phone (0131) 243 9387 or check website. **Facilities:** 🅿 🍴 licensed ♿ (some paths difficult) toilets for disabled shop 🐶 (ex guide dogs) 🌱

Highland - Inverclyde

🏛 ROSEMARKIE   Map 14 NH75
GROAM HOUSE MUSEUM
High St IV10 8UF (Turn off A9 at Tote onto A832)
☎ 01381 620961 & 01381 621309
📠 01381 621730
e-mail: groamhouse@ecosse.net

Opened in 1980, this community museum explores the history, culture and crafts of the mysterious Picts, who faded from history over a thousand years ago. Visitors can see the Rosemarkie Stones, large slabs that show Pictish carvings; paintings, a replica Pictish harp, and a collection of photographs of Pictish stones all over the country.
Times: Open 29 Mar-7 Apr, daily 2-4.30; May-Sep Mon-Sat 10-5, Sun 2-4.30; Oct-Apr 2-4 Sat & Sun. Other times by prior appointment. **Fee:** Free. **Facilities:** 🅿 shop ✖ (ex guide dogs) ⚑

🏛 STRATHPEFFER   Map 14 NH45
HIGHLAND MUSEUM OF CHILDHOOD
The Old Station IV14 9DH (take A9 N of Inverness, then the Tore rdbt, follow signs to Dingwall. Strathpeffer 5m W of Dingwall on A834)
☎ 01997 421031   📠 01997 421031
e-mail: info@hmoc.freeserve.co.uk   **2 for 1**

Located in a renovated Victorian railway station of 1885, the museum tells the story of childhood in the Highlands amongst the crofters and townsfolk; a way of life recorded in oral testimony, displays, and evocative photographs. An award-winning video, "A Century of Highland Childhood" is shown. There are also doll and toy collections.
Times: Open Apr-Oct, daily 10-5, (Sun 2-5) also Jul & Aug evenings open to 7pm. Other times by arrangement. **Fee:** £1.50 (ch, pen & students £1). Family ticket £3.50 (2ad+3ch) **Facilities:** 🅿 🍴 ♿ (tape tour with induction loop for partially sighted) shop ✖ (ex guide dogs) ⚑

🏛 TORRIDON   Map 14 NG85
TORRIDON COUNTRYSIDE CENTRE
The Mains IV22 2EZ (N of A896)
☎ 01445 791221   📠 01445 791378
e-mail: aclipson@nts.scot.demon.co.uk

Set amid some of Scotland's finest mountain scenery, the centre offers audio-visual presentations on the local wildlife. At The Mains nearby there are deer to be seen.
Times: Open - Countryside Centre May-29 Sep, daily 10-6. Estate and Deer Museum daily all year. **Fee:** Admission free to NTS members. For other details please phone (0131) 243 9387 or check website.
Facilities: 🅿 ♿ toilets for disabled ⚑

🏛 WICK   Map 15 ND34
CAITHNESS GLASS FACTORY & VISITOR CENTRE
Airport Industrial Estate KW1 5BP (on N side of Wick, beside airport on A99 to John O'Groats)
☎ 01955 602286   📠 01955 605200
e-mail: visitor@caithnessglass.co.uk

All aspects of glassmaking are on view, from the initial processing of the raw materials to the finished article.
Times: Open all year, Factory shop & Restaurant Mon-Sat 9-5 (Sun, Etr-Dec 11-5). Glassmaking Mon-Fri 9-4.30. **Fee:** Free. **Facilities:** 🅿 ✖ licensed ♿ toilets for disabled shop ✖ ex guide dogs ⚑

CASTLE OF OLD WICK
(1m S)
☎ 0131 668 8800   📠 0131 668 8888

A ruined four-storey square tower that is probably from the 12th century. It is also known as Castle Oliphant.
Times: Open except when adjoining rifle range is in use. **Fee:** Free.
Facilities: ✖ ⚑

WICK HERITAGE CENTRE
20 Bank Row KW1 5HS (close to the harbour)
☎ 01955 605393   📠 01955 605393

The heritage centre is near the harbour in a complex of eight houses, yards and outbuildings. The centre illustrates local history from Neolithic times to the herring fishing industry. In addition, there is a complete working 19th-century lighthouse, and the famous Johnston collection of photographs.
Times: Open Jun-Sep, Mon-Sat 10-5. (Closed Sun). **Fee:** * £2 (ch 50p). **Facilities:** 🅿 ♿ toilets for disabled

INVERCLYDE

🏛 GREENOCK   Map 10 NS27
McLEAN MUSEUM & ART GALLERY
15 Kelly St PA16 8JX (close to Greenock West Railway Station and Greenock Bus Station)
☎ 01475 715624   📠 01475 715626

James Watt was born in Greenock, and various exhibits connected with him are shown. The museum also has an art collection, and displays on shipping, local and natural history, Egyptology and ethnography.
Times: Open all year, Mon-Sat 10-5. (Closed local & national PH).
Fee: Free. **Facilities:** 🅿 (200mtrs) ♿ (induction loop) toilets for disabled shop ✖ (ex guide & service dogs)

Inverclyde - Midlothian - Moray 327

🏛 PORT GLASGOW   Map 10 NS37
NEWARK CASTLE
PA14 5NH (In Port Glasgow on A8)
☎ 01475 741858

The one-time house of the Maxwells, dating from the 15th and 17th centuries. The courtyard and hall are preserved. Fine turrets and the remains of painted ceilings can be seen, and the hall carries an inscription of 1597.
Times: Open Apr-Sep, daily 9.30-6.30. **Fee:** * £2.20 (ch 75p, concessions £1.60). **Facilities:** 🅿 shop 🏴

MIDLOTHIAN

🏛 CRICHTON   Map 11 NT36
CRICHTON CASTLE
EH37 5QH (2.5m SW of Pathhead, off A68)
☎ 01875 320017

The castle dates back to the 14th century, but most of what remains today was built over the following 300 years. A notable feature is the 16th-century wing built by the Earl of Bothwell in Italian style, with an arcade below.
Times: Open Apr-Sep, daily 9.30-6.30. **Fee:** * £2 (ch 75p, concessions £1.50). **Facilities:** 🅿 🏴

🏛 DALKEITH   Map 11 NT36
EDINBURGH BUTTERFLY & INSECT WORLD
Dobbies Garden World, Lasswade EH18 1AZ (0.5m S of Edinburgh city bypass at Gilmerton junct or Sherrifhall rdbt)
☎ 0131 663 4932
📠 0131 654 2774   **2 for 1**
e-mail: info@edinburgh-butterfly-world.co.uk

Richly coloured butterflies from all over the world can be seen flying among exotic rainforest plants, trees and flowers. The tropical pools are filled with giant waterlilies and colourful fish, and are surrounded by lush vegetation. Also scorpions, leaf-cutting ants, beetles, tarantulas and other remarkable creatures. There is a unique honeybee display and daily insect handling sessions.
Times: Open Summer daily 9.30-5.30; winter daily 10-5. (Closed 25-26 Dec & 1 Jan). **Fee:** * £4.35 (ch, concessions & students £3.35). Family ticket £13.50 (2ad+2ch). Party 10+. **Facilities:** 🅿 🍴 ♿ toilets for disabled shop garden centre ✈ (ex guide dogs) 🏴

🏛 NEWTONGRANGE   Map 11 NT36
SCOTTISH MINING MUSEUM
Lady Victoria Colliery EH22 4QN (10m S of Edinburgh City on A7, signposted from Edinburgh City bypass)
☎ 0131 663 7519
📠 0131 654 1618   **2 for 1**
e-mail: enquiries@scottishminingmuseum.com

Based at Scotland's National Coalmining Museum offering an outstanding visit to Britains' finest Victorian colliery. Guided tours with miners, magic helmets,

exhibitions, theatres, interactive displays and a visit to the coal face. Home to Scotland's largest steam engine.
Times: Open all year, daily 10-5. **Fee:** * £4 (ch & concessions £2.20). Family ticket £10. Party 20+. **Facilities:** 🅿 🍴 ♿ (Tactile Opportunities) toilets for disabled shop ✈ (ex guide dogs) 🏴

🏛 PENICUIK   Map 11 NT26
'THE GLASSHOUSE' AT EDINBURGH CRYSTAL
Eastfield EH26 8HB (on A701 to Peebles)
☎ 01968 675128   **2 for 1**
📠 01968 674847
e-mail: visitorcentre@edinburgh-crystal.co.uk

Watch skilled craftsmen as they take molten crystal and turn it into intricately decorated glassware. Not only can you talk to the craftsmen but there is also video footage, story boards, artefacts and audio listening posts to help you understand the 300-year-old history of glassmaking. The shop includes the largest selection of Edinburgh crystal plus seconds at bargain prices.
Times: Open Mon-Sat 10-5, Sun 11-5. **Fee:** Tours £3 (concessions £2). Family ticket £7.50. Party 12+. **Facilities:** 🅿 🍴 ♿ (ramp to first floor) toilets for disabled shop ✈ (ex guide dogs) 🏴

MORAY

🏛 BALLINDALLOCH   Map 15 NJ13
THE GLENLIVET DISTILLERY
AB37 9DB (off B9008 10m N of Tomintoul)
☎ 01542 783220 📠 01542 783218
e-mail: linda.brown@chivas.com

The visitor centre includes a guided tour of the whisky production facilities and a chance to see inside the vast bonded warehouses where the spirit matures. The multimedia exhibition and interactive presentations communicate the unique history, and traditions of Glenlivet Scotch Whisky.
Times: Open Apr-Oct, Mon-Sat 10-4, Sun 12.30-4. **Fee:** * £3 for over 18's which includes minimum £2 voucher redeemable in distillery shop against the purchase of a 70cl bottle of whisky. This charge covers entry to exhibition, guided tour of Distillery & a free dram of whisky. (ch18 free, under 8's not admitted to production areas)
Facilities: 🅿 🍴 ♿ cafeteria toilets for disabled shop ✈ (ex guide dogs) 🏴

🏛 BRODIE CASTLE   Map 14 NH95
BRODIE CASTLE
IV36 2TE (4.5m W of Forres, off A96)
☎ 01309 641371 📠 01309 641600
e-mail: brodiecastle@nts.org.uk

The Brodie family lived here for hundreds of years before passing the castle to the NTS in 1980. It contains many treasures, including furniture, porcelain and paintings. The extensive grounds include a woodland walk and an adventure playground. Wheelchairs for disabled visitors are available. Please telephone for details of recitals, concerts, open air theatre etc.
Times: Open 25 Mar-29 Sep, Thu-Mon, 11-6. Grounds all year, daily, 9.30-sunset. **Fee:** admission free to NTS members. For other details please phone (0131) 243 9387 or check website. **Facilities:** 🅿 🍴 ♿ (audio tape & information sheet in Braille) toilets for disabled shop ✈ (ex guide dogs) ♥

Moray

🏛 BUCKIE　　　　　　　　　　　Map 15 NJ46
BUCKIE DRIFTER MARITIME HERITAGE CENTRE
Freuchny Rd AB56 1TT (off A98 at March Rd Industrial Estate. Follow road N to rdbt, straight ahead and follow road to left. Buckie Drifter car park is on right at bottom of hill)
☎ 01542 834646　📠 01542 835995
e-mail: buckie.drifter@moray.gov.uk

An exciting maritime heritage centre, where you can discover what life was like in the fishing communities of Moray District during the herring boom years of the 1890s and 1930s. Sign on as a crew member of a steam drifter and find out how to catch herring. Try your hand at packing fish in a barrel.
Times: Open end Mar-end Oct **Fee:** * £2.75 (concessions £1.75) Family ticket (2 adults & 3 children) £8. **Facilities:** 🅿 🍴 ♿ (car parking, touch display on lower floor) toilets for disabled shop ✖ (ex assistance dogs) 🐾

🏛 CRAIGELLACHIE　　　　　　Map 15 NJ24
SPEYSIDE COOPERAGE VISITOR CENTRE
Dufftown Rd AB38 9RS (1m S of Craigellachie on A941)
☎ 01340 871108　📠 01340 881437
e-mail: info@speyside-coopers.demon.co.uk

A working cooperage with unique visitor centre, where skilled coopers and their apprentices practise this ancient craft. Each year they repair around 100,000 oak casks which will be used to mature many different whiskies. The 'Acorn to Cask' exhibition traces the history and development of the coopering industry.
Times: Open all year, Mon-Fri 9.30-4. (Closed Xmas & New Year).
Fee: * £2.95 (ch £1.75 & pen £2.25). Family ticket £7.95. Party 15+.
Facilities: 🅿 🍴 ♿ (Special picnic table) toilets for disabled shop ✖ (ex guide dogs) 🐾

🏛 DUFFTOWN　　　　　　　　　Map 15 NJ34
BALVENIE CASTLE
AB55 4DH (On A941)
☎ 01340 820121

The ruined castle was the ancient stronghold of the Comyns, and became a stylish house in the 16th century.
Times: Open Apr-Sep, daily 9.30-6.30. **Fee:** * £1.50 (ch 50p, concessions £1.10). **Facilities:** 🅿 ♿ toilets for disabled 🏳

GLENFIDDICH DISTILLERY
AB55 4DH (N of town, off A941)
☎ 01340 820373　📠 01340 822083
Times: Open all year Mon-Fri 9.30-4.30, also Etr-mid Oct Sat 9.30-4.30, Sun 12-4.30. (Closed Xmas & New Year). **Facilities:** 🅿 ♿ (ramp access to production area & warehouse gallery) toilets for disabled shop ✖ (ex guide dogs) *Details not confirmed for 2003*

🏛 DUFFUS　　　　　　　　　　Map 15 NJ16
DUFFUS CASTLE
(off B9012)
☎ 0131 668 8800

The remains of the mighty motte-and-bailey castle are surrounded by a moat. Within the eight-acre bailey is a 15th-century hall, and the motte is crowned by a 14th-century tower.
Times: Open at all reasonable times. **Fee:** Free. **Facilities:** 🅿 ✖ 🏳

🏛 ELGIN　　　　　　　　　　Map 15 NJ26
ELGIN CATHEDRAL
North College St IV30 1EL
☎ 01343 547171

Founded in 1224, the cathedral was known as the Lantern of the North and the Glory of the Kingdom because of its beauty. In 1390 it was burnt, along with most of the town. Although it was rebuilt, it fell into ruin after the Reformation. The ruins are quite substantial, however, and there is still a good deal to admire, including the fine west towers and the octagonal chapter house.
Times: Open all year, Apr-Sep, daily 9.30-6.30; Oct-Mar, Mon-Sat 9.30-4.30, Sun 2-4.30. (Closed Thu pm, Fri in winter & 25-26 Dec). Telephone for 2003 details. **Fee:** * £2.80 (ch £1, concessions £2).
Facilities: 🅿 ♿ shop 🏳

ELGIN MUSEUM
1 High St IV30 1EQ (East end of High Street, opposite 'Safeway'. Follow brown heritage signs)
☎ 01343 543675　📠 01343 543675
e-mail: curator@elginmuseum.org.uk

This award-winning museum is internationally famous for its fossil fish and fossil reptiles, and for its Pictish stones. The displays relate to the natural and human history of Moray.
Times: Open Apr-Oct, Mon-Fri 10-5, Sat 11-4, Sun 2-5. May be closed for refurbishment early 2003 - phone for details. **Fee:** * £2 (ch 50p, pen, students & UB40 £1). Family ticket £4.50. **Facilities:** 🅿 (50mtrs) ♿ (handrails, case displays at sitting level with large fonts) toilets for disabled shop ✖ (ex guide dogs)

PLUSCARDEN ABBEY
IV30 8UA (6m SW on unclass road)
☎ 01343 890257　📠 01343 890258
e-mail: monks@pluscardenabbey.org

The original monastery, founded by Alexander II in 1230, was burnt, probably by the Wolf of Badenoch who also destroyed Elgin Cathedral. It was restored in the 14th and 19th centuries, and reoccupied in 1948 by Benedictines from Prinknash. Once more a religious

continued

community, retreat facilities are available for men and women. All services (with Gregorian chant) are open to the public. Pluscarden Pentecost Lectures held annually on Tuesday, Wednesday and Thursday after Pentecost.
Times: Open all year, daily 4.45-8.30. **Fee:** Free. **Facilities:** P & (induction loop, ramps to shop, garden partially accessible) toilets for disabled shop garden centre

FOCHABERS Map 15 NJ35
BAXTERS HIGHLAND VILLAGE
IV32 7LD (1m W of Fochabers on A96)
☎ 01343 820666   📠 01343 821790
e-mail: highland.village@Baxters.co.uk

The Baxters food firm started here over 130 years ago and now sells its products in over 60 countries. Visitors can see the shop where the story began, watch an audio-visual display, and visit four shops. See the great hall, audio-visual theatre, cooking theatre and food tasting area.
Times: Open all year, Jan-Mar 10-5; Apr-Dec 9-5.30. **Fee:** Free.
Facilities: P ✗ licensed & (parking facilities) toilets for disabled shop ✗ (ex guide dogs) ☕

FOCHABERS FOLK MUSEUM
High St IV32 7EP
☎ 01343 821204   📠 01343 821291
Times: Open May-Sep 10.30-4. **Facilities:** P & shop ✗ Details not confirmed for 2003

FORRES Map 14 NJ05
DALLAS DHU DISTILLERY
IV36 2RR (1m S of Forres, off A940)
☎ 01309 676548

A perfectly preserved time capsule of the distiller's art. It was built in 1898 to supply malt whisky for Wright and Greig's 'Roderick Dhu' blend. Visitors are welcome to wander at will through this fine old Victorian distillery, or to take a guided tour, dram included.
Times: Open all year, Apr-Sep, daily 9.30-6.30; Oct-Mar, Mon-Sat 9.30-4.30, Sun 2-4.30. (Closed Thu pm, Fri in winter & 25-26 Dec). Telephone for 2003 details. **Fee:** * £3.30 (ch £1, concessions £2.50).phone for 2003 details **Facilities:** P & toilets for disabled shop ✗ ☕

FALCONER MUSEUM
Tolbooth St IV36 1PH (11 miles W of Elgin)
☎ 01309 673701   📠 01309 675863
e-mail: museums@moray.gov.uk

Founded by bequests made by two brothers, Alexander and Hugh Falconer. Hugh was a distinguished scientist, friend of Darwin, recipient of many honours and Vice-President of the Royal Society. On display are fossil mammals collected by him, and items relating to his involvement in the study of anthropology. Other displays are on local wildlife, geology, archaeology and history. Also you can see the Forres Quincentennial Time Capsule.
Times: Open all year - Apr-Oct, Mon-Sat 10-5; Nov-Mar, Mon-Thu 11-12.30 & 1-3.30. (Closed Good Fri & May Day). **Fee:** Free.
Facilities: P & (induction loop system) shop ✗ (ex guide dogs)

SUENOS' STONE
☎ 0131 668 8800

The 20ft-high stone was elaborately carved in the 9th or 10th century, with a sculptured cross on one side and groups of warriors on the other. Why it stands here no one knows, but it may commemorate a victory in battle.
Times: Open - accessible at all times. **Fee:** Free. **Facilities:** P ✗ ♫

KEITH Map 15 NJ45
STRATHISLA DISTILLERY
Seafield Av AB55 5BS (follow A96 Aberdeen to Inverness road, Strathisla is signposted in town)
☎ 01542 783044   📠 01542 783039
e-mail: jeanett.grant@chivas.com

Tour the oldest distillery in the highlands, founded in 1786. Discover the art of the blender before sipping a dram in luxurious comfort.
Times: Open Apr-Oct, Mon-Sat 10-4, Sun 12.30-4 **Fee:** * £4 including £2 voucher redeemable in the distillery shop against the purchase of 70cl bottle of whisky. (ch18 free, children under 8 are not admitted to production areas, but are welcome in the centre) **Facilities:** P (access is very limited) shop ✗ (ex guide dogs) ☕

MARYPARK Map 15 NJ13
GLENFARCLAS DISTILLERY
AB37 9BD (4m W of Aberlour on A95 to Grantown-on-Spey)
☎ 01807 500245 & 500257   📠 01807 500234
e-mail: J&GGrant@glenfarclas.demon.co.uk
Times: Open Jan-Mar, Mon-Fri 10-4; Apr-Sep, Mon-Fri 10-5, Jul-Sep also open Sat 10-5; Oct-Dec, Mon-Fri 10-4. (Closed Sun). **Facilities:** P & (only visitor centre is accessible) toilets for disabled shop ✗ (ex guide dogs in vis. centre) Details not confirmed for 2003 ☕

ROTHES Map 15 NJ24
GLEN GRANT DISTILLERY
AB38 7BS (On A941, in Rothes)
☎ 01542 783318 & 783303   📠 01542 783304
e-mail: jennifer.robertson@chivas.com

Founded in 1840 in a sheltered glen by the two Grant brothers. Discover the secrets of the distillery, including the delightful Victorian garden originally created by Major Grant, and now restored to its former glory, where you can enjoy a dram.
Times: Open Apr-Oct, Mon-Sat 10-4, Sun 12.30-4. **Fee:** * £3 includes minimum £2 voucher redeemable in the distillery shop against 70cl bottle of whisky. **Facilities:** P & (reception centre & still house) toilets for disabled shop ✗ (ex guide dogs) ☕

SPEY BAY Map 15 NJ36
THE MORAY FIRTH WILDLIFE CENTRE
IV32 7PJ (off A96 onto B9014 at Fochabers, follow road approx 5m to village of Spey Bay. Turn left at Spey Bay Hotel and follow road for 500mtrs)
☎ 01343 820339   📠 01343 829109
e-mail: enquiries@mfwc.co.uk

Established in 1997, this family run visitor centre is

continued

330 Moray - North Ayrshire

housed in a former salmon fishing station at the mouth of the Spey. The centre contains exhibitions on dolphins, otters, birds, seals and other local wildlife, a gift shop and a restaurant. Visitors can take to sea on the "Dolphinicity", a survey boat that observes and records sightings of wildlife.
Times: Open Apr-Oct 10.30-5 **Fee:** Free. **Facilities:** P ⬛ ✕ ♿ toilets for disabled shop 🐕 (ex guide dogs) 🍴

TUGNET ICE HOUSE
Tugnet IV32 7PJ (8m E of Elgin on A96, then onto B9104 towards Spey Bay, establishment in 1m)
☎ 01309 673701 📠 01309 675863
e-mail: museums@moray.gov.uk

The largest ice house in Scotland, built in 1830.
Times: Please phone Mary Firth for details on 01343 820339. **Fee:** Free. **Facilities:** P 🐕 (ex guide dogs)

🏛 TOMINTOUL   Map 15 NJ11
TOMINTOUL MUSEUM
The Square AB37 9ET (on A939, 13m E of Grantown)
☎ 01309 673701 📠 01309 675863
e-mail: museums@moray.gov.uk

Situated in one of the highest villages in Britain, the museum features a reconstructed crofter's kitchen and smiddy, with other displays on the local wildlife, the story of Tomintoul, and the local skiing industry.
Times: Open 25 Mar-May, Mon-Fri 9.30-12 & 2-4; Jun-Aug, Mon-Sat, 9.30-12 & 2-4.30; 1 Sep-28 Sep, Mon-Sat, 9.30-12 & 2-4; 30 Sep-25 Oct, Mon-Fri, 9.30-12 & 2-4. Closed May Day & Good Friday. **Fee:** Free. **Facilities:** P ♿ (handling display for visually impaired) shop 🐕 (ex guide dogs)

NORTH AYRSHIRE

🏛 IRVINE   Map 10 NS34
THE BIG IDEA
The Harbourside KA12 8XX (Turn off A78 Irvine & follow signs for Irvine Harbourside & The Big Idea. The Big Idea on right)
☎ 08708 404030 📠 08708 403130   `2 for 1`
e-mail: net@bigidea.org.uk

The Big Idea is a permanent Millennium exhibition on the Ardeer Peninsula linked to Irvine harbourside by a retractable pedestrian bridge. It features 100 years of Nobel Laureates, and 1,000 years of invention and creative genius. Visitors can explore the history of mankind's inventions, creations and innovations.
Times: Open Mon-Sun, from 10am. Closed 25 Dec & 1 Jan. Please phone for exact opening times. **Fee:** £7.95 (ch, pen & concessions £5.95). Family ticket (2 adults & 2 ch) £24. **Facilities:** P ⬛ ♿ (wheelchairs) toilets for disabled shop 🐕 (ex guide dogs or outside) 🍴

SCOTTISH MARITIME MUSEUM
Harbourside KA12 8QE (Follow AA signs from Irvine)
☎ 01294 278283 📠 01294 313211
Times: Open all year, daily 10-5, (ex Xmas & New Year). **Facilities:** P ⬛ ♿ (audio tapes for blind) toilets for disabled shop 🐕 (ex guide dogs) *Details not confirmed for 2003* 🍴

VENNEL GALLERY
10 Glasgow Vennel KA12 0BD
☎ 01294 275059 📠 01294 275059
e-mail: vennel@globalnet.co.uk

The Vennel Gallery has a reputation for exciting and varied exhibitions, ranging from international to local artists. Behind the museum is the Heckling Shop where Robert Burns, Scotland's most famous poet, spent part of his youth learning the trade of flax dressing. In addition to the audio-visual programme on Burns, there is a reconstruction of his lodgings at No.4 Glasgow Vennel, Irvine.
Times: Open all year Thu-Sun 10-1 & 2-5 **Fee:** Free. **Facilities:** P (residential area) ♿ shop 🐕 (ex guide dogs)

🏛 LARGS   Map 10 NS25
KELBURN CASTLE AND COUNTRY CENTRE
Fairlie KA29 0BE (on A78 2m S of Largs)
☎ 01475 568685   `2 for 1`
📠 01475 568121
e-mail: admin@kelburncountrycentre.com

Historic home of the Earls of Glasgow, Kelburn is famous for its romantic Glen, family gardens, unique trees and spectacular views over the Firth of Clyde. Glen walks, riding and trekking centre, adventure course, activity workshop, Kelburn Story Cartoon Exhibition and a family museum. The "Secret Forest" at the centre, Scotland's most unusual attraction, is a chance to explore the Giant's Castle, maze of the Green Man and secret grotto.
Times: Open all year, Etr-end Oct, daily 10-6; Nov-Mar, Grounds only. **Fee:** £4.50 (concessions £3). Family tickets £13. **Facilities:** P ⬛ ✕ licensed ♿ (Ranger service to assist disabled) toilets for disabled shop 🍴

VIKINGAR!
Greenock Rd KA30 8QL (Opposite RNLI lifeboat stn on A78, 0.5m into Largs)
☎ 01475 689777 📠 01475 689444
e-mail: anyone@vikingar.co.uk
Times: Open daily, Apr-Sep, Mon-Fri & Sun 10.30-5.30, Sat 12.30-3.30; Oct-Mar, Mon-Fri & Sun 10.30-3.30, Sat 10.30-3.30; Nov & Feb, wknds only, Sat 12.30-3.30, Sun 10.30-3.30. (Closed Dec & Jan).
Facilities: P ⬛ ♿ toilets for disabled shop 🐕 (ex guide dogs) *Details not confirmed for 2003* 🍴

🏛 SALTCOATS   Map 10 NS24
NORTH AYRSHIRE MUSEUM
Manse St, Kirkgate KA21 5AA
☎ 01294 464174 📠 01294 464174
e-mail: namuseum@globalnet.co.uk

This museum is housed in an 18th-century church, and features a rich variety of artefacts from the North Ayrshire area, including archaeological and social history material. There is a continuing programme of temporary exhibitions.
Times: Open all year, Mon-Sat (ex Wed) 10-1 & 2-5. **Fee:** Free. **Facilities:** P (100mtrs) ♿ toilets for disabled shop 🐕 (ex guide dogs)

NORTH LANARKSHIRE

⛨ COATBRIDGE   Map 11 NS76
SUMMERLEE HERITAGE TRUST
Heritage Way, West Canal St ML5 1QD (In town centre, adjacent to Coatbridge central station)
☎ 01236 431261   📠 01236 440429

A 20-acre museum of social and industrial history centering on the remains of the Summerlee Ironworks which were put into blast in the 1830s. The exhibition hall features displays of social and industrial history including working machinery and recreated workshop interiors. Outside, Summerlee operates the only working tram in Scotland, a coal mine and reconstructed miners' rows with interiors dating from 1840.
Times: Open daily 10-5. (Closed 25-26 Dec & 1-2 Jan). Nov-Mar 10-4.
Fee: Free. **Facilities:** 🅿 💺 ♿ (wheelchair available & staff assistance) toilets for disabled shop ✖ (ex guide dogs)

⛨ MOTHERWELL   Map 11 NS75
MOTHERWELL HERITAGE CENTRE
High Rd ML1 3HU (M74 junct 6, A723 for town centre. At top of hill, turn left, before railway bridge)
☎ 01698 251000   📠 01698 268867

This award-winning audio-visual experince, 'Technopolis', traces the history of the area from Roman times to the rise of 19th-century industry and the post-industrial era. There is also a fine viewing tower, an exhibition gallery and family history research facilities. A mixed programme of community events and touring exhibitions occur throughout the year.
Times: Open Wed-Sat 10-5 (Thu 10-7), Sun 12-5. **Fee:** Free.
Facilities: 🅿 ♿ toilets for disabled shop ✖ (ex guide dogs)

PERTH & KINROSS

⛨ ABERFELDY   Map 14 NN84
DEWAR'S WORLD OF WHISKY
Aberfeldy Distillery PH15 2EB (from A9 turn off for Aberfeldy on A827 at Ballinluig)   **2 for 1**
☎ 01887 822010   📠 01887 822012
e-mail: enquiries@dewarsworldofwhisky

Tradition and the latest technology are combined here to tell the story of Dewar's White Label Whisky. Visitors are able to sample the product in the Nosing and Tasting Bar, and have a guided tour of the Aberfeldy distillery, where they can see traditional techniques being employed by skilled craftsmen.
Times: Open Apr-Oct, Mon-Sat 10-6, Sun noon-4; Nov-Mar, Mon-Fri 10-4. (Closed Xmas & New Year). **Fee:** * £3.95 (ch £2.50, concession £3). Family ticket £10. Party by arrangement. **Facilities:** 🅿 💺 ♿ (visitor centre only accessible) toilets for disabled shop ✖ (ex guide dogs) 🍴

⛨ BLAIR ATHOLL   Map 14 NN86
BLAIR CASTLE
PH18 5TL (7m NW of Pitlochry, off A9)
☎ 01796 481207   📠 01796 481487
e-mail: office@blair-castle.co.uk

Home of the Dukes of Atholl and the Atholl Highlanders, the Duke's unique private army. The castle dates back to the 13th century but was altered in the 18th, and later given a castellated exterior. The oldest part is Cumming's Tower, built in about 1270. There are paintings, Jacobite relics, lace, tapestries, and Masonic regalia. The extensive grounds include a deer park, and a restored 18th-century walled garden and children's play area. Events are held throughout the year, including the annual parade of the Duke's Private Army (ring for details).
Times: Open Apr-25 Oct, daily 10-6 (9.30-6 Jul-Aug) Last admission 5. Winter tours by arrangement only. **Fee:** * £6.50 (ch £4, £5.50). Family ticket £16.75. Party. **Facilities:** 🅿 💺 ✖ licensed ♿ (toilets not suitable for severely disabled, parking) shop ✖ (ex guide dogs) 🍴

⛨ BRUAR   Map 14 NN86
CLAN DONNACHAIDH (ROBERTSON) MUSEUM
PH18 5TW (approx 4m N of Blair Atholl, on B8079)
☎ 01796 483264   📠 01796 483338
e-mail: donkey3@freenetname.co.uk
Times: Open Apr-Oct, Mon-Sat 10-5, Sun 11-5 (Jun-Aug closes at 5.30). **Facilities:** 🅿 ♿ shop ✖ (ex guide dogs) *Details not confirmed for 2003*

⛨ CRIEFF   Map 11 NN82
INNERPEFFRAY LIBRARY
PH7 3RF (4.5m SE on B8062)
☎ 01764 652819
e-mail: library@innerpeff.fsnet.co.uk

This is Scotland's oldest free lending library. It was founded in 1680 and is still open every day except Thursdays. It is housed in a late 18th-century building, and contains a notable collection of bibles and rare books. Adjacent is St Mary's Chapel, the original site for the library and the Drummond family burial place.
Times: Open all year, Mon-Wed & Fri-Sat 10-12.45 & 2-4.45, Sun 2-4. (Closed Thu). Nov-Feb appointment only. **Fee:** £2.50 (ch under 15 50p) **Facilities:** 🅿 💺 ✖ (ex guide dogs)

Perth & Kinross

The Famous Grouse Experience
The Hosh PH7 4HA (1.5m NW off A85)
☎ 01764 656565 📠 01764 654366
2 for 1
e-mail: glenturret@highlanddistillers.co.uk

A trip to Crieff is incomplete without a visit to The Famous Grouse Experience, set in Scotland's oldest, most visited and award-winning distillery. Opened in July 2002, this new attraction is a fun and interesting day out which combines the traditional distillery visit with a unique exciting sensory experience. Spend a relaxing few hours exploring the history of the brand. Test your senses and see if you have what it takes to become a 'Whisky Nose'. Have lunch, a snack or even a barbecue at the family restaurant. Visit the well-stocked shop or enjoy a peaceful woodland walk over The Brig O' Dram.
Times: Open Feb-Dec, Mon-Sat 9.30-6 (last tour 4.30), Sun 12-6 (last tour 4.30); Jan, Mon-Fri 11.30-4 (last tour 2.30). (Closed 25-26 Dec & 1-2 Jan). **Fee:** * Distillery visit, grouse experience show £6, (ch £3) Family £16. **Facilities:** 🅿 🍴 ✕ licensed ♿ Lifts in all areas toilets for disabled shop ✕ (ex guide dogs) 🎁

DUNKELD
Map 11 NO04
The Ell Shop & Little Houses
The Cross PH8 0AN (off A9, 15m N of Perth)
☎ 01350 727460
e-mail: dunkeld@nts.org.uk

The National Trust owns two rows of 20 houses in Dunkeld, and has preserved their 17th/18th-century character. They are not open to the public, but there is a display and audio-visual show in the Information Centre.
Times: Open Ell Shop 25 Mar-Sep, Mon-Sat, 10-5.30, Sun 12.30-5.30. Oct-24 Dec, Mon-Sat 10-4.30, Sun 12.30-4.30. **Fee:** Free. **Facilities:** 🅿 (300yds) ♿ toilets for disabled shop ✕ 🎁

GLENGOULANDIE DEER PARK
Map 14 NN75
Glengoulandie Deer Park
PH16 5NL (8m NW of Aberfeldy on B846)
☎ 01887 830261 📠 01887 830261
e-mail: helenmcadam@supanet.com
Times: Open May-Oct, 9am-1hr before sunset. **Facilities:** 🅿 (charged) shop ✕ Details not confirmed for 2003

KILLIECRANKIE
Map 14 NN96
Killiecrankie Visitor Centre
NTS Visitor Centre PH16 5LG (3m N of Pitlochry on B8079)
☎ 01796 473233 📠 01796 473233
e-mail: killiecrankie@nts.org.uk

The visitor centre features an exhibition on the battle of 1689, when the Jacobite army routed the English, although the Jacobite leader, 'Bonnie Dundee', was mortally wounded in the attack. The wooded gorge is a notable beauty spot, admired by Queen Victoria, and there are some splendid walks.
Times: Visitor Centre: 25 Mar-Jun & 2 Sep-31 Oct, daily 10-5.30, Jul-1 Sep, daily 9.30-7. Site: open all year daily. **Fee:** Admission free to NTS members. For other details please phone (0131) 243 9387 or check website. **Facilities:** 🅿 🍴 ♿ (visitor centre only) toilets for disabled shop 🎁

KINROSS
Map 11 NO10
Kinross House Gardens
KY13 8ET (M90 (Edinburgh to Perth), junct 6 to Kinross, and signposted in village)
☎ 01577 862900 📠 01577 863372
e-mail: jm@kinrosshouse.com

Yew hedges, roses and herbaceous borders are the elegant attractions of these formal gardens. The 17th-century house was built by Sir William Bruce, but is not generally open to the public.
Times: Gardens only open Apr-Sep, daily 10-7. **Fee:** * £2 (ch 50p). **Facilities:** 🅿 ♿ ✕ (ex guide dogs)

Loch Leven Castle
Castle Island KY13 7AR (on an island in Loch Leven accessible by boat from Kinross)
☎ 01786 450000

Mary, Queen of Scots was imprisoned here in this five-storey castle in 1567 - she escaped 11 months later and gave the 14th-century castle its special place in history.
Times: Open Apr-Sep, daily 9.30-6.30. Telephone for 2003 details. **Fee:** * £3.30 (ch £1.20, concessions £2.50). Charge includes ferry trip. **Facilities:** 🅿 shop ✕ 🎁

RSPB Nature Reserve Vane Farm
By Loch Leven KY13 9LX (on S shore of Loch Leven, entered off B9097 to Glenrothes, 2m E M90 junct 5)
☎ 01577 862355 📠 01577 862013
2 for 1
e-mail: vane.farm@rspb.org.uk

Well placed beside Loch Leven, with a nature trail and hides overlooking the Loch and a woodland trail with stunning panoramic views. Noted for its pink-footed geese. The area also attracts whooper swans, greylag geese and great spotted woodpeckers amongst others. Details of special events are available from the Visitors Centre.
Times: Open daily, 10-5. **Fee:** £3 (ch 50p, concessions £2). Family £6 (2ad+all ch). Members free. **Facilities:** 🅿 🍴 ♿ (ramps, shop, coffee shop & observation room accessible) toilets for disabled shop ✕ (ex guide dogs) 🎁

MILNATHORT
Map 11 NO10
Burleigh Castle
KY13 7XZ
☎ 0131 668 8800

Dating from 1582, this tower house has an enclosed courtyard and roofed angle tower.
Times: Open at all reasonable times. **Fee:** Free. **Facilities:** ✕ 🎁

MUTHILL
Map 11 NN81
Drummond Castle Gardens
PH7 4HZ (2m S of Crieff on A822)
☎ 01764 681257 & 681433 📠 01764 681550
e-mail: thegardens@drummondcastle.sol.co.uk

The gardens of Drummond Castle were originally laid out in 1630 by John Drummond, 2nd Earl of Perth. In 1830, the parterre was changed to an Italian style. The

continued

multi-faceted sundial was designed by John Mylne, Master Mason to Charles I. These are Scotland's Largest formal gardens and amongst the finest in Europe.

Times: Open Gardens May-Oct, daily 2-6 (Last admission 5pm). Also Etr for 4 days. **Fee:** £3.50 (ch £1.50 & pen £2.50). **Facilities:** P & toilets for disabled shop

PERTH Map 11 NO12
BLACK WATCH REGIMENTAL MUSEUM
Balhousie Castle, Hay St PH1 5HR (Follow signs to Perth & Black Watch Museum, approach via Dunkeld Road)
☎ 0131 310 8530   📠 01738 643245
e-mail: rhq@theblackwatch.co.uk

The treasures of the 42nd/73rd Highland Regiment from 1739 to the present day are on show in this museum, together with paintings, silver, colours, uniforms and weapons.
Times: Open all year. May-Sep, Mon-Sat 10-4.30 (Closed last Sat in Jun); Oct-Apr, Mon-Fri, 10-3.30 (Closed 23 Dec-6 Jan). Other times & Parties 16+ by appointment. **Fee:** Donations. **Facilities:** P & (1 bay parking for disabled) shop ✈ (ex guide dogs)

BRANKLYN GARDEN
116 Dundee Rd PH2 7BB (on A85)
☎ 01738 625535
e-mail: aclipson@nts.scot.demon.co.uk

The gardens cover two acres and are noted for their collections of rhododendrons, shrubs and alpines. Garden tours and botanical painting courses are held.
Times: Daily, 9.30-6 **Fee:** Admission free to NTS members. For other details please phone (0131) 243 9387 or check website. **Facilities:** P ✈ (ex guide dogs)

CAITHNESS GLASS FACTORY & VISITOR CENTRE
Inveralmond Industrial Est PH1 3TZ (on Perth Western Bypass, A9, at Inveralmond)
☎ 01738 637373   📠 01738 492300
e-mail: visitor@caithnessglass.co.uk
Times: Open all year, Factory shop & restaurant Mon-Sat 9-5, Sun 10-5 (Dec-Feb 12-5). Glassmaking Mon-Fri 9-4.30. **Fee:** Free. **Facilities:** P ✈ licensed & (wheelchair available) toilets for disabled shop ✈ (ex guide dogs)

Drummond Castle Gardens Perthshire

Scotland's most important formal gardens, among the finest in Europe. The terraces overlook a magnificent parterre celebrating the saltire and family heraldry, surrounding the famous multiplex sundial by John Milne, Master Mason to Charles I.

Tel: 01764 681257/433
Fax: 01764 681550
Email: thegardens@drummondcastle.sol.co.uk

Open Easter weekend, then daily May 1st to October 31st, 2pm-6pm (last entry 5pm).

HUNTINGTOWER CASTLE
PH1 3JL (2m W)
☎ 01738 627231

Formerly known as Ruthven Castle and famous as the scene of the so-called `Raid of Ruthven' in 1582, this structure was built in the 15th and 16th centuries and features a painted ceiling.
Times: Open all year, Apr-Sep, daily 9.30-6.30; Oct-Mar, Mon-Sat 9.30-4.30, Sun 2-4.30. (Closed Thu pm, Fri in winter & 25-26 Dec). **Fee:** * £2.20 (ch 75p, concessions £1.60). **Facilities:** P shop ✈

PERTH MUSEUM & ART GALLERY
78 George St PH1 5LB (centrally situated)
☎ 01738 632488   📠 01738 443505
e-mail: museum@pkc.gov.uk

This purpose-built museum houses collections of fine and applied art, social and local history, natural history and archaeology. Temporary exhibitions are held throughout the year.
Times: Open all year, Mon-Sat 10-5. (Closed Xmas-New Year). **Fee:** Free. **Facilities:** P (adjacent) & toilets for disabled shop ✈ (ex guide dogs)

PITLOCHRY Map 14 NN95
EDRADOUR DISTILLERY
PH16 5JP (2.5m E of Pitlochry on A924)
☎ 01796 472095   📠 01796 472002
e-mail: lwilliamson@campbell-distillers.co.uk

It was in 1825 that a group of local farmers founded

continued

Perth & Kinross - Renfrewshire

Edradour, naming it after the bubbling burn that runs through it. It is Scotland's smallest distillery and is virtually unchanged since Victorian times. Have a dram of whisky while watching an audio-visual in the malt barn and then take a guided tour through the distillery itself.
Times: Open, early Mar-end Oct, Mon-Sat 9.30-5, Sun 12-5. Winter months, Mon-Sat 10-4, shop only. Tours by arrangement in winter months. **Fee:** Free. **Facilities:** P & toilets for disabled shop ✱ (ex guide & hearing dogs)

FASKALLY
(1m N on the B8019)
☎ 01350 727284   ▤ 01350 728635
e-mail: peter.fullarton@forestry.gsi.gov.uk
Times: Open all year-dawn to dusk. **Facilities:** P & (smooth, level path around Loch Dunmore, 700mtrs) toilets for disabled 🚲 *Details not confirmed for 2003*

SCOTTISH & SOUTHERN ENERGY VISITOR CENTRE, DAM & FISH PASS
PH16 5ND (Turn off A9, 24m N of Perth)
☎ 01796 473152   ▤ 01882 634 709

The visitor centre features an exhibition showing how electricity is brought from the power station to the customer, and there is access to the turbine viewing gallery. The salmon ladder viewing chamber allows you to see the fish as they travel upstream to their spawning ground.
Times: Open Apr-Oct, daily 10-5.30. **Fee:** * £2 (ch £1, concessions £1.20). Family ticket £4. **Facilities:** P & (monitor viewing of salmon fish pass) toilets for disabled shop ✱ (ex guide dogs) 🍴

QUEEN'S VIEW   Map 14 NN85
QUEEN'S VIEW VISITOR CENTRE
PH16 5NR (7m W of Pitlochry on B8019)
☎ 01350 727284   ▤ 01350 728635
e-mail: peter.fullarton@forestry.gsi.gov.uk
Times: Open Apr-Oct, daily 10-6. **Facilities:** P (charged) 🍴 & toilets for disabled shop *Details not confirmed for 2003* 🍴

SCONE   Map 11 NO12
SCONE PALACE
PH2 6BD (2m NE of Perth on A93)
☎ 01738 552300   ▤ 01738 552588   `2 for 1`
e-mail: visits@scone-palace.co.uk

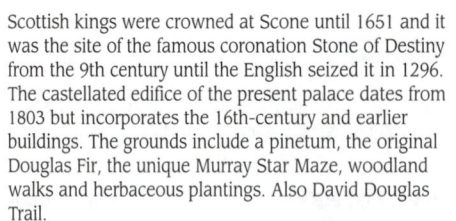

Scottish kings were crowned at Scone until 1651 and it was the site of the famous coronation Stone of Destiny from the 9th century until the English seized it in 1296. The castellated edifice of the present palace dates from 1803 but incorporates the 16th-century and earlier buildings. The grounds include a pinetum, the original Douglas Fir, the unique Murray Star Maze, woodland walks and herbaceous plantings. Also David Douglas Trail.
Times: Open Apr-Oct. **Fee:** * Palace & Grounds £6.20 (ch £3.60, students & pen £5.30). Family ticket £20, Season ticket £15. Grounds only £3.10 (ch £1.70, students and pen £2.50) Family £17. **Facilities:** P 🍴 ✕ licensed & toilets for disabled shop 🍴

WEEM   Map 14 NN84
CASTLE MENZIES
PH15 2JD (Follow signs from A9)
☎ 01887 820982   ▤ 01887 820982
e-mail: menziesclan@tesco.net

Restored seat of the Chiefs of Clan Menzies, and a fine example of a 16th-century Z-plan fortified tower house. Prince Charles Edward Stuart stayed here briefly on his way to Culloden in 1746. The whole of the 16th-century building can be explored, and there's a small clan museum.
Times: Open Apr-13 Oct, Mon-Sat 10.30-5, Sun 2-5. **Fee:** £3.50 (ch £2, concessions £3). **Facilities:** P & toilets for disabled shop ✱ (ex guide dogs)

RENFREWSHIRE

KILBARCHAN   Map 10 NS46
WEAVER'S COTTAGE
The Cross PA10 2JG (off A737, 12m SW of Glasgow)
☎ 01505 705588
e-mail: aclipson@nts.scot.demon.co.uk

The weaving craft is regularly demonstrated at this delightful 18th-century cottage museum, and there is a collection of weaving equipment and other domestic utensils.
Times: Open 25 Mar-27 Oct, daily, 1-5 **Fee:** Admission free to NTS members. For other details please phone (0131) 243 9387 or check website. **Facilities:** P ✱ (ex guide dogs) 🍴

LANGBANK   Map 10 NS37
FINLAYSTONE COUNTRY ESTATE
PA14 6TJ (on A8 W of Langbank, 10m W of Glasgow Airport, follow Thistle signs)
☎ 01475 540505   ▤ 01475 540285
e-mail: info@finlaystone.co.uk
Times: Open all year. Woodland & Gardens daily, 10-5. **Facilities:** P 🍴 & (lift to second floor pathways for wheelchairs) toilets for disabled shop *Details not confirmed for 2003*

LOCHWINNOCH   Map 10 NS35
LOCHWINNOCH COMMUNITY MUSEUM
High St PA12 4AB
☎ 01505 842615   ▤ 0141 889 9240
Times: Open all year, Mon 10-1, 2-5 & 6-8; Sat 10-1 & 2-5. **Facilities:** P & ✱ (ex guide dogs) *Details not confirmed for 2003*

RSPB LOCHWINNOCH NATURE RESERVE
Largs Rd PA12 4JF (on A760, Largs road, opposite Lochwinnoch station, 16m SW of Glasgow)
☎ 01505 842663   ▤ 01505 843026
e-mail: Lochwinnoch@rspb.org.uk

The reserve, part of Clyde Muirshiel Regional Park and a Site of Special Scientific Interest, comprises two shallow lochs fringed by marsh which in turn is fringed

continued

by scrub and woodland. There are two trails leading to three hides and a visitor centre with a viewing. **Times:** Open all year, daily 10-5. (Closed Xmas & New Year). **Fee:** * £2 (ch 50p, concessions £1). Family ticket £4. **Facilities:** P & (wheelchair available, access to 3 hides) toilets for disabled shop ✗

PAISLEY   Map 11 NS46
COATS OBSERVATORY
49 Oakshaw St West PA1 2DE (M8 junct 27, 28 or 29)
☎ 0141 889 2013   ≣ 0141 889 9240
Times: Open all year, Tue-Sat 10-5, Sun 2-5. Last entry 15 minutes before closing. **Facilities:** P 150yds (meters/limited street parking) shop ✗ (ex guide dogs) *Details not confirmed for 2003*

PAISLEY MUSEUM & ART GALLERIES
High St PA1 2BA
☎ 0141 889 3151   ≣ 0141 889 9240
Times: Open all year, Tue-Sat 10-5, Sun 2-5. BH 10-5. **Facilities:** P (200yds) & (parking on site) toilets for disabled shop ✗ (ex guide dogs) *Details not confirmed for 2003*

SCOTTISH BORDERS

COLDSTREAM   Map 12 NT84
HIRSEL
Douglas & Angus Estates, Estate Office, The Hirsel TD12 4LP (0.5m W on A697)
☎ 01890 882834 & 882965   ≣ 01890 882834
Times: Garden & Grounds open all year, daylight hours. Museum 10-5. Craft Centre Mon-Fri, 10-5, wknds noon-5. **Facilities:** P (charged) ⌂ & toilets for disabled shop ✗ *Details not confirmed for 2003*

DRYBURGH   Map 12 NT53
DRYBURGH ABBEY
TD6 0RQ (5m SE of Melrose on B6404)
☎ 01835 822381

The abbey was one of the Border monasteries founded by David I, and stands in a lovely setting on the River Tweed. The ruins are equally beautiful, and the church has the graves of Sir Walter Scott and Earl Haig.
Times: Open all year, Apr-Sep, daily 9.30-6.30; Oct-Mar, Mon-Sat 9.30-4.30, Sun 2-4.30. (Closed 25-26 Dec). Telephone for 2003 details. **Fee:** * £2.80 (ch £1, concessions £2). Telephone for 2003 details **Facilities:** P & shop ✗ ▯

DUNS   Map 12 NT75
JIM CLARK ROOM
44 Newtown St TD11 3AU
☎ 01361 883960   ≣ 01361 884104
Times: Open Etr-Sep, Mon-Sat 10.30-1 & 2-4.30, Sun 2-4; Oct, Mon-Sat 1-4. **Facilities:** P (on street) & (ramps, wheelchair space, large print notices etc) shop ✗ (ex guide dogs) *Details not confirmed for 2003*

Renfrewshire - Scottish Borders   335

MANDERSTON
TD11 3PP (2m E of Duns on A6105)
☎ 01361 883450   ≣ 01361 882010
e-mail: palmer@manderston.co.uk

This grandest of grand houses gives a fascinating picture of Edwardian life above and below stairs. Completely remodelled for the millionaire racehorse owner Sir James Miller, the architect was told to spare no expense, and so the house boasts the world's only silver staircase. The staterooms are magnificent, and there are fine formal gardens, with a woodland garden and lakeside walks.
Times: Open mid May-end Sep, Thu & Sun 2-50 (also late May & Aug English BH Mons). **Fee:** * £6.50 (ch £3) gardens only: £3.50 (ch £1.50) **Facilities:** P ⌂ & shop ✗ (ex guide dogs & in gardens)

EYEMOUTH   Map 12 NT96
EYEMOUTH MUSEUM
Auld Kirk, Manse Rd TD14 5JE (Turn off A1 onto A1107, follow signs to town centre. Museum in town centre)
☎ 018907 50678   **2 for 1**

The museum was opened in 1981 as a memorial to the 129 local fishermen lost in the Great Fishing Disaster of 1881. Its main feature is the 15ft Eyemouth tapestry, which was made for the centenary. There are also displays on local history.
Times: Open Apr-Jun & Sep, Mon-Sat 10-5, Sun 1-4; Jul-Aug, Mon-Sat 10-5; Sun 1-5; Oct, Mon-Sat 10-4, (closed Sun). **Fee:** * £2 (concessions £1.50). Accompanied ch free. Party. **Facilities:** P (250yds) (45min on street outside) & shop

GALASHIELS   Map 12 NT43
LOCHCARRON OF SCOTLAND VISITOR CENTRE
Waverley Mill, Huddersfield St TD1 3BA (On A7, follow signs to mill)
☎ 01896 752091 & 751100   **2 for 1**
≣ 01896 758833
e-mail: quality@lochcarron.com

The museum brings the town's past to life and the focal point is a display on the woollen industry. Guided tours of the mill take about 40 minutes.
Times: Open all year, Mon-Sat 9-5, Sun (Jun-Sep) 12-5. Mill tours Mon-Thu at 10.30, 11.30, 1.30 & 2.30, Fri am only. **Fee:** Museum free. Mill tour £2.50 (ch 14 free). **Facilities:** P & toilets for disabled shop ✗

GORDON   Map 12 NT64
MELLERSTAIN HOUSE
TD3 6LG (signposted on A6089 Kelso-Gordon road, 1m W)
☎ 01573 410225   ≣ 01573 410636
e-mail: enquiries@mellerstain.com

One of Scotland's finest Georgian houses, begun by William Adam and completed by his son Robert in the 1770s. It has beautiful plasterwork, period furniture and pictures, terraced gardens and a lake.
Times: Open Etr & May-Sep, Sun-Fri 12.30-5 (Last admission 4.30pm). & wknds in Oct **Fee:** * £5.50 (ch £3, pen £5) Party 20+. **Facilities:** P ⌂ & shop garden centre ✗ (ex guide dogs) ▯

Scottish Borders

HERMITAGE Map 12 NY59
Hermitage Castle
TD9 0LU (5.5m NE of Newcastleton, on B6399)
☎ 01387 376222

A vast, eerie ruin of the 14th and 15th centuries, associated with the de Soulis, the Douglases and Mary, Queen of Scots. Much restored in the 19th century.
Times: Open Apr-Sep, daily 9.30-6.30. Telephone for 2003 details.
Fee: * £2 (ch 75p, concessions £1.50). **Facilities:** P & ♫

INNERLEITHEN Map 11 NT33
Robert Smail's Printing Works
7/9 High St EH44 6HA
☎ 01896 830206
e-mail: smails@nts.org.uk

These buildings contain a Victorian office, a paper store with reconstructed waterwheel, a composing room and a press room. The machinery is in full working order and visitors may view the printer at work and experience typesetting in the compositing room.
Times: Open 25 Mar-28 Jun & 2 Sep-27 Oct, Thu-Mon 12-5, Sun 1-5. 29 Jun-1 Sep, Thu-Mon 10-6, Sun 1-5 **Fee:** Admission free for NTS members. For other details please phone (0131) 243 9387 or check website. **Facilities:** P (300yds) & shop ✈ (ex guide dogs) ♯

JEDBURGH Map 12 NT62
Jedburgh Abbey
☎ 01835 863925

Standing as the most complete of the Border monasteries (although it has been sacked and rebuilt many times) Jedburgh Abbey has been described as 'the most perfect and beautiful example of the Saxon and early Gothic in Scotland'. David I founded it as a priory in the 12th century and remains of some of the domestic buildings have been uncovered during excavations.
Times: Open all year, Apr-Sep, daily 9.30-6.30; Oct-Mar, Mon-Sat 9.30-4.30, Sun 2-4.30. (Closed 25-26 Dec). **Fee:** * £3.30 (ch £1.20, concessions £2.50). **Facilities:** P & (limited access) toilets for disabled shop ✈ ♫

KELSO Map 12 NT73
Floors Castle
Roxburghe Estates Office TD5 7SF (from town centre follow Roxburghe Street to main gates)
☎ 01573 223333 ≣ 01573 226056
e-mail: marketing@floorscastle.com

2 for 1

The home of the 10th Duke of Roxburghe, the Castle's lived-in atmosphere enhances the superb collection of French furniture, tapestries and paintings. The house was designed by William Adam in 1721 and enjoys a magnificent setting overlooking the River Tweed and the Cheviot Hills beyond.
Times: Open 5 Apr-26 Oct, daily 10-4.30. (last admission 4). **Fee:** £5.75 (ch £3.25, pen & students £4.75). Family ticket £15. Group rates for 20+. **Facilities:** P ⌘ ✗ licensed & (lift) toilets for disabled shop garden centre ⚘

KELSO ABBEY
☎ 0131 668 8800

Founded by David I in 1128 and probably the greatest of the four famous Border abbeys, Kelso became extremely wealthy and acquired extensive lands. In 1545 it served as a fortress when the town was attacked by the Earl of Hertford, but now only fragments of the once-imposing abbey church give any clue to its long history.
Times: Open at any reasonable time. **Fee:** Free. **Facilities:** & ♫

LAUDER Map 12 NT54
Thirlestane Castle
TD2 6RU (off A68, S of Lauder)
☎ 01578 722430 ≣ 01578 722761
e-mail: admin@thirlestanecastle.co.uk

One of the seven "Great Houses of Scotland" this fairy-tale castle has been the home of the Maitland family, the Earls of Lauderdale, since the 12th century. Some of the most splendid plasterwork ceilings in Britain may be seen in the 17th-century state rooms. The family nurseries house a sizeable collection of antique toys and dolls. Vaulted dungeon display. The informal riverside grounds, with their views of the grouse moors, include a woodland walk, picnic tables and adventure playground.
Times: Open Apr-Oct **Fee:** * £5.30. Family ticket £13.50. Grounds only £1.50. **Facilities:** P ⌘ shop ✈ (ex guide dogs) ♫

MELROSE Map 12 NT53
Abbotsford
TD6 9BQ (2m W off A6091, on B6360)
☎ 01896 752043 ≣ 01896 752916

Set on the River Tweed, Sir Walter Scott's romantic mansion remains much the same as it was in his day. Inside there are many mementoes and relics of his remarkable life and also his historical collections, armouries and library, with some 9,000 volumes. Scott built the mansion between 1811 and 1822, and lived here until his death ten years after its completion.
Times: Open daily from 3rd Mon in Mar-Oct, Mon-Sat 9.30-5. Sun in Mar-May & Oct 2-5. Sun Jun-Sep 9.30-5. **Fee:** * £4 (ch £2). Party £3.20 (ch £1.60). **Facilities:** P ⌘ & (parking at private entrance) toilets for disabled shop ✈ (ex guide dogs & hearing dogs)

Harmony Garden
St Mary's Rd TD6 9LJ (Opposite Melrose Abbey)
☎ 01721 722502 ≣ 01721 724700

Set around the early 19th century Harmony Hall (not open to visitor's), this attractive walled garden has magnificent views of Melrose Abbey and the Eildon Hills. The garden comprises lawns, herbaceous and mixed borders, vegetable and fruit areas, and a rich display of spring bulbs.
Times: Open 25 Mar-27 Oct, Mon-Sat 10-6, Sun 1-5 **Fee:** Admission free for NTS members. For othe price details please phone (0131) 243 9387 or check website **Facilities:** P & ✈ ♯

Scottish Borders

MELROSE ABBEY & ABBEY MUSEUM
TD6 9LG
☎ 01896 822562

The ruin of this Cistercian abbey is probably one of Scotland's finest, and has been given added glamour by its connection with Sir Walter Scott. The abbey was repeatedly wrecked during the Scottish wars of independence, but parts survive from the 14th century. The heart of Robert the Bruce is buried somewhere within the church.
Times: Open all year,1 Apr-Sep, daily 9.30-6; Oct-Jan, Mon-Sat 9.30-6 (Closed 25-26 Dec). Telephone for 2003 details. **Fee:** * £3.30 (ch £1.20, concessions £2.50). Telephone for 2003 details **Facilities:** P & shop ✻ ♫

PRIORWOOD GARDEN & DRIED FLOWER SHOP
TD6 9PX (off A6091, in Melrose, adjacent to abbey. On National Cycle Route 1)
☎ 01896 822493   📠 01896 822965
e-mail: priorwooddriedflowers@nts.org.uk

This small garden specialises in flowers suitable for drying. It is formally designed with herbaceous and everlasting annual borders, and the attractive orchard has a display of 'apples through the ages'. Dried flowers are on sale in the shop.
Times: Open 25 Mar-24 Dec, Mon-Sat 10-5, Sun 1-5 **Fee:** Admission free for NTS members. For other details please phone (0131) 243 9387 or check website **Facilities:** P & (ramps, paths) shop ♥

🏛 PEEBLES   Map 11 NT23
KAILZIE GARDENS
EH45 9HT (2.5m SE on B7062)
☎ 01721 720007   📠 01721 720007

These extensive grounds, with their fine old trees, provide a burnside walk flanked by bulbs, rhododendrons and azaleas. A walled garden contains herbaceous, shrub rose borders, greenhouses and a formal rose garden. A garden for all seasons, don't miss the snowdrops. A large stocked trout pond and rod hire available, and an 18-hole putting green. Newly open bait pond.
Times: Open 25 Mar-Oct, daily 11-5.30. Grounds close 5.30pm. Garden open all year. **Fee:** mid Mar-Jun £2.50, Jun-Oct £3 (end Oct-mid Mar £2 honesty box) ch 5-12 80p **Facilities:** P ☕ ✕ licensed & (ramps in garden) toilets for disabled shop

NEIDPATH CASTLE
EH45 8NW (0.5m of Peebles W on A72)
☎ 01721 720333
e-mail: keith.roxburgh@eidosnet.uk   **2 for 1**

Occupying a spectacular position on the Tweed, this 14th-century stronghold was adapted to 17th-century living; it contains a rock-hewn well, a pit prison, a small museum, and a tartan display. There are fine walks and a picnic area.
Times: Open Etr, May BH's, mid Jun-mid Sep Mon-Sat 10.30-4.30, Sun 12.30-4.30 **Fee:** £3 (ch £1, concessions £2.50). Family ticket £7.50. Party 20+. **Facilities:** P (charged) shop

🏛 SELKIRK   Map 12 NT42
BOWHILL HOUSE AND COUNTRY PARK
TD7 5ET (3m W of Selkirk off A708)
☎ 01750 22204   📠 01750 22204
e-mail: bht@buccleuch.com

An outstanding collection of pictures, including works by Van Dyck, Canaletto, Reynolds, Gainsborough and Claude Lorraine, are displayed here. Memorabilia and relics of people such as Queen Victoria and Sir Walter Scott, and a restored Victorian kitchen add further interest inside the house. Outside, the wooded grounds are perfect for walking. A small theatre provides a full programme of music and drama.
Times: Open, Park: Apr-Aug daily 12-5 (ex Fri). House & park: Jul, daily 1-4.30. **Fee:** House & grounds £4.50 (ch under 5 & wheelchair users free, pen & groups £4). Grounds only £1. **Facilities:** P ☕ ✕ licensed & (guided tours for the blind) toilets for disabled shop (Jul) ✻ (ex in park on leads) ☕

HALLIWELLS HOUSE MUSEUM
Halliwells Close, Market Place TD7 4BC (off A7 in town centre)
☎ 01750 20096   📠 01750 23282
e-mail: museums@scotborders.gov.uk
Times: Open Apr-Oct, Mon-Sat 10-5 (Jul & Aug until 6), Sun 2-4.
Facilities: P (charged) & toilets for disabled shop ✻ (ex guide dogs) Details not confirmed for 2003

SIR WALTER SCOTT'S COURTROOM
Market Place TD7 4BT (on A7 in town centre)
☎ 01750 20096   📠 01750 23282
e-mail: museums@scotborders.gov.uk
Times: Open Apr-Sep, Sat 10-4, Jun-Sep, Sun 2-4; Oct, Mon-Sat 1-4.
Facilities: P (100mtrs) (30min on street, car park 50p for 2hrs) ☕ shop ✻ (ex guide dogs) Details not confirmed for 2003

🏛 SMAILHOLM   Map 12 NT63
SMAILHOLM TOWER
TD5 7RT (6m W of Kelso on B6937)
☎ 01573 460365

An outstanding example of a classic Border tower-house, probably erected in the 15th century. It is 57ft high and well preserved. The tower houses an exhibition of dolls and a display based on Sir Walter Scott's book *'Minstrels of the Border'*.
Times: Open Apr-Sep, daily 9.30-6.30; Oct-Mar, Sat-Sun only. (Closed 25-26 Dec). Telephone for 2003 details. **Fee:** * £2 (ch 75p, concessions £1.50). Telephone for 2003 details **Facilities:** P shop ✻ ♫

🏛 STOBO   Map 11 NT13
DAWYCK BOTANIC GARDEN
EH45 9JU (8m SW of Peebles on B712)
☎ 01721 760254   📠 01721 760214
e-mail: info@rbge.org.uk

From the landscaped walks of this historic arboretum an impressive collection of mature specimen trees can be seen - some over 40mtrs tall and including the unique Dawyck beech-stand. Notable features include the Swiss Bridge, a fine estate chapel and

continued

338 Scottish Borders - South Ayrshire

stonework/terracing produced by Italian craftsmen in the 1820s.
Times: Open daily 14 Feb-16 Nov Feb & Nov 10-4. Mar-Oct 10-5. Apr-Sep 10-6 **Fee:** £3 (ch £1, concessions £2.50). Family ticket £7.
Facilities: 🅿 💷 ♿ toilets for disabled shop garden centre ✈ (ex guide dogs) 🍴

🏛 TRAQUAIR   Map 11 NT33
TRAQUAIR HOUSE
EH44 6PW (At Innerleithen take B709, house is 1m S of Innerleithen)
☎ 01896 830323 & 830785   📠 01896 830639
e-mail: enquiries@traquair.co.uk

Said to be Scotland's oldest inhabited house, dating back to the 12th century, 27 Scottish monarchs have stayed at Traquair House. William the Lion Heart held court here, and the house has associations with Mary, Queen of Scots and the Jacobite risings. The Bear Gates were closed in 1745, not to be reopened until the Stuarts should once again ascend the throne. There is croquet, a maze and woodland walks by the River Tweed, craft workshops and a children's mini adventure playground. Also a brewery museum and shop, and antique shop.
Times: Open 12 Apr-Oct. **Fee:** £5.60 (ch £3.10 pen £5.30) Family £16.50 (2ad+3ch). Grounds only £2.50 (ch £1.25). **Facilities:** 🅿 💷 ✗ licensed ♿ toilets for disabled shop (must be on lead) 🍴

SOUTH AYRSHIRE

🏛 ALLOWAY   Map 10 NS31
BURNS NATIONAL HERITAGE PARK
Murdoch's Lone KA7 4PQ (2m S of Ayr)   **2 for 1**
☎ 01292 443700   📠 01292 441750

The birthplace of Robert Burns, Scotland's National Poet. An introduction to the life of Robert Burns, with an audio-visual presentation – a multi-screen 3D experience describing the Tale of Tam O'Shanter. This attraction consists of the museum, Burn's Cottage, visitor centre, tranquil landscaped gardens and historical monuments. Please telephone for details.
Times: Open all year, Apr-Sep 9.30-5.30, Oct-Mar 10-5. **Fee:** * Adult passport £5 (pen & ch passport £2.50). **Facilities:** 🅿 💷 ✗ licensed ♿ (wheelchair available) toilets for disabled shop ✈ (ex guide & hearing dogs) 🍴

🏛 BARGANY
See Old Dailly

🏛 CULZEAN CASTLE   Map 10 NS21
CULZEAN CASTLE & COUNTRY PARK
KA19 8LE (4m W of Maybole, off A77)
☎ 01655 884455   📠 01655 884503
e-mail: culzean@nts.org.uk

This 18th-century castle stands on a cliff in spacious grounds and was designed by Robert Adam for the Earl of Cassillis. It is noted for its oval staircase, circular drawing room and plasterwork. The Eisenhower Room explores the American general's links with Culzean. The 563-acre country park has a wide range of attractions - shoreline, woodland walks, parkland, an adventure playground and gardens.
Times: Castle: 25 Mar-27 Oct, daily 10-5, 2 Nov-22 Dec, Sat/Sun 10-4. Park: open all year 9.30-sunset. **Fee:** Admission free to NTS members. For other details please phone (0131) 243 9387 or check website.
Facilities: 🅿 💷 ✗ licensed ♿ (wheelchairs, lift in castle, braille guides) toilets for disabled shop garden centre (ex castle, ex guide dogs) 🍴

🏛 KIRKOSWALD   Map 10 NS20
SOUTER JOHNNIE'S COTTAGE
Main Rd KA19 8HY (on A77, 4m SW of Maybole)
☎ 01655 760603
e-mail: aclipson@nts.scot.demon.co.uk

'Souter' means cobbler and the village cobbler who lived in this 18th-century cottage was the inspiration for Burns' character Souter Johnnie, in his ballad "Tam O'Shanter". The cottage is now a Burns museum and life-size stone figures of the poet's characters can be seen in the restored ale-house in the cottage garden.
Times: 25 Mar-27 Oct, daily 11.30-5 **Fee:** Admission free to NTS members. For other details please phone (0131) 243 9387 or check website. **Facilities:** 🅿 (75yds) ♿ (only one small step into cottage) ✈ (ex guide dogs) 🍴

🏛 MAYBOLE   Map 10 NS20
CROSSRAGUEL ABBEY
KA19 5HQ (2m S)
☎ 01655 883113

The extensive remains of this 13th-century Cluniac monastery are impressive and architecturally important. The monastery was founded by Duncan, Earl of Carrick and the church, claustral buildings, abbot's house and an imposing castellated gatehouse can be seen.
Times: Open Apr-Sep, daily 9.30-6.30. Telephone for 2003 details. **Fee:** * £2 (ch 75p, concessions £1.50). Telephone for 2003 details **Facilities:** 🅿 ✈ 🍴

🏛 OLD DAILLY   Map 10 NX29
BARGANY GARDENS
KA26 9PH (4m NE on B734 from Girvan)   **2 for 1**
☎ 01465 871249   📠 01465 871282

Woodland walks with a fine show of azaleas and rhododendrons. Plants on sale from the gardens.
Times: Open Gardens Sat, Sun & Mon, May weekends only 10-5. **Fee:** * £2 (ch under 12 free). **Facilities:** 🅿 ♿ (only rock garden not accessible)

🏛 TARBOLTON   Map 10 NS42
BACHELORS' CLUB
Sandgate St KA5 5RB (on B744, 7.5m NE of Ayr)
☎ 01292 541940

In this 17th-century thatched house, Robert Burns and his friends formed a debating club in 1780. Burns attended dancing lessons and was initiated into freemasonry here in 1781. The house is furnished in the period.
Times: Open 25 Mar-27 Oct, daily 1-5 **Fee:** Admission free for NTS members. For other details please phone (0131) 243 9387 or check website. **Facilities:** 🅿 (in village) ♿ ✈ (ex guide dogs) 🍴

South Lanarkshire

BIGGAR
Map 11 NT03

GLADSTONE COURT MUSEUM
ML12 6DT (entrance by 113 High St)
☎ 01899 221573 & 221050
🖷 01899 221050
e-mail: margaret@bmtrust.freeserve.co.uk

2 for 1

An old-fashioned village street is portrayed in this museum, which is set out in a century-old coach-house. On display are reconstructed shops, complete with old signs and advertisements - a bank, telephone exchange, photographer's booth and other interesting glimpses into the recent past.
Times: Open Etr-Oct, Mon-Sat 10.30-5, Sun 2-5. **Fee:** * £2 (ch £1, pen £1.50). Family ticket £4. Party £1.25 each. **Facilities:** P & shop ✈ (ex guide dogs)

GREENHILL COVENANTERS HOUSE
Burn Braes ML12 6DT (On A702, 30 miles from Edinburgh)
☎ 01899 221572 & 221050 🖷 01899 221050
e-mail: margaret@bmtrust.freserve.co.uk

2 for 1

This 17th-century farmhouse was brought, stone by stone, ten miles from Wiston and reconstructed at Biggar. It has relics of the turbulent 'Covenanting' period, when men and women defended the right to worship in Presbyterian style. Audio presentations.
Times: Open mid May-Sep, wknds only 2-5. **Fee:** * £1 (ch 50p, pen 70p). Family ticket £2.50. Party 70p each. **Facilities:** P & ✈ (ex guide dogs)

MOAT PARK HERITAGE CENTRE
ML12 6DT (On A702 30m from Edinburgh)
☎ 01899 221050 🖷 01899 221050
e-mail: margaret@bmtrust.co.uk

2 for 1

The centre illustrates the history, archaeology and geology of the Upper Clyde and Tweed valleys with interesting displays.
Times: Open all year, Apr-Oct, daily 10.30-5, Sun 2-5; Nov-Feb, wkdays during office hours. Other times by prior arrangement. **Fee:** * £2 (ch £1, pen £1.50). Family ticket £4. Party £1.25 each. **Facilities:** P & (upper floor with assistance on request) toilets for disabled shop ✈ (ex guide dogs)

BLANTYRE
Map 11 NS65

DAVID LIVINGSTONE CENTRE
165 Station Rd G72 9BY (M74 junct 5 onto A725, then A724, follow signs for Blantyre, right at lights. Centre at foot of hill)
☎ 01698 823140 🖷 01698 821424

Share the adventurous life of Scotland's greatest explorer, from his childhood in the Blantyre Mills to his explorations in the heart of Africa, dramatically illustrated in the historic tenement where he was born. Various events are planned throughout the season.
Times: Open 25 Mar-24 Dec, Mon-Sat 10-5, Sun 12.30-5 **Fee:** Admission free to NTS members. For other details please phone (0131) 243 9377 or check website. **Facilities:** P & toilets for disabled shop ✈ (ex guide dogs/lead grounds) ⚑

BOTHWELL
Map 11 NS75

BOTHWELL CASTLE
G71 8BL (approach from Uddingston off B7071)
☎ 01698 816894

Besieged, captured and 'knocked about' several times in the Scottish-English wars, the castle is a splendid ruin. Archibald the Grim built the curtain wall; later, in 1786, the Duke of Buccleuch carved graffiti - a coronet and initials - beside a basement well.
Times: Open all year, Apr-Sep, daily 9.30-6.30; Oct- Mar, Mon-Sat 9.30-4.30, Sun 2-4.30. (Closed Thu pm, Fri & Sun am in winter). Telephone for 2003 details. **Fee:** * £2 (ch 75p, concessions £1.50). **Facilities:** P shop ⚑

EAST KILBRIDE
Map 11 NS65

MUSEUM OF SCOTTISH COUNTRY LIFE
Wester Kittochside G76 9HR (From Glasgow take A749 to East Kilbride. From Edinburgh follow M8 to Glasgow, turn off junct 6 on A725 to East Kilbride. Kittochside is signposted before East Kilbride)
☎ 01355 224 181 🖷 01355 571290
e-mail: kittochside@nms.ac.uk

A fascinating museum built on a 170-acre farm and offering an insight into the working lives of people in rural Scotland. The museum runs a programme of events throughout the year, demonstrating its working collection and contrasting modern and traditional farming methods.
Times: Open daily 10-5 (Closed 25/26 Dec & 1/2 Jan). **Fee:** £3 (ch under 18 free, concessions £1.50). **Facilities:** P 🍴 & (disabled parking, exhibition building is fully accessible) toilets for disabled shop ✈ (ex guide dogs) ⚑

HAMILTON
Map 11 NS75

CHATELHERAULT
Ferniegair ML3 7UE (2.5km SE of Hamilton on A72 Hamilton-Larkhall/Lanark Clyde Valley tourist route)
☎ 01698 426213 🖷 01698 421532

Designed as a hunting lodge by William Adam in 1732, Chatelherault, built of unusual pink sandstone, has been described as a gem of Scottish architecture. Situated close to the motorway, there is a visitor's centre, shop and adventure playground. Also a herd of white Cadzow cattle.
Times: Open all year, Mon-Sat 10-5, Sun 12-5. House closed all day Fri. **Fee:** Free. **Facilities:** P 🍴 & (ramps, parking, large print guide) toilets for disabled shop garden centre ✈ (ex in grounds & guide dogs) ⚑

LOW PARKS MUSEUM
129 Muir St ML3 6BJ (By Asda superstore, off M74 junct 6)
☎ 01698 328232 🖷 01698 328412

The museum tells the story of Hamilton and the Clyde Valley, created by linking the former District Museum and The Cameronians (Scottish Rifles) Museum. Housed in the town's oldest building, dating from 1696, the museum features a restored 18th-century assembly

continued

South Lanarkshire - Stirling

room and exhibitions on Hamilton Palace and The Covenanters.
Times: Open Mon-Sat 10-5, Sun 12-5. **Fee:** Free. **Facilities:** P & shop ✈ (ex guide dogs)

NEW LANARK   Map 11 NS84
NEW LANARK VISITOR CENTRE
New Lanark Visitor Centre, Mill 3, New Lanark Mills ML11 9DB (signposted from all major routes)
☎ 01555 661345 📠 01555 66538
e-mail: trust@newlanark.org

Founded in 1785, New Lanark became well known in the early 19th century as a model community managed by enlightened industrialist and educational reformer Robert Owen. Surrounded by woodland and situated close to the Falls of Clyde, this unusual heritage site explores the philosophies of Robert Owen, using theatre, interactive displays, and the 'New Millennium Experience', a magical chair ride through history.
Times: Open daily 11-5 ex Xmas Day & New Years Day. **Fee:** * £4.95 (ch, concessions £3.95) family ticket (2ad+2ch) £14.95 **Facilities:** P ⚒ ✗ licensed & ramps, disabled parking toilets for disabled shop ⚓

UDDINGSTON   Map 11 NS66
GLASGOW ZOOPARK
Calderpark G71 7RZ
☎ 0141 771 1185, 771 1186 & 771 1187
📠 0141 771 2615
Times: Open all year, daily 10-5 (or 6pm depending on season).
Facilities: P (charged) ⚒ & (key for toilet at gate) toilets for disabled shop ✈ (ex guide dogs) *Details not confirmed for 2003*

STIRLING

BANNOCKBURN   Map 11 NS89
BANNOCKBURN HERITAGE CENTRE
Glasgow Rd FK7 0LJ (2m S of Stirling off M80/M9 junct 9)
☎ 01786 812664 📠 01786 810892

The Heritage Centre stands close to what is traditionally believed to have been Robert the Bruce's command post before the 1314 Battle of Bannockburn, a famous victory for the Scots and a turning point in Scottish history.
Times: Site open all year, daily. **Fee:** Free. **Facilities:** P & (Induction loop for the hard of hearing) toilets for disabled shop (Closed 1-10 Nov) ✈ (ex site only) ♨

BLAIR DRUMMOND   Map 11 NS79
BLAIR DRUMMOND SAFARI & LEISURE PARK
FK9 4UR (M9 junct 10, 4m along A84 towards Callander)
☎ 01786 841456 & 841396 📠 01786 841491
e-mail: enquiries@safari-park.co.uk
Times: Open Apr-1 Oct, daily 10-5.30. Last admission 4.30. **Facilities:** P ⚒ ✗ licensed & (special menus & waitress service if booked in advance) toilets for disabled shop ✈ (ex guide dogs) *Details not confirmed for 2003*

CALLANDER   Map 11 NN60
ROB ROY AND TROSSACHS VISITOR CENTRE
Ancaster Square FK17 8ED (on A84)
☎ 01877 330342 📠 01877 330784   **2 for 1**
e-mail: robroyet@aillst.ossian.net

The fascinating story of Scotland's most famous outlaw, Rob Roy MacGregor is vividly portrayed through an exciting multi-media theatre and explained in the carefully researched 'Life and Times' exhibition. Also full tourist information centre covering the beautiful Trossachs area, Scottish bookshops and specially themed souvenirs. Evening entertainment, including traditional Scottish music evenings, celidhs and illustrated talks, is arranged 6 nights a week from June to October; telephone for details. School pack available.
Times: Open Mar-Dec daily; Mar-May & Oct-Dec 10-5; Jun 9.30-10; Jul-Aug 9-10, Sep 10-6. Jan & Feb wknds only 11-4.30. **Fee:** £2.90 (ch £1.05, student £2.40 & pen £2.05). Family ticket £6.35 **Facilities:** P & toilets for disabled shop ✈ (ex guide dogs) ♨

CAUSEWAYHEAD   Map 11 NS89
NATIONAL WALLACE MONUMENT
Abbey Craig, Hillfoots Rd FK8 2AD (Accessed from A907, Stirling to Alloa road)
☎ 01786 472140 📠 01786 461322

The 220ft tower was completed in 1869, and Sir William Wallace's two-handed sword is preserved inside. Seven battlefields and a fine view towards the Highlands can be seen in one of the most awe inspiring views in Scotland. Exhibitions on three floors.
Times: Open all year daily. Jan-Feb & Nov-Dec, 10.30-4; Mar-May & Oct, 10-5; Jun 10-6; Jul-Aug 9.30-6.30.Sep 9.30-5 **Fee:** £3.95 (ch & pen £2.75, student £3). Family ticket £10.75 **Facilities:** P ⚒ (accessible visitors pavillion at foot of hill) shop ✈ (ex guide dogs) ♨

DOUNE   Map 11 NN70
DOUNE CASTLE
FK16 6EA (8m S of Callander on A84)
☎ 01786 841742

The 14th-century stronghold with its two fine towers has been restored. It stands on the banks of the River Teith, and is associated with 'Bonnie' Prince Charlie and Sir Walter Scott.
Times: Open all year, Apr-Sep, daily 9.30-6.30; Oct-Mar, Mon-Sat 9.30-4.30, Sun 2-4.30. (Closed Thu pm, Fri in winter & 25-26 Dec). Telephone for 2003 details **Fee:** * £2.80 (ch £1, concessions £2). Telephone for 2003 details **Facilities:** P shop ♦

KILLIN   Map 11 NN53
BREADALBANE FOLKLORE CENTRE
Falls of Dochart FK21 8XE (on A82, turn right at Crianlarich onto A85 towards Perth/Stirling. Then take A827 to Killin)
☎ 01567 820254 📠 01567 820764   **2 for 1**

Overlooking the beautiful Falls of Dochart, the Centre gives a fascinating insight into the legends of Breadalbane - Scotland's 'high country'. Learn of the magical deeds of St Fillan and hear tales of mystical giants, ancient prophesies, traditional folklore and clan

continued

Stirling - West Dunbartonshire

history. Housed in historic St Fillans Mill which features a restored waterwheel. Tourist information and gift shop.
Times: Open Mar-May & Oct, daily 10-5; Jun & Sep, daily 10-6; Jul-Aug, daily 9.30-6.30. Feb wknds only 10-4. (Closed Nov-Jan). **Fee:** £1.55 (concessions £1.05, ch under 5 free). Family £3.05 **Facilities:** P (30 mtrs) & toilets for disabled shop ✕ (ex guide dogs)

PORT OF MENTEITH Map 11 NN50
INCHMAHOME PRIORY
FK8 3RA (4m E of Aberfoyle, off A81)
☎ 01877 385294

Walter Comyn founded this Augustinian house in 1238, and it became famous as the retreat of the infant Mary, Queen of Scots in 1547. The ruins of the church and cloisters are situated on an island in the Lake of Monteith.
Times: Open Apr-Sep, daily 9.30-6.30. Ferry subject to cancellation in adverse weather conditions. **Fee:** * £3.30 (ch £1.20, concessions £2.50). Admission charge includes ferry trip. **Facilities:** P shop

STIRLING Map 11 NS79
MAR'S WARK
Broad St FK8 1EE
☎ 0131 668 8800

Now partly ruined, this Renaissance-style mansion was built in 1570 by the 1st Earl of Mar, Regent of Scotland. With its gatehouse enriched with sculptures, it is one of several fine buildings on the road to Stirling Castle. The Earls of Mar lived there until the 6th Earl fled the country after leading the 1715 Jacobite Rebellion.
Times: Open all reasonable times. **Fee:** Free. **Facilities:**

MUSEUM OF ARGYLL & SUTHERLAND HIGHLANDERS
The Castle FK8 1EH (museum is within Stirling Castle)
☎ 01786 475165   01786 446038
e-mail: museum@argylls.co.uk

Situated in the King's Old Building in Stirling Castle, the museum tells the history of the Regiment from 1794 to the present day. Displays include uniforms, medals, silver, paintings, colours, pipe banners, and commentaries.
Times: Open Etr-Sep, Mon-Sat 10-5.30, Sun 11-5; Oct-Etr, Mon-Sun 10-4. **Fee:** Entry to museum free but entry fee to castle. **Facilities:** P (castle esplanade) shop ✕

OLD TOWN JAIL
Saint John St FK8 1EA (follow signs for castle up the hill, jail on left at top of Saint John's St)
☎ 01786 450050   01786 471301   **2 for 1**
e-mail: otjva@aillst.ossian.net

Built in 1847 to replace the old Tolbooth jail, this is an outstanding example of Victorian architecture. A living history performance means the visitor can learn about the daily life of the prisoners and the strict regime practised in the prison.
Times: Open daily, Oct-Mar 9.30-4.30; Nov-Feb 9.30-3.30, **Fee:** £3.95 (concessions £2.75, student £3). Family ticket £10.75 **Facilities:** P & (lift to viewpoint) toilets for disabled shop ✕ (ex guide dogs)

ROYAL BURGH OF STIRLING VISITOR CENTRE
Castle Esplanade FK8 1EH (next to Stirling Castle)
☎ 01786 479901 & 462517   01786 451881

A colourful introduction to Royal Stirling. For centuries, Stirling lay at the centre of Scotland's turbulent history, from the Wars of Independence, through the reign of the Stuart monarchs to a medieval burgh.
Times: Open all year, Jan-Mar & Nov-Dec 9.30-5; Apr-Jun & Sep-Oct 9.30-6.; Jul-Aug, 9-6; **Fee:** Free. **Facilities:** P & (Induction loop for the hard of hearing) toilets for disabled shop ✕ (ex guide dogs)

SMITH ART GALLERY & MUSEUM
Dumbarton Rd FK8 2RQ (M9 junct 10, follow Stirling Castle signs)
☎ 01786 471917   01786 449523
e-mail: museum@smithartgallery.demon.co.uk

This award-winning museum and gallery presents a variety of exhibitions drawing on its own rich collections and works from elsewhere. A range of programmes and events take place, ring for details.
Times: Open all year, Tue-Sat 10.30-5, Sun 2-5 (Closed Mon, 25-26 Dec & 1 Jan). **Fee:** Free. **Facilities:** P 🅿 & (wheelchair lift, induction loop in theatre) toilets for disabled shop

STIRLING CASTLE
Upper Castle Hill FK8 1EJ
☎ 01786 450000

Sitting on top of a 250ft rock, Stirling Castle has a strategic position on the Firth of Forth. As a result it has been the scene of many events in Scotland's history. James II was born at the castle in 1430. Mary, Queen of Scots spent some years here, and it was James IV's childhood home. Among its finest features are the splendid Renaissance palace built by James V, and the Chapel Royal, rebuilt by James VI.
Times: Open all year, Apr-Sep, daily 9.30-6; Oct-Mar, daily 9.30-4.15. Last ticket sold 45 mins prior to closing time. Telephone for 2003 details. **Fee:** * £7 (ch £2, concessions £5). **Facilities:** P (charged) ✕ licensed & toilets for disabled shop ✕

WEST DUNBARTONSHIRE

BALLOCH Map 10 NS38
BALLOCH CASTLE COUNTRY PARK
G83 8LX (A82 for Dumbartonshire, Balloch from Glasgow. A811 for Balloch from Stirling)
☎ 01389 758216   01389 720922
Times: Open: Visitor Centre, Apr-Oct daily 10-5.45. Country Park open all year, 8-dusk. **Facilities:** P 🅿 & toilets for disabled shop Details not confirmed for 2003

DUMBARTON
Dumbarton Castle　　　　　　Map 10 NS37
G82 1JJ
☎ 01389 732167

The castle, set on the 240ft Dumbarton Rock above the River Clyde, dominates the town (the capital of the Celtic kingdom of Strathclyde) and commands spectacular views. Most of what can be seen today dates from the 18th and 19th centuries, but there are a few earlier remains.
Times: Open all year, Apr-Sep, daily 10-6.30. Oct-Mar, Sun 2-4.30. Telephone for 2003 details. **Fee:** * £2.20 (ch £1, concessions £2). Telephone for 2003 details **Facilities:** P shop ✖ ♫

WEST LOTHIAN

LINLITHGOW
Blackness Castle　　　　　　Map 11 NS97
EH49 7AL (4m NE)
☎ 01506 834807

Once, this was one of the most important fortresses in Scotland. Used as a state prison during covenanting time and in the late 19th century as a powder magazine, it was one of four castles left fortified by the Articles of Union. Most impressive are the massive 17th-century artillery emplacements.
Times: Open all year, Apr-Sep, daily 9.30-6.30; Oct-Mar, Mon-Sat 9.30-4.30, Sun 2-4.30. (Closed Thu pm, Fri & Sun am in winter). Telephone for 2003 details. **Fee:** * £2.20 (ch 75p, concessions £1.60). **Facilities:** P shop ♫

House of The Binns
EH49 7NA (4m E of Linlithgow off A904)
☎ 01506 834255
e-mail: houseofthebinns@nts.org.uk

An example of changing architectural tastes from 1612 onwards, this house reflects the transition from fortified stronghold to spacious mansion. The original three-storey building, with small windows and twin turrets, evolved into a fine crenellated house with beautiful moulded plaster ceilings - the ancestral home of the Dalyell family. There is a magnificent display of snowdrops and daffodils in spring.
Times: House: May-29 Sep, Sat-Mon 1-5. Parkland: 25 Mar-27 Oct, daily 10-7, 28 Oct-24 Mar, daily 10-4. **Fee:** admission free to NTS members. For other details please phone (0131) 243 9387 or check website **Facilities:** P ♿ (braille sheets) ✖ (ex guide dogs) ♨

Linlithgow Palace
EH49 7AL (off M9)
☎ 01506 842896

The magnificent ruin of a great Royal Palace, set in its own park or `peel'. All the Stewart kings lived here, and work commissioned by James I, III, IV, and VI can be seen. The great hall and the chapel are particularly fine. James V was born here in 1512 and Mary, Queen of Scots in 1542.
Times: Open all year, Apr-Sep, daily 9.30-6.30; Oct-Mar, Mon-Sat 9.30-4.30, Sun 2-4.30. (Closed 25-26 Dec). Telephone for 2003 details. **Fee:** * £2.85 (ch £1, concessions £2). Telephone for 2003 details. **Facilities:** P shop ✖ ♫

LIVINGSTON　　　　　　Map 11 NT06
Almond Valley Heritage Centre
Millfield EH54 7AR (2m from M8 junct 3)
☎ 01506 414957　📠 01506 497771
e-mail: info@almondvalley.co.uk

A combination of fun and educational potential ideal for children, Almond Valley has a petting zoo of farm animals, an interactive museum on the shale oil industry, a narrow gauge railway, and tractor rides. Special events throughout the year. Ring for details.
Times: Open all year, daily 10-5 **Fee:** * £2.80 (ch £1.60) **Facilities:** P 🍽 ♿ toilets for disabled shop 🛒

The Scottish Islands

Both beautiful and daunting, the islands around the Scottish coast reward the braver traveller with incredible unspoilt landscapes, and the satisfaction of journeying to them.

Lewis, Skye and Mull are the largest of the islands, but there are countless others, some of them are tiny, like the sparsely populated Scarp (2500 acres) or the furthest south of the Outer Hebrides, Berneray, which is only 500 acres. The furthest north is Shetland, which is 110 miles north-east of Scotland's north coast. The traditions of this group of islands are more Viking than Scottish, as is demonstrated by Lerwick's annual celebration, the fire feast of 'Up-Helly-Aa'. Held on the last Tuesday of January, the festival is an adaptation of a Norse feast, Uphalliday, marking the end of Yule and the long winter nights. A replica of a 30ft Viking galley is hauled through the streets and ceremonially burned as a prelude to a night of revelry.

Lewis and Harris form a single island that, together with the Uists, Benbecula and Barra, provides a 150-mile long storm-break for the Inner Hebrides and the Western Highlands. Though thousands of people live on Lewis and Harris, the island nevertheless contains huge areas of emptiness. What is not peat-bog and water is mostly rock. The seas are cold, unsurprisingly, but the white sands are lovely to walk on, and there are a number of standing stones near Callanish.

From the sea, Skye's cloud-cap can be seen long before its dark mountains climb over the horizon; so the Norsemen called it Skuyo, 'Isle of Clouds'. Composed mainly of moutain and moor, Skye is a gathering of peninsulas, where crofting is still the main occupation.

Top: Loch Scridain on the Isle of Mull.

Scottish Islands (Arran, Bute, Great Cumbrae)

ARRAN, ISLE OF

🏛 BRODICK   Map 10 NS03
BRODICK CASTLE, GARDEN & COUNTRY PARK
KA27 8HY (Ferry from Ardrossan-Brodick. From N end of Arran-Kintyre frequent in Summer, limited in winter)
☎ 01770 302202 & 302462   📠 01770 302312
e-mail: brodick@nts.org.uk

The site has been fortified since Viking times, but the present castle dating from the 13th century was a stronghold of the Dukes of Hamilton. Splendid silver, fine porcelain and paintings acquired by generations of owners can be seen, including many sporting pictures and trophies. There is a magnificent woodland garden, started by the Duchess of Montrose in 1923, world famous for its rhododendrons and azaleas.
Times: Open 25 Mar-27 Oct, daily 10-5. Park: open all year, daily 9.30-sunset **Fee:** Admission free to NTS members. For other details please phone (0131) 243 9287 or check website. **Facilities:** 🅿 ✗ ♿ (Braille sheets, motorised buggy, wheelchairs & stairlift) toilets for disabled shop 🐕 (ex guide dogs) 🍴

ISLE OF ARRAN HERITAGE MUSEUM
Rosaburn KA27 8DP (Right at Brodick Pier, approx 1m)
☎ 01770 302636
e-mail: tom.macleod@arranmuseum.co.uk

The setting is an 18th-century croft farm, including a cottage restored to its pre-1920 state and a `smiddy' where a blacksmith worked until the late 1960s. There are also occasional demonstrations of horseshoeing, sheepshearing, weaving and spinning, a veteran car rally and a golf tournament - please ring for details.
Times: Open Apr-Oct, daily 10.30-4.30. **Fee:** * £2.25 (ch £1, pen £1.25) Family £6. **Facilities:** 🅿 ☕ ♿ shop

🏛 LOCHRANZA   Map 10 NR95
ISLE OF ARRAN DISTILLERY VISITOR CENTRE
KA27 8HJ (from Brodick Ferry Terminal take coast road N for 14 m. Distillery located on edge of village of Lochranza)
☎ 01770 830264   **2 for 1**
📠 01770 830364
e-mail: visitorcentre@arranwhisky.com

Located amidst beautiful surroundings, the distillery was built to revive the dormant traditions of Arran single malt whisky production. After a guided tour of the distillery, visitors can now taste some of the first whiskies to be ready after production began in 1995.
Times: Open daily Mar-Oct; Nov-Dec, open 4 days a week. (Closed Jan). **Fee:** £3.50 (ch under 12 free, pen/student £2.50). Party 20+. **Facilities:** 🅿 ✗ licensed ♿ (ex working distillery, chair lift in visitor centre) toilets for disabled shop 🐕 (ex guide dogs) 🍷

BUTE, ISLE OF

🏛 ROTHESAY   Map 10 NS06
ARDENCRAIG
PA20 9HA (1m off A844, S of Rothesay)
☎ 01700 504225   📠 01700 504225
e-mail: allan.macdonald@argyll-bute.co.uk

Times: Open May-Sep. **Facilities:** 🅿 ☕ ♿ 🐕 (ex guide dogs) *Details not confirmed for 2003*

BUTE MUSEUM
Stuart St PA20 0BR (Behind the castle)
☎ 01700 502033 (contact) & 505067 (museum)
e-mail: thomas.clegg@btinternet.com
Times: Open all year, Apr-Sep, Mon-Sat 10.30-4.30, Sun 2.30-4.30; Oct-Mar, Tue-Sat 2.30-4.30 (Closed Sun & Mon). **Facilities:** 🅿 ♿ (touch table for blind, ramps) shop 🐕 (ex guide dogs) *Details not confirmed for 2003*

ROTHESAY CASTLE
PA20 0DA
☎ 01700 502691

The focal point of Rothesay is this 13th-century castle. It has lofty curtain walls defended by drum towers that enclose a circular courtyard.
Times: Open all year, Apr-Sep, daily 9.30-6.30; Oct-Mar, Mon-Sat 9.30-4.30, Sun 2-4.30. (Closed Thu pm, Fri in winter & 25-26 Dec). **Fee:** * £2.20 (ch 75p, concessions £1.60). **Facilities:** 🅿 shop 🎧

GREAT CUMBRAE ISLAND

🏛 MILLPORT   Map 10 NS15
MUSEUM OF THE CUMBRAES
Garrison House KA28 0DG (Ferry to Millport, from Largs Cal-Mac Terminal. Bus meets each ferry)
☎ 01475 531191   📠 01294 464174
e-mail: namuseum@globalinet.co.uk

A small museum which displays the history and life of the Cumbraes. Along with artefacts from the collection, the museum displays a major exhibition each summer. There is also a fine collection of local photographs.
Times: Open Jun-Sep, Mon-Sat 11-1 & 1.30-5. **Fee:** Free. **Facilities:** 🅿 (50mtrs) ♿ shop 🐕 (ex guide dogs)

LEWIS, ISLE OF

ARNOL   Map 13 NB34
BLACK HOUSE MUSEUM
PA86 9DB (11m NW of Stornoway on A858)
☎ 01851 710395

A traditional Hebridean dwelling, built without mortar, and roofed with thatch on a timber framework. It has a central peat fire in the kitchen, no chimney and a byre under the same roof.
Times: Open all year, Apr-Sep, Mon-Sat 9.30-6.30; Oct-Mar, Mon-Thu & Sat 9.30-4.30. (Closed 25-26 Dec). Telephone for 2003 details. **Fee:** * £2.80 (ch £1, concessions £2). **Facilities:** P & toilets for disabled shop

CALLANISH   Map 13 NB23
CALLANISH STANDING STONES
PA86 9DY (12m W of Stornoway off A859)
☎ 01851 621422

An avenue of 19 monoliths leads north from a circle of 13 stones with rows of more stones fanning out to south, east and west. Probably constructed between 3000 and 1500BC, this is a unique cruciform of megaliths.
Times: Site accessible at all times. Visitor Centre open Apr-Sep, Mon-Sat 10-7; Oct-Mar, Mon-Sat 10-4. **Fee:** *Prices not confirmed for 2003*. **Facilities:** P ✗ & toilets for disabled shop

CARLOWAY   Map 13 NB24
DUN CARLOWAY BROCH
(1.5m S of Carloway)
☎ 0131 668 8800

Brochs are late-prehistoric circular stone towers, and their origins are mysterious. One of the best examples can be seen at Dun Carloway, where the tower still stands about 30ft high.
Times: Open at all reasonable times. **Fee:** Free. **Facilities:** P

MULL, ISLE OF

CRAIGNURE   Map 10 NM73
MULL & WEST HIGHLAND NARROW GAUGE RAILWAY
Craignure (old pier) Station PA65 6AY
☎ 01680 812494 (in season) or 01680 300389
✉ 01680 300595
Times: Open 9 Apr-20 Oct. **Facilities:** P & (provision to carry person seated in wheelchair on trains) shop *Details not confirmed for 2003*

TOROSAY CASTLE & GARDENS
PA65 6AY (1.5m S of Ferry Terminal at Craignure)
☎ 01680 812421 ✉ 01680 812470
e-mail: torosay@aol.com

The Scottish baronial architecture of this Victorian castle is complemented by the magnificent setting, and inside the house there are displays of portraits and wildlife pictures, family scrapbooks and a study of the Antarctic. The gardens include a statue walk and water

Ardencraig
Gardens & Aviaries
Rothesay – Isle of Bute

Ardencraig Gardens on the beautiful Island of Bute where you can sit and enjoy the sunshine in peace and tranquillity with views overlooking the Firth of Clyde.

You can reach the gardens by car, bus, or a leisurely stroll through the Skipper's woods.

Argyll & Bute Council

garden, an avenue of Australian gum trees, and an Oriental garden. Within the grounds there is a narrow gauge steam and diesel railway, a weaver's workshop and a silversmiths.
Times: Open end Mar-end Oct, daily 10.30-5. Gardens all year. **Fee:** House & Gardens: £5 (ch £1.75, student & pen £4) Family £12. Gardens only: £4 (ch £1.25, student & pen £3) Family £8. **Facilities:** P & toilets for disabled shop garden centre

ORKNEY

BIRSAY   Map 16 HY22
EARL'S PALACE
KW15 1PD
☎ 0131 668 8800

The gaunt remains of the residence of the 16th-century Earl of Orkney, constructed round a courtyard.
Times: Open at all reasonable times. **Fee:** Free. **Facilities:** ✗

DOUNBY   Map 16 HY22
BROUGH OF BIRSAY
(6m NW)
☎ 0131 668 8800

This ruined Romanesque church stands next to the remains of a Norse village. The nave, chancel and semicircular apse can be seen, along with claustral buildings. Crossings must be made on foot at low-water - there is no boat.
Times: Open at all reasonable times. **Fee:** Free. **Facilities:**

Scottish Islands (Orkney)

CLICK MILL
(NE of village, off B9057)
☎ 0131 668 8800

This is an example of the rare Orcadian horizontal watermill, and is in working condition.
Times: Open at all reasonable time. **Fee:** Free. **Facilities:** ℙ

SKARA BRAE
KW16 3LR (19m W of Kirkwall on B9056)
☎ 01856 841815

Engulfed in drift sand, this remarkable group of well-preserved Stone Age dwellings is the most outstanding survivor of its kind in Britain. Stone furniture and a fireplace can be seen.
Times: Open all year, Apr-Sep, daily 9.30-6.30; Oct-Mar, Mon-Sat 9.30-4.30, Sun 2-4.30. (Closed 25-26 Dec). **Fee:** * Summer: £4.50 (ch £1.30, concessions £3.30); Winter: £3.50 (ch £1.20, concessions £2.60). **Facilities:** P ✕ & toilets for disabled shop ✱ ℙ

🏛 FINSTOWN   Map 16 HY31
MAES HOWE CHAMBERED CAIRN
(9m W of Kirkwall, on A965)
☎ 01856 761606

The masonry of Britain's finest megalithic tomb is in a remarkably good state of preservation. Dating from neolithic times, it contains Viking carvings and runes.
Times: Open all year, Apr-Sep, daily 9.30-6.30; Oct-Mar, Mon-Sat 9.30-4.30, Sun 2-4.30. (Closed Sun am in winter & 25-26 Dec). **Fee:** * £2.80 (ch £1, concessions £2). **Facilities:** P ✕ shop ✱ ℙ

STENNESS STANDING STONES
(3m SW off A965)
☎ 0131 668 8800

Dating back to the second millennium BC, the remains of this stone circle are near the Ring of Brogar - a splendid circle of upright stones surrounded by a ditch.
Times: Open at any reasonable time. **Fee:** Free. **Facilities:** P ℙ

🏛 HARRAY   Map 16 HY31
CORRIGALL FARM & KIRBUSTER MUSEUM
KW17 2JR
☎ 01856 771411 & 771268   ▤ 01856 874615

The museum consists of two Orkney farmhouses with outbuildings. Kirbuster (Birsay) has the last surviving example of a `Firehoose' with its central hearth; Corrigall (Harray) represents an improved farmhouse and steading of the late 1800s.
Times: Open Mar-Oct, Mon-Sat 10.30-1 & 2-5, Sun 2-7. **Fee:** Free. **Facilities:** P & shop ✱ (ex guide dogs)

🏛 KIRKWALL   Map 16 HY41
BISHOP'S & EARL'S PALACES
KW15 1PD (In Kirkwall on A960)
☎ 01856 875461

The Bishop's Palace is a hall-house of the 12th century, later much altered, with a round tower built by Bishop Reid in 1541-48. A later addition was made by the notorious Patrick Stewart, Earl of Orkney, who built the adjacent Earl's Palace between 1600 and 1607 in a splendid Renaissance style.
Times: Open Apr-Sep, daily 9.30-6.30. Telephone for 2003 details.
Fee: * £2 (ch 75p, concessions £1.50). joint entry ticket for all Orkney monuments **Facilities:** shop ℙ

SCAPA FLOW VISITOR CENTRE & MUSEUM
KW15 1DH (on A964 to Howton)
☎ 01856 873191   ▤ 01856 871560
e-mail: museum@orkney.gov.uk

Also known as the Lyness Interpretation Centre, this fascinating museum is home to a large collection of military equipment used in the defence of the Orkneys during the First and Second World Wars. There are also guns salvaged from the German ships scuppered in WWII. Visitors arrive at the island after a short boat trip from the Orkney mainland.
Times: Open all year: Mon-Fri 9-4.30 (mid May-Oct also Sat, Sun 10.30-3.30) **Fee:** Free. **Facilities:** P 🍴 & toilets for disabled shop ✱ (ex guide dogs) ☕

THE ORKNEY MUSEUM
Broad St KW15 1DH
☎ 01856 873191   ▤ 01856 874616

One of the finest vernacular town houses in Scotland, this 16th-century building now contains a museum of Orkney history, including the islands' fascinating archaeology.
Times: Open, Oct-Mar Mon-Sat, 10.30-12.30 & 1.30-5, Apr-Sep, 10.30-5 Mon-Sat. **Fee:** Free. **Facilities:** P (50yds) & shop ✱ (ex guide dogs) ☕

🏛 STROMNESS   Map 16 HY20
ORKNEY MARITIME & NATURAL HISTORY MUSEUM
52 Alfred St KW16 3DF
☎ 01856 850025   `2 for 1`

The museum focuses on Orkney's broad maritime connections, including fishing, whaling, the Hudson's Bay Company, the German Fleet in Scapa Flow, and the award-winning Pilot's House extension. The Natural History Gallery is fully restored, displaying a fine collection of curios and rare and interesting exhibits.
Times: Open Apr-Sep, Mon-Sun 10-5; Oct-Mar, Mon-Sat 11-3.30. (Closed Xmas, New Year & 3 wks Feb-Mar). **Fee:** £2.50 (ch 50p con £2). Family ticket £5. **Facilities:** P (50yds) & toilets for disabled shop ✱ (ex guide dogs)

PIER ARTS CENTRE
KW16 3AA
☎ 01856 850209   ▤ 01856 851462
e-mail: info@pierartscentre.com
Times: Open all year, Tue-Sat 10.30-12.30 & 1.30-5. **Facilities:** P (100yds) & shop ✱ (ex guide dogs) *Details not confirmed for 2003*

WESTRAY   Map 16 HY44
NOLTLAND CASTLE
☎ 0131 668 8800

Started in the 16th century, this ruined castle was never completed. It has a fine hall, vaulted kitchen and a notable winding staircase.
Times: Open all reasonable times. Application to key keeper. **Fee:** Free. **Facilities:** ✸ ♫

SHETLAND

LERWICK   Map 16 HU44
CLICKHIMIN
ZE1 0QX (1m SW)
☎ 0131 668 8800

The remains of a prehistoric settlement that was fortified at the beginning of the Iron Age with a stone-built fort. The site was occupied for over 1000 years. The remains include a partially demolished broch (round tower) which still stands to a height of 17ft.
Times: Open at all reasonable time. **Fee:** Free. **Facilities:** ♫

FORT CHARLOTTE
ZE1 0JN (overlooking harbour)
☎ 0131 668 8800

An artillery fort, begun in 1665 to protect the Sound of Bressay during the Anglo-Dutch War. The Dutch burned the fort in 1673, together with the town of Lerwick. It was repaired in 1781 during the American War of Independence. The fort is pentagonal with high walls and seaward-facing gunports.
Times: Open at all reasonable time. **Fee:** Free. **Facilities:** ♫

SHETLAND MUSEUM
Lower Hillhead ZE1 0EL
☎ 01595 695057 📠 01595 696729
e-mail: shetland.museum@sic.shetland.gov.uk

The massive brass propeller blade outside the building is from the 17,000-ton liner *Oceanic*, wrecked off Foula in 1914. The archaeology gallery covers Neolithic burials, axe-making, Bronze Age houses, Iron Age farming and domestic life. There are also agricultural and social history displays, including peat-working, corn harvest, local businesses, medals, bootmaking and Shetland weddings. Changing displays of local contemporary art.
Times: Open all year Mon, Wed, Fri 10-7, Tue, Thu, Sat 10-5. **Fee:** Free. **Facilities:** 🅿 ♿ (lift, wheelchair available) toilets for disabled shop ✸ (ex guide dogs) ♫

MOUSA ISLAND   Map 16 HU42
MOUSA BROCH
(Accessible by boat from Sandwick)
☎ 0131 668 8800

This broch is the best-preserved example of an Iron Age drystone tower in Scotland. The tower is nearly complete and rises to a height of 40ft. The outer and inner walls both contain staircases that may be climbed to the parapet.
Times: Open at all reasonable time. **Fee:** Free. **Facilities:** ♫

(Orkney, Shetland, Skye) Scottish Islands   347

SCALLOWAY   Map 16 HU33
SCALLOWAY CASTLE
ZE1 0TP
☎ 0131 668 8800

The ruins of a castle designed on the medieval two-step plan. The castle was actually built in 1600 by Patrick Stewart, Earl of Orkney. When the Earl, who was renowned for his cruelty, was executed in 1615, the castle fell into disuse.
Times: Open at all reasonable time. **Fee:** Free. **Facilities:** 🅿 ♫

SUMBURGH   Map 16 HU30
JARLSHOF PREHISTORIC SITE
(At Sumburgh Head, approx 22m S of Lerwick)
☎ 01950 460112

One of the most remarkable archaeological sites in Europe. There are remains of Bronze Age, Iron Age and Viking settlements as well as a medieval farm. There is also a 16th-century Laird's House, once the home of the Earls Robert and Patrick Stewart, and the basis of 'Jarlshof' in Sir Walter Scott's novel *The Pirate*.
Times: Open Apr-Sep, daily 9.30-6.30. **Fee:** * £3 (ch £1, concessions £2.20). **Facilities:** 🅿 shop ♫

SKYE, ISLE OF

ARMADALE   Map 13 NG60
ARMADALE CASTLE GARDENS & MUSEUM OF THE ISLES
IV45 8RS (16m S of Broadford on A851. Signposted with Clan Donald Centre or Armadale Castle Gardens & Museum of the Isles. Easily reached by Skye Bridge or the Mallaig A830 to Armdale Ferry)
☎ 01471 844305 & 844227   **2 for 1**
📠 01471 844275
e-mail: office@cland.demon.co.uk

Armadale Castle and Gardens were built in 1815 as the home of Lord Macdonald. The warming effect of the Gulf Stream allows exotic trees and plants to flourish. Within the 40 acres of gardens is the Museum of the Isles, where visitors can discover the history of the Highlands.
Times: Open daily 9.30-5.30. Garden & Museum open Apr-Oct. **Fee:** £4.50 (concessions £3). Family ticket £14. Group 8+ **Facilities:** 🅿 ♨ ✗ licensed ♿ (wheelchairs available) toilets for disabled shop (on lead) ♫

DUNVEGAN   Map 13 NG24
DUNVEGAN CASTLE
IV55 8WF (Follow A87 over Skye Bridge. Turn onto A863 at Sligachan, continue on road to Dunvegan Castle)
☎ 01470 521206 📠 01470 521205
e-mail: info@dunvegancastle.com
Times: Open mid Mar-end Oct, Mon-Sun 10-5.30 (last admission 5pm). Winter opening: Nov-mid Mar, Castle & Gardens Mon-Sun 11-4, last admission 3.30pm. **Facilities:** 🅿 ♨ ✗ licensed (restaurant has ramps for wheelchair access) shop ✸ (ex guide dogs & in grounds)
Details not confirmed for 2003 ♫

Need to find the perfect place?

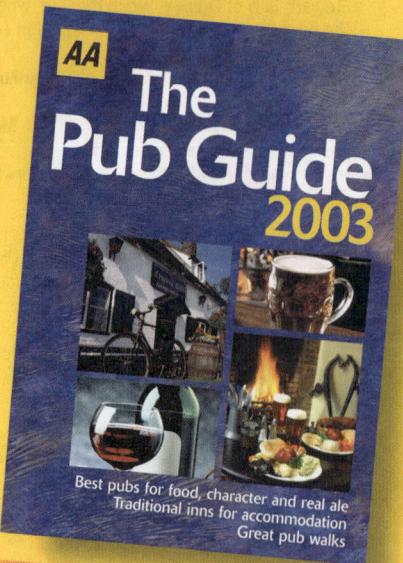

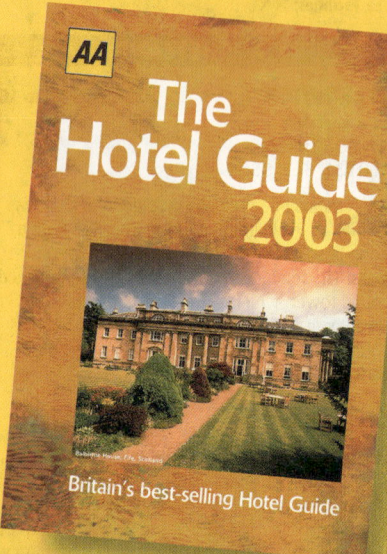

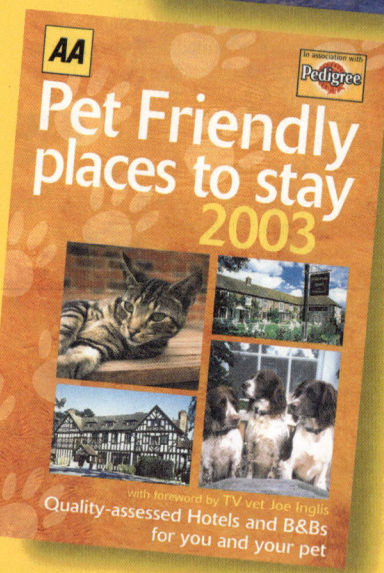

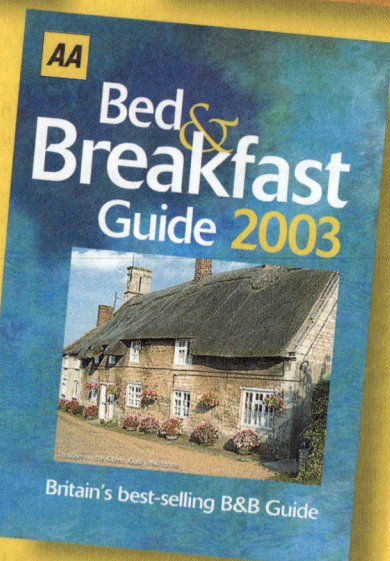

The Pub Guide 2003
Best pubs for food, character and real ale
Traditional inns for accommodation
Great pub walks

The Hotel Guide 2003
Britain's best-selling Hotel Guide

Pet Friendly places to stay 2003
in association with Pedigree
with foreword by TV vet Joe Inglis
Quality-assessed Hotels and B&Bs for you and your pet

Bed & Breakfast Guide 2003
Britain's best-selling B&B Guide

New editions on sale now!

Available from all good bookshops, via our internet site: www.theAA.com or by calling 01206 255800

The Pass of Llanberis

Wales
EVENTS & FESTIVALS

March
24th-30th Wrexham Science Festival, Wrexham
26th Conwy Seed Fair, High Street, Conwy (horticultural fair)

April
tbc Country Music Festival, North Wales Theatre, Promenade, Llandudno, Conwy

May
23rd-1st June Hay Festival of Literature
24th-1st June Beaumaris Festival, Beaumaris, Anglesey
24th-9th June St David's Cathedral Festival, St David's, Pembrokeshire
25th-26th North Wales Garden Festival & Woodland Festival, Bodelwyddan Castle, St Asaph
tbc Celtic Challenge, a bi-annual rowing race across the Irish Sea
tbc Wrexham Arts Festival, Wrexham

June
23rd May-1st Hay Festival of Literature
24th May-1st Beaumaris Festival, Anglesey
24th May-9th St David's Cathedral Festival, St David's, Pembrokeshire
21st Three Peaks Yacht Race, Barmouth, Gwynedd
tbc Llandudno Festival

July
4th-6th North Wales Bluegrass Festival, Llandudno, Conwy
8th-13th Llangollen International Musical Eisteddfod, International Pavilion, Abbey Road, Llangollen, Denbighshire
12th Annual Mountain Bike Bog Snorkelling World Championships, Llanwrtyd Wells (various venues)
17th-26th Welsh Proms, St Davidís Hall, The Hayes, Cardiff
19th-26th Fishguard International Music Festival, Pembrokeshire
21st-24th Royal Welsh Show, Royal Welsh Showground, Builth Wells
tbc Abertawe/Swansea Festival of Young Musicians
tbc Gower Music Festival (various venues) Gower, Swansea

August
2nd-9th Royal National Eisteddfod of Wales, Montgomery & the Marches, held at Meifod, Powys

3rd-9th Victorian Week, Talyllyn Railway, Tywyn, Gwynedd
8th-10th Brecon Jazz Festival (various venues), Brecon, Powys
9th Chepstow Agricultural Show, Chepstow Racecourse, Chepstow
9th Llangurig & District Show, Tynymaes, Llangurig, Powys
12th-13th Anglesey County Show, Mona, Anglesey
16th-24th Llandrindod Wells Victorian Festival, Powys
19th-21st Pembrokeshire County Show, Haverfordwest
20th Vale of Glamorgan Agricultural Show, Fonmon
23rd Denbigh Flower Show, Lon Felin Field, Denbigh
24th-25th North Wales Summer Garden Festival & Woodland Festival, Bodelwyddan Castle, St Asaph
28th Monmouthshire Show, Vauxhall Fields, Monmouth, Monmouthshire
tbc Brecon County Show
tbc Conwy River Festival, Harbour, Conwy

September
13th Conwy Honey Fair, Conwy High Street
13th Usk Show, Gwernesney, Monmouthshire
20th-27th Tenby Arts Festival, Pembrokeshire
tbc Barmouth Art Festival, Barmouth, Gwynedd
tbc Llangollen Hot Air Balloon Festival, International Pavilion, Abbey Road, Llangollen, Denbighshire
tbc North Wales International Music Festival, St Asaph, Denbighshire

October
10th-12th Anglesey Oyster Fair, Anglesey (provisional)
27th-9th Nov Dylan Thomas - The Celebration, Dylan Thomas Centre, Somerset Place Swansea
tbc Bala Autumn Fair Day, Bala, Gwynedd
tbc Cardigan Festival of Walks, Cardigan, Pembrokeshire

November
27th Oct-9th Dylan Thomas - The Celebration, Dylan Thomas Centre, Somerset Place Swansea
tbc Gwyl Ffilm Ryngwladol Cymru - International Film Festival Wales, Market House, Market Road, Cardiff

December
tbc Royal Welsh Agricultural Winter Fair, Royal Welsh Showground, Builth Wells

BRIDGEND

🏰 BRIDGEND   Map 03 SS97
NEWCASTLE
☎ 01656 659515
Times: Open - accessible throughout the year. Key keeper arrangement. **Facilities:** 🅿 ✕ ♿ *Details not confirmed for 2003*

🏰 COITY   Map 03 SS98
COITY CASTLE
CF35 6BG
☎ 01656 652021
Times: Open all year, at all times. Key keeper arrangement.
Facilities: 🅿 ✕ ♿ *Details not confirmed for 2003*

CAERPHILLY

🏰 CAERPHILLY   Map 03 ST18
CAERPHILLY CASTLE
CF8 1JL (on A469)
☎ 029 2088 3143

The concentrically planned castle was begun in 1268 by Gilbert de Clare and completed in 1326. It is the largest in Wales, and has extensive land and water defences. A unique feature is the ruined tower - the victim of subsidence - which manages to out-lean even Pisa! The south dam platform, once a tournament-field, now displays replica medieval siege-engines.
Times: Open: 27 Mar-May daily 9.30-5, Jun-29 Sep daily 9.30-6, 30 Sep-27 Oct daily 9.30-5. 28 Oct-26 Mar Mon-Sat 9.30-4, Sun 11-4.
Fee: * £2.50 (ch 5-16, pen & students £2). Family ticket £7. **Facilities:** 🅿 ♿ shop ✕ ♿ 🚻

LLANCAIACH FAWR MANOR
Gelligaer Rd, Nelson CF46 6ER (M4 junct 32, A470 to Merthyr Tydfil. Towards Ystrad Mynach A472 follow brown heritage signs)
☎ 01443 412248   📠 01443 412688
e-mail: allens@caerphilly.gov.uk

Step back in time to the Civil War period at this fascinating living history museum. The year is 1645 and visitors are invited into the Manor to meet the servants of 'Colonel' Edward Prichard - from the puritanical to the gossipy.
Times: Open Mon-Fri 10-3.30 (last admission), Sat & Sun 10-4.30. (Closed Mon, Nov-Feb & 24 Dec-2 Jan). **Fee:** £4.50 (ch & concessions £3). Family ticket £12. **Facilities:** 🅿 ♿ ✕ licensed ♿ (personal stereo, photo album & braille map) toilets for disabled shop ✕ (ex guide dogs) 🚻

🏰 CWMCARN   Map 03 ST29
CWMCARN FOREST DRIVE
Nantcarn Rd NP11 7FA (8m N of Newport on A467, M4 junct 28, follow brown heritage signs)
☎ 01495 272001   📠 01495 272001
e-mail: tourism@caerphilly.gov.uk

A seven-mile scenic drive with spectacular views over the Bristol Channel and surrounding countryside. Facilities include barbecues, picnic and play areas, and forest and mountain walks. Special events are held throughout the year, please ring for details.

Times: Open Forest Drive: Etr-Oct. Visitor Centre: all year except between Xmas & New Year. **Fee:** * Cars & Motorcycles £3, Minibus £6, Coaches £20. **Facilities:** 🅿 ♿ ♿ toilets for disabled shop

CARDIFF

🏰 CARDIFF   Map 03 ST17
CARDIFF CASTLE
Castle St CF10 3RB (Follow signs to city centre. From M4, A48 & A470)
☎ 029 2087 8100   📠 029 2023 1417
e-mail: cardiffcastle@cardiff.gov.uk

The Norman castle was built on the site of a Roman fort, and Roman walls, some 10ft thick, can still be seen. There is also a Norman keep and a 13th-century tower. The character of the castle comes from its transformation in the 19th century, when the immensely rich 3rd Marquess of Bute employed William Burges to restore and rebuild it. Together they created a romantic fantasy of a medieval castle. Also here are the military museums of the Royal Regiment of Wales and Queen's Dragoon Guards.
Times: Open all year, daily (ex 25-26 Dec & 1 Jan) including guided tours, Mar-Oct, 9.30-6 (last tour 5pm); Nov-Feb, 9.30-5.30 (last tour 3.45pm). Royal Regiment of Wales Museum closed Tue. Queen's Dragoon Guards Museum closed Fri. **Fee:** Full conducted tour, military museums, green, Roman Wall & Norman Keep £5.50 (ch & pen £3.30). Roman Wall, Norman Keep, & military museum £2.75 (ch & pen £1.70). **Facilities:** 🅿 (200 yds) ♿ ♿ (access to Castle Green & Museum) toilets for disabled shop ✕ (ex in grounds & guide dogs)

DYFFRYN GARDENS
St Nicholas CF5 6SU (6m W of city centre off A48)
☎ 029 2059 3328   📠 029 2059 1966
Times: Open all year, 10-dusk **Facilities:** 🅿 ♿ ♿ (wheelchairs for hire, parking) toilets for disabled shop garden centre *Details not confirmed for 2003* 🚻

Llandaff Cathedral

Llandaff CF5 2YF (A48 off M4 follow signs to Llantrisant then signs to Llandaff Cathedral)
☎ 02920 564554 📠 02920 564554
e-mail: office@llandaffcathedral.org.uk

A medieval cathedral begun in the 12th century on the site of an early Christian place of worship. The cathedral was severely damaged during the bombing raids on Cardiff during World War II. The interior is dominated by a modernistic post-war 'Christ in Majesty' sculpture by Epstein.
Times: Open all year, daily. **Fee:** Donations appreciated **Facilities:** 🅿 🍴 ✕ ♿ (Wheelchair available) toilets for disabled shop 🐕 (ex guide dogs) ☕

Millennium Stadium Tours

Millenium Stadium, West Gate St, Gate 3 CF10 1JA (M4 junct 32, take A470 to Cardiff city centre. West Gate Street is opposite Cardiff Castle) **2 for 1**
☎ 029 2082 2228 📠 029 2082 2228

In the late 1990s this massive stadium was completed as part of an effort to revitalise Welsh fortunes. It replaced Cardiff Arms Park, and now hosts major music events, exhibitions, and international rugby and soccer matches. Its capacity of around 75,000 and its retractable roof makes it unique in Europe. The current home of five controlling bodies; Welsh Rugby, Welsh Football, English Football ASS, Football league (English) & British Speedway.
Times: Open Mon - Sat, 10-5; Sun 10-4. **Fee:** £5 (ch up to 16 £2.50, ch under 5 free, concessions £3). Party 20+. **Facilities:** 🅿 Opposite gate 3 ♿ (lifts escalators disabled parking) toilets for disabled shop 🐕 (ex guide dogs) ☕

National Museum & Gallery Cardiff

Cathays Park CF10 3NP (In Cardiff's Civic Centre, 5 mins walk from the city centre, 20 mins walk from Cardiff's bus and train station. Off M4 junct 32)
☎ 029 2039 7951 📠 029 2037 3219
e-mail: post@nmgw.ac.uk

This establishment is unique amongst British museums and galleries in its range of art and science displays. 'The Evolution of Wales' exhibition takes visitors on a spectacular 4,600-million-year journey, tracing the world from beginning of time and the development of Wales. There are displays of Bronze Age gold, early Christian monuments, Celtic treasures, silver, coins and medals, ceramics, fossils and minerals. A significant collection of French Impressionist paintings sits alongside the work of Welsh artists, past and present in the elegant art galleries.
Times: Open all year, Tue-Sun 10-5. Closed Mon (ex BHs) & 24-26 Dec. **Fee:** Free. **Facilities:** 🅿 (charged) 🍴 ✕ licensed ♿ (wheelchair available) Tel 0292057 3509 for access guide toilets for disabled shop 🐕 (ex guide dogs)

Techniquest

Stuart St CF10 5BW (M4 junct 33, follow A4232 to Cardiff Bay)
☎ 029 2047 5475 📠 029 2048 2517 **2 for 1**
e-mail: info@techniquest.org

Located in the heart of the Cardiff Bay redevelopment area, visitors of all ages will find science and technology made accessible at this discovery science centre. Launch a hot air balloon, see yourself on television. Fascinating and educational fun.
Times: Open all year (ex Xmas), Mon-Fri 9.30-4.30; Sat-Sun & BH's 10.30-5, school holidays 9.30-5. **Fee:** £6.50 (ch 5-16 & con £4.50). Family ticket £18 (2ad+3ch). Friend season ticket £47. Groups 10+
Facilities: 🅿 (50mtrs) 🍴 ♿ (lift, hearing loop & audio tapes) toilets for disabled shop 🐕 (ex guide dogs) ☕

🏛 ST FAGANS Map 03 ST17
Museum of Welsh Life

CF5 6XB (4m W of Cardiff, 3m from M4 junct 33, on A4232)
☎ 029 2057 3500 📠 029 2057 3490
e-mail: mwl@nmgw.ac.uk

A stroll around the indoor galleries and 100 acres of beautiful grounds will give you a fascinating insight into how people in Wales have lived, worked and spent their leisure hours since Celtic times. You can see people practising the traditional means of earning a living, the animals they kept and at certain times of year, the ways in which they celebrated the seasons.
Times: Open all year daily, 10-5. Closed 24-26 Dec. **Fee:** Free.
Facilities: 🅿 🍴 ✕ licensed ♿ (wheelchairs available on a 'first come-first served' basis) toilets for disabled shop 🐕 (ex in grounds if on lead)

🏛 TONGWYNLAIS Map 03 ST18
Castell Coch

CF4 7YS (A470 to Tongwynlais junction, then B4262 to castle on top of hill)
☎ 029 2081 0101

'Castell Coch' is Welsh for red castle, an appropriate name for this fairy-tale building with its red sandstone walls and conical towers. The castle was originally built in the 13th century but fell into ruins, and the present

continued

castle is a late 19th-century creation. Inside, the castle is decorated in fantasy style.
Times: Open: 31 Mar-May 9.30-5; Jun-29 Sep 9.30-6; 30 Sep-29 Oct daily 9.30-5; 30 Oct-31 Mar Mon-Sat 9.30-4, Sun 11-4. **Fee:** * £3 (ch 5-16, pen & students £2.50). Family ticket £8.50. **Facilities:** P shop ✈ ♿ ☕

CARMARTHENSHIRE

♨ ABERGWILI   Map 02 SN42
CARMARTHENSHIRE COUNTY MUSEUM
SA31 2JG (2m E of Carmarthen, just off A40, at Abergwili rdbt)
☎ 01267 231691   📠 01267 223840
e-mail: cdelaney@carmarthenshire.gov.uk

Housed in the old palace of the Bishop of St David's and set in seven acres of grounds, the museum offers a wide range of local subjects to explore, from geology and prehistory to butter making, Welsh furniture and folk art. Temporary exhibitions are held.
Times: Open all year, Mon-Sat 10-4.30. (Closed Xmas-New Year).
Fee: Free. **Facilities:** P 🍴 ♿ toilets for disabled shop ✈ (ex guide dogs)

♨ CARREG CENNEN CASTLE   Map 03 SN61
CARREG CENNEN CASTLE
SA19 6UA (unclassified road from A483 to Trapp village)
☎ 01558 822291

A steep path leads up to the castle, which is spectacularly sited on a limestone crag. It was first built as a stronghold of the native Welsh and then rebuilt in the late 13th century. Most remarkable among the impressive remains is a mysterious passage, cut into the side of the cliff and lit by loopholes. The farm at the site has a rare breeds centre.
Times: Open all year, Apr-Oct, daily 9.30-7.30; Nov-Mar, daily, 9.30-dusk. Closed 25 Dec **Fee:** * £3 (ch 5-16, pen & students £2.50, disabled free). Family ticket £8.50. **Facilities:** P 🍴 shop ✈ ☕

♨ DRE-FACH FELINDRE   Map 02 SN33
MUSEUM OF THE WELSH WOOLLEN INDUSTRY
SA44 5UP (16m W of Carmarthen off A484, 4m E of Newcastle Emlyn)
☎ 01559 370929   📠 01559 371592

The museum is housed in the former Cambrian Mills and has a comprehensive display tracing the evolution of the industry from its beginnings to the present day. Demonstrations of the fleece to fabric process are given on 19th-century textile machinery. Following re-development work, details regarding facilities, disabled access etc may change. Please telephone the museum before visit to confirm details.
Times: Open all year, Apr-Sep, Mon-Sat 10-5; Oct-Mar, Mon-Fri 10-5. (Closed 24-26 Dec & 1 Jan). May vary, please call in advance. Museum being refurbished reopens Easter 2003. **Fee:** Free. **Facilities:** P 🍴 ♿ (Wheelchair access to ground floor & ample seating) toilets for disabled shop garden centre ☕

♨ DRYSLWYN   Map 02 SN52
DRYSLWYN CASTLE
(on B4279)
☎ 029 2050 0200
Times: Open - entrance by arrangement with Dryslwyn Farm.
Facilities: P ✈ ☕ *Details not confirmed for 2003*

♨ KIDWELLY   Map 02 SN40
KIDWELLY CASTLE
SA17 5BQ (via A484)
☎ 01554 890104

This is an outstanding example of late 13th-century castle design, with its `walls within walls' defensive system. There were later additions made to the building, the chapel dating from about 1400. Of particular interest are two vast circular ovens.
Times: Open: 27 Mar-31 May daily 9.30-5; 1 Jun-29 Sep daily 9.30-6; 30 Sep-27 Oct daily 9.30-5; 28 Oct-31 Mar Mon-Sat 9.30-4, Sun 11-4.
Fee: * £2.50 (ch 5-16, pen & students £2). Family ticket £7. **Facilities:** P ♿ toilets for disabled shop ✈ ☕

KIDWELLY INDUSTRIAL MUSEUM
Broadford SA17 4LW (signposted from Kidwelly by-pass)
☎ 01554 891078

Two of the great industries of Wales are represented in this museum: tinplate and coal mining. The original buildings and machinery of the Kidwelly tinplate works, where tinplate was hand made, are now on display to the public. There is also an exhibition of coal mining with pit-head gear and a winding engine, while the more general history of the area is shown in a separate exhibition.
Times: Open Etr, Jun-Sep, PH wknds, Mon-Fri 10-5, Sat-Sun 2-5. Last admission 4pm (5pm Jul-Aug). Other times by arrangement for parties only. **Fee:** Free. **Facilities:** P 🍴 ♿ toilets for disabled shop ✈ (ex in grounds)

♨ LAUGHARNE   Map 02 SN31
DYLAN THOMAS' BOAT HOUSE
Dylans Walk SA33 4SD (14m SW of Carmarthen)
☎ 01994 427420   📠 01554 747501

Under Milk Wood was written here by Wales's most

continued

Carmarthenshire

prolific 20th-century poet and writer. Set on the 'heron priested' shore of the Taf estuary, the house contains original furniture, family photographs, an art gallery and displays on the life and works of Dylan Thomas.
Times: Open all year, May-Oct & Etr wknd, daily 10-5.30 (Last admission 5); Nov-Apr, daily 10.30-3.30 (Last admission 3). **Fee:** * £3 (ch under 7 free, ch over 7 £1, concessions £2). Family and group rates available. **Facilities:** P (200yds) 🍴 (not accessible for wheelchairs) shop ✱ (ex guide dogs)

LAUGHARNE CASTLE
King St SA33 4SA (on A4066)
☎ 01994 427906

This picturesque Castle stands on a low ridge overlooking the wide Taff Estuary. A medieval fortress converted into an Elizabethan mansion, it suffered a civil war siege and later became the backdrop for elaborate Victorian gardens, now recreated. Laugharne Castle has also inspired two modern writers - Richard Hughes and Dylan Thomas.
Times: Open: 27 Mar-29 Sep daily 10-5 (Closed at all other times ex Strata Florida Abbey, Valle Crucis Abbey & Whit which are open sites). **Fee:** * £2.50 (ch 5-16, pen & students £2). Family ticket £7. **Facilities:** P (150 mtrs) ♿ toilets for disabled shop ✱ ✡

🏛 LLANARTHNE   Map 02 SN52
NATIONAL BOTANIC GARDEN OF WALES
Middleton Hall SA32 8HG (8m E of Carmarthen on A48 (M4), dedicated intersection - signed)
☎ 01558 667134   📠 01558 667138

Set amongst 568 acres of parkland in the beautiful Towy Valley the Gardens' centrepiece is the Great Glasshouse, an amazing tilted glass dome with a six-metre ravine. The Mediterranean landscape enables the visitor to experience the aftermath of an Australian bush fire, pause in an olive grove or wander through Fuchsia collections from Chile. A 220mtr herbaceous broad walk forms the spine of the garden and leads children's play area and our 360-surround screen cinema to the Old Stables Courtyard. Here there are art exhibitions, a gift shop and a restaurant. Land train tours will take the visitor around the necklace of lakes, which surround the central garden.
Times: Opening mid May 10-6.30, Jun-Aug 10-7. Sep-Oct 10-5.30, Nov-Dec 10-4.30. Last admission 1hr before closing time. (Closed 25 Dec). **Fee:** * £6.50 (ch 5-16 £3, concessions £5). Family £16. Carer with wheelchair user/blind visitor free. **Facilities:** P 🍴 ✱ licensed ♿ toilets for disabled shop garden centre ✱ (ex guide dogs)

🏛 LLANDEILO   Map 03 SN62
DINEFWR PARK
SA19 6RT (off A40, on the western outskirts of Llandeilo)
☎ 01558 823902   📠 01558 822036
Times: Open Apr-Oct, daily (ex Tue & Wed) 11-4.30. Last admission 30 mins before closing. **Facilities:** P (charged) 🍴 ♿ toilets for disabled ✱ (ex outer park on lead) 🐾 Details not confirmed for 2003

🏛 LLANELLI   Map 02 SN50
WWT LLANELLI
Penclacwydd, Llwynhendy SA14 9SH (3m E of Llanelli, off A484)
☎ 01554 741087   📠 01554 741087   **2 for 1**
e-mail: wwtllanelli@aol.com

A wide variety of wild birds, including oystercatchers, redshanks, curlews, little egrets and occasionally ospreys, can be seen here during the right season. The grounds are beautifully landscaped, and include CCTV transmitting pictures of wild birds on the reserve, a wetland craft area and a flock of colourful Caribbean Flamingos. Facilities for the disabled include easy access on level paths, special viewing areas and wheelchair loan.
Times: Open summer 9.30-5, winter 9.30-4.30. (Closed 24-25 Dec). **Fee:** * £5.50 (ch £3.50, pen £4.50). Family £14.50 **Facilities:** P 🍴 ✱ ♿ toilets for disabled shop ✱ (ex guide/hearing dogs)

🏛 LLANGATHEN   Map 02 SN52
ABERGLASNEY GARDENS
SA32 8QH (4m W of Llandeilo, follow signs from A40)
☎ 01558 668998   📠 01558 668998
e-mail: info@aberglasney.org.uk

With a history stretching back to the 15th century, Aberglasney was reworked by the 17th-century Bishop of St David's, the 18th-century poet, John Dyer and the 19th-century surgeon John Walters Phillips. Falling into disrepair through the 20th century, the house and its gardens were eventually rescued in 1995, and are now largely restored to their original Jacobean splendour. A mysterious and beautiful day out.
Times: Open all year, Apr-Oct, daily 10-6 (last entry 5); Nov-Mar, Mon-Fri & 1st Sun of month 10.30-3. **Fee:** * £5 (ch & disabled £2.50, pen £4). Party 10+ **Facilities:** P ✱ licensed ♿ (wheelchairs available) toilets for disabled ✱ (ex guide dogs)

🏛 LLANSTEFFAN   Map 02 SN31
LLANSTEFFAN CASTLE
(off B4312)
☎ 01267 241756
Times: Open - access throughout the year. **Facilities:** ✱ ✡ Details not confirmed for 2003

Carmarthenshire – Ceredigion

🏛 PUMSAINT Map 03 SN64
DOLAUCOTHI GOLD MINES
SA19 8RR (on A482, signposted)
☎ 01558 650359   📠 01558 822036
e-mail: penpeb@Smpt.NTrust.org.uk
Times: Open 14 Apr-17 Sep, daily 10-5. Guided underground tours daily. **Facilities:** 🅿 💺 ♿ toilets for disabled shop 🐾 *Details not confirmed for 2003* 🎧

CEREDIGION

🏛 ABERAERON Map 02 SN46
LLANERCHAERON
SA48 8DG (2.5m E of Aberaeron off A482)
☎ 01545 570200   📠 01545 571759
Times: Open early Apr-late Oct, Thu-Sun & BH Mons 11-5. Last admission 30 mins before closing. Park open all year dawn to dusk. **Facilities:** 🅿 ♿ toilets for disabled ✖ (ex on lead) 🐾 *Details not confirmed for 2003*

🏛 ABERYSTWYTH Map 06 SN58
NATIONAL LIBRARY OF WALES
Penglais Hill SY23 3BU (off Penglais Hill, A487 in the northern area of Aberystwyth)
☎ 01970 632800, 623834 & 623837   📠 01970 615709
e-mail: holi@llgc.org.uk
Times: Open all year, exhibitions, library & reading rooms Mon-Fri 9.30-6, Sat until 5. (Closed BH's & first wk Oct). **Facilities:** 🅿 💺 ♿ toilets for disabled shop ✖ *Details not confirmed for 2003*

🏛 CAPEL BANGOR Map 06 SN68
RHEIDOL HYDRO ELECTRIC POWER STATION & VISITOR CENTRE
Cwm Rheidol SY23 3NF (off A44 at Capel Bangor)
☎ 01970 880667   📠 01970 880670
Times: Open Apr-Oct, daily 10-4 for free tours of the Power Station, fish farm & visitor centre. **Facilities:** 🅿 💺 ♿ toilets for disabled *Details not confirmed for 2003*

🏛 CENARTH Map 02 SN24
THE NATIONAL CORACLE CENTRE
Cenarth Falls SA38 9JL (on A484 between Carmarthen and Cardigan, centre of Cenarth village, beside bridge and river)
☎ 01239 710980
e-mail: martinfowler@btconnect.com   **2 for 1**

Situated by the beautiful Cenarth Falls, this fascinating museum has a unique collection from all over the world, including Tibet, India, Iraq, Vietnam, and North America. Cenarth has long been a centre for coracle fishing, coracle rides are often available in village during summer holiday. Look out for the salmon leap by the flour mill.
Times: Open Etr-Oct, Sun- Fri 10.30-5.30. All other times by appointment. **Fee:** £3 (ch £1, concessions £2.50) **Facilities:** 🅿 💺 ♿ shop 🎧

🏛 EGLWYSFACH Map 06 SN69
RSPB NATURE RESERVE
Cae'r Berllan SY20 8TA (6m S of Machynlleth on A487 in Eglwys-Fach. Signposted from main road)
☎ 01654 781265   📠 01654 781328

The mixture of different habitats is home to an abundance of birds and wildlife. The saltmarshes in winter support the only regular wintering flock of greenland white-fronted geese in England and Wales in addition to peregrines, hen harriers and merlins. The sessile oak woodland is home to pied flycatchers, wood warblers, redstarts in the summer but woodpeckers, nut hatches, red kites, sparrow hawks and buzzards are here all year round. Otters, polecats, 30 butterfly and 15 dragonfly species are also present.
Times: Open daily, 9am-9pm (or sunset if earlier). Visitor Centre: Apr-Oct 9-5 daily; Nov-Mar 10-4 (wknds only) **Fee:** £3.50 (ch £1, concessions £2.50) Family £7 RSPB members free. **Facilities:** 🅿 ♿ ✖ (ex guide dogs) 🎧

🏛 FELINWYNT Map 02 SN25
FELINWYNT RAINFOREST & BUTTERFLY CENTRE
Rhosmaen SA43 1RT (from A487 Blaenannerch Airfield turning, turn onto B4333. Signposted 6m N of Cardigan)
☎ 01239 810882   📠 01239 810465   **2 for 1**
e-mail: dandjdevereux@btinternet.com

A chance to wander amongst free-flying exotic butterflies accompanied by the recorded wildlife sounds of the Peruvian Amazon. A waterfall, ponds and streams contribute to a humid tropical atmosphere and provide a habitat for fish and native amphibians. See the exhibition of rainforests of Peru and around the world. Free paper and crayons to borrow for children.
Times: Open daily Etr-Oct. Open wknds till xmas **Fee:** £3.75 (ch 4-14 £1.50, pen £3.50) **Facilities:** 🅿 💺 ♿ shop ✖ (ex guide dogs) 🎧

🏛 STRATA FLORIDA Map 03 SN76
STRATA FLORIDA ABBEY
SY25 6BT (unclassified road from Pontrhydfendigaid, reached from B4340)
☎ 01974 831261

Little remains of the Cistercian abbey founded in 1164, except the ruined church and cloister. Strata Florida was an important centre of learning in the Middle Ages, and it is believed that the 14th-century poet Dafyd ap Gwilym was buried here.
Times: Open 27 Mar-29 Sep, daily 10-5; Site open rest of year 10-4 daily **Fee:** * £2 (ch 5-16, pen & students £1.50). Family ticket £5.50. **Facilities:** 🅿 ♿ shop ✖ ☕ 🎧

CONWY

BETWS-Y-COED Map 06 SH75
CONWY VALLEY RAILWAY MUSEUM
Old Goods Yard LL24 0AL (signed from A5 into Old Church Rd, adjacent to train station)
☎ 01690 710568   01690 710132
Times: Open Etr-Oct, daily 10-5.30, then wknds until Mar. Museum, large model & gift shop also open on Mon & Tue in winter period.
Facilities: P ⚹ ♿ (ramps & clearances for wheelchairs) toilets for disabled shop *Details not confirmed for 2003*

CERRIGYDRUDION Map 06 SH94
LLYN BRENIG VISITOR CENTRE
LL21 9TT (on B4501 between Denbigh & Cerrigydrudion)
☎ 01490 420463   01490 420694
e-mail: llyn.brenig@clwrcymru.com

The 1800-acre estate has a unique archaeological trail and round-the-lake walk of 10 miles. A hide is available and disabled anglers are catered for with a specially adapted fishing boat and an annual open day. The centre has an exhibition on archaeology, history and conservation and an audio-visual programme.
Times: Open mid Mar-Oct, daily 9-5. **Fee:** Free. **Facilities:** P (charged) ⚹ ♿ (boats for disabled & fishing open days) toilets for disabled shop ✘ (ex guide dogs)

CONWY Map 06 SH77
ABERCONWY HOUSE
LL32 8AY (At junction of Castle St & High St)
☎ 01492 592246   01492 585153
Times: Open 29 Mar-Oct, Wed-Mon 11-5. Last admission 30 mins before closing. **Facilities:** P (100yds & 0.5 mile) shop ✘ (ex guide dogs) 🐕 *Details not confirmed for 2003*

CONWY CASTLE
LL32 8AY (by A55 or B5106)
☎ 01492 592358

The castle is a magnificent fortress, built 1283-7 by Edward I. There is an exhibition on castle chapels on the ground floor of the Chapel Tower. The castle forms part of the same defensive system as the extensive town walls, which are among the most complete in Europe.
Times: Open: 27 Mar-31 May, daily 9.30-5; 1 Jun-29 Sep, daily 9.30-6; 30 Sep-27 Oct, 9.30-5; 28 Oct-31 Mar, Mon-Sat 9.30-4, Sun 11-4. **Fee:** * £3.50 (ch 5-16, pen & students £3). Family ticket £10. Joint ticket for both monuments: £6.50 (ch 5-16, pen & students £5.50) Family £18.50. **Facilities:** P ♿ toilets for disabled shop ✘ ⚹

CONWY SUSPENSION BRIDGE
LL32 8LO (adjacent to Conwy Castle)
☎ 01492 573282
Times: Open Jul-Aug, daily 10-5; 29 Mar-Jun & Sep-Oct, Wed-Mon 10-5. **Facilities:** P ♿ ✘ 🐕 *Details not confirmed for 2003*

PLAS MAWR
High St LL32 8DE
☎ 01492 593413

Plas Mawr is an excellent example of an Elizabethan town mansion, and is practically the same as when it was built between 1570 and 1580. Temporary exhibitions are held here.
Times: Open 27 Mar-May daily 9.30-5; Jun-1 Sep daily 9.30-6; 2 Sep-29 Sep daily 9.30-5; 30 Sep-27 Oct daily 9.30-4 **Fee:** * £4.50 (ch, pen & students £3.50). Family £12.50. Joint ticket for both monuments available £6.50 (ch, pen & students £5.50) family £18.50.
Facilities: shop ⚹

SMALLEST HOUSE
The Quay LL32 8BB (leave A55 at Conwy signpost, through town, at bottom of High St for the quay, turn left)
☎ 01492 593484   01492 593484 **2 for 1**

The `Guinness Book of Records' lists this as the smallest house in Britain. Just 6ft wide by 10ft high, it is furnished in the style of a mid-Victorian Welsh cottage.
Times: Open Apr-May & Oct 10-5; Jun & Sep, 10-6; Jul & Aug 10-9 or 9.30. **Fee:** 50p (ch under 16 30p, under 5yrs free admission).
Facilities: P (100 yds) ♿ shop

DOLWYDDELAN Map 06 SH75
DOLWYDDELAN CASTLE
LL25 0EJ (on A470 Blaenau Ffestiniog to Betws-y-Coed)
☎ 01690 750366

The castle is reputed to be the birthplace of Llywelyn the Great. It was captured in 1283 by Edward I, who immediately began strengthening it for his own purposes. A restored keep of around 1200, and a 13th-century curtain wall can be seen. An exhibition on the castles of the Welsh Princes is located in the keep.
Times: Open all year, 27 Mar-30 Oct, daily 9.30-6.30; 31 Oct-26 Mar, Mon-Sat 9.30-4 & Sun 11-4. (Closed 24-26 Dec & 1 Jan). **Fee:** * £2 (ch 5-16, pen & students £1.50). Family ticket £5.50 **Facilities:** P ✘ ⚹

LLANDUDNO JUNCTION Map 06 SH77
RSPB NATURE RESERVE
LL31 9XZ (off A55, signposted)
☎ 01492 584091   01492 584091
Times: Open daily, 10-5 (or sunset if earlier). **Facilities:** P ♿ (wheelchair available) toilets for disabled shop ✘ (ex guide dogs) *Details not confirmed for 2003* ⚹

LLANRWST Map 06 SH86
GWYDYR UCHAF CHAPEL
(0.5m SW off B5106)
☎ 01492 640578
Times: Open any reasonable time. **Facilities:** P ✘ 🚗 ⚹ *Details not confirmed for 2003*

PENMACHNO
Map 06 SH75
TY MAWR WYBRNANT
LL25 0HJ (From A5 3m S of Betws-y-Coed take B4406 to Penmachno. House is 2.5m NW of Penmachno by forest road)
☎ 01690 760213
Times: Open 30 Mar-Sep, Thu-Sun & BH Mons 12-5; Oct, Thu, Fri & Sun 12-4. Last admission 30 mins before closing. **Facilities:** P ✕ (ex in grounds) 🚐 (minibus access only) ✻ *Details not confirmed for 2003*

TAL-Y-CAFN
Map 06 SH77
BODNANT GARDEN
LL28 5RE (8m S of Llandudno & Colwyn Bay off A470. Also signposted from A55 junct 19)
☎ 01492 650460   📧 01492 650448

Set above the River Conwy with beautiful views over Snowdonia, these gardens are a delight. Five Italian style terraces were constructed below the house - on the lowest terrace is a canal pool with an open-air yew hedge stage and a reconstructed Pin Mill. The garden is renowned for its collections of magnolias, camellias, rhododendrons and azaleas and the famous Laburnum Arch. Contact for details of open air theatre.
Times: Open mid Mar-2 Nov, daily 10-5 (last admission half hour before closing) **Fee:** * £5.20 (ch £2.60). Party 20+ **Facilities:** P ☕ ♿ (ramps to gardens, wheelchairs & braille guides) toilets for disabled shop garden centre ✕ (ex guide dogs) ✻ 🐕

TREFRIW
Map 06 SH76
TREFRIW WOOLLEN MILLS
LL27 0NQ (on B5106 in centre of Trefriw, 5m N of Betws-y-Coed)
☎ 01492 640462   📧 01492 641821
e-mail: info@trefriw-woollen-mills.co.uk

Established in 1859, the mill is situated beside the fast-flowing Afon Crafnant, which drives two hydro-electric turbines to power the looms. All the machinery of woollen manufacture can be seen here: blending, carding, spinning, dyeing, warping and weaving. In the Weaver's Garden, there are plants traditionally used in the textile industry, mainly for dyeing. Hand-spinning demonstrations.
Times: Mill open Etr-Oct, Mon-Fri 10-5. Weaving demonstrations & turbine house: open all year, Mon-Fri 10-5. **Fee:** Free. **Facilities:** P (35yds) ☕ ♿ (access to shop, cafe, weaving & turbine house) shop

DENBIGHSHIRE

BODELWYDDAN
Map 06 SJ07
BODELWYDDAN CASTLE
LL18 5YA (adjacent to A55, near St Asaph)
☎ 01745 584060   📧 01745 584563
e-mail: bodelwyddan-castle.co.uk
Times: Open Nov-Mar Tue-Thu & Sat-Sun, 10.30-4; Apr-Jun Sat-Thu, 10.30-5; Jul-Aug daily 10.30-5; Sep-Oct Sat-Thu, 10.30-5. **Facilities:** P ☕ ♿ (lift to first floor & braille & audio guides) toilets for disabled shop ✕ (ex guide dogs) *Details not confirmed for 2003* 🐕

CORWEN
Map 06 SJ04
EWE-PHORIA SHEEPDOG CENTRE
Glanrafon, Llangwm LL21 0PE (Turn off A5 to Llangwm, follow signs)
☎ 01490 460369
e-mail: info@ewe-phoria.co.uk

Ewe-Phoria is an Agri-Theatre and Sheepdog Centre that details the life and work of the shepherd on a traditional Welsh farm. The Agri-Theatre has unusual living displays of sheep with accompanying lectures on their history and breed, while outside sheepdog handlers put their dogs through their paces.
Times: Open Etr-end Oct, Tue-Fri & Sun. Closed Sat & Mon ex BH's
Fee: * £3.95 (ch £2.95, concessions £3.25) **Facilities:** P ☕ ✕ licensed ♿ toilets for disabled shop ✕ (ex guide dogs) 🐕

PEN-Y-BRYN FARM PARK
LL21 9PP (off A5 onto B5105. 5m from Cerrigydrudion)
☎ 01490 420244 & 📧 01490 420244

Proudly catering to all ages, Pen-y-Bryn Park has a petting zoo, falconry, and 'Solo', its very own llama.
Times: Open Etr-Oct, Tue-Sun & BH's, 10-5 **Fee:** * £3 (ch, pen £2.50) Family ticket £10 **Facilities:** P ☕ ♿ toilets for disabled shop garden centre

RUG CHAPEL
Rug LL21 9BT
☎ 01490 412025

Rug Chapel was built in 1637 for Colonel William Salusbury, famous Civil War defender of Denbigh Castle. A rare little altered example of a 17th-century private chapel, it reflects the Colonel's High Church religious views. Prettily set in a wooded landscape, the chapel's modest exterior gives little hint of the interior where local artists and carvers were given a free reign, with some spectacular results.
Times: Open late Mar-late Sep, Wed-Sun 10-5. (Closed Winter, Mon & Tue, ex BH wknds). **Fee:** * £2 (ch 5-16, pen & students £1.50). Family ticket £5.50. **Facilities:** P ♿ toilets for disabled shop ✕ 🐕 🐕

Denbighshire

DENBIGH   Map 06 SJ06
DENBIGH CASTLE
(via A525, A543 & B5382)
☎ 01745 813385

The castle was begun by Henry de Lacy in 1282 and has an inspiring and impressive gatehouse, with a trio of towers and a superb archway, which is surmounted by a figure believed to be that of Edward I.
Times: Open: 27 Mar-29 Sep, Mon-Fri 10-5.30, Sat/Sun 9.30-5.30 (open site at all other times) **Fee:** * £2 (ch 5-16, pen & students £1.50). Family ticket £5.50. **Facilities:** P & shop ✈ ✤ ⛴

LLANGOLLEN   Map 07 SJ24
DOCTOR WHO EXHIBITION & MODEL RAILWAY WORLD
Lower Dee Exhibition Centre LL20 8RX (from Llangollen Bridge, 500yds on road towards Wrexham)
☎ 01978 860584 📠 01978 861928   **2 for 1**
e-mail: dapol.drwho@btinternet.com

The world's largest collection of Doctor Who items direct from the BBC, original costumes, models and Hall of Monsters, also 'Bessie', the Doctor's car. Model Railway World illustrates the history of model railways, from the earliest hand-made models of the 1920s up to the present day, as well as working layouts of various sizes, and examples of rolling stock from around the world. Dapol Toy Factory is also on site, visitors can watch toys being made.
Times: Open 10-5. (Closed 25/26 Dec & 1 Jan). **Fee:** * Doctor Who Experience £5.95 (ch £3.75). Family ticket £15.95; Model Railway World £4.75 (ch £3.75). Family ticket £13.50; Combination ticket to all attractions £9 (ch £6). Family ticket £24.95. **Facilities:** P 🍴 shop ✈ (ex guide dogs) ⛴

HORSE DRAWN BOATS CENTRE
The Wharf, Wharf Hill LL20 8TA (From A5 turn onto Llangollen High St, across river bridge to T-junction. The wharf on hill facing)
☎ 01978 860702 & 01691 690322
📠 01978 860702
e-mail: sue@horsedrawnboats.co.uk

Take a horsedrawn boat trip along the beautiful Vale of Llangollen, and visit the museum, which illustrates the heyday of canals in Britain. The displays include working and static models, photographs, murals and slides. There is also a narrowboat trip that crosses Pontcysyllte Aqueduct, the largest navigable aqueduct in the world.
Times: Open Etr-end Oct, daily. May closed Thu, closed Fri in Oct. **Fee:** Horse Drawn Boat Trip from £4 (ch £2.50). Family ticket £11. Narrowboat Trip £7 (ch £6). **Facilities:** P (400 yds) 🍴 & (alighting/pick-up point available) toilets for disabled shop ⛴

LLANGOLLEN RAILWAY
Abbey Rd LL20 8SN (off A5 at Llangollen traffic lights onto A539 cross river bridge. Station on left at T-junct)
☎ 01978 860979 & 860951 (timetable)
📠 01978 869247
e-mail: office@llangollen-railway.co.uk

Heritage Railway featuring steam and classic diesel services along the picturesque Dee Valley. The journey consists of a 15-mile roundtrip between Llangollen and Carrog. A special coach for the disabled is available on some services. Please contact for more information.
Times: Open - station wknds, reduced services off peak, daily services Jun-Oct. Principally steam hauled, diesel trains please refer to timetable for off peak services. **Fee:** * Station Free, except for special event days when charge of £1 (ch 50p) this is deducted from fare if travelling; 2nd class return fare for full journey £8 (ch £3.80, pen £5.50) Family ticket £18 (2 adult & 2 ch). **Facilities:** P (400yds) 🍴 & (special coach for disabled on some trains, notice required) toilets for disabled shop (at Llangollen only) ⛴

PLAS NEWYDD
Hill St LL20 8AW (Follow brown heritage signs from A5, close to Grapes public house in Llangollen)
☎ 01978 861314 📠 01824 708258
e-mail: rose.mcmahon@denbighshire.gov.uk

The 'Ladies of Llangollen', Lady Eleanor Butler and Sarah Ponsonby, lived here from 1780 to 1831. The original stained-glass windows, carved panels, and domestic miscellany of two lives are exhibited along with prints, pictures and letters.
Times: Open Apr-Oct, daily, 10-5. **Fee:** * £2.50 (ch £1.25). Family £6. Party 20+. **Facilities:** P & toilets for disabled ✈ (ex guide dogs or in grounds)

VALLE CRUCIS ABBEY
LL29 8DD (on B5103, off A5 W of Llangollen)
☎ 01978 860326

Set in a deep, narrow valley, the abbey was founded for the Cistercians in 1201 by Madog ap Gruffydd. Substantial remains of the church can be seen, and some beautifully carved grave slabs have been found. There is a small exhibition on the Cistercian monks and the abbey.
Times: Open 27 Mar-29 Sep daily 10-5, Winter opening site 10-4 daily. **Fee:** * £2 (ch 5-16, pen & students £1.50). Family ticket £5.50.
Facilities: P & shop ✈ ✤ ⛴

RHUDDLAN   Map 06 SJ07
RHUDDLAN CASTLE
LL18 5AD
☎ 01745 590777

The castle was begun by Edward I in 1277, on a simple 'diamond' plan with round towers linked by sections of 9ft-thick curtain wall. The moat was linked to a deep-water canal, allowing Edward's ships to sail from the sea right up to the castle.
Times: Open 27 Mar-29 Sep, daily 10-5. (Closed at all other times ex for Strata Florida Abbey, Valle Crucis Abbey & Whit which are open sites). **Fee:** * £2 (ch 5-16, pen & students £1.50). Family ticket £5.50.
Facilities: P & shop ✈ ✤ ⛴

FLINTSHIRE

EWLOE Map 07 SJ26
EWLOE CASTLE
(NW of village on B5125)
Times: Open at all times. **Facilities:** ✈ ✛ *Details not confirmed for 2003*

FLINT Map 07 SJ27
FLINT CASTLE
CH6 5PH
☎ 01352 733078
Times: Open at all times. **Facilities:** 🅿 ✈ ✛ *Details not confirmed for 2003*

HOLYWELL Map 07 SJ17
BASINGWERK ABBEY
Greenfield Valley Heritage Pk, Greenfield CH8 7GH
☎ 01352 714172
Times: Open all year, daily 9-6. **Facilities:** 🅿 ✈ ♿ (disabled facilities in Heritage Park) toilets for disabled shop ✈ ✛ *Details not confirmed for 2003*

GREENFIELD VALLEY HERITAGE PARK
Greenfield Rd CH8 7GH
☎ 01352 714172 📠 01352 714791
e-mail: info@greenfieldvalley.com

This fascinating park covers one and a half miles of woodlands, reservoirs, ancient monuments and industrial history. Among the multitude of sights are a footpath that was once a railway line, the remnants of a number of mills relating to the copper industry, an environment centre, the shrine of St Winefride's Well, and Basingwerk Abbey.
Times: Park open all year. Museum & farm 23 Mar-Oct 10-4.30 **Fee:** * Museum & farm £2.50 (ch £1.50, concessions £2). Park free.
Facilities: 🅿 ☕ ♿ ramps to enter buildings toilets for disabled shop

GWYNEDD

BANGOR Map 06 SH57
PENRHYN CASTLE
LL57 4HN (1m E at Bangor, at Llandegai on A5122, just off A55)
☎ 01248 353084 📠 01248 371281 **2 for 1**
e-mail: ppemsn@smtp.ntrust.org.uk

The splendid castle with its towers and battlements was commissioned in 1827 as a sumptuous family home. Notable rooms include the great hall, the library and the dining room, which is covered with neo-Norman decoration. There is a slate bed weighing over a ton, and a decorated brass bed made for Edward VII at the then huge cost of £600.
Times: Open 22 Mar-5 Nov, daily (ex Tue) Castle 12-5pm. Grounds and stableblock exhibitions 11-5 (Jul & Aug 10-5.30). Last admission 4.30pm. Last audio tour 4pm. **Fee:** * All inclusive ticket: £6 (ch £3). Family ticket £15. Party 15+ £5 pp. Grounds & stableblock only £4 (ch £2). **Facilities:** 🅿 ✈ licensed ♿ (wheelchairs & golf buggies pre bookable) toilets for disabled shop 🐕

BEDDGELERT Map 06 SH54
SYGUN COPPER MINE
LL55 4NE (1m E of Beddgelert on A498)
☎ 01766 510100 📠 01766 510102
e-mail: sygunmine@aol.com

On a self-guided audio-visual underground tour, visitors can explore the workings of this 19th-century copper mine, where magnificent stalactite and stalagmite formations can be seen. Audio-visual presentation and a display of artefacts found during excavations.
Times: Open daily mid Feb-mid Nov Mon-Fri 10-5, Sat 10-4, Sun 11-5
Fee: * £4.95 (ch £3.25, pen £4.25). **Facilities:** 🅿 ☕ ♿ wide access toilets for disabled shop

BLAENAU FFESTINIOG Map 06 SH74
HYDRO CENTRE FFESTINIOG
Ffestiniog Hydro Centre, First Hydro Company, Tan-Y-Grisiau LL41 3TP (off A496)
☎ 01766 830465 📠 01766 833472
e-mail: robertsb@fhc.co.uk
Times: Open Etr-Oct, Sun-Fri, 10-4.30. Other times by prior arrangement. **Facilities:** 🅿 ☕ shop ✈ (ex guide dogs) *Details not confirmed for 2003*

LLECHWEDD SLATE CAVERNS
LL41 3NB (25m from A55 N Wales Expressway S on A470. 10m from A5 junct with A470. Beside A470)
☎ 01766 830306 📠 01766 831260
e-mail: llechwedd@aol.com
Times: Open all year, daily from 10am. Last tour 5.15 (Oct-Feb 4.15). (Closed 25-26 Dec & 1 Jan). **Facilities:** 🅿 ☕ ✈ licensed ♿ toilets for disabled shop (also Victorian shops in the Village) ✈ (ex on surface) *Details not confirmed for 2003*

CAERNARFON Map 06 SH46
CAERNARFON CASTLE
LL55 2AY
☎ 01286 677617

Edward I began building the castle and extensive town walls in 1283 after defeating the last independent ruler of Wales. Completed in 1328, it has unusual polygonal towers, notably the 10-sided Eagle Tower. There is a

continued

theory that these features were copied from the walls of Constantinople, to reflect a tradition that Constantine was born nearby. Edward I's son and heir was born and presented to the Welsh people here, setting a precedent that was followed in 1969, when Prince Charles was invested as Prince of Wales.
Times: Open 27 Mar-31 May, daily 9.30-5; 1 Jun-29 Sep, daily, 9.30-6; 30 Sep-29 Oct, daily 9.30-5; 30 Oct-Mar, Mon-Sat 9.30-4, Sun 11-4.
Fee: * £4.50 (ch 5-16, pen & students £3.50, disabled free). Family ticket £12.50. **Facilities:** P shop ✈ ☺ ▾

SEGONTIUM ROMAN MUSEUM
Beddgelert Rd LL55 2LN (on A4085 towards Beddgelert, approx 1m from Caernarfon)
☎ 01286 675625   ◫ 01286 678416
e-mail: post@nmgw.ac.uk

This museum tells the story of the conquest and occupation of Wales by the Romans and displays the finds from the auxiliary fort of Segontium, one of the most famous in Britain. You can combine a visit to the museum with exploration of the site of the Roman Fort, which is in the care of Cadw: Welsh Historic Monuments. The discoveries displayed vividly portray the daily life of the soldiers.
Times: Open Etr-Oct Mon-Sat 10-5, Sun 2-5, Nov-Mar Mon-Sat 10-4, Sun 2-4 **Fee:** Free. **Facilities:** P ✈ (ex guide dogs) ▾

🏛 CRICCIETH   Map 06 SH43
CRICCIETH CASTLE
LL52 0DP (off A497)
☎ 01766 522227

The castle dates from the 13th century and was taken and destroyed by Owain Glyndwr in 1404. Evidence of a fierce fire can still be seen. The gatehouse leading to the inner ward remains impressive.
Times: Open 27 Mar-May, daily 10-5; Jun-29 Sep, daily 10-6. (Open site at all other times). **Fee:** * £2.50 (ch 5-16, pen & students £2). Family ticket £7. **Facilities:** P shop ✈ ☺ ▾

🏛 CYMER ABBEY   Map 06 SH71
CYMER ABBEY
(2m NW of Dolgellau on A494)
☎ 01341 422854
Times: Open all year, early Apr-Oct, daily 9.30-6; Nov-Mar, daily 9.30-4. (Closed 24-26 Dec & 1 Jan) **Facilities:** P ♿ ✈ ☺ Details not confirmed for 2003 ▾

🏛 FAIRBOURNE   Map 06 SH61
FAIRBOURNE RAILWAY
Beach Rd LL38 2PZ (on A493 follow signs for Fairbourne)
☎ 01341 250362
◫ 01341 250240   `2 for 1`
e-mail: enquiries@fairbourne-railway.co.uk

One of the most unusual of Wales' 'little trains'; built in 1890 as a horse-drawn railway to carry building materials, it was later converted to steam, and now covers two-and-a-half miles. Its route passes one of the loveliest beaches in Wales, with views of the beautiful Mawddach Estuary.
Times: Open early/mid Apr-mid/late Sep, times vary according to season and events. Trains will run during Oct half term holiday and Santa Specials at Xmas. **Fee:** * Return £6.10 (ch £3.75, pen £5.30), family £15.80 (2 adults & 2 ch). **Facilities:** P 🍴 shop Details not confirmed for 2003 ▾

🏛 GROESLON   Map 06 SH45
INIGO JONES SLATEWORKS
LL54 7ST (on A487, 6m S of Caernarfon)
☎ 01286 830242   ◫ 01286 831247   `2 for 1`
e-mail: slate@inigojones.co.uk

Inigo Jones was established in 1861 primarily to make school writing slates. Today the company uses the same material to make architectural, monumental and craft products. A self-guided audio/video tour takes visitors round the slate workshops, and displays the various processes used in the extraction and working of Welsh slate.
Times: Open daily, summer wkdays 9-5, wknds 10-5; winter wkdays 9-5, Sat am 9-12. **Fee:** * £3.80 (ch & pen £3) **Facilities:** P 🍴 ♿ toilets for disabled shop (ex guide dogs) ▾

🏛 HARLECH   Map 06 SH53
HARLECH CASTLE
LL46 2YH (from A496)
☎ 01766 780552

Harlech Castle was built in 1283-81 by Edward I, with a sheer drop to the sea on one side. Owain Glyndwr starved the castle into submission in 1404 and made it his court and campaigning base. Later, the defence of the castle in the Wars of the Roses inspired the song *Men of Harlech*. Today the sea has slipped away, and the castle's great walls and round towers stand above the dunes.
Times: Open 27 Mar-31 May, daily 9.30-5; Jun-29 Sep, daily 9.30-6; 30 Sep-27 Oct, daily 9.30-5; 28 Oct-31 Mar, Mon-Sat 9.30-4, Sun 11-4.
Fee: * £3 (ch 5-16, pen & students £2). Family ticket £8. **Facilities:** P (disabled spaces in car park) shop ✈ ☺ ▾

🏛 LLANBERIS   Map 06 SH56
DOLBADARN CASTLE
LL55 4UD (A4086)
Times: Open any reasonable time. **Facilities:** P ✈ ☺ Details not confirmed for 2003 ▾

LLANBERIS LAKE RAILWAY
Padam Country Park LL55 4TY (off A4086 at Llanberis)
☎ 01286 870549   ◫ 01286 870549
e-mail: info@lake-railway.co.uk

Steam locomotives dating from 1889 to 1948 carry passengers on a four-mile return journey along the shore of Padarn Lake. The terminal station is adjacent to the Welsh Slate Museum, in the Padarn Country Park. The railway was formerly used to carry slate.
Times: Open Etr-late Oct. Trains run frequently Sun-Fri (Sat in Jul & Aug), 11-4.30 in peak season. Send for free timetable. **Fee:** * £4.50 (ch £3). Family ticket available. Reduced rates for groups. **Facilities:** P (charged) 🍴 ♿ (Disabled carriage available) toilets for disabled shop ✈ ▾

Gwynedd

Snowdon Mountain Railway
LL55 4TY (on A4086, Caernarfon to Capel Curig road. 7.5m from Caernarfon)
☎ 0870 4580033 📠 01286 872518
e-mail: enquiries@snowdonrailway.co.uk

The journey of just over four-and-a-half miles takes passengers more than 3000ft up to the summit of Snowdon; breathtaking views include, on a clear day, the Isle of Man and the Wicklow Mountains in Ireland. The round trip to the summit and back takes two and a half hours including a half hour at the summit.
Times: Open 15 Mar-5 Nov, daily from 9am (weather permitting).
Fee: Return £18 (ch £13), early bird discount on 9 & 9.30 trains.
Facilities: P (charged) 🍴 ♿ (some carriages suitable for wheelchairs - must notify) toilets for disabled shop ✈ (ex guide dogs)

Welsh Slate Museum
Gilfach Ddu, Padarn Country Park LL55 4TY (0.25m off A4086. The Museum is within Padarn Country Park)
☎ 01286 870630 📠 01286 871906
e-mail: slate@nmgw.ac.uk

Set among the towering quarries at Llanberis, the Welsh Slate Museum is a living, working site located in the original workshops of Dinorwig Quarry, which once employed 15,000 men and boys. You can see the foundry, smithy, workshops and mess room which make up the old quarry, and view original machinery, much of which is still in working order.
Times: Open Etr-Oct, daily 10-5; Nov-Etr, Sun-Fri 10-4. **Fee:** Free.
Facilities: P (charged) 🍴 ♿ (all parts accessible except patten loft) toilets for disabled shop

🏛 LLANFIHANGEL-Y-PENNANT
Map 06 SH60

Castell-y-Bere
☎ 029 2050 0200
Times: Open all reasonable times. **Facilities:** ✈ ♿ Details not confirmed for 2003

🏛 LLANGYBI
Map 06 SH44

St Cybi's Well
☎ 01766 810047
Times: Open at all times. **Facilities:** ♿ ✈ ♿ Details not confirmed for 2003

🏛 LLANUWCHLLYN
Map 06 SH83

Bala Lake Railway
The Station LL23 7DD (off A494 Bala to Dolgellau road)
☎ 01678 540666 📠 01678 540535 **2 for 1**

Steam locomotives which once worked in the slate quarries of North Wales now haul passenger coaches for four-and-a-half miles from Llanuwchllyn Station along the lake to Bala. The railway has one of the few remaining double-twist lever-locking framed GWR signal boxes, installed in 1896. Some of the coaches are open and some closed, so passengers can enjoy the beautiful views of the lake and mountains in all weathers.

Times: Open Etr-29 Sep, daily (except certain Mon & Fri in Apr, May, Jun & Sep) **Fee:** * £6.70 return (pen £6.20). Family ticket £16 (2ad+2ch) **Facilities:** P 🍴 ♿ (wheelchairs can be taken on train) shop

🏛 LLANYSTUMDWY
Map 06 SH43

Lloyd George Museum & Highgate Victorian Cottage
LL52 0SH (on A497 between Pwllheli & Criccieth)
☎ 01766 522071 📠 01766 522071
e-mail: amgueddfeydd-museums@gwynedd.gov.uk

Explore the life and times of David Lloyd George in this museum. His boyhood home is recreated as it would have been when he lived there between 1864 and 1880, along with his Uncle Lloyd's shoemaking workshop.
Times: Open Etr, daily 10-5; May, Mon-Fri 10.30-5; Jun-Sep daily 10.30-5; Oct, Mon-Fri, 11-4. Other times by appointment, telephone 01286 679098 for details. **Fee:** * £3 (ch & pen £2). Family ticket £7.
Facilities: P ♿ (induction loop in audio visual theatre, shop & cottage) toilets for disabled shop ✈ (ex guide dogs)

🏛 PENARTH FAWR
Map 06 SH43

Penarth Fawr
(3.5m NE of Pwllheli off A497)
☎ 01766 810880
Times: Open at all times. **Facilities:** ♿ ✈ ♿ Details not confirmed for 2003

🏛 PLAS-YN-RHIW
Map 06 SH22

Plas-yn-Rhiw
LL53 8AB (12m from Pwllheli signposted from B4413 to Aberdaron)
☎ 01758 780219
Times: Open Mar-14 May, Thu-Mon noon-5; mid May-Oct, Wed-Mon noon-5. **Facilities:** P ♿ (braille guides/scented plants) toilets for disabled shop ✈ 🚲 Details not confirmed for 2003

PORTHMADOG Map 06 SH53
FFESTINIOG RAILWAY
Harbour Station LL49 9NF (SE end of town, on A487)
☎ 01766 512340 📠 01766 514576
e-mail: info@festrail.co.uk
Times: Open late Mar-early Nov, daily service and also 26 Dec-1 Jan. Limited service Nov-Dec (most days). Limited service Feb & Mar.
Facilities: P (charged) ✘ licensed ♿ (Wheelchair ramps) toilets for disabled shop (closed 24/25 Dec) *Details not confirmed for 2003* 🏷

PORTMEIRION Map 06 SH53
PORTMEIRION
LL48 6ET (Off A487 at Minffordd)
☎ 01766 770000 📠 01766 771331 **2 for 1**
e-mail: info@portmeirion-village.com

Welsh architect Sir Clough Williams Ellis built his fairy-tale, Italianate village on a rocky, tree-clad peninsula on the shores of Cardigan Bay. A bell-tower, castle and lighthouse mingle with a watch-tower, grottoes and cobbled squares among pastel-shaded picturesque cottages let as holiday accommodation. The 60-acre Gwyllt Gardens include miles of dense woodland paths and are famous for their fine displays of rhododendrons, azaleas, hydrangeas and sub-tropical flora. There is a mile of sandy beach and a playground for children.
Times: Open all year, daily 9.30-5.30. **Fee:** * £5.30 (ch £2.60, pen £4.20). Party 15+. **Facilities:** P 💷 ✘ licensed ♿ toilets for disabled shop garden centre ✈ (ex guide dogs) 🏷

TYWYN Map 06 SH50
TALYLLYN RAILWAY
Wharf Station LL36 9EY (A493 Machynlleth to Dolgellau for Tywyn station, B4405 for Abergynolwyn)
☎ 01654 710472 📠 01654 711755
e-mail: enquiries@talyllyn.co.uk
Times: Open Sun mid Feb-Mar, daily; Apr-early Nov & 26 Dec-1 Jan. Ring for timetable. **Facilities:** P (charged) 💷 ♿ (prior notice useful) toilets for disabled shop *Details not confirmed for 2003* 🏷

Y FELINHELI Map 06 SH56
GREENWOOD CENTRE
LL56 4QN (leave A55 at A5 junct, follow Llanberis signs onto B4366, signposted from next rdbt)
☎ 01248 670076 📠 01248 670069 **2 for 1**
e-mail: info@greenwood-centre.co.uk

This forest park provides a wide range of exciting activities for the whole family. Try the Great Green Run - the longest slide in Wales, shoot a real longbow, build dens in the woods and saw a log. Try the Jungle Boat Adventure and explore the rainforest. There are also large interactive exhibitions in the oak-framed great hall.
Times: Open daily mid Mar-end Oct 10-5.30 (Sep/Oct 10-5 & Sun 11-5) **Fee:** * Varies with time of year. £3.95-£5.50 (ch & pen £2.95-£4.95). Family ticket £12.10-£17.50. Party. **Facilities:** P 💷 ♿ (grounds partly accessible) toilets for disabled shop 🏷

Gwynedd – Isle of Anglesey 361

ISLE OF ANGLESEY

BEAUMARIS Map 06 SH67
BEAUMARIS CASTLE
LL58 8AP
☎ 01248 810361

Beaumaris was built by Edward I and took from 1295 to 1312 to complete. In later centuries it was plundered for its lead, timber and stone. Despite this it remains one of the most impressive and complete castles built by Edward I. It has a perfectly symmetrical, concentric plan, with a square inner bailey and curtain walls, round corner towers and D-shaped towers in between.
Times: Open: 27 Mar-May daily 9.30-5, Jun-29 Sep daily 9.30-6, 30 Sep-27 Oct daily 9.30-5, 28 Oct-26 Mar Mon-Sat 9.30-4, Sun 11-4.
Fee: * £3 (ch u5 free, ch 5-16, pen & students £2.50). Family ticket £8.50. Party 15+ 10% discount. **Facilities:** P ♿ shop ✈ 🏷

BEAUMARIS GAOL & COURTHOUSE
Steeple Ln LL58 8EW
☎ 01248 810921 & 724444 📠 01248 750282

With its treadmill and grim cells, the gaol is a vivid reminder of the tough penalties exacted by 19th-century law. The courthouse, built in 1614 and renovated early in the 19th century, is a unique example of an early Welsh court.
Times: Open Etr-Sep, daily 10.30-5. Other times by arrangement only.
Fee: * Gaol £2.75 (ch, pen £1.75). Courthouse £1.50 (ch, pen £1). Combined ticket £3.50 (ch & pen £2.50). Family ticket £7.75.
Facilities: P (500yds) ♿ (narrow gates may restrict some wheelchairs) shop ✈ (ex guide dogs)

MUSEUM OF CHILDHOOD
1 Castle St LL58 8AP (Opp Beaumaris Castle)
☎ 01248 712498 📠 01248 716869
Times: Open daily 10.30-5.30, Sun 12-5. Last admission 4.30, Sun 4. (Closed Nov-2nd wk Mar). **Facilities:** P (50yds) ♿ shop ✈ (ex guide dogs) *Details not confirmed for 2003*

BRYNCELLI DDU Map 06 SH57
BRYN CELLI DDU BURIAL CHAMBER
(3m W of Menai Bridge off A4080)
☎ 029 2050 0200
Times: Open at all times. **Facilities:** P ✈ ☉ *Details not confirmed for 2003*

BRYNSIENCYN Map 06 SH46
ANGLESEY SEA ZOO
LL61 6TQ (take 1st turning off Britannia Bridge then follow Lobster signs along A4080 to zoo)
☎ 01248 430411 📠 01248 430213
e-mail: fishandfun@seazoo.demon.co.uk

This attraction contains a shipwreck bristling with conger eels, a lobster hatchery, a seahorse nursery, crashing waves and the enchanting fish forest.
Times: Open 16 Mar-3 Nov 10-6. Last admission 1hr before site closes. **Fee:** £5.95 (ch, student & UB40 £4.95, pen £5.50). Family ticket £14.95-£21.95. Party 10+. Please telephone to confirm 2003 prices. **Facilities:** P 💷 ✘ licensed ♿ (2 wheelchairs available) toilets for disabled shop ✈ (ex guide dogs) 🏷

Foel Farm Park
Foel Farm LL61 6TQ (Left off A55 onto A5/A4080 to Llanfairpwllgwyngyll. Left on A4080 to Brynsiencyn. Follow signs)
☎ 01248 430646 ▤ 01248 430066
e-mail: foelfarm@btinternet.com

Children will love this friendly farm experience, where they can meet animals big and small, and take tractor and trailer rides. The park also contains a luxury handmade chocolate business, a bistro and bar.
Times: Open daily Mar-Oct 10.30-5.30; wknds Nov-Feb 10.30-4.30. Also open half term Feb **Fee:** * £4.25 (ch 4-16 £3.25, sen £3.45)
Facilities: ℗ 🍴 ✕ licensed ♿ toilets for disabled shop 🐕 ex guide dogs 🚌

HOLYHEAD Map 06 SH28
RSBP Nature Reserve South Stack
South Stack LL65 1YH (A5 or A55 to Holyhead then follow brown heritage signs)
☎ 01407 764973 ▤ 01407 764973

High cliffs with caves and offshore stacks, backed by the maritime heathland, make this an ideal reserve to watch seabirds. Live video pictures of breeding seabirds are shown in the summer. Choughs, guillemots, razorbills, fulmars and puffins may be seen.
Times: Open: Visitor Centre daily, Apr-mid Sep, 11-5. Reserve open daily at all times. **Fee:** Free. **Facilities:** ℗

LLANALLGO Map 06 SH58
Din Llugwy Ancient Village
(1m NW off A5025)
Times: Open at all times. **Facilities:** 🐕 ⊕ Details not confirmed for 2003

PLAS NEWYDD Map 06 SH56
Plas Newydd
LL61 6DQ (2m S of Llanfairpwll, on A4080)
☎ 01248 714795 ▤ 01248 713673   **2 for 1**
e-mail: ppnmsn@smtp.ntrust.org.uk

Set amidst breathtakingly beautiful scenery and with spectacular views of Snowdonia, this elegant 18th-century house was built by James Wyatt and is an interesting mix of Classical and Gothic. The interior, restyled in the 1930s, is famous for its association with Rex Whistler, whose largest painting is here. A military museum contains campaign relics of the 1st Marquess of Anglesea. There is a fine spring garden and Australasian arboretum. Access to a marine walk on the Menai Strait.
Times: Open Apr-Oct, Sat-Wed. House 12-5; Garden 11-5.30. Last admission 4.30. **Fee:** * £4.60 (ch £2.30). Family £11.50 (2ad+3ch). Parties **Facilities:** ℗ ✕ licensed ♿ (Close parking, wheelchairs, garden shuttle, braille guide) toilets for disabled shop 🐕 (ex guide dogs) 🏛

MERTHYR TYDFIL

⛰ MERTHYR TYDFIL Map 03 SO00
Brecon Mountain Railway
Pant Station Dowlais CF48 2UP (Follow the Mountain Railway Signs from A470 or A465 N of Merthyr Tydfil)
☎ 01685 722988 ▤ 01685 384854

This narrow-gauge railway follows part of an old British Rail route which closed in 1964 when the iron industry in South Wales fell into decline. The present route starts at Pant Station and continues for 3.5 miles through the beautiful scenery of the Brecon Beacons National Park, as far as Taf Fechan reservoir. The train is pulled by a vintage steam locomotive.
Times: Opening times on application to The Brecon Mountain Railway, Pant Station, Merthyr Tydfil. **Fee:** Fares are under review, please ring for details. **Facilities:** ℗ 🍴 ✕ licensed ♿ (adapted carriage) toilets for disabled shop 🚌

Cyfarthfa Castle Museum & Art Gallery
Cyfarthfa Park CF47 8RE (off A470, N towards Brecon, follow brown heritage signs)
☎ 01685 723112 ▤ 01685 723112
e-mail: museum@cyfarthfapark.freeserve.co.uk

Set in wooded parkland beside a lake, this imposing Gothic mansion now houses a superb museum and art gallery. Providing a fascinating glimpse into 3,000 years of history, the museum displays wonderful collections of fine art, social history and objects from around the world.
Times: Open Apr-Sep: Mon-Sun 10-5.30, Oct-Mar, Tue-Fri 10-4, Sat-Sun 12-4. **Fee:** Free. **Facilities:** ℗ 🍴 ♿ (stair lift & wheelchair available) toilets for disabled shop 🐕 (ex guide dogs)

MONMOUTHSHIRE

⛰ CAERWENT Map 03 ST49
Caerwent Roman Town
(off A48)
☎ 029 2050 0200
Times: Open - access throughout the year. **Facilities:** 🐕 ⊕ Details not confirmed for 2003

⛰ CALDICOT Map 03 ST48
Caldicot Castle, Museum & Countryside Park
Church Rd NP26 4HU (From M4 junct 23A onto B4245. From M48 take junct 2 & follow A48 & B4245)
☎ 01291 420241
▤ 01291 435094   **2 for 1**
e-mail: caldicotcastle@monmouthshire.gov.uk

Caldicot Castle's well-preserved fortifications were founded by the Normans and fully developed by the late 14th century. Restored as a family home the castle offers the chance to explore medieval walls and towers

continued

Monmouthshire

in a setting of tranquil gardens and wooded country parkland.

Times: Open Mar-Oct, daily 11-5. Fee: £3 (ch, pen, student & disabled £1.50). Family (2ad+3ch) £8.50 Party 15+. Facilities: P 🍴 ♿ (taped tour, level trails, induction loop) toilets for disabled shop 💳

CHEPSTOW   Map 03 ST59
CHEPSTOW CASTLE
NP6 5EZ
☎ 01291 624065

Built by William FitzOsbern, Chepstow is the first recorded Norman stone castle. The castle was strengthened in the following centuries, but was not besieged (as far as is known) until the Civil War. The remains of the domestic rooms and the massive gatehouse are still impressive, as are the walls and towers.
Times: Open 27 Mar-31 May, daily 9.30-5; 1 Jun-29 Sep, daily 9.30-6; 30 Sep-27 Oct, daily 9.30-5; 28 Oct- 31 Mar, Mon-Sat 9.30-4, Sun 11-4. Fee: * £3 (ch 5-16, pen & students £2). Family ticket £8. Facilities: P ♿ shop ✖ ✿ 💳

GROSMONT   Map 03 SO42
GROSMONT CASTLE
(on B4347)
☎ 01981 240301
Times: Open - access throughout the year. Facilities: ♿ ✖ ✿ Details not confirmed for 2003

LLANTHONY   Map 03 SO22
LLANTHONY PRIORY
☎ 029 2050 0200
Times: Open - access throughout the year. Facilities: P ♿ toilets for disabled ✖ ✿ Details not confirmed for 2003

LLANTILIO CROSSENNY   Map 03 SO31
HEN GWRT
(off B4233)
☎ 029 2050 0200
Times: Open - access throughout the year. Facilities: ✖ 🚗 ✿ Details not confirmed for 2003

MONMOUTH   Map 03 SO51
NELSON MUSEUM & LOCAL HISTORY CENTRE
New Market Hall, Priory St NP25 3XA (Town centre)
☎ 01600 713519   📠 01600 775001
e-mail:
nelsonmuseum@monmouthshire.gov.uk

Times: Open all year, Mon-Sat 10-1 & 2-5; Sun 2-5. (Closed Xmas & New Year). Facilities: P (200yds) (small daily charge) ♿ shop ✖ (ex guide dogs) Details not confirmed for 2003 💳

RAGLAN   Map 03 SO40
RAGLAN CASTLE
NP5 2BT (signposted off A40)
☎ 01291 690228

This magnificent 15th-century castle is noted for its 'Yellow Tower of Gwent'. Built by Sir William ap Thomas it was destroyed during the civil war after a long siege. The ruins are still impressive however, and the castle's history is illustrated in an exhibition.
Times: Open 26 Mar-31 May, daily 9.30-5; 26 1 Jun-29 Sep, daily 9.30-6; 30 Sep-27 Oct, daily 9.30-5; 28 Oct-Mar, Mon-Sat 9.30-4, Sun 11-4. Fee: * £2.50 (ch 5-16, pen & students £2). Family ticket £7. Facilities: P ♿ shop ✖ ✿ 💳

SKENFRITH   Map 03 SO42
SKENFRITH CASTLE
☎ 029 2050 0200
Times: Open - access throughout the year. Key keeper arrangement.
Facilities: P ✖ ✿ 🐕 Details not confirmed for 2003

TINTERN   Map 03 SO50
TINTERN ABBEY
NP6 6SE (via A466)
☎ 01291 689251

The ruins of this Cistercian monastery church are still surprisingly intact. The monastery was established in 1131 and became increasingly wealthy well into the 15th century. During the Dissolution, the monastery was closed and most of the buildings were completely

continued

destroyed. During the 18th century many poets and artists came to see the ruins and recorded their impressions.
Times: Open: 26 Mar-25 May daily 9.30-5; Jun-29 Sep daily 9.30-6; 30 Sep-27 Oct daily 9.30-5; 28 Oct-25 Mar Mon-Sat 9.30; Sun 11-4.
Fee: * £2.50 (ch 5-16, pen & students £2). Family ticket £7. **Facilities:** P & toilets for disabled shop

USK
Map 03 SO30
USK RURAL LIFE MUSEUM
Malt Barn, New Market St NP15 1AU
☎ 01291 673777
Times: Open Apr-Oct, daily 10-5 (ex Sat & Sun am) Last admission 4.30. Winter hours contact the Museum. **Facilities:** P & (special tape recording of tour for deaf) shop *Details not confirmed for 2003*

WHITE CASTLE
Map 03 SO31
WHITE CASTLE
NP7 8UD (7m NE of Abergavenny, unclass road N of B4233)
☎ 01600 780380

The impressive 12th to 13th-century moated stronghold was built by Hubert de Burgh to defend the Welsh Marches. Substantial remains of walls, towers and a gatehouse can be seen. This is the finest of a trio of castles, the others being at Skenfrith and Grosmont.
Times: Open all year, late 27 Mar-29 Sep, daily 10-5; site open rest of year. 10-4 **Fee:** * £2 (ch 5-16, pen & students £1.50). Family ticket £5.50. **Facilities:** P &

NEATH PORT TALBOT

ABERDULAIS
Map 03 SS79
ABERDULAIS FALLS
SA10 8EU (from M4 junct 43, take A465, signposted Vale of Neath)
☎ 01639 636674   01639 645069
Times: Open: March: Sat & Sun 11am-4pm only. Apr-Oct Mon-Fri 10am-5pm, Sat, Sun & Bank Hols 11am-6pm. **Facilities:** P & (lifts for disabled to view falls) toilets for disabled shop *Details not confirmed for 2003*

CRYNANT
Map 03 SN70
CEFN COED COLLIERY MUSEUM
SA10 8SN (1m S of Crynant, on A4109)
☎ 01639 750556   01639 750556

The museum is on the site of a former working colliery, and tells the story of mining in the Dulais Valley. A steam-winding engine has been kept and is now operated by electricity, and there is also a simulated underground mining gallery, boilerhouse, compressor house, and exhibition area. Outdoor exhibits include a stationary colliery locomotive. Forest walks and picnic sites nearby. Exhibitions relating to the coal mining industry are held on a regular basis.
Times: Open daily, Apr-Oct 10.30-5; Nov-Mar, groups welcome by prior arrangement. **Fee:** Free. **Facilities:** P & toilets for disabled shop

CYNONVILLE
Map 03 SS89
SOUTH WALES MINERS MUSEUM
Afan Argoed Country Park SA13 3HG (on A4107 6m NE of Port Talbot, leave M4 at junct 40)
☎ 01639 850564 & 850875   01639 850446
e-mail: boast@boastm.fsnet.co.uk

The picturesquely placed museum gives a vivid picture of mining life, with coal faces, pit gear and miners' equipment. Guided tours of the museum on request. The country park has forest walks and picnic areas, and a visitor centre.
Times: Open all year daily, Apr-Sep 10.30-5 (Sat & Sun 10.30-6); Oct-Feb 10.30-4 (Sat & Sun 10.30-5). Closed Xmas week **Fee:** * £1.20 (ch & pen 60p). Concessionary rate for advance bookings. **Facilities:** P (charged) ✕ & (mechanical & manual wheel chairs on request) toilets for disabled shop (ex guide dogs)

NEATH
Map 03 SS79
GNOLL ESTATE COUNTRY PARK
SA11 3BS (follow brown heritage signs from town centre)
☎ 01639 635808   01639 635694

The extensively landscaped Gnoll Estate offers tranquil woodland walks, picnic areas, stunning views, children's play areas, adventure playground, 9-hole golf course, and coarse fishing. Varied programme of events and school holiday activities.
Times: Open all year - Country park; Vistor centre, daily from 10am. (Closed Xmas wk). **Fee:** Free. **Facilities:** P & (w/chair, designated parking) toilets for disabled shop (ex on lead)

NEATH ABBEY
SA10 7DW
☎ 01639 812387
Times: Open at all times. Key keeper arrangement. **Facilities:** P & *Details not confirmed for 2003*

NEWPORT

CAERLEON
Map 03 ST39
CAERLEON ROMAN BATHS
NP6 1AE (on B4236)
☎ 01663 422518

Caerleon was an important Roman military base, with accommodation for thousands of men. The foundations of barrack lines and parts of the ramparts can be seen, with remains of the cookhouse, latrines and baths. The amphitheatre nearby is one of the best examples in Britain.
Times: Open 27 Mar-28 Oct, daily 9.30-5; 29 Oct-31 Mar, Mon-Sat 9.30-5, Sun 1-5. **Fee:** * £2 (ch 5-16, pen & students £1.50, disabled free). Family ticket £5.50. **Facilities:** P & shop

ROMAN LEGIONARY MUSEUM
High St NP18 1AE (Near Newport, 20min from M4)
☎ 01633 423134   01633 422869
e-mail: rlm@nmgw.ac.uk

The museum illustrates the history of Roman Caerleon
continued

and the daily life of its garrison. On display are arms, armour and equipment, with a collection of engraved gemstones, a labyrinth mosaic and finds from the legionary base at Usk. Please telephone for details of children's holiday activities.
Times: Open all year: Mon-Sat 10-5, Sun 2-5. **Fee:** Free. **Facilities:** P (100yds) & toilets for disabled shop ✈ (ex guide dogs)

🏛 NEWPORT   Map 03 ST38
TREDEGAR HOUSE & PARK
Coedkernew NP1 9YW (2m W, signposted from A48/M4 junct 28)
☎ 01633 815880 📠 01633 815895
e-mail: tredegar.house@newport.gov.uk
Times: Open Good Fri-Sep, Wed-Sun & BHs 11-4. (All week in Aug, wknds only in Oct). Special Hallowe'en & Xmas opening. Also open for group visits at other times. **Facilities:** P (charged) 🍴 ✕ licensed & (wheelchairs for loan) toilets for disabled shop ✈ (ex grounds & guide dogs) *Details not confirmed for 2003* 🚩

🏛 PENHOW   Map 03 ST49
PENHOW CASTLE
NP26 3AD (on A48 between Newport & Chepstow. Use M4 junct 24)
☎ 01633 400800 📠 01633 400990   **2 for 1**
e-mail: info@penhowcastle.com

The oldest inhabited castle in Wales, originally a small border fortress. The building presents a fascinating picture of castle life through nine centuries. Rooms include the Norman bedchamber, the 15th-century Great Hall with its fine screen and minstrels' gallery, the elegant dining room with original panelling and the cosy Victorian housekeeper's room. Please ring for details of special events.
Times: Open Good Fri-end Sep, Wed-Sun & BH 10-5.15 last admission; "Candlelit Tours" by arrangement; Aug open daily; Winter Wed 10-4 Sun 1-4. (Closed Jan-Feb). **Fee:** * £3.80 (ch £2.60). Family ticket £10.50. Party 20+ 10% discount. **Facilities:** P & (audio-tours for blind) shop ✈ (ex guide dogs)

PEMBROKESHIRE

🏛 AMROTH   Map 02 SN10
COLBY WOODLAND GARDEN
SA67 8PP (1.5 miles inland from Amroth beside Carmarthen Bay, follow brown signs from A477)
☎ 01834 811885
Times: Open Apr-Oct, daily 10-5. Walled garden Apr-30 Oct 11-5.
Facilities: P 🍴 & (Limited due to terrain) toilets for disabled shop garden centre 🐾 *Details not confirmed for 2003* 🚩

🏛 CAREW   Map 02 SN00
CAREW CASTLE & TIDAL MILL
SA70 8SL (on A4075, just off A477 Pembroke to Kilgetty rd)
☎ 01646 651782 📠 01646 651782
e-mail: enquiries@carewcastle.com

This magnificent Norman castle has royal links with Henry Tudor and was the setting for the Great Tournament of 1507. Nearby is the Carew Cross (Cadw),

an impressive 13ft Celtic cross dating from the 11th century. Carew Mill is one of only four restored tidal mills in Britain, with records dating back to 1558.
Times: Open Apr-2 Nov 2003 daily 10-5 **Fee:** * £2.80 (ch & pen £1.90). Family ticket £7.50. Single ticket (castle or mill) £1.90 (ch £1.50). **Facilities:** P & toilets for disabled shop 🚩

🏛 CILGERRAN   Map 02 SN14
CILGERRAN CASTLE
SA43 2SF (off A484 & A478)
☎ 01239 615007

Set above a gorge of the River Teifi - famed for its coracle fishermen - Cilgerran Castle dates from the 11th to 13th centuries. It decayed gradually after the Civil War, but its great round towers and high walls give a vivid impression of its former strength.
Times: Open 27 Mar-26 Oct, daily 9.30-6.30;27Oct-31 Mar, daily 9.30-4. **Fee:** * £2.50 (ch 5-16, pen & students £2). Family ticket £7.
Facilities: & shop ✈ ✚ 🚩

🏛 CRYMYCH   Map 02 SN13
CASTELL HENLLYS FORT
Pant-Glas, Meline SA41 3UT (Off A487 between Eglwyswrw and Newport)
☎ 01239 891319 📠 01239 891319
e-mail: enquiries@
castellhenlyss.pembrokeshire.org.uk

This Iron Age hill fort is set in the beautiful Pembrokeshire Coast National Park. Excavations began in 1981 and three roundhouses have been reconstructed, another has been completed and is the largest on the site. A Celtic roundhouse has been constructed by original methods using hazel wattle walls, oak rafters and a thatched conical roof. A forge, smithy, and looms can be seen, with other attractions such as trails and a herb garden. Please telephone for details of special events.
Times: Open Apr-early Nov, daily 10-5. Last entry 4.30 **Fee:** * £2.80 (ch & pen £1.90) Family £7.10. **Facilities:** P & toilets for disabled shop 🚩

🏛 FISHGUARD   Map 02 SM93
OCEANLAB
The Parrog, Goodwick SA64 0DE (Take A40 to Fishguard, turning at the bypass, following signs for Oceanlab and Stenaline ferry terminal)
☎ 01348 874737 📠 01348 872528
e-mail: ocean_lab01@hotmail.com

Overlooking the Pembrokeshire coastline, OceanLab is a multifunctional centre which aims to provide a fun filled experience for the family. A deep-sea adventure takes the visitor back in time to see marine creatures that lived in the distant past. There is also a hands-on ocean quest exhibition, a soft play area and a cybercafé.
Times: Open Etr-Oct 10-6, winter opening 10-5 **Fee:** Telephone for details **Facilities:** P 🍴 & toilets for disabled shop ✈ (ex guide dogs) 🚩

LAMPHEY
Map 02 SN00
LAMPHEY BISHOP'S PALACE
SA71 5NT (off A4139)
☎ 01646 672224

This ruined 13th-century palace once belonged to the Bishops of St David's.
Times: Open all year, daily 10-5. ex 25 Dec **Fee:** * £2.50 (ch 5-16, pen & students £2, disabled free). Family ticket £7. **Facilities:** P & toilets for disabled shop ✈ ⊕ ▇

LLANYCEFN
Map 02 SN02
PENRHOS COTTAGE
SA66 7XT (Near Maenclochog & Llanycefn, N of Haverfordwest)
☎ 01437 760460   ▤ 01437 760460
2 for 1

Local tradition has it that cottages built overnight on common land could be claimed by the builders, together with the ground a stone's throw away from the door. This thatched cottage is an example, built with help from friends and family; and it gives an insight into traditional Welsh country life.
Times: Open mid May-Sep Mon-Fri, by appointment only. Tel: 01437 731328. **Fee:** Free. **Facilities:** P (roadside) & shop ✈ (ex in grounds or guide dogs)

LLAWHADEN
Map 02 SN01
LLAWHADEN CASTLE
☎ 01437 541201
Times: Open at all times. Key keeper arrangement. **Facilities:** & ✈ ⊕ Details not confirmed for 2003

NARBERTH
Map 02 SN11
OAKWOOD PARK
Canaston Bridge SA67 8DE (M4 W junct 49, take A48 to Carmarthen, signposted)
☎ 0870 124 00 44 & 0845 345 56 67
▤ 01834 891408
e-mail: enquiries@oakwood-leisure.com
Times: Open daily 12 Apr-Sep, from 10. **Facilities:** P ▇ ✗ licensed & (wheelchair hire, special access to some rides) toilets for disabled shop ✈ (ex guide dogs) Details not confirmed for 2003

NEWPORT
Map 02 SN03
PENTRE IFAN BURIAL CHAMBER
(3m SE from B4329 or A487)
☎ 029 2050 0200
Times: Open - access throughout the year. **Facilities:** ✈ ⊕ Details not confirmed for 2003

PEMBROKE
Map 02 SM90
THE MUSEUM OF THE HOME
7 Westgate Hill SA71 4LB (Opposite Pembroke Castle)
☎ 01646 681200
2 for 1

A pleasant domestic setting provides an opportunity to view some of the objects that have been part of everyday life over the past 300 years.
Times: Open May-Sep, Mon-Thu 11-5, other times by arrangement. **Fee:** £1.20 (ch & pen 90p). **Facilities:** P (100 yds) (Public Pay & Display) ✈

PEMBROKE CASTLE
SA71 4LA (W end of main street)
☎ 01646 681510 684585   ▤ 01646 622260
e-mail: pembroke.castle@talk21.com

The birthplace of the first Tudor king, Henry VII, Pembroke Castle is a well-preserved Norman fortress with an impressive 75ft circular keep. The Great Gatehouse is home to a number of exhibitions tracing the history of medieval life at the castle. Beneath the Northern Hall is a vast cavern, once occupied by Stone Age cave dwellers and later used as a food and boat store by the Normans. Exploring from the top of the many lofty towers to the bottom of the vast cavern beneath makes it an exhilarating visit for all ages. Also the Brass Rubbing Centre where your own special souvenir can be made.
Times: Open all year, daily, Apr-Sep 9.30-6; Mar & Oct 10-5; Nov-Feb, 10.30-4.30; (Closed 24-26 Dec & 1 Jan). **Fee:** £3 (ch under 16 & pen £2, ch under 5 & wheelchairs free). Family ticket £8. **Facilities:** P (200 yds) ▇ & toilets for disabled shop ▇

ST DAVID'S
Map 02 SM72
ST DAVIDS BISHOP'S PALACE
SA62 6PE (on A487)
☎ 01437 720517

These extensive and impressive ruins are all that remain of the principal residence of the Bishops of St David's. The palace shares a quiet valley with the cathedral, which was almost certainly built on the site of a monastery founded in the 6th century by St David. The Bishop's Palace houses an exhibition: `Lords of the Palace'.
Times: Open: 27 Mar-May daily 9.30-5; Jun-29 Sep daily 9.30-6; 30 Sep-27 Oct daily 9.30-5; 28 Oct-26 Mar Mon-Sat 9.30-4, Sun 11-4.
Fee: * £2 (ch 5-16, pen & students £1.50). Family ticket £5.50.
Facilities: P & toilets for disabled shop ✈ ⊕ ▇

ST DAVIDS CATHEDRAL
The Close SA62 6PE
☎ 01437 720202   ▤ 01437 721885
e-mail: adminstrator@stdavidscathedral.org.uk

Begun 1181 on the reputed site of St David's 6th century monastic settlement. The present building was

continued

Pembrokeshire – Powys

altered during the 12th to the 14th centuries and again in the 16th. The ceilings of oak, painted wood and stone vaulting are of considerable interest.

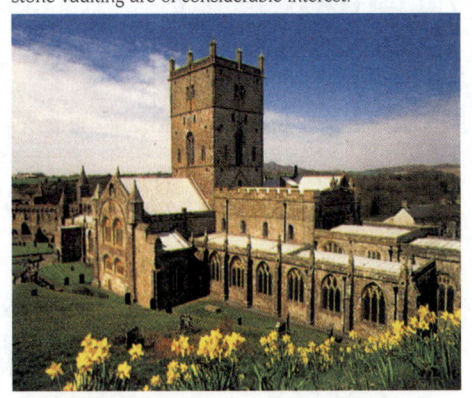

Times: Open all year 8.30-6. **Fee:** Free - Suggested donation of £2. **Facilities:** P (300yds) 🍴 ♿ (hearing loop) toilets for disabled shop ✈ (ex guide dogs) ☕

ST FLORENCE   Map 02 SN00
MANOR HOUSE WILDLIFE & LEISURE PARK
Ivy Tower SA70 8RJ (on B4318 between Tenby & St Florence)
☎ 01646 651201   📠 01646 651201   `2 for 1`

The park is set in 35 acres of delightful wooded grounds and award-winning gardens. The wildlife includes exotic birds, reptiles and fish. Also a pets' corner, a children's playground with free rides on an astraglide slide, and roundabouts. Other attractions include a natural history museum, a go-kart track, model railway exhibition. Daily falconry displays. Telephone for details of displays and animal feeding times.
Times: Open Etr-end Sep, daily 10-6. Please telephone for late opening Jul & Aug. **Fee:** £4.20 (ch £3.50, pen £4, disabled/helpers £2.50) Family ticket £14.50 (2ad + 2ch). Party 20+. **Facilities:** P 🍴 ♿ toilets for disabled shop ✈ ☕

SCOLTON   Map 02 SM92
SCOLTON VISITOR CENTRE
SA62 5QL (5m N of Haverfordwest, on B4329)
☎ 01437 731328 (Mus) & 731457 (Park)
📠 01437 731743   `2 for 1`

Scolton Manor Museum is situated in Scolton Country Park. The early Victorian mansion, refurbished stables and the exhibition hall illustrate the history and natural history of Pembrokeshire. There are new displays in the house and stables, plus a 'Pembrokeshire Railways' exhibition. The 60-acre grounds, partly a nature reserve, have fine specimen trees and shrubs. Environmentally friendly Visitor Centre, alternative

energy and woodland displays, guided walks and children's play areas.
Times: Open; Museum Apr-Oct, Tue-Sun & BH's 10.30-1 & 1.30-5.30; Country Park all year ex 25 & 26 Dec, Etr-Sep 10-7, Oct-Etr 10-6. **Fee:** * Museum: £2 (ch £1, concessions £1.50). Country Park car park £1 all day. **Facilities:** P (charged) 🍴 ♿ (disabled parking area near house) toilets for disabled shop ✈ (ex guide dogs & in grounds)

🏛 TENBY   Map 02 SN10
TENBY MUSEUM & ART GALLERY
Castle Hill SA70 7BP (Near the centre of town on Castle Hill, above the harbour)
☎ 01834 842809   📠 01834 842809
e-mail: tenbymuseum@hotmail.com

The museum is situated on Castle Hill. It covers the local heritage from prehistory to the present in galleries devoted to archaeology, geology, maritime history, natural history, militaria and bygones. The art galleries concentrate on local associations with an important collection of works by Augustus John, Gwen John and others.
Times: Open all year, Etr-Oct, daily 10-5; Nov-Etr, Mon-Fri 10-5. **Fee:** £2 (ch £1, concessions £1.50). Family ticket £4.50. **Facilities:** P (10 mins walk) ♿ (lifts, levelled floors, ramps) toilets for disabled shop ✈ (ex guide dogs)

TUDOR MERCHANT'S HOUSE
Quay Hill SA70 7BX
☎ 01834 842279
Times: Open 2 Apr-Sep, Mon-Tue, Thu-Sat 10-5, Sun 1-5. Dec Mon-Tue, Thu-Fri 10-3, Sun 12-3. **Facilities:** P (500yds) (no coaches nearby) ♿ (garden could be accessed) ✈ (ex guide or small dogs) 🚭
Details not confirmed for 2003

POWYS

🏛 ABERCRAF   Map 03 SN81
DAN-YR-OGOF THE NATIONAL SHOWCAVES CENTRE FOR WALES
SA9 1GJ (M4 junct 45, midway between Swansea & Brecon on A4067)
☎ 01639 730284 & 730801   📠 01639 730293
e-mail: info@showcaves.co.uk

This award-winning attraction includes three separate caves, dinosaur park, Iron Age Farm, museum, shire horse centre and covered children's play area.
Times: Open Apr-Oct, daily from 10am. Please telephone for Oct. **Fee:** * £7.80 (ch £4.80). Group rates 15+ **Facilities:** P 🍴 shop ☕

🏛 BERRIEW   Map 07 SJ10
GLANSEVERN HALL GARDENS
Glansevern SY21 8AH (on A483 between Welshpool and Newtown)
☎ 01686 640200   📠 01686 640829

Built in the Greek Revival style for Arthur Davies Owen, who chose a romantically positioned site on the banks of the River Severn. The current owners have developed the gardens, respecting the plantings and features of the past, and added a vast collection of new

continued

Powys

and interesting species. There are many fine and unusual trees, a lakeside walk, water gardens and a rock garden with lamp-lit grotto.
Times: Open May-Sep, BH Mon, Fri-Sat 2-6. Parties other dates by arrangement **Fee:** £3 (pen £2, ch under 15 free). **Facilities:** P 🅿 & (most areas accessible) shop garden centre

BRECON   Map 03 SO02
BRECKNOCK MUSEUM & ART GALLERY
Captain's Walk LD3 7DW (Near centre of town at junct of The Watton & Glamorgan St)   **2 for 1**
☎ 01874 624121   ≣ 01874 611281
e-mail: brecknock.museum@powys.gov.uk

A wealth of local history is explored at the museum, which has archaeological and historical exhibits, with sections on folk life, decorative arts and natural history. Victorian Assize Court is interpreted with life-size figures, sound and light and there is one of the finest collections of Welsh Lovespoons. The museum also runs a lively programme of Welsh contemporary art exhibitions.
Times: Open all year, Mon-Fri 10-5, Sat 10-1 & 2-5 (2-5 Nov-Feb); also open Sun 12-5 Apr-Sep. (Closed Good Fri, 25-26 Dec & New Year's Day). **Fee:** Free. **Facilities:** P & (limited parking, must be accompanied by able-bodied) toilets for disabled shop ✈ (ex guide dogs) 🛍

SOUTH WALES BORDERERS (24TH REGIMENT) MUSEUM
The Barracks, The Watton LD3 7EB (close to town centre, well signed)
☎ 01874 613310   ≣ 01874 613275
e-mail: swb@rrw.org.uk

The museum of the South Wales Borderers and Monmouthshire Regiment, which was raised in 1689 and has been awarded 23 Victoria Crosses. Amongst the collections is the Zulu War Room, devoted to the war in particular to the events at Rorke's Drift, 1879, when 121 men fought 4500 Zulus.
Times: Open all year, Apr-Sep daily; Oct-Mar, Mon-Fri 9-5. (Closed Xmas & New Year). **Fee:** £3 (ch up to 16 free). **Facilities:** P (town centre) & toilets for disabled shop ✈ (ex guide dogs) 🛍

LLANFAIR CAEREINION   Map 06 SJ10
WELSHPOOL & LLANFAIR LIGHT RAILWAY
SY21 0SF (beside A458, Shrewsbury-Dollgellau road)
☎ 01938 810441   ≣ 01938 810861
e-mail: info@wllr.org.uk

The Llanfair Railway is one of the Great Little Trains of Wales. It offers a 16-mile round trip through glorious scenery by narrrow-gauge steam train. The line is home to a collection of engines and coaches from all round the world. Please ring for details of special events.
Times: Open weekends Etr-end Oct, daily during holiday periods phone for timetable enquiries. **Fee:** * £8.50 return (ch £1, pen £7.50). **Facilities:** P 🅿 & (three coaches adapted for wheelchairs) toilets for disabled shop 🛍

MACHYNLLETH   Map 06 SH70
CELTICA
Y Plas, Aberystwyth Rd SY20 8ER (2 mins walk S of town clock. Car park entrance off Aberystwyth Rd)
☎ 01654 702702   ≣ 01654 703604
e-mail: celtica@celtica.wales.com
Times: Open daily 10-6 (last show starts 4.40). Evening opening for pre-booked groups. (Closed 1 Jan, & 14-18 Jan) **Facilities:** P 🅿 ✕ licensed & (Lift & ramps to public areas; Induction loop) toilets for disabled shop ✈ (ex guide dogs) Details not confirmed for 2003 🛍

CENTRE FOR ALTERNATIVE TECHNOLOGY
SY20 9AZ (2.5m N on A487)
☎ 01654 702400   ≣ 01654 702782
e-mail: help@catinfo.demon.co.uk
Times: Open Mar-Oct; 10-5.30; Nov-Feb; 11-4. (Closed 23-26 Dec & 5-23 Jan). **Facilities:** P 🅿 (wheelchair available) shop ✈ (ex guide dogs) Details not confirmed for 2003 🛍

KING ARTHUR'S LABYRINTH
Corris SY20 9RF (on A487 between Machynlleth and Dolgellau)
☎ 01654 761584   ≣ 01654 761575
e-mail: king.arthurs.labyrinth@corris-wales.co.uk

A subterranean storybook, a boat ride through the great waterfall and into the Labyrinth of tunnels and caverns carved into the ancient rocks of Wales. Tales of King Arthur and other legends are re-told as you walk through this underground setting.
Times: Open Apr-2 Nov 2003, daily 10-5 **Fee:** * £4.70 (ch £3.30, pen £4.15). Prices for 2003 to be confirmed. **Facilities:** P 🅿 & toilets for disabled shop 🛍

MONTGOMERY   Map 03 SO29
MONTGOMERY CASTLE
☎ 029 2050 0200
Times: Open all year, any reasonable time. **Facilities:** & ✈ ✥ Details not confirmed for 2003

PRESTEIGNE   Map 03 SO36
THE JUDGE'S LODGING
Broad St LD8 2AD (In centre of town, off B4362, signed from A44 & A49)
☎ 01544 260650   ≣ 01544 260652   **2 for 1**
e-mail: info@judgeslodging.org.uk

A restored Victorian town house with integral courtroom, cells and service areas - step back into the 1860s, accompanied by an 'evesdropping' audiotour of voices from the past. Explore the fascinating world of

continued

Powys – Rhondda Cynon Taff – Swansea   **369**

the Victorian judges, their servents & felonious guests at this award-winning, 'hands on' historic house.

Times: Open daily, Mar-Oct 10-6; Nov-Dec Wed-Sun 10-4. Closed Jan-Feb. **Fee:** £3.95 (ch & concessions £2.95). Family £12. Party rates available. **Facilities:** P (200mtrs) & (lift, disabled pack for inacessible items) shop ✈ (ex guide dogs)

TRETOWER   Map 03 SO12
TRETOWER COURT & CASTLE
NP8 2RF (3m NW of Crickhowell, off A479)
☎ 01874 730279

The castle is a substantial ruin of an 11th-century motte and bailey, with a three-storey tower and 9ft-thick walls. Nearby is the Court, a 14th-century fortified manor house which has been altered and extended over the years. The two buildings show the shift from medieval castle to more domestic accommodation over the centuries.
Times: Open early-late Mar, daily 10-4; late Mar-late May & early Sep-late Oct, daily 10-5; early Jun-early Sep, daily 10-6. **Fee:** * £2.50 (ch 5-16, pen & students £2). Family ticket £7. **Facilities:** P & toilets for disabled shop ✈ ⊙

WELSHPOOL   Map 07 SJ20
POWIS CASTLE
SY21 8RF (1m S of Welshpool, signposted off A483)
☎ 01938 551920   📠 01938 554336
e-mail: ppcmsn@smtp.ntrust.org.uk
Times: Castle & museum open: Apr-Jun and Sep-Oct, Wed-Sun 1-5; Jul-Aug Tue-Sun 1-5; Open all Bank Hol's in season. Garden is open same days as castle and museum 11-6. Last admission to all parts is 30 mins before closing. **Facilities:** P ✗ licensed (photos of interior available from tearoom) shop garden centre ✈ (ex guide dogs) ✿
Details not confirmed for 2003

RHONDDA CYNON TAFF

TREHAFOD   Map 03 ST09
RHONDDA HERITAGE PARK
Lewis Merthyr Colliery, Coed Cae Rd CF37 7NP (between Pontypridd & Porth, off A470; follow brown heritage signs from M4 junct 32)
☎ 01443 682036   📠 01443 687420   **2 for 1**
e-mail: reception@rhonddaheritagepark.com

Based at the Lewis Merthyr Colliery, the Heritage Park is a fascinating 'living history' attraction. You can take the Cage Ride to 'Pit Bottom' and explore the underground workings of a 1950's pit, guided by men who were miners themselves. There are children's activities, an art gallery and a museum illustrating living conditions in the Rhondda Valley. Special events throughout the year, phone for details.
Times: Open all year, daily 10-6. (Closed Mon from Oct-Etr). Last admission 4.30pm. (Closed 25 Dec-2 Jan). **Fee:** * £5.60 (ch £4.30, pen £4.95). Family ticket £16.50. **Facilities:** P 💺 ✗ licensed & (Wheelchair available, accessible parking, lifts) toilets for disabled shop ✈ (ex guide dogs)

SWANSEA

LLANRHIDIAN   Map 02 SS49
WEOBLEY CASTLE
SA3 1HB (from B4271 or B4295)
☎ 01792 390012

A 12th to 14th-century fortified manor house with an exhibition on the history of Weobley and other historic sites on the Gower peninsula.
Times: Open all year, 27 Mar-30 Oct 9.30-6; 31 Oct-Mar daily 9.30-5. Closed 24-26 Dec & 1 Jan **Fee:** * £2 (ch 5-16, pen & students £1.50). Family ticket £5.50. **Facilities:** P & shop ✈ ⊙

OXWICH   Map 02 SS48
OXWICH CASTLE
SA3 1NG (A4118 from Swansea)
☎ 01792 390359

Situated on the Gower peninsula, this Tudor mansion is a striking testament in stone to the pride and ambitions of the Mansel dynasty of Welsh gentry. The E-shaped wing houses an exhibition on historical Gower and 'Chieftains and Princes of Wales'.
Times: Open 27 Mar-29 Sep, daily 10-5 (Closed at all other times ex Strata Florida Abbey, Valle Crucis Abbey and Whit which are open sites). **Fee:** * £2 (ch 5-16, pen & students £1.50). Family ticket £5.50.
Facilities: P & (Radar key toilet) toilets for disabled ✈ ⊙

PARKMILL   Map 02 SS58
GOWER HERITAGE CENTRE
Y Felin Ddwr SA3 2EH (Follow signs for South Gower on A4118 W from Swansea. W side of Parkmill village)
☎ 01792 371206   📠 01792 371471   **2 for 1**
e-mail: info@gowerheritagecentre.sagehost.co.uk

Based around a 12th-century water-powered cornmill, the site also contains a number of craft workshops, a

continued

Swansea – Torfaen

museum and a miller's cottage, all set in attractive countryside in an Area of Outstanding Natural Beauty.

Gower Heritage Centre

Times: Open daily, Mar-Oct 10-6; Nov-Feb 10-5. (Closed 25 Dec).
Fee: * £3.50 (ch, students & pen £2.20). Family ticket £17.50. Party.
Facilities: 🅿 🍴 ♿ (ramp entrance access) toilets for disabled shop 🐕

SWANSEA   Map 03 SS69
GLYNN VIVIAN ART GALLERY
Alexandra Rd SA1 5DZ (Turn off M4 junct 42 along Fabian Way A483 up Wind St. Turn left at train station opposite library)
☎ 01792 655006 & 651738   📠 01792 651713
e-mail: glynn.vivian.gallery@business.ntl.com
Times: Open all year, Tue-Sun & BH Mon 10-5. (Closed 25, 26 Dec & 1 Jan). **Facilities:** 🅿 (200 yds, NCP) ♿ toilets for disabled shop 🐕 (ex guide dogs, hearing dogs) *Details not confirmed for 2003* 🏷

SWANSEA MARITIME & INDUSTRIAL MUSEUM
Museum Square, Maritime Quarter SA1 1SN (M4 junct 42, on main rd into Swansea city centre)
☎ 01792 650351 & 470321   📠 01792 654200
e-mail: swansea.maritime.museum@swansea.gov.uk
Times: Open all year, Tue-Sun 10-5.(last admission 4.45pm). Closed Mon except BH Mon, 25-26 Dec & 1 Jan. **Facilities:** 🅿 (50yds) (charged) 🍴 ♿ shop 🐕 (ex guide dogs) *Details not confirmed for 2003* 🏷

TORFAEN

BLAENAVON   Map 03 SO20
BIG PIT NATIONAL MINING MUSEUM OF WALES
NP4 9XP (M4 junct 26 or 25, follow signs along A4042 & A4043 to Pontypool & Blaenavon. Signposted off A465)
☎ 01495 790311   📠 01495 792618
e-mail: bigpit@nmgw.ac.uk

The Real Underground Experience! Big Pit is the UK's leading mining museum. It is a real colliery and was the place of work for hundreds of men, woman and children for over 200 years. A daily struggle to extract the precious mineral that stoked furnaces and lit household fires across the world.
Times: Open Mid Feb-End Nov, daily 9.30-5, telephone to confirm
Fee: Free. **Facilities:** 🅿 🍴 ♿ (underground tours by prior arrangement) toilets for disabled shop (not on underground tours)

BLAENAVON IRONWORKS
North St
☎ 01495 792615

The Blaenavon Ironworks were a milestone in the history of the Industrial Revolution. Constructed in 1788-99, they were the first purpose-built, multi-furnace ironworks in Wales. By 1796, Blaenavon was the second largest ironworks in Wales, eventually closing down in 1904.
Times: Open 27 Mar-31 Oct, daily 9.30-4.30. For details of opening outside this period, telephone 01633 648081. **Fee:** * £2 (ch 5-16, pen & students £1.50). Family ticket £5.50 **Facilities:** 🅿 🐕 ♿ 🏷

CWMBRAN   Map 03 ST29
GREENMEADOW COMMUNITY FARM
Greenforge Way NP44 5AJ (Follow signs for Cwmbran then brown heritage signs (with sheep on) to farm)
☎ 01633 862202   📠 01633 489332   **2 for 1**
e-mail: greenmeadow_community_farm@compuserve.com

This is one of Wales' leading tourist attractions - a community farm that was built during the 1980s on land threatened by developers. There are milking demonstrations, tractor and trailer rides, a dragon adventure play area, a farm trail, a nature trail and lots more. Phone for details of lambing weekends, shearing, country fair and agricultural shows, Halloween and Christmas events.
Times: Open summer 10-6, winter 10-4. (Closed 25 Dec). **Fee:** Adult £3.50 (ch £2.75) Family (2ad+3ch) £14 **Facilities:** 🅿 🍴 ♿ (tractor & trailer rides for wheelchair users) toilets for disabled shop 🏷

VALE OF GLAMORGAN

🏛 BARRY Map 03 ST16
WELSH HAWKING CENTRE
Weycock Rd CF62 3AA (on A4226)
☎ 01446 734687   📄 01446 739320   `2 for 1`

There are over 200 birds of prey here, including eagles, hawks, owls, buzzards and falcons. They can be seen and photographed in the mews and some of the breeding aviaries. There are flying demonstrations at regular intervals during the day. A variety of tame, friendly animals, such as pigs, lambs and rabbits will delight younger visitors.
Times: Open end Mar-end Sep, daily 10.30-5, 1hr before dusk in winter. **Fee:** £5 (ch & pen £3). **Facilities:** 🅿 🍴 ♿ toilets for disabled shop ✂ 🐕

🏛 OGMORE Map 03 SS87
OGMORE CASTLE
☎ 01656 653435
Times: Open - access throughout the year. Key keeper arrangement.
Facilities: 🅿 ♿ ✂ ✜ Details not confirmed for 2003

🏛 PENARTH Map 03 ST17
COSMESTON LAKES COUNTRY PARK & MEDIEVAL VILLAGE
Cosmeston Lakes Country Park, Lavernock Rd CF64 5UY (on B4267 between Barry and Penarth, close to M4 junct 33)
☎ 029 2070 1678   📄 029 2070 8686
e-mail: ncoles@valeofglamorgan.gov.uk

Deserted during the plagues and famines of the 14th century, the original village was rediscovered through archaeological excavations. The buildings have been faithfully reconstructed on the excavated remains, creating a living museum of medieval village life. Special events throughout the year include re-enactments and Living History.
Times: Open all year, daily 11-5 in Summer, 11-4 in Winter. (Closed 25 Dec). Country park open at all times. **Fee:** Entry to Village £3, (concessions £2) Family ticket £7.50. Entry to Country Park is free.
Facilities: 🅿 🍽 ✗ ♿ (access ramps) toilets for disabled shop

🏛 ST HILARY Map 03 ST07
OLD BEAUPRE CASTLE
(1m SW, off A48)
☎ 01446 773034
Times: Open - access throughout the year. Key keeper arrangement.
Facilities: 🅿 ✂ ✜ Details not confirmed for 2003

WREXHAM

🏛 CHIRK Map 07 SJ23
CHIRK CASTLE
LL14 5AF (8m S of Wrexham, signposted off A483)
☎ 01691 777701   📄 01691 774706
e-mail: pcwmsn@smtp.ntrust.org.uk
Times: Open 29 Mar-Sep, Wed-Sun & BH Mon 12-5 (castle), 11-6 (gardens); Oct, Wed-Sun 12-4 (castle), 11-5 (gardens). Last admission 30 mins before closing. **Facilities:** 🅿 ✗ licensed ♿ (stairclimber) toilets for disabled shop ✂ (ex guide dogs) 🐕 Details not confirmed for 2003

🏛 WREXHAM Map 07 SJ35
ERDDIG
LL13 0YT (off A525, 2m S of Wrexham & A483/A5152 Oswestry road)
☎ 01978 355314   📄 01978 313333
Times: Open 25 Mar-1 Nov, Sat-Wed (open Good Fri), house 12-5, garden 11-6 (Jul-Aug gardens 10-6); Oct-1 Nov, Sat-Wed, house 12-4, garden 11-5. **Facilities:** 🅿 ✗ licensed ♿ toilets for disabled shop garden centre ✂ (ex guidance dogs) 🐕 Details not confirmed for 2003

`2 for 1` This symbol indicates which attractions have chosen to participate in our new 2-for-1 voucher scheme.

Northern Ireland

The six counties of Ulster are part of the United Kingdom. The greater part of its 1.6 million inhabitants are Protestants, descendants of an influx of settlers from England and Scotland in the 17th century.

Despite well-publicized tensions, the province has consistently drawn tourists, not so much to the cities which are more interesting than attractive, but for the scenery.

The most popular landscapes are linked by the 430 mile (700km) Ulster Way, which would take an intrepid walker though all six counties, taking in the Glens of Antrim with its woods, waterfalls and ruins, and the remarkable Giant's Causeway. Further south near the border with the Republic, the Ulster Way meanders through the Mountains of Mourne, rather gaunt, steep granite hills (highest point Slieve Donard, 2795 ft (852m)). Less strenuous stretches explore the beautiful Lough Erne.

Belfast is more attractive than news reports may have led you to imagine, with its parks, castle, meadows and botanical gardens.

After Belfast, the second city is Londonderry, or Derry, depending on your perspective. The city walls stand virtually complete, a reminder of the siege of 1688 when the Apprentice Boys locked out James II's army. From the walls you can view the sweep of the River Foyle.

Downpatrick, the market town of Down, claims to be the burial place of St Patrick, the patron saint of Ireland. His life is commemorated in the cathedral, and in the converted jail.

For lakes, islands, caves, castles and grand houses, Enniskillen is the place to go. Perched on an island between the Upper and Lower Lough Erne, it offers boat trips, angling, water sports and easy rambling.

Top: Dunluce Castle, Co Antrim

EVENTS & FESTIVALS

March
17th St Patrick's Day Parade, Armagh, County Armagh & other locations

June
tbc Fleadh Amhrám agus Rince, Ballycastle, Co Antrim
tbc Ulster Scottish Pipe Band Championships, Belfast
tbc Waterfront Festival, Carrickfergus, Co Antrim (funfair, circus, spectacle)
27th-29th Hookers Regatta, Portaferry, Co Down (traditional Irish sailing boats)

July
14th The Sham Fight, Scarva, Co Down (joust between William of Orange & James II)
tbc American Independence Day Celebrations, Ulster American Folk Park, Co Tyrone

August
25th-26th Oul' Lammas Fair, Ballycastle, Co Antrim (traditional fair from 1606)
tbc Maiden of the Mournes Festival, Co Down (folk, country & western)

September
tbc Oyster Festival, Hillsborough, Co Down

October
24th-9th Nov Belfast Festival at Queens, Belfast (major arts festival)

November
27th-7th Dec Cinemagic International Film Festival for Young People, Belfast
24th Oct-9th Belfast Festival

Belfast – Co Antrim

BELFAST

🏛 BELFAST Map 01 D5
BELFAST ZOOLOGICAL GARDENS
Antrim Rd BT36 7PN (6m N, on A6)
☎ 028 9077 6277 📠 028 9037 0578
e-mail: strongej@belfastcity.gov.uk

The 50-acre zoo has a dramatic setting on the face of Cave Hill, enjoying spectacular views. Attractions include the award-winning primate house (gorillas and chimpanzees), penguin enclosure, free-flight aviary, African enclosure, and underwater viewing of sealions and penguins. There are also red pandas, free-ranging lemurs and a group of very rare spectacled bears.
Times: Open all year (ex 25 Dec), daily Apr-Sep 10-5; Oct-Mar 10-2.30. **Fee:** * Summer: £6 (ch £3), Winter: £5 (£2.50) **Facilities:** P 🍴 ♿ (free admission & reserved parking) toilets for disabled shop 🐕 (ex guide dogs)

BOTANIC GARDENS
Stranmillis Rd BT7 1JP
☎ 028 9032 4902 📠 028 9023 7070
e-mail: maxwellr@belfastcity.gov.uk
Times: Open all year, Park daily 8-dusk. Tropical Ravine and Palmhouse Mon-Fri 10-12.30 & 1-5 (summer), closes 4.30 (winter); wknds open 1-5 (summer), 1-4 (winter). **Facilities:** P (street) ♿ Details not confirmed for 2003

GIANT'S RING
(0.75m S of Shaws Bridge)
☎ 028 9023 5000 📠 028 9031 0288
Times: Open all times. **Facilities:** P Details not confirmed for 2003

ULSTER MUSEUM
Botanic Gardens BT9 5AB (M1/M2 to Balmoral exit)
☎ 028 9038 3000 📠 028 9038 3003
Times: Open all year, Mon-Fri 10-5, Sat 1-5, Sun 2-5. Tel for details of Xmas closures. **Facilities:** P (100yds on street) (Clearway 8-9.30 & 4.30-6) 🍴 ♿ (all galleries except one. Loop system, wheelchair lifts) toilets for disabled shop 🐕 (ex guide dogs) Details not confirmed for 2003

W5 AT ODYSSEY
2 Queens Quay BT3 9QQ
☎ 028 9046 7700 📠 028 9046 7707 `2 for 1`

W5 investigates Who? What? Where? When? Why?... and that pretty much sums up the intent behind Ireland's first purpose built discovery centre. Visitors of any age will want to get their hands on interactive science and technology displays that include the laser harp, the fog knife, microscopes, robots and computers. W5 is part of a massive Millennium Landmark Project in the heart of Belfast.
Times: Open all year ex 25-26 Dec & 12 Jul. Mon-Sat 10-6, Sun 12-6. **Fee:** * £5.50 (ch £3.50, concessions £4). Family ticket £15. **Facilities:** P (charged) 🍴 licensed ♿ (hearing loop) toilets for disabled shop 🐕 (ex guide dogs)

CO ANTRIM

🏛 ANTRIM Map 01 D5
ANTRIM ROUND TOWER
BT41 1BJ (N of town)
☎ 028 9023 5000 📠 028 9031 0288
Times: Open all year. **Facilities:** P ♿ Details not confirmed for 2003

🏛 BALLYCASTLE Map 01 D6
BONAMARGY FRIARY
(E of town, at golf course)
☎ 028 9023 5000 📠 028 9031 0288
Times: Open all year. **Facilities:** P ♿ 🚗 Details not confirmed for 2003

🏛 BALLYLUMFORD Map 01 D5
BALLYLUMFORD DOLMEN
(on B90 on NW tip of Island Magee)
☎ 028 9023 5000 📠 028 9031 0288
Times: Open all year. **Facilities:** ♿ Details not confirmed for 2003

🏛 BALLYMENA Map 01 D5
ECOS MILLENNIUM ENVIRONMENTAL CENTRE
Ecos Centre, Kernohams Ln, Broughshane Rd BT43 7QA (follow signs from M2 bypass at Ballymena)
☎ 028 2566 4400 📠 028 2563 8984
e-mail: info@ecoscentre.com

Ecos is an alternative environmental centre, which allows visitors to explore alternative means of energy production, including electricity generated using wood, wind and sun, recycling, and alternative technologies such as willow coppicing. Plenty of hands-on fun and educational potential.
Times: Open all year ex 24 Dec-1 Jan. Please phone for opening dates **Fee:** * £4 (ch, concessions £3). Family ticket £12.50 **Facilities:** P 🍴 ♿ toilets for disabled shop 🐕 ex guide dogs

HARRYVILLE MOTTE
(N bank of river Braid)
☎ 028 9023 5000 📠 028 9031 0288
Times: Open all year. **Facilities:** P ♿ 🚗 Details not confirmed for 2003

🏛 BALLYMONEY Map 01 C6
LESLIE HILL OPEN FARM
Leslie Hill BT53 6QL (1m NW of Ballymoney on MacFin Rd)
☎ 028 2766 6803 📠 028 2766 6803 `2 for 1`

An 18th-century estate with a Georgian house, magnificent period farm buildings, and fine grounds with paths, lakes and trees. Attractions include an extensive collection of rare breeds, poultry, horsedrawn machinery and carriages, exhibition rooms, a museum, working forge, deer park, walled garden and an adventure playground.
Times: Open Jul-Aug Mon-Sat 11-6, Sun 2-6; Jun Sat-Sun & BH's 2-6; Etr-May, Sun & BH's 2-6, open all Etr wk 11-6. **Fee:** * £2.90 (ch £1.90). Family ticket £8.50. **Facilities:** P 🍴 ♿ (ramps) toilets for disabled shop garden centre 🐕 (ex on leads)

Co Antrim

BUSHMILLS Map 01 C6
OLD BUSHMILLS DISTILLERY
BT57 8XH (on the Castlecatt road)
☎ 028 2073 1521 028 2073 1339
e-mail: scroskery@idl.ie

Old Bushmills was granted its licence in 1608 and is the oldest licenced whiskey distillery in the world. There's a guided tour, and afterwards you can take part in a comparative tasting session and become a whiskey expert!
Times: Open Apr-Oct, Mon-Sat 9.30-5.30, Sun 12-5.30, last tour 4pm; Nov-Mar, Mon-Fri 5 tours daily, 10.30, 11.30, 1.30, 2.30 & 3.30. Sat & Sun 3 tours, 1.30, 2.30, 3.30. Closed July 12, Xmas & New Year. **Fee:** * £3.95 (pen & student £3.50, accompanied ch £2) Family ticket £11.
Facilities: P X licensed & (audio visual theatre, shops & restaurant) toilets for disabled shop ✈ (ex guide dogs)

CARRICK-A-REDE Map 01 D6
CARRICK-A-REDE ROPE BRIDGE AND LARRYBANE VISITORS CENTRE
(E of Ballintoy on B15)
☎ 028 2073 1582 & 2073 2143
 028 2073 2963   2 for 1
e-mail: carrickarede@ntrust.org.uk

This shaky rope bridge, 80ft above the sea, bridges the 60ft gap between cliffs and a small rocky island. It owes its existence to the salmon who regularly make the dash through the chasm and get netted for their efforts. The bridge has been put across the gap each spring and dismantled every autumn for the last 300 years.
Times: Bridge open Spring-early Sep, daily 10-6; Jul-Aug, daily 10-8. Visitor centre & Tea room open May, wknds & BHs 1-5; Jun-Aug daily 12-6. **Fee:** * £3 per car, minibuses £6, coach £10 & motorbike £1.50
Facilities: P (charged) & (information centre) toilets for disabled

CARRICKFERGUS Map 01 D5
CARRICKFERGUS CASTLE
BT38 7BG (on N shore of Belfast Lough)
☎ 028 9335 1273 028 9336 5190
Times: Open all year, Apr-Sep, weekday 10-6, Sun 2-6; Oct-Mar closes at 4. **Facilities:** P & toilets for disabled shop ✈ Details not confirmed for 2003

TOWN WALLS
☎ 028 9023 5000 028 9031 0288
Times: Visible at all times. **Facilities:** P & Details not confirmed for 2003

CHURCHTOWN Map 01 D5
CRANFIELD CHURCH
(3.75m SW of Randalstown)
☎ 028 9023 5000 028 9031 0288
Times: Open all year. **Facilities:** P & Details not confirmed for 2003

GIANT'S CAUSEWAY Map 01 C6
GIANT'S CAUSEWAY CENTRE
44 Causeway Rd BT57 8SU (2m N of Bushmills on B146)
☎ 028 2073 1855 028 2073 2537
e-mail: causewaytic@hotmail.com
Times: Open all year, daily 10-4 (6pm Jun & Sep-Oct; 7pm Jul-Aug).
Facilities: P (charged) X & (mini bus transport with wheelchair hoist, reserved parking) toilets for disabled shop ✈ (ex guide dogs) Details not confirmed for 2003

LARNE Map 01 D5
OLDERFLEET CASTLE
☎ 028 9023 5000 028 9031 0288
Times: Open at all times. **Facilities:** Details not confirmed for 2003

LISBURN Map 01 D5
DUNEIGHT MOTTE AND BAILEY
(2.3m S beside Ravernet River)
☎ 028 9023 5000 028 9031 0288
Times: Open all year. **Facilities:** Details not confirmed for 2003

IRISH LINEN CENTRE & LISBURN MUSEUM
Market Square BT28 1AG (signposted both in and outside the town centre)
☎ 028 9266 3377 028 9267 2624
e-mail: irishlinencentre@lisburn.gov.uk

The centre tells the story of the Irish linen industry past and present. The recreation of individual factory scenes brings the past to life and a series of imaginative hands-on activities describe the linen manufacturing processes. The Museum has a range of temporary exhibitions of local interest.
Times: Open all year, Mon-Sat, 9.30-5. **Fee:** Free. **Facilities:** P (200mtrs) (limited for disabled and coaches) & (lift, induction loop, staff trained in sign language) toilets for disabled shop ✈ (ex guide dogs)

PORTBALLINTRAE Map 01 C6
DUNLUCE CASTLE
(off A2)
☎ 028 2073 1938 028 2031 8288
Times: Open all year, Apr-Sep, weekdays 10-7, Sun 2-7; Oct-Mar, Tue-Sat 10-4, Sun 2-4. **Facilities:** P & toilets for disabled shop Details not confirmed for 2003

TEMPLEPATRICK Map 01 D5
PATTERSONS SPADE MILL
751 Antrim Rd BT39 0AP (2m SE of Templepatrick on A6)
☎ 028 9443 3619 028 9443 3619   2 for 1

This is the last surviving water-driven spade mill in Ireland. It has been completely restored by the National Trust and is now back in production.
Times: Open Etr, Apr-May & Sep, wknds 2-6; Jun-Aug, daily 2-6, also on BHs. **Fee:** * £3.50 (ch £1.50). Family Ticket £8.50. Groups £2 each.
Facilities: P & (ramps wheelchair available) toilets for disabled

Co Antrim – Co Armagh

TEMPLETOWN MAUSOLEUM
BT39 (in Castle Upton graveyard on A6, Belfast-Antrim road)

Situated in the graveyard of Castle Upton, this family mausoleum is in the shape of a triumphal arch and was designed by Robert Adam.
Times: Open daily during daylight hours. **Fee:** Free. **Facilities:**

CO ARMAGH

ARMAGH
Map 01 C5
ARMAGH COUNTY MUSEUM
The Mall East BT61 9BE (on the Mall, in the centre of Armagh City)
☎ 028 3752 3070   028 3752 2631
e-mail: acm.um@nics.gov.uk

Housed in a 19th-century schoolhouse, this museum contains an art gallery and library, as well as a collection of local folkcrafts and natural history. Special events are planned thoughout the year.
Times: Open all year, Mon-Fri 10-5, Sat 10-1 & 2-5. **Fee:** Free. **Facilities:** P & (entrance, ramp & lift for disabled) toilets for disabled shop ✈ (ex guide dogs)

ARMAGH FRIARY
(SE edge of town)
☎ 028 9023 5000   028 9031 0288
Times: Open all year. **Facilities:** P & Details not confirmed for 2003

ARMAGH PLANETARIUM
College Hill BT61 9DB (on main Armagh-Belfast road close to mall, Armagh city centre)
☎ 028 3752 3689 & 3752 4725
  028 3752 6187
e-mail: ktl@armagh-planetarium.co.uk
Times: Open all year, Hall of Astronomy Mon-Fri 10-4.45, shows daily at 3. Also open Sat & Sun 1.15-4.45, shows every Sat 2, 3 & 4. Additional shows during Etr, Xmas & BH's. (Closed Sun). **Facilities:** P & (Loop system in theatre) toilets for disabled shop ✈ (ex guide dogs) Details not confirmed for 2003

NAVAN CENTRE
Killylea Rd BT60 4LD (2m W on A28)
☎ 028 3752 5550   028 3752 2323
e-mail: navan@enterprise.net
Times: Open all year Mon-Fri 10-5, Sat 11-5, Sun 12-5. (Closed Xmas week). **Facilities:** P ⌂ & (loop for hearing aids, parking) toilets for disabled shop ✈ (ex guide dogs) Details not confirmed for 2003

PALACE STABLES HERITAGE CENTRE
The Palace Demesne BT60 4EL (off Friary Road beside council offices)
☎ 028 3752 9629   028 3752 9630   **2 for 1**
e-mail: stables@armagh.gov.uk

This picturesque Georgian building, set around a cobbled courtyard, has been lovingly restored and now houses a heritage centre. A daily Georgian interpretation is provided by authentic costumed characters. Special events include the Easter Georgian Festival, and an antiques and collectibles fair on the last Sunday of each month.
Times: Open all year, Jul-Aug, Mon-Sat 10-5.30, Sun 1-5.30; Sep-Apr, Mon-Sat 10-5, Sun 2-5. Last tour 1hr before closing. **Fee:** Telephone for admission prices. **Facilities:** P ✗ licensed & (ramps & Lift in stables) toilets for disabled shop

ST PATRICK'S TRIAN
40 English St BT61 7BA
☎ 028 37 521801   028 37 510180
e-mail: info@armagh.gov.uk

This award-winning attraction incorporates three different exhibitions. 'The Armagh Story' traces the city's history; 'Patrick's Testament' examines Armagh's association with Ireland's patron saint; and 'The Land of Lilliput' where a giant tells the story of *Gulliver's Travels*.
Times: Open all year, Mon-Sat 10-5, Sun 2-5; Jul-Aug, Mon-Sat 10-5. Last tour 1hr before closing. **Fee:** * £3.75 (ch £2, pen & student £2.75). Family ticket £9.50. **Facilities:** P (charged) ✗ licensed & (specially designed for disabled) toilets for disabled shop ✈ (ex guide dogs)

CAMLOUGH
Map 01 D5
KILLEVY CHURCHES
(3m S lower eastern slopes of Slieve Gullion)
☎ 028 9023 5000   028 9031 0288
Times: Open all year. **Facilities:** & Details not confirmed for 2003

JONESBOROUGH
Map 01 D5
KILNASAGGART INSCRIBED STONE
(1.25m S)
☎ 028 9023 5000   028 9031 0288
Times: Open all year. **Facilities:** P Details not confirmed for 2003

MOY
Map 01 C5
ARGORY
Derrycaw Rd BT71 6NA (3m NE)
☎ 028 8778 4753   028 8778 9598   **2 for 1**
e-mail: argory@ntrust.org.uk

Originally the home of the McGeough family, this

continued

Co Armagh – Co Down

Regency house is situated on a hillside overlooking the Blackwater River. The house is full of period furniture and bric-a-brac. Of particular interest is the very unusual acetylene lighting, installed by the family in 1906.
Times: Grounds: Open Oct-Apr daily 10-4; May-Sep daily 10-8. House: 16 Mar-May & Sep 12-6 at wkds & BH. June-Aug open daily (from 1pm in Jun) **Fee:** * Grounds £2 per car. House Tour £4 (ch £10) Family £10. Party **Facilities:** P (charged) ⬛ ♿ (special parking facilities, wheelchair available) toilets for disabled shop ✱ (ex guide dogs) ✿ 🍴

NEWRY   Map 01 D5
MOYRY CASTLE
(7.5m S)
☎ 028 9023 5000   📠 028 9031 0288
Times: Open all year **Facilities:** Details not confirmed for 2003

OXFORD ISLAND   Map 01 D5
LOUGH NEAGH DISCOVERY CENTRE
Oxford Island National Nature, Reserve BT66 6NJ (signposted from M1, exit 10)
☎ 028 3832 2205   📠 028 3834 7438
e-mail: oxford.island@craigavon.gov.uk

Learn about the history and wildlife of the Lough through a series of exciting audio-visual shows, interactive games and an exhibition, then experience the Island for yourself. In a spectacular setting on the water's edge, discover natural history, wildlife, family walks and much more.
Times: Open Apr-Sep, Mon-Sat 10-6; Sun 10-7, Oct-Mar, Wed-Sun 10-5. **Fee:** Telephone for admission prices. **Facilities:** P ⬛ ♿ (grounds accessible in part, bird watching hides) toilets for disabled shop ✱ (ex guide dogs) 🍴

PORTADOWN   Map 01 D5
ARDRESS HOUSE
64 Ardress Rd, Annaghmore BT62 1SQ (7m W on B28)
☎ 028 3885 1236   📠 028 3885 1236
e-mail: ardress@ntrust.org.uk

A plain 17th-century house, transformed around 1770 by its visionary architect-owner George Ensor, who added elegant wings and superb Adamesque plasterwork. The house has a fine picture gallery on loan from the Earl of Castlestewart. The grounds are beautifully unspoilt and there is a farmyard with livestock and a display of farm implements.
Times: Open Etr, daily; Apr-May & Sep, wknds & BH's, Jun-Aug, daily 2-6. **Fee:** * House, grounds & farm £2.70 (ch £1.35). Family ticket £6.75. Party **Facilities:** P ♿ toilets for disabled shop ✱ (ex guide dogs) ✿ 🍴

TYNAN   Map 01 C5
VILLAGE CROSS
☎ 028 9023 5000   📠 028 9031 0288
Times: Open all year **Facilities:** P ♿ Details not confirmed for 2003

CO DOWN

ARDGLASS   Map 01 D5
JORDAN'S CASTLE
☎ 028 9023 5000   📠 028 9031 0288
Times: Open Jul-Aug; Tue-Sat 10-7, Sun 2-7. Other times on request.
Facilities: ✱ Details not confirmed for 2003

BALLYWALTER   Map 01 D5
GREY ABBEY
(on east edge of village)
☎ 028 9023 5000   📠 028 9031 0288
Times: Open Apr-Sep; Tue-Sat 10-7, Sun 2-7. **Facilities:** P ♿ toilets for disabled Details not confirmed for 2003

CASTLEWELLAN   Map 01 D5
DRUMENA CASHEL
(2.25m SW)
☎ 028 9023 5000   📠 028 9031 0288
Times: Open all times **Facilities:** P Details not confirmed for 2003

COMBER   Map 01 D5
WWT CASTLE ESPIE
Ballydrain Rd BT23 6EA (3m S of Comber, 13m SE of Belfast. Signed from A22 Comber-Killyleagh-Downpatrick road)
☎ 02891 874146   📠 02891 873857   **2 for 1**
e-mail: castleespie@wwt.org.uk

Home to the largest collection of wildfowl in Ireland. Comfortable hides enable you to watch the splendour of migratory waders and wildfowl. Beautiful landscaped gardens, a taxidermy collection and fine paintings by wildlife artists can also be seen. Thousands of birds migrate to the reserve in winter and birdwatch mornings are held on the last Thursday of every month. The Centre's effluent is treated in a reed bed filtration system which can be seen on one walk.
Times: Open all year; summer, Mon-Sat 10.30-5, Sun 11.30-5.30; In July, Aug, spring & summer BH the centre will close at 5.30pm. Winter Nov-Feb Mon-fri 11-4 Sat & Sun 11-4.30. **Fee:** * £3.90 (ch under 4 free, ch £2.50, pen & concessions £3.10). Family ticket £10 Party 12+ **Facilities:** P ✱ ♿ (hides have wheelchair platforms) toilets for disabled shop ✱ (ex guide/hearing dogs) 🍴

DONAGHADEE   Map 01 D5
BALLYCOPELAND WINDMILL
(1m W, on B172)
☎ 028 9186 1413   📠 028 9131 0288
Times: Open all year Apr-Sep, Tue-Sat 10-7, Sun 2-7; Oct-Mar, Sat 10-4, Sun 2-4. **Facilities:** P shop ✱ Details not confirmed for 2003

DOWNPATRICK   Map 01 D5
DOWN COUNTY MUSEUM
The Mall BT30 6AH (follow brown heritage signs)
☎ 028 4461 5218   📠 028 4461 5590
e-mail: museum@downdc.gov.uk

The museum is located in the restored buildings of the 18th-century county gaol. In addition to restored cells that tell the stories of some of the prisoners, there are

continued

Co Down

exhibitions on the history of County Down. Plus temporary exhibits, events, tea-room and shop.
Times: Open all year, Mon-Fri 10-5, wknds 1-5; **Fee:** Free. **Facilities:** P (100yds) 🚗 ♿ (wheelchair available, handling boxes on application) toilets for disabled shop 🐕 (ex guide dogs)

INCH ABBEY
(0.75m NW off A7)
☎ 028 9023 5000 📠 028 9031 0288
Times: Open Apr-Sep 10-7, Sun 2-7. Oct-Mar free access. **Facilities:** P ♿ *Details not confirmed for 2003*

LOUGHINISLAND CHURCHES
(4m W)
☎ 028 9023 5000 📠 028 9031 0288
Times: Open all times **Facilities:** P ♿ 🚗 *Details not confirmed for 2003*

MOUND OF DOWN
(on the Quoile Marshes, from Mount Crescent)
☎ 028 9023 5000 📠 028 9031 0288
Times: Open all times **Facilities:** P *Details not confirmed for 2003*

THE ST PATRICK CENTRE
St Patrick Visitor Centre, Market St BT30 6LZ
☎ 028 4461 9000 📠 028 4461 9111
e-mail: director@saintpatrickcentre.com

This 21st-century multimedia, interactive, audio-visual feast is dedicated to the fascinating story of Ireland's Patron Saint, Saint Patrick, who brought Christianity to Ireland in the 5th century. The Centre is located beside the saint's grave.
Times: Open all year Oct-Mar, Mon-Sat, 10-5 & St Patricks Day 9.30-7; Apr-May & Sep, Mon-Sat 9.30-5.30, Sun 1-5.30, Jun-Aug Mon-Sat 9.30-7, Sun10-6 **Fee:** £4.50 (ch £2.25, concessions £3) family ticket (2ad+2ch) £11 groups 25+ **Facilities:** P 🍽 ✕ ♿ lifts+w/chairs toilets for disabled shop garden centre 🐕 ex guide dogs 🎧

STRUELL WELLS
(1.5m E)
☎ 028 9023 5000 📠 028 9031 0288
Times: Open all times **Facilities:** P 🚗 *Details not confirmed for 2003*

🏛 DROMARA   Map 01 D5
LEGANANNY DOLMEN
(4m S)
☎ 028 9023 5000 📠 028 9031 0288
Times: Open at all times **Facilities:** ♿ 🚗 *Details not confirmed for 2003*

🏛 HILLSBOROUGH   Map 01 D5
HILLSBOROUGH FORT
☎ 028 9268 3285 📠 028 9031 0288
Times: Open all year; Apr-Sep, Tue-Sat 10-7, Sun 2-7; Oct-Mar, Tue-Fri 10-4, Sat 10-4, Sun 2-4., **Facilities:** P ♿ *Details not confirmed for 2003*

🏛 KILKEEL   Map 01 D4
GREENCASTLE
(4m SW)
☎ 028 9023 5000 📠 028 9031 0288
Times: Open Jul-Aug, Tue-Sat 10-7, Sun 2-7. **Facilities:** P ♿ *Details not confirmed for 2003*

🏛 KILLINCHY   Map 01 D5
SKETRICK CASTLE
(3m E on W tip of Sketrick Islands)
☎ 028 9023 5000 📠 028 9031 0288
Times: Open at all times. **Facilities:** P ♿ *Details not confirmed for 2003*

🏛 NEWCASTLE   Map 01 D5
DUNDRUM CASTLE
(4m N)
☎ 028 9023 5000 📠 028 9031 0288
Times: Open Apr-Sep, Tue-Sat 10-7, Sun 2-7. **Facilities:** P ♿ toilets for disabled *Details not confirmed for 2003*

MAGHERA CHURCH
(2m NNW)
☎ 028 9023 5000 📠 028 9031 0288
Times: Open all year. **Facilities:** P ♿ *Details not confirmed for 2003*

🏛 NEWTOWNARDS   Map 01 D5
MOUNT STEWART HOUSE, GARDEN & TEMPLE OF THE WINDS
Greyabbey BT22 2AD (5m SE off A20)
☎ 028 4278 8387 📠 028 4278 8569   **2 for 1**
e-mail: mountstewart@ntrust.org.uk

On the east shore of Strangford Lough, this 18th-century house was the work of three architects. In the inspired gardens, which are now a nominated World Heritage site, many rare and subtropical trees thrive. Located by the shore is the Temple of the Winds, built by James 'Athenian' Stuart in 1782 for the first Marquess.
Times: Lakeside Gardens & Walks: Oct-Apr, daily 10-4; May-Sep daily 10-8; Formal Gardens: Mar 16-18, 23-24 & 29-31, Apr, daily 10-4, May-Sep daily 10-5 & Oct Wknds 10-4. House: Mar 16-18, 23-24 & 29-31, Apr wknds, Jun-Sep daily & Oct wknds. Temple of the Winds: Apr-Oct wknds 2-5. **Fee:** * House Garden & Temple: £4.75 (ch £2.25). Family ticket £9.75. Garden: £4 (ch £2) Group 15+. Garden only £3.75 (ch £2). Family £8.50. Party **Facilities:** P 🍽 ✕ licensed ♿ (4 wheelchairs (2 electric) available) toilets for disabled shop 🐾 🎧

SCRABO TOWER
Scrabo Country Park, 203A Scrabo Rd BT23 4SJ (1m W)
☎ 028 9181 1491 📠 028 9182 0695
Times: Open Etr, May-Sep, Sat-Thu 11-6.30. Country park open all year, daily, 11-6.30. **Facilities:** P shop 🐕 *Details not confirmed for 2003*

Co Down – Co Fermanagh

PORTAFERRY   Map 01 D5
EXPLORIS AQUARIUM
The Rope Walk, Castle St BT22 1NZ (A20 or A2 or A25 to Strangford Ferry Service)
☎ 028 4272 8062   028 4272 8396
e-mail: info@ards-council.gov.uk

Exploris Aquarium is Northern Ireland's only public aquarium and now includes a seal sanctuary. Situated on the shores of Strangford Lough it houses some of Europe's finest displays. The Open Sea Tank holds 250 tonnes of sea water, and the Shoaling Ring, where visitors are surrounded by hundreds of fish, is a tank 6m in diameter. The complex includes a park with duck pond, picnic area, children's playground, caravan site, woodland and bowling green.
Times: Open all year, Mon-Fri 10-6, Sat 11-6, Sun 1-6. (Sep-Feb closing 1 hr earlier). **Fee:** * £5.40 (concessions £3.20). Family £15. **Facilities:** P (2 lifts within complex) toilets for disabled shop (ex guide dogs)

SAINTFIELD   Map 01 D5
ROWALLANE GARDEN
BT24 7LH (1m S of Saintfield on A7)
☎ 028 9751 0131   028 9751 1242   2 for 1
e-mail: rowallane@ntrust.org.uk

Beautiful and exotic 52-acre gardens, started by the Rev John Moore in 1860, containing exquisite plants from all over the world. They are particularly noted for their rhododendrons and azaleas and for the wonderful floral displays in spring and summer. There are monthly demonstrations on The Art of the Gardener.
Times: Open Oct-Apr, 10-4; May-Sep, 10-8. Closed Dec 24-1 Jan. **Fee:** * £3 (ch £1.25) Family £7, groups £2 each. **Facilities:** P (parking facilities) toilets for disabled (ex on leads)

STRANGFORD   Map 01 D5
AUDLEY'S CASTLE
(1.5m W by shore of Strangford Lough)
☎ 028 9023 0560   028 9031 0288
Times: Open Apr-Sep, daily 10-7. **Facilities:** P Details not confirmed for 2003

CASTLE WARD
BT30 7LS (0.5m W of Strangford village on A25)
☎ 028 4488 1204   028 4488 1729   2 for 1
e-mail: castleward@ntrust.org.uk

The curious diversity of styles in this house is due to the fact that its owner and his wife could never agree; so classical themes and a more elaborate Gothic look were both incorporated. The servants' living quarters are reached by an underground passage. Gardens, complete with a small lake and classical summerhouse, are richly planted and especially beautiful in spring.
Times: House open Jun-Aug, daily 12-6; May 1-6 daily (ex Tue); Apr, wknds & BHs 12-6. **Fee:** * House £4.50 (ch £1.75). Family £3.50. Party. Grounds (Mar-Oct) car £3, Coach £15 & Horsebox £5. **Facilities:** P (charged) (wheelchair available, may be driven to house) toilets for disabled shop

STRANGFORD CASTLE
☎ 028 9023 5000   028 9031 0288
Times: Visable from outside. **Facilities:** Details not confirmed for 2003

WARRENPOINT   Map 01 D5
NARROW WATER CASTLE
(1m NW)
☎ 028 9023 5000   028 9031 0288
Times: Open Jul-Aug, Tue-Sat 10-7, Sun 2-7. **Facilities:** P Details not confirmed for 2003

CO FERMANAGH

BELLEEK   Map 01 B5
BELLEEK POTTERY
3 Main St BT93 3FY (Take A46 from Ennisuilla to Belleek. Pottery at entrance to village)
☎ 028 6865 9300   028 6865 8625   2 for 1
e-mail: visitorcentre@belleek.ie

Known worldwide for its fine Parian china, Ireland's oldest pottery was started in 1857 by the Caldwell family. Meet the craftspeople at work whilst touring the Pottery and visit the museum, which has exhibits dating back over 140 years.
Times: Open all year, Apr-Sep, Mon-Fri 9-6; Sat; 10-6 & Sun Apr-Jun & Sep 2-6; Sun, Jul & Aug 11-6; Oct-Mar Mon-Fri 9-5.30; Sat; Closed wknds except Oct, Sat 10-5.30 & Sun 2-6. **Fee:** Guided tours £2.50 (ch under 12 free, pen £1.50). **Facilities:** P (2 wheelchairs) toilets for disabled shop (ex guide dogs)

CASTLE ARCHDALE BAY   Map 01 C5
WHITE ISLAND CHURCH
(in Castle Archdale Bay; ferry from marina)
☎ 028 9023 5000   028 9031 0288
Times: Open Jul-Aug, Tue-Sat 10-7, Sun 2-7. **Facilities:** P Details not confirmed for 2003

DERRYGONNELLY   Map 01 C5
TULLY CASTLE
(3m N, on W shore of Lower Lough Erne)
☎ 028 9023 5000   028 9031 0288
Times: Open Apr-Sep Tue-Sat 10-7, Sun 2-7; Oct-Mar 10-4.(2-4 Sun). **Facilities:** P Details not confirmed for 2003

ENNISKILLEN   Map 01 C5
Castle Coole
BT74 (1.5m SE on A4)
☎ 028 6632 2690   ≡ 028 6632 5665
e-mail: castlecoole@ntrust.org.uk

2 for 1

No expense was spared in the building of this mansion. James Wyatt was the architect, the lovely plasterwork ceilings were by Joseph Rose, and the chimneypieces the work of Richard Westmacott. Vast amounts of Portland stone were specially imported, together with an Italian expert in stonework. The house is filled with beautiful Regency furniture.
Times: Grounds, Oct-Apr 10-4; May-Sep 10-8. House 12-6, mid Mar-May 7 Sep open wknds & BH. Jun, Wed-Sun; Jul-Aug, daily. **Fee:** * Grounds £2 car. House Tour £3.50 (ch £1.75). Family ticket £8.50. Party **Facilities:** 🅿 ⬛ ♿ (may be driven to house) toilets for disabled shop ✈ (ex in park & guide dogs) 🚲 ☕

Devenish Island
(2m N)
☎ 028 9023 5000   ≡ 028 9031 0288
Times: Open Apr-Sep, Tue-Sat 10-7, Sun 2-7. **Facilities:** 🅿 shop ✈ Details not confirmed for 2003

Enniskillen Castle
BT74 7HL
☎ 028 6632 2711
Times: Open all year Mon 2-5, Tue/Fri 10-5 (closed 1-2, Oct-Apr), Sat 2-5 May-Aug, Sun 2-5 Jul-Aug, all day BH's. **Facilities:** 🅿 ♿ shop ✈ Details not confirmed for 2003

Florence Court
BT92 1DB (8m SW of Enniskillen via A4 & A32)
☎ 028 6634 8249   ≡ 028 6634 8873
e-mail: florencecourt@ntrust.org.uk

2 for 1

An 18th-century mansion overlooking wild and beautiful scenery towards the Mountains of Cuilcagh. The interior of the house, particularly noted for its flamboyant rococo plasterwork, was gutted by fire in 1955, but has been miraculously restored. There are pleasure grounds with an Ice House, Summer House, Water Powered Sawmill and also a walled garden.
Times: Open daily. Grounds, Oct-Apr 10-4; May-Sep 10-8; House, daily Jun-Aug, 12-6; Apr, May & Sep, wknds. **Fee:** * £3.50 (ch £1.75). Family ticket £8.50. Group £3 each. **Facilities:** 🅿 (charged) ⬛ ♿ (electric wheelchair available & wheelchair path) toilets for disabled shop 🚲 ☕

Marble Arch Caves
Marlbank Scenic Loop BT92 1EW (off A4 Enniskillen-Sligo road)
☎ 028 6634 8855   ≡ 028 6634 8928
e-mail: mac@fermanagh.gov.uk
Times: Open late Mar-Sep. From 10 daily. **Facilities:** 🅿 ⬛ ♿ toilets for disabled shop ✈ (ex guide dogs) Details not confirmed for 2003 ☕

Monea Castle
(6m NW)
☎ 028 9023 5000   ≡ 028 9031 0288
Times: Open at any reasonable time. **Facilities:** 🅿 ♿ Details not confirmed for 2003

The Sheelin Irish Lace Museum
Ballanaleck BT92 2BA (from Enniskillen take A4 onto A509. Thatched Sheelin restaurant on left after 3m, museum in restaurant car park)
☎ 028 6634 8052   ≡ 028 6634 8200
e-mail: rosemary.cathcart@virgin.net

The Irish Lace Museum has the largest and most comprehensive display of antique lace anywhere in Ireland. There are around 140 exhibits, representing the five main types of Irish lace: Inishmacsaint Needlelace, Crochet, Limerick, Carrickmacross, and Youghal Needlelace. The history of the Irish lace-making industry is described, and antique items can be bought in the museum shop.
Times: Open Mon-Sat 10-6. **Fee:** £2.50 (ch under 14 £1). Party 15+ £1.50 each. **Facilities:** 🅿 ✖ licensed ♿ (toilets for disabled in restaurant) shop ✈ (ex guide dogs) ☕

LISNASKEA   Map 01 C5
Castle Balfour
☎ 028 9023 5000   ≡ 028 9031 0288
Times: Open at all times. **Facilities:** 🅿 ♿ Details not confirmed for 2003

NEWTOWNBUTLER   Map 01 C5
Crom Estate
BT92 8AP (3m W)
☎ 028 6773 8118   ≡ 028 6773 8118
e-mail: crom@ntrust.org.uk

2 for 1

Featuring 770 hectares of woodland, parkland and wetland, the Crom Estate is one of Northern Ireland's most important conservation areas. Nature trails are signposted through woodlands to the ruins of the old castle, and past the old boat house and picturesque summer house. Day tickets for pike fishing and boat hire are available from the Visitor Centre.
Times: Open Jul & Aug 10-8, Sep daily 10-6, Sun open 12 noon. **Fee:** * Car £4, boat £4, minibus £12, coach £25 **Facilities:** 🅿 (charged) ⬛ ♿ toilets for disabled shop 🚲 ☕

CO LONDONDERRY

COLERAINE   Map 01 C6
Hezlett House
107 Sea Rd, Castlerock BT51 4TN (5m W on Coleraine/Downhill coast road)
☎ 028 7084 8567   ≡ 02870 848567
e-mail: downcastle@ntrust.org.uk

2 for 1

A low, thatched cottage built around 1690 with an interesting cruck truss roof, constructed by using pairs of curved timbers to form arches and infilling around

continued

this frame with clay, rubble and other locally available materials.
Times: Open 16 Mar-May, 12-5, wknds & BH, Jun-Aug, daily (ex Tue), Sep wknds only. **Fee:** * £2 (ch 90p). Family ticket £5. Party **Facilities:** P ✈ (ex in gardens) ♨

Mount Sandel
(1.25m SSE)
☎ 028 9023 0560 📠 028 9031 0288
Times: Open at all times. **Facilities:** P ♿ *Details not confirmed for 2003*

COOKSTOWN   Map 01 C5
Tullaghoge Fort
(2m S)
☎ 028 9023 5000 📠 028 9031 0288
Times: Open at all times. **Facilities:** P *Details not confirmed for 2003*

Wellbrook Beetling Mill
20 Wellbrook Rd, Corkhill BT80 9RY (4m W, 0.5m off A505)
☎ 028 86748210 028 86751735   **2 for 1**
e-mail: wellbrook@ntrust.org.uk

This 18th-century water-powered linen mill was used for bleaching and, until 1961, for finishing Irish linen. Beetling was the name given to the final process in linen making, when the material was beaten by 30 or so hammers (beetles) to achieve a smooth and slightly shiny finish.
Times: Open 16 Mar-Jun wknds & BHs, Jul-Aug daily, Sep wknds.
Fee: * £2.50 (ch £1.25). Family £5.50. Party **Facilities:** P ♿ toilets for disabled shop ✈ (ex on lead) ♨

DOWNHILL   Map 01 C6
Mussenden Temple Bishop's Gate and Black Glen
Mussenden Rd BT51 4RP (1m W of Castlerock off A2)
☎ 028 7084 8728 📠 028 7084 8728
e-mail: downhillcastle@ntrust.org.uk

Spectacularly placed on a cliff edge overlooking the Atlantic, this perfect 18th-century rotunda was modelled on the Temple of Vesta at Tivoli. Visitors entering by the Bishop's Gate can enjoy a beautiful glen walk up to the headland where the temple stands.
Times: Downhill; open dusk-dawn daily all year. Temple; 11-6, 17 Mar-May & wknds. Hezlett; 12-5, 16 May-May, wknds & BH, Jun-Aug daily (ex Tue), Sep wknds. **Fee:** Free. **Facilities:** P ♿ ♨

DUNGIVEN   Map 01 C5
Banagher Church
(2m SW)
☎ 028 9023 5000 📠 028 9031 0288
Times: Open at all times. **Facilities:** P ♿ *Details not confirmed for 2003*

Dungiven Priory
(SE of town overlooking River Roe)
☎ 028 9023 5000 📠 028 9031 0288
Times: Open - Church at all times, chancel only when caretaker available. Check at house at end of lane. **Facilities:** P ♿ *Details not confirmed for 2003*

LIMAVADY   Map 01 C6
Rough Fort
(1m W off A2)

Early Christian rath.
Times: Open at all times. **Fee:** Free. **Facilities:** 🚗 ♨

LONDONDERRY   Map 01 C5
City Walls
☎ 028 9023 5000 📠 028 9031 0288
Times: Open all times. **Facilities:** P (charged) ♿ *Details not confirmed for 2003*

Foyle Valley Railway Museum
Foyle Rd BT48 6SQ
☎ 028 7126 5234 📠 028 7137 7633   **2 for 1**
Times: Open all year, Apr-Sep Mon-Sat 10-5, Sun 2-5; Oct-Mar Mon-Sat 10-4. **Facilities:** P ♿ toilets for disabled shop garden centre ✈ *Details not confirmed for 2003*

Tower Museum
Union Hall Place BT48 6LU (directly behind the city wall, facing the guildhall)
☎ 028 7137 2411 📠 028 7137 7633   **2 for 1**
e-mail: towermuseum@dnet.co.uk

This exhibition recounts the history of Londonderry from pre-historic times to the present day using real artefacts, theatrical displays and eleven audio-visual programmes showing the spread of Irish monasticism, the famous Siege of Derry and the road to the partition of Ireland.
Times: Open all year, Sep-Jun Tue-Sat 10-5. Jul-Aug Mon-Sat 10-5, Sun 2-5. Also open all BH Mons. **Fee:** * £4.20 (pen, UB40s, students £1.60) Family ticket £8.50. **Facilities:** P (300 yds) ♿ toilets for disabled shop ✈ (ex guide dogs) 🍴

MAGHERA   Map 01 C5
Maghera Church
(E approach to the town)
☎ 028 9023 5000 📠 028 9031 0288
Times: Key from Leisure Centre. **Facilities:** P ♿ *Details not confirmed for 2003*

MONEYMORE   Map 01 C5
Springhill
BT45 7NQ (1m from Moneymore on B18 to Coagh)
☎ 028 8674 8210 & 8674 7927   **2 for 1**
📠 028 8674 8210
e-mail: springhill@ntrust.org.uk

This pleasingly symmetrical manor house dates back to the 17th century. Today much of the family furniture, books and bric-a-brac have been retained. Outside, the laundry, stables, brewhouse, and old dovecote make

continued

Co Londonderry – Co Tyrone

interesting viewing, as does the excellent costume museum. **Times:** Open 16 Mar-Jun, 12-6 wknds & BH, Jul -Aug daily, Sep wknds only. **Fee:** * £3.50 (ch £1.75). Family ticket £7.25. Party **Facilities:** P 🍴 ♿ (photograph album of first floor available) toilets for disabled shop 🐕 (ex on leads) 🎁

CO TYRONE

🏛 ARDBOE Map 01 C5
ARDBOE CROSS
(off B73)
☎ 028 9023 5000   📠 028 9031 0288
Times: Open at all times. **Facilities:** P ♿ *Details not confirmed for 2003*

🏛 BALLYGAWLEY Map 01 C5
U S GRANT ANCESTRAL HOMESTEAD & VISITOR CENTRE
Dergenagh, 190 Ballygawley Rd BT70 1TW (off A4, 2m on Dergenagh road, signposted)
☎ 028 8555 7133   📠 028 8555 7133
e-mail: killymaddy@nitic.net

Ancestral homestead of Ulysses S Grant, 18th President of the United States of America. The homestead and farmyard have been restored to the style and appearance of a mid 19th-century Irish smallholding. There is an audio visual display in centre telling of the Ulster American connections and an American civil war presentation. Also a children's play area, purpose-built barbecue and picnic tables, and butterfly garden.
Times: Open Etr-Sep, Tue-Sat 12-5, Sun 2-6. Other times by arrangement. (Closed 25-26 Dec & 1 Jan). **Fee:** £1 (ch & concessions 50p). Party 10+ **Facilities:** P 🍴 ♿ (wide doorway to audio-visual area/entrances/exits) shop 🐕 (ex guide dogs)

🏛 BEAGHMORE Map 01 C5
BEAGHMORE STONE CIRCLES AND ALIGNMENTS
☎ 028 9023 5000   📠 028 9031 0288
Times: Open at all times. **Facilities:** P ♿ *Details not confirmed for 2003*

🏛 BENBURB Map 01 C5
BENBURB CASTLE
☎ 028 9023 5000   📠 028 9031 0288
Times: Castle grounds open at all times. Special arrangements, made in advance, necessary for access to flanker tower. **Facilities:** P ♿ 🐕 *Details not confirmed for 2003*

🏛 CASTLECAULFIELD Map 01 C5
CASTLE CAULFIELD
☎ 028 9023 5000   📠 028 9031 0288
Times: Open at all times. **Facilities:** P ♿ *Details not confirmed for 2003*

🏛 DUNGANNON Map 01 C5
TYRONE CRYSTAL VISITOR CENTRE
Killybrackey BT71 6TT (M1 junct 14/A45 to t-junct, turn left towards Dungannon, Centre 2.5m on left. Signposted)
☎ 028 8772 5335   📠 028 8772 6260
e-mail: info@tyronecrystal.com

Crystal making in Tyrone is a comparatively modern enterprise, dating from the days of Benjamin Edwards in the 1770s. Tyrone Crystal is hand-cut, and visitors can see this craft on guided tours of the factory. The new spacious visitor centre and facilities contribute to the fascinating insight of Tyrone Crystal.
Times: Visitor Centre Mon-Sat 9-6, Sun1-5; Tour times Mon-Fri 11, 12, 2, 3pm. Sat tours prior booking only **Fee:** * £2 for tour. Visitor Centre free. **Facilities:** P 🍴 ♿ Disabled parking spaces toilets for disabled shop 🐕 (ex guide dogs) 🎁

🏛 NEWTOWNSTEWART Map 01 C5
HARRY AVERY'S CASTLE
(0.75m SW)
☎ 028 9023 5000   📠 028 9031 0288
Times: Open at all times. **Facilities:** 🐕 🍴 *Details not confirmed for 2003*

🏛 OMAGH Map 01 C5
ULSTER AMERICAN FOLK PARK
BT78 5QY (5m NW Omagh on the NW passage route)
☎ 028 8224 3292   📠 028 8224 2241   **2 for 1**
e-mail: uafp@iol.ie

An outdoor museum that traces the history of Ulster's links with America and the emigration of Ulster residents to the US during the 18th and 19th centuries. The 70-acre site is divided into two parts - Old World and New World. There are demonstrations of Old and New World crafts, and a visitor centre, with exhibitions and audio-visual presentations. The Centre for Emigration Studies is based here, with a research library and emigration database - please ring for details.
Times: Open Etr-Sep, daily 10.30-6, Sun & BH 11-6.30; Oct-Etr Mon-Fri 10.30-5. Last admission 1hr 30mins before closing. **Fee:** * £4 (ch & pen £2.50). Family ticket £10. Children under 5yrs free.
Facilities: P 🍴 🍽 ♿ toilets for disabled shop 🐕 (ex guide dogs) 🎁

ULSTER HISTORY PARK
Cullion BT79 7SU (7m on B48)
☎ 028 8164 8188   📠 028 8164 8011
e-mail: uhp@omagh.gov.uk

The story of settlement in Ireland, told with the aid of full-scale models of the houses and monuments built through the ages. Exhibitions and audio-visual presentations expand the theme.
Times: Open all year, Jul-Aug daily 10-6.30; Apr-Jun & Sep, daily 10-5.30; Oct-Mar, Mon-Fri 10-5. **Fee:** * £3.75 (ch, students, pen & registered disabled £2.50). Family ticket (2 adults & 2 ch) £12. Group 15+ **Facilities:** P 🍴 ♿ toilets for disabled shop 🐕 (ex guide dogs) 🎁

STEWARTSTOWN
Map 01 C5

MOUNTJOY CASTLE
Magheralamfield (3m SE, off B161)
☎ 028 9023 5000   028 9031 0288
Times: Open at all times. **Facilities:** P *Details not confirmed for 2003*

STRABANE
Map 01 C5

GRAY'S PRINTING PRESS
49 Main St BT82 8AU
☎ 028 7188 4094

`2 for 1`

Strabane was once an important printing and book-publishing centre, the only relic of this is a small shop in Main Street which now houses a museum illustrating the history of Strabane. The Print Museum, in a separate building, contains three 19th-century presses and shows the development of printing techniques over 150 years.
Times: Open Apr-Sep, Tue-Sat 2-5. Other times by prior arrangement.
Fee: * £2.50 (ch £1.50). Family ticket £5.50. Party **Facilities:** P (100yds) ♿ ✈ (ex guide dogs) ✻

Republic of Ireland

No visitor comes here without preconceptions, and while some of these will be confirmed, there are always plenty of surprises.

To be sure it is green - the Emerald Isle is no misnomer - and you're never far from water, from the craggy Atlantic coast, the countless loughs, rivers and bogs, to the regular falls of rain, or Irish mist. And then there are the people.

Certainly this country with its tiny population has brought us an abundance of world-class literary figures, and you will meet the same love of words and ideas in any street, shop or pub. Music too seems to run in the veins - listening to an Irish band, it soon becomes clear that the musicians are playing as much for their own pleasure as for the tourists'. However, this is no quaint backwater; the Republic has enthusiastically embraced its European identity, and has now exchanged the Punt for the Euro.

Where to go? It would be hard to miss out on elegant, cosmopolitan Dublin, and in the south there's Cork, vying with the capital for business and cultural supremacy. To explore the west, head for Galway, where Gaelic is still spoken by many inhabitants as a first language, and inland you will not be disappointed by the craft studios and restaurants of Kilkenny.

Further afield there is no end of opportunity for fishing, golfing, walking and relaxing. You can find a quiet charm everwhere you visit, but there are some strikingly unique attractions. The Burren is a naturalist's joy, with exotic flora in every crevice of its strange rockscape, and Newgrange is one of Europe's most important and mysterious prehistoric sites. In many ways similar to England's Stonehenge, this amazing dome of earth and stone was built some five thousand years ago, and is 250 feet in diameter. Like much of Ireland, it is beautiful, mysteriously spiritual, and fascinating.

Top: cottage near Rosmuck

EVENTS & FESTIVALS

March
tbc Feis Ceoil, Dublin
tbc St Patrick's Festival

April
tbc Dublin Film Festival
tbc Pan Celtic International Festival, Kilkenny Castle

May
1st-4th Cork International Choral Festival, Co Cork
tbc Dundalk International Maytime Festival, Co Louth
tbc Fleadh Nua, Ennis, Co Clare
tbc Listowel Writers Week, Listowel, Co Kerry

June
16th Bloomday (James Joyce Festival), Dublin
25th-5th July Enniscorthy Strawberry Fair, Co Wexford
tbc The Cat Laughs, comedy festival, Co Kilkenny

July
tbc Galway International Arts Festival, Co Galway

August
6th-10th Dublin Horse Show, Ballsbridge, Dublin
8th-17th Kilkenny Arts Festival, Co Kilkenny
tbc Fleadh Cheoil na hEireann, Enniscorthy (Irish music)

September
25th-28th Galway International Oyster Festival, Co Galway
29th-11th Oct Dublin Theatre Festival (various venues)

October
16th-2nd Nov Wexford Festival Opera, Co Wexford
tbc Cork Jazz Festival, Co Cork

CO CLARE

BALLYVAUGHAN Map 01 B3
AILLWEE CAVE
(3m S of Ballyvaughan. Signposted from Galway and Ennis)
☎ 065 7077036 & 7077067   065 7077107
e-mail: aillwee@eircom.net

An underground network of caves beneath the world famous Burren. Guided tours take you through large caverns, over bridged chasms and alongside thunderous waterfalls. There is a craftshop, a dairy where cheese is made, a speciality food shop and a tea room. Santa uses the cave as a workshop around Christmas time, while Easter sees a massive egg hunt in the woods.
Times: Open all year from 10am. **Fee:** * €7.50 (ch €4.50, student & pen €6). Family ticket €21-€24. **Facilities:** P ⬛ ✗ licensed ♿ toilets for disabled shop 🐕

BUNRATTY Map 01 B3
BUNRATTY CASTLE & FOLK PARK
(8 miles from Limerick city on N18 road to Ennis)
☎ 061 361511 & 360788   061 361020
e-mail: liddyt@shannon-dev.ie
Times: Open all year, daily 9.30-5.30 (last admission 4.30pm). Folk Park also open Jun-Aug 9-6.30 (last admission 5.30pm). Last admission to Castle 4pm all year. Closed Good Friday & 24-26 Dec.
Facilities: P ⬛ ✗ licensed ♿ toilets for disabled shop *Details not confirmed for 2003*

LISCANNOR Map 01 B3
CLIFFS OF MOHER VISITORS CENTRE
(6m NW of Lahinch)
☎ 065 81565 & 061 360788   061 361020
e-mail: liddyt@shannon-dev.ie
Times: Open all year, 9.30-5.30 June-Aug 9-8pm (subject to weather conditions). Visitor centre closed Good Friday & 23-27 Dec. O'Briens Tower 9.30-5.30. **Facilities:** P (charged) ⬛ ♿ toilets for disabled shop *Details not confirmed for 2003*

QUIN Map 01 B3
THE CRAGGAUNOWEN BRONZE AGE PROJECT
(signed from N18, 10km N from Sixmilebridge)
☎ 061 367178 & 360788   061 361020
e-mail: liddyt@shannon-dev.ie
Times: Open Apr-Oct daily 10-6 (last admission 5pm). **Facilities:** P ⬛ ♿ toilets for disabled shop *Details not confirmed for 2003*

CO CORK

BALLINCOLLIG Map 01 B2
BALLINCOLLIG GUNPOWDER MILLS HERITAGE CENTRE
(on Cork/Killarney road)
☎ 021 4874430   021 4874836
e-mail: ballinco@indigo.ie
Times: Open daily, 25 Apr-Sep 10-6. Last tour at 5.15pm. **Facilities:** P ⬛ ♿ toilets for disabled shop 🐕 (ex guide dogs) *Details not confirmed for 2003*

BLARNEY Map 01 B2
BLARNEY CASTLE & ROCK CLOSE
(5m from Cork on main road towards Limerick)
☎ 021 4385252 & 4385669   021 4381518
e-mail: info@blarneyc.iol.ie

The site of the famous Blarney Stone, known the world over for the eloquence it is said to impart to those who kiss it. The stone is in the upper tower of the castle, and, held by your feet, you must lean backwards down the inside of the battlements in order to receive the gift of the gab.
Times: Open - Blarney Castle & Rock Close, Jun-Jul Mon-Sat 9-7.30; Aug Mon-Sat 9-7.30; May Mon-Sat 9-7; Sep Mon-Sat 9-6.30; Apr & Oct Mon-Sat 9-sunset; summer Sun 9.30-5.30; winter Sun 9.30-sunset. Blarney House & Gardens Jun-mid Sep Mon-Sat noon-6. **Fee:** * Blarney Castle & Rock Close €5.50 (ch €2, pen & students €4). Family ticket (2ad+2ch €11.50) **Facilities:** P ♿ shop 🐕 (ex guide dogs)

CARRIGTWOHILL (CARRIGTOHILL) Map 01 B2
FOTA ARBORETUM & GARDENS
Fota Estate
☎ 021 4812728   021 4812728
Times: Open Mar-Oct, daily 10-6; Nov-Feb, daily 10-5. (Closed 25 Dec). **Facilities:** P (charged) ♿ toilets for disabled 🐕 (ex on lead) *Details not confirmed for 2003*

FOTA WILDLIFE PARK
Fota Estate (situated 10km E of Cork City. Take the Cobh road from N25 Cork - Waterford road)
☎ 021 4812678   021 4812744
e-mail: info@fotawildlife.ie

Times: Open all year 17 Mar-Sep daily, 10-6 (Sun 11-6) Oct-17 Mar wkends only. Last admission 5. **Facilities:** P (charged) ✗ ♿ (Ramps where required) toilets for disabled shop 🐕 *Details not confirmed for 2003*

Co Cork **385**

CLONAKILTY   Map 01 B2
WEST CORK MODEL VILLAGE RAILWAY
Inchydoney Rd (From Cork N71 West Cork left at junct for Inchydoney Island, signposted at road junction. Village is on Bay side of Clonakilty)
☎ 023 33224
e-mail: modelvillage@eircom.net

This miniature world depicts Irish towns as they were in the 1940s, with models of the West Cork Railway and various animated scenes. The tea room is set in authentic railway carriages that overlook picturesque Clonakilty Bay.
Times: Open Feb-Oct daily 11-5, daily 11-5; Jul-Aug, daily, extended hours 10-6. **Fee:** * €5 (ch €2.50, concessions €4). Family ticket €13, Party 12+. **Facilities:** P ⬛ & toilets for disabled shop ✖ (ex guide dogs) 🦮

COBH   Map 01 B2
THE QUEENTOWN STORY
Cobh Railway Station (Off N25, follow signs for Cobh. Centre is located at Deepwater Quay, adjacent to Train Station)
☎ 021 4813591   ▣ 021 4813595
e-mail: info@cobhheritage.com

A dramatic exhibition of the origins, history and legends of Cobh. Between 1848 and 1950 over 3 million Irish people were deported from Cobh on convict ships. Visitors can explore the conditions onboard these vessels and learn about the harbour's connections with the *Lusitania* and the *Titanic*.
Times: Mar-Nov 10-6. Last admission 5pm. Nov-Mar 10-5. Last admission 4pm **Fee:** €5 (ch12 €2.50, pen & students €4). Family ticket €15.50 **Facilities:** P ⬛ ✖ & toilets for disabled shop ✖ (ex guide dogs) 🦮

CORK   Map 01 B2
CORK CITY GAOL
Convent Av, Sundays Well (Off Sunday's Well Rd)
☎ 021 4305022   ▣ 021 4307330
e-mail: corkgaol@indigo.ie

A restored 19th-century prison building. Furnished cells, lifelike characters and sound effects combine to allow visitors to experience day-to-day life for prisoners and the gaoler. There is an audio-visual presentation of the social history of Cork City. Individual sound tours are available in a number of languages. The Radio Museum Experience is located in the restored 1920's broadcasting studio, home to Cork's first radio station, 6CK. Unfortunately the 1st and 2nd floors are not accessible to wheelchair users.
Times: Open Mar-Oct, daily 9.30-6; Nov-Feb, daily 10-5. Last admission 1hr before closing. **Fee:** * €5 (ch €3, concessions €4) Family ticket €14 **Facilities:** P & (customer care policy - individual attention) toilets for disabled shop ✖ (ex guide dogs)

CORK PUBLIC MUSEUM
Fitzgerald Park, Mardyke (N of University College)
☎ 021 427 0679   ▣ 021 427 0931
e-mail: museum@corkcorp.ie

Displays illustrating the history of the city are housed in this museum. The collections cover the economic, social and municipal history from the Mesolithic period. There are fine collections of Cork Silver and Glass and Youghal Needlepoint Lace.
Times: Open all year, Jun-Aug Mon-Fri 11-1 & 2.15-6, Sun 3-5; Sep-May Mon-Fri 11-1 & 2.15-5, Sun 3-5. (Closed Sat, BH wknds & PH)
Fee: Mon-Fri free; Sun, Family €3 individual €1.50. Students, pen & unwaged free **Facilities:** P (100 yds) shop ✖ (ex guide dogs)

GLENGARRIFF   Map 01 B2
GARINISH ISLAND
(1.5km boat trip from Glengarriff)
☎ 027 63040   ▣ 027 63149
Times: Open Jul-Aug, Mon-Sat 9.30-6.30, Sun 11-7; Apr-Jun & Sep, Mon-Sat 10-6.30, Sun 1-7; Mar & Oct, Mon-Sat 10-4.30, Sun 1-5. Last landing 1 hour before closing. Charge made by boat operators.
Facilities: ⬛ & (minimal due to boat access) toilets for disabled ✖ (ex on leads) *Details not confirmed for 2003*

KINSALE   Map 01 B2
CHARLES FORT
☎ 021 772263   ▣ 021 774347
e-mail: info@heritageireland.ie
Times: Open all year, mid Mar-Oct, daily 10-6; Nov-mid Mar, Sat-Sun 10-5, wkdays by arrangement. Last admission 45 minutes before closing. **Facilities:** P ⬛ & toilets for disabled ✖ (ex guide dogs) *Details not confirmed for 2003*

DESMOND CASTLE
Cork St
☎ 021 774855
Times: Open mid Jun-early Oct, daily 10-6; mid Apr-mid Jun, Tue-Sun & BH Mon 10-6. Last admission 45 mins before closing. **Facilities:** P ✖ (ex guide dogs) *Details not confirmed for 2003*

MIDLETON   Map 01 C2
OLD MIDLETON DISTILLERY
(At the E end of the main street on left. Well signposted)
☎ 021 4613594   ▣ 021 4613642

A tour of the Old Midleton Distillery consists of a 15-minute audio/visual presentation, then a 35-minute

continued

guided tour of the Old Distillery and then back to the Jameson Bar for a whiskey tasting - minerals are available for children. The guided tour and audio-visual aids are available in seven languages.
Times: Open Nov-Mar 10-6 tours 11.30, 2.30 & 4. Mar-Nov 9-6 tours on demand. **Fee:** €5.75 (ch €2.50). Family ticket (2ad + 3ch) €15.
Facilities: P ⬛ ✗ licensed & toilets for disabled shop ✱ (ex certain areas/guide dogs) ⬛

CO DONEGAL

ARDARA   Map 01 B5
ARDARA HERITAGE CENTRE
The Diamond
☎ 075 41704   ≣ 075 41381
Times: Open Apr-Sep, 10-6. **Facilities:** P ⬛ ✗ & toilets for disabled shop ✱ (ex guide dogs) *Details not confirmed for 2003*

BALLYSHANNON   Map 01 B5
THE WATER WHEELS
Abbey Assaroe (cross Abbey River on Rossnowlagh Rd, next turning left & follow signs)
☎ 072 51580

Abbey Assaroe was founded by Cistercian Monks from Boyle Abbey in the late 12th century. The Cistercians excelled in water engineering and canalised the river to turn water wheels for mechanical power. Two restored 12th-century mills, one is used as a coffee shop and restaurant; the other houses a small museum related to the history of the Cistercians.
Times: Open Apr-Nov, daily 10.30-6.30 **Fee:** Free. **Facilities:** P ⬛ ✗ licensed & toilets for disabled shop garden centre ⬛

DONEGAL   Map 01 B5
DONEGAL CASTLE
☎ 073 22405   ≣ 073 22436
Times: Open mid Mar-mid Oct, daily 9.30-6.30 (last admission 5.45).
Facilities: P ✱ (ex guide dogs) *Details not confirmed for 2003*

LETTERKENNY   Map 01 C5
GLEBE HOUSE & GALLERY
Churchill (signposted from Letterkenny)
☎ 074 37071   ≣ 074 37521
Times: Open Etr & mid May-Sep, Sat-Thu 11-6.30. (Last tour of house 5.30). **Facilities:** P ⬛ & toilets for disabled ✱ (ex guide dogs) *Details not confirmed for 2003*

GLENVEAGH NATIONAL PARK & CASTLE
Churchill (left off N56 onto L77))
☎ 074 37090 & 37262   ≣ 074 37072
e-mail: cbrady@eaglea.ie

Over 40,000 acres of mountains, glens, lakes and woods. A Scottish-style castle is surrounded by one of the finest gardens in Ireland, contrasting with the rugged surroundings.

Times: Open daily mid Mar-early Nov, 10-5 **Fee:** Park: free Castle: €2.50 (ch & students €1.20, pen €1.90, family ticket €6.35).
Facilities: P ⬛ ✗ & toilets for disabled ✱ (ex guide dogs)

LIFFORD   Map 01 C5
CAVANACOR HISTORIC HOUSE & ART GALLERY
Ballindrait (1.5m from town off N14 Strabane/Letterkenny road)
☎ 074 41139   ≣ 074 41143
e-mail: joannaok7@hotmail.com

Built in the early 1600s and commanding a view of the Clonleigh Valley and the River Deele, Cavanacor House is the ancestral home of James Knox Polk, 11th President of the USA (1845-1849). King James II dined under the sycamore tree in front of the house in 1689. There are over 10 acres of landscaped gardens and an old-fashioned walled garden. The Art Gallery will feature exhibitions of new work by national and international artists. Please ring for details.
Times: Open Etr & Jul-Aug Tue-Sat 12-6, Sun 2-6. Art gallery open all year **Fee:** €5 (ch & pen €4.50). **Facilities:** P ⬛ ✗ & shop ⬛

CO DUBLIN

BALBRIGGAN   Map 01 D4
ARDGILLAN CASTLE
(Pass Airport & Swords rdbt, take R127 & follow signs)
☎ 01 8492212   ≣ 01 8492786

A large and elegant country manor house built in 1738, set in 194 acres of parkland, overlooking the sea and coast as far as the Mourne Mountains. There is a permanent exhibition of the 17th-century 'Down Survey' maps and various temporary exhibitions. Tours of the Gardens (June, July and August) begin at 3.30pm every Thursday.
Times: Open Apr-Sep, Tue-Sun & BH's 11-6 (daily Jul-Aug); Oct-Mar, Wed-Sun & BH's 11-4.30. (Closed 23 Dec-1 Jan). **Fee:** * €4 (pen & students €3). Family ticket €9. **Facilities:** P ⬛ & toilets for disabled shop ✱ (ex guide dogs)

Co Dublin

DONABATE Map 01 D4
NEWBRIDGE HOUSE AND TRADITIONAL FARM
☎ 01 8436534 & 8462184   📠 01 8462537
Times: Open Apr-Sep Tue-Sat 10-5, Sun & PH 2-6; Oct-Mar Sat-Sun & PH 2-5. Parties at other times by arrangement. **Facilities:** P ⌐ shop ✱ *Details not confirmed for 2003*

DUBLIN Map 01 D4
THE CASINO
off Malahide Rd, Marino (5km N of city centre)
☎ 01 8331618   📠 01 8331618
Times: Open Jun-Sep, daily 10-6; May & Oct, daily 10-5; Apr, Sun, Thu & BH's 12-5; Feb, Mar & Nov, Sun, Thu & BH's 12-4. Last admission 45 mins before closing. (Closed Dec & Jan). **Facilities:** P ⌐ ✱ (ex guide dogs) *Details not confirmed for 2003*

THE CHESTER BEATTY LIBRARY
Clock Tower, Dublin Castle (10 walk from Trinity College, up Dame St towards Christ Church Cathedral)
☎ 01 4070750   📠 01 4070760
e-mail: info@cbl.ie
Times: Open all year Sat 11-5 & Sun 1-5; May-Sep, Mon-Fri 10-5; Oct-Apr Tue-Fri, 10-5. (Closed Good Friday, BH Mons, 25-26 Dec & 1 Jan). **Facilities:** P (5mins walk) ✕ ⌐ toilets for disabled shop garden centre ✱ (ex guide dogs) *Details not confirmed for 2003*

CHRIST CHURCH CATHEDRAL
Christchurch Place (at the top end of Dame St)
☎ 01 6778099   📠 01 6798991
e-mail: welcome@cccdub.ie

Founded in 1030, the present building dates from 1180 with a major restoration in the 1870s. The crypt is the second largest medieval crypt in Britain or Ireland. There are daily services and choral services on Sundays and during the week.
Times: Open all year 9.45-5. **Fee:** Requested donation €3 **Facilities:** P (100yds) ⌐ for access to crypt advance notice required shop ✱ (ex guide dogs)

DRIMNAGH CASTLE
Long Mile Rd, Drimnagh DL12 (from Dame St, left at Christchurch Cathedral into Patrick St, right into Cork St. Through Dolphins Barn up to Crumlin Rd, past Halfway House at junction. Situated 500 yards on right)
☎ 01 4502530 & 4508927   📠 01 4508927
e-mail: drimnaghcastle@eircom.net

The last surviving medieval castle in Ireland with a flooded moat, Drimnagh dates back to the 13th century and was inhabited until 1954. The Castle consists of a restored Great Hall and medieval undercroft, a tall battlement tower and lookout posts, and other separate buildings including stables, an old coach house and a folly. One of the most attractive features of Drimnagh is the garden, a formal 17th-century layout with box hedges, yews and mop heads.
Times: Open Apr-Oct. Wed & wknds 12-5; Nov-Mar, Sun 2-5. Last Tour 4.15 **Fee:** * €3.50 (ch €2.50, pen & students €3). Groups 20+ €2.50 each. **Facilities:** P ⌐ (gravel courtyard and garden. steps) ✱ (ex guide dogs)

DUBLIN CASTLE
Dame St
☎ 01 6777129   📠 01 6797831
Times: Open all year, Mon-Fri 10-5, Sat-Sun & BH 2-5. (Closed 24-26 Dec & Good Fri). **Facilities:** P ✕ ⌐ toilets for disabled *Details not confirmed for 2003*

DUBLINIA
St Michael's Hill, Christ Church
☎ 01 6794611   📠 01 6797116
e-mail: info@dvblinia.ie

The story of medieval Dublin. Housed in the former Synod Hall beside Christ Church Cathedral and developed by the Medieval Trust, DVBLINIA recreates the period from the arrival of Strongbow and the Anglo-Normans in 1170 to the closure of the monasteries by Henry VIII in 1540.
Times: Open Apr-Sep 10-5; Oct-Mar, Mon-Sat 11-4, Sun & BH 10-4.30. (Closed 24-26 Dec). **Fee:** * €5.75 (ch €4.25 concession €4.50). Family ticket (2ad + 3ch) €15 **Facilities:** P (100yds) ⌐ ⌐ (2 floors accessible, but bridge and tower are not) toilets for disabled shop ✱ (ex guide dogs)

DUBLIN WRITERS MUSEUM
18 Parnell Square North
☎ 01 8722077   📠 01 8722231
e-mail: writers@dublintourism.ie
Times: Open all year, Mon-Sat 10-5 & Sun & BH 11-5. Jun-Aug, Mon-Fri 10-6pm. **Facilities:** P (200 yds) (Metered) ⌐ ✕ licensed shop ✱ (ex guide dogs) *Details not confirmed for 2003*

DUBLIN ZOO
Phoenix Park (10mins bus ride from City Centre)
☎ 01 474 8900   📠 01 6771660
e-mail: info@dublinzoo.ie

Dublin Zoo first opened to the public in 1830, making it one of the oldest zoos in the world and has consistently been Ireland's favourite attraction. The new 'African Plains' is the biggest single development undertaken by the zoo. This 30-acre development has doubled the size of the zoo and provides spacious new areas for African species. Dublin Zoo is a modern zoo with conservation, education & study as its mission. The majority of the animals at the zoo have been born and bred in zoos and are part of global breeding programmes to ensure their continued survival.
Times: Open Mar-Oct, Mon-Sat 9.30-6, Sun 10.30-6; Nov-Feb, daily 10.30-dusk. **Fee:** * €10.10 (ch & pen €6.30, ch under 3 free, student & unwaged €7.70). Family tickets from €29.40 **Facilities:** P ⌐ ✕ licensed ⌐ (Wheelchairs are available) toilets for disabled shop ✱

> € Don't forget that the Republic of Ireland now uses the Euro as its currency

Co Dublin

GUINNESS STOREHOUSE
St James's Gate (Located next to James' St)
☎ 01 4084800   📠 01 4084965
e-mail: guinness-storehouse@guinness.com

Established in 1876 the Storehouse remained crammed with hopsacks until 1957, then it was converted and now is a hi-tech, 21st-century mix of arts centre, conference facilities, restaurant and bar. Find out about the history of Guinness and sample a glass.
Times: Open daily 9.30-5. (Closed 24-26 Dec, 1 Jan & Good Fri).
Fee: €13.50 (ch 6-12 €3, students & pen €6.50); family ticket (2 adults & 2 ch) €28. **Facilities:** P ⬛ ✕ ♿ toilets for disabled shop ✈ (ex guide dogs) ☕

HOWTH CASTLE RHODODENDRON GARDENS
Howth (9m NE of Dublin city centre, by coast road to Howth. Signposted for Deer Park Hotel)
☎ 01 8322624 & 8322256   📠 01 8392405
e-mail: sales@deerpark.iol.ie
Times: Open all year, daily 8am-dusk. (Closed 25 Dec). **Facilities:** P ♿ (steep hills unsuitable, ramped entrance) toilets for disabled ✈ (ex guide dogs) Details not confirmed for 2003 ☕

HUGH LANE MUNICIPAL GALLERY OF MODERN ART
Charlemont House, Parnell Square
☎ 01 8741903   📠 01 8722182
e-mail: info@hughlane.ie
Times: Open all year, Tue-Thu 9.30-6, Fri-Sat 9.30-5, Sun 11-5. Late night opening Thu until 8, Apr-Aug only. (Closed Mon, Good Fri & 24-25 Dec). **Facilities:** P (100 metres) (meter parking) ⬛ ♿ (Ramp & reserved parking) toilets for disabled shop ✈ (ex guide dogs) Details not confirmed for 2003

IRISH MUSEUM OF MODERN ART
Royal Hospital, Kilmainham (from city centre pass Heuston Station, 1st left on St John's Rd)
☎ 01 612 9900   📠 01 612 9999
e-mail: info@modernart.ie
Times: Open all year Tue-Sat 10-5.30, Sun & BH's 12-5.30. (Closed 24-26 & 31 Dec & Good Fri). **Facilities:** P ⬛ ♿ (wheelchair available) toilets for disabled shop ✈ (ex guide dogs) Details not confirmed for 2003

JAMES JOYCE CENTRE
35 North Great George's St (near O'Connel Street and Parnell Square)
☎ 01 8788547   📠 01 8788488
e-mail: joycecen@iol.ie

Situated in a beautifully restored 18th-century Georgian town house, the Centre is dedicated to the promotion of a greater interest in, and understanding of, the life and works of Joyce. There is a library open to visitors, exhibition rooms, videos and tapes.
Times: Open all year, Mon-Sat 9.30-5, Sun 12.30-5. (Closed Good Fri & 24-26 Dec). **Fee:** * €4.50 (ch free). Family ticket €12.50 **Facilities:** P (200 mtrs) ⬛ ♿ toilets for disabled shop ✈ (ex guide dogs) ☕

KILMAINHAM GAOL
Inchicore Rd
☎ 01 4535984   📠 01 4532037
Times: Access by guided tour only. Open Apr-Sep, daily 9.30-6 (last tour 4.45); Oct-Mar, Mon-Fri 9.30-5 (last tour 4), Sun 10-6 (last tour 4.45). **Facilities:** P (on street parking only) ⬛ ♿ (tours available by prior appointment) toilets for disabled ✈ Details not confirmed for 2003

MARSH'S LIBRARY
St Patrick's Close (beside St Patrick Cathedral)
☎ 01 4543511   📠 01 4543511
e-mail: keeper@marshlibrary.ie

The first public library in Ireland, dating from 1701. Designed by William Robinson, the interior has been unchanged for 300 years. The collection is of approximately 25,000 volumes of 16th, 17th and early 18th century books.
Times: Open Mon & Wed-Fri, 10-1 & 2-5; Sat 10.30-1. **Fee:** * €2.50 (students & pen €1.25, ch free). **Facilities:** P ✈ 🅿

NATIONAL BOTANIC GARDENS
Glasnevin (on Botanic Road, between N1 and N2)
☎ 01 8374388 & 8377596   📠 01 8360080
Times: Open all year, summer Mon-Sat 9-6, Sun 11-6; winter Mon-Sat 10-4.30, Sun 11-4.30. **Facilities:** P ♿ (Wheelchair available) toilets for disabled ✈ (ex guide dogs) Details not confirmed for 2003

NATIONAL GALLERY OF IRELAND
Merrion Square (5 mins walk from Pearse Station)
☎ 01 6615133   📠 01 6615372
e-mail: artgall@eircom.net
Times: Open Mon-Sat 9.30-5.30 (Thu 9.30-8.30), Sun 12-5.30. (Closed 24-26 Dec & Good Fri). **Facilities:** P (5 mins walk) (meter parking, 2hrs max) ⬛ ✕ licensed ♿ (braille/audio tours, lifts, ramps, parking bay) toilets for disabled shop ✈ Details not confirmed for 2003

NATIONAL LIBRARY OF IRELAND
Kildare St
☎ 01 6030200   📠 01 6766690
e-mail: info@nli.ie
Times: Open: Mon-Wed 10-9, Thu-Fri 10-5 & Sat 10-1. (Closed Sun, Xmas-New Year, Etr & BH's). **Facilities:** ♿ toilets for disabled shop ✈ (ex guide dogs) 🅿 Details not confirmed for 2003

NATIONAL PHOTOGRAPHIC ARCHIVE
Meeting House Square, Temple Bar
☎ 01 6030200   📠 01 6777451
e-mail: photoarchive@nli.ie
Times: Open all year, Mon-Fri 10-5; Sat 10-2 exhibition area only. (Closed BH's). **Facilities:** ♿ toilets for disabled shop ✈ (ex guide dogs) Details not confirmed for 2003 ☕

NATURAL HISTORY MUSEUM
Merrion St
☎ 01 6777444   📠 01 6766116
Times: Open Tue-Sat 10-5, Sun 2-5. **Facilities:** P (parking meters wkdays) ♿ ✈ Details not confirmed for 2003

Co Dublin – Co Galway

NEWMAN HOUSE
University College Dublin, 86 St Stephens Green (South side of St Stephen's Green)
☎ 01 7067422 & 4757255   01 7067211

Newman House consists of two superb Georgian town houses, containing some of Ireland's finest 18th-century plasterwork and decoration. As the founding home of University College Dublin in 1854, the house has been associated with many famous literary and historical figures, including John Henry Newman, Gerard Manley Hopkins and James Joyce.
Times: Open Jun-Aug, Tue-Fri 12-5, Sat 2-5. Tours, Tue-Fri; 12,2,3 & 4; Sat 2,3 & 4. At other times tours by prior arrangement only. **Fee:** * €4 (concessions €3). **Facilities:** P (100yds) ✖ licensed ✈ (ex guide dogs)

NUMBER TWENTY NINE
29 Lower Fitzwilliam St (on the corner of Lower Fitzwilliam St & Upper Mount Sq)
☎ 01 7026165   01 7027796
e-mail: numbertwentynine@mail.esb.ie

Number Twenty-Nine is an exhibition of the home life of a middle-class merchant family in Dublin, in the late 18th and early 19th century.
Times: Open all year, Tue-Sat 10-5, Sun 2-5. (Closed Mon & 2 wks prior to Xmas). **Fee:** €3.15 (ch under 16 free, other concessions €1.25). **Facilities:** P (on street 1 hour meter) 🍴 shop ✈

PHOENIX PARK VISITOR CENTRE
Phoenix Park
☎ 01 6770095   01 8205584
Times: Open all year; Jun-Sep, daily 10-6; Apr-May, daily 9.30-5.30; mid-end Mar & Oct, daily 9.30-5; Jan-mid Mar & Nov-Dec, Sat & Sun 9.30-4.30. Last admission 45 mins before closing. **Facilities:** P 🍴 ♿ toilets for disabled ✈ (ex guide dogs) *Details not confirmed for 2003*

GEORGE BERNARD SHAW HOUSE
33 Synge St
☎ 01 4750854 & 8722077   01 8722231
e-mail: dublin-tourism@msn.com
Times: Open May-Oct, Mon-Sat 10-5, Sun & PH's 11-5. **Facilities:** P (charged) shop garden centre ✈ (ex guide dogs) *Details not confirmed for 2003*

🚂 DUN LAOGHAIRE   Map 01 D4
JAMES JOYCE TOWER
Joyce Tower, Sandycove (1m SE Dun Laoghaire by coast road to Sandycove Point or turn off main Dun Laoghaire-Dalkey road)
☎ 01 2809265 & 8722077   2809365
e-mail: joycetower@dublintourism.ie

Built by the British as a defence against a possible invasion by Napoleon, the tower has walls approximately 8ft thick and an original entrance door 13ft above the ground. The tower was once the temporary home of James Joyce, who depicted this setting in the opening scene of *'Ulysses'*. The structure is now a museum devoted to the author. Bloomsday, the day in 1904 on which all the action of *'Ulysses'* is set, is celebrated annually on 16th June. On this day,

the museum is open from 8-6 for visits, readings from *'Ulysses'* and performances of various kinds, Edwardian costume is encouraged.
Times: Open Apr-Oct, Mon-Sat 10-1 & 2-5, Sun & BHs 2-6; Nov-Mar by arrangement. **Fee:** * €5.50 (ch 3-11 €3, pen, students & ch 12-17 €5). Family ticket €15. Parties 20+. **Facilities:** P (100yds) ♿ shop ✈ (ex guide dogs) 🍴

🚂 MALAHIDE   Map 01 D4
FRY MODEL RAILWAY
Malahide Castle Demesne
☎ 01 8463779 & 8462184   01 8463723
e-mail: fryrailway@dublintourism.ie

The Fry Model Railway is a rare collection of `O' gauge trains and trams, depicting the history of Irish rail transport from the first train that ran in 1834. Cyril Fry began to build his model collection in his attic, in the late 1920s. All the models are built to scale, and they are now housed in a purpose-built setting adjacent to Malahide Castle.
Times: Open all year, Apr-Sep, Mon-Sat 10-5, Sun & PH 2-6; Nov-Mar Sat-Sun & PH 2-5. Parties at other times by arrangement. Closed 1-2pm **Fee:** * €5.50 (ch €3, concessions €5). Family ticket €15. Combined ticket for related attractions available. **Facilities:** P ♿ shop ✈ 🍴

MALAHIDE CASTLE
(From Dublin city centre follow signs for Malahide, then approaching the village, main entrance to castle is signposted to right)
☎ 01 8462184 & 8462516   01 8462537
e-mail: malahidecastle@dublintourism.ie

One of Ireland's oldest castles, this romantic and beautiful structure, set in 250 acres of grounds, has changed very little in 800 years. Tours offer views of Irish period furniture and historical portrait collections. Additional paintings from the National Gallery depict figures from Irish life over the last few centuries.
Times: Open all year, Apr-Oct, Mon-Sat 10-5, Sun & PH 11-6; Nov-Mar, Mon-Sat 10-5, Sun & BH 11-5. (Closed for tours 12.45-2). **Fee:** * €5.50 (ch €3, concessions €5). Family ticket €15. Combined tickets for related attractions available. **Facilities:** P 🍴 ✖ licensed shop ✈ 🍴

CO GALWAY

🚂 GALWAY   Map 01 B3
ATLANTAQUARIA
Galway Atlantaquaria, Salthill (Follow signs for Salthill, over Wolfe Tone Bridge, along Fr Griffin Rd, White Sand Rd & along The Promenade)
☎ 091 585100   091584360
e-mail: atlantaquaria@eircom.net

Concentrating on the native Irish marine ecosystem, the Galway Atlantiquaria contains some 170 species of fish and sealife, and features both fresh and saltwater exhibits.
Times: Open Apr, May, Jun & Sep daily 10-5; Jul & Aug daily 10-8; Oct-Dec, Jan-Mar Wed-Sun 10-5. Closed Mon & Tue. **Fee:** * €7 (ch 3-14 €4, student, pen €5) family ticket (1ad+2ch) €15, (2ad+2ch)€21 **Facilities:** P 🍴 ✖ ♿ special discounts toilets for disabled shop ✈ (ex guide dogs) 🍴

Galway City Museum
Spanish Arch
☎ 091 567641 ✉ 091 567641
Times: Open all year daily, Mar-Oct 10-5.15. Nov-Feb 2-4, times under review. **Facilities:** P (100yds) (parking discs required) ♿ ✈ (ex guide dogs) *Details not confirmed for 2003*

Nora Barnacle House Museum
Bowling Green (close to St Nicholas Collegiate Church, in city centre)
☎ 091 564743

The smallest museum in Ireland, this tiny turn-of-century house was the home Nora Barnacle, companion, wife and lifelong inspiration of James Joyce. It was here in 1909, sitting at the kitchen table that Joyce first met his darling's mother. Letters, photographs and other exhibits of the lives of James Joyce & Nora Barnacle make a visit here a unique experience.
Times: Open Jun-Aug, Wed-Fri during summer months. Opening times may vary. **Fee:** * €2.50 (students €2). **Facilities:** P (100yds) (disc parking)

Royal Tara China Visitor Centre
Tara Hall, Mervue (Follow the N6 from the Galway Tourist office. At rndbt take 2nd left and at the lights turn right)
☎ 091 705602 ✉ 091 757574
e-mail: visitor@royal-tara.com

Royal Tara China visitor centre, located minutes from the city centre, operates from a 17th-century Mansion. Free factory tours, five factory showrooms and coffee shop. No admission charge.
Times: Open all year, 9-6 (9-8 Jul-Sep, 9-9 Dec). Guided factory tours Mon-Fri 9.30-3.30. **Fee:** Free. **Facilities:** P 🍽 ✈ licensed ♿ all facilities accessible for disabled toilets for disabled shop ✈ (ex guide dogs) 👨‍🍳

✱ An asterisk by an entry indicates that the prices shown are for 2002 only. Please contact the attraction for up-to-date price information.

Are there any great Days Out that we've missed? Use the Readers' Report form at the back of the book to tell us about them

---

♿ GORT   Map 01 B3
Thoor Ballylee
(1km off N18, 1km off N66)
☎ 091 631436 & 537733 ✉ 091 631436

This tower house is the former home of the poet William Butler Yeats and this is where he completed most of his literary works. The tower, which has been restored to appear exactly as it was when he lived there, houses an Interpretative Centre with audio-visual presentations and displays of his work.
Times: Open 31 May-Sep 10-6 Mon-Sat **Fee:** * €5 (ch €1, pen & students €4.50). Family ticket €10. Party. **Facilities:** P ♿ (audio-visual presentation) toilets for disabled shop ✈ (ex guide dogs) 👨‍🍳

♿ KINVARRA   Map 01 B3
Dunguaire Castle
☎ 091 37108 & 061 360788 ✉ 061 361020
e-mail: liddyt@shannon-dev.ie
Times: Open May-mid Oct, daily 9.30-5.30 (last admission 4.30pm).
Facilities: P shop ✈ (ex guide dogs) *Details not confirmed for 2003* 👨‍🍳

♿ PORTUMNA   Map 01 B3
Portumna Castle & Gardens
☎ 0509 41658
Times: Open mid Apr-Sep, daily 9.30-6.30. **Facilities:** P ♿ (access limited) ✈ (ex guide dogs) *Details not confirmed for 2003*

♿ ROUNDSTONE   Map 01 A4
Roundstone Music, Crafts & Fashion
Craft Centre (Take N59 Galway to Clifden road. Turn left at Roundstone sign, 7m to village. Roundstone Music at the top of village)
☎ 095 35875 ✉ 095 35980
e-mail: bodhran@iol.ie

The Roundstone Music Craft is located within the walls of an old Franciscan Monastery. Here you can see Ireland's oldest craft – the Bodhran being made and regular talks and demonstrations are given. The 1st *Riverdance* stage drums were made here and are still on display in the Craftsman's Craftshop. There is an outdoor picnic area alongside the bell tower in a beautiful location by the water where the dolphins swim up to the wall in summer.
Times: Open Apr-Oct 9.30-6, Jul-Sep 9-7, Winter 6 days 9.30-6. **Fee:** Free. **Facilities:** P 🍽 ♿ toilets for disabled shop

---

CO KERRY

♿ CASTLEISLAND   Map 01 B2
Crag Cave
(1m N, signposted off N21)
☎ 066 7141244 ✉ 066 7142352
e-mail: info@cragcave.com

Crag Cave is one of the longest surveyed cave systems in Ireland, with a total length of 3.81km. It is a spectacular world, where pale forests of stalagmites

continued

and stalactites, thousands of years old, throw eerie shadows around vast echoing caverns complemented by dramatic sound and lighting effects. Tours last about 30 minutes.
Times: Open daily, mid Mar-1 Nov 10-6 (Jul-Aug until 6.30). Last tour 30 minutes before closing time. **Fee:** * €5.50 (ch €3.25, pen & students €4.50). Family ticket €15.50 **Facilities:** P ⌂ ✗ licensed ♿ (ramp to visitor centre) toilets for disabled shop ✈ (ex guide dogs) ⚑

DUNQUIN Map 01 A2
THE BLASKET CENTRE
(10m W of Dingle town, on Slea Head Drive)
☎ 066 9156444 & 9156371   📠 066 9156446
e-mail: mdemordha@eolga.ie
Times: Open daily, Etr-late Oct 10-6 (7 Jul-Aug). Open on request all year for groups over 30. Last admission 45mins before closing.
Facilities: P ⌂ ✗ licensed ♿ (reserved parking) toilets for disabled ✈ (ex guide dogs) *Details not confirmed for 2003*

KILLARNEY Map 01 B2
KILLARNEY TRANSPORT MUSEUM
Scotts Hotel Gardens (centre of town, opposite railway station)
☎ 064 34677 📠 064 32638

A unique collection of Irish veteran, vintage and classic cars, motorcycles, bicycles, carriages and fire engines. Exhibits include the 1907 Silver Stream, reputed to be the rarest car in the world, it was designed and built by an Irishman and he only made one!
Times: Open Apr, May, Sep & Oct 11-5. Jun, Jul & Aug 10-6 **Fee:** €4 (ch €2.50, students & pen €2.50). Family ticket €10.50-€12. Wheelchair visitors free. Party. **Facilities:** P ⌂ ✗ licensed ♿ shop

MUCKROSS HOUSE, GARDENS & TRADITIONAL FARMS
Muckross (4m on Kenmare Road)
☎ 066 31440 & 35571 📠 066 33926
e-mail: mucros@iol.ie
Times: Open Jul-Aug, daily 9-7; 17 Mar-Jun & Sep-Oct, 9-6; Nov-16 Mar 9-5.30. **Facilities:** P ✗ licensed ♿ toilets for disabled shop ✈ (ex guide dogs) *Details not confirmed for 2003* ⚑

TRALEE Map 01 A2
KERRY THE KINGDOM MUSEUM
Ashe Memorial Hall, Denny St (Town centre, follow signs for museum & tourist information office)
☎ 066 712 7777 📠 066 712 7444
e-mail: info@kerrymuseum.com
Times: Open daily, 17 Mar-20 Dec. Mar-Oct 10-5.30, Nov-Dec noon-4.
Facilities: P ⌂ ♿ (special time car through Medieval Experience) toilets for disabled shop ✈ (ex guide dogs) *Details not confirmed for 2003* ⚑

VALENTIA ISLAND Map 01 A2
THE SKELLIG EXPERIENCE
(Ring of Kerry Road, signed after Cahersiveen then Valentia bridge or ferry from Rena Rd Point)
☎ 066 9476306 📠 066 9476351
e-mail: info@skelligexperience.com

The Skellig Rocks are renowned for their scenery, sea bird colonies, lighthouses, Early Christian monastic architecture and rich underwater life. The two islands - Skellig Michael and Small Skellig - stand like fairytale castles in the Atlantic Ocean, rising to 218 metres and their steep cliffs plunging 50 metres below the sea. The Heritage Centre, (on Valentia Island, reached from the mainland via a bridge), tells the story of the Skellig Islands in an exciting multimedia exhibition. Cruises around harbour.
Times: Open 25 Mar-Jun & Sep 10-7, Jul-Aug 9.30-7 (last tour 6.15). Oct-mid Nov, Sun-Thu 10-5.30. **Fee:** €4.40 (ch €2.20, pen & student €3.80). Family ticket €10. **Facilities:** P ⌂ ♿ toilets for disabled shop ✈ (ex guide dogs) ⚑

CO KILDARE

CELBRIDGE Map 01 D4
CASTLETOWN
(13m from Dublin, follow signs to Celbridge from N4)
☎ 01 6288252 📠 01 6271811
e-mail: castletown@ealga.ie
Times: Open Etr Day-Sep Mon-Fri 10-6, Sat-Sun & BH 1-6; Oct Mon-Fri 10-5, Sun & BH 1-5; Nov Sun 1-5. Restoration continues.
Facilities: P ⌂ ♿ toilets for disabled ✈ (ex guide dogs) *Details not confirmed for 2003*

KILDARE Map 01 C3
JAPANESE GARDENS
Irish National Stud, Tully (Off N7)
☎ 045 521617 & 522763 📠 045 522964
e-mail: japenesegardens@eircom.net

Situated in the grounds of the Irish National Stud, the gardens were established by Lord Wavertree between 1906 and 1910, and symbolise 'The Life of Man' in a Japanese-style landscape. You can also visit the Horse Museum which includes the skeleton of Arkle. The Commemorative Millennium Garden of St Fiachra seeks to capture the power of the Irish landscape in its rawest state, that of rock and water.
Times: Open 12 Feb-12 Nov, daily 9.30-6, last admission 5. **Fee:** €8.50 (ch under 12 €4.50, students & pen €6.50). Family ticket €18 **Facilities:** P ✗ licensed ♿ (all parts of stud accessible, only small part of gardens) toilets for disabled shop ✈ (ex on lead) ⚑

Counties Kilkenny, Limerick, Longford, Mayo, Monaghan

CO KILKENNY

KILKENNY Map 01 C3
KILKENNY CASTLE
☎ 056 21450 📠 056 63488
Times: Open all year - Jun-Sep, daily 10-7; Apr-May, daily 10.30-5; Oct-Mar, Tue-Sat 10.30-12.45 & 2-5, Sun 11-12.45 & 2-5. Last tour 45mins before closing. (Closed Xmas & Good Fri). **Facilities:** P (charged) ☕ & shop ✱ (ex guide dogs) *Details not confirmed for 2003*

CO LIMERICK

FOYNES Map 01 B3
FOYNES FLYING BOAT MUSEUM
(on N69 in Village of Foynes, 23m from Limerick city)
☎ 069 65416 📠 069 65416
e-mail: famm@eircom.net

The museum recalls the era of the flying boats during the 1930s and early 1940s when Foynes was an important airport for air traffic between the United States and Europe. There is a comprehensive range of exhibits, graphic illustrations and a 1940's style cinema featuring a 17-minute film - all original footage from the 30s and 40s. This is where Irish coffee was first invented by chef, Joe Sheridan, in 1942.
Times: Open 31 Mar-Oct, daily 10-6. Last admissions 5.15pm. **Fee:** * €4.50 (ch €2.50, student €3.50). Family ticket €11. **Facilities:** P ☕ & toilets for disabled shop ✱ (ex guide dogs)

HOLYCROSS Map 01 C3
LOUGH GUR STONE AGE CENTRE
Bruff Rd (17 km S of Limerick City, off R512 to Kilmallock)
☎ 061 385186 & 061 360788 📠 061 361020
e-mail: liddyt@shannon-dev.ie
Times: Open May-Sep, daily 10-6 (last admission 5pm) **Facilities:** P ☕ & shop ✱ (ex guide dogs) *Details not confirmed for 2003*

KILCORNAN Map 01 B3
CELTIC PARK & GARDENS
(N69 Limerick to Tralee road)
☎ 061 394243

Located on an original Celtic settlement in one of the most important Cromwellian plantations in the south-west of Ireland. As you walk through the park there's plenty to see, including a church built in 1250, a Mass rock, dolmen, a stone circle, lake dwellings, cooking site, Celtic tomb and a fine example of a ring fort. The gardens contain over 1000 roses, flowering shrubs, a rockery, herbaceous borders, shrubbery, large pool and colonnades.
Times: Open mid Mar-Oct, daily 9.30-6. **Fee:** €5 (€4 pen & students, ch under 12 free accompanied by parent). **Facilities:** P ☕ shop

LIMERICK Map 01 B3
KING JOHN'S CASTLE
Nicholas St
☎ 061 411201 & 360788 📠 061 361020
e-mail: liddyt@shannon-dev.ie
Times: Open Apr-Oct daily 9.30-5.30 (last admission 4.30); Jul & Aug open until 6pm; Nov-Mar 10.30-4.30 (last admission 3.30pm).
Facilities: P ☕ & (lifts and ramps) toilets for disabled shop ✱ (ex guide dogs) *Details not confirmed for 2003*

THE HUNT MUSEUM
The Custom House, Rutland St (a short walk from Arthur's Quay)
☎ 061 312833 📠 061 312834
e-mail: info@huntmuseum.com

On show at the Hunt Museum is one of Ireland's finest private collections of art and antiquities. Reflecting Ireland's Celtic past as well as masterworks by Da Vinci and Renoir. Set in an 18th-century customs house beside the broad majestic Shannon.
Times: Open daily Mon-Sat 10-5, Sun 2-5. **Fee:** * €5.70 (ch €2.80, concessions €4.45). Family ticket €14. Party. **Facilities:** P (50mtrs) (parking discs for street parking) ☕ ✱ licensed & toilets for disabled shop ✱ (ex guide dogs)

CO LONGFORD

KEENAGH Map 01 C4
CORLEA TRACKWAY VISITOR CENTRE
(Off R397, 3km from village)
☎ 043 22386 📠 043 22442
Times: Open Apr-1 Oct, daily 10-6. Last admission 45 mins before closing. **Facilities:** P ☕ & toilets for disabled ✱ (ex guide dogs) *Details not confirmed for 2003*

CO MAYO

BALLYCASTLE Map 01 B5
CÉIDE FIELDS
(5m W on R314)
☎ 096 43325 📠 096 43261
Times: Open Jun-Sep, daily 9.30-6.30; mid Mar-May & Oct, daily 10-5; Nov, daily 10-4.30; other times by arrangement. **Facilities:** P ☕ & toilets for disabled ✱ (ex guide dogs) *Details not confirmed for 2003*

CO MONAGHAN

INNISKEEN Map 01 C4
PATRICK KAVANAGH RURAL & LITERARY RESOURCE CENTRE
Candlefort (From Dundalk: Take R178 (ignore sign on right for Inniskeen). Continue on to Conlon's Pub and turn right for Inniskeen)
☎ 042 78560 📠 042 78560
e-mail: infoatpkc@eircom.net

Birthplace of Patrick Kavanagh, one of Ireland's foremost 20th-century poets. The village grew around the ancient monastery of St Daig MacCairill, founded by 562, and its strong, 10th-century round tower still stands. The centre, housed in the former parish church,

continued

Counties Monaghan, Offaly, Roscommon, Tipperary, Waterford

chronicles the ancient history of the region and its role in developing Kavanagh's work.
Times: Open all year, Tue-Fri 11-5, wknds & BH's 2-6. (Closed Oct-May, wknds & BH's Dec-16 Mar) **Fee:** * €4 (ch 12 free, concessions €2). Kavanagh trail guide Map available €0.65. Kavanagh Country Tours - a guided tour with live performances lasting 90 mins, advance booking essential €7.50 including admission to centre.
Facilities: P ⛽ & toilets for disabled shop

MONAGHAN   Map 01 C5
MONAGHAN COUNTY MUSEUM
1-2 Hill St (near town centre, opposite Tourist Information Office)
☎ (047) 82928   📠 047 71189
e-mail: comuseum@mongkancoco.ie

This is an award-winning museum of local archaeology, history, arts and crafts. Throughout the year various special exhibitions take place.
Times: Open Tue-Fri 10-1 & 2-5 Sat 11-1 & 2-5, closed Sun & Mon **Fee:** Free. **Facilities:** P (near town centre) (restricted on street parking) & ✈

CO OFFALY

BIRR   Map 01 C3
BIRR CASTLE DEMESNE
(In Birr Town square take exit beside Bank of Ireland and bear right. Turn left entrance is on right, car park on left)
☎ 0509 20336   📠 0509 21583
e-mail: info@birrcastle.com
Times: Open all year, 9am-6pm. **Facilities:** P (charged) ⛽ & toilets for disabled shop garden centre (on leads at all times) *Details not confirmed for 2003*

CO ROSCOMMON

BOYLE   Map 01 B4
KING HOUSE
(in town centre, 1km from N4)
☎ 079 63242   📠 079 63243
e-mail: kinghouseboyle@hotmail.com

King House is a magnificently restored Georgian Mansion built around 1730 by Sir Henry King, whose family were one of the most powerful and wealthy in Ireland. After its first life as a home, King House became a military barracks to the famous Connaught Rangers from 1788-1922. In more recent years King House has also been a barracks for the National Irish Army. Today visitors can explore King House and delve into the dramatic episodes of its history with stories of tragic Irish romance, runaway lovers, a duel of honour, a murder trial and feats of bravery and hardship in war.
Times: Open Apr-Sep, daily 10-6 (last admission 5). Pre-booked groups welcome all year round, telephone for details. **Fee:** €4 (ch €2.50, pen & student €3.50). Family ticket €10. Party **Facilities:** P ⛽ ✕ & (lift to all areas, ramps, wide doors) toilets for disabled shop ✈ (ex guide dogs)

STROKESTOWN   Map 01 C4
STROKESTOWN PARK HOUSE GARDEN & FAMINE MUSEUM
Strokestown Park
☎ 078 33013   📠 078 33712
e-mail: info@strokestownpark.ie
Times: Open Apr-Oct, daily 11-5.30. All other times, group bookings only. **Facilities:** P ✕ licensed & (Access for ramps) toilets for disabled shop *Details not confirmed for 2003*

CO TIPPERARY

CAHIR   Map 01 C3
SWISS COTTAGE
Kilcommon (1m from town on Ardfinnan road)
☎ 052 41144   📠 052 42324
Times: Open mid Mar-Apr & Oct-Nov, Tue-Sun 10-1 & 2-4.30; May-Sep, daily 10-6. Last admission 30mins before closing. **Facilities:** P ✈ (ex guide dog) *Details not confirmed for 2003*

CASHEL   Map 01 C3
BRÚ BORÚ HERITAGE CENTRE
☎ 062 61122   📠 062 62700
e-mail: bruboru@comhaltas.com

At the foot of the Rock of Cashel, a 4th-century stone fort, this Heritage Centre is dedicated to the study and celebration of native Irish music, song, dance, story telling, theatre and Celtic studies. There's a Folk Theatre where three performances are held daily in the summer, and in the evening, banquets evoke the Court of Brian Ború, 11th-century High King of Ireland with songs, poems and sagas.
Times: Open Jan-May & Oct-Dec, Mon-Fri 9-5; Jun-Sep Tue-Sat 9-11, Sun-Mon 9-5.30. **Fee:** * Admission to centre free. Night show €13. Exhibition, 'Sounds of History' €5 **Facilities:** P (charged) ⛽ ✕ licensed & (wheelchair bay in theatre) toilets for disabled shop ✈ (ex guide dogs)

CO WATERFORD

LISMORE   Map 01 C2
LISMORE CASTLE GARDENS
(On Dungarvan rd N72 just centre of Lismore)
☎ 058 54424   📠 058 54896
e-mail: lismoreestates@eircom.net

Lismore Castle is the Irish home of the Duke of Devonshire. The beautifully situated walled and woodland gardens contain a fine collection of camelias, magnolias and other shrubs, and a remarkable Yew Walk.
Times: Open 16 Mar-29 Sep, daily 1.45-4.45. (Open at 11 during Jul & Aug). **Fee:** * €4 (ch under 16 €2). Party 20+. **Facilities:** P & (some of grounds are accessible) *Details not confirmed for 2003*

WATERFORD
Map 01 C2

WATERFORD CRYSTAL VISITOR CENTRE
(on N25, 1m from city centre)
☎ 051 73311 ▤ 051 78539
Times: Tours of factory: Apr-Oct, daily 8.30-4, gallery daily 8.30-6; Nov-Feb, Mon-Fri 9-3.15, gallery 9-5. **Facilities:** P ⬛ ✗ ♿ (special tours on request) toilets for disabled shop ✈ *Details not confirmed for 2003* ❦

CO WEXFORD

FERRYCARRIG
Map 01 D3

IRISH NATIONAL HERITAGE PARK
(3m from Wexford, on N11)
☎ 053 20733 ▤ 053 20911
e-mail: info@inhp.com

Fourteen historical sites set in a magnificent 35-acre mature forest explaining Ireland's history from the Stone and Bronze Ages, through the Celtic period and concluding with the Vikings and Normans. Among the exhibits are a reconstructed Mesolithic camp, a Viking boatyard with two full size ships and a Norman motte and bailey. Please ring for details of special events.
Times: Open Nov-Mar daily 9.30-5.30. Mar-Nov 9.30-6.30 Last admission 5. Allow 1.5 hour for visit. **Fee:** * €7 (pen & students €5.50). Family ticket €17.50. Group rates available on request. **Facilities:** P ⬛ ✗ licensed ♿ toilets for disabled shop ✈ (ex guide dogs) ❦

NEW ROSS
Map 01 C3

DUNBRODY ABBEY VISITORS CENTRE
Dunbrody Abbey, Campile (10m from New Ross at the base of the Hook Peninsular)
☎ 051 88603

The visitor centre is based around the Abbey itself and Dunbrody Castle. There is an intriguing yew hedge maze with 1,550 yew trees and a museum. In addition there is a golf pitch and putt course with competitions organised twice a month, and a local craft centre.
Times: Open Apr-Sep 10-6 (7pm Jul-Aug). **Fee:** * €2, Family ticket €5. Maze/Golf €3, (ch €1.50). Family €7.50. **Facilities:** P ⬛ ♿ shop garden centre (specialising in conifers & shrubs)

JOHN F KENNEDY ARBORETUM
(12km S of New Ross, off R733)
☎ 051 388171 ▤ 051 388172
Times: Open daily, May-Aug 10-8; Apr & Sep 10-6.30; Oct-Mar 10-5. Last admission 45 mins before closing. (Closed Good Fri & 25 Dec). **Facilities:** P ⬛ ♿ toilets for disabled shop (dogs on lead) *Details not confirmed for 2003*

WEXFORD
Map 01 D3

THE IRISH AGRICULTURAL MUSEUM
Johnstown Castle Old Farmyard (4m SW of Wexford town, signposted off N25)
☎ 053 42888 ▤ 053 42213
e-mail: aosullivan@johnstown.teagasc.ie

This museum has displays on rural transport, farming and the activities of the farmyard and farmhouse; and includes a large exhibition on the history of the potato and the Great Famine (1845-49). Large scale replicas of different workshops, including a blacksmith, cooper and basket worker, and include displays on dairying, cycling, and sugar-beet harvesting and a collection of Irish country furniture. Permanent exhibitions on gardening and the Ferguson System.
Times: Open all year, Jun-Aug Mon-Fri 9-5 & Sat-Sun 11-5; Apr-May & Sep-14 Nov Mon-Fri 9-12.30 & 1.30-5, Sat-Sun 2-5; 15 Nov-Mar Mon-Fri 9-12.30 & 1.30-5 (Closed 25 Dec-2 Jan). **Fee:** €5 (ch & students €3). Family ticket €5. Parking charge May-Sep. **Facilities:** P (charged) ⬛ ♿ toilets for disabled shop ✈ (ex small dogs)

JOHNSTOWN CASTLE GARDENS
Johnstown Castle (4m SW of Wexford town, signposted off N25)
☎ 053 42888 ▤ 053 42004
Times: Open all year, daily 9-5.30. (Closed 25 Dec). **Facilities:** P ⬛ ♿ toilets for disabled *Details not confirmed for 2003*

WEXFORD WILDFOWL RESERVE
North Slob (take coast road over bridge for 3km, signs show turning on right)
☎ 053 23129 ▤ 053 24785
e-mail: cwilson@ealga.ie
Times: Open all year, 15 Apr-Sep 9-6; Oct-14 Apr 10-5. **Facilities:** P ♿ toilets for disabled ✈ (ex guide dogs) *Details not confirmed for 2003*

CO WICKLOW

ENNISKERRY
Map 01 D4

POWERSCOURT GARDENS EXHIBITION
Powerscourt Estate (just off N11 S of Bray, next to Enniskerry)
☎ 01 204 6000 ▤ 01 204 6900
e-mail: gardens@powerscourt.ie

Begun by Richard Wingfield in the 1740s, the gardens are a blend of formal plantings, sweeping terraces, statuary and ornamental lakes together with secret hollows, rambling walks and walled gardens. The house itself incorporates an exhibition which traces the history of the estate, and tells the story of the disastrous fire of 1974 which gutted the house.
Times: Open - Gardens Mar-Oct daily 9.30-5.30; Nov-Feb daily 9.30-dusk. Waterfall Mar-Oct daily 9.30-7; Nov-Feb daily 10.30-dusk.(Please check winter opening times as they are subject to change. Closed 25-26 Dec). **Fee:** * Gardens & House exhibition: €6 (ch €3, students €5) House only €2 (ch €1, students €1.50) Gardens only €4 (ch €2, students €3.50) Waterfall €2.50 (ch €1.50, students €2). Winter rates are cheaper. **Facilities:** P ⬛ ✗ licensed ♿ (Lift to first floor, Wheelchair available) toilets for disabled shop garden centre ❦

KILQUADE   Map 01 D3
NATIONAL GARDEN EXHIBITIONS CENTRE
Calumet Nurseries (7m S of Bray - turn off N11 at Kilpcddcr)
☎ 01 2819890   ▤ 01 2810359
e-mail: calumet@clubi.ie

There are 20 different gardens designed by some of Ireland's leading landscapers and designers. Lectures throughout the year and guided tours during summer. Ring for details and a calender of events. All plants are clearly labelled.
Times: Open Feb-22 Dec, Mon-Sat 10-6, Sun 1-6. **Fee:** * €4.50 (ch under 16 free, pen €3.50). Group rates available. **Facilities:** 🅿 ☕ ♿ shop garden centre ✈ (ex guide dogs) 💳

RATHDRUM   Map 01 D3
AVONDALE HOUSE & FOREST PARK
(1.6km S of town. R752 off N11)
☎ 0404 46111   ▤ 0404 46111
e-mail: costelloe_j@coillte.ie
Times: House: 17 Mar-Oct, 11-6. Outside of these dates group bookings by appointment. Last admission 1 hour before closure. (Closed Good Fri). Park: Open daily. **Facilities:** 🅿 (charged) ✖ licensed ♿ (Special carpark & one forest trail accessible) shop ✈ (ex guide dogs & on lead) *Details not confirmed for 2003* 💳

County Maps

The county map shown here will help you identify the counties within each county. You can look up each county in the guide using the county names at the top of each page. To find towns featured in the guide use the atlas and the index.

England

1. Bedfordshire
2. Berkshire
3. Bristol
4. Buckinghamshire
5. Cambridgeshire
6. Greater Manchester
7. Herefordshire
8. Hertfordshire
9. Leicestershire
10. Northamptonshire
11. Nottinghamshire
12. Rutland
13. Staffordshire
14. Warwickshire
15. West Midlands
16. Worcestershire

Scotland

17. City of Glasgow
18. Clackmannanshire
19. East Ayrshire
20. East Dunbartonshire
21. East Renfrewshire
22. Perth & Kinross
23. Renfrewshire
24. South Lanarkshire
25. West Dunbartonshire

Wales

26. Blaenau Gwent
27. Bridgend
28. Caerphilly
29. Denbighshire
30. Flintshire
31. Merthyr Tydfil
32. Monmouthshire
33. Neath Port Talbot
34. Newport
35. Rhondda Cynon Taff
36. Torfaen
37. Vale of Glamorgan
38. Wrexham

Western Isles
Orkney Islands
Shetland Islands
Highland
Moray
Aberdeen City
Aberdeenshire
SCOTLAND
Angus
Perth & Kinross
Argyll & Bute
Stirling
Dundee City
Fife
East Lothian
North Ayrshire
24
19
Borders (Scottish)
South Ayrshire
Dumfries & Galloway
Argyll & Bute
Stirling
18
22
Fife
25
20
Falkirk
Inverclyde
23
17
North Lanarkshire
West Lothian
City of Edinburgh
Midlothian
North Ayrshire
21
19
South Lanarkshire
Borders (Scottish)
Northumberland
Tyne & Wear
Durham
Cumbria
Isle of Man
North Yorkshire
East Riding of Yorkshire
Lancashire
West Yorkshire
Isle of Anglesey
6
South Yorkshire
Merseyside
Conwy
30
Cheshire
Derbyshire
11
Lincolnshire
29
38
ENGLAND
Gwynedd
13
Norfolk
Shropshire
9
12
WALES
15
5
Ceredigion
Powys
14
10
Suffolk
7
16
1
Pembrokeshire
Carmarthenshire
8
Essex
Gloucestershire
4
Swansea
Oxfordshire
Greater London
31
26
32
3
2
33
35
36
Wiltshire
Surrey
Kent
28
34
27
Cardiff
Somerset
Hampshire
37
West Sussex
East Sussex
Devon
Dorset
Isle of Wight
Cornwall
0
20
40
60
80
100 miles
0
20
40
60
80
100
120
140
160 kilometres
Isles of Scilly
Guernsey
Jersey

KEY TO ATLAS

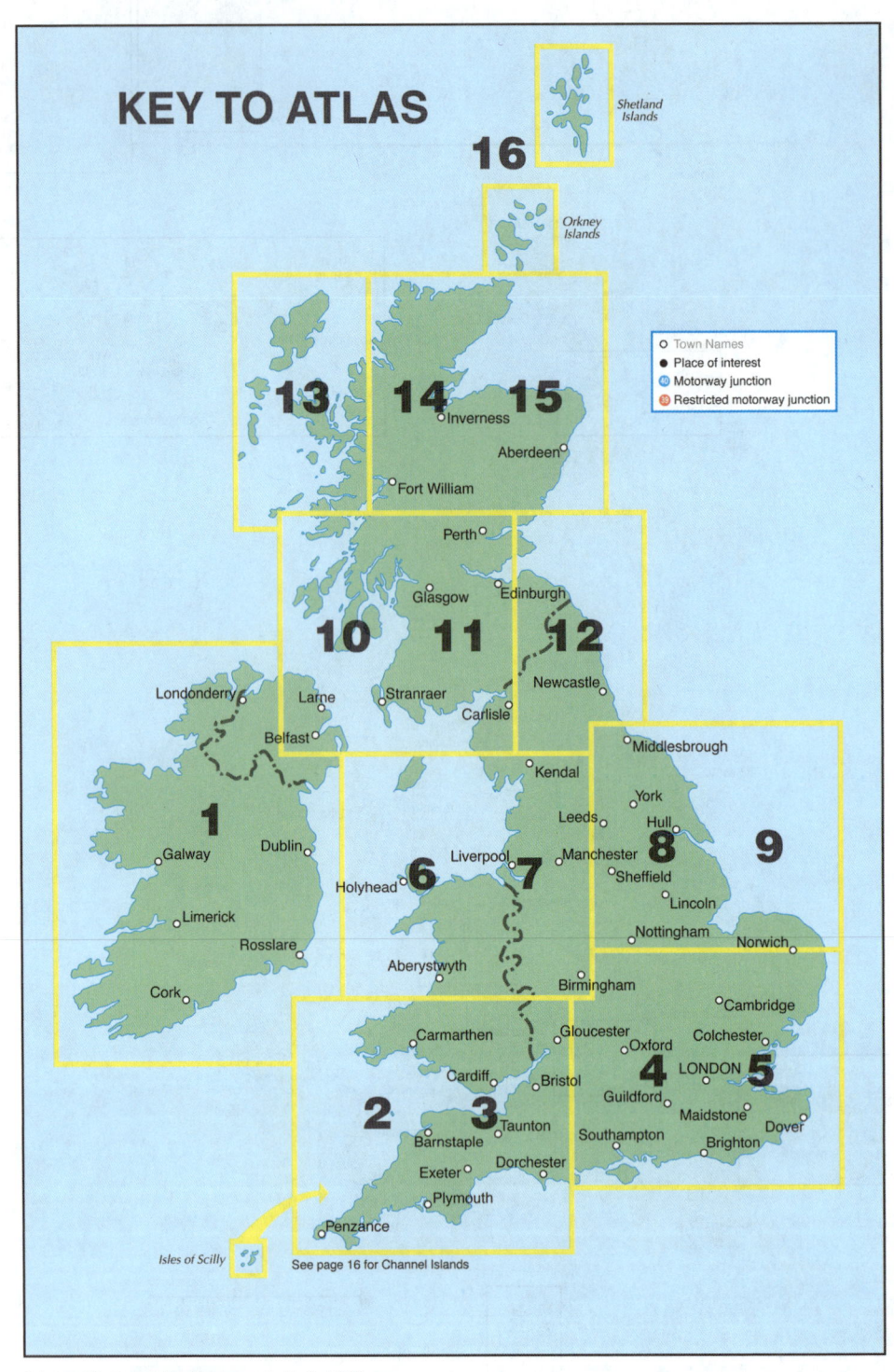

1
A
B
C
D
6
5
4
3
2
1
Rathlin Island
Giant's Causeway
Carrick-a-Rede
Portballintrae
Ballycastle
Bushmills
Downhill
Coleraine
Limavady
Ballymoney
Tory Island
LONDONDERRY
Aran Island
Letterkenny
Dungiven
Ballymena
Larne
Lifford
Maghera
Ballylumford
Templepatrick
Narin
Ardara
Strabane
Churchtown
Antrim
Carrickfergus
Moneymore
Beaghmore
BELFAST
Donaghadee
Newtownstewart
Ardboe
Donegal
Omagh
Cookstown
Oxford Island
Newtownards
Comber
Castle Archdale Bay
Stewartstown
Lisburn
Ballywalter
Saintfield
Hillsborough
Ballyshannon
Castlecaulfield
Killinchy
Ballygawley
Moy
Portadown
Portaferry
Belleek
Benburb
Dromara
Strangford
Derrygonnelly
Enniskillen
Tynan
Armagh
Castlewellan
Downpatrick
Ballycastle
Monaghan
Ardglass
Camlough
Newry
Newcastle
SLIGO
Lisnaskea
Warrenpoint
Newtownbutler
Clones
Jonesborough
Kilkeel
Inniskeen
DUNDALK
Ballina
Cavan
Achill
Boyle
Ardee
Castlebar
Drogheda
Clare
Westport
Castlerea
Strokestown
Inishturk
Longford
Balbriggan
Inishbofin
Roscommon
Navan
Keenagh
Mullingar
Donabate
Lambay
Tuam
Malahide
DUBLIN
Roundstone
Celbridge
ATHLONE
DUN LAOGHAIRE
Enniskerry
GALWAY
BRAY
Gorumna Island
Kildare
Naas
Ballyvaughan
Kinvarra
Birr
PORT LAOISE
Kilquade
Inishmore
Gort
Portumna
Wicklow
Rathdrum
Liscannor
CARLOW
Ennis
Arklow
Quin
Holycross
KILKENNY
Bunratty
LIMERICK
Foynes
Kilcornan
Cashel
New Ross
Tipperary
Ferrycarrig
Cahir
WEXFORD
CLONMEL
Rosslare
TRALEE
WATERFORD
Castleisland
Lismore
Great Blasket Island
Dunquin
Killarney
Blarney
Midleton
CORK
Valentia Island
Kenmare
Ballincollig
Cobh
Carrigtohill
Glengarriff
Kinsale
Bantry
Clonakilty
1 Dungannon
Dursey
Clear
Town Names
Place of Interest
0 20 40 miles
0 20 40 60 kilometres
M1
M2
M4
M7
M9
M11
M50
N15
N16
N17
N4
N26
N2
N3
N6
N7
N8
N9
N18
N20
N21
N22
N24
N25
A4
A5
A6
A32
A36

2

Legend
- ○ Town Names
- ● Places of Interest
- BLAE G — Blaenau Gwent
- BRDGND — Bridgend
- CAERPH — Caerphilly
- MYR TD — Merthyr Tydfil
- NEWPT — Newport
- RHONDD — Rhondda Cynon Taff
- TORFN — Torfaen
- V GLAM — Vale of Glamorgan

Places (Wales / Pembrokeshire / Carmarthenshire)
Aberaeron, Felinwynt, Cardigan, Cilgerran, Cenarth, Strumble Head, Newport, Fishguard, Dre-Fach Felindre, Llanycefn, Crymych, St David's, Ramsey Island, PEMBROKESHIRE, Scolton, Carmarthen, Abergwili, Llangathen, Dryslwyn, St Brides Bay, Llawhaden, St Clears, Llanarthne, Skomer Island, Narberth, Laugharne, Llansteffan, Skokholm Island, Milford Haven, Amroth, Kidwelly, Carew, St Florence, Pembroke, Lamphey, Tenby, Llanelli, Caldey Island, Carmarthen Bay, Llanrhidian, Oxwich, Parkmill

CERED, SN, CARMARTHEN, SWAN, SM

SW Inset (Cornwall)
Goonhavern, ST AUSTELL, Probus, Truro, Pentewan, Zennor, St Ives, Pool, Gorran, Chysauster Ancient Village, Godolphin Cross, Trelissick Garden, Marazion, Wendron, St Mawes, Sancreed, Penzance, Falmouth, Mawnan Smith, Land's End, Helston, Gweek, Mount's Bay, Lizard Point

Cornwall / Devon
Ilfracombe, Combe Martin, Arlington, Lundy, Hartland Point, Appledore, Barnstaple, Clovelly, Great Torrington, Bude, Okehampton, Tintagel, Launceston, Lydford, Camelford, Trevose Head, Padstow, CORNWALL, Morwellham, Tavistock, Isles of Scilly, St Mary's, Wadebridge, Bodmin, Bodmin Moor, Calstock, Yelverton, Tredinnick, Dobwalls, Buckland Abbey, Newquay, Lanhydrock, Liskeard, PLYMOUTH, Plympton, Trerice, Restormel, Lanreath, Fowey, Looe, Torpoint, Yealmpton, SEE INSET, Dodman Point

SS, SX

For continuation pages refer to numbered arrows

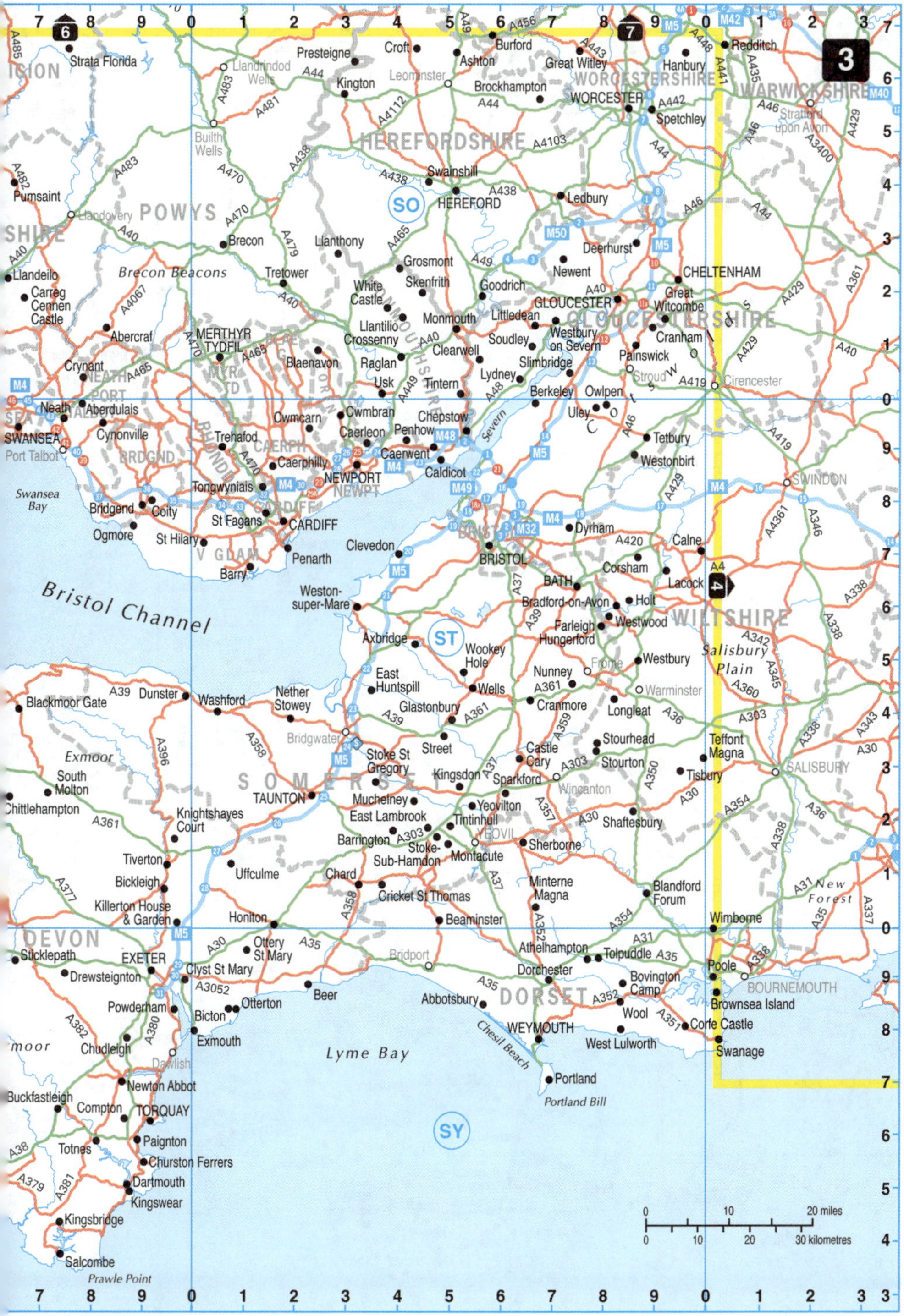
3
Redditch
Hanbury
WARWICKSHIRE
WORCESTERSHIRE
Strata Florida
Presteigne
Croft
Burford
Ashton
Great Witley
Llandrindod Wells
Kington
Leominster
Brockhampton
WORCESTER
Spetchley
Stratford upon Avon
Builth Wells
HEREFORDSHIRE
Swainshill
HEREFORD
Ledbury
Pumsaint
Llandovery
POWYS
SO
Brecon
Llanthony
Grosmont
Deerhurst
Newent
CHELTENHAM
Llandeilo
Carreg Cennen Castle
Brecon Beacons
Tretower
White Castle
Skenfrith
Goodrich
GLOUCESTER
Great Witcombe
GLOUCESTERSHIRE
Abercraf
MERTHYR TYDFIL
Llantilio Crossenny
Monmouth
Littledean
Soudley
Westbury on Severn
Cranham
Painswick
Blaenavon
Raglan
Clearwell
Slimbridge
Crynant
Usk
Tintern
Lydney
Stroud
Cirencester
Neath
Aberdulais
Berkeley
Owlpen
Uley
SWANSEA
Cynonville
Cwmcarn
Cwmbran
Caerleon
Penhow
Chepstow
Tetbury
Port Talbot
Trehafod
Caerwent
Westonbirt
Caerphilly
NEWPORT
Caldicot
SWINDON
Swansea Bay
Tongwynlais
Bridgend
Coity
St Fagans
CARDIFF
Dyrham
Ogmore
St Hilary
Clevedon
Calne
Penarth
BRISTOL
Corsham
Barry
BATH
Lacock
Bristol Channel
Weston-super-Mare
Bradford-on-Avon
Holt
Farleigh Hungerford
Westwood
WILTSHIRE
Axbridge
ST
Wookey Hole
Frome
Westbury
Salisbury Plain
East Huntspill
Wells
Nunney
Warminster
Blackmoor Gate
Dunster
Washford
Nether Stowey
Glastonbury
Cranmore
Longleat
Bridgwater
Stourhead
Teffont Magna
Exmoor
Stoke St Gregory
Street
Castle Cary
Stourton
SALISBURY
South Molton
SOMERSET
Kingsdon
Sparkford
Tisbury
Chittlehampton
TAUNTON
Muchelney
Yeovilton
Wincanton
East Lambrook
Tintinhull
Shaftesbury
Knightshayes Court
YEOVIL
Barrington
Stoke-Sub-Hamdon
Montacute
Sherborne
Tiverton
Uffculme
Chard
Minterne Magna
Blandford Forum
New Forest
Bickleigh
Cricket St Thomas
Killerton House & Garden
Honiton
Beaminster
Wimborne
DEVON
Sticklepath
EXETER
Ottery St Mary
Bridport
Athelhampton
Tolpuddle
Poole
Drewsteignton
Clyst St Mary
Dorchester
Bovington Camp
BOURNEMOUTH
Beer
Abbotsbury
DORSET
Brownsea Island
Powderham
Otterton
Bicton
Wool
Corfe Castle
WEYMOUTH
Exmouth
Chesil Beach
West Lulworth
Swanage
Chudleigh
Lyme Bay
Dawlish
Portland
Newton Abbot
Portland Bill
Buckfastleigh
Compton
TORQUAY
SY
Paignton
Totnes
Churston Ferrers
Dartmouth
Kingswear
Kingsbridge
Salcombe
Prawle Point
0 10 20 miles
0 10 20 30 kilometres

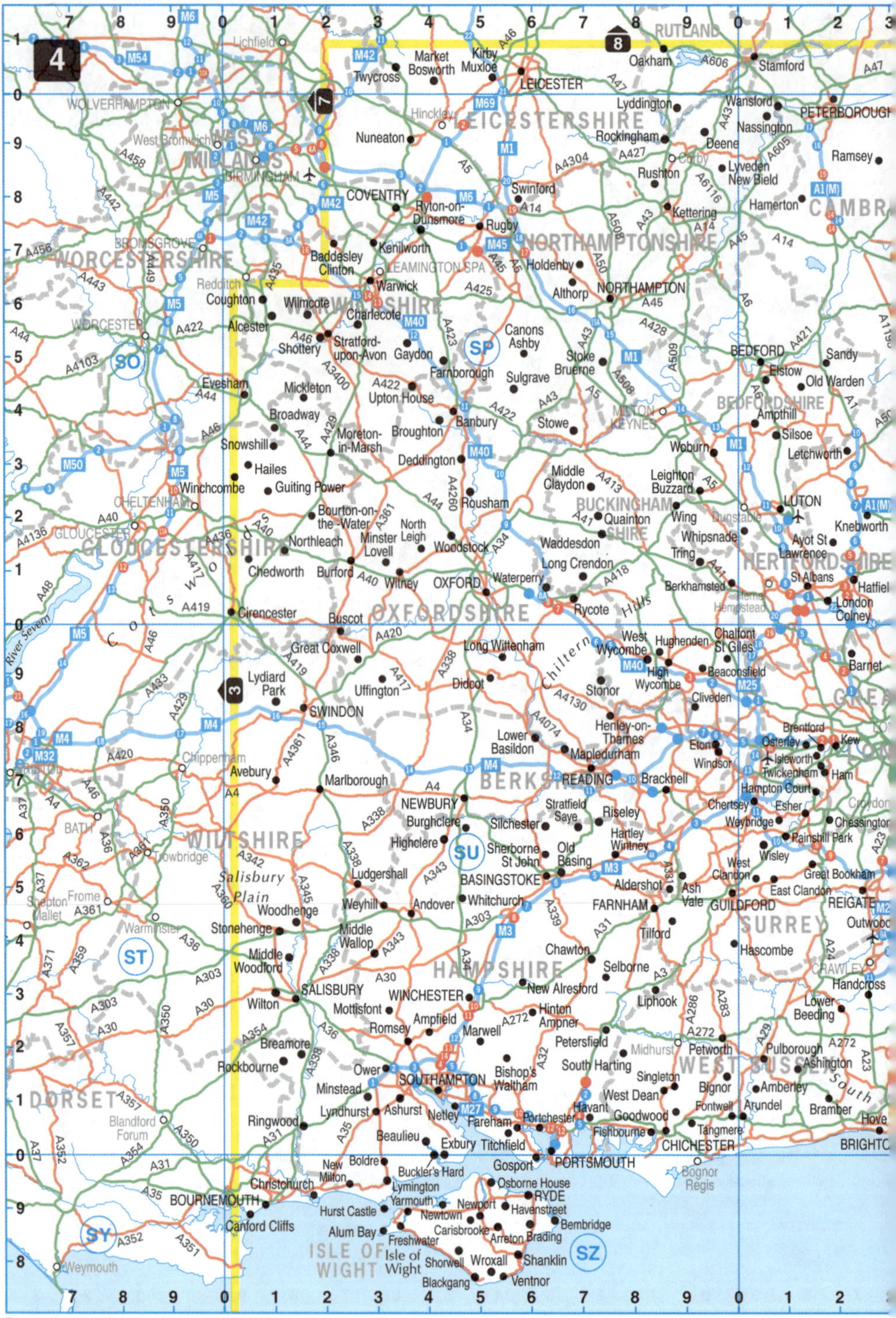

For continuation pages refer to numbered arrows

5
NORFOLK
Oxborough
NORWICH
GREAT YARMOUTH
Reedham
Burgh Castle
St Olaves
LOWESTOFT
March
Welney
Weeting
Grimes Graves
Banham
Bungay
Beccles
Flixton
Suffolk Wildlife Park
Ely
Thetford
Euston
Bressingham
Southwold
DGESHIRE
West Stow
SUFFOLK
Saxtead Green
Westleton
Saxmundham
Lode
Newmarket
BURY ST EDMUNDS
Framlingham
Leiston
CAMBRIDGE
Horringer
Easton
Stowmarket
Wimpole
TL
Lavenham
Orford
Long Melford
Woodbridge
Orford Ness
TM
Cavendish
Duxford
Linton
Lindsey
IPSWICH
Saffron Walden
Castle Hedingham
Sudbury
Audley End
Felixstowe
Newport
Mistley
Harwich
Stansted
The Naze
Braintree
Coggeshall
COLCHESTER
Layer Marney
CLACTON-ON-SEA
Ware
ESSEX
Harlow
CHELMSFORD
Waltham Abbey
Enfield
Foulness Island
Basildon
Hadleigh
SOUTHEND-ON-SEA
R Thames
Tilbury
Sheerness
Isle of Sheppey
Bexley
Chislehurst
Upnor
Swanley
ROCHESTER
Reculver
Birchington
Broadstairs
Eynsford
Gillingham
Chatham
Sittingbourne
Ramsgate
Downe
Borough Green
Aylesford
Faversham
Fordwich
Minster-in-Thanet
Richborough
Brasted
Westerham
Sevenoaks
Ightham
West Malling
Maidstone
North Downs
CANTERBURY
Bekesbourne
Deal
Godstone
Chartwell
Chiddingstone
Beltring
KENT
Swingfield Minnis
TR
Hever
Penshurst
CHANNEL TUNNEL TERMINAL
ASHFORD
East Grinstead
TUNBRIDGE WELLS
Sissinghurst
Dover
Biddenden
Hawkinge
Groombridge Place
Lamberhurst
Goudhurst
Lympne
Folkestone
Ardingly
TQ
Rolvenden
Hythe
Sheffield Park
Burwash
Bodiam
Smallhythe
Dymchurch
Strait of Dover
Haywards Heath
Sheffield Park Station
Northiam
Lydd
Halland
EAST SUSSEX
Rye
Dungeness
Herstmonceux
Battle
Lewes
Glynde
Hailsham
Downs
Firle
HASTINGS
Alfriston
Pevensey
Newhaven
EASTBOURNE
Beachy Head
TV
Town Names
Place of Interest
0 10 20 miles
0 10 20 30 kilometres

For continuation pages refer to numbered arrows

7
12
8
4
3
North York Moors
Yorkshire Dales
THE PENNINES
CUMBRIA
NORTH YORKSHIRE
LANCASHIRE
WEST YORKSHIRE
GREATER MANCHESTER
SOUTH YORKSHIRE
MERSEYSIDE
CHESHIRE
DERBYSHIRE
NOTTINGHAMSHIRE
STAFFORDSHIRE
LEICESTERSHIRE
SHROPSHIRE
WEST MIDLANDS
FLINTS
WREXHAM
Peak District
SD
SE
SJ
SK
SO
SP
Ambleside
Troutbeck
Hawkshead
Windermere
Hardknott Castle
Coniston
Bowness-on-Windermere
Near Sawrey
Kendal
Lakeside
Sizergh
Sedbergh
Levens
Kirkby Lonsdale
Silverdale
Leighton Hall
Holker
Dalton-in-Furness
BARROW-IN-FURNESS
Isle of Walney
MORECAMBE
LANCASTER
Clapham
Richmond
Scotch Corner
Castle Bolton
Hawes
Aysgarth
Middleham
Northallerton
Thirsk
Ripon
Malton
Pateley Bridge
Grassington
Malham
Parcevall Hall Gardens
Harrogate
YORK
Skipton
Ilkley
Fleetwood
Clitheroe
Whalley
Padiham
Keighley
Haworth
BRADFORD
LEEDS
Selby
Blackpool
Salmesbury
PRESTON
Blackburn
Halifax
Lytham St Anne's
Leyland
Turton Bottoms
Rossendale
Goole
Pontefract
Wakefield
Dewsbury
Southport
Rufford
Chorley
HUDDERSFIELD
Martin Mere
Charnock Richard
Bury
Barnsley
Wigan
Prestwich
Oldham
Uppermill
DONCASTER
MANCHESTER
Ashton-under-Lyne
Bootle
St Helens
Salford
Stalybridge
Wallasey
LIVERPOOL
Prescot
Stockport
SHEFFIELD
BIRKENHEAD
Altrincham
Warrington
Bramhall
Castleton
Port Sunlight
Speke
Widnes
Styal
Disley
Holywell
Neston
Runcorn
Knutsford
Nether Alderley
Ellesmere Port
Northwich
Capesthorne
MACCLESFIELD
Buxton
Flint
Ewloe
Mouldsworth
Jodrell Bank
Gawsworth
CHESTER
Beeston
Biddulph
Matlock
Scholar Green
Cheddleton
WREXHAM
Cholmondeley
Nantwich
Newcastle-under-Lyme
STOKE-ON-TRENT
Alton
Ashbourne
Llangollen
Whitchurch
Willoughbridge
NOTTINGHAM
Chirk
DERBY
Uttoxeter
Sudbury
Oswestry
Weston-under-Redcastle
Hodnet
Moreton Corbet
Burton upon Trent
STAFFORD
Shugborough
LOUGHBOROUGH
Haughmond Abbey
Lilleshall
SHREWSBURY
Weston Park
Cannock
Lichfield
Whittington
Oakham
Welshpool
Atcham
Wroxeter
TELFORD
Boscobel
Moseley
Wall
LEICESTER
Acton Burnell
Buildwas
Ironbridge
Benthall
Cosford
Tamworth
Berriew
WOLVERHAMPTON
Much Wenlock
Walsall
Middleton
Montgomery
Halfpenny Green
Himley
West Bromwich
Nuneaton
Quatt
Dudley
BIRMINGHAM
Lydbury North
Craven Arms
Stourbridge
Bournville
COVENTRY
Stokesay
Kidderminster
Solihull
Stone
Ludlow
Bewdley
Packwood House
Bromsgrove
M6
M55
M65
M61
M66
M62
M621
M58
M60
M53
M56
M1
M18
M180
M181
A1(M)
M42
M54
M5
M69
M45
M40
A685
A683
A684
A6108
A593
A590
A6
A65
A683
A59
A682
A6068
A629
A640
A635
A628
A616
A57
A623
A6
A621
A619
A61
A515
A53
A523
A52
A50
A516
A518
A51
A519
A34
A38
A5
A444
A42
A453
A6
A46
A607
A606
A47
A447
A5199
A4304
A427
A508
A14
A45
A46
A456
A4117
A4113
A488
A49
A489
A458
A442
A454
A495
A483
A41
A528
A53
A49
A525
A534
A541
A556
A533
A500
A51
A5
A55
A565
A570
A19
A167
A168
A170
A172
A169
A64
A58
A63
A163
A614
A161
A159
A631
A156
A620
A619
A616
A614
A60
A617
A6097
A1
A38
A52
A607
A606
A5
A6003

For continuation pages refer to numbered arrows

9

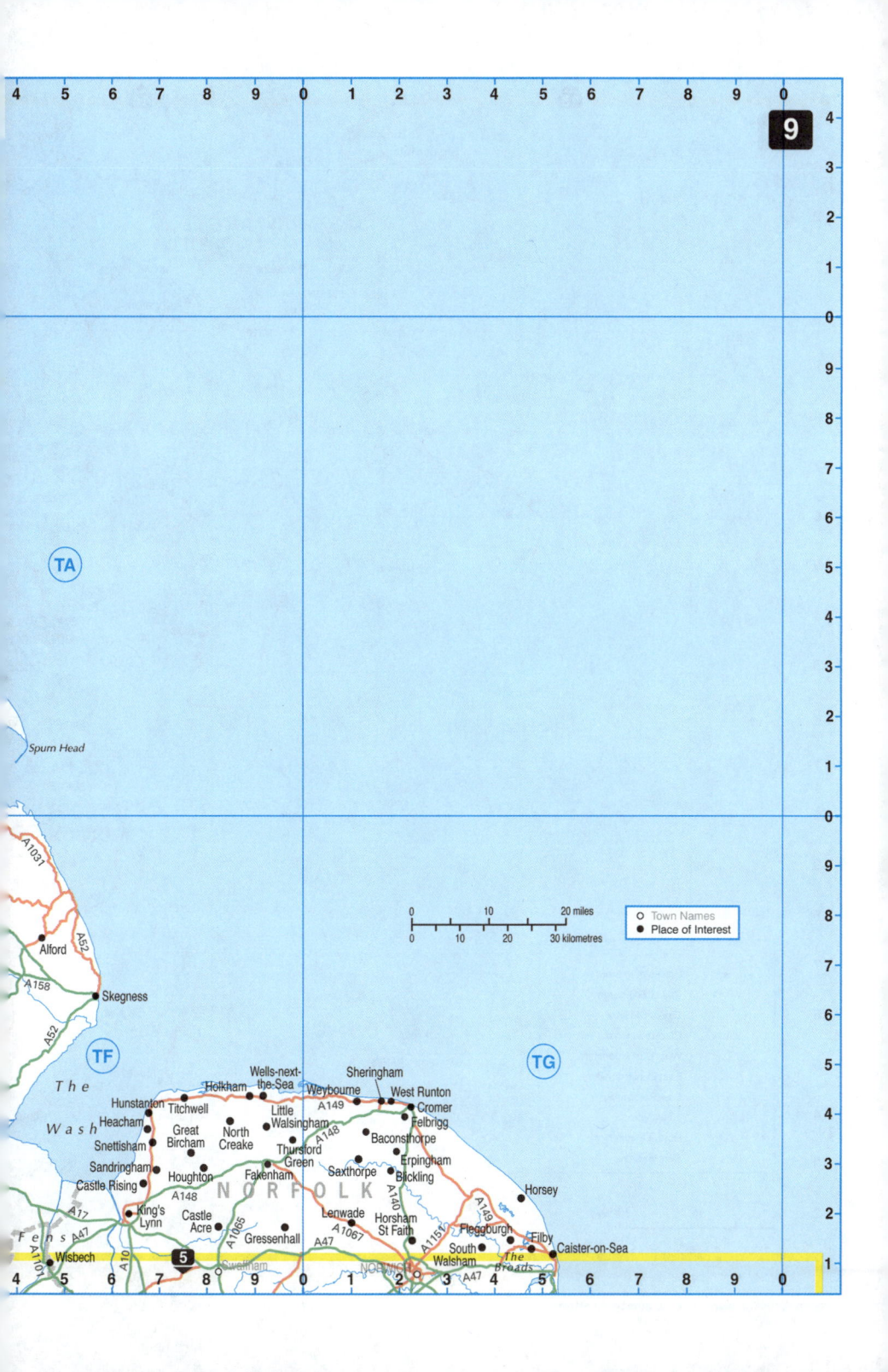

TA

TF

Spurn Head

A1031
Alford
A52
A158
Skegness
A17
The Wash
Hunstanton Titchwell Holkham Wells-next-the-Sea Weybourne Sheringham West Runton Cromer
Heacham
Snettisham Great Bircham North Creake Little Walsingham A149 Baconsthorpe Felbrigg
Sandringham Houghton Thursford Green Saxthorpe Erpingham
Castle Rising A148 Fakenham Bickling
King's Lynn Castle Acre A1065 Lenwade A140 Horsey
Wisbech A10 5 Swaffham Gressenhall A1067 Horsham St Faith A1151 Fleggburgh Filby Caister-on-Sea
Fens A47 South Walsham The Broads
NORFOLK
NORWICH

TG

0 10 20 miles
0 10 20 30 kilometres

○ Town Names
● Place of Interest

10

Argyll and Bute

Tiree, Ulva, Isle of Mull, Craignure, Lismore, Barcaldine, Iona, Firth of Lorne, Oban, Taynuilt, Lochawe, Crianlarich, Luing, Arduaine, Inveraray, Scarba, Carnassarie Castle, Auchindrain, Arrochar, Colonsay, Kilmartin, Oronsay, Benmore, Balloch, Jura, Greenock, Dumbarton, Sound of Jura, Port Glasgow, Langbank, Rothesay, Kilbarchan, Coul Point, Islay, Largs, Lochwinnoch, Sound of Bute, Millport

North Ayrshire

Gigha, Gigha Island, Lochranza, Kilbrannan Sound, Saltcoats, Arran, Brodick, Irvine, Kilmarnock, Holy I, Firth of Clyde, Tarbolton, Kintyre, Campbeltown, Ayr, Alloway, Culzean Castle, Maybole, Kirkoswald, Mull of Kintyre, Old Dailly

South Ayrshire

Ailsa Craig, North Channel, Stranraer, Glenluce, Portpatrick, Loch Ryan, Ardwell, Luce Bay, Port Logan, Mull of Galloway, Whithorn

Legend

○ Town Names
● Places of Interest

C EDIN	City of Edinburgh
C GLAS	City of Glasgow
CLACKS	Clackmannanshire
W DUNS	West Dunbartonshire
E DUNS	East Dunbartonshire
E RENS	East Renfrewshire
INVER	Inverclyde
N LANS	North Lanarkshire
RENS	Renfrewshire

Scale: 0–20 miles / 0–30 kilometres

For continuation pages refer to numbered arrows

11
15
7
12
PERTH AND KINROSS
DUNDEE CITY
FIFE
STIRLING
CLACKS
EAST LOTHIAN
MIDLOTHIAN
SOUTH LANARKSHIRE
EAST AYRSHIRE
BORDERS (SCOTTISH)
DUMFRIES AND GALLOWAY
NORTHUMBERLAND
CUMBRIA
DURHAM
NORTH SEA
NN
NO
NS
NT
NX
NY
Killin
Dunkeld
Scone
PERTH
DUNDEE
Arbroath
Crieff
Muthill
Cupar
St Andrews
St Andrews Bay
Fife Ness
Firth of Tay
Callander
Milnathort
Kinross
Falkland
Doune
Blair Drummond
Port of Menteith
Causewayhead
Alva
Dollar
Alloa
STIRLING
Bannockburn
Dunfermline
Aberdour
KIRKCALDY
Burntisland
Culross
Bo'ness
North Queensferry
South Queensferry
Firth of Forth
Isle of May
Birkhill
Falkirk
Linlithgow
EDINBURGH
Prestonpans
Dunbar
Inveresk
Dalkeith
Gogar
Livingston
Balerno
Newtongrange
Crichton
Penicuik
Milngavie
Bearsden
GLASGOW
Coatbridge
Paisley
Uddingston
Bothwell
Blantyre
Motherwell
East Kilbride
Hamilton
St Abb's Head
Lammermuir Hills
Berwick-upon-Tweed
Holy Island
Peebles
Stobo
New Lanark
Biggar
Innerleithen
Traquair
Galashiels
Uplands
Galston
Coldstream
Kelso
Jedburgh
The Cheviot Hills
Hawick
Wanlockhead
Sanquhar
Alnwick
Southern
Thornhill
Moniaive
Otterburn
Morpeth
DUMFRIES
Drumcoltran Tower
New Abbey
Ruthwell
Caerlaverock
Castle Douglas
Creetown
Palnackie
Cardoness Castle
Kirkcudbright
Wigtown Bay
Dundrennan
Abbey Head
Solway Firth
Burrow Head
CARLISLE
Corbridge
Hexham
Consett
Cockermouth
Bassenthwaite
WORKINGTON
Keswick
Penrith
North Head
Lake District
Grasmere
Rydal
Point of Ayre
M9
M80
M73
M8
M77
M74
M90
A74(M)
M6
A1
A7
A66
A68
A69
A70
A71
A72
A73
A76
A77
A84
A85
A90
A91
A92
A94
A9
A198
A697
A698
A702
A701
A708
A709
A710
A711
A712
A713
A6105
A6112
A6089
A6088
A1107
A689
A686
A688
A691
A695
A696
A595
A596
A5086
A591
A826
A827
A822
A823
A914
A915
A917
A80
A81
A811
A706
A703
A721
A726
A75

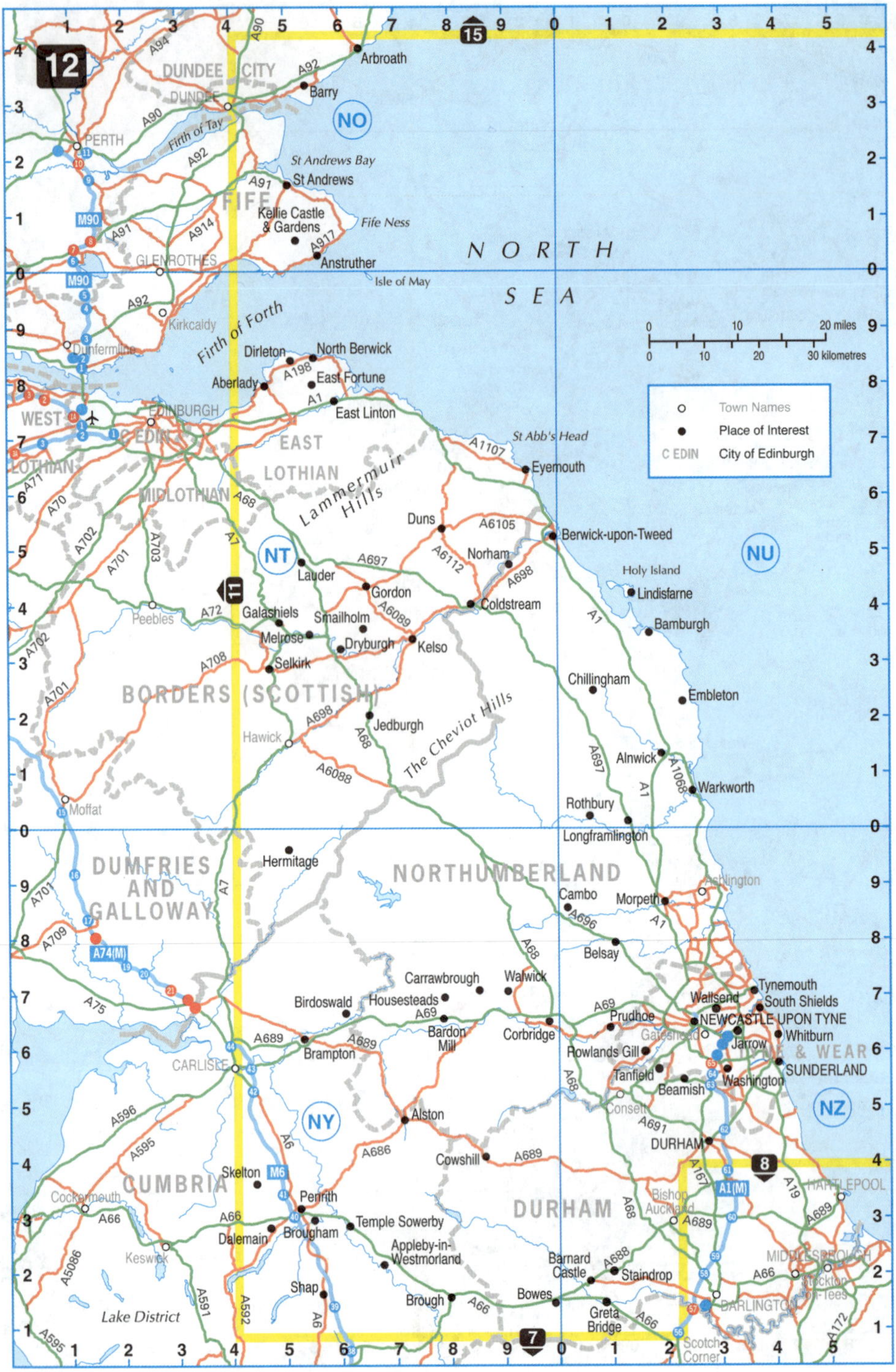

For continuation pages refer to numbered arrows

Town Names
Place of Interest
0 10 20 miles
0 10 20 30 kilometres
NA
NB
NF
NG
NL
NM
Rudha Rhobhanais (Butt of Lewis)
Port Nis (Port of Ness)
A857
Arnol
Carloway
Callanish
Steornabhagh (Stornoway)
Broad Bay
Tolsta Head
Eye Peninsula
Gallan Head
A858
A859
Scarp
Isle of Lewis
The Minch
Point of Stoer
Summer Isles
Greenstone Point
Rudha Reidh
WESTERN ISLES
Outer Hebrides
Taransay
Tairbeart (Tarbert)
Toe Head
Shiant Islands
Pabbay
Harris
Sound of Harris
Uibhist a Tuath (North Uist)
A867
Loch nam Madadh (Lochmaddy)
The Little Minch
A832
Gairloch
14
Uig
A87
Dunvegan Head
Beinn na Faoghla (Benbecula)
Rona
Sound of Raasay
Inner Sound
Raasay
Dunvegan
A896
A890
Uibhist a Deas (South Uist)
A865
Rudha Hallagro
A863
Sconser
Scalpay
Kyle of Lochalsh
Dornie
Isle of Skye
Sound of Barra
Eriskay
Canna
Cuillin
A851
Armadale
Sound of Sleat
Barra
A888
Rum
Sound
Mallaig
Eigg
Mingulay
A830
Muck
Sound of Arisaig
Inner Hebrides
Coll
A861
A848
Sound of Mull
A884
Loch Linnhe
Tiree
10

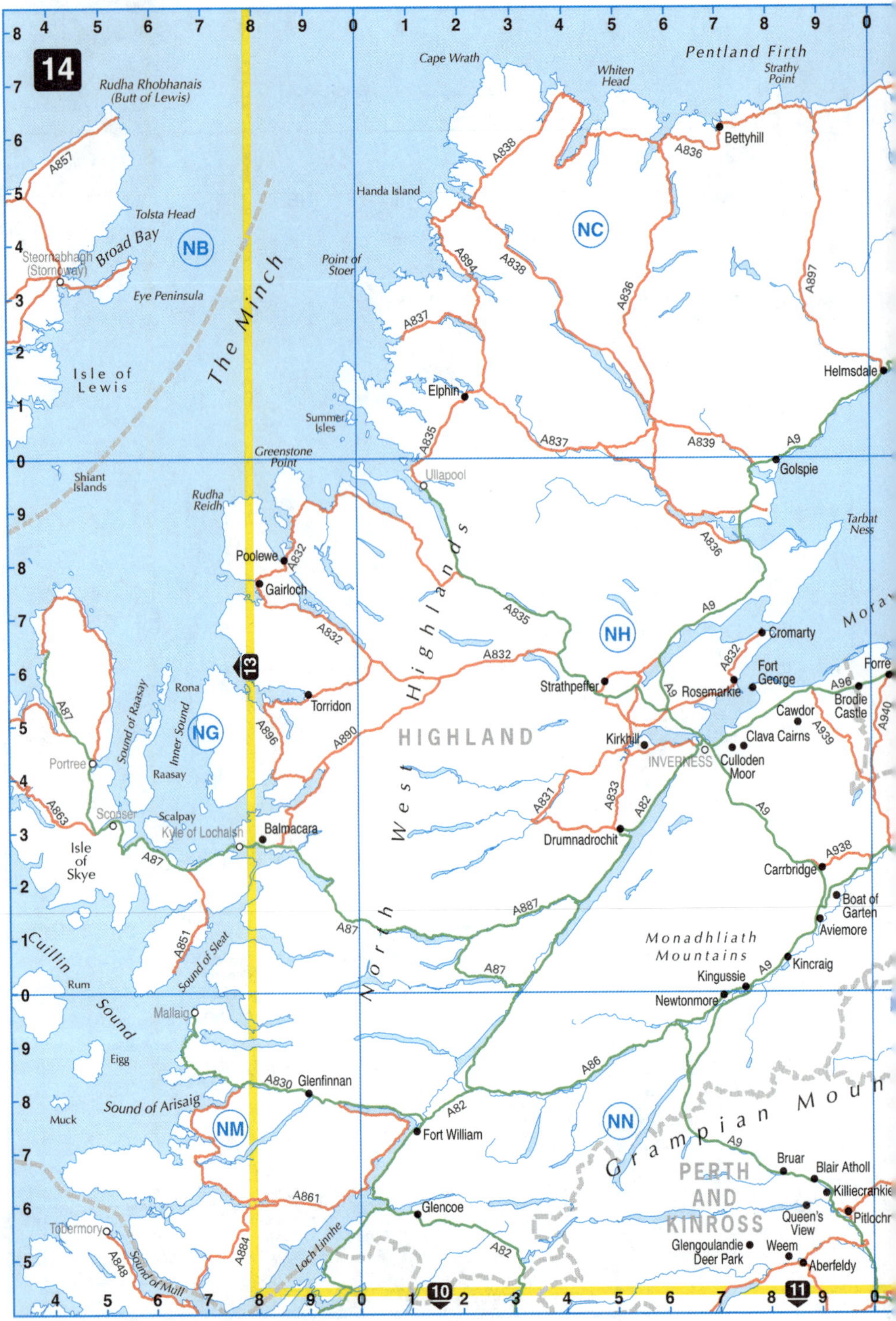

For continuation pages refer to numbered arrows

15
Dunnet Head
Island of Stroma
Duncansby Head
Thurso
A836
A9
Noss Head
Wick
A99
ND
Dunbeath
Firth
Duffus
Spey Bay
Buckie
Banff
Macduff
Fraserburgh
A98
A90
Elgin
Fochabers
NJ
A95
A941
A96
MORAY
Rothes
Keith
Turriff
A950
Mintlaw
Old Deer
Peterhead
NK
Craigellachie
Huntly
A97
A947
A952
Marypark
A95 Dufftown
A920
Methlick
Ballindalloch
Rhynie
Pitmedden
Oyne
ABERDEENSHIRE
Tomintoul
Kildrummy
Alford
Inverurie
Kemnay
A944
A939
ABERDEEN CITY
ABERDEEN
Corgarff
A980
Peterculter
A93
Maryculter
Braemar
Balmoral
Banchory
Crathes
A957
Stonehaven
Town Names
Place of Interest
A92
Fettercairn
NO
Edzell
ANGUS
Brechin
A935
Montrose
Kirriemuir
A926
A932
Glamis
Forfar
A933
Lunan Bay
A924
Arbroath
12
0 10 20 miles
0 10 20 30 kilometres

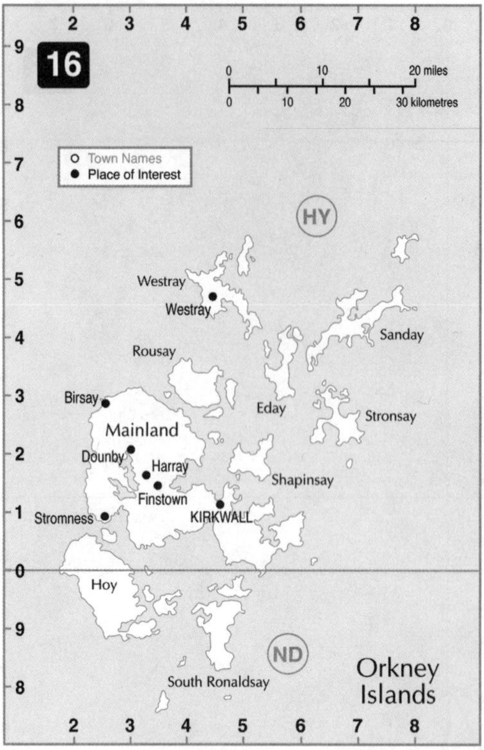
16
0 10 20 miles
0 10 20 30 kilometres
Town Names
Place of Interest
HY
Westray
Westray
Sanday
Rousay
Birsay
Eday
Stronsay
Mainland
Dounby
Harray
Shapinsay
Finstown
Stromness
KIRKWALL
Hoy
ND
South Ronaldsay
Orkney Islands

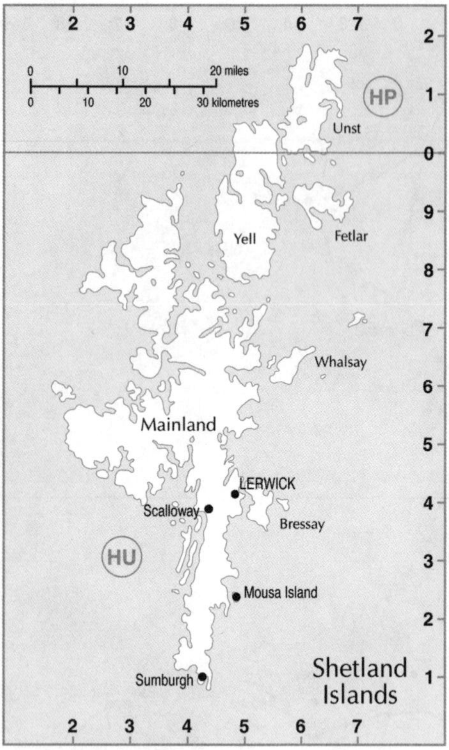
0 10 20 miles
0 10 20 30 kilometres
HP
Unst
Yell
Fetlar
Whalsay
Mainland
LERWICK
Scalloway
Bressay
HU
Mousa Island
Sumburgh
Shetland Islands

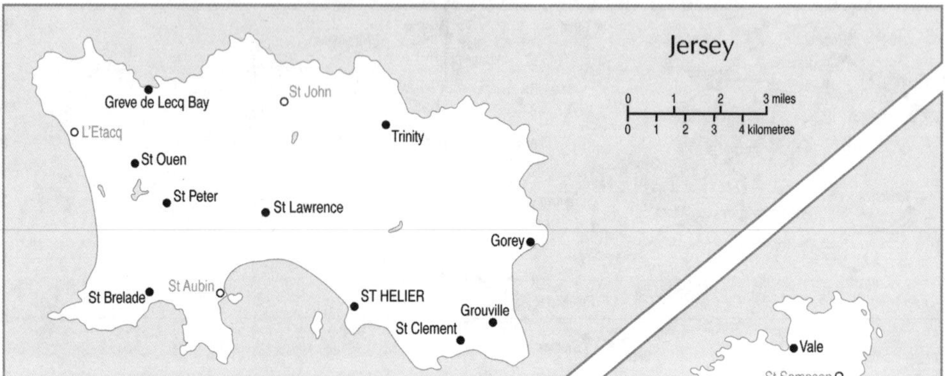
Jersey
0 1 2 3 miles
0 1 2 3 4 kilometres
Greve de Lecq Bay
St John
L'Etacq
Trinity
St Ouen
St Peter
St Lawrence
Gorey
St Brelade
St Aubin
ST HELIER
Grouville
St Clement

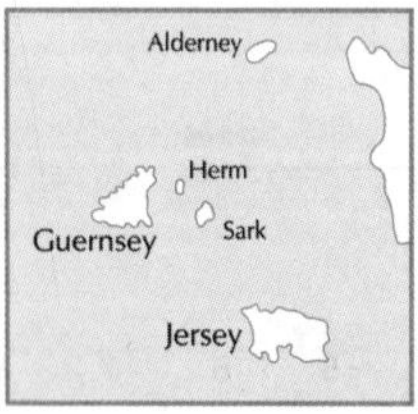
Alderney
Herm
Guernsey
Sark
Jersey

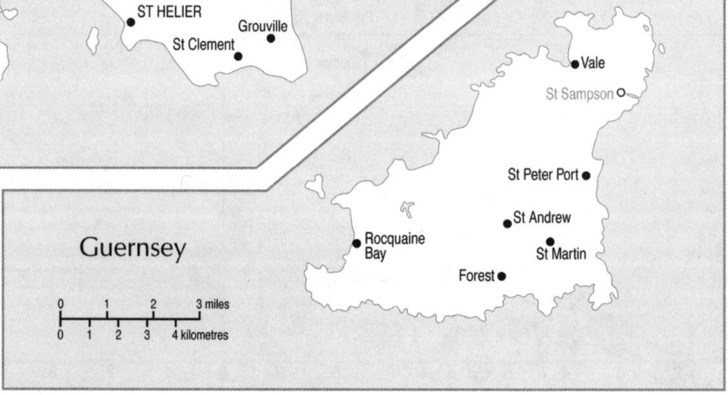
Vale
St Sampson
St Peter Port
St Andrew
Guernsey
Rocquaine Bay
St Martin
Forest
0 1 2 3 miles
0 1 2 3 4 kilometres

Need to find the perfect place?

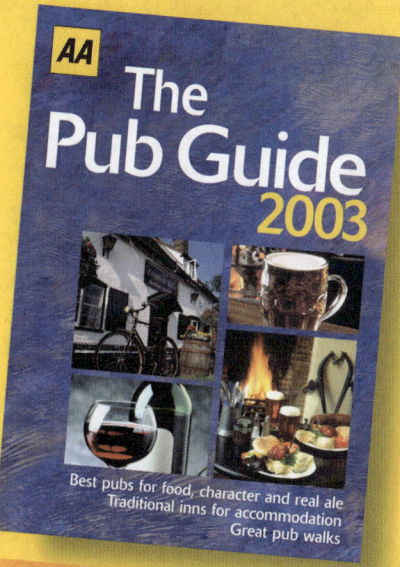

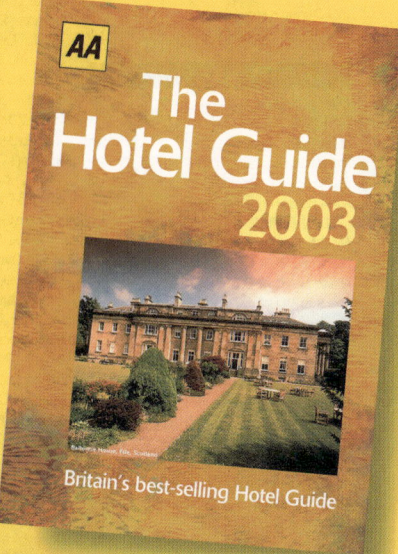

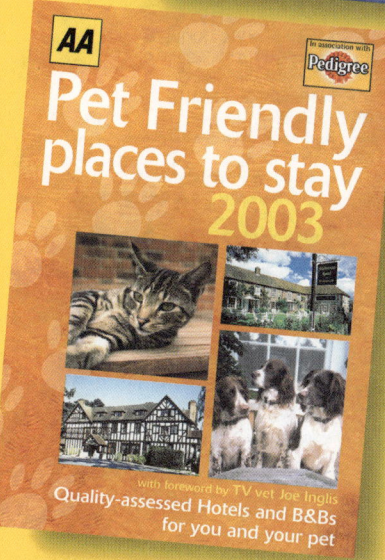

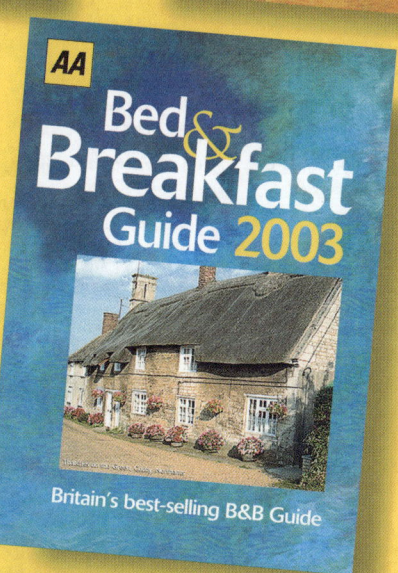

The Pub Guide 2003
Best pubs for food, character and real ale
Traditional inns for accommodation
Great pub walks

The Hotel Guide 2003
Britain's best-selling Hotel Guide

Pet Friendly places to stay 2003
Quality-assessed Hotels and B&Bs for you and your pet
with foreword by TV vet Joe Inglis

Bed & Breakfast Guide 2003
Britain's best-selling B&B Guide

New editions on sale now!

Available from all good bookshops, via our internet site: www.theAA.com or by calling 01206 255800

Index

0-9

1066 Battle of Hastings Abbey & Battlefield BATTLE	226
1066 Story in Hastings Castle HASTINGS & ST LEONARDS	229

A

A Day at the Wells TUNBRIDGE WELLS (ROYAL)	127
Abbey House Museum LEEDS	285
Abbey Pumping Station LEICESTER	134
Abbot Hall Art Gallery KENDAL	50
Abbot House Heritage Centre DUNFERMLINE	320
Abbotsbury Swannery ABBOTSBURY	71
Abbotsford MELROSE	336
Aberconwy House CONWY	355
Aberdeen Art Gallery ABERDEEN	297
Aberdeen Maritime Museum ABERDEEN	297
Aberdeenshire Farming Museum MINTLAW	299-300
Aberdour Castle ABERDOUR	319
Aberdulais Falls ABERDULAIS	364
Aberglasney Gardens LLANGATHEN	353
Achamore Gardens GIGHA ISLAND	303
Acorn Bank Garden TEMPLE SOWERBY	52
Acton Burnell Castle ACTON BURNELL	198
African Violet Centre KING'S LYNN	172
Aillwee Cave BALLYVAUGHAN	384
Airborne Forces Museum ALDERSHOT	97
Aldershot Military Museum ALDERSHOT	97
Alexander Keiller Museum AVEBURY	255
Alford Valley Railway ALFORD	297
Alfred East Gallery KETTERING	178
Alfriston Clergy House ALFRISTON	226
Allhallows Museum HONITON	65
Alloa Tower ALLOA	310
Almond Valley Heritage Centre LIVINGSTON	342
Almonry Heritage Centre EVESHAM	261
Alnwick Castle ALNWICK	181
Althorp ALTHORP	178
Alton Towers ALTON	209
Amberley Working Museum AMBERLEY	232
American Adventure Theme Park ILKESTON	58
American Museum BATH	202
Ancient House Museum THETFORD	175
Andrew Carnegie Birthplace Museum DUNFERMLINE	320
Anglesey Abbey LODE	28-29
Anglesey Sea Zoo BRYNSIENCYN	361
Angus Folk Museum GLAMIS	301
Anne Hathaway's Cottage SHOTTERY	242
Anne of Cleves House LEWES	229
Antony House TORPOINT	44
Antrim Round Tower ANTRIM	373
Appleby Castle APPLEBY-IN-WESTMORLAND	47
Appuldurcombe House WROXALL	253
Apsley House, The Wellington Museum LONDON W1	142
Aquarium of the Lakes LAKESIDE	51
Arbeia Roman Fort & Museum SOUTH SHIELDS	237
Arbroath Abbey ARBROATH	301
Arbroath Museum ARBROATH	301
Arbury Hall NUNEATON	241
Arbuthnot Museum & Art Gallery PETERHEAD	300
ARC, The YORK	276
Archaeolink OYNE	300
Ardara Heritage Centre ARDARA	386
Ardboe Cross ARDBOE	381
Ardencraig ROTHESAY	344
Ardgillan Castle BALBRIGGAN	386
Ardress House PORTADOWN	376
Arduaine Garden ARDUAINE	302
Ardwell House Gardens ARDWELL	311
Argory MOY	375-376
Argyll Forest Park ARROCHAR	302
Arkwright's Cromford Mill CROMFORD	57
Arley Hall & Gardens NORTHWICH	36
Arlington Court ARLINGTON	62
Armadale Castle Gardens & Museum of the Isles ARMADALE	347
Armagh County Museum ARMAGH	375
Armagh Friary ARMAGH	375
Armagh Planetarium ARMAGH	375
Armitt Museum AMBLESIDE	47
Army Medical Services Museum ASH VALE	221
Arnolfini BRISTOL	20
Arundel Castle ARUNDEL	232
Ascott WING	25
Ash End House Childrens Farm MIDDLETON	241
Ashby-de-la-Zouch Castle ASHBY-DE-LA-ZOUCH	134
Ashmolean Museum of Art & Archaeology OXFORD	192
Astley Cheetham Art Gallery STALYBRIDGE	95
Astley Hall Museum & Art Gallery CHORLEY	129
Aston Hall BIRMINGHAM	246
At-Bristol BRISTOL	20
Athelhampton House & Gardens ATHELHAMPTON	71
Atkinson Art Gallery SOUTHPORT	167
Atlantaquaria GALWAY	389
Attingham Park ATCHAM	198
Auchindrain Township-Open Air Museum AUCHINDRAIN	302
Auckland Castle BISHOP AUCKLAND	78
Audley End House & Gardens AUDLEY END	82
Audley's Castle STRANGFORD	378
Avebury Manor AVEBURY	255
Avoncroft Museum of Historic Buildings BROMSGROVE	261
Avondale House & Forest Park RATHDRUM	395
Aylesford Priory AYLESFORD	117

B

Babbacombe Model Village TORQUAY	68
Bachelors' Club TARBOLTON	338
Baconsthorpe Castle BACONSTHORPE	169
Baddesley Clinton Hall BADDESLEY CLINTON	240
Bala Lake Railway LLANUWCHLLYN	360
Ballincollig Gunpowder Mills Heritage Centre BALLINCOLLIG	384
Balloch Castle Country Park BALLOCH	341
Ballycopeland Windmill DONAGHADEE	376
Ballylumford Dolmen BALLYLUMFORD	373
Balmacara Estate & Lochalsh Woodland Garden BALMACARA	322
Balmoral Castle Grounds & Exhibition BALMORAL	297
Balvenie Castle DUFFTOWN	328
Bamburgh Castle BAMBURGH	181
Banagher Church DUNGIVEN	380
Banbury Museum BANBURY	190
Banchory Museum BANCHORY	298
Banff Museum BANFF	298
Banham Zoo BANHAM	169
Bank of England Museum LONDON EC2	142
Bankfield Museum HALIFAX	283
Bankside Gallery LONDON SE1	142
Bannockburn Heritage Centre BANNOCKBURN	340
Banqueting House at Whitehall Palace LONDON SW1	142
Barbara Hepworth Museum & Sculpture Gallery ST IVES	43
Barcaldine Castle BARCALDINE	302-303
Bargany Gardens OLD DAILLY	338
Barnard Castle BARNARD CASTLE	78
Barrington Court Garden BARRINGTON	202
Barry Water Mill BARRY	301
Basildon Park LOWER BASILDON	17
Basing House OLD BASING	102-3
Basingwerk Abbey HOLYWELL	358
Bass Museum BURTON UPON TRENT	209
Bateman's BURWASH	227
Bath Abbey BATH	202
Bath Postal Museum BATH	202
Batsford Arboretum MORETON-IN-MARSH	89
Battle Museum of Local History BATTLE	226
Battle of Britain Memorial Flight Visitor Centre CONINGSBY	138
Battlefield Line MARKET BOSWORTH	135
Baxters Highland Village FOCHABERS	329
Bayard's Cove Fort DARTMOUTH	64
Bayham Abbey LAMBERHURST	123
BBC Television Centre Tours LONDON W12	142-3
Beaghmore Stone Circles and Alignments BEAGHMORE	381
Beale Park LOWER BASILDON	17
Beamish, The North of England Open Air Museum BEAMISH	78
Bear Museum & Steiff Club Store PETERSFIELD	103
Beatles Story, The LIVERPOOL	163
Beatrix Potter Gallery HAWKSHEAD	50
Beaulieu : National Motor Museum BEAULIEU	98
Beaumaris Castle BEAUMARIS	361
Beaumaris Gaol & Courthouse BEAUMARIS	361
Bedale Museum BEDALE	269
Bede House LYDDINGTON	196
Bedes World & St Paul's Church JARROW	237
Bedford Museum BEDFORD	14
Beeston Castle BEESTON	32
Bekonscot Model Village BEACONSFIELD	23
Belfast Zoological Gardens BELFAST	373
Belgrave Hall & Gardens LEICESTER	134
Bell Tower of All Saint's Church INVERARAY	303
Belleek Pottery BELLEEK	378
Belsay Hall, Castle and Gardens BELSAY	181
Belton House Park & Gardens BELTON	138
Belvoir Castle BELVOIR	134
Bembridge Windmill BEMBRIDGE	251
Benburb Castle BENBURB	381
Beningbrough Hall BENINGBROUGH	269
Benmore Botanic Garden BENMORE	303
Benthall Hall BENTHALL	198

Index

Bentley Wildfowl & Motor Museum HALLAND	228	Borde Hill Garden HAYWARDS HEATH	234	Buckfast Butterfly Farm & Dartmoor Otter Sanctuary BUCKFASTLEIGH	63
Berkeley Castle BERKELEY	86	Borthwick Institute of Historical Research YORK	276	Buckie Drifter Maritime Heritage Centre BUCKIE	328
Berkhamsted Castle BERKHAMSTED	112	Boscobel House and The Royal Oak BOSCOBEL	198	Buckingham Palace LONDON SW1	143
Berney Arms Windmill BURGH CASTLE	169	Bosworth Battlefield Visitor Centre & Country Park MARKET BOSWORTH	135-136	Buckinghamshire Railway Centre QUAINTON	24
Berrington Hall ASHTON	109			Buckland Abbey BUCKLAND ABBEY	63
Berwick Barracks, Museum & Art Complex BERWICK-UPON-TWEED	181	Botanic Gardens BELFAST	373	Bucklers Hard Village & Maritime Museum BUCKLERS HARD	99
Beth Chatto Gardens COLCHESTER	83	Bothwell Castle BOTHWELL	339	Buckleys Yesterday's World BATTLE	226
Bickleigh Castle BICKLEIGH	62	Bowden House Ghostly Tales & The British Photographic Museum TOTNES	69	Building of Bath Museum, The BATH	202
Bicton Park Botanical Gardens BICTON	62	Bowes Castle BOWES	79	Buildwas Abbey BUILDWAS	198
Biddenden Vineyards & Cider Works BIDDENDEN	117	Bowes Museum BARNARD CASTLE	78	Bunratty Castle & Folk Park BUNRATTY	384
Biddulph Grange Garden BIDDULPH	209	Bowhill House & Country Park SELKIRK	337	Burford House Gardens BURFORD	198
Big Idea, The IRVINE	330	Bowood House & Gardens CALNE	255	Burghley House STAMFORD	140
Big Pit National Mining Museum of Wales BLAENAVON	370	Bradford Industrial Museum and Horses at Work BRADFORD	283	Burleigh Castle MILNATHORT	332
Bignor Roman Villa & Museum BIGNOR	233	Bradley Manor NEWTON ABBOT	66	Burnby Hall Garden & Museum Trust POCKLINGTON	267
Bircham Windmill GREAT BIRCHAM	170	Bramall Hall & Park BRAMHALL	93	Burns House DUMFRIES	312
Birdland Park & Gardens BOURTON-ON-THE-WATER	86	Bramber Castle BRAMBER	233	Burns Mausoleum DUMFRIES	312
Birdoswald Roman Fort BIRDOSWALD	47	Bramham Park BRAMHAM	283	Burns National Heritage Park ALLOWAY	338
Birdworld & Underwaterworld FARNHAM	221	Brander Museum HUNTLY	298	Burntisland Edwardian Fair Museum BURNTISLAND	319-320
Birkenhead Priory BIRKENHEAD	163	Branklyn Garden PERTH	333	Burrell Collection GLASGOW	308
Birkhill Fireclay Mine BIRKHILL	318	Brantwood CONISTON	49	Burton Agnes Hall BURTON AGNES	266
Birmingham Botanical Gardens & Glasshouses BIRMINGHAM	246	Brass Rubbing Centre EDINBURGH	304	Burton Constable Hall SPROATLEY	267
Birmingham Museum & Art Gallery BIRMINGHAM	246	Braxton Gardens LYMINGTON	101	Buscot Park BUSCOT	190
		Breadalbane Folklore Centre KILLIN	340-341	Bute Museum ROTHESAY	344
Birr Castle Demesne BIRR	393	Breamore House & Countryside Museum BREAMORE	98-99	Butterfly & Wildlife Park SPALDING	139-140
Bishop's & Earl's Palaces KIRKWALL	346	Brecknock Museum & Art Gallery BRECON	368	Butterfly Centre SWINGFIELD MINNIS	126
Bishops' House SHEFFIELD	281	Brecon Mountain Railway MERTHYR TYDFIL	362	Butterfly Farm STRATFORD-UPON-AVON	242
Bishop's Palace, The WELLS	207	Bressingham Steam Museum & Gardens BRESSINGHAM	169	'Bygones' TORQUAY	69
Bishop's Waltham Palace BISHOP'S WALTHAM	98	Brewhouse Yard Museum NOTTINGHAM	186	Byland Abbey COXWOLD	269
Black Country Living Museum DUDLEY	248	Bridewell Museum NORWICH	173		
Black House Museum ARNOL	345	Brimham Rocks BRIMHAM	269	**C**	
Black Watch Regimental Museum PERTH	333	Brinkburn Priory LONGFRAMLINGTON	183	C M Booth Collection of Historic Vehicles ROLVENDEN	126
Blackgang Chine Fantasy Park BLACKGANG	251	Bristol City Museum & Art Gallery BRISTOL	20	Cabinet War Rooms LONDON SW1	143
Blackness Castle LINLITHGOW	342	Bristol Industrial Museum BRISTOL	20	Cadbury World BOURNVILLE	247
Blackpool Zoo Park BLACKPOOL	129	Bristol Zoo Gardens BRISTOL	20	Cadhay OTTERY ST MARY	67
Blackwell The Arts & Crafts House BOWNESS-ON-WINDERMERE	47	British Airways London Eye LONDON SE1	142	Caerhays Castle Gardens GORRAN	39
Blaenavon Ironworks BLAENAVON	370	British Commercial Vehicle Museum LEYLAND	130	Caerlaverock Castle CAERLAVEROCK	311
Blair Castle BLAIR ATHOLL	331	British Cycling Museum CAMELFORD	38	Caerleon Roman Baths CAERLEON	364
Blair Drummond Safari & Leisure Park BLAIR DRUMMOND	340	British Engineerium-Museum of Steam & Mechanical Antiquities HOVE	229	Caernarfon Castle CAERNARFON	358-359
				Caerphilly Castle CAERPHILLY	350
Blaise Castle House Museum BRISTOL	20	British Golf Museum ST ANDREWS	321	Caerwent Roman Town CAERWENT	362
Blarney Castle & Rock Close BLARNEY	384	British Lawnmower Museum SOUTHPORT	167	Caithness Glass Factory & Visitor Centre WICK	326
Blasket Centre DUNQUIN	391	British Museum LONDON WC1	143	Caithness Glass Factory & Visitor Centre PERTH	333
Bleak House Dickens Maritime & Smuggling BROADSTAIRS	117	Broadlands ROMSEY	105	Caithness Glass Visitor Centre OBAN	304
		Broadway Tower & Animal Park BROADWAY	261	Caldicot Castle & Country Park CALDICOT	362-363
Blenheim Palace WOODSTOCK	194	Brodick Castle, Garden & Country Park BRODICK	344	Calke Abbey CALKE	55
Blickling Hall BLICKLING	169	Brodie Castle BRODIE CASTLE	327	Callanish Standing Stones CALLANISH	345
Blue Planet Aquarium ELLESMERE PORT	33	Brodsworth Hall & Gardens DONCASTER	280	Callendar House FALKIRK	319
Blue Reef Aquarium NEWQUAY	41	Brokerswood Country Park WESTBURY	259	Calleva Museum SILCHESTER	105
Bluebell Railway SHEFFIELD PARK STATION	230	Bronte Parsonage Museum HAWORTH	284	Cambridge & County Folk Museum CAMBRIDGE	27
Blue-John Cavern & Mine CASTLETON	55	Brooklands Museum WEYBRIDGE	224	Cambridge University Botanic Garden CAMBRIDGE	27
Boat Museum ELLESMERE PORT	33	Brough Castle BROUGH	48		
Bodelwyddan Castle BODELWYDDAN	356	Brough of Birsay DOUNBY	345	Camelot Theme Park CHARNOCK RICHARD	129
Bodiam Castle BODIAM	226	Brougham Castle BROUGHAM	48	Camera Obscura EDINBURGH	304
Bodnant Garden TAL-Y-CAFN	356	Broughton Castle BROUGHTON	190	Camperdown Country Park DUNDEE	315
Bohunt Manor LIPHOOK	101	Broughton House & Garden KIRKCUDBRIGHT	313	Canal Museum STOKE BRUERNE	179
Bolling Hall BRADFORD	283	Broughty Castle Museum DUNDEE	315	Canons Ashby House CANONS ASHBY	178
Bolsover Castle BOLSOVER	55	Brownsea Island BROWNSEA ISLAND	71	Canonteign Falls CHUDLEIGH	63
Bolton Castle CASTLE BOLTON	269	Bru Boru Heritage Centre CASHEL	393	Canterbury Roman Museum CANTERBURY	118
Bonamargy Friary BALLYCASTLE	373	Bruisyard Wines & Herbs SAXMUNDHAM	218	Canterbury Tales CANTERBURY	118
Bonawe Iron Furnace TAYNUILT	304	Bryn Celli Ddu Burial Chamber BRYNCELLI DDU	361	Canterbury West Gate Museum CANTERBURY	118
Bo'ness & Kinneil Railway BO'NESS	318	Buckfast Abbey BUCKFASTLEIGH	63	Capesthorne Hall CAPESTHORNE	32
Booth Museum of Natural History BRIGHTON	226				

Captain Cook Birthplace Museum MIDDLESBROUGH	272	
Cardiff Castle CARDIFF	350	
Cardoness Castle CARDONESS CASTLE	311	
Carew Castle & Tidal Mill CAREW	365	
Carisbrooke Castle CARISBROOKE	252	
Carlisle Castle & Border Regiments Museum CARLISLE	48	
Carlisle Cathedral CARLISLE	48	
Carlyle's House LONDON SW3	143	
Carmarthenshire County Museum ABERGWILI	352	
Carn Euny Ancient Village SANCREED	43	
Carnassarie Castle CARNASSARIE CASTLE	303	
Carnegie Museum INVERURIE	299	
Carreg Cennen Castle CARREG CENNEN CASTLE	352	
Carrick-a-Rede Rope Bridge and Larrybane Visitors Centre CARRICK-A-REDE	374	
Carrickfergus Castle CARRICKFERGUS	374	
Cartwright Hall Art Gallery BRADFORD	283	
Casino, The DUBLIN	387	
Castell Coch TONGWYNLAIS	351-352	
Castell Henllys Fort CRYMYCH	365	
Castell-y-Bere LLANFIHANGEL-Y-PENNANT	360	
Castle NORHAM	183	
Castle MORETON CORBET	199	
Castle & Visitor Centre ST ANDREWS	321	
Castle Acre Priory & Castle CASTLE ACRE	169	
Castle Balfour LISNASKEA	379	
Castle Campbell DOLLAR	311	
Castle Caulfield CASTLECAULFIELD	381	
Castle Coole ENNISKILLEN	379	
Castle Cornet ST PETER PORT	289	
Castle Drogo DREWSTEIGNTON	64	
Castle Fraser KEMNAY	299	
Castle Howard MALTON	271	
Castle Kennedy Gardens STRANRAER	314	
Castle Menzies WEEM	334	
Castle Museum NOTTINGHAM	186	
Castle of Old Wick WICK	326	
Castle Rising Castle CASTLE RISING	170	
Castle Rushen CASTLETOWN	294	
Castle Ward STRANGFORD	378	
Castle, The BURGH CASTLE	169	
Castle, White Horse & Dragon Hill UFFINGTON	193	
Castletown CELBRIDGE	391	
Catalyst Science Discovery Centre WIDNES	36	
Cathedral GLASGOW	308	
Cathedral (& Museum) ST ANDREWS	321	
Cavanacor Historic House & Art Gallery LIFFORD	386	
Caves of Nottingham NOTTINGHAM	186	
Cawdor Castle CAWDOR	322	
Cecil Higgins Art Gallery BEDFORD	14	
Cefn Coed Colliery Museum CRYNANT	364	
Céide Fields BALLYCASTLE	392	
Celtic Park & Gardens KILCORNAN	392	
Celtica MACHYNLLETH	368	
Central Art Gallery ASHTON-UNDER-LYNE	93	
Central Library LIVERPOOL	163	
Centre for Alternative Technology MACHYNLLETH	368	
Centre for Life NEWCASTLE UPON TYNE	237	
Ceramica STOKE-ON-TRENT	211	
Channel Islands Military Museum ST OUEN	292	
Charlecote Park CHARLECOTE	240	
Charles Dickens' Birthplace Museum PORTSMOUTH	103	
Charles Dickens Centre ROCHESTER	126	
Charles Dickens Museum LONDON WC1	143	

Charles Fort KINSALE	385	
Charlestown Shipwreck & Heritage Centre ST AUSTELL	42-43	
Chartwell CHARTWELL	119	
Chatelherault HAMILTON	339	
Chatsworth CHATSWORTH	56	
Chavenage House TETBURY	91	
Cheddleton Flint Mill CHEDDLETON	209	
Chedworth Roman Villa CHEDWORTH	86	
Chelsea Physic Garden LONDON SW3	143	
Cheltenham Art Gallery & Museum CHELTENHAM	86	
Chepstow Castle CHEPSTOW	363	
Cheshire Military Museum CHESTER	32	
Chessington World of Adventures CHESSINGTON	158	
Chester Beatty Library DUBLIN	387	
Chester Cathedral CHESTER	32	
Chester Visitor Centre CHESTER	32	
Chester Zoo CHESTER	32	
Chesters Roman Fort WALWICK	183	
Chichester Cathedral CHICHESTER	233	
Chiddingstone Castle CHIDDINGSTONE	119	
Chilford Hall Vineyard LINTON	28	
Chillingham Castle CHILLINGHAM	182	
Chillingham Wild Cattle Park CHILLINGHAM	182	
Chiltern Open Air Museum CHALFONT ST GILES	23	
China Clay Museum - Wheal Martyn ST AUSTELL	43	
Chirk Castle CHIRK	371	
Chislehurst Caves CHISLEHURST	158	
Chiswick House LONDON W4	144	
Cholmondeley Castle Gardens CHOLMONDELEY	33	
Christ Church Cathedral DUBLIN	387	
Christchurch Castle & Norman House CHRISTCHURCH	72	
Christchurch Mansion IPSWICH	216	
Church Farm Museum SKEGNESS	139	
Churnet Valley Railway CHEDDLETON	209	
Chysauster Ancient Village CHYSAUSTER ANCIENT VILLAGE	38	
Cider Museum & King Offa Distillery HEREFORD	109	
Cilgerran Castle CILGERRAN	365	
City Art Centre EDINBURGH	304	
City Art Gallery MANCHESTER	93	
City Art Gallery LEEDS	285	
City Museum & Art Gallery PLYMOUTH	67	
City Museum & Art Gallery GLOUCESTER	88	
City Museum & Art Gallery WORCESTER	263	
City Museum & Records Office PORTSMOUTH	103	
City Museum (also 15 Castle Hill) LANCASTER	129	
City of Norwich Aviation Museum HORSHAM ST FAITH	172	
City Walls LONDONDERRY	380	
Clan Donnachaidh (Robertson) Museum BRUAR	331	
Clan Macpherson House & Museum NEWTONMORE	325	
Clandon Park WEST CLANDON	223	
Clapham National Park Centre CLAPHAM	269	
Clava Cairns CLAVA CAIRNS	322	
Claydon House MIDDLE CLAYDON	24	
Clearwell Caves Ancient Iron Mines CLEARWELL	87	
Cleeve Abbey WASHFORD	206-207	
Clevedon Court CLEVEDON	204	
Click Mill DOUNBY	346	
Clickhimin LERWICK	347	

Cliffe Castle Museum & Gallery KEIGHLEY	284	
Clifford's Tower YORK	276	
Cliffs of Moher Visitor Centre LISCANNOR	384	
Clifton Park Museum ROTHERHAM	281	
Clitheroe Castle Museum CLITHEROE	129	
Cliveden CLIVEDEN	23	
Clock Tower ST ALBANS	113	
Clouds Hill BOVINGTON CAMP	71	
Clumber Park WORKSOP	188	
Clydebuilt GLASGOW	308-309	
Coats Observatory PAISLEY	335	
Cobbaton Combat Collection CHITTLEHAMPTON	63	
Cogges Manor Farm Museum WITNEY	194	
Coity Castle COITY	350	
Colby Woodland Garden AMROTH	365	
Colchester Castle Museum COLCHESTER	83	
Colchester Zoo COLCHESTER	83	
Coldharbour Mill Working Wool Museum UFFCULME	69	
Coleridge Cottage NETHER STOWEY	205	
Coleton Fishacre House & Garden KINGSWEAR	65	
Colne Valley Railway & Museum CASTLE HEDINGHAM	82	
Colour Museum BRADFORD	283	
Combe Martin Wildlife & Dinosaur Park COMBE MARTIN	64	
Commandery, The WORCESTER	263	
Commonwealth Institute LONDON W8	144	
Compton Acres Gardens CANFORD CLIFFS	72	
Compton Castle COMPTON	64	
Conisbrough Castle CONISBROUGH	280	
Conkers MOIRA	136	
Conservation Centre LIVERPOOL	163	
Conwy Castle CONWY	355	
Conwy Suspension Bridge CONWY	355	
Conwy Valley Railway Museum BETWS-Y-COED	355	
Cookworthy Museum of Rural Life KINGSBRIDGE	65	
Corbridge Roman Station CORBRIDGE	182	
Corfe Castle CORFE CASTLE	72	
Corfe Castle Museum CORFE CASTLE	72	
Corgarff Castle CORGARFF	298	
Corinium Museum CIRENCESTER	87	
Cork City Gaol CORK	385	
Cork Public Museum CORK	385	
Corlea Trackway Visitor Centre KEENAGH	392	
Cornish Mines & Engines POOL	42	
Corrigall Farm & Kirbuster Museum HARRAY	346	
Corsham Court CORSHAM	255-256	
Cosmeston Lakes Country Park & Medieval Village PENARTH	371	
Cotehele CALSTOCK	38	
Cotswold Falconry Centre MORETON-IN-MARSH	89	
Cotswold Farm Park GUITING POWER	88-89	
Cotswold Heritage Centre NORTHLEACH	90	
Cotswold Wildlife Park BURFORD	190	
Coughton Court COUGHTON	240	
Courtauld Gallery LONDON WC2	144	
Courthouse LONG CRENDON	24	
Courts, The HOLT	256	
Coventry Cathedral & Visitor Centre COVENTRY	247	
Crabble Corn Mill DOVER	120	
Crag Cave CASTLEISLAND	390-391	
Craggaunowen Bronze Age Project QUIN	384	
Cragside ROTHBURY	183	
Craigmillar Castle EDINBURGH	304	
Cranfield Church CHURCHTOWN	374	

Index 419

Crathes Castle & Gardens CRATHES	298
Creake Abbey NORTH CREAKE	173
Crealy Adventure Park CLYST ST MARY	63
Creetown Gem Rock Museum CREETOWN	312
Cregneash Village Folk Museum CREGNEISH	294
Creswell Crags Visitor Centre CRESWELL	56-57
Criccieth Castle CRICCIETH	359
Crich Tramway Village CRICH	57
Crichton Castle CRICHTON	327
Croft Castle CROFT	109
Crofton Beam Engines MARLBOROUGH	257
Crom Estate NEWTOWNBUTLER	379
Crossraguel Abbey MAYBOLE	338
Cruachan Power Station LOCHAWE	303-304
Cruickshank Botanic Garden ABERDEEN	297
Culloden Battlefield CULLODEN MOOR	323
Culross Palace, Town House & The Study CULROSS	320
Culzean Castle & Country Park CULZEAN CASTLE	338
Cumberland Pencil Museum GRETA BRIDGE	50
Cuming Museum LONDON SE17	144
Curraghs Wild Life Park BALLAUGH	294
Cutty Sark Clipper Ship LONDON SE10	144
Cwmcarn Forest Drive & Visitor Centre CWMCARN	350
Cyfarthfa Castle Museum & Art Gallery MERTHYR TYDFIL	362
Cymer Abbey CYMER ABBEY	359

D

Dairy Land Farm World NEWQUAY	41
Dalemain DALEMAIN	49
Dales Countryside Museum Centre HAWES	270
Dali Universe LONDON SE1	144
Dallas Dhu Distillery FORRES	329
Dalmeny House SOUTH QUEENSFERRY	308
Dan-Yr-Ogof The National Showcaves Centre for Wales ABERCRAF	367
Dapdune Wharf GUILDFORD	222
Darlington Railway Centre & Museum DARLINGTON	79
Dartington Crystal GREAT TORRINGTON	65
Dartmouth Castle DARTMOUTH	64
David Livingstone Centre BLANTYRE	339
Dawyck Botanic Garden STOBO	337-338
D-Day Museum & Overlord Embroidery PORTSMOUTH	104
de Havilland Aircraft Heritage Centre LONDON COLNEY	113
Deal Castle DEAL	119
Dean Forest Railway LYDNEY	89
Dean Gallery EDINBURGH	304
Dean Heritage Centre SOUDLEY	91
Deddington Castle DEDDINGTON	190
Deene Park DEENE	178
Deep Sea Adventure & Sharky's Play Zone WEYMOUTH	75
Deep Sea World NORTH QUEENSFERRY	321
Deep, The HULL	267
Deer Abbey OLD DEER	300
Denbigh Castle DENBIGH	357
Denby Pottery Visitor Centre DENBY	57
Denmans Garden FONTWELL	233
Derby Museum & Art Gallery DERBY	57
Design Museum LONDON SE1	144-145
Desmond Castle KINSALE	385
Deva Roman Experience CHESTER	33
Devenish Island ENNISKILLEN	379
Dewar's World of Whisky ABERFELDY	331

Dick Institute Museum & Art Galleries KILMARNOCK	316-317
Dickens House Museum BROADSTAIRS	118
Didcot Railway Centre DIDCOT	190
Dimbola Lodge FRESHWATER	252
Din Llugwy Ancient Village LLANALLGO	362
Dinefwr Park LLANDEILO	353
Dinosaur Adventure Park LENWADE	172
Dinosaur Museum DORCHESTER	72
Dirleton Castle DIRLETON	317
Discovery Point & RRS Discovery DUNDEE	316
Dobwalls Family Adventure Park DOBWALLS	38
Doctor Who Exhibition & Model Railway World LLANGOLLEN	357
Dolaucothi Gold Mines PUMSAINT	354
Dolbadarn Castle LLANBERIS	359
Dolphin Sailing Barge Museum SITTINGBOURNE	126
Dolwyddelan Castle DOLWYDDELAN	355
Doncaster Museum & Art Gallery DONCASTER	280
Donegal Castle DONEGAL	386
Donington Grand Prix Collection CASTLE DONINGTON	134
Donington le Heath Manor House DONINGTON LE HEATH	134
Dorney Court ETON	17
Dorothy Clive Garden, The WILLOUGHBRIDGE	213
Dorset County Museum DORCHESTER	72
Dorset Teddy Bear Museum DORCHESTER	72
Doune Castle DOUNE	340
Dove Cottage & The Wordsworth Museum GRASMERE	50
Dover Castle & Secret Wartime Tunnels DOVER	120
Down County Museum DOWNPATRICK	376-377
Down House - Home of Charles Darwin DOWNE	159
Dr Johnson's House LONDON EC4	145
Drayton Manor Family Theme Park TAMWORTH	212
Drimnagh Castle DUBLIN	387
Druidstone Park & Art Park CANTERBURY	118
Drum Castle PETERCULTER	297
Drumcoltran Tower DRUMCOLTRAN TOWER	312
Drumena Cashel CASTLEWELLAN	376
Drumlanrig Castle THORNHILL	314
Drummond Castle Gardens MUTHILL	332-333
Drusillas Park ALFRISTON	226
Dryburgh Abbey DRYBURGH	335
Dryslwyn Castle DRYSLWYN	352
Dublin Castle DUBLIN	387
Dublin Writers Museum DUBLIN	387
Dublin Zoo DUBLIN	387
Dublinia DUBLIN	387
Dudley Zoo & Castle DUDLEY	248
Dudmaston QUATT	199
Duff House BANFF	298
Duffus Castle DUFFUS	328
Dulwich Picture Gallery LONDON SE21	145
Dumbarton Castle DUMBARTON	342
Dumfries Museum & Camera Obscura DUMFRIES	312
Dun Carloway Broch CARLOWAY	345
Dunadd Fort KILMARTIN	303
Dunbrody Abbey Visitors Centre NEW ROSS	394
Duncombe Park HELMSLEY	270-271
Dundrennan Abbey DUNDRENNAN	312
Dundrum Castle NEWCASTLE	377
Duneight Motte and Bailey LISBURN	374

Dunfermline Abbey DUNFERMLINE	320
Dungeness Power Stations' Visitor Centre DUNGENESS	120
Dungiven Priory DUNGIVEN	380
Dunguaire Castle KINVARRA	390
Dunham Massey ALTRINCHAM	93
Dunluce Castle PORTBALLINTRAE	374
Dunnottar Castle STONEHAVEN	300
Dunrobin Castle GOLSPIE	324
Dunstaffnage Castle OBAN	304
Dunstanburgh Castle EMBLETON	182
Dunster Castle DUNSTER	204
Dunvegan Castle DUNVEGAN	347
Durban House Heritage Centre EASTWOOD	185
Durham Cathedral DURHAM	79
Durham Light Infantry Museum & Durham Art Gallery DURHAM	79
Durrell Wildlife Conservation Trust TRINITY	292
Dyffryn Gardens CARDIFF	350
Dylan Thomas' Boat House LAUGHARNE	352-353
Dynamic Earth EDINBURGH	305
Dyrham Park DYRHAM	87

E

Earl's Palace BIRSAY	345
Earth Centre DONCASTER	280
Easby Abbey EASBY	270
East Anglia Transport Museum LOWESTOFT	217
East Lambrook Manor Garden EAST LAMBROOK	204
East Riddlesden Hall KEIGHLEY	284
East Somerset Railway CRANMORE	204
Eastney Beam Engine House PORTSMOUTH	104
Eastnor Castle LEDBURY	110
Easton Farm Park EASTON	215
Ecos Millennium Environmental Centre BALLYMENA	373
Eden Camp Modern History Theme Museum MALTON	272
Eden Project ST AUSTELL	43
Edinburgh Butterfly & Insect World DALKEITH	327
Edinburgh Castle EDINBURGH	305
Edinburgh Zoo EDINBURGH	305
Edradour Distillery PITLOCHRY	333-334
Edzell Castle EDZELL	301
Egglestone Abbey BARNARD CASTLE	78
Elgar Birthplace Museum WORCESTER	263
Elgin Cathedral ELGIN	328
Elgin Museum ELGIN	328
Elizabeth Castle ST HELIER	291
Elizabethan House Museum GREAT YARMOUTH	170-171
Ell Shop & Little Houses DUNKELD	332
Eltham Palace House & Gardens LONDON SE9	145
Ely Cathedral ELY	28
Emmetts Garden BRASTED	117
Enniskillen Castle ENNISKILLEN	379
Erasmus Darwin Centre LICHFIELD	210
Erddig WREXHAM	371
Etruria Industrial Museum STOKE-ON-TRENT	211
Eureka! The Museum for Children HALIFAX	283
Euston Hall EUSTON	215
Ewe-Phoria Shepdog Centre CORWEN	356
Ewloe Castle EWLOE	358
Exbury Gardens & Railway EXBURY	99-100
Exmoor Zoological Park BLACKMOOR GATE	62
Exploris Aquarium PORTAFERRY	378
Explosion! Museum of Naval Firepower GOSPORT	100

Index

Eyam Hall EYAM	58	
Eyemouth Museum EYEMOUTH	335	
Eynsford Castle EYNSFORD	120	

F

Fairbourne Railway FAIRBOURNE	359
Fairfax House YORK	276
Fairhaven Woodland & Water Garden SOUTH WALSHAM	174-175
Falconer Museum FORRES	329
Falconry Centre STOURBRIDGE	248
Falkland Palace & Garden FALKLAND	320
Famous Grouse Experience CRIEFF	332
Farleigh Hungerford Castle FARLEIGH HUNGERFORD	205
Farmer Giles Farmstead TEFFONT MAGNA	258-259
Farnborough Hall FARNBOROUGH	240
Farnham Castle Keep FARNHAM	221
Faskally PITLOCHRY	334
Fasque FETTERCAIRN	298
Felbrigg Hall FELBRIGG	170
Felinwynt Rainforest & Butterfly Centre FELINWYNT	354
Fenton House LONDON NW3	145
Ffestiniog Railway PORTHMADOG	361
Finch Foundry STICKLEPATH	68
Finchale Priory DURHAM	79
Finchcocks GOUDHURST	121
Finkley Down Farm Park ANDOVER	97
Finlaystone Country Estate LANGBANK	334
Firepower LONDON SE18	145
Firle Place FIRLE	228
Fishbourne Roman Palace FISHBOURNE	233
Fitzwilliam Museum CAMBRIDGE	27
Flambards Village Theme Park HELSTON	39-40
Flamingo Land Theme Park & Zoo KIRBY MISPERTON	271
Fleet Air Arm Museum YEOVILTON	207
Fleur de Lis Heritage Centre FAVERSHAM	120
Flint Castle FLINT	358
Floors Castle KELSO	336
Florence Court ENNISKILLEN	386
Florence Nightingale Museum LONDON SE1	146
Flying Flowers ST LAWRENCE	291
Fochabers Folk Museum FOCHABERS	329
Foel Farm Park BRYNSIENCYN	362
Folk Museum GLOUCESTER	88
Forde Abbey CHARD	204
Forge Mill Needle Museum & Bordesley Abbey Visitor Centre REDDITCH	262
Fort Amherst CHATHAM	119
Fort Charlotte LERWICK	347
Fort George FORT GEORGE	323
Fort Grey and Shipwreck Museum ROCQUAINE BAY	289
Forty Hall Museum ENFIELD	145
Fota Arboretum & Gardens CARRIGTWOHILL	384
Fota Wildlife Park CARRIGTWOHILL	384
Fountains Abbey & Studley Royal RIPON	275
Foyle Valley Railway Museum LONDONDERRY	380
Foynes Flying Boat Museum FOYNES	392
Framlingham Castle FRAMLINGHAM	215
Freud Museum LONDON NW3	146
Frogmore House WINDSOR	18
Frontierland - Family Park MORECAMBE	130
Fry Model Railway MALAHIDE	389
Furness Abbey BARROW-IN-FURNESS	47
Furzey Gardens MINSTEAD	102

Fyvie Castle TURRIFF	301

G

Gainsborough's House SUDBURY	218
Gairloch Heritage Museum GAIRLOCH	324
Galleries of Justice NOTTINGHAM	186
Gallery of Costume MANCHESTER	93
Gallery of Modern Art GLASGOW	309
Galway City Museum GALWAY	390
Gardens of The Rose (Royal National Rose Society) ST ALBANS	114
Garinish Island GLENGARRIFF	385
Gawsworth Hall GAWSWORTH	33-34
Gawthorpe Hall PADIHAM	131
Geffrye Museum LONDON E2	146
General Register House EDINBURGH	305
George Bernard Shaw House DUBLIN	389
Georgian House BRISTOL	20
Georgian House EDINBURGH	305
German Military Underground Hospital & Ammunition Store ST ANDREW	289
German Occupation Museum FOREST	289
German Underground Hospital ST LAWRENCE	291-292
Giant's Causeway Centre GIANT'S CAUSEWAY	374
Giant's Ring BELFAST	373
Gibside ROWLANDS GILL	237
Gilbert Collection LONDON WC2	146
Gilbert White's House & The Oates Museum SELBORNE	105
Gisborough Priory GUISBOROUGH	270
Gladstone Court Museum BIGGAR	339
Gladstone Working Pottery Museum STOKE-ON-TRENT	211
Gladstone's Land EDINBURGH	305
Glamis Castle GLAMIS	302
Glansevern Hall Gardens BERRIEW	367-368
Glasgow Art Gallery & Museum GLASGOW	309
Glasgow Botanic Gardens GLASGOW	309
Glasgow Science Centre GLASGOW	309
Glasgow Zoopark UDDINGSTON	340
Glasshouse, The at Edinburgh Crystal PENICUIK	327
Glastonbury Abbey GLASTONBURY	205
Glebe House & Gallery LETTERKENNY	386
Glen Grant Distillery ROTHES	329
Glencoe & North Lorn Folk Museum GLENCOE	324
Glencoe Visitor Centre GLENCOE	324
Glendurgan MAWNAN SMITH	41
Glenfarclas Distillery MARYPARK	329
Glenfiddich Distillery DUFFTOWN	328
Glenfinnan Monument GLENFINNAN	324
Glengoulandie Deer Park GLENGOULANDIE DEER PARK	332
Glenlivet Distillery BALLINDALLOCH	327
Glenluce Abbey GLENLUCE	312-313
Glenveagh National Park & Castle LETTERKENNY	386
Glenwhan Gardens STRANRAER	314
Glynde Place GLYNDE	228
Glynn Vivian Art Gallery SWANSEA	370
Gnoll Estate Country Park NEATH	364
Godolphin House GODOLPHIN CROSS	39
Godstone Farm GODSTONE	221
Golden Hinde Educational Museum LONDON SE1	146
Goodrich Castle GOODRICH	109
Goodwood House GOODWOOD	234
Gordon Highlanders Museum ABERDEEN	297

Gorhambury ST ALBANS	114
Gower Heritage Centre PARKMILL	369-370
Grace Darling Museum BAMBURGH	181
Grand National Experience LIVERPOOL	163-164
Gray's Printing Press STRABANE	382
Great Central Railway LOUGHBOROUGH	135
Great Chalfield Manor BRADFORD-ON-AVON	255
Great Comp Garden BOROUGH GREEN	117
Great Coxwell Barn GREAT COXWELL	191
Great Dixter NORTHIAM	230
Great Hall WINCHESTER	107
Great Laxey Wheel & Mines Trail LAXEY	295
Green Howards Museum RICHMOND	274
Greenbank Garden GLASGOW	309
Greencastle KILKEEL	377
Greenfield Valley Heriatge Park HOLYWELL	358
Greenhill Covenanters House BIGGAR	339
Greenmeadow Community Farm CWMBRAN	370
Greenway Garden CHURSTON FERRERS	63
Greenwood Centre Y FELINHELI	361
Greve de Lecq Barracks GREVE DE LECQ BAY	291
Grey Abbey BALLYWALTER	376
Greys Court HENLEY-ON-THAMES	191
Grimes Graves GRIMES GRAVES	171
Grimsthorpe Castle GRIMSTHORPE	138
Groam House Museum ROSEMARKIE	326
Groombridge Place Gardens & Enchanted Forest GROOMBRIDGE PLACE	122
Grosmont Castle GROSMONT	363
Grove The' Rural Life Museum RAMSEY	295
Guernsey Museum & Art Gallery ST PETER PORT	289
Guildford Castle GUILDFORD	222
Guildford House Gallery GUILDFORD	222
Guildhall TOTNES	69
Guildhall EXETER	64
Guildhall YORK	276
Guildhall Museum CARLISLE	48
Guildhall Museum ROCHESTER	126
Guildhall, The LONDON EC2	146
Guinness Storehouse DUBLIN	388
Gurkha Museum WINCHESTER	106-107
Gwydyr Uchaf Chapel LLANRWST	355

H

Haddo House METHLICK	299
Haddon Hall HADDON HALL	58
Hadleigh Castle HADLEIGH	83
Hadspen Garden & Nursery CASTLE CARY	204
Hailes Abbey HAILES	89
Hailes Castle EAST LINTON	318
Halfpenny Green Vineyards HALFPENNY GREEN	209-210
Hall Place BEXLEY	158
Halliwells House Museum SELKIRK	337
Hall's Croft STRATFORD-UPON-AVON	242
Ham House HAM	159
Hamerton Zoo Park HAMERTON	28
Hampton Court Palace HAMPTON COURT	159-160
Hamptonne Country Life Museum ST LAWRENCE	292
Hanbury Hall HANBURY	261-262
Hancock Museum NEWCASTLE UPON TYNE	237
Handel House Museum LONDON W1	147
Harcourt Arboretum OXFORD	192
Hardknott Castle Roman Fort HARDKNOTT CASTLE ROMAN FORT	50
Hardwick Old Hall HARDWICK HALL	58
Hardy's Cottage DORCHESTER	73

Index

Hare Hill MACCLESFIELD	34	
Harewood House & Bird Garden HAREWOOD	284	
Harlech Castle HARLECH	359	
Harlow Museum HARLOW	83	
Harmony Garden MELROSE	336	
Harris Museum & Art Gallery PRESTON	131	
Harry Avery's Castle NEWTOWNSTEWART	381	
Harryville Motte BALLYMENA	373	
Hartlepool Historic Quay HARTLEPOOL	79	
Harveys Wine Cellars BRISTOL	21	
Harwich Redoubt Fort HARWICH	83	
Haseley Manor ARRETON	251	
Hatchlands Park EAST CLANDON	221	
Hatfield House, Park and Gardens HATFIELD	112	
Haughmond Abbey HAUGHMOND ABBEY	199	
Hawford Dovecote WORCESTER	263	
Hawk Conservancy and Country Park WEYHILL	106	
Hawkstone Historic Park & Follies WESTON-UNDER-REDCASTLE	200	
Haynes Motor Museum SPARKFORD	206	
Heale Gardens, Plant Centre & Shop MIDDLE WOODFORD	257	
Heaton Hall PRESTWICH	94	
Hedgehog Hospital at Prickly Ball Farm NEWTON ABBOT	66	
Hedingham Castle CASTLE HEDINGHAM	82	
Heights of Abraham Cable Cars, Caverns & Hilltop Park MATLOCK BATH	59	
Helicopter Museum WESTON-SUPER-MARE	207	
Helmsley Castle HELMSLEY	271	
Hen Gwrt LLANTILIO CROSSENNY	363	
Henry Blogg Museum CROMER	170	
Herbert Art Gallery & Museum COVENTRY	247	
Hereford Cathedral HEREFORD	109	
Hergest Croft Gardens KINGTON	109	
Heritage Motor Centre GAYDON	240-241	
Hermitage Castle HERMITAGE	336	
Hestercombe Gardens TAUNTON	206	
Hever Castle & Gardens HEVER	122	
Hezlett House COLERAINE	379-380	
Hidcote Manor Garden MICKLETON	89	
Highclere Castle & Gardens HIGHCLERE	101	
Highgate Cemetery LONDON N6	147	
Highland & Rare Breeds Farm ELPHIN	323	
Highland Folk Museum KINGUSSIE	325	
Highland Folk Museum NEWTONMORE	325	
Highland Museum of Childhood STRATHPEFFER	326	
Highland Mysteryworld GLENCOE	324	
Highland Wildlife Park KINCRAIG	325	
Hill of Tarvit Mansionhouse & Garden CUPAR	320	
Hill Top NEAR SAWREY	51	
Hillsborough Fort HILLSBOROUGH	377	
Himley Hall & Park HIMLEY	210	
Hinton Ampner Garden HINTON AMPNER	101	
Hirsel, The COLDSTREAM	335	
Historic Dockyard, The CHATHAM	119	
Historic Warships BIRKENHEAD	163	
HM Customs & Excise National Museum LIVERPOOL	164	
HM Frigate Unicorn DUNDEE	316	
HMS Belfast LONDON SE1	147	
HMS Trincomalee HARTLEPOOL	79-80	
Hodnet Hall Gardens HODNET	199	
Hogarth's House LONDON W4	147	
Holburne Museum of Art BATH	202	
Holdenby House, Gardens & Falconry Centre HOLDENBY	178	
Holker Hall & Gardens HOLKER	50	

Holkham Hall & Bygones Museum HOLKHAM	171-172	
Holly Gate Cactus Garden ASHINGTON	232	
Hollycombe Steam Collection LIPHOOK	101	
Holst Birthplace Museum CHELTENHAM	87	
Hoo Farm Animal Kingdom TELFORD	200	
Hop Farm & Country Park BELTRING	117	
Hopetoun House SOUTH QUEENSFERRY	308	
Horniman Museum & Gardens LONDON SE23	147	
Hornsea Museum HORNSEA	266	
Horse Drawn Boats Centre LLANGOLLEN	357	
Horsey Windpump HORSEY	172	
Hospital of St Cross WINCHESTER	107	
Houghton Hall HOUGHTON	172	
Houghton House AMPTHILL	14	
House for an Art Lover GLASGOW	309	
House of Dun MONTROSE	302	
House of Manannan PEEL	295	
House of The Binns LINLITHGOW	342	
House on the Hill Museum Adventure STANSTED	84	
Household Cavalry Museum WINDSOR	18	
Houses of Parliament LONDON SW1	147	
Housesteads Roman Fort HOUSESTEADS	182-183	
How We Lived Then Museum of Shops & Social History EASTBOURNE	227	
Howletts Wild Animal Park BEKESBOURNE	117	
Howth Castle Rhododendron Gardens DUBLIN	388	
Hugh Lane Municipal Gallery of Modern Art DUBLIN	388	
Hugh Miller's Cottage CROMARTY	322	
Hughenden Manor HUGHENDEN	23	
Hunt Museum LIMERICK	392	
Hunterian Art Gallery GLASGOW	309	
Hunterian Museum GLASGOW	309	
Huntingtower Castle PERTH	333	
Huntly Castle HUNTLY	298	
Hurst Castle HURST CASTLE	101	
Hutchesons' Hall GLASGOW	309	
Hutton-in-the-Forest SKELTON	52	
Hydro Centre Ffestiniog BLAENAU FFESTINIOG	358	

I

Ickworth House, Park & Gardens HORRINGER	216
Ightham Mote IGHTHAM	123
Ilfracombe Museum ILFRACOMBE	65
Imperial War Museum LONDON SE1	147
Imperial War Museum Duxford DUXFORD	27
Inch Abbey DOWNPATRICK	377
Inchcolm Abbey SOUTH QUEENSFERRY	308
Inchmahome Priory PORT OF MENTEITH	341
Industrial Museum DERBY	57
Inigo Jones Slateworks GROESLON	359
Innerpeffray Library CRIEFF	331
Inveraray Castle INVERARAY	303
Inveraray Jail INVERARAY	303
Inveresk Lodge Garden INVERESK	318
Inverewe Garden POOLEWE	325
Inverlochy Castle FORT WILLIAM	324
Ipswich Museum IPSWICH	216
Irish Agricultural Museum WEXFORD	394
Irish Linen Centre & Lisburn Museum LISBURN	374
Irish Museum of Modern Art DUBLIN	388
Irish National Heritage Park FERRYCARRIG	394
Ironbridge Gorge Museums IRONBRIDGE	199

Isle of Arran Distillery Visitor Centre LOCHRANZA	344	
Isle of Arran Heritage Museum BRODICK	344	
Isle of Wight Steam Railway HAVENSTREET	252	
Isle of Wight Wax Works BRADING	251	

J

J M Barrie's Birthplace KIRRIEMUIR	302
Jaguar Daimler Heritage Centre COVENTRY	247
James Gilbert Rugby Football Museum RUGBY	242
James Joyce Centre DUBLIN	388
James Joyce Tower DUN LAOGHAIRE	389
Jane Austen's House CHAWTON	99
Japanese Gardens KILDARE	391
Jarlshof Prehistoric & Norse Settlement SUMBURGH	347
Jedburgh Abbey JEDBURGH	336
Jenner Museum BERKELEY	86
Jennings Brewery Tour COCKERMOUTH	48
Jersey Lavender Farm ST BRELADE	291
Jersey Museum ST HELIER	291
Jewellery Quarter Discovery Centre BIRMINGHAM	246
Jewish Museum LONDON N3	147
Jewish Museum LONDON NW1	148
Jewry Wall Museum & Site LEICESTER	134
Jim Clark Room DUNS	335
Jodrell Bank Science Centre, Planetarium & Arboretum JODRELL BANK SCIENCE CENTRE	34
John Dony Field Centre LUTON	14
John F Kennedy Arboretum NEW ROSS	394
John Knox House EDINBURGH	305
John Rylands Library MANCHESTER	93
John Wesley's Chapel (The New Room) BRISTOL	21
Johnstown Castle Gardens WEXFORD	394
Jordan's Castle ARDGLASS	376
JORVIK, The Viking City YORK	276-277
Judge's Lodging, The PRESTEIGNE	368-369

K

Kailzie Gardens PEEBLES	337
Keats House LONDON NW3	148
Kedleston Hall KEDLESTON HALL	59
Keighley & Worth Valley Railway & Museum HAWORTH	284
Keith Harding's World of Mechanical Music NORTHLEACH	90
Kelburn Castle and Country Centre LARGS	330
Kelham Island Museum SHEFFIELD	281
Kellie Castle & Garden KELLIE CASTLE & GARDENS	321
Kelso Abbey KELSO	336
Kempt Tower Visitor Centre ST OUEN	292
Kendal Museum KENDAL	50
Kenilworth Castle KENILWORTH	241
Kensington Palace State Apartments & Royal Ceremonial Dress Collection LONDON W8	148
Kent Battle of Britain Museum HAWKINGE	122
Kents Cavern TORQUAY	69
Kentwell Hall LONG MELFORD	216-217
Kenwood LONDON NW3	148
Kerry The Kingdom Museum TRALEE	391
Keswick Museum & Art Gallery KESWICK	51
Kew Bridge Steam Museum BRENTFORD	158
Kew Gardens (Royal Botanic Gardens) KEW	160
Kew Palace KEW	160

Index

Kidwelly Castle KIDWELLY	352	
Kidwelly Industrial Museum KIDWELLY	352	
Kiftsgate Court Garden MICKLETON	89	
Kildrummy Castle KILDRUMMY	299	
Kildrummy Castle Gardens KILDRUMMY	299	
Kilkenny Castle KILKENNY	392	
Killarney Transport Museum KILLARNEY	391	
Killerton House & Garden		
KILLERTON HOUSE & GARDEN	65	
Killevy Churches CAMLOUGH	375	
Killhope Lead Mining Museum COWSHILL	79	
Killiecrankie Visitor Centre KILLIECRANKIE	332	
Kilmainham Gaol DUBLIN	388	
Kilnasaggart Inscribed Stone		
JONESBOROUGH	375	
King Arthur's Labyrinth MACHYNLLETH	368	
King House BOYLE	393	
King John's Castle LIMERICK	392	
King John's Hunting Lodge AXBRIDGE	202	
King's Lynn Arts Centre KING'S LYNN	172	
King's Royal Hussars Regimental Museum		
WINCHESTER	107	
Kingston Lacy House, Garden & Park		
WIMBORNE	75	
Kinneil Museum & Roman Fortlet BO'NESS	319	
Kinross House Gardens KINROSS	332	
Kirby Hall DEENE	178	
Kirby Muxloe Castle KIRBY MUXLOE	134	
Kirkcaldy Museum & Art Gallery KIRKCALDY	321	
Kirkham Priory KIRKHAM	271	
Kirkstall Abbey LEEDS	285	
Knaresborough Castle & Museum		
KNARESBOROUGH	271	
Knebworth House, Gardens & Country Park		
KNEBWORTH	112	
Knightshayes Court KNIGHTSHAYES COURT	66	
Knole SEVENOAKS	126	
Knoll Gardens & Nursery WIMBORNE	75	
Knowsley Safari Park PRESCOT	166	

L

La Hougue Bie GROUVILLE	291	
Lace Centre NOTTINGHAM	186	
Lackham Countryside Centre LACOCK	256	
Lacock Abbey LACOCK	256	
Lady Lever Art Gallery PORT SUNLIGHT	166	
Laidhay Croft Museum DUNBEATH	323	
Lake District Visitor Centre at Brockhole		
WINDERMERE	53	
Lakeland Sheep & Wool Centre		
COCKERMOUTH	49	
Lamb House RYE	230	
Lamphey Bishop's Palace LAMPHEY	366	
Lancaster Maritime Museum LANCASTER	130	
Landmark Forest Heritage Park CARRBRIDGE	322	
Lanercost Priory BRAMPTON	48	
Lanhydrock LANHYDROCK	40	
Lanreath Farm & Folk Museum LANREATH	40	
Laugharne Castle LAUGHARNE	353	
Launceston Castle LAUNCESTON	40	
Launceston Steam Railway LAUNCESTON	40	
Lauriston Castle EDINBURGH	305	
Lavenham Guildhall LAVENHAM	216	
Layer Marney Tower LAYER MARNEY	83	
Le Moulin de Quetivel ST PETER	292	
Lee Valley Park Farms WALTHAM ABBEY	84	
Leeds Castle MAIDSTONE	124	
Leeds Industrial Museum at Armley Mills		
LEEDS	285	
Legananny Dolmen DROMARA	377	

LEGOLAND Windsor WINDSOR	18	
Leicestershire Museum & Art Gallery		
LEICESTER	135	
Leighton Buzzard Railway		
LEIGHTON BUZZARD	14	
Leighton Hall LEIGHTON HALL	130	
Leighton House Museum & Art Gallery		
LONDON W14	148	
Leiston Abbey LEISTON	216	
Leith Hall & Garden RHYNIE	300	
Leonardslee Gardens LOWER BEEDING	234	
Leslie Hill Open Farm BALLYMONEY	373	
Levens Hall LEVENS	51	
Lewes Castle & Barbican House Museum		
LEWES	229	
Lichfield Cathedral LICHFIELD	210	
Lichfield Heritage Centre LICHFIELD	210	
Lightwater Valley Theme Park		
NORTH STAINLEY	273	
Lilleshall Abbey LILLESHALL	199	
Lilliput Antique Doll & Toy Museum BRADING	251	
Lincoln Castle LINCOLN	139	
Lindisfarne Castle		
HOLY ISLAND [LINDISFARNE]	182	
Lindisfarne Priory		
HOLY ISLAND [LINDISFARNE]	182	
Linley Sambourne House LONDON W8	148	
Linlithgow Palace LINLITHGOW	342	
Linton Zoological Gardens LINTON	28	
Lismore Castle Gardens LISMORE	393	
Little Moreton Hall SCHOLAR GREEN	36	
Littledean Hall LITTLEDEAN	89	
Liverpool Football Club Museum and Stadium		
Tour LIVERPOOL	164	
Liverpool University Botanic Gardens (Ness		
Gardens) NESTON	35	
Living Legend, The ST PETER	292	
Llanberis Lake Railway LLANBERIS	359	
Llancaiach Fawr Manor CAERPHILLY	350	
Llandaff Cathedral CARDIFF	351	
Llanerchaeron ABERAERON	354	
Llangollen Railway LLANGOLLEN	357	
Llansteffan Castle LLANSTEFFAN	353	
Llanthony Priory LLANTHONY	363	
Llawhaden Castle LLAWHADEN	366	
Llechwedd Slate Caverns		
BLAENAU FFESTINIOG	358	
Lloyd George Museum & Highgate Cottage		
LLANYSTUMDWY	360	
Llyn Brenig Visitor Centre CERRIGYDRUDION	355	
Loch Leven Castle KINROSS	332	
Lochcarron of Scotland Visitor Centre		
GALASHIELS	335	
Lochwinnoch Community Museum		
LOCHWINNOCH	334	
Logan Botanic Garden PORT LOGAN	314	
London Aquarium LONDON SE1	148-149	
London Canal Museum LONDON N1	149	
London Dungeon LONDON SE1	149	
London Planetarium LONDON NW1	149	
London Wetland Centre LONDON SW13	149	
London Zoo LONDON NW1	149	
London's Transport Museum LONDON WC2	149	
Long Shop Museum LEISTON	216	
Longdown Activity Farm ASHURST	98	
Longleat LONGLEAT	256	
Longthorpe Tower PETERBOROUGH	29	
Look Out Discovery Centre BRACKNELL	17	
Lord's Tour & M.C.C. Museum		
LONDON NW8	149-150	
Loseley Park GUILDFORD	222	

Lost Gardens of Heligan PENTEWAN	42	
Lotherton Hall LOTHERTON HALL	286	
Loudoun Castle Theme Park GALSTON	316	
Lough Gur Stone Age Centre HOLYCROSS	392	
Lough Neagh Discovery Centre		
OXFORD ISLAND	376	
Loughinisland Churches DOWNPATRICK	377	
Low Parks Museum HAMILTON	339-340	
Lower Brockhampton BROCKHAMPTON	109	
Lowry, The SALFORD	94-95	
Ludgershall Castle LUDGERSHALL	256	
Ludlow Castle LUDLOW	199	
Lullingstone Castle EYNSFORD	120	
Lullingstone Roman Villa EYNSFORD	120	
Lulworth Castle WEST LULWORTH	75	
Lunt Roman Fort COVENTRY	247	
Luton Museum & Gallery LUTON	14-15	
Lydford Castle LYDFORD	66	
Lydford Gorge LYDFORD	66	
Lydiard Park LYDIARD PARK	256	
Lyme Park DISLEY	33	
Lynn Museum KING'S LYNN	172	
Lytes Cary Manor KINGSDON	205	
Lyveden New Bield LYVEDEN NEW BIELD	178	

M

Macclesfield Silk Museum MACCLESFIELD	34-35	
Macduff Marine Aquarium MACDUFF	299	
MacLellan's Castle KIRKCUDBRIGHT	313	
Madame Tussaud's LONDON NW1	150	
Maes Howe Chambered Cairn FINSTOWN	346	
Maghera Church NEWCASTLE	377	
Maghera Church MAGHERA	380	
Magna Science Adventure Centre		
ROTHERHAM	281	
Maiden Castle DORCHESTER	73	
Maidstone Museum & Bentlif Art Gallery		
MAIDSTONE	124	
Maister House HULL	266	
Malahide Castle MALAHIDE	389	
Malham National Park Centre MALHAM	271	
Mall Galleries LONDON SW1	150	
Malleny Garden BALERNO	304	
Malton Museum MALTON	272	
Manchester Museum MANCHESTER	94	
Manchester United Museum & Tour Centre		
MANCHESTER	94	
Manderston DUNS	335	
Mannington Gardens & Countryside		
SAXTHORPE	174	
Manor House Gallery & Museum ILKLEY	284	
Manor House Museum BURY ST EDMUNDS	215	
Manor House Museum ALFORD	138	
Manor House Wildlife & Leisure Park		
ST FLORENCE	367	
Manx Museum DOUGLAS	294	
Mapledurham House MAPLEDURHAM	191	
Mapledurham Watermill MAPLEDURHAM	191	
Mapperton BEAMINSTER	71	
Marble Arch Caves ENNISKILLEN	379	
Marble Hill House TWICKENHAM	160-161	
Maritime Heritage Centre BRISTOL	21	
Maritime Museum RAMSGATE	125	
Maritime Museum GREAT YARMOUTH	171	
Maritime Museum LOWESTOFT	217	
Maritime Museum HULL	266-267	
Maritime Museum & Occupation Tapestry Gallery		
ST HELIER	291	
Mar's Wark STIRLING	341	
Marsh's Library DUBLIN	388	

Index

Martello Tower DYMCHURCH	120	Motherwell Heritage Centre MOTHERWELL	331	Museum of Scotland EDINBURGH	306	
Marwell Zoological Park MARWELL	102	Mottisfont Abbey Garden MOTTISFONT	102	Museum of Scottish Country Life		
Marwood Hill Gardens BARNSTAPLE	62	Mouldsworth Motor Museum		EAST KILBRIDE	339	
Mary Arden's House and the Shakespeare		MOULDSWORTH	35	Museum of South Yorkshire Life Cusworth Hall		
Countryside Museum WILMCOTE	244	Mound of Down DOWNPATRICK	377	CUSWORTH	280	
Maxwelton House Trust MONIAIVE	313	Mount Edgcumbe House & Country Park		Museum of St Albans ST ALBANS	114	
McLean Museum & Art Gallery GREENOCK	326	TORPOINT	44	Museum of the Cumbraes MILLPORT	344	
McLellan Galleries GLASGOW	309	Mount Grace Priory OSMOTHERLEY	273	Museum of the History of Science OXFORD	192	
McManus Galleries DUNDEE	316	Mount Sandel COLERAINE	380	Museum of the History of Smuggling		
Mechanical Music & Doll Collection		Mount Stewart House, Garden & Temple of the		VENTNOR	253	
CHICHESTER	233	Winds NEWTOWNARDS	377	Museum of the Home PEMBROKE	366	
Medieval Hall (Discover Salisbury) SALISBURY	257	Mountfitchet Castle & Norman Village		Museum of The Manchester Regiment		
Meffan Art Gallery & Museum FORFAR	301	STANSTED	84	ASHTON-UNDER-LYNE	93	
Melbourne Hall & Gardens MELBOURNE	59	Mountjoy Castle MOUNTJOY	382	Museum of The Order of St John		
Melford Hall LONG MELFORD	217	Mousa Broch MOUSA ISLAND	347	LONDON EC1	150	
Mellerstain House GORDON	335	Moyry Castle NEWRY	376	Museum of the Welsh Woollen Industry		
Melrose Abbey & Abbey Museum MELROSE	337	Moyse's Hall Museum BURY ST EDMUNDS	215	DRE-FACH FELINDRE	352	
Merchant Adventurers' Hall YORK	277	Much Wenlock Priory MUCH WENLOCK	199	Museum of Transport MANCHESTER	94	
Merchant's House Museum PLYMOUTH	67	Muchelney Abbey MUCHELNEY	205	Museum of Transport GLASGOW	310	
Merrivale Model Village GREAT YARMOUTH	171	Muckleburgh Collection WEYBOURNE	176	Museum of Welsh Life ST FAGANS	351	
Merseyside Maritime Museum LIVERPOOL	164	Muckross House, Gardens & Traditional Farms		Museum of Worcester Porcelain WORCESTER	264	
Metropolitan Cathedral of Christ the King		KILLARNEY	391	Museums of the Royal College of Surgeons		
LIVERPOOL	164	Mugdock Country Park MILNGAVIE	317	LONDON WC2	150-151	
Michelham Priory HAILSHAM	228	Mull & West Highland Narrow Gauge Railway		Musical Museum BRENTFORD	158	
Middle Temple Hall LONDON EC4	150	CRAIGNURE	345	Mussenden Temple Bishop's Gate and Black Glen		
Middleham Castle MIDDLEHAM	272	Muncaster Castle, Gardens & Owl Centre		DOWNHILL	380	
Middleton Hall MIDDLETON	241	MUNCASTER	51	Myreton Motor Museum ABERLADY	317	
Middleton Railway LEEDS	285	Museum & Art Gallery LETCHWORTH	112			
Middleton Top Engine House MIDDLETON	59	Museum & Art Gallery BRIGHTON	227	**N**		
Midland Railway Centre RIPLEY	60	Museum & Art Gallery DUDLEY	248			
Milestones - Hampshire's Living History Museum		Museum & Winter Gardens		Narrow Water Castle WARRENPOINT	378	
BASINGSTOKE	98	SUNDERLAND	237-238	National Army Museum LONDON SW3	151	
Military Museum BODMIN	38	Museum of Antiquities		National Birds of Prey Centre NEWENT	90	
Military Museum of Devon & Dorset		NEWCASTLE UPON TYNE	237	National Botanic Garden of Wales		
DORCHESTER	73	Museum of Archaeology SOUTHAMPTON	106	LLANARTHNE	353	
Milky Way Adventure Park CLOVELLY	63	Museum of Argyll & Sutherland Highlanders		National Botanic Gardens DUBLIN	388	
Mill Trail Visitor Centre ALVA	311	STIRLING	341	National Coal Mining Museum For England		
Millennium Galleries SHEFFIELD	281	Museum of Army Flying MIDDLE WALLOP	102	WAKEFIELD	286	
Millennium Stadium Tours CARDIFF	351	Museum of Army Transport BEVERLEY	266	National Coracle Centre CENARTH	354	
Millgate Museum NEWARK-ON-TRENT	185	Museum of Bath at Work BATH	202-203	National Fishing Heritage Centre GRIMSBY	138	
Mills Observatory DUNDEE	316	Museum of British Road Transport COVENTRY	248	National Football Museum PRESTON	131	
Milton's Cottage CHALFONT ST GILES	23	Museum of Canterbury CANTERBURY	118-119	National Gallery LONDON WC2	151	
Minster Abbey MINSTER-IN-THANET	125	Museum of Childhood BEAUMARIS	361	National Gallery of Ireland DUBLIN	388	
Minster Lovell Hall & Dovecot		Museum of Childhood EDINBURGH	305-306	National Gallery of Scotland EDINBURGH	306	
MINSTER LOVELL	191-192	Museum of Childhood at Bethnal Green		National Garden Exhibitions Centre		
Minterne Gardens MINTERNE MAGNA	73	LONDON E2	150	KILQUADE	395	
Mirehouse KESWICK	51	Museum of Costume BATH	203	National Glass Centre SUNDERLAND	238	
Mistley Towers MISTLEY	83	Museum of Costume & Textiles		National Horseracing Museum and Tours		
Moat Park Heritage Centre BIGGAR	339	NOTTINGHAM	186	NEWMARKET	217-218	
Model Village BOURTON-ON-THE-WATER	86	Museum of Dartmoor Life OKEHAMPTON	66	National Library of Ireland DUBLIN	388	
Mole Hall Wildlife Park NEWPORT	84	Museum of Domestic Design & Architecture		National Library of Wales ABERYSTWYTH	354	
Mompesson House SALISBURY	257	BARNET	158	National Maritime Museum LONDON SE10	151	
Monaghan County Museum MONAGHAN	393	Museum of East Anglian Life STOWMARKET	218	National Maritime Museum Cornwall		
Monea Castle ENNISKILLEN	379	Museum of Edinburgh EDINBURGH	306	FALMOUTH	38	
Moniack Castle (Highland Winery) KIRKHILL	325	Museum of English Rural Life READING	17	National Motorcycle Museum SOLIHULL	248	
Monk Bretton Priory BARNSLEY	280	Museum of Flight EAST FORTUNE	317-318	National Museum & Gallery Cardiff CARDIFF	351	
Monkey Sanctuary LOOE	40	Museum of Garden History LONDON SE1	150	National Museum of Photography, Film &		
Monkey World WOOL	76	Museum of Hartlepool HARTLEPOOL	80	Television BRADFORD	283	
Mont Orgueil Castle GOREY	291	Museum of Kent Life MAIDSTONE	124-125	National Park Centre SEDBERGH	52	
Montacute House MONTACUTE	205	Museum of Lakeland Life KENDAL	51	National Park Centre AYSGARTH	269	
Montgomery Castle MONTGOMERY	368	Museum of Lead Mining WANLOCKHEAD	315	National Park Centre GRASSINGTON	270	
Montrose Museum & Art Gallery MONTROSE	302	Museum of Lincolnshire Life LINCOLN	139	National Photographic Archive DUBLIN	388	
Monument, The LONDON EC3	150	Museum of Liverpool Life LIVERPOOL	164	National Portrait Gallery LONDON WC2	151	
Moors Centre DANBY	269	Museum of Local Life WORCESTER	263	National Railway Museum YORK	277	
Moors Valley Country Park RINGWOOD	105	Museum of London LONDON EC2	150	National Seal Sanctuary GWEEK	39	
Moot Hall ELSTOW	14	Museum of Nottingham Lace NOTTINGHAM	187	National Shire Horse Centre YEALMPTON	69	
Moray Firth Wildlife Centre SPEY BAY	329-330	Museum of Oxford OXFORD	192	National Space Centre LEICESTER	135	
Morpeth Chantry Bagpipe Museum MORPETH	183	Museum of Rugby & Twickenham Stadium Tours		National Wallace Monument		
Morton Manor BRADING	251-252	TWICKENHAM	161	CAUSEWAYHEAD	340	
Morwellham Quay MORWELLHAM	66	Museum of Science and Industry in Manchester		National War Museum of Scotland		
Moseley Old Hall MOSELEY	210-211	MANCHESTER	94	EDINBURGH	306	

National Waterways Museum GLOUCESTER		88
National Wildflower Centre LIVERPOOL		166
Natural History Museum LONDON SW7		151
Natural History Museum NOTTINGHAM		187
Natural History Museum DUBLIN		388
Natural History Museum & Butterfly House PORTSMOUTH		104
Nature in Art GLOUCESTER		88
Nautical Museum CASTLETOWN		294
Navan Centre ARMAGH		375
Neath Abbey NEATH		364
Needles Old Battery ALUM BAY		251
Needles Park ALUM BAY		251
Neidpath Castle PEEBLES		337
Nelson Monument EDINBURGH		306
Nelson Museum & Local History Centre MONMOUTH		363
Nene Valley Railway WANSFORD		29
Nether Alderley Mill NETHER ALDERLEY		36
Netley Abbey NETLEY		102
New Abbey Corn Mill NEW ABBEY		313
New Art Gallery Walsall WALSALL		249
New Forest Museum & Visitor Centre LYNDHURST		101
New Lanark Visitor Centre NEW LANARK		340
New Place / Nash's House STRATFORD-UPON-AVON		242-243
New Pleasurewood Hills LOWESTOFT		217
Newark Air Museum NEWARK-ON-TRENT		185
Newark Castle PORT GLASGOW		327
Newarke Houses LEICESTER		135
Newbridge House and Traditional Farm DONABATE		387
Newby Hall & Gardens NEWBY HALL & GARDENS		272-273
Newcastle BRIDGEND		350
Newman House DUBLIN		389
Newquay Zoo NEWQUAY		41
Newstead Abbey NEWSTEAD		186
No 1 Royal Crescent BATH		203
Noltland Castle WESTRAY		347
Nora Barnacle House Museum GALWAY		390
Norfolk & Suffolk Aviation Museum FLIXTON		215
Norfolk Lavender HEACHAM		171
Norfolk Rural Life Museum & Union Farm GRESSENHALL		171
Norfolk Shire Horse Centre WEST RUNTON		176
Norman Manor House BURTON AGNES		266
Normanby Hall Country Park SCUNTHORPE		139
North Ayrshire Museum SALTCOATS		330
North Devon Maritime Museum APPLEDORE		62
North Leigh Roman Villa NORTH LEIGH		192
North Norfolk Railway SHERINGHAM		174
North Somerset Museum WESTON-SUPER-MARE		207
North Yorkshire Moors Railway PICKERING		274
Northampton Museum & Art Gallery NORTHAMPTON		179
Norton Conyers Hall RIPON		275
Norton Priory Museum & Gardens RUNCORN		36
Norwich Castle Museum NORWICH		173
Norwich Cathedral NORWICH		173
Nostell Priory NOSTELL PRIORY		286
Nottingham Industrial Museum NOTTINGHAM		187
Number Twenty Nine DUBLIN		389
Nunney Castle NUNNEY		205
Nunnington Hall NUNNINGTON		273
Nunwell House & Gardens BRADING		252
Nymans Garden HANDCROSS		234

O

Oakham Castle OAKHAM		196
Oakwell Hall OAKWELL HALL		286
Oakwood Park NARBERTH		366
Observatory Science Centre HERSTMONCEUX		229
Oceanarium BOURNEMOUTH		71
OceanLab FISHGUARD		365
Odda's Chapel DEERHURST		87
Official Loch Ness Monster Exhibition Centre DRUMNADROCHIT		323
Ogmore Castle OGMORE		371
Okehampton Castle OKEHAMPTON		66
Old Beaupre Castle ST HILARY		371
Old Bridge House Museum DUMFRIES		312
Old Bushmills Distillery BUSHMILLS		374
Old Grammar School CASTLETOWN		294
Old Hall GAINSBOROUGH		138
Old House HEREFORD		109
Old House of Keys CASTLETOWN		294
Old Merchant's House GREAT YARMOUTH		171
Old Midleton Distillery MIDLETON		385-386
Old Oswestry Hill Fort OSWESTRY		199
Old Rectory EPWORTH		138
Old Royal Observatory LONDON SE10		151
Old Sarum SALISBURY		257
Old Town Hall NEWTOWN		252
Old Town Hall Museum of Local History HASTINGS & ST LEONARDS		228
Old Town Jail STIRLING		341
Old Wardour Castle TISBURY		259
Olderfleet Castle LARNE		374
Oliver Cromwell's House ELY		28
Orchardton Tower PALNACKIE		313
Orford Castle ORFORD		218
Oriental Museum DURHAM		79
Orkney Maritime & Natural History Museum STROMNESS		346
Orkney Museum KIRKWALL		346
Orleans House Gallery TWICKENHAM		161
Ormesby Hall ORMESBY		273
Osborne House OSBORNE HOUSE		253
Osterley Park House OSTERLEY		160
Otter Trust BUNGAY		215
Otterton Mill Centre OTTERTON		66
Outwood Windmill OUTWOOD		222-223
Overbecks Museum & Garden SALCOMBE		68
Owlpen Manor OWLPEN		90
Oxburgh Hall OXBOROUGH		173-174
Oxford Story, The OXFORD		192
Oxford University Museum of Natural History OXFORD		192-193
Oxfordshire Museum WOODSTOCK		194
Oxwich Castle OXWICH		369

P

Packwood House PACKWOOD HOUSE		241
Paignton & Dartmouth Steam Railway PAIGNTON		67
Paignton Zoo Environmental Park PAIGNTON		67
Painshill Landscape Garden PAINSHILL PARK		223
Painswick Rococo Garden PAINSWICK		90
Paisley Museum & Art Galleries PAISLEY		335
Palace of Holyroodhouse EDINBURGH		306
Palace Stables Heritage Centre ARMAGH		375
Pallant House Gallery CHICHESTER		233
Paradise Mill MACCLESFIELD		35
Paradise Park & Gardens NEWHAVEN		230
Parcevall Gardens PARCEVALL HALL GARDENS		273

Parham House & Gardens PULBOROUGH		234
Park Farm SNETTISHAM		174
Parliament House EDINBURGH		306
Patrick Kavanagh Rural & Literary Centre INNISKEEN		392-393
Pattersons Spade Mill TEMPLEPATRICK		374
Paultons Park OWER		103
Paxton House BERWICK-UPON-TWEED		181
Paycocke's COGGESHALL		82
Peak Cavern CASTLETON		56
Peak District Mining Museum MATLOCK BATH		59
Pearoom, The HECKINGTON		138
Peckover House & Garden WISBECH		30
Pecorama Pleasure Gardens BEER		62
Peel Castle PEEL		295
Pembroke Castle PEMBROKE		366
Penarth Fawr PENARTH FAWR		360
Pencarrow BODMIN		38
Pendennis Castle FALMOUTH		38
Pendon Museum LONG WITTENHAM		191
Penhow Castle PENHOW		365
Penrhos Cottage LLANYCEFN		366
Penrhyn Castle BANGOR		358
Penshurst Place & Gardens PENSHURST		125
Penstorpe Waterfowl Park & Nature Reserve FAKENHAM		170
Pentre Ifan Burial Chamber NEWPORT		366
Pen-Y-Bryn Farm Park CORWEN		356
People's Palace GLASGOW		310
People's Story, The EDINBURGH		306
Perth Museum & Art Gallery PERTH		333
Peterborough Cathedral PETERBOROUGH		29
Petrie Museum of Egyptian Archaeology LONDON WC1		151
Pettitts Animal Adventure Park REEDHAM		174
Petworth House & Park PETWORTH		234
Pevensey Castle PEVENSEY		230
Peveril Castle CASTLETON		56
Phoenix Park Visitor Centre DUBLIN		389
Pickering Castle PICKERING		274
Pickford's House Museum of Georgian Life & Costume DERBY		58
Pictavia Visitor Centre BRECHIN		301
Piece Hall HALIFAX		284
Pier Arts Centre STROMNESS		346
Pitmedden Garden PITMEDDEN		300
Pitt Rivers Museum OXFORD		193
Pittencrieff House Museum DUNFERMLINE		320
Plas Mawr CONWY		355
Plas Newydd LLANGOLLEN		357
Plas Newydd PLAS NEWYDD		362
Plas yn Rhiw PLAS YN RHIW		360
Pleasure Island Theme Park CLEETHORPES		138
Pleasureland SOUTHPORT		167
Pluscarden Abbey ELGIN		328-329
Plymouth Dome PLYMOUTH		67
Poldark Mine and Heritage Complex WENDRON		45
Polesden Lacey GREAT BOOKHAM		222
Pollock's Toy Museum LONDON W1		152
Pollok House GLASGOW		310
Poole's Cavern (Buxton Country Park) BUXTON		55
Port Lympne Wild Animal Park, Mansion & Garden LYMPNE		124
Portchester Castle PORTCHESTER		103
Portland Basin Museum ASHTON-UNDER-LYNE		93
Portland Castle PORTLAND		73
Portland Museum PORTLAND		73
Portmeirion PORTMEIRION		361
Portsmouth Historic Dockyard PORTSMOUTH		104

Index

Portumna Castle & Gardens PORTUMNA	390
Potteries Museum & Art Gallery, The STOKE-ON-TRENT	211-212
Powderham Castle POWDERHAM	68
Powell-Cotton Museum, Quex House & Gardens BIRCHINGTON	117
Powerscourt Gardens & House Exhibition ENNISKERRY	394
Powis Castle WELSHPOOL	369
Prebendal Manor House NASSINGTON	178
Prescot Museum PRESCOT	166
Preston Manor BRIGHTON	227
Preston Mill & Phantassie Doocot EAST LINTON	318
Prestongrange Museum PRESTONPANS	318
Prideaux Place PADSTOW	42
Priest's House Museum and Garden WIMBORNE	76
Prinknash Abbey and Pottery CRANHAM	87
Prinknash Bird & Deer Park CRANHAM	87
Priorwood Garden & Dried Flower Shop MELROSE	337
Provand's Lordship GLASGOW	310
Provost Skene's House ABERDEEN	297
Prudhoe Castle PRUDHOE	183
Public Record Office Museum KEW	160

Q

Quarry Bank Mill & Styal Estate STYAL	36
Quebec House WESTERHAM	127
Queen Charlotte's Cottage KEW	160
Queen's Gallery LONDON SW1	152
Queens House LONDON SE10	152
Queen's Own Highlanders Regimental Museum Collection FORT GEORGE	323-324
Queen's View Visitor Centre QUEEN'S VIEW	334
Queensferry Museum SOUTH QUEENSFERRY	308
Queentown Story, The COBH	385
Quince Honey Farm SOUTH MOLTON	68

R

Raby Castle STAINDROP	80
Raglan Castle RAGLAN	363
Ragley Hall ALCESTER	240
Ramsey Abbey Gatehouse RAMSEY	29
Rangers House (The Wernher Collection) LONDON SE3	152
Ravenglass & Eskdale Railway RAVENGLASS	52
Record Office for Leicestershire, Leicester & Rutland LEICESTER	135
Reculver Towers & Roman Fort RECULVER	125
Red House GOMERSAL	283
Red House Museum & Gardens CHRISTCHURCH	72
Red Lodge BRISTOL	21
Redoubt Fortress and Museum EASTBOURNE	228
Reigate Priory Museum REIGATE	223
Restormel Castle RESTORMEL	42
Revolution House OLD WHITTINGTON	60
Rheidol Hydro Power Station & Visitor Centre CAPEL BANGOR	354
Rhondda Heritage Park TREHAFOD	369
RHS Garden Hyde Hall CHELMSFORD	82
RHS Garden Rosemoor GREAT TORRINGTON	65
RHS Garden Wisley WISLEY	224
RHS Garden, Harlow Carr HARROGATE	270
Rhuddlan Castle RHUDDLAN	357
Richborough Castle RICHBOROUGH	126
Richmond Castle RICHMOND	274
Rievaulx Abbey RIEVAULX	274

Rievaulx Terrace & Temples RIEVAULX	274
Ripley Castle RIPLEY	274-275
River & Rowing Museum HENLEY-ON-THAMES	191
RNLI Zetland Museum REDCAR	274
Rob Roy and Trossachs Visitor Centre CALLANDER	340
Robert Burns Centre DUMFRIES	312
Robert Opie Collection-Museum of Advertising & Packaging GLOUCESTER	88
Robert Smail's Printing Works INNERLEITHEN	336
Robin Hill Country Park ARRETON	251
Roche Abbey MALTBY	280
Rochester Castle ROCHESTER	126
Rockbourne Roman Villa ROCKBOURNE	105
Rockingham Castle ROCKINGHAM	179
Roman Bath-House BEARSDEN	317
Roman Baths & Pump Room BATH	203
Roman City WROXETER	200
Roman Legionary Museum CAERLEON	364-365
Roman Painted House DOVER	120
Roman Theatre of Verulamium ST ALBANS	114
Roman Town CAISTER-ON-SEA	169
Roman Town ALDBOROUGH	269
Roman Villa NEWPORT	252
Roman Wall (Mithraic Temple) CARRAWBROUGH	182
Romney Hythe & Dymchurch Railway HYTHE	122-123
Rothesay Castle ROTHESAY	344
Rough Castle FALKIRK	319
Rough Fort LIMAVADY	380
Roundstone Music, Crafts & Fashion ROUNDSTONE	390
Rousham House ROUSHAM	193
Rousse Tower VALE	289
Rowallane Garden SAINTFIELD	378
Royal Academy Of Arts LONDON W1	152
Royal Air Force Museum COSFORD	198
Royal Air Force Museum LONDON NW9	152
Royal Armouries Fort Nelson FAREHAM	100
Royal Armouries Museum LEEDS	285
Royal Botanic Garden Edinburgh EDINBURGH	306-307
Royal Burgh of Stirling Visitor Centre STIRLING	341
Royal Citadel PLYMOUTH	67
Royal Cornwall Museum TRURO	44-45
Royal Crown Derby Visitor Centre DERBY	58
Royal Doulton Visitor Centre STOKE-ON-TRENT	211
Royal Engineers Museum GILLINGHAM	121
Royal Hampshire Regiment Museum & Memorial Garden WINCHESTER	107
Royal Marines Museum PORTSMOUTH	104
Royal Mews LONDON SW1	152
Royal Museum EDINBURGH	307
Royal Museum & Art Gallery with Buffs Museum CANTERBURY	119
Royal Naval College LONDON SE10	154
Royal Navy Submarine Museum & HMS Alliance GOSPORT	100
Royal Norfolk Regimental Museum NORWICH	173
Royal Observatory Visitor Centre EDINBURGH	307
Royal Pavilion BRIGHTON	227
Royal Pump Room Museum HARROGATE	270
Royal Shakespeare Company Collection STRATFORD-UPON-AVON	243
Royal Signals Museum BLANDFORD FORUM	71
Royal Tara China Visitor Centre GALWAY	390
Royal Yacht Britannia EDINBURGH	307

RSPB Lochwinnoch Nature Reserve LOCHWINNOCH	334-335
RSPB Nature Reserve LLANDUDNO JUNCTION	355
RSPB Nature Reserve SANDY	15
RSPB Nature Reserve LYDD	123
RSPB Nature Reserve SILVERDALE	132
RSPB Nature Reserve TITCHWELL	175
RSPB Nature Reserve BEMPTON	266
RSPB Nature Reserve FAIRBURN	270
RSPB Nature Reserve EGLWYSFACH	354
RSPB Nature Reserve Abernethy Forest BOAT OF GARTEN	322
RSPB Nature Reserve Minsmere WESTLETON	219
RSPB Nature Reserve Radipole Lake WEYMOUTH	75
RSPB Nature Reserve South Stack HOLYHEAD	362
RSPB Nature Reserve Vane Farm KINROSS	332
RSPB Pulborough Brooks Nature Reserve PULBOROUGH	235
Rufford Abbey and Country Park OLLERTON	188
Rufford Old Hall RUFFORD	131
Rug Chapel CORWEN	356
Rural Life Centre TILFORD	223
Rushen Abbey BALLASALLA	294
Ruskin Museum CONISTON	49
Russian Submarine FOLKESTONE	121
Ruthven Barracks KINGUSSIE	325
Ruthwell Cross RUTHWELL	314
Rutland County Museum OAKHAM	196
Rycote Chapel RYCOTE	193
Rydal Mount RYDAL	52
Rye Castle Museum RYE	230
Ryton Organic Gardens RYTON-ON-DUNSMORE	242

S

Saddleworth Museum & Art Gallery UPPERMILL	95
Saffron Walden Museum SAFFRON WALDEN	84
Sainsbury Centre for Visual Arts NORWICH	173
Salford Museum & Art Gallery SALFORD	95
Salisbury & South Wiltshire Museum SALISBURY	257
Salisbury Cathedral SALISBURY	257
Sally Lunn's Refreshment House & Museum BATH	203
Salt Museum NORTHWICH	36
Saltburn Smugglers Heritage Centre SALTBURN-BY-THE-SEA	275
Saltram PLYMPTON	68
Samares Manor ST CLEMENT	291
Samlesbury Hall SAMLESBURY	131
Sammy Miller Mototcycle Museum NEW MILTON	102
Samuel Johnson Birthplace Museum LICHFIELD	210
Sandham Memorial Chapel BURGHCLERE	99
Sandringham House, Grounds, Museum & Country Park SANDRINGHAM	174
Sanquhar Tolbooth Museum SANQUHAR	314
Sarehole Mill BIRMINGHAM	246
Satrosphere (Hands-On Science & Technology Centre) ABERDEEN	297
Sausmarez Manor ST MARTIN	289
Savill Garden (Windsor Great Park) WINDSOR	18
Savings Banks Museum RUTHWELL	314
Saxtead Green Post Mill SAXTEAD GREEN	218
Scalloway Castle SCALLOWAY	347

Entry	Page
Scapa Flow Visitor Centre & Museum KIRKWALL	346
Scarborough Castle SCARBOROUGH	275
Science Museum LONDON SW7	154
Scolton Visitor Centre SCOLTON	367
Scone Palace SCONE	334
Scotch Whisky Heritage Centre EDINBURGH	307
Scotney Castle Garden LAMBERHURST	123
Scott Polar Research Institute Museum CAMBRIDGE	27
Scottish & Southern Energy Visitor Centre, Dam & Fish Pass PITLOCHRY	334
Scottish Deer Centre CUPAR	320
Scottish Fisheries Museum ANSTRUTHER	319
Scottish Maritime Museum IRVINE	330
Scottish Mining Museum NEWTONGRANGE	327
Scottish National Gallery of Modern Art EDINBURGH	307
Scottish National Portrait Gallery EDINBURGH	307
Scottish Seabird Centre NORTH BERWICK	318
Scottish Sealife & Marine Sanctuary BARCALDINE	303
Scott's Grotto WARE	115
Scrabo Tower NEWTOWNARDS	377
Sea Life & Marine Sanctuary SCARBOROUGH	275
Sea Life Aquarium & Marine Sanctuary HUNSTANTON	172
Sea Life Centre BRIGHTON	227
Sea Life Park WEYMOUTH	75
Secret World-Badger & Wildlife Reserve Centre EAST HUNTSPILL	204
Segedunum Roman Fort, Baths & Museum WALLSEND	238
Segontium Roman Museum CAERNARFON	359
Sellafield Visitors Centre SELLAFIELD	52
Selly Manor Museum BIRMINGHAM	246
Severn Valley Railway BEWDLEY	261
Severn Valley Railway KIDDERMINSTER	262
Sewerby Hall & Gardens BRIDLINGTON	267
Sezincote MORETON-IN-MARSH	90
Shaftesbury Abbey Museum & Garden SHAFTESBURY	74
Shakespeare's Birthplace STRATFORD-UPON-AVON	244
Shakespeare's Globe Exhibition and Theatre Tour LONDON SE1	154
Shambellie House Museum of Costume NEW ABBEY	313
Shambles NEWENT	90
Shanklin Chine SHANKLIN	253
Shap Abbey SHAP	52
Shaw's Corner AYOT ST LAWRENCE	112
Sheelin Irish Lace Museum ENNISKILLEN	379
Sheffield Park Garden SHEFFIELD PARK	230
Sherborne Castle SHERBORNE	74
Sherborne Museum SHERBORNE	74
Sherborne Old Castle SHERBORNE	74
Sherwood Forest Country Park & Visitor Centre EDWINSTOWE	185
Shetland Museum LERWICK	347
Shibden Hall HALIFAX	284
Shire Hall LANCASTER	130
Shire Hall Gallery STAFFORD	211
Shires Family Adventure Park TREDINNICK	44
Shoe Museum STREET	206
Shrewsbury Castle and Shropshire Regimental Museum SHREWSBURY	200
Shrewsbury Quest SHREWSBURY	200
Shropshire Hills Discovery Centre CRAVEN ARMS	198
Shugborough Estate SHUGBOROUGH	211
Shuttleworth Collection OLD WARDEN	15
Sir Harold Hillier Gardens & Arboretum AMPFIELD	97
Sir John Soane's Museum LONDON WC2	154
Sir Walter Scott's Courtroom SELKIRK	337
Sissinghurst Castle Garden SISSINGHURST	126
Sizergh Castle & Garden SIZERGH	52
Skara Brae DOUNBY	346
Skegness Natureland Seal Sanctuary SKEGNESS	139
Skellig Experience VALENTIA ISLAND	391
Skenfrith Castle SKENFRITH	363
Sketrick Castle KILLINCHY	377
Skipton Castle SKIPTON	275-276
Smailholm Tower SMAILHOLM	337
Smallest House CONWY	355
Smallythe Place SMALLHYTHE	126
Smith Art Gallery & Museum STIRLING	341
Smugglers Adventure HASTINGS & ST LEONARDS	228-229
Snaefell Mountain Railway DOUGLAS	295
Snibston Discovery Park COALVILLE	134
Snowdon Mountain Railway LLANBERIS	360
Snowshill Manor SNOWSHILL	91
Soho House BIRMINGHAM	247
Souter Johnnie's Cottage KIRKOSWALD	338
Souter Lighthouse WHITBURN	238
South Lakes Wild Animal Park DALTON-IN-FURNESS	49
South London Gallery LONDON SE5	154
South Tynedale Railway ALSTON	47
South Wales Borderers (24th Regiment) Museum BRECON	368
South Wales Miners Museum CYNONVILLE	364
Southampton City Art Gallery SOUTHAMPTON	106
Southampton Maritime Museum SOUTHAMPTON	106
Southend Museum, Planetarium & Discovery Centre SOUTHEND-ON-SEA	84
Southport Zoo & Conservation Trust SOUTHPORT	167
Southsea Castle PORTSMOUTH	104
Southwark Cathedral LONDON SE1	155
Spalding Tropical Forest SPALDING	140
Speedwell Cavern CASTLETON	56
Speke Hall SPEKE	167
Spetchley Park Gardens SPETCHLEY	262-263
Speyside Cooperage Visitor Centre CRAIGELLACHIE	328
Spinners BOLDRE	98
Spitbank Fort PORTSMOUTH	105
Spode STOKE-ON-TRENT	211
Springfields Gardens SPALDING	140
Springhill MONEYMORE	380-381
Squerryes Court Manor House & Gardens WESTERHAM	127
SS Great Britain BRISTOL	21
St Albans Cathedral ST ALBANS	114
St Andrews Aquarium ST ANDREWS	321
St Augustine's Abbey CANTERBURY	119
St Catherine's Castle FOWEY	39
St Cybi's Well LLANGYBI	360
St Davids Bishop's Palace ST DAVID'S	366
St Davids Cathedral ST DAVID'S	366-367
St Edmund Hall OXFORD	193
St George's Chapel WINDSOR	18
St James's Chapel LINDSEY	216
St Leonard's Tower WEST MALLING	127
St Mawes Castle ST MAWES	43
St Michael's Mount MARAZION	41
St Mungo Religious Life & Art Museum GLASGOW	310
St Nicholas' Priory EXETER	64
St Olaves Priory ST OLAVES	174
St Patrick Centre DOWNPATRICK	377
St Patrick's Trian ARMAGH	375
St Paul's Cathedral LONDON EC4	154
St Williams College YORK	277
Staffordshire Regiment Museum, Whittington Barracks WHITTINGTON	213
Stained Glass Museum ELY	28
Stamford Museum STAMFORD	140
Stamford Shakespeare Company STAMFORD	140
Standen EAST GRINSTEAD	233
Stanford Hall SWINFORD	136
Stapehill Abbey WIMBORNE	76
Stapeley Water Gardens NANTWICH	35
Staunton Country Park HAVANT	100-101
Steam - Museum of The Great Western Railway SWINDON	258
Steam Yacht Gondola CONISTON	49
Stenness Standing Stones FINSTOWN	346
Stewartry Museum KIRKCUDBRIGHT	313
Stirling Castle STIRLING	341
Stockwood Craft Museum & Gardens LUTON	15
Stoke sub Hamdon Priory STOKE SUB HAMDON	206
Stokesay Castle STOKESAY	200
Stone House Cottage Gardens STONE	263
Stonehenge STONEHENGE	258
Stoneleigh Abbey KENILWORTH	241
Stonor House & Park STONOR	193
Storybook Glen MARYCULTER	299
Stourhead Garden & House STOURHEAD	258
Stourton House Flower Garden STOURTON	258
Stowe House STOWE	24
Stowe Landscape Gardens STOWE	24
Strangford Castle STRANGFORD	378
Strata Florida Abbey STRATA FLORIDA	354
Stratfield Saye House STRATFIELD SAYE	106
Strathisla Distillery KEITH	329
Strathnaver Museum BETTYHILL	322
Strathspey Steam Railway AVIEMORE	322
Streetlife - Hull Museum of Transport HULL	267
Strokestown Park House Garden & Famine Museum STROKESTOWN	393
Struell Wells DOWNPATRICK	377
Stump Cross Caverns PATELEY BRIDGE	273-274
Sudbury Hall SUDBURY	60
Sudeley Castle & Gardens WINCHCOMBE	91
Sue Ryder Foundation Museum CAVENDISH	215
Suenos' Stone FORRES	329
Suffolk Wildlife Park SUFFOLK WILDLIFE PARK	219
Sulgrave Manor SULGRAVE	179
Summerlee Heritage Park COATBRIDGE	331
Suntrap Garden GOGAR	308
Sutton House LONDON E9	155
Sutton Park SUTTON-ON-THE-FOREST	276
Swanage Railway SWANAGE	74
Swansea Maritime & Industrial Museum SWANSEA	370
Sweetheart Abbey NEW ABBEY	313
Swiss Cottage CAHIR	393
Sygun Copper Mine BEDDGELERT	358
Syon House ISLEWORTH	160
Syon Park ISLEWORTH	160

T

Entry	Page
Tabley House KNUTSFORD	34
Tales of Robin Hood NOTTINGHAM	187

Index

Tall Ship at Glasgow Harbour GLASGOW	310
Talyllyn Railway TYWYN	361
Tamworth Castle TAMWORTH	212
Tanfield Railway TANFIELD	80
Tangmere Military Aviation Museum Trust TANGMERE	235
Tank Museum BOVINGTON CAMP	71
Tantallon Castle NORTH BERWICK	318
Tate Britain LONDON SW1	155
Tate Liverpool LIVERPOOL	166
Tate Modern LONDON SE1	155
Tate St Ives ST IVES	43
Tattershall Castle TATTERSHALL	140
Tatton Park KNUTSFORD	34
Techniquest CARDIFF	351
Teddy Bear Museum STRATFORD-UPON-AVON	244
Temple Mine MATLOCK BATH	59
Temple Newsam House & Park LEEDS	285
Templetown Mausoleum TEMPLEPATRICK	375
Tenby Museum and Art Gallery TENBY	367
Tenement House GLASGOW	310
Thackray Museum LEEDS	285-286
Thames Barrier Visitors Centre LONDON SE18	155
Theakston Brewery & Visitor Centre MASHAM	272
Theatre Museum LONDON WC2	155
Thetford Priory THETFORD	175
Thirlestane Castle LAUDER	336
Thoor Ballylee GORT	390
Thornton Abbey THORNTON	140
Thorpe Park CHERTSEY	221
Threave Castle CASTLE DOUGLAS	311
Threave Garden & Estate CASTLE DOUGLAS	311
Thrigby Hall Wildlife Gardens FILBY	170
Thursford Collection THURSFORD GREEN	175
Thwaite Mills Watermill LEEDS	286
Tilbury Fort TILBURY	84
Timespan HELMSDALE	325
Timothy Hackworth Victorian & Railway Museum SHILDON	80
Tintagel Castle TINTAGEL	43-44
Tintern Abbey TINTERN	363-364
Tintinhull House Garden TINTINHULL	206
Titchfield Abbey TITCHFIELD	106
Tithe Barn BRADFORD-ON-AVON	255
Tiverton Castle TIVERTON	68
Tiverton Museum of Mid Devon Life TIVERTON	68
Tolbooth Art Centre KIRKCUDBRIGHT	313
Tolbooth Museum STONEHAVEN	300
Tolhouse Museum GREAT YARMOUTH	171
Tolpuddle Martyrs Museum TOLPUDDLE	74
Tolquhon Castle PITMEDDEN	300
Tolson Memorial Museum HUDDERSFIELD	284
Tom Leonard Mining Museum SKINNINGROVE	275
Tomintoul Museum TOMINTOUL	330
Torosay Castle & Gardens CRAIGNURE	345
Torre Abbey Historic House & Gallery TORQUAY	69
Torridon Countryside Centre TORRIDON	326
Totnes Castle TOTNES	69
Totnes Museum TOTNES	69
Tower Bridge Experience LONDON SE1	155
Tower Museum LONDONDERRY	380
Tower of London LONDON EC3	156
Town Hall FORDWICH	121
Town Walls CARRICKFERGUS	374
Townend TROUTBECK [NEAR WINDERMERE]	53
Toy & Teddy Bear Museum LYTHAM ST ANNES	130
Traquair House TRAQUAIR	338

Treak Cliff Cavern CASTLETON	56
Treasurer's House YORK	277
Trebah Garden MAWNAN SMITH	41
Tredegar House & Park NEWPORT	365
Trefriw Woollen Mills TREFRIW	356
Trelissick Garden TRELISSICK GARDEN	44
Trengwainton Garden PENZANCE	42
Trerice TRERICE	44
Tretower Court & Castle TRETOWER	369
Trevarno Estate Garden & Museum of Gardening HELSTON	40
Trewithen Gardens PROBUS	42
Triangular Lodge RUSHTON	179
Tropical World LEEDS	286
Tropiquaria Animal and Adventure Park WASHFORD	207
Trotters World of Animals BASSENTHWAITE	47
Truggery, The HERSTMONCEUX	229
Tuckers Maltings NEWTON ABBOT	66
Tudor House Museum SOUTHAMPTON	106
Tudor Merchant's House TENBY	367
Tugnet Ice House SPEY BAY	330
Tullaghoge Fort COOKSTOWN	380
Tullie House Museum & Art Gallery CARLISLE	48
Tully Castle DERRYGONNELLY	378
Tunbridge Wells Museum and Art Gallery TUNBRIDGE WELLS (ROYAL)	127
Turton Tower TURTON BOTTOMS	132
Tutankhamun Exhibition DORCHESTER	73
Twycross Zoo Park TWYCROSS	136
Ty Mawr Wybrnant PENMACHNO	356
Tynemouth Castle & Priory TYNEMOUTH	238
Tyrone Crystal Visitor Centre DUNGANNON	381
Tyrwhitt Drake Museum of Carriages MAIDSTONE	125

U

U S Grant Ancestral Homestead & Visitor Centre BALLYGAWLEY	381
Uley Tumulus ULEY	91
Ulster American Folk Park OMAGH	381
Ulster History Park OMAGH	381
Ulster Museum BELFAST	373
University Museum of Archaeology & Anthropology CAMBRIDGE	27
University of Glasgow Visitor Centre GLASGOW	310
University of Leicester Harold Martin BotanicGarden LEICESTER	135
University of Oxford Botanic Garden OXFORD	193
Upnor Castle UPNOR	127
Uppark SOUTH HARTING	235
Upton House UPTON HOUSE	244
Urquhart Castle DRUMNADROCHIT	323
Usher Gallery LINCOLN	139
Usk Rural Life Museum USK	364

V

Valle Crucis Abbey LLANGOLLEN	357
Vennel Gallery IRVINE	330
Verdant Works DUNDEE	316
Verulamium Museum ST ALBANS	114
Victoria and Albert Museum LONDON SW7	156
Vikingar! LARGS	330
Village Cross TYNAN	376
Village, The FLEGGBURGH	170
Vina Cooke Museum of Dolls & Bygone Childhood NEWARK-ON-TRENT	186
Vindolanda (Chesterholm) BARDON MILL	181
Vinopolis, City of Wine LONDON SE1	156

Vyne, The SHERBORNE ST JOHN	105

W

W5 at Odyssey BELFAST	373
Waddesdon Manor WADDESDON	25
Wakefield Art Gallery WAKEFIELD	286
Wakehurst Place & Millennium Seed Bank ARDINGLY	232
Walcot Hall LYDBURY NORTH	199
Walker Art Gallery LIVERPOOL	166
Wall Roman Site WALL	212
Wallace Collection LONDON W1	156
Wallington House Walled Garden & Grounds CAMBO	181-182
Walmer Castle DEAL	119
Walsall Leather Museum WALSALL	249
Walsingham Abbey Grounds & Shirehall Museum LITTLE WALSINGHAM	172-173
Walter Rothschild Zoological Museum TRING	115
Waltham Abbey Gatehouse, Bridge & Entrance to Cloisters WALTHAM ABBEY	84
Warkworth Castle WARKWORTH	183
Warkworth Hermitage WARKWORTH	183
Warren Lodge THETFORD	175
Warwick Castle WARWICK	244
Warwickshire Yeomanry Museum WARWICK	244
Washington Old Hall WASHINGTON	238
Water Wheels BALLYSHANNON	386
Watercress Line ALRESFORD	97
Waterford Crystal Visitor Centre WATERFORD	394
Waterfront Museum & Scaplen's Court POOLE	73
Watermouth Castle & Family Theme Park ILFRACOMBE	65
Waterperry Gardens WATERPERRY	193
Wayside Folk Museum ZENNOR	45
Weald & Downland Open Air Museum SINGLETON	235
Weaver's Cottage KILBARCHAN	334
Wedgwood Visitor Centre STOKE-ON-TRENT	212
Weeting Castle WEETING	175
Weir Gardens SWAINSHILL	110
Wellbrook Beetling Mill COOKSTOWN	380
Wellington Country Park RISELEY	17
Wells & Walsingham Light Railway WELLS-NEXT-THE-SEA	175
Welsh Hawking Centre BARRY	371
Welsh Slate Museum LLANBERIS	360
Welshpool & Llanfair Light Railway LLANFAIR CAEREINION	368
Weobley Castle LLANRHIDIAN	369
Wesley's Chapel, House & Museum Of Methodism LONDON EC1	156
West Berkshire Museum NEWBURY	17
West Cork Model Village Railway CLONAKILTY	385
West Dean Gardens WEST DEAN	235
West Green House Gardens HARTLEY WINTNEY	100
West Highland Museum FORT WILLIAM	324
West Midland Safari & Leisure Park BEWDLEY	261
West Register House EDINBURGH	307
West Stow Anglo Saxon Village WEST STOW	219
West Wycombe Caves WEST WYCOMBE	25
West Wycombe Park WEST WYCOMBE	25
Westbury Court Garden WESTBURY-ON-SEVERN	91
Westminster Abbey LONDON SW1	156-157
Westminster Cathedral LONDON SW1	157
Westminster Hall LONDON SW1	157
Weston Park WESTON PARK	212
Westonbirt Arboretum WESTONBIRT	91

Index

Westwood Manor WESTWOOD	259	
Wetheriggs Country Pottery PENRITH	51	
Wetlands Waterfowl Reserve & Exotic Bird Park SUTTON-CUM-LOUND	188	
Wexford Wildfowl Reserve WEXFORD	394	
Whalley Abbey WHALLEY	132	
Whipsnade Wild Animal Park WHIPSNADE	15	
Whitaker Park & Rossendale Museum ROSSENDALE	131	
Whitby Abbey WHITBY	276	
Whitchurch Silk Mill WHITCHURCH	106	
White Castle WHITE CASTLE	364	
White Island Church CASTLE ARCHDALE BAY	378	
White Post Modern Farm Centre FARNSFIELD	185	
Whiteladies Priory (St Leonards Priory) BOSCOBEL	198	
Whithorn - Cradle of Christianity WHITHORN	315	
Whithorn Priory WHITHORN	315	
Whitworth Art Gallery MANCHESTER	94	
Wick Heritage Centre WICK	326	
Wigan Pier WIGAN	95	
Wightwick Manor WOLVERHAMPTON	249	
Wilberforce House HULL	267	
Wildlife Park at Cricket St Thomas CRICKET ST THOMAS	204	
William Morris Gallery LONDON E17	157	
Williamson Art Gallery & Museum BIRKENHEAD	163	
Willow & Wetlands Visitor Centre STOKE ST GREGORY	206	
Wilton House WILTON [NEAR SALISBURY]	259	
Wimbledon Lawn Tennis Museum LONDON SW19	157	
Wimpole Hall WIMPOLE	29-30	
Wimpole Home Farm WIMPOLE	30	
Winchester Cathedral WINCHESTER	107	
Winchester City Mill WINCHESTER	107	
Winchester City Museum WINCHESTER	107	
Winchester College WINCHESTER	107	
Wind in the Willows ROWSLEY	60	
Windermere Steamboat Centre WINDERMERE	53	
Windsor Castle WINDSOR	18	
Winkworth Arboretum HASCOMBE	222	
Winston Churchill's Britain at War Experience LONDON SE1	157	
Wirksworth Heritage Centre WIRKSWORTH	60	
Wisbech & Fenland Museum WISBECH	30	
Wish Tower Puppet Museum EASTBOURNE	228	
Witcombe Roman Villa GREAT WITCOMBE	88	
Witley Court WITLEY COURT	261	
Woburn Abbey WOBURN	15	
Woburn Safari Park WOBURN	15	
Wollaton Hall & Park NOTTINGHAM	187-188	
Wolterton Park ERPINGHAM	170	
Woodbridge Tide Mill WOODBRIDGE	219	
Woodhenge WOODHENGE	259	
Woodlands Leisure Park DARTMOUTH	64	
Wookey Hole Caves & Papermill WOOKEY HOLE	207	
Woolsthorpe Manor WOOLSTHORPE	140	
Worcester Cathedral WORCESTER	264	
Worcestershire County Museum KIDDERMINSTER	262	
Wordsworth House COCKERMOUTH	49	
Working Silk Mill BRAINTREE	82	
World in Miniature GOONHAVERN	39	
World of Country Life EXMOUTH	64-65	
World of Robin Hood HAUGHTON	185	
Wrest Park House & Gardens SILSOE	15	
Writers' Museum EDINBURGH	307-308	
WWT Arundel ARUNDEL	232	
WWT Caerlaverock CAERLAVEROCK	311	
WWT Castle Espie COMBER	376	
WWT Llanelli LLANELLI	353	
WWT Martin Mere MARTIN MERE	130	
WWT Slimbridge SLIMBRIDGE	90-91	
WWT Washington WASHINGTON	238	
WWT Welney WELNEY	176	
Wycombe Local History & Chair Museum HIGH WYCOMBE	23	
Wygston's House Museum of Costume LEICESTER	135	

Y

Yafford Water Mill Farm Park SHORWELL	253
Yarmouth Castle YARMOUTH	253
Yelverton Paperweight Centre YELVERTON	69
York Castle Museum YORK	277
York City Art Gallery YORK	277
York Dungeon YORK	277-278
York Minster YORK	278
York Model Railway YORK	278
Yorkshire Air Museum & Allied Air Forces Memorial ELVINGTON	270
Yorkshire Carriage Museum AYSGARTH	269
Yorkshire Museum YORK	278
Yorkshire Sculpture Park WEST BRETTON	287

Acknowledgments – Days Out Guide 2003

The Automobile Association would like to thank the following libraries and associations for their assistance in the preparation of this book: Longleat Enterprises Ltd 8t, 11c; Monkey World 9c, 11br, National Seal Sanctuary 10c; Nova Development Corp. 2, 3tr, 4br, 8c, 8b, 9t, 10t, 11t

The remaining photographs are held in the Association's own library (AA PHOTO LIBRARY) with contributions from: Stuart Abrahams 290; Adrian Baker 21, 201; Peter Baker 37, 54, 61, 70, 184, 231; Stuart Bates 293; Jeff Beazley 77, 129; M Birkitt 13, 30, 81, 133, 137, 177, 195b, 196, 239; Ian Burgum 108, 394b; Chris Coe 166, 225, 272; Steve Day 53, 85, 162, 189, 254, 296b, 383; Michael Diggin 382; Richard Elliott 343t; Eric Ellington 343b; Derek Forss 26, 214; Caroline Jones 16, 22, 31, 111, 115, 197; Max Jourdan 3bc, 11bl, 11bc, 141; Cameron Lees 46, 180, 236; Tom Mackie 3bl, 5t, 5t, 6t; S & O Mathews 176; Graham Matthews 4bc; John Millar 3t, 5bl, 220; John Morrison 278; Roger Moss 45; John Mottishaw 92, 287; Rich Newton 19; Hugh Palmer 110, 260, 264; Andrew Perkins 168; Tony Souter 96; Rupert Tenison 5br; Wyn Voysey 250, 288; Ronald Weir 349t; Jonathon Welsh 208, 245, 249; Stephen Whitehorne 1, 4bl, 296t; Peter Wilson 265, 268, 279, 282.

Readers' Reports

If you have enjoyed a visit to an attraction that is not included in our guide, and you think it should be, please contact us by e-mail at:

lifestyleguides@theAA.com

or by post at:

Days Out Guide, Lifestyle Guides, 15th Floor, Fanum House, Basing View, Basingstoke, Hants, RG21 4EA